American Casebook Series
Hornbook Series and Basic Legal Texts
Nutshell Series

of

WEST PUBLISHING COMPANY
P.O. Box 43526
St. Paul, Minnesota 55164
June, 1984

ACCOUNTING

Faris' Law and Accounting in a Nutshell, 377 pages, 1984 (Text)

Fiflis, Kripke and Foster's Teaching Materials on Accounting for Business Lawyers, 3rd Ed., 838 pages, 1984 (Casebook)

Siegel and Siegel's Accounting and Financial Disclosure: A Guide to Basic Concepts, 259 pages, 1983 (Text)

ADMINISTRATIVE LAW

Davis' Cases, Text and Problems on Administrative Law, 6th Ed., 683 pages, 1977 (Casebook)

Davis' Basic Text on Administrative Law, 3rd Ed., 617 pages, 1972 (Text)

Davis' Police Discretion, 176 pages, 1975 (Text)

Gellhorn and Boyer's Administrative Law and Process in a Nutshell, 2nd Ed., 445 pages, 1981 (Text)

Mashaw and Merrill's Introduction to the American Public Law System, 1095 pages, 1975, with 1980 Supplement (Casebook)

Robinson, Gellhorn and Bruff's The Administrative Process, 2nd Ed., 959 pages, 1980, with 1983 Supplement (Casebook)

ADMIRALTY

Healy and Sharpe's Cases and Materials on Admiralty, 875 pages, 1974 (Casebook)

Maraist's Admiralty in a Nutshell, 390 pages, 1983 (Text)

Sohn and Gustafson's Law of the Sea in a Nutshell, 264 pages, 1984 (Text)

AGENCY—PARTNERSHIP

Fessler's Alternatives to Incorporation for Persons in Quest of Profit, 258 pages, 1980 (Casebook)

AGENCY—PARTNERSHIP—Continued

Henn's Cases and Materials on Agency, Partnership and Other Unincorporated Business Enterprises, 2nd Ed., approximately 400 pages, 1985 (Casebook)

Reuschlein and Gregory's Hornbook on the Law of Agency and Partnership, 625 pages, 1979, with 1981 pocket part (Text)

Seavey, Reuschlein and Hall's Cases on Agency and Partnership, 599 pages, 1962 (Casebook)

Selected Corporation and Partnership Statutes and Forms, 556 pages, 1982

Steffen and Kerr's Cases and Materials on Agency-Partnership, 4th Ed., 859 pages, 1980 (Casebook)

Steffen's Agency-Partnership in a Nutshell, 364 pages, 1977 (Text)

AMERICAN INDIAN LAW

Canby's American Indian Law in a Nutshell, 288 pages, 1981 (Text)

Getches, Rosenfelt and Wilkinson's Cases on Federal Indian Law, 660 pages, 1979, with 1983 Supplement (Casebook)

ANTITRUST LAW

Gellhorn's Antitrust Law and Economics in a Nutshell, 2nd Ed., 425 pages, 1981 (Text)

Gifford and Raskind's Cases and Materials on Antitrust, 694 pages, 1983 (Casebook)

Hovenkamp's Economics and Federal Antitrust Law, Student Ed., approximately 375 pages, 1985 (Text)

Oppenheim, Weston and McCarthy's Cases and Comments on Federal Antitrust Laws, 4th Ed., 1168 pages, 1981 (Casebook)

Posner and Easterbrook's Cases and Economic Notes on Antitrust, 2nd Ed., 1077 pages, 1981, with 1984–85 Supplement (Casebook)

LAW SCHOOL PUBLICATIONS—Continued

ANTITRUST LAW—Continued

Sullivan's Hornbook of the Law of Antitrust, 886 pages, 1977 (Text)

See also Regulated Industries, Trade Regulation

ART LAW

DuBoff's Art Law in a Nutshell, 335 pages, 1984 (Text)

BANKING LAW

Lovett's Banking and Financial Institutions in a Nutshell, 409 pages, 1984 (Text)

Symons and White's Teaching Materials on Banking Law, 2nd Ed., approximately 943 pages, 1984 (Casebook)

BUSINESS PLANNING

Epstein and Scheinfeld's Teaching Materials on Business Reorganization Under the Bankruptcy Code, 216 pages, 1980 (Casebook)

Painter's Problems and Materials in Business Planning, 2nd Ed., 1008 pages, 1984 (Casebook)

Selected Securities and Business Planning Statutes, Rules and Forms, 485 pages, 1982

CIVIL PROCEDURE

Casad's Res Judicata in a Nutshell, 310 pages, 1976 (text)

Cound, Friedenthal and Miller's Cases and Materials on Civil Procedure, 3rd Ed., 1147 pages, 1980 with 1984 Supplement (Casebook)

Ehrenzweig, Louisell and Hazard's Jurisdiction in a Nutshell, 4th Ed., 232 pages, 1980 (Text)

Federal Rules of Civil-Appellate-Criminal Procedure—West Law School Edition, approximately 477 pages, 1984

Hodges, Jones and Elliott's Cases and Materials on Texas Trial and Appellate Procedure, 2nd Ed., 745 pages, 1974 (Casebook)

Hodges, Jones and Elliott's Cases and Materials on the Judicial Process Prior to Trial in Texas, 2nd Ed., 871 pages, 1977 (Casebook)

Kane's Civil Procedure in a Nutshell, 271 pages, 1979 (Text)

Karlen's Procedure Before Trial in a Nutshell, 258 pages, 1972 (Text)

Karlen, Meisenholder, Stevens and Vestal's Cases on Civil Procedure, 923 pages, 1975 (Casebook)

Koffler and Reppy's Hornbook on Common Law Pleading, 663 pages, 1969 (Text)

Park's Computer-Aided Exercises on Civil Procedure, 2nd Ed., 167 pages, 1983 (Coursebook)

CIVIL PROCEDURE—Continued

Siegel's Hornbook on New York Practice, 1011 pages, 1978 with 1981–82 Pocket Part (Text)

See also Federal Jurisdiction and Procedure

CIVIL RIGHTS

Abernathy's Cases and Materials on Civil Rights, 660 pages, 1980 (Casebook)

Cohen's Cases on the Law of Deprivation of Liberty: A Study in Social Control, 755 pages, 1980 (Casebook)

Lockhart, Kamisar and Choper's Cases on Constitutional Rights and Liberties, 5th Ed., 1298 pages plus Appendix, 1981, with 1984 Supplement (Casebook)—reprint from Lockhart, et al. Cases on Constitutional Law, 5th Ed., 1980

Vieira's Civil Rights in a Nutshell, 279 pages, 1978 (Text)

COMMERCIAL LAW

Bailey's Secured Transactions in a Nutshell, 2nd Ed., 391 pages, 1981 (Text)

Epstein and Martin's Basic Uniform Commercial Code Teaching Materials, 2nd Ed., 667 pages, 1983 (Casebook)

Henson's Hornbook on Secured Transactions Under the U.C.C., 2nd Ed., 504 pages, 1979 with 1979 P.P. (Text)

Murray's Commercial Law, Problems and Materials, 366 pages, 1975 (Coursebook)

Nordstrom and Clovis' Problems and Materials on Commercial Paper, 458 pages, 1972 (Casebook)

Nordstrom and Lattin's Problems and Materials on Sales and Secured Transactions, 809 pages, 1968 (Casebook)

Nordstrom, Murray and Clovis' Problems and Materials on Sales, 515 pages, 1982 (Casebook)

Nordstrom's Hornbook on Sales, 600 pages, 1970 (Text)

Selected Commercial Statutes, 1379 pages, 1983

Speidel, Summers and White's Teaching Materials on Commercial and Consumer Law, 3rd Ed., 1490 pages, 1981 (Casebook)

Stockton's Sales in a Nutshell, 2nd Ed., 370 pages, 1981 (Text)

Stone's Uniform Commercial Code in a Nutshell, 2nd Ed., approximately 500 pages, 1984 (Text)

Uniform Commercial Code, Official Text with Comments, 994 pages, 1978

UCC Article 9, Reprint from 1962 Code, 128 pages, 1976

UCC Article 9, 1972 Amendments, 304 pages, 1978

Weber and Speidel's Commercial Paper in a Nutshell, 3rd Ed., 404 pages, 1982 (Text)

LAW SCHOOL PUBLICATIONS—Continued

COMMERCIAL LAW—Continued

White and Summers' Hornbook on the Uniform Commercial Code, 2nd Ed., 1250 pages, 1980 (Text)

COMMUNITY PROPERTY

Mennell's Community Property in a Nutshell, 447 pages, 1982 (Text)

Verrall and Bird's Cases and Materials on California Community Property, 4th Ed., 549 pages, 1983 (Casebook)

COMPARATIVE LAW

Barton, Gibbs, Li and Merryman's Law in Radically Different Cultures, 960 pages, 1983 (Casebook)

Glendon, Gordon, and Osakwe's Comparative Legal Traditions in a Nutshell, 402 pages, 1982 (Text)

Langbein's Comparative Criminal Procedure: Germany, 172 pages, 1977 (Casebook)

COMPUTERS AND LAW

Mason's An Introduction to the Use of Computers in Law, 223 pages, 1984 (Text)

CONFLICT OF LAWS

Cramton, Currie and Kay's Cases-Comments-Questions on Conflict of Laws, 3rd Ed., 1026 pages, 1981 (Casebook)

Scoles and Hay's Hornbook on Conflict of Laws, Student Ed., 1085 pages, 1982 (Text)

Scoles and Weintraub's Cases and Materials on Conflict of Laws, 2nd Ed., 966 pages, 1972, with 1978 Supplement (Casebook)

Siegel's Conflicts in a Nutshell, 469 pages, 1982 (Text)

CONSTITUTIONAL LAW

Engdahl's Constitutional Power in a Nutshell: Federal and State, 411 pages, 1974 (Text)

Lockhart, Kamisar and Choper's Cases-Comments-Questions on Constitutional Law, 5th Ed., 1705 pages plus Appendix, 1980, with 1984 Supplement (Casebook)

Lockhart, Kamisar and Choper's Cases-Comments-Questions on the American Constitution, 5th Ed., 1185 pages plus Appendix, 1981, with 1984 Supplement (Casebook)—reprint from Lockhart, et al. Cases on Constitutional Law, 5th Ed., 1980

Manning's The Law of Church-State Relations in a Nutshell, 305 pages, 1981 (Text)

Miller's Presidential Power in a Nutshell, 328 pages, 1977 (Text)

CONSTITUTIONAL LAW—Continued

Nowak, Rotunda and Young's Hornbook on Constitutional Law, 2nd Ed., Student Ed., 1172 pages, 1983 (Text)

Rotunda's Modern Constitutional Law: Cases and Notes, 1034 pages, 1981, with 1984 Supplement (Casebook)

Williams' Constitutional Analysis in a Nutshell, 388 pages, 1979 (Text)

See also Civil Rights

CONSUMER LAW

Epstein and Nickles' Consumer Law in a Nutshell, 2nd Ed., 418 pages, 1981 (Text)

McCall's Consumer Protection, Cases, Notes and Materials, 594 pages, 1977, with 1977 Statutory Supplement (Casebook)

Selected Commercial Statutes, 1379 pages, 1983

Spanogle and Rohner's Cases and Materials on Consumer Law, 693 pages, 1979, with 1982 Supplement (Casebook)

See also Commercial Law

CONTRACTS

Calamari & Perillo's Cases and Problems on Contracts, 1061 pages, 1978 (Casebook)

Calamari and Perillo's Hornbook on Contracts, 2nd Ed., 878 pages, 1977 (Text)

Corbin's Text on Contracts, One Volume Student Edition, 1224 pages, 1952 (Text)

Fessler and Loiseaux's Cases and Materials on Contracts, 837 pages, 1982 (Casebook)

Freedman's Cases and Materials on Contracts, 658 pages, 1973 (Casebook)

Friedman's Contract Remedies in a Nutshell, 323 pages, 1981 (Text)

Fuller and Eisenberg's Cases on Basic Contract Law, 4th Ed., 1203 pages, 1981 (Casebook)

Hamilton, Rau and Weintraub's Cases and Materials on Contracts, 830 pages, 1984 (Casebook)

Jackson and Bollinger's Cases on Contract Law in Modern Society, 2nd Ed., 1329 pages, 1980 (Casebook)

Keyes' Government Contracts in a Nutshell, 423 pages, 1979 (Text)

Reitz's Cases on Contracts as Basic Commercial Law, 763 pages, 1975 (Casebook)

Schaber and Rohwer's Contracts in a Nutshell, 2nd Ed., 425 pages, 1984 (Text)

COPYRIGHT

See Patent and Copyright Law

CORPORATIONS

Hamilton's Cases on Corporations—Including Partnerships and Limited Partnerships, 2nd Ed., 1108 pages, 1981, with 1981 Statutory Supplement and 1984 Supplement (Casebook)

LAW SCHOOL PUBLICATIONS—Continued

CORPORATIONS—Continued

Hamilton's Law of Corporations in a Nutshell, 379 pages, 1980 (Text)

Henn's Cases on Corporations, 1279 pages, 1974, with 1980 Supplement (Casebook)

Henn and Alexander's Hornbook on Corporations, 3rd Ed., Student Ed., 1371 pages, 1983 (Text)

Jennings and Buxbaum's Cases and Materials on Corporations, 5th Ed., 1180 pages, 1979 (Casebook)

Selected Corporation and Partnership Statutes, Regulations and Forms, 556 pages, 1982

Solomon, Stevenson and Schwartz' Materials and Problems on the Law and Policies on Corporations, 1172 pages, 1982 with 1984 Supplement (Casebook)

CORPORATE FINANCE

Hamilton's Cases and Materials on Corporate Finance, 895 pages, 1984 (Casebook)

CORRECTIONS

Krantz's Cases and Materials on the Law of Corrections and Prisoners' Rights, 2nd Ed., 735 pages, 1981, with 1982 Supplement (Casebook)

Krantz's Law of Corrections and Prisoners' Rights in a Nutshell, 2nd Ed., 384 pages, 1983 (Text)

Popper's Post-Conviction Remedies in a Nutshell, 360 pages, 1978 (Text)

Robbins' Cases and Materials on Post Conviction Remedies, 506 pages, 1982 (Casebook)

Rubin's Law of Criminal Corrections, 2nd Ed., 873 pages, 1973, with 1978 Supplement (Text)

CREDITOR'S RIGHTS

Bankruptcy Code and Rules, Law School Ed., 438 pages, 1984

Epstein's Debtor-Creditor Law in a Nutshell, 2nd Ed., 324 pages, 1980 (Text)

Epstein and Landers' Debtors and Creditors: Cases and Materials, 2nd Ed., 689 pages, 1982 (Casebook)

Epstein and Sheinfeld's Teaching Materials on Business Reorganization Under the Bankruptcy Code, 216 pages, 1980 (Casebook)

Riesenfeld's Cases and Materials on Creditors' Remedies and Debtors' Protection, 3rd Ed., 810 pages, 1979 with 1979 Statutory Supplement and 1981 Case Supplement (Casebook)

CRIMINAL LAW AND CRIMINAL PROCEDURE

Cohen and Gobert's Problems in Criminal Law, 297 pages, 1976 (Problem book)

CRIMINAL LAW AND CRIMINAL PROCEDURE—Continued

Davis' Police Discretion, 176 pages, 1975 (Text)

Dix and Sharlot's Cases and Materials on Criminal Law, 2nd Ed., 771 pages, 1979 (Casebook)

Federal Rules of Civil-Appellate-Criminal Procedure—West Law School Edition, approximately 477 pages, 1984

Grano's Problems in Criminal Procedure, 2nd Ed., 176 pages, 1981 (Problem book)

Israel and LaFave's Criminal Procedure in a Nutshell, 3rd Ed., 438 pages, 1980 (Text)

Johnson's Cases, Materials and Text on Substantive Criminal Law in its Procedural Context, 2nd Ed., 956 pages, 1980 (Casebook)

Kamisar, LaFave and Israel's Cases, Comments and Questions on Modern Criminal Procedure, 5th ed., 1635 pages plus Appendix, 1980 with 1984 Supplement (Casebook)

Kamisar, LaFave and Israel's Cases, Comments and Questions on Basic Criminal Procedure, 5th Ed., 869 pages, 1980 with 1984 Supplement (Casebook)—reprint from Kamisar, et al. Modern Criminal Procedure, 5th ed., 1980

LaFave's Modern Criminal Law: Cases, Comments and Questions, 789 pages, 1978 (Casebook)

LaFave and Israel's Hornbook on Criminal Procedure, Student Ed., approximately 1300 pages, 1985 (Text)

LaFave and Scott's Hornbook on Criminal Law, 763 pages, 1972 (Text)

Langbein's Comparative Criminal Procedure: Germany, 172 pages, 1977 (Casebook)

Loewy's Criminal Law in a Nutshell, 302 pages, 1975 (Text)

Saltzburg's American Criminal Procedure, Cases and Commentary, 2nd Ed., 1193 pages, 1984 with 1984 Supplement (Casebook)

Uviller's The Processes of Criminal Justice: Investigation and Adjudication, 2nd Ed., 1384 pages, 1979 with 1979 Statutory Supplement and 1983 Update (Casebook)

Uviller's The Processes of Criminal Justice: Adjudication, 2nd Ed., 730 pages, 1979. Soft-cover reprint from Uviller's The Processes of Criminal Justice: Investigation and Adjudication, 2nd Ed. (Casebook)

Uviller's The Processes of Criminal Justice: Investigation, 2nd Ed., 655 pages, 1979. Soft-cover reprint from Uviller's The Processes of Criminal Justice: Investigation and Adjudication, 2nd Ed. (Casebook)

LAW SCHOOL PUBLICATIONS—Continued

CRIMINAL LAW AND CRIMINAL PROCEDURE—Continued

Vorenberg's Cases on Criminal Law and Procedure, 2nd Ed., 1088 pages, 1981 (Casebook)

See also Corrections, Juvenile Justice

DECEDENTS ESTATES

See Trusts and Estates

DOMESTIC RELATIONS

Clark's Cases and Problems on Domestic Relations, 3rd Ed., 1153 pages, 1980 (Casebook)

Clark's Hornbook on Domestic Relations, 754 pages, 1968 (Text)

Krause's Cases and Materials on Family Law, 2nd Ed., 1221 pages, 1983 (Casebook)

Krause's Family Law in a Nutshell, 400 pages, 1977 (Text)

Krauskopf's Cases on Property Division at Marriage Dissolution, 250 pages, 1984 (Casebook)

ECONOMICS, LAW AND

Goetz' Cases and Materials on Law and Economics, 547 pages, 1984 (Casebook)

Manne's The Economics of Legal Relationships—Readings in the Theory of Property Rights, 660 pages, 1975 (Text)

See also Antitrust, Regulated Industries

EDUCATION LAW

Alexander and Alexander's The Law of Schools, Students and Teachers in a Nutshell, 409 pages, 1984 (Text)   .

Morris' The Constitution and American Education, 2nd Ed., 992 pages, 1980 (Casebook)

EMPLOYMENT DISCRIMINATION

Player's Cases and Materials on Employment Discrimination Law, 2nd Ed., 782 pages, 1984 (Casebook)

Player's Federal Law of Employment Discrimination in a Nutshell, 2nd Ed., 402 pages, 1981 (Text)

See also Women and the Law

ENERGY AND NATURAL RESOURCES LAW

Rodgers' Cases and Materials on Energy and Natural Resources Law, 2nd Ed., 877 pages, 1983 (Casebook)

Selected Environmental Law Statutes, 758 pages, 1984

Tomain's Energy Law in a Nutshell, 338 pages, 1981 (Text)

See also Environmental Law, Oil and Gas, Water Law

ENVIRONMENTAL LAW

Bonine and McGarity's Cases and Materials on the Law of Environment and Pollution, 1076 pages, 1984 (Casebook)

Findley and Farber's Cases and Materials on Environmental Law, 738 pages, 1981, with 1983 Supplement (Casebook)

Findley and Farber's Environmental Law in a Nutshell, 343 pages, 1983 (Text)

Rodgers' Hornbook on Environmental Law, 956 pages, 1977 (Text)

Selected Environmental Law Statutes, 758 pages, 1984

See also Energy and Natural Resources Law, Water Law

EQUITY

See Remedies

ESTATES

See Trusts and Estates

ESTATE PLANNING

Kurtz' Cases, Materials and Problems on Family Estate Planning, 853 pages, 1983 (Casebook)

Lynn's Introduction to Estate Planning, in a Nutshell, 3rd Ed., 370 pages, 1983 (Text)

See also Taxation

EVIDENCE

Broun and Meisenholder's Problems in Evidence, 2nd Ed., 304 pages, 1981 (Problem book)

Cleary and Strong's Cases, Materials and Problems on Evidence, 3rd Ed., 1143 pages, 1981 (Casebook)

Federal Rules of Evidence for United States Courts and Magistrates, approximately 325 pages, 1984

Graham's Federal Rules of Evidence in a Nutshell, 429 pages, 1981 (Text)

Kimball's Programmed Materials on Problems in Evidence, 380 pages, 1978 (Problem book)

Lempert and Saltzburg's A Modern Approach to Evidence: Text, Problems, Transcripts and Cases, 2nd Ed., 1296 pages, 1983 (Casebook)

Lilly's Introduction to the Law of Evidence, 486 pages, 1978 (Text)

McCormick, Elliott and Sutton's Cases and Materials on Evidence, 5th Ed., 1212 pages, 1981 (Casebook)

McCormick's Hornbook on Evidence, 3rd Ed., Student Ed., 1155 pages, 1984 (Text)

Rothstein's Evidence, State and Federal Rules in a Nutshell, 2nd Ed., 514 pages, 1981 (Text)

LAW SCHOOL PUBLICATIONS—Continued

EVIDENCE—Continued

Saltzburg's Evidence Supplement: Rules, Statutes, Commentary, 245 pages, 1980 (Casebook Supplement)

FEDERAL JURISDICTION AND PROCEDURE

Currie's Cases and Materials on Federal Courts, 3rd Ed., 1042 pages, 1982 (Casebook)

Currie's Federal Jurisdiction in a Nutshell, 2nd Ed., 258 pages, 1981 (Text)

Federal Rules of Civil-Appellate-Criminal Procedure—West Law School Edition, approximately 477 pages, 1984

Forrester and Moye's Cases and Materials on Federal Jurisdiction and Procedure, 3rd Ed., 917 pages, 1977 with 1981 Supplement (Casebook)

Redish's Cases, Comments and Questions on Federal Courts, 878 pages, 1983 (Casebook)

Vetri and Merrill's Federal Courts, Problems and Materials, 2nd Ed., 232 pages, 1984

Wright's Hornbook on Federal Courts, 4th Ed., Student Ed., 870 pages, 1983 (Text)

FUTURE INTERESTS

See Trusts and Estates

IMMIGRATION LAW

Weissbrodt's Immigration Law and Procedure in a Nutshell, 345 pages, 1984 (Text)

INDIAN LAW

See American Indian Law

INSURANCE

Dobbyn's Insurance Law in a Nutshell, 281 pages, 1981 (Text)

Keeton's Cases on Basic Insurance Law, 2nd Ed., 1086 pages, 1977

Keeton's Basic Text on Insurance Law, 712 pages, 1971 (Text)

Keeton's Case Supplement to Keeton's Basic Text on Insurance Law, 334 pages, 1978 (Casebook)

Keeton's Programmed Problems in Insurance Law, 243 pages, 1972 (Text Supplement)

York and Whelan's Cases, Materials and Problems on Insurance Law, 715 pages, 1982 (Casebook)

INTERNATIONAL LAW

Henkin, Pugh, Schachter and Smit's Cases and Materials on International Law, 2nd Ed., 1152 pages, 1980, with Documents Supplement (Casebook)

INTERNATIONAL LAW—Continued

Jackson's Legal Problems of International Economic Relations, 1097 pages, 1977, with Documents Supplement (Casebook)

Kirgis' International Organizations in Their Legal Setting, 1016 pages, 1977, with 1981 Supplement (Casebook)

Weston, Falk and D'Amato's International Law and World Order—A Problem Oriented Coursebook, 1195 pages, 1980, with Documents Supplement (Casebook)

Wilson's International Business Transactions in a Nutshell, 2nd Ed., 476 pages, 1984 (Text)

INTERVIEWING AND COUNSELING

Binder and Price's Interviewing and Counseling, 232 pages, 1977 (Text)

Shaffer's Interviewing and Counseling in a Nutshell, 353 pages, 1976 (Text)

INTRODUCTION TO LAW

Dobbyn's So You Want to go to Law School, Revised First Edition, 206 pages, 1976 (Text)

Hegland's Introduction to the Study and Practice of Law in a Nutshell, 418 pages, 1983 (Text)

Kinyon's Introduction to Law Study and Law Examinations in a Nutshell, 389 pages, 1971 (Text)

See also Legal Method and Legal System

JUDICIAL ADMINISTRATION

Carrington, Meador and Rosenberg's Justice on Appeal, 263 pages, 1976 (Casebook)

Nelson's Cases and Materials on Judicial Administration and the Administration of Justice, 1032 pages, 1974 (Casebook)

JURISPRUDENCE

Christie's Text and Readings on Jurisprudence—The Philosophy of Law, 1056 pages, 1973 (Casebook)

JUVENILE JUSTICE

Fox's Cases and Materials on Modern Juvenile Justice, 2nd Ed., 960 pages, 1981 (Casebook)

Fox's Juvenile Courts in a Nutshell, 3rd Ed., 291 pages, 1984 (Text)

LABOR LAW

Gorman's Basic Text on Labor Law—Unionization and Collective Bargaining, 914 pages, 1976 (Text)

Leslie's Labor Law in a Nutshell, 403 pages, 1979 (Text)

Nolan's Labor Arbitration Law and Practice in a Nutshell, 358 pages, 1979 (Text)

LAW SCHOOL PUBLICATIONS—Continued

LABOR LAW—Continued

Oberer, Hanslowe and Andersen's Cases and Materials on Labor Law—Collective Bargaining in a Free Society, 2nd Ed., 1168 pages, 1979, with 1979 Statutory Supplement and 1982 Case Supplement (Casebook)

See also Employment Discrimination, Social Legislation

LAND FINANCE

See Real Estate Transactions

LAND USE

Hagman's Cases on Public Planning and Control of Urban and Land Development, 2nd Ed., 1301 pages, 1980 (Casebook)

Hagman's Hornbook on Urban Planning and Land Development Control Law, 706 pages, 1971 (Text)

Wright and Gitelman's Cases and Materials on Land Use, 3rd Ed., 1300 pages, 1982 (Casebook)

Wright and Webber's Land Use in a Nutshell, 316 pages, 1978 (Text)

LEGAL HISTORY

Presser and Zainaldin's Cases on Law and American History, 855 pages, 1980 (Casebook)

See also Legal Method and Legal System

LEGAL METHOD AND LEGAL SYSTEM

Aldisert's Readings, Materials and Cases in the Judicial Process, 948 pages, 1976 (Casebook)

Bodenheimer, Oakley and Love's Readings and Cases on an Introduction to the Anglo-American Legal System, 161 pages, 1980 (Casebook)

Davies and Lawry's Institutions and Methods of the Law—Introductory Teaching Materials, 547 pages, 1982 (Casebook)

Dvorkin, Himmelstein and Lesnick's Becoming a Lawyer: A Humanistic Perspective on Legal Education and Professionalism, 211 pages, 1981 (Text)

Fryer and Orentlicher's Cases and Materials on Legal Method and Legal System, 1043 pages, 1967 (Casebook)

Greenberg's Judicial Process and Social Change, 666 pages, 1977 (Coursebook)

Kelso and Kelso's Studying Law: An Introduction, 587 pages, 1984 (Coursebook)

Kempin's Historical Introduction to Anglo-American Law in a Nutshell, 2nd Ed., 280 pages, 1973 (Text)

Kimball's Historical Introduction to the Legal System, 610 pages, 1966 (Casebook)

Mashaw and Merrill's Introduction to the American Public Law System, 1095 pages, 1975, with 1980 Supplement (Casebook)

LEGAL METHOD AND LEGAL SYSTEM—Continued

Murphy's Cases and Materials on Introduction to Law—Legal Process and Procedure, 772 pages, 1977 (Casebook)

Reynolds' Judicial Process in a Nutshell, 292 pages, 1980 (Text)

See also Legal Research and Writing

LEGAL PROFESSION

Aronson's Problems in Professional Responsibility, 280 pages, 1978 (Problem book)

Aronson and Weckstein's Professional Responsibility in a Nutshell, 399 pages, 1980 (Text)

Mellinkoff's The Conscience of a Lawyer, 304 pages, 1973 (Text)

Mellinkoff's Lawyers and the System of Justice, 983 pages, 1976 (Casebook)

Pirsig and Kirwin's Cases and Materials on Professional Responsibility, 4th Ed., approximately 650 pages, 1984 (Casebook)

Schwartz and Wydick's Problems in Legal Ethics, 285 pages, 1983 (Casebook)

Selected Statutes, Rules and Standards on the Legal Profession, approximately 260 pages, Revised 1984

Smith's Preventing Legal Malpractice, 142 pages, 1981 (Text)

LEGAL RESEARCH AND WRITING

Cohen's Legal Research in a Nutshell, 4th Ed., approximately 425 pages, 1984 (Text)

Cohen and Berring's How to Find the Law, 8th Ed., 790 pages, 1983. Problem book by Foster and Kelly available (Casebook)

Cohen and Berring's Finding the Law, 8th Ed., Abridged Ed., 556 pages, 1984 (Casebook)

Dickerson's Materials on Legal Drafting, 425 pages, 1981 (Casebook)

Felsenfeld and Siegel's Writing Contracts in Plain English, 290 pages, 1981 (Text)

Gopen's Writing From a Legal Perspective, 225 pages, 1981 (Text)

Mellinkoff's Legal Writing—Sense and Nonsense, 242 pages, 1982 (Text)

Rombauer's Legal Problem Solving—Analysis, Research and Writing, 4th Ed., 424 pages, 1983 (Coursebook)

Squires and Rombauer's Legal Writing in a Nutshell, 294 pages, 1982 (Text)

Statsky's Legal Research, Writing and Analysis, 2nd Ed., 167 pages, 1982 (Coursebook)

Statsky's Legislative Analysis: How to Use Statutes and Regulations, 2nd Ed., 217 pages, 1984 (Text)

Statsky and Wernet's Case Analysis and Fundamentals of Legal Writing, 2nd Ed., 441 pages, 1984 (Text)

LAW SCHOOL PUBLICATIONS—Continued

LEGAL RESEARCH AND WRITING—Continued

Teply's Programmed Materials on Legal Research and Citation, 334 pages, 1982. Student Library Exercises available (Coursebook)

Weihofen's Legal Writing Style, 2nd Ed., 332 pages, 1980 (Text)

LEGISLATION

Davies' Legislative Law and Process in a Nutshell, 279 pages, 1975 (Text)

Nutting and Dickerson's Cases and Materials on Legislation, 5th Ed., 744 pages, 1978 (Casebook)

Statsky's Legislative Analysis: How to Use Statutes and Regulations, 2nd Ed., 217 pages, 1984 (Text)

LOCAL GOVERNMENT

McCarthy's Local Government Law in a Nutshell, 2nd Ed., 404 pages, 1983 (Text)

Michelman and Sandalow's Cases-Comments-Questions on Government in Urban Areas, 1216 pages, 1970, with 1972 Supplement (Casebook)

Reynolds' Hornbook on Local Government Law, 860 pages, 1982 (Text)

Valente's Cases and Materials on Local Government Law, 2nd Ed., 980 pages, 1980 with 1982 Supplement (Casebook)

MASS COMMUNICATION LAW

Gillmor and Barron's Cases and Comment on Mass Communication Law, 4th Ed., 1076 pages, 1984 (Casebook)

Ginsburg's Regulation of Broadcasting: Law and Policy Towards Radio, Television and Cable Communications, 741 pages, 1979, with 1983 Supplement (Casebook)

Zuckman and Gayne's Mass Communications Law in a Nutshell, 2nd Ed., 473 pages, 1983 (Text)

MEDICINE, LAW AND

King's The Law of Medical Malpractice in a Nutshell, 340 pages, 1977 (Text)

Shapiro and Spece's Problems, Cases and Materials on Bioethics and Law, 892 pages, 1981 (Casebook)

Sharpe, Fiscina and Head's Cases on Law and Medicine, 882 pages, 1978 (Casebook)

MILITARY LAW

Shanor and Terrell's Military Law in a Nutshell, 378 pages, 1980 (Text)

MORTGAGES

See Real Estate Transactions

NATURAL RESOURCES LAW

See Energy and Natural Resources Law, Environmental Law, Oil and Gas, Water Law

NEGOTIATION

Edwards and White's Problems, Readings and Materials on the Lawyer as a Negotiator, 484 pages, 1977 (Casebook)

Williams' Legal Negotiation and Settlement, 207 pages, 1983 (Coursebook)

OFFICE PRACTICE

Hegland's Trial and Practice Skills in a Nutshell, 346 pages, 1978 (Text)

Strong and Clark's Law Office Management, 424 pages, 1974 (Casebook)

See also Computers and Law, Interviewing and Counseling, Negotiation

OIL AND GAS

Hemingway's Hornbook on Oil and Gas, 2nd Ed., Student Ed., 543 pages, 1983 (Text)

Huie, Woodward and Smith's Cases and Materials on Oil and Gas, 2nd Ed., 955 pages, 1972 (Casebook)

Lowe's Oil and Gas Law in a Nutshell, 443 pages, 1983 (Text)

See also Energy and Natural Resources Law

PARTNERSHIP

See Agency—Partnership

PATENT AND COPYRIGHT LAW

Choate and Francis' Cases and Materials on Patent Law, 2nd Ed., 1110 pages, 1981 (Casebook)

Miller and Davis' Intellectual Property—Patents, Trademarks and Copyright in a Nutshell, 428 pages, 1983 (Text)

Nimmer's Cases on Copyright and Other Aspects of Law Pertaining to Literary, Musical and Artistic Works, 2nd Ed., 1023 pages, 1979 (Casebook)

POVERTY LAW

Brudno's Poverty, Inequality, and the Law: Cases-Commentary-Analysis, 934 pages, 1976 (Casebook)

LaFrance, Schroeder, Bennett and Boyd's Hornbook on Law of the Poor, 558 pages, 1973 (Text)

See also Social Legislation

PRODUCTS LIABILITY

Noel and Phillips' Cases on Products Liability, 2nd Ed., 821 pages, 1982 (Casebook)

Noel and Phillips' Products Liability in a Nutshell, 2nd Ed., 341 pages, 1981 (Text)

PROPERTY

Aigler, Smith and Tefft's Cases on Property, 2 volumes, 1339 pages, 1960 (Casebook)

Bernhardt's Real Property in a Nutshell, 2nd Ed., 448 pages, 1981 (Text)

Boyer's Survey of the Law of Property, 766 pages, 1981 (Text)

LAW SCHOOL PUBLICATIONS—Continued

PROPERTY—Continued

Browder, Cunningham and Smith's Cases on Basic Property Law, 4th Ed., 1431 pages, 1984 (Casebook)

Bruce, Ely and Bostick's Cases and Materials on Modern Property Law, 1004 pages, 1984 (Casebook)

Burby's Hornbook on Real Property, 3rd Ed., 490 pages, 1965 (Text)

Burke's Personal Property in a Nutshell, 322 pages, 1983 (Text)

Chused's A Modern Approach to Property: Cases-Notes-Materials, 1069 pages, 1978 with 1980 Supplement (Casebook)

Cohen's Materials for a Basic Course in Property, 526 pages, 1978 (Casebook)

Cunningham, Whitman and Stoebuck's Hornbook on the Law of Property, Student Ed., 916 pages, 1984 (Text)

Donahue, Kauper and Martin's Cases on Property, 2nd Ed., 1362 pages, 1983 (Casebook)

Hill's Landlord and Tenant Law in a Nutshell, 319 pages, 1979 (Text)

Moynihan's Introduction to Real Property, 254 pages, 1962 (Text)

Phipps' Titles in a Nutshell, 277 pages, 1968 (Text)

Uniform Land Transactions Act, Uniform Simplification of Land Transfers Act, Uniform Condominium Act, 1977 Official Text with Comments, 462 pages, 1978

See also Real Estate Transactions, Land Use

REAL ESTATE TRANSACTIONS

Bruce's Real Estate Finance in a Nutshell, 2nd Ed., approximately 300 pages, 1985 (Text)

Maxwell, Riesenfeld, Hetland and Warren's Cases on California Security Transactions in Land, 3rd Ed., 728 pages, 1984 (Casebook)

Nelson and Whitman's Cases on Real Estate Transfer, Finance and Development, 2nd Ed., 1114 pages, 1981, with 1983 Supplement (Casebook)

Osborne's Cases and Materials on Secured Transactions, 559 pages, 1967 (Casebook)

Osborne, Nelson and Whitman's Hornbook on Real Estate Finance Law, 3rd Ed., 885 pages, 1979 (Text)

REGULATED INDUSTRIES

Gellhorn and Pierce's Regulated Industries in a Nutshell, 394 pages, 1982 (Text)

Morgan's Cases and Materials on Economic Regulation of Business, 830 pages, 1976, with 1978 Supplement (Casebook)

REGULATED INDUSTRIES—Continued

Pozen's Financial Institutions: Cases, Materials and Problems on Investment Management, 844 pages, 1978 (Casebook)

See also Mass Communication Law, Banking Law

REMEDIES

Dobbs' Hornbook on Remedies, 1067 pages, 1973 (Text)

Dobbs' Problems in Remedies, 137 pages, 1974 (Problem book)

Dobbyn's Injunctions in a Nutshell, 264 pages, 1974 (Text)

Friedman's Contract Remedies in a Nutshell, 323 pages, 1981 (Text)

Leavell, Love and Nelson's Cases and Materials on Equitable Remedies and Restitution, 3rd Ed., 704 pages, 1980 (Casebook)

McCormick's Hornbook on Damages, 811 pages, 1935 (Text)

O'Connell's Remedies in a Nutshell, 2nd Ed., approximately 330 pages, 1984 (Text)

York and Bauman's Cases and Materials on Remedies, 4th Ed., approximately 1200 pages, 1985 (Casebook)

REVIEW MATERIALS

Ballantine's Problems

Black Letter Series

Smith's Review Series

West's Review Covering Multistate Subjects

SECURITIES REGULATION

Hazen's Hornbook on The Law of Securities Regulation, approximately 520 pages, 1984 (Text)

Ratner's Securities Regulation: Materials for a Basic Course, 2nd Ed., 1050 pages, 1980 with 1982 Supplement (Casebook)

Ratner's Securities Regulation in a Nutshell, 2nd Ed., 322 pages, 1982 (Text)

Selected Securities and Business Planning Statutes, Rules and Forms, 485 pages, 1982

SOCIAL LEGISLATION

Hood and Hardy's Workers' Compensation and Employee Protection Laws in a Nutshell, 274 pages, 1984 (Text)

LaFrance's Welfare Law: Structure and Entitlement in a Nutshell, 455 pages, 1979 (Text)

Malone, Plant and Little's Cases on Workers' Compensation and Employment Rights, 2nd Ed., 951 pages, 1980 (Casebook)

See also Poverty Law

TAXATION

Dodge's Federal Taxation of Estates, Trusts and Gifts: Principles and Planning, 771 pages, 1981 with 1982 Supplement (Casebook)

LAW SCHOOL PUBLICATIONS—Continued

TAXATION—Continued

Garbis and Struntz' Cases and Materials on Tax Procedure and Tax Fraud, 829 pages, 1982 with 1984 Supplement (Casebook)

Gunn's Cases and Materials on Federal Income Taxation of Individuals, 785 pages, 1981 with 1983 Supplement (Casebook)

Hellerstein and Hellerstein's Cases on State and Local Taxation, 4th Ed., 1041 pages, 1978 with 1982 Supplement (Casebook)

Kahn's Handbook on Basic Corporate Taxation, 3rd Ed., Student Ed., 614 pages, 1981 with 1983 Supplement (Text)

Kahn and Gann's Corporate Taxation and Taxation of Partnerships and Partners, 2nd Ed., approximately 1300 pages, 1984 (Casebook)

Kragen and McNulty's Cases and Materials on Federal Income Taxation, Vol. I: Taxation of Individuals, 3rd Ed., 1283 pages, 1979 with 1983 Supplement (Casebook)

Kragen and McNulty's Cases and Materials on Federal Income Taxation, Vol. II: Taxation of Corporations, Shareholders, Partnerships and Partners, 3rd Ed., 989 pages, 1981 with 1983 Supplement (Casebook)

McNulty's Federal Estate and Gift Taxation in a Nutshell, 3rd Ed., 509 pages, 1983 (Text)

McNulty's Federal Income Taxation of Individuals in a Nutshell, 3rd Ed., 487 pages, 1983 (Text)

Posin's Hornbook on Federal Income Taxation of Individuals, Student Ed., 491 pages, 1983 (Text)

Rice and Solomon's Problems and Materials in Federal Income Taxation, 3rd Ed., 670 pages, 1979 (Casebook)

Rose and Raskind's Advanced Federal Income Taxation: Corporate Transactions—Cases, Materials and Problems, 955 pages, 1978 (Casebook)

Selected Federal Taxation Statutes and Regulations, 1255 pages, 1983

Sobeloff and Weidenbruch's Federal Income Taxation of Corporations and Stockholders in a Nutshell, 362 pages, 1981 (Text)

TORTS

Christie's Cases and Materials on the Law of Torts, 1264 pages, 1983 (Casebook)

Green, Pedrick, Rahl, Thode, Hawkins, Smith and Treece's Cases and Materials on Torts, 2nd Ed., 1360 pages, 1977 (Casebook)

Green, Pedrick, Rahl, Thode, Hawkins, Smith, and Treece's Advanced Torts: Injuries to Business, Political and Family Interests, 2nd Ed., 544 pages, 1977 (Casebook)—reprint from Green, et al. Cases and Materials on Torts, 2nd Ed., 1977

TORTS—Continued

Keeton, Keeton, Sargentich and Steiner's Cases and Materials on Torts, and Accident Law, 1360 pages, 1983 (Casebook)

Kionka's Torts in a Nutshell: Injuries to Persons and Property, 434 pages, 1977 (Text)

Malone's Torts in a Nutshell: Injuries to Family, Social and Trade Relations, 358 pages, 1979 (Text)

Prosser and Keeton's Hornbook on Torts, 5th Ed., Student Ed., 1286 pages, 1984 (Text)

Shapo's Cases on Tort and Compensation Law, 1244 pages, 1976 (Casebook)

See also Products Liability

TRADE REGULATION

McManis' Unfair Trade Practices in a Nutshell, 444 pages, 1982 (Text)

Oppenheim, Weston, Maggs and Schechter's Cases and Materials on Unfair Trade Practices and Consumer Protection, 4th Ed., 1038 pages, 1983 (Casebook)

See also Antitrust, Regulated Industries

TRIAL AND APPELLATE ADVOCACY

Appellate Advocacy, Handbook of, 249 pages, 1980 (Text)

Bergman's Trial Advocacy in a Nutshell, 402 pages, 1979 (Text)

Binder and Bergman's Fact Investigation: From Hypothesis to Proof, 354 pages, 1984 (Coursebook)

Goldberg's The First Trial (Where Do I Sit?, What Do I Say?) in a Nutshell, 396 pages, 1982 (Text)

Hegland's Trial and Practice Skills in a Nutshell, 346 pages, 1978 (Text)

Hornstein's Appellate Advocacy in a Nutshell, 325 pages, 1984 (Text)

Jeans' Handbook on Trial Advocacy, Student Ed., 473 pages, 1975 (Text)

McElhaney's Effective Litigation, 457 pages, 1974 (Casebook)

Nolan's Cases and Materials on Trial Practice, 518 pages, 1981 (Casebook)

Parnell and Shellhaas' Cases, Exercises and Problems for Trial Advocacy, 171 pages, 1982 (Coursebook)

Sonsteng, Haydock and Boyd's The Trialbook: A Total System for Preparation and Presentation of a Case, Student Ed., approximately 400 pages, 1984 (Coursebook)

TRUSTS AND ESTATES

Atkinson's Hornbook on Wills, 2nd Ed., 975 pages, 1953 (Text)

Averill's Uniform Probate Code in a Nutshell, 425 pages, 1978 (Text)

Bogert's Hornbook on Trusts, 5th Ed., 726 pages, 1973 (Text)

Clark, Lusky and Murphy's Cases and Materials on Gratuitous Transfers, 2nd Ed., 1102 pages, 1977 (Casebook)

LAW SCHOOL PUBLICATIONS—Continued

TRUSTS AND ESTATES—Continued

Gulliver's Cases and Materials on Future Interests, 624 pages, 1959 (Casebook)

Gulliver's Introduction to the Law of Future Interests, 87 pages, 1959 (Casebook)—reprint from Gulliver's Cases and Materials on Future Interests, 1959

McGovern's Cases and Materials on Wills, Trusts and Future Interests: An Introduction to Estate Planning, 750 pages, 1983 (Casebook)

Mennell's Cases and Materials on California Decedent's Estates, 566 pages, 1973 (Casebook)

Mennell's Wills and Trusts in a Nutshell, 392 pages, 1979 (Text)

Powell's The Law of Future Interests in California, 91 pages, 1980 (Text)

Simes' Hornbook on Future Interests, 2nd Ed., 355 pages, 1966 (Text)

Turrentine's Cases and Text on Wills and Administration, 2nd Ed., 483 pages, 1962 (Casebook)

Uniform Probate Code, 5th Ed., Official Text With Comments, 384 pages, 1977

Waggoner's Future Interests in a Nutshell, 361 pages, 1981 (Text)

WATER LAW

Getches' Water Law in a Nutshell, 439 pages, 1984 (Text)

Trelease's Cases and Materials on Water Law, 3rd Ed., 833 pages, 1979, with 1984 Supplement (Casebook)

See also Energy and Natural Resources Law, Environmental Law

WILLS

See Trusts and Estates

WOMEN AND THE LAW

Kay's Text, Cases and Materials on Sex-Based Discrimination, 2nd Ed., 1045 pages, 1981, with 1983 Supplement (Casebook)

Thomas' Sex Discrimination in a Nutshell, 399 pages, 1982 (Text)

See also Employment Discrimination

WORKERS' COMPENSATION

See Social Legislation

THE LAW OF
FEDERAL COURTS

By

CHARLES ALAN WRIGHT

William B. Bates Chair for the Administration of Justice
The University of Texas

FOURTH EDITION

HORNBOOK SERIES

STUDENT EDITION

ST. PAUL, MINN.
WEST PUBLISHING CO.
1983

COPYRIGHT © 1963, 1970, 1976 By WEST PUBLISHING CO.

COPYRIGHT © 1983 By WEST PUBLISHING CO.
50 West Kellogg Boulevard
P.O. Box 3526
St. Paul, Minnesota 55165

Library of Congress Cataloging in Publication Data

Wright, Charles Alan.
Handbook of the law of federal courts.

(Hornbook series, Student Edition)
Includes index.
1. Jurisdiction—United States. 2. Procedure (Law)—
United States. I. Title. II. Series.
KF8840.W7 1983   347.73'2   83–1189
                       347.3071

ISBN 0-314-71354-9

Wright Law Fed.Cts. 4th Ed. HB
1st Reprint—1984

PREFACE TO FOURTH EDITION

The law on the jurisdiction and procedure of the federal courts, and the complications that come from their relations to the courts of the states and from the frequent need for federal courts to look to state law, continues to be one of the most rapidly changing fields in American law. This book was originally published in 1963. New editions were necessary in 1970 and 1976 and it is clear that yet another edition is now required, in order to bring before the reader the more recent cases and commentary as well as the important changes that have been made by statutes and rules.

Indeed this Fourth Edition contains two entirely new sections that have no counterpart in earlier editions. Civil rights litigation had been increasingly discussed in the Second and Third Editions, in connection with how general doctrines apply to that particular class of cases, but it is now obvious that the explosive growth in civil rights cases has made this one of the most important branches of the work of the federal courts; a new section 22A has been added to bring together in one place highlights of the learning on that subject. In addition, crowded dockets have led to an increased interest in the use of claim and issue preclusion, or res judicata as it used to be called, to prevent repetitive litigation. The Supreme Court has spoken on preclusion in a number of recent cases, and it is a subject with particular complexities in a federal system. It is examined in section 100A.

As in the past, this book makes frequent references to the multivolume Treatise on Federal Practice and Procedure, which I have been writing in collaboration with Professors Arthur R. Miller, Edward H. Cooper, Kenneth W. Graham, and Mary Kay Kane. Those who wish more detail on matters discussed here will find it by going to the cited portions of the Treatise. The citations to the Treatise omit its full title, and show only volume number, the authors of the volume in question, the unit of the Treatise to which the citation is being made —Criminal, Civil, Jurisdiction, or Evidence—and then the particular reference within the volume. (A citation to Criminal 2d or Civil 2d is to one of the volumes of those units for which a Second Edition now is in print.) In addition, so many references are made in this book to the American Law Institute Study of Division of Jurisdiction between State and Federal Courts (Official Draft, 1969) that a short form of reference, "ALI Study," has been used.

The manuscript of this Fourth Edition went to the publisher in August, 1982, and in general the book covers only those decisions and other materials that were available to me prior to that date. It has been possible to incorporate, however, a few more recent matters of importance. In particular, the Act of January 12, 1983, amending Civil Rule 4 and making major changes in how process is served in federal civil actions, has been taken into account in sections 64 and 65.

One of my students, Donald J. Piller, read all of the manuscript for this edition, and pointed out many places where revision was needed if the book were to be understandable to law students. I am very grateful to him for that assistance.

In the Preface to the First Edition I suggested that the needs of law students are far different from those of lawyers and judges and said that this work was intended for students. It was and is. But I underestimated the extent to which all of us in the legal profession remain students throughout our lives, and it has been highly gratifying to me to see the extent to which courts and lawyers have found the earlier editions of the book useful.

The Preface to the First Edition is not retained in this edition simply as a monument to my own failure to appreciate the needs of lawyers and judges. A more important reason is to preserve what I said then about my dear friends and mentors, Charles E. Clark and Charles T. McCormick. The First Edition of this book was published in September, 1963. Before the end of that year both Judge Clark and Dean McCormick were dead. I miss them very much.

But now another person who was important both to me and this book is gone. My dear friend and colleague, Bernie Ward, died on May 7, 1982, at much too young an age. The important place he had in the minds and the hearts of all those who care about what he called "the Article III judges" is described in the memorial tributes to him at 61 Texas L.Rev. 1 (1982). As my own contribution to that collection shows, he had a very special place with me. I counted on him constantly to help me work my way through complicated problems, and his wisdom—always presented with his marvelous wit—had a marked impact on every edition of this book from the Second Edition on. He often twitted me over the fact that the book did not say enough about civil rights cases. See, for example, 61 Texas L.Rev. 43, 46. He was extremely pleased to hear that I had decided to include in this edition a new section on that subject, and it was a matter of great regret that by the time that section was written his health was such that I could not burden him by asking him to read the draft. His wide knowledge and keen insight would undoubtedly have greatly improved the section. It is a matter of even greater regret that he did not recover from that illness and will never see the finished work.

With gratitude and with love, this Fourth Edition is dedicated to the memory of Bernard J. Ward.

CHARLES ALAN WRIGHT

Austin, Texas
February, 1983

PREFACE TO FIRST EDITION

This book is intended to provide for law students a comprehensive textual discussion of the jurisdiction and procedure of the federal courts. I have been greatly aided in preparing the book by my recent reexamination of these subjects in the course of doing my revision of the Barron & Holtzoff Treatise. The availability of the Treatise has been helpful, too, since it has made it possible to confine case citations to the more important precedents, while referring the reader interested in exhaustive citation to the Treatise. This book, however, is not a mere abridgement of the Treatise. The needs, as I conceive them, of the law student are so far different from those of the lawyer and the judge, for whom the Treatise was written, that it has been necessary to write for the student an entirely new book. The Treatise endeavors to state accurately and completely what the law is. This book, written for a student audience, is more concerned with why the law is as it is, and whether existing doctrine works as satisfactorily as it should. Thus, though there are occasional passages where I have borrowed what I have already said in the Treatise, the great bulk of the book is freshly written and based on fresh research.

The organization of the book is generally similar to that of the casebooks on this subject by Forrester and Currier, and by McCormick, Chadbourn, and Wright, though the subject of procedure in the federal courts is given more attention here than in those casebooks, and is intended to be useful by students taking courses which emphasize federal procedure, or procedure in a state with rules modelled on the Federal Rules. Necessarily the discussion here is primarily about civil cases, though I have endeavored to suggest a few of the problems which arise in criminal cases, and to indicate that not all of the business of the federal courts is civil. Like everyone who has worked in this field in the last decade, I have been influenced by the great work of scholarship produced by Professors Hart and Wechsler. Their insistence that the problems of federal jurisdiction be considered in terms of their effect on our system of federalism, rather than as purely technical exercises, is especially congenial to one whose professional concerns are with the federal courts and with constitutional law, and I am hopeful that some of that emphasis appears in the pages which follow.

My debts are many. I have acquired many valuable insights into the working of the federal courts from my brilliant and experienced colleagues on the Advisory Committee on Civil Rules. Dean W. Page Keeton has been a source of great encouragement, and has provided facilities and teaching arrangements conducive to scholarship. Three of

PREFACE TO FIRST EDITION

my former students, Bert B. Adkins, Jr., Buford P. Berry, and Thomas S. Terrell, have kindly read the manuscript, and pointed out many places where revision was necessary if the book was to meet the needs and the understanding of law students.

But to two men I owe an overwhelming debt. Each has been my friend and my collaborator. Each, through his scholarly work and his effort for reform, has done much to shape the federal court system as we know it. From each I have learned much. As an inadequate token of my gratitude to, and admiration for, these great men, this book is respectfully dedicated to Charles E. Clark and Charles T. McCormick, with the hope that they will not find it unworthy.

CHARLES ALAN WRIGHT

Austin, Texas
June, 1963

SUMMARY OF CONTENTS

*

TABLE OF CONTENTS

TABLE OF CONTENTS

CHAPTER 5. JURISDICTIONAL AMOUNT

CHAPTER 6. REMOVAL JURISDICTION AND PROCEDURE

CHAPTER 7. VENUE

CHAPTER 8. THE RELATIONS OF STATE AND FEDERAL COURTS

CHAPTER 9. THE LAW APPLIED BY THE FEDERAL COURTS

TABLE OF CONTENTS

CHAPTER 10. PROCEDURE IN THE DISTRICT COURTS

A. INTRODUCTION

TABLE OF CONTENTS

F. TRIALS

G. JUDGMENT

CHAPTER 11. THE APPELLATE JURISDICTION OF THE COURTS OF APPEALS

CHAPTER 12. THE APPELLATE JURISDICTION OF THE SUPREME COURT

CHAPTER 13. THE ORIGINAL JURISDICTION OF THE SUPREME COURT

HANDBOOK
OF THE LAW OF
FEDERAL COURTS

*

CHAPTER 1

THE FEDERAL JUDICIAL SYSTEM

Analysis

§ 1. The Historical Bases [1]

Any study of the federal courts in the latter part of the 20th century necessarily must begin with two 18th century landmarks—Article III of the Constitution and the Judiciary Act of 1789. Changes, indeed important changes, there surely have been, but the decisions made at the very beginning of the republic as to the nature of the federal judicial system have a marked imprint on even the most routine case to this day.

The necessity for constant resort to the Constitution in understanding the federal judicial system is obvious. The federal courts cannot be given authority beyond that conferred by the Constitution. This was recognized in the first case to hold an Act of Congress unconstitutional, the landmark decision in Marbury v. Madison,[2] where the Supreme Court held invalid a statute that purported to grant to it original jurisdiction beyond that defined in the Constitution. Although there is dispute as to which provisions of the Constitution are to be looked to in determining the power of the federal courts,[3] it is beyond challenge that the Constitution does mark the limits.[4]

In a more far-reaching sense, questions of federal jurisdiction are questions of constitutional law. In 1864 former Justice Benjamin Curtis made the still-timely reminder: "Let it be remembered, also, for just now we may be in some danger of forgetting it, that ques-

---

[§ 1]

1. The classic study of the history of the federal judiciary, somewhat misleadingly titled, is Frankfurter & Landis, The Business of the Supreme Court, 1928. Warren, New Light on the History of the Federal Judiciary Act of 1789, 1923, 37 Harv.L.Rev. 49, is definitive on the subject it treats, and has been extremely influential. See also Hart & Wechsler, The Federal Courts and the Federal System, Bator,

Mishkin, Shapiro & Wechsler ed. 1973, pp. 1–63; Frank, Historical Bases of the Federal Judicial System, 1948, 13 Law & Contemp.Probs. 3. The deliberations of the Constitutional Convention will be found in Farrand, The Records of the Federal Convention, rev. ed. 1937.

2. 1803, 1 Cranch 137, 2 L.Ed. 60.

3. See §§ 11, 20 below.

4. See § 8 below.

tions of jurisdiction were questions of power as between the United States and the several States." [5]   There is a recurring temptation to view questions of federal jurisdiction as if they were simple procedural questions, to be resolved in whatever fashion will best serve the desirable goal of efficient judicial administration.   Settled doctrine does give some play to such considerations.[6]   But when it is remembered that the delicate balance of a federal system is at stake, and that expansion of the jurisdiction of the federal courts diminishes the power of the states, it is apparent that efficiency cannot be the sole or the controlling consideration.

The Constitutional Convention had no difficulty in agreeing to the novel proposal of a federal judiciary.   Randolph's resolution "that a National Judiciary be established" was unanimously adopted early in the convention.[7]   There was more disagreement as to the form such a judiciary should take.   Though the Committee of the Whole had at first approved the proposition that such a judiciary should consist of one supreme tribunal and of inferior tribunals,[8] this came under attack from those who argued that an additional set of courts was an unnecessary expense, and that it would be sufficient to have all cases decided in the state courts in the first instance, with appeal to the supreme national court.   A motion to strike out the provision for inferior tribunals prevailed by a vote of five states to four, with two states divided.[9]   Wilson and Madison then put forward a compromise. They moved that the national legislature be empowered to institute inferior tribunals, and noted the distinction between establishing such tribunals absolutely and giving a discretion to the legislature to establish or not establish them.   This motion prevailed, by a vote of eight states to two, with one divided,[10] and this compromise formed the basis for the language later used in the Constitution itself.

The decisions of the convention as to appointment, tenure, and compensation of judges were of importance—and with regard to the first, quite controversial—but the other principal decision that had to be made in the Constitution was the scope of the judicial power to be granted to the national courts.   On this subject, unfortunately, the records of the convention are unilluminating, and it is not possible to say what motivated the Framers in including particular grants of jurisdiction in § 2 of Article III.   Perhaps most easily explained are the grants of admiralty jurisdiction and of jurisdiction over cases between two or more states.   Maritime commerce was at that time the principal business activity of the states.   The need for uniformity in such cases was deeply felt, and it was recognized also that admiralty

5.   Curtis, Notice of the Death of Chief Justice Taney, Proceedings in Circuit Court of the United States for the First Circuit, 1864, p. 9.

6.   See §§ 9, 19 below.   Cf. Aldinger v. Howard, 1976, 96 S.Ct. 2413, 2420, 427 U.S. 1, 14–15, 49 L.Ed.2d 276.

7.   1 Farrand, The Records of the Federal Convention, rev.ed. 1937, p. 104.

8.   Id. at 104–105, 119.

9.   Id. at 124–125.

10.   Id. at 125.

cases normally arise outside the borders of any state, and that they may involve relations with other nations. For all these reasons, in Hamilton's phrase, even "the most bigoted idolizers of State authority have not thus far shown a disposition to deny the national judiciary the cognizance of maritime causes." [11] Similarly the grant of jurisdiction over controversies between states was responsive to experience. There had been such disputes, principally over borders, and there was a felt need for a tribunal to resolve them. The jurisdiction thus granted may perhaps be thought of as a transfer to the national judiciary of a power exercised by the Privy Council prior to the revolution.

A number of the other jurisdictional clauses can be justified by the need of the national government to enforce its laws and to collect its revenues—thus the jurisdiction over cases arising under the Constitution or laws of the United States and over cases to which the United States shall be a party—and to speak for all the nation in dealings with foreign governments and peoples—thus the jurisdiction over cases arising under treaties, or affecting ambassadors, other public ministers or consuls, or between states, or their citizens, and foreign states, citizens, or subjects.

The greatest mystery, and the most heated controversy, surrounds the diversity jurisdiction, permitting the national courts to hear suits between citizens of different states, and between a state and citizens of another state. As will be seen later,[12] there is to this day no consensus as to the historical justification or the contemporary need for diversity jurisdiction, though it was accepted without question at the Constitutional Convention.

The judicial article of the Constitution was the center of much argument in the ratification debates. Five of the Federalists Papers, Nos. 78–82, are devoted to the judiciary. Though the basic idea of a national judiciary did not come under attack, many of the state ratifying conventions proposed amendments regarding the courts. The proposals that trial by jury be guaranteed in civil as well as in criminal cases, and that appellate review be limited to questions of law, were incorporated by the First Congress in the Seventh Amendment. Attempts to do away with diversity jurisdiction, and to take away the authority to establish inferior federal courts, were unsuccessful.

The other great landmark, the Judiciary Act of 1789 [13]—or the First Judiciary Act as it is often called—has acquired a status almost as exalted as the Constitution itself. The act itself, primarily drafted by Oliver Ellsworth, though much criticized in the early days of the Republic, is now universally regarded as "a great law." [14] But the act has a special authority of its own, not only because of its intrinsic

---

11. The Federalist No. 80, at 502, Wright ed. 1961 (Hamilton).

12. See § 23 below.

13. Act of Sept. 24, 1789, 1 Stat. 73.

14. Frankfurter & Landis, note 1 above, at p. 4.

merit, but because of the circumstances of its enactment. The Supreme Court has noted that the act "was passed by the first congress assembled under the constitution, many of whose members had taken part in framing that instrument, and is contemporaneous and weighty evidence of its true meaning." [15] The most significant aspect of the First Judiciary Act is that the power to create inferior federal courts was immediately exercised. As it had in the Constitutional Convention and in the ratification debates, the necessity for such courts aroused warm controversy, but in the end Congress proceeded to create not one set of inferior courts but two. It created for each state at least one district court. Finally it created three circuit courts. Judges were provided for the Supreme Court and for the district courts, but the circuit courts were given no judges of their own. Instead the circuit court was to hold two sessions each year at each district within the circuit, with the court made up of two justices of the Supreme Court, and the district judge for the district.

The district courts were entirely courts of original jurisdiction, authorized to entertain admiralty cases, minor criminal cases, and some other rather limited classes of cases. The circuit courts had both original and appellate jurisdiction. They were the court of original jurisdiction in diversity cases, most criminal cases, and larger cases to which the United States was a party. They had appellate jurisdiction over the district courts in civil cases where the amount in controversy exceeded $50 and in admiralty cases where the amount in controversy exceeded $300. The Supreme Court had some original jurisdiction, as the Constitution provided, and had appellate jurisdiction over the circuit courts in civil cases where the amount in controversy exceeded $2,000, and over the state courts in cases raising a federal question. There was no review in the Supreme Court of federal criminal cases.

Certain features of the First Judiciary Act deserve special comment. It was argued in Congress that there was a duty to confer on the federal courts the full judicial power granted by the Constitution. This view was rejected by Congress, and indeed at no time in history has the entire judicial power been vested in the federal courts.

It is interesting that Congress proceeded immediately to give the circuit courts jurisdiction in diversity cases, but that no jurisdiction was conferred on the lower courts in cases arising under the Constitution or laws of the United States. Except for a grant in 1801 that lasted little more than a year, not until 1875 was there a general grant of federal question jurisdiction; such cases could only be brought in the state courts.

The First Judiciary Act introduced the device of removal from state to federal courts, a device not mentioned in the Constitution. Subject to a jurisdictional amount of $500, the privilege of removing

---

15. Wisconsin v. Pelican Ins. Co., 1888,
    8 S.Ct. 1370, 1378, 127 U.S. 265, 297, 32
    L.Ed. 239.

to the circuit court a case commenced in state court was given to alien defendants, defendants in diversity cases where the plaintiff was a citizen of the state in which suit was brought, and to either party in cases involving title to land where the parties were relying on grants from different states.

Section 34 of the act is well known as the Rules of Decision Act. It provided that, except as otherwise required by federal law, "the laws of the several states" should be regarded as rules of decision in trials at common law in the federal courts in cases where they applied. Probably no statute regarding the federal courts has led to such difficulty.[16]

Finally, section 25 of the First Judiciary Act gave the Supreme Court appellate jurisdiction over final judgments of the highest state courts in certain cases involving federal questions.

The least satisfactory feature of the First Judiciary Act was the requirement that the Supreme Court justices "ride circuit" and participate in the proceedings of the circuit courts. As early as 1792 Chief Justice Jay and his associates joined in a memorial to the President in which they protested that the task of circuit riding was "too burdensome." Congress gave some relief in 1793 by providing that only one justice, rather than two, need attend each session of a circuit court,[17] but more than a century was to go by before the Supreme Court justices were entirely relieved of this burden.

There was, indeed, an earlier attempt to give complete relief. In the dying days of the Adams administration Congress passed the short-lived "Midnight Judges Act,"[18] which, so we are told on high authority, "combined thoughtful concern for the federal judiciary with selfish concern for the Federalist party."[19]

The 1801 Act put an end to circuit riding by the Supreme Court justices, and authorized the appointment of sixteen new circuit judges, so that each circuit court thereafter would consist of three judges appointed to that court. In addition the act purported to give the circuit courts jurisdiction in all cases to which the judicial power of the United States extended, subject in some cases to a jurisdictional amount of $400. Adams, before leaving office, promptly appointed deserving Federalists to the sixteen judicial posts thus created. The new administration and Congress lost little time in repealing the 1801 Act,[20] despite the argument, never judicially tested, that it was unconstitutional to abolish judgeships to which the Constitution gives life tenure. The 1802 legislation repealing the "Midnight Judges Act" did expand the number of circuits, and it contained a provision that

16. See §§ 54–60 below.

17. Act of March 2, 1793, 1 Stat. 333.

18. Act of Feb. 13, 1801, 2 Stat. 89. See Turner, Midnight Judges, 1961, 109 U.Pa.L.Rev. 494; Surrency, The Judiciary Act of 1801, 1958, 2 Am.J.Leg.Hist. 53.

19. Frankfurter & Landis, note 1 above, at p. 25.

20. Act of March 8, 1802, 2 Stat. 132.

circuit court might be held by a single judge. Thus, while the justices of the Supreme Court were not relieved directly of the burden of circuit riding, the pressure of their other duties was such that increasingly the circuit court was held by a single district judge.

Though changes were constantly being made in details of the organization and jurisdiction of the federal courts, only a few developments need be noticed here. In 1869 Congress authorized the appointment of one circuit judge for each of the circuits, and provided that a Supreme Court justice need sit with the circuit court only once every two years in each district within his circuit.[21] Legislation in 1875 finally gave the federal courts original jurisdiction, in terms very nearly as broad as the constitutional grant, to cases arising under the Constitution, laws, or treaties of the United States.[22] Thus for the first time general federal question jurisdiction was conferred, though in prior years particular statutes had authorized jurisdiction in some classes of federal question cases. The same statute also broadened diversity jurisdiction. The expanded jurisdiction naturally caused increased congestion in the courts, which an increase of the jurisdictional amount to $2,000 in 1887 failed to check. The time had come for a more drastic reshaping of the judicial structure.

Such a reshaping came with the adoption in 1891 of the Evarts Act.[23] This statute created for each circuit a circuit court of appeals, and authorized the appointment of an additional circuit judge for each circuit. The new circuit court of appeals was to consist of three judges, the two circuit judges and either a justice of the Supreme Court or one of the district judges from within the circuit. An important change, however, was the provision that no judge was to sit on an appeal in a case that he had heard below. Prior to 1891 it happened not infrequently that on appeal from the district court to the circuit court the district judge who had decided against appellant in the district court would be found hearing the appeal.

The Evarts Act retained both the district courts and the circuit courts as nisi prius courts, but it did abolish the appellate jurisdiction of the circuit courts. Thus there were still to be two baseline courts, with varying jurisdiction, but appeal from each was either to the circuit court of appeals or to the Supreme Court. The act provided for direct review in the Supreme Court of certain cases of an important nature. Other cases were to be appealed to the circuit court of appeals. In some classes of cases, notably diversity and admiralty, the decision of the circuit court of appeals was final, unless that court certified a question to the Supreme Court or the Supreme Court granted the discretionary writ of certiorari to bring the case up for further review. In other cases there was appeal as of right to the Supreme Court from the decision of the circuit court of appeals.

21. Act of April 10, 1869, 16 Stat. 44.   23. Act of March 3, 1891, 26 Stat. 826.
22. Act of March 3, 1875, 18 Stat. 470.
    See § 22 below.

With the adoption in 1911 of a Judicial Code,[24] the circuit courts were finally abolished. A source of complaint and controversy from their establishment in 1789, they had been quite unnecessary since the adoption of the Evarts Act in 1891. In 1911 their jurisdiction was transferred to the district courts. The Judicial Code of that year also increased the jurisdictional amount for most cases in the district court, this time to $3,000.

One last landmark must be mentioned. This was the "Judges' Bill," so-called because it was drafted by a committee of Supreme Court justices, adopted by Congress in 1925.[25] This act was intended to reduce the burden on the Supreme Court. It did this in two ways. Direct review in the Supreme Court of decisions of the district courts was eliminated, except in a very few classes of cases of particular importance and urgency. The principle of discretionary review in the Supreme Court by use of the writ of certiorari, first introduced by the Evarts Act, was greatly expanded. With regard both to the circuit courts of appeals and the state appellate courts, the Supreme Court was given discretion whether to hear the case, except in compelling instances where a state court has rejected a claim based on the supremacy of federal law, or where a federal court has held unconstitutional a state statute.

Changes continue to be made at virtually every session of Congress in the laws regulating the federal judiciary. The Judicial Code was recodified in 1948, while 1958 produced important enactments increasing the jurisdictional amount to $10,000, redefining corporate citizenship, and allowing for discretionary interlocutory appeals from the district courts to the courts of appeals. The requirement of an amount in controversy for federal question cases, always largely illusory, was greatly reduced in application in 1976 and abolished entirely in 1980. Another 1980 statute provides for the first time a means other than impeachment for investigating and resolving allegations that a federal judge has been unable to discharge efficiently all the duties of his office or has engaged in conduct inconsistent with the effective and expeditious administration of the courts.[26] But with the passage of the Judges' Bill in 1925, the federal court structure took on essentially the form that it has to this day. Its resemblance to the structure originally provided in 1789 is quite clear.

The pressures of docket congestion have caused many thoughtful persons and groups to think that the time has come for reexamination of the organization of the federal courts and for restructuring similar to the changes that occurred in the Evarts Act of 1891 and the Judges' Bill in 1925. Although there have been numerous provocative

24. Act of March 3, 1911, 36 Stat. 1087.

25. Act of Feb. 13, 1925, 43 Stat. 936.

26. 28 U.S.C.A. § 372(c). See Re, Judicial Independence and Accountability: The Judicial Councils Reform and Judicial Conduct and Disability Act of 1980, 1981, 8 N.Ky.L.Rev. 221; Neisser, The New Federal Judicial Discipline Act: Some Questions Congress Didn't Answer, 1981, 65 Judicature 142.

proposals to this end,[27] there is not yet agreement on whether fundamental changes are needed or what they should be.

§ 2. The District Courts [1]

The general court of original jurisdiction in the federal system is the United States District Court. The statutes divide the nation, including the District of Columbia and Puerto Rico, into 91 districts, in each of which there is established a district court. Other courts similarly named are created for the Canal Zone, Guam, the Virgin Islands, and the Northern Mariana Islands. The statutes specify with great particularity the borders of a district, and where within the district court is to be held.[2]

Following the example set in the First Judiciary Act and consistently adhered to since, districts do not—with one insignificant exception [3]—extend across state lines. Thus a state will constitute at least one judicial district, and many states are divided into two, three, or even, in the case of California, New York, and Texas, four districts. Many districts are further subdivided into divisions, but the divisions are of very little importance except as a rather frail limit on where within a district an action must be commenced.

The formation within a state of districts, and of divisions within districts, has not been an entirely rational process. There is no immediately apparent reason, for example, why Mississippi should be divided into two districts, which in turn are subdivided into four and five divisions, while the entire state of Massachusetts, with twice as many district judges, constitutes a single district and single division.

The statute authorizes 507 district judges to sit in the 91 district courts.[4] Though there is still one district with only a single judge,

27. E.g., ALI Study; Commission on Revision of the Federal Court Appellate System, Structure and Internal Procedures: Recommendations for Change, June 1975, reprinted 67 F.R.D. 195; Hruska, The National Court of Appeals: An Analysis of Viewpoints, 1975, 9 Creighton L.Rev. 286; Report of the Study Group on the Caseload of the Supreme Court, 1972, reprinted 57 F.R.D. 573; Friendly, Federal Jurisdiction: A General View, 1973; Haworth & Meador, A Proposed New Federal Intermediate Appellate Court, 1979, 12 U.Mich.J.L.Ref. 201; Hufstedler, Comity and the Constitution: The Changing Role of the Federal Judiciary, 1972, 47 N.Y.U.L.Rev. 841. Other materials on this subject are collected in 13 Wright, Miller & Cooper, Jurisdiction § 3510.

[§ 2]

1. Clark, Adjudication to Administration: A Statistical Analysis of Federal District Courts in the Twentieth Century, 1981, 55 S.Cal.L.Rev. 65; Steckler, The Future of the Federal District Courts, 1978, 11 Ind.L.Rev. 523; Judd, The Expanding Jurisdiction of the Federal Courts, 1974, 60 A.B.A.J. 938; Acheson, Professional Responsibility and the Workload of the Federal District Courts, 1964, 52 Geo.L.J. 542; Surrency, Federal District Court Judges and the History of Their Courts, 1966, 40 F.R.D. 139. The latter article has a history of each district and of the judges who have served in it.

2. 28 U.S.C.A. §§ 81–131.

3. The District Court for the District of Wyoming includes all of that state and such portions of Yellowstone National Park as are within Montana and Idaho.

4. 28 U.S.C.A. § 133.

most districts have two or more judges, ranging up to the 27 judges authorized for the Southern District of New York. Normally a single judge will sit in a case pending before the district court,[5] and it is the function of the chief judge of the district to apportion the business of the court among the judges, where there is more than one, in accordance with such rules and orders as the court may have made.[6] There are certain exceptional cases, dealt with elsewhere,[7] that call for the creation of a statutory three-judge court, made up of at least one circuit judge and the remainder district judges.

In addition, the statutes do not forbid, and some districts follow, the practice of having all the judges of the court sit en banc in important matters.[8] Finally in some districts, on procedural questions and others where a uniform practice within the district is especially desirable, the judge hearing the case will state in his opinion that he has shown the opinion to the other judges and they concur therein.[9]

The Federal Magistrates Act of 1968 creates United States magistrates to assist the district courts.[10] The statute specifies some of the functions that magistrates can perform and allows a district court to assign to the magistrate "such additional duties as are not inconsistent with the Constitution and laws of the United States."[11] The statute has been amended several times since adoption to broaden the duties that can be entrusted to magistrates.[12]

---

5. 28 U.S.C.A. § 132(c).

6. 28 U.S.C.A. § 137.

7. See § 50 below.

8. E.g., U. S. v. Anaya, D.C.Fla.1980, 509 F.Supp. 289; Hickman v. Taylor, D.C.Pa.1945, 4 F.R.D. 479.

In other cases a panel of judges, but not all of the judges of the district, may be named in order to establish uniformity within the district on recurring questions. E.g., Close v. Calmar S. S. Corp., D.C.Pa.1968, 44 F.R.D. 398, 401 n. 3.

9. E.g., Slomberg v. Pennabaker, D.C. Pa.1967, 42 F.R.D. 8, 12; Dziwanoski v. Ocean Carriers Corp., D.C.Md.1960, 26 F.R.D. 595, 599; U. S. v. Napela, D.C.N.Y.1928, 28 F.2d 898, 904.

10. 28 U.S.C.A. §§ 631–639.

11. 28 U.S.C.A. § 636(a), (b). See U. S. v. Raddatz, 1980, 100 S.Ct. 2406, 447 U.S. 667, 65 L.Ed.2d 424; Mathews v. Weber, 1976, 96 S.Ct. 549, 423 U.S. 261, 46 L.Ed.2d 483.

See generally Peterson, The Federal Magistrates Act: A New Dimension in the Implementation of Justice, 1970, 56 Iowa L.Rev. 62; Tushnet, Invitation to a Wedding: Some Thoughts on Article III and a Problem of Statutory Construction, 1975, 60 Iowa L.Rev. 937; Note, Masters and Magistrates in the Federal Courts, 1975, 88 Harv.L.Rev. 779; Note, The Validity of United States Magistrates' Criminal Jurisdiction, 1974, 60 Va.L.Rev. 697; Comment, An Adjudicative Role for Federal Magistrates in Civil Cases, 1973, 40 U.Chi.L.Rev. 584.

12. 28 U.S.C.A. § 636. See Puro, Goldman & Padawer-Singer, The Evolving Role of U. S. Magistrates in the District Courts, 1981, 64 Judicature 436; Margolis, U. S. Magistrates Get Broader Powers, 1980, 66 A.B.A.J. 322; Aug, The Magistrate Act of 1979: From a Magistrate's Perspective, 1980, 49 U.Cin.L.Rev. 363; McCabe, The Federal Magistrate Act of 1979, 1979, 16 Harv.J.Legis. 343; Note, Article III Constraints and the Expanding Civil Jurisdiction of Federal Magistrates: A Dissenting View, 1979, 88 Yale L.J. 1023.

§ 3. The Courts of Appeals [1]

The creation of the circuit courts of appeals in 1891, after a century of discontent with the prior structure of the courts, was described above.[2] These courts were renamed by the 1948 Judicial Code, and are now properly known as the United States Court of Appeals for the _____ Circuit.

The work of the courts of appeals is principally appellate, reviewing cases from the district courts, although the courts also have jurisdiction to review orders of many administrative agencies, and to issue original writs in appropriate cases.[3] In the year ended June 30, 1981, 21,391 appeals were filed with the courts of appeals from decisions of the district courts, 465 appeals were filed from bankruptcy courts, 706 original proceedings were commenced, and 3,800 applications were filed for review of orders of administrative agencies, for a total of 26,362 cases of all types.[4]

There are now 13 courts of appeals, one for the District of Columbia, 11 for numbered circuits that include anywhere from three to ten states and territories, and, created in 1982, the Court of Appeals for the Federal Circuit.[5] Normally cases are heard by a division of the court constituting three judges.[6] The number of judges appointed for each court of appeals ranges from four to 23,[7] and in addition the Supreme Court justice allotted as circuit justice for the circuit, and other judges or justices designated or assigned, are competent to sit on the court.[8] In particular, the chief judge of the court of appeals may designate and assign a district judge within the circuit to sit as a member of the court of appeals at a specific time,[9] and this power is frequently utilized.

The statute specifies the places within the circuit where the court is to sit during the year, but there is an increasing tendency, with improved methods of transportation, to centralize the work of a par-

---

[§ 3]

1. See Howard, Courts of Appeals in the Federal Judicial System, 1981; Lay, A Proposal for Discretionary Review in Federal Courts of Appeals, 1981, 34 Sw.L.J. 1151; Wasby, Inconsistency in the United States Courts of Appeals: Dimensions and Mechanisms for Resolution, 1979, 32 Vand.L.Rev. 1343; Friendly, The "Law of the Circuit" and All That, 1972, 46 St. John's L.Rev. 406; Hufstedler, New Blocks for Old Pyramids: Reshaping the Judicial System, 1971, 44 S.Cal.L.Rev. 901; Note, Supervisory Power in the United States Court of Appeals, 1978, 63 Corn. L.Rev. 642; Note, The Second Circuit: Federal Judicial Administration in Microcosm, 1963, 63 Col.L.Rev. 874.

2. See § 1 above.

3. As to the jurisdiction of the courts of appeals, see §§ 101–104 below, and see 15 Wright, Miller & Cooper, Jurisdiction §§ 3901–3919, 16 id. §§ 3920–3944.

4. Ann.Rep., Director of the Administrative Office of the United States Courts, 1981, Table B–3.

5. 28 U.S.C.A. § 41.

6. 28 U.S.C.A. § 46(c).

7. 28 U.S.C.A. § 44(a).

8. 28 U.S.C.A. § 43(b). See Oberman, Coping with Rising Caseload: A New Model of Appellate Review, 1980, 46 Brooklyn L.Rev. 841; Green & Atkins, Designated Judges: How Well Do They Perform?, 1978, 61 Judicature 358.

9. 28 U.S.C.A. § 292(a).

ticular circuit at one place, and to hold most, or all, of the sessions of the court at that place.

By statute, a majority of the circuit judges of the circuit who are in active service may order a hearing or a rehearing before the court en banc.[10] Prior to 1953 this power was exercised in some circuits, but ignored in others. In that year the Supreme Court held that each circuit should establish a clear procedure for determining when en banc hearings would be had, and cautioned against indiscriminate refusal to order such hearings.[11] That decision has led to more frequent use of the en banc procedure,[12] which has the advantage, in the unusual case to which it is suited, of avoiding conflicts of view within a circuit and promoting finality of decision in the courts of appeals.[13]

A statute, which seems to state an obvious truth but which changed the prior practice when it was first adopted in 1891, provides that no judge shall hear or determine an appeal from the decision of a case or issue tried by him.[14]

The Federal Rules of Appellate Procedure were adopted in 1968 and have been amended several times since. These had the salutary purpose of making procedures in the various courts of appeals largely uniform, rather than leaving appellate procedure, as in the past, to be regulated by rules of each of the courts of appeals.[15] That goal has been made largely illusory by the subsequent adoption of lengthy and inconsistent local rules in each circuit.[16]

The last two decades have seen a sudden and sharp increase in the workload of the courts of appeals that poses a major crisis in judicial administration. The number of cases commenced in all of the courts of appeals increased moderately from 2830 in 1950 to 3899 in 1960.

---

10. 28 U.S.C.A. § 46(c). The statute codified the decision in Textile Mills Securities Corp. v. Commissioner, 1943, 62 S.Ct. 272, 314 U.S. 326, 86 L.Ed. 249, that the courts of appeals had power to hold rehearings en banc.

See also Appellate Rule 35.

11. Western Pac. R. Corp. v. Western Pac. R. Co., 1953, 73 S.Ct. 656, 345 U.S. 247, 97 L.Ed. 986.

See also Shenker v. Baltimore & O. R. Co., 1963, 83 S.Ct. 1667, 1670, 374 U.S. 1, 4–5, 10 L.Ed.2d 709, emphasizing the discretion each circuit has in fashioning its own administrative machinery for determining when to hear a matter en banc. But there is no discretion to ignore clear requirements of the statute. Moody v. Albemarle Paper Co., 1974, 94 S.Ct. 2513, 417 U.S. 622, 41 L.Ed.2d 358.

12. See Louisell & Degnan, Rehearing in American Appellate Courts, 1960, 25 F.R.D. 143, 160–163.

13. Maris, Hearing and Rehearing Cases in Banc, 1954, 14 F.R.D. 91, 96. See generally Note, En Banc Review in Federal Circuit Courts: A Reassessment, 1974, 72 Mich.L.Rev. 1637; Comment, In Banc Procedure in the United States Court of Appeals, 1974, 43 Ford. L.Rev. 401; 16 Wright, Miller & Cooper, Jurisdiction § 3981.

14. 28 U.S.C.A. § 47. There is an interesting discussion of the statute in Swann v. Charlotte-Mecklenburg Bd. of Educ., C.A.4th, 1970, 431 F.2d 135 (Craven, J.). See also 13 Wright, Miller & Cooper, Jurisdiction § 3545.

15. See Ward, The Federal Rules of Appellate Procedure, 1968, 54 A.B.A.J. 661.

16. See 16 Wright, Miller & Cooper, Jurisdiction § 3945.

By 1970, it was 11,662 and there was a further increase to 26,362 by 1981. Congress has provided for additional judgeships, so that there are now 144 judgeships on the 13 courts of appeals compared with 68 in 1960. The Fifth Circuit, which had grown to 26 judgeships, was split in 1981 after years of discussion, and a new Eleventh Circuit created in the three easternmost states of the former Fifth Circuit.[17] The Ninth Circuit, with 23 judgeships, is now an obvious candidate for a split, but with 44% of its business coming from California it is hard to know how it can be split without taking on a local rather than a national character.[18]

Even without counting the 12 judges who have become judges of the newly-formed Court of Appeals for the Federal Circuit, the number of court of appeals judges has increased 94% since 1960, but the number of filings in the courts of appeals has multiplied more than nine times in the same period. In 1960 41.6 cases were filed for each authorized judgeship. In 1981 the number was 199.7. To cope with this vast volume of business the courts have had to restrict or eliminate oral argument in many cases, limit publication of opinions, and adopt other innovations to dispose of more cases more quickly.[19]

§ 4. The Supreme Court [1]

The Supreme Court, alone among the federal courts, is created directly by the Constitution, rather than by choice of Congress. It

17. Act of Oct. 14, 1980, Pub.L. 96–452, 94 Stat. 1994. See Heflin, Fifth Circuit Court of Appeals Reorganization Act of 1980—Overdue Relief for an Overworked Court, 1981, 11 Cum.L.Rev. 597; Reavley, The Split of the Fifth Circuit: Update and Finis, 1981, 12 Texas Tech L.Rev. 1; Wisdom, Requiem for a Great Court, 1980, 26 Loy.L. Rev. 787; Wright, The Overloaded Fifth Circuit: A Crisis in Judicial Administration, 1964, 42 Texas L.Rev. 949.

The new court has held that decisions of the former Fifth Circuit will be binding precedent unless overruled by the Eleventh Circuit sitting en banc. Bonner v. City of Prichard, C.A.11th, 1981, 661 F.2d 1206; Baker, A Postscript on Precedent in the Divided Fifth Circuit, 1982, 36 Sw.L.J. 725.

18. Hellman, Legal Problems of Dividing a State between Federal Judicial Circuits, 1974, 122 U.Pa.L.Rev. 1188.

See also the two reports of the Commission on Revision of the Federal Court Appellate System. They are The Geographical Boundaries of the Several Judicial Circuits: Recommendations for Change, December 1973, reprinted 62 F.R.D. 223, and Structure and Internal

Procedures: Recommendations for Change, June 1975, reprinted 67 F.R.D. 195.

19. See § 104 below. See also Carrington, Ceremony and Realism: Demise of Appellate Procedure, 1980, 66 A.B.A.J. 863; Godbold, Improvements in Appellate Procedure: Better Use of Available Facilities, 1980, 66 A.B.A.J. 863.

[§ 4]

1. The literature about the Supreme Court is vast—and fascinating. See, e.g., Warren, The Supreme Court in United States History, 1922; Hughes, The Supreme Court of the United States, 1928; Frankfurter & Landis, The Business of the Supreme Court, 1928; Rodell, Nine Men, 1955; Westin, The Anatomy of a Constitutional Law Case, 1958; Frank, Marble Palace, 1958; Freund, The Supreme Court of the United States, 1961; Westin, The Supreme Court—Views from Inside, 1961.

A good feel for how the Supreme Court functions may be obtained from three extremely readable books about particular cases and groups of cases: Prettyman, Death and the Supreme Court,

consists at the present time of the Chief Justice of the United States and eight associate justices.[2]

The Court has not always had a total membership of nine. The First Judiciary Act created a Court with six members. This was increased to seven in 1807, to nine in 1837, and to ten in 1864. An 1866 statute, enacted to prevent Andrew Johnson from making any appointments to the Court, provided that no vacancy should be filled until the number of associate justices was reduced to six, but before enough deaths had occurred to accomplish this object, an 1869 statute was passed setting the size of the Court at nine, where it has since remained. In 1937 President Roosevelt proposed a bill that would have authorized the appointment of an additional justice for each sitting justice over 70 years of age, up to a maximum of 15 justices. The bitter fight that led to the defeat of this "court-packing" plan, as it was regarded, has given the notion of a nine-man Court such sanctity that it is unlikely that the size will again be changed.

The Supreme Court sits in Washington, D. C., in an annual term that begins on the first Monday in October and in recent years has normally ended in the first week of July. Six justices constitute a quorum, and there have been cases in which the Court has been unable to act because of inability to muster six justices who were not, for some reason, disqualified or unwilling to sit on a case. In one such situation Congress has given relief. Where a case comes to the Court on direct appeal from a district court, and there is no quorum, the case may be remitted to the court of appeals for the circuit including the district in which the case arose, and this court may make a final decision.[3] The provision for a quorum of six has led to some criticism in another direction. It means that in some cases a majority of only four justices may reverse a court below, and indeed even hold a statute unconstitutional. There has been a suggestion, never adopted, to prevent such situations by providing for summoning lower court judges to sit with the Supreme Court to make a full bench of

1961; Lewis, Gideon's Trumpet, 1964; and Friendly, Minnesota Rag, 1981.

Even to cite a select bibliography of law review articles about the Court would be an impossible task. One article, however, though its conclusions are extremely controversial, deserves mention because of the detailed picture it gives of the work of the Court. Hart, The Time Chart of the Justices, 1959, 73 Harv.L.Rev. 84. Other recent articles of interest include: Rehnquist, The Supreme Court: Past and Present, 1973, 59 A.B.A.J. 361; Cannon, Administrative Change and the Supreme Court, 1974, 57 Judicature 334; Hellman, The Business of the Supreme Court under the Judiciary Act of 1925:

The Plenary Docket in the 1970's, 1978, 91 Harv.L.Rev. 1709.

2.   28 U.S.C.A. § 1.

3.   28 U.S.C.A. § 2109. Apparently the statute has only been utilized in one case. U. S. v. Aluminum Co. of America, 1944, 64 S.Ct. 1281, 322 U.S. 716, 88 L.Ed. 1557.

If a case comes to the Supreme Court other than by direct review of a district court, and a quorum cannot be mustered, the same statute provides that the judgment of the court below is affirmed with the same effect as affirmance by an equally-divided court. Sloan v. Nixon, 1974, 95 S.Ct. 218, 419 U.S. 958, 42 L.Ed.2d 174.

nine.[4] The Supreme Court is not authorized to sit in divisions. All the qualified justices participate in each decision of the Court.

The Supreme Court has a limited original jurisdiction, and also exercises appellate jurisdiction, both by appeal and by the discretionary writ of certiorari, over the district courts, the courts of appeals, and the highest courts of the states.[5] In the 1980–1981 Term, the Court disposed of 4,280 cases. Of these 3,967 were disposed of by denial or dismissal of appeals and petitions for review, while 313 cases were determined on the merits. In 159 cases the Court disposed of a matter with a full opinion. Of these 89 were civil actions from inferior federal courts, eight were federal criminal cases, four were federal habeas corpus cases, 21 were civil actions from state courts, 15 were state criminal cases, and one was a case in the Court's original jurisdiction.[6]

There is, of course, no direct review of decisions of the Supreme Court. The late Justice Jackson observed: "We are not final because we are infallible, but we are infallible only because we are final." [7] In some instances, however, decisions of the Supreme Court do not finally resolve a controversy, though they dispose of the particular case. Decisions turning on statutory construction are subject to change in the statute by Congress, while in four instances the Constitution has been amended to overcome Supreme Court decisions.[8]

§ 5. Specialized Courts

Although the Supreme Court, the courts of appeals, and the district courts are from any standpoint the most important federal courts, and the courts to which the balance of this book is almost exclusively devoted, there are certain specialized courts that deserve brief mention. The exact status of these courts, and of the judges thereof, has been a troublesome matter, and will be considered in a later section.[1]

In geographical areas governed by Congress, and not a part of a state, there is a need for tribunals to exercise local jurisdiction, of the sort usually performed by state courts, as well as jurisdiction of a federal nature. In the District of Columbia, under the District of Co-

4. See Carrington, The Problem of Minority Decision, 1958, 44 A.B.A.J. 137.

5. See §§ 105–110 below.
There is now widespread support for a statute that would end the distinction between appeal and certiorari and bring all cases to the court by certiorari. See Gressman, Requiem for the Supreme Court's Obligatory Jurisdiction, 1979, 65 A.B.A.J. 1325.

6. The Supreme Court—1980 Term, 1981, 95 Harv.L.Rev. 91, 342–345.

See Report of the Study Group on the Caseload of the Supreme Court, December 1972, reprinted 57 F.R.D. 573; Casper & Posner, A Study of the Supreme Court's Caseload, 1974. 3 J.Legal Studies 339.

7. Brown v. Allen, 1953, 73 S.Ct. 397, 427, 344 U.S. 443, 540, 97 L.Ed. 469.

8. 13 Wright, Miller & Cooper, Jurisdiction § 3507 n. 14.

[§ 5]

1. See § 11 below.

lumbia Court Reform and Criminal Procedure Act of 1970,[2] what formerly were the Court of General Session, the Juvenile Court, and the District of Columbia Tax Court were consolidated into a single court known as the Superior Court, with jurisdiction of civil and criminal matters of a local nature similar to the state court systems in the 50 states. The District of Columbia Court of Appeals—not to be confused with the United States Court of Appeals for the District of Columbia Circuit—is the appellate court for the local system of courts and its decisions are reviewable in the Supreme Court in the same manner as decisions of the highest court of a state.[3] The District Court for the District of Columbia and the United States Court of Appeals for the District of Columbia Circuit hear only federal matters of the kind heard by federal courts in the states.

The District Courts of the Canal Zone, the Virgin Islands, Guam, and the Northern Mariana Islands have a dual jurisdiction. In addition to federal jurisdiction they have practically the same scope as state courts of general jurisdiction.[4] The District Court for the District of Puerto Rico is rather different. It is defined by statute as a "court of the United States" though it has certain additional jurisdiction.[5] Puerto Rico has a system of courts of its own, and decisions of the Supreme Court of Puerto Rico are reviewed by the United States Supreme Court in a fashion similar to review of a state court.[6]

The other specialized courts have traditionally been limited to particular subject matters. The oldest of these, the Court of Claims, was established in 1855. Until 1982, when it was merged with the Court of Customs and Patent Appeals to form the new Court of Appeals for the Federal Circuit, it was a court of seven judges, sitting in divisions of three. It had nationwide jurisdiction and sat in Washington.[7] It had jurisdiction, in some instances concurrent with the district courts, to hear such claims against the United States as the Con-

2. Pub.L. 91–358, 84 Stat. 473; D.C. Code, tit. 11. See Symposium, The Modernization of Justice in the District of Columbia, 1971, 20 Amer.U.L.Rev. 237, 621; 14 Wright, Miller & Cooper, Jurisdiction § 3681.

3. 28 U.S.C.A. § 1257.

4. Canal Zone: 7 C.Z.Code § 23–26; Virgin Islands: 48 U.S.C.A. § 1406; Guam: 48 U.S.C.A. § 1424; Northern Marianas, 48 U.S.C.A. § 1694.

It has been held, however, that because of the peculiar language of 48 U.S.C.A. § 1424 the District Court for Guam cannot exercise diversity jurisdiction. Chase Manhattan Bank v. South Acres Development Co., 1978, 98 S.Ct. 544, 434 U.S. 236, 54 L.Ed.2d 501.

5. 28 U.S.C.A. § 451; 48 U.S.C.A. § 863. The statutes were amended in

1966 to give life tenure to judges subsequently appointed to that court. 28 U.S.C.A. § 134(a). See generally U. S. v. Montanez, C.A.2d, 1967, 371 F.2d 79, certiorari denied 88 S.Ct. 147, 389 U.S. 884, 19 L.Ed.2d 181. See 17 Wright, Miller & Cooper, Jurisdiction § 4106.

6. 28 U.S.C.A. § 1258.

7. 28 U.S.C.A. §§ 171–175; Ellison, United States Court of Claims: Keeper of the Nation's Conscience for One Hundred Years, 1956, 24 Geo.Wash.L. Rev. 251; McNamara, The Court of Claims: Its Development and Present Role in the Unified Court System, 1965, 40 St. John's L.Rev. 1; Symposium, The United States Court of Claims, 1967, 55 Geo.L.J. 573.

stitution or statutes permit to be maintained.[8]　Initially it was held that decisions of the Court of Claims could not be reviewed by the Supreme Court, since the earliest statutes permitted the Secretary of the Treasury to revise the court's judgment.[9]　The provision for revision of the judgment was stricken in 1866, and it became established that, so long as the Court of Claims was performing a judicial function, its decisions were reviewable by the Supreme Court.[10]　In the court year ending September 30, 1980, the Court of Claims disposed of 571 petitions in which nearly $1.3 billion was claimed.[11]

The Court of Customs and Patent Appeals was created in 1909 to take over specialized litigation that at that time was swamping the Second Circuit, into which most imports come.[12]　At the time of its merger with the Court of Claims in 1982 into the new Court of Appeals for the Federal Circuit, the Court of Customs and Patent Appeals consisted of five judges.　The judges had their official station in Washington, D. C., but the jurisdiction ran throughout the nation and the court could sit at such times and places as it fixed by rule.[13]　It had jurisdiction to review certain determinations of the Court of International Trade (formerly known as the Customs Court), decisions of the Board of Appeals and the Board of Patent Interferences of the Patent Office as to patent applications and interferences, decisions of the Commissioner of Patents as to trademark applications, the findings of the United States International Trade Commission as to unfair practices in import trade, certain findings of the Secretary of Commerce about tariffs, and certain appeals under the Plant Variety Protection Act.[14]　In the year ended June 30, 1980, the court disposed

8.　28 U.S.C.A. §§ 1491–1506.　See 17 Wright, Miller & Cooper, Jurisdiction § 4101.

The Court of Claims and the district courts had concurrent jurisdiction of tax refund actions, for example.　28 U.S.C.A. § 1346(a)(1).　The average amount involved in a tax refund suit in the Court of Claims was approximately $400,000 while in the district courts it is less than $70,000.

In a suit under the Tucker Act, neither the Court of Claims nor a district court could give equitable or declaratory relief.　Richardson v. Morris, 1973, 93 S.Ct. 629, 409 U.S. 464, 34 L.Ed.2d 647.　However, the Court of Claims could issue declaratory relief where it was tied and subordinate to a monetary award.　Ellis v. U. S., Ct.Cl.1979, 610 F.2d 760.

9.　Gordon v. U. S., 1865, 2 Wall. 561, 117 U.S. 697, 17 L.Ed. 921 (the important opinion of Chief Justice Taney, who died before the decision was handed down, appears only in 117 U.S.　See § 11 n. 12 below).

10.　Pope v. U. S., 1944, 65 S.Ct. 16, 23, 323 U.S. 1, 12–14, 89 L.Ed. 3.

11.　Ann.Rep., Director of the Administrative Office of the United States Courts, 1980, pp. 568–569.

12.　Frankfurter and Landis, The Business of the Supreme Court, 1928, pp. 148–152; Graham, Court of Customs and Patent Appeals: Its History, Functions and Jurisdiction, 1932, 1 Fed.B.A. J. 33.

As created in 1909 it was the Court of Customs Appeals.　Its jurisdiction was enlarged and its name changed in 1929.

13.　28 U.S.C.A. §§ 211–216, 456.

14.　28 U.S.C.A. §§ 1541–1545.　The constitutionality of the jurisdiction to review decisions of the International Trade Commission, purportedly granted by 28 U.S.C.A. § 1543, is highly doubtful.　See Glidden Co. v. Zdanok, 1962, 82 S.Ct. 1459, 1488–1490, 1492–1493, 370 U.S. 530, 579–583, 587–589, 8 L.Ed.2d 671; 17 Wright, Miller & Cooper, Jurisdiction § 4104.

of 41 cases involving customs and international trade and 128 patents cases.[15]

A change in the structure of these two courts was made in 1982. A new court, the United States Court of Appeals for the Federal Circuit, was given the appellate jurisdiction of the Court of Claims and the Court of Customs and Patent Appeals. Another new court, the United States Claims Court, was created to assume the trial jurisdiction of the Court of Claims.[16]

The Customs Court was established as such in 1926, replacing the former Board of General Appraisers. Its name was changed again in 1980 to the Court of International Trade, and its jurisdiction redefined to create a comprehensive system of judicial review of civil actions arising from import transactions and to avoid jurisdictional conflicts that had been caused previously by the ill-defined division of jurisdiction between the former Customs Court and the federal district courts.[17] The court has nine judges, and its offices are in New York, but it may sit at any place within the jurisdiction of the United States.[18] During the year ended June 30, 1980, the former Customs Court disposed of 6,636 cases.[19]

For many years the Tax Court of the United States was not a court at all, despite its name, but was an administrative agency and a part of the executive branch of the government. Its name and status were changed by a 1969 statute. It is now the United States Tax Court and is a court of record under Article I of the Constitution rather than an executive agency.[20] However the Court of Military

See Gholz, Patent and Trademark Jurisdiction of the Court of Customs and Patent Appeals, 1972, 40 Geo.Wash.L. Rev. 416.

15. Ann.Rep., Director of the Administrative Office of the United States Courts, 1980, p. 567.

16. Act of April 2, 1982, Pub.L. 97–164, 96 Stat. 25, tit. 1. See Schwartz, Two New Federal Courts, 1982, 68 A.B.A.J. 1091.

In addition to the jurisdiction previously exercised by the two courts it succeeded, the Court of Appeals for the Federal Circuit was given exclusive jurisdiction of appeals from district courts throughout the country in cases arising under the laws relating to patents or plant variety protection and in cases against the United States, except for Tort Claims Act cases and internal revenue cases. 28 U.S.C.A. § 1295.

The new United States Claims Court, an Article I court, was given the trial jurisdiction of the former Court of Claims, which had largely been exercised by commissioners of that court, but it is also given jurisdiction, which

the Court of Claims never had, to grant declaratory judgments and give equitable relief in controversies within its jurisdiction. 28 U.S.C.A. § 1491(a) (2), (3).

17. 28 U.S.C.A. §§ 1581–1585; See Cohen, The New United States Court of International Trade, 1981, 20 Col.J. Transnational L. 277; Comment, Customs Court Act of 1980: An Evaluation and Analysis, 1981, 4 Hamline L.Rev. 537; 17 Wright, Miller & Cooper, Jurisdiction § 4103.

18. 28 U.S.C.A. §§ 251–257.

19. Ann.Rep., Director of the Administrative Office of the United States Courts, 1980, p. 566.

20. 26 U.S.C.A. (I.R.C.1954) § 7441, as amended by Act of Dec. 30, 1969, Pub. L. 91–172, § 951, 83 Stat. 487. See Petition of Benjamin, D.C.La.1971, 52 F.R.D. 407; Note, Recent Legislative Changes in the Constitutional Status of the United States Tax Court and the Courts of the District of Columbia, 1973 Wash.U.L.Q. 381. The constitutionality of making the Tax Court a legislative court was upheld in Stix

Appeals, and the courts-martial it reviews, remain a part of the government of the armed forces, and are entirely separate from the judiciary.[21]

Some specialized courts that existed in the past have been abolished. The Commerce Court, with jurisdiction to review decisions of the Interstate Commerce Commission, was established in 1910, over strong congressional opposition. It was saved from extinction only by a presidential veto in 1912, and in 1913, with a new administration in power, was abolished. A number of cases in which the court was reversed by the Supreme Court, and a fear, widely voiced before its creation and never quieted, that it would incline too much in favor of the railroads and against the public interest, led to abolition of the court.[22]

The Emergency Court of Appeals was created during the second world war to review orders of the Price Control Administrator. With the end of price control, there was no continued need for such a court, and it was abolished, except for concluding pending cases, in 1953.[23] However, in 1971 Congress created a Temporary Emergency Court of Appeals, staffed by judges of the existing federal courts, to hear all appeals in cases arising out of the then-current price-wage regulation.[24] Another special court is created by § 209 of the Regional Rail Reorganization Act of 1973. That court, composed of three designated federal judges, has exclusive jurisdiction to review the final system plan called for by that statute.[25]

Neither the two Emergency Courts of Appeals nor the special railroad court have had judges of their own, but were made up of sitting judges designated for part-time duty on those courts. There may be some significance to this beyond the history of these particular courts. Very few specialized courts have been created since the de-

Friedman & Co., Inc. v. Coyle, C.A.8th, 1972, 467 F.2d 474.

See Dubroff, The United States Tax Court: An Historical Analysis, 1975, 40 Albany L.J. 7; 17 Wright, Miller & Cooper, Jurisdiction § 4102.

21.   10 U.S.C.A. § 867; Dynes v. Hoover, 1857, 20 How. 65, 79, 15 L.Ed. 838; O'Callahan v. Parker, 1969, 89 S.Ct. 1683, 1686–1687, 395 U.S. 258, 265, 23 L.Ed.2d 291; Willis, The United States Court of Military Appeals: Its Origin, Operation and Future, 1972, 55 Military L.Rev. 39; Willis, The Constitution, The United States Court of Military Appeals and the Future, 1972, 57 Military L.Rev. 27.

22.   Frankfurter & Landis, The Business of the Supreme Court, 1928, pp. 153–174; Dix, The Death of the Commerce Court: A Study in Institutional Weakness, 1964, 8 Am.J.Leg.Hist. 238.

23.   50 App.U.S.C.A. § 2166.

24.   Act of Dec. 22, 1971, Pub.L. 92–210, § 211(b), 85 Stat. 743. The program of controls was ended in 1974. See 12 U.S.C.A. § 1904 note. However, the court has been given jurisdiction under other statutes. See 17 Wright, Miller & Cooper, Jurisdiction § 4105. See also Wiechmann & Heinzer, An Unappealing Dilemma: Searching for the Appellate Jurisdiction of the Temporary Emergency Court of Appeals, 1982, 3 U.Bridgeport L.Rev. 305.

25.   45 U.S.C.A. § 719. See 17 Wright, Miller & Cooper, Jurisdiction § 4106. The constitutionality of the statute creating the court was upheld in Blanchette v. Connecticut Gen. Ins. Corp., 1974, 95 S.Ct. 335, 419 U.S. 102, 42 L.Ed.2d 320.

mise of the Commerce Court in 1913. The Court of Appeals for the Federal Circuit and the United States Claims Court assumed jurisdiction that had already been vested in specialized courts. The Custom Court, now known as the Court of International Trade, was a formalization of an agency that had a long history. The Emergency Court of Appeals, and its 1971 successor, merely centralized in one place litigation of a type that otherwise could have been brought anywhere in the country, and it was made up of judges who were not appointed solely for that purpose. The same things may be said of the court created by the Regional Rail Reorganization Act.

Since 1913 Congress has resisted the many pressures, which continue to this day,[26] for creation of new courts with specialized subject-matter jurisdiction. The history of the Commerce Court may have given rise to a feeling, whether or not justified, that it is more desirable to use judges who hear all types of cases than to create a special tribunal with judges who hear only that kind of case.

§ 6. The Judicial Code

In 1911, after 12 years' work, the first Judicial Code was adopted, as an attempt to unify the previously scattered provisions relating to the business of the federal courts.[1] With the passage of time frequent amendments to these provisions suggested the desirability of a new code. The Judicial Code of 1948, which appears as Title 28 in the United States Code, is the product of this labor.[2] The Code has been warmly praised on eminent authority. The Supreme Court has said: "This was scarcely hasty, ill-considered legislation. To the contrary, it received close and prolonged study. Five years of Congressional attention supports the Code. And from the start, Congress obtained the most eminent expert assistance available. The spadework was entrusted to two lawbook-publishing firms, the staffs of which had unique experience in statutory codification and revision. They formed an advisory committee, including distinguished judges and members of the bar, and obtained the services of special consultants. Furthermore, an advisory committee was appointed by the Judicial Conference. And to assist with matters relating to the jurisdiction of this Court, Chief Justice Stone appointed an advisory committee, consisting of himself and Justices Frankfurter and Douglas."[3]

26. See 13 Wright, Miller & Cooper, Jurisdiction § 3508.

See generally Jordan, Specialized Courts: A Choice?, 1981, 76 Nw.U.L.Rev. 745.

[§ 6]

1. Frankfurter & Landis, The Business of the Supreme Court, 1928, pp. 130–145.

2. See Barron, The Judicial Code—1948 Revision, 1949, 8 F.R.D. 439; Holtzoff, The New Federal Judicial Code, 1949, 8 F.R.D. 343; Maris, New Federal Judicial Code, 1948, 34 A.B.A.J. 863.

The legislative history of the 1948 Code is collected in Legislative History of Title 28, United States Code "Judiciary and Judicial Procedure," Mersky & Jacobstein eds. 1971.

3. Ex parte Collett, 1949, 69 S.Ct. 944, 949–950, 337 U.S. 55, 65–66, 93 L.Ed. 1207.

The 1948 Code is accompanied by Reviser's Notes,[4] which have been given great weight by the Supreme Court in determining the meaning of the Code.[5]

Despite the praise that the 1948 Code has received, there is no unanimity of professional opinion on this subject. Indeed it has been called everything from "a masterpiece of legislative draftsmanship" [6] to "one of the worst pieces of draftsmanship in all history." [7] An Amendatory Act in 1949 corrected numerous errors in the original Code.

In 1959 in an address to the American Law Institute Chief Justice Warren said that it "is essential that we achieve a proper jurisdictional balance between the Federal and State Court systems, assigning to each system those cases most appropriate in the light of the basic principles of federalism." He suggested that it would be desirable if the Institute would undertake such a study. Work was begun in 1960 and the task was completed in 1968.[8] It proposes to repeal the chapters of the Judicial Code dealing with jurisdiction of the district courts, venue, and removal, and to substitute new statutory provisions. In addition changes in other portions of the Judicial Code are proposed. Although the ALI Study has influenced thinking about the federal courts, and some of the specifics of its proposals have borne legislative fruit, time and increasing dockets have made part of its recommendations no longer appropriate, and it would not now be desirable, even if it were possible, to have it adopted in its entirety by Congress.

4. The Historical Notes in 28 U.S.C.A. contain the Reviser's Notes to the 1948 Code.

5. Ex parte Collett, note 3 above; Fourco Glass Co. v. Transmirra Products Corp., 1957, 77 S.Ct. 787, 353 U.S. 222, 1 L.Ed.2d 786. In the latter case Justice Harlan protested that the "Notes have been given undue weight." 77 S.Ct. at 792, 353 U.S. at 229.

6. Holtzoff, The New Federal Judicial Code, 1949, 8 F.R.D. 343, 344.

7. Book Note, 1951, 36 Minn.L.Rev. 117, 118; Wright, Foreword, in Legislative History of Title 28, United States Code "Judiciary and Judicial Procedure," Mersky & Jacobstein eds., 1971, p. iii. There are substantive criticisms of the 1948 Code in Wechsler, Federal Jurisdiction and the Revision of the Judicial Code, 1948, 13 Law & Contemp.Prob. 216, and in Keeffe et al., Venue and Removal Jokers in the New Federal Judicial Code, 1952, 38 Va.L.Rev. 569. See also Keeffe, Twenty-Nine Distinct Damnations of the Federal Practice—And a National Ministry of Justice, 1954, 7 Vand.L.Rev. 636.

8. American Law Institute, Study of the Division of Jurisdiction between State and Federal Courts, Official Draft, 1969 (cited hereafter as ALI Study). See Field, Jurisdiction of Federal Courts—A Summary of American Law Institute Proposals, 1969, 46 F.R.D. 141. There is a critical examination of the proposals in Currie, The Federal Courts and the American Law Institute, 1968–1969, 36 U.Chi.L.Rev. 1, 268. They are defended in Wright, Restructuring Federal Jurisdiction: The American Law Institute Proposals, 1969, 26 Wash. & Lee L.Rev. 185.

See generally Symposium, An Analysis of the ALI's Approach to the State-Federal Jurisdiction Dilemma, 1972, 21 Amer.U.L.Rev. 287; Fraser, Proposed Revision of the Jurisdiction of the Federal District Courts, 1974, 8 Valp.U.L. Rev. 189.

Though the Judicial Codes, both of 1911 and 1948, have largely been responsive to professional suggestions and drafted for the legal profession, statutes regulating the judiciary can hardly avoid political and sectional pressures. This was true of the Midnight Judges Act of 1801, and the repeal of that act a year later.[9] It continues to be true today, and explains much that otherwise would be obscure in the Code.

9. See § 1 above.

CHAPTER 2

THE JUDICIAL POWER OF THE
UNITED STATES

Analysis

§ 7. Courts of Limited Jurisdiction [1]

It is a principle of first importance that the federal courts are courts of limited jurisdiction. Most state courts are courts of general jurisdiction, and the presumption is that they have jurisdiction over a particular controversy unless a showing is made to the contrary. The federal courts, on the other hand, cannot be courts of general jurisdiction. They are empowered to hear only such cases as are within the judicial power of the United States, as defined in the Constitution, and have been entrusted to them by a jurisdictional grant by Congress.

Because of this unusual nature of the federal courts, and because it would not be simply wrong but indeed an unconstitutional invasion of the powers reserved to the states if those courts were to entertain cases not within their jurisdiction, the rule is well settled that the party seeking to invoke the jurisdiction of a federal court must demonstrate that the case is within the competence of such a court. The presumption is that the court lacks jurisdiction in a particular case until it has been demonstrated that jurisdiction over the subject matter exists.[2]

To rebut this presumption against jurisdiction, the facts that disclose the existence of jurisdiction must be affirmatively alleged.[3] If

[§ 7]

1. 13 Wright, Miller & Cooper, Jurisdiction § 3522.

2. Turner v. President, Directors and Co. of the Bank of North America, 1799, 4 Dall. 8, 1 L.Ed. 718.

3. Bingham v. Cabot, 1798, 3 Dall. 382, 1 L.Ed. 646. As to how jurisdiction is pleaded, see § 69 below.

these facts are challenged, the burden is on the party claiming jurisdiction to demonstrate that jurisdiction of the subject matter exists.[4] But what if the parties fail to raise any jurisdictional question? The rule is that the parties cannot confer on a federal court jurisdiction that has not been vested in the court by the Constitution and Congress. The parties cannot waive lack of jurisdiction, whether by express consent,[5] or by conduct,[6] nor yet even by estoppel.[7] The court, whether trial or appellate, is obliged to notice want of jurisdiction on its own motion,[8] and it may well happen that the party who has invoked the jurisdiction of the federal court will be unhappy with the result he achieves there and will challenge the jurisdiction at a late stage of the proceedings after he has lost on the merits.[9] Such a harsh rule could hardly be defended as a sensible regulation of procedure, and can only be justified by the delicate problems of federal-state relations that are involved.[10]

4. McNutt v. General Motors Acceptance Corp., 1935, 56 S.Ct. 780, 298 U.S. 178, 80 L.Ed. 1135.

5. Jackson v. Ashton, 1834, 8 Pet. 148, 8 L.Ed. 898; Sosna v. Iowa, 1975, 95 S.Ct. 553, 556–557, 419 U.S. 393, 398, 42 L.Ed.2d 532. The rule has been said to be "[g]raven in stone" and "enforced with draconian zeal." Reale International, Inc. v. Federal Republic of Nigeria, C.A.2d, 1981, 647 F.2d 330, 331–332.

6. Dred Scott v. Sandford, 1857, 19 How. 393, 15 L.Ed. 691 (defendant pleaded over after his plea in abatement, challenging jurisdiction, had been overruled); Mitchell v. Maurer, 1934, 55 S.Ct. 162, 293 U.S. 237, 79 L.Ed. 338 (party never raised lack of jurisdiction in any court); Goldstone v. Payne, C.C.A.2d, 1938, 94 F.2d 855 (party who counterclaimed in federal court allowed to assert lack of jurisdiction after losing on merits).

7. Mansfield, C. & L. M. Ry. v. Swan, 1884, 4 S.Ct. 510, 111 U.S. 379, 28 L.Ed. 462; Amco Constr. Co. v. Mississippi State Bldg. Comm., C.A.5th, 1979, 602 F.2d 730.

8. Mansfield, C. & L. M. Ry. v. Swan, 1884, 4 S.Ct. 510, 111 U.S. 379, 28 L.Ed. 462; Cameron v. Hodges, 1888, 8 S.Ct. 1154, 127 U.S. 322, 32 L.Ed. 132; Louisville & N. R. Co. v. Mottley, 1908, 29 S.Ct. 42, 211 U.S. 149, 53 L.Ed. 126; Sumner v. Mata, 1981, 101 S.Ct. 764, 769 n. 2, 449 U.S. 539, 547 n. 2, 66 L.Ed.2d 722.

9. E.g., American Fire & Cas. Co. v. Finn, 1951, 71 S.Ct. 534, 341 U.S. 6, 95 L.Ed. 702 (party who removed case to federal court, and successfully resisted plaintiff's attempts to have it remanded, can raise want of jurisdiction after verdict for plaintiff). See also Santos v. Alaska Bar Assn., C.A.9th, 1980, 618 F.2d 575; Sadat v. Mertes, C.A.7th, 1980, 615 F.2d 1176, 1188–1189.

But a final judgment has res judicata effect even though there was a jurisdictional defect that the parties did not raise. See § 16 below.

10. The doctrine is criticized in the provocative article, Morse, Judicial Self-Denial and Judicial Activism: The Personality of the Original Jurisdiction of the District Courts, 1954, 3 Clev.-Mar. L.Rev. 101, 1955, 4 Clev.-Mar.L.Rev. 7. See also Note, 1960, 7 Utah L.Rev. 258.

Professor Dobbs also is critical of the rule that jurisdiction over the subject matter cannot be obtained by consent. His penetrating study of the history of the rule demonstrates that it was not until the middle of the nineteenth century, when textwriters began to generalize broadly from more limited views dating back to Bracton and Lord Coke, that such a rule become thoroughly settled in the common law. Dobbs, The Decline of Jurisdiction by Consent, 1961, 40 N.C.L.Rev. 49. See also Dobbs, Beyond Bootstrap: Foreclosing the Issue of Subject-Matter Jurisdiction Before Final Judgment, 1967, 51 Minn.L.Rev. 491. It seems clear, however, that this has long been accepted as the rule for the federal courts.

This doctrine is embodied in the Federal Rules of Civil Procedure. Most defects are waived if the party fails to assert them at the time specified by the rules, but it is specifically provided that "whenever it appears by suggestion of the parties or otherwise that the court lacks jurisdiction of the subject matter, the court shall dismiss the action." [11]

A well-known case, if sound, would have made serious inroads on the doctrine just described. In a diversity case defendant challenged the existence of diversity, and the case was set for a preliminary hearing on this issue. Before the date set for the hearing, the parties filed a stipulation that the court had jurisdiction, and so the hearing was not held. Twenty-three months later, after the parties had made extensive preparation for trial, and after the statute of limitations had run on plaintiff's claim, defendant, at the pretrial conference, once more asserted lack of jurisdiction, and presented facts that showed conclusively that there was a want of diversity. The trial court dismissed the action, but the Third Circuit reversed. [12] The basis of the decision is not entirely clear. The court relied on cases that have held that after jurisdiction has been challenged, and the court on inquiry has held that jurisdiction exists, the issue cannot be relitigated. [13] Though the Third Circuit said that defendant's stipulation that jurisdiction existed was equivalent to inquiry and a finding by the court, it may be questioned whether the action of the parties can be so readily equated to a determination by the court. The Third Circuit also argued that the belated assertion of lack of jurisdiction amounted in effect to an attempt to amend the answer. It is discretionary whether to accept amendments to the pleadings, and the court said it would be an abuse of discretion to permit such an amendment in the circumstances before it. This argument seems to assume that the court has discretion to hear a case where jurisdiction is not present, a very questionable assumption. Finally it was said that "a defendant may not play fast and loose with the judicial machinery and deceive the courts." [14] The argument is appealing, but the answer to it may lie in the suggestion of the Seventh Circuit, sustaining a similarly belated challenge to jurisdiction, that while an intentional failure to raise the jurisdictional question in the beginning would be reprehensible, the remedy for such conduct would be disciplinary action by the court rather than an assumption of jurisdiction which the court does not have. [15]

11.　Fed.R.Civ.P. 12(h)(3).

12.　Di Frischia v. New York Central R. Co., C.A.3d, 1960, 279 F.2d 141, noted 1960, 7 Utah L.Rev. 258, 1961, 15 U.Miami L.Q. 315. The result of the case is supported in Stephens, Estoppel to Deny Federal Jurisdiction—Klee and Di Frischia Break Ground, 1963, 68 Dick.L.Rev. 47.

13.　Price v. Greenway, C.A.3d, 1948, 167 F.2d 196; Murphy v. Sun Oil Co., C.C.A.5th, 1936, 86 F.2d 895, certiorari denied 57 S.Ct. 754, 300 U.S. 683, 81 L.Ed. 886.

14.　279 F.2d at 144.

15.　Page v. Wright, C.C.A.7th, 1940, 116 F.2d 449, 455. See also Basso v. Utah Power & Light Co., C.A.7th, 1974, 495

The matter seems to be settled, contrary to the view of the Third Circuit, by a recent Supreme Court decision. On the third day of trial in a wrongful death action the party being sued, which had admitted the jurisdictional allegations in the complaint, disclosed for the first time that its principal place of business was in Iowa, not in Nebraska as alleged in the complaint, and that diversity did not exist. The district court thought it had discretion to finish the trial, and a substantial verdict was returned for plaintiff. The Eighth Circuit affirmed, saying that "the most elementary considerations of judicial fairness" precluded the belated challenge to jurisdiction, particularly since there seemed a good possibility that the statute of limitations would now bar action in state court.[16] The Supreme Court reversed. In a curt footnote it said: "Our holding is that the District Court lacked power to entertain the respondent's lawsuit against the petitioner. Thus, the asserted inequity in the respondent's alleged concealment of its citizenship is irrelevant. Federal judicial power does not depend upon 'prior action or conduct of the parties.' " [17]

Undoubtedly Congress has power to ameliorate, if not to abolish altogether, the doctrine that a jurisdictional defect must be noticed at any time. If the defect is that the case is not within the statutory grant of jurisdiction, as where the jurisdictional amount is not satisfied, Congress, having created the statutory limitation, may determine at what stage of the case it can be asserted. The matter is more difficult if the defect is that the case does not fall within the constitutional grant of judicial power. Even here, however, a tenable argument may be made that the "necessary and proper" clause of the Constitution gives Congress power to avoid wasteful burdens on the courts by setting a time limit for raising jurisdictional questions. This is the view of the American Law Institute. It has proposed a statute providing that no federal court shall consider a jurisdictional defect, except in certain specified circumstances, after the trial on the merits has begun or the district court has made a decision dispositive of the merits.[18]

It is important to understand that the present section is concerned solely with jurisdiction over the subject matter. Jurisdiction over the person is a waivable defect, which must be asserted by the party who

F.2d 906; Knee v. Chemical Leaman Tank Lines, Inc., D.C.Pa.1968, 293 F.Supp. 1094.

"The Di Frischia decision has received considerable attention from the commentators * * *, but has been ignored, criticized, or limited to its facts and distinguished by the federal courts." Sadat v. Mertes, C.A.7th, 1980, 615 F.2d 1176, 1189.

16. Kroger v. Owen Equipment & Erection Co., C.A.8th, 1977, 558 F.2d 417, 427.

17. Owen Equipment & Erection Co. v. Kroger, 1978, 98 S.Ct. 2396, 2404 n. 21, 437 U.S. 365, 377 n. 21, 57 L.Ed.2d 274.

18. ALI Study, § 1386. The proposal is criticized as both "too broad and too narrow" by Dobbs, Beyond Bootstrap: Foreclosing the Issue of Subject-Matter Jurisdiction Before Final Judgment, 1967, 51 Minn.L.Rev. 491, 527.

would take advantage of it.[19] And a distinction must be drawn between lack of jurisdiction and want of merits. A court may have jurisdiction over a case even though the case is one to which there is no merit.[20] The jurisdiction of the federal courts is dependent on the subject matter of the action or the status of the parties to it; it is not dependent on the merits of the case.

§ 8. Constitutional Basis of the Judicial Power

Article III, section 2 of the Constitution provides in part: "The judicial Power shall extend to all Cases, in Law and Equity, arising under this Constitution, the Laws of the United States, and Treaties made, or which shall be made, under their Authority;—to all Cases affecting Ambassadors, other public Ministers and Consuls;—to all Cases of admiralty and maritime jurisdiction;—to Controversies to which the United States shall be a party;—to Controversies between two or more States;—between a State and Citizens of another State;—between Citizens of different States;—between Citizens of the same State claiming Lands under Grants of different States, and between a State, or the Citizens thereof, and foreign States, Citizens or Subjects.

"In all Cases affecting Ambassadors, other public Ministers and Consuls, and those in which a State shall be a party, the Supreme Court shall have original Jurisdiction. In all the other cases before mentioned, the Supreme Court shall have appellate Jurisdiction, both as to Law and Fact, with such Exceptions, and under such Regulations as the Congress shall make."

The quoted provision is the primary, if not the exclusive, source of power for the federal courts. In 1809 the Supreme Court decided the case of Hodgson v. Bowerbank.[1] In that case the record showed that the plaintiffs were English citizens, and thus aliens, but did not show the citizenship of the defendants. The First Judiciary Act provided for jurisdiction in all suits in which an alien was a party, and it was argued accordingly that since the plaintiffs were aliens, the citizenship of the defendants was immaterial. Not so, said Chief Justice Marshall, for the Court. "Turn to the article of the Constitution of the United States, for the statute cannot extend the jurisdiction beyond the limits of the Constitution." Since the Constitution does not authorize jurisdiction in all cases to which an alien is a party, but only to cases "between a State, or the citizens thereof, and foreign States, citizens, or subjects," there was no jurisdiction, where the citizenship

19. Fed.R.Civ.P. 12(h)(1); Petrowski v. Hawkeye-Sec. Ins. Co., 1956, 76 S.Ct. 490, 350 U.S. 495, 100 L.Ed. 639.

20. Venner v. Great Northern Ry. Co., 1908, 28 S.Ct. 328, 209 U.S. 24, 52 L.Ed. 666; Duke Power Co. v. Carolina Environmental Study Group, Inc., 1978, 98 S.Ct. 2620, 2629, 438 U.S. 59, 70–72, 57 L.Ed.2d 595.

[§ 8]

1. 1809, 5 Cranch 303, 3 L.Ed. 108.

of the defendants was not shown, even though the statute purported to confer jurisdiction.

The Court cited no authority for this proposition, nor did it need to do so. The landmark case of Marbury v. Madison,[2] decided six years before, had held unconstitutional so much of a section of the First Judiciary Act as purported to give the Supreme Court original jurisdiction in a case admittedly within the judicial power of the United States but not within the definition of original jurisdiction in the second paragraph of Article III, section 2. If, as there held, Congress cannot distribute the judicial power of the federal courts among the various federal courts except as provided by the Constitution, then it appears to be an a fortiori proposition that Congress cannot give federal courts jurisdiction in cases not within the Constitutional definition of the judicial power.[3]

This principle, that the jurisdiction of the federal courts cannot extend beyond that given by the Constitution, would seem to be fundamental. It has, however, been subject to some inroads. Thus the Constitution does not in terms permit the removal of cases from state court to federal court. Yet the First Judiciary Act, and all since, have authorized this in particular circumstances, and where the case is one within the judicial power of the United States, the provision for removal has been held to be an appropriate exercise of the congressional power to make laws "necessary and proper" for carrying out the tasks delegated to the national government.[4] There are some matters that cannot be independently asserted in a federal court, because they do not come within the judicial power of the United States, but that may, as a matter of procedural convenience, be raised as "ancillary" to a matter that is properly being heard by the federal court.[5] Finally there has been some recent contention that Congress is not confined to Article Three in conferring jurisdiction on the federal courts, but may also give to those courts jurisdiction as to any matter within the legislative powers of Congress, set out in Article One. This contention is discussed later.[6]

2. 1803, 1 Cranch 137, 2 L.Ed. 60.

3. It has recently been argued that Hodgson represented merely a narrow interpretation of § 11 of the Judiciary Act of 1789, rather than a holding that § 11 was unconstitutional insofar as it purported to give the federal courts jurisdiction of all suits to which an alien was a party. Mahoney, A Historical Note on Hodgson v. Bowerbank, 1982, 49 U.Chi.L.Rev. 725. The latter view is described, at 733, as "[t]he Hart-Wechsler-Wright revisionist interpretation of Hodgson's significance * * *." The important point of Hodgson, however, is its recognition that a statute cannot extend the jurisdiction beyond the limits of the Constitution. Whether the Court then interpreted the statute narrowly, because it would be unconstitutional if construed literally, or whether it held the statute pro tanto unconstitutional, seems to the present author a question of semantics.

4. Tennessee v. Davis, 1880, 100 U.S. 257, 25 L.Ed. 648.

5. See § 9 below.

6. See § 11 below. See also § 20 below.

§ 9. Ancillary Jurisdiction [1]

The most important instance in which the federal courts hear cases over which no jurisdiction is conferred on them, in terms, by the Constitution, or by the statutes, is where the ill-defined concept of "ancillary jurisdiction" can be brought into play. By this concept it is held that a district court acquires jurisdiction of a case or controversy as an entirety, and may, as an incident to disposition of a matter properly before it, possess jurisdiction to decide other matters raised by the case of which it could not take cognizance were they independently presented. Thus if the court has jurisdiction of the principal action, it may hear also any ancillary proceeding therein, regardless of the citizenship of the parties, the amount in controversy, or any other factor that would normally determine jurisdiction.[2]

That there should be such an ancillary jurisdiction is, in some instances, virtually a matter of necessity. This is illustrated by the leading case of Freeman v. Howe.[3] In an action properly in federal court on the basis of diversity, Freeman, the United States marshal, seized certain railroad cars under writs of attachment. The mortgagees of the railroad then brought an action of replevin against Freeman in a state court, and had judgment there. On review of the state court decision, the Supreme Court held that a state court has no authority to interfere with property that is under control of the federal court. Such a holding is inevitable, if an unseemly conflict between courts is to be avoided and if the federal court is indeed to function as a court. But the mortgagees argued that to bar their action in state court would be to leave them remediless, since, as to them, there was no diversity and they could not proceed to assert their claim against the property in federal court. The Supreme Court said that this was a misapprehension. It said that any party whose interests are affected by the action in federal court in which that court has taken control of the property may assert his claim to the property in federal court, and that such a claim would be ancillary and dependent, supplementary merely to the original suit out of which it had arisen, and maintained without reference to the citizenship or residence of the parties.

[§ 9]

1. 13 Wright, Miller & Cooper, Jurisdiction § 3523; Garvey, The Limits of Ancillary Jurisdiction, 1979, 57 Texas L.Rev. 697; Fraser, Jurisdiction of the Federal Courts of Actions Involving Multiple Claims, 1977, 76 F.R.D. 525; Goldberg, The Influence of Procedural Rules on Federal Jurisdiction, 1976, 28 Stan.L.Rev. 395; Baker, Toward a Relaxed View of Federal Ancillary and Pendent Jurisdiction, 1972, 33 U.Pitts. L.Rev. 659; Note, Federal Civil Procedure: Limiting Ancillary Jurisdiction, 1979, 31 U.Fla.L.Rev. 442; Comment, Limiting Federal Ancillary and Pendent Jurisdiction in Diversity Cases, 1979, 64 Iowa L.Rev. 930.

2. Krippendorf v. Hyde, 1884, 4 S.Ct. 27, 110 U.S. 276, 28 L.Ed. 145; Iowa v. Union Asphalt & Roadoils, Inc., C.A. 8th, 1969, 409 F.2d 1239; Compton v. Jesup, C.C.A.6th, 1895, 68 F. 263; and cases cited 13 Wright, Miller & Cooper, Jurisdiction § 3523 n. 2.

3. 1860, 24 How. 450, 16 L.Ed. 749. See the discussion of this case in Aldinger v. Howard, 1976, 96 S.Ct. 2413, 2418–2419, 427 U.S. 1, 10–11, 49 L.Ed. 2d 276.

Once it is agreed that a state court cannot interfere with property in the control of the federal court, the notion of ancillary jurisdiction put forward in Freeman v. Howe cannot be avoided. Unless the federal court has ancillary jurisdiction to hear the claims of all persons to the property, regardless of their citizenship, some persons, with a valid claim to the property, would be deprived of any forum in which to press that claim.[4] Most of the early cases of ancillary jurisdiction were of this type.

In addition to the cases in which property was under the control of the court, there was a group of cases holding that the federal court has jurisdiction to do those acts that it must do in order properly to effectuate its judgment on a matter as to which it has jurisdiction. Thus it may enjoin relitigation in state courts of issues already determined in a federal action, and issue such other writs as are needed to make its judgment effective.[5] This jurisdiction, too, is required if the federal court is to make effective disposition of cases properly before it.

If this were the total extent of ancillary jurisdiction, it would be a concept of importance but of limited usefulness. As late as 1925 the Supreme Court said "no controversy can be regarded as dependent or ancillary unless it has direct relation to property or assets actually or constructively drawn into the court's possession or control by the principal suit."[6] Literally this was not true. There were obscure earlier cases in which ancillary jurisdiction had been exercised though it did not involve property controlled by the court, nor was it needed to effectuate the judgment.[7] But it is significant that the Supreme Court thought that ancillary jurisdiction was so limited.

The major expansion of ancillary jurisdiction rests on a case decided in 1926. In Moore v. New York Cotton Exchange [8] there was no diversity. Plaintiff's claim was properly in federal court, since it alleged a violation of the Sherman Act. Defendant asserted a counterclaim, compulsory under the Equity Rules of 1912 since it arose out of the same transaction as did plaintiff's claim, asking for an injunction. The counterclaim did not involve a federal question. It was held, nevertheless, that after the plaintiff's claim had been dismissed on the merits, the court could go ahead and award the injunction sought by the counterclaim. The Moore case did not use the term

4. Aldinger v. Howard, 1976, 96 S.Ct. 2413, 2419 n. 7, 427 U.S. 1, 11 n. 7, 49 L.Ed.2d 276.

5. Supreme Tribe of Ben-Hur v. Cauble, 1921, 41 S.Ct. 338, 255 U.S. 356, 65 L.Ed. 673. See § 47 below. See also Board of County Commrs. v. U. S. ex rel. Moulton, 1884, 5 S.Ct. 108, 112 U.S. 217, 28 L.Ed. 698.

6. Fulton Nat. Bank of Atlanta v. Hozier, 1925, 45 S.Ct. 261, 262, 267 U.S. 276, 280, 69 L.Ed. 609.

7. Dewey v. West Fairmont Gas Coal Co., 1887, 8 S.Ct. 148, 123 U.S. 329, 31 L.Ed. 179; Partridge v. Phoenix Mut. Life Ins. Co., 1872, 15 Wall. 573, 580, 21 L.Ed. 229. See also Barney v. Latham, 1881, 103 U.S. 205, 26 L.Ed. 514.

8. 1926, 46 S.Ct. 367, 270 U.S. 593, 70 L.Ed. 750.

"ancillary jurisdiction" nor did it cite to the earlier cases in which that concept had been applied. Indeed the Court cited no cases, and gave very little explanation of why the federal court had jurisdiction to hear the counterclaim. It said only: "So close is the connection between the case sought to be stated in the bill and that set up in the counterclaim that it only needs the failure of the former to establish a foundation for the latter; but the relief afforded by the dismissal of the bill is not complete without an injunction restraining appellant from continuing to obtain by stealthy appropriation what the court had held it could not have by judicial compulsion." [9] The result is a convenient one. When parties have conflicting claims arising from a single transaction, it is undesirable to require that the litigation be divided between state and federal court. But there is a difference between allowing ancillary jurisdiction to do those things that are a necessity if the court is to function as a court, as the earlier cases had permitted, and allowing ancillary jurisdiction to do those things that are merely procedurally convenient.

The Federal Rules of Civil Procedure, adopted in 1938, broadened prior provisions for joinder of claims and joinder of parties. Many of these joinder rules would be of limited utility if they were subject to the ordinary rules of jurisdiction and venue, yet the rules themselves cannot extend jurisdiction or venue. Following the lead of the Moore case, the federal courts have employed the concept of ancillary jurisdiction in an effort to balance federal jurisdictional requirements with the liberal provisions of the rules as to joinder.[10] Since it was not until 1978 that the Supreme Court spoke significantly on the permissible scope of ancillary jurisdiction under the rules, there was disagreement on how far it extended.

The 1978 decision was in Owen Equipment & Erection Co. v. Kroger.[11] The Court there rejected the notion that a "common nucleus of operative fact" is enough for the exercise of ancillary jurisdiction.[12] The test, the Court said, is "not mere factual similarity but logical dependence." [13] It went on to emphasize that "ancillary jurisdiction typically involves claims by a defending party haled into court against his will, or by another person whose rights might be irretriev-

---

9. 46 S.Ct. at 371, 270 U.S. at 610.

10. Revere Copper & Brass Inc. v. Aetna Cas. & Sur. Co., C.A.5th, 1970, 426 F.2d 709, 716–717; Brandt v. Olson, D.C.Iowa 1959, 179 F.Supp. 363, 370. See Goldberg, note 1 above.

11. 1976, 96 S.Ct. 2413, 427 U.S. 1, 49 L.Ed.2d 276. See Brill, Federal Rule of Civil Procedure 14 and Ancillary Jurisdiction, 1980, 59 Neb.L.Rev. 631; Berch, The Erection of a Barrier Against Assertion of Ancillary Claims: An Examination of Owen Equipment and Erection Company v. Kroger, 1979 Ariz.St.L.J. 253; Note, Critique—Ancillary and Pendent Party Jurisdiction in the Aftermath of Owen Equipment & Erection Co. v. Kroger, 1979, 28 Drake L.Rev. 758; Note, Ancillary Jurisdiction: The Kroger Approach and The Federal Rules, 1979, 28 Emory L.J. 463.

12. 98 S.Ct. at 2403, 437 U.S. at 374–375.

13. 98 S.Ct. at 2404, 437 U.S. at 376.

ably lost unless he could assert them in an ongoing action in a federal court." [14]

The permissibility of ancillary jurisdiction will be considered with regard to particular rules in later sections. The following statements probably represent a present consensus, though there is no unanimity on many of them, and some rules may need to be reappraised in the light of Owen Equipment.

Ancillary jurisdiction permits courts to hear compulsory counter-claims, under Rule 13(a), and to bring in additional parties to respond to a compulsory counterclaim under Rule 13(h), but permissive counter-claims, under Rule 13(b), require independent jurisdictional grounds.[15] Cross-claims, under Rule 13(g), are ancillary.[16] Implead-er of a third party defendant under Rule 14 falls within ancillary jurisdiction.[17] Ancillary jurisdiction does not apply to joinder of claims, under Rule 18, except where the federal and nonfederal claims are so closely related as to amount to separate grounds in support of a single cause of action.[18] Ancillary jurisdiction is available in interplead-er, under Rule 22.[19] Intervention as of right, under Rule 24(a), comes within the court's ancillary jurisdiction, but permissive intervention, under Rule 24(b), does not.[20]

Until recently it had been thought to be the law that ancillary jurisdiction had no application to joinder of parties under Rule 20, and that no matter how closely related the matters might be, a party whose citizenship was wrong or whose claim was for less than the jurisdictional amount could not be joined in a suit with a party who satisfied federal jurisdictional requirements. There were, however, departures from that orthodoxy. By analogy to the concept of "pendent jurisdiction," which permits a nonfederal claim to be heard if it is closely related to a federal claim,[21] some courts and commentators developed a notion of "pendent parties." [22] This problem takes different forms in different contexts and is discussed in each of these contexts in subsequent sections. For now it is enough to say that Owen Equipment itself rejects the notion that a pendent party concept can be used to overcome the requirement of complete diversity,[23] that that concept cannot be used to avoid the rule on amount in controversy,[24] and that in Aldinger v. Howard [25] the Supreme Court took a

---

14. 98 S.Ct. at 2404, 437 U.S. at 376.

15. See § 79 below.

16. See § 80 below.

17. See § 76 below.

18. See §§ 19, 78 below.

19. See § 74 below.

20. See § 75 below.

21. See § 19 below. The distinction between "pendent jurisdiction" and "ancillary jurisdiction" is defined in Corporacion Venezolana de Fomento v. Vintero Sales Corp., D.C.N.Y.1979, 477 F.Supp. 615, 622 n. 13.

22. Currie, Pendent Parties, 1978, 45 U.Chi.L.Rev. 753; Fortune, Pendent Jurisdiction—The Problem of "Pendenting Parties," 1972, 34 U.Pitt. L.Rev. 1.

23. 98 S.Ct. at 2402–2404, 437 U.S. at 373–377. See § 24 below.

24. Zahn v. International Paper Co., 1973, 94 S.Ct. 505, 414 U.S. 291, 38 L.Ed.2d 511. See § 36 below.

25. 1976, 96 S.Ct. 2413, 427 U.S. 1, 49 L.Ed.2d 276.

guarded view on use of the concept to allow joinder of one claim against one party with a second claim, for which there is no independent jurisdictional ground, against a second party, but the Court did not close the door entirely on that possibility.[26]

It is usually held that where ancillary jurisdiction suffices to allow a claim, or a party without independent jurisdictional grounds, it is also unnecessary to satisfy the venue statutes with regard to that claim or party. Though there have been cases to the contrary,[27] it would seem that if procedural convenience is enough to avoid the constitutional limitations on the jurisdiction of the federal court, it should suffice also to dispense with the purely statutory requirements as to venue.[28]

In general the ancillary concept does not avoid the requirement that the party to be brought in must be served with process within the territorial limits set out in Rule 4(f).[29] One interesting problem in this area, however, has not yet been resolved by the courts. Where out-of-state service is possible under a federal statute allowing such service for particular claims, does the process also bring the party into court to respond to a claim, joined with the statutory claim, as to which, if sued on independently, out-of-state service would be improper? Though the matter is not settled,[30] it would seem that where the claims are sufficiently related to come within the ancillary jurisdiction concept, the process should be regarded as sufficient to bring the party into court to respond to both claims.[31]

§ 10. Congressional Control of Jurisdiction [1]

In section 8 it was seen that, in general, the jurisdiction of the federal courts must find its basis in Article III of the Constitution.

26. See § 19 below.

27. Lewis v. United Air Lines Transport Corp., D.C.Conn.1939, 29 F.Supp. 112; King v. Shepherd, D.C.Ark.1938, 26 F.Supp. 357; Habina v. M. A. Henry Co., D.C.N.Y.1948, 8 F.R.D. 52.

28. Haile v. Henderson Nat. Bank, C.A. 6th, 1981, 657 F.2d 816, 822 n. 6; Lesnik v. Public Industrials Corp., C.C.A. 2d, 1944, 144 F.2d 968, 974–977; Herndon v. Herndon, D.C.Tex.1980, 491 F.Supp. 53; 6 Wright & Miller, Civil § 1445. But see Note, Ancillary Process and Venue in the Federal Courts, 1960, 73 Harv.L.Rev. 1164.

29. Donnely v. Copeland Intra Lenses, Inc., D.C.N.Y.1980, 87 F.R.D. 80; U. S. v. Rhoades, D.C.Colo.1953, 14 F.R.D. 373.

30. See 4 Wright & Miller, Civil § 1125.

31. E.g., International Controls Corp. v. Vesco, C.A.2d, 1979, 593 F.2d 166, 175 n. 5, certiorari denied 99 S.Ct. 2884, 442 U.S. 941, 61 L.Ed.2d 311; Robinson v.

Penn Central Co., C.A.3d, 1973, 484 F.2d 553; Mills, Pendent Jurisdiction and Extraterritorial Service Under the Federal Securities Law, 1970, 70 Col.L. Rev. 423; Note, 1982, 51 Fordham L.Rev. 127; ALI Study, § 1313(a). But see, e.g., Wilensky v. Standard Beryllium Corp., D.C.Mass.1964, 228 F.Supp. 703, 705–706; Ferguson, Pendent Personal Jurisdiction in the Federal Courts, 1965, 11 Vill.L.Rev. 56.

[§ 10]

1. 13 Wright, Miller & Cooper, Jurisdiction §§ 3525, 3526; Redish, Federal Jurisdiction: Tensions in the Allocation of Judicial Power, 1980, pp. 7–34; Berger, Congress v. Supreme Court, 1969, pp. 225–296; Harris, The Judicial Power of the United States, 1940, c. 2; Hart, The Power of Congress to Limit the Jurisdiction of Federal Courts: An Exercise in Dialectic, 1953, 66 Harv.L.Rev. 1362; Ratner, Congressional Power over the Appellate Jurisdiction of the Supreme

The present section is concerned with the extent to which the judicial power granted by the Constitution is subject to control by Congress.

The question is most readily answered with regard to the original jurisdiction of the Supreme Court. Although the First Congress, in the Judiciary Act of 1789, undertook to set forth that jurisdiction, it has always been understood that the constitutional language is, in this regard, self-executing, and that Congress cannot take that jurisdiction away from the Supreme Court.[2] Congress cannot expand the original jurisdiction of the Supreme Court, even to cases otherwise within the judicial power of the United States,[3] nor can it deny such jurisdiction. It can, however, provide that the jurisdiction of the Supreme Court in cases within the grant of original jurisdiction, be concurrent with the district courts,[4] and can give appellate jurisdiction in cases that might also fall within the original jurisdiction of the Supreme Court.[5]

The extent of congressional control of the appellate jurisdiction of the Supreme Court and of the lower federal courts has not been the subject of many court decisions. It has, however, aroused much debate and scholarly writing when legislation has been proposed that would limit jurisdiction as a means of depriving the federal courts of authority in fields in which their decisions have been controversial.

Court, 1960, 109 U.Pa.L.Rev. 157; Merry, Scope of the Supreme Court's Appellate Jurisdiction: Historical Basis, 1962, 47 Minn.L.Rev. 53; Strong, Rx for a Nagging Constitutional Headache, 1971, 8 San Diego L.Rev. 246; Keeffe & Warlick, Article III: Where Are You Now that We Need You?, 1976, 62 A.B.A.J. 246; Redish & Woods, Congressional Power to Control the Jurisdiction of Lower Federal Courts: A Critical Review and a New Synthesis, 1975, 124 U.Pa.L.Rev. 45; McGowan, Federal Jurisdiction: Legislative and Judicial Change, 1978, 28 Case W.Res.L.Rev. 517; Symposium, Limiting Federal Court Jurisdiction, 1981, 65 Judicature 177; Sager, Foreword: Constitutional Limitations on Congress' Authority to Regulate the Jurisdiction of the Federal Courts, 1981, 95 Harv.L.Rev. 17; Young, Congressional Regulation of Federal Courts' Jurisdiction and Processes: United States v. Klein Revisited, 1981 Wis.L.Rev. 1189; Redish, Constitutional Limitations on Congressional Power to Control Federal Jurisdiction: A Reaction to Professor Sager, 1982, 77 Nw.U.L.Rev. 143; Auerbach, The Unconstitutionality of Congressional Proposals to Limit the Jurisdiction of Federal Courts, 1982, 47 Mo.L.Rev. 47;

Meserve, Limiting Jurisdiction and Remedies of Federal Courts, 1982, 68 A.B.A.J. 159; Anderson, The Government of Courts: The Power of Congress under Article III, 1982, 68 A.B. A.J. 686.

2. Chisholm v. Georgia, 1793, 2 Dall. 419, 1 L.Ed. 440; Florida v. Georgia, 1854, 17 How. 478, 15 L.Ed. 181; Kentucky v. Dennison, 1860, 24 How. 66, 16 L.Ed. 717; California v. Arizona, 1979, 99 S.Ct. 919, 440 U.S. 59, 59 L.Ed.2d 144; 17 Wright, Miller & Cooper, Jurisdiction § 4043.

3. Marbury v. Madison, 1803, 1 Cranch 137, 2 L.Ed. 60; Wisconsin v. Pelican Ins. Co. of New Orleans, 1888, 8 S.Ct. 1370, 1379, 127 U.S. 265, 300, 32 L.Ed. 239.

4. Ohio v. Wyandotte Chemicals Corp., 1971, 91 S.Ct. 1005, 401 U.S. 493, 28 L.Ed.2d 256; Ames v. Kansas ex rel. Johnston, 1884, 4 S.Ct. 437, 111 U.S. 449, 28 L.Ed. 482; U. S. v. California, C.A.9th, 1964, 328 F.2d 729, certiorari denied 85 S.Ct. 34, 379 U.S. 817, 13 L.Ed.2d 29. Congress has in fact done this ever since 1789. See 28 U.S.C.A. §§ 1251, 1351. See §§ 109, 110 below.

5. Cohens v. Virginia, 1821, 6 Wheat. 264, 5 L.Ed. 257.

In the 1950s the issue was subversion; in the early 1980s it is such matters as abortion, school prayer, and busing.

The Constitution, after defining the original jurisdiction of the Supreme Court, provides that in all other cases within the judicial power of the United States, "the supreme Court shall have appellate Jurisdiction, both as to Law and Fact, with such Exceptions, and under such Regulations as the Congress shall make." The power to make exceptions in this jurisdiction was tested in the famous case of Ex parte McCardle.[6] An Act of 1867 gave the Supreme Court appellate jurisdiction in habeas corpus cases. Prior to that time there was no such jurisdiction on appeal, though the Supreme Court could issue original writs of habeas corpus and certiorari, and review a denial of habeas corpus below by this means. McCardle was a civilian, held for trial by a military commission in Mississippi pursuant to Reconstruction statutes. The circuit court denied his application for habeas corpus, and he appealed. In 1868, while the case was pending before the Supreme Court, Congress, apprehensive lest the Supreme Court would grant the writ and thus invalidate much of the Reconstruction legislation, passed an amendatory statute, taking away the appellate jurisdiction of the Supreme Court in habeas corpus cases. The Supreme Court held that the 1868 legislation deprived it of jurisdiction. It considered that this was a legitimate exercise of the congressional power to make exceptions to appellate jurisdiction, and that it was immaterial that the act was passed after the Supreme Court had already taken jurisdiction of the case. This case has long been read as giving Congress full control over the Supreme Court's appellate jurisdiction, but of late there has been some suggestion that this is reading too much into the McCardle decision, and that Congress does not have power to make such exceptions as will destroy the essential role of the Supreme Court in the constitutional plan.[7] This reading, for which there is little or no direct authority, is fortified by the fact that shortly after the McCardle case it was held that the Supreme Court could still issue original writs of habeas corpus and certiorari, and thus review in a case like McCardle's.[8] The argument is that the essential role of the Supreme Court is not destroyed when, as in 1868, one means of approach is taken away but another is left open. To deprive litigants altogether of access to the Supreme Court in cases

6. 1868, 7 Wall. 506, 19 L.Ed. 264. See Van Alstyne, A Critical Guide to Ex Parte McCardle, 1973, 15 Ariz.L.Rev. 229.

7. Sager, note 1 above, at 42–68. Brant, Appellate Jurisdiction: Congressional Abuse of the Exceptions Clause, 1973 Ore.L.Rev. 3; Ratner, note 1 above, Hart, note 1 above, at 1365. See also Merry, note 1 above, arguing that congressional control of the Supreme Court's appellate jurisdiction was intended to extend only to questions of fact, not questions of law.

In a dissenting opinion in Glidden Co. v. Zdanok, 1962, 82 S.Ct. 1459, 1501 n. 11, 370 U.S. 530, 605, 8 L.Ed.2d 671, Justices Douglas and Black say "there is a serious question whether the McCardle case could command a majority view today."

8. Ex parte Yerger, 1869, 8 Wall. 85, 19 L.Ed. 332.

involving the supremacy of federal law would, on this approach, be invalid.

The orthodox view, however, is that Congress possesses plenary power to confer or withhold appellate jurisdiction.[9] Even those who subscribe to this traditional view of congressional power may still conclude, however, that Congress may not violate other provisions of the Constitution in controlling appellate jurisdiction.[10] Thus it can be argued that a jurisdictional statute that acted as an arbitrary or invidious exclusion of a class of litigants or that purported to prevent Supreme Court review of a class of cases involving constitutional rights because of dissatisfaction with the Court's past decisions in that field of law would be unconstitutional.[11]

Congress has a considerable discretion in dealing with the jurisdiction of the lower federal courts. It can provide a particular court for hearing certain questions and deny all other courts the power to consider that question,[12] even to the point of precluding raising the invalidity of a regulation as a defense in a criminal action, where there was a court provided in which the invalidity of the regulation might have been asserted.[13] Congress can provide that cases within the judicial power shall come to the federal courts by removal, rather than in their original jurisdiction.[14] It can take away from the courts power to grant a particular remedy or to enforce a particular kind of contract.[15]

From the First Judiciary Act to the present, Congress has provided that in certain instances the jurisdiction of the federal courts shall be exclusive of the courts of the several states,[16] though federal jurisdiction is not exclusive unless Congress chooses to make it so, either

9.   Abraham, A "Self-Inflicted Wound?", 1981, 65 Judicature 179; Rice, The Constitutional Basis for the Proposals in Congress Today, 1981, 65 Judicature 190; Anderson, The Power of Congress to Limit the Appellate Jurisdiction of the Supreme Court, 1981 Det. C.L.L.Rev. 753; Van Alstyne, note 6 above; Wechsler, The Courts and the Constitution, 1965, 65 Col.L.Rev. 1001, 1005.

10.   Meserve, note 1 above, Taylor, The Unconstitutionality of Current Legislative Proposals, 1981, 65 Judicature 199; Van Alstyne, note 6 above.

11.   See Taylor, note 10 above; Sager, note 1 above, at 68–80.

The case of U. S. v. Klein, 1872, 13 Wall. 128, 20 L.Ed. 519, lends some support to this thesis, but the decision is cryptic, and there is much argument on how far it goes. See Young, note 1 above.

12.   Lockerty v. Phillips, 1943, 63 S.Ct. 1019, 319 U.S. 182, 87 L.Ed. 1339.

13.   Yakus v. U. S., 1944, 64 S.Ct. 660, 321 U.S. 414, 88 L.Ed. 834.

14.   Tennessee v. Davis, 1880, 100 U.S. 257, 25 L.Ed. 648; Martin v. Wyzanski, D.C.Mass.1967, 262 F.Supp. 925.

15.   Lauf v. E. G. Shinner & Co., 1938, 58 S.Ct. 578, 303 U.S. 323, 82 L.Ed. 872; Chrisman v. Sisters of St. Joseph of Peace, C.A.9th, 1974, 506 F.2d 308.

But see Meserve, note 1 above, Sager, note 1 above at 80–88; Rotunda, Congressional Power to Restrict the Jurisdiction of the Lower Federal Courts and the Problem of School Busing, 1976, 64 Geo.L.J. 839.

16.   13 Wright, Miller & Cooper, Jurisdiction § 3527. The constitutionality of this practice was thought beyond serious question in The Moses Taylor, 1867, 4 Wall. 411, 18 L.Ed. 397.

expressly or by fair implication.[17]   At present the most significant areas in which Congress has made federal jurisdiction exclusive are bankruptcy proceedings,[18] patent and copyright cases,[19] cases involving fines, penalties, forfeitures, or seizures, under laws of the United States,[20] and crimes against the United States,[21] though there are some others.[22]   The statute purports to give the federal courts exclusive jurisdiction of cases of admiralty and maritime jurisdiction,[23] but by virtue of the "saving to suitors" clause in the statute, in fact federal jurisdiction is exclusive only in limitation of liability proceedings and in maritime actions in rem.[24]

Though a wide power in Congress to regulate the jurisdiction of the federal courts has never been challenged, there has been discussion from 1789 on about whether Congress is required to vest all of the judicial power defined in Article III, § 2, in some federal court. On this question at least four positions are possible: (1) the constitutional grant is self-executing, and if there is some part of the judicial power not vested by Congress, the courts can hear such cases on the basis of the Constitution alone; (2) the constitutional language is mandatory, and Congress should vest the whole of the judicial power, but the duty is not enforcible if Congress should fail to act; (3) Congress has discretion in deciding whether or not to give to the federal courts any part of the constitutional judicial power, save that the grant of original jurisdiction to the Supreme Court is self-executing; (4) though Congress has a wide discretion in granting or refusing to grant jurisdiction, there are due process limitations on this discretion. Scholarly and judicial support can be found for each of these views.

17. Claflin v. Houseman, 1876, 93 U.S. 130, 23 L.Ed. 833; Charles Dowd Box Co. v. Courtney, 1962, 82 S.Ct. 519, 523, 368 U.S. 502, 507–508, 7 L.Ed.2d 483.   Redish & Muench, Adjudication of Federal Causes of Action in State Court, 1976, 75 Mich.L.Rev. 311; Note, Exclusive Jurisdiction of the Federal Courts in Private Civil Actions, 1957, 70 Harv.L.Rev. 509.

18. 28 U.S.C.A. § 1334; 13A Wright, Miller & Cooper, Jurisdiction 2d § 3570.

19. 28 U.S.C.A. § 1338(a); 13 Wright, Miller & Cooper, Jurisdiction § 3582; Cooper, State Law of Patent Exploitation, 1972, 56 Minn.L.Rev. 313; Chisum, The Allocation of Jurisdiction between State and Federal Courts in Patent Litigation, 1971, 46 Wash.L. Rev. 633.

20. 28 U.S.C.A. §§ 1355, 1356; 13 Wright, Miller & Cooper, Jurisdiction § 3578. The ALI Study, pp. 184–186, proposes repeal of these provisions.

21. 18 U.S.C.A. § 3231.

22. 28 U.S.C.A. §§ 1351 (consuls and vice-consuls as defendants), 1583 (review of decisions of collectors of customs); 1346 (United States as defendant). In the last of these categories it is only by implication that federal jurisdiction is exclusive.

Some provisions for exclusive federal jurisdiction appear outside the Judicial Code. See, e.g., 15 U.S.C.A. §§ 15, 26 (antitrust actions), 15 U.S.C.A. § 78aa (cases under the Securities Exchange act), 15 U.S.C.A. § 717u (violations of the Natural Gas Act), and 40 U.S.C.A. § 270(b) (suits on bonds under the Miller Act).

See Dickinson, Exclusive Federal Jurisdiction and the Role of the States in Securities Regulation, 1980, 65 Iowa L.Rev. 1201; Note, The Securities Exchange Act and the Rule of Exclusive Federal Jurisdiction, 1979, 89 Yale L.J. 95.

23. 28 U.S.C.A. § 1333.

24. See 14 Wright, Miller & Cooper, Jurisdiction § 3672; ALI Study, pp. 234–239; Black, Admiralty Jurisdiction: Critique and Suggestions, 1950, 50 Col.L.Rev. 259, 266–267.

The difficulty on this point was felt in the first Congress. "The crucial contest in the enactment of the Judiciary Act," Charles Warren tells us, was between the broad pro-Constitution men who believed that Congress had no power to withhold from the federal courts any of the judicial power granted by the Constitution, and the narrow pro-Constitution men who were anxious to give the federal courts as little jurisdiction as possible.[25]   Though the jurisdictional grants that were made in the First Judiciary Act are patently a compromise between these two positions, the fact is that Congress did not grant to the federal courts the full judicial power of the United States.   There was no general grant of "federal question" jurisdiction, jurisdictional amount requirements barred access to federal court for small cases otherwise within the judicial power, and the troublesome "assignee clause" denied jurisdiction, though there was diversity between the parties of record, in some cases where the plaintiff was an assignee of a claim originally owned by a person who, for want of diversity, could not have sued in federal court.

The constitutionality of the decision of the first Congress might have been thought settled in 1799.[26]   A case came to the Supreme Court in which the indorsee of a note had sued, and diversity existed between him and the defendants, but the record did not show the citizenship of the indorsers of the note.   At the oral argument it was asserted that the citizenship of the indorsers was immaterial; since there was citizenship between the parties of record, the constitutional requirement was satisfied, and Congress lacked power to limit that jurisdiction by the assignee clause.   Chief Justice Ellsworth expressed his doubt as to how far the argument could be carried, and Justice Chase expressed his view more strongly: "The notion has frequently been entertained, that the federal courts derive their judicial power immediately from the constitution; but the political truth is, that the disposal of the judicial power (except in a few specified instances) belongs to Congress.   If Congress has given the power to this court, we possess it, not otherwise; and if Congress has not given the power to us, or to any other court, it still remains at the legislative disposal.   Besides, Congress is not bound, and it would, perhaps, be inexpedient, to enlarge the jurisdiction of the federal courts, to every subject, in every form, which the constitution might warrant." [27]   Though the opinion of the Court, holding the suit must fail for want of allegations as to the citizenship of the indorsers, does not discuss the constitutional question, it was necessarily present in the case, and, in view of the oral argument, cannot be thought to have been overlooked.

25. Warren, New Light on the History of the Federal Judiciary Act of 1789, 1923, 37 Harv.L.Rev. 49, 65–70.

26. Turner v. The President, Directors, and Co. of the Bank of North America, 1799, 4 Dall. 8, 1 L.Ed. 718.

27. 4 Dall. at 10.

A different answer was given, however, by Justice Story, speaking for the Court in 1816, in the supremely important case of Martin v. Hunter's Lessee.[28] The language of Article III, he said, "is manifestly designed to be mandatory upon the legislature. Its obligatory force is so imperative that Congress could not, without a violation of its duty, have refused to carry it into operation. The judicial power of the United States shall be vested (not may be vested) in one supreme court, and in such inferior courts as Congress may, from time to time, ordain and establish. * * * The judicial power must, therefore, be vested in some court, by Congress; and to suppose that it was not an obligation binding on them, but might, at their pleasure, be omitted or declined, is to suppose that, under the sanction of the constitution they might defeat the constitution itself; a construction which would lead to such a result cannot be sound. * * * If, then, it is the duty of Congress to vest the judicial power of the United States, it is a duty to vest the whole judicial power. The language, if imperative as to one part, is imperative as to all." [29]

Despite this strong statement, Justice Story apparently believed that the Constitution, though mandatory, was not self-executing. Sitting at circuit two years later, he marvelled at the fact that the jurisdiction conferred by Congress fell so far short of the constitutional extent, but held nevertheless that the court had no jurisdiction not given by some statute.[30]

Justice Story's view was not to prevail. At least since 1845 it has been frequently stated by the Supreme Court that "the judicial power of the United States, although it has its origin in the Constitution, is (except in enumerated instances, applicable exclusively to this court) dependent for its distribution and organization, and for the modes of its exercise, entirely upon the action of Congress, who possess the sole power of creating the tribunals (inferior to the Supreme Court), for the exercise of the judicial power, and of investing them with jurisdiction either limited, concurrent, or exclusive, and of withholding jurisdiction from them in the exact degrees and character which to Congress may seem proper for the public good." [31]

There is so much authority for the proposition that Congress is free to grant or withhold the judicial power that it might seem unnecessary to belabor the point. Yet lingering doubts remain. In 1949 the Court of Appeals for the District of Columbia asserted that it is compulsory upon Congress to confer the whole of the judicial power upon some federal court, and that if a case arises under the Constitu-

28.   1816, 1 Wheat. 304, 4 L.Ed. 97.

29.   1 Wheat. at 328–330.

30.   White v. Fenner, C.C.D.R.I.1818, 29 F.Cas. 1015 (No. 17,547).

31.   Cary v. Curtis, 1845, 3 How. 236, 245, 11 L.Ed. 576. To the same effect, see Sheldon v. Sill, 1850, 8 How. 441, 12 L.Ed. 1147; Plaquemines Tropical Fruit Co. v. Henderson, 1898, 18 S.Ct. 685, 170 U.S. 511, 42 L.Ed. 1126; Kline v. Burke Constr. Co., 1922, 43 S.Ct. 79, 260 U.S. 226, 67 L.Ed. 226; Lockerty v. Phillips, 1943, 63 S.Ct. 1019, 319 U.S. 182, 87 L.Ed. 1339; Palmore v. U. S., 1973, 93 S.Ct. 1670, 1678, 411 U.S. 389, 400–402, 36 L.Ed.2d 342.

tion, laws, or treaties of the United States, jurisdiction to entertain it is in some district court by compulsion of the Constitution itself.[32] That decision was reversed, though on other grounds,[33] but it is interesting that a court at so late a date was willing to take a position which went even beyond Story's. Yet the position is supported by some modern writers.[34] Further there are other writers who recognize the general authority of Congress in this area, but who suggest that there are due process limits on the congressional power.[35] A decision of the Second Circuit lends supports to this thesis, saying that "while Congress has the undoubted power to give, withhold, and restrict the jurisdiction of the courts other than the Supreme Court, it must not so exercise that power as to deprive any person of life, liberty, or property without due process of law or take private property without just compensation." [36] If there is any limit on Congress, this is probably the maximum limit. Nearly two centuries of history stand in the way of those who would claim that Congress must vest the entire judicial power.

§ 11. "Constitutional" and "Legislative" Courts [1]

Article III, § 1, of the Constitution provides: "The judicial Power of the United States, shall be vested in one supreme Court, and in such inferior Courts as the Congress may from time to time ordain and establish. The Judges, both of the supreme and inferior Courts, shall hold their Offices during good Behaviour, and shall, at stated Times, receive for their Services a Compensation which shall not be diminished during their Continuance in Office." This would seem to be a very clear declaration that the judicial power, as defined in the

---

32. Eisentrager v. Forrestal, D.C.Cir. 1949, 174 F.2d 961, 966.

33. Johnson v. Eisentrager, 1950, 70 S.Ct. 936, 339 U.S. 763, 94 L.Ed. 1255.

34. 1 Crosskey, Politics and the Constitution in the History of the United States, 1953, pp. 610–620; Howland, Shall Federal Jurisdiction of Controversies Between Citizens of Different States be Preserved?, 1932, 18 A.B.A.J. 499; Eisenberg, Congressional Authority to Restrict Lower Federal Court Jurisdiction, 1974, 83 Yale L.J. 498.

35. Pritchett, The Political Offender and the Warren Court, 1958, pp. 65–69; Taylor, note 10 above; Sager, note 1 above; Redish, note 1 above.

36. Battaglia v. General Motors Corp., C.A.2d, 1948, 169 F.2d 254, 257, certiorari denied 69 S.Ct. 236, 335 U.S. 887, 93 L.Ed. 425.

Several district courts held that Congress cannot constitutionally require more than $10,000 to be in controversy if the effect is to bar any judicial review of a constitutional claim. Cortright v. Resor, D.C.N.Y.1971, 325 F.Supp. 797, 808–811; West End Neighborhood Corp. v. Stans, D.C.D.C.1970, 312 F.Supp. 1066, 1068; Murray v. Vaughn, D.C.R.I.1969, 300 F.Supp. 688, 695–696. The courts of appeals held to the contrary. Goldsmith v. Sutherland, C.A.6th, 1970, 426 F.2d 1395, certiorari denied 91 S.Ct. 353, 400 U.S. 960, 27 L.Ed.2d 270; Spock v. David, C.A.3d, 1972, 469 F.2d 1047; McGaw v. Farrow, C.A.4th, 1973, 472 F.2d 952.

[§ 11]

1. 13 Wright, Miller & Cooper, Jurisdiction § 3528; Redish, Federal Jurisdiction: Tensions in the Allocation of Judicial Power, 1980, pp. 35–51; Gallagher & Kutcher, Quis Custodiet Custodes? The Case Against Article I Courts, 1976, 22 Loy.L.Rev. 301.

following section of Article III, can only be conferred on courts where the judges enjoy tenure for good behavior, and assurance against diminution of salary, protections that the Framers, and all succeeding generations,[2] have thought of vital importance in preserving judicial independence. It would seem also to follow that the holding of the Court, through Marshall, in Hodgson v. Bowerbank,[3] is applicable to all courts created by Congress, and that such courts cannot hear a case that is beyond the judicial power of the United States.[4] The historical development, however, has been much more complicated than these seemingly obvious propositions would suggest.

Difficulty begins in 1828, in the case of American Insurance Co. v. Canter.[5] The case came from the territory of Florida. Acts of Congress had created for that territory two Superior courts, with judges to serve for four-year terms, and had authorized the territorial legislature to create courts inferior to the Superior Courts. One such inferior court, created by the territorial legislature, was the "wreckers court" at Key West, consisting of a notary and five temporary members. This court had jurisdiction over salvage matters, and the members of the court were paid a fee dependent on the value of the salvage. A certain ship was wrecked on the coast of Florida, part of the cargo was salvaged, and a judicial sale of the cargo was had on the order of the wreckers court. At that sale, David Canter purchased 356 bales of cotton. Subsequently he shipped the cotton to Charleston, where suit was brought claiming it by the insurance company, which had succeeded to the claims of the owners of the cargo. If the sale in Key West was lawful, Canter had good title to the cotton. If the sale was invalid, the insurance company's claim to the cotton had to be sustained.

In attacking the sale at Key West, the insurance company argued that a sale of salvaged cargo was within admiralty jurisdiction, that the judicial power of the United States extended to all cases of admiralty and maritime jurisdiction, and that accordingly this portion of the judicial power could only be conferred on the Superior Courts,

---

2. The Federalist No. 78, at 494–496, No. 79, at 497, Wright ed. 1961 (Hamilton).

The meaning of the tenure provision is considered in Kramer & Barron, The Constitutionality of Removal and Mandatory Retirement Procedures for the Federal Judiciary: The Meaning of "During Good Behavior," 1967, 35 Geo. Wash.L.Rev. 455. See also Re, Judicial Independence and Accountability: The Judicial Councils Reform and Judicial Conduct and Disability Act of 1980, 1981, 8 N.Ky.L.Rev. 221; Close, Good Behavior Tenure and Judicial Power, 1978, 9 Seton Hall L.Rev. 208.

"The very point of the tenure guarantee of Article III is to release federal judges from any debts of gratitude running to the President who appointed them. As one Justice told a new colleague worried about pressures from former associates, 'Yes, but you are here now.'" Hobson v. Hansen, D.C.D.C. 1967, 265 F.Supp. 902, 931 n. 50 (Wright, J., dissenting).

3. 1809, 5 Cranch 303, 3 L.Ed. 108. See § 8 above at notes 1 to 3.

4. See § 8 above.

5. 1828, 1 Pet. 511, 7 L.Ed. 242.

which Congress had established, and not on the wreckers court, which was not a court established by Congress. To this argument Chief Justice Marshall made a famous answer: "We have only to pursue this subject one step further, to perceive that this provision of the Constitution does not apply to it. The next sentence declares that 'the judges both of the supreme and inferior courts, shall hold their offices during good behavior.' The judges of the Superior Courts of Florida hold their offices for four years. These courts, then, are not Constitutional courts, in which the judicial power conferred by the Constitution on the general government can be deposited. They are incapable of receiving it. They are legislative courts, created in virtue of the general right of sovereignty which exists in the government, or in virtue of that clause which enables Congress to make all needful rules and regulations, respecting the territory belonging to the United States. The jurisdiction with which they are invested, is not a part of that judicial power which is defined in the 3d article of the Constitution, but is conferred by Congress, in the execution of those general powers which that body possesses over the territories of the United States. Although admiralty jurisdiction can be exercised in the States in those courts only which are established in pursuance of the 3d article of the Constitution, the same limitation does not extend to the territories. In legislating for them, Congress exercises the combined powers of the general and of a State government." [6]

Thus David Canter was allowed to keep the cotton he had purchased at Key West, a result that seems quite just, but it was settled that territorial courts are not created pursuant to Article III of the Constitution, a doctrine of doubtful soundness. Accordingly it was later held that the salary of a territorial judge may be reduced,[7] and that he may be removed from office regardless of good behavior before the expiration of his statutory term.[8] In some of the territories Congress had provided that the judges were to hold office during good behavior, but even this was not enough to alter the status of the court. The grant of tenure was thought to be a matter of legislative grace rather than constitutional compulsion.[9]

Although Marshall had said that the jurisdiction of the territorial courts is not a part of the judicial power of the United States, it has been held from the earliest times that the Supreme Court may review decisions of a territorial court.[10] How the same case can involve the

6. 1 Pet. at 546.

7. U. S. v. Fisher, 1883, 3 S.Ct. 154, 109 U.S. 143, 27 L.Ed. 885.

8. McAllister v. U. S., 1891, 11 S.Ct. 949, 141 U.S. 174, 35 L.Ed. 693.

9. Ibid., 11 S.Ct. at 953, 141 U.S. at 186; see Glidden Co. v. Zdanok, 1962, 82 S.Ct. 1459, 1471, 370 U.S. 530, 548, 8 L.Ed.2d 671.

10. E.g., Durousseau v. U. S., 1810, 10 U.S. (6 Cranch) 307, 3 L.Ed. 232. See, e.g., 28 U.S.C.A. § 1252, permitting direct appeal to the Supreme Court in certain instances from the United States District Court for the District of the Canal Zone, the District Court of Guam and the District Court of the Virgin Islands, and any court of record of Puerto Rico.

judicial power of the United States when it reaches the Supreme Court, but not be within the judicial power when it is tried in the territorial court, is but one of the conceptual problems to which the "legislative court" fiction gives rise.

From 1828 to 1923, the notion of a "legislative court" was confined to territorial courts and other courts beyond the limits of the United States.[11] There was a brief flurry with regard to the Court of Claims. When it was created in 1855, it had no power to enter judgments, but only to report its findings to Congress. In 1863, however, it was empowered to render final judgment, with a right of appeal to the Supreme Court in certain cases. Nevertheless the Supreme Court construed one section of the 1863 act as leaving it in the discretion of the Secretary of the Treasury whether to pay judgments that the Court of Claims had entered. The Supreme Court refused to hear appeals from the Court of Claims, on the ground that the authority in the Secretary of the Treasury to revise decisions of the court denied to the Court of Claims judicial power.[12] The offensive section was quickly repealed, and thereafter the Supreme Court took jurisdiction on appeals from the Court of Claims.[13] In later years the Supreme Court seemed to have no doubt but that the Court of Claims was a "constitutional" court, created under Article III.[14]

The modern expansion of the "legislative court" concept began in 1923, when the Supreme Court refused to hear an appeal from the Court of Appeals of the District of Columbia in a case involving utility rates. The Court held that the relevant statute required the District of Columbia courts to assume legislative or administrative duties in these cases.[15] Such duties could be imposed on the District of Columbia courts, it was held, since they were created pursuant to the power of Congress over the District under Article I, § 8, of the Constitution, but the Supreme Court, created as it is under Article III, could not review a matter that was not judicial in nature.[16] A similar result was reached seven years later with regard to review of decisions of the District of Columbia courts involving orders of the Federal Radio Commission.[17]

11. E.g., In re Ross, 1891, 11 S.Ct. 897, 140 U.S. 453, 35 L.Ed. 581 (consular court).

12. Gordon v. U. S., 1864, 2 Wall. 561, 17 L.Ed. 921. The draft opinion of Chief Justice Taney, prepared before his death and before reargument of the Gordon case, was ordered published many years later, 117 U.S. 697, and has been much cited, but cannot be regarded as the opinion of the Court in that case. Indeed in U. S. v. Jones, 1886, 7 S.Ct. 283, 119 U.S. 477, 30 L.Ed. 440, the Court found in its records the opinion of Chief Justice Chase in Gordon, which differs from that published in 1864.

13. DeGroot v. U. S., 1866, 5 Wall. 419, 18 L.Ed. 700; U. S. v. Jones, 1886, 7 S.Ct. 283, 119 U.S. 477, 30 L.Ed. 440; Pope v. U. S., 1944, 65 S.Ct. 16, 323 U.S. 1, 89 L.Ed. 3.

14. U. S. v. Union Pac. R. Co., 1878, 98 U.S. 569, 603, 25 L.Ed. 143; Miles v. Graham, 1925, 45 S.Ct. 601, 268 U.S. 501, 1067.

15. See § 15 below.

16. Keller v. Potomac Elec. Power Co., 1923, 43 S.Ct. 445, 261 U.S. 428, 67 L.Ed. 731.

17. Federal Radio Comm. v. General Elec. Co., 1930, 50 S.Ct. 389, 281 U.S. 464, 74 L.Ed. 969.

The whole question of "legislative courts" was fully discussed in 1929 by Justice Van Devanter, for a unanimous Court, in Ex parte Bakelite Corporation.[18] The case involved the status of the Court of Customs Appeals—later known as the Court of Customs and Patent Appeals and in 1982 merged into the Court of Appeals for the Federal Circuit. This Court had been created in 1909 to hear appeals from the Board of General Appraisers—later known as the Customs Court and, since 1980, as the Court of International Trade—in cases involving duty, which had previously been heard by the circuit courts. The statute creating the court set no limit on the tenure of the judges. In 1922, however, it was given further jurisdiction to review findings of the Tariff Commission on certain matters that must ultimately be decided by the President, and that are fairly clearly not "cases or controversies" in the Article III sense.[19] When one such case came before the Court of Customs Appeals, a writ of prohibition was sought in the Supreme Court to restrain it from hearing it, on the ground that as a constitutional court it could not give what was, in effect, an advisory opinion. The Court held, however, that the Court of Customs Appeals was not a "constitutional court," and thus that it could hear the matter before it whether or not it was within the judicial power of the United States. Justice Van Devanter reviewed all the special courts, and declared in extended dicta that the courts in the District of Columbia and the Court of Claims were all "legislative courts."[20] He found that the Court of Customs Appeals was a "legislative court" because its jurisdiction included "nothing which inherently or necessarily requires judicial determination, but only matters the determination of which may be, and at times has been, committed exclusively to executive officers."[21] He refused to ascribe any importance to the fact that the statute creating the Court of Customs Appeals apparently gave life tenure to the judges, saying that that argument "mistakenly assumes that whether a court is of one class or the other depends on the intention of Congress, whereas the true test lies in the power under which the court was created and in the jurisdiction conferred."[22]

The next step came in companion cases decided in 1933. A year earlier Congress had purported to reduce the salaries of judges, but had excepted from the reduction "judges whose compensation may not, under the Constitution, be diminished during their continuance in office." Suit was brought by judges of the Court of Appeals and the Supreme Court of the District of Columbia, and by judges of the Court of Claims, contending that the act did not apply to them since their salaries were constitutionally protected. In O'Donoghue v. United States[23] it was held, over three dissents, that this was true as

18. 1929, 49 S.Ct. 411, 279 U.S. 438, 73 L.Ed. 789.

19. See § 12 below.

20. 49 S.Ct. at 413–415, 279 U.S. at 450–455.

21. 49 S.Ct. at 416, 279 U.S. at 458.

22. 49 S.Ct. at 416, 279 U.S. at 459.

23. 1933, 53 S.Ct. 740, 289 U.S. 516, 77 L.Ed. 1356.

to the District of Columbia judges. The statement four years before in the Bakelite case, that those courts were "legislative," was dismissed by Justice Sutherland as "made incidentally, by way of illustration merely and without discussion or elaboration, * * * [and] not necessary to the decision."[24] Instead a new theology was announced by which the courts in the District were "hybrid." They were "constitutional courts," created under Article III of the Constitution, and endowed with the judicial power of the United States, and accordingly their judges enjoyed the protections of Article III. But at the same time "the clause giving plenary power of legislation over the District enables Congress to confer such jurisdiction in addition to the federal jurisdiction which the District courts exercise under article 3."[25]

In the companion case, Williams v. United States,[26] Justice Sutherland spoke for a unanimous Court in holding that the Court of Claims was a "legislative court" and that the salary of its judges could be diminished. The result was not unexpected, but the reasoning, in the phrase of two distinguished writers, "introduced intellectual chaos."[27] The dictum in the Bakelite case about the Court of Claims was given much weight. Though it was conceded that the views there expressed were "not strictly necessary to the decision, * * * they are elucidated and fortified by reasoning and illustration, and, moreover, are the result of a careful review of the entire matter."[28] The numerous earlier expressions that the Court of Claims was a "constitutional" court were rejected as "clearly obiter dicta."[29]

The principal difficulty in the way of Justice Sutherland's conclusion that the Court of Claims does not exercise the judicial power of the United States was the provision in Article III, § 2, that that judicial power extends to "Controversies to which the United States shall be a party." The United States is a party to every case in the Court of Claims. Justice Sutherland was equal to this difficulty. He argued, on dubious historical grounds, that in 1787 suit againt the sovereign was unknown, and that the Framers therefore must have meant to extend the judicial power only to "controversies to which the United States shall be a party plaintiff or petitioner."[30] Thus suits against the United States were not within the constitutionally-defined judicial power, and the Court of Claims, hearing such suits, must necessarily be a "legislative," not a "constitutional" court.

On this construction, it may well be asked how the Supreme Court was able to entertain in its original jurisdiction a suit by a state

24. 53 S.Ct. at 750, 289 U.S. at 550.

25. 53 S.Ct. at 748, 289 U.S. at 546.

26. 1933, 53 S.Ct. 751, 289 U.S. 553, 77 L.Ed. 1372.

27. Hart & Wechsler, The Federal Courts and the Federal System, 1953, p. 237.

28. 53 S.Ct. at 756, 289 U.S. at 571.

29. 53 S.Ct. at 756, 289 U.S. at 568.

30. 53 S.Ct. at 759, 289 U.S. at 577.

against the United States, to which the latter had consented.[31]   It is also not clear why a suit against the United States, authorized by federal statute, is not a case arising under the Constitution, laws, or treaties of the United States.[32]

At this stage in the development of the "legislative court" doctrine, confusion reigned.   There were no dependable criteria for identifying the nature of a particular court,[33] and its conceptual basis led inevitably to contradictions.   As an example, the Tucker Act of 1887 gave the Court of Claims and the district courts concurrent jurisdiction over actions against the United States in particular situations, provided the amount sued for was not in excess of $10,000.[34]   Logically it would seem that such a suit either is or is not an exercise of the judicial power of the United States.   If it is, then the Court of Claims—held in the Williams case to be a "legislative court"—should not be able to hear it, for Marshall had declared in the Canter case that "legislative courts" are "incapable of receiving" the judicial power.   On the other hand, if a Tucker Act case does not involve the judicial power of the United States, a district court should not be able to hear it, for Marshall had declared in Hodgson v. Bowerbank that a court created under Article III could not be given jurisdiction beyond the judicial power as there defined.   Perhaps it is possible for a particular case to be either within or without the judicial power, depending on the court it is in.   This would escape the dilemma just posed, and would be consistent with the decisions permitting review in the Supreme Court of cases coming from the territorial courts or other "legislative courts."   But if the analysis of the Williams case is accepted, cases under the Tucker Act, the Federal Tort Claims Act, or other suits to which the United States has consented, are not within the Article III judicial power, and it is very unclear how they may be heard in the district courts.

Three justices thought they had an answer to the problem last stated, which they put forward in 1949 in the remarkable case of National Mutual Insurance Co. of District of Columbia v. Tidewater Transfer Co., Inc.[35]   The case is more fully considered in a later sec-

31. Minnesota v. Hitchcock, 1902, 22 S.Ct. 650, 654, 655, 185 U.S. 373, 384, 386, 46 L.Ed. 954; cf. U. S. v. Louisiana, 1887, 8 S.Ct. 17, 18, 123 U.S. 32, 35, 31 L.Ed. 69.

32. Justice Jackson was later to offer this explanation: "Moreover, the Tucker Act simply opens those courts to plaintiffs already possessed of a cause of action. If that is sufficient to make the case one arising under the laws of the United States, the same is true of this suit and all others like it." National Mut. Ins. Co. v. Tidewater Transfer Co., Inc., 1949, 69 S.Ct. 1173, 1178

n. 22, 337 U.S. 582, 594 n. 22, 93 L.Ed. 1556. In the same case, however Justice Rutledge took the position that the cases in question do "arise under" the laws of the United States. 69 S.Ct. at 1187, 337 U.S. at 610.

33. The best article on the subject in this period, fully developing the difficulties, is Watson, Concept of the Legislative Court: A Constitutional Fiction, 1942, 10 Geo.Wash.L.Rev. 799.

34. See 28 U.S.C.A. § 1346(a)(2).

35. 1949, 69 S.Ct. 1173, 337 U.S. 582, 93 L.Ed. 1556.

tion.[36] For present purposes it is enough to note that Justice Jackson, in an opinion concurred in by Justices Black and Burton, was willing to extend the logic of the O'Donoghue case and make all of the courts created under Article III into "hybrid" courts. He concluded that "where Congress in the exercise of its powers under Art. I finds it necessary to provide those on whom its power is exerted with access to some kind of court or tribunal for determination of controversies that are within the traditional concept of the justiciable, it may open the regular federal courts to them regardless of lack of diversity of citizenship." [37] So long as the regular federal courts were not asked to participate in any legislative, administrative, political or other nonjudicial function or to render any advisory opinion,[38] Congress could give them, on this view, jurisdiction in any case in which Congress has legislative power under Article I.[39]

In the National Mutual Insurance case the other six justices rejected Jackson's argument that the district courts could be made into "hybrid" courts. The statute in question, which treated citizens of the District of Columbia as if they were citizens of a state for purposes of diversity,[40] was upheld, however. Two other justices, though disagreeing with Jackson's argument, voted to uphold the statute on a different line of reasoning, rejected by their seven brethren.

During the 1950s statutes were passed in which Congress declared the Court of Claims, the Customs Court, and the Court of Customs and Patent Appeals to be courts "established under Article III of the Constitution of the United States." [41] The effect of these declarations was not free from doubt. In the Bakelite case Justice Van Devanter had said that whether a court is "constitutional" or "legislative" does not depend on the intention of Congress. Further, the Court of Claims and the Court of Customs and Patent Appeals, at least, continued to have jurisdiction to give what amounted to advisory opinions in some cases,[42] and such jurisdiction was difficult to reconcile with the concept of a "constitutional" court.

The current status of the Court of Claims and the Court of Customs and Patent Appeals came before the Supreme Court in 1962 in two cases decided under the name of Glidden Company v. Zdanok.[43]

36. See § 24 below.

37. 69 S.Ct. at 1182, 337 U.S. at 600.

38. See 69 S.Ct. at 1177, 337 U.S. at 591.

39. Compare the similar, but more sophisticated, argument for "protective jurisdiction," discussed in § 20 below.

40. The present form of the statute is 28 U.S.C.A. § 1332(d).

41. 28 U.S.C.A. § 171, as amended by Act of July 28, 1953, c. 253, § 1, 67 Stat. 226 (Court of Claims); 28 U.S. C.A. § 251, as amended by Act of July 14, 1956, c. 589, § 1, 70 Stat. 532 (Customs Court); 28 U.S.C.A. § 211, as amended by Act of Aug. 25, 1958, Pub. L. 85–755, § 1, 72 Stat. 848 (Court of Customs and Patent Appeals).

42. Note, The Constitutional Status of the Court of Claims, 1955, 68 Harv.L. Rev. 527.

43. 1962, 82 S.Ct. 1459, 370 U.S. 530, 8 L.Ed.2d 671, noted 1962, 76 Harv.L. Rev. 160, 37 Tul.L.Rev. 144.

The cases arose because of the statutory power to assign judges of one court to sit with another.[44]   Under these statutes a retired judge of the Court of Customs and Patent Appeals had been designated by the Chief Justice to sit in the District Court for the District of Columbia, and, while there, had presided over a criminal trial in which the defendant was convicted.   Similarly a judge of the Court of Claims had been designated to sit with the Court of Appeals for the Second Circuit, and had cast the deciding vote in an important case.   Though there was no suggestion that either of these judges had in any way shown a lack of the judicial independence that Article III, § 1, is intended to secure, it was argued that as judges of "legislative" courts they could not be assigned temporarily for service with a "constitutional" court.

In the Glidden case the Supreme Court held that the Court of Claims and the Court of Customs and Patent Appeals are "constitutional" courts and that the assignment of judges or retired judges of these courts to sit with courts that are clearly "constitutional" is valid.   Unfortunately the justices in the majority reached this result on varying grounds, so that there is no authoritative answer as to why this is so.   Seven justices participated in the decision in Glidden.   Justice Harlan, speaking for himself and Justices Brennan and Stewart, concluded that the Bakelite and Williams decisions were erroneous and should be overruled, and thus held that the courts in question have always been "constitutional" courts.   The other four justices participating, however, declared expressly that Bakelite and Williams should not be overruled.   Justice Clark, for himself and Chief Justice Warren, reached the same result as did Justice Harlan by relying on the recent statutes declaring the congressional intention to treat these as "constitutional" courts.   In this view, the Court of Claims became a "constitutional" court in 1953, and the Court of Customs and Patent Appeals achieved this status in 1958.[45]   Justice Harlan recognized these congressional declarations as "persuasive evidence" [46] but did not rest his opinion on them.   Justice Douglas, in a dissenting opinion for himself and Justice Black, rejected both of these lines of argument, and would have held that the courts in question were still "legislative" in nature.

Both of the opinions for the justices in the majority recognized that the jurisdiction of the Court of Claims to hear matters on reference from Congress and report to that body [47] and the jurisdiction of the Court of Customs and Patent Appeals to review Tariff Commission findings in proceedings relating to unfair practices in the import

44.   28 U.S.C.A. § 293(a).

45.   82 S.Ct. at 1491–1492, 370 U.S. at 586–587.

46.   82 S.Ct. at 1469, 370 U.S. at 542.

47.   28 U.S.C.A. §§ 1492, 2509.   These statutes were amended in 1966 to provide that congressional reference cases be heard by the chief commissioner of the Court of Claims rather than by the court itself.   Act of Oct. 15, 1966, Pub. L. 89–681, 80 Stat. 958.

trade [48] may well go beyond the judicial power that can be given to a "constitutional" court. Justice Clark's opinion asserted flatly that such matters are not within the judicial power, while Justice Harlan noted the doubt but put off definitive decision until such a case shall arise. In any event, both opinions regarded this as a very small portion of the business of the courts in question, insufficient to alter the basic character of the courts as "constitutional," and indicated that if such jurisdiction is not within the judicial power, then the courts should refuse to entertain such cases.[49]

Even if the varying opinions in Glidden meant that there was still no clear analytical answer as to when a court is "legislative," the result in the case apparently restored the situation that existed prior to 1923. The Court of Claims and the Court of Customs and Patent Appeals were definitely "constitutional" courts, as is the Court of Appeals for the Federal Circuit, into which they have now been merged. The same seems true of what is now the Court of International Trade and was formerly the Customs Court.[50] The 1956 statute declaring it to have been established under Article III, together with the composition and jurisdiction of the court, satisfied the tests applied by Justice Black, while it also meets Justice Harlan's stated test that "whether a tribunal is to be recognized as one created under Article III depends basically upon whether its establishing legislation complies with the limitations of that article; whether, in other words, its business is the federal business there specified and its judges and judgments are allowed the independence there expressly or impliedly made requisite." [51]

There was nothing said in the Glidden case altering the decision in O'Donoghue that the courts in the District of Columbia are "hybrid," but the statutes giving "administrative" jurisdiction to those courts, which led to this classification of them, have long since been repealed,[52] and the 1970 reorganization of the court system in the Dis-

---

48. 28 U.S.C.A. § 1543. The relevant statutes were amended in 1975 to provide for review of what has been redesignated as the International Trade Commission only after the possibility of presidential revision of the determinations of the Commission has passed. See 19 U.S.C.A. § 1337(c). This should obviate the difficulties noted in the Glidden case.

49. After the Glidden decision, and prior to the 1966 legislation described note 47 above, the Court of Claims refused to accept jurisdiction of new congressional reference cases, but it passed on those that had been referred prior to Glidden. Armiger et al. Estates v. U. S., 1964, 339 F.2d 625, 627 n. 1, 168 Ct. Cl. 379. See Note, The Court of Claims and Congressional Referrals, 1965, 51 Va.L.Rev. 486.

50. See Eastern State Petroleum Corp. v. Rogers, D.C.Cir.1960, 280 F.2d 611, 614.

51. 82 S.Ct. at 1474, 370 U.S. at 552.

52. 82 S.Ct. at 1488 n. 53, 370 U.S. at 580 n. 53.

A statute authorizing the judges of the District Court for the District of Columbia to appoint members of the board of education was sustained, over a strong dissent, in Hobson v. Hansen, D.C.D.C.1967, 265 F.Supp. 902, with the majority relying on the "hybrid" nature of the court. The statute was amended the following year to take this power away from the judges and provide for election of the school board. D.C.Code, 31–101(a), as amended by Act of April 22, 1968, Pub. L. 90–292, 82 Stat. 101.

trict of Columbia has given jurisdiction of local matters to a local system of courts.[53] These local courts are "legislative" courts,[54] but the United States District Court for the District of Columbia and the United States Court of Appeals for the District of Columbia Circuit are now "constitutional."

Since 1969 the United States Tax Court has been a "legislative" court, created under Article 1 of the Constitution.[55] The Court of Military Appeals is not a part of the judiciary at all, but is a military tribunal, created pursuant to the Article 1 power to make rules for the government and regulation of the land and naval forces.[56]

The other remaining "legislative" courts are the district courts for Guam, the Virgin Islands, the Northern Mariana Islands, and the Canal Zone.[57] Whether the necessity that is thought to have required the development in 1828 of the concept of "legislative" courts for the territories still exists may well be questioned.[58] If judicial independence is of vital importance in the states, it is hard to see why it is not equally valuable in the territories.[59] The district judges there try persons for crimes against the United States. They hear civil cases in which the United States is a party. They should be able to decide such cases fearlessly and impartially, without being dependent upon the Department of Justice for their continued tenure. Unfortunately instances are not unknown of territorial judges who have not been reappointed, under circumstances where it appears that they have been denied reappointment because of decisions displeasing to the appointing authority.[60] So long as these judges have limited tenure, the possibility of such abuse, or apparent abuse, will persist. The granting to these judges of tenure during good behavior, as was recently done for Puerto Rico,[61] would be desirable.

There have been questions of the extent to which the judicial power of the United States may validly be exercised by United States

53. See § 5 n. 2 above.

54. Palmore v. U. S., 1973, 93 S.Ct. 1670, 411 U.S. 389, 36 L.Ed.2d 342. See Keeffe & Warlick, Article III: Where Are You Now That We Need You?, 1976, 62 A.B.A.J. 240; Comment, Palmore v. United States: The Interrelationship of Article I and Article III of the Constitution 1973, 23 Amer.U.L. Rev. 119.

55. 26 U.S.C.A. (I.R.C.1954) § 7441, as amended by Act of Dec. 30, 1969, Pub. L. 91–172, § 951, 83 Stat. 487. See § 5 n. 20 above.

56. See § 5 n. 21 above.

57. That "legislative" courts are still possible in the territories is held in U. S. v. Montanez, C.A.2d, 1967, 371 F.2d 79, certiorari denied 88 S.Ct. 147, 389 U.S. 884, 19 L.Ed.2d 181. See also

Sablan v. Santos, C.A.9th, 1980, 634 F.2d 1153; Rose v. McNamara, C.A.1967, 375 F.2d 924, 126 U.S.App. D.C. 179, certiorari denied 88 S.Ct. 70, 389 U.S. 856, 19 L.Ed.2d 121.

58. The question is left open in Justice Harlan's opinion in the Glidden case. See 82 S.Ct. at 1472 n. 19, 370 U.S. at 548 n. 19.

59. Loring, Judicial Power and Territorial Judges, 1955, 7 Hastings L.J. 62. See U. S. v. Montanez, C.A.2d, 1967, 371 F.2d 79, 84, certiorari denied 88 S.Ct. 147, 389 U.S. 884, 19 L.Ed.2d 181.

60. See Metzger, Why I Am No Longer A Judge, 1953, 177 The Nation 52.

61. 28 U.S.C.A. § 134(a), as amended by Act of Sept. 12, 1966, Pub.L. No. 89–571, 80 Stat. 764.

magistrates, who serve for an eight-year term,[62] and these questions have been sharpened by 1979 amendments to the Magistrates' Act enlarging the powers of magistrates.[63]   These questions will now have to be examined in the light of the Court's 1982 decision in Northern Pipeline Construction Co. v. Marathon Pipe Line Co.,[64] in which the Court again struggled with the metaphysics of "constitutional" and "legislative" courts, this time in the context of bankruptcy courts.

Until 1978 the district courts acted as bankruptcy courts.   Although proceedings were generally conducted before referees in bankruptcy, the district court could withdraw a case from a referee and the final order of a referee was appealable to the district court. The Bankruptcy Act of 1978 made drastic changes in that scheme.   It established "in each judicial district, as an adjunct to the district court for such district, a bankruptcy court which shall be a court of record known as the United States Bankruptcy Court for the district." [65]   The judges of the new courts were to serve 14-year terms, they were removable by the judicial council of the circuit, and salaries were not protected against diminution.[66]   By any test these were not Article III courts.   Their jurisdiction, however, was sweeping.   They were authorized to hear all civil proceedings arising under Title 11, the bankruptcy title, "or arising in or related to cases under title 11." [67]   The Northern Pipeline case itself was a state-created claim for damages for breach of contract and warranty, brought in a bankruptcy court because Northern Pipeline had earlier filed a petition for reorganization.

Although it was held that an Article I court could not hear a claim such as Northern Pipeline's claim against Marathon, the Court was as badly fragmented in reaching this result as it had been in the National Mutual Insurance case and the Glidden case.   Justice Brennan wrote the lead opinion, but he spoke only for a plurality of the Court, since only Justices Marshall, Blackmun, and Stevens joined his opinion.   Justice Brennan undertook to rationalize the earlier cases as establishing a "constitutional command that the judicial power of the United States must be vested in Art. III courts," except for "three narrow situations not subject to the command, each recognizing a circumstance in which the grant of power to the Legislative and Executive Branches was historically and constitutionally so exceptional that

---

62.   28 U.S.C.A. § 631(e).   See § 2 n. 11.

63.   Comment, Article III Limits on Article I Courts: The Constitutionality of the Bankruptcy Court and the 1979 Magistrate Act, 1980, 80 Col.L.Rev. 560; Note, Article III Constraints and the Expanding Civil Jurisdiction of Federal Magistrates: A Dissenting View, 1979, 88 Yale L.J. 1023.

64.   1982, 102 S.Ct. 2858, ___ U.S. ___, 73 L.Ed.2d 598.

65.   28 U.S.C.A. § 151(a).

66.   28 U.S.C.A. §§ 152–154.

67.   28 U.S.C.A. § 1471(b).   The bankruptcy judges were also given power of hold jury trials, 28 U.S.C.A. § 1480, to issue declaratory judgments, 28 U.S. C.A. § 2201, and to issue writs of habeas corpus under certain circumstances, 28 U.S.C.A. § 2256.

the congressional assertion of a power to create legislative courts was consistent with, rather than threatening to, the constitutional mandate of separation of powers." [68]

The first of these three exceptions involved the courts in the territories and in the District of Columbia. In these geographical areas, in which no state operated as sovereign, Congress was to exercise the general powers of government.[69] Next were the cases upholding the military system of courts martial. "It too involves a constitutional grant of power that has been historically understood as giving the political branches of Government extraordinary control over the precise subject matter at issue." [70]

Finally Justice Brennan considered a group of cases in which the Court had upheld the constitutionality of legislative courts and administrative agencies created by Congress to adjudicate cases involving "public rights." [71] This "public rights" doctrine, he said, may be explained in part by reference to the principle of sovereign immunity, but it also draws upon the principle of separation of powers, and an historical understanding that certain prerogatives were reserved to the political branches of government. "The understanding of these cases is that the Framers expected that Congress would be free to commit such matters completely to non-judicial executive determination, and that as a result there can be no constitutional objection to Congress' employing the less drastic expedient of committing their determination to a legislative court or an administrative agency." [72] The "public rights" doctrine, he said, is limited to matters arising between the government and others and cannot extend to a case such as the Northern Pipeline case, involving the liability of one individual to another.[73]

To Justice Brennan, and the three others who joined him, none of the three exceptions to the command of Article III were present in the case before them. They rejected also the argument that Congress is free to use "legislative" courts whenever it thinks this expedient in exercising its Article I powers. Language in an earlier case that the requirements of Article III must "give way to accommodate plenary grants of power to Congress to legislate with respect to specialized areas having particularized needs and warranting distinctive treatment" [74] was read by them as referring only to geographic areas, rather than to specialized subject matter.[75] The plurality opinion also rejected the argument that the bankruptcy court was merely an

---

68. 102 S.Ct. at 2867–2868, ___ U.S. at ___.

69. 102 S.Ct. at 2868, ___ U.S. at ___.

70. 102 S.Ct. at 2869, ___ U.S. at ___.

71. 102 S.Ct. at 2869–2871, ___ U.S. ___. The "public rights" doctrine has its origin in Murray's Lessee v. Hoboken Land & Improvement Co., 1855, 18 How. 272, 284, 15 L.Ed. 372.

72. 102 S.Ct. at 2870, ___ U.S. at ___.

73. 102 S.Ct. at 2870–2871, ___ U.S. at ___.

74. Palmore v. U. S., 1973, 93 S.Ct. 1670, 1681, 411 U.S. 389, 407–408, 36 L.Ed.2d 342.

75. 102 S.Ct. at 2872–2874, ___ U.S. at ___–___.

"adjunct" to the district court and that the delegation of certain adjudicative functions to the bankruptcy court was accordingly consistent with the principle that the judicial power of the United States must be vested in Article III courts.[76]

Justices Rehnquist and O'Connor concurred in the judgment only. In an opinion by Justice Rehnquist, they agreed that Marathon could not constitutionally be compelled to defend a state-created claim for damages by a private plaintiff before a court whose judges do not have the tenure and salary protection of Article III. They thought that was all that it was necessary to decide in the case before them, and that in this area of law, "with its frequently arcane distinctions and confusing precedents,"[77] it was especially important that the Court not decide more of a constitutional question than is absolutely necessary. They found it unnecessary to decide whether the Court's earlier decisions on "constitutional" and "legislative" courts "support a general proposition and three tidy exceptions, as the plurality believes, or whether instead they are but landmarks on a judicial 'darkling plain' where ignorant armies have clashed by night, as Justice White apparently believes them to be."[78] Thus the concurring opinion leaves open the possibility that the bankruptcy courts could be given jurisdiction to hear private lawsuits on federally-created claims.

Justice White dissented at length, joined by Chief Justice Burger and Justice Powell.[79] He concluded that "[t]here is no difference in principle between the work that Congress may assign to an Article I court and that which the Constitution assigns to Article III courts. * * * Article III is not to be read out of the Constitution; rather, it should be read as expressing one value that must be balanced against competing constitutional values and legislative responsibilities. This Court retains the final word on how that balance is to be struck."[80] In the case of the bankruptcy courts he would have held that the reform of the bankruptcy system Congress was attempting was important enough, and the safeguard provided by allowing appellate review in Article III courts was sufficient, to justify striking the balance in favor of allowing use of Article I courts.[81]

That is the present status of the question of "constitutional" and "legislative" courts. In his plurality opinion in Glidden Justice Harlan wrote that this distinction "has been productive of much confusion and controversy."[82] Neither the confusion nor the controversy have ended in the ensuing 20 years.

---

76. 102 S.Ct. at 2874–2880, ___ U.S. at ___–___.

77. 102 S.Ct. at 2881, ___ U.S. at ___.

78. 102 S.Ct. at 2881, ___ U.S. at ___.

79. There is also a brief separate dissent by Chief Justice Burger.

80. 102 S.Ct. at 2893, ___ U.S. at ___.

81. 102 S.Ct. at 2894–2896, ___ U.S. at ___–___.

82. 82 S.Ct. at 1464, 370 U.S. at 534.

§ 12. "Case or Controversy"—In General [1]

The judicial power of the United States, according to the Constitution, extends to "all Cases" of three designated types, and to "Controversies" of six other types. The courts of the United States do not sit to decide questions of law presented in a vacuum, but only such questions as arise in a "case or controversy." The two terms can be used interchangeably, for, we are authoritatively told, a "controversy," if distinguishable at all from a "case," is distinguishable only in that it is a less comprehensive term, and includes only suits of a civil nature.[2]

What is a "case or controversy" that is justiciable in the federal courts? The answer of Chief Justice Hughes is classic if cryptic. He said: "A 'controversy' in this sense must be one that is appropriate for judicial determination. A justiciable controversy is thus distinguished from a difference or dispute of a hypothetical character; from one that is academic or moot. The controversy must be definite and concrete, touching the legal relations of parties having adverse legal interests. It must be a real and substantial controversy admitting of specific relief through a decree of a conclusive character, as distinguished from an opinion advising what the law would be upon a hypothetical state of facts." [3] Unfortunately, as has been pointed out,[4] this definition, though often quoted, turns upon labels that the Court had used in the past to describe cases before it, and the labels themselves are elastic, inconstant, and imprecise.

In a later case, Chief Justice Warren said of the "case or controversy" requirement that "those two words have an iceberg quality, containing beneath their surface simplicity submerged complexities which go to the very heart of our constitutional form of government. Embodied in the words 'cases' and 'controversies' are two complementary but somewhat different limitations. In part those words limit the business of federal courts to questions presented in an adversary context and in a form historically viewed as capable of resolution through the judicial process. And in part those words define

[§ 12]

1. 13 Wright, Miller & Cooper, Jurisdiction § 3529; Radcliffe, The Case-or-Controversy Provision, 1978; Varat, Variable Justiciability and the Duke Power Case, 1980, 58 Texas L.Rev. 273; Singer, Justiciability and Recent Supreme Court Cases, 1969, 21 Ala.L. Rev. 229.

2. Aetna Life Ins. Co. v. Haworth, 1937, 57 S.Ct. 461, 463, 300 U.S. 227, 239, 81 L.Ed. 617, quoting from Re Pacific Ry. Comm., C.C.D.Cal.1887, 32 F. 241, 255.

3. Aetna Life Ins. Co. v. Haworth, 1937, 57 S.Ct. 461, 464, 300 U.S. 229, 240–241, 81 L.Ed. 617 (citations omitted).

4. Public Serv. Comm. of Utah v. Wycoff Co., 1952, 73 S.Ct. 236, 239–240, 344 U.S. 237, 242, 97 L.Ed. 291. See Note, 1962, 62 Col.L.Rev. 106, 108.
   " * * * The standards by which cases and controversies are distinguished from claims premature or insufficiently adverse are not susceptible of ready application to a particular case. The considerations, while catholic, are not concrete." McCahill v. Borough of Fox Chapel, C.A.3d, 1971, 438 F.2d 213, 215.

the role assigned to the judiciary in a tripartite allocation of power to assure that the federal courts will not intrude into areas committed to the other branches of government. Justiciability is the term of art employed to give expression to this dual limitation placed upon federal courts by the case and controversy doctrine." [5]

It should also be noted that the limitation to "case or controversy" is intimately related to the doctrine of judicial review. In Marbury v. Madison [6] it was central to Chief Justice Marshall's argument that a court has power to declare a statute unconstitutional only as a consequence of the power of the court to decide a case properly before it. Unconstitutional statutes there may be, but unless they are involved in a case properly susceptible of judicial determination, the courts have no power to pronounce that they are unconstitutional. The reluctance of courts to pass on constitutional issues unless absolutely necessary has led to a rigorous set of rules as to what constitutes a justiciable "case or controversy."

Whether the decisions on justiciability are cast in terms of Article III limitations on judicial power or in terms of wise refusal to exercise acknowledged power, there are few clear rules. This area of the law is a "conceptual morass." [7] The precedents are sufficiently malleable to afford ample opportunity for courts to avoid decision on justiciability grounds simply because decision is thought inconvenient. This has led to continuing debate on the extent to which courts should in fact be free to avoid awkward decisions on grounds of "prudence" falling somewhere between implementation of strict principle and mere caprice.[8]

In private litigation there is, in fact, very little difficulty. Now that the dispute over whether the federal courts can render declaratory judgments has been satisfactorily resolved, most private litigation is of a nature clearly meeting the tests of justiciability. The main body of law on "case or controversy" comes from cases raising questions of constitutionality of statutes, or cases seeking judicial review of administrative action. For this reason this subject is usually treated with care in courses and treatises on constitutional law and administrative law, and may be more summarily considered here.

5. Flast v. Cohen, 1968, 88 S.Ct. 1942, 1949–1950, 392 U.S. 83, 94, 95, 20 L.Ed. 2d 947.

6. 1803, 1 Cranch 137, 2 L.Ed. 60.

7. Haitian Refugee Center v. Civiletti, D.C.Fla.1980, 503 F.Supp. 442, 461.

8. Compare Bickel, The Supreme Court 1960 Term: Foreword: The Passive Virtues, 1961, 75 Harv.L.Rev. 40, with Wechsler, Toward Neutral Principles of Constitutional Law, 1959, 73 Harv.L. Rev. 1, Gunther, The Subtle Vices of the "Passive Virtues"—A Comment on Principle and Expediency in Judicial Review, 1964, 64 Col.L.Rev. 1, and Varat, note 1 above.

See also Brilmayer, The Jurisprudence of Article III: Perspectives on the "Case or Controversy" Requirement, 1979, 93 Harv.L.Rev. 297; Tushnet, The Sociology of Article III: A Response to Professor Brilmayer, 1980, 93 Harv.L.Rev. 1698; Brilmayer, A Reply, 1980, 93 Harv.L.Rev. 1727.

It is easy to understand, for example, why moot cases are held to be beyond the judicial power.[9] There is no case or controversy once the matter has been resolved. The Court, particularly in recent years, has had considerable difficulty in deciding when a case is moot. The former doctrine that a criminal case is moot after the defendant has served his sentence has, after much backing and filling, succumbed to the recognition of "the obvious fact of life that most criminal convictions do in fact entail adverse collateral legal consequences. The mere 'possibility' that this will be the case is enough to preserve a criminal case from ending 'ignominiously in the limbo of mootness.' "[10]

There is a useful escape from the mootness rule in the doctrine that if an issue is "capable of repetition, yet evading review" the courts may decide the case though the particular circumstances that gave rise to it have come to an end.[11] The stated doctrine is that this escape can be used only if two elements are combined: the challenged action was in its duration too short to be fully litigated prior to its cessation or expiration; and there was a reasonable expectation that the same complaining party would be subjected to the same action again.[12] In applying this principle, however, the Court has

9. E.g., California v. San Pablo & T. R. Co., 1893, 13 S.Ct. 876, 149 U.S. 308, 37 L.Ed. 747; A. L. Mechling Barge Lines, Inc. v. U. S., 1961, 82 S.Ct. 337, 368 U.S. 324, 7 L.Ed.2d 317.

A party's emotional involvement in knowing whether conduct was wrongful is not enough to save a case from mootness. Ashcroft v. Mattis, 1977, 97 S.Ct. 1739, 431 U.S. 171, 52 L.Ed.2d 219.

A case may be dismissed as moot even though the parties are agreed that it is not moot. Murphy v. Hunt, 1982, 102 S.Ct. 1181, ___ U.S. ___, 71 L.Ed.2d 353; DeFunis v. Odegaard, 1974, 94 S.Ct. 1704, 416 U.S. 312, 40 L.Ed.2d 164.

See generally 13 Wright, Miller & Cooper, Jurisdiction § 3533; Kates & Barber, Mootness in Judicial Proceedings: Toward a Coherent Theory, 1974, 62 Calif.L.Rev. 1385; Comment, A Search for Principles of Mootness in the Federal Courts, 1976, 54 Texas L.Rev. 1289; Note, The Mootness Doctrine in the Supreme Court, 1974, 88 Harv.L. Rev. 373; Note, Exceptions to the Prohibition Against Considering Moot Questions, 1968, 17 De Paul L.Rev. 590.

10. Sibron v. New York, 1968, 88 S.Ct. 1889, 1899, 392 U.S. 40, 55, 20 L.Ed.2d

917. See also: Carafas v. LaVallee, 1968, 88 S.Ct. 1556, 391 U.S. 234, 20 L.Ed.2d 554; Jones v. Cunningham, 1963, 83 S.Ct. 373, 371 U.S. 236, 9 L.Ed.2d 285; U. S. v. Morgan, 1954, 74 S.Ct. 247, 346 U.S. 502, 98 L.Ed. 248.

The collateral consequences doctrine allows review at the instance of the state as well as of the defendant. Pennsylvania v. Mimms, 1977, 98 S.Ct. 330, 434 U.S. 106, 54 L.Ed.2d 331, on remand 1978, 385 A.2d 334, 477 Pa. 553.

Nonstatutory consequences, such as employment prospects or the sentence imposed in a future criminal proceeding, are not enough to prevent mootness. Lane v. Williams, 1982, 102 S.Ct. 1322, ___ U.S. ___, 71 L.Ed.2d 508.

11. Southern Pac. Terminal Co. v. ICC, 1911, 31 S.Ct. 279, 283, 219 U.S. 498, 515, 55 L.Ed. 310. See Roe v. Wade, 1973, 93 S.Ct. 705, 712–713, 410 U.S. 113, 124–125, 35 L.Ed.2d 147, holding that the natural termination of a pregnancy did not moot an action challenging the restrictions on abortions. See also Nebraska Press Assn. v. Stuart, 1976, 96 S.Ct. 2791, 427 U.S. 539, 49 L.Ed.2d 683.

12. Murphy v. Hunt, 1982, 102 S.Ct. 1181, ___ U.S. ___, 71 L.Ed.2d 353; Weinstein v. Bradford, 1975, 96 S.Ct. 347, 423 U.S. 147, 46 L.Ed.2d 350.

drawn distinctions too subtle for many observers,[13] and it has not yet clearly defined the extent to which an even broader escape from the usual rules of mootness may be available if a suit was brought as a class action.[14]

It is held also that the courts will not hear collusive cases.[15] Though the rule is not in terms so confined, it is principally applied in constitutional cases, on the notion that "it never was the thought that, by means of a friendly suit, a party beaten in the legislature could transfer to the courts an inquiry as to the constitutionality of the legislative act." [16] Even here application of the rule has not always been rigid—some of the most famous constitutional decisions have come in what now seem to have been collusive cases.[17] Nor is it fatal to the existence of a case or controversy that a party has deliberately provoked a test case.[18]

The rule against collusive litigation does not mean—though it is sometimes stated as if it meant—that the parties must actually disagree. A court has jurisdiction to render judgment by default or on a plea of guilty.[19] It may order naturalization of an alien though no one challenges the alien's petition.[20] But if one party is financing and controlling both sides of the litigation, the court should deem the suit collusive. If both litigants desire precisely the same result there is no case or controversy within the meaning of Article III.[21] The same result is reached if one party refuses to take a position on the merits and merely asks that a matter be resolved.[22]

When the authors of the Constitution restricted the federal courts to determination of cases and controversies, presumably they had in mind that the business of the courts should be the kind of judicial business with which they were familiar in the English courts. Indeed

---

13. Compare, for example, the 5–4 decisions one week apart, reaching opposite results though the later case does not cite the earlier, in Super Tire Engineering Co. v. McCorkle, 1974, 94 S.Ct. 1694, 416 U.S. 115, 40 L.Ed.2d 1, and DeFunis v. Odegaard, 1974, 94 S.Ct. 1704, 416 U.S. 312, 40 L.Ed.2d 164.

14. Compare Deposit Guar. Nat. Bank v. Roper, 1980, 100 S.Ct. 1166, 445 U.S. 326, 63 L.Ed.2d 427, with Sosna v. Iowa, 1975, 95 S.Ct. 553, 419 U.S. 393, 42 L.Ed.2d 532.

15. Lord v. Veazie, 1850, 8 How. 251, 12 L.Ed. 1067; 13 Wright, Miller & Cooper, Jurisdiction § 3530.

16. Chicago & G. T. Ry. Co. v. Wellman, 1892, 12 S.Ct. 400, 402, 143 U.S. 339, 345, 36 L.Ed. 176. See also U. S. v. Johnson, 1943, 63 S.Ct. 1075, 319 U.S. 302, 87 L.Ed. 1413.

17. E.g., Fletcher v. Peck, 1810, 6 Cranch 87, 3 L.Ed. 162; Dred Scott v.

Sandford, 1857, 19 How. 393, 16 L.Ed. 691.

18. Havens Realty Corp. v. Coleman, 1982, 102 S.Ct. 1114, ___ U.S. ___, 71 L.Ed.2d 214; Evers v. Dwyer, 1958, 79 S.Ct. 178, 358 U.S. 202, 3 L.Ed.2d 222.

19. See In re Metropolitan Ry. Receivership, 1907, 28 S.Ct. 219, 208 U.S. 90, 52 L.Ed. 403.

20. Tutun v. U. S., 1926, 46 S.Ct. 425, 270 U.S. 568, 70 L.Ed. 738. See Note, Judicial Determinations in Nonadversary Proceedings, 1959, 72 Harv.L.Rev. 723.

21. Moore v. Charlotte-Mecklenburg Bd. of Educ., 1971, 91 S.Ct. 1292, 402 U.S. 47, 28 L.Ed.2d 590. But cf. GTE Sylvania, Inc. v. Consumers Union, 1980, 100 S.Ct. 1194, 445 U.S. 375, 63 L.Ed.2d 467.

22. Princeton Univ. v. Schmid, 1982, 102 S.Ct. 867, ___ U.S. ___, 70 L.Ed.2d 865.

a member of the Court has observed that "a court will not decide a question unless the nature of the action challenged, the kind of injury inflicted, and the relationship between the parties are such that judicial determination is consonant with what was, generally speaking, the business of the Colonial courts and the courts of Westminster when the Constitution was framed." [23] Yet the oldest and most consistent thread in the federal law of justiciability is that the federal courts will not give advisory opinions, though at least by 1770 the power of the English judges to give advisory opinions was well recognized.[24] Thus the refusal to give advisory opinions must be based on "the implicit policies embodied in Article III, and not history alone." [25] It recognizes the risk that comes from passing on abstract questions rather than limiting decisions to concrete cases in which a question is precisely framed by a clash of genuine adversary argument exploring every aspect of the issue.[26]

The rule against advisory opinions was first enunciated in 1793. Secretary of State Jefferson submitted to the Supreme Court 29 questions dealing with international law, neutrality, and the construction of the French and British treaties. In its reply to President Washington, the Court said that the separation of powers contemplated by the Constitution, and the fact that the Supreme Court is a court of last resort, afforded strong arguments against the propriety of an extra-judicial decision of the questions.[27] Very shortly thereafter a similar rule was established for the trial courts. A 1792 statute provided that disabled veterans of the Revolutionary War wishing to be put on the pension list should apply to the circuit court, which would determine whether the applicant was in fact a veteran, and disabled, and then would certify to the Secretary of War that the applicant should be put on the pension lists at a stated amount. The Secretary of War on receiving such a certificate was to put the applicant on the pension list unless he had cause to suspect imposition or mistake. The circuit courts to which such petitions were presented, on which five of the Supreme Court justices sat, uniformly refused to entertain such petitions, on the grounds that the business was not properly judicial in nature, and that the power of the Secretary of War to sus-

23. Frankfurter, J., concurring in Joint Anti-Fascist Refugee Committee v. Mc-Grath, 1951, 71 S.Ct. 624, 637, 341 U.S. 123, 150, 95 L.Ed. 817. See also Coleman v. Miller, 1939, 59 S.Ct. 972, 985, 307 U.S. 433, 460, 83 L.Ed. 1385 (separate opinion of Frankfurter, J.).

24. Frankfurter, 1 Encyc. of the Social Sciences, 1937, p. 476, quoted in 3 Davis, Administrative Law Treatise, 1958, pp. 127–128.

25. Flast v. Cohen, 1968, 88 S.Ct. 1942, 1950, 392 U.S. 83, 95, 20 L.Ed.2d 947.

26. U. S. v. Fruehauf, 1961, 81 S.Ct. 547, 554, 365 U.S. 146, 157, 5 L.Ed.2d

476. See also Golden v. Zwickler, 1969, 89 S.Ct. 956, 394 U.S. 103, 22 L.Ed.2d 113.

See 13 Wright, Miller & Cooper, Jurisdiction § 3529; Weinstein, Rendering Advisory Opinions—Do We, Should We?, 1970, 54 Judicature 140; Frankfurter, A Note on Advisory Opinions, 1924, 37 Harv.L.Rev. 1002; Note, The Case for an Advisory Function in the Federal Judiciary, 1962, 50 Geo.L.J. 785.

27. 3 Correspondence and Public Papers of John Jay, 1890, pp. 488–489.

pend the decision deprived the proceeding of the finality requisite to a judgment of a court.[28]

The rule against advisory opinions has had modern importance in casting doubt, now resolved, on the power of the federal judiciary to give declaratory judgments. Muskrat v. United States,[29] decided in 1911, involved a statute authorizing certain named Indians to bring a test suit against the United States to determine whether a 1906 statute, broadening the class of Indians who were to be allotted certain lands, was an unconstitutional modification of a 1902 statute allotting the lands. Suit was to be brought in the Court of Claims with review in the Supreme Court. The Supreme Court held that there was no case or controversy in the constitutional sense, relying on the debatable assertion that the United States, the named defendant, had no interest adverse to the plaintiffs, and on the notion that since in a legal sense the judgment could not be executed, it amounted in fact to no more than an expression of opinion upon the validity of the statutes in question.[30]

The case of Willing v. Chicago Auditorium Association [31] in 1928 purported to be a suit in the nature of a bill to remove a cloud upon title by the lessee of real estate. The lessee desired to tear down an unprofitable auditorium on the land and erect an office building in its stead. The lessor had indicated informally that to do so would violate the lease, and the lessee desired to determine this question before demolishing the auditorium. The Supreme Court held that this was not a proper case for a bill to remove a cloud on title, but added the dictum that "what the plaintiff seeks is simply a declaratory judgment. To grant that relief is beyond the power conferred upon the federal judiciary." [32]

When the issue was finally presented squarely to the Supreme Court, it ignored its past doubts and recognized that where there is an actual controversy between real parties, the constitutional requisites of jurisdiction are met even though the judgment is declaratory and cannot be executed. Thus in 1933 it held that review of an action

---

28. Hayburn's Case, 1796, 2 Dall. 409, 1 L.Ed. 436. For a similar ruling in a different context, see U. S. v. Ferreira, 1852, 13 How. 40, 14 L.Ed. 42.

29. 1911, 31 S.Ct. 250, 219 U.S. 346, 55 L.Ed. 246.

30. 31 S.Ct. at 256, 219 U.S. at 362.
The merits of the Indians' claim were decided the following year in Gritts v. Fisher, 1912, 32 S.Ct. 580, 224 U.S. 640, 56 L.Ed. 928, an action for an injunction against the Secretary of the Interior.

31. 1928, 48 S.Ct. 507, 277 U.S. 274, 72 L.Ed. 880.

32. 48 S.Ct. at 509, 277 U.S. at 289. Justice Stone concurred in the result but objected to the quoted dictum as "very similar itself to a declaratory judgment to the effect that we could not constitutionally be authorized to give such judgments—but is, in addition, prospective, unasked, and unauthorized under any statute." 48 S.Ct. at 510, 277 U.S. at 291.

A similarly hostile attitude toward declaratory judgments was shown in Liberty Warehouse Co. v. Grannis, 1927, 47 S.Ct. 282, 273 U.S. 70, 71 L.Ed. 541. But cf. Fidelity Nat. Bank & Trust Co. v. Swope, 1927, 47 S.Ct. 511, 274 U.S. 123, 71 L.Ed. 959.

brought under a state declaratory judgment statute was within the judicial power, saying that "the Constitution does not require that the case or controversy should be presented by traditional forms of procedure, invoking only traditional remedies. The judiciary clause of the Constitution defined and limited judicial power, not the particular method by which that power might be invoked. It did not crystallize into changeless form the procedure of 1789 as the only possible means for presenting a case or controversy otherwise cognizable by the federal courts." [33] This decision led to the enactment of a federal statute authorizing declaratory judgments in the following year, and the validity of this statute too was upheld.[34] There are sometimes still difficulties in determining whether a particular controversy is appropriate for issuance of a declaratory judgment, and the Court is particularly loath to allow important constitutional questions to be litigated by this procedure,[35] but the declaratory judgment is now a familiar and often-used tool of the federal courts.[36]

§ 13.   "Case or Controversy"—Standing to Litigate [1]

The law of standing, the Supreme Court says, is a "complicated specialty of federal jurisdiction, the solution of whose problems is in any event more or less determined by the specific circumstances of

---

33. Nashville, C. & St. L. Ry. Co. v. Wallace, 1933, 53 S.Ct. 345, 348, 288 U.S. 249, 264, 77 L.Ed. 730.

34. Aetna Life Ins. Co. v. Haworth, 1937, 57 S.Ct. 461, 300 U.S. 227, 81 L.Ed. 617.

35. See, e.g., Electric Bond & Share Co. v. S. E. C., 1938, 58 S.Ct. 678, 303 U.S. 419, 82 L.Ed. 936; United Public Workers v. Mitchell, 1947, 67 S.Ct. 556, 330 U.S. 75, 91 L.Ed. 754; International Longshoremen's and Warehousemen's Union Local 37 v. Boyd, 1954, 74 S.Ct. 447, 347 U.S. 222, 98 L.Ed. 650; Steffel v. Thompson, 1974, 94 S.Ct. 1209, 1216 n. 10, 115 U.S. 452, 459 n. 10, 39 L.Ed. 2d 505; Ellis v. Dyson, 1975, 95 S.Ct. 1691, 421 U.S. 426, 44 L.Ed.2d 274.

A declaratory judgment action by a doctor and several of his patients, challenging a state statute that prohibited him from giving them needed advice as to contraceptives, was held not justiciable where past history led the Court to believe there was no likelihood that the statute would be enforced. Poe v. Ullman, 1961, 81 S.Ct. 1752, 367 U.S. 497, 6 L.Ed.2d 989. See Comment, Threat of Enforcement—Prerequisite of a Justiciable Controversy, 1962, 62 Col.L. Rev. 106. Subsequently the state brought a criminal action against the

doctor and another who had openly violated the statute, and the law was held unconstitutional. Griswold v. Connecticut, 1965, 85 S.Ct. 1678, 381 U.S. 479, 14 L.Ed.2d 510.

36. See § 100 below.

[§ 13]

1. 13 Wright, Miller, & Cooper, Jurisdiction § 3531; Davis, Administrative Law of the Seventies, 1976, c. 22; Varat, Variable Justiciability and the Duke Power Case, 1980, 58 Texas L.Rev. 273; Brilmayer, The Jurisprudence of Article III: Perspectives on the "Case or Controversy" Requirement, 1979, 93 Harv.L.Rev. 297; Tushnet, The Sociology of Article III: A Response to Professor Brilmayer, 1980, 93 Harv.L.Rev. 1698; Brilmayer, A Reply, 1980, 93 Harv.L.Rev. 1727; Tushnet, The New Law of Standing: A Plea for Abandonment, 1977, 62 Corn. L.Rev. 663; Scott, Standing in the Supreme Court—A Functional Analysis, 1973, 86 Harv.L.Rev. 645; Monaghan, Constitutional Adjudication: The Who and When, 1973, 82 Yale L.J. 1363; Jaffe, The Citizen as Litigant in Public Actions: The Non-Hohfeldian or Ideological Plaintiff, 1968, 116 U.Pa.L.Rev. 1033.

individual situations *   *   * ." [2] The description of this problem as a "specialty of federal jurisdiction" has caused difficulty. State courts must and do have a body of law determining who has standing to litigate particular matters. One leading writer has taken the view that standing is a specialty of federal jurisdiction only in the sense that the federal law of standing involves artificialities that the states have wisely refused to follow.[3] The phrase can, however, be understood in a different sense. Since standing to sue is an element of the federal constitutional concept of "case or controversy," perhaps the Supreme Court meant to say only that on such questions the federal courts must reach their own decisions without regard to what the state law in point may be.[4]

The law of standing is almost exclusively concerned with such public law questions as determinations of constitutionality and review of administrative or other governmental action. In theory, of course, it is not so limited. The person suing for breach of contract or for a tort must satisfy the court that he has standing to bring such a suit, but in practice such suits are brought only by a person harmed by the supposed wrong, and his standing to sue is self-evident. It is only where the question is of a public nature that the interested bystander is likely to attempt suit.

The law of standing has experienced rapid and repeated change in the years since 1968. The Court has vacillated on whether it is desirable to relax the requirement of standing, although in general the recent cases have been more restrictive than those earlier in that period. About all that is certain on the subject is that the last word has not yet been written. In a 1982 decision, Valley Forge Christian College v. Americans United for Separation of Church and State, Inc.,[5] almost the only noncontroversial statement the Court made was: "We need not mince words when we say that the concept of 'Art. III standing' has not been defined with complete consistency in all of the various cases decided by this Court which have discussed it, nor when we say that this very fact is probable proof that the concept cannot be reduced to a one-sentence or one-paragraph definition." [6]

The best known Supreme Court decision on standing, prior to 1968, was Frothingham v. Mellon,[7] often referred to as Massachusetts v. Mellon, a related case that the Court decided in the same

2. U. S. ex rel. Chapman v. FPC, 1953, 73 S.Ct. 609, 612, 345 U.S. 153, 156, 97 L.Ed. 918.

"Generalizations about standing to sue are largely worthless as such." Association of Data Processing Serv. Organizations, Inc. v. Camp, 1970, 90 S.Ct. 827, 829, 397 U.S. 150, 151, 25 L.Ed.2d 184.

3. Davis, Administrative Law Treatise, 1958, p. 210. See also Scanwell Laboratories, Inc. v. Shaffer, C.A.1970, 424

F.2d 859, 861–862, 137 U.S.App.D.C. 371.

4. Village of Arlington Heights v. Metropolitan Housing Development Corp., 1977, 97 S.Ct. 555, 561 n. 8, 429 U.S. 252, 262 n. 8, 50 L.Ed.2d 450.

5. 1982, 102 S.Ct. 752, ___ U.S. ___, 70 L.Ed.2d 700, noted 1982, 28 Loy.L.Rev. 653, 12 Seton Hall L.Rev. 865.

6. 102 S.Ct. at 760, ___ U.S. at ___.

7. 1923, 43 S.Ct. 597, 262 U.S. 447, 67 L.Ed. 1078.

opinion. Mrs. Frothingham, alleging that she was a taxpayer of the United States, sued to restrain payments from the Treasury to the several states that chose to participate in a program created by the Maternity Act of 1921. Her claim was that the federal government lacked power to appropriate money for the reduction of maternal and infant mortality, and that such appropriations would cause an unconstitutional increase in her future taxes. The Court never reached the merits of her attack on the statute, for it held that she lacked what is now called standing to make such a challenge. The Court recognized that it had entertained suits by a municipal taxpayer, but held that the case of a federal taxpayer is far different, since his interest in the federal revenue is shared with millions of others, is comparatively minute and indeterminable, and the effect on future taxation of any particular payment is remote, fluctuating, and uncertain. The Court also was alarmed at the prospect that to allow such a suit would mean that any federal taxpayer could challenge the validity of any federal expenditure. Finally the Court stated that its power to declare statutes unconstitutional exists only where the statute is involved in a justiciable case, and that to present such a case the plaintiff "must be able to show, not only that the statute is invalid, but that he has sustained or is immediately in danger of sustaining some direct injury as the result of its enforcement, and not merely that he suffers in some indefinite way in common with people generally."[8]

The Frothingham decision, taken together with the decision in the companion case that a state cannot challenge the constitutionality of a federal expenditure,[9] had the effect of taking the spending power beyond the scope of judicial review. Though the case was thus of the first importance, and perhaps at the time salutary in result, neither its reasoning nor its result found much favor with later commentators. They noted that states almost universally permit review of gov-

---

As is was common in the earlier standing cases, the term "standing" is not used in the opinion. "The word *standing* is rather recent in the basic judicial vocabulary and does not appear to have been commonly used until the middle of our own century. No authority that I have found introduces the term with proper explanations and apologies and announces that henceforth *standing* should be used to describe who may be heard by a judge. Nor was there any sudden adoption by tacit consent. The word appears here and there, spreading very gradually with no discernible pattern. Judges and lawyers found themselves using the term and did not ask why they did so or where it came from." Vining, Legal Identity, 1978, p. 55.

8. 43 S.Ct. at 601, 262 U.S. at 488.

9. See § 14 below.

On the standing of a state to sue parens patriae, see also Pennsylvania v. New Jersey, 1976, 96 S.Ct. 2333, 426 U.S. 660, 49 L.Ed.2d 124; Hawaii v. Standard Oil Co. of California, 1972, 92 S.Ct. 885, 405 U.S. 251, 31 L.Ed.2d 184; Pennsylvania by Shapp v. Kleppe, C.A. 1976, 533 F.2d 668, 174 U.S.App.D.C. 441, certiorari denied 97 S.Ct. 485, 429 U.S. 977, 50 L.Ed.2d 584, noted 1976, 26 Cath.U.L.Rev. 168; Strausberg, The Standing of a State as Parens Patriae To Sue the Federal Government, 1976, 35 Fed.Bar J. 1; Comment, State Standing to Challenge Federal Administrative Action: A Re-Examination of the Parens Patriae Doctrine, 1977, 125 U.Pa.L.Rev. 1069.

ernmental spending at the instance of local or state taxpayers.[10] The distinction drawn in Frothingham between federal and municipal taxpayers, based on the size of their interest, seemed unrealistic at a time when certain large corporations pay in taxes as much as 2% of the entire federal revenue, and thus have an interest of twenty million dollars in, for example, a billion dollar spending program. Sums of this nature, far exceeding the amount likely to be at stake in a suit by a municipal taxpayer, did not seem to fit the Court's description of "comparatively minute." Further it was argued that it would be better to permit a suit, and have the constitutionality of a particular expenditure determined on its merits, than to have the matter go by default.

The heaviest pressure on the Frothingham rule, however, was based on wholly practical rather than theoretical considerations. There was considerable uncertainty about the extent to which the First Amendment permits Congress to provide financial aid to educational institutions operated in the interest of a particular religious group. Both those who favored such aid and those who opposed it were eager to have some means by which the constitutionality of this kind of aid might be tested, since each side thought its constitutional arguments would be vindicated, and a resolution of the matter would affect the willingness of Congress to make such appropriations. Several times bills passed the Senate that purported to grant standing to a variety of interested persons and institutions to challenge grants of this kind, but these bills never became law.

The Supreme Court resolved the problem in 1968 in Flast v. Cohen.[11] A taxpayers' action challenged the allegedly unconstitutional expenditure of federal funds under the Elementary and Secondary Education Act of 1965. The appropriations involved under that act were used to finance instruction in reading, arithmetic, and other subjects in religious schools, and to purchase textbooks for use in those schools. The district court dismissed the action on the authority of Frothingham, but the Supreme Court reversed. The Court did not overrule Frothingham, as the commentators had urged. Instead it distinguished Frothingham by recognizing a qualification on what had seemed to be a broad ban against suits by federal taxpayers to challenge federal appropriations.

The Court drew a distinction that had not always been clearly made in earlier cases between whether a plaintiff is a proper party to

10. See Comment, Taxpayers' Suits—A Survey and Summary, 1960, 69 Yale L.J. 895.

11. 1968, 88 S.Ct. 1942, 392 U.S. 83, 20 L.Ed.2d 947. The decision, and the vagaries that it left in the law of standing generally, were criticized by Professor Davis in a typically thoughtful and thought-provoking article. Davis, Standing: Taxpayers and Others, 1968, 35 U.Chi.L.Rev. 601. See also the witty exchange: Bittker, The Case of the Fictitious Taxpayer: The Federal Taxpayer's Suit Twenty Years After Flast v. Cohen, 1969, 36 U.Chi.L.Rev. 364; Davis, The Case of the Real Taxpayer: A Reply to Professor Bittker, 1969, 36 U.Chi.L.Rev. 375.

request an adjudication of a particular issue and whether the issue itself is justiciable. In terms of constitutional limitation, "the question of standing is related only to whether the dispute sought to be adjudicated will be presented in an adversary context and in a form historically viewed as capable of judicial resolution." [12] On this analysis there is no absolute bar to suits by federal taxpayers, and the question is whether the circumstances are such that a federal taxpayer has the personal stake and interest necessary to give the litigation the concreteness required by Article III. This, Chief Justice Warren wrote for the Court, depends on "whether there is a logical nexus between the status asserted and the claim sought to be adjudicated." [13]

To establish the required nexus between his status and his claim, a taxpayer challenging a federal appropriation must show two things. "First, the taxpayer must establish a logical link between that status and the type of legislative enactment attacked. Thus, a taxpayer will be a proper party to allege the unconstitutionality only of exercises of congressional power under the taxing and spending clause of Art. I, § 8, of the Constitution. It will not be sufficient to allege an incidental expenditure of tax funds in the administration of an essentially regulatory statute. * * * Secondly the taxpayer must establish a nexus between that status and the precise nature of the constitutional infringement alleged. Under this requirement, the taxpayer must show that the challenged enactment exceeds specific constitutional limitations imposed upon the exercise of the congressional taxing and spending power and not simply that the enactment is generally beyond the powers delegated to Congress by Art. I, § 8." [14]

Both the plaintiffs in the Flast case and Mrs. Frothingham met the first test, since both were attacking a federal spending program rather than a regulatory statute. The Flast plaintiffs met the second test as well, since the Establishment Clause of the First Amendment "operates as a specific constitutional limitation upon the exercise by Congress of the taxing and spending power * * *." [15] Mrs.

---

12. 88 S.Ct. at 1953, 392 U.S. at 101.

13. 88 S.Ct. at 1953, 392 U.S. at 101. The Court here cited McGowan v. Maryland, 1961, 81 S.Ct. 1101, 1107–1108, 366 U.S. 420, 429–430, 6 L.Ed.2d 393, in which it was held that merchants attacking a Sunday closing law on the ground that it caused them economic injury had standing to claim that the law violated the Establishment Clause of the First Amendment but could not press a claim under the Free Exercise Clause.

Although the reference in Flast to McGowan would have suggested that the nexus requirement is of general applicability, the court has since said it applies only in taxpayer cases. Duke Power Co. v. Carolina Enviromental Study Group, Inc., 1978, 98 S.Ct. 2620, 2633, 438 U.S. 59, 78–79, 57 L.Ed.2d 595.

14. 88 S.Ct. at 1954, 392 U.S. at 102.

15. 88 S.Ct. at 1954–1955, 392 U.S. at 102–106.

In Richardson v. Kennedy, D.C.Pa.1970, 313 F.Supp. 1282, affirmed 1971, 91 S.Ct. 868, 401 U.S. 901, 27 L.Ed.2d 800, it was held that a taxpayer does not have standing to challenge increase of congressional salaries by a commission, since the authority for the payment of congressional salaries comes from Article I, § 6, rather than Article I, § 8, of the Constitution, and Article

Frothingham failed the second test since the constitutional provisions on which she relied, the Tenth Amendment and the Due Process Clause of the Fifth Amendment, are not specific limitations on the taxing and spending power. The Court did not decide whether any provision of the Constitution other than the Establishment Clause is a specific limitation on the taxing and spending power. That was left to be "determined only in the context of future cases." [16]

A bare majority of the Court accepted all that was said in Flast. Justices Stewart and Fortas, in concurring opinions, thought that standing should be recognized only in Establishment Clause cases, and that the possibility that it exists in other cases should not have been opened. Justices Douglas and Harlan thought that the twofold test of standing announced by the majority would not prove durable, and that the opinion signalled the eventual demise of the Frothingham rule. Justice Douglas, who would welcome such an outcome, concurred in the result. Justice Harlan, thinking Frothingham a wise limitation on the federal courts, dissented.

In general the Court has remained true to the other aspect of the rule recognized in Frothingham, and has entertained suits by local taxpayers challenging local expenditures.[17] There was an important qualification announced, however, in the Doremus case in 1952.[18] This was an attack by state and municipal taxpayers on a state statute requiring the reading of a portion of the Old Testament at the beginning of each school day. The state court entertained the suit and held the statute valid, but the Supreme Court dismissed an appeal on the ground that the plaintiffs lacked standing. It held that a taxpayer's suit could be heard only if it was a good-faith pocketbook action, and that in the case before it, where there was no measurable disbursement of school funds because of the activity complained of, the plaintiff was not seeking to litigate a direct dollars-and-cents injury but only a religious difference.

A case decided the same day as Doremus illustrates strikingly the vagaries in the law of standing. In Adler v. Board of Education [19] the challenge was to a New York statute directing the state board of regents to make regulations looking to the elimination of subversive teachers from the public schools. The plaintiffs in the suit attacking

I, § 6 is not a specific limitation on the taxing and spending power.

The Flast tests were also held not satisfied in U. S. v. Richardson, 1974, 94 S.Ct. 2940, 418 U.S. 166, 41 L.Ed.2d 678, Schlesinger v. Reservists Committee to Stop the War, 1974, 94 S.Ct. 2925, 418 U.S. 208, 41 L.Ed.2d 706, and the Valley Forge Christian College case, all discussed in the text below.

16.   88 S.Ct. at 1955, 392 U.S. at 105.

17.   E.g., Everson v. Board of Educ., 1947, 67 S.Ct. 504, 330 U.S. 1, 91 L.Ed.

711, (taxpayer had standing to challenge use of public funds for transportation to parochial schools). The Court has also accepted, without comment on the standing question, suit by a state taxpayer challenging a state statute. Wieman v. Updegraff, 1952, 73 S.Ct. 215, 344 U.S. 183, 97 L.Ed. 216.

18.   Doremus v. Board of Educ., 1952, 72 S.Ct. 394, 342 U.S. 429, 96 L.Ed. 475.

19.   1952, 72 S.Ct. 380, 342 U.S. 485, 96 L.Ed. 517.

the statute included variously taxpayers, parents of school children, and teachers. The teachers did not show that they were in the class sought to be reached by the statute, and, on precedent,[20] probably lacked standing. The standing of the parents seems even more problematical. Parents may well have standing to challenge school activities that injure their children in an unconstitutional way,[21] but in the vivid phrase of one justice, "it is like catching butterflies without a net to try to find a legal interest" in the parent's desire to have his child educated in a school where the teachers are free from unconstitutional restraint.[22] Finally the taxpayers would seem barred by the doctrine announced that day in the Doremus case, for as in that case, they could show no measurable pocketbook injury.

The striking thing about the Adler decision is not that the Court decided the case on its merits; the standing of each of the classes of plaintiffs is at least arguable. But the Court never made the argument. It upheld the law on the merits, over a strong dissent on grounds of standing and ripeness, without ever discussing standing or even stating who the plaintiffs were.

As the Doremus and Adler cases show, the decisions on standing are not easy to reconcile on their facts. Nor has the theory on standing questions been much more satisfactory. It used to be said that to have standing the plaintiff must be able to demonstrate injury to a legally protected interest.[23] Such an approach is demonstrably circular: if the plaintiff is given standing to assert his claims, his interest

---

20. See United Public Workers v. Mitchell, 1946, 67 S.Ct. 556, 330 U.S. 75, 91 L.Ed. 754 (federal employees who alleged that they wished to participate in political activities, but had been advised that this would cause them to lose their jobs under the Hatch Act, lacked standing to challenge that act since they had not yet in fact violated it).

21. The Court has listened to attacks on school released-time programs brought by plaintiffs who sued as parents and as taxpayers. McCollum v. Board of Educ., 1948, 68 S.Ct. 461, 333 U.S. 203, 92 L.Ed. 649; Zorach v. Clauson, 1952, 72 S.Ct. 679, 343 U.S. 306, 96 L.Ed. 954. This was the basis for standing in Engel v. Vitale, 1962, 82 S.Ct. 1261, 370 U.S. 421, 8 L.Ed.2d 601, but that decision has been criticized for holding that the parents had standing. Sutherland, Establishment According to Engel, 1962, 76 Harv.L.Rev. 25. See also School Dist. of Abington Tp., Pa. v. Schempp, 1963, 83 S.Ct. 1560, 1572 n. 9, 374 U.S. 203, 224 n. 9, 10 L.Ed.2d 844. In the Valley Forge Christian College case the Court says: "The

plaintiffs in Schempp had standing not because their complaint rested on the Establishment Clause—for as Doremus demonstrated, that is insufficient—but because impressionable schoolchildren were subjected to unwelcome religious exercises or were forced to assume special burdens to avoid them." 102 S.Ct. at 766 n. 22, ___ U.S. at ___ n. 22.

22. 72 S.Ct. at 390, 342 U.S. at 502 (Frankfurter, J., dissenting).

23. Tennessee Elec. Power Co. v. Tennessee Val. Auth., 1938, 59 S.Ct. 366, 306 U.S. 118, 83 L.Ed. 543 (competing corporations lack standing to assert unconstitutionality of TVA); Alabama Power Co. v. Ickes, 1938, 58 S.Ct. 300, 302 U.S. 464, 82 L.Ed. 374 (competitors lack standing to challenge loans and grants to municipal corporations because "no violation of a right"); Perkins v. Lukens Steel Co., 1940, 60 S.Ct. 869, 310 U.S. 113, 84 L.Ed. 1108 (seller of goods to government has no legal right and cannot challenge administrative determination of wages government suppliers must pay).

is legally protected; if he is denied standing, his interest is not legally protected.

The requirement of a legal interest was rejected by the Supreme Court in 1970 in Association of Data Processing Service Organizations, Inc. v. Camp.[24] The Court held that sellers of data processing services have standing to challenge a ruling of the Comptroller of the Currency allowing national banks to provide services of that kind. The lower courts had denied standing on the ground that competitors had no legally protected interest. Although that view was based on an earlier Supreme Court decision,[25] the Court rejected it, saying: "The 'legal interest' test goes to the merits. The question of standing is different."[26] It announced a two-part test for standing. Standing exists if "the plaintiff alleges that the challenged action has caused him injury in fact, economic or otherwise,"[27] and if "the interest sought to be protected by the complainant is arguably within the zone of interest to be protected or regulated by the statute or constitutional guarantee in question."[28]

In a companion case this test was applied to hold that tenant farmers receiving benefits under the upland cotton program had standing to challenge a regulation that, so they alleged, gave their landlord an opportunity to require them to assign their benefits to the landlord in advance as a condition to obtaining a lease to work the land.[29] Justices Brennan and White concurred in the result in both cases but dissented from the test that the Court announced for standing. They argued that the first part of the Court's test, injury in fact, is all that ought to be required and that the second part of the test, showing that the interest sought to be protected is arguably within the zone of interests protected or regulated by the statute, invites an inquiry into the merits that is unnecessary and inappropriate on the question of standing.[30]

24. 1970, 90 S.Ct. 827, 397 U.S. 150, 25 L.Ed.2d 184.

25. Tennessee Elec. Power Co. v. TVA, 1938, 59 S.Ct. 366, 369, 306 U.S. 118, 137–138, 83 L.Ed. 543. See also the other cases cited n. 21 above.

26. 90 S.Ct. at 830, 397 U.S. at 153.

27. 90 S.Ct. at 829, 397 U.S. at 152.

28. 90 S.Ct. at 830, 397 U.S. at 153.

29. Barlow v. Collins, 1970, 90 S.Ct. 832, 397 U.S. 159, 25 L.Ed.2d 192. In that case the Court said that "the tenant farmers are clearly within the zone of interests protected by the Act." 90 S.Ct. at 836, 397 U.S. at 164. The Court never discussed, as the Data Processing test seems to require, why or how the particular "interest sought to be protected by the" tenant farmers was within the zone protected by the statute. See Davis, The Liberalized

Law of Standing, 1970, 37 U.Chi.L.Rev. 450, 454–456.

See also Arnold Tours, Inc. v. Camp, 1970, 91 S.Ct. 158, 400 U.S. 45, 27 L.Ed.2d 179, holding that travel agents have standing to challenge a ruling by the Comptroller of Currency that national banks may provide travel services for their customers. The court of appeals, applying the Data Processing standard, thought that the travel agents lacked standing because there was no evidence that Congress was specifically concerned with the competitive interests of travel agencies. C.A. 1st, 1970, 428 F.2d 359. The Supreme Court said that Data Processing gives standing to businessmen who compete with national banks in any field other than the performance of bank services.

30. 90 S.Ct. at 838, 397 U.S. at 159.

The Court has continued to write frequently about standing. Though the later decisions go both ways, on the whole they suggest that the movement to broaden the standing concept has slowed down, though it has not stopped. In Sierra Club v. Morton [31] in 1972, the Court ruled explicitly that noneconomic injury, such as recreational use or aesthetic appreciation, was enough for standing but held that the Sierra Club lacked standing, despite its longstanding interest and concern in the protection of natural resources and its great litigating experience, since it failed to allege that either it or its members would be in any way affected by the challenged action in their use of the area they sought to protect.[32]

The major change in the direction of denying standing came in companion 1974 decisions in United States v. Richardson [33] and Schlesinger v. Reservists Committee to Stop the War.[34] Those cases, building heavily on a renewed emphasis on separation of powers principles, make it clear that a direct injury, and not merely a general interest common to all members of the public, is required for standing. Neither as a citizen nor as a taxpayer may one invoke judicial review simply to vindicate a belief in the need for lawful conduct by Congress or public officials. Finally, the fact that if the present plaintiff is not allowed to litigate, no one can do so, is not regarded as an argument for finding that the present plaintiff has standing. Instead that fact supports the view that the issue is one to be resolved through the political processes rather than in the courts.[35]

The 1976 decision in Simon v. Eastern Kentucky Welfare Rights Organization [36] built on two earlier cases [37] in giving new emphasis to the causal connection between plaintiff's asserted injury and defend-

---

31. 1972, 92 S.Ct. 1361, 405 U.S. 727, 31 L.Ed.2d 636. See Baude, Sierra Club v. Morton: Standing Trees in a Thicket of Justiciability, 1973, 48 Ind.L.Rev. 197; Sax, Standing to Sue: A Critical Review of the Mineral King Decisions, 1973, 13 Nat.Res.J. 76.

See also U. S. v. S.C.R.A.P., 1973, 93 S.Ct. 2405, 412 U.S. 669, 37 L.Ed.2d 254.

32. As the Supreme Court had indicated, the remedy was easily found in amendment of the complaint on remand. Sierra Club v. Morton, D.C.Cal. 1972, 348 F.Supp. 219.

33. 1974, 94 S.Ct. 2940, 418 U.S. 166, 41 L.Ed.2d 678.

34. 1974, 94 S.Ct. 2925, 418 U.S. 208, 41 L.Ed.2d 706.

35. The Richardson and Schlesinger cases are discussed in 13 Wright, Miller & Cooper, Jurisdiction § 3531. Note, Recent Standing Cases and a Possible Alternative Approach, 1975, 27 Hast.L.J. 213.

The Valley Forge Christian College case again rejects the argument that plaintiffs must have standing because if they do not, no one does. "This view would convert standing into a requirement that must be observed only when satisfied." 102 S.Ct. at 767, ___ U.S. at ___.

36. 1976, 96 S.Ct. 1917, 426 U.S. 26, 48 L.Ed.2d 450, noted 1977, 13 Wake Forest L.Rev. 602. The decision is severely criticized in Davis, Standing, 1976, 1977, 72 Nw.U.L.Rev. 69.

One question inevitably raised by Simon, but not yet resolved, is the extent to which the pleadings are determinative of standing or whether this preliminary issue of standing can be contested by motion for summary judgment. See 96 S.Ct. at 1927 n. 25, 426 U.S. at 45 n. 25; Haven Realty Corp. v. Coleman, 1982, 102 S.Ct. 1114, 1123–1124, ___ U.S. ___, ___, 71 L.Ed.2d 214, and the concurring opinion of Powell, J., 102 S.Ct. at

---

37. See note 37 on page 68.

ant's challenged action. Suit was brought against the Secretary of the Treasury challenging a new IRS regulation that allowed hospitals to qualify as charitable, and thus for contributions to them to be deductible, although they did not furnish service except in emergencies to indigents. The plaintiffs were low-income individuals and organizations representing them who claimed that they had been refused treatment, because of their indigency, at hospitals enjoying favorable tax treatment under the new regulation. A plaintiff, the Court thought, has standing only if he "has shown an injury to himself that is likely to be redressed by a favorable decision." [38] That test was not met in this case because the Court found it purely speculative whether the injury to the plaintiffs in not receiving free medical care could be traced to the IRS regulation and whether, if the regulation were changed, hospitals would not do without charitable contributions rather than take on the burden of caring for the indigent. [39] "Speculative inferences are necessary to connect their injury to the challenged actions of petitioners. Moreover, the complaint suggests no substantial likelihood that victory in this suit would result in respondents' receiving the hospital treatment they desire." [40]

In Simon, as in the earlier cases from which it took the requirements that the injury be traceable to defendant's conduct and that the injury was likely to be redressed by a favorable decision, these requirements led to holdings that standing did not exist. In subsequent cases the Court has found these requirements satisfied and upheld standing [41] or it has simply ignored these requirements. [42] Even so the requirements have been mentioned so often in the cases that by 1982 in the Valley Forge Christian College case the Court was able to announce as settled law that "at an irreducible minimum, Art. III requires the party who invokes the court's authority to 'show that he personally has suffered some actual or threatened injury as a result of the putatively illegal conduct of the defendant,' and that the injury 'fairly can be traced to the challenged action' and 'is likely to be redressed by a favorable decision.' " [43]

1126–1127, ___ U.S. at ___; Roberts, Fact Pleading, Notice Pleading, and Standing, 1980, 65 Corn.L.Rev. 390.

37. Linda R. S. v. Richard D., 1973, 93 S.Ct. 1146, 410 U.S. 614, 35 L.Ed.2d 536; Warth v. Seldin, 1975, 95 S.Ct. 2197, 422 U.S. 490, 45 L.Ed.2d 343.

38. 96 S.Ct. at 1924, 426 U.S. at 38.

39. Nationwide private philanthropy accounts for only 4% of private hospital revenues. 96 S.Ct. at 1927, 426 U.S. at 43.

40. 96 S.Ct. at 1927–1928, 426 U.S. at 45–46.

41. Village of Arlington Heights v. Metropolitan Housing Development Corp., 1977, 97 S.Ct. 555, 429 U.S. 252, 50 L.Ed.2d 450; Duke Power Co. v. Caro-

lina Environmental Study Group, 1978, 98 S.Ct. 2620, 438 U.S. 59, 57 L.Ed.2d 595; Watt v. Energy Action Educational Foundation, 1981, 102 S.Ct. 205, 454 U.S. 151, 70 L.Ed.2d 309.

See Nichol, Causation as a Standing Requirement: The Unprincipled Use of Judicial Restraint, 1981, 69 Ky.L.J. 185.

42. Orr v. Orr, 1979, 99 S.Ct. 1102, 440 U.S. 268, 59 L.Ed.2d 306.

43. 102 S.Ct. at 758, ___ U.S. at ___ (citations omitted).

The quoted passage seems to suggest that ability to trace the injury to the challenged action and the likelihood of redress are but two facets of a single causation requirement. Indeed in Duke

In the Valley Forge Christian College case it was the requirement of injury in fact, rather than the causation requirements, that was held fatal to standing. A statute allows a cabinet member to dispose of surplus government property without charge to tax exempt educational institutions. What had been a military hospital was turned over under that statute to a sectarian college. An organization dedicated to separation of church and state, along with several of its employees, challenged the conveyance on the ground that it was aid to religion in violation of the Establishment Clause.

The Supreme Court held that plaintiffs lacked standing. After a lengthy exposition of the principles concerning standing that have developed from the time of Frothingham, and of the reasons for rules of standing, the Court first rejected plaintiffs' argument that they had standing as taxpayers. Flast, it said, had created only a limited exception to the Frothingham principle that taxpayers do not have standing. That exception, under the first test of Flast, applies only where the challenge is to an exercise of the taxing and spending powers of Article I, § 8 of the Constitution. Here the property transfer challenged was an exercise of the power of Congress under Article IV, § 3, to dispose of property of the United States, and Flast had no application.

Nor could plaintiffs claim standing as citizens. Their claim that they had suffered a particular and concrete injury to a personal constitutional right was not enough for standing. "Although they claim that the Constitution has been violated, they claim nothing else. They fail to identify any personal injury suffered by the plaintiffs *as a consequence* of the alleged constitutional error, other than the psychological consequence presumably produced by observation of conduct with which one disagrees." [44] The Court reiterated its prior holdings that standing may be predicated on noneconomic injury,[45] but said that these plaintiffs had not alleged any injury of any kind, economic or otherwise, sufficient to confer standing. The Court, rejecting the views of four dissenters, could find no principled basis for

---

Power Co. v. Carolina Environmental Study Group, 1978, 98 S.Ct. 2620, 2631, 438 U.S. 59, 74, 57 L.Ed.2d 595, the Court says that these are but two ways of putting the same thing.

Other cases, however, seem to view the constitutional limits on standing as a three-part test, of which "distinct and palpable injury" is the first prong and the requirements that it be fairly traceable and be redressable are the second and third prongs. Watt v. Energy Action Educational Foundation, 1981, 102 S.Ct. 205, 212, 454 U.S. 151, 160, 70 L.Ed.2d 309; Theriault v. Brennan, C.A.1st, 1981, 641 F.2d 28, 31.

In the article cited note 40 above Professor Nichol argues, at 199, that "a substantial correlation exists between the concerns for directness of injury and redressability," but that "both their aims and modes of analysis are distinct."

44. 102 S.Ct. at 765, ___ U.S. at ___ (emphasis in original).

45. Duke Power Co. v. Carolina Environmental Study Group, 1978, 98 S.Ct. 2620, 2630, 438 U.S. 59, 73–74, 57 L.Ed. 2d 595 ("environmental and aesthetic consequences"); U. S. v. S.C.R.A.P., 1973, 93 S.Ct. 2405, 2415–2416, 412 U.S. 669, 686–688, 37 L.Ed.2d 254.

a special judicial role, and thus a lesser requirement of standing, in enforcing the Establishment Clause than for other provisions of the Constitution.[46]

In recent years almost no discussion of standing by the Supreme Court has been complete without its reference to the observation in Baker v. Carr that "the gist of the question of standing" is whether the plaintiffs have alleged "such a personal stake in the outcome of the controversy as to assure that concrete adverseness which sharpens the presentation of issues upon which the court so largely depends for illumination of difficult constitutional questions."[47] Despite the frequent reiteration of this language, the rules the Court has announced have little relation to that stated test. It is as unrealistic to place emphasis on a plaintiff's status as taxpayer, when the amount of his dollars going to finance a challenged program is minute and will be exacted by the government in any event, as it is to suppose that the Sierra Club will not bring concrete adverseness to its presentation of issues whether or not any of its members have ever used a particular area.[48] That concrete adverseness is not itself a test of standing was clearly stated in the Valley Forge Christian College case, where the Court said that "standing is not measured by the intensity of the litigant's interest or the fervor of his advocacy."[49] Concrete adverseness, on this view, is the anticipated consequence of proceedings commenced by one who has been injured in fact, and is not a permissible substitute for the showing of injury itself.

What has been said thus far has concerned the Article III limitations on standing. Even when the Article III requirements are met, "a plaintiff may still lack standing under the prudential principles by which the judiciary seeks to avoid deciding questions of broad social import where no individual rights would be vindicated and to limit access to the federal courts to those litigants best suited to assert a particular claim."[50] Three such prudential rules have been identified.[51] These are that the plaintiff's interest must come within the

---

46. 102 S.Ct. at 764–768, ___ U.S. at ___–___.

47. 1962, 82 S.Ct. 691, 703, 369 U.S. 186, 204, 7 L.Ed.2d 663.

48. An organization may sue in its own right if it shows concrete and demonstrable injury to its activities, and a consequent drain on its resources, rather than merely, as in Sierra Club, a setback to the organization's abstract social interests. Havens Realty Corp. v. Coleman, 1982, 102 S.Ct. 1114, 1124–1125, ___ U.S. ___, 71 L.Ed.2d 214.

To have standing to sue on behalf of its members it must show that: "(a) its members would otherwise have standing to sue in their own right; (b) the interests it seeks to protect are germane to the organization's purpose; and (c) neither the claim asserted nor the relief requested requires the participation of individual members in the lawsuit." Hunt v. Washington State Apple Advertising Comm., 1977, 97 S.Ct. 2434, 2441, 432 U.S. 333, 343, 53 L.Ed.2d 383, noted 1978, 64 Iowa L.Rev. 121.

49. 102 S.Ct. at 765, ___ U.S. at ___.

50. Gladstone, Realtors v. Village of Bellwood, 1979, 99 S.Ct. 1601, 1608, 441 U.S. 91, 99–100, 60 L.Ed.2d 66.

51. Ibid. See also Valley Forge Christian College, 102 S.Ct. 759–760, ___ U.S. at ___.

"zone of interests" arguably protected or regulated by the law in question,[52] that the courts will not hear "generalized grievances" shared in substantially equal measure by all or a large class of citizens,[53] and that plaintiff must assert his own legal interests rather than those of third parties.

A well-known example of the third of these limitations is Tileston v. Ullman,[54] holding that a physician, seeking a declaratory judgment that a statute preventing him from giving advice as to contraceptives was unconstitutional, could not rely on his patients' right to life, which the statute supposedly threatened. Many other cases announce a similar rule. Nevertheless "this rule has not been imposed uniformly as a firm constitutional restriction on federal court jurisdiction."[55] Indeed when the statute involving contraceptives came before the Court in a criminal prosecution of a doctor, he was allowed to assert the constitutional rights of his patients. The Court distinguished Tileston v. Ullman, on the ground that it was a declaratory judgment action in which the requirements of standing should be strict, while the case before it was a criminal prosecution, and the doctor, charged as an accessory, should have standing to assert that the offense he was charged with assisting cannot constitutionally be made a crime.[56]

In one striking case, a white person was suing for specific performance of his contract to sell real estate to a black person. The defense was that a city ordinance barred black persons from the area

A lower court has now recognized a fourth prudential rule in a situation that has not yet come to the Supreme Court. It was held in Riegle v. Federal Open Market Committee, C.A.1981, 656 F.2d 873, 211 U.S.App.D.C. 284, that ordinary rules of standing will determine whether a member of Congress can attack the constitutionality of a federal statute or the legitimacy of executive action, but that separation of powers considerations would be taken into account as a matter of equitable discretion in determining whether to decide the merits of the case. See also McGowan, Congressmen in Courts: The New Plaintiffs, 1981, 15 Ga.L.Rev. 241; Note, Congressional Access to the Federal Courts, 1977, 90 Harv.L.Rev. 1632.

52. Association of Data Processing Serv. Organizations v. Camp, 1970, 90 S.Ct. 827, 830, 397 U.S. 150, 153, 25 L.Ed.2d 184.

The failure of the Supreme Court to refer to "zone of interests" in Duke Power Co. v. Carolina Environmental Study Group, 1978, 98 S.Ct. 2620, 438 U.S. 59, 57 L.Ed.2d 595, caused some speculation that the limitation had been abandoned, but it is referred to as one of the prudential limitations in both of the cases cited note 50 above. The lower courts continue to enforce the limit, while lamenting its amorphous nature. Control Data Corp. v. Baldrige, C.A. 1981, 655 F.2d 283, 170 U.S.App.D.C. 210; Marshall & Ilsley Corp. v. Heimann, C.A.7th, 1981, 652 F.2d 685, 693–698.

53. See the discussion in the text above of the Schlesinger and Richardson cases.

54. 1943, 63 S.Ct. 493, 318 U.S. 44, 87 L.Ed. 603.

See also Laird v. Tatum, 1972, 92 S.Ct. 2318, 408 U.S. 1, 33 L.Ed.2d 154; Moose Lodge No. 107 v. Irvis, 1972, 92 S.Ct. 1965, 1968, 407 U.S. 163, 166, 32 L.Ed.2d 627.

55. Flast v. Cohen, 1968, 88 S.Ct. 1942, 1952, n. 20, 392 U.S. 83, 90 n. 20, 20 L.Ed.2d 947.

56. Griswold v. Connecticut, 1965, 85 S.Ct. 1678, 1679–1680, 381 U.S. 479, 481, 14 L.Ed.2d 510.

See also Eisenstadt v. Baird, 1972, 92 S.Ct. 1029, 405 U.S. 438, 31 L.Ed.2d 349.

in question. Such an ordinance violates the equal protection clause of the Fourteenth Amendment but here the black defendant, whose constitutional rights were violated by the ordinance, was relying on it as a defense, while the white person, whose constitutional rights were not hurt by the ordinance, was claiming it to be unconstitutional. The challenge was permitted, however.[57] Similar cases are well known. A parochial school was allowed to attack a statute that would have required public education for all children, though the constitutional rights involved were those of children and their parents.[58] Organizations have been allowed to put forward the constitutional rights of their members.[59] A school board was allowed to obtain an injunction barring conduct that would have interfered with the right of school children to be free from segregation.[60] A white defendant has been allowed to assert, as a defense in an action for damages for breach of a racially restrictive covenant, that to enforce the covenant would be unconstitutional state action, although it was clearly recognized that the constitutional right involved was not that of the defendant, but of unidentified non-whites who, in the future, would find it more difficult to buy property if their vendor would be required to respond in damages.[61] These cases were all explainable on the ground, made explicit in the restrictive covenant case, that the rule against relying on the rights of others is merely a rule of self-restraint, not part of the constitutional requirement of standing, and should not be applied where, as in those cases, it would be difficult if not impossible for the persons whose rights were asserted to present their grievance before any court.[62] Because the rule is not constitutionally required, and because it is concerned with the arguments a litigant can make rather than with his right to be in court at all, the Supreme Court has now followed the lead of commentators in referring to this rule as one of "jus tertii" rather than of standing.[63]

The rule against relying on jus tertii has been markedly relaxed in recent years. Physicians have been allowed to assert the rights of their patients in challenging a statute to limit abortions.[64] A seller of 3.2% beer has been allowed to assert that men aged 18 to 20 have the same right to purchase that beverage as do women in the same age

57. Buchanan v. Warley, 1917, 38 S.Ct. 16, 245 U.S. 60, 62 L.Ed. 149.

58. Pierce v. Society of Sisters, 1925, 45 S.Ct. 571, 268 U.S. 510, 69 L.Ed. 1070.

59. Joint Anti-Fascist Refugee Committee v. McGrath, 1951, 71 S.Ct. 624, 341 U.S. 123, 95 L.Ed. 817; National Assn. for the Advancement of Colored People v. Alabama ex rel. Patterson, 1958, 78 S.Ct. 1163, 1170, 357 U.S. 449, 458–460, 2 L.Ed.2d 1488.
See also note 48 above.

60. Brewer v. Hoxie Sch. Dist. No. 46, C.A.8th, 1956, 238 F.2d 91, 104–105.

61. Barrows v. Jackson, 1953, 73 S.Ct. 1031, 346 U.S. 249, 97 L.Ed. 1586.

62. 73 S.Ct. at 1034–1035, 346 U.S. at 255–257.

63. Craig v. Boren, 1976, 97 S.Ct. 451, 455, 429 U.S. 190, 193, 50 L.Ed.2d 397, rehearing denied 1977, 97 S.Ct. 1161, 429 U.S. 1124, 51 L.Ed.2d 574. See Sedler, Standing to Assert Constitutional Jus Tertii in the Supreme Court, 1962, 71 Yale L.J. 599; Note, Standing to Assert Constitutional Jus Tertii, 1974, 88 Harv.L.Rev. 423.

64. Singleton v. Wulff, 1976, 96 S.Ct. 2868, 428 U.S. 106, 49 L.Ed.2d 826.

group.[65] A mail-order seller of contraceptives has been allowed to raise the privacy rights of potential customers.[66] The Court seems to have moved close to, if indeed it has not already adopted, a general rule that either party to a relationship that is regulated or prohibited by statute will be allowed to raise the rights of the other.[67]

Closely related to the rule that one may not, save in exceptional cases, assert the rights of another is the rule that a defendant cannot claim a statute is unconstitutional in some of its reaches if the statute is constitutional as applied to him.[68] Nor, if he is required by the statute to do some particular act, can he defend on the ground that if he does so, he will in the future be exposed to some sanction that cannot validly be imposed.[69] The court in these cases will treat the present requirement as separable, and will leave to a later day the validity of the provisions not immediately in question.

To the propositions just stated there are, however, either limits or exceptions, depending on how they are viewed. The statute may be so broad in its scope that defendant will be allowed to assert that it is void for vagueness, even though it may clearly and constitutionally reach his case.[70] Particularly in the First Amendment area, there has been an inclination to consider the validity of the statute on its face, rather than as applied to the particular case, probably because of the threat a broad statute is thought to pose of inhibiting free expression.[71] The Court will entertain challenges to a statute as overbroad

---

65. Craig v. Boren, 1976, 97 S.Ct. 451, 429 U.S. 190, 50 L.Ed.2d 397.

66. Carey v. Population Services Intl., 1977, 97 S.Ct. 2010, 431 U.S. 678, 52 L.Ed.2d 675.

67. The party who goes to court must still satisfy the Article III requirements, despite the closeness of the relationship, by showing injury in fact and causation. Akron Center for Reproductive Health, Inc. v. City of Akron, C.A.6th, 1981, 651 F.2d 1198, 1210–1211.

68. Yazoo & M. V. R. R. v. Jackson Vinegar Co., 1912, 33 S.Ct. 40, 226 U.S. 217, 57 L.Ed. 193; U. S. v. Raines, 1960, 80 S.Ct. 519, 522–524, 362 U.S. 17, 21–24, 4 L.Ed.2d 524. Stern, Separability and Separability Clauses in The Supreme Court, 1937, 51 Harv.L.Rev. 76.

69. Communist Party of the U. S. v. Subversive Activities Control Bd., 1961, 81 S.Ct. 1357, 1396–1402, 367 U.S 1, 69–81, 6 L.Ed.2d 625; Electric Bond & Share Co. v. SEC, 1938, 58 S.Ct. 678, 303 U.S. 419, 82 L.Ed. 936.

70. See Lanzetta v. New Jersey, 1939, 59 S.Ct. 618, 306 U.S. 451, 83 L.Ed.

888; U. S. v. Cohen Grocery Co., 1921, 41 S.Ct. 298, 255 U.S. 81, 65 L.Ed. 516; U. S. v. Reese, 1876, 92 U.S. 214, 23 L.Ed. 563; Amsterdam, The Void for Vagueness Doctrine in the Supreme Court, 1960, 109 U.Pa.L.Rev. 67.

71. Thornhill v. Alabama, 1940, 60 S.Ct. 736, 310 U.S. 88, 84 L.Ed. 1093; Winters v. New York, 1948, 68 S.Ct. 665, 333 U.S. 507, 92 L.Ed. 840; National Assn. for Advancement of Colored People v. Button, 1963, 83 S.Ct. 328, 371 U.S. 415, 9 L.Ed.2d 405.

The farthest extension of this doctrine came in Dombrowski v. Pfister, 1965, 85 S.Ct. 1116, 1121, 380 U.S. 479, 487, 14 L.Ed.2d 22. The Court seemed to withdraw substantially from this aspect of Dombrowski, as from others, in Younger v. Harris, 1971, 91 S.Ct. 746, 753–755, 401 U.S. 37, 50–53, 27 L.Ed.2d 669. But those cases involved special considerations of federalism, and the rules stated in the text seem well accepted when the problem of federal interference with state proceedings is not present.

if the statute regulates pure speech.[72] It is more reluctant to hear this kind of challenge to a statute that primarily regulates conduct and not merely speech, even if the First Amendment may protect some of the activity condemned by the statute.[73]

There are two important respects in which the prudential rules about standing differ from the Article III limitations on standing. First, the Court itself is free to disregard one of the prudential rules when it thinks it appropriate to do so. The jus tertii rule, in particular, has often been disregarded by the Court in cases that seemed to it proper.[74] Second, Congress is free to grant standing, if it chooses, to the full limits of Article III. If Congress has done so, the courts lack authority to create prudential barriers to standing in suits brought under a statute in which Congress has done this.[75]

§ 14. "Case or Controversy"—Political Questions [1]

No branch of the law of justiciability is in such disarray as the doctrine of the "political question." Judge Carl McGowan has said that "the recent history of the doctrine has been one of judicial indifference and scathing scholarly attack." [2] Professor Louis Henkin

---

72. Schad v. Borough of Mount Ephraim, 1981, 101 S.Ct. 2176, 452 U.S. 61, 68 L.Ed.2d 671; Village of Schaumburg v. Citizens for a Better Environment, 1980, 100 S.Ct. 826, 444 U.S. 620, 63 L.Ed.2d 73; Bigelow v. Virginia, 1975, 95 S.Ct. 2222, 421 U.S. 809, 44 L.Ed.2d 600; Lewis v. City of New Orleans, 1974, 94 S.Ct. 970, 415 U.S. 130, 39 L.Ed.2d 214.

73. Broadrick v. Oklahoma, 1973, 93 S.Ct. 2908, 413 U.S. 601, 37 L.Ed.2d 830. The distinction drawn in Broadrick was applied in Parker v. Levy, 1974, 94 S.Ct. 2547, 417 U.S. 733, 41 L.Ed.2d 439, and in Young v. American Mini Theatres, Inc., 1976, 96 S.Ct. 2440, 427 U.S. 50, 49 L.Ed.2d 310.

74. E.g., Duke Power Co. v. Carolina Environmental Study Group, 1978, 98 S.Ct. 2620, 2634–2635, 438 U.S. 59, 80–82, 57 L.Ed.2d 595. See also text above at notes 57 to 66.

75. It has been held that Congress did this in §§ 810 and 812 of the Fair Housing Act of 1968, 42 U.S.C.A. §§ 3610, 3612. Havens Realty Corp. v. Coleman, 1982, 102 S.Ct. 1114, ___ U.S. ___, 71 L.Ed.2d 214; Gladstone, Realtors v. Village of Bellwood, 1979, 99 S.Ct. 1601, 441 U.S. 91, 60 L.Ed.2d 66; Trafficante v. Metropolitan Life Ins. Co., 1972, 93 S.Ct. 364, 409 U.S. 205, 34 L.Ed.2d 415.

Many other Acts of Congress appear on their face to contain very broad grants of standing.

[§ 14]

1. 13 Wright, Miller & Cooper, Jurisdiction § 3534; Strum, The Supreme Court and "Political Questions": A Study in Judicial Evasion, 1974; Henkin, Is There a "Political Question" Doctrine?, 1976, 85 Yale L.J. 597; Jackson, The Political Question Doctrine: Where Does It Stand after Powell v. McCormack, O'Brien v. Brown, and Gilligan v. Morgan?, 1973, 44 U.Colo.L.Rev. 477; Tigar, Judicial Power, The "Political Question Doctrine," and Foreign Relations, 1970, 17 U.C.L.A.L.Rev. 1135; Bean, The Supreme Court and the Political Question: Affirmation or Abdication?, 1969, 71 W.Va.L.Rev. 97; Yokota, Political Questions and Judicial Review: A Comparison, 1968, 43 Wash.L.Rev. 1031; Scharpf, Judicial Review and the Political Question: A Functional Analysis, 1966, 75 Yale L.J. 517; Tollett, Political Questions and the Law, 1965, 42 U.Det.L.J. 439.

2. McGowan, Congressmen in Court: The New Plaintiffs, 1981, 15 Ga.L.Rev. 241, 256.

has asked the heretical question whether there is any such doctrine.[3] Even those who accept the existence of the doctrine recognize that there is no workable definition of characteristics that distinguish political questions from justiciable questions, and that the category of political questions is "more amenable to description by infinite itemization than by generalization."[4]

Yet the notion that there are political questions that courts are not to decide has ancient roots in American law, and the Supreme Court still seems to take that notion seriously, even if today it rarely finds any cases that fit within the category. In the happy figure of speech Zechariah Chafee devised in another context, it may be said of political questions: "They are at least as real as Santa Clauses in department stores before Christmas. We have to know what to do about them even if we believe they ought not to be there."[5]

The political question doctrine goes back to the great case of Marbury v. Madison.[6] Chief Justice Marshall there expressed the view that the courts will not entertain political questions even though such questions involve actual controversies. The non-justiciability of a political question is founded primarily on the doctrine of separation of powers and the policy of judicial self-restraint. The relationship between the judiciary and the other branches of the federal government gives rise to the political question, and whether a matter has been committed by the Constitution to another branch of the government is decided by the Court.[7]

Modern political question analysis derives from the classic legislative apportionment decision in 1962 in Baker v. Carr.[8] Justice Brennan there repeatedly emphasized that the concern underlying the doctrine is that of separating the proper sphere of federal judicial power from the appropriate spheres of federal executive and legislative power. After examining several categories of matters that had been regarded as political questions, he summarized the relevant considerations: "Prominent on the surface of any case held to involve a political question is found a textually demonstrable constitutional commitment of the issue to a coordinate political department; or a lack of judicially discoverable and manageable standards for resolving it; or the impossibility of deciding without an initial policy determination of a kind clearly for nonjudicial discretion; or the impossibility of a court's undertaking independent resolution without expressing lack of the respect due coordinate branches of government; or an unusual need for unquestioning adherence to a political decision already made;

3. Henkin, note 1 above. See also Tigar, note 1 above, at 1163; Cox, The Role of Congress in Constitutional Determinations, 1971, 40 U.Cin.L.Rev. 199, 201.

4. Frank, Political Questions, in Supreme Court & Supreme Law, Cahn ed. 1954, p. 36.

5. Chafee, Some Problems of Equity, 1950, p. 374.

6. 1803, 1 Cranch 137, 164–166, 2 L.Ed. 60.

7. Id.

8. 1962, 82 S.Ct. 691, 369 U.S. 186, 7 L.Ed.2d 663.

or the potentiality of embarrassment from multifarious pronouncements by various departments on one question." [9]

As has been pointed out by several commentators, the doctrine, as
summarized by Justice Brennan, contains at least three theoretical
strands.[10] The Baker formulation lists six factors, at least one of
which must be unmistakably present in a case before it is dismissed
as a political question. The first factor—a textually demonstrable
commitment to another branch—is the classical view that the Court
must decide all cases and issues before it unless, as a matter of constitutional interpretation, the Constitution itself has committed the
determination of the issue to another branch of government.[11] the
second and third factors—lack of judicially discoverable standards
and involvement of the judiciary in nonjudicial policy determinations—suggest a functional approach.[12] The final three factors—lack
of respect for other branches, need for adherence to a political decision already made, and possibility of embarrassment—all seem to be
prudential considerations.[13] These six factors, and these three possible approaches, have been mingled in various proportions in the uses
that have been made of the political question doctrine over the years.

The clearest example of a nonjusticiable political question is a
claim resting on the provision in Article IV, § 4, that the United
States shall guarantee every state a republican form of government.
Either because this is a textually demonstrable constitutional commitment of the issue to a coordinate political department,[14] or, as suggested in Baker v. Carr, for lack of judicially manageable standards,[15]
it is accepted that such claims are nonjusticiable. In Luther v. Borden [16] the Court refused to decide which group was the legitimate
government of Rhode Island, relying on this ground, and since then
the Court has consistently refused to resort to the guaranty clause as
a constitutional source for invalidating state action.[17] It has also held

9. 82 S.Ct. at 710, 369 U.S. at 217.

10. Tribe, American Constitutional Law,
1978, p. 71 n. 1; Gunther, Constitutional Law—Cases and Materials, 10th ed.
1980, pp. 449–450, 1688–1690; Thomas
& Thomas, Presidential War-Making
Power: A Political Question?, 1981, 35
Sw.L.J. 879, 882.

11. Wechsler, Toward Neutral Princi-
ples of Constitutional Law, 1959, 73
Harv.L.Rev. 1, 7–9; Weston, Political
Questions, 1925, 38 Harv.L.Rev. 296.

12. Nowak, Rotunda & Young, Constitutional Law, 1978, pp. 110–111;
Scharpf, note 1 above.

13. Bickel, The Least Dangerous
Branch, 1962, pp. 23–28, 69–71; Bickel,
The Supreme Court, 1960 Term: Fore-
word: The Passive Virtues, 1961, 75
Harv.L.Rev. 40, 46, 75; Finkelstein, Ju-
dicial Self-Limitation, 1924, 37 Harv.L.

Rev. 338, 361; Finkelstein, Some Further Notes on Judicial Self-Limitation,
1926, 39 Harv.L.Rev. 221.

14. " 'The United States shall guarantee' plausibly refers to the political
branches, and it is not implausible to
read it as excluding monitoring and enforcement by the courts. If so, we
may have a unique constitutional
clause excluding the courts; but that
hardly adds up to a 'political question
doctrine.' " Henkin, note 1 above, at
609.

15. 82 S.Ct. at 713, 369 U.S. at 223.

16. 1849, 7 How. 1, 12 L.Ed. 581.

17. See, e.g., Mountain Timber Co. v.
Washington, 1917, 37 S.Ct. 260, 243
U.S. 219, 61 L.Ed. 685; Pacific States
Tel. & Tel. Co. v. Oregon, 1911, 32
S.Ct. 224, 223 U.S. 118, 56 L.Ed. 377;
Taylor & Marshall v. Beckham (No. 1),

that a challenge to congressional action on the ground that it is inconsistent with the guaranty clause presents no justiciable question.[18] However, the nonjusticiability of claims resting on the guaranty clause does not mean that similar questions will not be heard if other provisions of the Constitution, such as the equal protection clause, are in issue.[19]

A great many questions involving political rights are not political questions. The objection that a suit charging racial discrimination in conducting Democratic party primary elections in Texas involved a political question, for instance, was curtly rejected as "little more than a play on words." [20] But in Colegrove v. Green [21] three of the seven justices who sat agreed that malapportionment of congressional districts in a state was political and thus nonjusticiable. The concurring Justice disagreed with this reasoning, but concurred in the result on the ground that it would be inequitable to issue an injunction. For the next 16 years other attacks on apportionments and similar state laws were, with one exception, unsuccessful, though a variety of grounds were used by the Court to reach such results.[22] This was changed in 1962 by the decision in Baker v. Carr. In that case plaintiffs, qualified voters from populous counties in Tennessee, sued in federal court, claiming that the existing apportionment of the state legislature provided inequality of representation, and that the resulting discrimination was a violation of equal protection of the laws. The district court dismissed the complaint for lack of jurisdiction of the subject matter and for want of a justiciable issue. The Supreme Court reversed, holding that the district court had jurisdiction of the subject matter and that a claim that the apportionment of a state legislature denied equal protection presented a justiciable issue.

Since Baker v. Carr the Court has passed on a variety of issues that previously would have been thought not to be justiciable: the standard for apportioning seats in Congress,[23] a state legislature,[24] or

1900, 20 S.Ct. 890, 178 U.S. 548, 44 L.Ed. 1187.

18. Georgia v. Stanton, 1867, 6 Wall. 50, 18 L.Ed. 721.

19. Baker, 82 S.Ct. at 716, 369 U.S. at 228.

20. Nixon v. Herndon, 1927, 47 S.Ct. 446, 447, 273 U.S. 536, 540, 71 L.Ed. 759.

21. 1946, 66 S.Ct. 1198, 328 U.S. 549, 90 L.Ed. 1432.

22. E.g., Cox v. Peters, 1952, 72 S.Ct. 559, 342 U.S. 936, 96 L.Ed. 697 (per curiam) (want of a substantial federal question); South v. Peters, 1950, 70 S.Ct. 641, 339 U.S. 276, 94 L.Ed. 834 (want of equity); Colegrove v. Barrett, 1947, 67 S.Ct. 973, 330 U.S. 804, 91 L.Ed. 1262 (per curiam) (want of equity). Only in Gomillion v. Lightfoot, 1960, 81 S.Ct. 125, 364 U.S. 339, 5 L.Ed.2d 110, was relief granted. In Gomillion the plaintiffs complained of affirmative legislative action that deprived them of their vote. The decision was based on discriminatory treatment of a racial minority which violated the Fifteenth Amendment.

23. Wesberry v. Sanders, 1964, 84 S.Ct. 526, 376 U.S. 1, 11 L.Ed.2d 481.

24. Reynolds v. Sims, 1964, 84 S.Ct. 1362, 377 U.S. 533, 12 L.Ed.2d 506; Lucas v. Forty-Fourth Gen. Assembly, 1964, 84 S.Ct. 1459, 377 U.S. 713, 12 L.Ed.2d 632.

a local governing board; [25] the method by which a state chooses a governor if no candidate has a majority of the popular vote; [26] the refusal by the House of Representatives or by a state legislature to seat a person elected to that body; [27] the hurdles a state may properly impose on an attempt by a new political party to win a place on the ballot; [28] the validity of state procedures for recounting votes in an election for the United States Senate; [29] the use of government jobs for political patronage; [30] and whether majorities of both city voters and county voters can be required in approving amendments to a county charter.[31] The Court has left open, however, the possibility that decisions of the national political parties about representation in their national conventions are political questions.[32]

Possibly the most difficult and important of these cases is the decision in Powell v. McCormack,[33] in which it was held that the House of Representatives had erred in refusing to seat Congressman-elect Adam Clayton Powell. It was strongly argued that there was a "textually demonstrable commitment of the issue to a coordinate political department" in Article I, § 5, of the Constitution, providing that "Each House shall be the Judge of the * * * Qualifications of its own Members." The Court concluded, however, that this was "at most a 'textually demonstrable commitment' to Congress to judge only the qualifications expressly set forth in the Constitution." [34] Since it was conceded that Powell met the qualifications expressly set forth, and was not excluded for failure to meet those, the Court held that this exclusion on other purported grounds of disqualification was justiciable.

In Baker v. Carr the Court said "it is error to suppose that every case or controversy which touches foreign relations lies beyond judicial cognizance." [35] At the same time it recognized that many such

25. Avery v. Midland County, Texas, 1968, 88 S.Ct. 1114, 390 U.S. 474, 20 L.Ed.2d 45.

26. Fortson v. Morris, 1966, 87 S.Ct. 446, 385 U.S. 231, 17 L.Ed.2d 330.

27. Powell v. McCormack, 1969, 89 S.Ct. 1944, 395 U.S. 486, 23 L.Ed.2d 491; Bond v. Floyd, 1966, 87 S.Ct. 339, 385 U.S. 116, 17 L.Ed.2d 235.

28. Williams v. Rhodes, 1968, 89 S.Ct. 5, 393 U.S. 23, 21 L.Ed.2d 24.

29. Roudebush v. Hartke, 1972, 92 S.Ct. 804, 405 U.S. 15, 31 L.Ed.2d 1.

The Court said, however, that which candidate is entitled to be seated in the Senate is a nonjusticiable political question. 92 S.Ct. at 807, 405 U.S. at 19.

30. Elrod v. Burns, 1976, 96 S.Ct. 2673, 427 U.S. 347, 49 L.Ed.2d 547.

31. Town of Lockport v. Citizens for Community Action at the Local Level,

Inc., 1977, 97 S.Ct. 1047, 430 U.S. 259, 51 L.Ed.2d 313.

32. Cousins v. Wigoda, 1975, 95 S.Ct. 541, 419 U.S. 477, 42 L.Ed.2d 595. See also O'Brien v. Brown, 1972, 92 S.Ct. 2718, 409 U.S. 1, 34 L.Ed.2d 1. See Rotunda, Constitutional and Statutory Restrictions on Political Parties in the Wake of Cousins v. Wigoda, 1975, 53 Texas L.Rev. 935, 960–962; Kester, Constitutional Restrictions on Political Parties, 1974, 60 Va.L.Rev. 735, 781–783; Comment, Judicial Intervention in Political Party Disputes: The Political Thicket Reconsidered, 1975, 22 U.C.L.A.L.Rev. 622.

33. 1969, 89 S.Ct. 1944, 395 U.S. 486, 23 L.Ed.2d 491.

34. 89 S.Ct. at 1978, 395 U.S. at 548.

35. 82 S.Ct. at 707, 369 U.S. at 211.

See also Henkin, Foreign Affairs and the Constitution, 1972, pp. 210–216;

cases are political questions because they "turn on standards that defy judicial application, or involve the exercise of a discretion demonstrably committed to the executive or legislature" or "uniquely demand single-voiced statement of the Government's views." [36]

The recent case of Goldwater v. Carter [37] is of particular interest. Senator Goldwater and others challenged the power of President Carter to terminate the mutual defense treaty with Taiwan without either a two-thirds vote of the Senate or a majority vote of each house of Congress. The court of appeals held for the President. [38] The Supreme Court summarily vacated the judgment of the court of appeals and directed that the action be dismissed. Two justices would have set the case down for oral argument, and one concurred in the result without explanation, but the other six all spoke to the application to the case of the political question doctrine. To Justice Rehnquist, with whom three others joined, the case was a nonjusticiable political question. The Constitution says how a treaty must be ratified, but is silent on how it may be terminated, and since different methods of termination might be appropriate for different treaties, the matter should be settled by political standards rather than by having a rule laid down by the courts. The fact that foreign relations were involved strengthened his conclusion. Justice Powell agreed that the case should be dismissed, but on the ground that it was not yet ripe for decision because neither the Senate nor the House had rejected the President's claim of power to terminate. [39] He rejected the view, however, that it was a political question, arguing that there was no textually demonstrable commitment to another branch, judicially manageable standards could be discovered, and the case touched foreign affairs only at the stage of resolving the constitutional division of power between Congress and the President. Justice Brennan would have affirmed the court of appeals. He thought it already well settled that the Constitution commits to the President alone the power to recognize, and withdraw recognition from, foreign regimes, [40] and that a court could properly decide that abrogation of the defense treaty was a necessary incident to recognition of the Peking government.

Scharpf, note 1 above; Tigar, note 1 above.

36. 82 S.Ct. at 707, 369 U.S. at 211.
See particularly Chicago & Southern Air Lines, Inc. v. Waterman S. S. Corp., 1948, 68 S.Ct. 431, 333 U.S. 103, 92 L.Ed. 568; U. S. v. Curtiss-Wright Export Corp., 1936, 57 S.Ct. 216, 299 U.S. 304, 81 L.Ed. 255.

37. 1979, 100 S.Ct. 533, 444 U.S. 996, 62 L.Ed.2d 428.

38. Goldwater v. Carter, C.A.1979, 617 F.2d 697, 199 U.S.App.D.C. 115. The court of appeals also held that the plaintiffs had standing, an issue not reached by any of the opinions in the Supreme Court. See § 13 n. 50.

39. On ripeness generally, see 13 Wright, Miller & Cooper, Jurisdiction § 3532.

40. See U. S. v. Pink, 1942, 62 S.Ct. 552, 315 U.S. 203, 86 L.Ed. 796.

An area closely related to foreign relations was involved in Commercial Trust Co. v. Miller.[41] War with Germany was officially ended by a joint resolution of Congress with the approval of the President in July of 1921. In August a proclamation of peace was issued. Subsequently the Alien Property Custodian sought to seize a trust fund held for the benefit of a German citizen, relying on his powers under the Trading with the Enemy Act. The Act provided that it continued in effect, and all property subject to it should remain under the control of the United States, until the German government had made acceptable provision for the satisfaction of all claims, but it was argued that the end of the war should end the Custodian's power. The Court rejected this argument, saying: "the power which declared the necessity is the power to declare its cessation, and what the cessation requires. The power is legislative." [42] Thus it appears that the Court will not review the determination of the political departments as to when the exigencies produced by war have ended.

More than 70 lawsuits were brought challenging American military involvement in Viet Nam and Southeast Asia. Reasoning by the courts varied widely, but the striking fact is that in no case was the involvement held unconstitutional and that most of the courts refused to reach the merits of the constitutional issue by finding that the suits raised a political question or were otherwise nonjusticiable.[43]

The processes by which statutes or constitutional amendments are adopted have been thought to be political and nonjusticiable. The leading case is Coleman v. Miller,[44] where it was held that Congress, rather than the Court, can decide how long a proposed amendment to the Constitution remains open for adoption, and what effect a prior rejection has on the power of a state to ratify such an amendment. The pendency of the proposed Equal Rights Amendment produced a rich literature on whether Coleman v. Miller remains the law and on what the answers should be to the questions left unresolved in Coleman if they should be found to be justiciable.[45]

41. 1923, 43 S.Ct. 486, 262 U.S. 51, 67 L.Ed. 858.

42. 43 S.Ct. at 488–489, 262 U.S. 51. But cf. Chastleton Corp. v. Sinclair, 1924, 44 S.Ct. 405, 264 U.S. 543, 68 L.Ed. 841.

43. See Thomas & Thomas, note 10 above; Firmage, The War Powers and the Political Question Doctrine, 1977, 49 U.Colo.L.Rev. 65.

44. 1939, 59 S.Ct. 972, 307 U.S. 433, 83 L.Ed. 1385. See also Leser v. Garnett, 1922, 42 S.Ct. 217, 258 U.S. 130, 66 L.Ed. 505; Field v. Clark, 1892, 12 S.Ct. 495, 143 U.S. 649, 36 L.Ed. 294. But cf. Gardner v. Collector, 1867, 6 Wall. 499, 18 L.Ed. 890.

But in Dyer v. Blair, D.C.Ill.1975, 390 F.Supp. 1291, the political question doctrine was held not to bar a suit seeking to establish that a vote of a majority in the state legislature constituted effective ratification of a federal constitutional amendment in the face of a local requirement that ratification must be by a three-fifths vote.

45. Ginsburg, Ratification of the Equal Rights Amendment: A Question of Time, 1979, 57 Texas L.Rev. 919; Elder, Article V, Justiciability, and the Equal Rights Amendment, 1978, 31 Okla.L.Rev. 63; Kanowitz & Klinger, Can a State Rescind Its Equal Rights Amendment Ratification: Who Decides and How?, 1977, 28 Hastings L.J. 979; Note, Article V: Political Questions and Sensible Answers, 1979, 57 Texas L.Rev. 1259; Comment, Rescinding

A famous case had held that a contention by a state that the federal government has exceeded its powers under the Constitution is political, not judicial, in character.[46] The Court, without any reasoned explanation, has since departed from this rule and heard challenges by states to Acts of Congress dealing with the right to vote.[47]

To a distinguished commentator one of the few issues committed by the constitutional text to another branch of government, and thus wholly excluded from judicial review, was the impeachment process.[48] The Constitution gives the House of Representatives "the sole Power of Impeachment" and the Senate "the sole Power to try all impeachments."[49] The events of 1972 to 1974 caused some to doubt even this, and to assert that the courts could intervene in at least some aspects of the impeachment process.[50] Most commentators, however, have adhered to the orthodox view that the courts have no role to play with regard to impeachment.[51]

Clearly the political question doctrine has shrunken in scope since Baker v. Carr and Powell v. McCormack. It is not yet dead. In one case a lower court referred to "the diminished vitality of the political question doctrine" and entertained a suit requiring judicial surveillance over the training and weaponry of the National Guard. The Supreme Court tartly responded that "because this doctrine has been held inapplicable to certain carefully delineated situations, it is no reason for federal courts to assume its demise."[52] It found in the constitutional language that states are to train the militia "according to the discipline prescribed by Congress" a textual commitment of the question to a coordinate branch of the federal government.[53]

Ratification of Proposed Constitutional Amendments—A Question for the Court, 1977, 37 La.L.Rev. 896.

Coleman v. Miller, at least by way of dictum, supported the view that a state, once having ratified, cannot later rescind its ratification. That question too was mooted in the materials just cited.

46. Massachusetts v. Mellon, 1923, 43 S.Ct. 597, 262 U.S. 447, 67 L.Ed. 1078.

See the discussion of this question in the dissent in Massachusetts v. Laird, 1970, 91 S.Ct. 128, 129–135, 400 U.S. 886, 887–900, 27 L.Ed.2d 130.

47. South Carolina v. Katzenbach, 1966, 86 S.Ct. 803, 383 U.S. 301, 15 L.Ed.2d 769. See Bickel, The Voting Rights Cases, 1966, Sup.Ct.Rev. 79, 80–92. A similar case was heard in Oregon v. Mitchell, 1970, 91 S.Ct. 260, 400 U.S. 112, 27 L.Ed.2d 272.

48. Wechsler, note 11 above, at 8.

49. Const., Art. I, §§ 2, 3.

50. Berger, Impeachment: The Constitutional Problem, 1973.

51. Black, Impeachment: A Handbook, 1974; Nowak, Rotunda & Young, Constitutional Law, 1978, pp. 109–110; Gunther, Judicial Hegemony and Legislative Autonomy: The Nixon Case and the Impeachment Process, 1974, 22 U.C.L.A.L.Rev. 30.

52. Gilligan v. Morgan, 1973, 93 S.Ct. 2440, 2446, 413 U.S. 1, 11, 37 L.Ed.2d 407.

53. See also Goldwater v. Carter, note 38 above, where, as discussed in the text above, four of the six justices who addressed the issue were prepared to dismiss the case as a nonjusticiable political question.

§ 15.   "Case or Controversy"—Administrative Questions [1]

Another limitation on the jurisdiction of the federal courts is that they cannot exercise administrative, or legislative, power. This limitation is a requirement of Article III, since it extends the judicial power only to "cases or controversies." The necessity for distinguishing judicial from legislative or administrative power usually arises when a court is called upon to review action taken by agencies or lower courts. Where the scope of review could be unlimited, the early cases indicated that the nature of the power the court would exercise on review was determined by the nature of the function performed by the lower tribunal. It was established that the nature of the function performed below depends not on the character of the tribunal but on the character of the proceedings before it.[2] If the lower tribunal is a court, but has performed a legislative function, no review can be had in a "constitutional" court.[3]

There is no established formula for deciding whether a certain proceeding or function is, by its nature, judicial or administrative.[4] The distinction has been determined case by case in terms of traditional concepts of judicial and administrative or legislative matters,[5] and is not easy to trace. It is often said that if a tribunal has discretion as to whether it will issue an order or grant a privilege its function is administrative.[6] There is no exercise of discretion, however, when a court applies the standards of a statute.[7] Naturalization proceedings in a district court are similar to licensing proceedings in administrative agencies: a petition for citizenship is submitted to the court, and the court then decides whether the petitioner has complied with the terms of the statute. Yet naturalization proceedings are held to be judicial.[8] Similarly an order of a state court denying a license to practice law has been held reviewable in the United States

---

[§ 15]

1.   13 Wright, Miller & Cooper, Jurisdiction § 3535.

2.   Prentis v. Atlantic Coast Line Co., 1908, 29 S.Ct. 67, 211 U.S. 210, 53 L.Ed. 150.

3.   Federal Radio Comm. v. General Elec. Co., 1930, 50 S.Ct. 389, 281 U.S. 464, 74 L.Ed. 969. As to the meaning of a "constitutional" court, see § 11 above.

In Chandler v. Judicial Council of the Tenth Circuit, 1970, 90 S.Ct. 1648, 398 U.S. 74, 26 L.Ed.2d 100, noted 1971, 51 B.U.L.Rev. 106, the Court considered, but did not decide, whether action by a circuit Judicial Council limiting the cases that a district judge could hear was "judicial" action, reviewable on mandamus from the Supreme Court, or

was "administrative," and not reviewable in an original proceeding in the Supreme Court.

4.   But see the formula offered by Justice Holmes in Prentis v. Atlantic Coast Line Co., 1908, 29 S.Ct. 67, 69, 211 U.S. 210, 226, 53 L.Ed. 150.

5.   See United Steelworkers of America v. U. S., 1959, 80 S.Ct. 1, 4, 185, 361 U.S. 39, 43, 60, 4 L.Ed.2d 12.

6.   E.g., R.C., 1949, 62 Harv.L.Rev. 1067, 1069.

7.   Ullman v. U. S., 1956, 76 S.Ct. 497, 350 U.S. 422, 100 L.Ed. 511; U. S. v. First City Nat. Bank of Houston, 1967, 87 S.Ct. 1088, 1093–1094, 386 U.S. 361, 369–370, 18 L.Ed.2d 151.

8.   Tutun v. U. S., 1926, 46 S.Ct. 425, 270 U.S. 568, 70 L.Ed. 738.

Supreme Court.[9] It may well be that it is easier to find "judicial" action where the proceedings involve important human rights.

In Keller v. Potomac Electric Power Co.[10] it was held that the Supreme Court could not review a decision of the Court of Appeals for the District of Columbia involving public utility rates, since the court of appeals had, by statute, such broad power in cases coming to it from the Public Utilities Commission that its action was thought administrative rather than judicial. Again in the first Federal Radio Commission case,[11] review was refused by the Supreme Court since the court below was authorized by statute to revise or alter licensing orders of the Commission as the court might deem just. This made the proceedings in the Court of Appeals for the District of Columbia "administrative." Later Congress amended the statute so that review of orders of the Radio Commission was confined to questions of law, with findings of fact by the Commission to be upheld if supported by substantial evidence. In the second Federal Radio Commission case [12] the Supreme Court held that it could now hear cases in which the court below had passed on orders of the commission, since the proceedings below were now "judicial." Application of the substantial evidence test was considered a legal question on the theory that a capricious order of the Commission would be outside the authority conferred on it by statute. This is the reasoning on which all review of administrative determinations [13] is now justified. Although the proceedings before the agency may be "administrative," the courts can review "judicial" questions.

A 1966 statute allows the Comptroller of the Currency to permit certain bank mergers if he finds them justified by standards set out in the statute. If an antitrust proceeding is later brought attacking the merger, the court is to apply these same standards but it is to "review de novo the issues presented." [14] The Supreme Court held that this did not require the courts to perform nonjudicial tasks, and that it is valid, on the ground that "the courts are not left at large as planning agencies" and that the standards to be applied are familiar ones, and within "the area of judicial competence." [15] After this deci-

---

9. In re Summers, 1945, 65 S.Ct. 1307, 325 U.S. 561, 89 L.Ed.2d 1795; Dasher v. Supreme Court of Texas, C.A.5th, 1981, 658 F.2d 1045, 1049–1050.

But an order by the District of Columbia Court of Appeals denying petitions that it waive one of its requirements for admission to the bar was held to be administrative rather than judicial. Feldman v. Garner, C.A.1981, 661 F.2d 1295, 1310–1320, 213 U.S.App.D.C. 119, certiorari denied 102 S.Ct. 3481, ___ U.S. ___, 73 L.Ed.2d 1365.

10. 1923, 43 S.Ct. 445, 261 U.S. 428, 67 L.Ed. 731.

11. 1930, 50 S.Ct. 389, 281 U.S. 464, 74 L.Ed. 969.

12. 1933, 53 S.Ct. 627, 289 U.S. 266, 77 L.Ed. 1166.

13. See § 103 below.

14. 12 U.S.C.A. § 1828(c)(7).

15. U. S. v. First City Nat. Bank of Houston, 1967, 87 S.Ct. 1088, 1094, 386 U.S. 361, 369–370, 18 L.Ed.2d 251.

See also Chandler v. Roudebush, 1976, 96 S.Ct. 1949, 425 U.S. 840, 48 L.Ed.2d 416.

sion, it is hard to see what vitality, if any, is left in the first Federal Radio case.

§ 16. Jurisdiction to Determine Jurisdiction [1]

"Jurisdiction to determine jurisdiction" refers to the power of a court to determine whether it has jurisdiction over the parties to and subject matter of a suit. If the jurisdiction of a federal court is questioned, the court has the power, subject to review, to determine the jurisdictional issue.[2] Questions have arisen, however, about the effect of a court's finding that it has jurisdiction in a particular case.

It used to be said that a judgment or order entered by a court is open to direct or collateral attack upon the ground that the court entering the judgment lacked jurisdiction of either the parties or the subject matter.[3] However, it is now held that if a party appears before a court to contest its jurisdiction in personam, a finding that jurisdiction exists will bind the party, and he cannot later collaterally attack that court's judgment upon the basis of lack of personal jurisdiction.[4] The finding of jurisdiction is considered to be res judicata of the issue.

More difficult theoretical problems are encountered when the question is of a court's jurisdiction of the subject matter of a suit. The rule has been that a court's determination that it has subject matter jurisdiction is res judicata of the issue, if the jurisdictional question was actually litigated and expressly decided.[5] This rule was expanded in Chicot County Drainage District v. Baxter State Bank.[6]

[§ 16]

1. 13 Wright, Miller & Cooper, Jurisdiction §§ 3536, 3537; Moore, Collateral Attack on Subject Matter Jurisdiction: A Critique of the Restatement (Second) of Judgments, 1981, 66 Corn.L.Rev. 534; Dobbs, The Validation of Void Judgments: The Bootstrap Principle, 1967, 53 Va.L.Rev. 1003; Dobbs, The Scope of Bootstrap, 1967, 53 Va.L.Rev. 1241; Dobbs, The Decline of Jurisdiction by Consent, 1961, 40 N.C.L.Rev. 49; Boskey & Braucher, Jurisdiction and Collateral Attack, 1940, 40 Col.L. Rev. 1006; Note, Filling the Void: Judicial Power and Jurisdictional Attacks on Judgments, 1977, 87 Yale L.J. 164.

2. U. S. v. United Mine Workers of America, 1947, 67 S.Ct. 677, 330 U.S. 258, 91 L.Ed. 884.

3. See § 7 above; Comment, 1939, 39 Col.L.Rev. 274. For criticism of the unhistorical basis of the orthodox rule, see Dobbs, The Decline of Jurisdiction by Consent, 1961, 40 N.C.L.Rev. 49.

4. Restatement Second of Judgments, 1982, § 10(2); American Sur. Co. v. Baldwin, 1932, 53 S.Ct. 98, 287 U.S. 156, 77 L.Ed. 231; Baldwin v. Iowa State Traveling Men's Assn., 1931, 51 S.Ct. 517, 283 U.S. 522, 75 L.Ed. 1244. See McCormick v. Sullivant, 1824, 10 Wheat. 192, 6 L.Ed. 300; 18 Wright, Miller & Cooper, Jurisdiction § 4430.

5. Stoll v. Gottlieb, 1938, 59 S.Ct. 134, 305 U.S. 165, 83 L.Ed. 104. For Professor Chafee's comments on the case, see Chafee, Some Problems of Equity, 1950, p. 319, n. 42. See also Davis v. Davis, 1938, 59 S.Ct. 3, 305 U.S. 32, 83 L.Ed. 26; Durfee v. Duke, 1963, 84 S.Ct. 242, 375 U.S. 106, 11 L.Ed.2d 186, noted 1964, 18 Sw.L.J. 500; Independence Mortg. Trust v. White, D.C.Or. 1978, 446 F.Supp. 120.

6. 1940, 60 S.Ct. 317, 308 U.S. 371, 84 L.Ed. 329. See also Boskey & Braucher, Jurisdiction and Collateral Attack, 1940, 40 Col.L.Rev. 1006; Comment, The Applicability of Res Judicata to Determinations of "Subject Matter" Jurisdiction in Conflict of Laws Cases, 1963, 11 Kan.L.Rev. 544.

There the parties collaterally attacking the judgment had not contested the jurisdiction in the original suit. Jurisdiction had been founded upon a federal statute later held unconstitutional. The Supreme Court held that the judgment was not subject to collateral attack. The later holding of unconstitutionality would not operate retroactively so as to render the judgment void,[7] and the judgment would be deemed to include a finding of jurisdiction. The result of the decision appears to be that, hereafter, a party who does not actually contest the jurisdiction will be bound by the judgment.[8]

The rule that a finding of jurisdiction is res judicata of the issue is subject to exception when the policy in favor of finality of judgments is outweighed by other factors.[9] Thus when a federal statute has vested exclusive jurisdiction of a particular type of case in the federal courts, the finding by a state court that it has jurisdiction over such a case will not preclude collateral attack upon the judgment rendered in the state court.[10] Similarly collateral attack is permitted on a judgment that violates the government's immunity from suit.[11]

Before it has determined whether it has jurisdiction of an action, a federal court may issue various orders, such as temporary restraining orders or preliminary injunctions. In the nineteenth century there was no speedy means for review of such orders, and no review at all of contempt convictions for violation of such orders except by habeas corpus. To fill this gap, the Supreme Court developed the notion that a decree issued by a court that lacked jurisdiction was void, permitting the person found guilty of contempt to go free on

This rule may have been expanded in Honneus v. Donovan, C.A.1st, 1982, 691 F.2d 1, where it was held that a default judgment could not later be challenged for lack of diversity.

7. In so holding the Court, 60 S.Ct. at 318, 308 U.S. at 374, expressly limited statements in Norton v. Shelby County, 1886, 6 S.Ct. 1121, 1125, 118 U.S. 425, 442, 30 L.Ed. 178, and Chicago, I. & L. R. Co. v. Hackett, 1913, 33 S.Ct. 581, 584, 228 U.S. 559, 566, 57 L.Ed. 966, that had indicated that a law held unconstitutional is inoperative and confers neither rights nor duties.

8. This is in accord with the general principle that res judicata applies not only to matters actually litigated but to all other matters that might have been presented to sustain or defeat the right asserted in the earlier proceeding. Cromwell v. County of Sac, 1877, 94 U.S. 351, 24 L.Ed. 195; Grubb v. Public Utilities Comm., 1930, 50 S.Ct. 374, 281 U.S. 470, 74 L.Ed. 972; Underwriters Nat. Assur. Co. v. North Carolina Life & Accident & Health Ins. Guar. Assn., 1982, 102 S.Ct. 1357, ___ U.S. ___, 71

L.Ed.2d 558. See Restatement Second of Judgments, 1982, § 12 comm. d, 18 Wright, Miller & Cooper, Jurisdiction § 4428; § 100A below.

9. Restatement Second of Judgments, 1982, § 12. See Moore, note 1 above, at 544–547, 554–560.

10. Kalb v. Feuerstein, 1940, 60 S.Ct. 343, 308 U.S. 433, 84 L.Ed. 370, conformed to 291 N.W. 840, 234 Wis. 507; Consolidated Rail Corp. v. Illinois, Spec.Ct.R.R.R.A.1976, 423 F.Supp. 941, 947–950, certiorari denied 1977, 97 S.Ct. 1111, 429 U.S. 1095, 51 L.Ed.2d 542.

11. U. S. v. U. S. Fidelity & Guar. Co., 1940, 60 S.Ct. 653, 309 U.S. 506, 84 L.Ed. 894.

The Supreme Court, however, has said of this case, and the Kalb case, note 10 above, that "in neither of these cases had the jurisdictional issues actually been litigated in the first forum." Durfee v. Duke, 1963, 84 S.Ct. 242, 247 n. 12, 375 U.S. 106, 114 n. 12, 11 L.Ed. 2d 186.

habeas corpus.[12] This notion that the orders of a court lacking jurisdiction of the merits were not binding was applied whether the order
granted substantive relief [13] or merely aimed to preserve the status
quo pending determination of the jurisdictional question.[14] One who
violated such an order could be punished for contempt only if the
court were ultimately found to possess jurisdiction of the merits.
The only exception to that test existed where the violation of the order operated in itself to defeat the jurisdiction of the court, such as
by making the case moot.[15]

The law on this point was apparently changed in United States v.
United Mine Workers of America.[16] The United States sued to restrain a strike in mines that had earlier been seized by the government. There was a serious question whether the Norris-LaGuardia
Act deprived the district court of jurisdiction to issue a temporary
restraining order in such a labor dispute. The defendants permitted
the strike notice to remain in effect and the strike to occur. The district court held the defendants to be in civil and criminal contempt of
court. As an alternative ground for affirmance of the conviction of
criminal contempt, the Supreme Court held that orders issued by the
district court must be obeyed until they are set aside, and their violation is punishable as criminal contempt, even if it is ultimately determined that the district court lacked jurisdiction to make the order.

12.   See Chafee, note 5 above, at pp.
337–363.

13.   Ex parte Fisk, 1884, 5 S.Ct. 724, 133
U.S. 713, 28 L.Ed. 1117; Ex parte Row-
land, 1881, 104 U.S. 604, 26 L.Ed. 861.
See Thomas v. Collins, 1945, 65 S.Ct.
315, 323 U.S. 516, 89 L.Ed. 430.

14.   Ex parte Sawyer, 1887, 8 S.Ct. 482,
124 U.S. 200, 31 L.Ed. 402, discussed
by Chafee, note 5 above, at pp.
337–343; Ex parte Ayers, 1887, 8 S.Ct.
164, 123 U.S. 443, 31 L.Ed. 216.

15.   U. S. v. Shipp, 1906, 27 S.Ct. 165,
203 U.S. 563, 51 L.Ed. 319. In that
case the Supreme Court had allowed an
appeal from denial of habeas corpus in
a state court, and had stayed all proceedings pending appeal. While the
appeal was pending, the prisoner was
taken from jail and lynched. Shipp,
the sheriff who was charged with contempt for conspiring with others to
permit the lynching, sought unsuccessfully to defend on the ground that the
Supreme Court had no jurisdiction to
issue a stay since the federal questions
on which relief was sought were frivolous and a mere pretense.
See also Griffin v. County Sch. Bd. of
Prince Edward Co., Va., C.A.4th, 1966,
363 F.2d 206, certiorari denied 87 S.Ct.

395, 385 U.S. 960, 17 L.Ed.2d 305, noted 1966, 52 Va.L.Rev. 1556, 1967, 24
Wash. & Lee L.Rev. 119. It is there
held that it is civil contempt to disburse
a fund at a time when the appellate
court has before it an application to
prevent such disbursement, although
no injunction has yet issued. There is
an interesting discussion of the case in
Rendleman, Compensatory Contempt
to Collect Money, 1980, 41 Ohio St.L.J.
625, 631–635.

16.   1947, 67 S.Ct. 677, 330 U.S. 258, 91
L.Ed. 884. See Chafee, note 5 above,
at pp. 364–380; Watt, Divine Right of
Government by Judiciary, 1947, 14
U.Chi.L.Rev. 409; Cox, The Void Order
and the Duty to Obey, 1948, 16 U.Chi.
L.Rev. 86; Rendleman, More on Void
Orders, 1973, 7 Ga.L.Rev. 246; Notes,
1947, 60 Harv.L.Rev. 811, 35 Ill.B.J.
414.

In Bethlehem Mines Corp. v. United Mine
Workers of America, C.A.3d, 1973, 476
F.2d 860, the rule of the United Mine
Workers case was extended to a finding of civil contempt where the union
had not also appealed from the underlying order it was found to have violated.

The view of the majority of the Supreme Court in the United Mine Workers case appeared to be that every court has the power to determine if it has the capacity to hear and decide the merits of the case before it. That power, or jurisdiction to determine jurisdiction, is of itself sufficient to give binding effect to the orders of the court issued to preserve the status quo, even though the court is ultimately found to lack jurisdiction of the merits. A party is bound to obey such orders until the jurisdictional question is determined. The only limitation to the binding effect of such orders is that the assertion of jurisdiction must not be "frivolous" but must possess some merit; the order need not be obeyed if the assertion of jurisdiction is only "frivolous."

The impact of the United Mine Workers decision was unclear. The order violated was one intended to preserve the status quo, and it could have been that the decision was limited to orders of that kind.[17] There were suggestions, however, that the decision might apply also to orders granting substantive relief.[18]

The authoritative effect of the United Mine Workers decision was also unclear. Only five of the nine justices thought there was a duty to obey an order if the court that issued it lacked jurisdiction, and since three of these five thought that the court below had jurisdiction of the case, there was, in Professor Chafee's phrase, "a lack of impressive solidity on this point." [19]

Subsequent decisions of the Supreme Court did not dispel all questions. In one case, In re Green,[20] a state court contempt conviction was set aside on finding that the state court lacked jurisdiction because the question involved was exclusively of federal concern. The United Mine Workers case was brushed aside in a footnote on the ground that it "involved a restraining order of a federal court and presented no question of pre-emption of a field by Congress where, if the federal policy is to prevail, federal power must be complete." [21] It is hard to see why the determination by Congress in the Norris-LaGuardia Act that federal courts are not to act is less puissant than

---

17. Stewart v. Dunn, C.A.5th, 1966, 363 F.2d 591, 598; U. S. v. Thompson, C.A.2d, 1963, 319 F.2d 665, 668; James, Book Review, 1965, 78 Harv.L. Rev. 1296, 1298.

As Professor James points out in the cited book review, this may well explain the cases in which an appellate court, without reference to the United Mine Workers case, has reversed contempt convictions of persons who have refused to comply with discovery orders, when the appellate court found issuance of the order was an abuse of discretion. E.g., Guilford Nat. Bank of Greensboro v. Southern Ry. Co., C.A. 4th, 1962, 297 F.2d 921; Hauger v. Chi-cago, R. I. & P. R. Co., C.A.7th, 1954, 216 F.2d 501; cf. Appeal of U. S. Securities & Exchange Comm., C.A.6th, 1955, 226 F.2d 501. But see Southern Ry. Co. v. Lanham, C.A.5th, 1969, 408 F.2d 348, 349–350 (Brown, J., dissenting).

18. Giancana v. Johnson, C.A.7th, 1964, 335 F.2d 372; Note, 1947, 35 Ill.B.J. 414.

19. Chafee, note 5 above, at p. 367.

20. 1962, 82 S.Ct. 1114, 369 U.S. 689, 8 L.Ed.2d 198, noted 1962, 57 Nw.U.L. Rev. 609.

21. 82 S.Ct. at 1117 n. 1, 369 U.S. at 692 n. 1.

its determination in the pre-emption area that state courts are not to act.

In Walker v. City of Birmingham [22] a bare majority of the Court upheld contempt convictions against the late Dr. Martin Luther King and a number of others for parading in violation of a temporary injunction issued by an Alabama state court. They had felt free to defy the injunction on the ground that it was unconstitutional. The Court agreed that "the breadth and vagueness of the injunction itself would * * * unquestionably be subject to substantial constitutional question," [23] and that the same was true of the city ordinance on parades that underlay the injunction. It held, however, that the state court undoubtedly had jurisdiction of the parties and the subject matter, and that the constitutional claims should have been presented to that court. The United Mine Workers case was cited once, at the end of a long string of cases.[24] The case of In re Green was distinguished on the ground that there the claim was that the state court was "without jurisdiction," and that: "The petitioner in Green, unlike the petitioners here, had attempted to challenge the validity of the injunction *before* violating it by promptly applying to the issuing court for an order vacating the injunction. The petitioner in Green had further offered to prove that the court issuing the injunction had agreed to its violation as an appropriate means of testing its validity." [25]

Finally in yet another case the Supreme Court recognized the possibility that a court may not wish to punish a person for violating an order subsequently held to be invalid.[26]

In fact, however, a sensible reconciliation of the Supreme Court cases on this point is possible. It would be that the validity of an order can be challenged in a contempt proceeding for violation of the order only if there was no opportunity for effective review of the order before it was violated. This view is suggested by the quoted passage from the Walker case. It emerges even more clearly from the decision in United States v. Ryan.[27] The holding in Ryan was that an order denying a motion to quash a grand jury subpoena duces tecum was not appealable. It was said that if the subpoena was unduly burdensome or otherwise unlawful, the party on whom it was served "may refuse to comply and litigate those questions in the event that contempt or similar proceedings are brought against him. Should his contentions be rejected at that time by the trial court they will then

22. 1967, 87 S.Ct. 1824, 388 U.S. 307, 18 L.Ed.2d 1210.

23. 87 S.Ct. at 1830, 388 U.S. at 317.

24. 87 S.Ct. at 1828 n. 5, 388 U.S. at 314 n. 5.

25. 87 S.Ct. at 1829, n. 6, 388 U.S. at 315 n. 6 (emphasis by the Court).

26. Donovan v. City of Dallas, 1964, 84 S.Ct. 1579, 1583, 377 U.S. 408, 414, 12 L.Ed.2d 409, on remand Tex.Civ.App. 1964, 384 S.W.2d 724. Dunn v. U. S., C.A.10th, 1968, 388 F.2d 511, is to the same effect.

27. 1971, 91 S.Ct. 1580, 402 U.S. 530, 29 L.Ed.2d 85.

be ripe for appellate review." [28]   In a footnote at that point in the opinion the Court said: "Walker v. Birmingham * * * is not to the contrary.   Our holding that the claims there sought to be asserted were not open on review of petitioners' contempt convictions was based upon the availability of review of those claims at an earlier stage." [29]   This is a clearer explanation of the Walker decision than the opinion in that case itself provides.

It should be noted that it is only a realistic opportunity for effective review that bars later challenge in a contempt proceeding.   In the Walker case the Court said that the matter would be in a different posture if the defendants had challenged the injunction in the Alabama courts "and had been met with delay or frustration of their constitutional claims." [30]   The Court pointed out that the injunction had issued ex parte, that if the court had been presented with defendant's contentions it might well have dissolved or modified the order, and that under Alabama procedure there was an expedited process of appellate review.[31]   By way of contrast, in the earlier case of In re Green, in which a contempt conviction was set aside because the temporary injunction that was violated should not have issued, the party held in contempt had sought unsuccessfully to have the trial court vacate the temporary injunction and, though the Supreme Court did not mention this in its opinion, it appears from the briefs in the case that state law did not permit appellate review of a temporary injunction.

That the key is the effectiveness of appellate review is also made clear by Maness v. Meyers,[32] where a contempt conviction was set aside because there was no effective way to test an order requiring a party to produce material that he thought would incriminate him except by refusing compliance and raising the issue on appeal of the conviction.

This interpretation of the United Mine Workers rule reconciles it also with the 19th century cases allowing challenge to an injunctive order by appeal from a contempt conviction.   As has been pointed out,[33] at the time they were decided there was no speedy or effective means for review of such orders.

28.   91 S.Ct. at 1582, 402 U.S. at 532.

29.   91 S.Ct. at 1582 n. 4, 402 U.S. at 532 n. 4.

30.   87 S.Ct. at 1831, 388 U.S. at 318.

31.   91 S.Ct. at 1831, 388 U.S. at 319.

32.   1975, 95 S.Ct. 584, 419 U.S. 449, 42 L.Ed.2d 574.

See also U. S. v. Dickinson, C.A.5th, 1972, 465 F.2d 496, 509–514, affirmed C.A.5th, 1973, 476 F.2d 373, certiorari denied 94 S.Ct. 270, 414 U.S. 979, 38 L.Ed.2d 223.

33.   See text at notes 12–15 above.

CHAPTER 3

FEDERAL QUESTION

Analysis

§ 17. The Meaning of "Arising Under" [1]

The Constitution provides that federal courts may be given jurisdiction over "Cases, in Law and Equity, arising under this Constitution, the Laws of the United States, and Treaties made, or which shall be made, under their authority." Cases that fall under this head of jurisdiction are usually spoken of as involving a "federal question." This jurisdiction was one of the principal reasons that the Constitution authorized Congress to create a system of inferior federal courts, but it was not until 1875 that Congress gave the federal courts general original jurisdiction over such cases.[2] The statute, first passed in that year and preserved substantially unchanged to the present, confers original jurisdiction on the federal courts over federal question cases in language virtually the same as the Constitu-

---

[§ 17]

1. 13 Wright, Miller & Cooper, Jurisdiction §§ 3561–3563; ALI Study, § 1311 and Commentary thereto. The following articles and commentaries are cited in chronological order for they represent something of a dialogue, in which each writer draws on and discusses the writings that have been published earlier: Forrester, The Nature of a Federal Question, 1942, 16 Tul.L.Rev. 363; Chadbourn & Levin, Original Jurisdiction of Federal Questions, 1942, 90 U.Pa.L.Rev. 639; Forrester, Federal Question Jurisdiction and Section 5, 1943, 18 Tul.L.Rev. 263; Note, Proposed Revision of Federal Question Jurisdiction, 1945, 40 Ill.L.Rev. 387; Bergman, Reappraisal of Federal Question Jurisdiction, 1946, 46 Mich.L. Rev. 17; Fraser, Some Problems in Federal Question Jurisdiction, 1950, 49 Mich.L.Rev. 73; Mishkin, The Federal

"Question" in the District Courts, 1953, 53 Col.L.Rev. 157; London, "Federal Question" Jurisdiction—A Snare and a Delusion, 1959, 57 Mich.L.Rev. 835; Cohen, The Broken Compass: the Requirement that a Case Arise "Directly" Under Federal Law, 1967, 115 U.Pa.L.Rev. 890; Aycock, Introduction to Certain Members of the Federal Question Family, 1970, 49 N.C.L.Rev. 1; Note, The Outer Limits of "Arising Under," 1979, 54 N.Y.U.L.Rev. 978.

2. Act of March 3, 1875, § 1, 18 Stat. 470. The history of the constitutional provision, and of the 1875 Act, are set out in the two articles by Dean Forrester cited note 1 above.

There had been a short-lived grant of this jurisdiction in the Midnight Judges Act of 1801, but this was promptly repealed a year later. See § 1 above.

tion.[3] The key phrase, both in the Constitution and in the statute, is "arises under." Though the meaning of this phrase has attracted the interest of such giants of the bench as Marshall, Waite, Bradley, the first Harlan, Holmes, Cardozo, and Frankfurter, and has been the subject of voluminous scholarly writing, it cannot be said that any clear test has yet been developed to determine which cases "arise under" the Constitution, laws, or treaties of the United States.[4]

Analysis must begin with Marshall's opinion in Osborn v. Bank of the United States.[5] The congressional act chartering the bank authorized it "to sue and be sued * * * in any Circuit Court of the United States." The bank brought suit to enjoin the state auditor of Ohio from collecting from it a tax alleged to be unconstitutional. In considering the jurisdictional question, Chief Justice Marshall first held that the authorization to "sue and be sued" was a grant by Congress to the federal courts of jurisdiction in all cases to which the bank was a party. Even this conclusion is debatable.[6] Assuming that conclusion, the question then occurred whether Congress had constitutional power to confer jurisdiction of such cases. Surely the power existed in the case actually before the Court, for the bank was asserting a claim under the federal Constitution, which would suffice for jurisdiction by any test. Marshall's opinion, however, undertakes to support the validity of the jurisdictional grant in all cases to which the bank might be a party, and discusses in detail the situation that would be presented if the bank were asserting a claim under the state law arising out of a contract.[7] Even here, it was held, federal question jurisdiction would exist. Since the bank is a mere creature of federal law, in every case the first question that presents itself must

3. 28 U.S.C.A. § 1331: "The district courts shall have original jurisdiction of all civil actions arising under the Constitution, laws, or treaties of the United States."

There are also many statutes granting jurisdiction in particular federal question cases. From 1875 to 1980 the general federal question statute had required a jurisdictional amount, most recently $10,000, and these other statutes were significant since they granted jurisdiction without regard to amount. See § 32 below. With the abolition in 1980 of the amount requirement in § 1331, the special statutes, which are scattered in chapter 85 of title 28, have lost their significance. It is clear, in any event, that "arising under" has the same meaning in these statutes as in § 1331. E.g., First Nat. Bank of Aberdeen v. Aberdeen Nat. Bank, C.A.8th, 1980, 627 F.2d 843, 849 n. 14; Maritime Serv. Corp. v. Sweet Brokerage De Puerto Rico, Inc., C.A. 1st, 1976, 537 F.2d 560, 561 n. 1.

In the year ended June 30, 1981, 72,514 of the 180,576 cases brought in the district courts were private "federal question" cases. Ann.Rep. of the Director of the Administrative Office of the U.S. Courts, 1981, Table C–2.

4. First Nat. Bank of Aberdeen v. Aberdeen Nat. Bank, C.A.8th, 1980, 627 F.2d 843, 849; Town of Greenhorn v. Baker County, C.A.9th, 1979, 596 F.2d 349, 351.

5. 1824, 9 Wheat. 738, 6 L.Ed. 204.

6. A more natural interpretation might have been that the charter gave the bank capacity to be a party to a suit but did not in itself create jurisdiction. This is the construction now placed on such language in charters. Bankers Trust Co. v. Texas & P. Ry. Co., 1916, 36 S.Ct. 569, 241 U.S. 295, 60 L.Ed. 1010.

7. Such a situation was in fact presented by the companion case of Bank of the U. S. v. Planter's Bank of Georgia, 1824, 9 Wheat. 904, 6 L.Ed. 244, decided on the authority of Osborn.

be whether this legal entity has a right to sue. Once this question is settled, it is of course unlikely that it would be raised in subsequent cases, but this, in Marshall's view, was immaterial. "The question forms an original ingredient in every cause. Whether it be in fact relied on or not, in the defence, it is still a part of the cause, and may be relied on." [8] Earlier in the opinion Marshall, in language heavily relied on by later judges, had seemed to say that federal question jurisdiction existed only when the title or right set up by the party might be defeated by one construction of the Constitution or law of the United States and sustained by the opposite construction,[9] but his later analysis, just described, demonstrates that this was not his position, and that jurisdiction would be present even in a case where no question of federal law is ever raised.

The Osborn decision took on importance after the 1875 statute gave the federal courts general original jurisdiction of federal question cases. At least until comparatively recent years, no decision construing the statute was complete without its reference to the Osborn case and its praise for Marshall's analysis there. What was not clearly perceived in the early cases construing the 1875 act, and has not always been kept in mind even in the later cases, is that there is a difference between construing the Constitution, as Marshall was obliged to do in Osborn, and construing a statute. The very expansive reading Marshall gave to the "cases arising under" language of the Constitution is appropriate in dealing with a constitution. It leaves room for Congress to grant such particular jurisdiction as may in the future be seen to be necessary. But to hold that the 1875 statute gives federal jurisdiction wherever some element of federal law is an "ingredient" of the cause of action would mean, for example, that virtually every case involving the title to land in the western states, where title descends from a grant from the United States, could be litigated in federal court. If Congress in fact meant to open the door of the federal courthouse to such a flood of litigation, the Osborn case shows that it had power to do so. Actually both the language of the 1875 statute, following so closely the constitutional language, and such skimpy legislative history as exists,[10] do support the view that Congress meant to give all the jurisdiction it could constitutionally confer, but this is not an inevitable conclusion, and the courts acted understandably in giving a restrictive reading to the statute. Regrettably, from the standpoint of clear analysis, they did so by a distor-

---

8. 9 Wheat. at 824, 6 L.Ed. at 224.

9. 9 Wheat. at 822, 6 L.Ed. at 224. In the earlier case of Cohens v. Virginia, 1821, 6 Wheat. 264, 379, 5 L.Ed. 257, 285, Marshall had written: "A case in law or equity consists of the right of the one party, as well as of the other, and may truly be said to arise under the constitution or a law of the United States, whenever its correct decision depends on the construction of either." In Cohens, however, Marshall was considering the appellate jurisdiction of the Supreme Court over state courts, which involves different considerations than does the original jurisdiction of the federal trial courts.

10. See Forrester, Federal Question Jurisdiction and Section 5, 1943, 18 Tul.L. Rev. 263, 276–280.

tion of the Osborn opinion, rather than by an overt recognition that their problem of statutory construction was not the same as Marshall's problem of interpreting the Constitution.

The point emerges most clearly in the Pacific Railroad Removal Cases,[11] decided in 1885, where the Court, through Justice Bradley, held that ordinary tort actions against railroads with federal charters were within the scope of the 1875 statute. Chief Justice Waite, dissenting, stated that "in my opinion congress did not intend to give the words 'arising under the constitution or laws of the United States,' in the act of 1875, the broad meaning they have when used by Chief Justice Marshall in the argument of the opinion in Osborn v. Bank of U. S." [12] The case itself is now regarded by the Supreme Court as an "unfortunate decision" [13] and has long since been effectively overruled by Congress.[14] But Waite himself, in decisions before and after the Pacific Railroad Removal Cases, was able to give a restrictive reading to the 1875 statute while purporting to apply the Osborn rule,[15] and later judges have done the same thing.[16]

When courts are unclear in formulating the question before them, it is not surprising if the answers are also wanting in clarity. The Osborn theory, that when federal law is an ingredient of the claim there is a federal question, has been rejected, in construing the statute. It is not easy to state what has been substituted in its stead. One line of decisions is symbolized by Justice Holmes' statement that "a suit arises under the law that creates the action." [17] Many cases

11. 1885, 5 S.Ct. 1113, 115 U.S. 1, 29 L.Ed. 319.

12. 5 S.Ct. at 1124, 115 U.S. at 24.

13. Romero v. International Terminal Operating Co., 1959, 79 S.Ct. 468, 484 n. 50, 358 U.S. 354, 379 n. 50, 3 L.Ed.2d 368.

14. 28 U.S.C.A. § 1349 provides that the district courts shall not have jurisdiction on the ground that a corporation was incorporated by Congress unless the United States owns more than half the capital stock of the corporation. See also 28 U.S.C.A. § 1348 (national banks).

The reasoning of Osborn and of the Pacific Railroad Removal Cases has been resurrected to support a holding that international organizations, authorized by statute "to institute judicial proceedings," may sue in federal court even on claims stemming from state law. International Refugee Organization v. Republic S. S. Corp., C.A.4th, 1951, 189 F.2d 858. See Notes, 1952, 61 Yale L.J. 111, 1958, 71 Harv.L.Rev. 1300, 1301–1306.

15. E.g., Gold-Washing & Water Co. v. Keyes, 1877, 96 U.S. 199, 24 L.Ed. 656;

Starin v. New York, 1885, 6 S.Ct. 28, 115 U.S. 248, 29 L.Ed. 388.

16. Thus Justice Stone, in People of Puerto Rico v. Russell & Co., 1933, 53 S.Ct. 447, 288 U.S. 476, 77 L.Ed. 903, and Justice Cardozo, in Gully v. First Nat. Bank in Meridian, 1936, 57 S.Ct. 96, 299 U.S. 109, 81 L.Ed. 70, felt obliged to express misgivings about the Osborn decision, rather than distinguishing it as involving a different question.

The distinction between the constitutional question and the statutory question is recognized in Shoshone Mining Co. v. Rutter, 1900, 20 S.Ct. 726, 177 U.S. 505, 44 L.Ed. 864, and in Romero v. International Terminal Operating Co., 1959, 79 S.Ct. 468, 484 n. 51, 358 U.S. 354, 379 n. 51, 3 L.Ed.2d 368: "Of course the many limitations which have been placed on jurisdiction under § 1331 are not limitations on the constitutional power of Congress to confer jurisdiction on the federal courts." See also Powell v. McCormack, 1969, 89 S.Ct. 1944, 1961, 395 U.S. 486, 515–516, 23 L.Ed.2d 491.

17. American Well Works Co. v. Layne & Bowler Co., 1916, 36 S.Ct. 585, 586,

can be explained by—or at least are consistent with—this test,[18] though of late it has been thought that the "Holmes' formula is more useful for inclusion than for the exclusion for which it was intended." [19]   There are surely other cases that cannot be reconciled with the test proposed by Holmes, cases in which federal question jurisdiction has been upheld although the action was created by state law,[20] and in which jurisdiction has been denied although federal law created the action.[21]

Other cases have said that "a suit to enforce a right which takes its origin in the laws of the United States is not necessarily, or for that reason alone, one arising under those laws, for a suit does not so arise unless it really and substantially involves a dispute or controversy respecting the validity, construction or effect of such a law, upon the determination of which the result depends." [22]   Such a test would be difficult, if not impossible, to apply, in view of the rule that jurisdiction must be determined from plaintiff's well-pleaded complaint.[23]   The complaint by itself can hardly disclose on what aspects of the case there will be dispute or controversy.   Such a test would be inconsistent, also, with those cases that hold that federal jurisdiction exists though defendant defaults, and thus controverts nothing,[24]

241 U.S. 257, 260, 60 L.Ed. 987 (no jurisdiction over suit for damages to business from defendant's statements that plaintiff was infringing defendant's patents).

18.   E.g., no jurisdiction: Albright v. Teas, 1883, 1 S.Ct. 550, 106 U.S. 613, 27 L.Ed. 295 (suit on a contract involving a patent); People of Puerto Rico v. Russell & Co., 1933, 53 S.Ct. 447, 288 U.S. 476, 77 L.Ed. 903 (federal law gave authority to bring suit but suit itself was under local law); Gully v. First Nat. Bank in Meridian, 1936, 57 S.Ct. 96, 299 U.S. 109, 81 L.Ed. 70 (suit to collect state taxes that could not be brought unless federal law granted permission).

Jurisdiction: Feibelman v. Packard, 1883, 3 S.Ct. 289, 109 U.S. 421, 27 L.Ed. 984 (suit on bond required by federal law); The Fair v. Kohler Die & Specialty Co., 1913, 33 S.Ct. 410, 228 U.S. 22, 57 L.Ed. 716 (suit for patent infringement); McGoon v. Northern Pac. Ry. Co., D.C.N.D.1913, 204 F. 998 (Interstate Commerce Act gave remedy).

19.   T. B. Harms Co. v. Eliscu, C.A.2d 1964, 339 F.2d 823, 827, certiorari denied 85 S.Ct. 1534, 381 U.S. 915, 14 L.Ed.2d 435.

The formula of Justice Holmes is sharply attacked in Note, The Outer Limits of "Arising Under," 1979, 54 N.Y.U.L. Rev. 978.

20.   Smith v. Kansas City Title & Trust Co., 1921, 41 S.Ct. 243, 255 U.S. 180, 65 L.Ed. 577 (suit to enjoin bank from investing in particular government bonds, on ground that Act of Congress authorizing the bonds was unconstitutional).

21.   Shoshone Mining Co. v. Rutter, 1900, 20 S.Ct. 726, 177 U.S. 505, 44 L.Ed. 864 (federal statute authorized suit to determine adverse claims to mining right, but no jurisdiction since local rules or customs were to govern result).   See also Roecker v. U. S., C.A. 5th, 1967, 379 F.2d 400, 407–408, certiorari denied 88 S.Ct. 563, 389 U.S. 1005, 19 L.Ed.2d 600.

22.   Shulthis v. McDougal, 1912, 32 S.Ct. 704, 706, 225 U.S. 561, 569, 56 L.Ed. 1205.   See also Gold-Washing & Water Co. v. Keyes, 1877, 96 U.S. 199, 203, 24 L.Ed. 656; Gully v. First Nat. Bank in Meridian, 1936, 57 S.Ct. 96, 98, 299 U.S. 109, 114, 81 L.Ed. 70.

23.   See § 18 below.

24.   E.g., The Fair v. Kohler Die & Specialty Co., 1913, 33 S.Ct. 410, 228 U.S. 22, 57 L.Ed. 716.   See ALI Study, pp. 486–487.

or that it exists though the only questions are fact questions and the application of the federal law is not in issue.[25]

In Gully v. First National Bank in Meridian,[26] Justice Cardozo, after repeating most of the earlier definitions of a federal question, cautioned against broad and abstract definitions and called for a common-sense accommodation of judgment to kaleidoscopic situations. "If we follow the ascent far enough, countless claims of right can be discovered to have their source or their operative limits in the provisions of a federal statute or in the Constitution itself with its circumambient restrictions upon legislative power. To set bounds to the pursuit, the courts have formulated the distinction between controversies that are basic and those that are collateral, between disputes that are necessary and those that are merely possible. We shall be lost in a maze if we put that compass by." [27]

There is little difficulty if federal law expressly creates a remedy. Here jurisdiction ordinarily will be found.[28] There is more difficulty if federal law creates a duty without in terms providing a remedy. In some cases it is held that a federal remedy can be implied from the duty and that this gives federal question jurisdiction.[29] Other cases refuse to imply a remedy and hold that the remedy, if any, is the creature of state law. On this view jurisdiction is denied.[30] Finally

25. E.g., McGoon v. Northern Pac. Ry. Co., D.C.N.D.1913, 204 F. 998, cited approvingly in Peyton v. Railway Exp. Agency, Inc., 1942, 62 S.Ct. 1171, 1172–1173, 316 U.S. 350, 352–353, 86 L.Ed. 1525. See also Townsend v. Boston & M. R. Co., D.C.Mass.1940, 35 F.Supp. 938.

26. 1936, 57 S.Ct. 96, 299 U.S. 109, 81 L.Ed. 70.

27. 57 S.Ct. at 100, 299 U.S. at 118.

"This is prose so beautiful that it seems almost profane to analyze it. Yet, committing the sacrilege will make it clear that as long as we are forbidden to look at both sides of the pleadings the distinction between 'controversies that are basic and those that are collateral, between disputes that are necessary and those that are merely possible' still have us without compass—lost in a maze." Chadbourn & Levin, Original Jurisdiction of Federal Questions, 1942, 90 U.Pa.L.Rev. 639, 671.

28. E.g., Feibelman v. Packard, 1883, 3 S.Ct. 289, 109 U.S. 421, 27 L.Ed. 984. But see the cases cited note 21 above.

29. E.g., Carlson v. Green, 1980, 100 S.Ct. 1468, 446 U.S. 14, 64 L.Ed.2d 15; Cannon v. University of Chicago, 1979, 99 S.Ct. 1946, 441 U.S. 677, 60 L.Ed.2d 560; Bivens v. Six Unknown Named Agents, 1971, 91 S.Ct. 1999, 403 U.S. 388, 29 L.Ed.2d 619; Tunstall v. Brotherhood of Locomotive Firemen & Enginemen, 1944, 65 S.Ct. 235, 323 U.S. 210, 89 L.Ed. 187, conformed to C.C.A.4th, 1945, 148 F.2d 403.

"When should a person injured by a violation of federal law be allowed to recover his damages in a federal court? This seemingly simple question has recently presented the Court with more difficulty than most substantive questions that come before us." Middlesex County Sewerage Auth. v. National Sea Clammers Assn., 1981, 101 S.Ct. 2615, 2617, 453 U.S. 1, 2, 69 L.Ed.2d 435 (Stevens, J., concurring in part).

The Court is more willing to imply a right of action from the Constitution than from an Act of Congress. Davis v. Passman, 1979, 99 S.Ct. 2264, 2274–2276, 442 U.S. 228, 239–243, 60 L.Ed.2d 846.

30. E.g., California v. Sierra Club, 1981, 101 S.Ct. 1775, 451 U.S. 287, 68 L.Ed. 2d 101; Cort v. Ash, 1975, 95 S.Ct. 2080, 422 U.S. 66, 45 L.Ed.2d 26; Wheeldin v. Wheeler, 1963, 83 S.Ct. 1441, 373 U.S. 647, 10 L.Ed.2d 605; Moore v. Chesapeake & O. Ry. Co., 1934, 54 S.Ct. 402, 291 U.S. 205, 78 L.Ed. 755.

Whether suits to enforce contracts contemplated by federal statutes set forth

there may be some room for finding federal jurisdiction though both the right and the remedy are state-created, if an important question of federal law is an essential element in the case.[31] In the absence of holdings applying this broader understanding of what is a federal question, which rests on a single old Supreme Court decision, it is difficult to say when or whether the scope of the jurisdiction will be expanded on this theory.

Professor Mishkin has distilled the course of decision here described into the succinct test that for original federal jurisdiction there must be "a substantial claim founded 'directly' upon federal law."[32] As definitions go—having in mind Cardozo's warning against their hazards—this seems as good as any, but it must be recognized that the books contain some results, and a good deal more language, inconsistent with it. Rather than attempting a test it might be wiser simply to recognize that "the existing doctrines as to when a case raises a federal question are neither analytical nor entirely logical,"[33] and that in the unusual case in which there is a debatable issue about federal question jurisdiction, pragmatic considerations must be taken into account.[34]

federal claims and whether private parties can sue in federal court to enforce these contractual rights turns on the intent of Congress. Jackson Transit Auth. v. Local Div. 1285, Amalgamated Transit Union, 1982, 102 S.Ct. 2202, ___ U.S. ___, 72 L.Ed.2d 639.

But if a claim that a remedy exists under federal law is not insubstantial or frivolous, this is enough for jurisdiction, and if it is decided that there is no remedy, dismissal should be on the merits rather than for want of jurisdiction. See § 18 at notes 21–22.

31. Judge Friendly's analysis in these terms in T. B. Harms Co. v. Eliscu, C.A.2d, 1964, 339 F.2d 823, 827, certiorari denied 85 S.Ct. 1534, 381 U.S. 915, 14 L.Ed.2d 435, has been accepted in dicta from several other courts. Mountain Fuel Supply Co. v. Johnson, C.A.10th, 1978, 586 F.2d 1375, 1381, certiorari denied 1979, 99 S.Ct. 2182, 441 U.S. 952, 60 L.Ed.2d 1058; Garrett v. Time-D. C., Inc., C.A.9th, 1974, 502 F.2d 627, 629, certiorari denied 95 S.Ct. 1569, 421 U.S. 913, 43 L.Ed.2d 778; Warrington Sewer Co. v. Tracy, C.A. 3d, 1972, 463 F.2d 771, 772. The only cases in which it has been relied on as the basis of a holding seem to be Stone & Webster Engineering Corp. v. Ilsley, C.A.2d, 1982, 690 F.2d 323, Christopher v. Cavallo, C.A.4th, 1981, 662 F.2d 1082, and Sweeney v. Abramovitz, D.C. Conn.1978, 449 F.Supp. 213. See also Note, cited note 19 above; Redish, Fed-

eral Jurisdiction: Tensions in the Allocation of Judicial Power, 1980, pp. 66–69. Professor Redish, like Judge Friendly, puts great emphasis on Smith v. Kansas City Title & Trust Co., 1921, 41 S.Ct. 243, 255 U.S. 180, 65 L.Ed. 577.

32. Mishkin, The Federal "Question" in the District Courts, 1953, 53 Col.L.Rev. 157, 165, 168.

The Mishkin formulation has been called "the most thoughtful distillation" in Keaukaha-Panaewa Community Assn. v. Hawaiian Homes Comm., C.A.9th, 1978, 588 F.2d 1216, 1225, certiorari denied 1979, 100 S.Ct. 49, 444 U.S. 826, 62 L.Ed.2d 33. See also e.g., Mescalero Apache Tribe v. Martinez, C.A.10th, 1975, 519 F.2d 479, 481; Johnston v. Byrd, C.A.5th, 1965, 354 F.2d 982, 984.

33. ALI Study, p. 179. See also Currie, The Federal Courts and the American Law Institute (Part II), 1969, 36 U.Chi. L.Rev. 268, 276–279.

34. Cohen, The Broken Compass: The Requirement that a Case Arise "Directly" Under Federal Law, 1967, 115 U.Pa.L.Rev. 890. Professor Cohen suggests, at 916, that the relevant pragmatic considerations include such matters as: "the extent of the caseload increase for federal trial courts if jurisdiction is recognized; the extent to which cases of this class will, in practice, turn on issues of state or federal law; the extent of the necessity for an

The federal law that will support federal question jurisdiction may be the Constitution, a statute of the United States, an administrative regulation, or a treaty.[35] There was once a contention that federal admiralty law is a "law of the United States" within the meaning of the jurisdictional statute, and thus that admiralty suits could be brought on the "law side" of the court, where trial is to a jury, rather than on the "admiralty side," where admittedly they can be brought [36] but where there is no jury. After conflicting decisions in the courts of appeals, the Supreme Court rejected this argument.[37] The decision is of general significance because of the clear recognition that the problem was to determine the intent of the draftsmen of the 1875 act, rather than to rely on constitutional conceptions. The decisions construing the statute would be more coherent if this distinction had always been observed.

Beyond this, however, the decision just mentioned states a rule confined to the esoteric area of admiralty and maritime jurisdiction. As had been anticipated,[38] it has now been held that "federal common law," when it exists,[39] is among the "laws of the United States" referred to in the jurisdictional statute, and that, except in the admiralty field, there is federal question jurisdiction of claims based on federal common law.[40]

expert federal tribunal to handle issues of state law that do arise; the extent of the necessity for a sympathetic federal tribunal in cases of this class." See also Redish, note 31 above, at 71.

The test stated in the text is applied in Barlow v. Marriott Corp., D.C.Md.1971, 328 F.Supp. 624, 627–628. It was held there that there is no federal question jurisdiction of a suit by employees contesting their employer's amendment of a profit-sharing trust even though the amendment may have disqualified the trust for exemption from federal taxes.

But the Note cited note 19 above says, at 980–981: "The jurisdictional grants do not invite ad hoc assessments of 'pragmatic need.'"

35. 13 Wright, Miller & Cooper, Jurisdiction § 3563.

36. On the admiralty jurisdiction of the federal courts, see 28 U.S.C.A. § 1333; 14 Wright, Miller & Cooper, Jurisdiction §§ 3671–3678; ALI Study, pp. 225–245; Robertson, Admiralty Procedure and Jurisdiction After the 1966 Unification, 1976, 74 Mich.L.Rev. 1627; Landers, by Sleight of Rule: Admiralty Unification and Ancillary and Pendent Jurisdiction, 1972, 51 Texas L.Rev. 50; Currie, note 33 above, at 286–289; Black, Admiralty Jurisdiction: Critique and Suggestions, 1950, 50 Col.L.Rev.

259; Symposium, 1969, 5 Willamette L.Rev. 367.

Admiralty jurisdiction extends to a collision between two recreational boats on navigable waters even though no commercial activity was involved. Foremost Ins. Co. v. Richardson, 1982, 102 S.Ct. 2654, ___ U.S. ___, 73 L.Ed.2d 300.

37. Romero v. International Terminal Operating Co., 1959, 79 S.Ct. 468, 358 U.S. 354, 3 L.Ed.2d 368. See Currie, The Silver Oar and All That: A Study of the Romero Case, 1959, 27 U.Chi.L. Rev. 1; Kurland, The Romero Case and Some Problems of Federal Jurisdiction, 1960, 73 Harv.L.Rev. 817; 14 Wright, Miller & Cooper, Jurisdiction § 3673.

38. See ALI Study, pp. 180–182; Kurland, The Romero Case and Some Problems of Federal Jurisdiction, 1960, 73 Harv.L.Rev. 817, 829–833; Comment, 1964, 74 Yale L.J. 325.

39. See § 60 below.

40. Illinois v. City of Milwaukee, 1972, 92 S.Ct. 1385, 406 U.S. 91, 31 L.Ed.2d 712, noted 1973, 49 Den.L.J. 609. See Comment, The Expansion of Federal Common Law and Federal Question Jurisdiction to Interstate Pollution, 1972, 10 Hous.L.Rev. 121.

Laws that are applicable exclusively to the District of Columbia are not "laws * * * of the United States" for purposes of federal question jurisdiction.[41] Although there has been uncertainty on the matter, it seems probable that a claim based on an interstate compact is within federal question jurisdiction,[42] and that the same is true of claims based on customary international law.[43]

It is not enough for federal question jurisdiction that federal law has been incorporated by reference in a state statute.[44] In the converse situation, in which an Act of Congress incorporates state law, the state law becomes federal law for purposes of federal question jurisdiction.[45]

§ 18. Determination From the Pleadings [1]

In the preceding section it was seen that the scope of the 1875 statute, conferring general original jurisdiction of federal question cases, was narrowed considerably from what the words of the statute might seem to suggest by restrictive definitions of what is a "case arising under" federal law. The scope of the jurisdiction was further narrowed by application of a rigid pleading rule that the federal question must appear on the face of the well-pleaded complaint.

The first Supreme Court decision to construe the 1875 statute applied such a rule, citing Chitty to determine what allegations are proper,[2] and the rule has been insisted upon ever since.

Because of this rule, it does not suffice for jurisdiction that the answer raises a federal question. If the basis for original federal question jurisdiction is that the federal courts have a special expertness in applying federal law, and that assertions of federal law will be received more hospitably in a federal court, it would seem that the

---

41. 28 U.S.C.A. § 1364. This is one of three sections all numbered § 1364 in the Judicial Code.

42. Jurisdiction was upheld in League to Save Lake Tahoe v. Tahoe Regional Planning Agency, C.A.9th, 1974, 507 F.2d 517, certiorari denied 95 S.Ct. 1398, 420 U.S. 974, 43 L.Ed.2d 654. This result is supported in Comment, Federal Question Jurisdiction to Interpret Interstate Compacts, 1975, 64 Geo.L.J. 87. See also Engdahl, Construction of Interstate Compacts: A Questionable Federal Question, 1965, 51 Va.L.Rev. 987, 1025.

43. ALI Study, p. 181; Filartiga v. Pena-Irala, C.A.2d, 1980, 630 F.2d 876; Chapalain Compagnie v. Standard Oil Co. (Indiana), D.C.Ill.1978, 467 F.Supp. 181; Note, Enforcement of International Human Rights in the Federal Courts After Filartiga v. Pena-Irala, 1981, 67 Va.L.Rev. 1379.

44. Nuclear Engineering Co. v. Scott, C.A.7th, 1981, 660 F.2d 241; United Air Lines v. Division of Indus. Safety, C.A.9th, 1980, 633 F.2d 814, certiorari denied 1981, 102 S.Ct. 485, 944 U.S. 454, 70 L.Ed.2d 255; Greene, Hybrid State Law in the Federal Courts, 1969, 83 Harv.L.Rev. 289, 322–325.

45. Willis v. Craig, C.A.9th, 1977, 555 F.2d 724; Haas v. Pittsburgh Nat. Bank, D.C.Pa.1973, 60 F.R.D. 604. But cf. Sylvane v. Whalen, D.C.N.Y. 1981, 506 F.Supp. 1355.

[§ 18]

1. 13 Wright, Miller & Cooper, Jurisdiction § 3566; ALI Study, pp. 169–172; Note, Necessity That Federal Question Appear in the Complaint, 1951, 8 Wash. & Lee L.Rev. 89.

2. Gold-Washing & Water Co. v. Keyes, 1877, 96 U.S. 199, 24 L.Ed. 656.

courts should have jurisdiction where there is some federal issue regardless of which pleading raises it. The rule to the contrary probably stems from the conceptual notion that unless the initial pleading is sufficient to invoke the jurisdiction of the court, the court lacks power to require responsive pleadings or take any other act in the case. The rule is an inconvenient one, expecially when, as seen in section 17, the existence of a federal question is said to depend on a genuine and present controversy. How a controversy can be found in plaintiff's pleading alone "still remains a mystery of the judicial process." [3]

Plaintiff's expectation that his opponent will raise a federal question cannot serve to bring the case to federal court. In 1871 the Louisville & Nashville Railroad settled a claim for damages that a Mr. and Mrs. Mottley had against it by agreeing to give the Mottleys free passes each year for the remainder of their lives. In 1906 an Act of Congress prohibited free transportation by railroads, and the following year the railroad did not give the Mottleys their pass. They sued in federal court for specific performance, alleging that the statute did not apply in the circumstances of their case, and that if it did it was unconstitutional. The Mottleys won in the trial court, but on appeal the Supreme Court held that the trial court had no jurisdiction.[4] "It is not enough," the Court said, "that the plaintiff alleges some anticipated defense to his cause of action, and asserts that the defense is invalidated by some provision of the Constitution of the United States. Although such allegations show that very likely, in the course of the litigation, a question under the Constitution would arise, they do not show that the suit, that is, the plaintiff's original cause of action, arises under the Constitution." [5] Thus the Mottleys were forced to begin anew in the state courts. Again they were successful below but the question as to the meaning and validity of the 1906 Act, though insufficient as a basis for original jurisdiction, did suffice to support appeal from the Kentucky courts to the United States Supreme Court, where, three years after their first appearance, they finally lost on the merits.[6] The case illustrates strikingly the proposition that original federal question jurisdiction is not coextensive with the constitutional grant of jurisdiction, but it also shows the practical inconvenience of the "well-pleaded complaint" rule.

3. Chadbourn & Levin, Original Jurisdiction of Federal Questions, 1942, 90 U.Pa.L.Rev. 639, 671.

It is proposed in Note, Proposed Revision of Federal Question Jurisdiction, 1945, 40 Ill.L.Rev. 387, that the statute be amended to permit consideration of all the pleadings in determining the existence of a federal question. Other writers have made similar proposals. Reasons for rejecting this view are stated in ALI Study, pp. 188–191, and in Stone v. Stone, D.C.Cal.1978, 450 F.Supp. 919, 922, affirmed C.A.9th, 1980, 632 F.2d 740. The Law Institute proposes instead to allow removal on the basis of a federal defense or counterclaim. ALI Study, § 1312(a).

4. Louisville & N. R. Co. v. Mottley, 1908, 29 S.Ct. 42, 211 U.S. 149, 53 L.Ed. 126.

5. 29 S.Ct. at 43, 211 U.S. at 152.

6. Louisville & N. R. Co. v. Mottley, 1911, 31 S.Ct. 265, 219 U.S. 467, 55 L.Ed. 297.

The plaintiff is not permitted to anticipate defenses in his complaint.[7] Nor can he win admission to federal court by allegations to support his own case that are not required by nice pleading rules. If title to land is in doubt because of some matter of federal law, there is federal jurisdiction to entertain a bill to remove a cloud on title[8] but not a suit to quiet title,[9] since allegations as to the nature of the cloud are proper in the first kind of action but improper in the second. An action to enjoin another from using land that, by federal law, is asserted to be plaintiff's raises a proper federal question,[10] but if plaintiff is out of possession, he has an adequate legal remedy in an action for ejectment, in which allegations as to the title of land are not proper, and he cannot invoke federal question jurisdiction.[11]

These subtle distinctions, dependent on long-forgotten lore as to the forms of action, are hard enough to apply in conventional law suits. There has been added uncertainty about how the rule about the well-pleaded complaint is to be applied in the new statutory action for a declaratory judgment.[12] There are two possibilities. The complaint in a declaratory judgment action may be judged on its own merits; if it reveals a federal claim, then jurisdiction will exist. But this, as will be seen, would permit some cases to be brought in federal court that could not be so brought absent the Declaratory Judgment Act. The alternative is to say that the declaratory action may be entertained in federal court only if the coercive action that would have been necessary, absent declaratory judgment procedure, might have been so brought.

There is no difficulty in an action to establish that plaintiff has an affirmative federal right. If the Jones Company brings an action for a declaratory judgment that its patent is valid and being infringed by

7. Phillips Petroleum Co. v. Texaco, Inc., 1974, 94 S.Ct. 1002, 415 U.S. 125, 39 L.Ed.2d 209.

8. Hopkins v. Walker, 1917, 37 S.Ct. 711, 244 U.S. 486, 61 L.Ed. 1270; New York v. White, C.A.2d, 1975, 528 F.2d 336.

9. Shulthis v. McDougal, 1912, 32 S.Ct. 704, 225 U.S. 561, 56 L.Ed. 1205; Marshall v. Desert Properties Co., C.C.A. 9th, 1939, 103 F.2d 551, certiorari denied 60 S.Ct. 74, 308 U.S. 563, 84 L.Ed. 473.

10. Lancaster v. Kathleen Oil Co., 1916, 36 S.Ct. 711, 241 U.S. 551, 60 L.Ed. 1161.

11. White v. Sparkill Realty Corp., 1930, 50 S.Ct. 186, 280 U.S. 500, 74 L.Ed. 578; Taylor v. Anderson, 1914, 34 S.Ct. 724, 234 U.S. 74, 58 L.Ed. 1218; Joy v. St. Louis, 1906, 26 S.Ct. 478, 201 U.S. 332, 50 L.Ed. 776; Heirs of Burat v. Board of Levee Commrs., C.A.5th, 1974, 496 F.2d 1336, certiorari denied

95 S.Ct. 625, 419 U.S. 1049, 42 L.Ed.2d 644.

The Supreme Court recognized this as the general rule but was able to create an exception where Indian tribes are claiming title. Oneida Indian Nation of New York State v. County of Oneida, 1974, 94 S.Ct. 772, 414 U.S. 661, 39 L.Ed.2d 73.

12. 10 Wright & Miller, Civil § 2767; Trautman, Federal Right Jurisdiction and the Declaratory Remedy, 1954, 7 Vand.L.Rev. 445; Comment, Federal Question Jurisdiction and the Declaratory Judgment Act, 1966 Ky.L.J. 150; Note, Federal Question Jurisdiction of the Federal Courts and the Declaratory Judgment Act, 1951, 4 Vand.L.Rev. 827; Mishkin, The Federal "Question" in the District Courts, 1953, 53 Col.L. Rev. 157, 177–184; Note, Declaratory Judgments, 1949, 62 Harv.L.Rev. 787, 802–803, 863, 864; R.C. 1968, 81 Harv. L.Rev. 1580.

a device manufactured by Smith, the federal claim necessarily appears on the face of the complaint, and if there were no declaratory judgment procedure, Jones Company could have brought a coercive action for damages or injunction.

The matter is somewhat more difficult where the suit is for a declaratory judgment that the other party does *not* have a federal right. If Jones Company does not sue, but merely threatens Smith, he will have a lively interest in determining whether the patent is valid and whether his device is infringing. Prior to the Declaratory Judgment Act, his action to resolve this question would not, absent diversity, have been within federal jurisdiction.[13] Nevertheless it seems now settled that Smith can sue for a declaratory judgment of invalidity or noninfringement.[14] Again the federal nature of the claim appears on the complaint for declaratory judgment. Here the precise issue could have been litigated in federal court in a coercive action brought by Jones Company, and this is thought to suffice, even though Smith could not have brought a coercive action.

The hardest situation is where a party seeks a declaration that he is immune, by virtue of federal law, from a non-federal claim that the other party may have. Suppose the controversy between the Louisville & Nashville Railroad and the Mottleys had arisen after passage of the Declaratory Judgment Act. Could the railroad sue in federal court for a declaratory judgment that the statute relieved it from its obligation to give Mr. and Mrs. Mottley a pass? On the narrow view it could not, for, absent the declaratory procedure, the federal claim would arise only as a defense to the passholder's common-law action for breach of contract, and the only possible coercive action, that by the Mottleys for specific performance, would raise no federal question.[15] The broader view would permit the declaratory action since in that suit the railroad's federal claim of an immunity to the common-law action would appear on the face of the railroad's complaint. Though this would mean that the federal courts were entertaining a suit not within their jurisdiction prior to passage of the Declaratory Judgment Act, this broad view has the merit of being far simpler to apply than the narrow view, and would be a sensible departure from the use of the old forms of action as tests for federal jurisdiction. Some lower courts had apparently adopted this view,[16] but there is

13. American Well Works Co. v. Layne & Bowler Co., 1916, 36 S.Ct. 585, 241 U.S. 257, 60 L.Ed. 987.

14. Hanes Corp. v. Millard, C.A.1976, 531 F.2d 585, 594 n. 8, 174 U.S.App. D.C. 253; E. Edelmann & Co. v. Triple-A Specialty Co., C.C.A.7th, 1937, 88 F.2d 852, certiorari denied 57 S.Ct. 673, 300 U.S. 680, 81 L.Ed. 884.

In Jewell Ridge Coal Corp. v. Local No. 6167, UMW, 1945, 65 S.Ct. 1063, 325 U.S. 161, 89 L.Ed. 1534, the Court considered, without discussion of any jurisdictional question, an action by an employer for a declaratory judgment that he was not liable to his employees under the Fair Labor Standards Act.

15. Louisville & N. R. Co. v. Mottley, 1908, 29 S.Ct. 42, 211 U.S. 149, 53 L.Ed. 126.

16. Zaconick v. City of Hollywood, D.C. Fla.1949, 85 F.Supp. 52, noted 1950, 3 Vand.L.Rev. 320. And see cases cited 10 Wright & Miller, Civil § 2767 n. 65.

strong language from the Supreme Court that it would "distort the limited procedural purpose of the Declaratory Judgment Act" to permit a party by "artful pleading" to anticipate a defense based on federal law and thus to bring a suit within federal jurisdiction that could not otherwise be heard in federal court.[17] These statements may have been dicta, but they do suggest that the narrow view will be adopted and a historical test used to measure federal jurisdiction in declaratory actions.[18] This does not preclude the possibility of change by legislation. The case put is within Article III, and the limitation to the "well-pleaded complaint," is only a construction of the jurisdictional statute.[19] Congress is free to provide by statute for the broader—and simpler—view.[20]

It has been seen that the federal question must appear in the complaint. A corollary rule is that federal jurisdiction exists if the complaint states a case arising under federal law, even though on the merits the party may have no federal right. If his claim is bad, then judgment is to be given against him on the merits, and even if the court is persuaded that federal law does not give the right the party claims, it is to dismiss for failure to state a claim on which relief can be granted rather than for want of jurisdiction.[21] Dismissal for want of jurisdiction is appropriate only if the federal claim is frivolous or a mere matter of form.[22]

17. Skelly Oil Co. v. Phillips Petroleum Co., 1950, 70 S.Ct. 876, 880, 339 U.S. 667, 673–674, 94 L.Ed. 1194. See dicta to the same effect in Public Serv. Comm. of Utah v. Wycoff Co., 1952, 73 S.Ct. 236, 242–243, 344 U.S. 237, 248–249, 97 L.Ed. 291. See also Note, Federal Jurisdiction over Declaratory Suits Challenging State Action, 1979, 79 Col.L.Rev. 983.

But see Stone & Webster Engineering Corp. v. Ilsley, C.A.2d, 1982, 690 F.2d 323, 327, and Justice White's dissent from the denial of certiorari in United Air Lines v. Division of Indus. Safety, 1981, 102 S.Ct. 485, 454 U.S. 255, 70 L.Ed.2d 255.

18. Monks v. Hetherington, C.A.10th, 1978, 573 F.2d 1164; Allegheny Airlines, Inc. v. Pennsylvania Public Util. Comm., C.A.3d, 1972, 465 F.2d 237, certiorari denied 1973, 93 S.Ct. 1367, 410 U.S. 943, 35 L.Ed.2d 609; McCorkle v. First Pennsylvania Banking & Trust Co., C.A.4th, 1972, 459 F.2d 243; Thiokol Chem. Corp. v. Burlington Indus., C.A.3d, 1971, 448 F.2d 1328, certiorari denied 1972, 92 S.Ct. 684, 404 U.S. 1019, 30 L.Ed.2d 668; First Federal Sav. & Loan Assn. v. McReynolds, D.C. Ky.1969, 297 F.Supp. 1159; Government Employees Ins. Co. v. LeBleu, D.C.La.1967, 272 F.Supp. 421, 427–428.

19. This is evidenced by the fact that the Supreme Court ultimately did pass on the merits of the Mottley case. See note 6 above.

20. The American Law Institute proposes that such legislation be adopted. ALI Study, § 1311(a).

21. Bell v. Hood, 1946, 66 S.Ct. 773, 327 U.S. 678, 90 L.Ed. 939. To the same effect see The Fair v. Kohler Die & Specialty Co., 1913, 33 S.Ct. 410, 228 U.S. 22, 57 L.Ed. 716; Montana-Dakota Utilities Co. v. Northwestern Public Serv. Co., 1951, 71 S.Ct. 692, 341 U.S. 246, 95 L.Ed. 912; Duke Power Co. v. Carolina Environmental Study Group, 1978, 98 S.Ct. 2620, 2629, 438 U.S. 59, 69, 57 L.Ed.2d 595; Jackson Transit Auth. v. Local Div. 1285, Amalgamated Transit Union, 1982, 102 S.Ct. 2202, 2206 n. 6, —— U.S. ——, —— n. 6, 72 L.Ed.2d 639.

Dissenting from the denial of certiorari in Yazoo County Indus. Development Corp. v. Suthoff, 1982, 102 S.Ct. 1032, —— U.S. ——, 71 L.Ed.2d 316, Justice Rehnquist has questioned the soundness of Bell v. Hood and whether its doctrine, described in the text, can be reconciled with Rule 12.

22. 13 Wright, Miller & Cooper, Jurisdiction § 3564; Hagans v. Lavine,

§ 19. Scope of the Jurisdiction [1]

In the Osborn case, Chief Justice Marshall observed that "when a question to which the judicial power of the Union is extended by the constitution, forms an ingredient of the original cause, it is in the power of congress to give the circuit courts jurisdiction of that cause, although other questions of fact or of law may be involved in it." [2] There could hardly be any other rule. When the Supreme Court is reviewing a state court decision it can and does confine its review to the federal question in the case,[3] but a court of original jurisdiction could not function, as Marshall recognized, unless it had power to decide all the questions that the case presents. This functional justification of the Osborn rule finds support also in the constitutional language, which grants jurisdiction over "cases" rather than over "questions."

The Osborn doctrine was expanded in Siler v. Louisville & Nashville R. Co.[4] A state order regulating rates was attacked as unauthorized by state law and as unconstitutional by federal law. The Supreme Court said: "The Federal questions as to the invalidity of the state statute because, as alleged, it was in violation of the Federal Constitution, gave the circuit court jurisdiction, and, having properly obtained it, that court had the right to decide all the questions in the

---

1974, 94 S.Ct. 1372, 1378–1379, 415 U.S. 528, 536–538, 39 L.Ed.2d 577; Bell v. Hood, 1946, 66 S.Ct. 773, 327 U.S. 678, 90 L.Ed. 939; Levering & Garrigues Co. v. Morrin, 1933, 53 S.Ct. 549, 550, 289 U.S. 103, 105, 77 L.Ed. 1062. See Seid, The Tail Wags the Dog: Hagans v. Lavine and Pendent Jurisdiction, 1975, 53 J.Urban Law 1.

[§ 19]

1. 13 Wright, Miller & Cooper, Jurisdiction § 3567; ALI Study, § 1313 and Commentary thereto; Schenkier, Ensuring Access to Federal Courts: A Revised Rationale for Pendent Jurisdiction, 1980, 75 Nw.U.L.Rev. 245; Fraser, Jurisdiction of the Federal Courts of Actions Involving Multiple Claims, 1978, 76 F.R.D. 525; Minahan, Pendent and Ancillary Jurisdiction of United States Federal District Courts, 1976, 10 Creighton L.Rev. 279; Sullivan, Pendent Jurisdiction: The Impact of Hagans and Moor, 1974, 7 Ind.L.Rev. 925; Baker, Toward a Relaxed View of Federal Ancillary and Pendent Jurisdiction, 1972, 33 U.Pitt.L.Rev. 759; Note, The Res Judicata Implications of Pendent Jurisdiction, 1981, 66 Cornell L.Rev. 608; Comment, Pendent and Ancillary Jurisdiction: Towards a Synthesis of Two Doctrines, 1975, 22 U.C. L.A.L.Rev. 1263.

See also the literature on pendent parties, cited note 32 below.

The Supreme Court has twice found it unnecessary to decide whether there are any principled differences between "pendent jurisdiction," discussed in this section, and "ancillary jurisdiction," discussed in § 9 above. Aldinger v. Howard, 1976, 96 S.Ct. 2413, 2420, 427 U.S. 1, 13, 49 L.Ed.2d 276; Owen Equipment & Erection Co. v. Kroger, 1978, 98 S.Ct. 2396, 2401 n. 8, 437 U.S. 365, 370, n. 8, 57 L.Ed.2d 274. Yet it seems convenient to keep the terms separate, with pendent jurisdiction referring to those claims asserted by plaintiffs in their complaints, while ancillary jurisdiction is used to refer to the joinder, ordinarily by a party other than the plaintiff, of additional claims and parties after the complaint has been filed. See U. S. v. Pioneer Lumber Treating Co., D.C.Wash.1980, 496 F.Supp. 199, 201; Corporacion Venezolana de Fomento v. Vintero Sales Corp., D.C.N.Y.1979, 477 F.Supp. 615, 622 n. 13.

2. Osborn v. Bank of United States, 1824, 9 Wheat. 738, 823, 6 L.Ed. 204.

3. See § 107 below.

4. 1909, 29 S.Ct. 451, 213 U.S. 175, 53 L.Ed. 753.

case, even though it decided the Federal questions adversely to the party raising them, or even if it omitted to decide them at all, but decided the case on local or state questions only." [5] In fact the state regulation was held invalid on state grounds, and the Court declared this preferable to an unnecessary determination of federal constitutional questions. This rule, that the federal court need not, and perhaps should not, decide the federal issues but may resolve the case entirely on state grounds is not, as the Osborn rule was, a rule of necessity. It is, however, a useful rule. It avoids decision of constitutional questions where possible, and it permits one lawsuit, rather than two, to resolve the entire controversy.

Finally in Hurn v. Oursler [6] the Court extended this rule of "pendent jurisdiction," as it is usually known, to situations where decision of state issues must be justified solely on the ground of procedural convenience. In that case plaintiffs were claiming that defendants had incorporated an idea from a play written by plaintiffs and shown to defendants in a play that defendants later wrote. Plaintiffs sought to enjoin infringement of their copyrighted play, unfair competition in unauthorized use of the copyrighted play, and unfair competition through interference with plaintiffs' rights in an uncopyrighted version of the play. The trial court, finding no copyright infringement, dismissed the first claim on its merits and then dismissed the other two claims, which raised no federal question, for want of jurisdiction. The Supreme Court considered that the Siler rule applied. It measured the scope of federal jurisdiction in terms of the elusive concept of a "cause of action." If a plaintiff presented "two distinct grounds," one state and one federal, "in support of a single cause of action," the federal court had jurisdiction of the entire claim, but if plaintiff's assertions amounted to "two separate and distinct causes of action," there was jurisdiction only over the federal "cause of action." [7]

Applying this test, the Court held that the claim of unfair competition with regard to the copyrighted play arose from the same cause of action as the claim of infringement of the copyrighted play, and thus was within the pendent federal jurisdiction. The claim with regard to the uncopyrighted version of the play was held to involve a separate and distinct cause of action not within the pendent jurisdiction principle. This illustrates the difficulty of a test centering on so elastic a yardstick as the extent of a "cause of action." It could be reasonably argued that a single cause of action encompassed the right to protection of the play in all its versions.

---

5. 29 S.Ct. at 454–455, 213 U.S. at 191.

In Schmidt v. Oakland Unified Sch. Dist., 1982, 102 S.Ct. 2612, ___ U.S. ___, 73 L.Ed.2d 245, it was held to have been an abuse of discretion to decide a case on federal constitutional grounds when it might have been decided on a pendent state ground.

6. 1933, 53 S.Ct. 586, 289 U.S. 238, 77 L.Ed. 1148.

7. 53 S.Ct. at 589, 289 U.S. at 245–246.

The indefiniteness of the Hurn v. Oursler test created difficulties, and uncertainty in application, among the lower courts. A test based on the concept of "cause of action" inevitably became "the source of considerable confusion"[8] and the application it received in many lower court cases was, as the Court later said, "unnecessarily grudging."[9] Although the Hurn doctrine was purportedly codified in the 1948 Judicial Code, the statute created problems of its own rather than solving old problems.[10]

Thus the Court returned to the subject in 1966 in the case of United Mine Workers v. Gibbs.[11] Gibbs sued the union in federal court, alleging that the union had brought improper pressure on his employer to discharge him. He asserted both a federal claim of violation of the Taft-Hartley Act and a state claim of unlawful conspiracy to interfere with his contract of employment. After verdict for Gibbs, the trial court held that he had failed to establish his federal claim, but entered judgment for him on the basis of the state claim. The union argued that the court lacked jurisdiction to give judgment on the state claim, but the Supreme Court, though holding for the union on the merits, expressly decided that there was pendent jurisdiction to decide the state claim.

The Court discarded the test of Hurn v. Oursler, cast in terms of "cause of action", and held that as a matter of constitutional power pendent jurisdiction exists whenever the state and federal claims "derive from a common nucleus of operative fact" and are such that a plaintiff "would ordinarily be expected to try them all in one judicial proceeding."[12]

The Court distinguished sharply, however, between constitutional power and discretionary exercise of that power. Even before Gibbs, some lower courts had recognized a discretion in the trial judge to refuse to hear a pendent state claim after dismissal of the federal claim if judicial economy would not be served by hearing the state claim.[13] The Court in Gibbs broadened the discretion to refuse to

---

8. United Mine Workers v. Gibbs, 1966, 86 S.Ct. 1130, 1138, 383 U.S. 715, 724, 16 L.Ed.2d 218.

9. United Mine Workers v. Gibbs, 1966, 86 S.Ct. 1130, 1139, 383 U.S. 715, 725, 16 L.Ed.2d 218.

10. 28 U.S.C.A. § 1338(b): "The district court shall have original jurisdiction of any civil action asserting a claim of unfair competition when joined with a substantial and related claim under the copyright, patent or trade-mark laws." See Note, The Doctrine of Hurn v. Oursler and the New Judicial Code, 1952, 37 Iowa L.Rev. 406.

11. 1966, 86 S.Ct. 1130, 383 U.S. 715, 16 L.Ed.2d 218.

12. 86 S.Ct. at 1138, 383 U.S. at 725.

One commentator reads the requirements of a common nucleus of fact and that the claims would ordinarily be expected to be tried in a single proceeding as alternatives, either of which creates power to hear the claim. Baker, note 1 above, at 764–765. The courts and the other commentators regard these as cumulative requirements, both of which must be satisfied. E.g., ALI Study, p. 210; Ferguson v. Mobil Oil Corp., D.C.N.Y.1978, 443 F.Supp. 1334, 1340, affirmed C.A.2d, 607 F.2d 995.

13. "Where the federal element which is the basis for jurisdiction is disposed of early in the case, as on the pleadings, it smacks of the tail wagging the dog to continue with a federal hearing of the state claim." McFaddin Exp., Inc. v.

hear the pendent claim. The trial court, it said, should look to "considerations of judicial economy, convenience and fairness of litigants" in exercising its discretion, and should avoid needless decisions of state law.[14] It appeared to require dismissal of the state claim if the federal claim, though substantial enough to confer jurisdiction, were dismissed before trial.[15] Even if this were not the case, the state claim should be dismissed without prejudice if the state issues substantially predominate,[16] or if the possibility of jury confusion would justify separating the state and federal claims for trial.[17] The argument is stronger for retaining the state claim if it is closely tied to questions of federal policy,[18] as was true in Gibbs itself where the scope of the state claim was limited by the federal doctrine of preemption.[19] The question of power to hear the pendent claim, the Court said, should ordinarily be resolved on the pleadings, but the discretion whether to dismiss the state claim exists throughout the case.[20]

The commentators and the lower courts read Gibbs as broadening the scope of pendent jurisdiction, a development that some applaud and others deplore,[21] but it was not inevitable that this would be its effect. It did give a broader reading to constitutional power than Hurn v. Oursler did. At the same time its emphasis that power need not be exercised wherever it exists, and its list of factors that should

---

Adley Corp., C.A.2d, 1965, 346 F.2d 424, 427, certiorari denied 86 S.Ct. 643, 382 U.S. 1026, 15 L.Ed.2d 539. See also Massachusetts Universalist Convention v. Hildreth & Rogers Co., C.A.1st, 1950, 183 F.2d 497, 501, relying on the comprehensive concurring opinion of Judge Magruder in Strachman v. Palmer, C.A.1st, 1949, 177 F.2d 427, 431–434.

14. 86 S.Ct. at 1139, 383 U.S. at 726.

15. 86 S.Ct. at 1139, 383 U.S. at 726.

But in Rosado v. Wyman, 1970, 90 S.Ct. 1207, 1212–1214, 397 U.S. 397, 402–405, 25 L.Ed.2d 442, it was held that a federal court has discretion to decide a claim within its pendent jurisdiction after the claim that gives it jurisdiction has become moot. In that case the Court said that pendent jurisdiction is based on "the commonsense policy" of "the conservation of judicial energy and the avoidance of multiplicity of litigation." 90 S.Ct. at 1214, 397 U.S. at 405.

Cases in which jurisdiction of pendent claims was retained although the federal claim was dismissed without trial are cited in 13 Wright, Miller & Cooper, Jurisdiction § 3567 n. 35.

In Weaver v. Marine Bank, C.A.3d, 1982, 683 F.2d 744, the court relied on a state statute to remand a pendent state claim to state court, rather than dismiss the claim, where it was found that the federal court lacked jurisdiction of the federal claim on the basis of which the action had been commenced in federal court.

16. 86 S.Ct. at 1139, 383 U.S. at 726–727.

The state claim can also be left undecided if it is not pressed until too late in the proceeding. Mayor of City of Philadelphia v. Educational Equality League, 1974, 94 S.Ct. 1323, 1336, 415 U.S. 605, 627, 39 L.Ed.2d 630.

17. 86 S.Ct. at 1139, 383 U.S. at 727.

See also Moor v. County of Alameda, 1973, 93 S.Ct. 1785, 1799, 411 U.S. 693, 716–717, 36 L.Ed.2d 596.

18. 86 S.Ct. at 1139, 383 U.S. at 727.

19. 86 S.Ct. at 1140, 383 U.S. at 729.

20. 86 S.Ct. at 1139, 383 U.S. at 727.

21. Compare Notes, 1968, 81 Harv.L. Rev. 657, and 1966, 44 Texas L.Rev. 1631, both mildly applauding, with Shakman, The New Pendent Jurisdiction of the Federal Courts, 1968, 20 Stan.L.Rev. 262, strongly deploring.

induce a court in its discretion to dismiss the state claim, might well have meant that fewer state claims would be heard in federal court as pendent to a federal claim than was previously the case.[22]

In 1974, however, in Hagans v. Lavine [23] the court seemed to encourage hearing pendent claims. It said: "it is evident from Gibbs that pendent state law claims are not always, or even almost always, to be dismissed and not adjudicated. On the contrary, given advantages of economy and convenience and no unfairness to litigants, Gibbs contemplates adjudication of these claims." [24] The Court also indicated that the argument for hearing the pendent claim is much stronger where, instead of being a state-created claim, the pendent claim is a federal claim that is not independently within federal jurisdiction because the amount in controversy is insufficient.[25] Finally the Court held that if the federal claim that gives jurisdiction raises a significant constitutional issue, the interest in avoiding unnecessary decision of constitutional questions suggests that ordinarily it is preferable to dispose of the case, if possible, by deciding the pendent claim, whether state or federal, rather than resolving the constitutional issue.[26]

Gibbs had presented a classic illustration of pendent jurisdiction. There was one plaintiff, one defendant, and a federal claim joined with a state-created claim. Hagans, as has been seen, broadened the application of pendent jurisdiction to include a federal claim for which no amount in controversy was required joined with a second federal claim that did not satisfy the amount requirement. Presumably that kind of pendent jurisdiction will now fade away again, since a 1980 amendment removed the amount requirement from the general federal question statute.[27]

There has been another, quite surprising, expansion of pendent jurisdiction since Gibbs on which the last word has not yet been written. Until Gibbs it had always been understood that the same parties must be involved for pendent jurisdiction to be used.[28] In 1971, however, the Second Circuit led the way in holding that pendent jurisdiction would allow taking jurisdiction of a state claim against one party if it were related closely enough to a federal claim against another

---

22. Compare ALI Study, § 1313. Although this is properly said, id. at 210, to be "consistent with the holding" in Gibbs, it reflects a rather different approach than does the language in Gibbs. It would, as a matter of statute, limit the power to entertain a pendent claim more narrowly than does Gibbs, but at the same time would restrict the discretion to dismiss the claim if power to hear it exists.

23. 1974, 94 S.Ct. 1372, 415 U.S. 528, 39 L.Ed.2d 577. There is a scathing criticism of the decision in Seid, The Tail Wags the Dog: Hagans v. Lavine and

Pendent Jurisdiction, 1975, 53 J.Urban Law 1.

24. 94 S.Ct. at 1383, 415 F.2d at 545–546.

25. 94 S.Ct. at 1385, 415 U.S. at 548.

26. 94 S.Ct. at 1383–1384, 415 U.S. at 546–547.

27. See § 32 below.

28. E.g., Wojtas v. Village of Niles, C.A. 7th, 1964, 334 F.2d 797, certiorari denied 1965, 85 S.Ct. 655, 379 U.S. 964, 13 L.Ed.2d 558; Note, 1968, 81 Harv.L. Rev. 657, 662–664.

party, even though there was no independent jurisdictional base for the state claim.[29]

This concept of "pendent parties," as it quickly came to be called, found favor with other lower courts and with the commentators.[30] The Supreme Court, which had once considered the validity of the concept "a subtle and complex question" that it would not then decide,[31] returned to the subject in 1976 in Aldinger v. Howard.[32] That was a suit in which a civil rights claim against county officials was joined with a state law claim against the county itself. There was no independent basis of jurisdiction against the county, since there was no diversity between it and the plaintiff and a municipal corporation, such as a county, was not then regarded as a "person" against whom an action would lie under the Civil Rights Act of 1871, 42 U.S.C.A. § 1983.[33] Thus the county could be retained as a defendant only if the concept of "pendent parties" is valid.

The Supreme Court approached the issue guardedly and refused to "formulate any general, all-encompassing jurisdictional rule." [34] It discerned important differences between the traditional pendent jurisdiction situation and that in which it is sought to add a completely new party, but believed that ultimately the question must be decided "upon the deductions which may be drawn from congressional statutes as to whether Congress wanted to grant this sort of jurisdiction to federal courts." [35] Since the Court then thought that Congress had clearly excluded counties from liability in § 1983, the general jurisdictional statutes should not be read as bringing a county back in as a "pendent party." The Court recognized that other statutory grants and other alignments of parties and claims might call for a different result, and it concluded with two observations: "If the new party sought to be impleaded is not otherwise subject to federal juris-

29. Astor-Honor, Inc. v. Grosset & Dunlap, Inc., C.A.2d, 1971, 441 F.2d 627; Leather's Best, Inc. v. S. S. Mormaclynx, C.A.2d 1971, 451 F.2d 800.

30. Fortune, Pendent Jurisdiction—the Problem of "Pendenting Parties," 1972, 34 U.Pitt.L.Rev. 1; Note, 1976, 62 Va.L.Rev. 194; Comment, 1974, 20 Loy.L.Rev. 176; Comment, 1973, 73 Col.L.Rev. 153.

31. Moor v. County of Alameda, 1973, 93 S.Ct. 1785, 1797–1799, 411 U.S. 693, 713–715, 36 L.Ed.2d 596.

32. 1976, 96 S.Ct. 2413, 427 U.S. 1, 49 L.Ed.2d 276.

See Currie, Pendent Parties, 1978, 45 U.Chi.L.Rev. 753; Note, Pendent Party Jurisdiction—Forcing the "Subtle and Complex Issue," 1978, 11 Loy.—L.A.L. Rev. 659; Note, Pendent Party Jurisdiction: The Demise of a Doctrine?, 1978, 27 Drake L.Rev. 361; Note, The Concept of Law-Tied Pendent Jurisdic-

tion: Gibbs and Aldinger Reconsidered, 1978, 87 Yale L.J. 627; Comment, Aldinger v. Howard and Pendent Jurisdiction, 1977, 77 Col.L.Rev. 127.

33. In Monell v. New York City Dept. of Social Services, 1978, 98 S.Ct. 2018, 436 U.S. 658, 56 L.Ed.2d 611, the Court overruled an earlier decision and held that a municipal corporation could be a "person" and suable under 42 U.S.C.A. § 1983. "But Monell in no way qualifies the holding of Aldinger that the jurisdictional questions presented in a case such as this one are statutory as well as constitutional, a point on which the dissenters in Aldinger agreed with the Court." Owen Equipment & Erection Co. v. Kroger, 1978, 98 S.Ct. 2396, 2402 n. 12, 437 U.S. 365, 372 n. 12, 57 L.Ed.2d 274.

34. 96 S.Ct. at 2419, 427 U.S. at 13.

35. 96 S.Ct. at 2421, 427 U.S. at 17.

diction, there is a more serious obstacle to the exercise of pendent jurisdiction than if parties already before the court are required to litigate a state law claim. Before it can be concluded that such jurisdiction exists, a federal court must satisfy itself not only that Art. III permits it, but that Congress in the statutes conferring jurisdiction has not expressly or by implication negated its existence." [36] Though the cases are not yet numerous, it is far from clear that Aldinger has had any significant impact. Aldinger itself had hinted that the pendent party concept might well be proper where the federal claim is one of which the federal courts have exclusive jurisdiction, so that "the argument of judicial economy and convenience can be coupled with the additional argument that *only* in a federal court may all of the claims be tried together." [37] The lower courts have continued to allow the joinder of a pendent party in those exclusive jurisdiction situations,[38] but they have not confined it to those situations.[39]

If a state claim is properly within the pendent jurisdiction of the federal court, it should not be ground for objection that venue would not be proper if that claim were sued on alone, or that personal jurisdiction has been obtained only by virtue of a federal statute allowing nationwide service on the federal claim. As was seen earlier, however,[40] to date the cases are divided on this point.

If a court determines to exercise pendent jurisdiction over a state-created claim, state substantive law is controlling on the pendent claim.[41]

---

36. 96 S.Ct. at 2422, 427 U.S. at 18.

37. 96 S.Ct. at 2422, 427 U.S. at 18.

38. Ortiz v. United States Government, C.A.1st, 1979, 595 F.2d 65; Dick Meyers Towing Serv., Inc. v. U. S., C.A.5th, 1978, 577 F.2d 1023; Johnston v. U. S., D.C.Kan.1982, 546 F.Supp. 879; Dumansky v. U. S., D.C.N.J.1980, 486 F.Supp. 1078; Obenshain v. Halliday, D.C.Va.1980, 504 F.Supp. 946; Ausland v. U. S., D.C.S.D.1980, 488 F.Supp. 426; Pearce v. U. S., D.C.Kan.1978, 450 F.Supp. 613; Maltais v. U. S., D.C.N.Y. 1977, 439 F.Supp. 540.

The statement in Aldinger about exclusive jurisdiction cases was rejected as "dictum," however, and a contrary result reached, in Ayala v. U. S., C.A.9th, 1977, 550 F.2d 1196, 1200, certiorari dismissed 1978, 98 S.Ct. 1635, 435 U.S. 982, 56 L.Ed.2d 76. See also Lamb v. U. S., D.C.Ga.1981, 526 F.Supp. 1117.

39. North Dakota v. Merchants Nat. Bank & Trust Co., C.A.8th, 1980, 634

F.2d 368; Boudreaux v. Puckett, C.A. 5th, 1980, 611 F.2d 1028; Transok Pipeline Co. v. Darks, C.A.10th, 1977, 565 F.2d 1150, certiorari denied 1978, 98 S.Ct. 1876, 435 U.S. 1006, 56 L.Ed.2d 388; De Maio v. Consolidated Rail Corp., D.C.N.Y.1980, 489 F.Supp. 315; Ford Motor Co. v. Wallensius Lines, D.C.Va.1979, 476 F.Supp. 1362.

But see Shields v. Consolidated Rail Corp., D.C.N.Y.1981, 530 F.Supp. 400; Lincoln Mfg. Co., Inc. v. Stern, D.C.Ill. 1981, 515 F.Supp. 21; Jong-Yul Lim v. International Institute of Metropolitan Detroit, Inc., D.C.Mich.1981, 510 F.Supp. 722; Brame v. Ray Bills Fin. Corp., D.C.N.Y.1979, 85 F.R.D. 568, 591–596; Wesley v. John Mullins & Sons, Inc., D.C.N.Y.1978, 444 F.Supp. 117.

40. See § 9 above.

41. Gibbs, 86 S.Ct. at 1139, 383 U.S. at 726.

§ 20. "Protective Jurisdiction"

As is seen elsewhere, in one well-known case three members of the Supreme Court took the view, rejected however by the other six, that Article I of the Constitution empowers Congress to confer on "constitutional" federal courts powers beyond those defined in Article III.[1] Since the rejection of that theory, commentators have put forward, and some judges have endorsed, a more subtle theory that would reach the same result while purporting to respect the limits of Article III. The theory, popularly known as "protective jurisdiction," is that, with regard to subjects where Congress has legislative power, it can pass a statute granting federal jurisdiction and that the jurisdictional statute is itself a "law of the United States" within Article III, even though Congress has not enacted any substantive rule of decision and thus state law is to be applied.[2] The argument has been of particular consequence with regard to § 301 of the Taft-Hartley Act,[3] which grants jurisdiction of suits for violation of labor-management contracts in industries affecting interstate commerce, but does not set out any rules of decisions for such suits. That particular controversy has now been resolved. In the Lincoln Mills case[4] a majority of the Supreme Court read § 301 as requiring the federal courts, in such cases, to fashion and apply a federal common law of labor-management contracts. Though this interpretation poses its own difficulties,[5] it obviates any jurisdictional problem, since federal law then provides both the right and the remedy, and the case is one of true federal question jurisdiction. Prior to the Lincoln Mills decision, however, the First Circuit, assuming that state law was to govern at least some of the issues in a § 301 case, found the statute nevertheless to be a valid exercise of "protective jurisdiction."[6] In the Lincoln Mills case itself, two members of the Court rejected the view that federal law was to be applied, but concurred in the result uphold-

[§ 20]

1. National Mut. Ins. Co. of Dist. of Columbia v. Tidewater Transfer Co., 1949, 69 S.Ct. 1173, 337 U.S. 582, 93 L.Ed. 1556, discussed § 11 above and § 24 below.

2. Wechsler, Federal Jurisdiction and the Revision of the Judicial Code, 1948, 13 L. & Contemp.Prob. 216, 224–225; Mishkin, The Federal "Question" Jurisdiction of the District Courts, 1953, 53 Col.L.Rev. 157, 184–196. Professor Wechsler apparently would allow a grant of such "protective jurisdiction" wherever Congress has substantive legislative power, while Professor Mishkin would limit such jurisdiction to those areas of the law where Congress has an articulated and active policy regulating a field.

This concept is the basis for proposed legislation that would allow the federal courts to hear consumer class actions that are governed by state law. The jurisdictional implications are discussed in Note, Protective Jurisdiction and Adoption as Alternative Techniques for Conferring Jurisdiction on Federal Courts in Consumer Class Actions, 1971, 69 Mich.L.Rev. 710.

3. 29 U.S.C.A. § 185.

4. Textile Workers Union of America v. Lincoln Mills of Alabama, 1957, 77 S.Ct. 912, 353 U.S. 448, 1 L.Ed.2d 972.

5. See Bickel & Wellington, Legislative Purpose and the Judicial Process: The Lincoln Mills Case, 1957, 71 Harv.L. Rev. 1.

6. International Broth. of Teamsters v. W. L. Mead, Inc., C.A.1st, 1956, 230 F.2d 576, 580–581.

ing § 301 on the "protective jurisdiction" theory.[7] Justice Frankfurter, on the other hand, in a dissenting opinion that considers the precedents and the arguments at great length, asserted that " 'protective jurisdiction,' once the label is discarded, cannot be justified under any view of the allowable scope to be given to Article III. * * * The theory must have as its sole justification a belief in the inadequacy of state tribunals in determininig state law. The Constitution reflects such a belief in the specific situation within which the Diversity Clause was confined. The intention to remedy such supposed defects was exhausted in this provision of Article III." [8] Thus there is as yet no definitive answer as to the validity of the "protective jurisdiction" theory and it remains in the realm of speculation.

The argument for "protective jurisdiction" rests on Chief Justice Marshall's opinion in the Osborn case,[9] where he said that Congress could authorize a bank chartered by it to sue in federal court though only state issues were involved, and on the line of cases permitting a trustee in bankruptcy to pursue in federal court a private cause of action arising under and wholly governed by state law.[10] It is true that in those cases there is, in the background at least, some federal right, other than the bare right to sue in federal court. The bank's very existence was as a creature of federal law; in the bankruptcy cases the trustee is an officer of a federal court, and his ancillary suit is a part of the whole bankruptcy process, itself governed by federal law. Nevertheless attempts to distinguish Osborn and the bankruptcy cases do not seem entirely successful.[11] Despite this, it is difficult to believe that the Court, if clearly confronted with the question, would accept the commentators' proposals for "protective jurisdiction" when to do so would have such drastic consequences on the accepted understanding of Article III as a limitation on the federal courts.[12]

7. Justices Harlan and Burton, concurring in the result, 77 S.Ct. at 920, 353 U.S. at 460.

8. 77 S.Ct. at 930, 353 U.S. at 474–475.

9. Osborn v. Bank of the United States, 1824, 9 Wheat. 738, 6 L.Ed. 204. See § 17 above.

10. Schumacher v. Beeler, 1934, 55 S.Ct. 230, 293 U.S. 367, 79 L.Ed. 433; Williams v. Austrian, 1947, 67 S.Ct. 1443, 331 U.S. 642, 91 L.Ed. 1718.

11. In his Lincoln Mills dissent, where he makes an extended effort to distinguish the cases, Justice Frankfurter is forced to conclude that there are "some elements of analytical similarity" between the Osborn case and the case before him, and that the bankruptcy cases do show at least "a superficial analogy." 77 S.Ct. at 934, 353 U.S. at 481–482. See also his dissent in National Mut. Ins. Co. of Dist. of Columbia v. Tidewater Transfer Co., 1949, 69 S.Ct. 1173, 1198 n. 3, 337 U.S. 582, 652 n. 3, 93 L.Ed. 1556, where he offers what seems a somewhat different distinction of the bankruptcy cases.

12. "There is, however, a technical problem with the protective-jurisdiction theory: What is the federal law under which the case arises? The only federal law in the picture is the federal law creating federal jurisdiction. To say that a case arises under federal law whenever a federal statute gives jurisdiction is to destroy all limitations on federal jurisdiction." Currie, Federal Jurisdiction in a Nutshell, 2d ed. 1981, p. 103. See also Redish, Federal Jurisdiction: Tensions in the Allocation of Judicial Power, 1980, pp. 59–63.

In one case the Second Circuit upheld a grant of protective jurisdiction without discussing the constitutional question

§ 21. Criminal Prosecutions

The federal district courts are given by statute original jurisdiction, exclusive of the courts of the states, of all offenses against the laws of the United States.[1] Thus they always have jurisdiction where a federal offense is charged, and in some few instances have jurisdiction, by removal from state court, of state criminal prosecutions.[2]

In 1812 the Supreme Court held that there are no federal common law crimes.[3] Recent scholarly research suggests considerable doubt about whether this holding was in accord with the intent of Congress when it passed the Judiciary Act of 1789,[4] but sound or unsound, the principle of no common law crimes is now well settled.[5] Since federal criminal prosecutions must, therefore, rest on an Act of Congress defining the crime, it is clear that all such cases "arise under" the laws of the United States, within the meaning of the constitutional grant of jurisdiction, and the state criminal prosecutions that come to the federal courts on removal do so because the circumstances under which the statutes provide for removal are enough to raise a federal question, within the meaning of the constitutional language even if not within the usual original federal question jurisdiction.[6]

Although the federal courts have exclusive jurisdiction of federal criminal prosecutions, the same act may constitute a federal crime and a state crime. In such a situation the offender may be prosecuted by both sovereigns, at least under the decisions to date.[7]

The federal statutes, notably in Title 18 of the United States Code, define a great many offenses that are crimes against the United States,[8] and criminal cases occupy much of the attention of the dis-

this raised. Ives v. W. T. Grant Co., C.A.2d 1975, 522 F.2d 749, noted 1976, 89 Harv.L.Rev. 998. In a later case the same court held that insofar as the Foreign Sovereign Immunities Act of 1976, 28 U.S.C.A. § 1330(a), purports to grant federal courts jurisdiction of a suit by an alien against a foreign state, when the governing law is not federal law, it is unconstitutional, since the "arising under" language of Article III, § 2, must be limited to cases arising under federal substantive law. Verlinden B. V. v. Central Bank of Nigeria, C.A.2d, 1981, 647 F.2d 320, certiorari granted 1982, 102 S.Ct. 997, ___ U.S. ___, 71 L.Ed.2d 291.

[§ 21]

1. 18 U.S.C.A. § 3231.

2. 28 U.S.C.A. §§ 1441, 1442a, 1443. In the year ended June 30, 1981, there were 22 criminal cases removed from state court to federal court. Ann.Rep. of the Director of the Administrative Office of the United States Courts, 1981, Table D–2.

3. U. S. v. Hudson & Goodwin, 1812, 7 Cranch 32, 3 L.Ed. 259. See also U. S. v. Collidge, 1816, 1 Wheat. 415, 4 L.Ed. 124.

4. Warren, New Light on the History of the Federal Judiciary Act of 1789, 1923, 37 Harv.L.Rev. 49, 73; 2 Crosskey, Politics and the Constitution in the History of the United States, 1953, pp. 763–784.

5. E.g., U. S. v. Eaton, 1892, 12 S.Ct. 764, 144 U.S. 677, 36 L.Ed. 591; U. S. v. George, 1913, 33 S.Ct. 412, 228 U.S. 14, 57 L.Ed. 712.

6. Tennessee v. Davis, 1879, 100 U.S. 257, 25 L.Ed. 648.

7. Bartkus v. Illinois, 1959, 79 S.Ct. 676, 359 U.S. 121, 3 L.Ed.2d 684; Abbate v. U. S., 1959, 79 S.Ct. 666, 359 U.S. 187, 3 L.Ed.2d 729; U. S. v. Nelligan, C.A. 5th, 1978, 573 F.2d 251.

8. See Schwartz, Federal Criminal Jurisdiction and Prosecutors' Discretion, 1948, 13 Law & Contemp.Prob. 64.

trict courts.[9] Special provision is made in the statutes for crimes committed on the high seas or in territories which are under the exclusive jurisdiction of the United States and where, therefore, there is no state criminal code to cover ordinary offenses.[10] A special District of Columbia Code performs the same function for that area. Further the so-called Assimilative Crimes Act, first adopted in 1825, provides that in areas within a state subject to federal jurisdiction if an act is committed that would be a crime by state law, it is also a crime by federal law.[11]

§ 22. Civil Actions to Which the United States Is a Party [1]

The most frequent litigant in the courts of the United States is the United States. It is a party in more than one-third of the civil cases in the district courts.[2]

If the United States is plaintiff to an action, there are no jurisdictional difficulties. The Constitution defines the judicial power as extending to "Controversies to which the United States shall be a Party," and a statute grants jurisdiction, except as otherwise provided, in "all civil actions, suits or proceedings commenced by the United States, or by any agency or officer thereof expressly authorized to sue by Act of Congress." [3]

The United States Code is filled with sections authorizing federal litigation in various kinds of cases, but the government can sue even if there is no specific authorization. In such cases, however, it must have some interest to be vindicated sufficient to give it standing. It cannot lend its name to a suit merely for the benefit of some private individual.[4] It is not required, however, that the government's interest be pecuniary or proprietary. "The obligations which it is under to promote the interest of all, and to prevent the wrongdoing of one resulting in injury to the general welfare, is often of itself sufficient to

9. In the year ended June 30, 1981, there were 30,355 criminal cases commenced in the district courts, as against 180,576 civil cases. Ann.Rep. of the Director of the Administrative Office of the United States Courts, 1981, Tables C–2, D–2.

10. 18 U.S.C.A. § 7.

11. 18 U.S.C.A. § 13. See U. S. v. Sharpnack, 1958, 78 S.Ct. 291, 355 U.S. 286, 2 L.Ed.2d 282, upholding the 1948 revision of this statute by which a continuing conformity to state law, rather than the assimilation of state law as of the date of enactment of the federal statute, is provided.

[§ 22]

1. 14 Wright, Miller & Cooper, Jurisdiction §§ 3651–3659.

2. In the year ended June 30, 1981, 180,576 civil cases were commenced in the district courts. The United States was a party plaintiff in 37,598 of these cases and defendant in 24,247 cases. Ann.Rep. of the Director of the Administrative Office of the U.S. Courts, 1981, Table C–2.

3. 28 U.S.C.A. § 1345. It was once argued that the United States could not sue for damages for wrongs done to it, and was confined to criminal proceedings against the wrongdoer, but this view was rejected in Cotton v. U. S., 1850, 11 How. 229, 13 L.Ed. 675.

4. U. S. v. San Jacinto Tin Co., 1888, 8 S.Ct. 850, 125 U.S. 273, 31 L.Ed. 747; U. S. v. Kuehn, C.A.7th, 1977, 562 F.2d 427.

give it a standing in court." [5]   If suit by the United States is expressly authorized by Act of Congress, there is no problem of standing; Congress has power to authorize the United States to be guardian of the public interest by bringing suit.[6]

The jurisdiction of the district courts in cases instituted by the United States is generally concurrent with the state courts, though if such actions are commenced in state court they may be removed by a nonresident defendant to federal court.[7] Suits involving seizures, or to recover fines, penalties, or forfeitures incurred under any Act of Congress, are exclusively in the jurisdiction of the district courts.[8]

Although it is commonly said that when the United States sues, it comes into court on an equality with private litigants,[9] in fact it en-

---

5. In re Debs, 1894, 15 S.Ct. 900, 906, 158 U.S. 564, 584, 39 L.Ed. 1092. See also Wyandotte Transp. Co. v. U. S., 1967, 88 S.Ct. 379, 389 U.S. 191, 19 L.Ed.2d 407; U. S. v. American Bell Tel. Co., 1888, 9 S.Ct. 90, 97, 128 U.S. 315, 367–368, 32 L.Ed. 450; U. S. v. Arlington County, C.A.4th, 1964, 326 F.2d 929, noted 1964, 64 Col.L.Rev. 951; Note, Nonstatutory Executive Authority to Bring Suit, 1972, 85 Harv.L.Rev. 1566.

It has been held that the United States has standing to seek to enjoin the practice of "sewer service," by which defendants bring state court actions against delinquent debtors and obtain default judgments on the basis of affidavits falsely reciting that service has been made. U. S. v. Brand Jewelers, Inc., D.C.N.Y.1970, 318 F.Supp. 1293, noted 1971, 37 Brooklyn L.Rev. 426, 84 Harv.L.Rev. 1930, 46 N.Y.U.L.Rev. 367, 20 J.Pub.L. 337, 24 Van.L.Rev. 829, 17 Wayne L.Rev. 1287, 1971 Wis. L.Rev. 665. The court based standing on the authority of the United States to remove large-scale burdens on interstate commerce and on the authority to correct wide-spread deprivations, by what amounts to state action, of the right not to be deprived of property without due process of law.

It has also been held that the United States has standing to seek invalidation of state miscegenation statutes, U. S. v. Brittain, D.C.Ala.1970, 319 F.Supp. 1658, to prevent a city from taxing property owned by a foreign government when the tax would violate a treaty obligation of the United States. U. S. v. City of Glen Cove, D.C.N.Y.1971, 322 F.Supp. 149, affirmed C.A.2d, 1971, 450 F.2d 884, and to protect national security, U. S. v. Marchetti, C.A.4th, 1972, 466 F.2d

1309, certiorari denied 1973, 93 S.Ct. 553, 409 U.S. 1063, 34 L.Ed.2d 516.

A more restrictive view has been taken in recent cases holding that in the absence of statutory authorization the United States lacks standing to sue to protect the constitutional rights of mentally retarded individuals in state mental hospitals. U. S. v. Mattson, C.A.9th, 1979, 600 F.2d 1295; U. S. v. Solomon, C.A.4th, 1977, 563 F.2d 1121. This result was changed by statute in 1980. 42 U.S.C.A. § 1997. It has been held also that the United States lacks standing to challenge allegedly unconstitutional practices of a city police department. U. S. v. City of Philadelphia, C.A.3d, 1980, 644 F.2d 187.

See generally Note, Fourteenth Amendment rights of Action in Favor of the United States, 1981, 61 B.U.L.Rev. 1159.

6. U. S. v. Raines, 1960, 80 S.Ct. 519, 526, 362 U.S. 17, 27, 4 L.Ed.2d 524 (civil rights action); U. S. Fidelity & Guar. Co. v. U. S., for Benefit of Kenyon, 1907, 27 S.Ct. 381, 204 U.S. 349, 51 L.Ed. 516 (suit in the name of the United States by a materialman on the bond of a contractor for public works).

7. 28 U.S.C.A. § 1441. See § 38 below.

It has been pointed out that the limitation that only a nonresident can remove makes no sense. Hart & Wechsler, The Federal Courts and the Federal System, Bator, Mishkin, Shapiro & Wechsler ed. 1973, p. 1294 n. 6.

The American Law Institute proposes not to allow removal of actions commenced by the United States in a state court. ALI Study, p. 257.

8. 28 U.S.C.A. §§ 1355, 1356.

9. E.g., Brent v. Bank of Washington, 1836, 10 Pet. 596, 614, 9 L.Ed. 547; U.

joys a number of advantages, both statutory and court-made,[10] of which perhaps the most important is that it is not bound by statutes of limitations save as Congress may have imposed them.[11] In 1966 a statute was enacted for the first time providing a general statute of limitations applicable to most actions brought by the United States or by a federal officer or agency.[12] Other statutory restrictions that would bar suit by a private litigant are held not to apply if suit is by the United States.[13]

More difficult problems arise when the United States is named as a party defendant, for such litigation is involved with the mysteries of sovereign immunity, and with a curiously conceptual approach to the nature of the jurisdiction.

It is now well settled—though for a century the rule was stated only in dicta—that the United States may not be sued without its consent.[14] Want of consent is a fundamental defect that may be asserted at any time, and that is not subject to estoppel.[15] If Congress has in fact consented to a particular kind of suit, the stated rule long has been that the consent is to be strictly interpreted,[16] but in recent years the Court has regarded the defense of sovereign immunity with

S. v. Stinson, 1905, 25 S.Ct. 426, 426–427, 197 U.S. 200, 205, 49 L.Ed. 724.

10. 14 Wright, Miller & Cooper, Jurisdiction § 3652. For example, the United States is given extra time to file an answer, Fed.R.Civ.Proc. 12(a), and to take an appeal, Fed.R.App.Proc. 4(a). Only recently was provision made for taxation of costs against the United States and the statute limits the taxable costs. 28 U.S.C.A. § 2412; 10 Wright & Miller, Civil § 2672. The United States enjoys special evidentiary privileges. 8 Wright & Miller, Civil § 2019. In a rescission action the United States is not required to make tender. Causey v. U. S., 1916, 36 S.Ct. 365, 240 U.S. 399, 60 L.Ed. 711. Fees and mileage need not be tendered to a witness subpoenaed on behalf of the United States or an officer or agency thereof. 28 U.S.C.A. § 1825; Fed.R. Civ.Proc. 45(c); Fed.R.Crim.Proc. 17(d).

11. U. S. v. Summerlin, 1940, 60 S.Ct. 1019, 310 U.S. 414, 84 L.Ed. 1283; Guaranty Trust Co. of New York v. U. S., 1938, 58 S.Ct. 785, 304 U.S. 126, 82 L.Ed. 1224.

12. 28 U.S.C.A. §§ 2415, 2416.

13. Department of Employment v. U. S., 1966, 87 S.Ct. 464, 466–467, 385 U.S. 355, 357–358, 17 L.Ed.2d 414 (Tax Injunction Act, 28 U.S.C.A. § 1341, inapplicable); Leiter Minerals, Inc. v. U. S., 1957, 77 S.Ct. 287, 352 U.S. 220, 1 L.Ed.2d 267 (Anti-Injunction Act, 28 U.S.C.A. § 2283, inapplicable).

14. U. S. v. Clarke, 1834, 8 Pet. 436, 444, 8 L.Ed. 1001; U. S. v. Tillou, 1867, 6 Wall. 484, 18 L.Ed. 920; U. S. v. Lee, 1882, 1 S.Ct. 240, 106 U.S. 196, 27 L.Ed. 171; Cunningham v. Macon & B. Ry. Co., 1883, 3 S.Ct. 292, 109 U.S. 446, 27 L.Ed. 992; Kansas v. U. S., 1907, 27 S.Ct. 388, 204 U.S. 331, 51 L.Ed. 510; Ickes v. Fox, 1937, 57 S.Ct. 412, 300 U.S. 82, 81 L.Ed. 525; Larson v. Domestic & Foreign Commerce Corp., 1949, 69 S.Ct. 1457, 337 U.S. 682, 93 L.Ed. 1628; U. S. v. Mitchell, 1980, 100 S.Ct. 1349, 445 U.S. 535, 63 L.Ed.2d 607.

15. Minnesota v. U. S., 1939, 59 S.Ct. 292, 305 U.S. 382, 83 L.Ed. 235; U. S. v. Rochelle, C.A.5th, 1966, 363 F.2d 225; Mellos v. Brownell, C.A.D.C.1958, 250 F.2d 35.

16. E.g., U. S. v. Sherwood, 1941, 61 S.Ct. 767, 771, 312 U.S. 584, 590, 85 L.Ed. 1058; Schillinger v. U. S., 1894, 15 S.Ct. 85, 86, 155 U.S. 163, 166, 39 L.Ed. 108.

"disfavor," [17] and has viewed more liberally waivers of such immunity.[18]

Over the years Congress has successively broadened the consent of the United States to be sued. The Court of Claims was created in 1855 to determine money claims against the government founded on Acts of Congress, or regulations of executive departments, or express or implied contracts with the government.[19] This jurisdiction was expanded in 1887 by the passage of the Tucker Act, which grants jurisdiction additionally in cases founded upon the Constitution, and in cases for damages, not sounding in tort, in respect of which the plaintiff would be entitled to redress in a civil action or in admiralty if the United States were suable.[20] Jurisdiction under the Tucker Act is in the Court of Claims or, if the claim does not exceed a certain amount, now $10,000, in the district court.

In 1946 the Federal Tort Claims Act was adopted.[21] Though it contains many exceptions, it recognizes the general principle that the United States should be liable for the negligence of government employees if a private person would be liable under the same circumstances.[22] Jurisdiction under this act is exclusively in the district courts.

In addition to the three statutes discussed, there are a great many other statutes, of less general import, by which the United States has consented to be sued.[23]

There is some authority holding that if the United States has brought an action, defendant may not assert a counterclaim, even

17. FHA v. Burr, 1940, 60 S.Ct. 488, 490, 309 U.S. 242, 245, 84 L.Ed. 724.

18. U. S. v. Yellow Cab Co., 1951, 71 S.Ct. 399, 404, 340 U.S. 543, 550, 95 L.Ed. 523. But see McMahon v. U. S., 1951, 72 S.Ct. 17, 19, 342 U.S. 25, 27, 96 L.Ed. 673.

19. Act of Feb. 24, 1855, 10 Stat. 612. See 17 Wright, Miller & Cooper, Jurisdiction § 4101.

20. Act of Mar. 3, 1887, 24 Stat. 505. For the present provisions of the Tucker Act, see 28 U.S.C.A. §§ 1346(a)(2), 1491. See 14 Wright, Miller & Cooper, Jurisdiction § 3657.

The Tucker Act is a jurisdictional statute only, and does not create any substantive right enforceable against the United States for money damages. U. S. v. Mitchell, 1980, 100 S.Ct. 1349, 449 U.S. 535, 63 L.Ed.2d 607, rehearing denied 100 S.Ct. 2979, 446 U.S. 992, 64 L.Ed. 2d 849.

21. Act of Aug. 2, 1946, Title IV, 60 Stat. 812, 842. The substantive grant of jurisdiction is now found in 28 U.S. C.A. § 1346(b). See also 28 U.S.C.A. §§ 1402(b), 1504, 2110, 2401, 2402, 2411, 2412, 2671–2680.

22. 14 Wright, Miller & Cooper, Jurisdiction § 3658.

23. 28 U.S.C.A. § 1346(a)(1) (suits to recover taxes); 46 U.S.C.A. §§ 741 et seq. (Suits in Admiralty Act); 46 U.S. C.A. §§ 781 et seq. (Public Vessels Act); 28 U.S.C.A. §§ 1347, 2409 (partition actions where United States is a tenant in common or joint tenant); 41 U.S.C.A. § 113(b) (suits on contracts); 28 U.S.C.A. § 1353 (rights to Indian lands); 42 U.S.C.A. § 405(c)(5)(g) (actions under Social Security Act). See 14 Wright, Miller & Cooper, Jurisdiction § 3656.

The United States has consented to be named as a party in affecting property on which it has a lien, 28 U.S.C.A. § 2410, but the statute is not a grant of jurisdiction and suit must be in state court unless there is some other basis of federal jurisdiction. See cases cited 14 Wright, Miller & Cooper, Jurisdiction § 3656 nn. 25–27.

though the counterclaim is such that an independent action on it could be brought against the United States.[24] The better view, supported by recent cases, is that if the government has waived immunity, it should make no difference whether the claim is brought as an independent action or asserted as a counterclaim.[25]

It would seem that there ought to be no jurisdictional difficulties if the United States has consented to be sued, since such cases appear to be within the constitutional definition, "Controversies to which the United States shall be a Party." So indeed the Court had said.[26] But in Williams v. United States [27] this natural reading was rejected, the judicial power was said to extend only to cases to which the United States is a party plaintiff, and suits against the government were regarded as not exercises of the constitutional judicial power at all. Some of the difficulties of this position have already been explored.[28] In particular, even if it be accepted that the clause of the Judiciary Article dealing with cases to which the United States is a party is inapplicable, cases under the Tucker Act, the Tort Claims Act, and similar legislation would seem to be cases "arising under" the laws of the United States, and thus within the constitutional judicial power.[29] Despite the conceptual difficulties introduced by the Williams opinion, the courts have not hesitated to accept jurisdiction of suits against the United States if consent has been given.[30]

There is no statute granting jurisdiction generally over actions against federal officers and agencies, and such actions must find independent grounds for jurisdiction.[31] Section 10 of the Administrative Procedure Act [32] was held not to be a grant of subject-matter

24. E.g., U. S. v. Patterson, C.A.5th, 1953, 206 F.2d 345; In re Greenstreet, Inc., C.A.7th, 1954, 209 F.2d 660; and cases cited 6 Wright & Miller, Civil § 1427 n. 10.

25. E.g., Frederick v. U. S., C.A.5th, 1967, 386 F.2d 481; U. S. v. Springfield, C.A.5th, 1960, 276 F.2d 798, 803–804; U. S. v. Silverton, C.A.1st, 1952, 200 F.2d 824; City of Newark v. U. S., C.A.3d, 1958, 254 F.2d 93; Thompson v. U. S., C.A.4th, 1957, 250 F.2d 43, 44; U. S. v. Summ, D.C.N.J. 1968, 282 F.Supp. 628; U. S. v. Southern Pac. Co., D.C.Cal.1962, 210 F.Supp. 760; U. S. v. Capital Transit Co., D.C. D.C.1952, 108 F.Supp. 348; and see 6 Wright & Miller, Civil § 1427, pp. 143–145.

See also § 79 below, discussing whether a claim otherwise barred by sovereign immunity, the statute of limitations, or some other reason can be used defensively in an action by the United States.

26. Minnesota v. Hitchcock, 1902, 22 S.Ct. 650, 654, 185 U.S. 373, 384, 46 L.Ed. 954.

This was also the view of Justice Harlan in the plurality opinion in Glidden Co. v. Zdanok, 1962, 82 S.Ct. 1459, 1480, 370 U.S. 530, 564, 8 L.Ed.2d 671.

27. 1933, 53 S.Ct. 751, 289 U.S. 553, 77 L.Ed. 1372.

28. See § 11 above.

29. The Court did not consider this possibility in the Williams case. Justice Jackson attempted to meet this argument in National Mut. Ins. Co. of Dist. of Columbia v. Tidewater Transfer Co., Inc., 1949, 69 S.Ct. 1173, 1178 n. 22, 337 U.S. 582, 93 L.Ed. 1556. See the contrary view of Justice Rutledge in the same case, 69 S.Ct. at 1187, 337 U.S. at 610.

30. See ALI Study, pp. 260–261.

31. 14 Wright, Miller & Cooper, Jurisdiction § 3655.

32. 5 U.S.C.A. §§ 701–706.

jurisdiction.[33] A suit against an officer in his official capacity will ordinarily arise under the Constitution or laws of the United States, but until recently 28 U.S.C.A. § 1331 required that more than $10,000 be in controversy.[34] Even if that requirement were satisfied, suit would often be barred by sovereign immunity. When property rights of the government are challenged, the Court, despite strong scholarly criticism,[35] has been firmly committed to the doctrine that suits, though in form against the officer, are in reality against the United States and thus barred by sovereign immunity,[36] except in the unlikely circumstance that the officer named as defendant is exceeding his statutory powers in holding the property or that his statutory powers are constitutionally void.

A 1962 statute eased the situation somewhat by granting the district courts original jurisdiction of any action in the nature of mandamus to compel an officer or employee of the United States or any agency thereof to perform a duty owed to the plaintiff.[37] Jurisdiction under the statute is "intricate, if not mazelike." [38] Although the statute led to decentralization of some kinds of litigation, including suits involving water rights, mineral rights, and grazing permits, most courts have allowed what has been called "mandamus medievalism" [39] to limit its application and it has not made significant inroads on sovereign immunity.[40]

Important changes were made, however, in 1976. Since that year no amount in controversy has been required in actions brought under

33. Califano v. Sanders, 1977, 97 S.Ct. 980, 430 U.S. 99, 51 L.Ed.2d 192.

34. See § 32 below.

35. Cramton, Nonstatutory Review of Federal Administrative Action: The Need for Statutory Reform of Sovereign Immunity, Subject Matter Jurisdiction, and Parties Defendant, 1970, 68 Mich.L.Rev. 387; Byse, Proposed Reforms in Federal "Nonstatutory" Judicial Review: Sovereign Immunity, Indispensable Parties, Mandamus, 1962, 75 Harv.L.Rev. 1479; Davis, Suing the Government by Falsely Pretending to Sue an Officer, 1962, 29 U.Chi.L.Rev. 435; Jaffe, Suits Against Governments and Officers, 1963, 77 Harv.L.Rev. 1, 209.

36. Larson v. Domestic & Foreign Commerce Corp., 1949, 69 S.Ct. 1457, 337 U.S. 682, 93 L.Ed. 1628; Malone v. Bowdoin, 1962, 82 S.Ct. 980, 369 U.S. 643, 8 L.Ed.2d 168; Dugan v. Rank, 1963, 83 S.Ct. 999, 372 U.S. 609, 10 L.Ed.2d 15; Hawaii v. Gordon, 1963, 83 S.Ct. 1052, 373 U.S. 57, 10 L.Ed.2d 191. Since the passage of the Tucker Act in 1887, compensation is now available if the officer has taken property that belongs to the plaintiff, and thus it is held that he is not acting unconstitutionally in holding the property. On this ground the once-leading case of U. S. v. Lee, 1882, 1 S.Ct. 240, 106 U.S. 196, 27 L.Ed. 171, which permitted an action of ejectment against the officer, is of no current relevance, since it was decided prior to enactment of the Tucker Act.

37. 28 U.S.C.A. § 1361, added by Act of Oct. 5, 1962, Pub.L. 87–748, § 1(a), 76 Stat. 744. The same act made liberal provisions for venue and service of process in actions against federal agencies, officers, and employees. 28 U.S.C.A. § 1391(e). See Cates, Venue in Corporate Suits against Federal Agencies and Officers, 1975, 60 Minn.L.Rev. 81.

38. Estate of Watson v. Blumenthal, C.A.2d, 1978, 586 F.2d 925, 934.

39. Davis, Administrative Law of the Seventies, 1976, p. 543.

40. Doe v. Civiletti, C.A.2d, 1980, 635 F.2d 88, 94. See 14 Wright, Miller & Cooper, Jurisdiction § 3655, pp. 189–202; French, The Frontiers of the Federal Mandamus Statute, 1976, 21 Vill.L.Rev. 637.

28 U.S.C.A. § 1331 against the United States, any agency thereof, or any officer or employee sued in his official capacity.[41] The same act amended 5 U.S.C.A. § 702 to provide that an action "seeking relief other than money damages and stating a claim that an agency or officer or employee thereof acted or failed to act in an official capacity or under color of legal authority shall not be dismissed nor relief therein be denied on the ground that it is against the United States or that the United States is an indispensable party." This is a waiver of sovereign immunity for nonstatutory review in suits brought under 28 U.S.C.A. § 1331.[42] The waiver does not apply to suits for money damages,[43] nor does it confer authority to grant relief if any other statute that grants consent to suit expressly or impliedly forbids the relief that is sought.[44]

§ 22A. Civil Rights Cases [1]

Almost all of this book is immediately relevant to civil rights cases. However they have become such an important, controversial, and distinctively federal class of cases that some of their major features will be pointed out here, with more detailed discussion, when it is appropriate, in other sections.

Although the principal civil rights statutes go back to the Reconstruction period, for many years they were rarely used.[2] This situation has changed dramatically in the last two decades. In 1961 there

---

41. 28 U.S.C.A. § 1331(a), as amended by Act of Oct. 21, 1976, Pub.L. 94–574, 90 Stat. 2721. Section 1331 was amended again in 1980 to remove the requirement of amount in controversy in all cases brought under the section. See § 32 below.

42. Warin v. Director, Dept. of Treasury, C.A.6th, 1982, 672 F.2d 590, citing cases to the same effect from the Third, Fifth, and Ninth Circuits.

Contra: Estate of Watson v. Blumenthal, C.A.2d, 1978, 586 F.2d 925, 932.

43. Laguna Hermosa Corp. v. Martin, C.A.9th, 1981, 643 F.2d 1376.

44. 5 U.S.C.A. § 702.

Thus the statute cannot be used to avoid the limitation in the Tucker Act that the Court of Claims has exclusive jurisdiction of contract claims for more than $10,000. Sea-Land Serv. Inc. v. Brown, C.A.3d, 1979, 600 F.2d 429, 432; American Science & Engineering Inc. v. Califano, C.A.1st, 1978, 571 F.2d 58.

[§ 22A]

1. 13 Wright, Miller & Cooper, Jurisdiction § 3573; Koury, Section 1983 and Civil Comity: Two for the Federalism Seesaw, 1979, 25 Loy.L.Rev. 659;

Schnapper, Civil Rights Litigation After Monell, 1979, 79 Col.L.Rev. 213; Glennon, Constitutional Liberty and Property: Federal Common Law and Section 1983, 1978, 51 So.Cal.L.Rev. 355; Yudof, Liability for Constitutional Torts and the Risk-Averse Public School Official, 1976, 49 So.Cal.L.Rev. 1322; Bristow, § 1983: An Analysis and Suggested Approach, 1975, 29 Ark. L.Rev. 255; McCormack, The Expansion of Federal Question Jurisdiction and the Prisoner Complaint Caseload, 1975 Wis.L.Rev. 523; McCormack, Federalism and Section 1983: Limitations on Judicial Enforcement of Constitutional Protections, 1974, 60 Va.L.Rev. 1, 250; Developments in the Law—Section 1983 and Federalism, 1977, 90 Harv.L.Rev. 1133.

2. Of the most important of the civil rights statutes, 42 U.S.C.A. § 1983, it has been said: "United States Code Annotated notes only 19 decisions under the section in its first 65 years on the statute books." Note, Limiting the Section 1983 Action in the Wake of Monroe v. Pape, 1969, 82 Harv.L.Rev. 1486 n. 4.

were 296 civil rights cases filed in federal courts, or barely half of one percent of all the civil cases commenced in that year.[3] In 1981, by contrast, there were 16,473 civil rights cases filed by federal and state prisoners (not including habeas corpus, motions to vacate, and similar attacks on a criminal conviction itself), and 15,419 civil rights cases by persons other than prisoners. Taken together these were more than one sixth of the civil cases commenced in that year.[4]

This tremendous increase in civil rights litigation is the result of several factors. In the first place, the time was ripe for it. The Supreme Court in interpreting the Constitution and Congress in legislating were broadening the categories of civil rights to which all persons are entitled, and, through holdings that various portions of the Bill of Rights are applicable to the states by virtue of the Fourteenth Amendment, the Court was expanding the rights enforceable against the states.

The other principal factor is a series of Supreme Court decisions removing what had been thought to be barriers against litigation under the Reconstruction civil rights statutes. The key case was Monroe v. Pape,[5] decided in 1961. It held that persons were acting "under color of" state law, and could be sued under 42 U.S.C.A. § 1983, although their acts were not authorized by the state and indeed were forbidden by the state. The net effect of Monroe, and of other important cases that have followed it, is that the door to the federal court is now open to those who think they have been denied federally-secured rights by persons acting under state law.[6] During the same period the Court has also been willing to imply a remedy for those denied constitutional rights under color of federal law.[7]

Other statutes with origins in Reconstruction have recently been revitalized and have significant uses today.[8] There are also impor-

3. Ann.Rep. of the Director of the Administrative Office of the U. S. Courts, 1961, Table C 2.

4. Ann.Rep. of the Director of the Administrative Office of the U. S. Courts, 1981, Tables 20, 21, 29.

5. 1961, 81 S.Ct. 473, 365 U.S. 167, 5 L.Ed.2d 492.

6. Although the Supreme Court has referred to § 1983 as providing "a uniquely federal remedy," Mitchum v. Foster, 1972, 92 S.Ct. 2151, 2160, 407 U.S. 225, 239, 32 L.Ed.2d 705, it is settled that a § 1983 action can be brought in state court. Martinez v. California, 1980, 100 S.Ct. 553, 558 n. 7, 444 U.S. 277, 283 n. 7, 62 L.Ed.2d 481.

7. The leading case is Bivens v. Six Unknown Named Agents of Federal Bureau of Narcotics, 1971, 91 S.Ct. 1999, 403 U.S. 388, 29 L.Ed.2d 619, on remand C.A.2d, 1972, 456 F.2d 1339, im-

plying a right of action for damages against federal officers for violation of the Fourth Amendment. A 1974 statute made the Federal Tort Claims Act applicable to such torts by federal investigative or law enforcement officers. 28 U.S.C.A. § 2680(h).

A victim of sex discrimination has a right of action for damages implied from the equal protection component of the due process clause of the Fifth Amendment. Davis v. Passman, 1979, 99 S.Ct. 2264, 442 U.S. 228, 60 L.Ed.2d 846.

An implied remedy is available for an alleged violation of Eighth Amendment rights even though the Federal Tort Claims Act provides a statutory remedy. Carlson v. Green, 1980, 100 S.Ct. 1468, 446 U.S. 14, 64 L.Ed.2d 15.

8. 42 U.S.C.A. § 1981 (equal rights under the law). See Runyon v. McCrary,

tant modern provisions, most of which come from the Civil Rights Act of 1964 and later statutes. Vital as these other statutes are, however, they take second place to 42 U.S.C.A. § 1983, the text of which is set out in the margin.[9] It and its jurisdictional counterpart, 28 U.S.C.A. § 1343(a), are derived from § 1 of the Ku Klux Klan Act of 1871.[10] Although Professor Chafee thought § 1983 an "unintelligible statute" and considered it "very queer to try to protect human rights in the middle of the Twentieth Century by a left-over from the days of General Grant," [11] endless pages of United States Reports have been filled with examination of the legislative history of the 1871 statute and of its codification in the Revised Statutes in 1874, and the answers that various majorities of the Court have found in these sources define the application today of the principal statute for the protection of civil rights.

Section 1983 provides a remedy for "any citizen of the United States or other person within the jurisdiction thereof." Thus it is available to all persons, whether they are citizens or not.[12]

The defendant in a § 1983 action must be a "person," and this has been construed as a term of art. In Monroe v. Pape it was first held, on the basis of the 1871 enactment, that a municipal corporation is not a "person" in this sense.[13] In 1978, however, in Monell v. Department of Social Services,[14] the Court reexamined the legislative history of the 1871 law, and concluded that its previous reading of that history had been erroneous.

1976, 96 S.Ct. 2586, 427 U.S. 160, 49 L.Ed.2d 415; Developments in the Law—Section 1981, 1980, 15 Harv.C. R.–C.L.L.Rev. 29.

42 U.S.C.A. § 1982 (property rights of citizens). See Jones v. Alfred H. Mayer Co., 1968, 88 S.Ct. 2186, 392 U.S. 409, 20 L.Ed.2d 1189.

42 U.S.C.A. § 1985 (conspiracy to interfere with civil rights). See Griffin v. Breckenridge, 1971, 91 S.Ct. 1790, 403 U.S. 88, 29 L.Ed.2d 338; Note, The Scope of Section 1985(3) Since Griffin v. Breckenridge, 1977, 45 Geo.Wash.L. Rev. 239.

9. "Every person who, under color of any statute, ordinance, regulation, custom, or usage, of any State or Territory or the District of Columbia, subjects, or causes to be subjected, any citizen of the United States or other person within the jurisdiction thereof to the deprivation of any rights, privileges, or immunities secured by the Constitution and laws, shall be liable to the party injured in an action at law, suit in equity, or other proper proceeding for redress. For the purposes of this section, any Act of Congress applicable exclusively to the District of Columbia shall be considered to be a statute of the District of Columbia." This is 42 U.S.C.A. § 1983 as it was amended in 1979 by the addition of the second sentence and the reference to the District of Columbia in what is now the first sentence.

10. Act of April 20, 1871, § 1, 17 Stat. 13. The 1871 statute was in turn derived from § 2 of the Civil Rights Act of 1866, 14 Stat. 27.

11. Chafee, Safeguarding Fundamental Human Rights, 1959, 27 Geo.Wash. L.Rev. 519, 526, 529.

12. Hague v. CIO, 1939, 59 S.Ct. 954, 307 U.S. 496, 83 L.Ed. 1423.

13. 81 S.Ct. at 484–486, 365 U.S. at 187–192.

14. 1978, 98 S.Ct. 2018, 436 U.S. 658, 56 L.Ed.2d 611. See Schnapper, note 1 above; Blum, From Monroe to Monell: Defining the Scope of Municipal Liability in Federal Courts, 1978, 51 Temp. L.Q. 409.

Under Monell a local government can be sued for monetary, declaratory, or injunctive relief, but only if the action that is alleged to be unconstitutional implements or executes "a policy statement, ordinance, regulation, or decision officially adopted and promulgated" by the officers of the corporation or has been taken "pursuant to governmental 'custom' even though such a custom has not received formal approval through the body's official decisionmaking channels." [15] A municipality "cannot be held liable *solely* because it employs a tortfeasor—or, in other words, a municipality cannot be held liable under § 1983 on a *respondeat superior* theory." [16]

Even after Monell a state may not be made a defendant in a § 1983 action. Wholly aside from whether it could be regarded as a "person," a state is protected by the Eleventh Amendment.[17]

For a person to be liable under § 1983 he must have acted under color of state law, or, in the more precise statutory term, "under color of any statute, ordinance, regulation, custom, or usage" of a state, territory, or the District of Columbia. It has been held that "custom, or usage" requires state involvement and is not simply a practice that reflects long-standing social habits, generally observed by the people in a locality. The custom or usage "must have the force of law by virtue of the persistent practices of state officials." [18]

Commonly the defendants in § 1983 actions will be municipal corporations or state or local officials exercising the authority of the state, but the statute is not limited to these bodies or functionaries. A private person who is a willful participant in a joint activity with the state is acting under color of state law.[19] As pointed out earlier, the major turning point in the construction of § 1983 came when Monroe v. Pape held that an action is "under color of" law even though it has not been authorized by the state and is indeed prohibit-

---

15. 98 S.Ct. at 2036, 436 U.S. at 690–691. See Note, Municipal Liability Under Section 1983: The Meaning of "Policy or Custom," 1979, 79 Col.L. Rev. 304.

16. 98 S.Ct. at 2036, 436 U.S. at 691 (emphasis in original). See Comment, Section 1983 Municipal Liability and the Doctrine of Respondeat Superior, 1979, 46 U.Chi.L.Rev. 935.

17. Quern v. Jordan, 1979, 99 S.Ct. 1139, 440 U.S. 332, 59 L.Ed.2d 358.

Local government units that are considered part of the state for Eleventh Amendment purposes also are protected. Monell, 98 S.Ct. at 2035 n. 54, 436 U.S. at 690, n. 54.

18. Adickes v. S. H. Kress & Co., 1970, 90 S.Ct. 1598, 1613, 398 U.S. 144, 167, 26 L.Ed.2d 142.

19. Lugar v. Edmondson Oil Co., 1982, 102 S.Ct. 2744, 2756, ___ U.S. ___, ___, 73 L.Ed.2d 482.

This is so even if the state official with whom private persons have conspired is a judge who is protected by judicial immunity. Dennis v. Sparks, 1980, 101 S.Ct. 183, 449 U.S. 24, 66 L.Ed.2d 185. See Note, Section 1983 Liability of Private Actors Who Conspire With Immune State Officials, 1980, 80 Col.L. Rev. 802.

But a warehouseman's proposed private sale of goods entrusted to him for storage, as permitted by the self-help provisions of the New York Uniform Commercial Code, was not "state action" as required for a federal civil rights action, absent any allegation of the participation of public officials. Flagg Bros., Inc. v. Brooks, 1978, 98 S.Ct. 1729, 436 U.S. 149, 56 L.Ed.2d 185.

ed by the state. Section 1983 reaches those "who carry a badge of authority of a State and represent it in some capacity, whether they act in accordance with their authority or misuse it." [20]

Section 1983 provides a remedy for deprivation of "any rights, privileges, or immunities secured by the Constitution and the laws * * *." Of course not every right is a product of the federal Constitution or laws, and those rights that come from the states, rather than from the federal government, are not properly the subject of a § 1983 action.[21]

The jurisdictional counterpart of § 1983, 28 U.S.C.A. § 1343(a)(3), does not use the broad term, "the laws," used in the substantive statute. It speaks instead of "any Act of Congress providing for equal rights of citizens or of all persons within the jurisdiction of the United States." Thus it was held that the Social Security Act is not a statute "providing for equal rights of citizens" and that § 1343(3) did not grant jurisdiction of a claim of deprivation of rights under the Act.[22] One year later, however, it was held that "the laws" in § 1983 is to be interpreted according to its plain language and that the substantive statute includes all federal statutes, rather than merely civil rights or equal protection laws. On this reasoning it was held that a claim under the Social Security Act comes within § 1983 although not within the jurisdictional statute, 28 U.S.C.A. § 1343(3).[23]

The significance of this was that § 1343(3) grants jurisdiction without regard to amount in controversy.[24] A suit under the Social Security Act itself, or under the Act as one of "the laws" referred to in § 1983, could have been brought in federal court under the general federal question statute, 28 U.S.C.A. § 1331, but until 1980 that statute required that more than $10,000 be in controversy, and this would

---

20. 81 S.Ct. at 476, 365 U.S. at 172.

A bare majority of the Court has said: "If the challenged conduct of respondents constitutes state action as delimited by our prior decisions, then that conduct was also action under color of state law and will support a suit under § 1983." Lugar v. Edmondson Oil Co., 1982, 102 S.Ct. 2744, 2753, ___ U.S. ___, ___, 73 L.Ed.2d 482.

21. Baker v. McCollan, 1979, 99 S.Ct. 2689, 443 U.S. 137, 61 L.Ed.2d 433, on remand C.A.5th, 601 F.2d 903 (false arrest); Paul v. Davis, 1976, 96 S.Ct. 1155, 424 U.S. 693, 47 L.Ed.2d 405, rehearing denied 96 S.Ct. 2194, 425 U.S. 985, 48 L.Ed.2d 811 (defamation).

22. Chapman v. Houston Welfare Rights Organization, 1979, 99 S.Ct. 1905, 441 U.S. 600, 60 L.Ed.2d 508. How the language in the two statutes came to differ is elaborately discussed in several opinions in this case.

23. Maine v. Thiboutot, 1980, 100 S.Ct. 2502, 448 U.S. 1, 65 L.Ed.2d 555.

24. For many years the conventional wisdom, derived from a separate opinion of Justice Stone in Hague v. CIO, 1939, 59 S.Ct. 954, 965–971, 307 U.S. 496, 518–532, 83 L.Ed. 1423, had been that § 1343(3) could be used only for personal rights, such as the right to vote and the rights of free expression, that could not be valued in dollars, and that § 1331 must be used, and the amount requirement satisfied, if the party were claiming a property right that could be given a dollars-and-cents value. This distinction was rejected, and § 1343(3) held applicable to property rights as well as personal rights, in Lynch v. Household Fin. Corp., 1972, 92 S.Ct. 1113, 405 U.S. 538, 31 L.Ed.2d 424. See § 37 below.

rarely be true of social security claims. Now that an amount in controversy is no longer required under § 1331, the difference in language between the substantive and jurisdictional statutes on civil rights is no longer of importance.[25]

The basic purpose of a damages award under § 1983 is to compensate persons for injuries caused by the deprivation of constitutional rights. Thus the common law rules of damages are to be adapted as needed to provide fair compensation for injuries.[26] The Civil Rights Attorneys' Fees Awards Act of 1976 allows the court, in its discretion, to award a reasonable attorney's fee to the prevailing party in civil rights actions.[27]

Under another Reconstruction statute, 42 U.S.C.A. § 1988, whenever the civil rights statutes "are deficient in the provisions necessary to furnish suitable remedies," the courts are to look to state law "so far as the same is not inconsistent with the Constitution and laws of the United States." Thus state law is looked to in determining the applicable period of limitations for a § 1983 action [28] and in determining whether the action abates on the death of the plaintiff.[29]

In Monroe v. Pape the Court held that state judicial remedies need not be exhausted before bringing a § 1983 action,[30] and two years later it seemed to say that there is also no need to exhaust state ad-

---

25. The holding that § 1983 includes all federal statutes might have ended the much-litigated question whether a remedy can be implied from a federal statute that does not give one in terms, see § 17 above at notes 29–30, since it could have been said that § 1983 is an express congressional authorization of private suits under all federal laws. But it was subsequently held that if the remedial devices provided in a particular statute are sufficiently comprehensive, they may suffice to demonstrate congressional intent to preclude the remedy of suits under § 1983. Middlesex County Sewerage Authority v. National Sea Clammers Assn., 1981, 101 S.Ct. 2615, 2625–2627, 453 U.S. 1, 19–21, 69 L.Ed.2d 435. See also Jackson Transit Auth. v. Local Div. 1285, Amalgamated Transit Union, 1982, 102 S.Ct. 2202, 2210 n. 12, ___ U.S. ___, ___ n. 12, 72 L.Ed.2d 639.

26. Carey v. Piphus, 1978, 98 S.Ct. 1042, 435 U.S. 247, 55 L.Ed.2d 252. See Note, Damage Awards for Constitutional Torts: A Reconsideration After Carey v. Piphus, 1980, 93 Harv.L.Rev. 966.

Punitive damages cannot be recovered against a municipality in a § 1983 case.

City of Newport v. Fact Concerts, Inc., 1981, 101 S.Ct. 2748, 453 U.S. 247, 69 L.Ed.2d 616.

27. 42 U.S.C.A. § 1988. See Note, Attorneys' Fees under Federal Civil Rights Legislation, 1979, 24 Vill.L.Rev. 215.

An attorney's fee can be awarded against a state, Hutto v. Finney, 1978, 98 S.Ct. 2565, 437 U.S. 678, 57 L.Ed.2d 522, and can be awarded in state court litigation. Maine v. Thiboutot, 1980, 100 S.Ct. 2502, 448 U.S. 1, 65 L.Ed.2d 555.

28. Board of Regents v. Tomanio, 1980, 100 S.Ct. 1790, 446 U.S. 478, 64 L.Ed. 2d 440.

It is argued that the courts have misunderstood § 1988, and that it was intended to apply only to state-created claims removed to federal court under 28 U.S.C.A. § 1443, in Eisenberg, State Law in Federal Civil Rights Cases: The Proper Scope of Section 1988, 1980, 128 U.Pa.L.Rev. 499.

29. Robertson v. Wegmann, 1978, 98 S.Ct. 1991, 436 U.S. 584, 56 L.Ed.2d 554, on remand C.A.5th, 1979, 591 F.2d 1208.

30. 81 S.Ct. at 482, 365 U.S. at 183.

ministrative remedies.[31] Although the Court subsequently made flat statements that exhaustion of administrative remedies is not required, there was much voiced dissatisfaction with this rule both on the Court itself and in the lower courts.[32] The Court gave full consideration to the question in 1982 in Patsy v. Board of Regents of State of Florida,[33] and there reaffirmed the rule that exhaustion is not required.

Even state judicial remedies may be significant in another way. There are circumstances in which the remedy that a state provides for a deprivation of liberty or property is sufficient to satisfy the requirements of due process, so that the deprivation is not a violation of the Fourteenth Amendment and thus is not cognizable under § 1983.[34]

Many civil rights cases either arise out of or are related to prior litigation in state court. Some commentators had argued, and some lower courts had held, that the usual rules about the preclusive effect of state court judgments did not apply to § 1983 suits.[35] In 1980, in Allen v. McCurry,[36] the Court found that the legislative history of § 1983 "does not in any clear way suggest that Congress intended to repeal or restrict the traditional doctrines of preclusion." [37] All that Allen actually holds is that issue preclusion—or collateral estoppel, as it used to be called—applies if an issue actually decided after a full and fair hearing in state court is raised subsequently in a § 1983 action. That holding, as well as some of the questions about preclusion left open by Allen, is explored elsewhere.[38]

A judge is immune from civil liability for acts done in the course of his judicial function, and this rule is not changed by the civil rights statutes.[39] Prosecutors also are absolutely immune, at least so far as damages are concerned,[40] and a public defender does not act under color of state law, so that the question of immunity does not arise.[41] Members of a legislative body are absolutely immune so long as they

31. McNeese v. Board of Educ., 1963, 83 S.Ct. 1433, 373 U.S. 668, 10 L.Ed.2d 622.

32. 17 Wright, Miller & Cooper, Jurisdiction § 4233.

33. 1982, 102 S.Ct. 2557, __ U.S. __, 73 L.Ed.2d 172.

34. Parratt v. Taylor, 1981, 101 S.Ct. 1908, 451 U.S. 527, 68 L.Ed.2d 420; Ingraham v. Wright, 1977, 97 S.Ct. 1401, 430 U.S. 651, 51 L.Ed.2d 711. See Kirby, Demoting 14th Amendment Claims to State Torts, 1982, 68 A.B.A.J. 166.

35. See 18 Wright, Miller & Cooper, Jurisdiction § 4471.

36. 1980, 101 S.Ct. 411, 449 U.S. 90, 66 L.Ed.2d 308.

37. 101 S.Ct. at 417, 449 U.S. at 98–99.

38. See § 100A below.

39. Stump v. Sparkman, 1978, 98 S.Ct. 1099, 435 U.S. 349, 55 L.Ed.2d 331; cf. Supreme Court of Virginia v. Consumers Union of United States, 1980, 100 S.Ct. 1967, 446 U.S. 719, 64 L.Ed.2d 641.

See Way, A Call for Limits to Judicial Immunity: Must Judges Be Kings in Their Courts?, 1981, 64 Judicature 390; Block, Stump v. Sparkman and the History of Judicial Immunity, 1980 Duke L.J. 879.

40. Imbler v. Pachtman, 1976, 96 S.Ct. 984, 424 U.S. 409, 47 L.Ed.2d 128. See Note, Delimiting the Scope of Prosecutorial Immunity from Section 1983 Damage Suits, 1977, 52 N.Y.U.L.Rev. 173.

41. Polk County v. Dodson, 1981, 102 S.Ct. 445, __ U.S. __, 70 L.Ed.2d 509.

are acting in a legislative capacity.[42] With regard to officers of the executive branch, a qualified immunity is available in varying scope, the variation being dependent upon the scope of discretion and responsibilities of the office and all the circumstances as they reasonably appear at the time of the action on which liability is sought to be based.[43] In those situations, however, in which Monell allows suit against a municipal corporation, it cannot defend on the ground that the good faith of its officers would have given them a qualified immunity if suit had been against them.[44]

The Anti-Injunction Act provides that a federal court may not grant an injunction to stay proceedings in a state court "except as expressly authorized by Act of Congress."[45] It has been held that § 1983 actions come within that exception,[46] but in so holding the Court made it clear that "we do not question or qualify in any way the principles of equity, comity, and federalism that must restrain a federal court when asked to enjoin a state court proceeding."[47] Lower courts had held that the more specific statutory prohibitions against enjoining state tax collections or state rate proceedings[48] are applicable even to actions brought under § 1983, but the Supreme Court found it unnecessary to decide that question, holding instead that the principle of comity barred a civil rights suit against state tax officials.[49]

But an appointed defense attorney in a federal criminal prosecution has no immunity from a malpractice suit. Ferri v. Ackerman, 1979, 100 S.Ct. 402, 444 U.S. 193, 62 L.Ed.2d 355, on remand 1980, 411 A.2d 213, 488 Pa. 113.

42. Lake Country Estates, Inc. v. Tahoe Regional Planning Agency, 1979, 99 S.Ct. 1171, 440 U.S. 391, 59 L.Ed.2d 401.

43. Procunier v. Navarette, 1978, 98 S.Ct. 855, 434 U.S. 555, 55 L.Ed.2d 24; Wood v. Strickland, 1975, 95 S.Ct. 992, 420 U.S. 308, 43 L.Ed.2d 214; Scheuer v. Rhodes, 1974, 94 S.Ct. 1683, 416 U.S. 232, 40 L.Ed.2d 90.

See Freed, Executive Official Immunity for Constitutional Violations: An Analysis and a Critique, 1977, 72 Nw.U.L. Rev. 526; Kattan, Knocking on Wood: Some Thoughts on the Immunities of State Officials to Civil Rights Damage Actions, 1977, 30 Vand.L.Rev. 941.

44. Owen v. City of Independence, 1980, 100 S.Ct. 1398, 445 U.S. 622, 63 L.Ed. 2d 673. See Levinson, Suing Political Subdivisions in Federal Court: From Edelman to Owen, 1980, 11 U.Tol.L. Rev. 829.

45. 28 U.S.C.A. § 2283. See § 47 below.

46. Mitchum v. Foster, 1972, 92 S.Ct. 2151, 407 U.S. 225, 32 L.Ed.2d 705.

47. 92 S.Ct. at 2162, 407 U.S. at 243.

See the discussion of the abstention doctrines, in § 52 below, and of "Our Federalism," in § 52A below.

See also Rizzo v. Goode, 1976, 96 S.Ct. 598, 423 U.S. 362, 46 L.Ed.2d 561.

48. 28 U.S.C.A. §§ 1341, 1342. See § 51 below.

49. Fair Assessment in Real Estate Assn., Inc. v. McNary, 1981, 102 S.Ct. 177, 454 U.S. 100, 70 L.Ed.2d 271.

CHAPTER 4

DIVERSITY OF CITIZENSHIP

Analysis

§ 23. Justifications of Diversity Jurisdiction

Ever since the First Judiciary Act, the federal courts have had original jurisdiction of so-called diversity cases, those involving a controversy between citizens of different states or between a citizen of a state and an alien.[1] This jurisdiction is retained today, subject to a jurisdictional amount of $10,000, in 28 U.S.C.A. § 1332. As was seen in section 1, neither the debates of the Constitutional Convention nor the records of the First Congress shed any substantial light on why such jurisdiction was granted by the Constitution or why the First Congress exercised its option to vest such jurisdiction. The diversity jurisdiction was the object of attack during the ratification debates, and, in the view of one historian, "the most astounding thing

---

[§ 23]

1. See generally 13 Wright, Miller & Cooper, Jurisdiction § 3601.

A distinction may be drawn between cases involving citizens of different states, properly referred to as diversity cases, and cases between a citizen of a state and an alien, properly referred to as alienage cases. For most purposes the distinction is unimportant, and in this book, as in the literature generally, the two classes of cases will usually be dealt with under the general head of diversity.

The Foreign Sovereign Immunities Act of 1976, Pub.L. 94–583, 90 Stat. 2891, is based in part on the constitutional grant of jurisdiction of suits between citizens of a state and foreign states. 28 U.S.C.A. § 1332(a)(4) grants jurisdiction of suits by a foreign state as

plaintiff against citizens of a state or of different states. 28 U.S.C.A. § 1330 grants jurisdiction of cases against foreign states. Other provisions added to Title 28 by the 1976 Act are § 1391(f) (venue in suits against foreign states), § 1441(d) (removal of suits against foreign states), and §§ 1602–1611 (defining "foreign state" and specifying when a foreign state is immune from jurisdiction). See Kane, Suing Foreign Sovereigns, A Procedural Compass, 1982, 34 Stan.L.Rev. 385.

In the year ended June 30, 1981, of 180,576 civil cases commenced in district courts, 45,444 were based on diversity. More than one-third of these were automobile accident or similar personal injury cases. Ann.Rep. of the Director of the Administrative Office of the U. S. Courts, 1981, Table C–2.

* * * is not the vigor of the attack but the apathy of the defense." [2]

The traditional explanation of the diversity jurisdiction is a fear that state courts would be prejudiced against those litigants from out of state. This explanation has the weighty support of Marshall: "However true the fact may be, that the tribunals of the states will administer justice as impartially as those of the nation, to parties of every description, it is not less true that the Constitution itself either entertains apprehensions on this subject, or views with such indulgence the possible fears and apprehensions of suitors, that it has established national tribunals for the decision of controversies between aliens and a citizen, or between citizens of different states." [3] This explanation for the grant of diversity jurisdiction has been disputed. One scholar concludes that in the period prior to the drafting of the Constitution there is no evidence of such prejudice by state courts,[4] while others, surveying the same period, conclude that it cannot be said that local prejudice was inconsequential.[5]

It might be thought that the historical origins of a jurisdiction that has been employed steadily for almost two centuries would be a subject of interest only to antiquarians. With regard to diversity, however, time has only exacerbated the controversy stirred at the time of the ratification debates. Thus the late Justice Jackson declared shortly before his death that "in my judgment the greatest contribution that Congress could make to the orderly administration of justice in the United States would be to abolish the jurisdiction of the federal courts which is based solely on the ground that the litigants are citizens of different states." [6] Justice Frankfurter, a longtime foe of diversity,[7] has referred to "the mounting mischief inflicted on the federal judicial system by the unjustifiable continuance of diversity litigation." [8] For at least the last 50 years the desirability of diversity jurisdiction has stirred continuing debate in the law reviews and in the halls of Congress.

The conditions that existed, or were feared to exist, in 1789 are irrelevant in determining the continued necessity for diversity jurisdiction. As the protagonists in this continuing controversy have rec-

---

2. Friendly, The Historic Basis of Diversity Jurisdiction, 1928, 41 Harv.L.Rev. 483, 487.

3. Bank of the United States v. Deveaux, 1809, 5 Cranch 61, 87, 3 L.Ed. 38.

4. Friendly, note 2 above.

5. Yntema & Jaffin, Preliminary Analysis of Concurrent Jurisdiction, 1931, 79 U.Pa.L.Rev. 869, 876. See also Frank, Historical Bases of the Federal Judicial System, 1948, 13 Law & Contemp. Prob. 1.

6. Jackson, The Supreme Court in the American System of Government, 1955, p. 38.

7. Frankfurter, Distribution of Judicial Power Between United States and State Courts, 1928, 13 Corn.L.Q. 499; Frankfurter, A Note on Diversity Jurisdiction—In Reply to Professor Yntema, 1931, 79 U.Pa.L.Rev. 1097.

8. Lumbermen's Mut. Cas. Co. v. Elbert, 1954, 75 S.Ct. 151, 155, 348 U.S. 48, 54, 99 L.Ed. 59 (concurring opinion).

ognized, the decision to retain or abolish such jurisdiction today must depend on the utility of the jurisdiction in today's society.

There are limits to the area of debate, though they are not always made explicit by the debaters. Even those who call for the complete abolition of diversity jurisdiction would hardly support its abandonment where, as with the Federal Interpleader Act,[9] it is a convenient means of providing a federal forum for cases of which no state court could obtain jurisdiction. Again the abolitionists probably would agree to removal of a diversity case where there is an actual showing of prejudice or local influence against the litigant from out of state,[10] though experience under earlier statutes containing such a provision suggest that such a showing is nearly impossible to make.[11]

On the other hand, even the strongest supporters of the retention of diversity recognize that the statutory scheme may require revision to prevent abuses. The fact that a corporation could carry on most or all of its business in a particular state, but still resort to the federal courts for litigation simply because it was incorporated elsewhere, was recognized by all as an abuse,[12] and has been ended by the definition of corporate citizenship that Congress adopted in 1958.[13] The supporters of diversity are divided, however, on other reforms that seem clearly required. They do not agree on the desirability of closing the doors of the federal court to a suit by a citizen of the forum state against a nonresident.[14] There is not even unanimity on the

9. 28 U.S.C.A. § 1335. See § 74 below. See also the proposals of the American Law Institute to use diversity as a basis for providing a federal forum in cases involving parties in many different states, cases that otherwise could not be heard in any court, ALI Study, §§ 2371–2376. These proposals are critically discussed in Note, ALI Proposals To Expand Federal Diversity Jurisdiction: Solution to Multiparty, Multistate Controversies? 1964, 48 Minn. L.Rev. 1109, and in Currie, The Federal Courts and the American Law Institute, 1968, 36 U.Chi.L.Rev. 1, 29–32.

10. See Ball, Revision of Federal Diversity Jurisdiction, 1933, 28 Ill.L.Rev. 356; Wechsler, Federal Jurisdiction and the Revision of the Judicial Code, 1948, 13 L. & Contemp.Prob. 216, 234–240.

11. Such provisions, dating back to the Act of March 2, 1867, 14 Stat. 558, were eliminated as unnecessary in the 1948 revision of the Judicial Code. The removal because of local prejudice in City of Detroit v. Detroit City Ry., C.C. Mich.1893, 54 F. 1, was on highly unusual facts.

12. The abuse was dramatized by Black & White Taxicab & Transfer Co. v.

Brown & Yellow Taxicab & Transfer Co., 1928, 48 S.Ct. 404, 276 U.S. 518, 72 L.Ed. 681, where a Kentucky corporation, simply by reincorporating in Tennessee, was able to gain access to federal court and thus, under the Swift v. Tyson rule, avoid Kentucky decisions which would have been unfavorable to its monopolistic designs.

13. 28 U.S.C.A. § 1332(c), as amended by Act of July 25, 1958, § 2, 72 Stat. 415. See § 27 below. For the purpose of the statute, see 13 Wright, Miller & Cooper, Jurisdiction § 3624. But see Phillips & Christensen, Should Corporations Be Regarded as Citizens Within the Diversity Jurisdiction Provisions?, 1962, 48 A.B.A.J. 435, which expresses some skepticism as to the 1958 amendment and argues against any further limitation on diversity with regard to corporations.

14. This is favored by Marbury, Why Should We Limit Federal Jurisdiction?, 1960, 46 A.B.A.J. 379, but opposed by Farage, Proposed Code Will Emasculate Diversity Jurisdiction, April/May 1966, Trial Magazine, p. 30, and Moore & Weckstein, Diversity Jurisdiction: Past, Present and Future, 1964, 43 Texas L.Rev. 1, 33–34, among others.

need to abolish the rule by which diversity is artificially created through the appointment of an out-of-state administrator or guardian to bring suit on behalf of one local person against another local person.[15]

Within the limits thus defined, the battle rages furiously. Some say diversity must go,[16] others argue for its retention,[17] while a third group says that it must be severely limited. The limitation usually proposed in the past has been that jurisdiction be denied where a citizen of a state is suing a corporation doing business in that state on a claim arising out of the corporation's activity in the state,[18] but one

15. Abolition of this rule is favored by Moore & Weckstein, note 14, above, at 35, but strongly opposed by Farage, note 14 above, at p. 20.

The rule is discussed in §§ 29, 31 below.

16. Ball, Revision of Federal Diversity Jurisdiction, 1933, 28 Ill.L.Rev. 356; Bork, Dealing with the Overload in Article III Courts, 1976, 70 F.R.D. 231, 236–237; Bratton, Diversity Jurisdiction: An Idea Whose Time Has Passed, 1976, 51 Ind.L.J. 347; Currie, The Federal Courts and the American Law Institute, 1968, 36 U.Chi.L.Rev. 1, 4–49; Frankfurter, Distribution of Judicial Power Between United States and State Courts, 1928, 13 Corn.L.Q. 499; Frankfurter, A Note on Diversity Jurisdiction—In Reply to Professor Yntema, 1931, 79 U.Pa.L.Rev. 1097; Haynsworth, Book Review, 1974, 87 Harv.L.Rev. 1082, 1089–1091; Hunter, Federal Diversity Jurisdiction: The Unnecessary Precaution, 1978, 46 UMKC L.Rev. 347; Jackson, The Supreme Court in the American System of Government, 1955, p. 38; Kastenmeier & Remington, Court Reform and Access to Justice: A Legislative Perspective, 1979, 16 Harv.J.Legis. 301, 311–318; Kurland, The Distribution of Judicial Power Between National and State Courts, 1958, 8 U.Chi.Law School Record 145; Rowe, Abolishing Diversity Jurisdiction: Positive Side Effects and Potential for Further Reforms, 1979, 92 Harv.L.Rev. 963; Sheran & Isaacman, State Cases Belong In State Courts, 1978, 12 Creighton L.Rev. 1; Wechsler, Federal Jurisdiction and the Revision of the Judicial Code, 1948, 13 L. & Contemp.Probs. 216, 234–240.

See also Feinberg, J., concurring in American Institute of Chemical Engineers v. Reber-Friel Co., C.A.2d, 1982, 682 F.2d 382, 392.

17. Brown, The Jurisdiction of the Federal Courts Based on Diversity of Citizenship, 1929, 78 U.Pa.L.Rev. 179; Farage, Proposed Code Will Emasculate Diversity Jurisdiction, April/May 1966, Trial Magazine, p. 30; Frank, The Case for Diversity Jurisdiction, 1979, 16 Harv.J.Legis. 403; Frank, For Maintaining Diversity Jurisdiction, 1963, 73 Yale L.J. 7; Howland, Shall Federal Jurisdiction of Controversies Between Citizens of Different States Be Preserved?, 1932, 18 A.B.A.J. 499; Marbury, Why Should We Limit Federal Diversity Jurisdiction?, 1960, 46 A.B. A.J. 379; Moore & Weckstein, Diversity Jurisdiction: Past, Present and Future, 1964, 43 Texas L.Rev. 1; Parker, The Federal Jurisdiction and Recent Attacks Upon It, 1932, 18 A.B.A.J. 433; Parker, Dual Sovereignty and the Federal Courts, 1956, 51 Nw.U.L.Rev. 407; Phillips & Christensen, Should Corporations Be Regarded as Citizens Within the Diversity Jurisdiction Provisions?, 1962, 48 A.B.A.J. 435; Wright, The Federal Courts and the Nature and Quality of State Law, 1967, 13 Wayne L.Rev. 317; Yntema, The Jurisdiction of the Federal Courts in Controversies Between Citizens of Different States, 1933, 19 A.B.A.J. 71, 149, 265.

18. Clark, Diversity of Citizenship Jurisdiction of the Federal Courts, 1933, 19 A.B.A.J. 499; Comment, Limiting Jurisdiction of Federal Courts—Comment by Members of Chicago University Law Faculty, 1932, 31 Mich.L.Rev. 59. This is apparently also the view of George Cochran Doub, though, after rejecting the conventional justifications of diversity, he is not explicit as to how much of the jurisdiction he would retain. See Doub, Time for Re-Evaluation: Shall We Curtail Diversity Jurisdiction?, 1958, 44 A.B.A.J. 243; Doub, The Federal Diversity Jurisdiction, 1959, 45 A.B.A.J. 1273.

The proposal with regard to corporations was originally put forward by Attor-

writer suggests barring from federal court all personal injury cases that arise solely under state law,[19] another would limit the jurisdiction to controversies between citizens and foreign states or foreign nations—alienage cases—and statutory interpleader actions,[20] and a third would allow each district to decide by local rule whether to eliminate or restrict diversity jurisdiction in that district.[21]

For a time the focus of the recent debate had been the recommendations made by the American Law Institute in its Study of Division of Jurisdiction between State and Federal Courts. These were a rather complex series of proposals that would have expanded jurisdiction in some respects but curtailed it in many more; the net effect would have been to reduce the volume of diversity litigation about in half. In particular, an individual who resides in a state or has his principal place of business there would not have been permitted to invoke diversity jurisdiction in that state, nor would a corporation or partnership with a "local establishment" in the state have been allowed to invoke diversity jurisdiction in an action arising out of activities of that establishment. These recommendations are based on the principle that "the function of the jurisdiction is to assure a high level of justice to the traveler or visitor from another state; when a person's involvement with a state is such as to eliminate any real risk of prejudice against him as a stranger and to make it unreasonable to heed any objection he might have to the quality of its judicial system, he should not be permitted to choose a federal forum, but should be required to litigate in the courts of the state."[22] This rationale, and the detailed recommendations based on it, were heavily attached and no longer figure significantly in the diversity debate.[23]

ney General William D. Mitchell, in the early '30s, as an alternative to the bill then sponsored by Senator Norris to abolish diversity jurisdiction entirely.

19. Meador, A New Approach to Limiting Diversity Jurisdiction, 1960, 46 A.B.A.J. 383.

20. Friendly, Federal Jurisdiction: A General View, 1973, pp. 139–152.

21. Shapiro, Federal Diversity Jurisdiction: A Survey and a Proposal, 1977, 91 Harv.L.Rev. 317. See also Bumiller, Choice of Forum in Diversity Cases: Analysis of a Survey and Implications for Reform, 1980, p. 29.

One district has taken a long step in this direction. It has announced that its judges are not able to try promptly all cases filed, and has divided cases into priority groups. The fourth and lowest priority is for cases that can be brought in either state or federal court, in which the court identifies FELA cases, diversity cases, and general federal question cases, "particularly civil rights cases brought under 42

U.S.C. § 1983." The court then speaks favorably of the willingness and ability of the state judges to try diversity cases. District of Minnesota, Policy Statement, Aug. 19, 1977.

22. ALI Study, p. 2.

Since the present author was one of the Reporters for the ALI Study, it is proper to note that he joined the Study after its work on diversity was virtually completed, and that he did not participate in the formulation of the diversity proposals. See Wright, Restructuring Federal Jurisdiction: The American Law Institute Proposals, 1969, 25 Wash. & Lee L.Rev. 185, 204.

23. The ALI proposals are criticized in the articles cited note 16 above by Currie and note 17 above by Farage, Frank, Moore & Weckstein, and Judge Wright. They are defended by Professor Richard H. Field, the Chief Reporter for the ALI Study, in Field, Diversity of Citizenship: A Response to Judge Wright, 1967, 13 Wayne L.Rev. 489. There is also an interesting debate be-

The arguments against diversity are not in themselves of great force. They rest primarily on the congestion that diversity cases are thought to cause for the federal courts, and on the inappropriateness of asking federal judges to decide these cases when, under the rule of Erie Railroad Co. v. Tompkins,[24] they are obliged to apply state law and thus are plunged into difficult questions on which only the state courts can speak authoritatively. It is thought, too, that judicial and legislative authority should be coextensive, and that for federal courts to decide cases arising under state law is an undesirable interference with state autonomy.[25] Finally it is said that the continuation of diversity jurisdiction diminishes the incentives and energies for reforming state courts of those influential groups who, by virtue of the diversity litigation, are able to avoid the state courts.[26] Though each of these arguments has force, they would not, singly or together, make a case for the abolition of diversity jurisdiction if that jurisdiction in fact serves some useful purpose in a federal system. Here is the crux of the controversy. Is there any continuing justification for diversity?

It is remarkable how little justification is offered in the literature, even by those who are friendly to diversity jurisdiction. This jurisdiction "is at least as traditionally federal as the Flag and the 4th of

tween Professor Field and John P. Frank in 1965, 17 S.C.L.Rev. 669. The present author, though having reservations about some aspects of the proposals, had urged their adoption. See Wright, note 21 above. However, the passage of time persuaded him that a more complete abolition of diversity is needed.

See generally Burdick, Diversity Jurisdiction under the American Law Institute Proposals: Its Purpose and Its Effect on State and Federal Courts, 1971, 48 N.D.L.Rev. 1.

For the view that time has passed the ALI proposals by, see Note, Eliminating Diversity Jurisdiction: A Short-Term Solution to a Long-Term Problem, 1978, 8 U.Tol.L.Rev. 896, 911–912.

24. 1938, 58 S.Ct. 817, 304 U.S. 64, 82 L.Ed. 1188.

On this particular phase of the argument, each side has sought to have it both ways. Prior to the Erie decision in 1938, the federal courts were free to apply "federal common law", see § 54 below, and this in itself was thought an argument against diversity jurisdiction. On the other hand, prior to 1938 the defenders of diversity argued that this very freedom of the federal courts led to a desirable uniformity of law,

while since 1938 they have been saying that diversity is harmless since state law is applied.

Judge J. Skelly Wright, in the article cited note 17 above, recognizes the difficulties that the Erie doctrine creates for diversity litigation. He suggests that this might be avoided by having Congress enact "if constitutionally permissible, a unitary federal substantive rule to govern every transaction and lawsuit, no matter where it arises or in what court, state or federal." 13 Wayne L.Rev. at 334.

See Hertz, Misreading the Erie Signs: The Downfall of Diversity, 1973, 61 Ky.L.J. 861.

25. ALI Study, p. 99.

A study of decisions in one circuit concludes that diversity jurisdiction is not in fact an intrusion on state autonomy because the state courts pay little heed, one way or the other, to federal decisions about state law. Note, The Effect of Diversity Jurisdiction on State Litigation, 1965, 40 Ind.L.J. 566.

26. See Frankfurter, J., concurring in Lumbermen's Mut. Cas. Co. v. Elbert, 1954, 75 S.Ct. 151, 158, 348 U.S. 48, 60, 99 L.Ed. 59.

See also ALI Study, pp. 458–459.

July," [27] and many of the writers who support diversity content themselves with asserting that the burden of proof is on those who would limit or abolish the jurisdiction.[28] This, of course, avoids, if indeed it does not beg, the key question of what utility diversity has today. Others of the defenders of diversity do undertake to justify its present value, but their arguments to this effect rarely rise beyond the level of mere assertion. Professor Yntema, himself friendly to diversity, wrote 30 years ago: "The theoretical arguments in favor of the maintenance of the federal diverse-citizenship jurisdiction, like the theories to the contrary which have just been considered, suffer from incomplete analysis of the problem and are in large part based upon general assumptions which have not been sufficiently verified." [29] This observation remains true today. It is necessary, therefore, to make an independent examination of the arguments that may justify retention of diversity jurisdiction.

The traditional explanation for the creation of diversity jurisdiction is, as has been seen, a fear that state courts would be prejudiced against those from out-of-state. Some of the defenders of diversity assert that such prejudice continues to be a danger.[30] But in a society infinitely more mobile than that of 1789, it is difficult to believe that prejudice against a litigant, merely because he is a citizen of a different state, is a significant factor. Juries may, regrettably, be subject to many kinds of prejudice. Race, religion, appearance, wealth, city as against country, home town as against another part of the state—all these are factors that may sway a jury. If litigants subject to any or all of these prejudices must take their chances with a state court, it is hard to defend provision of a federal forum to protect a person against such prejudice as may still be felt merely because the litigant is a citizen of another state.

27. Frank, Federal Diversity Jurisdiction—An Opposing View, 1965, 17 S.C.L.Rev. 677, 682.

28. This position is explicitly taken in the articles by Howland and by Marbury, cited note 17 above. It is also put forward by Frank, and by Moore & Weckstein, in their articles cited note 17 above, but those writers do not rest their case on this argument alone.

29. Yntema, The Jurisdiction of the Federal Courts in Controversies Between Citizens of Different States, 1933, 19 A.B.A.J. 71, 75.

30. See the articles by Brown and by Parker, cited note 17 above. A more sophisticated statement of the bias argument is advanced in ALI Study, pp. 105–110, to justify so much of the jurisdiction as it is there proposed to retain.

The scanty empirical evidence is inconclusive on the extent to which fear of prejudice is a factor in the decision to seek a federal forum. One study finds that it is a factor in only 4.3% of cases taken to federal court. Summers, Analysis of Factors that Influence Choice of Forum in Diversity Cases, 1962, 47 Iowa L.Rev. 933, 937–938. In another survey, however, 60.3% of the attorneys responding indicated that local prejudice against an out-of-state plaintiff is a factor leading to preference for a federal court when representing a plaintiff. Note, The Choice between State and Federal Court in Diversity Cases in Virginia, 1965, 51 Va. L.Rev. 178, 179. See also Goldman & Marks, Diversity Jurisdiction and Local Bias: A Preliminary Empirical Inquiry, 1980, 9 J.Leg.Studies 93.

Another argument, with respectable historical antecedents,[31] is that diversity jurisdiction is necessary in order to implement the constitutional guarantee that "the citizens of each State shall be entitled to all the privileges and immunities of citizens of the several States." [32] This argument has been characterized as "specious," [33] on the ground that abridgment of the privileges and immunities clause is in itself sufficient for federal question jurisdiction, and that diversity jurisdiction is not needed for this purpose.   In this connection, it is worthy of note that other federal systems have flourished without a diversity jurisdiction.

Another argument, again going back to Hamilton,[34] is that the federal courts are so much better than the state courts that it is desirable to channel as many cases as possible to federal court, or at least that those from out-of-state, who have no opportunity to work for the improvement of the state courts, should be spared from exposure to them.[35] There may be merit to this argument. Federal judges enjoy life tenure, they are free to comment on the evidence, and they sit with juries selected from a broader geographical area.[36] Not all lawyers would agree, however, that these differences lead to better justice, and though the prestige of the federal courts has generally been high, there have been long periods when these very procedural differences have led to suspicion of the federal courts as rich

---

31. See Hamilton in The Federalist No. 80, at 502, Wright ed. 1961. Perhaps this is the argument Justice Wayne had in mind when he wrote, in Dodge v. Woolsey, 1855, 18 How. 331, 354, 15 L.Ed. 401: "The foundation of the right of citizens of different states to sue each other in the courts of the United States, is not an unworthy jealousy of the impartiality of the state tribunals. It has a higher aim and purpose. It is to make the people think and feel, though residing in different states of the Union, that their relations to each other were protected by the strictest justice, administered in courts independent of all local control or connection with the subject matter of the controversy between the parties to a suit."

32. The argument is made today by Marbury, in the article cited note 17 above.

33. Friendly, The Historic Basis of Diversity Jurisdiction, 1928, 41 Harv. L.Rev. 483, 492 n. 44.

34. The Federalist No. 81, at 510, Wright ed. 1961 (Hamilton): " * * * every man may discover, that courts constituted like those of some of the States would be improper channels of the judicial authority of the Union."

35. This argument is made by Professors Moore & Weckstein, and by Judge Parker and by Judge Wright, in the articles cited note 17 above. The ALI Study, pp. 107–108, seems to accept so much of the argument as concerns persons from out-of-state.

See also the query in Currie, Federal Courts: Cases and Materials, 2d ed. 1975, p. 438. Whether this is "any more a perversion of constitutional authority than the common use of the commerce and tax powers to combat prostitution or child labor?"

36. It is argued that a federal court can better protect against bias because of "the advantages of federal procedure, Article III judges less exposed to local pressures than their state court counterparts, juries selected from wider geographical areas, review in appellate courts reflecting a multistate perspective, and more effective review by this Court."   United Steelworkers of America, AFL-CIO v. R. H. Bouligny, Inc., 1965, 86 S.Ct. 272, 275, 382 U.S. 145, 150, 15 L.Ed.2d 217. The Court was listing the advantages claimed by a party arguing before it and did not indicate whether it agreed with these arguments.

men's courts or defendants' courts. Further, arguments stemming from a supposed inferiority of state justice are insusceptible of proof and hardly politic to advance. There is, however, a somewhat related argument that the existence of concurrent state and federal jurisdiction acts as a spur to higher standards of justice in each system of courts.[37] It is hard to believe that already crowded state courts will feel a strong incentive in order to keep the comparative handful of cases where diversity exists and where, therefore, the litigants have a choice of forum. In addition, concurrent jurisdiction exists in any event over many federal question cases, and whatever benefits it may be thought to confer can be had from that phase of jurisdiction. Undoubtedly, so long as diversity exists, the choice of forum will be utilized for tactical purposes by particular litigants in particular cases, who think they may obtain an advantage from one forum or the other, but to the extent this exists, as it surely does,[38] it would seem more an abuse of concurrent jurisdiction than an argument for its retention.

It is argued also that there is no merit in transferring cases from congested federal courts to congested state courts, and that the practical consequence of abolition would be "to tell thousands upon thousands of American citizens to wait twice as long as before to have their suits disposed of, when it was already taking far too long."[39] Careful studies have shown, however, that because there are many more state judges than federal judges, abolition of diversity would have only a minimal impact on state court workloads.[40] The argument also fails to consider that the cases would take less judicial time to resolve in state courts of general jurisdiction than in federal courts, where preliminary determinations regarding the existence of diversity and of amount in controversy are often difficult and time-consuming without advancing decision on the merits of the case.[41]

---

37. Such an argument seems implicit in Hart, The Relations between State and Federal Law, 1954, 54 Col.L.Rev. 489. See especially pp. 513, 540.

It is stated explicitly by Judge Wright and Mr. Frank in their articles cited note 17 above.

38. The choice is clearly recognized as a purely tactical one in Kennedy, Federal Diversity Jurisdiction, 1961, 10 Kans.L. Rev. 47, 54. See also Summers, Analysis of Factors that Influence Choice of Forum in Diversity Cases, 1962, 47 Iowa L.Rev. 933; Note, The Choice between State and Federal Court in Diversity Cases in Virginia, 1965, 51 Va. L.Rev. 178.

39. Frank, The Case for Diversity Jurisdiction, 1979, 16 Harv.J.Legis. 403, 413.

40. Sheran & Isaacman, note 16 above, at 55–68. The same authors quote also at 51 n. 255 the 1977 resolution of the Conference of Chief Justices saying that the state courts "are able and willing" to assume all or part of the diversity jurisdiction now exercised by the federal courts.

The conclusion that the impact of abolition on the states would be minimal is supported also by Flango & Blair, The Relative Impact of Diversity Cases on State Trial Courts, 1978, 2 St. Court J. 20.

41. Rowe, note 16 above. A shorter version of the article appears as Rowe, Abolishing Diversity Jurisdiction: The Silver Lining, 1980, 66 A.B.A.J. 177.

Finally there is a comparatively new argument for diversity—though it may have been in the minds of the Framers [42]—that deserves consideration. As articulated by Chief Justice Taft, the argument is that "no single element in our governmental system has done so much to secure capital for the legitimate development of enterprises throughout the West and South as the existence of federal courts there, with a jurisdiction to hear diverse citizenship cases." [43] This argument at one time was endorsed by the Judicial Conference of the United States [44] and by many of the writers who support the retention of diversity.[45] If indeed diversity jurisdiction is an indispensable condition to the free flow of capital from one part of the nation to another, then diversity should be retained. It might seem at first glance that the merit of this argument is dependent on the other arguments—which we have seen to be of doubtful validity—for diversity. If, in fact, local prejudice will not be a significant factor, if state courts are as good as federal courts, then there is no apparent reason why the decisions of entrepreneurs to invest their funds in other parts of the country should be affected by the existence of recourse to the federal courts. On reflection, however, it will be apparent that this answer is insufficient, as most of those who have put forward the flow-of-capital argument recognize. The key question is not whether out-of-state investors will in fact receive fair treatment from state courts, but whether they think they will.[46] If abolition, or significant curtailment, of diversity jurisdiction would give rise to irrational fears by investors, and inhibit their willingness to invest in different parts of the country, then diversity serves a useful purpose

42. See Frank, Historical Bases of the Federal Judicial System, 1948, 13 Law & Contemp.Prob. 1.

43. Taft, Possible and Needed Reforms in the Administration of Justice in the Federal Courts, 1922, 47 A.B.A.Rep. 250, 258–259.

44. Report of the Judicial Conference of the United States, 1951, p. 27.

In recent years the Judicial Conference has repeatedly endorsed the complete abolition of general diversity jurisdiction. E.g., Report of the Judicial Conference of the United States, 1979, p. 66.

45. See the articles by Brown, Marbury, Moore & Weckstein, and Parker, cited note 17 above. See also Frank, note 39 above, at 410. The argument is most fully developed by Marbury, who says, at 380, that there is "value to our present-day economy in a system which guarantees to the citizen who moves beyond the borders of his own community the protecting mantle of the federal judiciary *   *   * enterprise is definitely encouraged by the fact that the federal courts are available under such circumstances."

46. Thus Chief Justice Taft, in the speech cited note 40 above, recognizes that "the material question is not so much whether the justice administered is actually impartial and fair, as it is whether it is thought to be so by those who are considering the wisdom of investing their capital in states where that capital is needed for the promotion of enterprises and industrial and commercial progress." Marbury, in the article cited note 17 above, says that his clients would be hesitant to invest in distant states without the assurance diversity jurisdiction provides, and then says, at 380: "I grant that if put to it to demonstrate a rational basis for that feeling, they might flounder a bit *   *   *. Perhaps what we are dealing with here is something that cannot be rationalized, but it is not for that reason less entitled to recognition." See also the article by Brown, cited note 17 above.

and should be retained. It is true that this proposition can never be proved short of "the heroic experiment of its abolition."[47] Nevertheless there is reason to believe that investors are now sufficiently national-minded, and that they are accustomed enough to investing abroad where they enjoy no protection from the federal courts, that it is no longer necessary to preserve diversity jurisdiction to comfort investors.[48]

It is unfortunate that the future of diversity jurisdiction is not likely to be resolved by objective consideration of the arguments for and against this head of jurisdiction. Any proposal to modify diversity meets immediate organized opposition from those who believe that they have a vested interest in preserving, for their own advantage, the widest possible choice of forum.[49]

In 1978 the House of Representatives twice voted by large margins to abolish general diversity jurisdiction. Neither bill reached a vote in the Senate.[50]

§ 24. Kinds of Diversity That Give Jurisdiction [1]

The constitutional grant of diversity jurisdiction extends "to Controversies * * * between Citizens of different states * * * and between a State, or the Citizens thereof, and foreign States, Citizens or Subjects."[2] This jurisdiction is conferred, subject to some

47. Yntema, The Jurisdiction of the Federal Courts in Controversies Between Citizens of Different States, 1933, 19 A.B.A.J. 71, 75.

48. It is worthy of note that the Reporters for the American Law Institute dismiss this argument for diversity without extended discussion—see ALI Study, pp. 105–106—and that their proposals for curtailment of diversity would deny its benefits in large measure to corporations that operate in many states.

49. See Kastenmeier & Remington, note 16 above, at 317–318; Wright, Procedural Reform: Its Limitations and Its Future, 1967, 1 Ga.L.Rev. 563, 576–577; Wright, Restructuring Federal Jurisdiction: The American Law Institute Proposals, 1969, 25 Wash. & Lee L.Rev. 185, 204–207.

"The only groups who still argue strongly for diversity jurisdiction are the Association of Trial Lawyers of America, whose members specialize in personal injury litigation, and corporate lawyers whose clients prefer the federal courts." Sheran & Isaacman, note 16 above, at 52.

A poll of lawyers showed that they opposed abolition of diversity by a 69–26% margin, with 5% undecided. On a more modest proposal to retain diversity for a nonresident defendant but eliminate it for a resident plaintiff, 58% were opposed, 33% in favor, and 9% undecided. Law Poll, 1980, 66 A.B. A.J. 148, 149.

50. 124 Cong.Rec. 5009, Feb. 28, 1978; 124 Cong.Rec. 33546, Oct. 4, 1978. See Kastenmeier & Remington, note 16 above, at 312.

[§ 24]

1. 13 Wright, Miller & Cooper, Jurisdiction §§ 3602–3605.

2. The Constitution also extends the judicial power to controversies "between Citizens of the same State claiming Lands under Grants of different States." It has been proposed that the statute implementing this grant of jurisdiction, 28 U.S.C.A. § 1354, be repealed on the ground that it is now obsolete. ALI Study, p. 411. Jurisdiction was based on conflicting grants of land from different states in Port of Portland v. Island in the Columbia River, D.C.Or.1971, 326 F.Supp. 291.

important changes, by § 1332 of the Judicial Code. In all cases in which that section of the code is relied on as the basis of jurisdiction, the amount in controversy must exceed $10,000.[3]

The typical case is that in which a citizen of Texas sues a citizen of New York. Here there is plainly diversity, but it is not clear that these facts in themselves should be enough for jurisdiction. Section 11 of the Judiciary Act of 1789 granted jurisdiction only where "the suit is between a citizen of the State where the suit is brought, and a citizen of another State." Thus in the example given, if suit were brought in the federal court in Pennsylvania, there would have been no jurisdiction under the 1789 statute, since neither of the parties would be a citizen of the state where the suit is brought. If the basis for diversity jurisdiction is fear of prejudice against the litigant from out of state,[4] there would seem no danger of such prejudice, and thus no reason for federal jurisdiction, where neither of the parties is a citizen of the forum state. This restriction was removed, however, in 1875, and ever since then jurisdiction has been granted where the suit is between "citizens of different States," regardless of where it is brought.[5] This leads to the further anomaly—which was true also under the 1789 formulation—that the Texas plaintiff can, if he is able to obtain service of process, bring suit against the New York citizen in the federal court in Texas. If the local prejudice rationalization for diversity jurisdiction is accepted, it is difficult to understand why a plaintiff who is a citizen of the forum state is able to resort to federal court.[6]

State citizenship is necessary for diversity jurisdiction. A person may be a citizen of the United States but domiciled abroad. Such a person is not a citizen of any state, and cannot sue or be sued in federal court on that basis, and since the person is not an alien, the alienage jurisdiction also cannot be invoked.[7] Nor can a person who has dual nationality, and who is a citizen of the United States but is regarded as a citizen also by another country, take advantage of alienage jurisdiction. A litigant in this position will be treated as though he possesses only United States citizenship.[8]

---

3. See §§ 32–37 below.

4. See § 23 above.

5. 28 U.S.C.A. § 1332(a)(1), carrying forward language that originally appeared in the Act of March 3, 1875, § 1, 18 Stat. 470.

6. The heart of the American Law Institute's proposals about diversity is to deny jurisdiction if the plaintiff is a citizen of the forum or otherwise closely associated with the forum. ALI Study, § 1302.

7. Sadat v. Mertes, C.A.7th, 1980, 615 F.2d 1176, 1180–1182; Smith v. Carter, C.A.5th, 1977, 545 F.2d 909, certiorari denied 97 S.Ct. 2677, 431 U.S. 955, 53

L.Ed.2d 272; Hammerstein v. Lyne, D.C.Mo.1912, 200 F. 165.

The converse situation cannot arise. A state may confer the benefits of state citizenship on anyone it thinks fit, but the power of naturalization is exclusively vested in Congress, and it is not possible for one who is not a citizen of the United States to be a citizen of a state for purposes of diversity. City of Minneapolis v. Reum, C.C.A.8th, 1893, 56 F. 576; Frick v. Lewis, C.C.A.6th, 1912, 195 F. 693, affirmed 1914, 34 S.Ct. 488, 233 U.S. 291, 58 L.Ed. 967.

8. Sadat v. Mertes, C.A.7th, 1980, 615 F.2d 1176, 1182–1188, noted 1981, 38

Jurisdiction is granted also where there is a suit between a citizen of a state and foreign states or citizens or subjects thereof.[9] Here it has never made any difference where the suit is brought, and probably should not, since there may be a real danger of prejudice, in any forum, against the alien. The 1789 Judiciary Act purported to extend jurisdiction to all suits in which an alien is a party. The Court at a very early date held that this was unconstitutional insofar as it might permit suit in federal courts between two aliens, while the Constitution only authorizes jurisdiction of suits between a citizen of a state and an alien.[10] The alien must be a citizen or subject of a foreign state; there is no jurisdiction if the suit is between a citizen of one of the United States and a person who is not a citizen either of the United States or of any other country.[11]

In an early decision the Court, speaking through Chief Justice Marshall, held that a citizen of the District of Columbia is not a citizen of a state, for purposes of diversity jurisdiction,[12] and the same result was later reached with regard to citizens of territories.[13] Marshall's opinion was unfortunately cryptic, for, after commenting on how extraordinary it was that the courts of the United States should be open to aliens, but not to those who resided in the District of Columbia, he said that "this is a subject for legislative, not for judicial

Wash. & Lee L.Rev. 77; Raphael v. Hertzberg, D.C.Cal.1979, 470 F.Supp. 984, appeal dismissed C.A.9th, 1980, 636 F.2d 1227; Currie, The Federal Courts and the American Law Institute, 1968, 36 U.Chi.L.Rev. 1, 10 n. 50.

But cf. Aguirre v. Nagel, D.C.Mich.1967, 270 F.Supp. 535, holding that plaintiff who was a citizen of Michigan and also of Mexico could sue a citizen of Michigan in federal court. The Aguirre case was purportedly followed in Robinson v. Anastasiou, D.C.Tex.1972, 339 F.Supp. 472, though that precedent was in fact irrelevant. The Robinson case was a suit by a citizen of Texas against a defendant who was a citizen of Greece—and perhaps also of Great Britain—and who was domiciled in Texas. The domicile of a party who is not a United States citizen is irrelevant and this was a simple case of a suit by a citizen of a state against an alien.

9. 28 U.S.C.A. § 1332(a)(2).

There is also jurisdiction of a suit between citizens of different states in which foreign countries or their citizens are additional parties. 28 U.S. C.A. § 1332(a)(3). See 13 Wright, Miller & Cooper, Jurisdiction § 3604. But this does not permit suit by an alien against a citizen of a state and a citizen of some other foreign country. Ed & Fred, Inc. v. Puritan Marine Ins. Un-

derwriters Corp., C.A.5th, 1975, 506 F.2d 757.

10. Hodgson v. Bowerbank, 1809, 5 Cranch 303, 3 L.Ed. 108. For the significance of this case, see § 8 above.

It has been held that the provision of the Foreign Sovereign Immunities Act that purports to allow suit by an alien against a foreign state, 28 U.S.C.A. § 1330, is unconstitutional for this reason. Verlinden B. V. v. Central Bank of Nigeria, C.A.2d, 1981, 647 F.2d 320, certiorari granted 1982, 102 S.Ct. 997, —— U.S. ——, 71 L.Ed.2d 291.

11. This at least is the holding of Blair Holdings Corp. v. Rubinstein, D.C.N.Y. 1955, 133 F.Supp. 496, and if there can actually be such a "man without a country," the decision appears sound. The Supreme Court may simply have overlooked this possibility in Sun Printing & Pub. Assn. v. Edwards, 1904, 24 S.Ct. 696, 194 U.S. 377, 48 L.Ed. 1027, where, in sustaining jurisdiction, it asserted that a person domiciled in Delaware must either be a citizen of Delaware or a citizen or subject of a foreign state.

12. Hepburn & Dundas v. Ellzey, 1804, 2 Cranch 445, 2 L.Ed. 332.

13. Corporation of New Orleans v. Winter, 1816, 1 Wheat. 91, 4 L.Ed. 44.

consideration." [14] This would seem to suggest that only the statute, rather than the Constitution, precluded diversity jurisdiction in suits between a citizen of the District of Columbia and a citizen of a state. This is a strange suggestion, since there was no significant difference between the language of the statute and that of the Constitution, but the alternative explanation of Marshall's statement is the strained argument that "constitutional amendment as well as statutory revision is for legislative, not judicial, consideration." [15]

Against this background Congress, in 1940, undertook to provide that citizens of the District of Columbia, and of the territories, should be regarded as citizens of a state for purposes of diversity jurisdiction.[16] Most of the lower courts thought this provision unconstitutional, but the Supreme Court, in the very unusual case of National Mutual Insurance Co. of District of Columbia v. Tidewater Transfer Co.[17] upheld the statute. Two justices thought that the older decisions should be overruled, and that citizens of the District of Columbia were citizens of a state within Article III of the Constitution. The other seven justices disagreed. Three justices, while of the view that these persons were not citizens of a state, voted to uphold the statute on the basis of the power of Congress, under Article I of the Constitution, to enact legislation for the inhabitants of the District of Columbia and the territories.[18] The other six justices rejected this line of argument. Nevertheless five justices altogether voted to uphold the statute, and it must now be regarded as valid,[19] even though seven and six justices respectively rejected the two lines of argument offered to support the statute.

The problems of diversity become more complex when there are multiple parties. Suppose that a citizen of Texas and a citizen of Oklahoma join as plaintiffs in a suit against a citizen of New York. Here it is settled that diversity exists, and that neither the statute

---

14. Hepburn & Dundas v. Ellzey, 1804, 2 Cranch 445, 453, 2 L.Ed. 332.

15. Jackson, J., in National Mut. Ins. Co. of Dist. of Columbia v. Tidewater Transfer Co., 1949, 69 S.Ct. 1173, 1175, 337 U.S. 582, 587, 93 L.Ed. 1556.

16. The 1940 statute conferred jurisdiction where suit "is between citizens of different States, or citizens of the District of Columbia, the Territory of Hawaii, or Alaska, and any State or Territory." Act of April 20, 1940, 54 Stat. 143. In its present form, as revised in the 1948 Judicial Code and consequently amended, the provision is: "The word 'States', as used in this section, includes the Territories, the District of Columbia, and the Commonwealth of Puerto Rico." 28 U.S.C.A. § 1332(d).

17. 1949, 69 S.Ct. 1173, 337 U.S. 582, 93 L.Ed. 1556, noted 1949, 2 Ala.L.Rev.

63, 4 Miami L.Q. 113, 28 N.C.L.Rev. 128, 1950, 50 Col.L.Rev. 535, 35 Corn. L.Q. 198, 19 Geo.Wash.L.Rev. 413, 4 Miami L.Q. 113, 48 Mich.L.Rev. 999, 3 Vand.L.Rev. 535.

18. See § 11 above.

19. In Americana of Puerto Rico, Inc. v. Kaplus, C.A.3d, 1966, 368 F.2d 431, so much of 28 U.S.C.A. § 1332(d) as provides that the Commonwealth of Puerto Rico is a "state" for purposes of diversity jurisdiction was upheld as a valid exercise of the power of Congress under Article IV, § 3, of the Constitution to make rules and regulations for United States territories.

See generally 13 Wright, Miller & Cooper, Jurisdiction § 3603.

nor the Constitution require that all the parties on one side be citizens of the same state.[20] But if the Texan and the Oklahoman join to bring suit against two defendants, one of whom is a citizen of New York but the other a citizen of Texas (or Oklahoma), there is no diversity jurisdiction. This is the rule of "complete diversity," first laid down by Chief Justice Marshall in the famous case of Strawbridge v. Curtiss.[21] A later justice was to write that, to the knowledge of several members of the Court, Marshall had repeatedly expressed regret that the decision in the Strawbridge case had been made, and had said that if the point of jurisdiction was an original one, the conclusion would be different.[22] Nevertheless, with one important exception, the complete diversity rule has since been consistently followed.[23] The exception was in interpleader cases, where the statute calls only for "two or more adverse claimants, of diverse citizenship." [24] The lower courts had held that "minimal diversity" was enough, and that jurisdiction existed if there were a claimant on each side from different states, even though all the other claimants on each side might be citizens of a single state.[25]

This application of the interpleader statute was valid only if Strawbridge v. Curtiss could be regarded as merely a construction of the diversity statute then in effect rather than a construction of the Constitution.[26] On its face the decision purported merely to construe the statute; though it is hard to find any significant difference between the language of the statute and that of the Constitution, there are other instances where statutory language, seemingly taken directly from Article III, has been given a narrower construction than the similar words in the Constitution itself.[27] To have held that the Constitution requires complete diversity would have had a debilitating effect on the interpleader act, and would have largely precluded the possibilities of using the diversity jurisdiction as a basis for providing a federal forum for other cases in which no state court could grant effective relief.[28] Even those most critical of diversity general-

20. Sweeney v. Carter Oil Co., 1905, 26 S.Ct. 55, 199 U.S. 252, 50 L.Ed. 178; Great Northern Ry. Co. v. Galbreath Cattle Co., 1926, 46 S.Ct. 439, 271 U.S. 99, 70 L.Ed. 854.

Prior to 1948 there was a question, never resolved, whether jurisdiction existed if an alien and a citizen of a state joined in a suit against a citizen of another state. See Ryan v. Ohmer, D.C.N.Y. 1916, 233 F. 165. The question was of purely statutory dimension, and was settled in the 1948 Code by an express grant of jurisdiction in such a situation. 28 U.S.C.A. § 1332(a)(3). See note 9 above.

21. 1806, 3 Cranch 267, 2 L.Ed. 435.

22. Louisville, C. & C. R. Co. v. Letson, 1844, 2 How. 497, 555, 11 L.Ed. 353.

23. See 13A Wright, Miller & Cooper, Jurisdiction 2d § 3605.

24. 28 U.S.C.A. § 1335(a)(1).

25. Haynes v. Felder, C.A.5th, 1957, 239 F.2d 868, and cases there cited. See § 74 below.

26. The question was specifically left open in Treinies v. Sunshine Mining Co., 1939, 60 S.Ct. 44, 47, 308 U.S. 66, 71–72, 84 L.Ed. 85. In Shields v. Barrow, 1855, 17 How. 130, 145, 15 L.Ed. 158, the Court talked as if complete diversity were constitutionally required, but the remark was not necessary to decision.

27. This is notably true with regard to federal question jurisdiction. See § 17 above.

28. See ALI Study, §§ 2371–2376.

ly have recognized and supported the potentialities of diversity for situations of the sort described,[29] and a construction barring this use of diversity would have been most unfortunate.

Fortunately when the Supreme Court finally decided this matter, it held that minimal diversity is enough to meet the requirement of the Constitution, and that the rule of Strawbridge v. Curtiss is merely a construction of the general diversity case. In 1967, in the case of State Farm Fire & Casualty Co. v. Tashire,[30] the Court, in an interpleader situation, raised the question of jurisdiction on its own motion. The Court had no difficulty in finding that Congress had intended to let minimal diversity suffice in interpleader, and in three sentences the Court resolved more than 150 years of controversy by holding that neither Article III, nor the Strawbridge case, barred Congress from doing so. " * * * Chief Justice Marshall there purported to construe only 'The words of the act of congress,' not the Constitution itself. And in a variety of contexts this Court and the lower courts have concluded that Article III poses no obstacle to the legislative extension of federal jurisdiction, founded on diversity, so long as any two adverse parties are not co-citizens. Accordingly, we conclude that the present case is properly in the federal courts." [31]

It must be kept clearly in mind that the Tashire case holds only that complete diversity is not required by the Constitution, and that Congress can permit less. It does not alter the established construction of the general diversity statute, and except where Congress, as in the interpleader statute, has authorized something less than complete diversity, Strawbridge v. Curtiss remains the controlling rule.[32]

A few district court cases relied on the then-evolving concept of "pendent parties" to entertain suits in which diversity was not complete.[33] Whatever the merits, or lack thereof, of that concept to bring in additional parties in cases in which there is a federal question [34] or to overcome problems of amount in controversy,[35] it is not

29. See § 23 above.

30. 1967, 87 S.Ct. 1199, 1203–1204, 386 U.S. 523, 530–531, 18 L.Ed.2d 270.

31. 87 S.Ct. at 1203–1204, 386 U.S. at 531. The Court indicated, id. at n. 7, that "full-dress arguments for the constitutionality of 'minimal diversity'" might be found in several cited lower-court opinions and in scholarly writings. See particularly Supporting Memorandum A in ALI Study, pp. 426–436, one of the sources cited by the Court.

32. Professor Currie believes that Strawbridge was wrongly decided and should be overruled by statute. Currie, The Federal Courts and the American Law Institute, 1968, 36 U.Chi.L. Rev. 1, 18–34.

33. Wittersheim v. General Transp. Services, Inc., D.C.Va.1974, 378 F.Supp. 762; Campbell v. Triangle Corp., D.C. Pa.1972, 336 F.Supp. 1002. Both of these cases rely on Borror v. Sharon Steel Co., C.A.3d, 1964, 327 F.2d 165, but that case is easily distinguishable, as the Third Circuit itself recognized in the Seyler case, note 36 below.

Cf. United Pac. Ins. Co. v. Capital Development Bd., D.C.Ill.1979, 482 F.Supp. 541.

34. See § 19 above.

35. See § 36 below.

properly used to avoid the longstanding requirement of complete diversity.[36]

§ 25. Exceptions From the Diversity Jurisdiction [1]

The diversity statute, 28 U.S.C.A. § 1332, purports to speak in very broad terms. If a suit is between citizens of different states, and the jurisdictional amount is satisfied, the district court has original jurisdiction. There are, however, limitations on the breadth of the jurisdiction thus seemingly conferred.

Thus it is provided by statute that there is no jurisdiction if a party, by assignment or otherwise, is improperly or collusively joined to invoke federal jurisdiction.[2] The rule is well-settled too that a federal court cannot entertain an in rem action if the property is already in the custody of a state court of competent jurisdiction;[3] the rule is based on considerations of comity but it is cast in terms of a limitation on the jurisdiction of the federal court.[4] The rapidly burgeoning abstention doctrines permit, and in some circumstances may require, a federal court to decline jurisdiction, or to postpone its exercise, even though the requirements of the diversity statute are satisfied.[5]

Finally there are two important areas, domestic relations cases and probate matters, where, by a judge-made exception to the statute, the federal courts will not act though diversity is present.[6] These two exceptions were first developed at a time when the diversity statute granted jurisdiction of "suits of a civil nature in law or in equity," and it was thought that the domestic relations and probate

---

36. Parker v. W. W. Moore & Sons, Inc., C.A.4th, 1975, 528 F.2d 764; Seyler v. Steuben Motors, Inc., C.A.3d, 1972, 462 F.2d 181; Grimandi v. Beech Aircraft Corp., D.C.Kan.1981, 512 F.Supp. 764; Burnside v. Sanders Assn., Inc., D.C. Tex.1980, 507 F.Supp. 165, affirmed C.A.5th, 1980, 643 F.2d 389; Wolgin v. Atlas United Financial Corp., D.C.Pa. 1975, 397 F.Supp. 1003; Carroll v. Protection Maritime Ins. Co., D.C.Mass. 1974, 377 F.Supp. 1294, 1298 n. 3, affirmed in part, reversed in part, C.A. 1st, 1975, 512 F.2d 4; Sherrell v. Mitchell Aero, Inc., D.C.Wis.1971, 340 F.Supp. 219.

See Bratton, Pendent Jurisdiction in Diversity Cases—Some Doubts, 1974, 11 San Diego L.Rev. 296; Fortune, Pendent Jurisdiction—The Problem of "Pendenting Parties," 1972, 34 U.Pitts. L.Rev. 1, 14–21. But see Comment, Pendent Jurisdiction and Minimal Diversity, 1973, 59 Iowa L.Rev. 179.

[§ 25]

1. 13 Wright, Miller & Cooper, Jurisdiction §§ 3609, 3610; Vestal & Foster, Implied Limitations on the Diversity Jurisdiction of Federal Courts, 1956, 41 Minn.L.Rev. 1.

2. 28 U.S.C.A. § 1359. See § 31 below.

3. Princess Lida of Thurn and Taxis v. Thompson, 1939, 59 S.Ct. 275, 305 U.S. 456, 83 L.Ed. 285; 14 Wright, Miller & Cooper, Jurisdiction § 3631.

4. Princess Lida of Thurn and Taxis v. Thompson, 1939, 59 S.Ct. 275, 281, 305 U.S. 456, 467–468, 83 L.Ed. 285. See also Porter v. Sabin, 1893, 13 S.Ct. 1008, 1010, 149 U.S. 473, 480, 37 L.Ed. 815; Wabash R. Co. v. Adelbert College, 1908, 28 S.Ct. 182, 187, 208 U.S. 38, 54, 52 L.Ed. 379; Lion Bonding & Sur. Co. v. Karatz, 1923, 43 S.Ct. 480, 484, 262 U.S. 77, 88–89, 67 L.Ed. 871.

5. See §§ 52, 52A below.

6. These limitations are inapplicable in the territories, and prior to the 1970 reorganization of the District of Columbia courts—see § 5 above—they were inapplicable there, but the basis of jurisdiction is not diversity in those places.

cases, being matters that would have been heard in the ecclesiastical courts, did not fit this description. The 1948 Judicial Code substituted the term "civil action" for the phrase used in the older statutes, but the exceptions have persisted. Today the exceptions may more rationally be defended on the ground that these are areas of the law in which the states have an especially strong interest and a well-developed competence for dealing with them.[7]

The exception with regard to domestic relations cases dates back to a dictum in an 1858 case. There the Court held that a wife could sue, on the basis of diversity, in a federal court in Wisconsin to enforce the decree of a New York state court that granted her a divorce and alimony, but it added: "We disclaim altogether any jurisdiction in the courts of the United States upon the subject of divorce, or for the allowance of alimony, either as an original proceeding in chancery or as an incident to divorce *a vinculo*, or to one from bed and board." [8] Such cases are apparently within the judicial power of the United States, for the Supreme Court has heard appeals in divorce actions from territorial courts,[9] but the 1858 dictum has been frequently applied as a general rule, which bars the federal courts not only from entertaining actions involving questions of matrimonial status [10] but also from hearing "domestic relations" cases where only property rights are involved.[11] Suit can be brought in a federal court to collect

7. Phillips, Nizer, Benjamin, Krim & Ballon v. Rosenstiel, C.A.2d, 1973, 490 F.2d 509, 512; Magaziner v. Montemuro, C.A.3d, 1972, 468 F.2d 782, 787; Buechold v. Ortiz, C.A.9th, 1968, 401 F.2d 371, 373; Kilduff v. Kilduff, D.C.N.Y.1979, 473 F.Supp. 873, 875.

8. Barber v. Barber, 1858, 21 How. 582, 584, 16 L.Ed. 226.

9. Simms v. Simms, 1899, 20 S.Ct. 58, 175 U.S. 162, 44 L.Ed. 115; De La Rama v. De La Rama, 1906, 26 S.Ct. 485, 201 U.S. 303, 50 L.Ed. 765.

10. Csibi v. Fustos, C.A.9th, 1982, 670 F.2d 134.

The most extreme case held that a state court had jurisdiction of an action for divorce against the consul of a foreign country, though normally the federal courts have exclusive jurisdiction of actions against consuls, 28 U.S.C.A. § 1351, on the ground that a federal court could not entertain the divorce action. Ohio ex rel. Popovici v. Agler, 1930, 50 S.Ct. 154, 280 U.S. 379, 74 L.Ed. 489.

See generally 13 Wright, Miller & Cooper, Jurisdiction § 3609.

A district court, in a decision critical of the whole line of cases establishing this exception, has held that a federal court may hear an action for a declaratory judgment that a foreign divorce is invalid. Spindel v. Spindel, D.C.N.Y. 1968, 283 F.Supp. 797, noted 1968, 72 Dick.L.Rev. 692, 54 Iowa L.Rev. 390, 28 Md.L.Rev. 376, 14 N.Y.L.F. 363. See also Vann v. Vann, D.C.Tenn.1968, 294 F.Supp. 193. But the views expressed in the Spindel case were not accepted by the Second Circuit. See Phillips, Nizer, Benjamin, Krim & Ballon v. Rosenstiel, C.A.2d, 1973, 490 F.2d 509.

11. Wilkins v. Rogers, C.A.4th, 1978, 581 F.2d 399; Linscott v. Linscott, D.C. Iowa 1951, 98 F.Supp. 802; Garberson v. Garberson, D.C.Iowa 1949, 82 F. Supp. 706; Albanese v. Richter, C.C.A.3d, 1947, 161 F.2d 688, certiorari denied 68 S.Ct. 49, 332 U.S. 782, 92 L.Ed. 365; Bercovitch v. Tanburn, D.C. N.Y.1952, 103 F.Supp. 62. These decisions are persuasively criticized by Vestal & Foster, note 1 above, at 29–31. Richie v. Richie, D.C.N.Y.1960, 186 F.Supp. 592, permitting suit to recover for breach of separation agreement by former husband, may be to the contrary, though the court states that certain of the cases above cited are distinguishable. And in Phillips, Nizer, Benjamin, Krim & Ballon v. Rosenstiel, C.A.2d, 1973, 490 F.2d 509, it

unpaid alimony under a state decree,[12] but jurisdiction has been declined even of tort actions if they arise out of an ongoing series of disputes centering around the marital relationship.[13] The federal courts also refuse to hear child custody cases, in line with the sweeping statement of the Supreme Court that "the whole subject of the domestic relations of husband and wife, parent and child, belongs to the laws of the States and not to the laws of the United States." [14]

The exception from the diversity jurisdiction as to probate matters [15] is far from absolute. It turns, instead, on unclear distinctions of the utmost subtlety. A federal court may not probate a will nor undertake the administration of an estate,[16] but if diversity or some other basis for jurisdiction is present, the federal court can entertain actions against administrators, executors, and other claimants in which plaintiffs seek to establish their claims against an estate so long as the federal court does not interfere with the probate proceedings or assume general jurisdiction of the probate or control of the property in the custody of the state court.[17] The federal action in such a case will establish the claimant's right in a fashion that will be binding in the state proceedings, but the federal court cannot order

was held that a federal court could hear a suit against a husband for legal services furnished his former wife.

12. Crouch v. Crouch, C.A.5th, 1978, 566 F.2d 486; Harrison v. Harrison, C.A.4th, 1954, 214 F.2d 571, certiorari denied 75 S.Ct. 217, 348 U.S. 896, 99 L.Ed. 704; Davis v. Davis, D.C.Pa. 1978, 452 F.Supp. 44.

The federal court will not take jurisdiction, however, if the state alimony order is not final. Morris v. Morris, C.A. 7th, 1960, 273 F.2d 678; Gonzales v. Gonzales, D.C.Pa.1947, 74 F.Supp. 883.

A suit for "palimony" is a contract action and not within the domestic relations exception. Anastasi v. Anastasi, D.C. N.J.1982, 532 F.Supp. 720.

13. Sutter v. Pitts, C.A.1st, 1981, 639 F.2d 842; Kilduff v. Kilduff, D.C.N.Y. 1979, 473 F.Supp. 873; Bacon v. Bacon, D.C.Or.1973, 365 F.Supp. 1019.

Jurisdiction exists, however, over a tort action against an estranged husband for removing a child from the home of its mother, to whom the state courts had awarded custody, since the tort of child enticement is not dependent on a present or past family relationship. Wasserman v. Wasserman, C.A.4th, 1982, 671 F.2d 832.

14. Ex parte Burrus, 1890, 10 S.Ct. 850, 853, 136 U.S. 586, 593–594, 34 L.Ed. 500 (federal court order granting

habeas corpus to obtain custody of a child was absolutely void, and could be disregarded with impunity); Hernstadt v. Hernstadt, C.A.2d 1967, 373 F.2d 316. For other cases to the same effect, see 13 Wright, Miller & Cooper, Jurisdiction § 3609 nn. 28–32.

See also Buechold v. Ortiz, C.A.9th, 1968, 401 F.2d 371 (no jurisdiction of case involving paternity and child support).

15. See 13 Wright, Miller & Cooper, Jurisdiction § 3610; Vestal & Foster, note 1 above, at 13–23; Comment, Federal Court Probate Proceedings, 1970, 45 Ind.L.J. 387; Note, Federal Jurisdiction in Matters Relating to Probate and Administration, 1930, 43 Harv.L.Rev. 462; Note, Federal Jurisdiction and Practice: Probate Matters, 1962, 15 Okl.L.Rev. 462.

16. In re Broderick's Will, 1875, 21 Wall. 503, 22 L.Ed. 599; Hook v. Payne, 1872, 14 Wall. 252, 20 L.Ed. 887; Byers v. McAuley, 1893, 13 S.Ct. 906, 149 U.S. 608, 37 L.Ed. 867; Turton v. Turton, C.A.5th, 1981, 644 F.2d 344.

17. Markham v. Allen, 1946, 66 S.Ct. 296, 326 U.S. 490, 90 L.Ed. 256; Waterman v. Canal-Louisiana Bank & Trust Co., 1909, 30 S.Ct. 10, 215 U.S. 33, 54 L.Ed. 80; Rice v. Rice Foundation, C.A. 7th, 1979, 610 F.2d 471; Lee v. Hunt, D.C.La.1977, 431 F.Supp. 371.

actual distribution of property in the custody of the state court nor give execution on its judgment.[18]

The state practice is controlling as to will contests. If the state permits an independent action to annul a will or to set aside a probate, such an action may be brought in federal court if jurisdictional requisites are met, but the federal court will not take jurisdiction if the state regards such contests as ancillary to the probate proceedings.[19] Federal courts will also entertain actions to construe wills or trusts,[20] and will hear suits seeking a personal judgment against an executor or administrator for fraud, but only if a final accounting has been made in the state probate proceeding.[21] A federal court has power to appoint or to remove a trustee,[22] but it may not interfere with property in the custody of a state court.[23]

§ 26.   The Meaning of Citizenship [1]

Diversity jurisdiction is dependent upon the citizenship of the parties. Though the Fourteenth Amendment declares that citizens of the United States are citizens "of the State wherein they reside," it is quite settled that mere residence in a state is not enough for purposes of diversity,[2] and that the more elusive concept of "domicile" is controlling.[3] A person's domicile is that place where he has his true, fixed, and permanent home and principal establishment, and to which he has the intention of returning whenever he is absent therefrom.[4]

---

18. Byers v. McAuley, 1893, 13 S.Ct. 906, 149 U.S. 608, 37 L.Ed. 867; Yonley v. Lavender, 1874, 21 Wall. 276, 22 L.Ed. 536.

19. Sutton v. English, 1918, 38 S.Ct. 254, 246 U.S. 199, 62 L.Ed. 664; Ledbetter v. Taylor, C.A.10th, 1966, 359 F.2d 760.

20. Colton v. Colton, 1888, 8 S.Ct. 1164, 127 U.S. 300, 32 L.Ed. 138; Fontain v. Ravenel, 1854, 17 How. 369, 15 L.Ed. 80.

21. Compare Lathan v. Edwards, C.C.A.5th, 1941, 121 F.2d 183, with Kittredge v. Stevens, C.C.A.1st, 1942, 126 F.2d 263, certiorari denied 63 S.Ct. 64, 317 U.S. 642, 87 L.Ed. 517. See 13 Wright, Miller & Cooper, Jurisdiction § 3610.

22. Burgess v. Murray, C.A.5th, 1952, 194 F.2d 131, 133.

23. Starr v. Rupp, C.A.6th, 1970, 421 F.2d 999. Kenney v. Kenney, C.A.1963, 314 F.2d 268, 114 U.S.App. D.C. 263; Beach v. Rome Trust Co., C.A.2d, 1959, 269 F.2d 367; In re Butler's Trust, D.C.Minn.1962, 201 F.Supp. 316.

[§ 26]

1. 13 Wright, Miller & Cooper, Jurisdiction §§ 3611–3613; Weckstein, Citizenship for Purposes of Diversity Jurisdiction, 1972, 26 Sw.L.J. 360.

2. Sun Printing & Pub. Assn. v. Edwards, 1904, 24 S.Ct. 696, 194 U.S. 377, 48 L.Ed. 1027.

3. 13 Wright, Miller & Cooper, Jurisdiction § 3612. Chicago & N. W. R. Co. v. Ohle, 1886, 6 S.Ct. 632, 117 U.S. 123, 29 L.Ed. 837; Reynolds v. Adden, 1890, 10 S.Ct. 843, 136 U.S. 348, 34 L.Ed. 360; Kaiser v. Loomis, C.A.6th, 1968, 391 F.2d 1007.

A federal test is applied in determining domicile for purposes of diversity. Sadat v. Mertes, C.A.7th, 1980, 615 F.2d 1176; Stifel v. Hopkins, C.A.6th, 1973, 477 F.2d 1116; Ziady v. Curley, C.A.4th, 1968, 396 F.2d 873, noted 1969, 71 W.Va.L.Rev. 420.

4. Stine v. Moore, C.A.5th, 1954, 213 F.2d 446, 448, paraphrasing the much-quoted definition in Story, Conflict of Laws, 8th ed. 1883, § 41. See also 13 Wright, Miller & Cooper, Jurisdiction § 3612.

The definition of "domicile" in Restatement, Conflict of Laws, 1934, § 9, is

A person may have a number of residences, but it is impossible for him to have more than one domicile.[5] The domicile of a child, at least until it is emancipated, has been thought to be that of its parents,[6] and similarly a married woman traditionally has acquired the domicile of her husband, though she may have a separate domicile if she is living apart from him.[7]

A citizen of the United States can change his domicile instantly. To do so, two elements are necessary. He must take up residence at the new domicile, and he must intend to remain there for the time at least. Neither the physical presence nor the intention to remain is alone sufficient.[8] He need not intend to remain permanently at the new domicile; [9] it is enough that he intends to make the new state his home and that he has no present intention of going elsewhere.[10] If

rather vaguer than that set forth in the text. See also Restatement Second of Conflict of Laws, 1971, §§ 11–23. One difficulty with this subject is the tendency to use cases and texts dealing with "domicile" in the law of conflicts as applicable to "domicile" for purposes of federal jurisdiction. The problem of what law to apply is surely a different problem from that of whether a litigant should have access to federal court, and it does not conduce to clarity of analysis to suppose that the same answers will suffice for different questions. The notion that conflicts of laws principles are determinative of "domicile" for purposes of diversity is rejected in Stifel v. Hopkins, C.A.6th, 1973, 477 F.2d 1116, 1124. And see Krasnov v. Dinan, C.A.3d, 1972, 465 F.2d 1298, 1300 n. 1. Instead those cases, and such other cases as Ziady v. Curley, C.A.4th, 1968, 396 F.2d 873, and Elliott v. Krear, D.C.Va. 1979, 466 F.Supp. 444, give attention to the policy of diversity jurisdiction to protect out-of-state litigants from bias, and look to whether a party is a stranger to a state who might be the victim of bias.

5. Harding v. Standard Oil Co., C.C.D. Ill.1910, 182 F. 421; Restatement Second of Conflict of Laws, 1971, § 11.

6. Delaware, L. & W. R. Co. v. Petrowsky, C.C.A.2d, 1918, 250 F. 554, 558–559, certiorari denied 38 S.Ct. 427, 247 U.S. 508, 62 L.Ed. 1241; cf. Bjornquist v. Boston & A. R. Co., C.C.A.1st, 1918, 250 F. 929. See Beale, The Domicile of an Infant, 1923, 8 Corn.L.Q. 103.

But see Ziady v. Curley, C.A.4th, 1968, 396 F.2d 873; Elliott v. Krear, D.C.Va. 1979, 466 F.Supp. 444; 13 Wright, Miller & Cooper, Jurisdiction § 3615.

7. 13 Wright, Miller & Cooper, Jurisdiction § 3614. Williamson v. Osenton, 1914, 34 S.Ct. 442, 232 U.S. 619, 58 L.Ed. 758; Napletana v. Hillsdale College, C.A.6th, 1967, 385 F.2d 871; Taylor v. Milam, D.C.Ark.1950, 89 F.Supp. 880 (a comprehensive opinion reflecting the modern trend to view the domicile of the wife on an independent basis).

But see Mas v. Perry, C.A.5th, 1974, 489 F.2d 1396, certiorari denied 95 S.Ct. 74, 419 U.S. 842, 42 L.Ed.2d 70.

8. 13 Wright, Miller & Cooper, Jurisdiction § 3613; Mitchell v. U. S., 1874, 21 Wall. 350, 22 L.Ed. 584; Sun Printing & Pub. Assn. v. Edwards, 1904, 24 S.Ct. 696, 194 U.S. 377, 48 L.Ed. 1027; Hawes v. Club Ecuestre El Comandante, C.A.1st, 1979, 598 F.2d 698; Hendry v. Masonite Corp., C.A.5th, 1972, 455 F.2d 955, certiorari denied 93 S.Ct. 464, 409 U.S. 1023, 34 L.Ed.2d 315.

9. Hawes v. Club Ecuestre El Comandante, C.A.1st, 1979, 598 F.2d 698; Hardin v. McAvoy, C.A.5th, 1954, 216 F.2d 399; Gallagher v. Philadelphia Transp. Co., C.A.3d, 1950, 185 F.2d 543; Brookley v. Ranson, D.C.Iowa 1974, 376 F.Supp. 195; 13 Wright, Miller & Cooper, Jurisdiction § 3613.

10. Chicago & N. W. R. Co. v. Ohle, 1886, 6 S.Ct. 632, 117 U.S. 123, 29 L.Ed. 837; Gilbert v. David, 1915, 35 S.Ct. 164, 235 U.S. 561, 59 L.Ed. 360; Milliken v. Tri-County Elec. Co-op., Inc., D.C.S.C.1966, 254 F.Supp. 302, 305, noted 1966, 18 S.C.L.Rev. 847; Anderson v. Splint Coal Corp., D.C.Ky. 1937, 20 F.Supp. 233. Compare Morris v. Gilmer, 1889, 9 S.Ct. 289, 129 U.S. 315, 32 L.Ed. 690, where a move to another state was ineffective to change domicile in view of the party's testimo-

these two elements are satisfied, it is immaterial that the motive for the change of domicile was to create diversity and gain access to federal court.[11]

The determination of whether a party has in fact made a bona fide change of domicile may, in the discretion of the court, be made either by the judge himself or by the jury.[12] The "normal and usual course" is for the judge to determine this question by himself,[13] and it is said that he cannot be charged with abuse of discretion in doing so.[14] In determining whether a party has intended to establish a domicile in the state to which he has moved, the factfinder will look to such circumstances as his declarations, exercise of political rights, payment of personal taxes, house or residence and place of business.[15]

§ 27.   Corporations and Other Associations [1]

When the Constitution was adopted, the private corporation was virtually unknown. One of the most interesting chapters in constitutional history has been the effort, frequently successful, to obtain for corporations the benefits extended by the Constitution to natural persons.[2] Among the benefits thus sought has been the right to invoke the diversity jurisdiction of the federal courts.

In 1809, when the Court was first faced with the problem in the Deveaux case, Chief Justice Marshall referred to the corporation as an "invisible, intangible, and artificial being," a "mere legal entity"

ny that whether he would return to the original state "depends altogether upon circumstances."

A citizen of Missouri who was studying at Ohio State and intended to remain in Ohio only as long as his studies required did not acquire an Ohio domicile. Holmes v. Sopuch, C.A.8th, 1981, 639 F.2d 431. See 13 Wright, Miller & Cooper, Jurisdiction § 3619.

11.   Williamson v. Osenton, 1914, 34 S.Ct. 442, 232 U.S. 619, 58 L.Ed. 758; Roorda v. Volkswagenwerk, A.G., D.C. S.C.1979, 481 F.Supp. 868.

12.   Gilbert v. David, 1915, 35 S.Ct. 164, 235 U.S. 561, 59 L.Ed. 360. On pleading and proof as to jurisdictional questions generally, see § 69 below.

13.   Hardin v. McAvoy, C.A.5th, 1954, 216 F.2d 399, 403. See also Holmes v. Sopuch, C.A.8th, 1981, 639 F.2d 431, and Sligh v. Doe, C.A.4th, 1979, 596 F.2d 1169, holding that the determination of domicile by the district judge is to be upheld unless clearly erroneous.

14.   Seideman v. Hamilton, C.A.3d, 1960, 275 F.2d 224, certiorari denied 80 S.Ct. 1258, 363 U.S. 820, 4 L.Ed.2d 1517.

15.   Mitchell v. U. S., 1874, 21 Wall. 350, 353, 22 L.Ed. 584. Illustrative cases holding that particular circumstances were or were not sufficient to establish a new domicile are cited in 13 Wright, Miller & Cooper, Jurisdiction § 3612.

[§ 27]

1.   13 Wright, Miller & Cooper, Jurisdiction §§ 3623–3630; Warren, Corporations and Diversity of Citizenship, 1933, 19 Va.L.Rev. 661; McGovney, A Supreme Court Fiction: Corporations in the Diverse Citizenship Jurisdiction of the Federal Courts, 1943, 56 Harv.L. Rev. 853, 1090, 1225; Green, Corporations as Persons, Citizens, and Possessors of Liberty, 1945, 94 U.Pa.L.Rev. 202; Moore & Weckstein, Corporations and Diversity of Citizenship Jurisdiction: A Supreme Court Fiction Revisited, 1964, 77 Harv.L.Rev. 1426.

2.   The classic work is Henderson, The Position of Foreign Corporations in American Constitutional Law, 1918.

which is "certainly not a citizen." [3]   In his view the citizenship of the members of the corporation would control.

This view did not long prevail. The increased use of the corporate device as a means of doing business and the desire of these corporations to resort to federal court proved irresistible. Thus in 1844, in the Letson case, the Court declared that a corporation chartered by a state is "entitled, for the purpose of suing and being sued, to be deemed a citizen of that state." [4]   Pressure from dissenting judges forced reexamination of this position ten years later, but while the rationale changed, the practical result remained the same. In Marshall v. Baltimore & Ohio R. Co.[5] the Court returned to Chief Justice Marshall's view that a corporation is an artificial being, that it cannot be a citizen and that the citizenship of the stockholders must control, but it then created a conclusive presumption that all of the stockholders of a corporation are citizens of the state of incorporation. Except as modified by a 1958 statute, to be discussed below, this proposition remains settled law.[6] Indeed it may have been extended, or at least carried to its logical limits. Thus there is a similar presumption that all of the stockholders of a corporation chartered by a foreign country are citizens of that country, and the corporation may come into federal court under the alienage jurisdiction.[7] Municipal corporations are regarded as citizens of the state in which they are located,[8] though the state itself is not a citizen for purposes of diversity.[9] National banks, not chartered by any state, are, by statute, to be "deemed citizens" of the states in which they are located,[10] and some courts have reached the same result with regard to other corporations chartered by the federal government with activity localized in a particular state.[11]

3. Bank of the United States v. Deveaux, 1809, 5 Cranch 61, 86, 3 L.Ed. 38.

4. Louisville, C. & C. R. Co. v. Letson, 1844, 2 How. 497, 555, 11 L.Ed. 353.

5. 1853, 16 How. 314, 14 L.Ed. 953.

6. The doctrine is "finally settled by repeated decisions of this court." St. Louis & S. F. Ry. Co. v. James, 1896, 16 S.Ct. 621, 624, 161 U.S. 545, 554, 40 L.Ed. 802. The Court also has spoken of the rule laid down in the Marshall case as "a compromise destined to endure for over a century." United Steelworkers of America v. R. H. Bouligny, Inc., 1965, 86 S.Ct. 272, 273, 382 U.S. 145, 148, 15 L.Ed.2d 217.

7. National S. S. Co. v. Tugman, 1882, 1 S.Ct. 58, 106 U.S. 118, 27 L.Ed. 87; Barrow S. S. Co. v. Kane, 1898, 18 S.Ct. 526, 170 U.S. 100, 42 L.Ed. 964.

8. Moor v. County of Alameda, 1973, 93 S.Ct. 1785, 1800–1802, 411 U.S. 693, 717–721, 36 L.Ed.2d 596; Illinois v. City of Milwaukee, 1972, 92 S.Ct. 1385, 1390, 406 U.S. 91, 97, 31 L.Ed.2d 712; Cowles v. Mercer County, 1868, 7 Wall. 118, 74 U.S. 118, 19 L.Ed. 86.

If suit against a governmental unit is in reality a suit against the state itself, the Eleventh Amendment deprives the court of jurisdiction. See § 46 below.

9. Postal Telegraph Cable Co. v. Alabama, 1894, 15 S.Ct. 192, 155 U.S. 482, 39 L.Ed. 231; Nuclear Engineering Co. v. Scott, C.A.7th, 1981, 660 F.2d 241, 250; 13 Wright, Miller & Cooper, Jurisdiction § 3602.

10. 28 U.S.C.A. § 1348; Walker v. Bank of America Nat. Trust & Sav. Assn., C.A.9th, 1959, 268 F.2d 16, certiorari denied 80 S.Ct. 211, 361 U.S. 903, 4 L.Ed.2d 158.

11. Feuchtwanger Corp. v. Lake Hiawatha Federal Credit Union, C.A.3d, 1959, 272 F.2d 453; Elwert v. Pacific First Federal Sav. & Loan Assn., D.C.Or. 1956, 138 F.Supp. 395. See Moore &

The conclusive presumption that all the stockholders of a corporation are citizens of the state of incorporation was dubious in 1854. Today it is clear that it is purest fiction. Marshall v. Baltimore & Ohio R. Co., and the doctrine that is based on it, have been severely criticized, as an expansion of federal jurisdiction by means of fiction.[12] It may be argued, however, that it is the Deveaux case, not the Marshall case, that is wrong. A corporation is an entity quite apart from its stockholders, an out-of-state corporation is as likely to be the object of local prejudice as is an out-of-state individual, and it may be said that it should have whatever protection a federal court can provide.[13] One's view on this question is very likely to be determined by his position as to the utility of diversity jurisdiction generally.[14]

Even those who favor permitting corporations to avail themselves of the diversity jurisdiction have recognized that it is an abuse of this jurisdiction when "a local institution, engaged in a local business and in many cases locally owned, is enabled to bring its litigation into the Federal courts simply because it has obtained a corporate charter from another State."[15] To prevent such abuse, and as part of a general purpose to limit diversity jurisdiction,[16] a 1958 statute provided that a corporation shall be deemed a citizen of any state in which it has been incorporated and of the state in which it has its principal place of business.[17] Arguments that the statute was unconstitutional were properly rejected by the courts as insubstantial.[18] The statute

Weckstein, Corporations and Diversity of Citizenship Jurisdiction; A Supreme Court Fiction Revisited, 1964, 77 Harv. L.Rev. 1426, 1436–1438. Contra: Hancock Financial Corp. v. Federal Sav. & Loan Ins. Corp., C.A.9th, 1974, 492 F.2d 1325; Rice v. Disabled American Veterans, D.C.D.C.1968, 295 F.Supp. 131.

See generally 13 Wright, Miller & Cooper, Jurisdiction § 3627.

12. See the articles by Warren and by McGovney cited note 1 above. A contrary view is expressed in Phillips & Christensen, Should Corporations Be Regarded as Citizens Within the Diversity Jurisdiction Provisions?, 1962, 48 A.B.A.J. 435.

The American Law Institute proposes to bar a corporation or other business association from invoking diversity jurisdiction in a state in which it has had, for two years, a "local establishment," as elaborately defined, in any action arising out of the activities of the local establishment. ALI Study, § 1302(b). One court has said that this proposal "makes a good deal of sense and is much more compatible with what little basis there is for diversity jurisdic-

tion." Asher v. Pacific Power & Light Co., D.C.Cal.1965, 249 F.Supp. 671, 678. Professors Moore & Weckstein, in the article cited note 1 above, say, at 1451, that the proposal is "not only unnecessary but unwise."

13. See the articles by Green and by Moore & Weckstein, cited note 1 above.

14. See § 23 above.

15. Sen.Rep. No. 1830, 85th Cong., 2d Sess., 1958, U.S.Code Cong. & Adm. News, pp. 3099, 3101–3102.

16. See 13 Wright, Miller & Cooper, Jurisdiction § 3624; Comment, Corporate Diversity of Citizenship Under 28 U.S.C. § 1332(c), 1974, 26 Baylor L.Rev. 211; Note, Federal Court Diversity Jurisdiction and the Corporation, 1972, 8 Tulsa L.J. 120.

17. 28 U.S.C.A. § 1332(c), as amended by Act of July 25, 1958, § 2, 72 Stat. 415. For the legislative history of the Act, see the Senate Report cited note 15 above.

18. E.g., Eldridge v. Richfield Oil Corp., D.C.Cal.1965, 247 F.Supp. 407, affirmed C.A.9th, 1966, 364 F.2d 909, certiorari denied 87 S.Ct. 750, 385 U.S. 1020, 17 L.Ed.2d 556.

does not give the pleader an option to allege the corporation's citizenship as being either that of the state of incorporation or that of the state where the principal place of business is located. Instead the corporation must be regarded as a citizen of both states. Thus where a corporation incorporated in Delaware and with its principal place of business in Ohio is a party to the suit, diversity is lacking if any adverse party is a citizen either of Delaware or of Ohio.[19]

Prior to the adoption of the 1958 statute, there was a vexing question in determining the citizenship of corporations incorporated in more than one state. The general rule was if such a corporation were a party to a lawsuit in one of the states in which it was incorporated, it would be considered, for diversity purposes, solely a citizen of that state. Thus if a citizen of Massachusetts sued a corporation incorporated both in New York and Massachusetts, diversity existed if the suit was brought in federal court in New York, where the corporation would be regarded as a citizen of New York, but if the suit were brought in federal court in Massachusetts, the corporation would be regarded as a Massachusetts citizen, and the suit dismissed for want of diversity.[20] Several courts and writers have suggested that this artificial rule has survived the 1958 reform,[21] but the sounder view is to the contrary. The matter would be clearcut if the 1958 statute had said that the corporation is to be deemed a citizen of "every" state in which it has been incorporated,[22] but this is the most logical, and surely the most desirable, meaning to ascribe to the phrase "any state" that Congress actually used.[23]

19. Canton v. Angelina Cas. Co., C.A.5th, 1960, 279 F.2d 553; Bender v. Hilton Riviera Corp., D.C.Puerto Rico 1973, 367 F.Supp. 380; Jaconski v. McCloskey & Co., D.C.Pa.1958, 167 F.Supp. 537.

20. Seavey v. Boston & M. R. Co., C.A.1st, 1952, 197 F.2d 485; Jacobson v. New York, N. H. & H. R. Co., C.A. 1st, 1953, 206 F.2d 153, affirmed per curiam, 1954, 74 S.Ct. 474, 347 U.S. 909, 98 L.Ed. 1067; cf. Patch v. Wabash R. Co., 1907, 28 S.Ct. 80, 207 U.S. 277, 52 L.Ed. 24. Contra: Gavin v. Hudson & M. R. Co., C.A.3d, 1950, 185 F.2d 104 (in the example given in the text, the Massachusetts plaintiff could treat the corporation as a New York citizen in whichever state he brought suit).

Professor Weckstein's exhaustive examination of the question recognizes that the Supreme Court had taken "seemingly irreconcilable positions," but concludes that the proposition stated in the text "may be accepted as the law as it existed prior to the 1958 Amendment." Weckstein, Multi-State Corporations and Diversity of Citizenship: A

Field Day for Fictions, 1964, 31 Tenn. L.Rev. 195, 198, 202. To Professor Currie this is "less certain." Currie, Federal Courts: Cases and Materials, 2d ed. 1975, p. 494. See also Currie, The Federal Courts and the American Law Institute, 1968, 36 U.Chi.L.Rev. 1, 39–43.

Under the former rule, a corporation was not considered as incorporated in a second state where the second state compelled the reincorporation as a condition of doing business. Southern R. Co. v. Allison, 1903, 23 S.Ct. 713, 190 U.S. 326, 47 L.Ed. 1078.

21. Hudak v. Port Auth. Trans-Hudson Corp., D.C.N.Y.1965, 238 F.Supp. 790; Majewski v. New York Central R. Co., D.C.Mich.1964, 227 F.Supp. 950; see Jaconski v. McCloskey & Co., D.C.Pa. 1958, 167 F.Supp. 537, 540; Friedenthal, New Limitations on Federal Jurisdiction, 1959, 11 Stan.L.Rev. 213, 236–241.

22. As in ALI Study, § 1301(b)(1).

23. Yancoskie v. Delaware River Port Auth., C.A.3d, 1975, 528 F.2d 722, 727 n. 17; Oslick v. Port Auth. of New

The legislative history of the 1958 statute indicates that the "principal place of business" of a corporation is to be determined by tests developed for the similar phrase in the Bankruptcy Act.[24] The determination of the principal place of business has not been as simple a matter as this might suggest. It is, in each case, a question of fact, and the court must consider such factors as the character of the corporation, its purposes, the kind of business in which it is engaged, and the situs of its operations.[25]

The early cases seemed to take two different views on how to determine the principal place of business of a corporation with significant activities in several states. On one view, the principal place of business was the place where a corporation's home office was located, since this was "the nerve center from which it radiates out to its constituent parts and from which its officers direct, control and coordinate all activities without regard to locale, in the furtherance of the corporate objective." [26] The "home office" test in itself could be variously applied, depending on whether the court looked to the executive offices, at which general policy decisions are made,[27] or to the place where day-to-day control of the business is exercised.[28]

York and New Jersey, D.C.N.Y.1979, 83 F.R.D. 494; French v. Clinchfield Coal Co., D.C.Del.1976, 407 F.Supp. 13; Evans-Hailey Co. v. Crane Co., D.C. Tenn.1962, 207 F.Supp. 193, appeal dismissed 1965, 86 S.Ct. 10, 382 U.S. 801, 15 L.Ed.2d 55; 13 Wright, Miller & Cooper, Jurisdiction § 2626; Weckstein, note 20 above, at 210–216; Comment, Corporate Diversity Jurisdiction: Voluntary Multiple Incorporation and the Forum Doctrine, 1977, 12 Gonz.L. Rev. 347; Note, Citizenship of Multi-State Corporations for Diversity Jurisdiction Purposes, 1963, 40 Iowa L.Rev. 410.

But cf. Rudisill v. Southern Ry. Co., D.C. N.C.1976, 424 F.Supp. 1102, affirmed C.A.4th, 1977, 548 F.2d 488, holding that a corporation is not to be regarded as a citizen of a state in which it was compelled to reincorporate as a condition of doing business in that state.

24. Moesser v. Crucible Steel Co. of America, D.C.Pa.1959, 173 F.Supp. 953. For the legislative history see the Senate Report cited note 15 above, and see Inland Rubber Corp. v. Triple A Tire Serv., Inc., D.C.N.Y.1963, 220 F.Supp. 490, 492–495. The phrase appears in the Bankruptcy Act at former 11 U.S.C.A. § 11 (11 U.S.C.A. § 109(a)). Cases construing the phrase in that Act are collected in the Appendix to Kelly v. U. S. Steel Corp., C.A.3d, 1960, 284 F.2d 850, 855. As the Kelly

case points out, at 852, though the question is one of fact, the relative significance of different facts is a question of law. Moore & Weckstein, in the article cited note 1 above, at 1439, are critical of the suggestion that the bankruptcy cases could be used as precedent since "ample precedent there was, but consistent precedent there was not."

25. Note, The Corporate Principal Place of Business: A Resolution and Revision, 1966, 34 Geo.Wash.L.Rev. 780; Comment, A Corporation's Principal Place of Business for Federal Diversity Jurisdiction, 1963, 38 N.Y.U.L.Rev. 148; Note, 1962, 47 Iowa L.Rev. 1151. The cases collected in 13 Wright, Miller & Cooper, Jurisdiction § 3625, illustrate the welter of views courts have taken and the variety of factors that have been considered.

26. Scot Typewriter Co. v. Underwood Corp., D.C.N.Y.1959, 170 F.Supp. 862, 865; Hughes v. United Engineers & Constr., Inc., D.C.N.Y.1959, 178 F.Supp. 895; Wear-Ever Aluminum, Inc. v. Sipos, D.C.N.Y.1960, 184 F.Supp. 364; Philip Morris, Inc. v. Sun Leasing Co., D.C.N.Y.1974, 371 F.Supp. 1233.

27, 28. See notes 27–28 on page 153.

The other view was that the principal place of business was the place where the corporation carried on the bulk of its activity, even though the home office, in either of the senses described above, was elsewhere.[29]

The essential difficulty is that the 1958 amendment is read, rightly so it seems, as meaning that every corporation must have one, but only one, "principal place of business."[30] This is highly unrealistic when applied to a far-flung corporate enterprise,[31] and the unreality of the process has given new vigor to those who urge that a corporation should be deemed a citizen of every state in which it has substantial local activity.[32] So long as the present statutory test is to be employed, reliance on the location of the home office simply on the ground that it is the "nerve center" gives too much weight to "a pleasant and alluring figure of speech."[33]

The courts have increasingly come to recognize that the earlier cases can be reconciled, in the light of their particular facts, and that a single rule can be applied. This looks to the place where the bulk of the corporate activity takes place, if there is any one state in which this is true, while resorting to the location of the home office only if the corporation's activities are dispersed among several states and no one state clearly predominates.[34]

27.   Sabo v. Standard Oil Co. of Indiana, C.A.7th, 1961, 295 F.2d 893; Mahoney v. Northwestern Bell Tel. Co., D.C. Neb.1966, 258 F.Supp. 500, affirmed C.A.8th, 1967, 377 F.2d 549; Scot Typewriter Co. v. Underwood Corp., D.C. N.Y.1959, 170 F.Supp. 862.

28.   Kelly v. U. S. Steel Corp., C.A.3d, 1960, 284 F.2d 850; Mattson v. Cuyuna Ore Co., D.C.Minn.1960, 180 F.Supp. 743; cf. Note, 1966, 34 Geo.Wash.L. Rev. 780.

29.   Anniston Soil Pipe Co. v. Central Foundry Co., C.A.5th, 1964, 329 F.2d 313; Bruner v. Marjec, Ind., D.C.Va. 1966, 250 F.Supp. 426; Foster v. Midland Valley R. Co., D.C.Okl.1965, 245 F.Supp. 60; Bullock v. Wiebe Constr. Co., D.C.Iowa 1965, 241 F.Supp. 961; Inland Rubber Corp. v. Triple A Tire Serv., Inc., D.C.N.Y.1963, 220 F.Supp. 490; Aron v. Indem. Ins. Co. of North America, D.C.Ill.1961, 200 F.Supp. 147; Clothier v. United Air Lines, Inc., D.C. N.Y.1961, 196 F.Supp. 435, noted 1962, 47 Iowa L.Rev. 1151.

30.   Celanese Corp. of America v. Vandalia Warehouse Corp., C.A.7th, 1970, 424 F.2d 1176; Egan v. American Airlines, Inc., C.A.2d, 1963, 324 F.2d

565; Campbell v. Associated Press, D.C.Pa.1963, 223 F.Supp. 151; Kaufman v. General Ins. Co. of America, D.C.Cal.1961, 192 F.Supp. 238.

31.   "The concept may get artificial in some cases as indeed it is in the case before us. This great corporation has fourteen divisions of the parent corporation and eleven principal subordinate companies. Its various manufacturing activities are spread over practically all the United States and extend to foreign countries. It has literally dozens of important places of business one of which we must pick out as the principal one because the statute says so." Kelly v. U. S. Steel Corp., C.A.3d, 1960, 284 F.2d 850, 853 (per Goodrich, J.).

32.   See § 23 above. See also the proposal of the American Law Institute, described note 12 above.

33.   Kelly v. U. S. Steel Corp., C.A.3d, 1960, 284 F.2d 850, 853.

34.   Toms v. Country Quality Meats, Inc., C.A.5th, 1980, 610 F.2d 313; Lugo-Vina v. Pueblo Intl., Inc., C.A.1st, 1978, 574 F.2d 41; Bialac v. Harsh Bldg. Co., C.A.9th, 1972, 463 F.2d 1185, certiorari denied 93 S.Ct. 558, 409 U.S.

Some cases have held that the 1958 amendment has no application to corporations chartered in foreign countries, and that such a corporation, as was true prior to 1958, is deemed to be a citizen only of the foreign country, regardless of where it has its principal place of business.[35] The problem was apparently not considered in drafting the amendment, and the result described is defensible as a matter of statutory construction. Nevertheless this is an unappealing result if it permits a corporation with its principal place of business in New York to invoke diversity in litigation with a New York citizen simply because the corporation is incorporated in Liberia rather than in Delaware.[36] More recent cases have avoided this result by holding that a foreign corporation is considered a citizen of the state or foreign state in which it has its principal place of business.[37]

The statutory definition of corporate citizenship was further amended in 1964 to provide that in a direct action against a liability insurer, to which the insured is not a party, the insurer shall be deemed to be a citizen of the state of which the insured is a citizen, as well as of its state of incorporation and of the state where it has its principal place of business.[38] This statute grew out of a problem that had led to clogged dockets in the federal courts in Louisiana. Because of the broad review of jury verdicts that the Louisiana practice permits, lawyers for plaintiffs in that state greatly preferred to be in federal court rather than in state court. They were able to convert what otherwise would have been a routine automobile accident case between two Louisiana citizens into a diversity action by taking ad-

1060, 34 L.Ed.2d 512, rehearing denied 93 S.Ct. 1355, 410 U.S. 948, 35 L.Ed.2d 615; Egan v. American Airlines, Inc., C.A.2d, 1963, 324 F.2d 565; Clinton v. Budd Co., D.C.Mich.1982, 543 F.Supp. 226; Mahoney v. Northwestern Bell Tel. Co., D.C.Neb.1966, 258 F.Supp. 500, affirmed C.A.8th, 377 F.2d 549; 13 Wright, Miller & Cooper, Jurisdiction § 3625.

35. E.g., Clarkson Co. v. Shaheen, C.A.2d, 1976, 544 F.2d 624, 628 n. 5; Salomon Englander y Cia, Ltda. v. Israel Discount Bank, Ltd., D.C.N.Y. 1980, 494 F.Supp. 914; cf. Eisenberg v. Commercial Union Assur. Co., D.C. N.Y.1960, 189 F.Supp. 500.

36. ALI Study, § 1301(b)(1); Moore & Weckstein, note 1 above, at 1435–1436.
The result described in the text, which the ALI proposal was specifically intended to avoid, was reached in Chemical Transp. Corp. v. Metropolitan Petroleum Corp., D.C.N.Y.1964, 246 F.Supp. 563.

37. Jerguson v. Blue Dot Investment, Inc., C.A.5th, 1981, 659 F.2d 31, certiorari denied 102 S.Ct. 2013, ___ U.S. ___,

72 L.Ed.2d 469; Trans World Hospital Supplies, Ltd. v. Hospital Corp. of America, D.C.Tenn.1982, 542 F.Supp. 869; Richmond Constr. Corp. v. Hilb, D.C.Fla.1980, 482 F.Supp. 1201; Bergen Shipping Co., Ltd. v. Japan Marine Services, Ltd., D.C.N.Y.1974, 386 F.Supp. 430; Southeast Guar. Trust Co. v. Rodman & Renshaw, Inc., D.C. Ill.1973, 358 F.Supp. 1001. See 13 Wright, Miller & Cooper, Jurisdiction § 3628.

The principal place of business within the United States will not be looked to if the foreign corporation has a more important place of business in some other country. Roby v. General Tire & Rubber Co., D.C.Md.1980, 500 F.Supp. 480; Arab Intl. Bank & Trust Co. v. National Westminster Bank Ltd., D.C.N.Y. 1979, 463 F.Supp. 1145.

38. 28 U.S.C.A. § 1332(c), as amended by Act of Aug. 14, 1964, Pub.L. 88–439, 78 Stat. 445. The statute is criticized by Weckstein, The 1964 Diversity Amendment: Congressional Indirect Action against State "Direct Action" Laws, 1965 Wis.L.Rev. 268.

vantage of the state statute permitting suit directly against the insurer without joinder of the insured.[39] If the defendant's insurer was incorporated and had its principal place of business in a state other than Louisiana, diversity was held to exist.[40] The statute has cured that problem, but it has raised problems of construction of its own, and there is as yet no agreement whether it should be literally applied or read as reaching only the situation that gave rise to it.[41]

The settled rule has long been that unincorporated associations do not enjoy the same fiction that is applied to corporations, and that when a partnership, a joint stock company, a labor union, the governing board of an institution, or some similar association is a party, the actual citizenship of each of its members must be considered in determining whether diversity exists.[42] This rule was followed even where local law permitted the association to sue or be sued as an entity, and declared that it was to be treated as if it were a corporation.[43] Some lower court cases evinced a willingness to depart from what had been the settled rule, and to treat an association as an entity for diversity purposes.[44] The Supreme Court, however, refused to

39. Only Louisiana and Wisconsin have such statutes. Wisconsin does not have the peculiarly broad scope of review that is had in Louisiana, and there is no indication that in Wisconsin the direct action statute was often used as a means of creating diversity. See Weckstein, note 38 above.

40. Lumbermen's Mut. Cas. Co. v. Elbert, 1954, 75 S.Ct. 151, 348 U.S. 48, 99 L.Ed. 59.

41. A number of cases have refused to apply the statute to suits against an insurer that were not the type Congress had in mind when it adopted the amendment: Henderson v. Selective Ins. Co., C.A.6th, 1966, 369 F.2d 143; White v. United States Fidelity & Guar. Co., C.A.1st, 1966, 356 F.2d 746; Watkins v. Allstate Ins. Co., D.C.Mich. 1980, 503 F.Supp. 848; Fiorentino v. Traveler's Ins. Co., D.C.Pa.1978, 448 F.Supp. 1364; Bishop v. Allstate Ins. Co., D.C.Ark.1970, 313 F.Supp. 875; Bourget v. Government Employees Ins. Co., D.C.Conn.1970, 313 F.Supp. 367. See 13 Wright, Miller & Cooper, Jurisdiction § 3629.
Litigation between an employee and his employer's compensation carrier has given particular difficulty. Compare Campbell v. Insurance Co. of North America, C.A.5th, 1977, 552 F.2d 604, with Aetna Cas. & Sur. Ins. Co. v. Greene, C.A.6th, 1979, 606 F.2d 123. See Wasson, Diversity Jurisdiction in Reverse Direct Actions: Section

1332(c) and the Need for Legislation Clarification, 1980, 68 Ky.L.J. 439; Note, Federal Diversity Jurisdiction in Direct Actions—A dispute over the Application of Section 1332(c), 1980, 29 U.Kan.L.Rev. 143.

42. 13 Wright, Miller & Cooper, Jurisdiction § 3630; Great Southern Fireproof Hotel Co. v. Jones, 1900, 20 S.Ct. 690, 177 U.S. 449, 44 L.Ed. 842 (partnership); Chapman v. Barney, 1889, 9 S.Ct. 426, 129 U.S. 677, 32 L.Ed. 800 (joint stock company); Thomas v. Board of Trustees of Ohio State Univ., 1904, 25 S.Ct. 24, 195 U.S. 207, 49 L.Ed. 160 (governing board); United Steelworkers of America v. R. H. Bouligny, Inc., 1965, 86 S.Ct. 272, 382 U.S. 145, 15 L.Ed.2d 217 (labor union).

43. Great Southern Fireproof Hotel Co. v. Jones, 1900, 20 S.Ct. 690, 177 U.S. 449, 44 L.Ed. 842.
Compare, however, People of Puerto Rico v. Russell & Co., Sucesores, S. en C., 1933, 53 S.Ct. 447, 288 U.S. 476, 77 L.Ed. 903, where a sociedad en comandita formed under Puerto Rican law was held to have so complete a "personality" under that law as to be treated as a corporation, for purposes of defeating diversity.

44. Mason v. American Exp. Co., C.A.2d, 1964, 334 F.2d 392; Van Sant v. American Exp. Co., C.A.3d, 1948, 169 F.2d 355; Comment, 1965 Duke L.J. 329; Note, 1959, 68 Yale L.J. 1182.

permit this. It recognized the appealing arguments for giving entity treatment to associations, but held that "pleas for extension of the diversity jurisdiction to hitherto uncovered broad categories of litigants ought to be made to the Congress and not to the courts." [45]

More recently, however, in Navarro Savings Association v. Lee,[46] the Court, rejecting many contrary decisions from the lower courts, held that the individual trustees of a business trust organized under Massachusetts law can invoke diversity jurisdiction on the basis of their own citizenship, without regard to the citizenship of the trust's beneficial shareholders. The Court chose to adhere to the rule, established since 1808, that the trustee of an express trust can sue on the basis of his own citizenship. Although a business trust differs from conventional trusts in some respects, and resembles a business enterprise, the trustees in this case were active trustees whose control over the assets held in their names was real and substantial, and this was thought decisive.

There is a division in the lower courts on whether to look to the citizenship of all the partners or only the general partners in the case of a limited partnership.[47] This issue will have to be reexamined in the light of Navarro.

In many cases it is possible to avoid the impact of the usual rule about unincorporated associations by bringing a class action for or against members of the association, naming as representatives of the class only those whose citizenship will produce diversity.[48]

§ 28. Time of Determination of Diversity [1]

Diversity is determined as of the commencement of the action.[2] If diversity existed between the parties at that date, it is not defeated

45. United Steelworkers of America v. R. H. Bouligny, Inc., 1965, 86 S.Ct. 272, 275, 382 U.S. 145, 150–151, 15 L.Ed.2d 217, noted 1966, 51 Cornell L.Q. 827, 34 Geo.Wash.L.Rev. 793, 7 Wm. & Mary L.Rev. 409.

The American Law Institute proposes to treat an association, if regarded as an entity under state law, as a citizen of the state in which it has its principal place of business, but to bar the association from invoking diversity jurisdiction in a state in which it has a "local establishment." ALI Study, §§ 1301(b) (2), 1302(b). See Comment, Unincorporated Associations: Diversity Jurisdiction and the ALI Proposal, 1965 Duke L.J. 329; Legislation Note, Federal Diversity Jurisdiction—Citizenship for Unincorporated Associations, 1966, 19 Vand.L.Rev. 984.

46. 1980, 100 S.Ct. 1779, 446 U.S. 458, 64 L.Ed.2d 425.

47. Compare Carlsberg Resources Corp. v. Cambria Sav. & Loan Assn., C.A.3d, 1977, 554 F.2d 1254 (all partners), with Colonial Realty Corp. v. Bache & Co., C.A.2d, 1966, 358 F.2d 178, certiorari denied 87 S.Ct. 40, 385 U.S. 817, 17 L.Ed.2d 56 (general partners). See Comment, Limited Partnerships and Federal Diversity Jurisdiction, 1978, 45 U.Chi.L.Rev. 384.

48. Rule 23.2. See § 72 below. See also 7A Wright & Miller, Civil § 1861.

[§ 28]

1. 13 Wright, Miller & Cooper, Jurisdiction § 3608.

2. Louisville, N. A. & C. R. Co. v. Louisville Trust Co., 1899, 19 S.Ct. 817, 174 U.S. 552, 43 L.Ed. 1081; Hoefferle Truck Sales, Inc. v. Divco-Wayne Corp., C.A.7th, 1975, 523 F.2d 543; Mullins v. Beatrice Pocahontas Co., C.A.4th, 1974, 489 F.2d 260.

because one of the parties later becomes a citizen of the same state as his opponent.[3] Nor will a change of parties, by intervention or substitution, divest the jurisdiction of the federal court.[4] By the same token, if there was no diversity when the action was commenced, it cannot be created by a change of domicile of one of the parties or other subsequent event,[5] although it may be that a new suit can then be commenced.

These principles apply only where the nature of the action remains the same. If the change in parties reflects a change in the nature of the action, the test of diversity must be met with regard to the parties to the altered action.[6] And in determining whether realignment of parties is required,[7] the position taken by a party during the litigation may be considered in determining how he should originally have been aligned.[8]

§ 29. Parties Considered in Determining Diversity [1]

It was seen earlier [2] that under the rule of Strawbridge v. Curtiss [3] complete diversity between the parties opposed in interest is a requisite of diversity jurisdiction, except as Congress has otherwise provided. In determining whether complete diversity exists, nominal or formal parties may be ignored.[4] Thus there is diversity despite the joinder of a party who has no interest in the controversy,[5] and the

3. Morgan's Heirs v. Morgan, 1817, 2 Wheat. 290, 15 U.S. 290, 4 L.Ed. 242; Johnston v. Cordell Nat. Bank, C.A. 10th, 1970, 421 F.2d 1310; Napletana v. Hillsdale College, C.A.6th, 1967, 385 F.2d 871.

4. Wichita R. & Light Co. v. Public Utilities Comm. of the State of Kansas, 1922, 43 S.Ct. 51, 260 U.S. 48, 67 L.Ed. 124 (intervention); Hardenbergh v. Ray, 1894, 14 S.Ct. 305, 151 U.S. 112, 38 L.Ed. 93 (substitution); and see 13 Wright, Miller & Cooper, Jurisdiction § 3608.

5. Field v. Volkswagenwerk AG, C.A.3d, 1980, 626 F.2d 293 (change of administratrix); Kendrick v. Kendrick, C.C.A.5th, 1927, 16 F.2d 744, certiorari denied 47 S.Ct. 472, 273 U.S. 758, 71 L.Ed. 877 (intervention); E. K. Carey Drilling Co. v. Murphy, D.C.Colo.1953, 113 F.Supp. 226 (change of domicile).

6. Grady v. Irvine, C.A.4th, 1958, 254 F.2d 224, certiorari denied 79 S.Ct. 30, 358 U.S. 819, 3 L.Ed.2d 60.

7. See § 30 below.

8. Reed v. Robilio, C.A.6th, 1967, 376 F.2d 392, 396; Green v. Green, C.A.7th, 1954, 218 F.2d 130, 144, certiorari denied 75 S.Ct. 606, 349 U.S. 917, 99 L.Ed. 1250; B. J. Van Ingen & Co., Inc. v. Burlington County Bridge Comm.,

D.C.N.J.1949, 83 F.Supp. 778, 788–789; Hellenthal v. John Hancock Mut. Life Ins. Co., D.C.Wash.1929, 31 F.2d 997, 998.

The subsequent events can be looked to, however, only insofar as they shed light on facts in existence at the time the action was commenced. American Motorists Ins. Co. v. Trane Co., C.A. 7th, 1981, 657 F.2d 146, 151 n. 3.

[§ 29]

1. 13 Wright, Miller & Cooper, Jurisdiction § 3606.

2. See § 24 above.

3. 1806, 3 Cranch 267, 2 L.Ed. 435.

4. Carneal v. Banks, 1825, 10 Wheat. 181, 6 L.Ed. 297; Salem Trust Co. v. Manufacturers' Fin. Co., 1924, 44 S.Ct. 266, 264 U.S. 182, 68 L.Ed. 628; Mayor and City Council of Baltimore v. Weinberg, D.C.Md.1961, 190 F.Supp. 140 (mortgagee whose mortgage had been satisfied before commencement of proceedings). On the significance of "John Doe" defendants, see § 31 below.

5. Salem Trust Co. v. Manufacturers' Fin. Co., 1924, 44 S.Ct. 266, 264 U.S. 182, 68 L.Ed. 628; Application of Blakeman, D.C.N.Y.1981, 512 F.Supp. 325.

fraudulent joinder of a defendant of the same citizenship as plaintiff will not defeat removal of an action.[6]

It is clear that the court may not disregard the citizenship of "indispensable" parties,[7] and indeed it is sometimes said too loosely that only the citizenship of "indispensable" parties will be considered. This is not the rule. Even though a party is merely proper, as, for example, a joint tortfeasor, if he has in fact been joined his citizenship must be considered,[8] although where the party is not "indispensable" it may be possible for plaintiff to have the action dismissed as to the co-citizen and thus perfect jurisdiction.[9] Where parties who are merely "proper" are involved, and they are not "needed for just adjudication" by the tests of Rule 19, a large measure of choice in shaping the action is thus left to the plaintiff.

It was noted above that nominal parties will be disregarded. In applying this rule, however, one who has the legal right to sue and to represent those having a beneficial interest in the recovery is not treated as a nominal party, and his citizenship, rather than the citizenship of those whom he represents, is looked to for determining diversity. This rule was so well established in early decisions [10] that by 1824 Chief Justice Marshall could announce as "the universally received construction" that "jurisdiction is neither given nor ousted by the relative situation of the parties concerned in interest, but by the relative situation of the parties named on the record." [11] In order to come within this rule, however, the representative must have actual powers with regard to the matter in litigation. Where the representative cannot prevent the institution or prosecution of the actions, or exercise any control over them, and is thus a mere conduit through whom the law affords a remedy to the persons aggrieved, the representative is treated as a nominal party, and the citizenship of the persons aggrieved is determinative.[12]

Similarly no diversity exists if the party of record is merely formal, and the real party is a citizen of the same state as his opponent. Miller & Lux v. East Side Canal & Irrigation Co., 1908, 29 S.Ct. 111, 211 U.S. 293, 53 L.Ed. 189.

6. See § 31 below at notes 51, 52.

7. Schuckman v. Rubenstein, C.C.A.6th, 1947, 164 F.2d 952; and cases cited 13 Wright, Miller & Cooper, Jurisdiction § 3606.

As to when the conclusory label "indispensable" is appropriate, see § 70 below.

8. Chicago, R. I. & P. R. Co. v. Dowell, 1913, 33 S.Ct. 684, 229 U.S. 102, 57 L.Ed. 1090 (removal); Carson v. Allied News Co., C.A.7th, 1975, 511 F.2d 22 (original jurisdiction); Iowa Public

Serv. Co. v. Medicine Bow Coal Co., C.A.8th, 1977, 556 F.2d 400 (removal); Dollar S.S. Lines v. Merz, C.C.A.9th, 1934, 68 F.2d 594 (original jurisdiction).

9. See § 69 below.

10. Chappedelaine v. Dechenaux, 1808, 4 Cranch 306, 307, 2 L.Ed. 629; Childress v. Emory, 1823, 8 Wheat. 642, 5 L.Ed. 705.

11. Osborn v. Bank of the United States, 1824, 9 Wheat. 738, 856, 6 L.Ed. 204.

12. The rule set out in the text is taken from Susquehanna & Wyoming Val. R. & Coal Co. v. Blatchford, 1870, 11 Wall. 172, 177, 20 L.Ed. 179. See also Kansas City, Mo. ex rel. Gemco, Inc. v. American Concrete Forms, Inc., D.C. Mo.1970, 318 F.Supp. 567.

Applying these two rules, if some officer is named as the formal obligee of a bond, for the benefit of private individuals, the citizenship of the individuals controls,[13] but the result is otherwise if the obligee has a real interest in the suit on the bond.[14] The citizenship of an active trustee, rather than that of the beneficiaries, is decisive,[15] but again a different result is reached with regard to a dry passive trustee who has only a naked legal title to the property.[16] Only the citizenship of the named representative in a class action is considered,[17] and this is the rule also in a suit by a receiver [18] or a subrogee.[19]

It was once accepted as the law that the executor or administrator of the estate of a decedent had control over litigation involving that estate, and it was, therefore, the citizenship of the representative, rather than the state of his appointment, or the citizenship of the deceased, or the citizenship of creditors, next of kin, or legatees that controlled for purposes of jurisdiction.[20] This rule was applied whether the result was to create jurisdiction that would otherwise be absent [21] or to defeat jurisdiction that would otherwise exist.[22]

13. Browne v. Strode, 1809, 5 Cranch 303, 3 L.Ed. 108; McNutt for Use of Leggett v. Bland, 1844, 2 How. 9, 11 L.Ed. 159; Howard v. U. S., 1902, 22 S.Ct. 543, 184 U.S. 676, 46 L.Ed. 754.

14. U. S. Fidelity & Guar. Co. v. U. S. for the Benefit of Kenyon, 1907, 27 S.Ct. 381, 204 U.S. 349, 51 L.Ed. 516.

15. Susquehanna & Wyoming Valley R. & Coal Co. v. Blatchford, 1870, 11 Wall. 172, 20 L.Ed. 179 (trustee under mortgage); Bullard v. City of Cisco, 1933, 54 S.Ct. 177, 290 U.S. 179, 78 L.Ed. 254 (bondholders' committee); Navarro Savings Assn. v. Lee, 1980, 100 S.Ct. 1779, 446 U.S. 458, 64 L.Ed. 2d 425 (business trust); County of Todd v. Loegering, C.A.8th, 1961, 297 F.2d 470 (trustee for the heirs under wrongful death statute).

16. Boon's Heirs v. Chiles, 1834, 8 Pet. 532, 8 L.Ed. 1034; Bogue v. Chicago, B. & Q. R. Co., D.C.Iowa 1912, 193 F. 728.

17. Snyder v. Harris, 1969, 89 S.Ct. 1053, 1059, 394 U.S. 332, 340, 22 L.Ed. 2d 319; 7 Wright & Miller, Jurisdiction § 1755.

18. Barber v. Powell, C.C.A.4th, 1943, 135 F.2d 728, certiorari denied 64 S.Ct. 56, 320 U.S. 752, 88 L.Ed. 447; Farlow v. Lea, C.C.D.Ohio, 1877, 8 Fed.Cas.No. 4,649.

The holding to the contrary in Chapman v. St. Louis & S. W. Ry. Co., D.C.Tex. 1947, 71 F.Supp. 1017, has been called "clearly wrong." Cohan & Tate, Manufacturing Federal Diversity Jurisdiction by the Appointment of Representatives: Its Legality and Propriety, 1956, 1 Vill.L.Rev. 201, 221.

19. City of New Orleans v. Gaines' Adm'r, 1891, 11 S.Ct. 428, 138 U.S. 595, 34 L.Ed. 1102.

20. Childress v. Emory, 1823, 8 Wheat. 642, 5 L.Ed. 705. See also notes 21 and 22 below.

The American Law Institute proposes, however, to have the representative of a decedent be deemed to be a citizen only of the state of which the decedent was a citizen. ALI Study, § 1301(b)(4). The ALI proposal has been much praised but not adopted. See § 31 n. 31 below.

21. Rice v. Houston, 1871, 13 Wall. 66, 20 L.Ed. 484; Lang v. Elm City Constr. Co., C.A.2d, 1963, 324 F.2d 235, noted 1964, 48 Minn.L.Rev. 785, 73 Yale L.J. 873; Deposit Guar. Bank & Trust Co. v. Burton, C.A.6th, 1967, 380 F.2d 346; Janzen v. Goos, C.A.8th, 1962, 302 F.2d 421; Erwin v. Barrow, C.A.10th, 1954, 217 F.2d 522.

22. Mecom v. Fitzsimmons Drilling Co., 1931, 52 S.Ct. 84, 284 U.S. 183, 76 L.Ed. 233; Hot Oil Serv., Inc. v. Hall, C.A.9th, 1966, 366 F.2d 295; Seymour v. Johnson, C.A.6th, 1956, 235 F.2d 181; Grady v. Irvine, C.A.4th, 1958, 254 F.2d 224, certiorari denied 79 S.Ct. 30, 358 U.S. 819, 3 L.Ed.2d 60.

These propositions are no longer the law. Beginning with the decision of the Third Circuit in 1968 in McSparran v. Weist,[23] an unbroken series of decisions from courts of appeals have refused to allow creation of jurisdiction by the appointment of an out-of-state representative whose only function is to give the appearance of diversity.[24] These decisions are discussed in a later section.[25]

Similarly in Miller v. Perry [26] the Fourth Circuit held that diversity was not defeated by the appointment of a resident ancillary administrator, as required by state law, and that jurisdiction existed because of diversity between the resident defendant and beneficiaries who were citizens of another state.

There has also been difficulty, and the law on the point is in the process of change, with regard to guardians. The rules had been that if a general guardian is empowered by state law to sue in his own name, his citizenship is controlling,[27] but that a guardian ad litem, whose responsibilities are only for a particular litigation, is merely a nominal party and the citizenship of the ward is looked to.[28] In line with the recent change in attitude toward out-of-state administrators, it now appears that if an out-of-state guardian, regardless of his powers, is appointed to create diversity, the citizenship of the guardian will be disregarded and the citizenship of the ward will control.[29]

23. C.A.3d, 1968, 402 F.2d 867, certiorari denied 89 S.Ct. 1739, 395 U.S. 903, 23 L.Ed.2d 217. The McSparran case itself involved an out-of-state guardian but the Third Circuit rejected any distinction between a guardian and the representative of a decedent's estate, 402 F.2d at 872, and overruled two of its earlier cases that had involved administrators.

24. Lester v. McFaddon, C.A.4th, 1969, 415 F.2d 1101; O'Brien v. AVCO Corp., C.A.2d, 1969, 425 F.2d 1030; Bass v. Texas Power & Light Co., C.A.5th, 1970, 432 F.2d 763, certiorari denied 91 S.Ct. 1194, 401 U.S. 975, 28 L.Ed.2d 324; Gilchrist v. Strong, D.C.Okl.1969, 299 F.Supp. 804. The principle was recognized, but a bona fide motive for the appointment of an out-of-state representative was found, in O'Brien v. Stover, C.A.8th, 1971, 443 F.2d 1013, and in Hackney v. Newman Memorial Hosp., Inc., C.A.10th, 1980, 621 F.2d 1069, certiorari denied 101 S.Ct. 397, 449 U.S. 982, 66 L.Ed.2d 244.

25. See § 31 below.

26 C.A.4th, 1972, 456 F.2d 63, noted 1972, 47 N.Y.U.L.Rev. 801.

27. "If in the state of the forum the general guardian has the right to bring suit in his own name as such guardian, and does so, he is to be treated as the party plaintiff so far as Federal Jurisdiction is concerned, even though suit might have been instituted in the name of the ward by guardian ad litem or next friend." Mexican Central Ry. Co. v. Eckman, 1903, 23 S.Ct. 211, 213, 187 U.S. 429, 434, 47 L.Ed. 245.

Citizenship of the ward controlled where state law did not permit guardian to sue in his own name. Martineau v. City of St. Paul, C.A.8th, 1949, 172 F.2d 777; Ansaldi v. Kennedy, D.C. Mass.1930, 41 F.2d 858.

28. Ziady v. Curley, C.A.4th, 1968, 396 F.2d 873; Appelt v. Whitty, C.A.7th, 1961, 286 F.2d 135; Blumenthal v. Craig, C.C.A.3d, 1897, 81 F. 320; Curry v. Maxson, D.C.Mo.1970, 318 F.Supp. 842; Hernandez v. Lucas, D.C.Tex. 1966, 254 F.Supp. 901; Blackwell v. Vance Trucking Co., D.C.S.C.1956, 139 F.Supp. 103.

29. McSparran v. Weist, C.A.3d, 1968, 402 F.2d 867, certiorari denied 89 S.Ct. 1739, 395 U.S. 903, 23 L.Ed.2d 217; Rogers v. Bates, C.A.8th, 1970, 431 F.2d 16; Bartnick v. Reader Co., C.A. 8th, 1973, 487 F.2d 1021. See § 31 below.

§ 30. Realignment of Parties [1]

In determining whether diversity jurisdiction exists, the alignment of the parties as plaintiffs and defendants in the pleadings is not conclusive. It is the duty of the court to "look beyond the pleadings, and arrange the parties according to their sides in the dispute." [2] Usually such realignment of the parties, where required, will have the effect of defeating jurisdiction,[3] but the rule works both ways and jurisdiction will be sustained, if there exists diversity when the parties are properly aligned, even though diversity is lacking on the face of the pleadings.[4]

In determining how the parties should be aligned, the courts look usually to the ultimate interests of each of the parties, and align those together who have the same ultimate interest. Thus in an action by one of the owners of land against the lessee of the land claiming a fraud upon the owners, the interest of the other owner is the same as the plaintiff, and she must be realigned as a plaintiff.[5] Where an insured tortfeasor brings an action against his insurer for a declaratory judgment as to his coverage and names the person suing him in tort as a defendant along with the insurer, the tort claimant will be realigned as a plaintiff, since he and the insured have an identical interest in having it held that the insurance covers the accident in question.[6] A similar analysis of the interests of the parties is made in other cases.[7] The ultimate interest test is not, however, the exclusive test. In a stockholders' derivative action where the corporation is alleged to be under control antagonistic to those bringing the suit, the corporation will be aligned as a defendant, even though any recovery in the suit will be for the benefit of the corporation and

---

[§ 30]

1. 13 Wright, Miller & Cooper, Jurisdiction § 3607.

2. City of Dawson v. Columbia Ave. Sav. Fund, Safe Deposit, Title & Trust Co., 1905, 25 S.Ct. 420, 421, 197 U.S. 178, 180, 49 L.Ed. 713.

3. E.g., Lee v. Lehigh Val. Coal Co., 1925, 45 S.Ct. 385, 267 U.S. 542, 69 L.Ed. 782; City of Indianapolis v. Chase Nat. Bank, 1941, 62 S.Ct. 15, 314 U.S. 63, 86 L.Ed. 47.

4. Pacific Ry. Co. v. Ketchum, 1879, 101 U.S. 289, 25 L.Ed. 932; Broidy v. State Mut. Life Assur. Co. of Worcester, Mass., C.A.2d, 1951, 186 F.2d 490; Thompson v. Bankers & Shippers Ins. Co. of New York, D.C.Miss.1979, 479 F.Supp. 956. Normally, as in the cases cited, realignment to create diversity will occur in a removed action where the removing party asks for realignment to justify the removal. This need not always be the case. When a party who should join as plaintiff refuses to

do so, he may be named as defendant, Fed.R.Civ.Proc. 19(a), 7 Wright & Miller, Civil § 1605, but should then be realigned as a plaintiff for jurisdictional purposes. Eikel v. States Marine Lines, Inc., C.A.5th, 1973, 473 F.2d 959; Standard Oil Co. of California v. Perkins, C.A.9th, 1965, 347 F.2d 379; cf. Perkins v. Standard Oil Co. of California, D.C.Or.1961, 29 F.R.D. 16; Dental Precision Shoulder v. L. D. Caulk Co., D.C.N.Y.1947, 7 F.R.D. 203.

5. Lee v. Lehigh Val. Coal Co., 1925, 45 S.Ct. 385, 267 U.S. 542, 69 L.Ed. 782; cf. Alexander v. Washington, C.A.5th, 1960, 274 F.2d 349.

6. Bonell v. General Acc. Fire & Life Assur. Corp., D.C.Cal.1958, 167 F.Supp. 384; cf. Farmer's Alliance Mut. Ins. Co. v. Jones, C.A.10th, 1978, 570 F.2d 1384, certiorari denied 99 S.Ct. 97, 439 U.S. 826, 58 L.Ed.2d 119.

7. See the cases set out in 13 Wright, Miller & Cooper, Jurisdiction § 3607 n. 7.

thus its ultimate interest is the same as the plaintiffs'.[8] This is done, seemingly, on the theory that the antagonism is sufficient to create the "collision of interest" said to be necessary.[9] The rules applicable to a stockholders' suit apply also to a suit by a beneficiary of a trust or estate seeking to enforce a claim of the trust or estate.[10]

Although questions of alignment are determined initially from the pleadings, the subsequent course of the litigation may reveal more clearly the position of the various parties and cast light on how they should have been originally aligned.[11]

The most difficult questions of realignment occur where the interests of a party are in accord with those of the plaintiffs in some respects and of the defendants in other respects. This was the problem in the well-known case of City of Indianapolis v. Chase National Bank.[12] The summary of the principles that govern in realignment cases set forth there has properly been regarded as definitive, though these principles are neither novel nor disputed by the four dissenting justices. The dispute turned, as is so often true, on the application of agreed principles to the facts at hand.

The bank, deemed a New York citizen, was trustee under a mortgage deed securing certain bonds issued by a gas company. The bank brought an action against the gas company, and the city of Indianapolis, both Indiana citizens, for a determination that the city had succeeded to the obligations of lessee on a lease from the gas company and that the lease was valid, and for overdue interest on the bonds. A bare majority of the Court held that in aligning parties it must look to the "primary and controlling matter in dispute," [13] which in the case before it was whether the city was bound by the lease. Since on this issue the gas company was united in interest with the bank, the majority held that the gas company should be realigned as a plaintiff and ordered dismissal for want of jurisdiction.[14] The four

8. Smith v. Sperling, 1957, 77 S.Ct. 1112, 354 U.S. 91, 1 L.Ed.2d 1205; Doctor v. Harrington, 1905, 25 S.Ct. 355, 196 U.S. 579, 49 L.Ed. 606; and see 7A Wright & Miller, Civil § 1822. See § 73 below.

9. City of Dawson v. Columbia Ave. Sav. Fund, Safe Deposit, Title & Trust Co., 1905, 25 S.Ct. 420, 421, 197 U.S. 178, 181, 49 L.Ed. 713.

But see Lewis v. Odell, C.A.2d, 1974, 503 F.2d 445, where the corporation was aligned as a plaintiff since the pleadings did not disclose any antagonism of the corporation to the derivative action.

10. Hamer v. New York Railways Co., 1917, 37 S.Ct. 511, 244 U.S. 266, 61 L.Ed. 1125; Reed v. Robilio, C.A.6th, 1967, 376 F.2d 392; Hellenthal v. John Hancock Mut. Life Ins. Co., D.C.Wash. 1929, 31 F.2d 997; see Goldstein v.

Groesbeck, C.C.A.2d, 1944, 142 F.2d 422, 425, certiorari denied 65 S.Ct. 36, 323 U.S. 737, 89 L.Ed. 590.

11. See § 28 n. 8 above.

12. 1941, 62 S.Ct. 15, 314 U.S. 63, 86 L.Ed. 47, noted 1942, 40 Mich.L.Rev. 1109, 7 Mo.L.Rev. 316, 90 U.Pa.L.Rev. 620, 15 So.Cal.L.Rev. 377, 28 Va.L.Rev. 549.

13. The quoted phrase is taken by the Court from Merchants Cotton-Press & Storage Co. v. Insurance Co. of North America, 1894, 14 S.Ct. 367, 373, 151 U.S. 368, 385, 38 L.Ed. 195.

14. The jurisdictional ruling seems the more technical because it came after years of litigation, and because three years earlier the Supreme Court had refused to review a decision of the circuit court of appeals, prior to trial on

dissenters, observing that the judgment below did hold the gas company liable for more than a million dollars, though it fixed primary liability on the city, objected to "the subtlety by which a judgment debtor is transfigured into a creditor for jurisdictional purposes." [15] They found a real controversy between the bank and the gas company as to the liability for interest, and rejected the notion that jurisdiction should turn on whether the court considers one issue to "dominate" another or to be more "actual" or "substantial" than the other. Both the majority and the dissenters relied in part on the earlier decision of Sutton v. English,[16] where it was held that in a suit to set aside testamentary dispositions and to distribute the property among the heirs, a defendant who, as a legatee, was interested adversely to the plaintiffs, should not be aligned as a plaintiff for jurisdictional purposes, even though, being also an heir, she would share in the relief if the plaintiffs were successful. To the majority the Sutton case was a clear holding that parties must be aligned according to their attitude toward the actual and substantial controversy,[17] while the dissenters found comfort in the fact that in Sutton it was held error to align one of the defendants with the plaintiff where her interest was adverse to the plaintiff on one out of four issues, although with the plaintiff as to three of the four.[18] The majority seem to have the better of it in their reading of the Sutton case. The issue on which the interest of the heir was adverse to that of the plaintiffs was whether she would take 100% of the estate, as residuary legatee, or 5% of the estate, as she would if the will were set aside. That she and the plaintiffs had a common interest on the other three claims, which, if successful, would have increased the size of the estate, was insignificant in comparison.[19]

It is obvious that reasonable arguments can be made either way in the City of Indianapolis situation. There is seeming merit in the view of the dissent that the alignment in the pleadings should be accepted if there is any real conflict between the parties there set on opposite sides, and that the court should not undertake to decide which issue dominates other issues, though the precedents do not support this view. It is also not clear that there was any conflict, except in the most formal sense, between the bank and the gas company in the

---

the merits, holding that diversity jurisdiction existed. Aggravating as this may seem, it is undoubtedly correct that the earlier denial of certiorari could not confer jurisdiction which Congress or the Constitution has denied. See § 7 above.

15. 62 S.Ct. at 21, 314 U.S. at 79.

16. 1918, 38 S.Ct. 254, 246 U.S. 199, 62 L.Ed. 664.

17. 62 S.Ct. at 19 n. 4, 314 U.S. at 75.

18. 62 S.Ct. at 23, 314 U.S. at 83.

19. See also Green v. Green, C.A.7th, 1954, 218 F.2d 130, certiorari denied 75

S.Ct. 606, 349 U.S. 917, 99 L.Ed. 1250, a suit by trust beneficiaries against the trustee for an accounting. It was held that the trustee's wife was properly aligned as a defendant, although she had a contingent interest in the trust. If the trustee won, upon his death his wife would inherit absolutely the amount he had allegedly misappropriated from the trust. If he lost, his death would give his wife a tenancy until death or remarriage in the income from one-half of that amount. Simple arithmetic shows where the wife's ultimate interest was.

actual case. Thus the case may stand for no more than a fairly arguable difference of view as to application of the law of alignment to a unique factual situation.[20]

§ 31.   Devices to Create or Defeat Diversity[1]

When there is a legitimate choice between a state and a federal forum for a particular action, the lawyer who has the choice quite properly will weigh what he conceives to be the tactical advantages and disadvantages of going to one court or the other.   Since 1938 there is, at least in theory, no longer any difference in the substantive law applied in the two sets of courts in diversity cases.[2]   The reputation the federal courts once had, whether or not deserved, of being unduly hospitable to corporations and to personal injury defendants is now dissipated.   But in choosing between a particular state court and a particular federal court for a particular case, there are still differences that to the lawyer seem significant.   In Louisiana tort claimants prefer federal court, because appellate review of jury verdicts is much more restrictive there than in the state courts.   In other areas, where the delay in reaching trial is much greater in federal court than in state court, it is the defendants in tort actions who seek to resort to federal court, and benefit from the attrition of delay, while claimants undertake to remain in the courts of the state.[3]   Differences between federal and state procedures may attract a litigant to one court or another.   He may wish to resort to federal court because of the liberal discovery techniques available there,[4] or he may prefer the state court if, as in many states, the judge no longer has the common law power to comment on the evidence, which federal judges still enjoy.   The reputation of the judges in the two courts, or folklore about the relative liberality or parsimony of juries in the two systems, may tip the balance one way or the other.

If a choice of forum exists, there is nothing improper in taking such tactical considerations as those mentioned into account in making that choice.   But so long as one court or the other provides, or seems to provide, an advantage, it is not unnatural that lawyers attempt to have the case tried in that forum even though the case appears to present no choice.   Thus the books are filled with cases in-

---

20. Thus of the law review commentaries cited in note 12 above, two (Michigan and Southern California) are approving, two (Missouri and Virginia) are critical, and one (Pennsylvania) is doubtful. The case is called "rigorous and debatable" by Hart & Wechsler, The Federal Courts and the Federal System, Bator, Mishkin, Shapiro & Wechsler ed. 1973, p. 1065.

[§ 31]

1. 14 Wright, Miller & Cooper, Jurisdiction §§ 3637–3642.

2. See chapter 9 below.

3. Frankfurter, J., in Lumbermen's Mut. Cas. Co. v. Elbert, 1954, 75 S.Ct. 151, 157, 348 U.S. 48, 58, 99 L.Ed. 59.

4. See, e.g., Mottolese v. Kaufman, C.A.2d 1949, 176 F.2d 301; Boggess v. Columbian Rope Co., D.C.N.Y.1958, 167 F.Supp. 854. See Kennedy, Federal Diversity Jurisdiction, 1961, 10 Kans.L.Rev. 47; Summers, Analysis of Factors that Influence Choice of Forum in Diversity Cases, 1962, 47 Iowa L.Rev. 933.

volving devices by which a particular party sought to create diversity, and thus get to federal court, or to prevent diversity, and thus keep the case in state court.

The First Congress, in the Judiciary Act of 1789, sought to outlaw one obvious device for manufacturing federal jurisdiction where it would not otherwise exist. A citizen of New Jersey has a claim, for the requisite amount, against another citizen of New Jersey. Seemingly he must sue in state court. But if, for some reason, he prefers to sue in federal court, he may well think of assigning his claim to a citizen of Pennsylvania, who will then sue on the basis of diversity and pay over the proceeds of the suit to his New Jersey friend. To prevent such a result, it was provided in Section 11 of the Judiciary Act of 1789 that the federal court was to have no jurisdiction of a suit on a promissory note, or other chose of action, in favor of an assignee, unless the suit could have been prosecuted in federal court if no assignment had been made.[5] With changes in language, this "assignee clause," as it was known, was a part of the law until 1948. The statute, even with—or perhaps because of—the successive amendments, was not well drafted. One commentator referred to its "obscure phraseology" as a "jumble of legislative jargon."[6] Its difficult language gave rise to a vast, and highly technical, body of decisions.[7] The clause reached some assigned claims but failed to reach others. If a particular assigned claim was within the ban of the assignee clause, suit in federal court was barred, though the assignment may have been entirely bona fide. If, on the other hand, the particular assignment did not fall within the highly artificial lines drawn by the statute and the decisions construing it, the assignee could sue in federal court even though the only purpose of the assignment was to create federal jurisdiction. Thus the statute no longer served to effectuate the purpose for which it was originally designed.

In the 1948 Judicial Code the assignee clause was dropped. In its stead the Reviser, building in part on § 37 of the 1911 Code,[8] provided, in 28 U.S.C.A. § 1359, that the district court should not have jurisdiction of a civil action "in which any party, by assignment or other-

---

5. The constitutionality of this partial withdrawal of jurisdiction was upheld in Turner v. The President, Directors, and Co. of the Bank of North America, 1799, 4 Dall. 8, 1 L.Ed. 718, and Sheldon v. Sill, 1850, 8 How. 441, 12 L.Ed. 1147. See § 10 above.

6. Comment, Chaos of Jurisdiction in the Federal District Courts, 1941, 35 Ill.L.Rev. 566, 569, 570. These strictures on the statute were quoted approvingly in the Reviser's Note to § 1359 of the 1948 Judicial Code.

7. See Dobie, Jurisdiction of the United States Courts as Affected by Assignment, 1920, 6 Va.L.Rev. 553.

8. Section 37, originally adopted as § 5 of the Act of March 3, 1875, 18 Stat. 472, required the court to dismiss or remand a suit whenever it appeared "that such suit does not really and substantially involve a dispute or controversy properly within the jurisdiction of said district court, or that the parties to said suit have been improperly or collusively made or joined, either as plaintiffs or defendants, for the purpose of creating a case cognizable or removable under this chapter * * * ."

wise, has been improperly or collusively made or joined to invoke the jurisdiction of such court." This would seem a potent barrier against the manufacture of diversity, whether by assignment or by any other device. The construction initially put on § 1359 by the courts, however, made the statute largely ineffective.

The leading case was Corabi v. Auto Racing, Inc.,[9] a unanimous opinion by the Third Circuit sitting en banc. The holding there was that diversity jurisdiction existed in a suit by a nonresident administrator, representing the estate of a resident, in a suit against a resident defendant. That result may be unattractive but could readily be explained on the basis of precedent,[10] and an unwillingness to look into the motives of the state court in appointing the nonresident as administrator. Unfortunately the court, in laying down what was to be for nearly a decade the authoritative construction of § 1359, turned to Webster's New International Dictionary, rather than to the purpose or history of the statute, to determine its meaning.[11] Many other courts followed the Third Circuit in its holding that a party's actions are not "improper" or "collusive" within the meaning of the statute, even though the sole motive was to gain access to federal court, if the actions were lawful in themselves.[12] The appointment of an administrator or general guardian of the proper citizenship to create diversity became very common,[13] and dubious assignments were held not to violate the ban of § 1359.[14]

9. C.A.3d, 1959, 264 F.2d 784.

10. See § 29 above.

11. 264 F.2d at 788.

12. Deposit Guar. Bank & Trust Co. v. Burton, C.A.6th, 1967, 380 F.2d 346; Lang v. Elm City Constr. Co., C.A.2d, 1963, 324 F.2d 235; Todd County v. Loegering, C.A.8th, 1961, 297 F.2d 470.

13. In Jamison v. Kammerer, C.A.3d, 1959, 264 F.2d 789, the court noted that the plaintiff administrator had been named administrator in 33 other cases in the court below "in order to create federal diversity jurisdiction," but held that jurisdiction existed nonetheless.

See also Kaufmann's Estate, Phila.Orphans' Ct., 1954, 87 Pa.D. & C. 401, 4 Fiduciary 253, where the court held that since verdicts in personal injury cases are higher in federal than in state court, it was in the interest of the ward for it to appoint a New Jersey resident as guardian in order to create diversity.

Although the situation in the Eastern District of Pennsylvania was clearly abnormal, 20.5% of all the original diversity actions pending in that court when a study was made were suits by out-of-state representatives against Pennsylvania defendants. ALI Study, p. 118.

This practice was sharply attacked. Cohan & Tate Manufacturing Federal Diversity Jurisdiction by the Appointment of Representatives: Its Legality and Propriety, 1956, 1 Vill.L.Rev. 201; Note, 1964, 73 Yale L.J. 873. The American Law Institute would put an end to it. ALI Study, §§ 1301(b)(4), 1307. The practice had, however, at least one defender. Farage, Proposed Code Will Emasculate Federal Jurisdiction, Trial Magazine, April/May 1966, p. 30, at 31–32.

14. Bradbury v. Dennis, C.A.10th, 1962, 310 F.2d 73, certiorari denied 83 S.Ct. 874, 372 U.S. 928, 9 L.Ed.2d 733, noted 1963, 14 Syracuse L.Rev. 687; City of Eufaula, Ala. v. Pappas, D.C.Ala.1963, 213 F.Supp. 749. But see Amar v. Garnier Enterprises, Inc., D.C.Cal.1966, 41 F.R.D. 211; Steinberg v. Toro, D.C. Puerto Rico 1951, 95 F.Supp. 791.

In 1968 Judge Thornberry, writing for the Fifth Circuit,[15] took a very different view. The holding there is that if an assignment does not divest the assignors of their interests in the lawsuit and was made only to create diversity, the assignment will be regarded as colorable and ineffective to create jurisdiction. Judge Thornberry was willing to accept the result of Corabi, and the other cases looking to the citizenship of a representative appointed by a state court, but he rejected the interpretation the Corabi case had given to § 1359, as well as the process by which that interpretation was reached.[16]

The Supreme Court agreed to review the Fifth Circuit case,[17] presumably to resolve the conflict between the Third and Fifth Circuits. Twelve days before the Court granted certiorari the conflict vanished. In McSparran v. Weist,[18] the Third Circuit, again sitting en banc, voted 4–2 to overrule Corabi. It now read § 1359 as meaning that "a nominal party designated simply for the purpose of creating diversity of citizenship, who has no real or substantial interest in the dispute or controversy, is improperly or collusively named." [19] The Third Circuit went even further than the Fifth Circuit had urged, since it applied its new rule to a court-appointed representative. It held that this did not amount to a collateral attack on the appointment by the state court, since the representative retains his capacity as such, but is merely a refusal to consider the citizenship of "a straw fiduciary" in determining the existence of diversity.

The rule announced by the Third Circuit in McSparran created its own problems both of meaning and of application. The McSparran case involved a guardian, and if the citizenship of the guardian is disregarded, it is easy to look to the citizenship of the ward. The court said, however, that the same rule should apply to "executors and administrators." [20] If it is so applied, should the court then look to the citizenship of the decedent or to that of the beneficiaries? Tenable arguments can be made both ways.[21] The problem of application

---

15. Caribbean Mills, Inc. v. Kramer, C.A.5th, 1968, 392 F.2d 387, affirmed 1969, 89 S.Ct. 1487, 394 U.S. 823, 23 L.Ed.2d 9.

Judge Leddy reached the same result as in Caribbean Mills in an equally fine opinion in Ferrara v. Philadelphia Labs., Inc., D.C.Vt.1967, noted 1968, 56 Geo.L.J. 1205, affirmed C.A.2d, 1968, 393 F.2d 934.

16. "By focusing on the literal meanings of the two words, the court virtually emasculated the statute * * *. If the statute is to have any utility, its meaning must be derived from the pre-revision statutes and cases, not from dictionary definitions of the individual words." 392 F.2d at 393.

17. 1968, 89 S.Ct. 99, 393 U.S. 819, 21 L.Ed.2d 91.

18. C.A.3d, 1968, 402 F.2d 867, certiorari denied 89 S.Ct. 1739, 395 U.S. 903, 23 L.Ed.2d 217, noted 1969, 73 Dick.L. Rev. 562, 20 Mercer L.Rev. 456, 44 N.Y.U.L.Rev. 212, 44 Notre Dame Law. 643, 47 Texas L.Rev. 1233.

19. 402 F.2d at 873.

20. 402 F.2d at 875.

21. The American Law Institute would look to the residence of the decedent. ALI Study, § 1301(b)(4). There is force in Professor Farage's objection that "the decedent is the only one in the whole wide world who literally has no interest in the proceedings * * *." Farage, note 13 above, at 32. Any other test, however, would be too difficult to administer. See Currie, The Federal Courts and the American

arose because McSparran did not hold that the citizenship of a representative is always immaterial but only if the appointment of a nonresident was an attempt to "manufacture" diversity. This was said to be a question of fact on which the plaintiff has the burden of proof.[22] A series of cases with a representative less transparent than a secretary to the plaintiff's attorney, in which the plaintiff will seek to prove some bona fide motive for the appointment, will be unedifying and wasteful.[23]

In Kramer v. Caribbean Mills, Inc.,[24] decided a few months after the McSparran case, the Supreme Court agreed with the view the Fifth Circuit had taken about § 1359 and its application to assignees. The Court held that an assignment for collection only and motivated by a desire to make diversity jurisdiction available falls within the "very core" of § 1359.[25] The Court found it unnecessary to reexamine its line of decisions holding that if the transfer of a claim is absolute, with the transferor retaining no interest in the subject matter, it is not "improperly or collusively made" regardless of the motive for the transfer.[26] The Court took note of McSparran, and of cases reaching a result contrary to McSparran with regard to administrators and guardians, but found it not necessary to consider that situation. It pointed out three respects in which cases involving court-appointed representatives differ from assignments, but said it was "not necessary to decide whether these distinctions amount to a difference for purposes of § 1359." [27]

Subsequent lower court cases have held with one voice that the distinctions about court-appointed representatives that the Court had noted in Kramer do not amount to a difference, and that if the purpose of appointing an out-of-state representative is to create diversity § 1359 bars federal jurisdiction.[28] In some instances proper motives have been found for the appointment of a representative from another state,[29] although the Fourth Circuit takes a more rigorous attitude

Law Institute, 1968, 36 U.Chi.L.Rev. 1, 16.

22.   402 F.2d at 875–876.

See also Groh v. Brooks, C.A.3d, 1970, 421 F.2d 589, 595, where the court attempted to make more explicit the factors that should be examined in deciding whether the citizenship of the representative is to control.

23.   See Silvious v. Helmick, D.C.W.Va. 1968, 291 F.Supp. 716, 720 n. 4; Comment, 1969, 44 N.Y.U.L.Rev. 212, 218–219.

24.   1969, 89 S.Ct. 1487, 394 U.S. 823, 23 L.Ed.2d 9.

25.   89 S.Ct. at 1491, 394 U.S. at 830.

26.   89 S.Ct. at 1490 n. 9, 394 U.S. at 828 n. 9.

27.   Id.

28.   Lester v. McFaddon, C.A.4th, 1969, 415 F.2d 1101; O'Brien v. AVCO Corp., C.A.2d, 1969, 425 F.2d 1030; Rogers v. Bates, C.A.8th, 1970, 431 F.2d 16; Bass v. Texas Power & Light Co., C.A.5th, 1970, 432 F.2d 763, certiorari denied 91 S.Ct. 1194, 401 U.S. 975, 28 L.Ed.2d 324; Bartnick v. Reader, C.A. 8th, 1973, 487 F.2d 1021; Gilchrist v. Strong, D.C.Okl.1969, 299 F.Supp. 804.

29.   O'Brien v. Stover, C.A.8th, 1971, 443 F.2d 1013; Joyce v. Seigel, C.A.3d, 1970, 429 F.2d 128; Bugbee v. Donahue, D.C.Wis.1980, 483 F.Supp. 1328; Majors v. Purnell's Pride, D.C.Miss. 1973, 360 F.Supp. 328.

The Tenth Circuit has held that even though the motive of changing the representative was to create diversity, it was effective for this purpose where

and holds that jurisdiction does not exist even though an appointment was not solely to create jurisdiction if the representative has no more than a nominal interest in the litigation.[30] If the circumstances are such that § 1359 applies and the citizenship of the representative is disregarded, the courts will look to the citizenship of the beneficiaries, in the case of an estate, or of the ward, in the case of a guardianship, to determine whether there is diversity.

The American Law Institute has what has been called "a better solution, one much more easily administered."[31] It would provide in all cases that the citizenship of a decedent, a minor, or an incompetent would be attributed to his representative.[32] This would eliminate all questions of motivation and would provide a simpler test for a decedent's estate than looking to the citizenship of the beneficiaries.

A party can gain access to federal court by changing his domicile to another state, chosen so that diversity will exist. Such a move will be effective, though it was motivated solely by a desire to sue in federal court,[33] but it must be a bona fide change of domicile and the party will not succeed if he plans to move back to his former home after the lawsuit is over.[34]

the successor representative was one of the beneficiaries of the estate and had a personal stake in the outcome. Hackney v. Newman Memorial Hosp., Inc., C.A.10th, 1980, 621 F.2d 1069, certiorari denied 101 S.Ct. 397, 449 U.S. 982, 66 L.Ed.2d 244.

30. Vaughan v. Southern Ry. Co., C.A.4th, 1976, 542 F.2d 641; Bishop v. Hendricks, C.A.4th, 1974, 495 F.2d 289, certiorari denied 95 S.Ct. 639, 419 U.S. 1056, 42 L.Ed.2d 653. See 14 Wright, Miller & Cooper, Jurisdiction § 3640, pp. 105–111.

The Fourth Circuit holds, however, that the citizenship of an executrix named by will is controlling, since the designation of an executrix from another state in a will cannot be a collusive attempt to manufacture diversity jurisdiction for a later wrongful death action and an executrix, as manager of the decedent's entire estate, has a greater stake in the controversy than an administrator named only to bring a death action. Sadler v. New Hanover Memorial Hosp., Inc., C.A.4th, 1978, 588 F.2d 914.

The Seventh Circuit applied the "nominal interest" test in unusual circumstances in Betar v. De Haviland Aircraft of Canada, Ltd., C.A.7th, 1979, 603 F.2d 30, certiorari denied 100 S.Ct. 1064, 444 U.S. 1098, 62 L.Ed.2d 785. The Public Administrator of Cook County, Illinois, was named administrator of the estate of a national of India, and he brought a wrongful death action in state court in Illinois against a Canadian corporation. Defendant sought to remove. It was held that since the beneficiaries of the estate could not have used the citizenship of the administrator, who had no personal stake in the case, to invoke original jurisdiction, defendant could not use that citizenship for removal. Since the beneficiaries were also Indian nationals, the suit was one between aliens and there was no federal jurisdiction.

31. Lester v. McFaddon, C.A.4th, 1969, 415 F.2d 1101, 1106. Chief Judge Haynsworth again referred to the ALI proposal as "a more satisfactory solution" in Miller v. Perry, C.A.4th, 1972, 456 F.2d 63, 68, discussed at n. 47 below. The Third Circuit has said that the ALI's proposal "has been praised by courts and commentators," but that "[i]n spite of such approbation, however, Congress has not yet enacted the proposal." Field v. Volkswagenwerk AG, C.A.3d, 1980, 626 F.2d 293, 303.

32. ALI Study, § 1301(b)(4).

33. Williamson v. Osenton, 1914, 34 S.Ct. 442, 232 U.S. 619, 58 L.Ed. 758. See § 26 above.

34. Morris v. Gilmer, 1889, 9 S.Ct. 289, 129 U.S. 315, 32 L.Ed. 690; O'Brien v. Delta Gas, Inc., D.C.La.1980, 486 F.Supp. 810. See § 26 above.

A corporation cannot get into federal court merely by transferring its claim to a subsidiary, incorporated in some other state chosen with diversity in mind,[35] but if the corporation in the original state is dissolved, and all the assets transferred to a corporation chartered by the new state, apparently this will be effective,[36] although, under the 1958 amendment to the law, the new corporation will also be deemed a citizen of the state in which it has its principal place of business.[37]

In class actions the court looks only to the citizenship of the named representatives of the class.[38] Thus where there is a large class and some members of the class are of such citizenship as to prevent diversity, a class action may be brought in which only persons of the right citizenship are named as representative of the class.[39] On the same principle, a stockholders' derivative suit may be brought in federal court if there can be found to act as plaintiff a qualified stockholder who is not a citizen of the same state as the corporation or the other named defendants.[40]

A party cannot create diversity where it would not otherwise exist by aligning the parties in the pleadings contrary to their real interests, since the court will realign the parties to determine the jurisdictional question.[41] Nor can the party avoid the requirement of complete diversity by failing to include as a party one whose citizenship would be wrong, if that party is "indispensable" to determination of the litigation.[42]

If the plaintiff's preference is for a state court, rather than a federal court, he may simply file his suit in state court. However, if diversity exists, and none of the defendants is a citizen of the state in which the suit is brought, the defendant or defendants may thwart plaintiff's choice by removal of the suit.[43] There are several devices by which plaintiff can avoid this; indeed he would seem to have more freedom here than he does when he is seeking to create diversity, since there is at least a statute, however ineffective it may have been in the past, purporting to bar collusive joinder to gain access to feder-

35. Miller & Lux v. East Side Canal & Irrigation Co., 1908, 29 S.Ct. 111, 211 U.S. 293, 53 L.Ed. 189; Southern Realty Inv. Co. v. Walker, 1909, 29 S.Ct. 211, 211 U.S. 603, 53 L.Ed. 346; Prudential Oil Corp. v. Phillips Petroleum Co., C.A.2d, 1976, 546 F.2d 469; Green & White Constr. Co. v. Cormat Constr. Co., D.C.Ill.1973, 361 F.Supp. 125; cf. Cahokia Sportservice, Inc. v. Cahokia Downs, Inc., D.C.Ill.1958, 165 F.Supp. 686 (assignment of lease by defendant to wholly-owned subsidiary corporation of same citizenship as plaintiff does not defeat diversity).

36. Black & White Taxicab & Transfer Co. v. Brown & Yellow Taxicab & Transfer Co., 1928, 48 S.Ct. 404, 276 U.S. 518, 72 L.Ed. 681. This decision has been the target of universal condemnation, as the worst example of the abuses of diversity possible under the rule of Swift v. Tyson, see § 54 below.

37. See § 27 above.

38. Snyder v. Harris, 1969, 89 S.Ct. 1053, 1059, 394 U.S. 332, 340, 22 L.Ed. 2d 319; Supreme Tribe of Ben Hur v. Cauble, 1921, 41 S.Ct. 338, 255 U.S. 356, 65 L.Ed. 673.

39. See § 72 below.

40. See § 73 below.

41. See § 30 above.

42. See § 70 below.

43. 28 U.S.C.A. § 1441(b); see § 38 below.

al court, while there is no statute barring collusive action to defeat federal jurisdiction.[44] Despite this, the courts are now "injecting a new note of realism into the determination of diversity jurisdiction," [45] and are refusing to allow artificial devices to be as effective as they formerly were in defeating diversity.

The device of choosing a personal representative of proper citizenship had been as effective to defeat diversity as it had been to create it. Indeed the leading case on this subject, Mecom v. Fitzsimmons Drilling Co.,[46] involved appointment of an administrator so chosen as to defeat removal. Smith, a citizen of Oklahoma, was killed, and his wife, also an Oklahoma citizen, was appointed administratrix of his estate by an Oklahoma probate court. She brought suit in an Oklahoma state court against a Louisiana corporation and certain individuals claimed to be liable for Smith's death. The corporation removed the case to federal court. After an unsuccessful motion to remand, Mrs. Smith dismissed her suit. Twice more she sued in state court, twice more the suit was removed, and twice more she dismissed. Thereupon Mrs. Smith resigned as administratrix, and one Mecom, a Louisiana citizen, was appointed administrator of Smith's estate by the probate court. Mecom did not know Mrs. Smith or her late husband, he knew of no assets in Louisiana, and he did not sign his own bond nor did he come to Oklahoma to be appointed. Instead he had agreed to serve as administrator solely as a favor to Mrs. Smith's attorney, and upon his appointment he immediately named Mrs. Smith as his state agent in Oklahoma. Suit was then brought in Mecom's name, for the wrongful death of Smith, in the Oklahoma state court. This suit also was removed, but after trial on the merits, with judgment for defendants, the Supreme Court held that the removal was improper, and that a motion to remand should have been granted. It stated the hitherto-settled rule that the citizenship of a personal representative, rather than those for whom he sues, is decisive; on this test there were Louisiana citizens on both sides of the suit and thus no diversity. The Court held that the rule was not altered by the fact that the administrator was appointed solely to defeat diversity, saying that the Mecom administrator could not be collaterally attacked because of the purposes and motives of the parties, when they practiced no fraud upon the court.

In 1972, however, in Miller v. Perry [47] the Fourth Circuit found that it was not bound by Mecom. The situation was somewhat differ-

---

44. "Section 1359, as its language clearly shows, expresses a policy against the creation of federal jurisdiction and not against its avoidance." McSparran v. Weist, C.A.3d, 1968, 402 F.2d 867, 875, certiorari denied 89 S.Ct. 1739, 395 U.S. 903, 23 L.Ed.2d 217. See also Herrick v. Pioneer Gas Products Co., D.C.Okl.1977, 429 F.Supp. 80.

45. Miller v. Perry, C.A.4th, 1972, 456 F.2d 63, 67.

46. 1931, 52 S.Ct. 84, 284 U.S. 183, 76 L.Ed. 233.

47. C.A.4th, 1972, 456 F.2d 63.

But see Herrick v. Pioneer Gas Products Co., D.C.Okl.1976, 429 F.Supp. 80, where the court felt compelled to follow Mecom rather than Miller v. Perry.

ent because there it was defendant, not plaintiff, who was seeking to avoid the federal court, but the principle seems much the same. The suit was a wrongful death action against North Carolina defendants. The deceased and all the beneficiaries were citizens of Florida, but in order to sue in federal court in North Carolina they were required to have as plaintiff an ancillary administrator who was a citizen of North Carolina. The Fourth Circuit held that the Supreme Court's decision in Kramer v. Caribbean Mills had recognized a need to reexamine Mecom and to give attention to the substantive relation of the administrator, the beneficiaries, and others to the controversy rather than blindly assuming that the citizenship of the ancillary administrator must control.

The specific holding of Miller is that state statutes requiring a noncitizen to appoint an in-state representative should not have the effect of depriving the noncitizen of the federal forum that Congress has made available. Thus Miller in itself would not require a different result in Mecom, where an out-of-state representative was freely chosen as plaintiff to prevent removal. But it seems beyond belief that a court that accepts Miller v. Perry would allow plaintiff to defeat an out-of-state defendant's statutory right to removal by the adroit choice for the purely nominal role of administrator of one whose citizenship will defeat diversity. Once again adoption of the legislation proposed by the American Law Institute would end all confusion and uncertainty in these matters.

Living litigants cannot defeat diversity by the choice of a personal representative, but a popular technique has been for plaintiff to assign his claim, or part of it, to a person who is a citizen of the same state as the defendant. Occasionally a district court balked, and pointed to the obvious truth that to allow removal to be defeated by this device "would make federal procedure a game in which the statutory rights of parties might be blocked by an adroit and cleverly designed maneuver of his adversary." [48] Much more often, however, the device worked and it seemed to be supported by several Supreme Court decisions.[49] But since 1969 there has been a definite trend in the district courts to hold that a partial assignment, at least, will be disregarded and will not defeat a right to remove that would otherwise exist.[50]

---

48. Phoenix Mut. Life Ins. Co. of Hartford, Conn. v. England, D.C.Mo.1938, 22 F.Supp. 284, 286.

49. Provident Sav. Life Assur. Soc'y of New York v. Ford, 1885, 5 S.Ct. 1104, 114 U.S. 635, 20 L.Ed. 261; Oakley v. Goodnow, 1886, 6 S.Ct. 944, 118 U.S. 43, 30 L.Ed. 61; Ridgeland Box Mfg. Co. v. Sinclair Ref. Co., D.C.S.C.1949, 82 F.Supp. 274 (assignment of ¹/₁₀₀ of claim); Krenzien v. United Services Life Ins. Co., D.C.Kan.1954, 121 F.Supp. 243, criticized 1954, 40 Va.L.

Rev. 803; Hair v. Savannah Steel Drum Corp., D.C.S.C.1955, 161 F.Supp. 654; Verschell v. Fireman's Fund Ins. Co., D.C.N.Y.1966, 257 F.Supp. 153.

50. Gentle v. Lamb-Weston, Inc., D.C. Me.1969, 302 F.Supp. 161, noted 1969, 83 Harv.L.Rev. 465; Carter v. Seaboard Coast Line R. Co., D.C.S.C.1970, 318 F.Supp. 368, noted 1971, 23 S.C. L.Q. 463; McClanahan v. Snodgrass, D.C.Miss.1970, 319 F.Supp. 913. Contra: Arant v. Stover, D.C.S.C.1969, 307 F.Supp. 144.

A fraudulent joinder as defendant of a person against whom plaintiff has no bona fide claim, but who is a citizen of the same state as plaintiff, will not defeat removal.[51] The joinder is not fraudulent within this rule, however, where plaintiff does have a claim against the co-citizen thus joined, even though this defendant may have no means with which to satisfy a judgment and may have been joined solely to prevent removal of the action.[52]

The practice, popular in some states and notably in California, of naming various "John Doe" defendants has created jurisdictional problems. In an action commenced in federal court, it seems reasonably clear that diversity does not exist unless plaintiff both pleads and proves that the John Does are citizens of some state other than plaintiff's state.[53] In a well-known case, the Supreme Court seemed

See 14 Wright, Miller & Cooper, Jurisdiction § 3641, pp. 113–116.

51. Wecker v. National Enameling & Stamping Co., 1907, 27 S.Ct. 184, 204 U.S. 176, 51 L.Ed. 430; Tedder v. F. M. C. Corp., C.A.5th, 1979, 590 F.2d 115; Smoot v. Chicago, R. I. & P. R. Co., C.A.10th, 1967, 378 F.2d 879; Dodd v. Fawcett Publications, Inc., C.A.10th, 1964, 329 F.2d 82; Covington v. Indemnity Ins. Co. of North America, C.A. 5th, 1958, 251 F.2d 930, certiorari denied 78 S.Ct. 1362, 357 U.S. 921, 2 L. Ed.2d 1365; Jacks v. Torrington Co., D.C.S.C.1966, 256 F.Supp. 282, 285–287; Tinney v. McClain, D.C.Tex. 1948, 76 F.Supp. 694; and cases cited 14 Wright, Miller & Cooper, Jurisdiction § 3641 n. 23.

As held in the Wecker case above, joinder is fraudulent, even though plaintiff had no actual knowledge of the facts which show that he had no bona fide claim against the joined defendant, if he has wilfully closed his eyes to information within his reach. Indeed in this context "fraudulent" has become "a term of art" that "in no way reflects on the integrity of plaintiff or her counsel." Newman v. Forward Lands, Inc., D.C.Pa.1976, 418 F.Supp. 134, 136 n. 1.

52. Pirie v. Tvedt, 1885, 5 S.Ct. 1034, 1161, 115 U.S. 41, 29 L.Ed. 331; Chicago, R. I. & P. R. Co. v. Schwyhart, 1913, 33 S.Ct. 250, 227 U.S. 184, 57 L.Ed. 473; Chicago, R. I. & P. R. Co. v. Dowell, 1913, 33 S.Ct. 684, 229 U.S. 102, 57 L.Ed. 1090; Bolstad v. Central Sur. & Ins. Corp., C.C.A.8th, 1948, 168 F.2d 927; Smith v. Southern Pac. Co., C.A.9th, 1951, 187 F.2d 397; Parks v. New York Times Co., C.A.5th, 1962, 308 F.2d 474; Frith v. Blazon-Flexible

Flyer, Inc., C.A.5th, 1975, 512 F.2d 899; Auto Ins. Agency, Inc. v. Interstate Agency, Inc., D.C.S.C.1981, 525 F.Supp. 1104; Nosonowitz v. Allegheny Beverage Corp., D.C.N.Y.1978, 463 F.Supp. 162. See also the statement of the test in Bobby Jones Garden Apartments, Inc. v. Suleski, C.A.5th, 1968, 391 F.2d 172.

"If under our dual court system a potential plaintiff has a choice between a state forum and a federal forum, it is his privilege to exercise that choice subject to legal limitations, and if he can avoid the federal forum by the device of properly joining a nondiverse defendant or a nondiverse co-plaintiff he is free to do so." Iowa Public Serv. Co. v. Medicine Bow Coal Co., C.A.8th, 1977, 556 F.2d 400, 406.

An evidentiary hearing on whether joinder is fraudulent is ordinarily improper. The court must resolve all disputed questions of fact from the pleadings and affidavits in favor of plaintiff and then determine whether there could possibly be a valid claim under state law against the defendant in question. B., Inc. v. Miller Brewing Co., C.A.5th, 1981, 663 F.2d 545.

53. Garter-Bare Co. v. Munsingwear, Inc., C.A.9th, 1980, 622 F.2d 416, 423; Molnar v. National Broadcasting Co., C.A.9th, 1956, 231 F.2d 684; Applegate v. Top Associates, Inc., D.C.N.Y.1969, 300 F.Supp. 51, affirmed C.A.2d, 1970, 425 F.2d 92; Johnson v. General Motors Corp., D.C.Va.1965, 242 F.Supp. 778; and cases cited 14 Wright, Miller & Cooper, Jurisdiction § 3642 n. 3.

But see Hannah v. Majors, D.C.Mo.1964, 35 F.R.D. 179. See also Sligh v. Doe, C.A.4th, 1979, 596 F.2d 1169.

to lay down a converse rule with regard to a case commenced in state court and sought to be removed. Plaintiff asserted a joint claim against the Pullman Company and one of its porters. The porter was named in the complaint as John Doe One, but his relation to the Pullman Company and his negligence as its servant were alleged. The Court held that to justify removal the Pullman Company was bound to show that the porter was a nonresident of plaintiff's state.[54] It would make federal jurisdiction more of a game than ever if removal could be defeated by the simple device of naming as a defendant a fictional John Doe. Thus the rule that the Ninth Circuit, the court principally confronted with the problem, seems to be working out is that where, so far as can be told from the complaint, the defendant Does are mere nominal and disinterested parties, who "live not and are accused of nothing," they can be disregarded in determining whether a case is removable.[55]

The proposals of the American Law Institute would put an end to problems of fraudulent joinder and of "John Doe" defendants, and would make it impossible to defeat removal even by proper joinder of a resident defendant, since they would allow any defendant who could have removed if sued upon alone to remove the entire action.[56]

A final device for defeating removal is to assert a claim for just less than the amount in controversy required for federal jurisdiction. The court will look to the amount actually claimed, not the amount that might have been claimed.[57] If the claim that could be made is for far more than the jurisdictional amount required, this device is a very expensive way of buying whatever tactical advantage there may be in remaining in state court.[58] If the plaintiff is willing to pay this

---

54. Pullman Co. v. Jenkins, 1939, 59 S.Ct. 347, 350, 305 U.S. 534, 540, 83 L.Ed. 334.

55. Grigg v. Southern Pac. Co., C.A.9th, 1957, 246 F.2d 613, 620; Southern Pac. Co. v. Haight, C.C.A.9th, 1942, 126 F.2d 900; Scurlock v. American President Lines, Ltd., D.C.Cal.1958, 162 F.Supp. 78; and cases cited 14 Wright, Miller & Cooper, Jurisdiction § 3642 n. 17. Hogan, California's Unique Doe Defendant Practice: A Fiction Stranger than Truth, 1977, 30 Stan.L.Rev. 51; See Comment, Unknown Parties: The John Doe Defendant, 1970 Law & Soc. Order 256. In applying this rule in Asher v. Pacific Power & Light Co., D.C.Cal.1965, 249 F.Supp. 671, 675, the court said: "we should not allow artificial devices to destroy the diversity jurisdiction of this Court."

If the Doe defendants are removed from the case, either by dismissal or by proceeding to trial without serving them, removal at that point is timely.

Preaseau v. Prudential Ins. Co. of America, C.A.9th, 1979, 591 F.2d 74.

56. ALI Study, § 1304(b).

57. Iowa Central Ry. Co. v. Bacon, 1915, 35 S.Ct. 357, 236 U.S. 305, 59 L.Ed. 591; Erwin v. Allied Van Lines, Inc., D.C.Ark.1965, 239 F.Supp. 144; and cases cited 14 Wright, Miller & Cooper, Jurisdiction § 3725 n. 12. Contra: Capps v. New Jellico Coal Co., D.C. Tenn.1950, 87 F.Supp. 369.

58. The device was more practical in the days before Erie R. Co. v. Tompkins, when different rules of law were applied in federal court than in state court. Thus in Brady v. Indemnity Ins. Co. of North America, C.C.A.6th, 1933, 68 F.2d 302, noted 1934, 12 N.Car.L.Rev. 390, it was to the plaintiff's advantage to sue for $2,999.99 in state court, where his claim would be good, rather than to sue for the full $15,000 face value of the insurance policy and have the case removed to federal court where a policy defense, re-

price, he must do so from the beginning. A reduction in the amount claimed after the suit has actually been removed will not defeat jurisdiction.[59]

garded as valid by the federal courts but void by the state courts, would have barred all recovery.

59. St. Paul Mercury Indem. Co. v. Red Cab Co., 1938, 58 S.Ct. 586, 303 U.S. 283, 82 L.Ed. 845, noted 1938, 51 Harv. L.Rev. 1108, 24 Va.L.Rev. 808, 1939, 37 Mich.L.Rev. 482; Albright v. R. J. Reynolds Tobacco Co., C.A.3d, 1976, 531 F.2d 132, certiorari denied 96 S.Ct. 2229, 426 U.S. 907, 48 L.Ed.2d 832; Marsh v. Tillie Lewis Foods, Inc., D.C. S.D.1966, 257 F.Supp. 645; Facella v. Home Fire & Marine Ins. Co. of California, D.C.Cal.1960, 184 F.Supp. 838; and cases cited 14 Wright, Miller & Cooper, Jurisdiction § 3725 n. 48.

CHAPTER 5

JURISDICTIONAL AMOUNT

Analysis

§ 32. When Jurisdictional Amount Is Necessary [1]

The Constitution makes no requirement that any particular amount be in controversy in order to invoke the jurisdiction of the federal courts. Nevertheless, since the earliest days of the Republic, there has been a requirement, in some classes of cases, that more than a certain minimum amount be in controversy to bring cases to the federal trial courts. The Judiciary Act of 1789 fixed this sum at $500, and it was increased to $2000 in 1887, $3000 in 1911, and to the present figure of $10,000 in 1958.[2] For jurisdiction to exist, where these requirements are applicable, the amount in controversy, exclusive of interest and costs, must exceed the stated sum.[3]

By these successive figures Congress has endeavored to require a jurisdictional amount "not so high as to convert the Federal courts into courts of big business nor so low as to fritter away their time in the trial of petty controversies." [4] An increase in the jurisdictional amount is intended to help reduce congestion in the federal courts, but its effect in this regard is problematical, particularly because in actions for unliquidated damages arising out of a tort, which make up a large part of the business of the courts, there is little to prevent plaintiffs from increasing their demand for judgment to meet the new jurisdictional test. Thus Chief Justice Warren has reported that while the increase from $3000 to $10,000 in 1958 "did result in a temporary reduction in the filing of private civil cases, the net effect on the workload has been very slight." [5]

[§ 32]

1. 14 Wright, Miller & Cooper, Jurisdiction § 3701.

2. Act of July 25, 1958, 72 Stat. 415, amending 28 U.S.C.A. §§ 1331 and 1332.

3. Clark v. National Travelers Life Ins. Co., C.A.6th, 1975, 518 F.2d 1167; Salkind v. Trafalgar Hosp., C.A.2d, 1963, 322 F.2d 947; Royal Ins. Co. of Liverpool, England v. Stoddard, C.C.A.8th, 1912, 201 F. 915.

4. Sen.Rep. No. 1830, 85th Cong., 2d Sess., 1958, p. 4; 1958 U.S. Code Congressional and Administrative News pp. 3099, 3101.

5. Warren, Address to the American Law Institute, 1960, 25 F.R.D. 213.

The Court has commented to the same effect. See Lynch v. Household Fin.

The $10,000 figure applies to diversity cases.[6] Until 1980 it purportedly applied to federal questions, although, as will be seen below, its application to such cases even before recent statutory amendments, was of limited importance. Other jurisdictional amounts apply to certain actions against the United States [7] and to statutory interpleader actions.[8] There are also some statutes that require an amount in controversy for particular federal question cases and that continue to apply despite the 1980 removal of an amount requirement from the general federal question statute. From 1789 to 1925 there were varying jurisdictional amounts required for appeal to the Supreme Court in some kinds of cases, but there is no longer any such requirement. It had long been the law that $500 or more had to be in controversy to appeal as of right to a court of appeals in a summary bankruptcy proceeding, but new bankruptcy legislation, adopted in 1978 and effective the following year, removed that requirement.[9]

From 1875, when the district courts were first given federal question jurisdiction by what is now 28 U.S.C.A. § 1331, until 1976, the statute purported to make the same requirement of amount in controversy for federal question cases as was made for diversity cases. There was much less to this than met the eye, since a long series of statutes, in terms otherwise parallel to the general federal question statute, granted jurisdiction without regard to amount in virtually all the areas that otherwise would have come under the general statute.[10] These statutes covered so much of the general federal ques-

---

Corp., 1972, 92 S.Ct. 1113, 1121 n. 18, 405 U.S. 538, 550 n. 18, 31 L.Ed.2d 424.

6.   28 U.S.C.A. § 1332.

7.   In cases against the United States not arising under the internal revenue laws nor out of a tort, the district courts have jurisdiction only if the amount does not exceed $10,000. Larger cases must go to the Court of Claims. 28 U.S.C.A. § 1346. See ALI Study, § 1322(a)(1), proposing that the limit be raised to $50,000.

There is a $1000 requirement for judicial review of decisions regarding payments for services under the medicare program. 42 U.S.C.A. § 1395ff.

8.   Statutory interpleader actions require that the amount in controversy exceed $500. 28 U.S.C.A. § 1335. It will be seen in § 74 below that there are also nonstatutory interpleader actions, where the usual $10,000 figure is applicable, if diversity is the basis of jurisdiction.

9.   The amount requirement had appeared in § 25a of the former Bankruptcy Act. The 1978 legislation, Pub.L. 95–598, omits that former section and creates a virtually incomprehensible scheme for appeals in bankruptcy. 16

Wright, Miller & Cooper, Jurisdiction § 3926. See also Levin, Bankruptcy Appeals, 1980, 58 N.C.L.Rev. 967.

10.   The following statutes all appear in 28 U.S.C.A.:

§ 1333 (admiralty, maritime, and prize cases).

§ 1334 (bankruptcy matters and proceedings; after 1984 this will cover only bankruptcy appeals).

§ 1336 (review of certain ICC orders).

§ 1337 (cases arising under any Act of Congress regulating commerce).

§ 1338 (patents, plant variety protection, copyrights, trademarks, and unfair competition).

§ 1339 (postal matters).

§ 1340 (internal revenue; customs duties).

§ 1343 (civil rights cases—see discussion in text below).

§ 1344 (election disputes).

§ 1350 (alien's action for tort).

§ 1351 (actions against consuls, vice consuls, and members of a diplomatic mission). See also § 1364.

tion jurisdiction that in 1958, when the jurisdictional amount was increased to $10,000, it was repeatedly asserted in the committee reports and supporting documents that "the only significant categories of 'Federal question' cases subject to the jurisdictional amount are suits under the Jones Act and suits contesting the constitutionality of State statutes." [11] It is highly doubtful whether the amount requirement extended even so far as that limited statement would suggest.

No case ever held that Jones Act actions had to meet the jurisdictional amount test of 28 U.S.C.A. § 1331. There were decisions that seemed to assume that the general federal question statute, § 1331, was the only jurisdictional basis for such suits,[12] but these cases did not so hold, and the assumption was a questionable one. The Jones Act,[13] which makes available to seamen the remedies given to railway employees by the Federal Employers' Liability Act,[14] rested, at least in part, on the power to regulate commerce,[15] and 28 U.S.C.A., granting jurisdiction without regard to amount in suits arising under any Act of Congress regulating commerce,[16] should have been held to cover Jones Act cases.[17]

§ 1352 (actions on bonds executed under federal law).

§ 1353 (cases involving Indian land allotments).

§ 1355 (actions to recover fines, penalties, or forfeitures incurred under federal law).

§ 1356 (seizures not within admiralty jurisdiction).

§ 1357 (injuries under certain federal laws).

§ 1362 (federal question actions by certain Indian tribes).

§ 1363 (actions to protect juror's employment rights).

A number of sections of 28 U.S.C.A. also grant jurisdiction without regard to amount in controversy of cases to which the United States is a party:

§ 1345 (United States as plaintiff).

§ 1346 (United States as defendant).

§ 1347 (partition actions where United States is joint tenant).

§ 1348 (actions by United States to wind up national banking associations).

§ 1349 (actions by or against corporations where United States owns more than one-half of the stock).

§ 1358 (eminent domain).

§ 1361 (action in nature of mandamus against a government officer or agency).

§ 1364 (certain suits by the Senate or a committee thereof—this is one of three sections numbered § 1364).

11. Sen.Rep. No. 1830, 85th Cong., 2d Sess., 1958, pp. 6, 15, 22; 1958 U.S. Code Congressional and Administrative News 3099, 3103, 3112–3113, 3122.

12. E.g., Wade v. Rogala, C.A.3d, 1959, 270 F.2d 280; Branic v. Wheeling Steel Corp., C.C.A.3d, 1945, 152 F.2d 887, certiorari denied 66 S.Ct. 902, 327 U.S. 801, 90 L.Ed. 1026; Turner v. Wilson Line of Massachusetts, Inc., D.C.Mass. 1956, 142 F.Supp. 264, affirmed C.A.1st, 1957, 242 F.2d 414; McDonald v. Cape Cod Trawling Corp., D.C.Mass. 1947, 71 F.Supp. 888; Rowley v. Sierra S. S. Co., D.C.Ohio 1942, 48 F.Supp. 193.

13. 46 U.S.C.A. § 688.

14. 45 U.S.C.A. § 51 et seq.

15. O'Donnell v. Great Lakes Dredge & Dock Co., 1943, 63 S.Ct. 488, 490, 318 U.S. 36, 39, 87 L.Ed. 596.

16. " * * * [T]o found jurisdiction upon § 1337, it is not requisite that the commerce clause be the exclusive source of Federal power; it suffices that it be a significant one." Murphy v. Colonial Federal Sav. & Loan Assn., C.A.2d, 1967, 388 F.2d 609, 615.

17. See note 17 on page 179.

There was equal difficulty in saying that an amount in controversy was required in suits contesting the constitutionality of state statutes. Many such cases come under 28 U.S.C.A. § 1343(a)(3), which gives jurisdiction, without regard to amount, of actions to redress the deprivation, under color of any state law, of any right, privilege, or immunity secured by the federal Constitution, or by any federal civil rights statute.[18] In a separate opinion in Hague v. CIO,[19] Justice Stone endeavored to draw the line between those actions that could be brought under § 1343(3), and required no jurisdictional amount, and those that must be brought under § 1331, where the jurisdictional amount was required, by saying that § 1343(3) covered those cases where the right involved was "inherently incapable of pecuniary valuation," such as the right to vote and the rights of free expression, while resort must be had to § 1331, and the amount in controversy test satisfied, where the party was claiming a property right that could be given a dollars-and-cents value.

This distinction between property rights and personal rights became increasingly a source of controversy [20] and it was finally rejected in 1972 in Lynch v. Household Finance Corp.[21] The Court, which was unanimous on this point, said that it had never adopted the property rights-personal liberties test for jurisdiction under 28 U.S. C.A. § 1343(3). It found that the distinction was not supported by the legislative history of the statutes that are now §§ 1343(3) and 1331, and noted "the virtual impossibility of applying" the distinction. Finally it said that "the dichotomy between personal liberties and property rights is a false one. Property does not have rights. People have rights. The right to enjoy property without unlawful deprivation, no less than the right to speak or the right to travel, is, in truth a 'personal' right, whether the 'property' in question be a welfare check, a home or a savings account." [22]

Even so, there were some federal question cases in which more than $10,000 continued to be required. The most important class of

As a matter of history it is probable that the statute that is now 28 U.S.C.A. § 1337 was intended to apply only to cases under the original Interstate Commerce Act, as it had been amended prior to 1910, but its language is not so confined and it has been applied much more broadly. See 13 Wright, Miller & Cooper, Jurisdiction § 3574.

17. Ballard v. Moore-McCormack Lines, Inc., D.C.N.Y.1968, 285 F.Supp. 290; Richardson v. St. Charles-St. John the Baptist Bridge and Ferry Auth., D.C. La.1967, 274 F.Supp. 764; Brown v. Sinclair Ref. Co., D.C.N.Y.1964, 227 F.Supp. 714.

18. See § 22A above. See also 13 Wright, Miller & Cooper, Jurisdiction § 3573.

19. 1939, 59 S.Ct. 954, 965–971, 307 U.S. 496, 518–532, 83 L.Ed. 1423.

20. See generally Comment, Federal Jurisdiction Under the Civil Rights Act— The Case Against the Personal-Property Rights Distinction, 1971, 17 Vill.L. Rev. 313. Note, The Property Rights Exception to Civil Rights Jurisdiction Under Section 1343(3), 1971, 49 N.C.L. Rev. 819; Note, Another and Hopefully Final Look at the Property-Personal Liberty Distinction of Section 1343(3), 1971, 24 Vand.L.Rev. 990; Comment, Section 1343(3) Jurisdiction and the Property-Personal Right Distinction, 1970 Duke L.J. 819.

21. 1972, 92 S.Ct. 1113, 405 U.S. 538, 31 L.Ed.2d 424.

22. 92 S.Ct. at 1122, 405 U.S. at 552.

cases was those challenging the validity of actions by federal officers.[23] Judge Medina was surely right when he called this "an unfortunate gap in the statutory jurisdiction of our federal courts." [24] This gap was much criticized by the commentators, who urged the courts to close it on their own.[25] Although some courts took a very relaxed view of what was needed to satisfy the statutory requirement in this class of cases,[26] most courts recognized that the gap was one "to be filled in by Congress" and "not by judicial legislation." [27]

A requirement of amount in controversy in federal question cases made no sense. The requirement was of extremely limited application, and when it did apply its effect was to deny a federal forum for cases in which the amount involved was small but for which the federal courts had a special expertness and a special interest.[28]

Congress took a long step toward ending this anomaly in 1976 when it amended § 1331 to provide that no amount in controversy was required in any action "brought against the United States, any agency thereof, or any officer or employee thereof in his official capacity." [29] This took care of by far the most important class of federal question cases in which the amount requirement had been an obstacle to suit. It did not do the whole job. More than $10,000 was still required if a suit against defendants other than federal officers was based on federal common law.[30] Challenges to state statutes did not come within § 1343(a)(3), and still required more than $10,000, if

23. E.g., Schlesinger v. Councilman, 1975, 95 S.Ct. 1300, 1306 n. 9, 420 U.S. 738 n. 9, 43 L.Ed.2d 591; Oestereich v. Selective Serv. System Local Bd. No. 11, 1968, 89 S.Ct. 414, 393 U.S. 233, 21 L.Ed.2d 402; King v. Morton, C.A.1975, 520 F.2d 1140, 172 U.S.App. D.C. 126; McGaw v. Farrow, C.A.4th, 1973, 472 F.2d 952.

24. Wolff v. Selective Serv. Local Bd. No. 16, C.A.2d, 1967, 372 F.2d 817, 826.

25. Weinberger, The Jurisdictional Amount Requirement of Section 1331 in Suits Against Federal Officers: Due Process Tensions, 1974, 46 U.Colo.L. Rev. 157; Burke, What Price Jurisdiction? The Jurisdictional Amount in Injunctive Suits against Federal Officials, 1973, 24 Hast.L.J. 215; Note, The Jurisdictional Amount Requirement and Actions to Enjoin Deprivations of Constitutional Rights by Federal Officials: The *Lynch*ing Effect, 1973, 17 How.L.J. 867; Note, The Constitutional Implications of the Jurisdictional Amount Provision in Injunction Suits Against Federal Officers, 1971, 71 Col. L.Rev. 1474; Comment, A Federal Question Question: Does Priceless Mean Worthless?, 1969, 14 St. Louis Univ.L.Rev. 268.

26. E.g., Spock v. David, C.A.3d, 1974, 502 F.2d 953, reversed on other grounds 1976, 96 S.Ct. 1211, 424 U.S. 828, 47 L.Ed.2d 505; Martin v. Schlesinger, D.C.Ala.1974, 371 F.Supp. 637; Schroth v. Warner, D.C.Hawaii 1973, 353 F.Supp. 1032; and see 14 Wright, Miller & Cooper, Jurisdiction § 3709.

The suggestion that a requirement of an amount in controversy is unconstitutional if its effect is to bar review of a constitutional claim—see § 10 n. 36 above—has been consistently rejected by the appellate courts.

27. McGaw v. Farrow, C.A.4th, 1973, 472 F.2d 952. See generally Comment, The Jurisdictional Amount in Controversy in Suits To Enforce Federal Rights, 1976, 54 Tex.L.Rev. 545.

28. See ALI Study § 1311(a), and Commentary at pp. 172–176; Wechsler, Federal Jurisdiction and the Revision of the Judicial Code, 1948, 13 Law & Contemp.Prob. 216, 225; Friedenthal, New Limitations on Federal Jurisdiction, 1959, 11 Stan.L.Rev. 213, 216–218.

29. Act of Oct. 21, 1976, Pub.L. 94–574, 90 Stat. 2721.

30. Illinois v. City of Milwaukee, 1972, 92 S.Ct. 1385, 406 U.S. 91, 31 L.Ed.2d

the basis of challenge was that a state statute was inconsistent with an Act of Congress other than one "providing for equal rights of citizens," [31] and this was probably the rule if the state statute were challenged on the basis of a constitutional provision other than the Fourteenth Amendment.[32]

Congress was persuaded that it had not gone far enough in its 1976 action, and in 1980 it amended § 1331 again to remove any requirement of amount from that general statute.[33] In those few instances where there is a special reason for excluding small federal claims from federal courts, an amount requirement has been separately stated.[34]

It has also been argued that the requirement of amount be abolished in diversity cases, largely because it is sometimes difficult to determine the amount involved.[35] There is enough uneasiness about diversity jurisdiction generally, however,[36] that it is hardly conceivable that Congress would expand the jurisdiction to open the federal court door to a multitude of small cases.

§ 33. Determination of the Amount in Controversy [1]

In the preceding section it was seen that the amount in controversy must exceed a specified sum, now generally $10,000, to give jurisdiction to the district court in diversity cases and a few other kinds of cases. The present section is concerned with the rules by which to determine whether the matter in controversy does exceed that amount. Considered here are the cases where plaintiff is suing defendant on a single claim, and where defendant will lose whatever

712. See T. B. Harms Co. v. Eliscu, C.A.2d, 1964, 339 F.2d 823, 828.

31. Social Security Act. Chapman v. Houston Welfare Rights Organization, 1979, 99 S.Ct. 1905, 441 U.S. 600, 60 L.Ed.2d 508.

32. See Hunt v. Washington State Apple Advertising Comm., 1977, 97 S.Ct. 2434, 2443–2444, 432 U.S. 333, 346–348, 53 L.Ed.2d 383.

33. Act of Dec. 1, 1980, Pub.L. 96–486, 94 Stat. 2369.

See Conklin, Federal Question Jurisdiction Amendments Act of 1980, 1980, 16 Gonz.L.Rev. 525.

34. The same law that removed the amount requirement from 28 U.S.C.A. § 1331 amended the Consumer Product Safety Act to require that more than $10,000 be in controversy in actions for damages under that statute. 15 U.S.C.A. § 2072.

More than $10,000 must now be in controversy in suits under 49 U.S.C.A. § 11707 for freight damage or loss resulting from shipments in interstate commerce. 28 U.S.C.A. §§ 1337, 1445(b), as amended in 1978.

At least $50,000 must be in controversy in suits under the Consumer Product Warranties Act. 15 U.S.C.A. § 2310(d).

35. Uxa, The Jurisdictional Amount: An Unreasonable Limitation on Diversity Jurisdiction, 1976, 65 Ill.B.J. 78; Currie, The Federal Courts and the American Law Institute (Part II), 1969, 36 U.Chi.L.Rev. 268, 292–298. The Institute proposes to retain the requirement in diversity cases. ALI Study, § 1301(a).

36. See § 23 above.

[§ 33]

1. 14 Wright, Miller & Cooper, Jurisdiction § 3702; Ilsen & Sardell, The Monetary Minimum in Federal Court Jurisdiction, 1955, 29 St. John's L.Rev. 1, 183; Note, Federal Jurisdictional Amount: Determination of the Matter in Controversy, 1960, 73 Harv.L.Rev. 1369.

plaintiff will gain by the judgment. In these simpler cases the problem is one of determining which elements are included in the "matter in controversy," and in valuing those elements. More complicated problems are considered in the remaining sections of this chapter.

Even in the simpler situations here discussed, the rules for measurement of the amount in controversy are complex. This is because of the two contradictory goals that the rules seek to achieve. The amount in controversy cannot be made dependent on the amount the plaintiff will ultimately recover. To do so would make jurisdiction turn on a guess by the trial court as to the final outcome, or would require a preliminary trial on jurisdiction that would duplicate the regular trial on the merits, or would demand a wasteful jurisdictional dismissal, after the case has been fully heard on the merits, because the final award was less than the jurisdictional amount. All these considerations argue in favor of looking to the amount claimed, rather than the amount that will be recovered. At the same time, jurisdiction cannot be determined solely by what the plaintiff has asked for. To do so would destroy the jurisdictional amount requirement, and would permit the party to create jurisdiction by a wholly frivolous claim. In short, the court should not entertain the suit if the claim for the jurisdictional amount is entirely without merit, but the court should not decide the merits of the case in making that determination.

Thus it is quite settled that jurisdiction is not lost because the award is for less than the jurisdictional amount.[2] Instead the amount in controversy is measured as of the time the action comes to the federal court. Subsequent events, even including a reduction in the amount sought by the plaintiff, cannot destroy jurisdiction that has once been acquired.[3] It is incumbent on plaintiff to allege a claim that satisfies the jurisdictional amount requirement,[4] and if this is put in issue, as by a motion to dismiss for want of jurisdiction, the burden is on plaintiff to satisfy the court that the requisite amount is in controversy.[5] Determination of the value of the matter in controversy is a federal question to be decided under federal standards, although

---

2. See Rosado v. Wyman, 1970, 90 S.Ct. 1207, 1214 n. 6, 397 U.S. 397, 405 n. 6, 25 L.Ed.2d 442; 14 Wright, Miller & Cooper, Jurisdiction § 3702 n. 35.

3. St. Paul Mercury Indem. Co. v. Red Cab Co., 1938, 58 S.Ct. 586, 303 U.S. 283, 82 L.Ed. 845, noted 1938, 51 Harv. L.Rev. 1108, 24 Va.L.Rev. 808, 1939, 37 Mich.L.Rev. 482; Worthams v. Atlanta Life Ins. Co., C.A.6th, 1976, 533 F.2d 994; Lynch v. Porter, C.A.8th, 1971, 446 F.2d 225, certiorari denied 92 S.Ct. 711, 404 U.S. 1047, 30 L.Ed.2d 739; Gulf Ref. Co. v. Price, C.A.5th, 1956,

232 F.2d 25; and cases cited 14 Wright, Miller & Cooper, Jurisdiction § 3702 n. 33.

4. On pleading jurisdiction, see § 69 below.

5. McNutt v. General Motors Acceptance Corp., 1935, 56 S.Ct. 780, 298 U.S. 178, 80 L.Ed. 1135; Opelika Nursing Home, Inc. v. Richardson, C.A.5th, 1971, 448 F.2d 658; and cases cited 14 Wright, Miller & Cooper, Jurisdiction § 3702 nn. 10, 11.

the federal court must look to state law to determine the nature and extent of the right to be enforced in a diversity case.[6]

How is the determination to be made of the amount in controversy where it has been challenged? If, as will usually be true, the issue of jurisdictional amount is closely tied to the merits of the cause, the court, it is said, should be reluctant to insist on evidence with respect thereto, lest, under the guise of determining jurisdiction, the merits of the controversy between the parties be summarily decided without the ordinary incidents of trial.[7] Indeed there is occasional support for the view that in actions at law the parties are entitled to demand that issues of jurisdictional fact be submitted to the jury.[8] This is not, however, the usual procedure. More commonly the court will look to the pleadings, and to such affidavits as may be submitted, and determine from these whether there is a substantial claim for an amount satisfying the statute.[9]

In making this examination, the court is guided by rules that have been developed to prevent this preliminary jurisdictional determination from depriving the party unfairly of a trial on the merits. In a leading case, the Supreme Court put the rule this way: "The rule governing dismissal for want of jurisdiction in cases brought in the federal courts is that, unless the law gives a different rule, the sum claimed by the plaintiff controls if the claim is apparently made in good faith. It must appear to a legal certainty that the claim is really for less than the jurisdictional amount to justify dismissal."[10] Thus in general the court looks to the sum demanded by plaintiff. It does not matter that on the face of the complaint there may appear a defense to part of the claim, since possibly defendant will not assert that defense.[11] Nor does it matter that defendant admits he is liable for the sum prayed for. Where there is a justiciable claim for a certain amount, there is a controversy, or dispute, between the parties within the meaning of the statute, even though the defendant does not controvert or dispute the claim. It is sufficient that he does not satisfy it.[12]

6. Horton v. Liberty Mut. Ins. Co., 1961, 81 S.Ct. 1570, 367 U.S. 348, 6 L.Ed.2d 890.

7. Smithers v. Smith, 1907, 27 S.Ct. 297, 204 U.S. 632, 51 L.Ed. 656; Continental Cas. Co. v. Department of Highways State of Louisiana, C.A.5th, 1967, 379 F.2d 673; Wade v. Rogala, C.A.3d, 1959, 270 F.2d 280; Fireman's Fund Ins. Co. v. Railway Exp. Agency, C.A. 6th, 1958, 253 F.2d 780.

8. Shaffer v. Coty, Inc., D.C.Cal.1960, 183 F.Supp. 662, 666–667. See Note, Trial by Jury of Preliminary Jurisdictional Facts in Federal Courts, 1963, 48 Iowa L.Rev. 471.

9. Columbia Pictures Corp. v. Rogers, D.C.W.Va.1949, 81 F.Supp. 580, noted 1949, 2 Vand.L.Rev. 705; Jamison v. Pennsylvania Power Co., D.C.Pa.1959, 172 F.Supp. 563; J. E. Sieben Constr. Co. Inc. v. City of Davenport, D.C.Iowa 1980, 494 F.Supp. 1035.

10. St. Paul Mercury Indem. Co. v. Red Cab Co., 1938, 58 S.Ct. 586, 590, 303 U.S. 283, 288, 82 L.Ed. 845.

11. Schunk v. Moline, Milburn & Stoddart Co., 1892, 13 S.Ct. 416, 147 U.S. 500, 37 L.Ed. 255; Zacharia v. Harbor Island Spa, C.A.2d, 1982, 684 F.2d 199.

12. In re Metropolitan Ry. Receivership, 1907, 28 S.Ct. 219, 208 U.S. 90, 107–108, 52 L.Ed. 403. When this case was decided the statutory phrase was "matter in dispute." This was changed to the present language,

The court may believe it highly unlikely that plaintiff will recover the amount demanded, but this is not enough to defeat jurisdiction, unless it appears to a legal certainty that plaintiff cannot recover the amount which he has demanded.[13] Thus suppose that plaintiff demands actual damages of $5000 and punitive damages of $20,000. If under the applicable rule of law, punitive damages are not recoverable, it can be said that there is a legal certainty that plaintiff will not recover the amount demanded, and the action will be dismissed.[14] if the relevant state law permits punitive damages on the facts alleged, the requisite amount is in controversy, even though it may be unlikely that the amount demanded will be had.[15] Cases from the courts of appeals suggest that jurisdiction exists also if the local law is not clear as to whether such damages are recoverable,[16] although it might be argued contrary to this that the court will have to resolve this legal question at some point in the case and might as well do it at the beginning.

It was said above that jurisdiction is lacking also if the claim is not made in good faith but is fictitious or colorable.[17] Though this is stated as something in addition to the legal certainty test, in fact it seems a mere variant of it, for unless it appears to a legal certainty that plaintiff cannot recover the sum for which he prays, how can it be held that his claim for that sum is not in good faith?[18] The most

"matter in controversy," in the Judicial Code of 1911, 36 Stat. 1091, presumably to codify this decision. See also Wheel Horse Sales, Inc. v. Spence, C.A. 10th, 1977, 566 F.2d 679; United Bonding Ins. Co. v. Parke, D.C.Mo.1968, 293 F.Supp. 1350; Jaros v. State Farm Mut. Auto. Ins. Co., D.C.La.1966, 261 F.Supp. 315.

13.   Barry v. Edmunds, 1886, 6 S.Ct. 501, 116 U.S. 550, 29 L.Ed. 729; Bell v. Preferred Life Assur. Soc'y, 1943, 64 S.Ct. 5, 320 U.S. 238, 88 L.Ed. 15; Weinberger v. Wiesenfeld, 1975, 95 S.Ct. 1225, 1230 n. 10, 420 U.S. 636, 642 n. 10, 43 L.Ed.2d 514; and cases cited 14 Wright, Miller & Cooper, Jurisdiction § 3702 n. 2.

14.   Kahal v. J. W. Wilson & Associates, Inc., C.A.1982, 673 F.2d 547, ___ U.S. App.D.C. ___; Wiggins v. North American Equitable Life Assurance Co., C.A.4th, 1981, 644 F.2d 1014; cf. Vance v. W. A. Vandercook Co., 1898, 18 S.Ct. 645, 170 U.S. 468, 42 L.Ed. 1111 (consequential damages not recoverable in claim and delivery action); Parmelee v. Ackerman, C.A.6th, 1958, 252 F.2d 721 (damages for emotional distress not recoverable); Bishop v. Byrne, D.C.W. Va.1967, 265 F.Supp. 460 (mental pain and suffering not recoverable); Diana v. Canada Dry Corp., D.C.Pa.1960, 189

F.Supp. 280 (loss of consortium not recoverable).

15.   Bell v. Preferred Life Assur. Soc'y, 1943, 64 S.Ct. 5, 320 U.S. 238, 88 L.Ed. 15.

But see Ehrenfeld v. Webber, D.C.Me. 1980, 499 F.Supp. 1283, 1291–1292, where the court found to a legal certainty that plaintiffs were entitled to at most $500 for punitive damages.

16.   Calhoun v. Kentucky-West Virginia Gas Co., C.A.6th, 1948, 166 F.2d 530; Columbia Pictures Corp. v. Grengs, C.A.7th, 1958, 257 F.2d 45. Contra: Nixon v. Loyal Order of Moose, Lodge No. 750, C.A.4th, 1960, 285 F.2d 250, criticized 1961, 63 W.Va.L.Rev. 365.

17.   See text at note 10 above; and cases cited in 14 Wright, Miller & Cooper, Jurisdiction § 3702 n. 80. Note, Good Faith Pleading of Jurisdictional Amount, 1963, 48 Iowa L.Rev. 426.

18.   "Thus, there is but one test: good faith and legal certainty are equivalents rather than two separate tests." Jones v. Landry, C.A.5th, 1967, 387 F.2d 102, 104.

Conversely plaintiff's good faith will not save him if it does appear to a legal certainty that he cannot recover the requisite amount. "This is not to say that plaintiff acted in deliberate bad

difficult cases are those in which plaintiff is suing for unliquidated damages from a tort, and the amount he is demanding seems far in excess of any reasonable verdict given the injuries alleged. In the past the prevailing view has been that a federal court should be reluctant to insist on a presentation of evidence regarding the jurisdictional question when it was interwoven with the merits, and that the cause should proceed to trial even if it appeared highly unlikely that plaintiff could recover the jurisdictional amount.[19] Recent decisions suggest that concern over the mounting federal caseload is causing a retreat from this position.[20] Although these decisions do not purport to change the legal certainty standard, they indicate that the courts are more willing than they have been in the past to scrutinize claims for more than $10,000 when only minor injuries to the plaintiff appear to be involved.[21]

When the jurisdictional amount was increased in 1958, the statutes were also amended to create a procedure apparently intended to meet the problem presented by such cases as those just described. It is now provided that if the plaintiff recovers less than $10,000, the court may refuse to allow him costs, and may impose costs against him.[22] The commentators were skeptical about the value of these provisions,[23] and the cases justify their skepticism. The courts have held that if plaintiff could reasonably have expected to recover a verdict for more than $10,000, and acted in good faith in claiming such an amount, he will be allowed costs even though he actually recovered less than $10,000.[24] On this construction, it is difficult to see

faith. Plaintiff may have felt that the insult fully warranted the $15,000 claimed. The question, however, is whether to anyone familiar with the applicable law this claim could objectively have been viewed as worth $10,000. The answer seems clearly in the negative." Jimenez Puig v. Avis Rent-A-Car System, C.A.1st, 1978, 574 F.2d 37. See also American Mut. Liab. Ins. Co. v. Campbell Lumber Mfg. Corp., D.C.Ga.1971, 329 F.Supp. 1283. But compare Tising v. Flanagan, D.C. Wis.1973, 360 F.Supp. 283.

19. Zunamon v. Brown, C.A.8th, 1969, 418 F.2d 883; Jones v. Landry, C.A.5th, 1967, 387 F.2d 102; Jaconski v. Avisun Corp., C.A.3d, 1966, 359 F.2d 931; Deutsch v. Hewes St. Realty Corp., C.A.2d, 1966, 359 F.2d 96, noted 1966, 35 U.Cin.L.Rev. 680, 35 Geo. Wash.L.Rev. 121, 4 Houston L.Rev. 328; Tullos v. Corley, C.A.6th, 1964, 337 F.2d 884; Wade v. Rogala, C.A.3d, 1959, 270 F.2d 280.

20. A leading case in the new direction is Nelson v. Keefer, C.A.3d, 1971, 451 F.2d 289, noted 1972, 47 N.Y.U.L.Rev. 349, 26 Sw.L.J. 461, 45 Temp.L.Q. 305.

See also Burns v. Anderson, C.A.5th, 1974, 502 F.2d 970; Sanders v. Hiser, C.A.8th, 1973, 479 F.2d 71; Starks v. Louisville & N. R. Co., C.A.5th, 1972, 468 F.2d 896; Ehrenfeld v. Webber, D.C.Me.1980, 499 F.Supp. 1283, 1291.

21. See 14 Wright, Miller & Cooper, Jurisdiction § 3707; Note, Determination of Federal Jurisdictional Amount in Suits on Unliquidated Claims, 1966, 64 Mich.L.Rev. 930.

22. 28 U.S.C.A. § 1332(b). The provision was invoked in McCord v. Moore-McCormack Lines, Inc., D.C.N.Y.1965, 242 F.Supp. 493; cf. Lutz v. McNair, D.C.Va.1964, 233 F.Supp. 871, affirmed C.A.4th, 1965, 340 F.2d 709.

23. Cowen, Federal Jurisdiction Amended, 1958, 44 Va.L.Rev. 971, 978 ("likely to create more problems than it solves"); comment, 1958 Amendment to the United States Judicial Code Relative to the Denial of Costs to a Plaintiff, 1961, 21 La.L.Rev. 783; Comment, 1958, 58 Col.L.Rev. 1287, 1291–1294.

24. Bochenek v. Germann, D.C.Mich. 1960, 191 F.Supp. 104; Stachon v. Hoxie, D.C.Mich.1960, 190 F.Supp. 185.

what the amended statutory provisions add, except perhaps the wisdom of hindsight, since if the claim is not made in good faith, it is subject to dismissal, even after trial.[25]

Plaintiff cannot satisfy the jurisdictional amount requirement by alleging, as part of his claim, something that is not actually a part of the matter in controversy. Side effects that the decision may have by way of stare decisis or collateral estoppel will not be considered.[26] Thus in a suit on bond coupons only the amount of the coupons is to be considered, even though the decision will be conclusive as to validity of the bonds themselves.[27] In a suit to restrain collection of a tax the jurisdictional amount must be satisfied by the tax that will be levied during the period of litigation; neither the capitalized value of the tax, nor the value of the right to conduct business free of the tax, is relevant.[28] In so ruling, the Supreme Court distinguished a case in which the matter in controversy was the validity of a permanent exemption by contract from a particular tax,[29] on the ground that the value of a contract providing permanent immunity from taxation is more than a limited number of the annual payments demanded.[30] The distinction has been criticised,[31] but is in accord with the cases, discussed below, involving installment payments. In the tax case, the Court also distinguished an earlier decision that had held, in a suit contesting the validity of an order of a state commission directing a railroad to construct and maintain an unremunerative spur track, that the amount in controversy was not merely the cost of installation of the track, but was the capitalized value of the annual costs that the track would impose on the railroad.[32] Again the distinction appears sound.

On a principle similar to that of the tax cases, it is held that where a taxpayer sues to prevent the issuance of municipal bonds, the tax that would be levied on plaintiff's property were the bonds issued,

25. City of Boulder v. Snyder, C.A.10th, 1968, 396 F.2d 853.

26. Healy v. Ratta, 1934, 54 S.Ct. 700, 292 U.S. 263, 78 L.Ed. 1248; and cases cited 14 Wright, Miller & Cooper, Jurisdiction § 3702 n. 44.

27. Town of Elgin v. Marshall, 1882, 1 S.Ct. 484, 106 U.S. 578, 27 L.Ed. 249.

28. Healy v. Ratta, 1934, 54 S.Ct. 700, 292 U.S. 263, 78 L.Ed. 1248; Clark v. Paul Gray, Inc., 1939, 59 S.Ct. 744, 306 U.S. 583, 83 L.Ed. 1001; May v. Supreme Court of State of Colorado, C.A. 10th, 1974, 508 F.2d 136.

The commuted value of future taxes may not be considered where it is merely "possible" that the taxpayer will suffer future harm in an amount sufficient to satisfy the statutory test. M & M Transp. Co. v. City of New York, C.A. 2d 1950, 186 F.2d 157.

29. Berryman v. Board of Trustees of Whitman College, 1912, 32 S.Ct. 147, 222 U.S. 334, 56 L.Ed. 225.

30. Healy v. Ratta, 1934, 54 S.Ct. 700, 704, 292 U.S. 263, 271, 78 L.Ed. 1248.

31. Note, 1934, 45 Harv.L.Rev. 95, 99; Comment, 1937, 25 Calif.L.Rev. 336, 344; Ilsen & Sardell, The Monetary Minimum in Federal Court Jurisdiction, 1955, 29 St.John's L.Rev. 1, 27.

32. Western & A. R. R. v. Railroad Comm., 1923, 43 S.Ct. 252, 261 U.S. 264, 67 L.Ed. 645, distinguished in Healy v. Ratta, 1934, 54 S.Ct. 700, 704, 292 U.S. 263, 271, 78 L.Ed. 1248.

rather than the value of the bond issue, is the amount in controversy.[33]

Where a business is threatened, either by a regulatory statute or by unfair competition, the stated rule is that the amount in controversy is the difference between the value of the business unregulated, or not subject to the competition, and its value under the regulation, or with the competition.[34] In making this determination, merely possible future harm is not to be considered,[35] but probable consequences will be taken into account.[36] If the statute seeks to impose a complete prohibition of the business, rather than mere regulation, then the entire value of the business furnishes the appropriate measure.[37] In determining the difference between the value of a regulated and an unregulated business, the cost of compliance with the regulation may be considered the amount in controversy.[38] In actions for unfair competition, or to restrain violation of "fair trade" prices, the value of the goodwill of the business is thought to be the relevant consideration,[39] and the amount expended in advertising is looked to in determining the value of the goodwill.[40] There is some suggestion in the literature that, as a matter of comity, a stricter standard of amount in controversy should be used where a state statute is challenged than where suit is between private parties,[41] but the Supreme Court has stated no such distinction and cites public and private cases interchangeably.[42]

33. Colvin v. City of Jacksonville, 1895, 15 S.Ct. 866, 158 U.S. 456, 39 L.Ed. 1053; Scott v. Frazier, 1920, 40 S.Ct. 503, 253 U.S. 243, 64 L.Ed. 883; Vraney v. Pinellas County, C.A.5th, 1958, 250 F.2d 617.

34. McNutt v. General Motors Acceptance Corp. of Ind., 1936, 56 S.Ct. 780, 298 U.S. 178, 80 L.Ed. 1135; KVOS, Inc. v. Associated Press, 1936, 57 S.Ct. 197, 299 U.S. 269, 81 L.Ed. 183; and cases cited 14 Wright, Miller & Cooper, Jurisdiction § 3708 nn. 4–6.

35. Pure Oil Co. v. Puritan Oil Co., D.C. Conn.1941, 39 F.Supp. 68, reversed on other grounds, C.C.A.2d, 1942, 127 F.2d 6. See also M & M Transp. Co. v. City of New York, C.A.2d, 1950, 186 F.2d 157.

36. Food Fair Stores v. Food Fair, C.A.1st, 1948, 177 F.2d 177, 184. See also Hunt v. New York Cotton Exchange, 1907, 27 S.Ct. 529, 205 U.S. 322, 51 L.Ed. 821; Bitterman v. Louisville & N. R. Co., 1907, 28 S.Ct. 91, 207 U.S. 205, 52 L.Ed. 171.

37. Gibbs v. Buck, 1939, 59 S.Ct. 725, 307 U.S. 66, 83 L.Ed. 1111.

38. Hunt v. Washington State Apple Advertising Comm., 1977, 97 S.Ct. 2434, 2443–2444, 432 U.S. 333, 346–348, 53 L.Ed.2d 383; Buck v. Gallagher, 1939, 59 S.Ct. 740, 307 U.S. 95, 83 L.Ed. 1128; Allway Taxi, Inc. v. City of New York, D.C.N.Y.1972, 340 F.Supp. 1120, affirmed C.A.2d, 1972, 468 F.2d 624.

39. Schering Corp. v. Sun Ray Drug Co., C.A.3d, 1963, 320 F.2d 72; Barrette v. City of Marinette, D.C.Wis. 1977, 440 F.Supp. 1277; Murphey v. G. C. Murphy Co., D.C.La.1963, 216 F.Supp. 124; Coca-Cola Co. v. Foods, Inc., D.C.S.D.1962, 220 F.Supp. 101; Parke, Davis & Co. v. Jarvis Drug Co., D.C.N.Y.1962, 208 F.Supp. 350.

40. Schering Corp. v. Sun Ray Drug Co., C.A.3d, 1963, 320 F.2d 72; American Plan Corp. v. State Loan & Fin. Corp., D.C.Del.1968, 278 F.Supp. 846; Johnson & Johnson v. Wagonfeld, D.C. N.Y.1960, 206 F.Supp. 30.

41. See Food Fair Stores v. Food Fair, C.A.1st, 1948, 177 F.2d 177, 184; Ilsen & Sardell, note 1 above, at 24–25; Comment, 1937, 37 Calif.L.Rev. 336; see Note, 1960, 73 Harv.L.Rev. 1369, 1375.

42. E.g., Hunt v. Washington State Apple Advertising Comm., 1977, 97 S.Ct. 2434, 2443–2444, 432 U.S. 333, 346–348, 53 L.Ed.2d 383.

Contracts calling for installment payments have been a source of particular difficulty. The holder of a policy of disability insurance claims that he is permanently disabled, and brings suit for the benefits due him. Though the cases are divided, the rule apparently is that only the amount of the installments due at the commencement of the suit may be taken into account, even though the judgment will be determinative of liability for future installments as they accrue.[43] The result is different where the entire contract is brought into issue, as where the insurer sues to cancel the policy for fraud.[44] By the same token, a declaratory judgment action as to the validity of a contract should bring into controversy the value of the whole contract.[45] Indeed where an insurer sought a declaratory judgment that it was not liable to defend its insured in a tort action, the amount in controversy was held satisfied, although the policy was for only $10,000, since the insurer would also be obliged to expend attorneys' fees in defense of its insured if it were bound under the policy.[46]

The Supreme Court has distinguished between those cases, just discussed, in which the judgment can only be for installments due at the time of suit, even though it has an estoppel effect as to future payments, and cases where the judgment will clearly and finally create an obligation to pay, over the years, a sum in excess of the jurisdictional amount, even though future events may alter or cut off the obligation. On such a distinction, the jurisdictional amount was held present in a suit under a state workmen's compensation statute

43. New York Life Ins. Co. v. Viglas, 1936, 56 S.Ct. 615, 297 U.S. 672, 80 L.Ed. 971; Beaman v. Pacific Mut. Life Ins. Co., C.A.4th, 1966, 369 F.2d 653; Keck v. Fidelity & Cas. Co. of New York, C.A.7th, 1966, 359 F.2d 840; White v. North American Acc. Ins. Co., C.A.10th, 1963, 316 F.2d 5; Cate v. Blue Cross & Blue Shield of Alabama, D.C.Tenn.1977, 434 F.Supp. 1187; Button v. Mutual Life Ins. Co. of New York, D.C.Ky.1943, 48 F.Supp. 168, noted 1943, 92 U.Pa.L.Rev. 211. Some of the earlier cases to the contrary are cited in the Button case.

In a removed action installments coming due between the filing of the suit and the petition for removal may be considered, Journal Pub. Co. v. General Cas. Co., C.A.9th, 1954, 210 F.2d 202, but the action must be remanded if the amount due on the date of removal was not sufficient, even though additional installments that have accrued after removal make the amount sufficient. Bowman v. Iowa State Travelers Mut. Assur. Co., D.C.Okl.1978, 449 F.Supp. 60; Strickland Transp. Co. v. Navajo Freight Lines, Inc., D.C.Tex. 1961, 199 F.Supp. 108.

44. Franklin Life Ins. Co. v. Johnson, C.C.A.10th, 1946, 157 F.2d 653; New York Life Ins. Co. v. Kaufman, C.C.A. 9th, 1935, 78 F.2d 398, certiorari denied 56 S.Ct. 149, 296 U.S. 626, 80 L.Ed. 445; cf. Duderwicz v. Sweetwater Sav. Assn., C.A.5th, 1979, 595 F.2d 1008 (forfeiture of interest because of usury); Morris v. Franklin Fire Ins. Co., C.C.A.9th, 1942, 130 F.2d 553 (reformation of policy).

45. Davis v. American Foundry Equipment Co., C.C.A.7th, 1938, 94 F.2d 441; Landers, Frary & Clark v. Vischer Products Co., C.A.7th, 1953, 201 F.2d 319; Aetna Cas. & Sur. Co. v. Yeatts, C.C.A.4th, 1938, 99 F.2d 665; Note, Declaratory Judgments, 1949, 62 Harv.L. Rev. 787, 801.

46. Allstate Ins. Co. v. Dillard, D.C.Pa. 1960, 190 F.Supp. 111.

A different result is reached if the declaratory action is against injured third persons rather than against the insured. Motorists Mut. Ins. Co. v. Simpson, C.A.7th, 1968, 404 F.2d 511.

where the judgment would create an obligation to make installment payments in the future, even though the obligation would be cut off upon the death or remarriage of the widow and the death or attainment of age 18 of the children.[47]

There appears to be a principle operating in the installment payment cases, though it is not clearly articulated by the courts. The proper rule is that the amount in controversy is the amount involved as a direct legal effect of the judgment; what that will be in a particular case depends on the applicable substantive law. In a suit for breach of a contract of employment, for example, some jurisdictions allow recovery only for the wages due at the time of filing suit, other jurisdictions require a single suit for the total breach, including wages not yet due, and still others give plaintiff an option either to sue for past-due wages or to treat the contract as totally breached. In a jurisdiction in the first group, only the wages due would be part of the amount in controversy. In one in the second group, the entire amount due under the contract, both past and future, would be in controversy, and in the third group the amount in controversy would depend on which of the alternative remedies plaintiff chooses to pursue.

If the right or matter in controversy cannot be translated into terms of money, there is no pecuniary amount in controversy.[48] Absolute certainty as to amount is not essential, however, and it is sufficient that there is a present probability that the value of the matter in controversy will exceed the jurisdictional amount.[49]

47. Aetna Cas. & Sur. Co. v. Flowers, 1947, 67 S.Ct. 798, 330 U.S. 464, 91 L.Ed. 1024, noted 1948, 36 Calif.L.Rev. 124. See also Williams v. Aetna Cas. & Sur. Ins. Co., D.C.Md.1980, 487 F.Supp. 44. A similar result was reached where suit was for statutory maintenance similar to alimony, Thompson v. Thompson, 1912, 33 S.Ct. 129, 226 U.S. 551, 57 L.Ed. 347, or to protect a contract providing for a life pension, Brotherhood of Locomotive Firemen & Enginemen v. Pinkston, 1934, 55 S.Ct. 1, 293 U.S. 96, 79 L.Ed. 219, or for social security benefits, Weinberger v. Wiesenfeld, 1975, 95 S.Ct. 1225, 1230 n. 10, 420 U.S. 636, 642 n. 10, 43 L.Ed.2d 514.

On the problem of installment payments, generally, see 14 Wright, Miller & Cooper, Jurisdiction § 3710.

48. Hague v. CIO, 1939, 59 S.Ct. 954, 307 U.S. 496, 83 L.Ed. 1423 (free speech); Barry v. Mercein, 1847, 5

How. 103, 12 L.Ed. 70 (custody of a child); Lister v. Commissioner Court, Navarro County, C.A.5th, 1978, 566 F.2d 490 (dilution of vote through reapportionment); Senate Select Committee on Presidential Campaign Activities v. Nixon, D.C.D.C.1973, 366 F.Supp. 51 (access to presidential tapes); and cases cited 14 Wright, Miller & Cooper, Jurisdiction § 3702 n. 63.

49. Wiley v. Sinkler, 1900, 21 S.Ct. 17, 179 U.S. 58, 45 L.Ed. 84; Aetna Cas. & Sur. Co. v. Flowers, 1947, 67 S.Ct. 798, 330 U.S. 464, 91 L.Ed. 1024; Bishop Clarkson Memorial Hosp. v. Reserve Life Ins. Co., C.A.8th, 1965, 350 F.2d 1006; and cases cited 14 Wright, Miller & Cooper, Jurisdiction § 3702 nn. 64, 65. An action is dismissed if its monetary value to plaintiff is pure conjecture. Kheel v. Port of New York Auth., C.A.2d, 1972, 457 F.2d 46, certiorari denied 93 S.Ct. 324, 409 U.S. 983, 34 L.Ed.2d 248.

In injunction actions, the amount in controversy is not the amount that plaintiff might recover at law, but the value of the right to be protected or the extent of the injury to be prevented.[50]

Plaintiff is master of his claim, and if he chooses to ask for less than the jurisdictional amount, only the sum he demands is in controversy and jurisdiction is absent, even though his underlying claim was of a value exceeding the statutory minimum.[51] Even though Rule 54(c), and similar provisions in a majority of the states, make the demand ineffective as a limitation on the amount recoverable in non-default cases, to hold, as a few cases suggest,[52] that this puts the requisite amount in controversy even though plaintiff has demanded less would make the requirement of an amount in controversy meaningless.[53]

§ 34. Viewpoint From Which Amount Is Measured [1]

It will sometimes happen, notably in suits for an injunction or to abate a nuisance, that the benefit to plaintiff will have a different value than the loss to defendant if the relief is granted. Which value represents the amount in controversy?

The leading case is so cryptic as to shed little, if any, light on the direction in which it leads. Mississippi & Missouri R. R. Co. v. Ward [2] was a suit by a steamboat owner for abatement of a bridge over the Mississippi River as a nuisance. Justice Catron disposed of the jurisdictional amount argument by saying: "But the want of a sufficient amount of damage having been sustained to give the Federal Courts

50. Mississippi & M. R. Co. v. Ward, 1862, 2 Black 485, 17 L.Ed. 311; City of Milwaukee v. Saxbe, C.A.7th, 1976, 546 F.2d 693, 702; 14 Wright, Miller & Cooper, Jurisdiction § 3708. See § 34 below.

51. Brady v. Indemnity Ins. Co. of North America, C.C.A.6th, 1933, 68 F.2d 302, noted 1934, 12 N.Car.L.Rev. 390; Sponholz v. Stanislaus, D.C.N.Y. 1976, 410 F.Supp. 286; Standard Acc. Ins. Co. v. Aguirre, D.C.Tex.1961, 199 F.Supp. 918; see § 31 above.

The principle was applied in debatable circumstances in Kansas City Philharmonic Assn. v. Greyhound Lines, Inc., D.C.Mo.1966, 257 F.Supp. 941. Plaintiff sued for $12,736 for damages caused it in transporting plaintiff's musicians. It admitted in the complaint that it owed defendant $2,784 for the transportation, and prayed for judgment in the amount of $9,952. It was held that the requisite amount was not in controversy, and the action was not removable, despite the argument that plaintiff was really seeking both judg-

ment for $9,952 and discharge from the admitted liability of $2,784.

The Kansas City Philharmonic case was not followed in Savarese v. Edrick Transfer & Storage, Inc., C.A.9th, 1975, 513 F.2d 140, where jurisdiction was held to exist when plaintiff sought recovery of $11,901.83 but asked that he be allowed to apply $2,578.41 he owed defendant against this recovery.

52. Campbell v. Jordan, D.C.S.C.1947, 73 F.Supp. 318; see Capps v. New Jellico Coal Co., D.C.Tenn.1950, 87 F.Supp. 369; Griffith v. Alabama By-Products Corp., D.C.Ala.1954, 120 F.Supp. 219.

53. Forest Laboratories, Inc. v. La Maur, Inc., D.C.Wis.1965, 236 F.Supp. 575. See ALI Study, pp. 343–348.

[§ 34]

1. 14 Wright, Miller & Cooper, Jurisdiction § 3703; Kennedy, Valuing Federal Matters in Controversy: Hohfeldian Analysis in Symbolic Logic, 1968, 35 Tenn.L.Rev. 423.

2. 1862, 2 Black 485, 17 L.Ed. 311.

jurisdiction, will not defeat the remedy, as the removal of the obstruction is the matter of controversy, and the value of the object must govern." [3] It is entirely unclear here whether the "value of the object" means the value of the bridge, the value of the plaintiff's steamboat business, the cost of removing the bridge, or the value of the plaintiff's right to be free of the obstruction. [4]

Dean Armistead M. Dobie, later a judge on the Fourth Circuit, argued very forcefully that the courts should look in such situations only to the benefit to the plaintiff, and this has become known as the "plaintiff viewpoint" rule. [5] It has attracted at least verbal support from some judges and writers, and indeed one distinguished court had declared that the "plaintiff viewpoint" rule is now "well settled." [6] The matter is not this clear. The principal Supreme Court decision relied on to support this view is Glenwood Light & Water Co. v. Mutual Light, Heat & Power Co. [7] In that case plaintiff sought to restrain the defendant from erecting poles and wires so as to injure the plaintiff's poles, wires, and business. The trial court, finding that the cost to defendant of removing its poles and wires would be less than the jurisdictional amount, dismissed for want of jurisdiction. The Supreme Court reversed, holding that plaintiff's right to operate its plant and conduct its business free from wrongful interference by defendant had a value in excess of the jurisdictional amount, and in strong language the Court said that the value of the protection of that right was determinative of the jurisdiction. Though the language here supports the "plaintiff viewpoint" rule, the holding, as in the other cases relied on by Dean Dobie, [8] is only that jurisdiction is present if the value to plaintiff exceeds the jurisdictional amount. This does not exclude the possibility that jurisdiction will also be present if the value to defendant is greater than the statutory requirement, even where the benefit to plaintiff is a lesser sum. Neither

3. 2 Black at 492.

4. See Judge Learned Hand's attempt to fathom the remark in M & M Transp. Co. v. City of New York, C.A. 2d, 1950, 186 F.2d 157, 158. And see the article by Kennedy, note 1 above.

5. Dobie, Jurisdictional Amount in the United States District Court, 1925, 38 Harv.L.Rev. 733.

"Dean Dobie, who is now a Judge of the Fourth Circuit Court of Appeals, calls this 'the plaintiff-viewpoint rule.' It is not always easy to apply." Associated Press v. Emmett, D.C.Cal.1942, 45 F.Supp. 907, 914.

6. Central Mexico Light & Power Co. v. Munch, C.C.A.2d, 1940, 116 F.2d 85, 87 (per Clark, J.). See also Alphonso v. Hillsborough County Aviation Auth., C.A.5th, 1962, 308 F.2d 724, 727; Massachusetts State Pharmaceutical Assn. v. Federal Prescription Serv., Inc., C.A.

8th, 1970, 431 F.2d 130; Kheel v. Port of New York Auth., C.A.2d, 1972, 457 F.2d 46, certiorari denied 93 S.Ct. 324, 409 U.S. 983, 34 L.Ed.2d 248; and cases cited 14 Wright, Miller & Cooper, Jurisdiction § 3703 n. 6. See also Ilsen & Sardell, The Monetary Minimum in Federal Court Jurisdiction, 1955, 29 St. John's L.Rev. 1, 183; Comment, 1939, 49 Yale L.J. 274; Note, 1950, 4 Vand.L. Rev. 146.

7. 1915, 36 S.Ct. 30, 239 U.S. 121, 60 L.Ed. 174.

8. Hunt v. New York Cotton Exchange, 1907, 27 S.Ct. 529, 205 U.S. 322, 51 L.Ed. 821; Bitterman v. Louisville & N. R. Co., 1907, 28 S.Ct. 91, 207 U.S. 205, 52 L.Ed. 171; Western & A. R. R. v. Railroad Comm. of Georgia, 1923, 43 S.Ct. 252, 261 U.S. 264, 67 L.Ed. 645. In each of these cases jurisdiction was held to exist.

Dean Dobie nor those who have accepted his view have pointed to any Supreme Court decision rejecting jurisdiction where the jurisdictional amount was satisfied from the defendant's viewpoint, but not from the plaintiff's. Only such a case can conclusively establish the "plaintiff viewpoint" rule. There are some such cases from the lower courts. In one case, plaintiff sought to enjoin defendant from breach of a covenant not to compete. The injunction, if granted, would close defendant's business, from which he was making an annual profit far in excess of $10,000. It was not shown, however, that plaintiff would benefit in an amount of more than $10,000 if defendant's business were shut down. The district court, applying the "plaintiff viewpoint" rule, held that plaintiff had not established that more than $10,000 was in controversy, and dismissed the case for want of jurisdiction.[9]

A very few lower court cases have suggested a different rule. These cases view the amount in controversy from the point of view of the party seeking to invoke federal jurisdiction, and thus look to the plaintiff's viewpoint in a case within the original jurisdiction, and to the defendant's viewpoint in a case brought to federal court by removal from state court.[10] There is an attraction to this rule, in that it would use the viewpoint of the party who has the burden of proof on jurisdiction. Nevertheless it would create the anomaly that a case brought in the original jurisdiction of the federal court could be dismissed for want of the requisite amount, but then removed to federal court by defendant if it were refiled in state court.[11]

There has been a distinct movement among the lower courts in recent years to yet a third rule. Under this rule jurisdiction is found if from the viewpoint of either plaintiff or defendant more than the statutory amount is involved. In a leading case to this effect individuals were suing a railroad to quiet title to water rights. It was stipulated that the rights in question were worth less than the jurisdictional amount to plaintiffs, but worth far more than the jurisdictional amount to the defendant railroad.[12] The court upheld jurisdiction, saying: "In determining the matter in controversy, we may look to the object sought to be accomplished by the plaintiff's complaint; the

---

9. Zep Mfg. Corp. v. Haber, D.C.Tex. 1962, 202 F.Supp. 847.

10. Family Motor Inn, Inc. v. L-K Enterprises Division Consol. Foods Corp., D.C.Ky.1973, 369 F.Supp. 766; Thomas v. General Elec. Co., D.C.Ky.1962, 207 F.Supp. 792; Martin v. City Water Co. of Chillicothe, Mo., D.C.Mo.1912, 197 F. 462, 466; Amelia Milling Co. v. Tennessee C., I. & R. Co., C.C.D.Ga.1903, 123 F. 811, 813; cf. Studebaker v. Salina Waterworks Co., D.C.Kan.1912, 195 F.Supp. 164.

11. See McCarty v. Amoco Pipeline Co., C.A.7th, 1979, 595 F.2d 389, 393.

12. Professor David Currie asks: "Does the apparent discrepancy in the value of a single right to the two parties result from a misconception of economics? If the water is worth only $1000 to the plaintiff, cannot the defendant buy it from him for $1000.01?" Currie, Federal Courts—Cases and Materials, 3d ed. 1982, p. 362. But the answer to the latter question will not always be "Yes," either because of stubbornness or because a right may have intangible value to a party, not included among the elements used in measuring the value of the right for purposes of amount in controversy.

test for determining the amount in controversy is the pecuniary result to either party which the judgment would directly produce." [13] A number of recent lower court cases are to the same effect,[14] and this seems the desirable rule, since the purpose of a jurisdictional amount, to keep trivial cases away from the court, is satisfied if the case is worth a large sum to either party.[15]

The rule that the court may look to the viewpoint of either party to see if the necessary amount is in controversy seems both sound and workable in the context of a single plaintiff suing a single defendant. The situation is quite different, however, if a number of plaintiffs are making separate and distinct claims against a defendant in a single suit. Here the rules on aggregation of claims [16] come into play, and there is no jurisdiction if the individual claims are for less than the required amount, even though the total detriment to defendant would exceed the sum specified in the statute.[17]

§ 35. Interest and Costs [1]

The present jurisdictional amount statutes, using language that has appeared unchanged in such statutes since 1887,[2] provide that the

13. Ronzio v. Denver & R. G. W. R. R., C.C.A.10th, 1940, 116 F.2d 604, 606.

14. Oklahoma Retail Grocers Assn. v. Wal-Mart Stores, Inc., C.A.10th, 1979, 605 F.2d 1155; McCarty v. Amoco Pipeline Co., C.A.7th, 1979, 595 F.2d 389; Smith v. Washington, C.A.1978, 593 F.2d 1097, 192 U.S.App.D.C. 443; Government Employees Ins. Co. v. Lally, C.A.4th, 1964, 327 F.2d 568; Ridder Bros., Inc. v. Blethen, C.C.A.9th, 1944, 142 F.2d 395; and cases cited 14 Wright, Miller & Cooper, Jurisdiction § 3704 n. 18.

A rather cryptic remark from the Supreme Court lends some support to this view. In Illinois v. City of Milwaukee, 1972, 92 S.Ct. 1385, 1390, 406 U.S. 91, 98, 31 L.Ed.2d 712, the Court's entire discussion of jurisdictional amount consisted of the citation of five authorities in support of the statement: "The considerable interests involved in the purity of interstate waters would seem to put beyond question the jurisdictional amount provided in § 1331(a)." The five authorities it cited were its own decisions in the Mississippi & Missouri Railroad case and the Glenwood Light & Water Co. case, the Ronzio case, this section of this text, and the Harvard Note cited in note 15. Since the two Supreme Court decisions raise, but do not answer, the question of viewpoint, and the Ronzio case, this text, and the Harvard Note all take the view that it

is enough if the requisite amount is in controversy from either viewpoint, the Court seems to be saying that that is the rule it was applying. Nevertheless, the passage is opaque and perhaps not too much should be read into it.

15. Note, The Jurisdictional Amount in Controversy Requirement: The Seventh Circuit Rejects the Plaintiff Viewpoint Rule, 1980, 29 De Paul L.Rev. 933; Note, The Jurisdictional Amount Requirement—Valuation from the Defendant's Perspective, 1978, 11 Loy.-L.A.L.Rev. 637; Note, Federal Jurisdictional Amount: Determination of the Matter in Controversy, 1960, 73 Harv. L.Rev. 1369.

16. See § 36 below.

17. Snow v. Ford Motor Co., C.A.9th, 1977, 561 F.2d 787; Lonnquist v. J. C. Penney Co., C.A.10th, 1970, 421 F.2d 597.

[§ 35]

1. 14 Wright, Miller & Cooper, Jurisdiction § 3712; Note, The "Interest" and "Costs" Excluded in Determining Federal Jurisdiction, 1960, 45 Iowa L.Rev. 832.

2. From 1789 to 1887, the statutes excluded only costs. "Interest" was added by Act of March 3, 1887, 24 Stat. 552.

matter in controversy is to be determined "exclusive of interest and costs."[3] There has not been much difficulty in deciding which costs are to be excluded. The only problem has been whether attorneys' fees, where they are allowed, are within the exclusion, and it is now quite settled that such fees are a part of the matter in controversy where they are provided for by contract,[4] or by state statute,[5] so long as the fee demanded is reasonable.[6] Where there is no legal authority for collection of an attorneys' fee, such a fee cannot be included in the jurisdictional amount.[7]

Interest is more complicated. The first case to come to the Supreme Court raising the question was Brown v. Webster.[8] In that case plaintiff sued for damages of $6000 for eviction from land to which defendant had given him a warranty deed. He had paid only $1200 for the land, and defendant claimed that the case did not satisfy the jurisdictional amount requirement of $2000 then in effect. Under the relevant state law, however, the damages in such an action were return of the purchase price with interest, and the purchase price, with interest from the time of purchase, came to more than $2000. On these facts the Court held that jurisdiction existed. It drew a distinction between "interest as such" and interest "as an instrumentality in arriving at the amount of damages to be awarded on the principal demand," and said that where, as in the case before it, the interest is an essential ingredient of the principal claim, rather than a mere accessory demand, it is not within the statutory exclusion of interest.

The apparent purpose of excluding interest in computing jurisdictional amount is to prevent plaintiff from delaying suit on his claim until the claim, with accruing interest, exceeds the statutory minimum.[9] Thus uniformly, under the rule of Brown v. Webster, interest is excluded if it is only an incident to the claim plaintiff is asserting[10]

3.   28 U.S.C.A. §§ 1332(a), 1337(a); 15 U.S.C.A. §§ 2072, 2310(d)(3)(B).

4.   Springstead v. Crawfordsville State Bank, 1913, 34 S.Ct. 195, 231 U.S. 541, 58 L.Ed. 354.

5.   Missouri State Life Ins. Co. v. Jones, 1933, 54 S.Ct. 133, 290 U.S. 199, 78 L.Ed. 267, noted 1934, 12 Texas L.Rev. 363; Velez v. Crown Life Ins. Co., C.A. 1st, 1979, 599 F.2d 471; and cases cited 14 Wright, Miller & Cooper, Jurisdiction § 3712 n. 5. It is immaterial that the statute may refer to the attorneys' fee as "costs."

6.   Colorado Life Co. v. Steele, C.C.A.8th, 1938, 95 F.2d 535; S. J. Groves & Sons Co. v. American Arbitration Assn., D.C.Minn.1978, 452 F.Supp. 121.

7.   Cupples Co. Mfrs. v. Farmers & Merchants State Bank, C.A.5th, 1968, 390 F.2d 184; Jacobs v. Tawes, C.A.4th, 1957, 250 F.2d 611. But cf. Mutual Benefit Health & Acc. Assn. v. Bowman, C.C.A.8th, 1938, 96 F.2d 7, vacated on other grounds, 1938, 58 S.Ct. 1056, 304 U.S. 549, 82 L.Ed. 1521, holding, somewhat dubiously, that a fee claimed in good faith is to be included even though in fact state law does not authorize such a fee. Compare § 33 above.

8.   1895, 15 S.Ct. 377, 156 U.S. 328, 39 L.Ed. 440.

9.   Brainin v. Melikian, C.A.3d, 1968, 396 F.2d 153, 155.

10.   Athan v. Hartford Fire Ins. Co., C.C.A.2d, 1934, 73 F.2d 66; Gilliland v. Colorado Life Co., D.C.Mo.1936, 15 F.Supp. 367; Moore v. Town Council of Edgefield, C.C.D.S.C.1887, 32 F. 498.

or if it arises solely by virtue of a delay in payment.[11] The interest is not excluded, however, if it is itself the basis of the suit. Thus where plaintiff is suing to collect on bond coupons, these coupons are the matter in controversy, even though they represent, in a sense, "interest." [12] Interest on the coupons themselves or on the bond, after maturity of either, is a different matter, and is excluded, as "interest," in computing the amount in controversy.[13] On similar reasoning it has been held that interest on a note prior to maturity, payable by terms of the note, is a part of the amount in controversy, though interest after maturity would not be.[14]

Finally there is the situation, typified by Brown v. Webster itself, where the interest is regarded as merely one of the elements of damage. Here again it is considered a part of the amount in controversy. Thus in a suit against a surety to recover on a supersedeas bond, by which the surety was bound to pay the judgment, interest, and costs, the amount in controversy is the whole sum due from the surety, since interest was merely an instrument in calculating the obligation of the bond.[15] Where the judgment in one action includes interest, the amount in controversy in a suit on the judgment is measured by the amount of that first judgment, including interest.[16]

The rules as to interest have been criticized by commentators.[17] They find the distinction between interest "as such" and interest as a principal claim unrealistic, and point out, with some justification, that the rule of Brown v. Webster with regard to interest as damages may open the door of federal court to adroit pleading, which asks simply for damages rather than for interest.[18]

11. Regan v. Marshall, C.A.1st, 1962, 309 F.2d 677; Albani v. D & R Truck Serv., Inc., D.C.Conn.1965, 248 F.Supp. 268.

12. Edwards v. Bates County, 1896, 16 S.Ct. 967, 163 U.S. 269, 41 L.Ed. 155.

13. Greene County v. Kortrecht, C.C.A.5th, 1897, 81 F. 241.

14. Bailey Employment System, Inc. v. Hahn, C.A.2d, 1981, 655 F.2d 473; Brainin v. Melikian, C.A.3d, 1968, 396 F.2d 153. The Brainin court refused to follow decisions to the contrary in Alropa Corp. v. Myers, D.C.Del.1944, 55 F.Supp. 936, and Fritchen v. Mueller, D.C.Kan.1928, 27 F.2d 167.

15. Fitchner v. American Sur. Co. of New York, D.C.Fla.1933, 2 F.Supp. 321.

16. San Juan Hotel Corp. v. Greenberg, D.C.N.Y.1980, 502 F.Supp. 34, affirmed C.A.2d, 646 F.2d 562; Phoenix Scotts-Sports v. Kadish, D.C.Alaska 1971, 321 F.Supp. 556.

17. See the Iowa Note, cited note 1 above; Note, 1946, 94 U.Pa.L.Rev. 401; Comment, 1936, 10 Tul.L.Rev. 289.

18. Thus in similar cases where plaintiff was suing on an insurance policy, jurisdiction was denied where his demand was for "$3,000 with interest thereon,"—the jurisdictional amount then being $3000—in Voorhees v. Aetna Life Ins. Co., D.C.N.J.1918, 250 F. 484, but sustained where plaintiff simply sued for damages, in the amount of the policy plus interest, for breach of the duty to pay. Continental Cas. Co. v. Spradlin, C.C.A.4th, 1909, 170 Fed. 322.

§ 36. Aggregation of Separate Claims [1]

The law on aggregation of claims to satisfy the requirement of amount in controversy is in a very unsatisfactory state. The traditional rules in this area evolved haphazardly and with little reasoning. They serve no apparent policy and "turn on a mystifying conceptual test." [2] There had been a strong tendency among the lower courts to liberalize the traditional rules, but this seems to have been met by Supreme Court decisions reemphasizing the old distinctions. Thus it is not altogether easy to say what the law is in this area, and it is quite hard to say why it is as it seems to be.

If a single plaintiff has two entirely unrelated claims against a single defendant, each for $6,000, he may sue in federal court since the aggregate of the claims exceeds $10,000. If two plaintiffs each have a $6,000 claim against a single defendant, they may not aggregate their claims, and may not sue in federal court, no matter how similar the claims may be, so long as the claims are regarded as "separate and distinct." Finally if one plaintiff has a claim for $11,000 and another plaintiff has a similar claim against the defendant for $6,000, the traditional rule—which had been under attack in the lower courts but has now been reaffirmed by the Supreme Court—is that the second plaintiff cannot join in the federal court suit of the first plaintiff but must litigate the matter all over again in state court. A good argument could be made that in each of these situations the result should be precisely opposite what it has traditionally been.

If a single plaintiff is suing a single defendant, Rule 18 permits the plaintiff to join as many claims as he may have against the defendant, regardless of their nature, and the value of all the claims is added together in determining whether the jurisdictional amount is met.[3] Ordinarily the claims are in fact closely related, but the statement of the rule in a multitude of decisions has never treated this as relevant to whether aggregation should be permissible. There is no apparent reason why plaintiff should be able to sue on two unrelated claims in federal court when neither claim would in itself be cognizable in federal court. The only virtue of the traditional rule is that it

[§ 36]

1. 14 Wright, Miller & Cooper, Jurisdiction § 3704; Riddell & Davis, Ancillary Jurisdiction and the Jurisdictional Amount Requirement, 1974, 50 Notre Dame Law. 346; Note, The Federal Jurisdictional Amount and Rule 20 Joinder of Parties: Aggregation of Claims, 1968, 53 Minn.L.Rev. 94.

2. Aetna Cas. & Sur. Co. v. Graves, D.C. La.1974, 381 F.Supp. 1159, 1162.

3. Crawford v. Neal, 1892, 12 S.Ct. 759, 144 U.S. 585, 36 L.Ed. 552; Griffin v. Red Run Lodge, Inc., C.A.4th, 1979, 610 F.2d 1198; Davis H. Elliott Co. v. Caribbean Utilities Co., C.A.6th, 1975, 513 F.2d 1176; Lynch v. Porter, C.A.8th, 1971, 446 F.2d 225, certiorari denied 92 S.Ct. 711, 404 U.S. 1047, 30 L.Ed.2d 739; and cases cited 14 Wright, Miller & Cooper, Jurisdiction § 3704 n. 6.

The same result is reached if a single plaintiff has two claims each of which is asserted jointly against multiple defendants. Litvak Meat Co. v. Baker, C.A.10th, 1971, 446 F.2d 329; Siegerist v. Blaw-Knox Co., C.A.8th, 1969, 414 F.2d 375, 381.

voids "the cumbersome inquiry into the necessary relationship between the claims." [4]

Thus a produce company converts apples that belong to three different apple growers. No one of the growers has a claim that meets the jurisdictional amount requirement, although the three taken together would do so. They cannot sue, individually or together, in federal court. But if a particular bank held a crop mortgage on the crops of each of the three growers, and has standing to sue by virtue of its lien, it can bring action against the produce company in federal court, since the claims it has under the three crop mortgages are aggregated where suit is brought by the single plaintiff.[5] Whether the apples were converted at one time or at different times and whether the issues are the same with regard to all three thefts are treated as immaterial.

The rule that if there are several parties their claims cannot be aggregated had its origin more than 150 years ago, at a time when joinder of parties was far less understood than it is today, and it was a construction of a statute regulating the appellate jurisdiction of the Supreme Court, rather than the original jurisdiction of the district courts.[6] The rule in its various ramifications was applied much later to determine whether there is original federal jurisdiction without any apparent realization that different policies might well be appropriate for original jurisdiction than for appellate jurisdiction.[7]

To the rule against aggregation of claims for or against multiple parties, there is a single exception: if the several parties have a common undivided interest and a single title or right is involved, the interests of co-parties may be added together in determining the amount in controversy.[8] Aggregation is not permitted if the claims

4. Currie, Federal Courts: Cases and Materials, 3d ed. 1982, p. 365.
5. Cashmere Val. Bank v. Pacific Fruit & Produce Co., Inc., D.C.Wash.1940, 33 F.Supp. 946. Cf. Bank of California Nat. Assn. v. Twin Harbors Lumber Co., C.A.9th, 1972, 465 F.2d 489.
6. Oliver v. Alexander, 1830, 6 Pet. 143, 8 L.Ed. 349.
7. Walter v. Northeastern R. Co., 1893, 13 S.Ct. 348, 147 U.S. 370, 37 L.Ed. 206; Wheless v. City of St. Louis, C.C.D.Mo.1899, 96 F. 865, 868–869, affirmed 1901, 21 S.Ct. 402, 180 U.S. 379, 45 L.Ed. 583. See Note, 1968, 53 Minn. L.Rev. 94, 102–105.
8. Troy Bank of Troy, Ind. v. G. A. Whitehead & Co., 1911, 32 S.Ct. 9, 222 U.S. 39, 56 L.Ed. 81 (holders of two notes, secured by a single vendor's lien, suing to assert the lien); Shields v. Thomas, 1854, 17 How. 3, 15 L.Ed. 93 (distributees of an estate against converter of estate); Texas & P. Ry.

Co. v. Gentry, 1896, 16 S.Ct. 1104, 163 U.S. 353, 41 L.Ed. 186 (action under wrongful death act by beneficiaries); Black v. Beame, C.A.2d, 1977, 550 F.2d 815 (right of family members to family services); Berman v. Narragansett Racing Assn., Inc., C.A.1st, 1969, 414 F.2d 311 (suit to require a fund to be created for benefit of a class); Phoenix Ins. Co. v. Woosley, C.A.10th, 1961, 287 F.2d 531 (creditors suing to collect fire insurance payable to their debtor); and see cases cited 14 Wright, Miller & Cooper, Jurisdiction § 3704 nn. 24–33.

The same rule applies where suit is against multiple defendants. McDaniel v. Traylor, 1905, 25 S.Ct. 369, 196 U.S. 415, 49 L.Ed. 533 (suit to set aside lien of judgments obtained fraudulently by defendants acting in concert); Sovereign Camp, Woodmen of the World v. O'Neill, 1924, 45 S.Ct. 49, 266 U.S. 292, 69 L.Ed. 293 (conspiracy by defendants).

for or against the various parties are considered several and distinct, and they may be so considered even though the claims arise from a single instrument or the parties have a community of interest.[9]

As the cases in the two preceding footnotes suggest, the distinction between a common undivided interest and several and distinct claims is something less than clear.[10] This is to be expected. Except in property law contexts, such terms as "common" and "several" are poor words for a test of jurisdiction—or anything else—since they "have little or no clear and ascertainable meaning." [11] Thus it is disappointing that the Supreme Court in Snyder v. Harris [12] should have vigorously endorsed the old test and declared it to be so firmly established that only Congress can change it. In doing so the Court said that "lower courts have developed largely workable standards for determining when claims are joint and common, and therefore entitled to be aggregated, and when they are separate and distinct and therefore not aggregable." [13] It would have been helpful if the Court had indicated what these standards are or where they are to be found.

In recent years there has been particular difficulty in applying this distinction to insurance cases. In one case an insurance company sued for a declaratory judgment of nonliability to a number of persons who had obtained judgments against its insured. The judgments collectively were for far more than the jurisdictional amount but no individual judgment was of that magnitude. The Fourth Circuit found that the defendants had a common or undivided interest as against the insurance company arising out of the single insurance policy, and sustained jurisdiction.[14] In a case shortly thereafter 47

9. Thomson v. Gaskill, 1942, 62 S.Ct. 673, 315 U.S. 442, 86 L.Ed. 951 (employees of a single defendant claiming employer had denied them rights under a collective bargaining contract); Pinel v. Pinel, 1916, 36 S.Ct. 416, 240 U.S. 594, 60 L.Ed. 817 (suit by two children claiming to have been omitted from father's will by mistake); Wheless v. City of St. Louis, 1901, 21 S.Ct. 402, 180 U.S. 379, 45 L.Ed. 583 (several owners of land suing to enjoin assessment for street improvements); Lion Bonding & Sur. Co. v. Karatz, 1923, 43 S.Ct. 480, 262 U.S. 77, 67 L.Ed. 871 (bill for appointment of receiver by several small creditors); Del Sesto v. Trans World Airlines, Inc., D.C.R.I.1962, 201 F.Supp. 879 (claim for personal injuries to minor joined with parent's claim for medical expenses incurred for minor's injuries); and see cases cited 14 Wright, Miller & Cooper, Jurisdiction § 3704 nn. 11–13, 16–23.

The rule is the same where suit is against multiple defendants. Walter v. Northeastern Ry. Co., 1893, 13 S.Ct.

348, 147 U.S. 370, 37 L.Ed. 206 (suit to enjoin several counties from collecting taxes); Davis v. Schwartz, 1895, 15 S.Ct. 237, 155 U.S. 631, 39 L.Ed. 289 (suit to set aside separate chattel mortgages executed to different mortgagees to secure different debts).

10. "Difficult it is to draw a general rule or a rationale from the decisions other than the broad rules stated above. Language to support either conclusion in a case such as the present one can be found." Dixon v. Northwestern Nat. Bank, D.C.Minn. 1967, 276 F.Supp. 96, 100.

11. Kaplan, Continuing Work of the Civil Committee: 1966 Amendments of the Federal Rules of Civil Procedure, 1967, 81 Harv.L.Rev. 356, 380.

12. 1969, 89 S.Ct. 1053, 394 U.S. 332, 22 L.Ed.2d 319.

13. 89 S.Ct. at 1059, 394 U.S. at 341.

14. Manufacturers Cas. Ins. Co. v. Coker, C.A.4th, 1955, 219 F.2d 631. This case is cited in Note, note 1 above, at 108–109, along with Raybould v. Man-

insurance companies, which had joined in issuance of a single policy of insurance to a railroad company, sued for a declaratory judgment that a loss suffered by the railroad was not within the coverage of the policy. The Tenth Circuit held that the claims against the various insurers were common, in the sense of a community of interest in the rights asserted, but not undivided in the sense that they constitute in their totality an integrated right. It refused to allow aggregation of the claims to measure the amount in controversy.[15]

In the Tenth Circuit case just discussed the potential liability of nine of the 47 insurers was for more than the required amount but this was not held sufficient to support jurisdiction with regard to those insurers with a smaller potential liability.[16] This suggests an additional, and vexing, problem of jurisdictional amount where multiple parties are involved. Suppose that one party has a claim for more than $10,000. Another party has a claim against the same defendant for less than $10,000, and his claim is technically "separate and distinct" though it is so closely related to the first party's claim that, as a matter of efficient judicial administration, they should be heard jointly. On these facts can the federal court hear the claim of the second party, when joined with that of the first party? This is a more appealing case for aggregation than the situations, heretofore considered, where no one of the individual claims satisfies the statute. In those other situations refusal to permit aggregation means that all the claims must be brought in state court where, presumably, they can be joined or otherwise conveniently tried. But in the situation now considered, the party with the claim for more than $10,000 has a statutory right to assert his claim in federal court and, if aggregation is not permitted, the party with the smaller claim must bring a wasteful independent suit in state court. The commentators have thought that in these circumstances the two parties should be permitted to join, with the larger claim satisfying the statutory requirement of jurisdictional amount for the entire suit and the smaller claim coming within the court's ancillary jurisdiction.[17] The weight of authority

cini-Fattore Co., D.C.Mich.1960, 186 F.Supp. 235 and Dixon v. Northwestern Nat. Bank, D.C.Minn.1967, 276 F.Supp. 96, as representing an "apparent attempt to expand the 'common and undivided' exception."

15. Aetna Ins. Co. v. Chicago, R. I. & P. R. Co., C.A.10th, 1956, 229 F.2d 584, noted 1957, 10 Okl.L.Rev. 92. To similar effect, see Niagara Fire Ins. Co. v. Dyess Furniture Co., Inc., C.A.5th, 1961, 292 F.2d 232; Jewell v. Grain Dealers Mut. Ins. Co., C.A.5th, 1961, 290 F.2d 11, criticised 1961, 64 W.Va.L. Rev. 87; cf. Ex parte Phoenix Ins. Co., 1886, 6 S.Ct. 772, 117 U.S. 367, 29 L.Ed. 923.

16. Indeed it did not support jurisdiction even for the nine. Since the action was one for a declaratory judgment, it was held that the court properly exercised its discretion in such an action— see § 100 below—to dismiss the entire suit so that the controversy could be resolved in a state court action in which all the insurers could be joined.

17. Comment, Pendent Jurisdiction in Diversity Cases, 1969, 30 U.Pitts.L. Rev. 607; Note, 1968, 30 U.Pitts.L.Rev. 413; Note, 1962, 27 Ind.L.J. 199; Recent Development, 1967, 66 Mich.L. Rev. 373; R.C., 1967, 81 Harv.L.Rev. 480; Case Comment, 1961, 64 W.Va.L. Rev. 87; cf. Note, 1968, 53 Minn.L.Rev.

had been to the contrary [18] but there was a distinct trend in recent years to apply the ancillary jurisdiction concept and to hold that the court has discretion to hear the insufficient claim joined with a claim for more than $10,000 if the claims are closely related and arise for the most part out of the same operative facts.[19] Many of the cases allowing the insufficient claim as within the ancillary jurisdiction have been cases involving claims by members of a single family arising out of a single accident. This is the strongest case for this result, and the American Law Institute has proposed a statutory codification of this approach limited to claims on behalf of members of a single family living in the same household.[20] But if, as is thought, the principle is sound, there seems no reason to limit it to family cases, since they differ from other cases only in degree; [21] the limitation poses serious problems of construction and could give rise to quite fortuitous results.[22]

The Supreme Court's decision in Snyder v. Harris cast grave doubt on this trend toward applying the ancillary jurisdiction principle to questions of aggregation, and its more recent decision in Zahn v. International Paper Co.[23] seems to be a death blow to that trend. In Snyder the Court had held that a class action cannot be maintained when no member of the class has a claim in the requisite amount. In Zahn it extended this to hold that even when the named plaintiffs have claims of more than $10,000, they cannot represent a class in which many of the members have claims for less than $10,000. The Court repeated its dogmatic pronouncement of a "rule that multiple plaintiffs with separate and distinct claims must each satisfy the jurisdictional-amount requirement," and said: "The rule has been applied to forbid aggregation of claims where none of the claimants satisfies the jurisdictional amount * * * . It also requires dismissal of those litigants whose claims do not satisfy the jurisdictional

94. As to "ancillary jurisdiction," see §§ 9, 19 above.

18. Clark v. Paul Gray, Inc., 1939, 59 S.Ct. 744, 306 U.S. 583, 83 L.Ed. 1001; and cases cited 14 Wright, Miller & Cooper, Jurisdiction § 3704 n. 46.

19. Niebuhr v. State Farm Mut. Auto. Ins. Co., C.A.10th, 1973, 486 F.2d 618; Beautytuft, Inc. v. Factory Ins. Assn., C.A.6th, 1970, 431 F.2d 1122; Hatridge v. Aetna Cas. & Sur. Co., C.A.8th, 1969, 415 F.2d 809; Stone v. Stone, C.A.4th, 1968, 405 F.2d 94, 96–99; Jacobson v. Atlantic City Hosp., C.A. 3d, 1968, 392 F.2d 149, noted 1968, 30 U.Pitts.L.Rev. 413; Wilson v. American Chain & Cable Co., C.A.3d, 1966, 364 F.2d 558, noted 1967, 16 Cath.U.L. Rev. 336, 66 Mich.L.Rev. 373; General Research, Inc. v. American Employers' Ins. Co., D.C.Mich.1968, 289 F.Supp. 735; Lucas v. Seagrave Corp., D.C. Minn.1967, 277 F.Supp. 338; Wiggs v. City of Tullahoma, D.C.Tenn.1966, 261 F.Supp. 821; Johns-Manville Sales Corp. v. Chicago Title & Trust Co., D.C.Ill.1966, 261 F.Supp. 905, noted 1967, 81 Harv.L.Rev. 480; and cases cited 14 Wright, Miller & Cooper, Jurisdiction § 3704 n. 47.

20. ALI Study, § 1301(e).

21. R.C., 1967, 81 Harv.L.Rev. 480, 481–482.

22. See Currie, The Federal Courts and the American Law Institute (Part II), 1969, 36 U.Chi.L.Rev. 268, 297.

23. 1974, 94 S.Ct. 505, 414 U.S. 291, 38 L.Ed.2d 511. See Riddell & Davis, note 1 above; Theis, Zahn v. International Paper Co.: The Non-Aggregation Rule in Jurisdictional Amount Cases, 1974, 35 La.L.Rev. 89.

amount, even though other litigants assert claims sufficient to invoke the jurisdiction of the federal court." [24]

Zahn cannot reasonably be read as applying only to class actions. Two of the three cases that the Court cited for the second sentence in the quoted passage are not even arguably class action cases. And it was only after stating these flat and "firmly rooted" rules against aggregation that the Court went on to say that the "same rules were applied to class actions * * *." [25]

Zahn is a puzzling case, particularly because of its failure even to consider the argument of three dissenters that recent principles of ancillary jurisdiction, which have been held to overcome the jurisdictional amount requirement in other contexts,[26] should do so also in connection with joinder of parties. A few lower courts have sought to distinguish Zahn and to apply ancillary jurisdiction in the situation being considered [27] but the distinctions seem unsound, as recognized by other lower courts that have held that a sufficient claim with regard to one party cannot carry with it jurisdiction of an insufficient claim with regard to another party.[28]

§ 37. Effect of Counterclaims[1]

The extent to which a counterclaim can be considered in determining the amount in controversy has never been satisfactorily answered by the courts, and a baffling 1961 decision of the Supreme Court only added to the difficulty. Here the issue will be examined as it appeared prior to 1961, and then consideration will be given to the 1961 decision and whatever implications it may have for this area of the law.

---

24. 94 S.Ct. at 508–509, 414 U.S. at 294–295.

25. 94 S.Ct. at 509, 414 U.S. at 296. See also Note, 1975 Wash.U.L.Q. 447, 457–458, agreeing that Zahn states a general rule and is not limited to class actions. But see Note, 1976, 62 Va.L. Rev. 194, 231–236.

26. See § 9 above.

27. In Uniroyal, Inc. v. Heller, D.C.N.Y. 1974, 65 F.R.D. 83, 88, it was held that ancillary jurisdiction can no longer be applied to plaintiffs but it can be applied against defendants. Nothing in Zahn or any prior decision supports such a distinction. In Afton Alps, Inc. v. U. S., D.C.Minn.1974, 392 F.Supp. 543, 546 n. 2, Zahn was read as applying only to a plaintiff class but not to named plaintiffs. The reasons for rejecting this distinction are stated in the text at note 25 above.

28. Hixon v. Sherwin-Williams Co., C.A.7th, 1982, 671 F.2d 1005; National

Ins. Underwriters v. Piper Aircraft Corp., C.A.10th, 1979, 595 F.2d 546, noted 1980, 58 Wash.U.L.Q. 497; Hughes Constr. Co. v. Rheem Mfg. Co., D.C.Miss.1980, 487 F.Supp. 345; Carr v. Mid-South Oxygen, Inc., D.C.Miss.1982, 543 F.Supp. 299; Alco Financial Services, Inc. v. Treasure Island Motor Inn, Inc., D.C.Ill.1979, 82 F.R.D. 735; Cass Clay, Inc. v. Northwestern Public Serv. Co., D.C.S.D.1974, 63 F.R.D. 34; and cases cited 14 Wright, Miller & Cooper, Jurisdiction § 3704 n. 52.

[§ 37]

1. 14 Wright, Miller & Cooper, Jurisdiction § 3706; Fraser, Ancillary Jurisdiction and the Joinder of Claims in the Federal Courts, 1963, 33 F.R.D. 27, 29–31. Feinberg, Establishing Federal Jurisdictional Amount by a Counterclaim, 1956, 21 Mo.L.Rev. 243.

In approaching the problem it is necessary to distinguish between counterclaims that arise out of the same transaction or occurrence as the plaintiff's claim, and that are, therefore, under Federal Rule 13(a) and similar rules and statutes in many states, compulsory, and counterclaims that do not arise out of the same transaction or occurrence and that are, under Rule 13(b) and corresponding state provisions, permissive.[2] It is also necessary to distinguish between cases brought originally in federal court and those brought in state court where removal to federal court is attempted.

The easiest situation is where plaintiff's claim is for more than $10,000. It is not necessary here to resort to the counterclaim to make up the jurisdictional amount, and the case can be heard in federal court, if other jurisdictional requirements are met, either originally or by removal. If the counterclaim is compulsory, it falls within the ancillary jurisdiction of the court and may be heard though it is for less than $10,000 or otherwise does not meet the usual tests for federal jurisdiction; a permissive counterclaim, on the other hand, must have an independent jurisdictional basis.[3]

The problem becomes more difficult where plaintiff sues in federal court on a claim for less than $10,000, and defendant counterclaims for a sum that, either by itself or when added to plaintiff's claim, would make the matter in controversy exceed $10,000. There are virtually no holdings on whether jurisdiction exists in these circumstances.[4] There are cases that contain dicta supporting aggregation

2. The counterclaim rules are discussed in § 79 below.

3. See § 79 below; 6 Wright & Miller, Civil §§ 1415, 1423, and cases there cited.

4. Roberts Mining and Milling Co. v. Schrader, C.C.A.9th, 1938, 95 F.2d 522, holds that jurisdiction exists in these circumstances where the counterclaim by itself is for more than the jurisdictional amount, though the original claim was insufficient. Compare Goldstone v. Payne, C.C.A.2d, 1938, 94 F.2d 855, certiorari denied 58 S.Ct. 1057, 304 U.S. 585, 82 L.Ed. 1547, where it was held that the counterclaim could not be added to the claim to determine the amount in controversy; the court left open what the result would be if the counterclaim by itself was for the jurisdictional amount, though strongly suggesting that jurisdiction would be denied even on those facts. In Home Life Ins. Co. v. Sipp, C.C.A.3d, 1926, 11 F.2d 474, there is a dictum that jurisdiction exists if the counterclaim, either by itself or added to the claim, is for the requisite amount, but the holding is against jurisdiction where

neither the claim nor the counterclaim is large enough to satisfy the statute, and the counterclaim represents a sum which will be deducted from plaintiff's recovery. Finally, as an alternative ground of decision in Liberty Mut. Ins. Co. v. Horton, C.A.5th, 1960, 275 F.2d 148, 152, the court applied what it termed "the long established rule" that the counterclaim and claim are to be aggregated in measuring the amount in controversy, but the affirmance of this decision by the Supreme Court, 1961, 81 S.Ct. 1570, 367 U.S. 348, 6 L.Ed.2d 890, as will be seen, made no reference to this ground.

Jurisdiction was denied in Motorists Mut. Ins. Co. v. Simpson, C.A.7th, 1968, 404 F.2d 511, in which plaintiff's claim was insufficient but defendant had asserted a counterclaim for more than $10,000. The critical fact there, however, was that defendant had objected to the jurisdiction of the federal court and only asserted the counterclaim, after her jurisdictional objection was overruled, because it was compulsory under Rule 13(a).

on such facts,[5] but it is difficult to believe that this can in fact be the rule, at least where the counterclaim is permissive only. The doctrine is well settled in many contexts that the original jurisdiction of the federal court can be invoked only on the basis of what is shown by the plaintiff's complaint, and to depart from that doctrine here would give the defendant the wholly novel privilege of choosing whether the federal court is to have subject matter jurisdiction of a case originally brought in that court. If the plaintiff's claim is for less than the jurisdictional amount, a motion to dismiss would have to be granted, and a default judgment would be of doubtful validity,[6] and yet if aggregation is permitted here, defendant could breathe life into the defective suit by asserting a counterclaim in the requisite amount.

Removal cases present quite a different problem. If plaintiff sues in state court for less than $10,000, and defendant counterclaims for more than $10,000, it is settled—wisely or not—that plaintiff cannot remove since the statute limits the privilege of removal to defendants.[7] Nor should defendant be able to remove where his counterclaim is permissive by state law. By hypothesis, his counterclaim bears no logical relation to plaintiff's claim against him, and he is entirely free to bring his independent action on the counterclaim in federal court. The cases so hold.[8] The cases are divided, however, on whether defendant can remove on these facts where the counterclaim is compulsory by state law.[9]

5. See Kirby v. American Soda Fountain Co., 1904, 24 S.Ct. 619, 621, 194 U.S. 141, 146, 48 L.Ed. 911; Ginsburg v. Pacific Mut. Life Ins. Co. of California, C.C.A.2d, 1934, 69 F.2d 97, 98; Central Commercial Co. v. Jones-Dusenbury Co., C.C.A.7th, 1918, 251 F. 13, 19; American Sheet & Tin Plate Co. v. Winzeler, D.C.Ohio 1915, 227 F. 321, 324. See also note 4 above.

6. See 18 Wright, Miller & Cooper, Jurisdiction § 4428.

7. Shamrock Oil & Gas Corp. v. Sheets, 1941, 61 S.Ct. 868, 313 U.S. 100, 85 L.Ed. 1214. Nor can the plaintiff remove by claiming that the counterclaim is a separate and independent cause of action, under 28 U.S.C.A. § 1441(c). Lee Foods Div. Consol. Grocers Corp. v. Bucy, D.C.Mo.1952, 105 F.Supp. 402, noted 1953, 53 Col.L.Rev. 282.

The American Law Institute proposes to permit removal on the basis of defendant's counterclaim. ALI Study, §§ 1304(c), (d), 1312(a)(3).

8. Merchants' Heat & Light Co. v. James B. Clow & Sons, 1907, 27 S.Ct. 285, 204 U.S. 286, 51 L.Ed. 488; Bryant Elec. Co. v. Joe Rainero Tile Co., Inc., D.C.Va.1979, 84 F.R.D. 120.

9. Removal permitted: Wheatley v. Martin, D.C.Ark.1945, 62 F.Supp. 109 (overruled by the Ingram case below); Lange v. Chicago, R. I. & P. R. Co., D.C.Iowa 1951, 99 F.Supp. 1; McLean Trucking Co. v. Carolina Scenic Stages, D.C.N.C.1951, 95 F.Supp. 437; National Upholstery Co. v. Corley, D.C.N.C. 1956, 144 F.Supp. 658; Congaree Broadcasters, Inc. v. TM Programming, Inc., D.C.S.C.1977, 436 F.Supp. 258.

Removal denied: Collins v. Faucett, D.C. Fla.1949, 87 F.Supp. 254; Barnes v. Parker, D.C.Mo.1954, 126 F.Supp. 649; Trullinger v. Rosenblum, D.C.Ark. 1955, 129 F.Supp. 12; Ingram v. Sterling, D.C.Ark.1956, 141 F.Supp. 786; Continental Carriers, Inc. v. Goodpasture, D.C.Ga.1959, 169 F.Supp. 602, noted 1959, 45 Va.L.Rev. 737; Hall v. Bowman, D.C.Mo.1959, 171 F.Supp. 454; Rudder v. Ohio State Life Ins. Co., D.C.Ky.1962, 208 F.Supp. 577; Burton Lines, Inc. v. Mansky, D.C.N.C. 1967, 265 F.Supp. 489; West Virginia State Bar v. Bostic, D.C.W.Va.1972, 351 F.Supp. 1118.

The practical consequence of denying removal in these circumstances is that a party who wins the race to the courthouse by asserting a small claim in state court can compel his opponent to litigate his own claim in that court, even though the opponent's claim is for far more than the amount required for federal jurisdiction. In one such case plaintiff sued in state court for $1,408.72. Defendant's counterclaim, compulsory by state law, was for $78,650.00.[10] Surely to permit plaintiff to force a state forum on defendant in such circumstances is undesirable, as even the judges who have reached this result concede.[11] If this is compelled by statute, then it must be followed, regardless of its desirability, but the courts so holding point to no specific statutory language that requires this result. The removal statutes themselves are silent about amount in controversy. The general diversity statute says only that the courts have jurisdiction "where the matter in controversy exceeds the sum or value of $10,000, exclusive of interest and costs." It would be perfectly consistent with the statute to hold that a claim that arises from the transaction sued on and that, by the relevant state law,[12] must either be asserted in the action or forever barred, is in controversy. There is another curiously conceptual argument in the cases that so to hold would be to permit state law to control removal, contrary to the usual principle that the right to remove is governed solely by federal law. But wherever, in a diversity case, amount in controversy is in question, it is the state law that is controlling, since it defines the elements for which recovery may be had, and prescribes the measure of damages.[13] Again state law is relevant on whether a claim is separate and independent from another claim so as to permit removal under 28 U.S.C.A. § 1441(c).[14] It seems fully in accord with these principles to say that the state law has the effect of putting in controversy defendant's claims arising out of the transaction sued on, and thus to permit removal if the counterclaim is for more than the jurisdictional amount.

10. National Upholstery Co. v. Corley, D.C.N.C.1956, 144 F.Supp. 658.

11. See Continental Carriers, Inc. v. Goodpasture, D.C.Ga.1959, 169 F.Supp. 602, 604, calling for remedial legislation to permit a contrary result, and the similar view expressed in the note on that case at 1959, 45 Va.L.Rev. 737. See also Rudder v. Ohio State Life Ins. Co., D.C.Ky.1962, 208 F.Supp. 577, 578.

12. The suggestion of Feinberg, Establishing Jurisdictional Amount by a Counterclaim, 1956, 21 Mo.L.Rev. 243, that the test should be whether the counterclaim is compulsory under the federal rules is unacceptable. It is state law, not the federal rules, that determines whether a speedy plaintiff can compel defendant to litigate in state court a claim for which he otherwise would have a federal forum. This is the evil to which the removal statutes are addressed.

The American Law Institute, however, would allow removal if defendant has a claim for more than $10,000 arising out of the same transaction or occurrence as the claim against him, without regard to whether the counterclaim is compulsory under state law. ALI Study, § 1304(d).

13. See § 33 n. 6 above.

14. See § 39 below.

Against this background, the surprising decision of the Supreme Court in 1961 in Horton v. Liberty Mutual Insurance Co.[15] can be examined. Horton asserted a claim before the Texas Industrial Accident Board for workmen's compensation of $14,035. The Board awarded him $1050. On the day the award was made, the insurer filed suit in federal court to set aside the award to Horton. The complaint alleged diversity, and asserted also that Horton had claimed, was claiming, and would claim $14,035, but that in fact he was not entitled to recover anything at all under Texas law. One week later Horton sued in state court to set aside the Board's award and to recover $14,035. Later he moved to dismiss the insurer's federal court action on the ground that the value of the "matter in controversy" was only $1050, and also filed, subject to his motion to dismiss, a conditional compulsory counterclaim for the $14,035. On these facts it was held, five to four, that the amount in controversy exceeded $10,000, and that federal jurisdiction existed.

The Supreme Court recognized the general rule that the amount in controversy is determined from the complaint, and noted the allegations in the complaint that Horton would claim $14,035. It said: "No denial of these allegations in the complaint has been made, no attempted disclaimer or surrender of any part of the original claim has been made by petitioner, and there has been no other showing, let alone a showing 'to a legal certainty,' of any lack of good faith on the part of the respondent in alleging that a $14,035 claim is in controversy. * * * The claim before the Board was $14,035; the state court suit asked that much; the conditional counterclaim in the federal court claims the same amount. Texas law under which this claim was created and has its being leaves the entire $14,035 claim open for adjudication in a de novo court trial, regardless of the award. Thus the record before us shows beyond a doubt that the award is challenged by both parties and is binding on neither; that petitioner claims more than $10,000 from the respondent and the respondent denies it should have to pay petitioner anything at all. No matter which party brings it into court, the controversy remains the same; it involves the same amount of money and is to be adjudicated and determined under the same rules. Unquestionably, therefore, the amount in controversy is in excess of $10,000." [16]

No further light has been shed on this case by later decisions, and it is difficult to the point of impossibility to state for what principle, if any, the decision stands. Is the Court, as its language suggests, really holding that good faith allegations in the complaint as to what the

---

15. 1961, 81 S.Ct. 1570, 367 U.S. 348, 6 L.Ed.2d 890, noted, usually critically, 1961, 11 DePaul L.Rev. 130, 36 Tul.L. Rev. 148, 1962, 11 Amer.U.L.Rev. 102, 1962 Duke L.J. 130, 22 La.L.Rev. 851, 46 Minn.L.Rev. 960, 23 Ohio St.L.J. 777. See the thoughtful Comment,

The Effect of the Horton Case on the Determination of the Amount in Controversy Under Statutes Limiting Federal Court Jurisdiction, 1962, 17 Rutgers L.Rev. 200.

16. 81 S.Ct. at 1573–1574, 367 U.S. at 353–354.

defendant will claim are to be considered in determining the matter in controversy? Such a holding would be contrary to the rule, developed in other contexts, that plaintiff cannot create federal jurisdiction by anticipating defenses that defendant may assert, but is held to his own well-pleaded claim.[17]

Is the Court saying that since Texas law reopens the entire controversy when court review of a compensation award is sought by either party, the whole amount that might potentially be awarded is the matter in controversy? Such a proposition may be tested by considering what would happen if Horton failed to answer the insurer's federal court complaint, and judgment went for the insurer by default. The judgment would simply set aside the Board's award of $1050. It is unusual to find the jurisdictional amount satisfied where plaintiff is given a judgment for precisely what he asked, and this judgment awards relief of little more than one-tenth the statutory amount. Yet if the Horton case means anything, surely such a judgment would not be void. Presumably the judgment on this analysis, would be valid because it would act as a bar against any later claim by Horton for the $14,035. To accept this proposition, however, would have far-reaching effect on the compulsory counterclaim cases. It would seem to mean that a person who suffers $1000 damage in an automobile accident could sue in federal court for that amount, if his opponent had potential damages of more than $10,000 from the same accident, since the opponent's claim would be barred by Rule 13(a) if he failed to assert it. This goes beyond anything either the cases or the commentators have heretofore suggested, since it would permit original jurisdiction, though plaintiff's own claim is for less than $10,000, not only where defendant has asserted a counterclaim for more than the statutory sum but also where he might have asserted a compulsory counterclaim for such amount, notwithstanding that he did not do so. Such an interpretation of Horton would also suggest, contrary to the present case authority,[18] that more than $10,000 is in controversy if plaintiff might have sued for a greater amount but chose to limit his demand to less than $10,000.

Is it decisive in the Horton case that Horton was in fact claiming $14,035, both in his state court action and in his conditional counterclaim in federal court? The Fifth Circuit has thought so, and has held no jurisdiction in such circumstances where the workman, in federal court, has asked for less than $10,000, though his original claim before the Board, or even his claim in his own state court action, was for more than that sum.[19] It is odd to make plaintiff's invocation of

---

17. Louisville & N. R. Co. v. Mottley, 1908, 29 S.Ct. 42, 211 U.S. 149, 53 L.Ed. 126; Gully v. First Nat. Bank in Meridian, 1936, 57 S.Ct. 96, 299 U.S. 109, 81 L.Ed. 70; see § 18 above.

18. See § 33 n. 51 above.

19. Hardware Mut. Cas. Co. v. McIntyre, C.A.5th, 1962, 304 F.2d 566, certiorari denied 83 S.Ct. 147, 371 U.S. 878, 9 L.Ed.2d 115, noted 1963, 41 Texas L.Rev. 587; Jekel v. Fireman's Fund Ins. Co., C.A.5th, 1963, 318 F.2d 321, noted 1963, 49 Corn.L.Q. 161; Insur-

federal jurisdiction dependent on what defendant subsequently decides to ask. It is even odder to make jurisdiction turn on the happenstance that the workman files his counterclaim, or brings an action in state court, before the federal court rules on his motion to dismiss. A motion to dismiss for want of jurisdiction can be made in advance of answer, and if it is successful, the defendant is not barred by the compulsory counterclaim rule from pressing his own claim in an independent suit.[20] If the decisive fact in Horton is that he actually has claimed the $14,035, the result in the case can be avoided simply by moving to dismiss for want of jurisdiction and waiting until that motion has been granted before bringing the state court action for the full amount,[21] or even by claiming more than $10,000 in a state court action while asking for less than $10,000 in the federal action.[22]

Perhaps the case is no more than a skirmish in the continuing battle between Texas employees, who prefer a state forum for their workmen's compensation actions, and insurers, who prefer the federal court.[23] The decision is of little importance if it states a rule confined to Texas workmen's compensation cases and motivated by the peculiarities of the Texas law as to judicial review of such cases.[24] If

ance Co. of North American v. Keeling, C.A.5th, 1966, 360 F.2d 88, certiorari denied 87 S.Ct. 91, 385 U.S. 840, 17 L.Ed.2d 73.

20. Lawhorn v. Atlantic Ref. Co., C.A.5th, 1962, 299 F.2d 353; cf. Martino v. McDonald's System, Inc., C.A.7th, 1979, 598 F.2d 1079, 1082, certiorari denied 100 S.Ct. 455, 444 U.S. 966, 62 L.Ed.2d 379; see § 79 below.

21. Jekel v. Fireman's Fund Ins. Co., C.A.5th, 1963, 318 F.2d 321.

22. Insurance Co. of North America v. Keeling, C.A.5th, 1966, 360 F.2d 88, certiorari denied 87 S.Ct. 91, 385 U.S. 840, 17 L.Ed.2d 73.

23. In 1958 Congress prohibited removal of state workmen's compensation cases. 28 U.S.C.A. § 1445(c). Prior to that time the insurers waited for the workman to bring suit, and then removed. The new statute dictated the new procedure that the dissenters in Horton described as "an unequal race to the courthouse door—a race which the insurers will invariably win, since they have resident counsel in Austin (the location of the Texas Industrial Accident Board) who quickly secure news of Board awards and are thus enabled to 'beat' the workman in the choice of forums." 81 S.Ct. at 1578, 367 U.S. at 362–363.

In Great American Ins. Co. v. Cacciola, D.C.Tex.1963, 213 F.Supp. 303, the insurer won the race to the courthouse by a scant six minutes.

The usual position of the parties was reversed in Kay v. Home Indem. Co., C.A.5th, 1964, 337 F.2d 898. There it was held that the employee's action in federal court to collect compensation should not be heard, though the ordinary requirements of federal jurisdiction were met, since the insurer had earlier sued in state court to set aside the award of compensation. See also Bryan v. Liberty Mut. Ins. Co., C.A.5th, 1969, 415 F.2d 314, certiorari denied 90 S.Ct. 972, 397 U.S. 950, 25 L.Ed.2d 131.

24. One court has said in terms that the holding in Horton was "required by the peculiar provisions of the Compensation Act of the State of Texas" and was not intended to overturn the doctrine of earlier cases about amount in controversy. Gordon v. Daigle, D.C. La.1964, 230 F.Supp. 819, 822.

There is evidence that the lower courts generally regard Horton as being so confined. When the case has been cited it either is in a Texas workmen's compensation case or it is for very familiar propositions relating to the basic principles of subject matter jurisdiction. A possible exception is Taylor v. Taylor, D.C.Va.1972, 339 F.Supp. 899,

Horton actually lays down a rule of general application, a great many cases will be needed to define that rule and to reconcile it with previously settled principles of federal jurisdiction.

in which, as an alternative ground for a decision that was otherwise soundly based, the court did read Horton as establishing a new and general principle.

CHAPTER 6

REMOVAL JURISDICTION AND PROCEDURE

Analysis

§ 38. Scope of the Removal Jurisdiction [1]

The right to remove a case from state to federal court is purely statutory, being dependent on the will of Congress.[2] It is quite an anomalous jurisdiction, giving a defendant, sued in a court of competent jurisdiction, the right to elect a forum of his own choosing. Such a procedure was unknown to the common law, nor is removal mentioned in the Constitution. Nevertheless there has been provision for removal of cases from state courts to federal courts from the First Judiciary Act, in 1789, to the present day, and the constitutionality of removal is entirely settled.[3]

The rather limited right to remove given in 1789 was expanded by a series of particular statutes. A great many such statutes were enacted in the aftermath of the Civil War, and these culminated in 1875 legislation that permitted removal, subject only to the then-required jurisdictional amount of $500, of virtually all cases within the constitutional judicial power.[4] This privilege was narrowed in 1887 by a statute that raised the jurisdictional amount to $2000, limited removal to defendants, and was construed as barring removal where defendant relied on federal law as his defense.[5] The present removal statute, 28 U.S.C.A. § 1441, is closely derived from the 1887 legislation.

[38]

1. 14 Wright, Miller & Cooper, Jurisdiction §§ 3721–3723, 3725–3729; Wills & Boyer, Proposed Changes in Federal Removal Jurisdiction and Procedure, 1948, 9 Ohio St.L.J. 257; Keeffe et al., Venue and Removal Jokers in the New Judicial Code, 1952, 38 Va.L.Rev. 569.

2. Gold-Washing & Water Co. v. Keyes, 1877, 96 U.S. 199, 24 L.Ed. 656; Finn v. American Fire & Cas. Co., C.A.5th, 1953, 207 F.2d 113, certiorari denied 74 S.Ct. 476, 347 U.S. 912, 98 L.Ed. 1069; and cases cited 14 Wright, Miller & Cooper, Jurisdiction § 3721 n. 2.

Removability is governed by federal law. Grubbs v. General Elec. Credit Corp.,

1972, 92 S.Ct. 1344, 405 U.S. 699, 31 L.Ed.2d 612.

3. Chicago & N. W. R. Co. v. Whitton's Admr., 1871, 13 Wall. 270, 20 L.Ed. 571; Tennessee v. Davis, 1879, 100 U.S. 257, 25 L.Ed. 648; Ames v. Kansas ex rel. Johnston, 1884, 4 S.Ct. 437, 111 U.S. 449, 28 L.Ed. 482. See Martin v. Hunter's Lessee, 1816, 1 Wheat. 304, 4 L.Ed. 97.

4. Act of March 3, 1875, c. 137, § 2, 18 Stat. 470.

5. Act of March 3, 1887, c. 373, 24 Stat. 552, corrected by Act of August 13, 1888, 25 Stat. 433. Removal is dealt with in § 2 of that Act. For the construction of the 1887 statute, see Ten-

In general, such actions as might originally have been brought in federal court may be removed thereto, though as will be subsequently seen, there are some respects in which the removal jurisdiction is broader, and some in which it is narrower, than the original jurisdiction of the federal courts. Though original jurisdiction and removal jurisdiction are thus linked, numerically the removal jurisdiction is invoked much less frequently than is the original jurisdiction.[6] Since removability is equated with original jurisdiction, the principles already developed as to existence of a federal question or diversity, and as to jurisdictional amount,[7] are equally relevant here, and need not be restated. There is a surface symmetry in setting out the same tests for removal and for original jurisdiction, but this leads to strange results in the federal question cases. Defendant can remove a case where the plaintiff relies on federal law for his claim, though the plaintiff is perfectly willing to entrust his federal claim to a state court, but neither party can take the case to federal court where defendant sets up federal law as a defense to a non-federal claim by plaintiff. This was the construction put on the 1887 statute by the Supreme Court many years ago, over a forceful dissent by the first Justice Harlan, and it is now so firmly entrenched that only a statutory amendment could change it.[8]

The general removal statute permits removal of "any civil action brought in a State court,"[9] though as will be seen later, special statutes permit certain non-civil proceedings to be removed. Perhaps the limitation to "civil actions" means no more than that criminal actions

nessee v. Union & Planters' Bank, 1894, 14 S.Ct. 654, 152 U.S. 454, 38 L.Ed. 511.

6. In the year ended June 30, 1981, 11,745 actions were removed from state court to federal court, as against 159,172 civil actions commenced in federal court. Ann.Rep. of the Director of the Administrative Office of the U. S. Courts, 1981, Table 16.

7. See §§ 17–22 (federal question), 23–31 (diversity), and 32–37 (jurisdictional amount), above. Particular reference is made to § 31, which considers devices to create or defeat diversity, since the devices to defeat diversity are primarily employed by plaintiffs who wish to shape their case so that it cannot be removed to federal court. See also 14 Wright, Miller & Cooper, Jurisdiction §§ 3722, 3723, 3725.

Where defendant seeks to remove on the basis both of diversity and a federal question, the removal will stand if either ground is well taken. Great Northern Ry. Co. v. Galbreath Cattle

Co., 1926, 46 S.Ct. 439, 271 U.S. 99, 70 L.Ed. 854.

There is a surprising suggestion in Albright v. R. J. Reynolds Tobacco Co., C.A.3d, 1976, 531 F.2d 132, 136, certiorari denied 96 S.Ct. 2229, 426 U.S. 907, 48 L.Ed.2d 832, that a "different, simpler" standard applies in measuring amount in controversy in a removed case than in a case commenced in federal court.

8. The American Law Institute proposes an amendment that would continue to allow defendant to remove if the complaint states a federal claim but that would allow either party to remove, with certain limitations, if defendant asserts a defense or counterclaim based on federal law. ALI Study, § 1312(a).

9. 28 U.S.C.A. § 1441(a). See Moore & VanDercreek, Federal Removal Jurisdiction—Civil Action Brought in a State Court, 1960, 14 Southwestern L.J. 297; 14 Wright, Miller & Cooper, Jurisdiction § 3721, pp. 524–529.

are not, except as specially provided by statute, removable.[10] Proceedings for garnishment,[11] condemnation,[12] or to compel arbitration or confirm or vacate an arbitration award,[13] are civil actions for this purpose. There is, however, a sensible judge-made limitation that proceedings that are ancillary to an action pending in state court cannot be removed, since it would be wasteful to have the appendage in federal court when the principal claim is being litigated in state court.[14] This has application particularly to garnishment and similar proceedings. The distinction is drawn between supplemental proceedings that are a mere mode of execution or of relief, inseparably connected with the original judgment or decree, and supplemental proceedings that in fact involve an independent controversy with some new and different party.[15] It had been thought that the state law must be looked to in order to determine the nature of the proceedings, and which branch of this rule they fall under. Many cases so held, but the more recent cases show a distinct trend toward regarding this as a question to be decided by federal law, with the state characterization regarded as weighty but not conclusive.[16]

10. Rand v. Arkansas, D.C.Ark.1961, 191 F.Supp. 20. See also Quinn v. A Book Named "Sixty Erotic Drawings From Juliette," D.C.Mass.1970, 316 F.Supp. 289. Similarly punishment for contempt is not removable. In re Heisig, D.C.Ill.1959, 178 F.Supp. 270.

11. Stoll v. Hawkeye Cas. Co. of Des Moines, Iowa, C.A.8th, 1950, 185 F.2d 96, noted 1951, 35 Minn.L.Rev. 675; Swanson v. Liberty Nat. Ins. Co., C.A. 9th, 1965, 353 F.2d 12.

12. Madisonville Traction Co. v. Saint Bernard Mining Co., 1905, 25 S.Ct. 251, 196 U.S. 239, 49 L.Ed. 462. Nice questions of timing arise as to the point in a condemnation proceeding at which it becomes a civil action, rather than merely administrative. See Chicago, R. I. & P. R. Co. v. Stude, 1954, 74 S.Ct. 290, 346 U.S. 574, 98 L.Ed. 317, noted 1955, 64 Yale L.J. 600; 12 Wright & Miller, Civil § 3055.

13. Johnson v. England, C.A.9th, 1966, 356 F.2d 44, certiorari denied 86 S.Ct. 1587, 384 U.S. 961, 16 L.Ed.2d 673; Lummus Co. v. Commonwealth Oil Ref. Co., D.C.N.Y.1961, 195 F.Supp. 47.

14. See Toney v. Maryland Cas. Co., D.C.Va.1939, 29 F.Supp. 785 (per Dobie, J.); Brucker v. Georgia Cas. Co., D.C.Mo.1926, 14 F.2d 688. The following cases hold particular proceedings to be ancillary, and not removable: Barrow v. Hunton, 1878, 99 U.S. 80, 25 L.Ed. 407 (proceeding to annul a judgment on the ground of irregularities); First Nat. Bank v. Turnbull

& Co., 1872, 16 Wall. 190, 21 L.Ed. 296 (petitions of claimants to property seized under execution); Lawrence v. Morgan's L. & T. Ry. & S. S. Co., 1887, 7 S.Ct. 1013, 121 U.S. 634, 30 L.Ed. 1018 (suit to enjoin the sale of land under an execution); Chappell v. Chappell, 1898, 39 A. 984, 86 Md. 532 (proceeding based on a divorce suit to recover alimony, counsel fees, and costs); Kerbow v. Kerbow, D.C.Tex. 1976, 421 F.Supp. 1253 (proceeding involving federal pension plan ancillary to a state divorce action); Buford & Co. v. Strother & Conklin, C.C.D.Iowa, 1881, 10 F. 406 (garnishment after judgment).

15. The rule was so stated by Judge Love in Buford & Co. v. Strother & Conklin, C.C.D.Iowa, 1881, 10 F. 406, 407–408, and since has been much quoted.

16. The following cases allow or refuse removal of garnishment proceedings depending on whether the state law views such proceedings as ancillary or independent: American Auto. Ins. Co. v. Freundt, C.C.A.7th, 1939, 103 F.2d 613 (refused—Illinois law); London & Lancashire Indem. Co. v. Courtney, C.C.A.10th, 1939, 106 F.2d 277 (allowed—Oklahoma law); Western Medical Properties v. Denver Opportunity, Inc., D.C.Colo.1980, 482 F.Supp. 1205 (refused—Colorado law); Toney v. Maryland Cas. Co., D.C.Va.1939, 29 F.Supp. 785 (refused—Virginia law); Joski v. Short, D.C.Wash.1939, 28

To be removable, the civil action must be pending in a state "court." A justice of the peace court, or a county board or court that is vested with judicial power, will suffice.[17] An appeal to the courts of a state from an administrative agency may be in the form of a civil action and thus removable.[18]

It is frequently said that jurisdiction on removal is derivative, and that if the state court had no jurisdiction, the federal court acquires none, and cannot even remand, but must dismiss for want of jurisdiction.[19] This doctrine may be justifiable conceptually, but the results to which it leads are often absurd. Thus a suit is brought in state court and removed to federal court. If it is determined that the case was one over which the federal courts have exclusive jurisdiction,[20] the federal court, remarkably enough, cannot hear the case. It must dismiss a case falling within its exclusive jurisdiction because the court from which the case was removed had no jurisdiction.[21]

F.Supp. 821 (refused—Washington law); Brucker v. Georgia Cas. Co., D.C.Mo.1926, 14 F.2d 688 (refused—Missouri law); Baker v. Duwamish Mill Co., C.C.D.Wash.1906, 149 F. 612 (allowed—Washington law).

It is held, however, in Stoll v. Hawkeye Cas. Co., C.A.8th, 1950, 185 F.2d 96, criticized 1951, 35 Minn.L.Rev. 675, in Randolph v. Employers Mut. Liab. Ins. Co., C.A.8th, 1958, 260 F.2d 461, and in Swanson v. Liberty Nat. Ins. Co., C.A.9th, 1965, 353 F.2d 12, that garnishment is a "civil action" and is removable regardless of how it is characterized under state law. State law is similarly rejected in Reed v. Bloom, D.C.Okl.1936, 15 F.Supp. 7, and in Clarise Sportswear Co. v. U & W Mfg. Co., D.C.Pa.1963, 223 F.Supp. 961. See Note, 1954, 7 Okla.L.Rev. 446.

17. Katz v. Herschel Mfg. Co., C.C.D. Neb.1906, 150 F. 684 (justice of the peace court); Cappetta v. Atlantic Ref. Co., D.C.Conn.1935, 12 F.Supp. 89 (the same); Drainage Dist. No. 19, Caldwell County, Mo. v. Chicago, M. & St. P. Ry. Co., D.C.Mo.1912, 198 F. 253.

A county board without judicial powers is not a court within the removal statute. Fuller v. Colfax County, C.C.D.Neb. 1882, 14 F. 177, Gurnee v. Brunswick, C.C.D.Va.1876, Fed.Cas.No.5,872.

18. Mississippi & Rum River Boom Co. v. Patterson, 1878, 98 U.S. 403, 25 L.Ed. 206; Floeter v. C. W. Transport, Inc., C.A.7th, 1979, 597 F.2d 1100; and cases cited 14 Wright, Miller & Cooper, Jurisdiction § 3721 n. 58. In such a case the matter may be sufficiently local that the federal court will abstain

and leave the parties to their state court remedies. See § 52 below.

19. Lambert Run Coal Co. v. Baltimore & O. R. Co., 1922, 42 S.Ct. 349, 258 U.S. 377, 66 L.Ed. 671; Venner v. Michigan Central R. Co., 1926, 46 S.Ct. 444, 271 U.S. 127, 70 L.Ed. 868; and cases cited 14 Wright, Miller & Cooper, Jurisdiction § 3721 n. 35.

In a mystifying footnote in Federated Dept. Stores, Inc. v. Moitie, 1981, 101 S.Ct. 2424, 2427 n. 2, 452 U.S. 394, 397 n. 2, 69 L.Ed.2d 103, the Court said that a case had been properly removed to federal court since at least some of the antitrust claims were federal in nature. That in itself raises questions, and is discussed at notes 40 to 48 below. But if that conclusion itself is correct, it would seem that the rule that removal jurisdiction is derivative, and that the federal courts have exclusive jurisdiction of federal antitrust claims, would have barred removal. Yet there is no mention of this latter problem in the majority's footnote or in the concurrence of Justice Blackmun or the dissent of Justice Brennan. See Salveson v. Western States Bankcard Assn., D.C.Cal.1981, 525 F.Supp. 566, 578–580, where a district court follows the derivative jurisdiction rule, despite the "shadow of doubt" about its vitality created by Moitie.

20. As to when federal courts have exclusive jurisdiction, see § 10 above.

21. General Inv. Co. v. Lake Shore & M. S. Ry. Co., 1922, 43 S.Ct. 106, 260 U.S. 261, 67 L.Ed. 244 (antitrust action); Washington v. American League of Professional Baseball Clubs, C.A.9th, 1972, 460 F.2d 654 (antitrust action);

It was said at the outset that removal jurisdiction is generally equated with original jurisdiction, but that there are some variations. Thus in addition to the general removal statute, there are certain other statutes authorizing removal, as where a federal officer is sued or prosecuted in a state court for acts done under color of office [22] or a federal employee is sued for injury caused by his operation of a motor vehicle within the scope of his employment.[23] There are other statutes of less general importance.[24] Either a civil action or a criminal prosecution may be removed by a defendant who cannot secure in state court civil rights guaranteed to him by the Constitution of the United States,[25] but it has been held that this allows removal only in "the rare situations where it can be clearly predicted by reason of the operation of a pervasive and explicit state or federal law that those rights will inevitably be denied by the very act of bringing the defendant to trial in the state court." [26] The fact that removal is authorized by special statutes of this kind does not of itself permit these actions to be commenced in federal court.[27]

Martinez v. Seaton, C.A.10th, 1961, 285 F.2d 587, certiorari denied 81 S.Ct. 1677, 366 U.S. 946, 6 L.Ed.2d 856 (Tort Claims Act case); Danielson v. Donmopray, D.C.Wyo.1932, 57 F.2d 565 (tort committed on federal enclave). See also Freeman v. Bee Machine Co., Inc., 1943, 63 S.Ct. 1146, 319 U.S. 448, 87 L.Ed. 1509; and cases cited 14 Wright, Miller & Cooper, Jurisdiction § 3722 n. 59. But see International Harvester Co. v. Long Mfg. Co., D.C.N.C.1964, 235 F.Supp. 223.

This result would be changed if the proposals of the American Law Institute are accepted. See ALI Study, §§ 1312(d), 1317(b), 1382(e).

22. 28 U.S.C.A. § 1442; Tennessee v. Davis, 1880, 100 U.S. 257, 25 L.Ed. 648; Willingham v. Morgan, 1969, 89 S.Ct. 1813, 395 U.S. 402, 23 L.Ed.2d 396; and 14 Wright, Miller & Cooper, Jurisdiction § 3727. Habeas corpus is also available in federal court in such cases to obtain relief from state custody. 28 U.S.C.A. § 2241(c)(2); In re Neagle, 1890, 10 S.Ct. 658, 135 U.S. 1, 34 L.Ed. 55. See § 53 below.

See ALI Study, § 1322(b).

23. 28 U.S.C.A. § 2679(d). See Comment, 1967, 115 U.Pa.L.Rev. 439, and cases cited 14 Wright, Miller & Cooper, Jurisdiction § 3727 n. 14.

24. 12 U.S.C.A. § 632 (certain actions arising out of international or foreign banking); 22 U.S.C.A. § 286g (actions involving the International Monetary Fund and the International Bank for Reconstruction and Development).

More general provision was made in 1976 when 28 U.S.C.A. § 1441(d) was added by amendment. This allows removal of any civil action brought in a state court against a foreign state, as defined in 28 U.S.C.A. § 1603(a). The statute generally parallels, however, the grant of original jurisdiction added at the same time as 28 U.S.C.A. § 1330(a).

25. 28 U.S.C.A. § 1443.

26. City of Greenwood, Miss. v. Peacock, 1966, 86 S.Ct. 1800, 1812, 384 U.S. 808, 828, 16 L.Ed.2d 944. See also Johnson v. Mississippi, 1975, 95 S.Ct. 1591, 421 U.S. 213, 44 L.Ed.2d 121. See 14 Wright, Miller & Cooper, Jurisdiction § 3728; Redish, Revitalizing Civil Rights Removal Jurisdiction, 1980, 64 Minn.L.Rev. 523.

Only a few cases are held to have met this exacting standard. Georgia v. Rachel, 1966, 86 S.Ct. 1783, 384 U.S. 780, 16 L.Ed.2d 925; cf. Achtenberg v. Mississippi, C.A.5th, 1968, 393 F.2d 468; Wyche v. Louisiana, C.A.5th, 1967, 394 F.2d 927; Whatley v. City of Vidalia, C.A.5th, 1968, 399 F.2d 521. See also White v. Wellington, C.A.2d, 1980, 627 F.2d 582, is one of the very few cases in which removal has been allowed under the second branch of 28 U.S.C.A. § 1443(2).

See ALI Study, §§ 1312(c), 1372(7), and Commentary thereto.

27. Martin v. Wyzanski, D.C.Mass.1967, 262 F.Supp. 925; Keppleman v. Upston, D.C.Cal.1949, 84 F.Supp. 478.

Removal jurisdiction is sometimes narrower than original jurisdiction, in part because of statutes expressly providing that particular actions, principally tort actions in which Congress wishes to give the plaintiff an absolute choice of forum, are not removable.[28]   The cases are about equally divided on whether the provision in the Fair Labor Standards Act [29] permitting suit to be "maintained" in any court of competent jurisdiction bars removal of such suits.[30]   There is some suggestion that maritime actions in state court under the "saving to suitors" clause of 28 U.S.C.A. § 1333 are not removable,[31] but it has long been established that these are in fact removable if there is an independent basis for federal jurisdiction such as diversity of citizenship and the requisite amount in controversy.[32]

An extremely important limitation on removal is that diversity cases are removable only if none of the parties in interest properly joined and served as defendants is a citizen of the state in which the action is brought.[33]   If jurisdiction is based on a federal question, there is no such limitation, and even a resident defendant may remove.[34]   Thus if a citizen of Utah sues a citizen of Texas in the state court in Texas, defendant cannot remove, if diversity is the only basis for federal jurisdiction.   The defendant could remove if suit were

---

28. 28 U.S.C.A. §§ 1445(a) (Federal Employers' Liability Act and Jones Act cases), 1445(b) (actions against carriers for delay, loss, or damage in shipments, where the matter in controversy is $10,000 or less), 1445(c) (workmen's compensation proceedings). It has been held also that actions under the Securities Act, 15 U.S.C.A. § 77v(a), to recover for misrepresentation are not removable. Wilko v. Swan, 1953, 74 S.Ct. 182, 346 U.S. 427, 98 L.Ed. 168. See generally 14 Wright, Miller & Cooper, Jurisdiction § 3729, and ALI Study, § 1312(b).

29. 29 U.S.C.A. § 216.

30. See ALI Study, § 1312(b)(1), and Commentary thereto. The cases each way are collected in 14 Wright, Miller & Cooper, Jurisdiction § 3729 nn. 29, 30.

31. Chambers-Liberty Counties Navigation Dist. v. Parker Bros. & Co., D.C. Tex.1967, 263 F.Supp. 602; Harbor Boating Club of Huntington, N. Y., Inc. v. Red Star Towing & Transp. Co., D.C.N.Y.1960, 179 F.Supp. 755. These cases rest on a dictum, for which no authority was cited, in Romero v. International Terminal Operating Co., 1959, 79 S.Ct. 468, 480, 358 U.S. 354, 371–372, 3 L.Ed.2d 368.

32. E.g., Safir v. Compagnie Generale Transatlantique, D.C.N.Y.1965, 241 F.Supp. 501; see Pacific Far East Line,

Inc. v. Ogden Corp., D.C.Cal.1977, 425 F.Supp. 1239, 1242–1243. See also ALI Study, pp. 239–243; Currie, The Silver Oar and All That: A Study of the Romero Case, 1959, 27 U.Chi.L.Rev. 1, 16 n. 57; 14 Wright, Miller & Cooper, Jurisdiction § 3674.

33. 28 U.S.C.A. § 1441(b); Martin v. Snyder, 1893, 13 S.Ct. 706, 148 U.S. 663, 37 L.Ed. 602; and cases cited 14 Wright, Miller & Cooper, Jurisdiction § 3723 n. 10.

It is held, however, that this limitation is not "jurisdictional" and that if plaintiff makes no timely motion to remand after removal by a resident defendant in a diversity case the objection that the case is not removable is waived. Woodward v. D. H. Overmyer Co., C.A. 2d, 1970, 428 F.2d 880, certiorari denied 91 S.Ct. 460, 400 U.S. 993, 27 L.Ed.2d 441; Handley-Mack Co. v. Godchaux Sugar Co., C.C.A.6th, 1924, 2 F.2d 435. See § 41 n. 5 below.

The American Law Institute would permit removal in a diversity case by any defendant who could have removed if sued alone, even though other defendants are joined whose presence, under existing law, would prevent removal. ALI Study, § 1304(b).

34. Crawford v. East Asiatic Co., D.C. Cal.1957, 156 F.Supp. 571. See 14 Wright, Miller & Cooper, Jurisdiction § 3722, p. 546.

brought in any other state. It will be noted in this instance that the plaintiff could have brought the case in federal court, in Texas or in Utah, originally. It is reasonable to deny a resident defendant access to the federal courts by removal, but the same logic would seem to preclude a resident plaintiff from invoking the original jurisdiction of the federal court.[35] Prior to 1948 the removal statutes used the term "resident," rather than the present term "citizen," in setting out this limitation on removal. The change in terms apparently now means that, contrary to the pre-1948 decisons, an alien resident in the state can remove though the citizen residing there has no such right.[36]

Generally the right of removal is decided by the pleadings, viewed as of the time whe the petition for removal is filed.[37] A case not removable when commenced may later become removable under some circumstances, as where the plaintiff has amended his pleadings to change the nature of the claim, or has dropped a party whose presence prevented diversity.[38] The plaintiff cannot, however, take action to defeat federal jurisdiction and force remand after the case has been properly removed.[39]

Plaintiff is master of his claim, and if he chooses not to assert a federal claim, though one is available to him, defendant cannot remove on the basis of a federal question.[40] Doubt is cast on this long-established rule, however, by Federated Department Stores, Inc. v. Moitie, in which the Supreme Court, following the lead of a few lower courts, endorsed what it called the "settled principle" that plaintiff cannot use "artful pleading" to avoid removal jurisdiction.[41] This is an area in which the distinctions are extremely subtle, "some courts have not strictly observed the restrictions on removal jurisdiction," [42] and it is likely that the last word has not yet been written.

35. See ALI Study, § 1302(a), and Commentary thereto.

36. Jacobson v. Malaxa, D.C.N.Y.1953, 113 F.Supp. 111; 14 Wright, Miller & Cooper, Jurisdiction § 3723, pp. 602–603.

37. American Fire & Cas. Co. v. Finn, 1951, 71 S.Ct. 534, 341 U.S. 6, 95 L.Ed. 702, 19 A.L.R.2d 738; and cases cited 14 Wright, Miller & Cooper, Jurisdiction § 3721 nn. 63–64, § 3723 nn. 11–14, § 3725 n. 8.

The application of this rule to installment payment cases is discussed in § 33 n. 43 above.

38. Great Northern Ry. Co. v. Alexander, 1918, 38 S.Ct. 237, 246 U.S. 276, 62 L.Ed. 713; and cases cited 14 Wright, Miller & Cooper, Jurisdiction § 3721 n. 71, § 3722 nn. 43–44, § 3723 nn. 21–23, § 3725 nn. 46–47.

39. St. Paul Mercury Indem. Co. v. Red Cab Co., 1938, 58 S.Ct. 586, 303 U.S. 283, 82 L.Ed. 845; Comstock v. Morgan, D.C.Mo.1958, 165 F.Supp. 798; and cases cited 14 Wright, Miller & Cooper, Jurisdiction § 3721 n. 73.

40. Great Northern Ry. Co. v. Alexander, 1918, 38 S.Ct. 237, 239, 246 U.S. 276, 282, 62 L.Ed. 713; La Chemise Lacoste v. Alligator Co., C.A.3d, 1974, 506 F.2d 339, certiorari denied 95 S.Ct. 1666, 421 U.S. 937, 44 L.Ed.2d 94; and 14 Wright, Miller & Cooper, § 3722, pp. 564–572.

41. 101 S.Ct. 2424, 2427 n. 2, 452 U.S. 394, 397 n. 2, 69 L.Ed.2d 103. This single footnote on jurisdiction, in a case otherwise entirely devoted to the effect of a former judgment, see § 100A below, has caused other uncertainties about the law of removal. See note 19 above.

42. 101 S.Ct. at 2433 n. 6, 452 U.S. at 410 n. 6 (Brennan, J., dissenting). Justice Brennan cited as an example In re Carter, C.A.5th, 1980, 618 F.2d 1093,

The rule that plaintiff is master of his claim works well enough if it is clear that remedies are available under both state and federal law for a particular course of conduct. If plaintiff chooses to pursue only the state remedy, that is his privilege and the case will not be removable as a federal question case. Often, however, it is contended that the state remedies have been preempted by federal law. The difficulty here is that "preemption" is used in the law in more than one sense. In many instances pre-existing state rights of action are cut off by federal law. In these situations preemption is a defense to the state claim, and the rule that jurisdiction must be based on the complaint rather than on defenses [43] is enough to defeat removal.[44] There are other situations, however, of which § 301 of the Taft-Hartley Act [45] is the most conspicuous, in which it is held that federal law has taken over an entire subject matter and made it inherently federal. An action can be brought in state court to enforce rights arising under a collective bargaining agreement in an industry affecting interstate commerce, but state courts are obliged to follow the decisional law developed by federal courts. Federal law in these labor cases is not merely a defense to a state contract theory, but is the basis of all rights of action under the contract. If state law has been preempted in this sense, so that a state right of action has been replaced by a federal right of action, plaintiff necessarily is stating a federal claim whether he wishes to do so or not, and the case is removable.[46]

1101, certiorari denied 1981, 101 S.Ct. 1410, 450 U.S. 949, 68 L.Ed.2d 378.

43. See § 18 above.

44. E.g., Illinois v. Kerr-McGee Chemical Corp., C.A.7th, 1982, 677 F.2d 571, certiorari denied 103 S.Ct. 469, ___ U.S. ___, ___ L.Ed.2d ___ (Atomic Energy Act arguably precludes a claim under state statutes dealing with nuclear waste); Madsen v. Prudential Federal Sav. & Loan Assn., C.A.10th, 1980, 635 F.2d 797 (federal banking regulation arguably defeats a state-created right of a borrower to recover interest on money held by the lender in an escrow account); First Nat. Bank of Aberdeen v. Aberdeen Nat. Bank, C.A.8th, 1980, 627 F.2d 843 (approval by Comptroller of the Currency of a name change by a national bank arguably defeats a claim that the new name is actionable unfair competition under state law); Eure v. NVF Co., D.C.N.C.1979, 481 F.Supp. 639 (Williams Act arguably bars suit for noncompliance with state takeover statute).

But see Gunter v. Ago Intl. B. V., D.C. Fla.1981, 533 F.Supp. 86 (holding that a suit under a state takeover statute is removable because of preemption by the Williams Act).

45. 29 U.S.C.A. § 185. See § 20 above.

46. Avco Corp. v. Aero Lodge No. 735, 1968, 88 S.Ct. 1235, 390 U.S. 557, 20 L.Ed.2d 126. Sheeran v. General Elec. Co., C.A.9th, 1979, 593 F.2d 93, certiorari denied 100 S.Ct. 143, 444 U.S. 868, 62 L.Ed.2d 93; cf. McKinney v. International Assn. of Machinists & Aerospace Workers, C.A.6th, 1980, 624 F.2d 745 (Railway Labor Act); American Synthetic Rubber Corp. v. Louisville & N. R. Co., C.A.6th, 1970, 422 F.2d 462 (state court action for negligence delivery of goods supplanted by the Carmack Amendment to the Interstate Commerce Act).

"Certainly in situations where preempting federal law provides the litigant, whose State claims have been preempted, with an alternative federal claim, * * * it is reasonable to assume that a litigant will choose to seek relief under federal law rather than abandon his claim altogether. Where, however, superseding federal law does not replace rights formerly granted by State law, it is illogical to say that the litigant's claim is really predicated on a body of law which grants him no rights." New York v. Local 1115 Joint Bd., D.C.N.Y.1976, 412 F.Supp. 720, 723.

The preemption cases are difficult enough, but a few cases, including notably the Supreme Court's decision in Moitie, seem to carry the "artful pleading" concept even farther. In Moitie the plaintiffs had earlier brought federal antitrust actions, which had been dismissed. They then brought actions in state court in which the allegations were quite similar to those in the earlier case, but purported to raise only state-law claims. It was in this context that the Court said that plaintiffs "had attempted to avoid removal jurisdiction by 'artfully' casting their 'essentially federal law claims' as state-law claims." [47] It has never been held that the federal antitrust laws preempt state law. A lower court has advanced the ingenious suggestion that the explanation of Moitie is that having once exercised their option to assert their claims as federal rather than state claims, plaintiffs could not later retreat from that decision to the prejudice of defendants, and that to allow plaintiffs to prosecute the same claims under state law in the second action would have been to impair the ability of defendants to assert the federal res judicata defense against those claims.[48] But a state court is competent to apply res judicata to protect a federal judgment and res judicata is ordinarily seen as a defense, which would not support removal. Thus the theories put forward by the lower court are not theories that have ever been accepted in the past as justifications for removal, nor were these theories articulated in Moitie.

Despite the usual rule that removability is determined as of the time when the petition for removal is filed, there is a long line of authority that diversity of citizenship, where it is the basis of jurisdiction, must exist at the time of filing the original action as well as at the time of petitioning for removal.[49] The purpose of this limitation is to prevent the defendant from acquiring a new domicile after commencement of the suit, and then removing on the basis of diversity. The reason for the limitation is inapplicable where the case has been dropped as to a nondiverse party after its original commencement, since this is action over which defendant has no control, and where such a nondiverse party is formally dropped on the record, the case then becomes removable.[50] Prior to 1949 it was settled that the case

47. 101 S.Ct. at 2427 n. 2, 452 U.S. at 397 n. 2.

48. Salveson v. Western States Bankcard Assn., D.C.Cal.1981, 525 F.Supp. 566, 575. The Salveson court suggests also, at 576–577, that the artful pleading doctrine applies if plaintiff, by failing to seek remand of his action to state court, accepts defendant's characterization of the claims as federal, e.g., Vitarroz v. Borden, Inc., C.A.2d, 1981, 644 F.2d 960, or if a state antitrust law applies to purely intrastate commerce, so that a complaint based on interstate transactions could only be based on the federal statute. E.g., In re Wiring Device Antitrust Litigation, D.C.N.Y. 1980, 498 F.Supp. 79.

49. Gibson v. Bruce, 1883, 2 S.Ct. 873, 108 U.S. 561, 27 L.Ed. 825; and cases cited 14 Wright, Miller & Cooper, Jurisdiction § 3723 n. 14.

50. Powers v. Chesapeake & O. Ry. Co., 1898, 18 S.Ct. 264, 169 U.S. 92, 42 L.Ed. 673; Yulee v. Vose, 1878, 99 U.S. 539, 25 L.Ed. 355; and cases cited 14 Wright, Miller & Cooper, Jurisdiction § 3723 n. 15. As to the requirement that the party be formally dropped on the record, see Stamm v. American Tel. & Tel. Co., D.C.Mo.1955, 129 F.Supp. 719.

did not become removable where the nondiverse party had been eliminated from the case by a directed verdict,[51] a distinction being drawn between subsequent action by a court, which did not make a case removable, and voluntary action by the plaintiff, which did. The distinction had merit, in that it prevented removal where the nondiverse party was eliminated by a court order that might be subject to reversal on appeal. It is questionable, however, whether the distinction has survived a 1949 amendment of the Judicial Code, which permits removal, if the case was not at first removable, upon "receipt by the defendant, through service, or otherwise, of a copy of an amended pleading, motion, order or other paper from which it may first be ascertained that the case is one which is or has become removable." [52] Read literally this would seem to allow removal when the resident defendant is eliminated by court order, and some cases have so held.[53] It seems very doubtful that Congress intended to abolish the former distinction between voluntary and involuntary action, though the legislative history is quite ambiguous, and most cases have held that the old distinction survives.[54]

The right of removal may be lost or waived, but the courts are slow to find such a waiver, even where the defendant had taken action in state court prior to seeking removal.[55] An old case seemed to say that a contract stipulating that the parties would not remove

51. Whitcomb v. Smithson, 1900, 20 S.Ct. 248, 175 U.S. 635, 44 L.Ed. 303; Great Northern Ry. Co. v. Alexander, 1918, 38 S.Ct. 237, 246 U.S. 276, 62 L.Ed. 713; and cases cited 14 Wright, Miller & Cooper, Jurisdiction § 3723 nn. 16–18.

52. 28 U.S.C.A. § 1446(b).

53. Lyon v. Illinois Central R. Co., D.C. Miss.1964, 228 F.Supp. 810; cf. Bradley v. Halliburton Oil Well Cementing Co., D.C.Okl.1951, 100 F.Supp. 913. See Comment, Federal Practice: Removal After Resident Defendant is Involuntarily Dismissed, 1964, 17 Okl.L. Rev. 336.

54. Weems v. Louis Dreyfus Corp., C.A.5th, 1967, 380 F.2d 545; Continental Oil Co. v. PPG Indus., Inc., D.C. Tex.1973, 355 F.Supp. 1183; Hearst Corp. v. Shopping Center Network, Inc., D.C.N.Y.1969, 307 F.Supp. 551; and cases cited 14 Wright, Miller & Cooper, Jurisdiction § 3723 n. 20.
In Comment, The Effect of Section 1446(b) on the Nonresident's Right to Remove, 1966, 115 U.Pa.L.Rev. 264, the view that the 1949 amendment changed the law is rejected, but it is argued that the voluntary-involuntary rule should be applied more flexibly

and with an eye to considerations of judicial administration.

Where plaintiff did not appeal dismissal of a defendant by court order, the dismissal became the functional equivalent of a voluntary dismissal, and removal was proper. Quinn v. Aetna Life & Cas. Co., C.A.2d, 1980, 616 F.2d 38.

55. The following conduct has been held not to waive the right to remove: appearance in state court, Collins Mfg. Co. v. Wickwire Spencer Steel Co., D.C. Mass.1926, 11 F.2d 196; taking depositions in state court, Duvall v. Wabash Ry. Co., D.C.Mo.1923, 9 F.2d 83; filing responsive pleadings, Baldwin v. Perdue, Inc., D.C.Va.1978, 451 F.Supp. 373; giving bond to release attachment, Purdy v. Wallace Muller & Co., C.C.D.Mass.1897, 81 F. 513; requesting an extension of time to answer, Malave v. Sun Life Assur. Co. of Canada, D.C.Puerto Rico 1975, 392 F.Supp. 51; and cases cited 14 Wright, Miller & Cooper, Jurisdiction § 3721 nn. 95, 96.

Voluntary filing of a cross-action in state court has been held to waive the right of removal. Briggs v. Miami Window Corp., D.C.Ga.1956, 158 F.Supp. 229.

cases to federal court would be invalid,[56] but the modern view is that such a contract is a valid waiver of the right to remove unless the contract is unreasonable or procured by duress.[57] After some vacillation it was finally held by the Supreme Court that a state may not restrict or limit the right to remove, even as a condition to doing business within its borders, and may not penalize a foreign corporation for exercising its removal right.[58]

It is said that the trend of the decisions is to restrict and limit the removal jurisdiction of the federal courts. Certainly there is ample case support for the proposition that removal statutes will be strictly construed.[59]

§ 39. Separate and Independent Claim or Cause of Action [1]

From 1789 to 1866 cases could be removed to federal court only where all of the defendants were citizens of states other than the states of which any plaintiff was a citizen. In other words, complete diversity was required, and all cases that were removable could have been brought originally in federal court. The Separable Controversy Act of 1866 [2] introduced into the law the notion that where, within the lawsuit, there was "a separable controversy between citizens of different states," this much of the suit could be removed, leaving the balance of the suit, in which citizens of the same state were on opposite sides, in the state court. The statutory language was changed in

56. Home Ins. Co. of New York v. Morse, 1874, 20 Wall. 445, 22 L.Ed. 365.

57. Wm. H. Muller & Co., Inc. v. Swedish American Line, Ltd., C.A.2d, 1955, 224 F.2d 806, 808, certiorari denied 76 S.Ct. 182, 350 U.S. 903, 100 L.Ed. 793; Monte v. Southern Delaware County Auth., C.A.3d, 1963, 321 F.2d 870; Perini Corp. v. Orion Ins. Co., D.C.Cal., 1971, 331 F.Supp. 453. Compare Wilson v. Continental Cas. Co., D.C.Mont. 1966, 255 F.Supp. 622 (contract enforced), with Hasek v. Certain Lloyd's Underwriters, D.C.Mo.1963, 228 F.Supp. 754 (contract unreasonable).

58. Terral v. Burke Constr. Co., 1922, 42 S.Ct. 188, 257 U.S. 529, 66 L.Ed. 352. This result had been indicated by the 1873 decision in the Home Ins. Co. case, note 56 above, but there was an unfortunate decision to the contrary in Security Mut. Life Ins. Co. v. Prewitt, 1906, 26 S.Ct. 619, 202 U.S. 246, 50 L.Ed. 1013, finally overruled in the Terral case.

59. Graves v. Corbin, 1890, 10 S.Ct. 196, 132 U.S. 571, 33 L.Ed. 462; Chicago, R. I. & P. R. Co. v. Stude, C.A.8th, 1953, 204 F.2d 116, affirmed 1953, 74 S.Ct.

290, 346 U.S. 574, 98 L.Ed. 317; Maurer v. International Typographical Union, D.C.Pa.1956, 139 F.Supp. 337; and cases cited 14 Wright, Miller & Cooper, Jurisdiction § 3721 nn. 78–82.

[§ 39]

1. 14 Wright, Miller & Cooper, Jurisdiction § 3724; Lewin, The Federal Courts' Hospitable Back Door—Removal of "Separate and Independent" Non-Federal Causes of Action, 1953, 66 Harv.L.Rev. 423; Duvall, Removal— The "Separate and Independent Claim", 1954, 7 Okla.L.Rev. 385; Moore & VanDercreek, Multi-party, Multi-claim Removal Problems: The Separate and Independent Claim under Section 1441(c), 1961, 46 Iowa L.Rev. 489; Cohen, Problems in the Removal of a "Separate and Independent Claim or Cause of Action", 1961, 46 Minn.L. Rev. 1; Note, Removal under Section 1441(c) of the Judicial Code, 1952, 52 Col.L.Rev. 101; Comment, Diversity Removal Where the Federal Court Would Not Have Original Jurisdiction: A Suggested Reform, 1966, 114 U.Pa. L.Rev. 709.

2. Act of July 27, 1866, 14 Stat. 306.

1875,[3] and the Court construed the changed language as meaning that where there was a separable controversy, the entire suit was to be removed.[4] The statutory provisions continued in this form substantially unchanged until 1948.

There developed from these statutes a very complex body of law.[5] Johnson, a citizen of California, brings suit in a California state court against Meyers, also a citizen of California, and Green, a citizen of Texas. Green wishes to remove. It was necessary, under the pre-1948 law, to decide whether the controversy between Johnson and Green was separate, or separable, or nonseparable from the controversy between Johnson and Meyers. If, for example, Johnson was claiming that Green and Meyers were jointly liable to him, the controversies were deemed nonseparable and the case could not be removed.[6] If the claim against Green was entirely separate from the claim against Meyers, as in condemnation actions, Green was permitted to remove the claim against him to federal court while the claim against Meyers stayed in state court.[7] Finally if the claims were not separate but merely separable, as where Johnson claimed that either Green or Meyers was liable to him, but he did not know which, Green could remove the entire case to federal court.[8] The distinctions thus suggested were surely confusing, but were not quite as irrational as they may appear. The notion behind the separable controversy doctrine was that if the claim against Green was capable of being wholly determined between Johnson and Green, then, since diversity existed between those two, Green should be able to resort to federal court; at the same time the claim against Green was not entirely separate from the claim against Meyers, and thus the whole suit should come to federal court to avoid duplicate litigation.

A substantial change was made in this scheme in the 1948 Judicial Code. Section 1441(c) of the Code provides: "Whenever a separate and independent claim or cause of action, which would be removable if sued upon alone, is joined with one or more otherwise non-removable claims or causes of action, the entire case may be removed and the district court may determine all issues therein, or, in its discretion, may remand all matters not otherwise within its original jurisdiction."

3. Act of March 3, 1875, 18 Stat. 470.

4. Barney v. Latham, 1880, 103 U.S. 205, 26 L.Ed. 514.

5. See Texas Employers' Ins. Assn. v. Felt, C.C.A.5th, 1945, 150 F.2d 227; Holmes, The Separable Controversy— A Federal Removal Concept, 1939, 12 Miss.L.J. 163; Keeffe & Lacey, The Separable Controversy—A Federal Concept, 1947, 33 Corn.L.Q. 261.

6. E.g., Pullman Co. v. Jenkins, 1939, 59 S.Ct. 347, 305 U.S. 534, 83 L.Ed. 334.

7. E.g., Pacific R. Removal Cases, 1885, 5 S.Ct. 1113, 115 U.S. 1, 29 L.Ed. 319; Alabama Power Co. v. Gregory Hill Gold Mining Co., D.C.Ala.1925, 5 F.2d 705.

8. E.g., Texas Employers' Ins. Assn. v. Felt, C.C.A.5th, 1945, 150 F.2d 227. A leading case, finding a separable controversy, is Barney v. Latham, 1880, 103 U.S. 205, 26 L.Ed. 514.

The stated purpose of the change in language embodied in § 1441(c) was simplification and advancement in the interests of justice.[9] This purpose was not achieved. One judge, after reviewing the decisions, declared "it is not an exaggeration to say that at least on the surface the field luxuriates in a riotous uncertainty."[10] The new statute as construed has led to at least as much confusion as did the statute it replaced, and has created additional problems of constitutionality.

The leading case on § 1441(c) is American Fire & Casualty Co. v. Finn.[11] In that case the Supreme Court discerned in the 1948 revision a further purpose, that of reducing the number of cases removable from state courts.[12] This purpose has been achieved. Only a small number of cases have been removed under § 1441(c) since the Supreme Court construed it in the Finn case, and a strong argument can be made that in permitting removal in those cases the district courts applied the statute erroneously, or that the removal was unconstitutional.

The Finn case was a suit by a Texas citizen against two foreign insurance companies and their local agent, also a Texas citizen, claiming in the alternative recovery for fire loss on one or the other of the policies, or that Reiss, the agent, was liable for having failed to keep the property insured. The insurers removed to federal court, relying on § 1441(c). After trial to a jury, judgment was entered for the amount of the loss against one of the insurance companies, while judgment was entered for the other company and the agent. The company against which judgment had been entered then sought to have judgment vacated on the ground that the action had been improperly removed, and that the federal court was without jurisdiction. This contention was upheld in the Supreme Court.[13]

In construing the statute, the Court was forced to plunge into the murky waters of what is a cause of action. After examining some language in its own decisions, and citing with approval Judge Clark's famous discussion of the subject,[14] the Court concluded that "where there is a single wrong to plaintiff, for which relief is sought, arising from an interlocked series of transactions, there is no separate and independent claim or cause of action under § 1441(c)."[15]

9. H.Rep. No. 308, Apr. 25, 1947, 80th Cong., 1st Sess., p. A. 134.

10. Harper v. Sonnabend, D.C.N.Y.1960, 182 F.Supp. 594, 595.

11. 1951, 71 S.Ct. 534, 341 U.S. 6, 95 L.Ed. 702.

12. 71 S.Ct. at 538, 341 U.S. at 9–10.

13. The insurer won the battle, but lost the war. On remand after the Supreme Court decision, plaintiff voluntarily dismissed as to the non-diverse party, Reiss, and the Fifth Circuit held that judgment could again be entered against the insurer on the basis of the former trial. Finn v. American Fire & Cas. Co., C.A.5th, 1953, 207 F.2d 113, certiorari denied 74 S.Ct. 476, 347 U.S. 912, 98 L.Ed. 1069.

14. Clark, Code Pleading, 2d ed. 1947, pp. 137 et seq., cited at 71 S.Ct. 540, n. 12, 341 U.S. 14, n. 12.

15. 71 S.Ct. at 540, 341 U.S. at 14.

Applying that test to the facts before it, the Court found removal improper. "The single wrong for which relief is sought is the failure to pay compensation for the loss on the property. Liability lay among three parties, but it was uncertain which one was responsible. * * * The facts in each portion of the complaint involve Reiss, the damage comes from a single incident. The allegations in which Reiss is a defendant involve substantially the same facts and transactions as do the allegations in the first portion of the complaint against the foreign insurance companies. It cannot be said that there are separate and independent claims for relief as § 1441(c) requires."[16]

Few, if any, diversity cases can properly be removed under this statute in the light of the construction placed on it in the Finn case.[17] Writing in 1961, Professor Cohen listed 24 such cases in which removal had been permitted but noted that there is substantial doubt as to the propriety of removal, evidenced by other cases denying removal in similar circumstances, in many of those cases.[18]

It is not surprising that few cases meet the Finn test. Under the most liberal state joinder rules, parties are not properly joined unless there is some question of law or fact common to all of them, and some claim asserted for or against all arising out of a single transac-

---

16. 71 S.Ct. at 540–541, 341 U.S. at 14, 16.

In Union Planters Nat. Bank of Memphis v. CBS, Inc., C.A.6th, 1977, 557 F.2d 84, recovery was not allowed although the claims against the defendants were based on different events and transactions, they relied on different legal theories, and they would have produced different measures of damage. But cf. National Sav. & Loan Assn. v. St. Paul Fire & Marine Ins. Co., D.C.Wis.1979, 84 F.R.D. 424.

17. See Chappell v. SCA Services, Inc., D.C.Ill.1982, 540 F.Supp. 1087, 1094; Thornton v. Allstate Ins. Co., D.C. Mich.1980, 492 F.Supp. 645, 648; El Dorado Springs R–2 Sch. Dist. v. Moos, D.C.Mo.1967, 264 F.Supp. 815, 818. But see Climax Chem. Co. v. C.F. Braun & Co., C.A.10th, 1966, 370 F.2d 616, 618–619, certiorari denied 87 S.Ct. 1287, 386 U.S. 981, 18 L.Ed.2d 231, where the court said: "We do not take such a morbid view. If the Court was sounding the death knell of section 1441(c) we believe it would have said so." The Climax Chemical case is noted 1967, 43 Notre Dame Law. 107, 46 Texas L.Rev. 102. And in Hermann v. Braniff Airways, Inc., D.C.N.Y.1969, 308 F.Supp. 1094, 1097, the court refused to follow what it called the "severely restrictive view" stated in the text.

18. Cohen, Problems in the Removal of a "Separate and Independent Claim or Cause of Action", 1961, 46 Minn.L.Rev. 1, 13 n. 54, 19 n. 76.

Cases permitting removal under § 1441(c) are described in 14 Wright, Miller & Cooper, Jurisdiction § 3724 nn. 42–46. Cases denying such removal are described id. at nn. 37–41.

Some cases have shown a greater willingness to find claims separate and independent when multiple plaintiffs have claims against a single defendant. E.g., Stokes v. Merrill Lynch, Pierce, Fenner & Smith, Inc., C.A.6th, 1975, 523 F.2d 433; Northside Iron & Metal Co. v. Dobson & Johnson, Inc., C.A.5th, 1973, 480 F.2d 798; Jong v. General Motors Corp., D.C.Cal.1973, 359 F.Supp. 223. This seems unsound. The claims of different plaintiffs are certainly "separate" but in the cases cited they were not "independent." Schwartz v. Merrill Lynch, Pierce, Fenner & Smith, D.C.Cal.1976, 424 F.Supp. 672; Lavan Petroleum Co. v. Underwriters at Lloyds, D.C.N.Y.1971, 334 F.Supp. 1069; Rosen v. Rozan, D.C. Mont.1959, 179 F.Supp. 829; Note, 1952, 52 Col.L.Rev. 101, 106–107; 14 Wright, Miller & Cooper, Jurisdiction § 3724, pp. 641–643.

tion or occurrence or series of transactions or occurrences.[19] The relation that the joinder-of-parties rules require is just the kind of relation that, according to the Finn case, bars resort to § 1441(c). It is true that, in the example given earlier, if Johnson of California has a claim against Meyers of California and Green of Texas on which they are properly joined as defendants, he may then join in the same lawsuit an entirely unrelated claim against Green.[20] This situation would meet the Finn test, and Green could remove under § 1441(c), but such cases appear so rarely in the courts that the utility of having a special and confusing statute to permit their removal may well be doubted. There was some doubt also as to the constitutionality of allowing such removal in the rare case of this type. Removal under § 1441(c) brings the entire case to federal court, including the claim on which California citizens are opposing parties. This occurred for nearly 75 years under the old separable controversy statute, and its constitutionality was little discussed and never denied.[21] Now that it has finally been established that complete diversity is not constitutionally required,[22] federal jurisdiction of Johnson's claim against Green and Meyers is defensible on the ground that § 1441(c) is a grant of jurisdiction over cases in which there is only partial diversity.[23]

The cases are quite divided on whether § 1441(c) applies only to claims joined by plaintiff or whether a third-party claim under Rule 14[24] can be the basis for removal in those rare instances in which it is in fact separate and independent from the main claim.[25] It seems rather drastic to force the plaintiff, whose choice of forum normally should be honored, to litigate in a federal court that he did not choose and one to which his adversary originally could not have removed, and if removal on the basis of a third-party claim is permissible at all, the main action should be remanded if plaintiff desires this.[26]

19. See § 71 below.
The holding in Leppard v. Jordan's Truck Line, D.C.S.C.1952, 110 F.Supp. 811, permitting removal under § 1441(c) on the basis of misjoined claims, seems clearly unsound. See the critical note, 1954, 67 Harv.L.Rev. 519.

20. See § 78 below.

21. The leading case on constitutionality of separable controversy removal relied on a theory of ancillary jurisdiction. Texas Employers' Ins. Assn. v. Felt, C.C.A.5th, 1945, 150 F.2d 227, noted 1946, 94 U.Pa.L.Rev. 239. This theory was of little help for § 1441(c), since that statute requires that the claims be entirely unrelated.

22. State Farm Fire & Cas. Co. v. Tashire, 1967, 87 S.Ct. 1199, 1203–1204, 386 U.S. 523, 530–531, 18 L.Ed.2d 270. See § 24 above.

23. Gallagher v. Continental Ins. Co., C.A.10th, 1974, 502 F.2d 827; Irving Trust Co. v. Century Export & Import, S.A., D.C.N.Y.1979, 464 F.Supp. 1232, 1237 n. 9; Twentieth Century-Fox Film Corp. v. Taylor, D.C.N.Y.1965, 239 F.Supp. 913, 918–921.

24. See § 76 below.

25. See cases cited 14 Wright, Miller & Cooper, Jurisdiction § 3724 nn. 58, 59.

26. E.g., Carl Heck Engineers v. Lafourche Parish Police Jury, C.A.5th, 1980, 622 F.2d 133; Peturis v. Fendley, D.C.Ala.1980, 496 F.Supp. 203; Wayrynen Funeral Home, Inc. v. J. G. Link & Co., D.C.Mont.1968, 279 F.Supp. 803. In Marsh Inv. Corp. v. Langford, D.C. La.1980, 494 F.Supp. 344, affirmed C.A.5th, 1981, 652 F.2d 583, plaintiff did not ask to have the main action remanded.

Prior to 1948, the separable controversy statute applied only to diversity cases. Section 1441(c), on the other hand, reaches any separate and independent claim or cause of action that would be removable if sued upon alone, and thus creates the possibility for the first time that a case may be removable where a federal question is joined with a separate claim of a non-federal nature, and diversity is absent. This situation can well arise, since, unlike the diversity cases, it can have reference to joinder of multiple claims by a single plaintiff against a single defendant. State rules on joinder of claims or causes of action would be relevant, and these, in the more liberal jurisdictions, permit such joinder even of completely unrelated claims. Removal of these federal question cases has its own problems, however.[27] It has been well established for years that federal courts can take jurisdiction of a non-federal claim if it is so closely related to a federal question as to be within the pendent jurisdiction of the federal court.[28] Such a case would be removable under 28 U.S.C.A. § 1441(b) without regard to separate and independent claims. In the leading case of Hurn v. Oursler,[29] the Supreme Court distinguished between those cases where the federal and non-federal claims are so closely related that both can come within federal jurisdiction, and cases where there is "a separate and distinct non-federal cause of action." Is a "separate and distinct" cause of action the same as the "separate and independent" cause of action for which the new statute calls? If it is, and there are some intimations that it may be,[30] then every case that includes a federal question will be removable. If the federal and the non-federal claims are separate and independent, the case will be removable under § 1441(c), while if they are not separate and independent, the case will be removable under § 1441(b) with the non-federal claim heard in the pendent jurisdiction of the federal court.[31]

27. Among them is the unresolved question of what happens when one of the two separate and independent claims is, by statute, expressly made non-removable. Compare Gamble v. Central of Georgia Ry. Co., C.A.5th, 1973, 486 F.2d 781, with Hages v. Aliquippa & Southern R. Co., D.C.Pa.1977, 427 F.Supp. 889. See 14 Wright, Miller & Cooper, Jurisdiction § 3724, pp. 654–655. There is considerable force in the argument that § 1441(c), unlike § 1441(a), does not have an "except as otherwise provided by law" restriction in it, and thus that removal should be allowed. See United States Indus., Inc. v. Gregg, D.C.Del.1972, 348 F.Supp. 1004, reversed on other grounds C.A.3d, 1976, 540 F.2d 142.

28. Hurn v. Oursler, 1933, 53 S.Ct. 586, 289 U.S. 238, 77 L.Ed. 1148; United Mine Workers of America v. Gibbs,

1966, 86 S.Ct. 1130, 383 U.S. 715, 16 L.Ed.2d 218. See § 19 above.

29. 1933, 53 S.Ct. 586, 589, 289 U.S. 238, 245–246, 77 L.Ed. 1148.

30. The language in American Fire & Cas. Co. v. Finn, 1951, 71 S.Ct. 534, 341 U.S. 6, 95 L.Ed. 702, is similar to that of Hurn v. Oursler, and indeed the Hurn case is cited in footnote 9 of the Finn case. The Finn case in turn was cited when the Court reformulated the pendent jurisdiction doctrine. United Mine Workers of America v. Gibbs, 1966, 86 S.Ct. 1130, 1137 n. 8, 383 U.S. 715, 723 n. 8, 16 L.Ed.2d 218.

31. This is the holding in Swift & Co. v. United Packinghouse Workers, D.C. Colo.1959, 177 F.Supp. 511. The statute is similarly interpreted in Cohen, note 1 above, at 25–34.

Such a result would be strange, but an even stranger result is reached if "separate and independent," for purposes of § 1441(c), means something more separate than the concept used as the measure of pendent jurisdiction. This approach would create a tripartite classification. If the two claims are closely enough related, the whole case is removable under § 1441(b). If the two claims are far enough removed, the whole case is removable under § 1441(c). But if the relation is too close for § 1441(c), while yet not close enough for § 1441(b), no part of the case is removable. This seems absurd, but reputable scholars have so read the statute.[32]

No matter which view is taken of the preceding question as to the interrelation of subsections (b) and (c) of the statute, the statute, if read literally, certainly means that there will be some cases where a federal court will have jurisdiction of a non-federal claim, though diversity is absent and though the claim bears no relation to any federal claim in the case. This poses a serious constitutional question. If the cases defining the pendent jurisdiction doctrine do so in terms of constitutional limits,[33] then the statute is unconstitutional when applied to the situation just described.

On the constitutional issues raised by § 1441(c), particularly in non-diversity cases, there has been a good deal of spirited writing by the commentators [34] but very little said by the courts.[35] Even if valid, the statute's utility is greatly outweighed by the confusion it has engendered.[36]

32. Lewin, note 1 above, at 441; Moore & VanDercreek, note 1 above, at 506 n. 81; Note, note 1 above, at 111–112.

33. The reformulation in United Mine Workers of America v. Gibbs, 1966, 86 S.Ct. 1130, 1138, 383 U.S. 715, 725, 16 L.Ed.2d 218, appears on its face to be a statement in terms of constitutional limits. Although the Court there abandons the language in Hurn about "causes of action," and looks instead to see whether the claims "derive from a common nucleus of operative fact" and whether a plaintiff would ordinarily be expected to try them all in one judicial proceeding, this does not seem to affect the analysis of § 1441(c) made in the text.

34. The article by Lewin, note 1 above, concludes that § 1441(c) is unconstitutional in nondiversity cases. Professors Moore and VanDercreek, in the article cited note 1 above, reject the attacks on the constitutionality of the statute as completely without substance. Professor Cohen, in the article cited note 1 above, finds the constitutional question difficult, but concludes that in Hurn v. Oursler the Court was

merely construing the jurisdictional statutes, and not defining the constitutional limits of ancillary jurisdiction, and thus reasons that the statute is valid. Green, Jurisdiction of United States District Courts in Multiple-Claim Cases, 1954, 7 Vand.L.Rev. 472, 489–493, makes a similar analysis. All of these discussions predate the Gibbs case, note 33 above.

35. In Stone v. Stone, D.C.Cal.1978, 450 F.Supp. 919, 934, affirmed C.A.9th, 1980, 632 F.2d 740, the court remanded the state claims to avoid what it called a "serious constitutional question."

36. See Cohen, note 1 above, at 41.
The American Law Institute would allow removal in diversity cases by any defendant who could have removed if sued upon alone. ALI Study, § 1304(b). For federal question cases it proposes to define explicitly the reach of pendent jurisdiction, id. at § 1313(a), and to require remand of all claims not within that reach. Id. at § .1313(b). This approach is regarded as preferable to that of § 1441(c) in Comment, 1966, 114 U.Pa.L.Rev. 709.

§ 40. Procedure for Removal [1]

The procedure for removal from state to federal court prior to 1948 [2] was not satisfactory. The petition for removal and the bond were filed in state court, and if the state court refused to allow removal, defendant had three courses of action available, none of them very reassuring. He could note his exception, litigate in state court, and on appeal, perhaps to the Supreme Court, contend that removal was erroneously denied. If he was successful in this contention, the case finally would go to federal court to be tried over again. A second possibility was to ignore the state proceedings and go ahead in federal court as if removal had been granted. The risk here was that the state judgment against him would be valid if it were ultimately determined that the state court was right in refusing removal. Finally he could litigate in both state and federal courts at the same time, surely a wasteful procedure. [3]

The 1948 Judicial Code has made a substantial improvement in the procedure for removal, and has virtually ended the conflicts described between state and federal jurisdiction. [4]

Procedure for removal is now spelled out in 28 U.S.C.A. § 1446. A defendant, wishing to remove, files with the federal district court for the district or division in which the action is pending a verified petition, setting out the facts that entitle him to removal, accompanied by a bond for costs and disbursements. The petition must usually be filed within 30 days after defendant receives the complaint. After he has filed the petition and bond with the federal court, the defendant gives written notice of removal to the plaintiff and files a copy of the petition with the state court. Upon the filing of the copy of the petition with the state court, the state court is prohibited by specific language from proceeding further with the case. Thus removal does not require leave from either the state or the federal court, although the propriety of removal may later be tested by motion to remand in federal court. [5] Conflict between the two systems of courts is eliminated because of the bar against further state proceedings after removal. So long as the case has not been remanded,

[§ 40]

1. 14 Wright, Miller & Cooper, Jurisdiction §§ 3730–3738; Brown, Removal Procedure Under the Revised Judicial Code, 1950, 19 U.Cin.L.Rev. 171; Note, Removal Procedure Under Revised Title 28, 1952, 4 Syracuse L.Rev. 118; Comment, Federal Procedure—Requirements and Procedure in the Removal Process, 1963, 16 Ala.L.Rev. 81.

2. See Brown, Procedure for Removal of Cases to Federal District Courts,

1946, 31 Iowa L.Rev. 354; Jones, Procedure in Removal of Causes, 1942, 18 Notre Dame Law. 95.

3. These procedures are outlined in Metropolitan Cas. Ins. Co. v. Stevens, 1941, 61 S.Ct. 715, 717–718, 312 U.S. 563, 567–568, 85 L.Ed. 1044.

4. See Notes, 1949, 98 U.Pa.L.Rev. 80, 1956, 9 Okla.L.Rev. 191.

5. See § 41 below.

any subsequent state action is void,[6] even if the case was removed improperly.[7]

Despite the general simplicity of the procedure for removal, some questions have arisen that require more detailed discussion. Only a defendant may remove a case. For purposes of removal, federal law determines who is the plaintiff and who is the defendant.[8] All defendants except purely nominal parties must join in the petition for removal,[9] except that defendants not served need not join,[10] and

---

6. 28 U.S.C.A. § 1446(e); National S. S. Co. v. Tugman, 1882, 1 S.Ct. 58, 106 U.S. 118, 27 L.Ed. 87; Kern v. Huidekoper, 1880, 103 U.S. 485, 26 L.Ed. 354; Heniford v. American Motors Sales Corp., D.C.S.C.1979, 471 F.Supp. 328, appeal dismissed without opinion C.A.4th, 1980, 622 F.2d 584; State v. Francis, 1964, 134 S.E.2d 681, 261 N.C. 358; Garden Homes, Inc. v. District Court of Somerville, Mass. 1957, 146 N.E.2d 372, 336 Mass. 432; Fire Assn. of Philadelphia v. General Handkerchief Corp., 1952, 107 N.E.2d 499, 304 N.Y. 382, noted 1953, 53 Col.L. Rev. 287, 66 Harv.L.Rev. 534; and cases cited 14 Wright, Miller & Cooper, Jurisdiction § 3737 nn. 7–10.

7. U. S. v. Ohio, Em.App.1973, 487 F.2d 936, 943, affirmed 1975, 95 S.Ct. 1792, 421 U.S. 542, 44 L.Ed.2d 363; South Carolina v. Moore, C.A.4th, 1971, 447 F.2d 1067; Hopson v. North American Ins. Co., 1951, 233 P.2d 799, 71 Idaho 461, 25 A.L.R.2d 1040; McCauley v. Consolidated Underwriters, Tex.Civ. App.1957, 301 S.W.2d 181, reversed on other grounds 1957, 304 S.W.2d 265, 157 Tex. 475; Artists' Representatives Assn., Inc. v. Haley, 1966, 274 N.Y.S.2d 442, 26 A.D.2d 918. See ALI Study, § 1383(a), and the Commentary thereon at pp. 357–360, proposing a means of escape from the rigidity of this rule.

In a criminal case, however, the filing of a petition for removal does not prevent the state court from proceeding further, except that a judgment of conviction shall not be entered unless the petition is denied. 28 U.S.C.A. § 1446(c) (3), as amended in 1977. Removable criminal cases are those against federal officers or members of the armed forces for acts done under color of office, and certain civil rights cases. 28 U.S.C.A. §§ 1442, 1442a, 1443. See § 38 above.

8. Mason City & Ft. D. R. Co. v. Boynton, 1907, 27 S.Ct. 321, 204 U.S. 570, 51 L.Ed. 629; Chicago, R. I. & P. R. Co. v. Stude, 1954, 74 S.Ct. 290, 346 U.S. 574, 98 L.Ed. 317; Note, 1953, 38 Iowa L.Rev. 575. See 14 Wright, Miller & Cooper, Jurisdiction § 3731.

The preceding cases hold that in a condemnation proceeding the condemnor is the plaintiff for purposes of removal, even though the landowner is denominated as plaintiff by the state statute permitting court review. It is not yet settled who is the plaintiff in an arbitration proceeding. Victorias Milling Co. v. Hugo Neu Corp., D.C.N.Y.1961, 196 F.Supp. 64, approved 1962, 75 Harv.L.Rev. 1438, holds that the party to the arbitration who first invokes judicial intervention is plaintiff for removal purposes. See also Irving S. Cohen, Inc. v. Glen Raven Cotton Mills, Inc., D.C.N.Y.1967, 263 F.Supp. 107. But see Minkoff v. Budget Dress Corp., D.C.N.Y.1960, 180 F.Supp. 818.

9. Chicago, R. I. & P. Ry. Co. v. Martin, 1900, 20 S.Ct. 854, 178 U.S. 245, 44 L.Ed. 1055; Padden v. Gallaher, D.C. Wis.1981, 513 F.Supp. 770. As to nominal parties, see Tri-Cities Newspapers, Inc. v. Tri-Cities Pressmen & Assistants' Local 349, C.A.5th, 1970, 427 F.2d 325. See generally cases cited 14 Wright, Miller & Cooper, Jurisdiction § 3731 nn. 7–12.

A party named as a defendant who should be realigned as a plaintiff, see § 30 above, need not join in a petition for removal. Sersted v. Midland-Ross Corp., D.C.Wis.1979, 471 F.Supp. 298.

10. Hughes Constr. Co. v. Rheem Mfg. Co., D.C.Miss.1980, 487 F.Supp. 345; S. E. Overton Co. v. International Broth. of Teamsters, Chauffeurs, Warehousemen & Helpers of America, AFL, D.C. Mich.1953, 115 F.Supp. 764.

Prior to 1948 it was held that nonresident defendants who had not been served need not join in the petition, but that a resident defendant must join, though not served, if there was to be removal. Pullman Co. v. Jenkins, 1939, 59 S.Ct. 347, 305 U.S. 534, 83 L.Ed. 334. There

where removal is on the basis of a separate and independent claim or cause of action under § 1441(c)—if there really can be such a case [11]—only the defendants involved in that claim need join.[12]

The venue for removed actions is the district and division in which the state court action is pending.[13] The general venue statutes are irrelevant in removed cases.

In general the petition for removal must be filed within 30 days after the receipt by the defendant, through service or otherwise, of a copy of the initial pleading setting forth the claim for relief upon which such action or proceeding is based, or within 30 days after the service of summons upon the defendant if such initial pleading has then been filed in court, and is not required to be served on the defendant, whichever period is shorter.[14] Time runs from the receipt of the complaint, rather than the date it is filed with the state court.[15] Receipt by a person authorized to accept process for the defendant is sufficient.[16] There was once some question about when the time be-

are some holdings, and some dicta, to this effect under the 1948 Code. Gratz v. Murchison, D.C.Del.1955, 130 F.Supp. 709; Wolsum v. J. W. Bateson Co., D.C.Mo.1960, 182 F.Supp. 879. But the language in § 1441(b) of the 1948 Code, providing that diversity cases "shall be removable only if none of the parties properly joined and served as defendants is a citizen of the State in which such action is brought," seems to imply that a resident defendant who has not been served can be ignored. See cases cited 14 Wright, Miller & Cooper, Jurisdiction § 3731 n. 16.

11. See the doubts expressed in § 39 above.

12. International Union of Operating Engineers v. Sletten Constr. Co., D.C. Mont.1974, 383 F.Supp. 855; Gratz v. Murchison, D.C.Del.1955, 130 F.Supp. 709.

All defendants need not join in the petition if a federal officer named as a defendant seeks removal under Ely Valley Mines, Inc. v. Hartford Acc. & Indem. Co., C.A.9th, 1981, 644 F.2d 1310, or if removal is under 28 U.S. C.A. § 1443(2). Bridgeport Educ. Assn. v. Zinner, D.C.Conn.1976, 415 F.Supp. 715.

13. 28 U.S.C.A. § 1441(a); Polizzi v. Cowles Magazines, 1953, 73 S.Ct. 900, 902, 345 U.S. 663, 665, 97 L.Ed. 1331; Minnesota Mining & Mfg. Co. v. Kirkevold, D.C.Minn.1980, 87 F.R.D. 317; 14 Wright, Miller & Cooper, Federal Practice and Procedure: Jurisdiction § 3726. But cf. Tanglewood Mall, Inc. v. Chase Manhattan Bank (Nat.

Assn.), D.C.Va.1974, 371 F.Supp. 722, affirmed C.A.4th, 1974, 508 F.2d 838, certiorari denied 95 S.Ct. 1954, 421 U.S. 965, 44 L.Ed.2d 452.

14. 28 U.S.C.A. § 1446(b); 14 Wright, Miller & Cooper, Jurisdiction § 3732.

Since 1978 a New York statute has required a summons served without a complaint to contain or have appended thereto a notice stating the nature of the action and the relief sought. Receipt of such a notice has been held sufficient to start the time for removal running even though the notice does not state the citizenship of the parties. DiMeglio v. Italia Crociere Internazionale, D.C.N.Y.1980, 502 F.Supp. 316. See also Keller v. Carr, D.C.Ark.1981, 534 F.Supp. 100.

The statutory provision is not entirely appropriate in states in which the initial pleading is not served on defendant but is filed in court after the service of process. See Raymond's, Inc. v. New Amsterdam Cas. Co., D.C.Mass.1966, 159 F.Supp. 212. Cf. ALI Study, § 1382(a).

15. Kulbeth v. Woolnought, D.C.Tex. 1971, 324 F.Supp. 908; and cases cited 14 Wright, Miller & Cooper, Jurisdiction § 3732 n. 3.

16. Percell's, Inc. v. Central Tel. Co., D.C.Minn.1980, 493 F.Supp. 156; Gobet v. Intercontinental Hotels Corp. (Ponce), D.C.Puerto Rico, 1960, 184 F.Supp. 171; Automatic Merchandising Corp. v. Zenga, D.C.Mass.1958, 159 F.Supp. 489; Allison v. Montgomery Ward & Co., D.C.N.H.1957, 159 F.Supp. 550.

gins to run if service is on a statutory agent, such as a state officer in a suit against a nonresident motorist. It is now settled that regardless of the niceties of state law as to when service is technically complete, the time for removal begins to run only when the party or his own appointed agent actually receives the process.[17]

There are certain exceptions to the usual 30-day limit on petitioning for removal.[18] Where defendant claims that a party has been fraudulently joined to prevent removal,[19] the petition is timely if it is filed within a reasonable time after defendant should have known that the joinder was fraudulent.[20] In addition, a 1949 amendment to the Code provides that where the case initially was not removable, the petition may be filed within 30 days after receipt by the defendant of an amended pleading, motion, order or other paper from which it may first be ascertained that the case is one that is or has become removable.[21] As has been pointed out earlier, the better view is that the reference to "order" in the 1949 amendment does not abolish the prior distinction by which voluntary action of the plaintiff would make a case removable, but a court order, dismissing, for example, as to a nondiverse party, would not.[22]

Ordinarily the amount demanded by the complaint is regarded as the amount in controversy.[23] This is true even where state law pro-

But see Barber v. Willis, D.C.Ga.1965, 246 F.Supp. 814.

17. E.g., Kurtz v. Harris, D.C.Tex.1965, 245 F.Supp. 752. As the Kurtz case points out, all of the cases to the contrary, except for one, have now been overruled by the courts that decided them.

18. Until 1977 28 U.S.C.A. § 1446(c) allowed a criminal case to be removed at any time before trial. This was susceptible of great abuse. South Carolina v. Moore, C.A.4th, 1971, 447 F.2d 1067; Note, Abuse of Procedure in Removal of State Criminal Prosecutions, 1971, 6 U.S.F.L.Rev. 117. As amended in 1977, the statute now requires the petition for removal to be filed not later than 30 days after the arraignment in state court, or before trial, whichever is earlier, although the court may, for good cause, allow it to be filed at a later time.

Foreign banking cases are removable at any time before trial. 12 U.S.C.A. § 632. Manas y Piniero v. Chase Manhattan Bank, N.A., D.C.N.Y.1978, 443 F.Supp. 418.

The 30-day period may be enlarged for good cause in suits against a foreign state under the Foreign Sovereign Immunities Act of 1976. 28 U.S.C.A. § 1441(d); Gray v. Permanent Mission

of the People's Republic of the Congo to the United Nations, D.C.N.Y.1978, 443 F.Supp. 816, affirmed without opinion C.A.2d, 1978, 580 F.2d 1044.

19. See § 31 above.

20. Parks v. New York Times Co., D.C. Ala.1961, 195 F.Supp. 919, reversed on other grounds C.A.5th, 1962, 308 F.2d 474.

21. 28 U.S.C.A. § 1446(b), as amended by the Act of May 24, 1949, c. 139, § 83, 63 Stat. 101. The corresponding section in the 1948 Code made the time run solely from the initial pleading, apparently overlooking the former law to the contrary.

If the case was removable originally, an amendment will not revive the right to remove unless it changes the original complaint so drastically that the purposes of the 30-day limit would not be served by enforcing it. Wilson v. Intercollegiate (Big Ten) Conference Athletic Assn., C.A.7th, 1982, 668 F.2d 962, certiorari denied 103 S.Ct. 70, ___ U.S. ___, 74 L.Ed.2d 70; 14 Wright, Miller & Cooper, Jurisdiction § 3732, pp. 725–729.

22. See § 38 above at n. 54.

23. In removal cases "there is a strong presumption that the plaintiff has not claimed a large amount in order to con-

vides that the relief ultimately given may exceed the demand for judgment.[24] But if the relief demanded is not limited to a money judgment the petition for removal may contain allegations as to the value of the matter in controversy.[25]

Difficult problems are caused for the federal courts and for litigants by the practice in a few states in which no demand for a specific sum is required.[26] Although it had been held that the time does not begin to run until it appears as a matter of record in the state proceeding that more than $10,000 is in controversy,[27] the courts are increasingly moving to the view that if defendant was adequately on notice that more than $10,000 is involved, he must immediately petition for removal and state in his petition that more than $10,000 is in controversy.[28]

The petition for removal must contain a short and plain statement of the facts that entitle the petitioners to removal, and must be verified.[29] A copy of all process, pleadings, and orders served upon the petitioners must accompany the petition.[30] Prior to the expiration of the 30-day period for removal, the petition may be freely amended, but the cases say that thereafter it can be amended only to state more specifically a ground for removal which is already imperfectly

fer jurisdiction on a federal court or that the parties have colluded to that end." St. Paul Mercury Indem. Co. v. Red Cab Co., 1938, 58 S.Ct. 586, 590, 303 U.S. 283, 290, 82 L.Ed. 845; Albright v. R. J. Reynolds Tobacco Co., C.A.3d, 1976, 531 F.2d 132.

24. See § 33 above at nn. 51–52.

25. Davenport v. Proctor & Gamble Mfg. Co., C.A.2d, 1947, 241 F.2d 511; Ronzio v. Denver & R. G. W. R. Co., C.A.10th, 1940, 116 F.2d 604; Perrin v. Tenneco Oil Co., D.C.Okl.1980, 505 F.Supp. 23; Dri Mark Products, Inc. v. Meyercord Co., D.C.N.Y.1961, 194 F.Supp. 536.

26. Gaitor v. Peninsular & Occidental S.S. Co., C.A.5th, 1961, 287 F.2d 252; Peacock v. American Ins. Co., D.C.Fla. 1966, 253 F.Supp. 624; Note, 1961, 15 U.Miami L.Rev. 415. See ALI Study, § 1381(c)(2); 14 Wright, Miller & Cooper, Jurisdiction § 3725, p. 666.

27. Bonnell v. Seaboard Air Line R. Co., D.C.Fla.1962, 202 F.Supp. 53; Fleming v. Colonial Stores, Inc., D.C.Fla.1968, 279 F.Supp. 933. See ALI Study, § 1382(d).

28. Mielke v. Allstate Ins. Co., D.C. Mich.1979, 472 F.Supp. 851; Lee v. Altamil Corp., D.C.Fla.1978, 457 F.Supp. 979; Horak v. Color Metal of Zurich, Switzerland, D.C.N.J.1968, 285 F.Supp. 603.

29. Though it is said that the requirement of a statement of "facts" is "a strict one," Gratz v. Murchison, D.C. Del.1955, 130 F.Supp. 709, and that a "mere conclusion" is insufficient, Smith v. Southern Pac. Co., C.A.9th, 1951, 187 F.2d 397, 400, certiorari denied 72 S.Ct. 42, 342 U.S. 823, 96 L.Ed. 622, the better rule is that "detailed grounds" are not required, Allman v. Hanley, C.A.5th, 1962, 302 F.2d 559, 562, and that the same liberal rules applied in testing the sufficiency of a pleading—see § 68 below—should apply also to a removal petition. Brown v. City of Meridian, C.A.5th, 1966, 356 F.2d 602, 606. See 14 Wright, Miller & Cooper, Jurisdiction § 3733.

Lack of verification is curable with reasonable promptitude. Nelson v. Peter Kiewit Sons' Co., D.C.N.J.1955, 130 F.Supp. 59; Henlopen Hotel Corp. v. Aetna Ins. Co., D.C.Del.1963, 213 F.Supp. 320.

30. 28 U.S.C.A. § 1446(a). Failure to attach copies of these papers has been held not to be a jurisdictional defect. Riehl v. National Mut. Ins. Co., C.A. 7th, 1967, 374 F.2d 739. Covington v. Indemnity Ins. Co. of North America, C.A.5th, 1958, 251 F.2d 930, certiorari denied 78 S.Ct. 1362, 357 U.S. 921, 2 L.Ed.2d 1365.

stated.[31] The application of this rule is not yet clearly settled where neither the complaint nor the petition allege the principal place of business of a corporate party, as has been required since 1958 to determine the existence of diversity jurisdiction.[32] Some cases refuse to allow amendment, after expiration of the 30 days, to show the principal place of business, but the cases to the contrary, which allow such an amendment even on appeal,[33] seem consistent with the general rule as to amendment just stated and with the statute permitting defective allegations of jurisdiction to be amended, upon terms, in the trial or appellate courts.[34]

There are cases that say that the grounds for removal must appear on the face of the complaint, unaided by reference to the other pleadings or to the petition for removal.[35] It is entirely clear, however, that this is not the rule. Thus the statutory provision that removal can be had within 30 days from receipt of the "amended pleading, motion, order or other paper" from which it first appears that the case is removable [36] shows that such papers may be considered in determining the removability of a case, and it is so held.[37] There are many other situations in which the requisite jurisdictional facts will not appear on the face of the complaint. Thus the citizenship of the parties will not normally be set forth in a state court complaint, and the defendant, seeking to remove on the basis of diversity, must be permitted to show these facts in his petition.[38] In some circumstances the complaint will not sufficiently disclose the jurisdictional amount, and the petition must be used for this purpose.[39] Allega-

31. Kinney v. Columbia Sav. & Loan Ass'n, 1903, 24 S.Ct. 30, 191 U.S. 78, 48 L.Ed. 103; Powers v. Chesapeake & O. R. Co., 1898, 18 S.Ct. 264, 169 U.S. 92, 42 L.Ed. 673; Carson v. Dunham, 1887, 7 S.Ct. 1030, 121 U.S. 421, 30 L.Ed. 992; McGuigan v. Roberts, D.C.N.Y. 1959, 170 F.Supp. 372 (amplifying amendment permitted); Gobet v. Intercontinental Hotels Corp. (Ponce), D.C. Puerto Rico, 1960, 184 F.Supp. 171 (amendment inconsistent with original petition not permitted); and cases cited 14 Wright, Miller & Cooper, Jurisdiction § 3733 n. 9.

32. 28 U.S.C.A. § 1332(c). See § 27 above.

33. E.g., Barrow Development Co. v. Fulton Ins. Co., C.A.9th, 1969, 418 F.2d 316; Hendrix v. New Amsterdam Cas. Co., C.A.10th, 1968, 390 F.2d 299; Firemen's Ins. Co. of Newark, N. J. v. Robbins Coal Co., C.A.5th, 1961, 288 F.2d 349, certiorari denied 82 S.Ct. 122, 368 U.S. 875, 7 L.Ed.2d 77; Stanley Elec. Contractors, Inc. v. Darin & Armstrong Co., D.C.Ky.1980, 486 F.Supp. 769. Contra: e.g., Richmond, F. & P. R. Co. v. Intermodal Services, Inc.,

D.C.Va.1981, 508 F.Supp. 804; Walsh v. American Airlines, Inc., D.C.Ky. 1967, 264 F.Supp. 514; Evans-Hailey Co. v. Crane Co., D.C.Tenn.1962, 207 F.Supp. 193, appeal dismissed 1965, 86 S.Ct. 10, 382 U.S. 801, 15 L.Ed.2d 55, criticised 1964, 42 Texas L.Rev. 398. See 14 Wright, Miller & Cooper, Jurisdiction § 3733, pp. 735–736.

34. 28 U.S.C.A. § 1653.

35. Patriot-News Co. v. Harrisburg Printing Pressmen, D.C.Pa.1961, 191 F.Supp. 568; and cases cited 14 Wright, Miller & Cooper, Jurisdiction § 3734 n. 3.

36. 28 U.S.C.A. § 1446(b).

37. Evangelical Lutheran Church v. Stanolind Oil & Gas Co., C.A.8th, 1958, 251 F.2d 412; Gilardi v. Atchison, T. & S. F. Ry. Co., D.C.Ill.1960, 189 F.Supp. 82.

38. Mattingly v. Northwestern Virginia R. Co., 1895, 15 S.Ct. 725, 158 U.S. 53, 39 L.Ed. 894; Eastern Metals Corp. v. Martin, D.C.N.Y.1960, 191 F.Supp. 245.

39. Davenport v. Proctor & Gamble Mfg. Co., C.A.2d, 1957, 241 F.2d 511; Gaitor v. Peninsular & Occidental S. S.

tions in the petition may be used to show that parties have been fraudulently joined to defeat removal.[40] These instances can be generalized, and the cases fully support a rule that the court is to consider the facts disclosed on the record as a whole in determining removability,[41] with the one qualification that the existence of a federal question must appear from the well-pleaded complaint, not from the answer.[42]

The petition must be accompanied by a bond,[43] written notice of the removal must be given to the adverse parties "promptly" after the filing of the petition and bond,[44] and a copy of the petition must be filed with the state court as soon thereafter as is practicable.[45] There is a general tendency to regard these steps as modal and formal, and thus to hold that defects with regard to them can be cured and do not defeat the jurisdiction of the federal court.[46] Plaintiff may also waive such defects if he proceeds in federal court with

Co., C.A.5th, 1961, 287 F.2d 252; Wright v. Continental Cas. Co., D.C. Fla.1978, 456 F.Supp. 1075; Studebaker v. Salina Waterworks Co., D.C.Kan. 1912, 195 F. 164; and cases cited 14 Wright, Miller & Cooper, Jurisdiction § 3734 n. 5.

40. Chesapeake & O. Ry. v. Cockrell, 1914, 34 S.Ct. 278, 232 U.S. 146, 58 L.Ed. 544; Smoot v. Chicago, R. I. & P. R. Co., C.A.10th, 1967, 378 F.2d 879.

41. Gay v. Ruff, 1934, 54 S.Ct. 608, 292 U.S. 25, 78 L.Ed. 1099; Villareal v. Brown Exp., Inc., C.A.5th, 1976, 529 F.2d 1219; and cases cited 14 Wright, Miller & Cooper, Jurisdiction § 3734 n. 9.

42. Tennessee v. Union & Planters' Bank, 1894, 14 S.Ct. 654, 152 U.S. 454, 38 L.Ed. 511. See §§ 18, 38 above.

This limitation is applicable only to removal of a general federal question under 28 U.S.C.A. § 1441. Where removal is sought under § 1442 on the ground that the case is against a federal officer, the petition for removal will establish the defense that makes the case removable. Poss v. Lieberman, D.C.N.Y.1960, 187 F.Supp. 841; Tennessee v. Keenan, D.C.Tenn.1936, 13 F.Supp. 784.

43. 28 U.S.C.A. § 1446(d). On the consequences of failing to file a proper bond within the time allowed for removal, compare Tucker v. Kerner, C.A. 7th, 1950, 186 F.2d 79, with Proteus Foods & Indus., Inc. v. Nippon Reizo Kabushiki Kaisha, D.C.N.Y.1967, 279 F.Supp. 876. See generally as to the bond, 14 Wright, Miller & Cooper, Jurisdiction § 3735. The American Law Institute proposes to abolish the requirement of a bond, ALI Study, p. 339.

44. 28 U.S.C.A. § 1446(e). As to what is prompt notice, see Barrett v. Southern Ry. Co., D.C.S.C.1975, 68 F.R.D. 413, 422; Coletti v. Ovaltine Food Products, D.C.Puerto Rico 1967, 274 F.Supp. 719; Kovell v. Pennsylvania R. Co., D.C.Ohio 1954, 129 F.Supp. 906; Jones v. Elliott, D.C.Va.1950, 94 F.Supp. 567; 14 Wright, Miller & Cooper, Jurisdiction § 3736.

45. 28 U.S.C.A. § 1446(e); Patterson v. Refinery Engineering Co., D.C.N.M. 1960, 183 F.Supp. 459.

46. Covington v. Indemnity Ins. Co. of North America, C.A.5th, 1958, 251 F.2d 930, certiorari denied 78 S.Ct. 1362, 357 U.S. 921, 2 L.Ed.2d 1365; Rock v. Manthei, D.C.Mo.1955, 129 F.Supp. 769 (bond); Hornung v. Master Tank & Welding Co., D.C.N.D.1957, 151 F.Supp. 169 (filing copy with state court); Heniford v. American Motors Sales Corp., D.C.S.C.1979, 471 F.Supp. 328, appeal dismissed without opinion C.A.4th, 1980, 622 F.2d 584 (notice to plaintiff given prior to filing with federal court). But cf. Merz v. Dixon, D.C.Kan.1951, 95 F.Supp. 193 (case remanded where notice to plaintiff, and to state court, were given before rather than after federal filing); State v. Butler, La.1981, 405 So.2d 836 (state court jurisdiction not defeated where notice was given to law clerk of state judge rather than to clerk of state court).

knowledge of the defect.[47]　Though there are some cases holding that removal is effective from the time the petition is filed with the federal court, and that the later steps work retroactively to vest jurisdiction in the federal court as of the earlier date,[48] it seems unfair to a state court to hold that it can be stripped of jurisdiction though it has no notice of this fact.　Accordingly the sounder rule is that removal is not effective until these later required steps have been taken.[49]

The federal court may protect its jurisdiction by issuing an injunction restraining further proceeding in the state court after removal has been effected.[50]

After removal the federal court may issue all necessary orders and process to bring before it all proper parties whether served by process issued by the state court or otherwise.[51]　Process or service may be completed or new process issued in the same manner as in cases originally filed in district court.[52]

A removed case proceeds according to federal procedural rules, as though it had originally been commenced in federal court,[53] and the federal court acquires full and exclusive jurisdiction.[54]　The complaint

47.　Parks v. Montgomery Ward & Co., C.A.10th, 1952, 198 F.2d 772; see Kramer v. Jarvis, D.C.Neb.1948, 81 F.Supp. 360; Note, 1954, 7 Okla.L.Rev. 468.

48.　First Nat. Bank in Little Rock v. Johnson & Johnson, D.C.Ark.1978, 455 F.Supp. 361; Barrett v. Southern Ry. Co., D.C.S.C.1975, 68 F.R.D. 413; Marsh v. Tillie Lewis Foods, Inc., D.C.S.D.1966, 257 F.Supp. 645; Corcoran v. Pan American World Airways, D.C.Mass.1961, 194 F.Supp. 840; Patterson v. Refinery Engineering Co., D.C.N.M. 1960, 183 F.Supp. 459.

49.　Beleos v. Life & Cas. Ins. Co. of Tennessee, D.C.S.C.1956, 161 F.Supp. 627; Cavanaugh v. Atchison, T. & S. F. Ry. Co., D.C.Mo.1952, 103 F.Supp. 855; see Donlan v. F. H. McGraw & Co., D.C.N.Y.1948, 81 F.Supp. 599, 600; ALI Study, § 1382(f); 14 Wright, Miller & Cooper, Jurisdiction § 3737.

There also are holdings that both courts have jurisdiction between the filing in federal court and the notice to the state court. Berberian v. Gibney, C.A. 1st, 1975, 514 F.2d 790; Howes v. Childers, D.C.Ky.1977, 426 F.Supp. 358.

50.　Frith v. Blazon-Flexible Flyer, Inc., C.A.5th, 1975, 512 F.2d 899; Lowe v. Jacobs, C.A.5th, 1957, 243 F.2d 432, certiorari denied 78 S.Ct. 65, 355 U.S. 842, 2 L.Ed.2d 52; Stoll v. Hawkeye Cas. Co. of Des Moines, Iowa, C.A.8th, 1950, 185 F.2d 96.

51.　28 U.S.C.A. § 1447(a); Gas Serv. Co. v. Hunt, C.A.10th, 1950, 183 F.2d 417; 14 Wright, Miller & Cooper, Jurisdiction § 3738.

52.　28 U.S.C.A. § 1448; Beecher v. Wallace, C.A.9th, 1967, 381 F.2d 372; Deason v. Groendyke Transport, Inc., D.C.Ark.1959, 176 F.Supp. 346; Hisel v. Chrysler Corp., D.C.Mo.1950, 90 F.Supp. 655; and cases cited 14 Wright, Miller & Cooper, Jurisdiction § 3738 n. 2.

This does not permit the federal court, however, to breathe life into a case that would be barred in state court for failure to serve process within the time provided by state law. Witherow v. Firestone Tire & Rubber Co., C.A.3d, 1976, 530 F.2d 160.

53.　Granny Goose Foods, Inc. v. Brotherhood of Teamsters & Auto Truck Drivers, 1974, 94 S.Ct. 1113, 1123, 415 U.S. 423, 437, 39 L.Ed.2d 435; and cases cited 14 Wright, Miller & Cooper, Jurisdiction § 3738 n. 6.

54.　French v. Hay, 1874, 89 U.S. (22 Wall.) 238, 22 L.Ed. 854; Drainage Dist. No. 17 of Mississippi County, Ark. v. Guardian Trust Co., C.C.A.8th, 1931, 52 F.2d 579, certiorari denied 52 S.Ct. 197, 284 U.S. 680, 76 L.Ed. 575; Texas Pipe Line Co. v. Ware, C.C.A. 8th, 1926, 15 F.2d 171, certiorari denied 47 S.Ct. 335, 273 U.S. 742, 71 L.Ed. 869.

may be amended after removal, even to add a claim that could not have been asserted in the state court action.[55] The orders of the state court are not conclusive, but they are binding until set aside.[56] Similarly an effective attachment of property in the state court, or a bond given prior to removal, remains effective after removal.[57]

Defendant waives nothing by removal. After removal he may move, in federal court, to dismiss the case, as for improper service, and the fact that he has removed does not act as a general consent to jurisdiction defeating the motion.[58] A party who has made an express demand for jury trial in state court need not repeat the demand after removal, and if the applicable state law in the court from which the case was removed does not require an express demand for jury trial, no demand is needed in federal court unless the court directs the parties after removal to make a demand if they desire trial by jury.[59]

§ 41.   Remand [1]

If at any time prior to final judgment it appears that a case was removed improvidently and without jurisdiction, the federal court must remand the case, and may order payment of costs by the removing party.[2] Since parties cannot confer jurisdiction on the federal

55. Freeman v. Bee Machine Co., Inc., 1943, 63 S.Ct. 1146, 319 U.S. 448, 87 L.Ed. 1509.

56. 28 U.S.C.A. § 1450; General Inv. Co. v. Lake Shore & M. S. Ry. Co., 1922, 43 S.Ct. 106, 260 U.S. 261, 67 L.Ed. 244; Hinckley v. Gilman, C. & S. R. Co., 1879, 100 U.S. 153, 25 L.Ed. 591; Daniels v. McKay Machine Co., C.A.7th, 1979, 607 F.2d 771; Coyle v. Skirvin, C.C.A.10th, 1942, 124 F.2d 934, certiorari denied 62 S.Ct. 1044, 316 U.S. 673, 86 L.Ed. 1748; Talley v. American Bakeries Co., D.C.Tenn.1954, 15 F.R.D. 391; and cases cited 14 Wright, Miller & Cooper, Jurisdiction § 3738 nn. 25–27.

A temporary restraining order issued before removal will not remain in force after removal any longer than it would have remained in effect under state law, and in no event will remain effective longer than the time limitations stated in Civil Rule 65(b), measured from the date of removal. Granny Goose Foods, Inc. v. Brotherhood of Teamsters & Auto Truck Drivers, 1974, 94 S.Ct. 1113, 415 U.S. 423, 39 L.Ed.2d 435.

57. 28 U.S.C.A. § 1450; Clark v. Wells, 1906, 27 S.Ct. 43, 203 U.S. 164, 51 L.Ed. 138; Rorick v. Devon Syndicate, 1939, 59 S.Ct. 877, 307 U.S. 299, 83

L.Ed. 1303; Tanko v. Saperstein, D.C. Ill.1957, 149 F.Supp. 317 (defective attachment perfected); and cases cited 14 Wright, Miller & Cooper, Jurisdiction § 3738 nn. 34–35.

58. George v. Lewis, D.C.Colo.1964, 228 F.Supp. 725; Sun-X Glass Tinting of Mid-Wisconsin, Inc. v. Sun-X Intern., Inc., D.C.Wis.1964, 227 F.Supp. 365. This was also the rule under the old law. Wabash Western Ry. v. Brow, 1896, 17 S.Ct. 126, 164 U.S. 271, 41 L.Ed. 431. See 14 Wright, Miller & Cooper, Jurisdiction § 3738 nn. 15–17.

59. Civil Rule 81(c); Myers v. U. S. Dist. Court, C.A.9th, 1980, 620 F.2d 741; Financial Bldg. Consultants, Inc. v. American Druggists Ins. Co., D.C.Ga. 1981, 91 F.R.D. 62; 9 Wright & Miller, Civil § 2319.

[§ 41]

1. 14 Wright, Miller & Cooper, Jurisdiction §§ 3739–3740.

2. 28 U.S.C.A. § 1447(c).

If the federal court is without jurisdiction, it must remand and cannot dismiss the case for plaintiff's misfeasance if the misfeasance did not involve solely the procedures connected with the district court's determination of whether it had subject-matter juris-

court by consent, the court may act on its own motion,[3] or on the motion of either party. Indeed even the party who petitioned for removal may move for remand after a verdict unsatisfactory to him.[4] But if at the time of trial or judgment the controversy is one over which the federal court could have entertained original jurisdiction, a removing defendant is estopped from protesting after judgment that there was no right to remove as an initial matter.[5]

The plaintiff may also move to remand for procedural irregularities in the removal, but in general such defects are curable, and in any event plaintiff must move promptly or he will be held to have waived his right to object to such defects.[6]

Section 1447(c) allows remand only if "the case was removed improvidently and without jurisdiction." The court may not remand a properly removed case merely because the court's docket is crowded.[7] If removal is proper, but the claim or party that was the basis for jurisdiction is eliminated from the case, it is discretionary with the court whether to hear other claims presented by the case or to remand the remaining claims and parties.[8]

Any issues of fact raised by a motion to remand are for the court alone to decide, with the removing party carrying the burden of proof.[9] If the court orders remand, that order is not reviewable on

diction. Davis v. Cluet, Peabody & Co., C.A.11th, 1982, 667 F.2d 1371.

3. Roby v. General Tire & Rubber Co., D.C.Md.1980, 500 F.Supp. 480; Matter of Marriage of Thompson, D.C.Tex. 1978, 450 F.Supp. 197; and cases cited 14 Wright, Miller & Cooper, Jurisdiction § 3739 n. 4.

4. American Fire & Cas. Co. v. Finn, 1951, 71 S.Ct. 534, 341 U.S. 6, 95 L.Ed. 702. For a full discussion of this case, see § 39 above.

5. Grubbs v. General Elec. Credit Corp., 1972, 92 S.Ct. 1344, 405 U.S. 699, 31 L.Ed.2d 612; Baggs v. Martin, 1900, 21 S.Ct. 109, 179 U.S. 206, 45 L.Ed. 155; and cases cited 14 Wright, Miller & Cooper, Jurisdiction § 3739 n. 9.

On this principle removal was upheld although it was plaintiff who removed the case and the amount in controversy was established only by defendant's counterclaim. Lockwood Corp. v. Black, C.A.5th, 1982, 669 F.2d 324.

6. See § 40 above; Woodward v. D. H. Overmyer Co., C.A.2d, 1970, 428 F.2d 880, certiorari denied 91 S.Ct. 460, 400 U.S. 993, 27 L.Ed.2d 441, described § 38 n. 33 above; Monaco v. Carey Canadian Mines, Ltd., D.C.Pa.1981, 514 F.Supp. 357.

Plaintiff who has made a general appearance in federal court is not estopped from moving to remand. In re Winn, 1909, 29 S.Ct. 515, 213 U.S. 458, 53 L.Ed. 873.

7. Thermtron Products, Inc. v. Hermansdorfer, 1976, 96 S.Ct. 584, 593, 423 U.S. 336, 351–352, 46 L.Ed.2d 542.

Nor may a properly removed case be remanded as a form of abstention. Ryan v. State Bd. of Elections, C.A.7th, 1981, 661 F.2d 1130, 1133–1134.

But see the astonishing case of Young v. Board of Educ. of Fremont County Sch. Dist., D.C.Colo.1976, 416 F.Supp. 1139.

8. In re Carter, C.A.5th, 1980, 618 F.2d 1093, certiorari denied 1981, 101 S.Ct. 1410, 450 U.S. 949, 67 L.Ed.2d 378; Watkins v. Grover, C.A.9th, 1974, 508 F.2d 920; Brough v. United Steelworkers of America, AFL–CIO, C.A.1st, 1971, 437 F.2d 748; see Comstock v. Morgan, D.C.Mo.1958, 165 F.Supp. 798.

9. Kansas City, Ft. S. & M. R. Co. v. Daughtry, 1891, 11 S.Ct. 306, 138 U.S. 298, 34 L.Ed. 963; Carson v. Dunham, 1887, 7 S.Ct. 1030, 121 U.S. 421, 30 L.Ed. 992; and cases cited 14 Wright, Miller & Cooper, Jurisdiction § 3739 nn. 15–16.

appeal or otherwise,[10] except in civil rights cases for which there is special statutory provision.[11] Even in the Supreme Court on review of a state court proceeding after remand, the propriety of the remand, in a non-civil rights case, cannot be questioned.[12] This ban on review is intended to spare litigants delay.[13] If the motion to remand is denied, on the other hand, the propriety of removal is reviewable on appeal from the final judgment in the case.[14] And if, on review from a final judgment, the court of appeals holds the case not removable, and orders remand, this order is not within the statutory ban and may be reviewed by the Supreme Court.[15]

There are limited exceptions to the usual rule of nonreviewability of remand orders. In an important recent case it was held that the ban on reviewability in § 1447(d) applies only if the remand is ordered on the grounds stated in § 1447(c). Thus mandamus will lie to set aside a remand order if the district court has not merely erred in applying the requisite provision for remand but has remanded a case on grounds not specified in the statute and not touching the propriety of the removal.[16] It also is held that if the court orders a party dis-

10. 28 U.S.C.A. § 1447(d); McKay Packers, Inc. v. Firemen's Ins. Co. of Newark, N. J., C.A.2d, 1953, 207 F.2d 955 (no appeal in federal court); Johnson Pub. Co. v. Davis, 1960, 124 So.2d 441, 271 Ala. 474 (not reviewable on appeal in state court); In re Bear River Drainage Dist., C.A.10th, 1959, 267 F.2d 849 (no interlocutory appeal under 28 U.S.C.A. § 1292(b)); Ex parte Pennsylvania Co., 1890, 11 S.Ct. 141, 137 U.S. 451, 34 L.Ed. 738 (mandamus will not lie); and cases cited 14 Wright, Miller & Cooper, Jurisdiction § 3740 n. 1.

11. 28 U.S.C.A. § 1447(d), as amended in 1964, permits review "by appeal or otherwise" if removal was sought under the provisions of 28 U.S.C.A. § 1443. Note, 1965, 43 N.C.L.Rev. 628.

12. Missouri Pac. R. Co. v. Fitzgerald, 1896, 16 S.Ct. 389, 396, 160 U.S. 556, 582, 40 L.Ed. 536; Metropolitan Cas. Ins. Co. v. Stevens, 1941, 61 S.Ct. 715, 718, 312 U.S. 563, 568–569, 85 L.Ed. 1044. But see Board of Educ. of City of New York v. City-Wide Committee for Integration of Schools, C.A.2d, 1965, 342 F.2d 284, 286.

13. U. S. v. Rice, 1946, 66 S.Ct. 835, 839, 327 U.S. 742, 751, 90 L.Ed. 982.

14. American Fire & Cas. Co. v. Finn, 1951, 71 S.Ct. 534, 341 U.S. 6, 95 L.Ed. 702; and cases cited 14 Wright, Miller & Cooper, Jurisdiction § 3740 n. 6.

Denial of remand is not an order from which an immediate appeal will lie, Poirrier v. Nicklos Drilling Co., C.A. 5th, 1981, 648 F.2d 1063, although on occasion an interlocutory appeal has been allowed under 28 U.S.C.A. § 1292(b). E.g., Climax Chem. Co. v. C. F. Braun & Co., C.A.10th, 1966, 370 F.2d 616; Central of Ga. Ry. Co. v. Riegel Textile Corp., C.A.5th, 1970, 426 F.2d 935.

The courts are divided on whether denial of remand can be raised on an appeal from a preliminary injunction. Compare La Chemise Lacoste v. Alligator Co., C.A.3d, 1974, 506 F.2d 339, certiorari denied (with three justices dissenting) 95 S.Ct. 1666, 421 U.S. 937, 44 L.Ed.2d 94, with Kysor Indus. Corp. v. Pet, Inc., C.A.6th, 1972, 459 F.2d 1010, certiorari denied 93 S.Ct. 314, 409 U.S. 980, 34 L.Ed.2d 243.

15. Gay v. Ruff, 1934, 54 S.Ct. 608, 292 U.S. 25, 78 L.Ed. 1099; Aetna Cas. & Sur. Co. v. Flowers, 1947, 67 S.Ct. 798, 330 U.S. 464, 91 L.Ed. 1024.

16. Thermtron Products, Inc. v. Hermansdorfer, 1974, 96 S.Ct. 584, 423 U.S. 336, 46 L.Ed.2d 542.

See Myers, Federal Appellate Review of Remand Orders: Expansion or Eradication?, 1977, 48 Miss.L.J. 741; Comment, 1977, 9 St. Mary's L.J. 274; Note, 1977 U.Ill.L.F. 1086.

missed and the dismissal leads to a remand it is still permissible to review the order of dismissal.[17]

A great many cases might be cited for the proposition that if federal jurisdiction is doubtful the case should be remanded. This rule rests on the inexpediency, if not unfairness, of exposing the plaintiff to the possibility that he will win a final judgment in federal court, only to have it determined that the court lacked jurisdiction.[18] The argument to the contrary is that since there is no means for reviewing a remand order, the district court should be cautious about remand, lest it deprive defendant of his right to a federal forum.[19] To this argument, Judge Hutcheson's answer is apposite: "I am not impressed by the assertion that some valuable right which is given him in the federal court will be taken from him by trial in the state court. As I understand the jurisprudence of this state, it operates with an eye to justice, just the same as that of the federal court."[20]

An order of remand ends the jurisdiction of the federal court.[21] The court is required to mail a certified copy of the order to the clerk of the state court, and upon receipt of this copy by the state court, the federal court is without power to vacate the order to remand, even if it be persuaded that the order was erroneous.[22]

17. Waco v. United States Fidelity & Guar. Co., 1934, 55 S.Ct. 6, 293 U.S. 140, 79 L.Ed. 244; Southeast Mortg. Co. v. Mullins, C.A.5th, 1975, 514 F.2d 747.

The Thermtron rule was held to allow review on mandamus in Three J Farms, Inc. v. Alton Box Bd. Co., C.A.4th, 1979, 609 F.2d 112, certiorari denied 100 S.Ct. 1090, 445 U.S. 911, 63 L.Ed. 2d 327. There is a more dubious extension of Thermtron in In re Carter, C.A. 5th, 1980, 618 F.2d 1093, certiorari denied 101 S.Ct. 1410, 450 U.S. 949, 67 L.Ed.2d 378. See Justice Rehnquist's dissent from the denial of certiorari in the Carter case.

The Thermtron exception was held inapplicable in Gravitt v. Southwestern Bell Tel. Co., 1977, 97 S.Ct. 1439, 430 U.S. 723, 52 L.Ed.2d 1, rehearing denied 97 S.Ct. 2941, 431 U.S. 975, 53 L.Ed.2d 1073, and in In re Weaver, C.A.5th, 1980, 610 F.2d 335, rehearing denied 615 F.2d 919.

18. Limbach Co. v. Renaissance Center Partnership, D.C.Pa.1978, 457 F.Supp. 347, 349; and cases cited 14 Wright, Miller & Cooper, Jurisdiction § 3739 n. 23.

19. See Boatmen's Bank of St. Louis, Mo. v. Fritzlen, C.C.A.8th, 1905, 135 F. 650, 653–655, certiorari denied 25 S.Ct. 803, 198 U.S. 586, 49 L.Ed. 1174; Vann v. Jackson, D.C.N.C.1958, 165 F.Supp.

377. There is a thoughtful discussion of the question, with the matter left open, in Minnesota v. Chicago & N. W. Ry. Co., D.C.Minn.1958, 174 F.Supp. 267.

20. Pabst v. Roxana Petroleum Co., D.C.Tex.1929, 30 F.2d 953, 954.

21. U. S. v. Rice, 1946, 66 S.Ct. 835, 327 U.S. 742, 90 L.Ed. 982; Board of Educ. of City of New York v. City-Wide Committee for Integration of Schools, C.A. 2d, 1965, 342 F.2d 284, 285.

But if a case was remanded because it was not then removable it may be removed later if subsequent events make it removable. Kulbeth v. Woolnought, D.C.Tex.1971, 324 F.Supp. 908. See also Dodd v. Fawcett Publications, Inc., C.A.10th, 1964, 329 F.2d 82.

22. Three J Farms, Inc. v. Alton Box Bd. Co., C.A.4th, 1979, 609 F.2d 112, certiorari denied 1980, 100 S.Ct. 1090, 445 U.S. 911, 63 L.Ed.2d 327; Federal Deposit Ins. Corp. v. Santiago Plaza, C.A.1st, 1979, 598 F.2d 634.

But if there is a right to appeal a remand order, as in civil rights cases, see note 11 above, a judge of the appeals court may stay the remand order after it has become effective in order to permit review. Board of Educ. of City of New York v. City-Wide Committee for Integration, C.A.2d, 1965, 342 F.2d 284, 285–286. Cf. ALI Study, § 1384(b).

CHAPTER 7

VENUE

Analysis

§ 42. Civil Cases [1]

Although the concept of venue—that there is a particular court or courts in which an action should be brought—is of ancient common law lineage,[2] it was not until 1887 that the federal courts had any significant venue requirements for civil actions. Until that time the relevant statute, with origins going back to the First Judiciary Act, permitted suit in any district where the defendant "is an inhabitant, or in which he shall be found * * *."[3] The latter clause meant that venue was proper in ordinary cases wherever service could be made on the defendant. The choice of place to sue was in fact not as broad for much of this period as this statute might indicate, since as has been seen,[4] from 1789 to 1875 the federal courts were given diversity jurisdiction only where one of the parties was a citizen of the state in which suit was brought. In 1887, as part of a general narrowing of access to federal court, the provision that suit might be brought in the district in which the defendant was found was omitted, and it was provided instead that suit should not be brought in "any other district than that whereof he is an inhabitant, but where the jurisdiction is founded only on the fact that the action is between citi-

---

[§ 42]

1. 15 Wright, Miller & Cooper, Jurisdiction §§ 3801–3829; Clermont, Restating Territorial Jurisdiction and Venue for State and Federal Courts, 1981, 66 Corn.L.Rev. 411; Foster, Judicial Economy: Fairness and Convenience of Place of Trial: Long-Arm Jurisdiction in District Courts, 1969, 47 F.R.D. 73; Currie, The Federal Courts and the American Law Institute (Part II), 1969, 36 U.Chi.L.Rev. 268, 299–307; Barrett, Venue and Service of Process in the Federal Courts—Suggestions for Reform, 1954, 7 Vand.L.Rev. 608; Keeffe et al., Venue and Removal Jokers in the New Federal Judicial Code, 1952, 38 Va.L.Rev. 569; Stevens, Venue Statutes: Diagnosis and Proposed Cure, 1951, 49 Mich.L.Rev. 307; Note, Venue, 1980, 31 S.C.L.Rev. 579.

2. Venue gave rise to one of the most famous of the fictions of the common law. Plaintiff suing for an assault that took place on the island of Minorca, many miles from England, was permitted to allege that the assault occurred "at Minorca, (to wit) at London aforesaid, in the parish of St. Mary le Bow, in the ward of Cheap." Defendant was not permitted to traverse the fictional "to wit" clause, and the allegation permitted suit to be brought in London. Mostyn v. Fabrigas, K.B. 1774, 1 Cowp. 161, 98 Eng.Rep. 1021.

3. Act of March 3, 1875, 18 Stat. 470, based on § 11 of the Act of Sept. 24, 1789, 1 Stat. 73, 78.

4. See § 24 above.

zens of different states, suit shall be brought only in the district of residence of either the plaintiff or the defendant." [5] Though the present statute speaks of "residence" while the 1887 statute used the term "inhabitant," the main outlines of the general venue statute did not change from 1887 until 1966, and even in the latter year the change was of modest dimension.

The distinction must be clearly understood between jurisdiction, which is the power to adjudicate, and venue, which relates to the place where judicial authority may be exercised, and which is intended for the convenience of the litigants. [6] It is possible for jurisdiction to exist though venue in a particular district is improper, and it is possible for a suit to be brought in the appropriate venue though it must be dismissed for lack of jurisdiction. The most important difference between venue and jurisdiction is that a party may consent to be sued in a district that otherwise would be an improper venue, [7] and he waives his objection to venue if he fails to assert it promptly. [8] This is in striking contrast to subject matter jurisdiction, which cannot be conferred by the parties, if it has not been granted by Congress, whether by consent, waiver, or estoppel. [9]

It is wholly settled by a long and unbroken line of authority that venue is controlled entirely by Acts of Congress and that the construction of these is a federal question. [10] Although some district courts, construing the 1966 amendment making the district in which the claim arose a proper venue, said that where a claim arises is to be determined by state law, the Supreme Court has now rebuffed that heresy and made it clear that this, like other questions of federal venue, is to be decided wholly by federal standards. [11]

The scheme of the general venue statutes as they stood prior to 1966 is easily described. If jurisdiction were founded "only" on diversity of citizenship, suit could be brought only in the district "where all plaintiffs or all defendants reside, while if" jurisdiction were based in whole or in part on the presence of a federal question,

---

5. Act of March 3, 1887, 24 Stat. 552, as corrected by the Act of August 13, 1888, 25 Stat. 433.

6. Neirbo Co. v. Bethlehem Shipbuilding Corp., 1939, 60 S.Ct. 153, 154, 308 U.S. 165, 167–168, 84 L.Ed. 167; 15 Wright, Miller & Cooper, Jurisdiction § 3801.

7. Consent to be sued in the courts of a state, and designation of an agent for the receipt of process, constitutes consent to venue in the federal courts in that state. Neirbo Co. v. Bethlehem Shipbuilding Corp., 1939, 60 S.Ct. 153, 308 U.S. 165, 84 L.Ed. 167.

8. Fed.R.Civ.Proc. 12(h); 15 Wright, Miller & Cooper, Jurisdiction §§ 3826,

3829; Locklin Waiver of Federal Venue Privilege, 1951, 4 Ala.L.Rev. 127.

9. See § 7 above.

10. 15 Wright, Miller & Cooper, Jurisdiction § 3803.

The only possible exception, never clearly resolved, is, as discussed below at notes 62–70, with regard to the concept of a "local action." But on that issue there is no Act of Congress involved, since the whole concept is a judgemade one, and in any event it is not clear that the concept goes to venue.

11. Leroy v. Great Western United Corp., 1979, 99 S.Ct. 2710, 2715 n. 15, 443 U.S. 173, 183 n. 15, 61 L.Ed.2d 464.

suit had to be brought in the district "where all defendants reside." [12] The word "only" in the statute with regard to diversity cases means what it says. Even though the stated basis of jurisdiction is diversity and diversity exists, the privilege to sue in the district of plaintiff's residence, given only in diversity cases, is inapplicable if there is a federal question presented in the complaint that would have supported jurisdiction.[13] The requirement that "all" plaintiffs or "all" defendants, as the case may be, must reside in the district is a codification of a result that the Supreme Court, perhaps unnecessarily, had reached under the 1887 statute, which was not explicit on venue for multiple-parties cases.[14]

In addition to satisfying the requirement of the general venue statutes in selection of a district, the suit must be brought in the division of the district where the party whose residence is being looked to for venue purposes resides.[15] If defendants reside in different divisions of the same district, suit may be brought in any of those divisions,[16] and if they reside in different districts in the same state, suit may be brought in any such district.[17] There is no corresponding provision for plaintiffs who reside in different districts in the same state suing on the basis of diversity.

At first glance this scheme might have seemed sensible enough, but on analysis it was difficult to avoid the conclusion that it was entirely irrational. It failed to promote the convenience of the parties, as venue statutes are intended to do, and it overlooked the distinctive functions and opportunities of a federal system of courts. The pre-1966 scheme had three principal weaknesses, and they were not wholly cured by the 1966 amendment.

1. Neither history nor logic explains why a wider choice of venue was and is available in diversity cases than in federal question cases. The distinction is the result of a Senate amendment to the House bill that led to the 1887 statute. There is nothing in the legislative history to shed light on it, and the probability is that it was entirely fortuitous.[18] Logically one would expect that if there is to be a difference,

---

12. 28 U.S.C.A. § 1391(a) (diversity); 28 U.S.C.A. § 1391(b) (federal question). See 15 Wright, Miller & Cooper, Jurisdiction § 3804.

13. Macon Grocery Co. v. Atlantic Coast Line R. Co., 1910, 30 S.Ct. 184, 215 U.S. 501, 54 L.Ed. 300; American Chem. Paint Co. v. Dow Chem. Co., C.C.A.6th, 1947, 161 F.2d 956.

14. Smith v. Lyon, 1889, 10 S.Ct. 303, 133 U.S. 315, 33 L.Ed. 635 (multiple plaintiffs); Camp v. Gress, 1919, 39 S.Ct. 478, 250 U.S. 308, 63 L.Ed. 997 (multiple defendants). See 15 Wright, Miller & Cooper, Jurisdiction § 3807.

15. 28 U.S.C.A. § 1393(a). The many problems that are created by the poor-

ly drafted provisions on divisions of a district are canvassed in 15 Wright, Miller & Cooper, Jurisdiction § 3809.

16. 28 U.S.C.A. § 1393(b).

17. 28 U.S.C.A. § 1392(a).

18. The House bill that led to the 1887 statute was intended to limit venue in diversity cases. It continued the authorization for suit wherever the defendant could be found, except in diversity cases, where only the district of residence of the plaintiff or the defendant would be proper. Thus it was an attempt to restore, through the venue provision, the bar against diversity suits between two non-citizens of the forum that, from 1789 to 1875, ap-

the wider choice would be in the federal question cases, since they are the cases for which the federal courts have a special competence. If fear of local prejudice is the basis for diversity jurisdiction, it is quite anomalous to give the diversity plaintiff the privilege of suing in the district where he resides.[19]

2.   The statutes frequently precluded suit in the most convenient district. Many times it would serve the convenience of the parties to sue in the district where the claim arose, but until 1966 the venue statutes prohibited this unless this district was also the residence of all the defendants or, in a diversity case, all the plaintiffs.[20]

3.   Suppose one defendant resided in New York City while another defendant resided just across the river in Newark. Unless venue objections were waived there was no way suit against these defendants on a federal question could be brought in a federal court, since there was no district in which all defendants resided. Nor could suit be brought against these two defendants on the basis of diversity if there were two plaintiffs residing in different states, or even in different districts within the same state. These cases involving multiple parties from different states are usually beyond the competence of any state tribunal and seem especially appropriate for a federal forum. Yet the venue statutes, ostensibly for the convenience of litigants, might in some such situations bar the parties from having their day in any court.

In part because these deficiencies in the present scheme of venue had become widely understood, and in part because modern means of transportation had minimized the inconvenience in going to another district to litigate, there was and is increasing professional pressure to ease venue requirements, permit nationwide service of process, and provide for easy transfer to the forum that will best serve the convenience of the parties and the court in the particular case.[21]

peared in the jurisdictional statute. The Senate struck the language permitting suit where the defendant might be found, and thus confined litigation to the district of which the defendant was an inhabitant except that plaintiff's residence was also proper in diversity cases. It seems most likely that the Senate wished to bar suit in a district merely because plaintiff was able to serve defendant there, and that it failed to see that the effect of this was to give diversity plaintiffs a wider choice of venue than was given plaintiffs in non-diversity cases. See 18 Cong.Rec. 1887, pp. 613, 2544–2546, 2651, 2672, 2721.

19.   The American Law Institute proposals do away with this anomaly. In general, they provide a similar choice of venue for diversity, ALI Study, § 1303, as for federal question, id. at

§ 1314, but the effective choice of forum is in fact broader in the federal question cases since nationwide service of process would be authorized. Id. at § 1314(c). Currie, note 1 above, at 299–307, is critical of the distinction between federal question cases and diversity cases in the ALI proposals.

20.   Thus a Wisconsin resident, injured in Florida, could not, prior to 1966, bring suit in the federal court in Florida against two defendants, one a resident of Florida and the other a resident of New Jersey. Dibble v. Cresse, C.A. 5th, 1959, 271 F.2d 426.

21.   E.g., Barrett, note 1 above, at 627–635; Currie, note 1 above, at 299–307; Keeffe et al., note 1 above, at 586–588. One author would abolish venue requirements entirely in federal question cases. Seidelson, Jurisdiction

In 1966 Congress responded to this pressure by amending the general venue statutes to provide that the district "in which the claim arose" is now a permissible alternative venue both in diversity and federal question cases.[22] This was a significant advance. It does not cure the anomaly that choice of venue is broader in diversity cases than in federal question cases, but, in theory at least, it should have resolved the second and third of the difficulties just described. Suit will be possible in the district in which the claim arose if that is the most convenient forum and there is at least one district that is a permissible venue for any federal action.[23] In many cases this will work as intended. Its effectiveness is limited, however, because even though the district in which the claim arose is now a proper venue, suit can in fact be brought there only if all defendants are subject to process from that district. This, in turn, generally will turn on the extent to which the state has an applicable long-arm statute.[24]

In addition, in actions with contacts in several states, there may be difficulty in determining that single district "in which the claim rose." The American Law Institute had proposed to allow suit in a district where "a substantial part of the events or omissions giving rise to the claim occurred, or a substantial part of property that is the subject of the action is situated." [25] This would have allowed plaintiff to choose, in the first instance, if a claim had logical ties to more than one district. But when the Supreme Court came to construe the 1966 language in Leroy v. Great Western United Corporation,[26] it said: "Without deciding whether this language adopts the occasionally fictive assumption that a claim may arise in only one district, it is absolutely clear that Congress did not intend to provide for venue at the residence of the plaintiff or to give that party an unfettered choice among a host of different districts. * * * [T]he broadest interpretation of the language of § 1391(b) that is even arguably acceptable is that in the unusual case in which it is not clear that the claim arose in only one specific district, a plaintiff may choose between those two (or conceivably even more) districts that with approximately equal plausibility—in terms of the availability of witnesses, the accessibility

of Federal Courts Hearing Federal Cases: An Examination of the Propriety of the Limitations Imposed by Venue Restrictions, 1968, 37 Geo.Wash.L. Rev. 82.

22. 28 U.S.C.A. § 1391(a), (b), as amended by Act of Nov. 2, 1966, Pub. L. 89–714, 80 Stat. 1111. The amendment repealed a more limited provision, adopted in 1963, applicable only to automobile cases.

23. The 1966 amendment was intended to close "venue gaps" in multiple-party situations. Brunette Machine Works, Ltd. v. Kockum Indus., Inc., 1972, 92 S.Ct. 1936, 1939 n. 8, 406 U.S. 706, 710 n. 8, 32 L.Ed.2d 428.

24. Note, Federal Venue Amendment— Service of Process, Erie and Other Limitations, 1967, 16 Cath.U.L.Rev. 297, 302–317.

This limitation prevented suit in the district in which a collision had occurred in Parham v. Edwards, D.C.Ga.1972, 346 F.Supp. 968, affirmed C.A.5th, 1973, 470 F.2d 1000.

25. ALI Study, §§ 1303(a)(1), 1314(a)(1), and Commentary thereto. Congress used the ALI language in a 1976 statute fixing venue for actions against foreign states. 28 U.S.C.A. § 1391(f) (1).

26. 1979, 99 S.Ct. 2710, 443 U.S. 173, 61 L.Ed.2d 464.

of other relevant evidence, and the convenience of the defendant (but *not* of the plaintiff)—may be assigned as the locus of the claim." [27]

The Leroy decision raises as many questions as it answers. The Court did not define the "unusual case" in which a claim may be said to arise in more than one district, and it is unclear whether the Court will be agreeable to any interpretation of the claim-arising language that does more than fill a "venue gap" in particular cases.[28] So long as the language adopted in 1966 remains unchanged, there will be unnecessary litigation about the place of suit.[29]

Thus while there has been substantial reform, further progress is possible, and it remains necessary to probe some of the mysteries that lurk within the easy language of 28 U.S.C.A. § 1391. The principal questions are the meaning of "residence" within the statute, and the determination of the proper venue where corporations or unincorporated associations are parties to a suit. In addition, the exceptions, both statutory and judge-made, to the usual venue rules must be explored.

Quite surprisingly, there is even a little uncertainty whether "residence," within the venue statutes, means the same thing as "citizen," within the diversity statute. Two courts have said that "citizenship" and "residence" are "related or cognate terms," and that the existence of citizenship is cogent evidence of residence, but that they "are not necessarily one and the same thing." [30] Other courts, however, have treated the two concepts as if they are indeed one and the same thing.[31] The question arises in its clearest form where a person maintains two homes. By hypothesis he may be a citizen of only one state. The courts that treat "citizenship" and "residence" as synonymous have refused to permit venue to be laid in the district where a home is located but where the party is not a citizen.[32] This view finds

27. 99 S.Ct. at 2717–2718, 443 U.S. at 184–185.

28. See Cheeseman v. Carey, D.C.N.Y. 1980, 485 F.Supp. 203, 212–214; Bastille Properties, Inc. v. Hometels of America, Inc., D.C.N.Y.1979, 476 F.Supp. 175, 180 n. 4; Note cited note 1 above, at 602–603.

29. See the welter of cases, and the absence of any coherent theory, discussed in 15 Wright, Miller & Cooper, Federal Practice and Procedure: Jurisdiction § 3806. See also Comment, Federal Venue: Locating the Place Where the Claim Arose, 1976, 54 Texas L.Rev. 392.

30. Townsend v. Bucyrus-Erie Co., C.C.A.10th, 1944, 144 F.2d 106, 108. See also Arley v. United Pac. Ins. Co., C.A.9th, 1967, 379 F.2d 183, 185 n. 1.

31. R. K. Mikesell Associates v. Grand River Dam Auth., D.C.Okl.1977, 442

F.Supp. 229; Lee v. Hunt, D.C.La.1976, 410 F.Supp. 329; Ott v. U. S. Bd. of Parole, D.C.Mo.1971, 324 F.Supp. 1034; Smith v. Murchison, D.C.N.Y.1970, 310 F.Supp. 1079; Champion Spark Plug Co. v. Karchmar, D.C.N.Y.1960, 180 F.Supp. 727; Schultz v. McAfee, D.C. Me.1958, 160 F.Supp. 210; Finger v. Masterson, D.C.S.C.1957, 152 F.Supp. 224. See also note 32 below.

32. MacNeil v. Whittemore, C.A.2d 1958, 254 F.2d 820; King v. Wall & Beaver St. Corp., C.C.A.D.C.1945, 145 F.2d 377, 79 U.S.App.D.C. 234; Koons v. Kaiser, D.C.N.Y.1950, 91 F.Supp. 511.

Contra: Arley v. United Pac. Ins. Co., C.A.9th, 1967, 379 F.2d 183, 185 n. 1; Townsend v. Bucyrus-Erie Co., C.C.A. 10th, 1944, 144 F.2d 106.

support in a Supreme Court dictum that equates "residence" and "citizenship" and says that the code used the former term, in speaking of venue, in order to avoid the anomaly of referring to a "citizen" of a district.[33] Probably this should be regarded as the authoritative view, although the considerations of convenience that underlie venue would seem to permit suit in the district where the party has his second home. On the view that "citizenship" and "residence" are the same thing, the court, when venue is challenged, will look to the same factors to determine the party's residence which are considered in determining his citizenship for purposes of diversity.[34]

The doctrines just stated with regard to residence do not apply where an alien is a party. An alien may be sued in any district.[35] Where he is plaintiff, suit must be in the district in which all defendants reside, or in which the claim arose, regardless of the basis of jurisdiction.[36]

For many years it was held that, for purposes of venue, a corporation was a resident only of the state in which it was incorporated, even though it did business or had an agent for service of process in some other state.[37] It was probably inevitable that the expanding economy of the nation and the nationwide activities of great corporations should eventually render intolerable a rule that restricted federal suits to the district of incorporation, especially if that district was remote from the scene of corporate activities. The Supreme Court took the first long step in changing the rule when it held, in the well-known case of Neirbo Co. v. Bethlehem Shipbuilding Corp.,[38] that a corporation that had complied with state law by designating an agent for the service of process had consented to be sued in federal court in that state despite any venue privilege it might otherwise have had. The Neirbo decision left many questions unanswered,[39] but the questions are now of little more than academic interest since Congress, in

33. Ex parte Shaw, 1892, 12 S.Ct. 935, 936, 145 U.S. 444, 447, 36 L.Ed. 768.

34. As to those factors, see § 26 above.

35. 28 U.S.C.A. § 1391(d). See Berger, Alien Venue: Neither Necessary nor Constitutional, 1976 N.Y.U.J.Intl.L. & Pol. 155.

This rule has been applied also to alien corporations. Brunette Machine Works, Ltd. v. Kockum Indus., Inc., 1972, 92 S.Ct. 1936, 406 U.S. 706, 32 L.Ed.2d 428.

36. Galveston, H. & S. A. R. Co. v. Gonzales, 1894, 14 S.Ct. 401, 151 U.S. 496, 38 L.Ed. 248; Du Roure v. Alvord, D.C.N.Y.1954, 120 F.Supp. 166; 15 Wright, Miller & Cooper, Jurisdiction § 3810.

See Comment, Federal Venue for Aliens: The Presumption of Nonresidency, 1973, 3 Calif.West.Int'l.L.J. 417.

37. Ex parte Shaw, 1892, 12 S.Ct. 935, 145 U.S. 444, 36 L.Ed. 768; In re Keasbey & Mattison Co., 1895, 16 S.Ct. 273, 160 U.S. 221, 40 L.Ed. 402; Southern Pac. Co. v. Denton, 1892, 13 S.Ct. 44, 146 U.S. 202, 36 L.Ed. 942.

Prior to 1887, when venue was proper wherever defendant was "found," it was held, after much vacillation, that a corporation was "found" in a district where it had a designated agent for service of process. Ex parte Schollenberger, 1877, 96 U.S. 369, 24 L.Ed. 853. This construction did not survive the 1887 amendment of the venue statute.

38. 1939, 60 S.Ct. 153, 308 U.S. 165, 84 L.Ed. 167. See Levin, Federal Venue in Actions Against Corporations, 1940, 15 Temp.L.Q. 92.

39. See Comment, The Aftermath of the Neirbo Case, 1948, 42 Ill.L.Rev. 780.

1948, adopted § 1391(c) of the Judicial Code. That section provides: "A corporation may be sued in any judicial district in which it is incorporated or licensed to do business or is doing business, and such judicial district shall be regarded as the residence of such corporation for venue purposes." [40] The statute builds on the Neirbo principle, but goes far beyond that decision in regarding a corporation, for purposes of venue, as a resident of any district in which it is doing business, whether or not it has designated an agent for receipt of process in that district.[41]

Section 1391(c) has created its own problems of interpretation. Prior to 1948 the rule was that a corporation incorporated within a state could be sued only in the district where it kept its principal office and transacted its general corporate business. It can be argued that this is no longer the law. Incorporation within a state licenses the corporation to do business throughout the state, and it can be argued that the corporation is licensed to do business, and may be sued, in each of the districts of the state. There is increasing adherence to this view in the cases.[42]

There is an even more complicated variant of the problem. Suppose a corporation is licensed to do business and actually doing business in every district in a state. Suppose further that an individual co-defendant resides in the Western District. May suit be brought against both defendants in the Eastern District? The argument in favor of allowing suit is that the corporate defendant is a resident of the Eastern District, and that § 1392(a), providing that where defendants reside in different districts of the same state suit may be brought in any such district, is applicable. The argument to the contrary is that, by virtue of § 1391(c), both defendants are residents of the Western District and thus § 1392(a) has no application. The cases are divided on this nice question.[43] The legislative history is

---

40. See generally 15 Wright, Miller & Cooper, Jurisdiction § 3811.

41. In the period between Neirbo and the adoption of § 1391(c), it was held that venue was improper as to a foreign corporation doing business within the state if it had not designated an agent for receipt of process even though state law required such a designation. Moss v. A. C. L. R. Co., C.C.A. 2d, 1945, 149 F.2d 701; Donahue v. M. A. Henry Co., D.C.N.Y.1948, 78 F.Supp. 91.

In another respect the statute clearly goes beyond the Neirbo rule. Under Neirbo the Supreme Court had held that though a corporation was amenable to suit where it had qualified to do business in a foreign state, it was not a "resident" of that district for purposes of the statute providing that where defendants resided in two or more districts of a single state, suit might be brought in any such district. Suttle v. Reich Bros. Co., 1948, 68 S.Ct. 587, 333 U.S. 163, 92 L.Ed. 614. Under § 1391(c) the rule of the Suttle case has been changed. See Robert E. Lee & Co. v. Veatch, C.A.4th, 1961, 301 F.2d 434, 438.

42. E.g., Davis v. Hill Engineering, Inc., C.A.5th, 1977, 549 F.2d 314, 322–323, rehearing denied 554 F.2d 1065; First Sec. Bank of Utah v. Aetna Cas. & Sur. Co., C.A.10th, 1976, 541 F.2d 869; Richards v. Upjohn Co., D.C.Mich.1976, 406 F.Supp. 405. See cases cited 15 Wright, Miller & Cooper, Jurisdiction § 3811 nn. 35–39.

43. Permitting suit in the Eastern District: PI, Inc. v. Valcour Imprinted Papers, Inc., D.C.N.Y.1979, 465 F.Supp. 1218; Hawkins v. National Basketball Assn., D.C.Pa.1968, 288 F.Supp. 614;

silent as to it. The language of § 1392(a) lends some support to the view that it does not apply, since it speaks of "defendants residing in different districts in the same state," but this is less clear-cut than if it was applicable only where there were "defendants residing in the state but not residents of the same district." Probably the strongest argument is one of policy. The evident purpose of § 1392(a), a statute with origins dating back to 1824, is to permit a single suit in a situation where two suits would otherwise be required. This purpose can be accomplished without resort to § 1392(a) in the hypothetical situation that has been posed, since a single suit can be brought in the Western District. There is no reason to bring the individual defendant, resident in the Western District, to defend a lawsuit in the Eastern District, when the suit can be heard in the Western District where both defendants reside.

A different result seems in order if one defendant resides in the Eastern District, one defendant resides in the Western District, and the claim arose in the Western District. Here it has been held, correctly it seems, that suit in the Eastern District is proper under the explicit and unambiguous language of § 1392(a).[44]

Another problem raised by § 1391(c) is whether its final language that "such judicial district shall be regarded as the residence of such corporation for venue purposes" defines residence for the purpose of special venue statutes that are couched in terms of residence. The Supreme Court, which was once equally divided on the question, has held that § 1391(c) is not to be read into the special venue statute for patent infringement cases, and that only the state of incorporation is the "residence" of a corporation sued for patent infringement.[45] But the Court reached a different result in a later case in which it held that the definition of residence in § 1391(c) does apply to the special venue provisions of the Jones Act.[46] The language of the later case suggests that the patent decision will be confined to its precise holding, and that the general provisions of the venue statutes will be held to supplement all other special venue statutes.[47]

Minter v. Fowler & Williams, Inc., D.C. Pa.1961, 194 F.Supp. 660; De George v. Mandata Poultry Co., D.C.Pa.1961, 196 F.Supp. 192; cf. Williams v. Hoyt, D.C.Tex.1974, 372 F.Supp. 1314.

Refusing to permit suit in the Eastern District: Mazzella v. Stineman, D.C.Pa. 1979, 472 F.Supp. 432; Johnson v. B. G. Coon Constr. Co., D.C.Pa.1960, 195 F.Supp. 197; Hawks v. Maryland & P. R. Co., D.C.Pa.1950, 90 F.Supp. 284.

44. Kirkland v. New York State Dept. of Correctional Services, D.C.N.Y.1973, 358 F.Supp. 1349.

45. Fourco Glass Co. v. Transmirra Products Corp., 1957, 77 S.Ct. 787, 353 U.S. 222, 1 L.Ed.2d 786. The special statute for patents is 28 U.S.C.A.

§ 1400(b). The American Law Institute proposes its repeal. See ALI Study, pp. 219–221.

46. Pure Oil Co. v. Suarez, 1966, 86 S.Ct. 1394, 384 U.S. 202, 16 L.Ed.2d 474. The Jones Act venue provision is 46 U.S.C.A. § 688.

47. Board of County Commrs. v. Wilshire Oil Co. of Texas, C.A.10th, 1975, 523 F.2d 125; Snyder v. Eastern Auto Distributors, Inc., C.A.4th, 1966, 357 F.2d 552, certiorari denied 86 S.Ct. 1889, 384 U.S. 987, 16 L.Ed.2d 1004; Philadelphia Housing Auth. v. American Radiator & Standard Sanitary Corp., D.C.Pa.1968, 291 F.Supp. 252; New York v. Morton Salt Co., D.C.Pa. 1967, 266 F.Supp. 570; Hoffman Mo-

The most natural reading of the special definition of corporate residence in § 1391(c), which says that "such judicial district shall be regarded as the residence of such corporation for venue purposes," is that it applies to corporate plaintiffs as well as corporate defendants. A majority of the early cases so held, but the Fourth Circuit in an important decision held that the statute applies only to corporate defendants and that a corporate plaintiff continues to reside only in the state and district of its incorporation.[48] Although the Supreme Court subsequently expressly refused to pass on the question, which it called "a difficult one, with far-reaching effects * * * ,"[49] there has been such significant support for the Fourth Circuit view since the Supreme Court decision that it now seems settled that § 1391(c) applies to corporate defendants only.[50]

Finally there is a question of what is meant by "doing business" in § 1391(c). The sensible answer to this question is to use the same test, and thus make applicable the body of law, employed in determining whether a corporation is doing business within the district for purposes of service of process,[51] recognizing, however, that the question of "doing business" for venue purposes is always a federal question, to be determined by federal standards,[52] while state law may be

tors Corp. v. Alfa Romeo S. p. A., D.C. N.Y.1965, 244 F.Supp. 70; and cases cited 15 Wright, Miller & Cooper, Jurisdiction § 3811 n. 21.

48. Robert E. Lee & Co. v. Veatch, C.A.4th, 1961, 301 F.2d 434, certiorari denied 83 S.Ct. 23, 371 U.S. 813, 9 L.Ed.2d 55, noted 1962, 48 Va.L.Rev. 968, 1963, 76 Harv.L.Rev. 641. This decision was followed in Carter-Beveridge Drilling Co. v. Hughes, C.A.5th, 1963, 323 F.2d 417.

49. Abbott Laboratories v. Gardner, 1967, 87 S.Ct. 1507, 1520 n. 20, 387 U.S. 136, 156 n. 20, 18 L.Ed.2d 681.

50. American Cyanamid Co. v. Hammond Lead Products, Inc., C.A.3d, 1974, 495 F.2d 1183; Manchester Modes, Inc. v. Schuman, C.A.2d, 1970, 426 F.2d 629; D C Electronics, Inc. v. Schlesinger, D.C.Ill.1974, 368 F.Supp. 1029; and cases cited 15 Wright, Miller & Cooper, Jurisdiction § 3811 n. 28. See Note, Federal Venue Over Corporations Under Section 1391(c): Plaintiff Corporations, the Judicial District Limitations, and "Doing Business," 1978, 12 Ga.L.Rev. 296, 301–302.

The first two editions of this text had taken the contrary view, but the decisions supporting the statement in the text had become so numerous by the time of the Third Edition that there was no choice save to yield to the weight of authority.

51. E.g., Fraley v. Chesapeake & O. R. Co., C.A.3d, 1968, 397 F.2d 1; Houston Fearless Corp. v. Teter, C.A.10th, 1963, 318 F.2d 822; and cases cited 15 Wright, Miller & Cooper, Jurisdiction § 3811 n. 45.

Other cases, however, hold that more is required to be "doing business" for purposes of venue than for amenability to process. See Honda Associates, Inc. v. Nozawa Trading, Inc., D.C.N.Y.1974, 374 F.Supp. 886; Scott Paper Co. v. Scott's Liquid Gold, Inc., D.C.Del.1974, 374 F.Supp. 184; and cases cited 15 Wright, Miller & Cooper, Jurisdiction § 3811 n. 46. See Note, cited note 50 above, at 308–322. See also Lansing & Castle, Venue in the Federal Courts under the "Doing Business" Provision of 28 U.S.C. § 1391(c): A Provision Subject to Reinterpretation? 1981, 16 U.Rich.L.Rev. 7.

For particular applications of the "doing business" concept in a § 1391(c) context, see 15 Wright, Miller & Cooper, Jurisdiction § 3811 nn. 47–67.

52. Frazier v. Alabama Motor Club, Inc., C.A.5th, 1965, 349 F.2d 456; Control Data Corp. v. Carolina Power & Light Co., D.C.N.Y.1967, 274 F.Supp. 336; Johnson v. Tri-State Motor Transit Co., D.C.Mo.1966, 263 F.Supp. 278; Rensing v. Turner Aviation Corp., D.C.Ill.1958, 166 F.Supp. 790.

controlling in determining a corporation's amenability to service of process.[53]

The law of venue for corporations has been seen not to be simple, even since the adoption of § 1391(c). The law of venue for unincorporated associations—partnerships, labor unions, and the like—has been even more complex. It must first be determined whether the association has capacity to sue or be sued as such. The question of capacity is resolved in accordance with the law of the state in which the suit is brought, except that such capacity exists, regardless of state law, where the suit involves a claimed right under the federal constitution or laws.[54] Even if the association has capacity to appear in court as such, it might still be held that the residences of the individual members of the association are determinative for venue purposes.[55] This view, once quite commonly accepted, was rejected in several notable cases, and unincorporated associations were assimilated to corporations for purposes of venue.[56] The latter view was finally adopted by the Supreme Court. It concluded that "it most nearly approximates the intent of Congress to recognize the reality of the multi-state, unincorporated association such as a labor union and to permit suit against that entity, like the analogous corporate entity, wherever it is 'doing business.' "[57]

All that has been said so far has been concerned with actions under the general venue statutes. A great many actions are governed by other venue provisions. Two of the most important exceptions are judge-made. The general venue statute, 28 U.S.C.A. § 1391(a), applies to "civil actions." The Supreme Court has held that the change of venue statute, 28 U.S.C.A. § 1404(a), which also refers to "civil actions," is applicable to actions in admiralty.[58] Yet there is no sign

53. See § 64 below.

54. Fed.R.Civ.Proc. 17(b); 6 Wright & Miller, Civil §§ 1561, 1564.

55. Champion Spark Plug Co. v. Karchmar, D.C.N.Y.1960, 180 F.Supp. 727; Harris Mfg. Co. v. Williams, D.C.Ark. 1957, 157 F.Supp. 779; cf. Koons v. Kaiser, D.C.N.Y.1950, 91 F.Supp. 511.

56. The path was broken by Judge Learned Hand in Sperry Products, Inc. v. Association of American Railroads, C.C.A.2d, 1942, 132 F.2d 408, certiorari denied 63 S.Ct. 1031, 319 U.S. 744, 87 L.Ed. 1700, noted 1943, 38 Ill.L.Rev. 208. The principle of that case was further developed in Rutland Ry. Corp. v. Brotherhood of Locomotive Engineers, C.A.2d, 1962, 307 F.2d 21, certiorari denied 83 S.Ct. 949, 372 U.S. 954, 9 L.Ed.2d 978.

57. Denver & R. G. W. R. Co. v. Brotherhood of R. Trainmen, 1967, 87 S.Ct. 1746, 1750, 387 U.S. 556, 562, 18 L.Ed. 2d 954, noted 1967, 36 U.Cin.L.Rev.

724, 1967 Duke L.J. 1064, 1968, 17 DePaul L.Rev. 455.

Congress had already provided in 1947 that in suits governed by the Taft-Hartley Act a labor organization may be sued in the district where it maintains its principal office or in the district where its duly authorized officers and agents are engaged in representing or acting for employee members. 29 U.S.C.A. § 185(c).

It is held in Penrod Drilling Co. v. Johnson, C.A.5th, 1969, 414 F.2d 1217, that the Brotherhood of Railroad Trainmen case is to be broadly construed, and is not limited to labor unions, and that for venue purposes a partnership is to be treated in the same fashion as unincorporated associations.

See generally 15 Wright, Miller & Cooper, Jurisdiction § 3812.

58. Continental Grain Co. v. The FBL–585, 1960, 80 S.Ct. 1470, 364 U.S. 19, 4 L.Ed.2d 1540.

that the ancient rule that admiralty suits are not subject to the general venue statutes [59] will be altered, and such suits continue to be subject only to the distinctive venue notions long applied in admiralty.[60] Indeed when admiralty suits were brought under the Rules of Civil Procedure in 1966 a special provision was made so that such suits can remain free from the general venue statutes while remaining subject to the transfer provisions of § 1404(a).[61]

Another judge-made exception, stemming from the common law, is the rule that "local actions" must be brought in the district where the res that is the subject matter of the action is located.[62] The general venue statutes are broad enough in terms to encompass local actions, but the special rule for such actions is ancient and well-settled,[63] and is recognized by other provisions in the statutes that make reference to local actions.[64] The requirement about local actions leads to some difficulty if the defendant is not subject to process in the state in which the property is located, but the difficulty is obviated in some, but not all, cases by a statute permitting service outside the state in actions to enforce a lien on or claim to, or to remove any incumbrance, lien or cloud upon the title to, property within the district.[65]

Attempts to define the distinction between a local action and a transitory action have been notoriously unsuccessful. A distinction based on the difference between actions in rem and actions in personam would make some sense. Chief Justice Marshall in 1811 said that this is where the line should be drawn but felt obliged by precedent to hold that certain in personam actions, such as an action for

---

59. Atkins v. Fibre Disintegrating Co., 1873, 18 Wall. 272, 21 L.Ed. 841; In re Louisville Underwriters, 1890, 10 S.Ct. 587, 134 U.S. 488, 33 L.Ed. 991.

60. See 15 Wright, Miller & Cooper, Jurisdiction § 3817. The American Law Institute, however, proposes to codify the liberal traditions of venue in admiralty. ALI Study, § 1318. Currie, note 1 supra, at 303, calls this decision by the Institute "wholly unacceptable."

61. Fed.R.Civ.Proc. 82.

62. See 15 Wright, Miller & Cooper, Jurisdiction § 3822; Note, Local Actions in the Federal Courts, 1957, 70 Harv.L. Rev. 708.

63. "The distinction between local and transitory actions is as old as actions themselves, and no one has ever supposed that laws which prescribed generally where one should be sued, included such suits as were local in their character, either by statute or the common law unless it was expressly so declared." Casey v. Adams, 1880, 102 U.S. 66, 67, 26 L.Ed. 52.

See also Livingston v. Jefferson, C.C.D. Va.1811, 15 Fed.Cas. 660, No. 8411 (per Marshall, C. J.); Greeley v. Lowe, 1894, 15 S.Ct. 24, 155 U.S. 58, 39 L.Ed. 69.

64. 28 U.S.C.A. § 1392(b) provides that local actions involving property located in different districts in the same state may be brought in any of such districts. See also 28 U.S.C.A. §§ 1392(a), 1393(a), which set out rules applicable to "any civil action, not of a local nature."

65. 28 U.S.C.A. § 1655. See 14 Wright, Miller & Cooper, Jurisdiction §§ 3632–3635 for full discussion of the statute.

The statute does not reach every action of a local nature. Thus it has been held that a suit to abate a nuisance must be brought in the district where the nuisance is located, and that such an action is beyond the scope of § 1655. Ladew v. Tennessee Copper Co., C.C.D.Tenn.1910, 179 F. 245, affirmed 31 S.Ct. 81, 218 U.S. 357, 54 L.Ed. 1069.

trespass q.c.f., were local actions, though the Chief Justice confessed the illogic of such a holding.[66] Thus there is no rationalizing principle that will accommodate the particular rules as to particular actions, and decision rests on the oddities of common law history rather than on policy considerations.[67]

It is not even clear whether the local action concept runs to the jurisdiction or the venue of the federal court. It is usually discussed as a matter of venue, but there are cases holding that the defect that the action was brought in a district other than where the property was located is non-waivable,[68] which would be true only if the defect is a matter of jurisdiction rather than of venue. It is also not clear whether a uniform federal rule applies in determining whether an action is local or transitory, or whether there must be resort to state law. Chief Justice Marshall was "decidedly of opinion" that the federal courts must decide this question for themselves,[69] and this view seems clearly preferable, but other cases, largely relying on later dicta erroneously describing what Marshall had held, have looked to state law in determining the nature of the action.[70]

Since 1979 there has been considerable interest, particularly on the part of certain Western senators, in changing the venue laws to

66. Livingston v. Jefferson, C.C.D.Va. 1811, 15 Fed.Cas. 660, No. 8411. This meant that unless Thomas Jefferson went to Louisiana, where the land was located, Livingston could not have his suit heard.

The American Law Institute proposes statutory language to provide that actions for trespass upon or harm to land are subject to the general venue statutes. ALI Study, § 1303(c). It characterizes this as a "modest" reform "that is long overdue." Id. at p. 139.

67. See Currie, The Constitution and the "Transitory" Cause of Action, 1959, 73 Harv.L.Rev. 36, 66–69. For holdings as to particular cases, see 15 Wright, Miller & Cooper, Jurisdiction § 3822 nn. 28–37.

68. Ellenwood v. Marietta Chair Co., 1895, 15 S.Ct. 771, 158 U.S. 105, 39 L.Ed. 913; Iselin v. Meng, C.A.5th, 1959, 269 F.2d 345, certiorari denied 80 S.Ct. 257, 361 U.S. 913, 4 L.Ed.2d 183; Minichiello Realty Associates, Inc. v. Britt, D.C.N.J.1978, 460 F.Supp. 896, affirmed without opinion C.A.3d, 1979, 605 F.2d 1196. See the cases both ways cited at 15 Wright, Miller & Cooper, Jurisdiction § 3822 nn. 18–19. See also Note, Local Actions in the Federal Courts, 1957, 70 Harv.L.Rev. 708, 712–713.

69. Livingston v. Jefferson, C.C.D.Va. 1811, 15 Fed.Cas. 660, 665, No. 8,411.

Accord: Illinois v. City of Milwaukee, C.A.7th, 1979, 599 F.2d 151, 157 n. 5, reversed on other grounds 1981, 101 S.Ct. 1784, 451 U.S. 304, 68 L.Ed.2d 114; Pasos v. Pan American Airways, Inc., C.A.2d, 1956, 229 F.2d 271.

70. The erroneous dicta is in Huntington v. Attrill, 1892, 13 S.Ct. 224, 228, 146 U.S. 657, 669–670, 36 L.Ed. 1123. Among recent cases holding that state law is controlling are: Chateau Lafayette Apartments, Inc. v. Meadow Brook Nat. Bank, C.A.5th, 1969, 416 F.2d 301, noted 1969 Duke L.Rev. 1304, 1970, 39 U.Cinc.L.Rev. 402; Still v. Rossville Crushed Stone Co., C.A.6th, 1966, 370 F.2d 324, certiorari denied 87 S.Ct. 2030, 387 U.S. 918, 18 L.Ed.2d 970; Landmark Tower Associates v. First Nat. Bank of Chicago, D.C.Fla.1977, 439 F.Supp. 195; Hasburgh v. Executive Aircraft Co., D.C.Mo.1964, 35 F.R.D. 354. In the Hasburgh case the court recognized that applying state law is a "theoretical error" but it felt bound to do so by the numerical weight of authority.

Fortunately in most cases there is no difference between federal law and the law of the state in which the court is held, and there is no need to distinguish between them. See the comprehensive opinion in Wheatley v. Phillips, D.C.N.C.1964, 228 F.Supp. 439.

shift venue in certain kinds of cases to the locality where the effects of the lawsuit are most directly felt.[71] These senators feel that the 1962 statute, allowing a very broad choice of venue in suits against federal officers and agencies,[72] has been abused "by some litigators, especially public interest law groups focusing on environmental issues and based in Washington, D.C."[73] and that actions have been taken "by judges in the Federal courts of the District of Columbia in cases which had little or no impact on the residents of Washington, but which deeply affected the lives of citizens living thousands of miles away from the Capital."[74] The proposals for change in this respect, some of which are limited to environmental cases while others would reach federal government litigation generally, should not be confused with the common law concept of "local" actions that has just been discussed.

There are a great many special venue statutes, both in the Judicial Code[75] and in other statutes that create particular rights to sue. Usually, though not invariably, these statutes broaden the choice of venue made available by the general venue statutes.[76] One important exception is the venue statute for patent infringement actions. It permits suit where the defendant resides or where he has committed acts of infringement and has a regular and established place of business.[77] Since the broad definition of corporate residence set out in 28 U.S.C.A. § 1391(c) has been held inapplicable to this special stat-

71. National Legal Center for the Public Interest, Venue at the Crossroads, 1982. This pamphlet contains articles by Senators DeConcini and Laxalt supporting these changes, and articles by Nicholas Yost and Professor David Currie expressing doubt whether it is possible to achieve the goal of the sponsors without imposing on courts and litigants the wasteful burden of an extensive preliminary trial to determine the appropriate place of trial.

72. 28 U.S.C.A. § 1391(e). See 15 Wright, Miller & Cooper, Jurisdiction § 3815; Cates, Venue in Corporate Suits Against Federal Agencies and Officers, 1975, 60 Minn.L.Rev. 81.

The statute was intended to provide a more convenient forum for individual plaintiffs in actions that are nominally against an individual officer, but are in reality against the government, and does not apply to actions brought against federal officials in their individual capacities. Stafford v. Briggs, 1980, 100 S.Ct. 774, 444 U.S. 527, 63 L.Ed.2d 1, noted 1980, 49 U.Cin.L.Rev. 675.

73. DeConcini, in National Legal Center for the Public Interest, note 71 above, at p. 7.

74. 128 Cong.Rec. S658 (daily ed. Feb. 9, 1982) (remarks of Sen. DeConcini).

75. 28 U.S.C.A. §§ 1394–1403.

76. See 15 Wright, Miller & Cooper, Jurisdiction §§ 3813 (national banks), 3814–3815 (United States or federal officers or agencies); 3816 (administrative matters), 3818 (antitrust), 3819 (copyright), 3820 (fines, penalties, seizures, and forfeitures), 3821 (internal revenue), 3824 (securities regulation), 3825 (miscellaneous cases).

Compare, however, the very restrictive statute on venue in suits against national banks, which has been held to control over broader, more general, venue statutes otherwise applicable. Radzanower v. Touche Ross & Co., 1976, 96 S.Ct. 1989, 426 U.S. 148, 48 L.Ed.2d 540. See 15 Wright, Miller & Cooper, Jurisdiction § 3813.

77. 28 U.S.C.A. § 1400(b); 15 Wright, Miller & Cooper, Jurisdiction § 3823; Wydick, Venue in Actions for Patent Infringement, 1973, 25 Stan.L.Rev. 551.

ute [78]—though not to other such special statutes [79]—a corporation cannot be sued for patent infringement in a state other than the state of its incorporation merely because it does business, or is licensed to do business, in that state.[80]

Not infrequently a contract will provide that suit on it may only be brought in the courts at a particular place. A provision of this kind will be enforced by the federal court, and venue restricted in this way, unless the provision is thought to be unreasonable in itself or in its possible effect on the rights of litigants.[81]

§ 43.   Criminal Cases [1]

In civil cases venue is a matter of convenience for the litigants. In criminal cases venue involves important considerations of policy, with deep historical roots, that are now expressed in a complicated interplay of constitutional provisions, statutes, and rules.

In 1769 Parliament, over the objection of those who said such a course would lead to war, proposed taking Americans to England or to another colony for trial in treason cases. Hearing of this, the Virginia House of Burgesses unanimously adopted the famous Virginia Resolves of May 16, 1769, in which they said that by such a proposal "the inestimable Privilege of being tried by a Jury from the Vicinage, as well as the Liberty of summoning and producing Witnesses on such Trial, will be taken away from the Party accused." [2] One of the grievances asserted against the King in the Declaration of Independence was "transporting us beyond the Seas for pretended offenses." The point was deemed so important by the founders that the right to be tried for crimes in the state where the crime was committed is protected not once but twice in the Constitution, in Article III, section 2, and in the Sixth Amendment. In an earlier era the place where a crime was committed was usually the place where the defendant lived, and the Supreme Court has spoken eloquently on several occa-

78. Fourco Glass Co. v. Transmirra Products Corp., 1957, 77 S.Ct. 787, 353 U.S. 222, 1 L.Ed.2d 786; Geriak, Fifteen Years of Fourco—The Needless Disputes Over Patent Venue, 1972, 24 Hast.L.J. 55.

79. Pure Oil Co. v. Suarez, 1966, 86 S.Ct. 1394, 1396, 384 U.S. 202, 205, 16 L.Ed.2d 474. See n. 47 above.

80. But an action by the alleged infringer for a declaratory judgment of noninfringement and of invalidity of the patent is not within 28 U.S.C.A. § 1400(b) and is governed by the general venue statutes. Emerson Elec. Co. v. Black & Decker Mfg. Co., C.A.8th, 1979, 606 F.2d 234; Dicar, Inc. v. L. E. Sauer Machine Co., Inc., D.C.N.J.1982, 530 F.Supp. 1083.

81. M/S Bremen v. Zapata Off-Shore Co., 1972, 92 S.Ct. 1907, 407 U.S. 1, 32 L.Ed.2d 513. See 15 Wright, Miller & Cooper, Jurisdiction § 3803.

[§ 43]

1. 2 Wright, Criminal 2d §§ 301–307; Kershen, Vicinage, 1976, 29 Okl.L.Rev. 801, 1977, 30 Okl.L.Rev. 1; Barber, Venue in Federal Criminal Cases: A Plea for Return to Principle, 1963, 42 Texas L.Rev. 39; Blume, The Place of Trial of Criminal Cases: Constitutional Vicinage and Venue, 1944, 43 Mich.L. Rev. 59.

2. Journals of the House of Burgesses of Virginia, 1766–1769, Kennedy ed. 1906, p. 214. See also Blume, note 1 above, at 63–65; Comment, 1967, 115 U.Pa.L.Rev. 399, 404–414.

sions about the importance of trying a criminal defendant in his home district.[3] "Questions of venue in criminal cases, therefore, are not merely matters of formal legal procedure. They raise deep issues of public policy in the light of which legislation must be construed. If an enactment of Congress equally permits the underlying spirit of the constitutional concern for trial in the vicinage to be respected rather than to be disrespected, construction should go in the direction of constitutional policy even though not commanded by it."[4]

The Court, however, has not been consistent in this view. The cases calling for placing venue, where possible, at the defendant's home are intermingled with cases deprecating that consideration and insisting that all that is required is trial at the place of the crime.[5]

Nor has Congress been any more consistent. In 1958 it passed a statute giving defendants in certain income tax cases an absolute right to trial at their residence, and did so, over objection by the Treasury and Justice Departments, because it recognized the difficulty to defendants required to stand trial away from home.[6] Yet three weeks later it amended the statute on mailing obscene matter to broaden the choice of venue and make it more likely that a defendant would not be tried where he resided.[7]

The constitutional command is reflected in Criminal Rule 18, which says that except as otherwise provided by statute or rule, criminal prosecutions are to be had in the district in which the crime was committed.[8] There are a number of special venue provisions, usually included in particular criminal statutes, but these are largely unnecessary, since Rule 18, and the general venue statutes, make ample provision for every type of case. One legitimate purpose of a special venue provision is to narrow the choice of venues that otherwise would be available. Thus it has always been the rule that the trial of offenses punishable by death shall be in the county where the offense was committed, where that can be done without great inconvenience.[9]

---

3. Hyde v. Shine, 1905, 25 S.Ct. 760, 762, 199 U.S. 62, 78, 50 L.Ed. 90; U. S. v. Johnson, 1944, 65 S.Ct. 249, 250–252, 323 U.S. 273, 275–278, 89 L.Ed. 236; U. S. v. Cores, 1958, 78 S.Ct. 875, 877, 356 U.S. 405, 407, 2 L.Ed.2d 873.

4. U. S. v. Johnson, 1944, 65 S.Ct. 249, 251, 323 U.S. 273, 276, 89 L.Ed. 236.

5. Johnston v. U. S., 1956, 76 S.Ct. 739, 742, 351 U.S. 215, 220–221, 100 L.Ed. 1097; Travis v. U. S., 1961, 81 S.Ct. 358, 360–361, 364 U.S. 631, 634, 5 L.Ed. 2d 340; Platt v. Minnesota Mining & Mfg. Co., 1964, 84 S.Ct. 769, 772, 376 U.S. 240, 245, 11 L.Ed.2d 674. These inconsistent lines of cases are fully discussed in 2 Wright, Criminal 2d § 301.

6. 18 U.S.C.A. § 3237(b), as amended by Act of Aug. 6, 1958, Pub.L. 85–595, 72 Stat. 512. For the legislative history, see 1958 U.S. Code Cong. & Adm.News 3261.

7. 18 U.S.C.A. § 1461, as amended by Act of Aug. 28, 1958, Pub.L. 85–796, § 1, 72 Stat. 962. See Comment, Multi-Venue and the Obscenity Statutes, 1967, 115 U.Pa.L.Rev. 399.

8. Until 1966 the rule also required that trial be in the division where the offense is committed. As amended in that year the rule now provides only that the court shall fix the place of trial within the district "with due regard to the convenience of the defendant and the witnesses." See 2 Wright, Criminal 2d § 305; U. S. v. Burns, C.A. 11th, 1981, 662 F.2d 1378; U. S. v. Florence, C.A.4th, 1972, 456 F.2d 46.

9. 18 U.S.C.A. § 3235.

Fugitive felons may be prosecuted only in the district where the original offense was committed, though under the general venue statute prosecution would have been possible in any district through which they passed in their flight.[10] Persons charged with using the mails in certain violations of the Internal Revenue Code are given a privilege to be tried in the district where they reside.[11]

The general principle that criminal trials are to be held where the offense was committed leaves three questions open. First, some offenses are committed on the high seas or otherwise not within any district. The Constitution authorized Congress to provide a rule for such cases, and it has provided that such offenses shall be tried in the district where the offender is found, or into which he is first brought.[12]

Second, in some cases it is not clear where the offense was committed. Statutes set out a rule for particular instances. Thus in cases of murder or manslaughter, where the injury was inflicted in one district and the victim died in another, the place of injury is declared to be the proper venue.[13] But in most such cases there is no statutory rule, and the courts have had to work out answers for themselves, with the rule being that the locus delicti must be determined from the nature of the crime alleged and the location of the act or acts constituting it.[14] It is now settled, for example, that a prosecution for conspiracy may be had in any district in which any act in furtherance thereof was committed by any of the conspirators.[15] The statute under which the prosecution is had must be studied carefully,

---

10. 18 U.S.C.A. § 1073.

11. 18 U.S.C.A. § 3237(b); U. S. v. DeMarco, D.C.D.C.1975, 394 F.Supp. 611. See also 18 U.S.C.A. § 3239 giving a right to persons charged with transmitting threatening communications to be tried in the district in which the matter mailed or otherwise transmitted was first set in motion.

12. 18 U.S.C.A. § 3238. See 2 Wright, Criminal 2d § 304; U. S. v. McRary, C.A.5th, 1980, 616 F.2d 181; U. S. v. Kampiles, C.A.7th, 1979, 609 F.2d 1233, certiorari denied 100 S.Ct. 2923, 446 U.S. 954, 64 L.Ed.2d 812.

If a provision added by amendment in 1963 is relied on, and the defendant is indicted before he is brought into the United States, he may be tried in the district in which he was indicted even if it is not the district in which he is first brought into the United States. U. S. v. Layton, D.C.Cal.1981, 519 F.Supp. 942, appeal dismissed C.A.9th, 645 F.2d 21.

13. 18 U.S.C.A. § 3236. Prior to the adoption of the statutory provision to this effect, cases had held that the place where the death occurred was the proper venue. U. S. v. Bladen, C.C.D.C.1809, 24 F.Cas. 1160, No. 14,605; cf. U. S. v. Davis, C.C.D.Mass. 1837, 25 F.Cas. 786, No. 14,932.

14. U. S. v. Anderson, 1946, 66 S.Ct. 1213, 1216, 328 U.S. 699, 703, 90 L.Ed. 1529. It was held here that refusal to submit to induction into the army was to be prosecuted at the place where the induction center was located, rather than at the place where the draft board was. See also Johnston v. U. S., 1956, 76 S.Ct. 739, 351 U.S. 215, 100 L.Ed. 1097. See 2 Wright, Criminal 2d § 302.

15. Hyde v. U. S., 1912, 32 S.Ct. 793, 225 U.S. 347, 56 L.Ed. 1114 (any overt act); Hyde v. Shine, 1905, 25 S.Ct. 760, 199 U.S. 62, 50 L.Ed. 90 (place of agreement); and cases cited 2 Wright, Criminal 2d § 303 nn. 11, 12. See Abrams, Conspiracy and Multi-Venue in Federal Criminal Prosecutions: The Crime Committed Formula, 1962, 9 UCLA L.Rev. 751.

with particular attention to the verb defining the offense.[16] Thus, where the statute makes it a crime to file a false affidavit, the crime is committed, and prosecution must be had, in the district where the affidavit was filed, even though it was executed in another district and mailed for filing.[17]

Finally there are some continuing offenses that are committed in more than one district. Except as otherwise expressly provided by statute, such offenses may be prosecuted in any district in which the offense was begun, continued, or completed.[18] Courts have gone even beyond the statute to hold that one who aids or abets a crime, though he may be prosecuted as a principal, can be tried not only in the district in which the substantive offense was committed, but also in the district in which he performed accessorial acts.[19] And the Second Circuit, in a notable opinion, has held that even where the mailings, which constituted the offense under the Securities Act, were in New York, the case could be tried in Alabama, where the scheme was hatched.[20]

There is obvious danger in those broad provisions and rulings as to venue, in that they make it possible to thwart the purpose of the constitutional requirement of trial in the vicinage. This is especially true as notions of vicarious participation in crime have become more expansive, and use of the mails or other means of interstate communication or transportation has become the touchstone of so many federal crimes. Thus suppose that two men in Key West devise a scheme that violates the Securities Act, or that may be used to defraud. The scheme is carried out entirely in the Key West area. One of the men writes a letter to Seattle in connection with the scheme. Not only this man, but also his associate who had nothing to do with

---

16. Dobie, Venue in Criminal Cases in the United States District Court, 1926, 12 Va.L.Rev. 287, 289; 2 Wright, Criminal 2d § 302.

17. Travis v. U. S., 1961, 81 S.Ct. 358, 364 U.S. 631, 5 L.Ed.2d 340. But see U. S. v. Herberman, C.A.5th, 1978, 583 F.2d 222, 225–227. For similar close analyses of the statutes under which particular prosecutions were brought, see Horner v. U. S., 1892, 12 S.Ct. 407, 143 U.S. 207, 36 L.Ed. 126; Burton v. U. S., 1905, 25 S.Ct. 243, 196 U.S. 283, 49 L.Ed. 482, 1906, 26 S.Ct. 688, 202 U.S. 344, 50 L.Ed. 1057; U. S. v. Lombardo, 1916, 36 S.Ct. 508, 241 U.S. 73, 60 L.Ed. 897; Newton v. U. S., C.C.A.4th, 1947, 162 F.2d 795, 796, certiorari denied 68 S.Ct. 650, 333 U.S. 848, 92 L.Ed. 1130. U. S. v. Walden, C.A.4th, 1972, 464 F.2d 1015.

Thus, there is division in the circuits on whether a defendant who shoots a witness to prevent him from testifying must be prosecuted for obstruction of justice in the district where the shooting occurred or the district where the witness was to have testified. See U. S. v. Barham, C.A.11th, 1982, 666 F.2d 521.

18. 18 U.S.C.A. § 3237(a). The constitutionality of such provisions was upheld in Armour Packing Co. v. U. S., 1908, 28 S.Ct. 428, 209 U.S. 56, 52 L.Ed. 681. See 2 Wright, Criminal 2d § 303.

19. U. S. v. Gillette, C.A.2d, 1951, 189 F.2d 449, certiorari denied 72 S.Ct. 49, 342 U.S. 827, 96 L.Ed. 625. See Abrams, note 15 above.

But the fact that an accessory performed acts in a district does not make it a proper venue for prosecution of his principal. U. S. v. Sweig, D.C.N.Y. 1970, 316 F.Supp. 1148, 1159–1162.

20. U. S. v. Cashin, C.A.2d, 1960, 281 F.2d 669.

the letter, can, if the government chooses, be prosecuted for their crime in Seattle, though it may be that neither one has ever been in that part of the country. The protection of the Constitution is vastly diluted when this is possible.[21] The remedy, however, is not to narrow criminal venue, but to permit easy transfer, if the government should choose to prosecute in the Western District of Washington, back to the Southern District of Florida, where the defendants reside, and where the witnesses and records are located. Criminal Rule 21(b) was intended to provide just such a procedure, and, as will be seen in the next section, it was amended in 1966 to overcome a strict judicial construction that had prevented it from accomplishing its purpose.

Venue is a fact that must be proved in a criminal case [22] though it need not be proved beyond a reasonable doubt, and the absence of direct proof of venue does not defeat conviction if the fact of venue is properly inferable from all the evidence.[23] Since venue is a privilege of the defendant, it may be waived if the defendant fails to object to an improper venue.[24]

§ 44. Change of Venue [1]

Provisions for change of venue have long been a commonplace in state jurisprudence. In the federal courts they are a novelty of the last three decades. Criminal Rules 21 and 22, effective in 1945, au-

21. "Plainly enough, such leeway not only opens the door to needless hardships to an accused by prosecution remote from home and from appropriate facilities for defense. It also leads to the appearance of abuses, if not to abuses, in the selection of what may be deemed a tribunal favorable to the prosecution." U. S. v. Johnson, 1944, 65 S.Ct. 249, 250, 323 U.S. 273, 275, 89 L.Ed. 236.

22. U. S. v. White, C.A.5th, 1980, 611 F.2d 531, certiorari denied 100 S.Ct. 2978, 446 U.S. 992, 64 L.Ed.2d 849; U. S. v. Jones, C.A.7th, 1949, 174 F.2d 746; and cases cited 2 Wright, Criminal 2d § 307 n. 2.

23. U. S. v. Martino, C.A.5th, 1981, 648 F.2d 367, 400; U. S. v. Kampiles, C.A.7th, 1979, 609 F.2d 1233, 1238, certiorari denied 1980, 100 S.Ct. 2923, 446 U.S. 954, 64 L.Ed.2d 812; and cases cited 2 Wright, Criminal 2d § 307 nn. 4–6.

24. E.g., U. S. v. Roberts, C.A.9th, 1980, 618 F.2d 530; U. S. v. Black Cloud, C.A.8th, 1979, 590 F.2d 270. See 2 Wright, Criminal 2d § 306.

[§ 44]

1. Civil cases: 15 Wright, Miller & Cooper, Jurisdiction §§ 3841–3855;

Kaufman, Observations on Transfers Under Section 1404(a) of the New Judicial Code, 1951, 10 F.R.D. 595; Kaufman, Further Observations on Transfers under Section 1404(a), 1956, 56 Col.L.Rev. 1; Black & Black, Injustices in the Federal Forum Non Conveniens Rule, 1953, 3 Utah L.Rev. 314; Korbel, Plaintiff's Right to Change of Venue in Federal Courts, 1960, 38 U.Det.L.J. 137; Masington, Venue in the Federal Courts—The Problem of the Inconvenient Forum, 1961, 15 U. Miami L.Rev. 237; Kitch, Section 1404(a) of the Judicial Code: In The Interest of Justice or Injustice?, 1965, 40 Ind.L.J. 99; Leathers, Dimensions of the Constitutional Obligation to Provide a Forum, 1974, 62 Ky.L.J. 1.

Criminal cases: 2 Wright, Criminal 2d §§ 341–347; Bailey & Golding, Remedies for Prejudicial Publicity—Change of Venue and Continuance in Federal Criminal Procedure, 1958, 18 Fed.B.J. 56; Barber, Venue in Federal Criminal Cases: A Plea for Return to Principle, 1963, 42 Texas L.Rev. 39; Note, The Efficacy of a Change of Venue in Protecting a Defendant's Right to an Impartial Jury, 1967, 42 Notre Dame Law. 925.

thorized change of venue to avoid prejudice or where the interests of justice so required. For civil cases § 1404(a) of the 1948 Judicial Code permitted transfer to a more convenient forum, while § 1406(a) provided transfer, as an alternative to dismissal, where the case is brought at an improper venue. Limited provisions for transfer of habeas corpus cases [2] and for pretrial proceedings in multidistrict litigation [3] have been added more recently. The provisions for criminal cases present fewer problems and will be considered first.

Criminal Rule 21(a) authorizes the court, on motion of a defendant, to transfer the case to another district if the court is satisfied that there exists in the district where the prosecution is pending so great a prejudice against the defendant that he cannot obtain a fair and impartial trial there.[4] Such motions have been granted in very few cases [5] and it is doubtful whether this rule will ever be much used. Given the size of federal judicial districts it is difficult to show that prejudice is so great that an impartial jury cannot be found, and the courts have been strict in demanding such a showing. Further, defendant has a constitutional right to be tried in the state where the offense was committed. Defendant can waive this right by moving to transfer to another state, but he is under no compulsion to do so. Since the Constitution gives him both the right to a fair trial and the right to a trial in the vicinage, he may insist upon both rights by moving for a continuance rather than for a transfer.[6]

As amended in 1966, Rule 21(b) provides that, on motion of a defendant, the court may transfer the proceeding as to him or any one

2. 28 U.S.C.A. § 2241(d), as amended in 1966, allows a habeas corpus action to be brought for a state prisoner either in the district in which he was convicted or the district in which he was confined, and allows for transfer from one district to the other "in furtherance of justice."

3. 28 U.S.C.A. § 1407, added to the Judicial Code in 1968, allows the temporary transfer of civil actions involving common questions of fact to a single district for purposes of coordinated pretrial proceedings, after which the actions are returned to their original districts for trial. Rules to implement the statute are set out at 65 F.R.D. 253. See 15 Wright, Miller & Cooper, Jurisdiction §§ 3861–3868; Herndon & Higginbotham, Complex Multidistrict Litigation—An Overview, 1979, 31 Baylor L.Rev. 33; Weigel, The Judicial Panel on Multidistrict Litigation, Transferor Courts and Transferee Courts, 1978, 78 F.R.D. 575, Kaminsky, The Judicial Panel on Multidistrict Litigation: Emerging Problems and Cur-

rent Trends of Decision, 1972, 23 Syracuse L.Rev. 817.

4. As amended in 1966, Rule 21(a) permits the court to determine for itself where to transfer a case, and the moving defendant cannot limit this choice. U. S. v. Marcello, D.C.La.1968, 280 F.Supp. 510, 520. See 2 Wright, Criminal 2d § 342 n. 2.

5. Eight reported cases in which a transfer was ordered under Criminal Rule 21(a) are cited in 2 Wright, Criminal 2d § 342 n. 18, while note 19 cites a multitude of cases in which a transfer motion has been denied.

6. Delaney v. U. S., C.A.1st, 1952, 199 F.2d 107. The courts, however, have been very reluctant to grant continuances sought on this ground. See Bailey & Golding, Remedies for Prejudicial Publicity—Change of Venue and Continuance in Federal Criminal Procedure, 1958, 18 Fed.B.J. 56; U. S. v. Marcello, D.C.La.1968, 280 F.Supp. 510, 519.

or more of the counts therein to any other district [7] "for the convenience of parties and witnesses, and in the interest of justice."[8] The former rule, which this replaced, was much more restrictive. It allowed transfer only of an offense that could be considered to have been committed in more than one district, and then permitted transfer only to another district in which the offense had been committed.[9] In addition, in a multi-count indictment only those counts that charged an offense in more than one district could be transferred,[10] and the courts were naturally reluctant to transfer part of a case while retaining the nontransferable counts.[11] For these reasons the former rule was not much used. The amendment did away with all of these limitations and gave the court ample power in every case to provide for trial in the most convenient forum if requested to do so by the defendant.[12] There is no indication, however, that transfers are being granted more liberally under the amended rule.

Section 1406(a) of the 1948 Code, as amended in 1949, provides that if a civil action is commenced in the wrong district or division, the court shall dismiss, but if it is in the interest of justice, the court may instead transfer the case to any district or division in which it could have been brought.[13] There are some instances in which dis-

---

7. Unlike Rule 21(a), Rule 21(b) does not provide for transfer to a district "whether or not such district is specified in the defendant's motion." Although the Advisory Committee Note to the amended rule suggests that the court has this power on Rule 21(b) motions, a strong argument can be made that on a 21(b) motion transfer can only be to a district to which defendant has requested transfer. See 2 Wright, Criminal 2d § 345.

8. Although the former Rule 21(b) spoke only of "in the interest of justice," there is no reason to believe that the added reference to the convenience of parties and witnesses makes any substantive change. Jones v. Gasch, C.A.1967, 404 F.2d 1231, 1236–1237, 131 U.S.App.D.C. 254, certiorari denied 88 S.Ct. 1414, 390 U.S. 1029, 20 L.Ed. 2d 286. Accordingly the factors to be considered listed by the Supreme Court under the old rule in Platt v. Minnesota Mining & Mfg. Co., 1964, 84 S.Ct. 769, 771, 376 U.S. 240, 243–244, 11 L.Ed.2d 674, should continue to be the relevant factors. For discussion of these factors and their application, see 2 Wright, Criminal 2d § 344.

9. 2 Wright, Criminal 2d § 343 n. 5.

10. U. S. v. Choate, C.A.5th, 1960, 276 F.2d 724.

11. See cases cited 2 Wright, Criminal 2d § 343 nn. 12, 13.

12. See U. S. v. Clark, D.C.N.Y.1973, 360 F.Supp. 936, mandamus refused C.A.2d, 1974, 481 F.2d 276; U. S. v. Herold, D.C.Wis.1970, 309 F.Supp. 997; U. S. v. Hinton, D.C.La.1967, 268 F.Supp. 728, 730; 1 Wright § 343. The rule is informatively discussed in Jones v. Gasch, C.A.1967, 404 F.2d 1231, 131 U.S.App.D.C. 254, certiorari denied 88 S.Ct. 1414, 390 U.S. 1029, 20 L.Ed.2d 286, in which a refusal to order transfer was upheld.

A defendant got an unexpected, but temporary, bonus from a transfer in U. S. v. Elkins, D.C.Cal.1975, 396 F.Supp. 314. A prosecution for mailing obscene matter had been transferred from Iowa, where the mailing was received, to California, from which it was sent. The California court ruled that despite the transfer the community standards of Iowa would continue to govern the case and, finding that a California jury would not know the Iowa community standard, dismissed the indictment. Subsequently the Eighth Circuit granted mandamus setting aside the transfer and requiring that the case be returned to Iowa for trial. U. S. v. McManus, C.A.8th, 1976, 535 F.2d 460, certiorari denied 97 S.Ct. 766, 429 U.S. 1052, 50 L.Ed.2d 769, noted 1977, 52 N.Y.U.L.Rev. 629.

13. 28 U.S.C.A. § 1406(a); 15 Wright, Miller & Cooper, Jurisdiction § 3827. As adopted in 1948, the statute re-

missal will still be ordered,[14] but more commonly transfer will be preferable, since it avoids the need of commencing a new action.[15] Transfer can be ordered only if the court in which the action was brought has jurisdiction of the subject matter of the action [16] but it is not necessary that it have in personam jurisdiction of the defendant.[17] The action can be transferred, and service made in the transferee district. The suit can only be transferred to a district in which venue is proper [18] and in which defendant is amenable to process.[19]

The most interesting, and most controversial, change of venue provision adopted for civil cases is 28 U.S.C.A. § 1404(a). It states: "For the convenience of parties and witnesses, in the interest of justice, a district court [20] may transfer any civil action to any other district or division where it might have been brought." One year earlier the Supreme Court had held that the doctrine of forum non conveniens was available in federal court, and that a court could dismiss a suit, though it had both personal and subject-matter jurisdiction, and the venue was properly laid, if there existed another forum so much more convenient for the parties and the courts that plaintiff's privilege of choosing his forum was outweighed.[21] Although the doctrine of forum non conveniens has flourished in the states since 1947,

quired transfer whenever a case was brought in the wrong venue. The 1949 amendment authorized dismissal unless the interests of justice required transfer.

14. E.g., Cook v. Fox, C.A.9th, 1976, 537 F.2d 370; Lowery v. Estelle, C.A.5th, 1976, 533 F.2d 265; Poe v. Kuyk, D.C. Del.1978, 448 F.Supp. 1231, affirmed C.A.3d, 1979, 591 F.2d 1336.

In most cases it will be the plaintiff who will wish transfer while the defendant will contend that the suit should be dismissed. See however Stevenson v. U. S., D.C.Tenn.1961, 197 F.Supp. 355, dismissing the case at plaintiff's request over defendant's motion to transfer.

15. E.g., Corke v. Sameiet M. S. Song of Norway, C.A.2d, 1978, 572 F.2d 77 (statute of limitations had run); Brenner v. Rubin, D.C.Mass.1965, 240 F.Supp. 467 (defendant had misled plaintiff about venue).

16. First Nat. Bank of Chicago v. United Air Lines, C.A.7th, 1951, 190 F.2d 493, reversed on other grounds, 1952, 72 S.Ct. 421, 342 U.S. 396, 96 L.Ed. 441; B. Heller & Co. v. First Spice Mfg. Corp., D.C.Ill.1959, 172 F.Supp. 46.

17. Goldlawr, Inc. v. Heiman, 1962, 82 S.Ct. 913, 369 U.S. 463, 8 L.Ed.2d 39. See Comment, Personal Jurisdiction Under Federal Change of Venue Statutes, 1962 Wis.L.Rev. 342.

18. Blackmar v. Guerre, C.A.5th, 1951, 190 F.2d 427, affirmed 1952, 72 S.Ct. 410, 342 U.S. 512, 96 L.Ed. 534; Westerman v. Grow, D.C.N.Y.1961, 198 F.Supp. 307.

Except under unusual circumstances the decision by the transferor court that venue is proper and service possible in the transferee court cannot be reconsidered by the transferee court. Hayman Cash Register Co. v. Sarokin, C.A.3d, 1982, 669 F.2d 162.

19. Johnson v. Helicopter & Airplane Services Corp., D.C.Md.1974, 389 F.Supp. 509, 523–525; Smith v. Murchison, D.C.N.Y.1970, 310 F.Supp. 1079, 1089–1090.

20. The language of the statute does not preclude an appellate court from effecting a transfer by direct order if unusual circumstances make this necessary. Koehring Co. v. Hyde Constr. Co., 1966, 86 S.Ct. 522, 382 U.S. 362, 15 L.Ed.2d 416.

21. Gulf Oil Corp. v. Gilbert, 1947, 67 S.Ct. 839, 330 U.S. 501, 91 L.Ed. 1055; Koster v. Lumbermens Mut. Cas. Co., 1947, 67 S.Ct. 828, 330 U.S. 518, 91 L.Ed. 1067.

See 15 Wright, Miller & Cooper, Jurisdiction § 3828; Barrett, The Doctrine of Forum Non Conveniens, 1947, 35 Calif. L.Rev. 380; Braucher, The Inconvenient Federal Forum, 1947, 60 Harv.L. Rev. 908.

it has largely been superseded in federal courts by the 1948 adoption of § 1404(a).[22]   Only in rare instances where the alternative forum is a state court or the court of a foreign country may the federal court now dismiss on grounds of forum non conveniens.[23]

Section 1404(a) has given rise to a veritable flood of litigation. Probably no issue of civil procedure gives rise to so many reported decisions, year after year, as does this seemingly simple statute. Most of the decisions merely illustrate how a court has weighed the various factors in determining whether to order transfer in a particular case on particular facts.[24]   There are some legal issues posed by the statute, however, that do appear in the cases.

One such issue was swiftly resolved by the Supreme Court.   It was contended that § 1404(a) should apply only to actions under the general venue statutes and not to those cases for which there is a special venue statute.   The Supreme Court rejected this argument, holding that the broad language "any civil action" meant what it said.[25]   Indeed even admiralty suits are subject to § 1404(a),[26] although they are not regarded as civil actions for purposes of the other general venue statutes.[27]   There has been disagreement in the cases as to whether an action in rem is transferable under the statute.   A Supreme Court decision allowing transfer of an action in which in rem and in personam admiralty proceedings were joined is probably best understood as resting on the Court's refusal to take seriously, in a § 1404(a) context, the archaic admiralty fiction by

22.   Collins v. American Auto. Ins. Co. of St. Louis, Missouri, C.A.2d, 1956, 230 F.2d 416, certiorari dismissed 77 S.Ct. 20, 352 U.S. 802, 1 L.Ed.2d 37; Watson v. DeFelice, D.C.D.C.1977, 428 F.Supp. 1276.

23.   E.g., Prack v. Weissinger, C.A.4th, 1960, 276 F.2d 446; and cases cited 15 Wright, Miller & Cooper, Jurisdiction § 3828 nn. 6–7.

For the standards to be applied in determining whether to dismiss in favor of a foreign country, see Piper Aircraft Co. v. Reyno, 1981, 102 S.Ct. 252, ___ U.S. ___, 70 L.Ed.2d 419, noted 1982, 23 S.Tex.L.J. 490; Alcoa S. S. Co., Inc. v. M/V Nordic Regent, C.A.2d, 1980, 654 F.2d 147.

24.   The flood of opinions with little or no precedential value is encouraged by those appellate courts that have urged trial courts to state their reasons for granting or denying a transfer motion: In re Pope, C.A.1978, 580 F.2d 620, 623, 188 U.S.App.D.C. 357; Starnes v. McGuire, C.A.1974, 512 F.2d 918, 934, 168 U.S.App.D.C. 4; Plum Tree, Inc. v. Stockment, C.A.3d, 1973, 488 F.2d 754, 756; Solomon v. Continental American

Life Ins. Co., C.A.3d, 1973, 472 F.2d 1043, 1048; cf. A. J. Indus., Inc. v. United States Dist. Court, C.A.9th, 1974, 503 F.2d 384, 389; Westinghouse Elec. Corp. v. Weigel, C.A.9th, 1970, 426 F.2d 1356, 1358.

25.   Ex parte Collett, 1949, 69 S.Ct. 944, 337 U.S. 55, 93 L.Ed. 1207 (FELA action); U. S. v. National City Lines, Inc., 1949, 69 S.Ct. 955, 337 U.S. 78, 93 L.Ed. 1226; 15 Wright, Miller & Cooper, Jurisdiction § 3843.   This result seems especially odd in the FELA cases, since the Code was presented to Congress as containing nothing of a controversial nature and the same Congress that enacted the Code then refused to adopt proposed legislation that would have limited the plaintiff's choice of forum in FELA cases.   See Pope v. Atlantic Coast Line R. Co., 1953, 73 S.Ct. 749, 753, 345 U.S. 379, 386–387, 97 L.Ed. 1094.

26.   Continental Grain Co. v. The FBL–585, 1960, 80 S.Ct. 1470, 364 U.S. 19, 4 L.Ed.2d 1540.

27.   Fed.R.Civ.Proc. 82, as amended in 1966.

which an action actually against the ship owner is pretended to be against the ship.[28] The lower courts, however, are reading that case as meaning that transfer is possible if in rem and in personam proceedings are joined,[29] and have come to hold that even an action purely in rem can be transferred, despite the conceptual argument that there is no other district in which an action in rem can be brought.[30]

The procedure for transfer under § 1404(a) has not given much difficulty. The motion for transfer may be made by any party, including the plaintiff,[31] though other limitations on the statute, discussed below severely limit the circumstances in which it would be of any use to a plaintiff. The motion may be made at any time, though delay in moving is a factor that will be considered in passing on the motion.[32] Once the motion has been granted and the papers lodged with the transferee court, the transferor court loses all jurisdiction over the case.[33] The case then proceeds in the transferee court as if it had been commenced, and all prior actions had, in that court.[34]

If the transfer was on motion of the defendant, the transferee court must apply the law that would have been applied in the transferor court, so that a change in forum will mean a change in courtrooms, but not a change of law.[35] This means that in passing on a

28. Continental Grain Co. v. The FBL–585, 1960, 80 S.Ct. 1470, 364 U.S. 19, 4 L.Ed.2d 1540.

29. Norfolk Shipbuilding & Drydock Corp. v. Motor Yacht La Belle Simone, D.C.Puerto Rico 1973, 371 F.Supp. 985; Jacobs v. Tenney, D.C.Del.1970, 316 F.Supp. 151. The same rule has been applied to an action quasi-in-rem. Ladson v. Kibble, D.C.N.Y.1969, 307 F.Supp. 11. See Comment, Transfer of Quasi in Rem Actions under 28 U.S. C.A. § 1404(a): A Study in the Interpretation of "Civil Action," 1964, 31 U.Chi.L.Rev. 373.

30. In re International Marine Towing, Inc., C.A.5th, 1980, 617 F.2d 362; Construction Aggregates Corp. v. S. S. Azalea City, D.C.N.J.1975, 399 F.Supp. 662.

31. E.g., Philip Carey Mfg. Co. v. Taylor, C.A.6th, 1961, 286 F.2d 782, certiorari denied 81 S.Ct. 1903, 366 U.S. 948, 6 L.Ed.2d 1242; Pruess v. Udall, C.A. D.C.1965, 359 F.2d 615, 123 U.S.App. D.C. 301; American Standard, Inc. v. Bendix Corp., D.C.Mo.1980, 487 F.Supp. 254; and cases cited 15 Wright, Miller & Cooper, Jurisdiction § 3844 n. 5. Some older cases were to the contrary but that view has no recent support. See also Korbel, Plaintiff's Right to Change of Venue in Federal Courts, 1960, 38 U.Det.L.J. 137.

32. McGraw-Edison Co. v. Van Pelt, C.A.8th, 1965, 350 F.2d 361; Nagle v. Pennsylvania R. Co., D.C.Ohio, 89 F.Supp. 822; and cases cited 15 Wright, Miller & Cooper, Jurisdiction § 3844 n. 18.

33. Starnes v. McGuire, C.A.1974, 512 F.2d 918, 923–925, 168 U.S.App.D.C. 4; cf. Sheldon v. Amperex Electronic Corp., D.C.N.Y.1971, 52 F.R.D. 1.

But the transferee court may acquire jurisdiction before the papers have physically reached it. Koehring Co. v. Hyde Constr. Co., 1966, 86 S.Ct. 522, 524 n. 4, 382 U.S. 362, 365 n. 4, 15 L.Ed.2d 416.

34. Magnetic Engineering & Mfg. Co. v. Dings Mfg. Co., C.A.2d, 1950, 178 F.2d 866. See 15 Wright, Miller & Cooper, Jurisdiction § 3846.

35. Van Dusen v. Barrack, 1964, 84 S.Ct. 805, 821, 376 U.S. 612, 639, 11 L.Ed.2d 945.

See Note, Choice of Law in Federal Court After Transfer of Venue, 1977, 63 Cornell L.Rev. 149.

Prior to the Van Dusen decision the courts were divided on this question and the problem was so complex that a leading scholar publicly retracted what he had earlier written on the subject. Compare Currie, Change of Venue and the Conflict of Laws, 1955, 22 U.Chi.L. Rev. 405, with Currie, Change of Ven-

motion to transfer the court must consider, as one of the factors in deciding whether to grant the motion, the effect that retaining the law of the transferor state will have. Thus if the law is unclear in the state in which the action is commenced, this argues against transfer, since a district judge in that state is presumably better able to fathom its law than is a district judge in the transferee state. Also the fact that the substantive law will not be changed by a transfer may cast doubt on the feasibility of consolidating the transferred case with other cases that were commenced in the court to which transfer is proposed, and may have an effect on the witnesses that will be necessary. All of this must be considered by the district court in passing on the transfer motion.[36]

The statute permits transfer only to another forum where the suit "might have been brought." The meaning of this limitation has caused much disagreement.[37] At a minimum it would seem to preclude transfer to a district that would not have been a proper venue for the action initially, at least in the absence of consent by the defendant. Courts were not agreed, however, as to whether the transferee forum must be one in which process could have been served on defendant. In the leading case of Foster-Milburn Co. v. Knight[38] Judge Learned Hand, speaking for the Second Circuit, held that a case could not be transferred on the motion of plaintiff to a district where defendants were not subject to process. Though the First Circuit rejected the Foster-Milburn rule as "a gloss" on the statute,[39] and the reasoning of the rule was carefully rebutted by an able district judge,[40] most courts accepted the rule, and the rigid limitation that it placed on the usefulness of § 1404(a).[41]

ue and the Conflict of Laws: A Retraction, 1960, 27 U.Chi.L.Rev. 341.

It has been held—deciding a question left open in the Van Dusen case, 84 S.Ct. at 821, 376 U.S. at 639–640—that the law of the transferor state will apply even though that state would have dismissed the action on the ground of forum non conveniens. In re Air Crash Disaster at Boston, Mass., D.C.Mass. 1975, 399 F.Supp. 1106, 1119–1122.

It is still not settled what law applies if transfer is on plaintiff's motion. The American Law Institute proposes that in that situation the transferee court should apply its own law. Compare ALI Study, § 1306(c), with id. at § 1305(c). It is so held in Carson v. U-Haul Co., C.A.6th, 1970, 434 F.2d 916. But see the Cornell Note cited above.

36. Van Dusen v. Barrack, 1964, 84 S.Ct. 805, 823–824, 376 U.S. 612, 643–646, 11 L.Ed.2d 945. See Popkin v. Eastern Air Lines, Inc., D.C.Pa.1966,

253 F.Supp. 244; and cases cited 15 Wright, Miller & Cooper, Jurisdiction § 3854 nn. 28–29.

37. 15 Wright, Miller & Cooper, Jurisdiction § 3845.

38. C.A.2d, 1950, 181 F.2d 949, criticised 1951, 60 Yale L.J. 183.

39. In re Josephson, C.A.1st, 1954, 218 F.2d 174, 185–186.

40. Kaufman, Further Observations on Transfers under Section 1404(a), 1956, 56 Col.L.Rev. 1, 15. See also Note, 1951, 60 Yale L.J. 183.

41. See cases cited 15 Wright, Miller & Cooper, Jurisdiction § 3845 n. 8. Indeed one court that had earlier held to the contrary, Otto v. Hirl, D.C.Iowa 1950, 89 F.Supp. 72, adopted the Foster-Milburn rule in preference to its own former view, Herzog v. Central Steel Tube Co., D.C.Iowa 1951, 98 F.Supp. 607.

A doctrine did develop among some courts—though rejected by others—that a defendant could have an action transferred to a district where venue would have been improper or he was not amenable to process since his motion for transfer waived any objection to venue or in personam jurisdiction in the transferee court. The Supreme Court repudiated this doctrine in Hoffman v. Blaski.[42] It held there that the words "might have been brought" direct the attention of the judge to the situation that existed when suit was instituted, and that they permit transfer only to a district where plaintiff would have had the right, independent of the wishes of the defendant, to bring the action. This clearly establishes that consent by the defendant will not permit transfer to a forum where the action could not originally have been commenced.[43] Though a few commentators suggested that Hoffman v. Blaski did not foreclose the Foster-Milburn issue, the rationale and language of the Hoffman opinion is such that any hope that the Foster-Milburn doctrine may yet be overruled seems wishful thinking, and the courts have uniformly so held.[44]

The commentators have been uniformly critical of Hoffman v. Blaski.[45] It is true, as the dissent demonstrates, that the result there is not inevitable from the language of the statute. Any other construction, however, would have converted the statute, intended in part to avoid forum shopping by plaintiffs, into a vehicle for forum shopping by defendant. Under the statute plaintiff must sue in the most convenient forum or he will find his suit transferred there, whether he consents or not. An opposite result in Hoffman would have meant that defendant sued, out of necessity, in a forum not the most convenient for all concerned would have had a choice either to consent to transfer or to insist that the litigation remain in the inconvenient forum.[46] To the extent that Hoffman and Foster-Milburn

---

42. 1960, 80 S.Ct. 1084, 363 U.S. 335, 4 L.Ed.2d 1254.

43. The reference, however, is only to where the suit "might have been brought" in terms of the federal laws delimiting where actions may be commenced. Neither the law of the transferee state concerning capacity of the plaintiff to sue nor Rule 17(b), defining capacity, are relevant. Van Dusen v. Barrack, 1964, 84 S.Ct. 805, 813, 376 U.S. 612, 624, 11 L.Ed.2d 945.

44. Relf v. Gasch, C.A.1975, 511 F.2d 804, 167 U.S.App.D.C. 238; Shutte v. Armco Steel Corp., C.A.3d, 1970, 431 F.2d 22, certiorari denied 91 S.Ct. 871, 401 U.S. 910, 27 L.Ed.2d 808; Cessna Aircraft Co. v. Brown, C.A.10th, 1965, 348 F.2d 689; and cases cited 15 Wright, Miller & Cooper, Jurisdiction § 3845 n. 20. The early hopes to the contrary were expressed in Notes, 1961, 46 Cornell L.Q. 318, 46 Iowa L.Rev. 661.

45. See Masington, Venue in the Federal Courts—The Problem of the Inconvenient Forum, 1961, U. Miami L.Rev. 237; Comment, 1962, 57 Nw.U.L.Rev. 456, Notes 1961, 46 Cornell L.Q. 318, 1961 Duke L.J. 349, 49 Geo.L.J. 765, 36 Ind.L.J. 344, 46 Iowa L.Rev. 661, 45 Minn.L.Rev. 680, 14 Vand.L.Rev. 646.

Some lower courts have not hidden their dislike for the Hoffman rule. See Schertenleib v. Traum, C.A.2d, 1978, 589 F.2d 1156, 1163; A. J. Indus., Inc. v. United States District Court, C.A. 9th, 1974, 503 F.2d 384, 387–389; Funnelcap, Inc. v. Orion Indus., Inc., D.C. Del.1975, 392 F.Supp. 938, 943–944; Ferri v. United Aircraft Corp., D.C. Conn.1973, 357 F.Supp. 814, 816.

46. See, for example, Gilpin v. Wilson, D.C.Ala.1957, 148 F.Supp. 493. Plaintiff resided in Tennessee, the accident for which suit was brought occurred in Tennessee, and every eyewitness to the accident and all of the doctors and

prevent some lawsuits from being tried at the most convenient place, the remedy is to strike the words "where it might have been brought" from the statute.[47]

The statute speaks only in the most general terms in setting out the standards to be considered in determining whether to grant or deny a § 1404(a) motion, and the matter is left generally in the discretion of the trial judge.[48] "At best," the Second Circuit says, "the judge must guess, and we should accept his guess unless it is too wild."[49] One court has endeavored to limit the discretion thus conferred on the trial court, saying "he is limited in his consideration to the three factors specifically mentioned in § 1404(a), and he may not properly be governed in his decision by any other factor or consideration."[50] Paradoxically that court went on to list eight factors, only one of which is mentioned in the statute, that persuaded it that the trial judge had erred in refusing to order transfer.[51] As this illustrates, a limitation to the three factors listed in the statute is unrealistic, except in the most general sense, since the factors mentioned are broad generalities that take on a variety of meanings in specific cases, and the statute gives no hint as to how these vast categories are to be weighed against each other.

nurses who treated plaintiff were residents of Tennessee. Nevertheless since defendant was not amenable to process in Tennessee and refused to consent to transfer there, the action had to remain in the Middle District of Alabama. This kind of insistence on the least convenient forum would not have been open to plaintiffs had Hoffman v. Blaski been decided the other way.

The problems of forum shopping by defendants were lessened by the 1966 amendment to § 1391(a), making the district "in which the claim arose" a proper venue. But that reform had not been enacted when Hoffman was decided, and the Supreme Court had to consider the consequences of its decision in terms of the venue statutes as they then existed. And even the 1966 amendment would not help in a case like the Gilpin case, discussed above, where the defendant was not amenable to process in the more convenient forum.

47. Thus a 1958 amendment to 28 U.S. C.A. § 1402, permitting transfer of actions by corporations for the recovery of taxes, does not contain the words "where it might have been brought" and transfer to any other federal court is permitted. See also Rule F(9) of the Supplemental Rules for Certain Admiralty and Maritime Claims for diversity cases, and Bankruptcy Rule 782.

The proposals of the American Law Institute would permit transfer on motion of the defendant to any district, ALI Study, § 1305(a), but would allow transfer on plaintiff's motion only to a district where venue would have been proper and defendant could have been served. Id. at § 1306(a). Thus a defendant, but not a plaintiff, could continue to insist on trial in an inconvenient forum. No such distinction is made in the proposals for federal question cases or cases to which the United States is a party. ALI Study, §§ 1315(a), 1327(a).

48. 15 Wright, Miller & Cooper, Jurisdiction § 3847.

49. Ford Motor Co. v. Ryan, C.A.2d 1950, 182 F.2d 329, 331, certiorari denied 71 S.Ct. 79, 340 U.S. 851, 95 L.Ed. 624. Later the same court spoke of the matter as "peculiarly one for the exercise of judgment by those in daily proximity to these delicate problems of trial litigation." Lykes Bros. S. S. Co., Inc. v. Sugarman, C.A.2d, 1959, 272 F.2d 679, 680.

50. Chicago, R. I. & P. R. Co. v. Igoe, C.A.7th, 1955, 220 F.2d 299, 302, certiorari denied 76 S.Ct. 49, 350 U.S. 822, 100 L.Ed. 735.

51. 220 F.2d at 304.

Though the Reviser's Notes to § 1404(a), on which the Supreme Court has consistently laid great stress, declare that the statute is drafted "in accordance with the doctrine of forum non conveniens," and in its earliest consideration of the statute the Court referred repeatedly to that doctrine,[52] it later held that § 1404(a) is something more than a mere codification of forum non conveniens and that transfer under the statute can be ordered on a lesser showing of inconvenience than would justify dismissal under forum non conveniens.[53]

The courts have recognized that plaintiff's venue privilege is still a factor to be considered, and that the burden is on the defendant to establish that another forum would be more convenient.[54] In determining where the suit is to be tried, they have looked, as the statute requires, to convenience of the parties,[55] convenience of witnesses,[56] and the interest of justice.[57] Usually the courts have insisted on documents showing that another forum would be more convenient, and have refused to order transfer on the basis of conclusory affidavits that trial where suit was brought would cause great expense and require importation of many witnesses. The courts have demanded that the moving party show what helpful testimony the distant witnesses would provide, and have taken into account that transportation companies, when defendants, have ready means to bring witnesses to the place of trial.[58] This same realistic approach has not always been displayed in determining what factors to consider. Some courts have refused to take into account the convenience of counsel [59] or the

---

52. Ex parte Collett, 1949, 69 S.Ct. 944, 337 U.S. 55, 93 L.Ed. 1207.

53. Norwood v. Kirkpatrick, 1955, 75 S.Ct. 544, 546, 349 U.S. 29, 32, 99 L.Ed. 789. In this rather surprising case, suit in Philadelphia by a Negro dining car employee who lived in that city was transferred to South Carolina, where the accident took place. Orthodox forum non conveniens doctrine would not have permitted dismissal where plaintiff sued in the district where he resided.

See also Piper Aircraft Co. v. Reyno, 1981, 102 S.Ct. 252, 264, ___ U.S. ___, ___, 70 L.Ed.2d 419.

Since a § 1404(a) motion and a motion to dismiss for forum non conveniens require "evaluations of similar, but by no means identical, objective criteria," a prior state court dismissal on grounds of forum non conveniens does not require a federal court sitting in the same state to order transfer. Parsons v. Chesapeake & O. Ry. Co., 1963, 84 S.Ct. 185, 375 U.S. 71, 11 L.Ed.2d 137.

54. 15 Wright, Miller & Cooper, Jurisdiction § 3848.

55. 15 Wright, Miller & Cooper, Jurisdiction § 3849.

56. 15 Wright, Miller & Cooper, Jurisdiction §§ 3851, 3853.

57. 15 Wright, Miller & Cooper, Jurisdiction § 3854.

58. E.g., Chicago, R. I. & P. R. Co. v. Hugh Breeding, Inc., C.A.10th, 1956, 232 F.2d 584; General Portland Cement Co. v. Perry, C.A.7th, 1954, 204 F.2d 316; Kaufman, Observations on Transfers Under Section 1404(a) of the New Judicial Code, 1951, 10 F.R.D. 595, 607; 15 Wright, Miller & Cooper, Jurisdiction § 3851.

59. E.g., Solomon v. Continental American Life Ins. Co., C.A.3d, 1973, 472 F.2d 1043, 1047; Chicago, R. I. & P. R. Co. v. Igoe, C.A.7th, 1955, 220 F.2d 299, 304, certiorari denied 76 S.Ct. 49, 350 U.S. 822, 100 L.Ed. 735. Contra: Miller v. National Broadcasting Co., D.C.Del.1956, 143 F.Supp. 78. See 15 Wright, Miller & Cooper, Jurisdiction § 3850.

availability of expert witnesses,[60] though these factors are relevant under forum non conveniens, and have not always viewed realistically racial prejudice where it is claimed to be a factor for or against transfer.[61]

An order granting or denying a § 1404(a) motion is not appealable as a final judgment, and ordinarily will not present a controlling question of law suitable for interlocutory review under 28 U.S.C.A. § 1292(b).[62] It is reviewable on appeal from a final judgment,[63] but by that time the matter will almost always be moot.[64] There have been many efforts to secure review by application for mandamus or prohibition. The use of such writs is proper where it is claimed that there was no power to make a transfer.[65] The circumstances under which the writs will be issued where it is claimed only that the trial court misapplied the statutory standards for transfer is a subject on which the decisions have been correctly said to be in "hopeless conflict." [66] Indeed there is such a variety of views that the decisions can only be considered circuit-by-circuit, [67] and even within a single circuit they are not always consistent. Nevertheless there has been "a growing recognition that 'it will be highly unfortunate if the result of an attempted procedural improvement is to subject parties to two lawsuits: first, prolonged litigation to determine the place where a case is to be tried; and, second, the merits of the alleged cause of action itself.' " [68] Accordingly there is a discernible tendency, despite

60. Compare Sypert v. Miner, C.A.7th, 1959, 266 F.2d 196 (refusing to consider expert witnesses), with Lykes Bros. S.S. Co., Inc. v. Sugarman, C.A.2d 1959, 272 F.2d 679, 681 (taking expert witnesses into account). See 15 Wright, Miller & Cooper, Jurisdiction § 3852.

61. Compare Kirk v. Spur Distributing Co., D.C.Del.1950, 95 F.Supp. 428, and Norwood v. Kirkpatrick, 1955, 75 S.Ct. 544, 349 U.S. 29, 99 L.Ed. 789, with Wilson v. Great Atlantic & Pac. Tea Co., D.C.Mo.1957, 156 F.Supp. 767.

See also Los Angeles Memorial Coliseum Comm. v. National Football League, D.C.Cal.1981, 89 F.R.D. 497. That was an antitrust action against the NFL seeking to make it possible for the Oakland Raiders to move to Los Angeles. A motion to transfer the suit, on the ground that jurors in Los Angeles would be prejudiced in favor of plaintiffs, was denied.

62. Ellicott Machine Corp. v. Modern Welding Co., Inc., C.A.4th, 1974, 502 F.2d 178; Garner v. Wolfinbarger, C.A. 5th, 1970, 433 F.2d 117; D'Ippolito v. American Oil Co., C.A.2d, 1968, 401 F.2d 764; and cases cited 15 Wright,

Miller & Cooper, Jurisdiction § 3855 nn. 1, 17–23.

63. E.g., Chicago, R. I. & P. R. Co. v. Hugh Breeding, Inc., C.A.10th, 1957, 247 F.2d 217, certiorari denied 78 S.Ct. 138, 355 U.S. 880, 2 L.Ed.2d 107. It should be noted that here the appellate court reversed the judgment below on other grounds and also reversed the trial court's refusal to transfer.

64. See In re Josephson, C.A.1st, 1954, 218 F.2d 174, 180; Note, Appealability of 1404(a) Orders: Mandamus Misapplied, 1957, 67 Yale L.J. 122, 124.

65. E.g., Hoffman v. Blaski, 1960, 80 S.Ct. 1084, 363 U.S. 335, 4 L.Ed.2d 1254; Van Dusen v. Barrack, 1964, 84 S.Ct. 805, 809 n. 3, 376 U.S. 612, 615, n. 3, 11 L.Ed.2d 945; and cases cited 15 Wright, Miller & Cooper, Jurisdiction § 3855 n. 24.

66. Clayton v. Warlick, C.A.4th, 1956, 232 F.2d 699, 703. See also Wilkins v. Erickson, C.A.8th, 1973, 484 F.2d 969, 971.

67. As is done in 15 Wright, Miller & Cooper, Jurisdiction § 3855.

68. Ellicott Machine Corp. v. Modern Welding Co., Inc., C.A.4th, 1974, 502

the differing reasons and formulations by the several courts of appeals, to restrict increasingly the possibility of interlocutory review.[69]

Section 1404(a) is an interesting experiment in judicial administration. It does not permit trial of every suit in the most convenient forum, but it is a step in that direction. The experiment cannot yet be pronounced a complete succes.[70]

F.2d 178, 181. The internal quotation is from All States Freight v. Modarelli, C.A.3d, 1952, 196 F.2d 1010, 1011–1012.

The American Law Institute accepts the views expressed in Judge Friendly's concurring opinion in A. Olinick & Sons v. Dempster Bros., Inc., C.A.2d, 1966, 365 F.2d 439, 445, and proposes to provide by statute that "the exercise of discretion by the district court on such a motion is not reviewable on appeal or otherwise." ALI Study, §§ 1305(a), 1306(a), 1315(a), 1327(a).

See Comment, Appellate Review of Sect. 1404(a) Orders—Misuse of an Extraordinary Writ, 1968, 1 J.Marsh.J. Prac. & Proc. 297.

69. Appellate review of forum non conveniens rulings is similar to that of § 1404(a) rulings. Castanho v. Jackson Marine, Inc., C.A.5th, 1981, 650 F.2d 546.

70. One critic has formed the harsh judgment that "it is better to bear with the small number of true hardship situations that would arise under a well drawn venue code than with the burdens which will inevitably result from a transfer provision like section 1404(a)." Kitch, Section 1404(a) of the Judicial Code: In the Interest of Justice or Injustice? 1965, 40 Ind.L.J. 99, 141–142. Professor Currie says that "the theory is good, but it is practically unworkable." Currie, The Federal Courts and the American Law Institute (Part II), 1969, 36 U.Chi.L.Rev. 268, 307.

See generally 15 Wright, Miller & Cooper, Jurisdiction § 3841.

CHAPTER 8

THE RELATIONS OF STATE AND FEDERAL COURTS

Analysis

§ 45. State Enforcement of Federal Law [1]

Congress has, beyond doubt, the power to give the federal courts exclusive jurisdiction of matters falling within the judicial power of the United States.[2] But unless Congress has made federal jurisdiction exclusive, either expressly or by fair implication, the state courts have concurrent jurisdiction with the federal courts, and a state court may entertain an action even though it is entirely based on a federal claim.[3]

At the Constitutional Convention, and in the framing of the Judiciary Act of 1789, the states-rights interests were opposed to the crea-

---

1. Redish & Muench, Adjudication of Federal Causes of Action in State Court, 1977, 75 Mich.L.Rev. 311; Cullison, State Courts, State Law, and Concurrent Jurisdiction of Federal Questions, 1963, 48 Iowa L.Rev. 230; Comment, State Court Jurisdiction Over Claims Arising Under Federal Law, 1982, 7 U.Day.L.Rev. 403; Note, State Enforcement of Federally Created Rights, 1960, 73 Harv.L.Rev. 1551.

2. See § 10 above; 13 Wright, Miller & Cooper, Jurisdiction 2d § 3527; Note, Exclusive Jurisdiction of the Federal Courts in Private Civil Actions, 1957, 70 Harv.L.Rev. 509; ALI Study, § 1311(b), and Commentary thereto.

3. "The general principle of state-court jurisdiction over cases arising under federal laws is straightforward: state courts may assume subject matter jurisdiction over a federal cause of action

absent provision by Congress to the contrary or disabling incompatibility between the federal claim and state-court adjudication." Gulf Offshore Co. v. Mobil Oil Corp., 1981, 101 S.Ct. 2870, 2875, 453 U.S. 473, 477–478, 69 L.Ed.2d 784. This rule dates back to Claflin v. Houseman, 1876, 93 U.S. 130, 136, 23 L.Ed. 833, where the Court drew heavily on the similar views about concurrent jurisdiction set forth in The Federalist, No. 82 (Hamilton).

In Redish & Muench, note 1 above, at 313–340, it is shown that the Claflin test has often been misunderstood by the courts and Congress, and an alternative test for determining whether federal jurisdiction is exclusive or concurrent is proposed. In the Gulf Offshore case, however, the Court ignored those criticisms, and was content merely to reaffirm the Claflin test.

tion of inferior federal courts, arguing that the state courts were sufficient to enforce federal law. This view, as has been seen, was rejected at that time.[4] As early as 1815 the states began to shift their ground, and to argue that they should not be required to entertain federal claims. For many years, though it was clear that the state courts could hear a federal claim, it was not clear whether they were required to do so. The question was finally resolved in the Second Employers' Liability Cases,[5] where it was held that claims arising under the Federal Employers' Liability Act could be enforced, as of right, in the courts of the states if their jurisdiction, as prescribed by local laws, was adequate to the occasion. The Connecticut court had held that enforcement of an FELA claim in state court was contrary to the policy of that state, but the Supreme Court found such reasoning quite inadmissible, holding that when Congress enacts a law it establishes a policy for all the states, which is as much the policy of Connecticut as if the act had emanated from its own legislature.

Some years later New York refused to entertain an FELA claim where the parties were Connecticut residents and the accident occurred in Connecticut, relying on a state statute that permitted actions by a nonresident against a foreign corporation only in certain classes of cases, of which the claim before it was not one. This refusal was held proper by the Supreme Court, which said "there is nothing in the Act of Congress that purports to force a duty upon such Courts as against an otherwise valid excuse."[6] It is not clear exactly what constitutes a "valid excuse." It is a valid excuse that the action falls within the state's conception of forum non conveniens, so long as the state applies that doctrine in all cases, regardless of their basis.[7]

It is not a valid excuse, however, that the statutes granting jurisdiction to the state court do not give it jurisdiction over a particular kind of action if the jurisdictional statutes discriminate against the claim in question because it is created by federal law. This was settled in McKnett v. St. Louis & San Francisco Railway Co.[8] An Alabama statute gave its courts jurisdiction over causes of action arising outside of the state if they were based on "common law or the statutes of another state." An FELA action was brought in Alabama for an injury that had occurred in Tennessee. The Alabama court refused to entertain the action, holding that the federal statute was neither part of the common law nor a statute of another state. A unanimous Supreme Court held that the Alabama statute, as so con-

4. See § 1 above.

5. 1912, 32 S.Ct. 169, 223 U.S. 1, 56 L.Ed. 327. These cases are also frequently cited under the name Mondou v. New York, N. H. & H. R. Co.

6. Douglas v. New York, N. H. & H. R. Co., 1929, 49 S.Ct. 355, 356, 279 U.S. 377, 388, 73 L.Ed. 747.

7. Missouri ex rel. Southern Ry. v. Mayfield, 1950, 71 S.Ct. 1, 340 U.S. 1, 95 L.Ed. 3.

8. 1934, 54 S.Ct. 690, 292 U.S. 230, 78 L.Ed. 1227, noted 1934, 48 Harv.L.Rev. 125. See also Comment, 1935, 33 Mich. L.Rev. 398.

strued, was unconstitutional and that Alabama was required to entertain the action. Since the Alabama court would have had jurisdiction
if the accident had occurred in Alabama, or, although the accident
occurred in Tennessee, if the defendant had been an Alabama corporation, the Supreme Court held that the ordinary jurisdiction of the
Alabama court was appropriate to enforce the federal claim. "The
denial of jurisdiction by the Alabama court is based solely upon the
source of law sought to be enforced. The plaintiff is cast out because he is suing to enforce a Federal Act. A state may not discriminate against rights arising under Federal laws." [9]

The cases considered thus far have involved what may be termed
remedial federal claims. Most state courts assumed, with support
from language in Supreme Court opinions and the writing of eminent
scholars, that they were under no duty to enforce federal penal statutes.[10] This was the reaction of the Rhode Island Supreme Court
when a case came to it in which a party sought treble damages for
sale of an automobile above the ceiling price. The Emergency Price
Control Act authorized such a suit for treble damages and provided
that the federal courts were to have jurisdiction of this kind of suit
"concurrently with State and Territorial courts." The Rhode Island
court reasoned that the treble damages provision was "a penal statute in the international sense," that a state need not enforce the penal laws of a government that is "foreign in the international sense,"
and that the United States was "foreign" to Rhode Island in the "private international" sense. From this syllogism, the court held that
suits for treble damages under this federal statute could not be maintained in the courts of the state.

The Supreme Court reversed unanimously, in Testa v. Katt.[11] It
could have reversed, on the basis of precedent, simply by holding that

9.   54 S.Ct. at 692, 292 U.S. at 234.

The McKnett principle, that there can be
no discrimination by the states against
federal claims, was applied by a state
court in an interesting situation. An
Illinois statute barred suit in the courts
of that state to recover damages for
deaths occurring outside Illinois. As
originally enacted the statute was non-
discriminatory. Later Supreme Court
decisions laid down the rule, however,
that, in view of the Full-Faith-and-
Credit Clause, Illinois could not refuse
to entertain actions brought under the
death acts of other states. The Illinois
Supreme Court held that "by the interplay of judicial decisions, instead of the
direct language of the statute," a discrimination against federal law had
been created, and that Illinois was constitutionally required to entertain an
FELA suit for a death occurring in Indiana. Allendorf v. Elgin, J. & E. R.

Co., 1956, 133 N.E.2d 288, 8 Ill.2d 164,
certiorari denied 77 S.Ct. 49, 352 U.S.
833, 1 L.Ed.2d 53.

10. See Warren, Federal Criminal Laws
and the State Courts, 1925, 38 Harv.L.
Rev. 545; Barnett, The Delegation of
Federal Jurisdiction to State Courts,
1909, 43 Am.L.Rev. 852, reprinted
1938, 3 Selected Essays on Constitutional Law 1202.

11. 1947, 67 S.Ct. 810, 330 U.S. 386, 91
L.Ed. 967. See Note, Utilization of
State Courts to Enforce Federal Penal
and Criminal Statutes: Development in
Judicial Federalism, 1947, 60 Harv.L.
Rev. 966.

The doctrine of this case and its prede-
cessors is questioned in Sandalow,
Henry v. Mississippi and the Adequate
State Ground: Proposals for a Revised
Doctrine, 1965 Sup.Ct.Rev. 187,
203–207.

the Emergency Price Control Act was remedial rather than penal.[12] Justice Black, speaking for the Court, chose instead to assume that the act was penal, and to hold that the states have no less duty to enforce federal penal statutes than they do to enforce federal remedial statutes. He relied heavily on the Supremacy Clause of Article VI, § 2, of the Constitution to reject the notion that the United States can be considered "foreign" to Rhode Island in any sense. Since it was conceded that the same type of claim arising under Rhode Island law would be enforced in the courts of that state, he found that they had jurisdiction adequate and appropriate under established local law to hear the action.

The Supreme Court has not yet considered whether Congress can require state courts to entertain federal claims when there is no analogous state-created right enforcible in the state courts. One commentator regards it as fortunate that ultimate questions such as this one do not often have to be faced.[13]

As recently as 1944, Justice Frankfurter could declare, in a concurring opinion, that when Congress does provide for enforcement of federal claims in state courts, it must "take the state courts as it finds them, subject to all the conditions for litigation in the state courts that the State has decreed for every other litigant who seeks access to its courts." [14] It is very doubtful whether a similar statement could be made today. Again most of the relevant law has been developed in FELA litigation.[15]

In Minneapolis & St. L. R. Co. v. Bombolis,[16] decided in 1916, the Supreme Court held that a unanimous verdict is not required of a state court jury hearing an FELA action, even though the Seventh

---

12. See Huntington v. Attrill, 1892, 13 S.Ct. 224, 230, 146 U.S. 657, 673–674, 36 L.Ed. 1123.

13. Hart, The Relations between State and Federal Law, 1954, 54 Col.L.Rev. 489, 507–508.

Note, State Enforcement of Federally Created Rights, 1960, 73 Harv.L.Rev. 1551, 1556, says that "at least in certain circumstances, a proper accommodation of the federal and state interests is not inconsistent with allowing Congress to impose upon state courts the duty to enforce non-analogous federally created rights."

But see Redish & Muench, note 1 above, at 350–351, where it is said that "none of the Supreme Court's state obligation cases explicitly employ the 'analogous state-created' terminology when addressing the valid excuse issue. In fact, there is serious question whether the doctrine is anything more than a product of commentators' unfounded speculation."

In Martinez v. California, 1980, 100 S.Ct. 553, 558 n. 7, 444 U.S. 277, 283 n. 7, 62 L.Ed.2d 481, the Court held that a state court may entertain a civil rights claim under 42 U.S.C.A. § 1983, and added: "We have never considered, however, the question whether a State *must* entertain a claim under § 1983. We note that where the same type of claim, if arising under state law, would be enforced in the state courts, the state courts are generally not free to refuse enforcement of the federal claim."

14. Brown v. Gerdes, 1944, 64 S.Ct. 487, 493, 321 U.S. 178, 190, 88 L.Ed. 659 (concurring opinion).

15. Hill, Substance and Procedure in State FELA Actions—The Converse of the Erie Problem?, 1956, 17 Ohio St. L.J. 384; Note, State Enforcement of Federally Created Rights, 1960, 73 Harv.L.Rev. 1551, 1561–1564.

16. 1916, 36 S.Ct. 595, 241 U.S. 211, 60 L.Ed. 961.

Amendment would require unanimity had suit been brought in federal court. The case was commonly understood as standing for the proposition that a litigant who chooses to assert his federal claim in state court gets the benefit of the federal substantive law but is obliged to accept the usual state procedure. In those earlier days there were opinions that raised doubt as to where to draw the line between substance and procedure, but there was no doubt that there was some area of procedure that the state could continue to regulate for itself even in federal claim cases. Perhaps this is still true today, but if so this area of procedure has become so shrunken as to fall within the maxim *de minimis*. Thus it is now held that in an FELA case the state cannot apply its usual rule that pleadings are to be construed strictly against the pleader, but instead must construe the pleading as liberally as possible in favor of the pleader.[17] If this is not procedure, it is hard to know what is. Again the Supreme Court has held that in an FELA case a state cannot follow its usual rule, with respectable equitable antecedents, that it is for the court to decide whether a release is invalid because of fraud, and instead must submit this question to the jury.[18] The Court in this latter case purports to distinguish the Bombolis case with the surprising suggestion that the state might abolish jury trial in all negligence cases, but that so long as it has not done so it cannot single out the one issue of fraudulent releases and deny the employee jury trial as to that issue. This is such a difficult distinction to defend that it may reasonably be doubted whether the Bombolis decision has any continuing authoritativeness beyond its particular facts.

Some commentators have read the cases just discussed as laying down a rule peculiar to FELA litigation, and have believed that in other types of cases the state courts can still apply state procedure to federal claims. It is certainly true that the Supreme Court has been astute to protect the rights of FELA plaintiffs. But even if the FELA cases are unique, they stand for the proposition that Congress

17. Brown v. Western Ry. of Alabama, 1949, 70 S.Ct. 105, 338 U.S. 294, 94 L.Ed. 100.

18. Dice v. Akron, C. & Y. R. Co., 1952, 72 S.Ct. 312, 342 U.S. 359, 96 L.Ed. 398.

See also Bowman v. Illinois Central R. Co., 1957, 142 N.E.2d 104, 11 Ill.2d 186, certiorari denied 78 S.Ct. 63, 355 U.S. 837, 2 L.Ed.2d 49, noted 1958, 71 Harv. L.Rev. 730, where the Illinois court held that the appellate courts of that state cannot order a new trial in an FELA case on the ground that the verdict is against the weight of the evidence—though they have the power to do so in common-law actions—since in the federal system only the trial court can order a new trial on this ground.

In Norfolk & W. Ry. Co. v. Liepelt, 1980, 100 S.Ct. 755, 444 U.S. 490, 62 L.Ed.2d 689, it was held that a state court in an FELA action must allow evidence of the income taxes that would have been payable on the decedent's future earnings, which seems clearly to go to the measure of damages and thus to be "substantive," and it was also held that the state court must give a cautionary instruction that the award of damages would not be subject to income taxation, a matter that two dissenters thought to be one of the "ordinary incidents of state procedure," which should be governed by state law.

has constitutional power to control the incidents of a state trial of a federal claim.[19]

Usually the federal law that a state court is called upon to enforce is statutory, but this need not always be the case. There is an expanding area of "federal common law," involving matters in which the federal interest is so strong that the federal courts are free to develop substantive rules to protect that interest.[20] When an issue of this nature arises in a state action, the state court must enforce the federal doctrine rather than its own law.[21]

§ 46. State Attempts to Limit Federal Jurisdiction [1]

Article III of the Constitution and the Acts of Congress made pursuant thereto define the jurisdiction of the federal courts. State statutes are irrelevant in this connection. The states have not attempted to extend the jurisdiction of the federal courts. Their persistent attempts to limit federal jurisdiction have been almost uniformly unsuccessful.

A key case is Railway Co. v. Whitton's Administrator.[2] The Wisconsin wrongful death statute provided that the right it created could be enforced only in a Wisconsin state court. Despite this limitation, it was held that a federal court could entertain a suit under the statute where diversity was present. Justice Field said for the Court: "Whenever a general rule as to property or personal rights, or injuries to either, is established by State legislation, its enforcement by a Federal court in a case between proper parties is a matter of course, and the jurisdiction of the court, in such case, is not subject to State limitation." [3]

---

19. See Note, Procedural Protection for Federal Rights in State Courts, 1961, 30 U.Cin.L.Rev. 184.

See also Gulf Offshore Co. v. Mobil Oil Corp., 1981, 101 S.Ct. 2870, 2879–2880, 453 U.S. 473, 485–488, 69 L.Ed.2d 784.

20. See § 60 below.

21. Free v. Bland, 1962, 82 S.Ct. 1089, 369 U.S. 663, 8 L.Ed.2d 180. See also Local 174, Teamsters, Chauffeurs, Warehousemen & Helpers of America v. Lucas Flour Co., 1962, 82 S.Ct. 571, 576–577, 369 U.S. 95, 102–104, 7 L.Ed. 2d 593, holding that the body of federal labor law that § 301(a) of the Taft-Hartley Act, 29 U.S.C.A. § 185(a), requires the federal courts to fashion is binding on the state courts.

See Comment, The State Courts and the Federal Common Law, 1963, 27 Alb.L. Rev. 73, which discusses also the interesting question of the weight state courts should give to decisions of lower federal courts when the state court is applying federal law. On that point,

see U. S. ex rel. Lawrence v. Woods, C.A.7th, 1970, 432 F.2d 1072, 1075–1076, certiorari denied 1971, 91 S.Ct. 1658, 402 U.S. 983, 29 L.Ed.2d 148, noted 1971, 25 Sw.L.J. 478, 24 Vand.L.Rev. 627.

[§ 46]

1. 17 Wright, Miller & Cooper, Jurisdiction §§ 4211–4213; Meador, State Law and the Federal Judicial Power, 1963, 49 Va.L.Rev. 1082.

2. 1871, 13 Wall. 270, 20 L.Ed. 571. The case is sometimes cited by the fuller title Chicago & N. W. R. Co. v. Whitton's Admr.

See also the earlier case of Suydam v. Broadnax, 1840, 14 Pet. 67, 10 L.Ed. 357, holding that a state statute providing that no suit should be commenced or sustained against an executor or administrator after the estate had been declared insolvent would not abate such a suit instituted in federal court.

3. 13 Wall. at 286.

In accord with this principle, the state cannot by statute bar removal of cases from state to federal court, even as a condition to permitting a foreign corporation to do business in the state.[4] It cannot defeat federal jurisdiction of a matter judicial in nature by confiding jurisdiction to a specialized state court, such as a probate court.[5]

Under the Eleventh Amendment a state is immune from suit in federal court unless it consents.[6] It can consent to suit in its own courts without waiving its Eleventh Amendment immunity.[7] The Eleventh Amendment does not provide immunity for counties and similar municipal corporations. These bodies are suable in federal court, even though the state statutes creating them purport to limit suit to state court.[8]

A few lower courts have held that the conformity to state law required in diversity cases by the Erie doctrine means that the federal

---

4. Home Ins. Co. v. Morse, 1874, 20 Wall. 445, 22 L.Ed. 365; Terral v. Burke Constr. Co., 1922, 42 S.Ct. 188, 257 U.S. 529, 66 L.Ed. 352. See § 38 above.

5. Payne v. Hook, 1869, 7 Wall. 425, 19 L.Ed. 260; McClellan v. Carland, 1910, 30 S.Ct. 501, 217 U.S. 268, 54 L.Ed. 762; Greyhound Lines, Inc. v. Lexington State Bank & Trust Co., C.A.8th, 1979, 604 F.2d 1151; Beach v. Rome Trust Co., C.A.2d, 1959, 269 F.2d 367; 13 Wright, Miller & Cooper, Jurisdiction § 3610.

A similar result was reached where a state statute provided that unlawful detainer actions be brought only before a magistrate. Rubel-Jones Agency, Inc. v. Jones, D.C.Mo.1958, 165 F.Supp. 652.

6. See generally 13 Wright, Miller & Cooper, Jurisdiction § 3524; Jacobs, The Eleventh Amendment and Sovereign Immunity, 1972; Redish, Federal Jurisdiction: Tensions in the Allocation of Judicial Power, 1980, c. 6; Field, The Eleventh Amendment and Other Sovereign Immunity Doctrines, 1978, 126 U.Pa.L.Rev. 515, 1203; Baker, Federalism and the Eleventh Amendment, 1977, 48 U.Colo.L.Rev. 139.

Consent need not be express. Implied consent was found where a state acted under an interstate compact that had been approved by Congress, Petty v. Tennessee-Missouri Bridge Comm., 1959, 79 S.Ct. 785, 359 U.S. 275, 3 L.Ed.2d 804, and where a state commenced operation of a railroad after enactment of the Federal Employers' Liability Act. Parden v. Terminal Ry., 1964, 84 S.Ct. 1207, 377 U.S. 184, 12 L.Ed.2d 333. See Comment, Sovereign

Immunity of States Engaged in Commercial Activities, 1965, 65 Col.L.Rev. 1086; Comment, Private Suits Against States in the Federal Courts, 1966, 33 U.Chi.L.Rev. 331. However, more recent cases have shown the Court reluctant to find an implied waiver of the Eleventh Amendment immunity. Employees of Dept. of Public Health & Welfare v. Department of Public Health & Welfare, 1973, 93 S.Ct. 1614, 411 U.S. 279, 36 L.Ed.2d 251; Edelman v. Jordan, 1974, 94 S.Ct. 1347, 415 U.S. 651, 39 L.Ed.2d 662.

Congress can remove a state's Eleventh Amendment immunity when Congress is legislating under § 5 of the Fourteenth Amendment. Fitzpatrick v. Bitzer, 1976, 96 S.Ct. 2666, 427 U.S. 445, 49 L.Ed.2d 614. See Note, Reconciling Federalism and Individual Rights: The Burger Court's Treatment of the Eleventh and Fourteenth Amendments, 1982, 68 Va.L.Rev. 865.

7. Smith v. Reeves, 1900, 20 S.Ct. 919, 178 U.S. 436, 44 L.Ed. 1140; Great Northern Life Ins. Co. v. Read, 1944, 64 S.Ct. 873, 322 U.S. 47, 88 L.Ed. 1121; Ford Motor Co. v. Department of Treasury of Indiana, 1945, 65 S.Ct. 347, 323 U.S. 459, 89 L.Ed. 389; Kennecott Copper Corp. v. State Tax Comm., 1946, 66 S.Ct. 745, 327 U.S. 573, 90 L.Ed. 862; Note, Waiver of State Immunity to Suit With Special Reference to Suits in Federal Courts, 1947, 45 Mich.L.Rev. 348.

8. Mount Healthy City Sch. Dist. v. Doyle, 1977, 97 S.Ct. 568, 429 U.S. 274, 50 L.Ed.2d 471; Lincoln County v. Luning, 1890, 10 S.Ct. 363, 133 U.S. 529, 33 L.Ed. 766.

court must honor a state statute that limits its waiver of tort immunity for governmental subdivisions only to suits brought in the state courts, or in a specialized state court.[9] The argument is unsound, and was effectively refuted by Judge Haynsworth, speaking for the Fourth Circuit, when he said: "It would be quite foreign to the Erie doctrine, however, to apply a state statute in such a way as to deny all relief in a federal court to a nonresident plaintiff on a cause of action which, clearly, the state courts would recognize and enforce. Erie requires that the federal court grant or withhold relief as the state courts would. It does not require relegation of the diversity jurisdiction to the mercies of the legislatures of fifty separate states." [10]

There is one respect in which the Erie doctrine does give the states a means of limiting indirectly federal jurisdiction. If a state closes its doors to a particular class of litigant or claim, a federal court, exercising diversity jurisdiction, cannot entertain a suit by such a litigant or on such a claim. The rule was contrary prior to the Erie case, [11] but Erie is said to have made the earlier decisions obsolete. In two controversial cases the Supreme Court held that a federal court cannot hear a case that the state court would not hear whether the right asserted is one created by another state [12] or by the forum state.[13] If the right is created by federal law, however, it can be heard in federal court regardless of whether the state has closed its

9. Markham v. City of Newport News, D.C.Va.1960,   184   F.Supp.   659, criticised 1961, 109 U.Pa.L.Rev. 428, reversed C.A.4th, 1961, 292 F.2d 711; Zeidner v. Wulforst, D.C.N.Y.1961, 197 F.Supp. 23, criticised 1962, 75 Harv.L. Rev. 1433; Kohlasch v. New York State Thruway Auth., D.C.N.Y.1978, 460 F.Supp. 956.

10. Markham v. City of Newport News, C.A.4th, 1961, 292 F.2d 711, 718, noted approvingly 1962, 48 Corn.L.Q. 192, 75 Harv.L.Rev. 1433, 23 U.Pitts.L.Rev. 800, 36 Tul.L.Rev. 351. To the same effect, see Baton Rouge Contracting Co. v. West Hatchie Drainage Dist., D.C.Miss.1968, 279 F.Supp. 430; S. J. Groves & Sons Co. v. New Jersey Turnpike Auth., D.C.N.J.1967, 268 F.Supp. 568; Sherman v. Ulmer, D.C. Pa.1961, 201 F.Supp. 660.

11. David Lupton's Sons v. Automobile Club of America, 1912, 32 S.Ct. 711, 225 U.S. 489, 56 L.Ed. 1177.

12. A federal court sitting in North Carolina could not entertain a suit for a deficiency judgment arising out of a Virginia mortgage where a state statute precluded deficiency judgments. Angel v. Bullington, 1947, 67 S.Ct. 657,

330 U.S. 183, 91 L.Ed. 832. See Meador, note 1 above, at 1088–1090; Farinholt, Angel v. Bullington: Twilight of Diversity Jurisdiction?, 1947, 26 N.C.L.Rev. 29; Note, 1947, 33 Va.L. Rev. 739.

13. Where a state statute bars suit in state court by a corporation that has not qualified to do business in that state, the federal court cannot hear a suit by the corporation, even though the state statute does not void the transaction on which suit is brought. Woods v. Interstate Realty Co., 1949, 69 S.Ct. 1235, 337 U.S. 535, 93 L.Ed. 1524. See Stewart, The Federal "Door-Closing" Doctrine, 1954, 11 Wash. & Lee L.Rev. 154.

See also Power City Communications, Inc. v. Calaveras Tel. Co., D.C.Cal. 1968, 280 F.Supp. 808. But cf. Avondale Shipyards, Inc. v. Propulsion Systems, Inc., D.C.La.1971, 53 F.R.D. 341, holding that Rule 13(a) requires assertion of a compulsory counterclaim and that this can be done even though the defendant would be barred from bringing suit, or asserting a counterclaim, on its claim because it has not qualified to do business in the state.

doors—or validly could close its doors [14]—to such a suit.[15]   Even in a
diversity case, the continued authoritativeness of the Supreme Court
decisions requiring "door-closing" statutes to be followed has been
doubted.[16]   The Fourth Circuit has held that a district court may entertain a suit by a nonresident against a foreign corporation on a
cause of action arising in another state despite a statutory bar to
such a suit in the state courts.[17]   It held that the state statute did not
embody any important policy that would be frustrated by the application of a different rule in federal court, and that the state interest
was outweighed by such countervailing federal considerations as the
grant of diversity jurisdiction to avoid discrimination against nonresidents, the policy of maximum enforcement in each state of rights created by sister states, and the federal interest in encouraging efficient
joinder in multiparty actions.[18]

    Since the states cannot limit the jurisdiction of the federal courts,
they cannot enjoin proceedings in federal courts, except to protect the
jurisdiction of the state court over property in its custody or under its
control.[19]   They cannot interfere with the continued prosecution of

---

14. See § 45 above.

15. Holmberg v. Ambrecht, 1946, 66
S.Ct. 582, 327 U.S. 392, 90 L.Ed. 743.
This distinction is stated, and the
Holmberg case cited to support it, in
Angel v. Bullington, 1947, 67 S.Ct. 657,
662, 330 U.S. 183, 192, 91 L.Ed. 832.

16. See the article by Dean Meador,
note 1 above.

But in Hanna v. Plumer, 1965, 85 S.Ct.
1136, 1143, 380 U.S. 460, 469, 14 L.Ed.
2d 8, the Court distinguished the case
before it from one in which "application of the state rule would wholly bar
recovery," and cited the Woods case,
note 13 above, as an example of such a
situation.

17. Szantay v. Beech Aircraft Corp.,
C.A.4th, 1965, 349 F.2d 60, noted 1965,
17 S.C.L.Rev. 631, 1966, 51 Corn.L.Q.
560.

See also Sun Sales Corp. v. Block Land,
Inc., C.A.3d, 1972, 456 F.2d 857, holding that a Pennsylvania statute barring
suit for services by an unlicensed real
estate broker could not bar a New
York firm not doing business in Pennsylvania from bringing a diversity action in Pennsylvania, and Foxco Indus.,
Ltd. v. Fabric World, Inc., C.A.5th,
1979, 595 F.2d 976, holding that a state
"door-closing" statute cannot be applied to a corporation if its activities in
the state are entirely in the course of
interstate commerce.

18. The case described in the text was
limited, however, in Bumgardner v.

Keene Corp., C.A.4th, 1979, 593 F.2d
572.   In the Bumgardner case the
plaintiff could have brought suit in
North Carolina, where he lived and
worked, and thus had an alternate forum in which he could gain full relief.
For this reason, it was held that the
countervailing federal considerations
that justified ignoring the South Carolina statute in the Szantay case, note
17 above, were not present.

See also McCollum Aviation, Inc. v. Cim
Associates, Inc., D.C.Fla.1977, 438
F.Supp. 245.

19. Donovan v. City of Dallas, 1964, 84
S.Ct. 1579, 377 U.S. 408, 12 L.Ed.2d
409.   See 17 Wright, Miller & Cooper,
Jurisdiction § 4212;   Arnold, State
Power To Enjoin Federal Court Proceedings, 1965, 51 Va.L.Rev. 59;   Comment, State Injunction of Proceedings
in Federal Courts, 1965, 75 Yale L.J.
150;   Comment, Anti-Suit Injunctions
Between State and Federal Courts,
1965, 32 U.Chi.L.Rev. 471.

The American Law Institute adopts the
view of the dissenters in the Donovan
case and would also allow an injunction
"where necessary to protect against
vexatious and harassing relitigation of
matters determined by an existing
judgment of the State court in a civil
action."   ALI Study, § 1373(2).

Even if a state action is in rem or quasi-
in-rem, the state court cannot enjoin a
federal in personam action.   Meridian
Investing & Development Corp. v. Sun-

pending federal actions nor can they bar commencement of a federal suit in the future.[20]

The state courts cannot interfere with the exercise of federal jurisdiction by granting habeas corpus for discharge of a person held in federal custody.[21] On a somewhat related issue, the Supreme Court never decided whether state courts can enjoin federal officers.[22] In the light of 1976 legislation making it always possible for such suits against federal officers to be brought in federal court, the principal argument for allowing state injunctions against federal officers has become moot.[23]

§ 47. Federal Injunctions Against State Proceedings [1]

For almost as long as there have been federal courts, there has been a statutory prohibition against issuance of a writ of injunction "to stay proceedings in any court of a state." First enacted in 1793,[2] for reasons that are obscure,[3] the statute was not significantly

coast Highland Corp., C.A.5th, 1980, 628 F.2d 370.

20. General Atomic Co. v. Felter, 1977, 98 S.Ct. 76, 434 U.S. 12, 54 L.Ed.2d 199. See also the same case 1978, 98 S.Ct. 1939, 436 U.S. 493, 56 L.Ed.2d 480.

It is argued in Hornstein & Magle, State Court Power to Enjoin Federal Judicial Proceedings: Donovan v. City of Dallas Revisited, 1982, 60 Wash.U.L.Q. 1, that a state court may enjoin commencement of a suit in federal court if the federal court would lack jurisdiction of the suit. In addition, the authors contend that in such a situation the determination by the state court that the federal courts would lack jurisdiction has preclusive effect and must be followed by the federal court if a party should defy the state court injunction and commence suit in federal court. The argument is novel, but ultimately unpersuasive.

21. Ableman v. Booth, 1859, 21 How. 506, 16 L.Ed. 169; Tarble's Case, 1872, 13 Wall. 397, 20 L.Ed. 597; Robb v. Connolly, 1884, 4 S.Ct. 544, 111 U.S. 624, 28 L.Ed. 542; see Eisentrager v. Forrestal, C.A.1949, 174 F.2d 961, 966, 84 U.S.App.D.C. 396.

See also Hagan, Ableman v. Booth, 1931, 17 A.B.A.J. 19; Warren, Federal and State Court Interference, 1930, 43 Harv.L.Rev. 345, 347–359.

If the United States consents, a state court may issue a writ of habeas corpus to bring a federal prisoner before the state court for trial. Ponzi v. Fessenden, 1922, 42 S.Ct. 309, 258 U.S.

254, 66 L.Ed. 607. See Smith v. Hooey, 1969, 89 S.Ct. 575, 393 U.S. 374, 21 L.Ed.2d 607.

22. Compare Arnold, The Power of State Courts to Enjoin Federal Officers, 1964, 73 Yale L.J. 1385, with Warren, Federal and State Court Interference, 1930, 43 Harv.L.Rev. 345, 358. It was held that the state court lacked this power in Pennsylvania Turnpike Comm. v. McGinnes, D.C.Pa.1959, 179 F.Supp. 578, affirmed C.A.3d, 1960, 278 F.2d 330, certiorari denied 81 S.Ct. 57, 364 U.S. 820, 5 L.Ed.2d 51.

23. See 17 Wright, Miller & Cooper, Jurisdiction § 4213.

[§ 47]

1. 17 Wright, Miller & Cooper, Jurisdiction §§ 4221–4226; ALI Study § 1372 and Commentary thereto; Mayton, Ersatz Federalism Under the Anti-Injunction Statute, 1978, 78 Col.L.Rev. 320; Redish, The Anti-Injunction Statute Reconsidered, 1977, 44 U.Chi.L.Rev. 717; Reaves & Golden, The Federal Anti-Injunction Statute in the Aftermath of Atlantic Coast Line Railroad, 1971, 5 Ga.L.Rev. 294.

2. Act of March 2, 1793, c. 22, § 5, 1 Stat. 334.

3. The possible theories are reviewed in Toucey v. New York Life Ins. Co., 1941, 62 S.Ct. 139, 142–143, 314 U.S. 118, 130–132, 86 L.Ed. 100. It is variously suggested that the statute stems from a 1790 report of Attorney General Edmund Randolph, that it was a response to the unpopular decision two weeks before in Chisholm v. Georgia,

changed in form until the revision of the Judicial Code in 1948.[4] Whatever may have motivated its original adoption, the statute has an important role in a federal system since it is well calculated "to prevent needless friction between state and federal courts." [5]

Until 1941, however, the effectiveness of the statute was diminished by restrictive construction and judge-made exceptions.[6] In that year, in the familiar case of Toucey v. New York Life Insurance Co.,[7] the Court changed its approach to construction of the statute. The precise issue in Toucey was whether an insurance company, which had successfully defended a claim against it in federal court, could enjoin relitigation of the claim in a state court by a person to whom the claimant had assigned his claim in order to defeat diversity and prevent removal. Could the federal courts use their injunctive power, despite the prohibition of the statute, "to save the defendants in the state proceedings the inconvenience of pleading and proving res judicata"? [8] Only seven years before the Court had unanimously held that a federal bankruptcy court could use its injunctive powers to save the bankrupt the inconvenience of pleading and proving discharge in bankruptcy in a later state action.[9] Other cases seemed to support the view that an injunction could issue against relitigation of a matter already decided in federal court.[10] Nevertheless in Toucey the answer was "No."

1793, 2 Dall. 419, 1 L.Ed. 440, holding that a state could be sued in federal court by a citizen of another state, or that it reflected the prevailing prejudices against equity jurisdiction. The legislative history is silent.

It has recently been suggested that the purpose of the 1793 statute was to bar injunctions, while allowing the use of common-law certiorari to stay state proceedings, Comment, Federal Court Stays of State Court Proceedings: A Re-Examination of Original Congressional Intent, 1971, 38 U.Chi.L.Rev. 612, or that it was intended to give single Justices authority to grant the writ of injunction, with the proviso that this authority not be used to stay a proceeding in state court. Mayton, note 1 above, at 332–338. These arguments are plausible, but it seems unlikely that the Court will abandon its firm perception of the intent of the statute if it should be persuaded that a change from a colon to a semicolon during the legislative process in 1793 was accidental rather than deliberate.

4. An express exception for cases where the bankruptcy laws authorized such an injunction was added in 1874. Rev. Stat. § 720. The provision was carried in this form as § 265 of the Judicial Code of 1911, formerly § 379 of 28 U.S.C.A. The present statute is 28 U.S.C.A. § 2283.

5. Oklahoma Packing Co. v. Oklahoma Gas & Elec. Co., 1940, 60 S.Ct. 215, 218, 309 U.S. 4, 9, 84 L.Ed. 447, 537.

See also Atlantic Coast Line R. Co. v. Brotherhood of Locomotive Engineers, 1970, 90 S.Ct. 1739, 1742–1743, 398 U.S. 281, 285–286, 26 L.Ed.2d 234.

6. For able discussions of this period in the history of the statute, see Durfee & Sloss, Federal Injunctions against Proceedings in State Courts: The Life History of a Statute, 1932, 30 Mich.L. Rev. 1145; Taylor & Willis, The Power of Federal Courts to Enjoin Proceedings in State Courts, 1933, 42 Yale L.J. 1169.

7. 1941, 62 S.Ct. 139, 314 U.S. 118, 86 L.Ed. 100.

8. 62 S.Ct. at 142, 314 U.S. at 129.

9. Local Loan Co. v. Hunt, 1934, 54 S.Ct. 695, 292 U.S. 234, 78 L.Ed. 1230. Though involving a discharged bankrupt, the case did not come within the statutory exception to the anti-injunction statute dealing with bankruptcy.

10. E.g., Looney v. Eastern Texas Ry. Co., 1918, 38 S.Ct. 460, 247 U.S. 214, 62 L.Ed. 1084; Supreme Tribe of Ben Hur v. Cauble, 1921, 41 S.Ct. 338, 255 U.S. 356, 65 L.Ed. 673.

Justice Frankfurter, speaking for the Court, did not confine himself to the precise issue raised by Toucey but dealt comprehensively with the history and meaning of the statute. He recognized that, in addition to the exception for certain bankruptcy matters specifically written into the statute in 1874, other statutes, dealing with removal of actions, limitation of shipowners' liability, interpleader, and relief for farmers under the Frazier-Lemke Act, authorized injunctions against state proceedings and had to be regarded as implied statutory exceptions to the anti-injunction statute. He was willing to acknowledge, however, only one non-statutory exception. The rule by this time was quite well settled that while in personam actions involving the same claim could proceed simultaneously in state and federal court, and the federal court was not to enjoin such a state action even though the federal action had been commenced first,[11] if the action was in rem the court first obtaining jurisdiction over the res could enjoin suits in other courts involving the same res.[12]

All other exceptions not justified by statute Justice Frankfurter rejected. There was a line of cases holding that enforcement of a judgment was not part of the state court "proceedings," and could be enjoined if the judgment had been obtained by fraud or if its enforcement was otherwise not in accord with equity and good conscience.[13] These cases were said to be "very doubtful," [14] but in any event had no application to the issue presented in Toucey. For the same reason he found it unnecessary to pass on cases holding that the statute did not bar an injunction against commencing a state action.[15] The opinion held clearly, however, that there was no exception for "relitigation" cases. Some of the cases thought to support such an exception were written off as actions in rem.[16] Of the cases that could not be so disposed, the Court said that "loose language and a sporadic, ill-considered decision cannot be held to have imbedded in our law a doctrine which so patently violates the expressed prohibition of Con-

11. Kline v. Burke Constr. Co., 1922, 43 S.Ct. 79, 260 U.S. 226, 67 L.Ed. 226, noted 1923, 36 Harv.L.Rev. 461; Vestal, Repetitive Litigation, 1960, 45 Iowa L.Rev. 525.

12. Hagan v. Lucas, 1836, 10 Pet. 400, 9 L.Ed. 470; Julian v. Central Trust Co., 1903, 24 S.Ct. 399, 193 U.S. 93, 48 L.Ed. 629; Lion Bonding & Surety Co. v. Karatz, 1923, 43 S.Ct. 480, 262 U.S. 77, 67 L.Ed. 871; see Kline v. Burke Constr. Co., 1922, 43 S.Ct. 79, 260 U.S. 226, 67 L.Ed. 226; Warren, Federal and State Court Interference, 1930, 43 Harv.L.Rev. 345, 359–366; 14 Wright, Miller & Cooper, Jurisdiction § 3631.

13. Marshall v. Holmes, 1891, 12 S.Ct. 62, 141 U.S. 589, 35 L.Ed. 870; Ex parte Simon, 1908, 28 S.Ct. 238, 208 U.S. 144, 52 L.Ed. 429; Wells Fargo & Co. v. Taylor, 1920, 41 S.Ct. 93, 254 U.S. 175, 65 L.Ed. 205; Note, Relief against State Judgments Obtained by Fraud, 1945, 54 Yale L.J. 687.

14. 62 S.Ct. at 145, 314 U.S. at 136.

15. Ex parte Young, 1908, 28 S.Ct. 441, 209 U.S. 123, 52 L.Ed. 714; cf. Hale v. Bimco Trading, Inc., 1939, 59 S.Ct. 526, 306 U.S. 375, 83 L.Ed. 771. This exception from the statute had been criticised as illogical in Warren, Federal and State Court Interference, 1930, 43 Harv.L.Rev. 345, 372–376.

16. Local Loan Co. v. Hunt, 1934, 54 S.Ct. 695, 292 U.S. 234, 78 L.Ed. 1230, discussed note 9 above, on which the dissenters placed heavy reliance, was thus disposed of by Justice Frankfurter, 62 S.Ct. at 145 n. 6, 314 U.S. at 135 n. 6.

gress." [17] The insurance company was not permitted to escape the inconvenience of pleading and proving res judicata in the state court.

Despite the care and comprehensiveness of the Toucey opinion, it proved unpersuasive to the authors of the 1948 Judicial Code. In the Reviser's Note to § 2283 the dissenting opinion in Toucey was spoken of favorably, and it was said that "the revised section restores the basic law as generally understood and interpreted prior to the Toucey decision." Section 2283, as adopted in 1948, says: "A court of the United States may not grant an injunction to stay proceedings in a State court except as expressly authorized by Act of Congress, or where necessary in aid of its jurisdiction, or to protect or effectuate its judgments."

The revised statute is not a model of clear draftsmanship.[18] The Supreme Court has often been called upon to construe it, and even with these constructions questions remain. In the first such case the issue was whether a federal court could enjoin a state court from restraining peaceful picketing, when the state court lacked jurisdiction to issue such a restraint since Congress had preempted the field and entrusted such matters to the National Labor Relations Board. The Court held that the federal court could not enjoin the state court.[19] With Justice Frankfurter again spokesman for the majority, the Court said that § 2283 "is not a statute conveying a broad general policy for appropriate ad hoc application. Legislative policy is here expressed in a clear-cut prohibition qualified only by specifically defined exceptions." [20] Two years later, however, the prohibition was thought to be something less than "clear-cut," and implied exceptions were discovered. The issue was whether § 2283 barred an injunction against state proceedings where the United States sought the injunction. The Court unanimously agreed that it did not. Justice Frank-

---

17. 62 S.Ct. at 147, 314 U.S. at 139.

18. "* * * [A]ny amendment should properly solve more questions than it raises. The proposed revision does not appear to have this virtue." Barrett, Federal Injunctions against Proceedings in State Courts, 1947, 35 Calif.L. Rev. 545, 563.

"* * * [T]he anti-injunction statute is rife with inadequacies and ambiguities." Redish, note 1 above, at 760.

Experience has shown that the 1948 revision "has not resolved the problems of interpretation, but rather seems to have generated new confusion." Comment, Anti-Suit Injunctions between State and Federal Courts, 1965, 32 U.Chi.L.Rev. 471, 482.

19. Amalgamated Clothing Workers v. Richman Bros., 1955, 75 S.Ct. 452, 348 U.S. 511, 99 L.Ed. 600. Such a federal injunction against enforcement of a state court injunction was held proper when sought by the Labor Board. Capital Serv., Inc. v. N L R B, 1954, 74 S.Ct. 699, 347 U.S. 501, 98 L.Ed. 887. Prior to the 1948 revision it had been held that the anti-injunction statute did not apply where Congress had preempted jurisdiction to the exclusion of state courts. Bowles v. Willingham, 1944, 64 S.Ct. 641, 321 U.S. 503, 88 L.Ed. 892. See also Kochery, Conflict of Jurisdiction: 28 U.S.C.A. § 2283 and Exclusive Jurisdiction, 1955, 4 Buff.L. Rev. 269; Comment, Power of a Federal Court to Enjoin State Court Action in Aid of Its Exclusive Jurisdiction, 1953, 48 Nw.U.L.Rev. 383.

See T. Smith & Son, Inc. v. Williams, C.A. 5th, 1960, 275 F.2d 397.

20. Amalgamated Clothing Workers v. Richman Bros., 1955, 75 S.Ct. 452, 455, 348 U.S. 511, 515–516, 99 L.Ed. 600.

furter, for the Court, referred to "the severe restrictions" of "an ambiguous statute," and said that "we cannot reasonably impute such a purpose to Congress from the general language of 28 U.S.C.A. § 2283 alone." [21]

This encouraged some lower courts to think that § 2283 was not a limitation on the jurisdiction of the federal court, but only a rule of comity that could be disregarded where necessary to prevent grave and irreparable injury.[22] But with or without § 2283, injunctions cannot issue save to prevent irreparable injury, and there would be no point in the statute if it meant no more than this.[23] Thus in 1970 the Supreme Court rejected the notion that the statute states only a rule of comity. Speaking through Justice Black, the Court held that the statute is "an absolute prohibition against enjoining state court proceedings, unless the injunction falls within one of three specifically defined exceptions." [24] It said further that the exceptions are not to be enlarged by loose statutory construction.[25]

Some things are clear under § 2283. Thus it is accepted that the prohibition against enjoining state court proceedings cannot be avoided by framing an injunction as a restraint on a party rather than directly on the state court.[26] It remains the rule, despite the doubts Toucey might have raised, that the statute does not prohibit an injunction against a state officer who is about to institute proceedings to enforce an unconstitutional statute.[27] The statute does not apply unless the state court is performing a judicial function.[28] Nor does it

21. Leiter Minerals v. U. S., 1957, 77 S.Ct. 287, 291, 352 U.S. 220, 226, 1 L.Ed.2d 267.

The Leiter Minerals exception was extended in NLRB v. Nash-Finch Co., 1971, 92 S.Ct. 373, 404 U.S. 138, 30 L.Ed.2d 328, where it was held that the Anti-Injunction Act does not bar the NLRB from suing in federal court to enjoin state proceedings on a matter preempted by federal law.

22. Baines v. City of Danville, C.A.4th, 1964, 337 F.2d 579, 593–594, certiorari denied 85 S.Ct. 1772, 381 U.S. 939, 14 L.Ed.2d 702. Machesky v. Bizzell, C.A. 5th, 1969, 414 F.2d 283, 287–291; Landry v. Daley, D.C.Ill.1967, 280 F.Supp. 929, 936.

23. Essanay Film Mfg. Co. v. Kane, 1922, 42 S.Ct. 318, 319, 258 U.S. 358, 361, 66 L.Ed. 658. See Comment, 1965, 32 U.Chi.L.Rev. 471, 484; Note, 1964, 50 Va.L.Rev. 1404, 1424–1426.

24. Atlantic Coast Line R. Co. v. Brotherhood of Locomotive Engineers, 1970, 90 S.Ct. 1739, 1743, 398 U.S. 281, 286, 26 L.Ed.2d 234, noted 1971, 46 Notre Dame Law. 616. See also Reaves & Golden, note 1 above.

25. 90 S.Ct. at 1743, 398 U.S. at 287.

26. Atlantic Coast Line R. Co. v. Brotherhood of Locomotive Engineers, 1970, 90 S.Ct. 1739, 1743, 398 U.S. 281, 287, 26 L.Ed.2d 234; Oklahoma Packing Co. v. Oklahoma Gas & Elec. Co., 1940, 60 S.Ct. 215, 218, 309 U.S. 4, 9, 84 L.Ed. 447.

27. Dombrowski v. Pfister, 1965, 85 S.Ct. 1116, 1119 n. 2, 380 U.S. 479, 484 n. 2, 14 L.Ed.2d 22.

The Seventh Circuit, speaking through Judge—now-Justice—Stevens held that an injunction may issue if there was no state action pending when the federal injunction was sought, even though the state action is commenced before the federal court acts on the request for an injunction. Barancik v. Investors Funding Corp. of New York, C.A.7th, 1973, 489 F.2d 933. The Sixth Circuit, however, has expressly refused to follow that decision. Roth v. Bank of the Com., C.A.6th, 1978, 583 F.2d 527, certiorari dismissed 1979, 99 S.Ct. 2852, 442 U.S. 925, 61 L.Ed.2d 292, noted 1980, 64 Minn.L.Rev. 830.

28. Prentis v. Atlantic Coast Line Co., 1908, 29 S.Ct. 67, 211 U.S. 210, 53

prevent a federal court from issuing a temporary stay while it determines whether § 2283 is applicable to the case.[29]

The first of the exceptions to § 2283 is "as expressly authorized by Act of Congress."[30] This does not mean that the Act of Congress must refer in terms to § 2283.[31] It is surely enough that it specifically says an injunction may be granted against a proceeding in a state court.[32] Probably it is enough that the Act of Congress permits a federal court to stay any proceeding, though it does not mention states specifically.[33] In Mitchum v. Foster[34] the Supreme Court said that the test is "whether an Act of Congress, clearly creating a federal right or remedy enforceable in a federal court of equity, could be given its intended scope only by the stay of a state court proceeding."[35] Applying that test the Court held that the legislative history of the civil rights statute, 42 U.S.C.A. § 1983, was enough to bring its authorization of "suit in equity" within this exception to the Anti-Injunction Act.[36]

Mitchum was not the last word on the application of the "expressly authorized" exception. The Court was sharply divided in 1977 in Vendo Company v. Lektro-Vend Corporation.[37] After the Supreme

L.Ed. 150; Roudebush v. Hartke, 1972, 92 S.Ct. 804, 405 U.S. 15, 31 L.Ed.2d 1; Lynch v. Household Fin. Corp., 1972, 92 S.Ct. 1113, 405 U.S. 538, 31 L.Ed.2d 424; Feldman v. Gardner, C.A.1981, 661 F.2d 1295, 213 U.S.App.D.C. 119. See 17 Wright, Miller & Cooper, Jurisdiction § 4222 at notes 21–24.

29. See Barancik v. Investors Funding Corp. of New York, C.A.7th, 1973, 489 F.2d 933, 937; ALI Study, p. 307; Note, 1964, 50 Va.L.Rev. 1404, 1426–1427.

30. 17 Wright, Miller & Cooper, Jurisdiction § 4224; Redish, note 1 above, at 726–743.

31. See Amalgamated Clothing Workers of America v. Richman Bros., 1955, 75 S.Ct. 452, 455, 348 U.S. 511, 516, 99 L.Ed. 600.

32. Thus see the interpleader statute, 28 U.S.C.A. § 2361, Pan American Fire & Cas. Co. v. Revere, D.C.La.1960, 188 F.Supp. 474, and the habeas corpus statute, 28 U.S.C.A. § 2251.

33. The provision in the Bankruptcy Act, 11 U.S.C.A. § 362, is to this effect, as had been the provision in the Frazier-Lemke Act, 49 Stat. 944.

The limitation of liability statute, 46 U.S.C.A. § 185, provides that "all claims and proceedings against the owner with respect to the matter in question shall cease." This is held to meet the "expressly authorized" test. Beal v. Waltz, C.A.5th, 1962, 309 F.2d 721, 724.

The provision of the removal statute that upon removal "the State court shall proceed no further" has always been understood to permit an injunction against further state proceedings. Frith v. Blazon-Flexible Flyer, Inc., C.A.5th, 1975, 512 F.2d 899, 901.

In Studebaker Corp. v. Gittlin, C.A.2d, 1966, 360 F.2d 692, the court was able to bring within the "expressly authorized" language an action by a private person to enjoin violation of Proxy Rules issued by the S.E.C., even though it is only by implication that a private person has any right of action whatever. The case is criticized in Redish, note 1 above, at 727–733.

Compare ALI Study, § 1372(1).

34. 1972, 92 S.Ct. 2151, 407 U.S. 225, 32 L.Ed.2d 705.

35. 92 S.Ct. at 2160, 407 U.S. at 238.

36. Considerations of comity may bar an injunction even when § 2283 does not apply. See § 52A below.

37. 1977, 97 S.Ct. 2881, 433 U.S. 623, 53 L.Ed.2d 1009, noted 1978, 44 Brooklyn L.Rev. 317, 56 N.C.L.Rev. 601. See Mayton, note 1 above, at 355, and Redish, note 1 above, at 739–743.

The Supreme Court had to act twice more before the injunction was finally dissolved. Vendo Co. v. Lektro-Vend Corp., 1978, 98 S.Ct. 702, 434 U.S. 25, 54 L.Ed.2d 659; In re Vendo Co., 1978, 98 S.Ct. 1660, 435 U.S. 994, 56 L.Ed.2d

Court had refused to review a substantial money judgment in a suit for breach of fiduciary duty, the losing defendant successfully moved in federal court for an injunction against collection of the state judgment on the ground that the state litigation had an anticompetitive purpose and violated the federal antitrust laws.

Although the Supreme Court held five-to-four that the injunction should not have issued, it did not agree on the reason. Three justices, in the plurality opinion of Justice Rehnquist, took the position that § 16 of the Clayton Act does not meet the second half of the Mitchum test, and thus is not within the exception to § 2283, since stay of a state action is not necessary to give § 16 its intended scope. The other two majority justices, in a concurring opinion by Justice Blackmun, thought that § 16 is an exception in narrowly limited circumstances, as where the state court proceedings are part of a pattern of baseless, repetitive claims that are being used as an anticompetitive device. The four dissenters, speaking through Justice Stevens, would have held that § 16 is always an expressly authorized exception and that even a single state court proceeding can be enjoined. Because the Court was so fragmented, the Vendo case sheds little light on when an injunction of state proceedings is "expressly authorized," and the lower courts continue to take varying views.[38]

The second exception allows a court to enjoin state proceedings "where necessary in aid of its jurisdiction."[39] This means, among other things, that the rule, recognized even in Toucey, remains, and a federal court can enjoin a later state action involving property in the custody of the federal court.[40] The corollary remains, however, that an injunction cannot issue to restrain a state action in personam involving the same subject matter from going on at the same time. This is true even though the state action raises a question of federal law,[41] or its findings may have a collateral estoppel effect in the federal action,[42] or it raises a claim that should be a compulsory counterclaim in the federal action.[43] The exception does not allow a federal

93. For the final resolution of the case, see Lektro-Vend Corp. v. Vendo Co., C.A.7th, 1981, 660 F.2d 255, certiorari denied 102 S.Ct. 1277, ___ U.S. ___, 71 L.Ed.2d 461.

38. Compare cases cited 17 Wright, Miller & Cooper, Jurisdiction § 4224 nn. 20, 21.

39. 17 Wright, Miller & Cooper, Jurisdiction § 4225.

40. Green v. Green, C.A.7th, 1958, 259 F.2d 229; De Korwin v. First Nat. Bank of Chicago, C.A.7th, 1959, 267 F.2d 337, certiorari denied 80 S.Ct. 369, 361 U.S. 931, 4 L.Ed.2d 352; Alabama Vermiculite Corp. v. Patterson, D.C.

S.C.1955, 149 F.Supp. 534; ALI Study, § 1372(3). See note 12 above.

41. Thiokol Chemical Corp. v. Burlington Indus., Inc., C.A.3d, 1971, 448 F.2d 1328, certiorari denied 1972, 92 S.Ct. 684, 404 U.S. 1019, 30 L.Ed.2d 668.

42. Signal Properties, Inc. v. Farha, C.A.5th, 1973, 482 F.2d 1136; Vernitron Corp. v. Benjamin, C.A.2d, 1971, 440 F.2d 105, certiorari denied 91 S.Ct. 1664, 402 U.S. 987, 29 L.Ed.2d 154.

43. Johnny's Pizza House, Inc. v. G & H Properties, Inc., D.C.La.1981, 524 F.Supp. 495; Carter v. Bedford, D.C. Ark.1976, 420 F.Supp. 927.

injunction of state proceedings merely because they involve issues presented in a federal in personam action.[44]

Commentators have urged that the "necessary in aid of its jurisdiction" exception be read more broadly, so that it would encompass more than the in rem situation.[45] There is a basis for such a broader reading in the Supreme Court's statement that both this and the third exception of § 2283 allow federal injunctive relief where this is "necessary to prevent a state court from so interfering with a federal court's consideration or disposition of a case as to seriously impair the federal court's flexibility and authority to decide that case."[46] There are a few scattered signs of such flexibility in the recent cases. In the school desegregation area the federal court typically takes a controversy in hand, modifying its orders as need be from time to time, and it has been held that it can enjoin state proceedings that would interfere with the federal court's continuing jurisdiction.[47] There are other cases like this that seem best viewed as analogous to the custody of property cases and thus within the second exception.[48]

---

44. In re Federal Skyway Cases, C.A.8th, 1982, 680 F.2d 1175, certiorari denied 103 S.Ct. 342, 342 U.S. ___, ___ L.Ed.2d ___; Carter v. Ogden Corp., C.A.5th, 1975, 524 F.2d 74; Hyde Constr. Co. v. Koehring Co., C.A.10th, 1968, 388 F.2d 501, certiorari denied 88 S.Ct. 1654, 391 U.S. 905, 20 L.Ed.2d 419; Billy Jack for Her, Inc. v. New York Coat, Suit, Dress, Rainwear and Allied Workers' Union, D.C.N.Y.1981, 515 F.Supp. 456.

45. Mayton, note 1 above, at 356–369; Redish, note 1 above, at 743–760.

46. American Coast Line R. Co. v. Brotherhood of Locomotive Engineers, 1970, 90 S.Ct. 1739, 1747, 398 U.S. 281, 295, 26 L.Ed.2d 234.

47. Swann v. Charlotte-Mecklenburg Bd. of Educ., C.A.4th, 1974, 501 F.2d 383; Oliver v. Kalamazoo Bd. of Educ., D.C.Mich.1981, 510 F.Supp. 1104; Grenchik v. Mandel, D.C.Md.1973, 373 F.Supp. 1298. See also Valley v. Rapides Parish Sch. Bd., C.A.5th, 1981, 646 F.2d 925, 943.

Since in these cases the federal court will typically have already made some orders, they may also be regarded as coming within the third exception to § 2283. E.g., Thomason v. Cooper, C.A.8th, 1958, 254 F.2d 808.

48. State Water Control Bd. v. Washington Suburban Sanitary Comm., C.A. 1981, 654 F.2d 802, 210 U.S.App.D.C. 87; Bekoff v. Clinton, D.C.N.Y.1972, 344 F.Supp. 642; Montgomery County Bd. of Educ. v. Shelton, D.C.Miss.1971, 327 F.Supp. 811; Moss v. Burkhart, D.C.Okl.1963, 220 F.Supp. 149, 162–163, affirmed 1964, 84 S.Ct. 1907, 378 U.S. 558, 12 L.Ed.2d 1026.

This principle would seem to apply to prevent conflicting state actions where many similar suits have been consolidated by the Judicial Panel on Multidistrict Litigation under 28 U.S.C.A. § 1407. The purpose of consolidation is to provide coordinated treatment of these complex cases, and, as in actions in rem and school desegregation cases, it is intolerable to have different orders coming from different courts. An injunction from the multidistrict court was upheld in In re Corrugated Container Antitrust Action Litigation, C.A.5th, 1981, 659 F.2d 1332, but on the basis that settlements that had already been reached were a "judgment" that could be protected under the third exception to § 2283. But see Alton Box Bd. Co. v. Esprit De Corp., C.A. 9th, 1982, 682 F.2d 1267.

The issue in In re Federal Skywalk Cases, C.A.8th, 1982, 680 F.2d 1175, certiorari denied 103 S.Ct. 342, ___ U.S. ___, ___ L.Ed.2d ___, was whether a Rule 23(b)(1) class action is barred since it effectively enjoins members of the plaintiff class from pursuing their individual claims in state court. The majority held that the class action was barred, but there is a strong dissent.

The third and last exception to § 2283 allows a federal court to stay state proceedings "to protect or effectuate its judgments." This overrules the specific holding of the Toucey case and allows use of an injunction to prevent relitigation that has gone to judgment in the federal court.[49] Although the commentators have thought that a federal injunction should not issue automatically in this situation, and that there should be some showing of irreparable injury and lack of an adequate remedy at law,[50] most cases do not seem to have imposed such a requirement.[51] In determining what is a "judgment" that can be protected under the third exception, Civil Rule 54(a), which defines "judgment" as "any order from which an appeal lies," provides a useful analogy. This would bring within the exception, and allow stays to issue to protect, interlocutory orders that are appealable as of right.[52]

If an injunction would be barred by § 2283, this should also bar the issuance of a declaratory judgment that would have the same effect as an injunction.[53] This problem is now of lessened importance, since most of the cases in which the issue arose involved challenges to official conduct, and most such cases are civil rights cases that, since 1972, have been held to come within the first exception to § 2283.

The "proceedings" in a state court that cannot be stayed include "execution issued on a judgment" and "any proceeding supplemental or ancillary taken with a view to making the suit or judgment effective." [54] If a state action has ended in a judgment requiring enforcement of a state statute, it may still be the law that this does not bar a federal court from enjoining enforcement of the statute on the suit of "strangers to the state court proceeding."[55] It is almost certainly not still the law that a federal court cannot enjoin the enforcement of a

49. 17 Wright, Miller & Cooper, Jurisdiction § 4226.

50. ALI Study, p. 306; Vestal, Protecting A Federal Court Judgment, 1975, 42 Tenn.L.Rev. 635, 661–671; Comment, Anti-Suit Injunctions between State and Federal Courts, 1965, 32 U.Chi.L.Rev. 471, 486.

51. See cases cited 17 Wright, Miller & Cooper, Jurisdiction § 4226 nn. 5, 12; Redish, note 1 above, at 723 n. 31.

But see Southern California Petroleum Corp. v. Harper, C.A.5th, 1960, 273 F.2d 715, 719; Texaco, Inc. v. Fiumara, D.C.Pa.1965, 248 F.Supp. 595, 597; and cases cited 17 Wright, Miller & Cooper, Jurisdiction § 4226 n. 34.

52. See § 102 below.

53. Regional Properties, Inc. v. Financial & Real Estate Consulting Co., C.A.5th, 1982, 678 F.2d 552, 565–567; Thiokol Chem. Corp. v. Burlington In-

dus., Inc., C.A.3d, 1971, 448 F.2d 1328, 1332, certiorari denied 1972, 92 S.Ct. 684, 404 U.S. 1019, 30 L.Ed.2d 668; Garrett v. Hoffman, D.C.Pa.1977, 441 F.Supp. 1151; and cases cited 17 Wright, Miller & Cooper, Jurisdiction § 4226 n. 11.

But see Note, The Federal Anti-Injunction Statute and Declaratory Judgments in Constitutional Litigation, 1970, 83 Harv.L.Rev. 1870.

54. Hill v. Martin, 1935, 56 S.Ct. 278, 282, 296 U.S. 393, 403, 80 L.Ed. 293; County of Imperial v. Munoz, 1980, 101 S.Ct. 289, 449 U.S. 54, 66 L.Ed.2d 258.

55. Hale v. Bimco Trading, Inc., 1939, 59 S.Ct. 526, 306 U.S. 375, 83 L.Ed. 771. For the present status of this rule, see County of Imperial v. Munoz, 1980, 101 S.Ct. 289, 449 U.S. 54, 66 L.Ed.2d 258, noted 1981, 8 Ohio N.L. Rev. 419. See also the same case on

state judgment that has been obtained by fraud or that is otherwise not in accord with equity and good conscience. The early cases that had allowed a federal injunction in these circumstances [56] cannot be comfortably fitted either with the later definition of "proceedings" that has now been developed or with the language of the exceptions to § 2283 in the 1948 revision.[57]

Even if an injunction against state proceedings is not barred by § 2283, it may still be refused. The various abstention doctrines may counsel that the federal court refrain from exercising its power to issue an injunction.[58] Special considerations of federalism restrict the use of injunctions that will interfere with state law enforcement.[59]

§ 48.   Federal Actions to Restrain State Officers [1]

It was pointed out in the first section of this book that questions as to the jurisdiction of the federal courts are not mere details of procedure, but go to the very heart of a federal system and affect the allocation of power between the United States and the several states. This is nowhere more strikingly illustrated than in the famous case of Ex parte Young,[2] and the doctrine that has been generated by that case.

In 1907 the Minnesota legislature passed a law reducing railroad rates, and providing very severe penalties for any railroad that failed to comply with the law. The day before the law was to take effect stockholders of nine railroads brought suits in federal court to enjoin the companies in which they held stock from complying with the law. They alleged that the rates prescribed by the new law were unjust,

remand, D.C.Cal.1981, 510 F.Supp. 879, affirmed C.A.9th, 1982, 667 F.2d 811, certiorari denied 103 S.Ct. 58, ___ U.S. ___, 74 L.Ed.2d 62.

56.   See notes 13 and 14 above.

57.   17 Wright, Miller & Cooper, Jurisdiction § 4223; ALI Study, pp. 51, 311–312; Warriner v. Fink, C.A.5th, 1962, 307 F.2d 933, certiorari denied 83 S.Ct. 937, 372 U.S. 943, 9 L.Ed.2d 969; Furnish v. Board of Medical Examiners, C.A.9th, 1958, 257 F.2d 520, certiorari denied 79 S.Ct. 123, 358 U.S. 882, 3 L.Ed.2d 111; Norwood v. Parenteau, C.A.8th, 1955, 228 F.2d 148, certiorari denied 76 S.Ct. 852, 351 U.S. 955, 100 L.Ed. 1478; cf. Manufacturers Record Pub. Co. v. Lauer, C.A.5th, 1959, 268 F.2d 187, certiorari denied 80 S.Ct. 258, 361 U.S. 913, 4 L.Ed.2d 184.

Contra: Alleghany Corp. v. Kirby, D.C. N.Y.1963, 218 F.Supp. 164, 169, affirmed C.A.2d, 1964, 333 F.2d 327, affirmed on rehearing C.A.2d, 1965, 340 F.2d 311, certiorari dismissed 86 S.Ct.

1250, 384 U.S. 28, 16 L.Ed.2d 335; Dowd v. Front Range Mines, D.C.Colo. 1965, 242 F.Supp. 591; Mayton, note 1 above, at 368–369; Note, 1961, 74 Harv.L.Rev. 726, 728.

58.   See § 52 below.

59.   See § 52A below.

[§ 48]

1.   17 Wright, Miller & Cooper, Jurisdiction §§ 4231, 4232; Jacobs, The Eleventh Amendment and Sovereign Immunity, 1972, c. 5; Field, The Eleventh Amendment and Other Sovereign Immunity Doctrines, 1978, 126 U.Pa.L. Rev. 515, 1203; Weick, Erosion of State Sovereign Immunity and the Eleventh Amendment by Federal Decisional Law, 1977, 10 Akron L.Rev. 583; Baker, Federalism and the Eleventh Amendment, 1977, 48 U.Colo.L.Rev. 139.

2.   1908, 28 S.Ct. 441, 209 U.S. 123, 52 L.Ed. 714.

unreasonable, and confiscatory, and would deprive the companies of their property without due process of law, contrary to the Fourteenth Amendment, but that the penalties under the law were such that the railroads, if not restrained, would comply with it. Among other de- fendants they included Edward T. Young, the Attorney General of Minnesota, and prayed that he be restrained from seeking to enforce the law. The federal court issued first a temporary restraining order and later a preliminary injunction, granting the relief the plaintiffs sought. This relief was given over Young's objection that the suit was in fact a suit against the state, to which the state had not consented, and thus barred by the Eleventh Amendment. The day after the preliminary injunction was issued Young sued in state court for a writ of mandamus against the railroads to compel them to comply with the new law. He was adjudged guilty of contempt for this action, fined $100, and ordered to jail until he dismissed the state mandamus proceeding. He then applied to the Supreme Court for a writ of habeas corpus to free him from the custody of the marshal. As the Supreme Court understood the issue, the contempt order was invalid, and habeas corpus should be granted, if the Eleventh Amendment prohibited the injunction against him that he had violated.[3]

The Supreme Court did not write on a clean slate in deciding Young's case. In 1793, in the unpopular decision of Chisholm v. Georgia,[4] it had held that the Constitution permitted a citizen of one state to sue another state in federal court, though the state had not consented to such suit. The Eleventh Amendment was ratified five years later to take away the judicial power of the federal courts in such cases,[5] and though in terms it does not so provide, it was construed as barring suits against a state without its consent even where, as in Young's case, the suit was brought by a citizen of the state and the basis of the jurisdiction was a claim under federal law.[6] In an early decision Chief Justice Marshall had construed the amendment as barring suit only where the state was formally a party of record,[7] but the principle embodied in the Eleventh Amendment was too vital to be restrained by such formalism and Marshall himself later construed the amendment as applying to a suit against the governor of a state where he was being sued in his official capacity.[8] Over the next half century the decisions were varying and uncertain. The

---

3. Compare U. S. v. United Mine Workers of America, 1947, 67 S.Ct. 677, 330 U.S. 258, 91 L.Ed. 884, discussed § 16 above.

4. 1793, 2 Dall. 419, 1 L.Ed. 440.

5. See 1 Warren, The Supreme Court in United States History, 2d ed. 1926, pp. 93–102; 13 Wright, Miller & Cooper, Jurisdiction 2d § 3524.

6. Hans v. Louisiana, 1890, 10 S.Ct. 504, 134 U.S. 1, 33 L.Ed. 842. See also Employees of Dept. of Public Health &

Welfare v. Department of Public Health & Welfare, 1973, 93 S.Ct. 1614, 1616, 411 U.S. 279, 280, 36 L.Ed.2d 251. This traditional understanding is challenged by Justice Brennan in his dissent in the case just cited. 93 S.Ct. at 1632–1637, 411 U.S. at 313–322.

7. Osborn v. Bank of the United States, 1824, 9 Wheat. 738, 846, 857, 6 L.Ed. 204.

8. Governor of Georgia v. Madrazo, 1828, 1 Pet. 110, 122–123, 7 L.Ed. 73.

Court undertook to rationalize them, and establish a rule on the subject, in 1887 in the case of In re Ayers.[9] The decision there was that suit against a state officer was not barred where his action, aside from any official authority claimed as its justification, was a wrong simply as an individual act, such as a trespass, but that if the act of the officer did not constitute an individual wrong and was something that only the state, through its officers, could do, the suit was in substance a suit against the state. The case would seem to be decisive of the Young litigation. Only a state can violate the Fourteenth Amendment. Only a state can compel railroads to charge particular rates. Indeed in the Ayers case the relief unsuccessfully sought was an injunction restraining state attorneys from bringing suits under a supposedly unconstitutional statute. The law was clouded between 1887 and 1908, when Young's case came to the Court, by decisions that, in dicta at least, suggested that the commencement of a suit to enforce an unconstitutional statute could be considered an actionable wrong similar to a trespass.[10]

Against this erratic background, the Court held that the injunction against Young was proper. Justice Peckham, for the Court, announced the rule that has since been repeatedly followed: [11] "The act to be enforced is alleged to be unconstitutional, and, if it be so, the use of the name of the state to enforce an unconstitutional act to the injury of the complainants is a proceeding without the authority of, and one which does not affect, the state in its sovereign or governmental capacity. It is simply an illegal act upon the part of a state official, in attempting by the use of the name of the state to enforce a legislative enactment which is void, because unconstitutional. If the act which the state Attorney General seeks to enforce be a violation of the federal Constitution, the officer in proceeding under such enactment comes into conflict with the superior authority of that Constitution, and he is in that case stripped of his official or representa-

---

9. 1887, 8 S.Ct. 164, 123 U.S. 443, 31 L.Ed. 216.

In a well-known later case, the Court purported to distinguish the Ayers case and to allow suit against a State Revenue Commissioner to enjoin him from collecting supposedly unconstitutional taxes. Ayers, the Court said, was not in point, because in that case there was no allegation that the challenged tax was a violation of constitutional rights, and thus the suit was directly against the state. Georgia R. & Banking Co. v. Redwine, 1952, 72 S.Ct. 321, 325, 342 U.S. 299, 306, 96 L.Ed. 335. The pleadings in the Ayers case, as well as the Court's opinion in that case, show that plaintiff was explicitly claiming that the tax challenged there impaired the obligation of his contract with the state

in violation of Art. I, § 10. See 17 Wright, Miller & Cooper, Jurisdiction § 4231 n. 11.

10. Reagan v. Farmers' Loan & Trust Co., 1894, 14 S.Ct. 1047, 154 U.S. 362, 38 L.Ed. 1014; Scott v. Donald, 1897, 17 S.Ct. 265, 266, 165 U.S. 58, 67, 41 L.Ed. 632; Smyth v. Ames, 1898, 18 S.Ct. 418, 169 U.S. 466, 42 L.Ed. 819; Prout v. Starr, 1903, 23 S.Ct. 398, 188 U.S. 537, 47 L.Ed. 584; Gunter v. Atlantic Coast Line R. Co., 1906, 26 S.Ct. 252, 200 U.S. 273, 50 L.Ed. 477; McNeill v. Southern R. Co., 1906, 26 S.Ct. 722, 202 U.S. 543, 50 L.Ed. 1142.

11. See Duker, Mr. Justice Rufus W. Peckham and the Case of Ex Parte Young: Lochnerizing Munn v. Illinois, 1980 B.Y.U.L.Rev. 539.

tive character and is subject in his person to the consequences of his individual conduct." [12]

Only the first Justice Harlan dissented. In a lengthy opinion he argued: "The suit was, as to the defendant Young, one against him as, and only because he was, Attorney General of Minnesota. No relief was sought against him individually but only in his capacity as Attorney General. And the manifest—indeed, the avowed and admitted—object of seeking such relief was to tie the hands of the state, so that it could not in any manner or by any mode of proceeding in its own courts test the validity of the statutes and orders in question. It would therefore seem clear that within the true meaning of the Eleventh Amendment the suit brought in the federal court was one, in legal effect, against the state." [13]

There is no doubt that the reality is as Justice Harlan stated it, and that everyone knew that the Court was engaging in fiction when it regarded the suit as one against an individual named Young rather than against the state of Minnesota.[14] The fiction has its own illogic. The Fourteenth Amendment runs only to the states; in order to have a right to relief under the amendment the plaintiff must be able to show that state action is involved in the denial of his rights.[15] It would have been possible to hold that the Fourteenth Amendment qualified the immunity from suit granted states by the Eleventh Amendment [16] but the Court expressly refused to so hold.[17] Instead it created the anomaly that enforcement of the Minnesota statute is state action for purposes of the Fourteenth Amendment but merely

12. 28 S.Ct. at 454, 209 U.S. at 159–160.

13. 28 S.Ct. at 459, 209 U.S. at 173–174.

14. "Of course, the Court well knew that the attorney general was still attorney general while he was enforcing the statute, and the Court well knew that the effect of enjoining the attorney general was to enjoin the state from carrying out the unconstitutional statute. From that day to this the false pretense made by the Court in Ex parte Young has been the mainstay in challenging governmental action through suits for injunctions and declaratory judgments." Davis, Suing the Government by Falsely Pretending to Sue an Officer, 1962, 29 U.Chi.L. Rev. 435, 437.

15. Civil Rights Cases, 1883, 3 S.Ct. 18, 109 U.S. 3, 27 L.Ed. 835. Lewis, The Meaning of State Action, 1960, 60 Calif.L.Rev. 1083. But cf. Williams, The Twilight of State Action, 1963, 41 Texas L.Rev. 347.

16. See Note, 1937, 50 Harv.L.Rev. 956, 961.

17. 28 S.Ct. at 450, 209 U.S. at 150.

If the Fourteenth Amendment does limit the Eleventh Amendment, then many subsequent cases in which a suit against the state itself on Fourteenth Amendment grounds has been held barred by the Eleventh Amendment were wrongly decided. But Justice Marshall, in his dissent in Edelman v. Jordan, 1974, 94 S.Ct. 1347, 1371 n. 2, 415 U.S. 651, 694, 39 L.Ed.2d 662, seems to regard this as still an open question. Even though the Fourteenth Amendment of its own force does not limit the Eleventh Amendment, Congress, in the exercise of its enforcement powers under § 5 of the Fourteenth Amendment, may take away a state's Eleventh Amendment immunity. Fitzpatrick v. Bitzer, 1976, 96 S.Ct. 2666, 427 U.S. 445, 49 L.Ed.2d 614.

the individual wrong of Edward T. Young for purposes of the Eleventh Amendment.[18]

What if the action of the state officer is beyond his authority as a matter of state law? A case prior to Ex parte Young had seemed to hold that an action unauthorized by state law could not be state action for purposes of the Fourteenth Amendment.[19] This decision has no continuing authority. It was settled five years after Ex parte Young that action by a state officer claiming to act under authority of the state can be enjoined, even if the state has not authorized such action.[20]

The effect of Ex parte Young is to bring within the scope of federal judicial review actions that might otherwise escape such review, and to subject the states to the restrictions of the United States Constitution that they might otherwise be able safely to ignore. If Ex parte Young had been decided the other way, there would have been no practicable means for the railroads to obtain a court determination of the new rates Minnesota wanted them to charge. The state could, of course, consent to suit, either in its own courts or in federal court, simply as a matter of grace, but even today most states have not done so. The railroads could have refused to obey the new law, and asserted its unconstitutionality as a defense to an action against them for its enforcement, but the state might have chosen to enforce the law by the criminal sanctions it supplied, and these were so severe that the railroads could not risk the possibility that they might lose and have to pay crushing fines.[21] In some situations, as where a state has failed to desegregate its schools, affirmative action is required of the state to fulfill its constitutional obligations, and there would not be even the possibility of raising the constitutional issue defensively. A doctrine could have been developed imposing on the

18. When the case was decided on the merits, it was discovered that Young had not committed a wrong after all, since the new rates required by the statute were held valid. Minnesota Rate Cases (Simpson v. Shepard), 1913, 33 S.Ct. 729, 230 U.S. 352, 57 L.Ed. 1511. Since he was not acting unconstitutionally in enforcing the rates, Young was not stripped of his state authority and the suit was in fact one against the state. But the ultimate outcome does not defeat the jurisdiction invoked by the complaint. E.g., Bell v. Hood, 1946, 66 S.Ct. 773, 327 U.S. 678, 90 L.Ed. 939; see § 18 nn. 17–18 above.

19. Barney v. City of New York, 1904, 24 S.Ct. 502, 193 U.S. 430, 48 L.Ed. 737. See Isseks, Jurisdiction of the Lower Federal Courts to Enjoin Unauthorized Action of State Officials, 1927, 40 Harv.L.Rev. 969.

20. Home Tel. & Tel. Co. v. City of Los Angeles, 1913, 33 S.Ct. 312, 227 U.S. 278, 57 L.Ed. 510. That case did not specifically overrule the Barney case, and it was possible, as in the article by Isseks cited note 19 above, to suppose that Barney retained some vitality. It was not until U. S. v. Raines, 1960, 80 S.Ct. 519, 525, 362 U.S. 17, 25–26, 4 L.Ed.2d 524, that it was expressly declared that "Barney must be regarded as having 'been worn away by the erosion of time,' * * * and of contrary authority."

21. Attempts to arrange a friendly test case might have floundered on the requirement of case or controversy. Chicago & G. T. Ry. Co. v. Wellman, 1892, 12 S.Ct. 400, 143 U.S. 339, 36 L.Ed. 176.

states a constitutional obligation to provide some remedy by which constitutional rights could be asserted—indeed a case decided the same day as Ex parte Young hints at such a doctrine [22]—but this would have either the advantage or the disadvantage, depending on how the matter is viewed, that the challenge would come in the first instance in a state court with review by the Supreme Court, rather than initially in the federal court.[23]

The fictional basis of Ex parte Young also limits the relief that can be afforded. A state officer can be enjoined from acting improperly in making welfare payments but he cannot be required to make restitution to those who have wrongfully been denied benefits in the past, since such an award would have to be paid from state funds, rather than from the pocket of the officer named as defendant, and would amount to an action for damages against the state, barred by the Eleventh Amendment. This is the 1974 holding in Edelman v. Jordan.[24] Edelman was reaffirmed five years later, with the Court saying that "[t]he distinction between that relief permissible under the doctrine of Ex parte Young and that found barred in Edelman was the difference between prospective relief on one hand and retrospective relief on the other." [25]

22. General Oil Co. v. Crain, 1908, 28 S.Ct. 475, 209 U.S. 211, 52 L.Ed. 754. It was held there that a state court decision denying jurisdiction to hear a federal challenge of a state statute has the effect of upholding the statute, and is reviewable in the United States Supreme Court. The doctrine of the Crain case may have been repudiated by Georgia R. & Banking Co. v. Musgrove, 1949, 69 S.Ct. 407, 335 U.S. 900, 93 L.Ed. 435. See 16 Wright, Miller & Cooper, Jurisdiction § 4024. On the duty of the states to enforce federal law, see generally § 45 above.

23. "If the railroads were required to take no active steps until they could bring a writ of error from this court to the Supreme Court of Appeals after a final judgment, they would come here with the facts already found against them. But the determination as to their rights turns almost wholly upon the facts to be found." Prentis v. Atlantic Coast Line Co., 1908, 29 S.Ct. 67, 70, 211 U.S. 210, 228, 53 L.Ed. 150 (per Holmes, J.).

Limiting the remedy to state courts would also expose litigants to delay if the state court chose not to act promptly. On the potentialities of such delay, see National Assn. for the Advancement of Colored People v. Alabama, 1959, 79 S.Ct. 1001, 360 U.S. 240, 3 L.Ed.2d 1205; National Assn. for the Advancement of Colored People v. Gal-

lion, 1961, 82 S.Ct. 4, 368 U.S. 16, 7 L.Ed.2d 85; National Assn. for the Advancement of Colored People v. Alabama ex rel. Flowers, 1964, 84 S.Ct. 1302, 377 U.S. 288, 12 L.Ed.2d 325.

24. 1974, 94 S.Ct. 1347, 415 U.S. 651, 39 L.Ed.2d 662.

But back payments can be ordered against a state if Congress, in the exercise of its powers under § 5 of the Fourteenth Amendment, has created a statutory remedy against a state. Fitzpatrick v. Bitzer, 1976, 96 S.Ct. 2666, 427 U.S. 445, 49 L.Ed.2d 614.

Lichtenstein, Retroactive Relief in the Federal Courts Since Edelman v. Jordan: A Trip Through the Twilight Zone, 1982, 32 Case W.Res.L.Rev. 364.

25. Quern v. Jordan, 1979, 99 S.Ct. 1139, 1143, 440 U.S. 332, 337, 59 L.Ed. 2d 358. The holding in Edelman was affirmed once again in Florida Dept. of Health & Rehabilitative Services v. Florida Nursing Home Assn., 1981, 101 S.Ct. 1032, 450 U.S. 147, 67 L.Ed.2d 132.

"However, it is not particularly responsive to argue, as the Court did, that there is a distinction for eleventh amendment purposes between prospective and retroactive relief, even though both may cause significant harm to state treasuries, because one is prospective and the other retroactive. The question before the Court was

The decision in Ex parte Young rests on purest fiction. It is illogical. It is only doubtfully in accord with the prior decisions. It was greeted with harsh criticism by the country when it was decided and for years thereafter.[26] For half a century Congress and the Court have vied in placing restrictions on the doctrine there announced.[27] Yet this case, ostensibly dealing only with the jurisdiction of the federal courts, remains a landmark in constitutional law.[28] In earlier years Ex parte Young was the foundation from which state utility regulation and welfare legislation were attacked. Today it provides the basis for forcing states to desegregate their schools [29] and reapportion their legislatures. Both lines of cases are highly controversial. Yet in perspective the doctrine of Ex parte Young seems indispensable to the establishment of constitutional government and the rule of law.

§ 49. Exhaustion of State Remedies [1]

The first limitation on the doctrine of Ex parte Young[2] was developed by the Supreme Court in the same year the Young case was decided. In Virginia the State Corporation Commission was authorized to fix railroad rates, with appeal to the Supreme Court of Appeals. The Supreme Court of Appeals was empowered to substitute its decision for that of the Corporation Commission, and to fix and determine the rates that might be charged. After a proceeding before the Corporation Commission, resulting in an order lowering rates, the railroads involved sued in federal court to enjoin the members of the Commission from taking any action to enforce the order. The principal contention of the state, on appeal from the injunction that was granted, was that the Commission was a "court" and that

whether this distinction actually made any practical difference; the Court seemed to concede that often it would not." Redish, Federal Jurisdiction: Tensions in the Allocation of Judicial Power, 1980, p. 158.

Even if the relief sought against a state officer is prospective only, the Young fiction is inapplicable, and the Eleventh Amendment bars the suit, unless the state officer is alleged to be acting contrary to federal or state law. Cory v. White, 1982, 102 S.Ct. 2325, ___ U.S. ___, 72 L.Ed.2d 694.

26. " * * * [T]he antagonism engendered by suits against officers was intense, verging in one instance, it was said, upon open rebellion. The outcry was reminiscent of that following the decision in Chisholm v. Georgia." Jacobs, note 1 above at 146.

27. The succeeding five sections examine restrictions on Ex parte Young.

28. "The authority and finality of Ex parte Young can hardly be overestimated." Hutcheson, A Case for Three Judges, 1934, 47 Harv.L.Rev. 795, 799 n. 9.

The Court has refused to overrule Ex parte Young at the request of those who think it allows too little protection to the states, Ray v. Atlantic Richfield Co., 1978, 98 S.Ct. 988, 994 n. 6, 435 U.S. 151, 156 n. 6, 55 L.Ed.2d 179, and of those who think Young provides too much protection. Alabama v. Pugh, 1978, 98 S.Ct. 3057, 438 U.S. 781, 57 L.Ed.2d 1114.

29. Griffin v. County Sch. Bd. of Prince Edward Co., 1964, 84 S.Ct. 1226, 1232, 377 U.S. 218, 228, 12 L.Ed.2d 256.

[§ 49]

1. 17 Wright, Miller & Cooper, Jurisdiction § 4233.

2. 1908, 28 S.Ct. 441, 209 U.S. 123, 52 L.Ed. 714, fully discussed § 48 above.

the Anti-Injunction Act [3] barred an injunction staying its proceedings. The Supreme Court rejected this argument, finding that the function of the Commission was "legislative," or as would now be said, "administrative," and thus that it was not functioning as a court.[4] It held, nevertheless, that the injunction action was premature. In view of the powers the Supreme Court of Appeals was granted by the Virginia statute, it was held that the state legislative process did not end until the Supreme Court of Appeals had reviewed the order of the Commission. As a matter of comity and equitable discretion, therefore, rather than as a limitation on jurisdiction, a federal court should not act until the state legislative process was concluded, since it could not lightly be supposed that the Supreme Court of Appeals would approve an unconstitutional order. If the order were finally approved, then an injunction in federal court would lie, and the decision of the Supreme Court of Appeals, since it was here functioning legislatively rather than judicially, would not be res judicata on the constitutional issue. A case a few years later added the limitation that if the review permitted in the state court was "judicial," rather than "legislative," the party need not resort to state court but could bring an action in federal court upon termination of the state administrative proceedings.[5]

The traditional rule can then be fairly simply stated. A litigant must normally exhaust state "legislative" or "administrative" remedies before challenging the state action in federal court.[6] He need not normally exhaust state "judicial" remedies.[7] The rationale for this distinction is that until the administrative process is complete, it cannot be certain that the party will need judicial relief, but when the case becomes appropriate for judicial determination, he may choose whether he wishes to resort to a state or federal court for such relief. The word "normally" is required in both branches of the rule. Even a state judicial remedy must be exhausted if a federal statute so pro-

---

3. See § 47 above.

4. Prentis v. Atlantic Coast Line Co., 1908, 29 S.Ct. 67, 211 U.S. 210, 53 L.Ed. 150.

5. Bacon v. Rutland R. Co., 1914, 34 S.Ct. 283, 232 U.S. 134, 58 L.Ed. 538. This case, like the Prentis case, note 4 above, was written by Justice Holmes.

If the state court in reviewing a commission order acts wholly judicially, its decision is res judicata and bars a subsequent federal court suit. State Corp. Comm. of Kansas v. Wichita Gas Co., 1934, 54 S.Ct. 321, 290 U.S. 561, 78 L.Ed. 500. See also Kremer v. Chemical Constr. Corp., 1982, 102 S.Ct. 1883, ___ U.S. ___, 72 L.Ed.2d 262.

6. Gilchrist v. Interborough Rapid Transit Co., 1929, 49 S.Ct. 282, 279 U.S. 159, 73 L.Ed. 652; Porter v. Investors

Syndicate, 1931, 52 S.Ct. 617, 286 U.S. 461, 76 L.Ed. 1226, adhered to 1932, 53 S.Ct. 132, 287 U.S. 346, 77 L.Ed. 354; Carson v. Warlick, C.A.4th, 1956, 238 F.2d 724, certiorari denied 77 S.Ct. 665, 353 U.S. 910, 1 L.Ed.2d 664; Baron v. O'Sullivan, C.A.3d, 1958, 258 F.2d 336.

7. City Bank Farmers' Trust Co. v. Schnader, 1934, 54 S.Ct. 259, 291 U.S. 24, 78 L.Ed. 628; Lane v. Wilson, 1939, 59 S.Ct. 872, 307 U.S. 268, 83 L.Ed. 1281; Amsley v. West Virginia Racing Comm., C.A.4th, 1967, 378 F.2d 815; Dove v. Parham, C.A.8th, 1960, 282 F.2d 256, 262.

But cf. Alabama Public Serv. Comm. v. Southern Ry. Co., 1951, 71 S.Ct. 762, 341 U.S. 341, 95 L.Ed. 1002, discussed § 52 below.

vides.[8] A state administrative remedy need not be exhausted if the remedy is inadequate.[9]

These rules must now be qualified in the light of cases in the last 15 years announcing different principles for civil rights actions under 42 U.S.C.A. § 1983. These recent cases are of particular importance since many of the cases developing the traditional rules were cases in which plaintiffs were claiming that states were unconstitutionally depriving them of their property, and it was not until 1972 that it was held that property rights were protected under § 1983.[10]

The leading case in the revitalization of § 1983, Monroe v. Pape,[11] announced the unexceptionable rule that state judicial remedies need not be exhausted before bringing a federal civil rights action. Two years later, in McNeese v. Board of Education,[12] the Court seemed to say that there is no need to exhaust state administrative remedies in § 1983 suits. McNeese may not have laid down such a rule,[13] particularly since much of the opinion was devoted to showing that the state administrative remedy in that case was inadequate. But the important fact is that the Supreme Court repeatedly relied on McNeese for the flat statement that exhaustion of administrative remedies is not required in § 1983 actions.[14]

There were cross-currents, however, in the Supreme Court decisions,[15] and members of the Supreme Court, as well as lower court

8. See 28 U.S.C.A. §§ 1341 (collection of state taxes), 1342 (utility rate orders), 2254 (habeas corpus). These are discussed in § 51 below.

See also 28 U.S.C.A. § 2254 (habeas corpus), discussed in § 53 below.

It may also be that the abstention doctrines or other considerations of federalism will suggest remitting the party to a state judicial remedy. See §§ 52, 52A below.

9. See Gibson v. Berryhill, 1973, 93 S.Ct. 1689, 411 U.S. 564, 36 L.Ed.2d 488 (question of adequacy of remedy identical with merits of suit); Smith v. Illinois Bell Tel. Co., 1926, 46 S.Ct. 408, 270 U.S. 587, 70 L.Ed. 747 (undue delay by agency); Montana Nat. Bank of Billings v. Yellowstone County, 1928, 48 S.Ct. 331, 276 U.S. 499, 72 L.Ed. 673 (agency action controlled by prior state court decision); Union Pac. R. Co. v. Board of Commrs. of Weld County, 1918, 38 S.Ct. 510, 247 U.S. 282, 62 L.Ed. 1110 (existence of remedy doubtful); Monongahela Connecting R. Co. v. Pennsylvania Public Util. Comm., C.A.3d, 1967, 373 F.2d 142 (inaction by agency); Kelly v. Board of Educ. of City of Nashville, D.C.Tenn.1958, 159 F.Supp. 272 (agency committed in advance to continue segregation).

10. Lynch v. Household Fin. Corp., 1972, 92 S.Ct. 1113, 405 U.S. 538, 31 L.Ed.2d 424. See § 22A.

11. 1961, 81 S.Ct. 473, 365 U.S. 167, 5 L.Ed.2d 492. Monroe is important because of its holding that state officers were acting under color of state law, within the meaning of § 1983, even though their acts were not authorized by the state and indeed were forbidden by the state.

12. 1963, 83 S.Ct. 1433, 373 U.S. 668, 10 L.Ed.2d 622.

13. See the analysis of McNeese and its progeny by Judge Friendly in Eisen v. Eastman, C.A.2d, 1969, 421 F.2d 560, 567–569.

14. See, e.g., Damico v. California, 1967, 88 S.Ct. 526, 389 U.S. 416, 19 L.Ed.2d 647; Wilwording v. Swenson, 1971, 92 S.Ct. 407, 404 U.S. 249, 30 L.Ed.2d 418; Steffel v. Thompson, 1974, 94 S.Ct. 1209, 1222, 415 U.S. 452, 472–473, 39 L.Ed.2d 505.

See generally Comment, Exhaustion of State Administrative Remedies in Section 1983 Cases, 1974, 41 U.Chi.L.Rev. 537.

15. The statutory requirement of exhaustion for habeas corpus actions cannot be avoided by casting the suit as a

judges, expressed dissatisfaction with the rule not requiring state administrative remedies to be exhausted before commencing a federal civil rights action. Nevertheless, when the Supreme Court was squarely faced with the question in 1972 in Patsy v. Board of Regents of Florida,[16] it held with only two dissents that this continues to be the rule.[17]

§ 50. The Three-Judge Court Acts [1]

An interesting, but increasingly unsatisfactory, feature in the federal courts, prior to its virtual abolition in 1976, was the use of special three-judge courts to hear constitutional cases. As a result of the resentment felt by the states to the doctrine of Ex parte Young,[2] there were legislative proposals to strip the federal courts of jurisdiction of suits challenging state laws. Congress chose instead, in 1910, a less drastic remedy. Statutes passed earlier in that decade dealing with certain antitrust actions of general public importance, and with suits to set aside orders of the Interstate Commerce Commission, had created a court of special dignity, composed of three judges, at least one of whom was a judge of the then-Circuit Court of Appeals, with direct appeal to the Supreme Court from the decision of the three-judge court.[3] Congress borrowed this device and made it applicable to suits in which an interlocutory injunction was sought against the enforcement of state statutes by state officers.[4] It was the thought of Congress that there would be less public resentment if enforcement of the state statute were stayed by three judges rather than one, and that the provision for direct appeal to the Supreme Court would provide speedy review.[5]

§ 1983 action, and a prisoner challenging the very fact or duration of his physical imprisonment, and seeking a determination that he is entitled to immediate or more speedy release from imprisonment, must first exhaust all state remedies, both administrative and judicial. Preiser v. Rodriguez, 1973, 93 S.Ct. 1827, 411 U.S. 475, 36 L.Ed.2d 439.

Under the doctrine of "Our Federalism" a litigant who wishes to challenge in federal court a state judgment adverse to him must first exhaust his state appellate remedies. Huffman v. Pursue, Ltd., 1975, 95 S.Ct. 1200, 420 U.S. 592, 43 L.Ed.2d 482. See § 52A below.

16. 1982, 102 S.Ct. 2557, ___ U.S. ___, 73 L.Ed.2d 172.

17. Chief Justice Burger and Justice Powell dissented. Justices Rehnquist and O'Connor, concurring, urged Congress to change the rule and require exhaustion.

[§ 50]

1. 17 Wright, Miller & Cooper, Jurisdiction §§ 4234, 4235; Williams, The New Three-Judge Courts of Reapportionment and Continuing Problems of Three-Judge-Court Procedure, 1977, 65 Geo.L.J. 971.

2. 1908, 28 S.Ct. 441, 209 U.S. 123, 52 L.Ed. 714, fully discussed § 48 above.

3. The use of three-judge courts in these classes of cases was ended by statutes adopted in 1974 and 1975. See Boskey & Gressman, Recent Reforms in the Federal Judicial Structure—Three-Judge District Courts and Appellate Review, 1975, 67 F.R.D. 135.

4. 36 Stat. 557. The statute was codified as § 266 of the 1911 Judicial Code, and until its repeal in 1976, was § 2281 of the 1948 Judicial Code.

5. See 1910, 42 Cong.Rec. 4847, 4853.

The 1910 statute was amended in 1913 to include cases in which it was sought to enjoin enforcement of an administrative order made by an administrative board or commission acting under a state statute.[6] Again it was amended in 1925 to require three judges for the hearing on a permanent injunction as well as on the application for an interlocutory injunction, and thus end the anomaly by which a single judge, on the final hearing, might overrule the determination of three judges at the hearing on the interlocutory injunction.[7] Finally when the statute was codified as § 2281 of the 1948 Judicial Code it was made applicable to any action in which either a preliminary injunction or a permanent injunction was sought.

In the meantime in 1937, as one of the few remnants of President Roosevelt's court reform proposals to be enacted, similar provision was made for a three-judge court and direct review in actions for injunctions against Acts of Congress claimed to be unconstitutional.[8] This provision did not reach attacks on federal administrative orders.[9] The procedure for three-judge court actions was the same whether a state statute or an Act of Congress was challenged.[10]

The three-judge court statutes placed a heavy burden on the federal judiciary. It was frequently difficult to summon a second district judge and a judge of the court of appeals. The direct appeal to the Supreme Court was contrary to the general scheme giving that Court substantial control over its own docket. For these reasons the Court had said that the statute was not "a measure of broad social policy to be construed with great liberality, but * * * an enactment technical in the strict sense of the term and to be applied as such."[11]

---

6. 37 Stat. 1013. It may have been that this amendment was unnecessary, since the original statute covered such situations. See Oklahoma Natural Gas Co. v. Russell, 1923, 43 S.Ct. 353, 354, 261 U.S. 290, 292, 67 L.Ed. 659.

7. 43 Stat. 936. The statute as thus amended was construed to mean that a three-judge court was required only where an application for an interlocutory injunction had been made and pressed. Smith v. Wilson, 1927, 47 S.Ct. 385, 273 U.S. 388, 71 L.Ed. 699. This was not true under the 1948 revision of the statute. See ALI Study, p. 322.

The procedural provisions of the statute were further amended in 1942, 56 Stat. 199, to define more clearly the powers of a single judge in an action for a three-judge court.

8. 50 Stat. 752. Until its repeal in 1976, this statute was § 2282 of the 1948 Judicial Code.

9. William Jameson & Co. v. Morgenthau, 1939, 59 S.Ct. 804, 307 U.S. 171, 83 L.Ed. 1189.

10. The procedure was and is set out in 28 U.S.C.A. § 2284. The provision for direct appeal to the Supreme Court is 28 U.S.C.A. § 1253. See § 105 below.

11. Phillips v. U. S., 1941, 61 S.Ct. 480, 483, 312 U.S. 246, 251, 85 L.Ed. 800. See also Ex parte Collins, 1928, 48 S.Ct. 585, 586, 277 U.S. 565, 567, 72 L.Ed. 990; Swift & Co. v. Wickham, 1965, 86 S.Ct. 258, 267–268, 382 U.S. 111, 128–129, 15 L.Ed.2d 194.

In recent years there had been a sharp increase in the number of cases heard by three-judge courts. The average number of such cases in the years 1955–1959 was 48.8 per year, and this increased to 95.6 in 1960–1964, 174.8 in 1965–1969, and to 280.4 in 1970–1976. The peak was in 1973, with 320 of these cases. See ALI Study, pp. 317–318, and Ann.Rep. of the Director of the Administrative Office of the U. S. Courts, 1976, p. 208.

For these reasons also, there was in recent years a strong movement to abolish three-judge courts, which succeeded in 1976.

As a result of the 1976 legislation, it is no longer necessary to examine the enormously complicated body of law that grew up around "this deceptively simple statute." [12] There was great confusion on when three judges were required and the rules on appellate review of orders by or about three-judge courts were so complex as to be virtually beyond belief. Under the 1976 legislation a three-judge court is now required only "when otherwise required by Act of Congress" or "when an action is filed challenging the constitutionality of the apportionment of congressional districts or the apportionment of any statewide legislative body." [13] The mention of when otherwise required by Act of Congress refers principally to certain provisions of the Civil Rights Act of 1964 and the Voting Rights Act of 1965 that require or permit a three-judge court.[14] There will be few of these cases, and recent experience demonstrates that the number of three-judge courts that will be needed for reapportionment cases is so small as to be insignificant.[15] Thus the numerical burden of three-judge courts is now virtually ended, and the problems of construction of the opaque provisions of the former statutes should also now be a thing of the past.

The 1976 legislation also clarifies procedural points, for those few three-judge courts that will now be convened, that had previously been unclear. Thus, it is now specified that the single judge before whom the action is filed must determine for himself whether three judges are required before notifying the chief judge of the circuit. The role of the chief judge is the merely ministerial one of designating the other two judges, at least one of whom shall be a circuit

12. Sardino v. Federal Reserve Bank of New York, C.A.2d, 1966, 361 F.2d 106, 114, certiorari denied 87 S.Ct. 203, 385 U.S. 898, 17 L.Ed.2d 130.

The Supreme Court had commented on "the opaque terms and prolix syntax" of these "very awkwardly drafted" statutes. Gonzalez v. Automatic Employees Credit Union, 1974, 95 S.Ct. 289, 293–294, 419 U.S. 90, 96–97, 42 L.Ed.2d 249.

13. 28 U.S.C.A. § 2284(a), as amended by Act of Aug. 12, 1976, Pub.L. 94–381, § 3, 90 Stat. 1119.

14. A three-judge court is mandatory in suits under §§ 4(a), 5, and 10 of the 1965 statute, 42 U.S.C.A. §§ 1973b(a), 1973c, 1973h(c). The Attorney General may request a three-judge court in actions under the public accommodations and equal employment provisions of the 1964 statute, 42 U.S.C.A. §§ 2000a–5(b), 2000e–6(b). Either the At-

torney General or the defendant may request a three-judge court in actions under the voting provisions of the 1964 statute, 42 U.S.C.A. § 1971g.

A few other statutes requiring a three-judge court are cited in 17 Wright, Miller & Cooper, Jurisdiction § 4235 n. 5.

15. In the fiscal years 1973–1977 a total of 35 reapportionment cases were heard by three-judge courts, or an average of seven cases per year. In 1972, however, there were 32 of these cases heard. Ann.Rep. of the Director of the Administrative Office of the U. S. Courts, 1977, table 36. Thus there may be a temporary increase in the number of these suits after a decennial census. On the other hand, it is not clear that all of the cases included in those figures were of bodies coming within the 1976 statute.

judge.[16] The single judge can dismiss the action for want of jurisdiction [17] or if the plaintiff lacks standing or the suit is otherwise not justiciable in the federal courts.[18] If irreparable damage will otherwise result, he may grant a temporary restraining order to remain in force until the three-judge court has heard the case, and he may conduct all proceedings except the trial. A single judge, however, may not appoint a master, or order a reference, or hear and determine any application for a preliminary or permanent injunction or motion to vacate such an injunction, or enter judgment on the merits.[19] Nor may a single judge abstain in favor of a state court.[20]

It is unclear whether the former rule that the requirement of three judges is jurisdictional, and must be applied even if the parties never raise the point,[21] remains the law. Section 2284(a) says a three-judge court "shall be convened" in the circumstances there listed, but the procedural provisions of § 2284(b) say that the three-judge court is to be designated "[u]pon the filing of a request for three judges." There is nothing in the legislative history to indicate what Congress intended on this point. The best result would be if the Supreme Court should hold that in all cases under § 2284(a) a request is required and that the three-judge provision is not jurisdictional.[22] But unless and until it does the cautious course for a lower court in a case within § 2284(a) would be to convene a three-judge court even without a request.

The 1976 legislation did not change the statutory provision that any party may appeal to the Supreme Court from an order granting or denying, after notice and hearing, an interlocutory or permanent injunction in an action required by Act of Congress to be heard and determined by a district court of three judges.[23] In the years immediately prior to 1976 the Court, in an effort to rid itself of as many direct appeals as possible had developed a bewildering and constantly

16. 28 U.S.C.A. § 2284(b)(1). For the previous uncertainty on the role of the chief judge of the circuit, see ALI Study, pp. 327–329.

17. Ex parte Poresky, 1934, 54 S.Ct. 3, 290 U.S. 30, 78 L.Ed. 152.

18. Gonzalez v. Automatic Employees Credit Union, 1974, 95 S.Ct. 289, 419 U.S. 90, 42 L.Ed.2d 249; Sharrow v. Fish, D.C.N.Y.1980, 501 F.Supp. 202.

19. 28 U.S.C.A. § 2284(b)(3). It is not clear what, if anything, remains of the rule, first announced in Bailey v. Patterson, 1962, 82 S.Ct. 549, 369 U.S. 31, 7 L.Ed.2d 512, that a single judge can grant an injunction in a case otherwise within the three-judge court statute, where the unconstitutionality of the practice challenged is obvious and patent. See 17 Wright, Miller & Cooper, Jurisdiction § 4235, pp. 399–401.

20. Ryan v. State Bd. of Elections, C.A. 7th, 1981, 661 F.2d 1130; and cases cited 17 Wright, Miller & Cooper, Jurisdiction § 4235 n. 67.

21. Kennedy v. Mendoza-Martinez, 1963, 83 S.Ct. 554, 559, 372 U.S. 144, 153, 9 L.Ed.2d 644; Goosby v. Osser, 1973, 93 S.Ct. 854, 861, 409 U.S. 512, 522–523, 35 L.Ed.2d 36; see McLucas v. DeChamplain, 1975, 95 S.Ct. 1365, 1370, 421 U.S. 21, 27–29, 43 L.Ed.2d 699.

22. 17 Wright, Miller & Cooper, Jurisdiction § 4235, pp. 392–394; Currie, Federal Jurisdiction in a Nutshell, 2d ed. 1981, p. 219; Williams, note 1 above, at 975. For a contrary view, see Stern & Gressman, Supreme Court Practice, 5th ed. 1978, pp. 131–133.

23. 28 U.S.C.A. § 1253.

changing variety of rules on what orders were directly appealable to it and what were reviewable in the courts of appeals. With three-judge courts now virtually eliminated, it is to be hoped that the provision for direct appeal will be given a straight forward reading shorn of the complications introduced by the recent cases.[24]

§ 51. Other Statutory Restrictions on Injunctions Against State Officers [1]

In addition to the three-judge court acts, there are three other federal statutes that restrict federal injunctions against state officers. As a part of the 1913 amendment of the 1910 three-judge court statute, it was provided that a three-judge court shall, before final hearing, stay any action pending therein to enjoin the enforcement of a state statute or order if it appears that a state court of competent jurisdiction has stayed proceedings under the statute or order pending the determination in the state court of an action to enforce the statute or order. It was further provided that if the state court action is not prosecuted diligently and in good faith, the three-judge court may, after notice to the state attorney general, vacate its stay.[2] The statute was virtually a dead letter,[3] and was repealed when three-judge courts were substantially abolished in 1976.[4]

A statute of much greater importance is the Johnson Act of 1934.[5] This statute deprives the district courts of jurisdiction to enjoin the operation of any order of a state administrative agency or rate-making body affecting rates chargeable by a public utility.[6] Four condi-

24. See 17 Wright, Miller & Cooper, Jurisdiction § 4040.

[§ 51]

1. 17 Wright, Miller & Cooper, Jurisdiction §§ 4236 (Johnson Act), 4237 (Tax Injunction Act).

2. Former 28 U.S.C.A. § 2284(5).

3. Such a stay was granted in Traffic Tel. Workers' Federation v. Driscoll, D.C.N.J.1947, 72 F.Supp. 499, appeal dismissed 1947, 68 S.Ct. 221, 332 U.S. 833, 92 L.Ed. 406, and Judge Hutcheson describes a few unreported cases in which this procedure has been followed. Hutcheson, A Case for Three Judges, 1934, 47 Harv.L.Rev. 795, 822–825. On the general disuse of the provision, see Pogue, State Determination of State Law and the Judicial Code, 1928, 41 Harv.L.Rev. 623.

A stay on this ground was refused in Bush v. Orleans Parish Sch. Bd., D.C.La.1960, 190 F.Supp. 861, affirmed 1961, 81 S.Ct. 754, 365 U.S. 569, 5 L.Ed.2d 806, and in Ramos v. Health and Social Services Bd., D.C.Wis.1967, 276 F.Supp. 474.

4. See § 50 above.

5. Act of May 14, 1934, 48 Stat. 775, codified as 28 U.S.C.A. § 1342. See Comment, Limitation of Lower Federal Court Jurisdiction Over Public Utility Rate Cases, 1934, 44 Yale L.J. 119; Note, The Johnson Act—A Return to State Independence, 1935, 30 Ill.L.Rev. 215.

6. The statute applies to rates fixed by a city ordinance. East Ohio Gas Co. v. City of Cleveland, D.C.Ohio 1937, 23 F.Supp. 965, affirmed C.C.A. 6th, 1938, 94 F.2d 443, certiorari denied 58 S.Ct. 761, 303 U.S. 657, 82 L.Ed. 1116; Hartford Consumer Activists Assn. v. Hausman, D.C.Conn.1974, 381 F.Supp. 1275.

Since the Johnson Act does not apply only to a "rate" but to "any order affecting rates," it reaches charges for late payment of utility bills. Tennyson v. Gas Serv. Co., C.A.10th, 1974, 506 F.2d 1135. It does not reach a city ordinance requiring property owners to connect to a new public water system and abandon a private state-approved

tions must be met for the statute to be applicable. (1) Jurisdiction must be based solely on diversity of citizenship or repugnance to the federal Constitution. (2) The order must not interfere with interstate commerce.[7] (3) The order must have been made after reasonable notice and hearing.[8] (4) There must be "a plain, speedy and efficient remedy" in the courts of the state.[9] Thus the statute channels normal rate litigation into state courts while leaving the federal courts free to exercise their equity powers where necessary to relieve against arbitrary action.[10]

The other statute, enacted in 1937, prohibits an injunction against the assessment, levy, or collection of any tax under state law where a plain, speedy, and efficient remedy may be had in the state courts.[11] Although the requirement of a plain, speedy, and efficient remedy does not mean that "every wrinkle of federal equity practice was codified, intact, by Congress,"[12] the Court has not been able to find a significant difference between the equitable requirement of remedies that are "plain, adequate, and complete" and the slightly different

water supply system. Shrader v. Horton, D.C.Va.1979, 471 F.Supp. 1236, affirmed on opinion below C.A.4th, 1980, 626 F.2d 1163.

The American Law Institute proposes to broaden the Johnson Act to include also orders affecting "the conservation, production, or use of minerals, water, or other like natural resource of the State." ALI Study, § 1371(b)(1).

7. The only reported cases in which it has been held that the order would interfere with interstate commerce, and thus that the Johnson Act did not apply on this ground, are Public Utilities Comm. of Ohio v. United Fuel Gas Co., 1943, 63 S.Ct. 369, 317 U.S. 456, 87 L.Ed. 396, and Tri-State Generation & Transmission Assn., Inc. v. Public Serv. Comm. of Wyoming, C.A.10th, 1969, 412 F.2d 115, certiorari denied 1970, 90 S.Ct. 1348, 397 U.S. 1043, 25 L.Ed.2d 654.

The American Law Institute proposes to remove this restriction and to provide instead that the statute applies if "the power of the State to make such order has not been superseded by any Act of Congress or administrative regulation thereunder." ALI Study, § 1371(b)(4).

8. Petroleum Exploration, Inc. v. Public Serv. Comm. of Kentucky, 1938, 58 S.Ct. 834, 304 U.S. 209, 82 L.Ed. 1294; City of El Paso v. Texas Cities Gas Co., C.C.A.5th, 1938, 100 F.2d 501, certiorari denied 59 S.Ct. 592, 306 U.S. 650, 83 L.Ed. 1049. The federal court, rather than the state, determines what is reasonable notice and hearing. City of

Meridian v. Mississippi Val. Gas Co., C.A.5th, 1954, 214 F.2d 525.

9. Doubt as to whether the state remedy is plain, speedy, and efficient will be resolved in favor of federal jurisdiction. Mountain States Power Co. v. Public Serv. Comm. of Montana, 1936, 57 S.Ct. 168, 299 U.S. 167, 81 L.Ed. 99; Driscoll v. Edison Light & Power Co., 1939, 59 S.Ct. 715, 307 U.S. 104, 83 L.Ed. 1134.

10. City of Meridian v. Mississippi Val. Gas Co., C.A.5th, 1954, 214 F.2d 525; Kansas-Nebraska Natural Gas Co. v. City of St. Edward, D.C.Neb.1955, 135 F.Supp. 629.

11. Act of Aug. 21, 1937, 50 Stat. 738, codified as 28 U.S.C.A. § 1341. A similar provision bars injunctions against the collection of federal taxes. 26 U.S. C.A. § 7421(a).

The Tax Injunction Act does not apply to suits challenging tax discrimination against railroad or motor carrier transportation property. 49 U.S.C.A. §§ 11503(c), 11503a(c).

On the meaning of "tax," see Robinson Protective Alarm Co. v. City of Philadelphia, C.A.3d, 1978, 581 F.2d 371. On the meaning of "assessment, levy, or collection," compare Wells v. Malloy, C.A.2d, 1975, 510 F.2d 74, on remand D.C.Vt., 402 F.Supp. 856, affirmed C.A.2d, 1976, 538 F.2d 317, with Huber Pontiac, Inc. v. Whitler, C.A. 7th, 1978, 585 F.2d 817.

12. Rosewell v. LaSalle Nat. Bank, 1981, 101 S.Ct. 1221, 1235, 450 U.S. 503, 525, 67 L.Ed.2d 464.

list of phrases in the Tax Injunction Act.[13] All that is required is a state court remedy that meets certain minimal procedural criteria.[14] The state remedy will not bar a federal injunction where it is unduly burdensome, as where the taxpayer would have had to file over 300 separate claims in 14 different counties.[15] A state remedy either in law or in equity will, if otherwise adequate, suffice to defeat jurisdiction.[16] Grave doubt as to the existence of the state remedy will permit the federal court to act.[17] But the state remedy, to satisfy this section, need not necessarily be the best remedy available or even equal to or better than the remedy that might be available in federal court.[18]

Neither statute in terms prohibits the granting of a declaratory judgment. The Supreme Court, without deciding whether the Tax Injunction Act bars a declaratory judgment as to state taxes, has held that the federal courts should abstain from giving such a judgment where there is a suitable state procedure for challenging the tax.[19] Similarly the Court, while recognizing that a suit challenging the refusal of a state agency to permit discontinuance of trains is not a rate order and thus not within the Johnson Act, has held that the federal courts should abstain from hearing such a suit where there is an adequate state judicial remedy.[20]

---

13. Fair Assessment in Real Estate Assn., Inc. v. McNary, 1981, 102 S.Ct. 177, 186 n. 8, 454 U.S. 100, 116 n. 8, 70 L.Ed.2d 271.

14. Rosewell v. LaSalle Nat. Bank, 1981, 101 S.Ct. 1221, 1228–1234, 450 U.S. 503, 512–524, 67 L.Ed.2d 464. The holding there is that a state remedy is plain, speedy, and efficient even though it is long-delayed and makes no provision for interest on refunds.

See also California v. Grace Brethren Church, 1982, 102 S.Ct. 2498, ___ U.S. ___, 73 L.Ed.2d 93.

15. Georgia R. & Banking Co. v. Redwine, 1952, 72 S.Ct. 321, 342 U.S. 299, 96 L.Ed. 335.

16. Garrett v. Bamford, C.A.3d, 1978, 582 F.2d 810, 820. This was stated expressly when the statute was adopted in 1937, but the words "at law or in equity" were dropped in the 1948 revision as "unnecessary."

A declaratory judgment can be a sufficient remedy. Tully v. Griffin, 1976, 97 S.Ct. 219, 429 U.S. 68, 50 L.Ed.2d 227.

17. Hillsborough Twp., Somerset County, New Jersey v. Cromwell, 1946, 66 S.Ct. 445, 326 U.S. 620, 90 L.Ed. 358; U. S. v. Livingston, D.C.S.C.1959, 179

F.Supp. 9, affirmed 1961, 80 S.Ct. 1611, 364 U.S. 281, 4 L.Ed.2d 1719.

18. See Bland v. McHann, C.A.5th, 1972, 463 F.2d 21, 29, 1973, certiorari denied 93 S.Ct. 1438, 410 U.S. 966, 35 L.Ed.2d 700; and cases cited 17 Wright, Miller & Cooper, Jurisdiction § 4237 n. 21.

19. Great Lakes Dredge & Dock Co. v. Huffman, 1943, 63 S.Ct. 1070, 319 U.S. 293, 87 L.Ed. 1407; see Lynch v. Household Fin. Corp., 1972, 92 S.Ct. 1113, 1117 n. 6, 405 U.S. 538, 542 n. 6, 31 L.Ed.2d 424.

The American Law Institute proposes to make both the Tax Injunction Act and the Johnson Act applicable in terms to actions for a declaratory judgment. ALI Study, § 1371(a), (b).

The question left open in the Great Lakes case was decided in California v. Grace Brethren Church, 1982, 102 S.Ct. 2498, ___ U.S. ___, 73 L.Ed.2d 93, and it was held that the Tax Injunction Act prohibits a declaratory judgment holding state tax laws unconstitutional.

20. Alabama Public Serv. Comm. v. Southern Ry. Co., 1951, 71 S.Ct. 762, 341 U.S. 341, 95 L.Ed. 1002.

See also Tennyson v. Gas Serv. Co., C.A. 10th, 1974, 506 F.2d 1135.

The Supreme Court recently heard a case in which taxpayers sued for damages under the civil rights statute, 42 U.S.C.A. § 1983, for alleged unconstitutional administration of a state tax system. The Court refrained from deciding whether the Tax Injunction Act, standing alone, barred the suit. Instead it held that the principle of comity bars taxpayers from asserting § 1983 actions against the validity of state tax systems in federal courts.[21]

Neither the Johnson Act nor the Tax Injunction Act applies to a suit brought by the United States.[22] Nor does the Tax Injunction Act apply to a suit between states in the original jurisdiction of the Supreme Court.[23]

§ 52. The Abstention Doctrines [1]

In 1824 Chief Justice Marshall said: "It is most true, that this court will not take jurisdiction if it should not; but it is equally true, that it must take jurisdiction, if it should. The judiciary cannot, as the legislature may, avoid a measure, because it approaches the confines of the constitution. * * * With whatever doubts, with whatever difficulties, a case may be attended, we must decide it, if it be brought before us. We have no more right to decline the exercise of jurisdiction which is given, than to usurp that which is not given. The one or the other would be treason to the constitution."[2]

It may be that there was never such a rule, uniformly applied, in the federal courts. It is clear that there is no such rule today. Since

---

21. Fair Assessment in Real Estate Assn., Inc. v. McNary, 1981, 102 S.Ct. 177, 454 U.S. 100, 70 L.Ed.2d 271. Four Justices rejected this use of comity, but agreed with the result because the taxpayers had failed to exhaust their administrative remedies.

It would seem to follow a fortiori that if a case comes within the terms of the Johnson Act or the Tax Injunction Act, the bar of those statutes is not escaped because suit is under § 1983.

22. Department of Employment v. U. S., 1966, 87 S.Ct. 464, 385 U.S. 355, 17 L.Ed.2d 414 (Tax Injunction Act); see U. S. v. Public Utilities Comm. of California, D.C.Cal.1956, 141 F.Supp. 168, affirmed 1958, 78 S.Ct. 146, 355 U.S. 534, 2 L.Ed.2d 470 (Johnson Act); ALI Study, § 1371(g).

Nor does § 1341 apply to a suit by an Indian tribe brought pursuant to 28 U.S. C.A. § 1362. Moe v. Confederated Salish & Kootenai Tribes, 1976, 96 S.Ct. 1634, 425 U.S. 463, 48 L.Ed.2d 96.

23. Maryland v. Louisiana, 1981, 101 S.Ct. 2114, 2128 n. 21, 451 U.S. 725, 745 n. 21, 68 L.Ed.2d 576.

[§ 52]

1. 17 Wright, Miller & Cooper, Jurisdiction §§ 4241–4248. Only the more recent writings on abstention are cited here. For earlier commentary, see 17 id. § 4241 n. 1.

Wells, The Role of Comity in the Law of Federal Courts, 1981, 60 N.C.L.Rev. 59; McMillan, Abstention—The Judiciary's Self-Inflicted Wound, 1978, 56 N.C.L.Rev. 527; Field, The Abstention Doctrine Today, 1977, 125 U.Pa.L.Rev. 590; Ashman, Alfini & Shapiro, Federal Abstention: New Perspectives on its Current Vitality, 1975, 46 Miss.L.J. 629; Bezanson, Abstention: The Supreme Court and Allocation of Judicial Power, 1974, 27 Vand.L.Rev. 1107; Pell, Abstention—A Primrose Path by Any Other Name, 1972, 21 DePaul L.Rev. 926.

2. Cohens v. Virginia, 1821, 6 Wheat. 264, 404, 5 L.Ed. 257. For a more recent expression to similar effect, see Willcox v. Consolidated Gas Co., 1909, 29 S.Ct. 192, 195, 212 U.S. 19, 40, 53 L.Ed. 382.

1941 there has been considerable recognition of circumstances under which a federal court may decline to proceed though it has jurisdiction under the Constitution and the statutes. The cases in which this has been recognized are usually referred to as establishing the "abstention doctrine," but it is more precise to refer to "abstention doctrines" since there are at least four distinguishable lines of cases, involving different factual situations, different procedural consequences, different support in the decisions of the Supreme Court, and different arguments for and against their validity.[3] Thus abstention is variously recognized: (1) to avoid decision of a federal constitutional question where the case may be disposed of on questions of state law; (2) to avoid needless conflict with the administration by a state of its own affairs; (3) to leave to the states the resolution of unsettled questions of state law; and (4) to ease the congestion of the federal court docket. These various doctrines overlap at times, and the courts have not always distinguished them clearly, but separate consideration of them will conduce to clarity of analysis.

The first of these doctrines, and the most clearly established, comes in cases where state action is being challenged in federal court as contrary to the federal constitution, and there are questions of state law that may be dispositive of the case. This is usually referred to as the Pullman doctrine, from the case of Railroad Commission of Texas v. Pullman Co.,[4] which is probably the first and surely the leading case supporting abstention in such circumstances. In that case the company was seeking to enjoin enforcement of an order of the Texas Railroad Commission, claiming that the order denied its rights under the Fourteenth Amendment and claiming also that Texas law did not give the Commission authority to make the order in question. It is settled that a federal court has jurisdiction to decide the ancillary state issues in such a case,[5] but the wisdom of exercising such jurisdiction is doubtful. A unanimous Court, speaking

3. The Supreme Court, the lower courts, and the commentators differ on how many abstention doctrines there are. Respectable support can be found for classifying the cases into two, three, four, or five categories. The number is of little significance, since the division is a mere organizational convenience. The present author has found the four-part division set forth in the text the most useful. On this view the "Our Federalism" cases, see § 52A below, are regarded as a special case of the second category, while certification is regarded as a procedural device that may be used in cases falling within the first and third categories.

4. 1941, 61 S.Ct. 643, 312 U.S. 496, 85 L.Ed. 971.

Abstention is a "judge-made doctrine * * *, first fashioned in 1941 in Railroad Commission of Texas v. Pullman Co." Zwickler v. Koota, 1967, 88 S.Ct. 391, 395, 389 U.S. 241, 248, 19 L.Ed.2d 444, on remand D.C.N.Y.1968, 290 F.Supp. 244, reversed 1969, 89 S.Ct. 956, 394 U.S. 103, 22 L.Ed.2d 113. For the history of the abstention doctrines, and how the Court has vacillated about them, see 17 Wright, Miller & Cooper, Jurisdiction § 4241.

5. Siler v. Louisville & N. R. Co., 1909, 29 S.Ct. 451, 213 U.S. 175, 53 L.Ed. 753. See also Schmidt v. Oakland Unified Sch. Dist., 1982, 102 S.Ct. 2612, ___ U.S. ___, 73 L.Ed.2d 245.

through Justice Frankfurter, said: "In this situation a federal court of equity is asked to decide an issue by making a tentative answer which may be displaced tomorrow by a state adjudication. * * * The resources of equity are equal to an adjustment that will avoid the waste of a tentative decision as well as the friction of a premature constitutional adjudication." [6] The Court ordered the trial court to abstain from deciding the case but to retain jurisdiction until the parties had had an opportunity to obtain from the state court a decision on the state issues involved. In this way the state court decides the state issues, and the federal court avoids deciding a federal constitutional question prematurely or unnecessarily, since if the state court should hold the order unauthorized as a matter of state law, there will be no need for the federal court to pass on the federal question.

Abstention of the Pullman type has been ordered by the Supreme Court in many cases, and usually with substantial unanimity.[7] It will not be ordered if the state law is clear on its face, or if its meaning has already been authoritatively decided by the state courts, or if the constitutional issue would not be avoided or changed no matter how the statute is construed. For abstention to be appropriate, the state law must be "fairly subject to an interpretation which will render unnecessary or substantially modify the federal constitutional question." [8] Abstention is not proper merely to give a state court the opportunity to hold that the statute violates the federal Constitution.[9] The issue is somewhat more complicated if the state statute is clear but there is a fair possibility that the state court may hold that the statute violates the state constitution. In these cases abstention is in order if the case may turn on the interpretation of some specialized

---

6. 61 S.Ct. at 645, 312 U.S. at 500. This view was anticipated by Isseks, Jurisdiction of the Lower Federal Courts to Enjoin Unauthorized Action of State Officials, 1927, 40 Harv.L.Rev. 969.

7. 17 Wright, Miller & Cooper, Jurisdiction § 4242; Field, Abstention in Constitutional Cases: The Scope of the Pullman Abstention Doctrine, 1974, 122 U.Pa.L.Rev. 1071.

See ALI Study, § 1371(c), where it is proposed to put this type of abstention, with some modifications, into statutory form.

8. Harman v. Forssenius, 1965, 85 S.Ct. 1177, 1182, 380 U.S. 528, 534–535, 14 L.Ed.2d 50, quoted in Babbitt v. United Farm Workers Nat. Union, 1979, 99 S.Ct. 2301, 2313, 442 U.S. 289, 306, 60 L.Ed.2d 895. See 17 Wright, Miller &

Cooper, Jurisdiction § 4242, pp. 455–460.

A claim that a state statute is unconstitutionally vague may call for abstention if the question is whether the statute applies to a particular person or a defined course of conduct, but abstention is not required if that claim is that persons to whom the statute plainly applies simply cannot understand what is required of them. Procunier v. Martinez, 1974, 94 S.Ct. 1800, 1805 n. 5, 416 U.S. 396, 401 n. 5, 40 L.Ed.2d 224.

9. The leading case is Wisconsin v. Constantineau, 1971, 91 S.Ct. 507, 400 U.S. 433, 27 L.Ed.2d 515. See also Zablocki v. Redhail, 1978, 98 S.Ct. 673, 677 n. 5, 434 U.S. 374, 379 n. 5, 54 L.Ed.2d 618; Douglas v. Seacoast Products, Inc., 1977, 97 S.Ct. 1740, 1744 n. 4, 431 U.S. 265, 271 n. 4, 52 L.Ed.2d 304.

state constitutional provision,[10] but not if "the state constitutional provision is the mirror of the federal one." [11]

The price of Pullman-type abstention is not cheap. In a number of well-known cases it has led to delays of many years before the case was finally decided on its merits [12] or limped to an inconclusive end.[13] This delay and expense can only be justified as the price that must be paid to satisfy the exigent demands of federalism and the vital policy of judicial review that dictates against unnecessary resolution of a federal constitutional issue. Experience with abstention has caused some to conclude that this is "an unnecessary price to pay for our federalism."[14] The Supreme Court itself has showed occasional signs of disenchantment with the practice it created in the Pullman case. In one case it said that "we also cannot ignore that abstention operates to require piecemeal adjudication in many courts * * * thereby delaying ultimate adjudication on the merits for an undue length of time," and held that "special circumstances" must exist to justify abstention.[15] In another case it held abstention un-

10. Harris County Commrs. Court v. Moore, 1975, 95 S.Ct. 870, 420 U.S. 77, 43 L.Ed.2d 32; Reetz v. Bozanich, 1970, 90 S.Ct. 788, 397 U.S. 82, 25 L.Ed.2d 68.

11. Herald Co. v. McNeal, C.A.8th, 1977, 553 F.2d 1125, 1130 n. 8. See Examining Bd. of Engineers, Architects & Surveyors v. Flores de Otero, 1976, 96 S.Ct. 2264, 2279, 426 U.S. 572, 598, 49 L.Ed.2d 65; Santa Fe Land Improvement Co. v. City of Chula Vista, C.A. 9th, 1979, 596 F.2d 838, 840 n. 3; White v. Edgar, Me.1974, 320 A.2d 668. But cf. Friendly, Federal Jurisdiction: A General View, 1973, p. 93.

12. E.g., Spector Motor Serv., Inc. v. O'Connor, 1951, 71 S.Ct. 508, 340 U.S. 602, 95 L.Ed. 573 (seven years); England v. Louisiana State Bd. of Medical Examiners, 1966, 86 S.Ct. 1924, 384 U.S. 885, 16 L.Ed.2d 998 (six years).

13. U. S. v. Leiter Minerals, Inc., 1965, 85 S.Ct. 1575, 381 U.S. 413, 14 L.Ed.2d 692 (dismissed as moot eight years after abstention ordered). See also the Government and Civic Employees case, described at ALI Study, p. 283, in which plaintiff abandoned the fight when five years of litigation, including two trips to the United States Supreme Court and two to the Alabama Supreme Court, had failed to produce a decision on the merits.

14. England v. Louisiana State Bd. of Medical Examiners, 1964, 84 S.Ct. 461,

470, 375 U.S. 411, 426, 11 L.Ed.2d 440 (Douglas, J., concurring). See also the view of a commentator that abstention has "a Bleak House aspect that in my mind is too high a price to pay for the gains in avoiding error, friction, and constitutional questions." Currie, The Federal Courts and the American Law Institute (Part II), 1969, 36 U.Chi.L. Rev. 268, 317.

15. Baggett v. Bullitt, 1964, 84 S.Ct. 1316, 1324–1326, 377 U.S. 360, 375–379, 12 L.Ed.2d 377.

The Court continues to require "special circumstances" to justify abstention, Kusper v. Pontikes, 1973, 94 S.Ct. 303, 306, 414 U.S. 51, 54, 38 L.Ed.2d 260, but is not reluctant to order abstention when it finds those circumstances present. E.g., Lake Carriers' Assn. v. MacMullan, 1972, 92 S.Ct. 1749, 406 U.S. 498, 32 L.Ed.2d 257; Harris County Commrs. Court v. Moore, 1975, 95 S.Ct. 870, 420 U.S. 77, 43 L.Ed.2d 32; Bellotti v. Baird, 1976, 96 S.Ct. 2857, 428 U.S. 132, 49 L.Ed.2d 844.

The delay that abstention will cause is a factor to be weighed against abstention if important interests will be harmed by the delay. Anderson v. Babb, C.A.4th, 1980, 632 F.2d 300; Lister v. Lucey, C.A.7th, 1978, 575 F.2d 1325, 1333, certiorari denied 99 S.Ct. 190, 439 U.S. 865, 58 L.Ed.2d 175; Field, note 7 above, at 1129–1134.

warranted where neither party had requested it and the litigation had already been long delayed.[16]

In the Pullman case the Supreme Court ordered the trial court to retain jurisdiction while the parties sought a state ruling on the state issues. Since retention of jurisdiction is usually [17] ordered in Pullman-type cases, the Court has defended abstention, saying "this principle does not, of course, involve the abdication of federal jurisdiction but only the postponement of its exercise * * *." [18] The implementation of this, however, has led to a complicated procedure. The Court first held that the federal constitutional objections must be presented to the state court, so that it may consider the issues of state law in the light of the constitutional claims.[19] But if the state court should decide the federal issues, on ordinary principles of res judicata this would be a binding determination, subject to review only in the Supreme Court, and there would be nothing left for the federal court to decide in the exercise of the jurisdiction it had retained. Since the Supreme Court cannot hear every case tendered to it, this would mean that many litigants would never have a hearing in a federal court though they were asserting claims based on federal law. As the Court said in England v. Louisiana State Board of Medical Examiners,[20] the possibility of review in the Supreme Court is an inadequate substitute for the determination by a district court to which the litigant has a statutory right. "This is true as to issues of law; it is especially true as to issues of fact. Limiting the litigant to review here would deny him the benefit of a federal trial court's role in constructing a record and making fact findings. How the facts are found will often dictate the decision of federal claims." [21] Thus in the England case the Court announced that though a litigant may submit all aspects of the case for a binding adjudication by the state court,[22]

---

16. Hostetter v. Idlewild Bon Voyage Liquor Corp., 1964, 84 S.Ct. 1293, 1296, 377 U.S. 324, 329, 12 L.Ed.2d 350. See also Mayor of City of Philadelphia v. Educational Equality League, 1974, 94 S.Ct. 1323, 1337, 415 U.S. 605, 628, 39 L.Ed.2d 630.

But a request from a party is not required and abstention may be raised by the court sua sponte. Bellotti v. Baird, 1976, 96 S.Ct. 2857, 2864 n. 10, 428 U.S. 132, 143 n. 10, 49 L.Ed.2d 844.

17. This is said to be the "proper course" in American Trial Lawyers Assn. v. New Jersey Supreme Court, 1973, 93 S.Ct. 627, 629, 409 U.S. 467, 469, 34 L.Ed.2d 651. Dismissal without prejudice may be ordered where retention of jurisdiction would interfere with obtaining a state court decision. Harris County Commrs. Court v. Moore, 1975, 95 S.Ct. 870, 878 n. 14, 420 U.S. 77, 88 n. 14, 43 L.Ed.2d 32.

18. Harrison v. National Assn. for the Advancement of Colored People, 1959, 79 S.Ct. 1025, 1030, 360 U.S. 167, 175, 3 L.Ed.2d 1152. See Allen v. McCurry, 1980, 101 S.Ct. 411, 418 n. 17, 449 U.S. 90, 101 n. 17, 66 L.Ed.2d 308.

On the procedural consequences of Pullman-type abstention generally, see 17 Wright, Miller & Cooper, Jurisdiction § 4243.

19. Government and Civic Employees Organizing Committee, CIO v. Windsor, 1957, 77 S.Ct. 838, 839, 353 U.S. 364, 366, 1 L.Ed.2d 894.

20. 1964, 84 S.Ct. 461, 375 U.S. 411, 11 L.Ed.2d 440.

21. 84 S.Ct. at 465, 375 U.S. at 416.

22. National Assn. for the Advancement of Colored People v. Button, 1963, 83 S.Ct. 328, 335, 371 U.S. 415, 427, 9 L.Ed.2d 405.

he is not required to do so. Any party may make on the state record a reservation to the disposition of the entire case by the state courts, by informing them that he is exposing his federal contentions only as a matter of information, and that he intends to return to the federal court for disposition of the federal contentions.[23]

There are two difficulties with the procedure announced in England. Many state courts will consider that if such a reservation is made, they are disabled from deciding the state issues since their decision would be a mere advisory opinion.[24] Even where the England procedure is acceptable to the state court, it invites the kind of shuttling back and forth between judicial systems that aggravates the delay inherently involved in abstention.[25] Given the state of the precedents at the time England was decided, the rule it announces was probably the best possible reconciliation of conflicting interests. If it were possible to start fresh, however, it would seem wiser to provide that, barring some unusual turn of events, a case should not return to the federal court after abstention has been ordered but should be fully and finally adjudicated by the state court with review possible in the Supreme Court. For this to be workable, it would be necessary also to provide that the federal court is not to abstain if the federal claims, and the issues of fact material to them, cannot be adequately protected by Supreme Court review of the state court decision.[26]

There are cases in which abstention is indicated under the Pullman doctrine, but in which the federal plaintiff will be seriously harmed if the state law is enforced while the state questions are being tested in the state court. Since the federal court is to retain jurisdiction rather than dismiss in these cases, it may give whatever interim relief is needed to protect the party during the period of abstention.[27]

---

23. 84 S.Ct. at 468, 375 U.S. at 421–422. See Liebenthal, A Dialogue on England: The England Case, Its Effect on the Abstention Doctrine, and Some Suggested Solutions, 1966, 18 West. Res.L.Rev. 157; 17 Wright, Miller & Cooper, Jurisdiction § 4243, pp. 476–480.

24. Cf. United Services Life Ins. Co. v. Delaney, Tex.1965, 396 S.W.2d 855, noted 1966, 20 Sw.L.J. 402, 44 Texas L.Rev. 1394; In re Richards, Me.1966, 223 A.2d 827. See Leiter Minerals, Inc., v. California Co., 1961, 132 So.2d 845, 241 La. 915, where the court said it was being asked to give an advisory opinion, but gave it anyhow as a matter of courtesy to, and respect for, the United States Supreme Court. Of course some state courts are free to give advisory opinions. See Sun Ins. Office, Ltd. v. Clay, Fla.1961, 133 So.2d

735. For discussion of the problems of justiciability that abstention poses for the state court, see Note, 1962, 40 Tex. L.Rev. 1041.

25. See notes 12 and 13 above.

26. The proposal in the text is that made by the American Law Institute. ALI Study, § 1371(c), (d). It is criticized in Redish, note 1 above, at pp. 255–256.

27. Babbitt v. United Farm Workers Nat. Union, 1979, 99 S.Ct. 2301, 2316 n. 18, 442 U.S. 289, 309 n. 18, 60 L.Ed.2d 895; Catrone v. Massachusetts State Racing Comm., C.A.1st, 1976, 535 F.2d 669; Deck House, Inc. v. New Jersey State Bd. of Architects, D.C.N.J.1982, 531 F.Supp. 633, 644–648; ALI Study, p. 261; Wells, Preliminary Injunctions and Abstention: Some Problems in Federalism, 1977, 63 Cornell L.Rev. 65.

A second type of abstention, which takes its name from the leading case of Burford v. Sun Oil Co.,[28] is Burford-type abstention. Its general thrust can be well captured by saying that abstention is ordered to avoid needless conflict with the administration by a state of its own affairs, though neither this nor any other attempt at defining the class of cases in which this type of abstention is proper is very precise. In Burford a sharply-divided Court held that the federal court should have dismissed the complaint in a case involving proration orders in Texas oil fields, on the ground that the issues involved a specialized aspect of a complicated regulatory system of local law, which should be left to the local administrative bodies and courts. Later the Court divided again in saying that a federal court should have declined jurisdiction of an action by a railroad challenging the order of a state regulatory commission refusing to permit discontinuance of certain trains. The railroad could have appealed from the commission's order to a state court, but had come instead to the federal court on the basis both of diversity of citizenship and of a federal question. The Supreme Court said: "As adequate state court review of an administrative order based upon predominantly local factors is available to appellee, intervention of a federal court is not necessary for the protection of federal rights." [29]

In Burford-type abstention, where the federal court defers to avoid interference with state activities, dismissal of the action, rather than retention of jurisdiction pending a state determination, is normally appropriate.[30] If the state court to which deference is thus shown prejudices any federal rights of the parties, this can be redressed by review of the state decision in the United States Supreme Court.

Two important cases, decided on the same day in 1959, must now be considered. It may be that they are only further examples of when Burford-type abstention is appropriate, but it is possible that they represent an extension of the third type of abstention, because of unsettled state law, which is yet to be discussed. Both cases grew out of state eminent domain proceedings. In County of Allegheny v.

---

28. 1943, 63 S.Ct. 1098, 319 U.S. 315, 87 L.Ed. 1424.

The strong feelings the Burford case produced within the Supreme Court are reported in Lash, From the Diaries of Felix Frankfurter, 1975, pp. 226–228.

29. Alabama Public Serv. Comm. v. Southern R. Co., 1951, 71 S.Ct. 762, 768, 341 U.S. 341, 349, 95 L.Ed. 1002.

30. 17 Wright, Miller & Cooper, Jurisdiction § 4245.

This is not inconsistent with ordering retention of jurisdiction simply against the possibility that something should prevent a prompt state court determination. Kaiser Steel Corp. v. W. S. Ranch Co., 1968, 88 S.Ct. 1753, 391 U.S. 593, 20 L.Ed.2d 835, noted 1969 Utah L.Rev. 196; ALI Study, § 1371(d). In the Kaiser Steel case, abstention was ordered so that the state courts could decide a novel question of water law of vital concern to a dry state such as New Mexico. This is probably best understood as Burford-type abstention, and it is so explained in a concurring opinion by three justices. The opinion of the Court is silent on the point. Cf. ALI Study, § 1371(b).

Frank Mashuda Co.,[31] the landowner brought an independent action of ouster, as the state law permitted, to challenge the validity of the taking, and brought it in federal court on the basis of diversity. Though the state law was regarded, rightly or not, as clearly settled, the district court, believing it should not interfere with the administration of the affairs of a political subdivision acting under color of state law, dismissed the action. In the other case, Louisiana Power & Light Co. v. City of Thibodaux,[32] the condemnee removed the condemnation action itself to federal court on the basis of diversity, and challenged the taking in that action. The state law here was regarded, rightly or not, as confused. The state statute seemed to permit the taking, but it was old and unconstrued by the courts, and an opinion of the state attorney general appeared to deny such a power. The trial judge, on his own motion, ordered the condemnation action stayed until the state court had had an opportunity to construe the statute relied on.

The cases are distinguishable in only two respects. In the Allegheny County case, the state law was thought to be clear; in the City of Thibodaux case, it was thought to be unclear. In the Allegheny County case, the trial court ordered the action dismissed, while in the other case it had merely ordered the federal action stayed. The Supreme Court held, 5–4, that it was error for the court in the Allegheny County case to dismiss the action and directed it to decide the case. At the same time the Court, by a vote of 6–3, upheld the stay of the federal action ordered in the City of Thibodaux. Perhaps the results can be reconciled on the basis of the two factual distinctions between the cases, but the opinions cannot be reconciled. The opinion in the City of Thibodaux case, upholding the stay, rested heavily on "the special nature of eminent domain" proceedings. A majority of the Court declared of eminent domain, "it is intimately involved with sovereign prerogative."[33] A majority of the same Court, on the same day, declared in the Allegheny County case that "surely eminent domain is no more mystically involved with 'sovereign prerogative' than"[34] a number of other matters on which abstention has been refused. Nor is difficulty dispelled by the fact that the dissenting opinion in City of Thibodaux is in all respects similar to, and in many passages taken verbatim from, the opinion for the Court in Allegheny County.

The two cases, taken together, do establish that an abstention doctrine can apply in eminent domain cases. Beyond this two explana-

31. 1959, 79 S.Ct. 1060, 360 U.S. 185, 3 L.Ed.2d 1163.

32. 1959, 79 S.Ct. 1070, 360 U.S. 25, 3 L.Ed.2d 1058.

33. 79 S.Ct. at 1073, 360 U.S. at 28.

In Crawford v. Courtney, C.A.4th, 1971, 451 F.2d 489, the court relied on the City of Thibodaux case, to hold that af-

ter a state court had decreed condemnation the federal court should abstain from entertaining a declaratory judgment action to decide who was entitled to the fund created by the condemnation.

34. 79 S.Ct. at 1064–1065, 360 U.S. at 190–192.

tions are possible. One is that abstention is proper in eminent domain cases where the state law is unsettled. If this explanation be sound, then the special nature of eminent domain proceedings, combined with difficulties of state law, will permit abstention though neither of the circumstances individually would suffice. An alternative explanation is that the grant of a stay in an eminent domain case is a matter of discretion for the trial court. This explanation has its own difficulties. As noted above, in Burford-type abstention, as contrasted with Pullman-type abstention, dismissal of the federal action, rather than a stay, is normally appropriate. Yet the Allegheny County case holds squarely that dismissal was erroneous while the City of Thibodaux case affirms a stay. Further, though the abstention doctrines have their origin in the discretion of equity judges, in the situations heretofore considered no discretion has been recognized. If the case was an appropriate one for abstention, then the trial judge committed reversible error by failure to abstain. Yet the majority opinion in City of Thibodaux speaks broadly of the district court "exercising a fair and well-considered judicial discretion in staying proceedings" [35] while the dissenters in the Allegheny County case argue that in view of peculiar circumstances of the case the trial judge had not "clearly abused his discretion." [36] That the Court may be willing to confide more to the discretion of the trial court in determining whether to abstain is suggested also by a decision two weeks after the cases just considered in which, in a Pullman-type situation, the Court ruled that reference to the state courts for construction of the state statute should not automatically be made, and remanded for the trial court to exercise its considered discretion.[37]

It may even be that attempts to explain the two decisions are a futile exercise. Seven of the nine members of the Court found the two cases indistinguishable, and would have reached the same result in both cases, though differing as to what that result should be. Thus any nice distinction that might have been drawn between the two cases probably would not have been acceptable to a majority of the Court.[38]

Perhaps the best that can be said about Burford-type abstention is that it may be appropriate if the state, as in Burford itself and in the

35. 79 S.Ct. at 1074, 360 U.S. at 30.

36. 79 S.Ct. at 1070, 360 U.S. at 25.

37. National Assn. for the Advancement of Colored People v. Bennett, 1959, 79 S.Ct. 1192, 360 U.S. 471, 3 L.Ed.2d 1375.

In his concurring opinion in England v. Louisiana State Bd. of Medical Examiners, 1964, 84 S.Ct. 461, 473, 375 U.S. 411, 432, 11 L.Ed.2d 440, Justice Douglas argues that Pullman-type abstention should be made "less of a mandatory and more a discretionary procedure." Abstention would always

be discretionary under the proposals of the American Law Institute. ALI Study, § 1371(c). See also Comment, The Exercise of the Abstention Doctrine and Its Consequences: A Clarification, 1968, 6 Duquesne L.Rev. 269.

38. See 17 Wright, Miller & Cooper, Jurisdiction § 4241, pp. 437–441; Redish, note 1 above, at pp. 240–243; Comment, Abstention by Federal Courts in Suits Challenging State Administrative Decisions: The Scope of the Burford Doctrine, 1979, 46 U.Chi.L.Rev. 971.

train discontinuance case, has a unified scheme for review of its administrative orders and federal intervention in cases in which diversity is present would have a disruptive effect on the state's efforts to establish a coherent policy on a matter of substantial public concern. This type of abstention is also proper if there is a difficult question of state law bearing on policy problems of substantial public importance transcending the result in the case at bar.[39]

All of the abstention cases prior to 1959 had involved equitable actions. It appeared in City of Thibodaux that the Court was about to demolish any such limitation on abstention when it said that the cases did not apply a technical rule of equity procedure but reflected a deeper policy derived from our federalism, but the Court went on in the same paragraph to emphasize that eminent domain is a special and peculiar kind of common law action and seemingly analogized eminent domain cases to equitable proceedings.[40] Nevertheless a year later, in Clay v. Sun Insurance Office Ltd.,[41] the Court actually ordered abstention in a common-law action to recover money from an insurance company, in a Pullman-type situation where the meaning of a state statute was deemed unclear and a supposedly difficult federal constitutional question would be raised if the statute applied to the suit before the Court.[42]

An important question, only recently resolved, is whether a third type of abstention is proper. All of the cases thus far considered have involved constitutional and statutory issues of a public nature. Is abstention appropriate in private litigation to avoid having to decide difficult questions of state law? In one early case it was held that a federal court should not have determined questions of state property law in a bankruptcy proceeding, but should have had the bankruptcy trustee bring an action in state court.[43] This case has

39. Colorado River Water Conservation Dist. v. U. S., 1976, 96 S.Ct. 1236, 1244–1245, 424 U.S. 800, 814–816, 47 L.Ed.2d 483, rehearing denied, 96 S.Ct. 2239, 426 U.S. 912, 48 L.Ed.2d 839. In the cited passage the Court now explains the City of Thibodaux case on the second of the grounds stated in the text. For cases in which the lower courts have thought Burford-type abstention was or was not proper, see 17 Wright, Miller & Cooper, Jurisdiction § 4245.

40. 79 S.Ct. at 1072, 360 U.S. at 28.

41. 1960, 80 S.Ct. 1222, 363 U.S. 207, 4 L.Ed.2d 1170. See Cardozo, Choosing and Declaring State Law: Deference to State Courts Versus Federal Responsibility, 1960, 55 Nw.U.L.Rev. 419.

42. Although four members of the Court, speaking through Justice Brennan, have recently sought to limit the "principle of comity" to cases "where a

federal court is asked to employ its historic powers as a court of equity," and have said somewhat grudgingly that "even assuming 'abstention' might have some application in actions at law," Fair Assessment in Real Estate Assn., Inc. v. McNary, 1981, 102 S.Ct. 177, 188 n. 3, 454 U.S. 100, 119 n. 3, 70 L.Ed.2d 271 (concurring opinion), other cases after Clay have ordered abstention in private damage actions. E.g., Fornaris v. Ridge Tool Co., 1970, 91 S.Ct. 156, 400 U.S. 41, 27 L.Ed.2d 174; United Gas Pipe Line Co. v. Ideal Cement Co., 1962, 82 S.Ct. 676, 369 U.S. 134, 7 L.Ed.2d 623. But see Liberty Curtin Concerned Parents v. Keystone Central Sch. Dist., D.C.Pa.1978, 81 F.R.D. 590, 597.

43. Thompson v. Magnolia Petroleum Co., 1940, 60 S.Ct. 628, 309 U.S. 478, 84 L.Ed. 876.

had no generative force outside the bankruptcy area and, at least until 1959, the rule seemed to be that the mere difficulty of determining state law did not justify abstention.

The leading case was Meredith v. City of Winter Haven.[44] In a diversity action seeking equitable relief, question was raised as to a city's power to issue certain bonds without a referendum. The trial court dismissed the action on the merits, but the court of appeals ordered that the dismissal be on abstention grounds. The Supreme Court reversed, and ordered the lower court to reinstate the complaint and to decide the case. Chief Justice Stone announced broadly that "the difficulties of ascertaining what the state courts may hereafter determine the state law to be do not in themselves afford a sufficient ground for a federal court to decline to exercise its jurisdiction to decide a case which is properly brought to it for decision." [45]

The Court frequently applied the Meredith principle, and refused to order abstention though a case presented difficult questions of state law.[46] The 1959 condemnation cases raised doubts. In City of Thibodaux the Court was at pains to say that the issue before it was "decisively different" from that involved in Meredith,[47] but the difference six Justices detected did not seem a persuasive distinction to everyone.[48] To the extent that City of Thibodaux and Allegheny County may have turned on the fact that the law was settled in one case and not in the other, they gave support to the notion that a federal court may or should leave to the states the decision of unsettled questions of state law. Yet four years after those cases the Court seemed to be at pains to reaffirm the Meredith principle.[49] The decisions of the lower courts were not entirely consistent. The Fifth Cir-

---

44. 1943, 64 S.Ct. 7, 320 U.S. 228, 88 L.Ed. 9.

45. 64 S.Ct. at 11, 320 U.S. at 235.

46. Markham v. Allen, 1946, 66 S.Ct. 296, 326 U.S. 490, 90 L.Ed. 256; Williams v. Green Bay & W. R. Co., 1946, 66 S.Ct. 284, 286, 326 U.S. 549, 553–554, 90 L.Ed. 311; Spiegel's Estate v. C. I. R., 1949, 69 S.Ct. 301, 335 U.S. 701, 93 L.Ed. 330; C. I. R. v. Church's Estate, 1949, 69 S.Ct. 322, 335 U.S. 632, 93 L.Ed. 288; Propper v. Clark, 1949, 69 S.Ct. 1333, 337 U.S. 472, 93 L.Ed. 1480; Sutton v. Leib, 1952, 72 S.Ct. 398, 342 U.S. 402, 96 L.Ed. 448.

But see Kaiser Steel Corp. v. W. S. Ranch Co., 1968, 88 S.Ct. 1753, 391 U.S. 593, 20 L.Ed.2d 835, discussed note 30 above.

47. 79 S.Ct. at 1072 n. 2, 360 U.S. at 27 n. 2.

48. The distinction was not persuasive to the dissenters in City of Thibodaux. See 79 S.Ct. at 1078 n. 4, 360 U.S. at 38 n. 4 (dissenting opinion).

In private correspondence at that time Justice Frankfurter, the spokesman for the majority in City of Thibodaux, expressed regret that he had joined in the Meredith decision. See 17 Wright, Miller & Cooper, Jurisdiction § 4241 n. 39.

49. In McNeese v. Board of Educ. for Community Sch. Dist. 187, Cahokia, Ill., 1963, 83 S.Ct. 1433, 1436 n. 5, 373 U.S. 668, 673 n. 5, 10 L.Ed.2d 622, the Court said: "Yet where Congress creates a head of federal jurisdiction which entails a responsibility to adjudicate the claim on the basis of state law, viz., diversity of citizenship, as was true in Meredith v. Winter Haven, 320 U.S. 228, we hold that difficulties and perplexities of state law are no reason for referral of the problem to the state court * * * ."

Meredith is also cited in Colorado River Water Conservation Dist. v. U. S., 1976, 96 S.Ct. 1236, 1245, 424 U.S. 800, 816, 47 L.Ed.2d 483, for the proposition that "the mere potential for conflict in

cuit, with scattered support elsewhere, thought abstention proper in a routine diversity case simply because the state law was unclear.[50] Other courts consistently rejected this view.[51]

The Clay case, discussed above, was unique in being the first decision in which the Supreme Court ordered abstention in a common-law action. It was unique also in that the Court ordered resort to the new device of certification of the state questions involved to the highest state court for decision. Florida had had on its books for some years a statute permitting a federal court of appeals to certify a question of Florida law to the Florida Supreme Court. The Florida statute had never been implemented by court rules setting up such a procedure, but after certification was ordered by the Supreme Court in the Clay case the Florida Supreme Court adopted such rules and determined the questions certified to it by the Fifth Circuit.[52] The Clay case itself was an example of Pullman-type abstention, since decision of the state issues might—though in the result it did not—obviate deciding a federal constitutional question.

The certification procedure has been regarded with quite an extraordinary enthusiasm by the commentators,[53] and half of the states now have followed Florida's lead and have made such a procedure

the results of adjudications, does not, without more, warrant staying exercise of federal jurisdiction."

50. The best-known Fifth Circuit case is United Services Life Ins. Co. v. Delaney, C.A.5th, 1964, 328 F.2d 483, certiorari denied 84 S.Ct. 1335, 377 U.S. 935, 12 L.Ed.2d 298. The case has been vigorously criticized. See Currie, note 14 above, at 313–314; Agata, Delaney, Diversity, and Delay: Abstention or Abdication, 1966, 4 Hous.L.Rev. 422, 447; Comments, 1964, 73 Yale L.J. 860, 1965 Duke L.J. 102. One commentator has suggested that the Fifth Circuit abstained in Delaney not because the state law was unclear but "because it did not believe the state law was what the state court had said it was." Comment, Abstention under Delaney: A Current Appraisal, 1971, 49 Texas L.Rev. 247, 258. There is a spirited defense of Delaney by Chief Judge John R. Brown of the Fifth Circuit, sitting by designation with the Tenth Circuit, in his separate opinion in W. S. Ranch Co. v. Kaiser Steel Corp., C.A.10th, 1967, 388 F.2d 257, 262, reversed 1968, 88 S.Ct. 1753, 391 U.S. 593, 20 L.Ed.2d 835.

See also White v. Husky Oil Co., D.C. Mont.1967, 266 F.Supp. 239; Richey v. Sumoge, D.C.Or.1969, 257 F.Supp. 32; A. F. L. Motors, Inc. v. Chrysler Corp., D.C.Wis.1960, 183 F.Supp. 56.

51. See cases cited in 17 Wright, Miller & Cooper, Jurisdiction § 4246 n. 28.

Indeed even the Fifth Circuit seems to have abandoned Delaney. Sayers v. Forsyth Bldg. Corp., C.A.5th, 1969, 417 F.2d 65, 72–74.

52. Sun Ins. Office, Ltd. v. Clay, Fla. 1961, 133 So.2d 735, noted 1962, 48 Iowa L.Rev. 185, 40 Tex.L.Rev. 1041.

The Fifth Circuit adhered to its earlier decision despite the answers to the certified questions provided by the Florida court. Sun Ins. Office, Ltd. v. Clay, C.A.5th, 1963, 319 F.2d 505. The Supreme Court, four years after first hearing the case, reversed the Fifth Circuit and held the Florida statute applicable. Clay v. Sun Ins. Office, Ltd., 1964, 84 S.Ct. 1197, 377 U.S. 179, 12 L.Ed.2d 229.

53. Kurland, Toward a Co-operative Judicial Federalism: The Federal Court Abstention Doctrine, 1959, 24 F.R.D. 481; Kaplan, Certification of Questions from Federal Appellate Courts to the Florida Supreme Court and Its Impact on the Abstention Doctrine, 1962, 16 U.Miami L.Rev. 413; McKusick, Certification: A Procedure for Cooperation Between State and Federal Courts, 1964, 16 U.Maine L.Rev. 33; Liebenthal, A Dialogue on England: The England Case, Its Effect on the Abstention Doctrine, and Some Suggested Solutions, 1966, 18 West.Res.L.

available.[54] In some states it is thought that for the state court to answer certified questions would be to give an impermissible advisory opinion,[55] while in other states the rule against advisory opinions limits the circumstances in which the court can answer certified questions.[56]

In the 1974 decision in Lehman Brothers v. Schein,[57] the Supreme Court gave strong endorsement to the use of certification in cases where state law is difficult to ascertain. The case was a private diversity case in New York that turned on an unsettled issue of Florida law. The Court vacated a decision of the case by the Second Circuit so that that court might reconsider whether to certify the question to the Florida Supreme Court. The Court restated the Meredith rule, that mere difficulty in ascertaining local law does not justify "remitting the parties to a state tribunal for the start of another lawsuit." [58] It then spoke warmly of certification. "We do not suggest that

Rev. 157; Lillich & Mundy, Federal Court Certification of Doubtful State Law Questions, 1971, 18 UCLA L.Rev. 888; Brown, Certification—Federalism in Action, 1977, 7 Cum.L.Rev. 455; Roth, Certified Questions from the Federal Courts: Review and Re-proposal, 1979, 34 U.Miami L.Rev. 1.

But see Cardozo, Choosing and Declaring State Law: Deference to State Courts Versus Federal Responsibility, 1960, 55 Nw.U.L.Rev. 419; Clark, Federal Procedural Reform and States' Rights; to a More Perfect Union, 1961, 40 Texas L.Rev. 211, 218–225; Mattis, Certification of Questions of State Law: An Impractical Tool in the Hands of the Federal Courts, 1969, 23 U.Miami L.Rev. 717.

54. The statutes and rules are cited, and their variations in matters of detail noted, in 17 Wright, Miller & Cooper, Jurisdiction § 4248 nn. 29–32. The Commissioners on Uniform State Laws approved in 1967 a Uniform Certification of Questions of Law Act. 12 U.L.A., pp. 49–56. See also ALI Study, § 1371(e).

55. The Florida court concluded that advisory opinions were permissible under the state constitution. Sun Ins. Office, Ltd. v. Clay, Fla.1961, 133 So.2d 735, 739–743.

The Washington certification statute was upheld by vote of 6–3. The majority thought that they were not being asked to give an advisory opinion, but held that they had power to give advisory opinions if this were what was involved. In re Elliot, 1968, 446 P.2d 347, 74 Wash.2d 600.

See note 24 above.

56. The usual rule is that the state court will not answer the certified question unless one of the possible answers it can give will be determinative of the case. Pan American Computer Corp. v. Data General Corp., 1982, ___ P.R. ___; White v. Edgar, Me.1974, 320 A.2d 668; In re Richards, Me.1966, 223 A.2d 827.

In Wyoming, however, the state court has taken the much more restrictive view that it will not answer a certified question until there is nothing left for the federal court to do but apply the state court's answer to the question and enter judgment consistent with the answer. Matter of Certified Question, Wyo.1976, 549 P.2d 1310, noted 1977, 12 Land & Water L.Rev. 337. See also the discussion of the Mississippi certification rule in Brewer v. Memphis Pub. Co., Inc., C.A.5th, 1980, 626 F.2d 1238, 1242 n. 5, rehearing denied 1981, 638 F.2d 247.

State courts have also refused to answer certified questions if they involve state constitutional provisions that mirror provisions of the federal Constitution. Pan American Computer Corp. v. Data General Corp., 1982, ___ P.R. ___; WXYZ, Inc. v. Hand, C.A.6th, 1981, 658 F.2d 420, 422 n. 3 (Michigan Supreme Court's action).

57. 1974, 94 S.Ct. 1741, 416 U.S. 386, 40 L.Ed.2d 215.

58. 94 S.Ct. at 1744, 416 U.S. at 386, 40 L.Ed.2d 215.

where there is doubt as to local law and where the certification procedure is available, resort to it is obligatory. It does of course in the
long run save time, energy, and resources and helps build a cooperative judicial federalism. Its use in a given case rests in the sound
discretion of the federal court." [59] Lower courts have accepted the
invitation of the Lehman Brothers case and have often certified unclear questions of state law to state courts where that procedure was
available, though they have not done so indiscriminately.[60]

Although there is still disagreement on the desirability of certification in cases of unclear state law, there is no such disagreement
about the value of certification in situations of the Pullman type.
The state law questions that are intertwined with federal constitutional issues in Pullman-type cases can be resolved more expeditiously by certification than by the traditional method of requiring a party
to commence a declaratory judgment action in the state trial court
and take the decision there to the highest court of the state. Thus
the availability of a certification procedure may tip the scales in favor
of having the state court first decide the state law questions in Pullman-type cases.[61]

The fourth, and presently the most disputed, of the abstention
doctrines concerns whether a federal court may stay or dismiss an
action on the sole ground that there is a similar action pending in
state court in which the controversy between the parties can be resolved. This may be regarded as abstention merely to serve the convenience of the federal courts or, to put a more prepossessing name
on it, to avoid duplicative litigation.

Of course the doctrine of forum non conveniens permits dismissal
in unusual cases.[62] If a state court has already taken jurisdiction of a

---

59. 94 S.Ct. at 1744, 416 U.S. at 386, 40
L.Ed.2d 215.

60. See cases cited 17 Wright, Miller &
Cooper, Jurisdiction § 4246 nn. 37, 38.

61. "Although we do not mean to inti-
mate that abstention would be improper in this case were certification not
possible, the availability of certification
greatly simplifies the analysis." Bellotti v. Baird, 1976, 96 S.Ct. 2857, 2868,
428 U.S. 132, 151, 49 L.Ed.2d 844, conformed to 1977, 360 N.E.2d 288, 371
Mass. 741, conformed to D.C.Mass.,
428 F.Supp. 854. See also Elkins v.
Moreno, 1978, 98 S.Ct. 1338, 1347 n. 15,
435 U.S. 647, 662 n. 15, 55 L.Ed.2d 614,
supplemented 1979, 99 S.Ct. 2044, 441
U.S. 458, 60 L.Ed.2d 354.

Certification has also been imaginatively
used in a habeas corpus case that was
analytically similar to a Pullman-type

case. Adams v. Murphy, C.A.5th,
1979, 598 F.2d 982. See the same case,
C.A.5th, 1981, 653 F.2d 224.

A leading scholar of Pullman-type abstention now concludes that "Pullman
abstention is not worth its costs" and
that it should be preserved only where
certification procedures are available.
Field, note 1 above, at 605–609.

Abstention of the traditional type has
been refused when the state court has
already refused to answer certified
questions in the case. WXYZ, Inc. v.
Hand, C.A.6th, 1981, 658 F.2d 420.

62. Piper Aircraft Co. v. Reyno, 1981,
102 S.Ct. 252, ___ U.S. ___, 70 L.Ed.2d
419. The enactment in 1948 of the
change of venue statute, 28 U.S.C.A. §
1404(a), see § 44 above, has left only
vestiges of this doctrine available in
federal court.

res, a federal court must decline jurisdiction.[63] If a state action is already pending in which all issues can be effectively determined, a federal court may refuse to entertain a declaratory judgment action,[64] but this rests on the special nature of declaratory judgment procedure and the fact that there is no need for that procedure in the situation outlined.[65] Also it is clear that a federal court can stay an action where the same issues are presented in an action pending in another federal court.[66]

Beyond the situations outlined, it had been thought to be the rule that the mere pendency of an action in personam in state court would not require, nor even permit, a federal court to refuse to hear an action or to stay an action, and that instead both state and federal actions should go forward until one of them resulted in a judgment that might be asserted as res judicata in the other.[67] Two decisions of the Second Circuit, and some cases elsewhere, cast doubt even on that proposition. In one a federal judge ordered a stay of a shareholder's action brought in federal court pending determination of a state suit in which nine similar actions had been consolidated. The Second Circuit upheld the stay, on condition that the defendants consent to discovery of the same scope in the state action as would be available in the federal action.[68] In the second case, a federal judge, relying solely on the fact of a crowded docket in his district, ordered a stay of a trademark infringement action pending determination of an earlier declaratory judgment action in state court that raised the same issues. The stay was upheld.[69]

Though these decisions had some support from commentators,[70] they seemed to go beyond anything required by the demands of federalism that are at the heart of the abstention doctrine.[71] At first the Second Circuit decisions were viewed skeptically by other courts, but

63. Princess Lida of Thurn and Taxis v. Thompson, 1939, 59 S.Ct. 270, 305 U.S. 456, 83 L.Ed. 285; 14 Wright, Miller & Cooper, Jurisdiction § 3631.

64. Brillhart v. Excess Ins. Co. of America, 1942, 62 S.Ct. 1173, 316 U.S. 491, 86 L.Ed. 1620. See § 100 below.

65. The Fifth Circuit has extended the doctrine of the Brillhart case, note 64 above, to permit a stay in ordinary equity suits in deference to a parallel state action. PPG Indus., Inc. v. Continental Oil Co., C.A.5th, 1973, 478 F.2d 674, noted 1973, 51 Texas L.Rev. 1252.

66. Kerotest Mfg. Co. v. C–O–Two Fire Equipment Co., 1952, 72 S.Ct. 219, 342 U.S. 180, 96 L.Ed. 200; Semmes Motors, Inc. v. Ford Motor Co., C.A.2d, 1970, 429 F.2d 1197.

67. McClellan v. Carland, 1910, 30 S.Ct. 501, 217 U.S. 268, 54 L.Ed. 762; see Kline v. Burke Constr. Co., 1922, 43

S.Ct. 79, 260 U.S. 226, 67 L.Ed. 226; Vestal, Repetitive Litigation, 1960, 45 Iowa L.Rev. 527; Note, Stays of Federal Proceedings in Deference to Concurrently Pending State Court Suits, 1960, 60 Col.L.Rev. 684.

68. Mottolese v. Kaufman, C.A.2d, 1949, 176 F.2d 301.

69. P. Beiersdorf & Co. v. McGohey, C.A.2d, 1951, 187 F.2d 14.

70. Kurland, Toward a Co-operative Judicial Federalism: The Federal Court Abstention Doctrine, 1960, 24 F.R.D. 481, 490–492; Notes, 1950, 59 Yale L.J. 978, 1952, 37 Minn.L.Rev. 46, 1960, 60 Col.L.Rev. 684.

71. Ashman, Alfini & Shapiro, note 1 above, at 652; Pell, note 1 above, at 950; Wright, The Abstention Doctrine Reconsidered, 1959, 37 Texas L.Rev. 815, 824; Comment, 1952, 19 U.Chi.L. Rev. 361.

in the years between 1967 and 1976, as federal courts felt increasing pressure on their dockets, the cases became more numerous in which federal courts actually stayed actions before them because of the pendency of a similar action in state court, or at least said that they had power to do so.[72]

The propriety of this type of abstention came to the Supreme Court in 1976 in Colorado River Water Conservation District v. United States.[73] In that case the Court stated the general rule that the pendency of an action in the state court is no bar to proceedings concerning the same matter in the federal court and that none of the abstention doctrines apply merely because there is a pending state action raising the same issue. But it did not make the general rule into an absolute. It concluded by saying "the circumstances permitting the dismissal of a federal suit due to the presence of a concurrent state proceeding for reasons of wise judicial administration are considerably more limited than the circumstances appropriate for abstention. The former circumstances, though exceptional, do nevertheless exist." [74] It found the case before it to be one of those exceptional cases in which a federal action should be dismissed in favor of a pending state action. Nevertheless, the factual situation in that case was so unusual, and the Court's emphasis on "the virtually unflagging obligation of the federal courts to exercise the jurisdiction given them" [75] and that only "exceptional" circumstances permit dismissals of this kind was so strong, that the case argues against, rather than for, the use of this practice in routine cases that some of the lower courts had recently endorsed.

Many of the lower courts had distinguished sharply between a dismissal and a stay and had held that only a stay was proper in these circumstances.[76] It would be wrong, however, to read Colorado River as speaking only to the propriety of dismissal. The distinction between a dismissal and a stay in this kind of case is extremely artificial. This is not like Pullman-type abstention, where it is expressly contemplated that the case may return to federal court for resolution of the federal issues after the state questions have been decided. The expectation when the fourth type of abstention has been invoked has always been that the controversy will be resolved in the state

---

72. 17 Wright, Miller & Cooper, Jurisdiction § 4247, pp. 508–514.

73. 1976, 96 S.Ct. 1236, 424 U.S. 800, 47 L.Ed.2d 438, noted 1977 Utah L.Rev. 315. See Comment, Federal Court Stays and Dismissal in Deference to Parallel State Court Proceedings: The Impact of Colorado River, 1977, 44 U.Chi.L.Rev. 641.

74. 96 S.Ct. at 1246, 424 U.S. at 818.
Doubt has been expressed on whether or why the Colorado River case was "exceptional." See Redish, note 1 above, at 251–252.

75. 96 S.Ct. at 1246, 424 U.S. at 818.

76. Weiner v. Shearson Hammill & Co., Inc., C.A.9th, 1975, 521 F.2d 817; Augustin v. Mughal, C.A.8th, 1975, 521 F.2d 1215; Ungar v. Mandell, C.A.2d, 1972, 471 F.2d 1163; Aetna State Bank v. Altheimer, C.A.7th, 1970, 430 F.2d 750.

proceeding, and that if the party returns to federal court after the state court action is over, the most that will be needed is to dispose of the federal suit on principles of claim or issue preclusion. For this reason, when the federal court orders a stay because of a pending state court proceeding, it is in practical effect a dismissal of the federal action.[77]

What had seemed the clear teaching of Colorado River, that a federal court cannot dismiss or stay a federal action in deference to a concurrent state proceeding save in "exceptional" circumstances, was muddied by the Court's decision two years later in Will v. Calvert Fire Insurance Co.[78] It was inevitable that Will would raise questions rather than answering them. The order the Supreme Court was reviewing in Will was grant of a writ of mandamus by the Seventh Circuit to require Judge Will to proceed immediately to consider Calvert's federal antitrust action, which he had stayed in deference to a state court contract action in which Calvert had raised the federal antitrust issues as a defense. This meant, first, that the case is complicated by questions about when mandamus may be used to review interlocutory orders of district courts.[79] Second, the federal action was one of which the federal courts have exclusive jurisdiction. There are significant questions, still unanswered, about whether any form of abstention is proper in an exclusive jurisdiction case [80] and also about how the usual rules of issue preclusion apply if a state court has decided issues that then arise in a case exclusively for the federal courts.[81] All of this would have been bad enough, but the case is further complicated by the fragmentation in the Court, so that the plurality opinion states a view that is expressly rejected by five of the Justices.

Although Justice Rehnquist, in the plurality opinion for himself and three others, purported to recognize the language in Colorado River about "the virtually unflagging obligation" of the federal courts to exercise the jurisdiction given them, he gave far more weight to the 1942 decision in the Brillhart case [82] as supporting the

77. Amdur v. Lizars, C.A.4th, 1967, 372 F.2d 103, 105–106.

78. 1978, 98 S.Ct. 2552, 437 U.S. 655, 57 L.Ed.2d 504, on remand C.A.7th, 586 F.2d 12, noted 1978, 49 Miss.L.J. 951, 1979, 10 St. Mary's L.J. 641, 24 Vill.L. Rev. 815. See Note, Abstention and Mandamus after Will v. Calvert Fire Ins. Co., 1979, 64 Cornell L.Rev. 566.

79. See § 102 below.

80. See Key v. Wise, C.A.5th, 1980, 629 F.2d 1049, and the dissent by three Justices from the denial of certiorari in that case, 102 S.Ct. 682, ___ U.S. ___, 70 L.Ed.2d 647. See also Note, Judicial Abstention and Exclusive Federal Jurisdiction: A Reconciliation, 1981, 67 Cornell L.Rev. 219.

81. See § 100A below; Note, The Collateral Estoppel Effect of Prior State Court Findings in Cases Within Exclusive Federal Jurisdiction, 1978, 91 Harv.L.Rev. 1281.

82. Brillhart v. Excess Ins. Co. of America, 1942, 62 S.Ct. 1173, 316 U.S. 491, 86 L.Ed. 1620. Brillhart was a suit for a declaratory judgment and has traditionally been read as supporting a wide discretion on whether to give declarations when there is other litigation pending in which a coercive judgment may be obtained. See notes 64 and 65 above. Brillhart is so understood by the dissenters in Will. 98 S.Ct. at 2562–2563, 437 U.S. at 670–672.

proposition that "the decision whether to defer to the concurrent jurisdiction of a state court is, in the last analysis, a matter committed to the District Court's discretion." [83] He also took the Seventh Circuit to task for treating the order staying the federal proceedings as equivalent to a dismissal. A stay was not the equivalent of a dismissal, he said, since Calvert remained free to urge Judge Will to reconsider on the basis of new information about the progress of the state case.[84] The fifth vote for reversal of the grant of mandamus came from Justice Blackmun. In a short concurring opinion he argued that Brillhart, a diversity case, had no application in a case turning on federal issues, and that in any event in Colorado River "the Court cut back on Mr. Justice Frankfurter's rather sweeping language in Brillhart." [85] Justice Blackmun joined in the result only because he thought issuance of mandamus was premature. Judge Will should be given an opportunity to reconsider the stay in the light of Colorado River.

Justice Brennan spoke for four members of the Court in his dissent. He detected in the plurality opinion "an ominous potential for the abdication of federal court jurisdiction * * * ." [86]

If the plurality opinion had spoken for the full Court, it would permit a greater discretion in deferring to state litigation than Colorado River had recognized. In addition, it would have seemed to ensure that when district judges do defer to state litigation they insulate themselves from appellate review so long as they are careful to use the language of stay rather than dismissal. But Justice Rehnquist did not speak for the Court. A clear majority of the Court—Justice Blackmun and the four dissenters—agreed on each of these propositions: (1) the Brillhart decision has no proper application in cases such as Will; (2) the Colorado River case continues to be authoritative on the circumstances in which a federal court may stay an action pending outcome of a state proceeding; and (3) mandamus can issue to vacate a stay that is not consistent with the teaching of Colorado River.[87] Many lower courts so understand the present state of the law, but there is much variation in the cases.[88]

---

83. 98 S.Ct. at 2558, 437 U.S. at 664.

84. 98 S.Ct. at 2559, 437 U.S. at 665.

85. 98 S.Ct. at 2560, 437 U.S. at 667.

86. 98 S.Ct. at 2561, 437 U.S. at 669.

87. This was how the case was read on remand. C.A.7th, 1978, 586 F.2d 12. Subsequently Judge Will reconsidered in the light of Colorado River and again ordered the federal action stayed. Calvert Fire Ins. Co. v. American Mut. Reinsurance Co., D.C.Ill.1978, 459 F.Supp. 859. This time the abstention order was affirmed, C.A.7th, 1979, 600 F.2d 1228, criticized 1980, 55 Notre Dame Law. 601.

88. Compare, e.g., Strode Publishers, Inc. v. Holtz, C.A.11th, 1982, 665 F.2d 333, with Giulini v. Blessing, C.A.2d, 1981, 654 F.2d 189. See cases cited 17 Wright, Miller & Cooper, Jurisdiction § 4247 n. 40.

§ 52A. "Our Federalism" [1]

There is no more controversial doctrine in the federal courts today than the doctrine of "Our Federalism," which teaches that federal courts must refrain from hearing constitutional challenges to state action under certain circumstances in which federal action is regarded as an improper intrusion on the right of a state to enforce its laws in its own courts. The doctrine is identified with the 1971 decision in Younger v. Harris,[2] though the Supreme Court has spoken a number of times since, and doubtless will have to speak often again, to resolve questions left open by Younger and its companion cases. The doctrine seems to be a special application of the abstention doctrines [3] but it has taken on such a robust life of its own that it is here discussed in a separate section.

The Younger case can only be understood against the background of the 1965 decision in Dombrowski v. Pfister.[4] The holding in Dombrowski was simple enough. Plaintiffs were held entitled to an injunction to prevent state officers from prosecuting them or threatening to prosecute them under a state statute that was so broad and vague that it interfered unconstitutionally with First Amendment rights. The holding seemed surprising, because to obtain this injunction plaintiffs had to overcome three hurdles: the Anti-Injunction

[§ 52A]

1. 17 Wright, Miller & Cooper, Jurisdiction §§ 5251–5255. The literature is immense, and tends to become quickly dated as new cases reshape the doctrine. It is cited in 17 id. § 4251 nn. 14, 37, and § 4252 n. 1. The following general discussions are current and helpful: Theis, Younger v. Harris: Federalism in Context, 1981, 33 Hastings L.J. 103; Wells, The Role of Comity in the Law of Federal Courts, 1981, 60 N.C.L.Rev. 59; Calhoun, Exhaustion Requirements in Younger-Type Actions: More Mud in Already Clouded Waters, 1980, 13 Ind.L.Rev. 521; Koury, Section 1983 and Civil Comity: Two for the Federalism Seesaw, 1979, 25 Loy.L.Rev. 659; Rosenfeld, The Place of State Courts in the Era of Younger v. Harris, 1979, 59 B.U.L.Rev. 597; Gibbons, Our Federalism, 1978, 12 Suff.U.L.Rev. 1087; McMillan, Abstention—The Judiciary's Self-Inflicted Wound, 1978, 56 N.C.L.Rev. 527; Redish, The Doctrine of Younger v. Harris: Deference in Search of a Rationale, 1978, 63 Cornell L.Rev. 463; Fiss, Dombrowski, 1977, 86 Yale L.J. 1103; Laycock, Federal Interference with State Prosecutions: The Need for Prospective Relief, 1977, Sup.Ct.Rev. 193; Soifer & Macgill, The Younger Doctrine: Reconstructing Reconstruction,

1977, 55 Texas L.Rev. 1141; Wilkinson, Anticipatory Vindication of Federal Constitutional Rights, 1977, 48 Albany L.Rev. 459; Weinberg, The New Judicial Federalism, 1977, 29 Stan.L.Rev. 1191; Zeigler, An Accommodation of the Younger Doctrine and the Duty of the Federal Courts To Enforce Constitutional Safeguards in the State Criminal Process, 1976, 125 U.Pa.L.Rev. 266; Whitten, Federal Declaratory and Injunctive Interference with State Court Proceedings: The Supreme Court and the Limits of Judicial Discretion, 1975, 53 N.C.L.Rev. 591; Wechsler, Federal Courts, State Criminal Law and the First Amendment, 1974, 49 N.Y.U.L. Rev. 740.

2. 1971, 91 S.Ct. 746, 401 U.S. 37, 27 L.Ed.2d 669.

3. It has repeatedly been so characterized by the Supreme Court, most recently in Middlesex County Ethics Committee v. Garden State Bar Assn., 1982, 102 S.Ct. 2515, 2523, ___ U.S. ___, ___, 73 L.Ed.2d 116. But see Hart & Wechsler, The Federal Courts and the Federal System, Bator, Mishkin, Shapiro & Wechsler, ed. 1973, p. 1043 n. 1.

4. 965, 85 S.Ct. 1116, 380 U.S. 479, 14 L.Ed.2d 22.

Act; the notion that equity will not interfere with enforcement of the criminal law; and the abstention doctrines. But when each of these was examined individually, the holding that it did not bar injunctive relief could be made to fit comfortably within prior learning.

At the time of Dombrowski it was still unsettled whether civil rights actions came within an exception to the Anti-Injunction Act, 28 U.S.C.A. § 2283, and indeed it was not until 1972 that it was held that they do.[5] But the settled rule has long been that the statute applies only to injunctions against pending proceedings and does not bar an injunction against the initiation of state proceedings in the future. On the facts of Dombrowski this rule was enough to avoid any problems with § 2283.[6]

It was necessary next to consider the practice, stemming from comity and the federal framework, that a federal equity court should not interfere with a state's good faith administration of its criminal laws. This practice has origins also in the traditional requirements for equitable relief. Even if a state statute is unconstitutional, a person charged under it normally has an adequate remedy at law by raising his constitutional defense in the state proceeding. Although this practice had frequently been followed in the federal courts,[7] it had never been stated as an absolute and both the statements of the practice and decisions under it had recognized that it could be departed from if necessary to prevent irreparable injury. In Dombrowski the Court thought that "the chilling effect upon the exercise of First Amendment rights may derive from the fact of the prosecution, unaffected by the prospect of its success or failure,"[8] and it found sufficient irreparable injury to justify equitable relief in the substantial loss or impairment of freedoms of expression that would occur if it were necessary to await disposition of the criminal actions in the state courts.[9]

Finally the Court held that the lower court had been in error in abstaining to await authoritative interpretation of the state statutes by the state court. It found the abstention doctrine inappropriate for cases where "statutes are justifiably attacked on their face as abridging free expression, or as applied for the purpose of discouraging protected activities."[10] Again it said that "abstention serves no legitimate purpose where a statute regulating speech is properly attacked

---

5. Mitchum v. Foster, 1972, 92 S.Ct. 2151, 407 U.S. 225, 32 L.Ed.2d 705. See § 47 above.

6. 85 S.Ct. at 1119 n. 2, 380 U.S. at 484, n. 2. But see Fiss, note 1 above, at 1109–1111.

7. The leading case was Douglas v. City of Jeannette, 1943, 63 S.Ct. 877, 319 U.S. 157, 87 L.Ed. 1324.

It has been argued, however, that in Dombrowski the Court overlooked many cases showing that injunctions against threatened prosecutions had issued routinely. Laycock, Federal Interference with State Prosecutions: The Cases Dombrowksi Forgot, 1979, 46 U.Chi.L.Rev. 636.

8. 85 S.Ct. at 1121, 380 U.S. at 487.

9. 85 S.Ct. at 1120–1122, 380 U.S. at 485–489.

10. 85 S.Ct. at 1122, 380 U.S. at 489–490.

on its face, and where, as here, the conduct charged in the indict-ments is not within the reach of an acceptable limiting construction readily to be anticipated as the result of a single criminal prosecution and is not the sort of 'hardcore' conduct that would obviously be pro-hibited under any construction." [11]   The formulations were new but the result was not. It had been well established that abstention is improper if the state statute is unconstitutional regardless of the con-struction the state court might give it.[12] The Court found this to be true in Dombrowski.

Between Dombrowski, in 1965, and Younger, in 1971, there was not much of significance from the Supreme Court on this subject. In-deed the little the Court did suggested a rather modest view of the Dombrowski holding.[13] Many litigants, however, thought that they discerned in Dombrowski a major change in federal-state relations. They read Dombrowski as meaning that every person prosecuted un-der state law for conduct arguably protected by the First Amendment could, by murmuring the words "chilling effect," halt the state prose-cution while a federal court, ordinarily of three judges, passed on the validity of the statute and the bona fides of the state law enforce-ment officers. Lower court cases in which litigants attempted to claim the benefit of what they understood to be the Dombrowski doc-trine numbered in the hundreds and went in every possible direc-tion.[14]

Those who had read a great deal into Dombrowski had their hopes dashed, and the Dombrowski decision itself was sharply limited, on February 23, 1971, when the Court announced its decisions in Young-er v. Harris [15] and five other cases, of which the most significant are Samuels v. Mackell,[16] Perez v. Ledesma,[17] and Boyle v. Landry.[18]

11. 85 S.Ct. at 1123–1124, 380 U.S. at 491–492.

12. See § 52 n. 9 above.

13. In Cameron v. Johnson, 1968, 88 S.Ct. 1335, 390 U.S. 611, 20 L.Ed.2d 182, the district court entered a declar-atory judgment that a state statute was valid on its face and, finding no bad faith in enforcement of the statute, refused injunctive relief. The Court, with two justices dissenting, affirmed both aspects of the decision below. In four other cases the Court, without opinion, summarily affirmed lower court decisions that had refused relief under Dombrowski.

In Zwickler v. Koota, 1967, 88 S.Ct. 391, 389 U.S. 241, 19 L.Ed.2d 444, the Court held that the rule against an injunction interfering with a state's enforcement of its criminal laws did not apply to a request for a declaratory judgment and that it was error for a lower court to abstain in a case challenging the con-stitutionality of a state statute prohib-iting anonymous election literature. On remand the district court entered a declaratory judgment but on a second appeal the Supreme Court vacated this on the ground that there was no longer an actual controversy in the circum-stances of the particular case. Golden v. Zwickler, 1969, 89 S.Ct. 956, 394 U.S. 103, 22 L.Ed.2d 113.

14. The state of the decisions at that point is carefully examined in Maraist, Federal Injunctive Relief Against State Court Proceedings: The Significance of Dombrowski, 1970, 48 Texas L.Rev. 535.

15. 1971, 91 S.Ct. 746, 401 U.S. 37, 27 L.Ed.2d 669.

16. 1971, 91 S.Ct. 764, 401 U.S. 66, 27 L.Ed.2d 688.

17. 1971, 91 S.Ct. 674, 401 U.S. 82, 27 L.Ed.2d 701.

18. See note 18 on page 323.

Five of the justices, speaking in every instance through Justice Black, announced a major retreat from Dombrowski. Three other justices, speaking through Justice Brennan, agreed in part with Justice Black. Justice Douglas opposed the retreat though he agreed with the result in one of the cases.

The Court in the Younger cases continued to leave open whether 28 U.S.C.A. § 2283 applied to civil rights actions.[19] Instead it held that relief was barred in all of these cases because of "the fundamental policy against federal intervention with state criminal proceedings"[20] and "the absence of the factors necessary under equitable principles to justify federal intervention."[21] The Court gave the name, "Our Federalism," to the concept of comity that was at the heart of its decisions. "Our Federalism," Justice Black wrote, represents "a system in which there is sensitivity to the legitimate interests of both State and National Governments, and in which the National Government, anxious though it may be to vindicate and protect federal rights and federal interests, always endeavors to do so in ways that will not unduly interfere with the legitimate activities of the States."[22]

The bare holding of the cases is that "a federal court should not enjoin a state criminal prosecution begun prior to the institution of the federal suit except in very unusual situations, where necessary to prevent immediate irreparable injury."[23] There is ordinarily no irreparable injury if the threat to plaintiff's federally protected rights can be eliminated by the defense of a single criminal prosecution, and "even irreparable injury is insufficient unless it is 'both great and immediate.' "[24] In a major change from what had been said in Dombrowski, the Court said that the possibility of a "chilling effect" on First Amendment freedoms does not by itself justify federal intervention.[25] Nor are federal courts to test the constitutionality of a state statute "on its face" and then enjoin all action to enforce the statute until the state can obtain court approval for a modified version.[26] A federal injunction can run against a pending state criminal prosecu-

The majority opinion in Perez adds very little to the other cases decided that day but Justice Brennan chose a separate opinion in that case as the vehicle for the major expression of his approach to the cases, a view shared by Justices White and Marshall.

18. 1971, 91 S.Ct. 758, 401 U.S. 77, 27 L.Ed.2d 696.

The other two cases of the Younger sextet were Dyson v. Stein, 1971, 91 S.Ct. 769, 401 U.S. 200, 27 L.Ed.2d 781, and Byrne v. Karalexis, 1971, 91 S.Ct. 777, 401 U.S. 216, 27 L.Ed.2d 792.

19. See note 5 above.

20. Younger, 91 S.Ct. at 751, 401 U.S. at 46.

21. Younger, 91 S.Ct. at 755, 401 U.S. at 54.

22. Younger, 91 S.Ct. at 750–751, 401 U.S. at 44.

23. Samuels, 91 S.Ct. at 766, 401 U.S. at 69.

24. Younger, 91 S.Ct. at 751, 401 U.S. at 46. The internal quotation is from Fenner v. Boykin, 1926, 46 S.Ct. 492, 493, 271 U.S. 240, 243, 70 L.Ed. 927, a precedent on which the Court relied heavily in Younger.

25. Younger, 91 S.Ct. at 753–754, 401 U.S. at 50–52.

26. Younger, 91 S.Ct. at 754–755, 401 U.S. at 52–54.

tion only on a "showing of bad faith, harassment, or any other unusual circumstance that would call for equitable relief."[27]

Several other important propositions were announced in that group of decisions. If injunctive relief against a pending state prosecution is barred because there is no showing of irreparable injury, declaratory relief should ordinarily be denied as well and the action should be dismissed without any consideration of the constitutionality of the state statute in question.[28] In addition, the Court tightened the rules on standing to challenge the constitutionality of state statutes. Persons who claim to be inhibited by a statute but who have not been indicted, arrested, or even threatened by the prosecutor lack standing since "persons having no fears of state prosecution except those that are imaginary or speculative, are not to be accepted as appropriate in such cases."[29] Finally, the Court reiterated the rule that a federal injunction is not to be used to test the validity of an arrest or the admissibility of evidence in a state criminal proceeding.[30]

In Younger the opinion of the Court purported to express no view about the circumstances under which federal courts may act if there is no state prosecution pending when the federal action is begun.[31] Nevertheless the principal precedent on which the Court relied held that an injunction should not have issued at the instance of one who had been threatened with criminal prosecution but who had not yet been arrested or otherwise formally charged.[32] The Court also referred approvingly to other cases "involving threatened prosecutions."[33]

The question that this seemed to leave open was largely resolved in 1974 in Steffel v. Thompson.[34] Justice Brennan, writing for the

---

27. Younger, 91 S.Ct. at 755, 401 U.S. at 54.

In Kugler v. Helfant, 1975, 95 S.Ct. 1524, 1531 n. 4, 421 U.S. 117, 125 n. 4, 44 L.Ed.2d 15, the Court agreed that the scope of the exception for other extraordinary circumstances "has been left largely undefined * * *." It pointed to Gibson v. Berryhill, 1973, 93 S.Ct. 1689, 411 U.S. 564, 36 L.Ed.2d 488, as a case that might be explained on that ground.

28. Samuels, 91 S.Ct. at 768, 401 U.S. at 73–74.

The holding in Samuels is inconsistent with Cameron v. Johnson, 1968, 88 S.Ct. 1335, 390 U.S. 611, 20 L.Ed.2d 182, discussed in note 13 above. In Cameron the Supreme Court affirmed grant of a declaratory judgment that a statute was valid on its face in circumstances in which an injunction would not lie. Samuels teaches clearly that in the Cameron situation the action should have been dismissed without

considering the declaratory judgment request. Cameron is not mentioned by the Court in Samuels.

29. Younger, 91 S.Ct. at 749, 401 U.S. at 42. See also Boyle, 91 S.Ct. at 760, 401 U.S. at 80–81.

30. Perez, 91 S.Ct. at 676–677, 401 U.S. at 83–85.

This was followed in Kugler v. Helfant, 1975, 95 S.Ct. 1524, 1533–1534, 421 U.S. 117, 128–131, 44 L.Ed.2d 15.

31. Younger, 91 S.Ct. at 749, 401 U.S. at 41. See also the concurring opinion of Justices Stewart and Harlan, 91 S.Ct. at 757, 401 U.S. at 54–55.

32. Fenner v. Boykin, 1926, 46 S.Ct. 492, 271 U.S. 240, 70 L.Ed. 927, discussed in Younger, 91 S.Ct. at 751, 401 U.S. at 45–46.

33. Younger, 91 S.Ct. at 751, 401 U.S. at 45. But see Laycock, note 7 above.

34. 1974, 94 S.Ct. 1209, 415 U.S. 452, 39 L.Ed.2d 505.

Court in Steffel, relied heavily on his separate opinion in Perez v. Ledesma for the proposition that declaratory relief is quite different from injunctive relief. Thus "regardless of whether injunctive relief may be appropriate, federal declaratory relief is not precluded when no state prosecution is pending and a federal plaintiff demonstrates a genuine threat of enforcement of a disputed state criminal statute, whether an attack is made on the constitutionality of the statute on its face or as applied." [35]

The Court was unanimous in Steffel,[36] and the result seems unavoidable. A person against whom state criminal charges are pending may vindicate his rights, if they exist, through the defense of a single criminal action, but the person against whom no charges are pending would have no remedy, except that provided by Steffel, to vindicate the constitutionality of the conduct in which he wishes to engage. Thus Steffel stands for "the sensible proposition that both a potential state defendant, threatened with prosecution but not charged, and the State itself, confronted by a possible violation of its criminal laws, may benefit from a procedure which provides for a declaration of rights without activation of the criminal process." [37]

Steffel laid heavy emphasis on the distinction between a declaratory judgment and an injunction, and purported not to decide whether an injunction could issue, without satisfying the Younger tests, if no state action is pending.[38] The following year, however, the Court held that in a case within the Steffel principle, in which no state action is pending, a preliminary injunction can issue, without satisfying the Younger tests, to preserve the status quo while the court considers whether to grant declaratory relief.[39] In a still later case the Court held that a permanent injunction could be given, as well as declaratory relief, if there is no pending prosecution and there is a clear showing that an injunction is necessary to afford adequate protection of constitutional rights.[40]

Thus whether a state action is pending is critical to the application of Younger. If a state criminal action is pending when the federal action is commenced, the federal court cannot give either injunctive or declaratory relief and must dismiss the action [41] except in the rare

35. 94 S.Ct. at 1223–1224, 415 U.S. at 475.

36. Concurring opinions by Justice White and by Justice Rehnquist, joined by the Chief Justice, do differ on the effect state officials must give to a declaration of unconstitutionality. 94 S.Ct. at 1224, 1225, 415 U.S. at 476, 478.

37. 94 S.Ct. at 1228, 415 U.S. at 484 (Rehnquist, J., concurring).

38. 94 S.Ct. at 1217–1218, 415 U.S. at 463.

39. Doran v. Salem Inn, Inc., 1975, 95 S.Ct. 2561, 2567–2568, 422 U.S. 922, 930–931, 45 L.Ed.2d 648.

40. Wooley v. Maynard, 1977, 97 S.Ct. 1428, 1434, 430 U.S. 705, 712, 51 L.Ed. 2d 752.

Compare Fiss, note 1 above, at 1143–1148 with Redish, Federal Jurisdiction: Tension in the Allocation of Judicial Power, 1980, pp. 311–314. See cases cited 17 Wright, Miller & Cooper, Jurisdiction § 4253 n. 21.

41. "Younger v. Harris contemplates the outright dismissal of the federal

case in which the Younger standard of bad faith, harassment, or other extraordinary circumstance is satisfied.[42]   But if the state action, though threatened, is not yet pending, the federal court can consider the request for the declaration without regard to the Younger restrictions and can also give at least preliminary injunctive relief if the usual equitable tests for that kind of relief are satisfied.[43]

Although the rules stated in the preceding paragraph continue to be valid, the cosmology of "Our Federalism" seems to require continuous refining,[44] and the application of those rules was significantly altered by two decisions in 1975.   In Hicks v. Miranda [45] a theater owner sued in federal court for declaratory and injunctive relief against a state obscenity statute.   At the time the federal action was brought state criminal charges were pending against two of the theater's employees and copies of a film had been seized.   The district court denied a temporary restraining order and requested convening of a three-judge court.   One day after service of the federal complaint was completed the state criminal charges were amended to include the theater owner as a defendant.

On these facts it was held, over the vigorous dissent of four justices, that the three-judge court erred in granting relief because the Younger tests had not been met and a state criminal proceeding was pending.   Even though the theater owner was not a party to the state proceedings at the time the federal action was brought, his interest and that of his employees was intertwined and the relief sought in federal court would have interfered with the pending state prosecution.[46]

But as a second, and more significant, ground for decision the Court held that "where state criminal proceedings are begun against

suit, and the presentation of all claims, both state and federal, to the state courts." Gibson v. Berryhill, 1973, 93 S.Ct. 1689, 1697, 411 U.S. 564, 577, 36 L.Ed.2d 488.

42. A rare instance in which the Court has found that the Younger standard was satisfied is Gibson v. Berryhill, 1973, 93 S.Ct. 1689, 1697, 411 U.S. 564, 577, 36 L.Ed.2d 488, where the state tribunal was found incompetent by reason of bias to adjudicate the issues. See note 27 above. See also Wall v. American Optometric Assn., Inc., D.C.Ga.1974, 379 F.Supp. 175, 185, affirmed without opinion 1974, 95 S.Ct. 166, 419 U.S. 888, 42 L.Ed.2d 134.

On the exceptions to Younger generally, which are almost never found applicable, see 17 Wright, Miller & Cooper, Jurisdiction § 4255.

43. The threat must be a real, rather than a speculative, one or plaintiffs will be held to lack standing, see note

29 above, and there will not be the actual controversy required by the Declaratory Judgment Act. See Steffel, 94 S.Ct. at 1215–1216, 415 U.S. at 458–460. See also O'Shea v. Littleton, 1974, 94 S.Ct. 669, 675–677, 414 U.S. 488, 493–499, 38 L.Ed.2d 674; and cases cited 17 Wright, Miller & Cooper, Jurisdiction § 4253 n. 25.

44. " * * * [A]s our cases abundantly illustrate, this area of law is in constant litigation, and it is an area through which our decisions have traced a path that may accurately be described as sinuous." Steffel, 94 S. Ct. at 1225, 415 U.S. at 479 (Rehnquist, J., concurring).

45. 1975, 95 S.Ct. 2281, 422 U.S. 332, 45 L.Ed.2d 223, noted 1976, 47 Miss.L.J. 143, 54 N.C.L.Rev. 247, 37 Ohio St.L.J. 205, 274 Kan.L.Rev. 739, 21 Vill.L.Rev. 317.

46. See cases cited 17 Wright, Miller & Cooper, Jurisdiction § 4252 n. 19.

the federal plaintiffs after the federal complaint is filed but before any proceedings of substance on the merits have taken place in the federal court, the principles of Younger v. Harris should apply in full force." [47] Thus the dividing line between Younger and Steffel continues to turn on the pendency of a state proceeding, but the commencement of the federal action is not the controlling date in determining whether a state action is pending. Instead the federal court is to make that determination when it is ready to commence "proceedings of substance on the merits." [48]

In the other case, Doran v. Salem Inn, Inc.,[49] three bar owners brought a federal action asking for a preliminary injunction and declaratory relief against a newly-enacted ordinance regulating the clothing of their waitresses and entertainers. Two of the bars complied with the ordinance until they were granted a preliminary injunction nearly a month later but the third bar disobeyed the ordinance and criminal proceedings were begun against it by the state one day after the federal action was filed. The Court held that while there may be circumstances in which legally distinct parties are so closely related that they should all be subject to the Younger considerations that govern any one of them, the case before it, where the bars were unrelated in terms of ownership and management, was not such a case.[50] Since there were never any criminal proceedings against the bars that had complied with the law, the grant of a preliminary injunction in their favor until final determination of their request for a declaration was upheld. This relief was denied, however, to the bar that had violated the ordinance. The federal litigation was "in an embryonic stage and no contested matter had been decided" [51] when criminal summonses issued against it, and its case was covered by the Younger rule.

The Court continues to use the Hicks formulation of "proceedings of substance on the merits," [52] though there is still much uncertainty on what the phrase means.[53] Hicks certainly means that the dividing line between Younger and Steffel is no longer drawn in terms of whether a state action was pending on the day the federal action was begun. It is true, as the dissenters in Hicks feared, that in many cases the state may be able to abort a federal action by commencing state court proceedings immediately after the federal action is filed. But this will not always be the case. As Doran shows, one who has

47. 95 S.Ct. at 2292, 422 U.S. at 349.

48. The majority did not define the quoted phrase and the dissenters found its meaning "a good deal less than apparent." 95 S.Ct. at 2294 n. 1, 422 U.S. at 353 n. 1.

49. 1975, 95 S.Ct. 2561, 422 U.S. 922, 45 L.Ed.2d 648.

50. See also U. S. v. Composite State Bd. of Medical Examiners, C.A.5th, 1981, 656 F.2d 131; New Jersey-Phila-delphia Presbytery v. New Jersey State Bd. of Higher Educ., C.A.3d, 1981, 654 F.2d 868; Bickham v. Lashof, C.A.7th, 1980, 620 F.2d 1238.

51. 95 S.Ct. at 2566, 422 U.S. at 927.

52. Middlesex County Ethics Committee v. Garden State Bar Assn., 1982, 102 S.Ct. 2515, 2524, ___ U.S. ___, ___, 73 L.Ed.2d 116.

53. See 17 Wright, Miller & Cooper, Jurisdiction § 4253, pp. 562–565.

not yet broken the law may commence a federal action and obtain a preliminary injunction so that he will not be subject to prosecution for violating the law while his attack on its constitutionality is being determined.

In 1975 the Court also spoke to another major question that had been left open in Younger and its companion cases. Those cases had all concerned interference with state criminal proceedings and shed no light on how far, if at all, "Our Federalism" restricts a federal court from interfering with civil actions in state courts in which the state, or its officer or agency, is seeking to enforce state laws.

That question came before the Court in Huffman v. Pursue, Ltd.[54] The state brought an action in state court under a statute providing that a place that exhibits obscene films is a nuisance and can be ordered closed for a year. Judgment was granted for the state. The theater did not appeal the state judgment but brought a federal action against the state authorities in which the federal court, without considering Younger, enjoined enforcement of the state court's judgment insofar as it barred the theater from showing films that had not been adjudged obscene. The Supreme Court held, six to three, that under these circumstances the federal injunction was improper unless the Younger test was satisfied. The Court found that it "need make no general pronouncements upon the applicability of Younger to all civil litigation," [55] since the state was a party to the nuisance action, it was brought in aid of and closely related to criminal statutes on obscenity, and thus the Court was dealing with "a state proceeding which in important respects is more akin to a criminal prosecution than are most civil cases." [56] Later cases, however, have broadened the rule announced in Huffman so that the Court can now say that the Younger rules "are fully applicable to noncriminal judicial proceedings when important state interests are involved." [57]

The theater in the Huffman case also sought to avoid application of Younger by arguing that there was no pending state proceeding since the action in the state trial court had gone to judgment and no appeal was taken. This argument was also rejected by the Court, which found that post-trial federal intervention would be if anything more offensive than intervention at an earlier stage. For this reason it held that Younger standards must be met to justify federal inter-

54. 1975, 95 S.Ct. 1200, 420 U.S. 592, 43 L.Ed.2d 482.

55. 95 S.Ct. at 1209, 420 U.S. at 605.

56. 95 S.Ct. at 1208, 420 U.S. at 603.

57. Middlesex County Ethics Committee v. Garden State Bar Assn., 1982, 102 S.Ct. 2515, 2521, ___ U.S. ___, ___, 73 L.Ed.2d 116 (disciplinary proceeding against an attorney). See also Moore v. Sims, 1979, 99 S.Ct. 2371, 442 U.S. 415, 60 L.Ed.2d 994 (child custody pro-

ceeding); Trainor v. Hernandez, 1977, 97 S.Ct. 1911, 431 U.S. 434, 52 L.Ed.2d 486, on remand D.C.Ill., 1978, 471 F.Supp. 516 (civil action by state to recover welfare payments wrongfully received); Juidice v. Vail, 1977, 97 S.Ct. 1211, 430 U.S. 327, 51 L.Ed.2d 376 (contempt proceeding for failure to obey court order in a private civil action).

See generally 17 Wright, Miller & Cooper, Jurisdiction § 4254.

vention in a state judicial proceeding as to which a losing litigant has not exhausted his state appellate remedies.[58]

This aspect of Huffman was distinguished two years later in Wooley v. Maynard.[59] Maynard had been convicted three times of violating a state statute by covering up the state motto, "Live Free or Die," on the license plate of his car. He did not appeal those convictions, but subsequently brought a federal action to enjoin future prosecutions for violating that statute. The Court found Huffman inapposite, since in Huffman the theater was seeking to prevent enforcement of the state court judgment, while Maynard was not seeking to have the record of his convictions expunged nor to annul any collateral effects those convictions might have, but instead was seeking purely prospective relief to preclude further prosecution under the statute.[60]

Although the exceptions to Younger that Justice Black discussed in that case have been found to be largely illusory,[61] there is one exception, probably implicit in Younger but not discussed there in terms, that is now well recognized. Federal intervention is proper if the federal claim is one that cannot be raised in the state action.[62]

Finally the Court has not limited considerations of "Our Federalism" to cases in which an injunction is being sought against the judicial branch of the state government. That concept must also be taken into account when relief is sought against those in charge of an executive branch of an agency of state or local government. Because of these considerations it was held error for a lower court to issue an injunction that sharply limited a police department's latitude in the dispatch of its internal affairs in an effort to provide prophylactic procedures to minimize misconduct by a handful of state employees.[63]

58.   95 S.Ct. at 1211, 420 U.S. at 610.

59.   1977, 97 S.Ct. 1428, 430 U.S. 705, 51 L.Ed.2d 752.

60.   97 S.Ct. at 1433, 430 U.S. at 710–711. See Fiss, note 1 above, at 1142, and Laycock, note 1 above, at 213–214.

If Maynard had raised his constitutional objection unsuccessfully in the state court proceeding, it would seem that he would be barred from a later federal action. Allen v. McCurry, 1980, 101 S.Ct. 411, 449 U.S. 90, 66 L.Ed.2d 308. See § 100A. The lower court in the Maynard case held that he was not barred since issue preclusion applies only to an issue actually litigated. Maynard v. Wooley, D.C.N.H.1976, 406 F.Supp. 1381, 1385 n. 6, affirmed 1977, 97 S.Ct. 1428, 430 U.S. 705, 51 L.Ed.2d 752.

61.   See note 42 above.

62.   Gerstein v. Pugh, 1975, 95 S.Ct. 854, 420 U.S. 103, 43 L.Ed.2d 54, on remand C.A.5th, 511 F.2d 528, on remand D.C.Fla., 1976, 422 F.Supp. 498. See also Trainor v. Hernandez, 1977, 97 S.Ct. 1911, 431 U.S. 434, 52 L.Ed.2d 486, on remand D.C.Ill.1978, 471 F.Supp. 516, and its aftermath, Quern v. Hernandez, 1979, 99 S.Ct. 1488, 440 U.S. 951, 59 L.Ed.2d 765, noted 1979, 28 De Paul L.Rev. 901.

This principle is recognized, but found inapplicable, in Middlesex County Ethics Committee v. Garden State Bar Assn., 1982, 102 S.Ct. 2515, ___ U.S. ___, 73 L.Ed.2d 116, and in Moore v. Sims, 1979, 99 S.Ct. 2371, 442 U.S. 415, 60 L.Ed.2d 994.

63.   Rizzo v. Goode, 1976, 96 S.Ct. 598, 423 U.S. 362, 46 L.Ed.2d 561.

The Younger rules also apply to bar interference in pending military court-martial proceedings. Schlesinger v.

In Younger Justice Black wrote that "this slogan, 'Our Federalism,' born in the early struggling days of our Union of States, occupies a highly important place in our Nation's history and its future." [64] The multitude of decisions in the years since he wrote confirms his prediction about the future but demonstrates also the difficulty in turning a slogan into workable and understandable legal rules.

§ 53. Habeas Corpus [1]

The writ of habeas corpus, by which the legal authority under which a person may be detained can be challenged, is of immemorial antiquity.[2] After a checkered career in which it was involved in the struggles between the common law courts and the Courts of Chancery and the Star Chamber, as well as in the conflicts between Parliament and the crown, the protection of the writ was firmly written into English law by the Habeas Corpus Act of 1679.[3] Today it is regarded as "perhaps the most important writ known to the constitutional law of England * * *." [4]

Its significance in the United States has been no less great. Article I, § 9, of the Constitution gives assurance that the privilege of the writ of habeas corpus shall not be suspended, unless when in cases of rebellion or invasion the public safety may require it,[5] and its use by the federal courts was authorized in § 14 of the Judiciary Act of 1789. The situations in which the writ might issue where extended in 1833 and 1842 to meet particular exigencies, but the great expansion came in 1867. Congress, anticipating difficulty in enforcing Reconstruction, authorized the federal courts to grant the writ "in all cases where any person may be restrained of his or her liberty in violation

Councilman, 1975, 95 S.Ct. 1300, 1313, 420 U.S. 738, 758, 43 L.Ed.2d 591.

64. Younger, 91 S.Ct. at 751, 401 U.S. at 44–45.

[§ 53]

1. 17 Wright, Miller & Cooper, Jurisdiction §§ 4261–4268; Duker, A Constitutional History of Habeas Corpus, 1980; Popper, Post-Conviction Remedies in a Nutshell, 1978; Michael, The "New" Federalism and the Burger Court's Deference to the States in Federal Habeas Proceedings, 1979, 64 Iowa L.Rev. 233; Soloff, Litigation and Relitigation: The Uncertain Status of Federal Habeas Corpus for State Prisoners, 1978, 6 Hofstra L.Rev. 297; Cobb, The Search for a New Equilibrium in Habeas Corpus Review: Resolution of Conflicting Values, 1978, 32 U.Miami L.Rev. 417; Cover & Aleinikoff, Dialetical Federalism: Habeas Corpus and the Court, 1977, 86 Yale L.J. 1035; Shapiro, Federal Habeas Corpus: A Study in Massachusetts, 1973, 87 Harv.L.Rev. 321; Gibbons, Waiver: The Quest for Functional Limitations on Habeas Corpus Jurisdiction, 1971, 2 Seton Hall L.Rev. 291; Friendly, Is Innocence Irrelevant? Collateral Attack on Criminal Judgments, 1970, 38 U.Chi.L.Rev. 142.

2. Duker, The English Origins of the Writ of Habeas Corpus: A Peculiar Path to Fame, 1978, 53 N.Y.U.L.Rev. 983; Glass, Historical Aspects of Habeas Corpus, 1934, 9 St. John's L.Rev. 55.

3. 31 Car. II, c. 2.

4. Secretary of State for Home Affairs v. O'Brien, [1923] A.C. 603, 609.

5. The implications of the Suspension Clause are considered in all three of the opinions in Swain v. Pressley, 1977, 97 S.Ct. 1224, 430 U.S. 372, 51 L.Ed.2d 411.

of the constitution, or of any treaty or law of the United States." [6]
The statutory provisions on habeas corpus appear as sections 2241 to
2255 of the 1948 Judicial Code. The recodification of that year set
out important procedural limitations and additional procedural
changes were added in 1966, but the scope of the writ, insofar as the
statutory language is concerned, has not been altered since 1867.

The "Great Writ," as it has been called by the Supreme Court
from John Marshall's day to this,[7] is available by statute in four different situations.[8] A little-used provision permits it to issue where a
foreign citizen is in custody for some act done under color of authority from his country and international law is involved.[9] It will issue
also where a person is held by a state for some act done pursuant to
federal authority,[10] but provisions for removal of such cases [11] diminish the need for habeas corpus in such situations. The writ will issue
to test the detention of any person held under custody of the United
States.[12] This provision, though still of much importance in non-crim-
inal cases,[13] is not of significance with regard to federal criminal prisoners. The writ will not issue to test the sufficiency of an indict

6. Act of Feb. 5, 1867, c. 28, § 1, 14 Stat. 385. Although the reason stated in the text seems the most likely, the legislative history is unclear and there is dispute about this. Mayers, The Habeas Corpus Act of 1867: The Supreme Court as Legal Historian, 1965, 33 U.Chi.L.Rev. 31.

7. See Ex parte Bollman, 1807, 4 Cranch 75, 95, 2 L.Ed. 554; Stone v. Powell, 1976, 96 S.Ct. 3037, 3042 n. 6, 428 U.S. 465, 474 n. 6, 49 L.Ed.2d 1067; Engle v. Isaac, 1982, 102 S.Ct. 1558, 1571, ___ U.S. ___, ___, 71 L.Ed.2d 783.

8. The "Great Writ" is the writ of habeas corpus ad subjiciendum. The statute also authorizes issuance of the writ to bring a person into court to tes-tify or for trial, 28 U.S.C.A. § 2241(c) (5), thus providing an analogue to the common law writs of habeas corpus ad prosequendum, testificandum, etc. Carbo v. U. S., 1961, 81 S.Ct. 338, 364 U.S. 611, 5 L.Ed.2d 329.

9. This provision—now 28 U.S.C.A. § 2241(c)(4)—was first added by Act of Aug. 29, 1842, c. 257, 5 Stat. 539. Eng-land had protested that the trial of a Canadian soldier for murder in the New York court, People v. McLeod, N.Y.1841, 25 Wend. 483, 37 Am.Dec. 328, was a violation of international law. The statute was designed to give jurisdiction of such matters to the fed-eral courts. Horn v. Mitchell, D.C. Mass.1915, 223 F. 549, affirmed C.C.A. 1st, 1916, 232 F. 819, appeal dismissed

1917, 37 S.Ct. 293, 243 U.S. 247, 61 L.Ed. 700.

It is arguable that the 1966 amendment of 28 U.S.C.A. § 2254(a) makes § 2241(c)(4) no longer available to state prisoners. If so, this was certainly in-advertent, but the provision has been used so rarely that its inadvertent re-peal, if this happened, is of little practi-cal consequence.

10. This provision—now 28 U.S.C.A. § 2241(c)(2)—was originally § 7 of the Force Act of 1833, 4 Stats. 634, and was the result of state imprisonment of federal marshals seeking to enforce the controversial Tariff Act. The most famous and colorful case involving this authorization for habeas corpus is In re Neagle, 1890, 10 S.Ct. 658, 135 U.S. 1, 34 L.Ed. 55. See Swisher, Stephen J. Field: Craftsman of the Law, 1930, pp. 321–361. The background of the Neagle case is also described in a fasci-nating book, Kroninger, Sarah and the Senator, 1964.

11. 28 U.S.C.A. §§ 1442, 1442a.

12. 28 U.S.C.A. § 2241(c)(1). This provi-sion stems from § 14 of the Judiciary Act of 1789, 1 Stat. 81.

13. For its use to challenge a deporta-tion order, a court-martial conviction, commitment to a mental hospital, deni-al of parole, and other matters, see 17 Wright, Miller & Cooper, Jurisdiction § 4261 n. 18.

ment,[14] and after the prisoners are convicted a statutory motion, covering the same scope as the writ of habeas corpus, is the remedy they must pursue.[15]

The most important part of the statute today is that provision, first adopted in 1867, authorizing issuance of the writ where persons are held in violation of the federal Constitution or laws,[16] which permits a federal court to order discharge of any person held by a state in violation of the supreme law of the land. The constitutionality of vesting this power in the federal courts is entirely settled.[17] The writ need not actually result in the discharge of the prisoner. Indeed in most cases grant of the writ is expressly made conditional in order that the state may retry the prisoner in a fashion meeting constitutional demands.[18]

It was once the law that the writ was not available unless it could potentially lead to discharge from custody under the sentence being attacked. This requirement has been considerably attenuated by the courts. A prisoner serving consecutive sentences is regarded as being "in custody" under any one of them, and may attack the validity of either the one he is serving or the one he is to serve in the future.[19] A prisoner being held as a multiple offender can use habeas corpus to challenge an earlier conviction that is being used to enhance his punishment on his latest conviction.[20] The writ may be used though the prisoner has been released on parole,[21] or is free on his own cognizance pending execution of sentence,[22] and even an unconditional re-

---

14. Riggins v. U. S., 1905, 26 S.Ct. 147, 199 U.S. 547, 50 L.Ed. 303.

15. 28 U.S.C.A. § 2255; U. S. v. Hayman, 1952, 72 S.Ct. 263, 342 U.S. 205, 96 L.Ed. 232; Hill v. U. S., 1962, 82 S.Ct. 468, 368 U.S. 424, 7 L.Ed.2d 417. For extended discussion of the vast litigation this statute has spawned, see 2 Wright Criminal 2d §§ 589–602. U. S. v. Frady, 1982, 102 S.Ct. 1584, ___ U.S. ___, 71 L.Ed.2d 816.

16. 28 U.S.C.A. § 2241(c)(3).

17. U. S. ex rel. Elliott v. Hendricks, C.A.3d, 1954, 213 F.2d 922, certiorari denied 75 S.Ct. 77, 348 U.S. 851, 99 L.Ed. 670. See Ex parte Royall, 1886, 6 S.Ct. 734, 739, 117 U.S. 241, 249, 29 L.Ed. 868; Frank v. Mangum, 1915, 35 S.Ct. 582, 588, 237 U.S. 309, 311, 59 L.Ed. 969.

18. E.g., Rogers v. Richmond, 1961, 81 S.Ct. 735, 365 U.S. 534, 5 L.Ed.2d 760; Irvin v. Dowd, 1961, 81 S.Ct. 1639, 366 U.S. 717, 6 L.Ed.2d 751.

19. Peyton v. Rowe, 1968, 88 S.Ct. 1549, 391 U.S. 54, 20 L.Ed.2d 426, overruling

McNally v. Hill, 1934, 55 S.Ct. 24, 293 U.S. 131, 79 L.Ed. 238.

See generally 17 Wright, Miller & Cooper, Jurisdiction § 4262; Smith, Federal Habeas Corpus: State Prisoners and the Concept of Custody, 1969, 4 U.Rich.L.Rev. 1; Note, Beyond Custody: Expanding Collateral Review of State Convictions, 1981, 14 U.Mich.J.L. Ref. 465.

20. Stubblefield v. Beto, C.A.5th, 1968, 399 F.2d 424, certiorari denied 89 S.Ct. 731, 393 U.S. 1072, 21 L.Ed.2d 715; Tucker v. Peyton, C.A.4th, 1966, 357 F.2d 115; U. S. ex rel. Durocher v. LaVallee, C.A.2d 1964, 330 F.2d 303, certiorari denied 84 S.Ct. 1921, 377 U.S. 998, 12 L.Ed.2d 1048. See also the extension of this principle in Cappetta v. Wainwright, C.A.5th, 1969, 406 F.2d 1238.

21. Jones v. Cunningham, 1963, 83 S.Ct. 373, 371 U.S. 236, 9 L.Ed.2d 285.

22. Hensley v. Municipal Court, 1973, 93 S.Ct. 1571, 411 U.S. 345, 36 L.Ed.2d 294.

lease does not make moot a pending application for habeas corpus.[23]
A prisoner in custody in one state against whom another state has a
detainer may challenge the sentence or indictment that is the basis
for the detainer by habeas corpus in federal court in either state.[24]

The statute permits granting of the writ "within their respective
jurisdictions" by the district court, a judge of a court of appeals, and
by the Supreme Court or a justice thereof.[25] In practice the application will normally be made to the district court; higher courts, and
judges thereof, are authorized to transfer to the district court any
application made to them.[26] By statute a state prisoner may seek
the writ either in the district in which he is being held or the district
in which he was convicted,[27] and the former rigid rule that both the
prisoner and the custodian must be within the territorial jurisdiction
of the court has been greatly watered down by decisions.[28]

The early concept of habeas corpus was that it guaranteed only
that all the proper legal processes had been used, "thus assuring only
a formalistic, check-list freedom." [29] The stated doctrine was that the
writ would issue only if the court that had committed the prisoner

23. Carafas v. LaVallee, 1968, 88 S.Ct.
1556, 391 U.S. 234, 20 L.Ed.2d 554,
overruling Parker v. Ellis, 1960, 80
S.Ct. 909, 362 U.S. 574, 4 L.Ed.2d 963.
See also Jago v. Van Curen, 1981, 102
S.Ct. 31, 36 n. 3, 454 U.S. 14, 21 n. 3, 70
L.Ed.2d 13.

This will not be true, however, if the pri-
or conviction has no collateral consequences. Lane v. Williams, 1982, 102
S.Ct. 1322, ____ U.S. ____, 71 L.Ed.2d
508.

24. Nelson v. George, 1970, 90 S.Ct.
1963, 399 U.S. 224, 26 L.Ed.2d 578
(state of custody); Braden v. 30th Judicial Circuit Court, 1973, 93 S.Ct. 1123,
410 U.S. 484, 35 L.Ed.2d 443 (state of
detainer). The Braden case suggests
that the state of detainer will ordinarily be the more convenient forum, and
that if the action is brought in the
state of custody it may be transferred
to the state of detainer under 28
U.S.C.A. § 1404(a).

25. 28 U.S.C.A. § 2241(a). The writ is
in aid of the appellate jurisdiction of
the higher courts, and thus the authorization for the Supreme Court to grant
it does not violate the constitutional
limits on the original jurisdiction of
that Court. Ex parte Siebold, 1879,
100 U.S. 371, 25 L.Ed. 717; Oaks, The
"Original" Writ of Habeas Corpus in
the Supreme Court, 1962 Sup.Ct.Rev.
153. See § 108 below.

26. 28 U.S.C.A. § 2241(b); Ex parte Abernathy, 1943, 64 S.Ct. 13, 320 U.S.

219, 88 L.Ed. 3; In re Tracy, 1919, 39
S.Ct. 374, 249 U.S. 551, 63 L.Ed. 768.
Whether an individual justice of the
Supreme Court may issue the writ is
an open question. Locks v. Command-
ing General, Sixth Army, 1968, 89 S.Ct.
31, 21 L.Ed.2d 78 (opinion of Circuit
Justice Douglas).

27. 28 U.S.C.A. § 2241(d), as amended
by Act of Sept. 19, 1966, Pub.L.
89–590, 80 Stat. 811. The court in
which the application is filed may
transfer it to the other district if this is
in the furtherance of justice.

28. Braden v. 30th Judicial Circuit
Court, 1973, 93 S.Ct. 1123, 410 U.S.
484, 35 L.Ed.2d 443; compare Strait v.
Laird, 1972, 92 S.Ct. 1693, 406 U.S.
341, 32 L.Ed.2d 141, with Schlanger v.
Seamans, 1971, 91 S.Ct. 995, 401 U.S.
487, 28 L.Ed.2d 251.

29. Note, 1948, 61 Harv.L.Rev. 657, 660.
But see Fay v. Noia, 1963, 83 S.Ct. 822,
830–831, 372 U.S. 391, 404–405, 9
L.Ed.2d 837, arguing that at common
law the writ was not narrowly limited
to jurisdictional questions. See
Bushell's Case, 1670, Vaughan, 135,
124 Eng.Rep. 1006. But see Justice
Powell's concurring opinion in
Schneckloth v. Bustamonte, 1973, 93
S.Ct. 2041, 2061, 412 U.S. 218, 254, 36
L.Ed.2d 854, on remand C.A.9th, 479
F.2d 1047.

lacked "jurisdiction" to do so.[30] The concept of jurisdictional defects was never entirely rigid, and a great expansion, beginning in 1923, has led to abandonment of the concept as a limit on habeas corpus. In 1923, in Moore v. Dempsey,[31] it was held that if a court was under the sway of mob rule, the proceedings, though formally entirely proper, would be a mere mask, depriving the court of jurisdiction, and that a prisoner convicted in such circumstances could attack his conviction by habeas corpus. A similar result was reached later where the conviction was allegedly obtained by the knowing use of perjured testimony.[32] In 1938 the Supreme Court held that a federal court that had jurisdiction at the outset of a trial "lost" jurisdiction during the course of the proceedings when it failed to provide the prisoner with counsel as the Sixth Amendment requires.[33] A similar doctrine was applied to state prisoners, and finally, in 1942, the Supreme Court abandoned the overstrained jurisdictional fiction and stated the reality: " *   *   * the use of the writ in the federal courts to test the constitutional validity of a conviction for crime is not restricted to those cases where the judgment of conviction is void for want of jurisdicton of the trial court to render it. It extends also to those exceptional cases where the conviction has been in disregard of the constitutional rights of the accused, and where the writ is the only effective means of preserving his rights." [34] Despite the language about "exceptional cases" in the passage just quoted, it is now clear that habeas corpus in a federal court is available whenever the state proceeding fails to meet the standards of procedural fairness that the Fourteenth Amendment requires of the states.[35]

There is an important limitation on the broad power of the federal courts to upset criminal convictions thus outlined. The Supreme Court had developed a doctrine that an application for habeas corpus should not be entertained until the prisoner had exhausted his state remedies.[36] This rule of comity was written into the statutes in 1948.[37] The Court first construed the statute to mean that the reme-

30. Ex parte Siebold, 1879, 100 U.S. 371, 25 L.Ed. 717. In this case it was held, however, that a court lacked jurisdiction if the statute creating the offense for which the prisoner was tried was unconstitutional.

31. 1923, 43 S.Ct. 265, 261 U.S. 86, 67 L.Ed. 543. See Waterman & Overton, Federal Habeas Corpus Statutes and Moore v. Dempsey, 1933, 1 U.Chi.L. Rev. 307; Waterman & Overton, The Aftermath of Moore v. Dempsey, 1933, 18 St. Louis L.Rev. 117.

32. Mooney v. Holohan, 1935, 55 S.Ct. 340, 294 U.S. 103, 79 L.Ed. 791.

33. Johnson v. Zerbst, 1938, 58 S.Ct. 1019, 1024, 304 U.S. 458, 468, 82 L.Ed. 1461.

34. Waley v. Johnston, 1942, 62 S.Ct. 964, 966, 316 U.S. 101, 104–105, 86 L.Ed. 1302.

35. See Hensley v. Municipal Court, 1973, 93 S.Ct. 1571, 1574, 411 U.S. 345, 349–350, 36 L.Ed.2d 294; Carafas v. LaVallee, 1968, 88 S.Ct. 1556, 1560, 391 U.S. 234, 238, 20 L.Ed.2d 554.

36. Ex parte Royall, 1886, 6 S.Ct. 734, 117 U.S. 241, 29 L.Ed. 868; Mooney v. Holohan, 1935, 55 S.Ct. 340, 343, 294 U.S. 103, 115, 79 L.Ed. 791; Ex parte Hawk, 1944, 64 S.Ct. 448, 321 U.S. 114, 88 L.Ed. 572; Slayton v. Smith, 1971, 92 S.Ct. 174, 404 U.S. 53, 30 L.Ed.2d 209.

37. 28 U.S.C.A. § 2254(b), (c). See 17 Wright, Miller & Cooper, Jurisdiction § 4264.

dies that must be exhausted normally included application to the Supreme Court to review the state proceedings, either by appeal or by certiorari as the case might be.[38] Though the prisoner was thus required to have sought Supreme Court review, denial of review by that Court was not to be given any weight by the district court on a later application for habeas corpus.[39] The wisdom of requiring a resort to the Supreme Court as a part of exhaustion of state remedies was always doubtful, and in 1963 the Court overruled the case that had read this requirement into the statute.[40] However, if the Supreme Court has decided the case, its judgment is conclusive in a later habeas corpus proceeding on all issues of fact or law that were actually adjudicated by the Court.[41]

The draftsman of the habeas corpus provisions incorporated in the 1948 revision of the Judicial Code had anticipated that the state remedies would not be deemed exhausted so long as the prisoner had the right to present his grievance again to the state by some state procedure.[42] The Supreme Court ruled to the contrary, holding squarely that the state remedies are exhausted when the constitutional contention has once been presented to the state courts, with, as then re-

The exhaustion requirement applies even though it is clear that the prisoner's constitutional rights were violated in the state proceeding. Duckworth v. Serrano, 1981, 102 S.Ct. 18, 454 U.S. 1, 70 L.Ed.2d 1.

The state remedy is not exhausted if the claim presented to the state court is not the same as that presented to the federal court. Picard v. Connor, 1971, 92 S.Ct. 509, 404 U.S. 270, 30 L.Ed.2d 438; Pitchess v. Davis, 1975, 95 S.Ct. 1748, 421 U.S. 482, 44 L.Ed.2d 317.

A federal court must dismiss a "mixed petition," one that contains some claims on which state remedies have been exhausted and others on which they have not been exhausted, and leave the prisoner with the choice of returning to state court to exhaust his claims or of amending or resubmitting the petition to present only the exhausted claims to the federal court. Rose v. Lundy, 1982, 102 S.Ct. 1198, ___ U.S. ___, 71 L.Ed.2d 379.

A state prisoner claiming that he is entitled to immediate or more speedy release from imprisonment cannot avoid the exhaustion requirement by framing his action as a civil rights action under 42 U.S.C.A. § 1983 but must proceed by habeas corpus. Preiser v. Rodriguez, 1973, 93 S.Ct. 1827, 411 U.S. 475, 36 L.Ed. 439. See Note, State Prisoners' Suits: Proper Forum, Choice of

Remedy, and Effect of Judgment, 1973, 51 Texas L.Rev. 1364.

38. Darr v. Burford, 1950, 70 S.Ct. 587, 339 U.S. 200, 94 L.Ed. 761. This may have been the rule prior to the 1948 codification. Ex parte Hawk, 1944, 64 S.Ct. 448, 321 U.S. 114, 88 L.Ed. 572; but cf. Wade v. Mayo, 1948, 68 S.Ct. 1270, 334 U.S. 672, 92 L.Ed. 1647.

39. Brown v. Allen, 1953, 73 S.Ct. 397, 344 U.S. 443, 97 L.Ed. 469, affirmed 73 S.Ct. 437, 344 U.S. 443, 97 L.Ed. 469. This is true even if the prisoner could have appealed as of right to the Supreme Court. County Court of Ulster County v. Allen, 1979, 99 S.Ct. 2213, 2220, n. 7, 442 U.S. 140, 149 n. 7, 60 L.Ed.2d 777.

40. Fay v. Noia, 1963, 83 S.Ct. 822, 847, 372 U.S. 391, 435, 9 L.Ed.2d 837.

41. 28 U.S.C.A. § 2244(c).

An affirmance by an equally divided Court is not an adjudication for this purpose. Neil v. Biggers, 1972, 93 S.Ct. 375, 409 U.S. 188, 34 L.Ed.2d 401. Neither is a denial of certiorari. But dismissal of an appeal for want of a substantial federal question is an adjudication. Howell v. Jones, C.A.5th, 1975, 516 F.2d 53; Connor v. Hutto, C.A.8th, 1975, 516 F.2d 853.

42. Parker, Limiting the Abuse of Habeas Corpus, 1948, 8 F.R.D. 171, 176.

quired, review sought, or excused, in the United States Supreme Court.[43] The draftsman had supposed that under this statute "there should be no more cases where proceedings of state courts, affirmed by the highest courts of the state, with denial of certiorari by the Supreme Court of the United States, will be reviewed by federal circuit or district judges." [44] The rule that only one state remedy need be exhausted has refuted such a hope. There are a great many such cases every year.

The requirement that state remedies be exhausted leads to the two most difficult problems with regard to federal habeas corpus for state prisoners. Though it appeared that they had been resolved in 1963, that resolution did not prove durable and there has been much subsequent change with regard to them. If the prisoner has been successful when he presented his constitutional contention to the state court, he will have been released, or retried, and has no need to resort to federal court. Applications for habeas corpus come, then, only where the state court has rejected the constitutional contention, or where for one reason or another it has failed to pass upon it. If the state court has held against the prisoner on his federal claim, what weight is to be given that determination in the subsequent federal proceedings? In a concurring opinion in Brown v. Allen,[45] which for 10 years was thought to be authoritative, Justice Frankfurter said that the federal judge could accept the determination of historic facts by the state court, unless there had been a "vital flaw" in the state factfinding process, but that the federal judge had to decide for himself mixed questions of law and fact as well as the application of constitutional principles to the facts as found. This formulation, though helpful, did not solve all questions as to the effect to be given the state determination.

Suppose a case in which a state defendant is convicted on the basis of a confession obtained after he was arrested but before he was brought before a magistrate. He contends, by analogy to the Mallory-McNabb rule once applicable in federal prosecutions,[46] that the use of such a confession against him is a violation of his rights under the Fourteenth Amendment. The contention is pressed and rejected by

43. Brown v. Allen, 1953, 73 S.Ct. 397, 402–404, 344 U.S. 443, 447–450, 97 L.Ed. 469.

A prisoner who has once exhausted his state remedies need not go back to the state court because an intervening decision by the state court makes it appear that it would now give the relief sought. Francisco v. Gathright, 1974, 95 S.Ct. 257, 419 U.S. 59, 42 L.Ed.2d 226.

Prisoners, who had unsuccessfully sought habeas corpus from the state courts, were not required to exhaust possible alternative state remedies before bringing a federal habeas corpus action. Wilwording v. Swenson, 1971, 92 S.Ct. 407, 404 U.S. 249, 30 L.Ed.2d 418.

44. Parker, note 42 above, at 178.

45. 1953, 73 S.Ct. 397, 446, 344 U.S. 443, 506–507, 97 L.Ed. 469.

46. 1 Wright, Criminal 2d §§ 72–75.

the state courts. He then applies to a federal district court for habeas corpus, raising the same contention.

Despite an occasional aberrational decision to the contrary, the historic rule applies that res judicata does not bar habeas corpus, and the mere fact that the contention has been presented to, and rejected by, the state courts does not prevent the federal court from giving relief.[47] If the state court has held that unreasonable delay in bringing an arrested person before a magistrate is no bar to the admissibility of confessions obtained in the interim, this construction of the Fourteenth Amendment raises a pure question of law that the federal judge is entirely free to decide for himself. Suppose, however, that the prisoner contends that the effect of holding him incommunicado after arrest was to produce coercion upon him, and make his confession involuntary. Such a contention would raise a mixed question of law and fact. The federal judge might accept the state court's finding as to the historical facts but would have to decide for himself whether on these facts an inference should be drawn that the confession was involuntary.[48]

The case becomes harder where the dispute goes solely to the historical facts. The prisoner, perhaps, has testified that he was held incommunicado for an extended period after arrest, but the police officers have denied this. If there was some "vital flaw" in the state process for finding the historical facts, as if the prisoner had not been given a fair opportunity to produce evidence to support his contention or the state court finding was contrary to uncontradicted evidence, the state finding could not be accepted by the federal court, which was required to make its own finding. In the absence of such a "vi-

---

47. Brown v. Allen, 1953, 73 S.Ct. 397, 408, 344 U.S. 443, 456, 97 L.Ed. 469; see Allen v. McCurry, 1980, 101 S.Ct. 411, 417 n. 12, 449 U.S. 90, 98 n. 12, 66 L.Ed.2d 308. See also Kelley, Finality and Habeas Corpus: Is the Rule That Res Judicata May Not Apply to Habeas Corpus or Motion to Vacate Still Viable?, 1975, 78 W.Va.L.Rev. 1.

Whether this was in fact the law prior to Brown v. Allen is a matter of dispute. In an interesting and scholarly article, Professor Bator contended that prior to Brown relief would lie for a state prisoner only if the state courts had failed to provide adequate corrective process. Bator, Finality in Criminal Law and Federal Habeas Corpus for State Prisoners, 1963, 76 Harv.L.Rev. 441. This analysis was persuasive to the dissenters in Fay v. Noia, 1963, 83 S.Ct. 822, 858–860, 372 U.S. 391, 457–461, 9 L.Ed.2d 837, but was rejected by the majority as "untenable." 83 S.Ct. at 839 n. 30, 372 U.S. at 421 n.

30. Professor Bator's view of history has been regarded more favorably in Oaks, Legal History in the High Court—Habeas Corpus, 1966, 64 Mich.L.Rev. 451, in Friendly, note 1 above, and in Justice Powell's concurring opinion (joined by two other justices) in Schneckloth v. Bustamonte, 1973, 93 S.Ct. 2041, 2059, 412 U.S. 218, 250, 36 L.Ed.2d 854. See also Stone v. Powell, 1976, 96 S.Ct. 3037, 3043 n.9, 428 U.S. 465, 476 n.9, 49 L.Ed.2d 1067, where the Court merely says: "There has been disagreement among scholars as to whether the result in Brown v. Allen was foreshadowed by the Court's decision in Moore v. Dempsey."

48. Cf. Leyra v. Denno, 1954, 74 S.Ct. 716, 347 U.S. 556, 98 L.Ed. 948.

This is still the rule. Sumner v. Mata, 1982, 102 S.Ct. 1303, ___ U.S. ___, 71 L.Ed.2d 480; Cuyler v. Sullivan, 1980, 100 S.Ct. 1708, 446 U.S. 335, 64 L.Ed.2d 333.

tal flaw," however, the federal court, under Brown v. Allen, was free to accept the state findings.[49] It was not, however, required to do so. Even without a "vital flaw," the district judge was at liberty if he saw fit to take testimony as to the facts.[50]

The Supreme Court undertook to shed light on these matters in 1963, in Townsend v. Sain.[51] The Court there was unanimous in holding that the federal court has the power to receive evidence and try the facts anew on a habeas corpus petition. The question is not whether the federal court may try the facts, but whether it must. The Court was unanimous also on the following statement as to when independent factfinding by the federal court is mandatory: "Where the facts are in dispute, the federal court on habeas corpus must hold an evidentiary hearing if the habeas applicant did not receive a full and fair evidentiary hearing in a state court, either at the time of the trial or in a collateral proceeding. In other words a federal evidentiary hearing is required unless the state-court trier of fact has after a full hearing reliably found the relevant facts." [52] Finally the Court was unanimous in holding that the district court is not limited to a study of the undisputed portions of the state court record.[53]

The decision in the Townsend case was by a vote of five to four, because of disagreement as to application of the announced standard on the facts of that case. The dissenters objected, also, to the majority's particularization of the general standard stated as to when independent factfinding is mandatory. The majority, believing that experience teaches that too general a standard, such as the "exceptional circumstances" and "vital flaw" tests of Brown v. Allen, did not give adequate guidance to the district courts, undertook to provide guidelines by listing six circumstances in which a federal evidentiary hearing was mandatory.[54] These were codified in somewhat different form in 1966.[55] The statute now provides that a determination of a

49. E.g., U. S. ex rel. Salemi v. Denno, C.A.2d, 1956, 235 F.2d 910; Thomas v. Eyman, C.A.9th, 1956, 235 F.2d 775.

50. U. S. ex rel. Rogers v. Richmond, 1958, 78 S.Ct. 1365, 357 U.S. 220, 2 L.Ed.2d 1361.

51. 1963, 83 S.Ct. 745, 372 U.S. 293, 9 L.Ed.2d 770.

52. 83 S.Ct. at 757, 372 U.S. at 293, 312–313. The Court states that this test supersedes, to the extent that there is any inconsistency, the tests set out in Brown v. Allen.

See also Smith v. Yeager, 1968, 89 S.Ct. 277, 393 U.S. 122, 21 L.Ed.2d 246.

A new hearing is not required unless the prisoner's version of the events, if true, would entitle him to relief. Procunier v. Atchley, 1971, 91 S.Ct. 485, 400 U.S. 446, 27 L.Ed.2d 524.

53. 83 S.Ct. at 761, 372 U.S. at 320.

54. 83 S.Ct. at 757, 372 U.S. at 313.

55. 28 U.S.C.A. § 2254(d), added by Act of Nov. 2, 1966, Pub.L. 89–711, 80 Stat. 1105.

Though Townsend lists six circumstances and the statute eight, the lists are not entirely overlapping on their face, and Townsend speaks of making a hearing mandatory while the statute is in terms of circumstances dispelling the presumption of correctness, it seems entirely clear that the statute is a determination by Congress that the Townsend guidelines "would be better understood and applied if they were codified in statutory form," White v. Swenson, D.C.Mo.1966, 261 F.Supp. 42, 61. See also Brewer v. Williams, 1977, 97 S.Ct. 1232, 1238, 430 U.S. 387, 395–396, 51 L.Ed.2d 424, rehearing de-

fact issue made by a state court after a hearing on the merits and evidenced by reliable and adequate written indicia is presumed to be correct, and the burden is on the petitioner to establish by convincing evidence that the determination is erroneous, unless one of eight specified circumstances exists. These circumstances are: "(1) that the merits of the factual dispute were not resolved in the State court hearing; (2) that the factfinding procedure employed by the State court was not adequate to afford a full and fair hearing; (3) that the material facts were not adequately developed at the State court hearing; (4) that the State court lacked jurisdiction of the subject matter or over the person of the applicant in the State court proceeding; (5) that the applicant was an indigent and the State court, in deprivation of his constitutional right, failed to appoint counsel to represent him in the State court proceeding; (6) that the applicant did not receive a full, fair, and adequate hearing in the State court proceeding; (7) that the applicant was otherwise denied due process of law in the State court proceeding; (8) or unless that part of the record of the State court proceeding in which the determination of such factual issue was made, pertinent to a determination of the sufficiency of the evidence to support such factual determination, is produced as provided for hereinafter, and the Federal court on a consideration of such part of the record as a whole concludes that such factual determination is not fairly supported by the record." Under the statute a state finding cannot be set aside merely on a preponderance of the evidence, and a federal court granting the writ must include in its opinion the reason that if found that one of the first seven factors were present, or the reason that it concluded that the state finding was not fairly supported by the record.[56]

Thus in the case earlier put, where there was conflicting evidence on whether the prisoner had been held incommunicado after arrest, the test will no longer be whether there was a "vital flaw" in the state process for finding the historical facts. Instead the test will be whether the prisoner received a full and fair evidentiary hearing in the state court, in the light of the principles announced in Townsend and with an eye to the circumstances specified in the statute.

If the state has not decided the federal claim, it will be because the prisoner has not asserted it properly in state court or because there is some adequate state ground that supports the conviction. On the problem of "an abortive state proceeding," the two Supreme Court decisions in point prior to 1963 were inconclusive. In Daniels

nied 97 S.Ct. 2200, 431 U.S. 925, 53 L.Ed.2d 240.

56. Sumner v. Mata, 1981, 101 S.Ct. 764, 449 U.S. 539, 66 L.Ed.2d 722. See also Sumner v. Mata, 1982, 102 S.Ct. 1303, ___ U.S. ___, 71 L.Ed.2d 480.

See generally 17 Wright, Miller & Cooper, Jurisdiction § 4265.

The failure of the state court specifically to articulate its credibility findings does not establish that the merits of the factual dispute were not resolved. LaVallee v. Delle Rose, 1973, 93 S.Ct. 1203, 410 U.S. 690, 35 L.Ed.2d 637.

v. Allen [57] the state defendants had filed their appeal papers in the state supreme court one day late, and that court had refused to pass on their meritorious claim that they had been denied federal constitutional rights. The United States Supreme Court held that the failure to perfect the appeal in accord with a reasonable state procedural requirement barred subsequent discharge on habeas corpus. In Irvin v. Dowd,[58] the state supreme court had held that the trial court had not erred in denying the prisoner's application for a new trial, since he had escaped the day before it was filed, but because the death sentence was involved the state court went on to consider and reject the federal constitutional claim. Four Supreme Court dissenters asserted that an adequate state ground sufficient to bar direct review by the Court was also sufficient to bar habeas corpus. The majority, holding that the application for habeas corpus should be considered on its merits,[59] avoided passing on this assertion directly by reading the state court opinion as resting decision entirely on the determination that the federal claim was without substance. Since the rule proposed by the dissenters in Irvin was not enunciated in terms in Daniel, nor rejected in terms by the majority in Irvin, the law on the point was not clear. The issue produced a spirited controversy in the law reviews [60] and was temporarily settled by the 1963 decision in Fay v. Noia.[61]

The Noia case was a particularly appealing one. Noia and two others were convicted of murder. Noia did not appeal. The other defendants appealed unsuccessfully. Fourteen years later one of the other defendants was discharged on federal habeas corpus when it was established that his confession had been coerced by "satanic practices." The following year the state court granted reargument of the appeal of Noia's second codefendant, and set his conviction aside on the same ground. Noia, whose conviction had been similarly coerced, then sought relief from the state court, but it was held there that his failure to appeal his conviction barred him from later attacking the conviction. He brought an action in federal court for habeas corpus. The state conceded that his rights under the Fourteenth Amendment had been denied, by use of the coerced confession, but relied on his failure to appeal as an adequate state ground precluding

---

57. 1953, 73 S.Ct. 397, 420–422, 344 U.S. 443, 482–487, 97 L.Ed. 469 (decided sub nom Brown v. Allen).

58. 1959, 79 S.Ct. 825, 359 U.S. 394, 3 L.Ed.2d 900.

59. When the case came back to the Supreme Court on the merits, it was held unanimously that Irvin had been unfairly convicted. Irvin v. Dowd, 1961, 81 S.Ct. 1639, 366 U.S. 717, 6 L.Ed.2d 751.

60. Hart, Foreword: The Time Chart of the Justices, 1959, 73 Harv.L.Rev. 84,

101–125; Arnold, Professor Hart's Theology, 1960, 73 Harv.L.Rev. 1298, 1304–1310; Reitz, Federal Habeas Corpus: Impact of an Abortive State Proceeding, 1961, 74 Harv.L.Rev. 315; Brennan, Federal Habeas Corpus and State Prisoners: An Exercise in Federalism, 1961, 7 Utah L.Rev. 423; R.C., 1962, 76 Harv.L.Rev. 411.

61. 1963, 83 S.Ct. 822, 372 U.S. 391, 9 L.Ed.2d 837.

relief, or as showing that he had not exhausted state remedies as required by the statute.

The Supreme Court disagreed. In a sweeping opinion by Justice Brennan, the Court held that federal courts have power to grant relief despite the applicant's failure to have pursued a state remedy not available to him at the time he seeks habeas corpus. The doctrine that a state procedural default is an adequate and independent state law ground barring direct review in the Supreme Court does not limit the power of a district court to grant habeas corpus. It held also that the statutory requirement of exhaustion of state remedies applies only to those still open to the applicant at the time he seeks federal habeas corpus, and does not include remedies he might have pursued in the past that are not still open. The Court recognized a discretion to refuse relief because of failure to comply with state procedures, but made it clear that such discretion is very limited. "If a habeas applicant, after consultation with competent counsel or otherwise, understandingly and knowingly forwent the privilege of seeking to vindicate his federal claims in the state courts, whether for strategic, tactical, or any other reasons that can fairly be described as the deliberate bypassing of state procedures, then it is open to the federal court on habeas to deny him all relief if the state courts refused to entertain his federal claims on the merits * * *. At all events we wish it clearly understood that the standard here put forth depends on the considered choice of the petitioner. * * * A choice made by counsel not participated in by the petitioner does not automatically bar relief. Nor does a state court's finding of waiver bar independent determination of the question by the federal courts on habeas, for waiver affecting federal rights is a federal question." [62]

Applying these principles to the case before it, the Court held that Noia's decision not to appeal—though made in consultation with counsel and based on a fear that at a second trial he might receive the death sentence, rather than life imprisonment—was not a deliberate bypassing of the state court system, and thus did not give the district court discretion to refuse to issue the writ.

To Justice Harlan, and two other dissenters, the Court, in Noia, had "turned its back on history and struck a heavy blow at the foundations of our federal system." [63] In their view the federal courts are constitutionally without power to order release of a prisoner where the validity of his conviction rests on an adequate and independent state ground.

---

62. 83 S.Ct. at 849, 372 U.S. at 439.

A deliberate bypass barred relief in Murch v. Mottram, 1972, 93 S.Ct. 71, 409 U.S. 41, 34 L.Ed.2d 194. Compare Humphrey v. Cady, 1972, 92 S.Ct. 1048, 405 U.S. 504, 31 L.Ed.2d 394.

63. 83 S.Ct. at 854, 372 U.S. at 449.

Echoes of the disagreement that divided the Court in Fay v. Noia were sounded in Henry v. Mississippi, 1965, 85 S.Ct. 564, 379 U.S. 443, 13 L.Ed.2d 408. See § 107 below.

Fay v. Noia was not to be the last word. The doctrine announced in Fay was decisively changed in 1977 in Wainwright v. Sykes,[64] but other cases between 1963 and 1977 provided the foundation on which the Court built in Wainwright. In Davis v. United States,[65] a 1973 decision involving a federal prisoner, the Court held that the deliberate bypass standard of Fay did not apply to a post-conviction motion challenging the composition of the grand jury. The motion was barred by Criminal Rule 12(b)(2), which provided that challenges of that kind must be made by motion before trial and that only "for cause shown" could a court grant relief from the waiver resulting from failure to make the motion at the time provided.[66] A similar attack on the makeup of a grand jury by a state prisoner was rejected in 1976 in Francis v. Henderson.[67] A state statute required such challenges to be made before trial. Although the Supreme Court recognized that a district court has power to entertain an application for habeas corpus in a case of that kind, it held that it would not be appropriate to exercise that power. Without any explanation of how the result could be reconciled with Fay v. Noia, the Court announced that in these circumstances collateral attack on a state conviction required "not only a showing of 'cause' for the defendant's failure to challenge the composition of the grand jury before trial, but also a showing of actual prejudice." [68]

In Wainwright v. Sykes habeas corpus was sought because of the introduction of inculpatory statements Sykes had made when allegedly he had not understood the Miranda warnings given him. No objection was made at trial to the introduction of the statements. The Court held that the failure to make a contemporaneous objection, as required by state procedure, could not be regarded as a deliberate bypass, but that it barred Sykes from habeas relief unless he could show cause for his failure to object and actual prejudice from admission of the statements. "To the extent that the dicta of Fay v. Noia may be thought to have laid down an all-inclusive rule rendering state timely objection rules ineffective to bar review of underlying federal claims in federal habeas proceedings—absent a 'knowing waiver' or a 'deliberate bypass' of the right to so object—its effect was limited by

---

64. 1977, 97 S.Ct. 2497, 433 U.S. 72, 53 L.Ed.2d 594.

65. 1973, 93 S.Ct. 1577, 411 U.S. 233, 36 L.Ed.2d 216.

66. What was Rule 12(b)(2) at the time of the Davis case is now divided between Rule 12(b) and Rule 12(f).

67. 1976, 96 S.Ct. 1708, 425 U.S. 536, 48 L.Ed.2d 149.

68. 96 S.Ct. at 1711, 425 U.S. at 542.

On the same day as Francis the Court held in Estelle v. Williams, 1976, 96 S.Ct. 1691, 425 U.S. 501, 48 L.Ed.2d 126, that a prisoner who was required to stand trial in his prison clothes could not obtain habeas corpus, because his failure to object in state court negated the presence of compulsion necessary to establish a constitutional violation.

Francis, which applied a different rule and barred a habeas challenge to the makeup of a grand jury."[69]

Wainwright leaves many questions unanswered.[70] The "cause" and "prejudice" test it announced surely applies to any failure to comply with a state rule requiring contemporaneous objection to events at the trial or prior to trial.[71] In Wainwright the Court said it was rejecting "the sweeping language of Fay v. Noia * * *, going far beyond the facts of the case eliciting it * * *," and expressly refrained from deciding whether failure to comply with state appeal procedures would bar habeas corpus and thus whether the holding of Fay is now overruled.[72] State law must be looked to in deciding if a contemporaneous objection is required,[73] and if a state court considers a defendant's constitutional claim and rejects it on the merits, despite failure to object or some other procedural default that might have made determination of the merits unnecessary, the federal court is free to consider the constitutional claim on habeas corpus.[74] The meaning of "cause" and of "prejudice" remains uncertain, although it has been held that the futility of presenting an objection to the state courts cannot alone constitute cause for a failure to object at trial, nor can the novelty of a constitutional claim if other defense counsel have perceived and litigated that claim.[75] Prejudice must be evaluated in the total context of the events at trial, and the party attacking a conviction must show not merely that the errors at his trial created a possibility of prejudice but that they worked to his actual and substantial disadvantage, infecting his entire trial with error of constitutional dimension.[76]

It had been thought that the use of illegally obtained evidence was not ground for collateral attack, whether on a motion under 28 U.S. C.A. § 2255 by a federal prisoner or on a habeas corpus application

---

69. 97 S.Ct. at 2505, 433 U.S. at 85.

70. See 17 Wright, Miller & Cooper, Jurisdiction § 4266; Goodman, Wainwright v. Sykes, The Lower Federal Courts Respond, 1979, 30 Hastings L.Rev. 1683; Kinnamon, Defenses to the Preclusive Rule of Wainwright v. Sykes, 1979, 28 Drake L.Rev. 571; Hill, The Forfeiture of Constitutional Rights in Criminal Cases, 1978, 78 Col.L.Rev. 1050; Rosenberg, Jettisoning Fay v. Noia: Procedural Defaults by Reasonably Incompetent Counsel, 1978, 62 Minn.L.Rev. 341; Spritzer, Criminal Waiver, Procedural Default and the Burger Court, 1978, 126 U.Pa.L.Rev. 473.

71. Spritzer, note 70 above, at 507–508. See, e.g., Sumner v. Mata, 1981, 101 S.Ct. 764, 769, 449 U.S. 539, 547, 66 L.Ed.2d 722; Lee v. Missouri, 1979, 99 S.Ct. 710, 439 U.S. 461, 58 L.Ed.2d 736.

72. 97 S.Ct. at 2507, 433 U.S. at 87–88.

73. Jenkins v. Anderson, 1980, 100 S.Ct. 2124, 2127 n. 1, 447 U.S. 231, 234 n. 1, 65 L.Ed.2d 86.

74. County Court of Ulster County v. Allen, 1979, 99 S.Ct. 2213, 2223, 442 U.S. 140, 154, 60 L.Ed.2d 777. See also Francis, 96 S.Ct. at 1711 n. 5, 425 U.S. at 542 n. 5.

75. Engle v. Isaac, 1982, 102 S.Ct. 1558, ___ U.S. ___, 71 L.Ed.2d 783.

76. U. S. v. Frady, 1982, 102 S.Ct. 1584, ___ U.S. ___, 71 L.Ed.2d 816. This case holds that the "cause" and "prejudice" test announced in Wainwright applies also to federal prisoners attacking a conviction under 28 U.S. C.A. § 2255.

by a state prisoner.[77]   Although the Supreme Court rejected his view in 1969,[78] it substantially returned to it in 1976, when it held, in Stone v. Powell,[79] that if the state "has provided an opportunity for full and fair litigation of a Fourth Amendment claim, a state prisoner may not be granted federal habeas corpus relief on the ground that evidence obtained in an unconstitutional search or seizure was introduced at his trial." [80]

It is possible that the Stone rule will be extended to constitutional violations other than the Fourth Amendment.   To date, at least, that has not happened, and in the one case in which the Court squarely confronted such an argument it refused to apply the Stone rationale to preclude habeas corpus on a claim of racial discrimination in the selection of the grand jury that indicted a state prisoner.[81]

Federal habeas corpus for state prisoners is, and always has been, a controversial and emotion-ridden subject.   In the last century there were protests against "the prostitution of the writ of habeas corpus, under which the decisions of the State courts are subjected to the superintendence of the Federal judges   *   *   *." [82]   As the scope of the writ has expanded, as the rights found to be protected by the Fourteenth Amendment have increased in number, so has the criticism of this jurisdiction mounted in volume.   There is an affront to state sensibilities when a single federal judge can order discharge of a prisoner whose conviction has been affirmed by the highest court of a state.   Thus it is not surprising that the Conference of Chief Justices has called for abolition of such jurisdiction, nor that the attorneys general of 41 states joined in a 1954 attempt to sweep aside nearly a century of history and precedent and have the habeas corpus statute itself, insofar as it applies to state prisoners, declared unconstitutional.[83]

Though there are a great many applications for habeas corpus, it is rare indeed to have the single federal judge set free the prisoner the state has convicted.   Comprehensive statistics are lacking, but

77.   Amsterdam, Search, Seizure, and Section 2255: A Comment, 1964, 112 U.Pa.L.Rev. 378; 2 Wright Criminal, 1969 ed., § 595 n. 57 and cases cited.

78.   Kaufman v. U. S., 1969, 89 S.Ct. 1068, 394 U.S. 217, 22 L.Ed.2d 227.

79.   1976, 96 S.Ct. 3037, 428 U.S. 465, 49 L.Ed.2d 1067.   See 17 Wright, Miller & Cooper, Jurisdiction § 4263; Halpern, Federal Habeas Corpus and the Mapp Exclusionary Rule After Stone v. Powell, 1982, 82 Col.L.Rev. 1; Comment, Development of Federal Habeas Corpus Since Stone v. Powell, 1979 Wis.L.Rev. 1145; Comment, Habeas Corpus After Stone v. Powell: The "Opportunity for Full and Fair Litiga-

tion" Standard, 1978, 13 Harv.C.R.-C.L.L.Rev. 521.

80.   96 S.Ct. at 3049, 428 U.S. at 489.

81.   Rose v. Mitchell, 1979, 99 S.Ct. 2993, 443 U.S. 545, 61 L.Ed.2d 739.

See Comment, Habeas Corpus and Due Process: Stone v. Powell Restricted, 1980, 17 Hous.L.Rev. 923.

82.   Note, Federal Abuses of the Writ of Habeas Corpus, 1898, 25 Am.L.Rev. 149, 153.

83.   U. S. ex rel. Elliott v. Hendricks, C.A.3d, 1954, 213 F.2d 922, certiorari denied 75 S.Ct. 77, 348 U.S. 851, 99 L.Ed. 670.

those that are available indicate that the writ is granted in at most 4% of the cases in which it is sought, and in many of these cases it is possible for the state to retry the petitioner.[84] The number of applications, however, puts a burden on the federal courts, and this burden has increased rapidly as procedural barriers to relief have been removed and Supreme Court decisions have broadened the substantive grounds on which relief is available. In 1953 Justice Jackson complained that "floods of stale, frivolous and repetitious petitions inundate the docket of the lower courts and swell our own." In a footnote at that point he noted that in the preceding year 541 petitions had been filed.[85] The number of petitions reached a peak of 9,063 in 1970 and seems now to have levelled off at about 7,800 per year.[86] Applications for habeas corpus or for other relief for prisoners, state and federal, now constitute the largest element of the civil caseload of the district courts.[87]

The great bulk of these applications are utterly unjustified, and it is easy to say, as Justice Jackson did, that "he who must search a haystack for a needle is likely to end up with the attitude that the needle is not worth the search."[88] To that attitude the classic answer has been that of Justice Walter V. Schaefer of the Illinois Supreme Court when he said "it is not a needle we are looking for in these stacks of paper, but the rights of a human being."[89] Nevertheless federal judges, fully sensitive to the importance of human rights, do feel the burden of processing this flood of applications[90] and the Supreme Court, while recognizing the honored position habeas corpus has in our jurisprudence, has gone on to point out that "the Great Writ entails significant costs."[91]

84. See 17 Wright, Miller & Cooper, Jurisdiction § 4261 n. 37.

85. Brown v. Allen, 1953, 73 S.Ct. 397, 425, 344 U.S. 443, 536, 97 L.Ed. 469 (concurring opinion).

86. Ann.Rep. of the Director of the Administrative Office of the United States Courts, 1981, p. 211. Figures for 1975 to 1981 are given there. Figures for earlier years can be found in similar tables in earlier reports.

87. Id. at 208–211. See also the statement of Chief Justice Burger, 1976, 62 A.B.A.J. 189, 190.

88. Brown v. Allen, 1953, 73 S.Ct. 397, 425, 344 U.S. 443, 537, 97 L.Ed. 469 (concurring opinion).

89. Schaefer, Federalism and State Criminal Procedure, 1956, 70 Harv.L. Rev. 1, 25.

90. Although many habeas corpus applications are considered in the first instance by a United States magistrate, 28 U.S.C.A. § 636(b)(1)(b), the magistrate can only make proposed findings of fact and recommendations, and the petition must finally be disposed of by a district judge. See 17 Wright, Miller & Cooper, Jurisdiction § 4268, pp. 712–713.

91. Engle v. Isaac, 1982, 102 S.Ct. 1558, 1571, ___ U.S. ___, ___, 71 L.Ed.2d 783. The Court itemized the costs: "Collateral review of a conviction extends the ordeal of trial for both society and the accused. * * * Liberal allowance of the writ, moreover, degrades the prominence of the trial itself. * * * [W]rits of habeas corpus frequently cost society the right to punish admitted offenders. * * * Federal intrusions into state criminal trials frustrate both the States' sovereign power to punish offenders and their good faith attempts to honor constitutional rights."

There have been many proposals over the years for legislation restricting habeas corpus, and the interest in such legislation appears to be growing.[92] In addition, the Supreme Court has shown a "historic willingness to overturn or modify its earlier views of the scope of the writ, even where the statutory language authorizing judicial action has remained unchanged."[93] In recent years states that have urged the Court to cut back on the scope of the writ have often found a receptive audience.

The scope of habeas corpus has never been static in the federal courts and further change seems likely. The Great Writ was long ago hailed as "the best and only sufficient defense of personal freedom"[94] and much more recently was described as "both the symbol and guardian of individual liberty."[95] But in recent years there has been increased support for the view that the writ must be saved from itself.[96]

92. E.g., ABA Standards for Criminal Justice, 2d ed. 1980, c. 22; Committee Report, Pending Legislation to Amend the Federal Habeas Corpus Statutes, 1980, 35 Record of N.Y.C.B.A. 124; see Note, Proposed Modification of Federal Habeas Corpus for State Prisoners—Reform or Revocation?, 1973, 61 Geo. L.J. 1221.

93. Wainwright, 97 S.Ct. at 2497, 433 U.S. at 81.

94. Ex parte Yerger, 1868, 8 Wall. 85, 95, 19 L.Ed. 332 (per Chase, C.J.).

95. Peyton v. Rowe, 1968, 88 S.Ct. 1549, 1551, 391 U.S. 54, 58, 20 L.Ed.2d 426 (per Warren, C.J.).

96. "There has been a halo about the 'Great Writ' that no one would wish to dim. Yet one must wonder whether the stretching of its use far beyond any justifiable purpose will not in the end weaken rather than strengthen the writ's vitality." Schneckloth v. Bustmonte, 1973, 93 S.Ct. 2041, 2072, 412 U.S. 218, 275, 36 L.Ed.2d 854 (Powell, J., concurring).

See also Friendly, note 1 above, at 143.

CHAPTER 9

THE LAW APPLIED BY THE
FEDERAL COURTS

Analysis

§ 54. The Rules of Decision Act and Swift v. Tyson [1]

Section 34 of the Judiciary Act of 1789 [2]—the famous Rules of Decision Act—provided that "the laws of the several states, except where the constitution, treaties, or statutes of the United States shall otherwise require or provide, shall be regarded as rules of decision in trials at common law in the courts of the United States in cases where they apply." The statute has remained substantially unchanged to this day.[3] No issue in the whole field of federal jurisprudence has been more difficult than determining the meaning of this statute.

The central question has been whether the decisions of state courts are "laws of the several states" within the meaning of the statute, and thus of controlling effect in some situations at least in the federal courts. Despite the claims of some commentators, it seems fair to say that the early decisions of this question were neither consistent nor considered,[4] and that the first attempt at a definitive answer was in 1842 in the celebrated case of Swift v. Tyson.[5] The precise issue in that case was whether a pre-existing debt was

---

[§ 54]

1. Zeigler, The Background of Erie, 1965, 17 S.C.L.Rev. 468; Jackson, The Rise and Fall of Swift v. Tyson, 1938, 24 A.B.A.J. 609; Teton, The Story of Swift v. Tyson, 1941, 35 Ill.L.Rev. 519; Keeffe, In Praise of Joseph Story, Swift v. Tyson and "The" True National Common Law, 1969, 18 Amer.U.L. Rev. 316; Note, Swift v. Tyson Exhumed, 1969, 79 Yale L.J. 284.

2. 1 Stat. 92.

3. As revised in 1948, some slight verbal changes were made in the statute which is now 28 U.S.C.A. § 1652, and

the phrase "civil actions" was substituted for "trials at common law."

4. The decisions prior to 1842 are reviewed in 2 Crosskey, Politics and the Constitution in the History of the United States, 1953, pp. 816–864. Compare Robinson v. Campbell, 1818, 3 Wheat. 212, 222–223, 4 L.Ed. 372, with Wheaton v. Peters, 1834, 8 Pet. 591, 658, 8 L.Ed. 1055.

5. 1842, 16 Pet. 1, 10 L.Ed. 865. Ironically the defendant's name, which was a household word to lawyers for a century, was apparently misspelled by the Supreme Court, and was in fact

good consideration for an endorsement of a bill of exchange so that the endorsee would be a holder in due course. Several decisions of the Supreme Court had regarded this as good consideration, but the New York decisions were unclear. Justice Story, speaking for the Court, assumed that the New York decisions would not regard this as good consideration, but held that an opposite result should be reached by a federal court sitting in a diversity case.

In determining whether the New York decisions were "laws" of that state within the Rules of Decision Act, Justice Story gave no consideration to the legislative history of the act, though, as will be seen, this was to be much argued at a later time. The bases of the decision were, rather, the normal meaning of the word "laws" and considerations of policy deemed of importance by the Court. On the first of these points, he said: "In the ordinary use of language it will hardly be contended that the decisions of courts constitute laws. They are, at most, only evidence of what the laws are, and are not of themselves laws." [6] He was not content to rest decision on this pronouncement as to the nature of law, but went on to distinguish between, on the one hand, matters of a local nature, including state statutes and the construction thereof, and decisions as to real estate and other immovable matters, and, on the other hand, questions of general commercial law, dependent not on "the decisions of the local tribunals, but in the general principles and doctrines of commercial jurisprudence." [7] When Justice Story went on to say that "the law respecting negotiable instruments may be truly declared" in terms of Cicero's remark that law cannot be one thing in Rome and another in Athens, he was being entirely consistent with his earlier views, expressed both on and off the bench, urging uniformity of law.[8]

Writing in 1928 of the progeny of Swift v. Tyson, Dean Dobie observed justly that "though the cases here are legion, these rules and their application are notoriously far from clear." [9] Since the doctrine of Swift v. Tyson is now a museum piece, it would not be worthwhile

---

"Tysen." See Teton, The Story of Swift v. Tyson, 1941, 35 Ill.L.Rev. 519, 530 n. 2. This is not the only example of misspelling in Supreme Court cases. The bank cashier in the great case of McCulloch v. Maryland, 1819, 4 Wheat. 316, 4 L.Ed. 579, actually spelled his name McCulloh. Lewis, Without Fear or Favor, 1965, p. 504 n. 163. The defendant in Dred Scott's case was John F. A. Sanford, but the case has gone into the books as Dred Scott v. Sandford, 1857, 19 How. 393, 15 L.Ed. 691. See Latham, The Dred Scott Decision, 1968, p. 26. The stubborn parents in Minersville Sch. Dist. v. Gobitis, 1940, 60 S.Ct. 1010, 310 U.S. 586, 84 L.Ed. 1375, were really named Gobitas. Harrell & Jones, Equal Justice Under Law, 1965, p. 85.

6. 16 Pet. at 18.

7. 16 Pet. at 19.

8. The quotation is 16 Pet. at 19. Twenty-seven years before Justice Story had made use of the same quotation from Cicero, only then it was prefaced with the words: "of the great system of maritime law it may be truly said * * *." DeLovio v. Bolt, C.C.D. Mass.1815, 7 Fed.Cas. 418, 443, No. 3776.

See also Teton, note 1 above. There is an engaging discussion of the intellectual underpinnings of Swift in the Yale Note, cited note 1 above.

9. Dobie, Federal Procedure, 1928, p. 558.

to develop the distinctions that the courts created in applying the doctrine. The dichotomy between matters of "general" law, which the federal courts were free to find for themselves, and matters of "local" law, on which state decisions were binding, proved particularly elusive. Though Swift v. Tyson might have been limited to questions of commercial law, it was not so limited, and it was ultimately held that federal courts were to decide for themselves questions of the law of torts.[10] Usually state law was respected on questions of real property, but even here the federal court was allowed to take its own view if the state decisions were thought to be unsettled.[11] In general state court decisions construing a state statute or constitution were followed in the federal courts, but it was held that such decisions need not be followed if they conflicted with an earlier federal construction of the statute or constitution,[12] or if the state decision had come down after the case had been tried in a lower federal court.[13] Finally, there is the controversial case of Gelpcke v. City of Dubuque.[14] Municipalities in Iowa had issued bonds to pay for stock in railroads building toward their towns. The Iowa Supreme Court initially held that such bonds were valid, but subsequently overruled itself and held that the bonds were invalid under the state constitution. Citizens of states other than Iowa sued on the bonds, and invoked the diversity jurisdiction of the federal court. The Supreme Court followed the earlier decisions and refused to be bound by the later ones holding the bonds invalid. The Court recognized that ordinarily the federal courts should follow state decisions construing state statutes or constitutions, but said there might be exceptions to the rule, and declared passionately: "We shall never immolate truth, justice, and the law, because a state tribunal has erected the altar and decreed the sacrifice."[15] On one level Gelpcke v. Dubuque may be thought inconsistent with Swift v. Tyson. If decisions of a court are not themselves law, as Justice Story had said, then the early Iowa decisions were entitled to no greater respect than the later decisions, and there was no basis for holding, as the Court was to hold, that bonds issued while the early decisions still stood were valid, but that bonds issued after the overruling decision were invalid. On another level, however, the Gelpcke case is consistent with the unarticulated assumption of Swift v. Tyson that the federal judiciary has the power, if not indeed the duty, to reach the result that appeals to it as just regardless of what the states may say.

Ultimately the doctrine of Swift v. Tyson was to come under heavy attack. As early as 1893 Justice Field, in a dissent, expressed "an abiding faith that this, like other errors, will, in the end 'die

---

10. E.g., Baltimore & O. R. Co. v. Baugh, 1893, 13 S.Ct. 914, 149 U.S. 368, 37 L.Ed. 772.

11. E.g., Kuhn v. Fairmont Coal Co., 1910, 30 S.Ct. 140, 215 U.S. 349, 54 L.Ed. 228.

12. E.g., Rowan v. Runnels, 1847, 5 How. 134, 12 L.Ed. 85.

13. E.g., Burgess v. Seligman, 1883, 2 S.Ct. 10, 107 U.S. 20, 27 L.Ed. 359.

14. 1863, 1 Wall. 175, 17 L.Ed. 520.

15. 1 Wall. at 206–207.

among its worshippers.' " [16]　The notion that decisions of a court are not "laws" was ridiculed by a new generation, which was prepared to accept the idea that judges do not merely find the law but in fact make it.[17]　Experience was said to show that independent determination by the federal courts of questions of general law had not promoted uniformity in the law.[18]　Professor Charles Warren uncovered evidence of an earlier draft of the Rules of Decision Act, which had said that "the Statute law of the several States in force for the time being and their unwritten or common law now in use, whether by adoption from the common law of England, the ancient statutes of the same or otherwise," should be rules of decision in federal court.　From this Professor Warren deduced that the phrase "laws of the several states," which was substituted by Oliver Ellsworth, in place of the quoted language, before the Act was adopted, was simply a shorthand expression of the same concept, and included decisions of state courts.[19]　Other commentators have been less confident that this is the inevitable conclusion from the facts found by Professor Warren.[20]

The hardest blow to Swift v. Tyson came with the 1928 decision in Black & White Taxicab Co. v. Brown & Yellow Taxicab Co.[21]　A Kentucky corporation had contracted with a railroad for the exclusive right to provide taxi service at a particular station.　Subsequently it wished to enjoin another Kentucky corporation from operating taxis at the station in violation of its exclusive right.　For 35 years, however, the law had been settled in the Kentucky state courts that such exclusive contracts were contrary to public policy and thus unenforcible.　The Kentucky corporation was, therefore, dissolved, a new cor-

16.　Baltimore & O. R. Co. v. Baugh, 1893, 13 S.Ct. 914, 928, 149 U.S. 368, 403, 37 L.Ed. 772.

17.　Gray, The Nature and Sources of the Law, 2d ed. 1927, c. x.; Kuhn v. Fairmont Coal Co., 1910, 30 S.Ct. 140, 147–148, 215 U.S. 349, 370–372, 54 L.Ed. 228 (dissenting opinion of Holmes, J.); Southern Pac. Co. v. Jensen, 1917, 37 S.Ct. 524, 531, 244 U.S. 205, 221, 61 L.Ed. 1086 (dissenting opinion of Holmes, J.).　But see Green, The Law as Precedent, Prophecy, and Principle: State Decisions in Federal Courts, 1924, 19 Ill.L.Rev. 217.

Other attacks on Swift from within and without the Court are cited in 19 Wright, Miller & Cooper, Jurisdiction § 4502 n. 22.

18.　2 Warren, The Supreme Court in United States History, Rev. ed. 1935, p. 89; Frankfurter, Distribution of Judicial Power Between Federal and State Courts, 1928, 13 Corn.L.Q. 499, 529 n. 150.　But cf. Yntema & Jaffin, Preliminary Analysis of Concurrent Jurisdiction, 1931, 79 U.Pa.L.Rev. 869, 881 n.

23; Keeffe et al., Weary Erie, 1949, 34 Corn.L.Q. 494, 504, 527–531.

19.　Warren, New Light on the History of the Federal Judiciary Act of 1789, 1923, 37 Harv.L.Rev. 49, 84–88.

20.　See Jackson, note 1 above, at 614; Shulman, The Demise of Swift v. Tyson, 1938, 47 Yale L.J. 1336, 1345; Teton, note 1 above, at 536–551; 2 Crosskey, Politics and the Constitution in the History of the United States, 1953, p. 867; Friendly, In Praise of Erie—And of the New Federal Common Law, 1964, 39 N.Y.U.L.Rev. 383, 389–391; Comment, 1956, 51 Nw.U.L.Rev. 338, 342 n. 26; Note, note 1 above, at 285 n. 8.

The language in the early draft would have required applying statutes "in force for the time being" but the common law "now in use" and would have precluded using state decisions subsequent to 1789.

21.　1928, 48 S.Ct. 404, 276 U.S. 518, 72 L.Ed. 681.

poration with the same name formed in Tennessee and the contract assigned to it, and suit for an injunction brought against the second taxi company in the federal court on the basis of diversity of citizenship. The Supreme Court upheld grant of the injunction, ruling that this was a question of general law on which Kentucky decisions were not binding, and that the common law permitted such an exclusive contract.

The result could easily have been avoided. The reincorporation in Tennessee in order to create diversity verged on fraud, and it was not necessary to hold that diversity jurisdiction could be so readily abused.[22] Even if jurisdiction were thought present, it would have been easy to classify the question of whether exclusive use may be granted for a particular piece of land as a question of "local" law on which the state could have the final say. The Court did not choose to follow either of these courses, and its decision upholding grant of the injunction provoked a famous dissent from Justice Holmes, in which he was joined by Justices Brandeis and Stone. In this dissent Holmes argued that the rule of Swift v. Tyson was "an unconstitutional assumption of powers by the Courts of the United States," insofar as it permitted the federal courts to declare rules of law in areas beyond the delegated powers of the federal government.[23] Justice Holmes said that Swift v. Tyson should be left undisturbed, but that its doctrine should not be allowed to spread into new fields.

The Black & White Taxicab case was greeted with widespread criticism, and during the next ten years the Supreme Court showed some tendency to retreat from the furthest extensions of the Swift v. Tyson rule. It deferred to state law under circumstances where earlier it would have taken a different view, and it said that as a matter of comity state law should be followed where a question was balanced with doubt.[24] Thus the Swift doctrine was narrowed, but the end did not come until 1938.

Cases in equity presented their own complications. The Judiciary Act of 1789 gave the federal courts equitable jurisdiction, though at that time many of the states did not have courts of equity, the Rules of Decision Act was limited by its express terms to "trials at common law," and the federal courts were required to conform their proce-

---

22. See § 31 above. Under a 1958 amendment to the statute diversity jurisdiction would no longer exist on the facts of this case, since even after reincorporating in Tennessee the company had its principal place of business in Kentucky. See 28 U.S.C.A. § 1332(c), discussed § 27 above.

23. 48 S.Ct. at 408–410, 276 U.S. at 532–536. That the doctrine of Swift v. Tyson was unconstitutional had been argued also by Justice Field in his dissent in Baltimore & O. R. Co. v. Baugh,

1893, 13 S.Ct. 914, 923, 149 U.S. 368, 401, 37 L.Ed. 772.

24. The most important case is Mutual Life Ins. Co. v. Johnson, 1934, 55 S.Ct. 154, 293 U.S. 335, 79 L.Ed. 398. See also Burns Mortg. Co. v. Fried, 1934, 54 S.Ct. 813, 292 U.S. 487, 78 L.Ed. 1380; Trainor v. Aetna Cas. & Sur. Co., 1933, 54 S.Ct. 1, 290 U.S. 47, 78 L.Ed. 162; Note, Some Recent Implications of Swift v. Tyson, 1935, 48 Harv.L.Rev. 979.

dure to that of the state in which they sat in actions at law, but not in proceedings in equity. There was good reason to believe that a system of federal equity jurisprudence independent of the states was intended,[25] and indeed the early decisions seemed to imply as much.[26] Later decisions developed a more subtle doctrine. State statutes defining substantive rights were to be followed by the federal court. The Rules of Decision Act was held applicable to such statutes, though it is limited to "trials at common law," on the theory that the Act was merely declaratory of the rule that would have existed without it.[27] A different result was reached where state statutes affected what came to be known as "equitable remedial rights." The federal court was free to refuse a remedy newly created by state statute,[28] and in equity, unlike law, could give a remedy that state law denied.[29]

§ 55. The Erie Doctrine [1]

In 1938 the Supreme Court of the United States decided what a member of the Court later called "one of the most important cases at

25. See 2 Crosskey, Politics and the Constitution in the History of the United States, 1953, pp. 877–902; Morse, The Substantive Equity Historically Applied by the United States Courts, 1949, 54 Dick.L.Rev. 10; Van Moschzisker, Equity Jurisdiction in the Federal Courts, 1927, 75 U.Pa.L.Rev. 287. For a contrary view, see Hill, The Erie Doctrine in Bankruptcy, 1953, 66 Harv. L.Rev. 1013, 1024–1035.

26. Robinson v. Campbell, 1818, 3 Wheat. 212, 4 L.Ed. 372; U. S. v. Howland, 1819, 4 Wheat. 108, 115, 4 L.Ed. 526; Livingston v. Story, 1835, 9 Pet. 632, 9 L.Ed. 255; Neves v. Scott, 1851, 13 How. 268, 14 L.Ed. 140.

27. Mason v. U. S., 1923, 43 S.Ct. 200, 260 U.S. 545, 67 L.Ed. 396.

28. The leading case is Pusey & Jones Co. v. Hanssen, 1923, 43 S.Ct. 454, 261 U.S. 491, 67 L.Ed. 763. See also Whitehead v. Shattuck, 1891, 11 S.Ct. 276, 138 U.S. 146, 34 L.Ed. 873; Scott v. Neely, 1891, 11 S.Ct. 712, 140 U.S. 106, 35 L.Ed. 358.

See generally 19 Wright, Miller & Cooper, Jurisdiction § 4513.

29. This appears very clearly in Guffey v. Smith, 1915, 35 S.Ct. 526, 237 U.S. 101, 59 L.Ed. 856. Under Illinois law holders under a particular kind of lease could not sue in ejectment against a trespasser operating under a subsequent lease, nor could they sue for an injunction, even though the remedy at law was inadequate. The Supreme Court held that a federal court must follow the state law, and refuse to al-

low ejectment, but that equitable relief, including an injunction, was available.

[§ 55]

1. See generally 19 Wright, Miller & Cooper Jurisdiction §§ 4503–4504.

The literature dealing with the subject of the present section, and the remaining sections of this chapter, is voluminous, and much of it is outdated by changes in the doctrine. Thus the writings of the commentators cited in this and subsequent sections of the chapter are those that the present author has found most helpful and of contemporary relevance.

There was a spirited exchange in the Harvard Law Review. See Ely, The Irrepressible Myth of Erie, 1974, 87 Harv.L.Rev. 693, and the commentaries thereon: Chayes, The Bead Game, 1974, 87 Harv.L.Rev. 741; Ely, The Necklace, 1974, 87 Harv.L.Rev. 753; Mishkin, The Thread, 1974, 87 Harv.L. Rev. 1682.

For another provocative debate, see: Redish & Phillips, Erie and the Rules of Decision Act: In Search of the Appropriate Dilemma, 1977, 91 Harv.L. Rev. 356; Westen & Lehman, Is There Life for Erie After the Death of Diversity?, 1980, 78 Mich.L.Rev. 311; Redish, Continuing the Erie Debate: A Response to Westen and Lehman, 1980, 78 Mich.L.Rev. 959; Westen, After "Life for Erie"—A Reply, 1980, 78 Mich.L.Rev. 971.

law in American legal history." [2] It hardly appeared to be such a case when it began. Harry Tompkins was walking along the right of way of the Erie Railroad at Hughestown, Pa. A train came by and he was hit by something that looked like a door projecting from one of the moving cars. Under at least one view of Pennsylvania law, the courts of that state would have regarded Tompkins as a trespasser, and held that the railroad would not be liable except for wanton or willful misconduct. The "general" law, recognized by the federal courts under Swift v. Tyson, gave Tompkins the status of a licensee, and imposed liability for ordinary negligence. Since the railroad was a New York corporation, and Tompkins was a citizen of Pennsylvania, he brought suit in federal court in New York City, and obtained a judgment for $30,000, which was affirmed by the Second Circuit. The railroad successfully petitioned for certiorari. In its brief in the Supreme Court the railroad said "we do not question the finality of the holding of this Court in Swift v. Tyson * * *" and the argument, both in the brief and orally, was that the Pennsylvania doctrine as to the duty owed those in Tompkins' position declared a Pennsylvania rule sufficiently "local" in nature to be controlling.

The decision in the case of Erie Railroad Company v. Tompkins [3] was handed down on April 25, 1938. "The question for decision," Justice Brandeis began his opinion for the Court, "is whether the oft-challenged doctrine of Swift v. Tyson shall now be disapproved." [4] Having posed this somewhat surprising question, Justice Brandeis was quick to answer it in the affirmative. In the first section of the opinion he referred to the "more recent research of a competent scholar," Professor Charles Warren, whose examination of the original document "established" that the construction given to the Rules of Decision Act in Swift v. Tyson and thereafter was "erroneous." [5] Section Two of the opinion argued that Swift v. Tyson had not produced the hoped-for uniformity and had introduced grave discrimination by noncitizens against citizens. These teachings of experience were not enough to justify overruling the Swift case. "If only a question of statutory construction were involved we should not be prepared to abandon a doctrine so widely applied throughout nearly a century. But the unconstitutionality of the course pursued has now

---

2. Black, Address, 1942, 13 Mo.B.J. 173, 174.

3. 1938, 58 S.Ct. 817, 304 U.S. 64, 82 L.Ed. 1188.

4. 58 S.Ct. at 818, 304 U.S. at 69.

Though the parties had not raised such a question, at oral argument Justice Brandeis had asked counsel's views of Swift v. Tyson. Hicks, Materials and Methods of Legal Research, 3d ed. 1942, p. 376. See Friendly, In Praise of Erie—And of the New Federal Common Law, 1964, 39 N.Y.U.L.Rev. 383, 399 n. 71.

For a highly entertaining and informative account of the lawsuit itself, including the underlying facts, the legal arguments and litigation strategies, and profiles of some of the lawyers and judges involved, see Younger, What Happened in Erie, 1978, 56 Texas L.Rev. 1011.

5. 58 S.Ct. at 819, 304 U.S. at 73. For discussion of what Professor Warren found, and whether it actually "established" anything, see § 54 above at notes 19 and 20.

been made clear, and compels us to do so." [6] This led to the third section of the opinion where the new rule was summarily stated: "Except in matters governed by the Federal Constitution or by acts of Congress, the law to be applied in any case is the law of the state. And whether the law of the state shall be declared by its Legislature. in a statute or by its highest court in a decision is not a matter of federal concern. There is no federal general common law. Congress has no power to declare substantive rules of common law applicable in a state whether they be local in their nature or 'general,' be they commercial law or a part of the law of torts. And no clause in the Constitution purports to confer such a power upon the federal courts." [7] These conclusions were supported by extensive quotations from earlier dissents by Justices Field and Holmes. Finally Justice Brandeis said: "In disapproving [the doctrine of Swift v. Tyson] we do not hold unconstitutional section 34 of the Federal Judiciary Act of 1789 or any other act of Congress. We merely declare that in applying the doctrine this Court and the lower courts have invaded rights which in our opinion are reserved by the Constitution to the several states." [8] The case was remanded to the Second Circuit to determine whether Pennsylvania law in fact was as the railroad contended, and on remand Tompkins ended up without his $30,000 judgment.[9]

Since Justice Cardozo was ill and took no part, only eight justices participated in the Erie decision. Four of the other justices joined in the opinion by Justice Brandeis. Justice Reed concurred in part.[10] He agreed with the disapproval of Swift v. Tyson, but said it was sufficient to hold that "the laws" in the Rules of Decision Act referred to state decisions as well as to state statutes. He thought it unnecessary to speak about the constitutionality of the Swift v. Tyson doctrine, and suggested that Article III of the Constitution and the Necessary and Proper Clause of Article I might indeed empower Congress to declare what rules of substantive law should govern the federal courts. Justices Butler and McReynolds dissented.[11] They argued against overruling Swift v. Tyson, and pointed out that Justice Field had acquiesced in the doctrine of that case after his one

---

6. 58 S.Ct. at 822, 304 U.S. at 77–78.

The sentence about statutory construction was put in the opinion at the insistence of Justice Stone. Mason, Harland Fiske Stone: Pillar of the Law, 1956, pp. 478–481. For his later view, see § 56 n. 4.

In view of this quite explicit sentence in Erie, it is surprising to have Justice Stevens say that Swift was overruled because it rested "upon a discredited interpretation of the relevant historical documents." Florida Dept. of Health & Rehabilitative Services v. Florida Nursing Home Assn., 1981, 101 S.Ct. 1032, 1035, 450 U.S. 147, 153, 67 L.Ed. 2d 132 (concurring opinion).

7. 58 S.Ct. at 822, 304 U.S. at 78.

8. 58 S.Ct. at 823, 304 U.S. at 79–80.

9. Tompkins v. Erie R. Co., C.C.A.2d 1938, 98 F.2d 49, certiorari denied 59 S.Ct. 108, 305 U.S. 637, 83 L.Ed. 410.

10. 58 S.Ct. at 828, 304 U.S. at 90–92.

11. 58 S.Ct. at 823–828,ʲ 304 U.S. at 80–90. Although their opinion is listed as a dissent in the reports, they would have reversed the decision below on the ground that Tompkins was guilty of contributory negligence as a matter of law.

famous protest, and that Justice Holmes, dissenting in the Black & White Taxicab case, had stated specifically that he would not disturb Swift v. Tyson, and argued only against extending its doctrine into new fields. They protested the Court's discussion of a constitutional question without having heard counsel on that question, and, with what must have been glee, observed that the Court had failed to follow a 1937 statute, one of the few vestiges of the "court-packing plan" to survive Congress, that required notice to the Attorney General and permission for him to participate whenever the constitutionality of an Act of Congress was questioned in the courts.

It is impossible to overstate the importance of the Erie decision. It announces no technical doctrine of procedure or jurisdiction, but goes to the heart of the relations between the federal government and the states, and returns to the states a power that had for nearly a century been exercised by the federal government. Nevertheless the decision attracted no popular attention when it was announced.[12] Lawyers, however, were quick to recognize its significance, and there has hardly been a civil case since Erie was decided that has not felt the effect of that decision.[13] In the process the law has gone far beyond the simple holding of Erie, to the point where one competent scholar refers to "the Erie jurisprudence that has developed a doctrine completely foreign to the decision that is its putative source."[14]

12. Though other decisions of the Supreme Court on April 25, 1938, received attention in the press the following day, no mention was made of the Erie case. On May 2d Justice Stone wrote to Arthur Krock, of the New York Times, prodding him on the matter, Mason, note 6 above, at 477, and Krock then wrote a column entitled "A Momentous Decision of the Supreme Court," Krock, N.Y.Times, May 3, 1938, p. 22, col. 5. Mr. Krock began his discussion by observing that if the Supreme Court had a publicity agent eight days would not have passed before the importance of the Erie decision became known. He followed this with another column, entitled "More about the Epochal Tompkins Decision," the next day. N.Y.Times, May 4, 1938, p. 22, col. 5. See also the Letter to the Editor, by someone who signed himself mysteriously "L.L.B.," defending the constitutional arguments relied on by Justice Brandeis in the Erie decision. N.Y.Times, May 7, 1938, p. 14, col. 6.

One close observer of the Court did not miss the Erie decision, nor its significance. In a letter of April 27, 1938, to President Roosevelt, Professor Frankfurter said: "I certainly didn't expect to live to see the day when the Court would announce, as they did on Mon-

day, that it itself has usurped power for nearly a hundred years. And think of not a single New York paper—at least none that I saw—having a nose for the significance of such a decision. How fluid it all makes the Constitution!" Freedman, Roosevelt and Frankfurter, 1967, p. 456.

13. "My senior colleague Judge Learned Hand has a way of startling counsel in these 'erieantompkinated' days by saying, as they approach that inevitable citation: 'I don't suppose a civil appeal can now be argued to us without counsel sooner or later quoting large portions of Erie Railroad v. Tompkins.'" Clark, State Law in the Federal Courts: The Brooding Omnipresence of Erie v. Tompkins, 1946, 55 Yale L.J. 267, 269.

For statistics on how often Erie had been referred to up to 1978, see Younger, note 4 above, at 1011–1012.

14. Boner, Erie v. Tompkins: A Study in Judicial Precedent: II, 1962, 40 Tex. L.Rev. 619, 625. Mrs. Boner also observes, at 635, that "its status rose to that of a jurisprudence, which has continued to gain stature until it is practically a religion. To its critics, the religion may be wearing a little thin, but

That doctrine is examined in the succeeding five sections, but three subsequent decisions of the Supreme Court in this area are of such landmark importance as to require special mention here.

The Erie doctrine was substantially redefined in 1945 in the case of Guaranty Trust Co. of New York v. York,[15] to the point where one writer observed that "the governing doctrine might be better described if it took its name from York rather than Erie." [16] The Guaranty Trust case was a suit in equity brought in federal court because of diversity. The issue was whether in such a suit a state statute of limitations, which would have barred the suit in state court, operated as a bar also in federal court. The federal court might be thought free to entertain the action, regardless of the state statute of limitations, if equitable actions are in some way free from the compulsion of Erie, or if a statute of limitation is a mere matter of procedure, not controlling in federal court, within the "substance-procedure" dichotomy that Erie seemed to endorse. The Court, with Justice Frankfurter speaking for five members,[17] rejected both of these possible escapes from following the state statute.

Though recognizing that in a sense federal equity is a separate legal system, the Court pointed out that the substantive right to be enforced is created by the state, and the federal courts, whether sitting in law or in equity, must respect state law, both statutory and court-made, as to that right. It was immaterial, the Court thought, that for some purposes statutes of limitation are treated as procedural rather than substantive. " *   *   * [S]ince a federal court adjudicating a state-created right solely because of the diversity of citizenship of the parties is for that purpose, in effect, only another court of the State, it cannot afford recovery if the right to recover is made unavailable by the State nor can it substantially affect the enforcement of the right as given by the State." [18] The Erie case, Justice Frankfurter wrote, "was not an endeavor to formulate scientific legal terminology. It expressed a policy that touches vitally the proper distribution of judicial power between State and federal courts. In essence, the intent of that decision was to insure that, in all cases where a federal court is exercising jurisdiction solely because of the diversity of citizenship of the parties, the outcome of the litigation in the federal court should be substantially the same, so far as legal rules determine the outcome of a litigation, as it would be if tried in a State court. The nub of the policy that underlies Erie R. Co. v. Tompkins is that for the same transaction the accident of a suit by a

heresy is still promptly and mercilessly eradicated."

15. 1945, 65 S.Ct. 1464, 326 U.S. 99, 89 L.Ed. 2079.

16. Kurland, Mr. Justice Frankfurter, The Supreme Court and the Erie Doctrine in Diversity Cases, 1957, 67 Yale L.J. 187–188.

17. Justices Rutledge and Murphy dissented. Justices Roberts and Douglas took no part.

18. 65 S.Ct. at 1469–1470, 326 U.S. at 108–109.

non-resident litigant in a federal court instead of in a State court a block away, should not lead to a substantially different result." [19] It is clear that a state statute that would completely bar recovery in a state court does significantly affect the outcome of the case, and, on the "outcome-determinative" test announced in Guaranty Trust, is binding in federal court.

For 13 years the lower courts struggled loyally with the rule of Guaranty Trust, but there were inevitable difficulties. Applied literally, very little would remain of the Federal Rules of Civil Procedure in diversity cases, for almost every procedural rule may have a substantial effect on the outcome of a case. If the test was not to be carried to its literal limits, however, there was confusion as to how far it was to go. Professor Henry Hart commented that "the principle having no readily apparent stopping place, the reach of the decisions is unclear." [20] In the view of Judge Charles E. Clark, the outcome-determinative test carried the very delicate question of federalism "to an absurd extreme." [21]

In 1958 the Supreme Court seemed to retreat from the rigorous view of Guaranty Trust in the case of Byrd v. Blue Ridge Rural Electric Cooperative, Inc.[22] As a defense to a diversity action for injuries resulting from negligence, defendant asserted that plaintiff was its employee for purposes of the South Carolina Workmen's Compensation Act, and that the act provided plaintiff's exclusive remedy. A state decision had held that this defense is to be passed on by the judge, rather than the jury. The Supreme Court held that, notwithstanding this state rule, in federal actions a jury must pass on this defense.

Justice Brennan, writing for six members of the Court,[23] said first that there was nothing to suggest that the South Carolina rule, leaving this issue for the judge rather than the jury, "was announced as an integral part of the special relationship created by the statute. Thus the requirement appears to be merely a form and mode of enforcing the immunity * * * and not a rule intended to be bound up with the definition of the rights and obligations of the parties." [24]

19. 65 S.Ct. at 1470, 326 U.S. at 109.

20. Hart, The Relations between State and Federal Law, 1954, 54 Col.L.Rev. 489, 512.

See also Judge Friendly's reference to "some overly enthusiastic expressions" in Guaranty Trust. Friendly, note 4 above, at 402.

21. Clark, Federal Procedural Reform and States' Rights; to a More Perfect Union, 1961, 40 Texas L.Rev. 211, 220.

22. 1958, 78 S.Ct. 893, 356 U.S. 525, 2 L.Ed.2d 953. See Smith, Blue Ridge

and Beyond: A Byrd's-Eye View of Federalism in Diversity Litigation, 1962, 36 Tul.L.Rev. 443.

23. Justice Whittaker dissented on this point. Justices Harlan and Frankfurter dissented on another issue and did not discuss the Erie features of the case.

24. 78 S.Ct. at 900, 356 U.S. at 536. See also Magenau v. Aetna Freight Lines, Inc., 1959, 79 S.Ct. 1184, 360 U.S. 273, 3 L.Ed.2d 1224.

The Court then went on to consider whether such a result was consistent with the rule of the Guaranty Trust case. It conceded that "were 'outcome' the only consideration, a strong case might appear for saying that the federal court should follow the state practice. But there are affirmative countervailing considerations at work here." [25] Such an affirmative countervailing consideration might have been found in the express command of the Seventh Amendment that actions at law are to be tried to a jury, but the Court was at pains to refrain from deciding whether the Seventh Amendment extends to a factual issue of statutory immunity when asserted as an affirmative defense in a common-law negligence action.[26] Instead it found "a strong federal policy against allowing state rules to disrupt the judge-jury relationship in the federal courts",[27] and held that this policy outweighed the general policy, enunciated in Guaranty Trust, that the outcome of a case should not be different because it is brought in a federal court rather than in the state court a block away. As a final ground for decision, the Court expressed doubt as to whether the difference between jury and court determination of an issue would in fact lead to a different outcome.

The Court came to grips with the scope of the Erie doctrine again in 1965 in Hanna v. Plumer.[28] The precise holding of that case was that substituted service on an executor by leaving the process at his usual place of abode, as authorized by Rule 4(d)(1), is sufficient even where a state statute requires in hand service on an executor within a specified period. In Hanna Chief Justice Warren, writing for the Court, accepted the teaching of Guaranty Trust that "Erie-type problems were not to be solved by reference to any traditional or common-sense substance-procedure distinction," [29] but he cited the Byrd case for the proposition that the outcome-determinative test "was never intended to serve as a talisman." [30] He read Guaranty Trust as holding only that the choice between federal and state law cannot be made "by application of any automatic, 'litmus paper' criterion, but rather by reference to the policies underlying the Erie rule." [31] These policies he found to be two: "discouragement of forum-shopping and avoidance of inequitable administration of the laws." [32] The Chief Justice went on to say that Erie is not the proper test when the question is governed by one of the Rules of Civil Procedure. If the

25. 78 S.Ct. at 900, 356 U.S. at 537.

26. 78 S.Ct. at 901 n. 10, 356 U.S. at 537 n. 10.

27. 78 S.Ct. at 901, 356 U.S. at 538.

28. 1965, 85 S.Ct. 1136, 380 U.S. 460, 14 L.Ed.2d 8. See Holtzoff, A Landmark in Federal Procedural Reform, 1965, 10 Vill.L.Rev. 701; McCoid, Hanna v. Plumer: The Erie Doctrine Changes Shape, 1965, 51 Va.L.Rev. 884; Stason, Choice of Law Within the Federal System: Erie versus Hanna, 1967, 52 Corn.L.Q. 377; Zabin, The Federal Rules in Diversity Cases: Erie in Retreat, 1967, 53 A.B.A.J. 266; Siegel, The Federal Rules in Diversity Cases: Erie Implemented, Not Retarded, 1968, 54 A.B.A.J. 172.

29. 85 S.Ct. at 1141, 380 U.S. at 465–466.

30. 85 S.Ct. at 1141, 380 U.S. at 466–467.

31. 85 S.Ct. at 1141, 380 U.S. at 467.

32. 85 S.Ct. at 1142, 380 U.S. at 468.

rule is valid when measured against the standards contained in the Enabling Act and the Constitution,[33] it is to be applied regardless of contrary state law.[34]

Lawyers commonly refer to "the Erie doctrine," and this practice will be followed in the present work. It is clear, however, that the doctrine today is not what was announced in 1938. All four of the cases here discussed accept the decisions of state courts as forming a part of the "laws" of the state. All four recognize that rights created by state law should be adjudicated in accordance with state law. They differ in their attempts to delineate the issues on which state law is to control and the issues on which the federal courts are free to decide legal points for themselves. This particular problem is examined further in section 59 below.

§ 56. The Erie Doctrine—The Constitutional Basis [1]

"If only a question of statutory construction were involved," Justice Brandeis wrote in Erie, "we should not be prepared to abandon a doctrine so widely applied throughout nearly a century. But the unconstitutionality of the course pursued has now been made clear, and compels us to do so."[2] Perhaps no aspect of the Erie decision so

33. In determining the validity of a rule, a court "need not wholly blind itself to the degree to which the Rule makes the character and result of the federal litigation stray from the course it would follow in state courts * * *." 85 S.Ct. at 1145, 380 U.S. at 473.

34. 85 S.Ct. at 1143–1145, 380 U.S. at 469–474.

Seven members of the Court joined in the opinion of the Chief Justice. Justice Black concurred in result. Justice Harlan wrote a separate concurring opinion. He recognized as "unquestionably true that up to now Erie and the cases following it have not succeeded in articulating a workable doctrine governing choice of law in diversity actions." 85 S.Ct. at 1145, 380 U.S. at 474. He thought, however, that the opinion of the Court erred by oversimplification and by making the rules of procedure inviolate. He thought the inquiry should be whether "the choice of rule would substantially affect those primary decisions respecting human conduct which our constitutional system leaves to state regulation." 85 S.Ct. at 1146, 380 U.S. at 476. See the elaboration of Justice Harlan's test in Note, The Law Applied in Diversity Cases: The Rules of Decision Act and the Erie Doctrine, 1976, 85 Yale L.J. 678, 692–700.

The court of appeals that was reversed in Hanna later concluded that the Supreme Court had misconstrued the state statute it held not controlling in Hanna. Because of this the court of appeals felt justified in giving Hanna a much narrower reading than its words seem to justify and that most people have given it. Marshall v. Mulrenin, C.A.1st, 1974, 508 F.2d 39, noted 1976, 50 N.Y.U.L.Rev. 952.

[§ 56]

1. 19 Wright, Miller & Cooper, Jurisdiction § 4505; Westen & Lehman, Is There Life for Erie after the Death of Diversity?, 1980, 78 Mich.L.Rev. 311, 338–344; Ely, The Irrepressible Myth of Erie, 1974, 87 Harv.L.Rev. 693, 700–706; Friendly, In Praise of Erie—And of the New Federal Common Law, 1964, 39 N.Y.U.L.Rev. 383, 394–398; Quigley, Congressional Repair of the Erie Derailment, 1962, 60 Mich.L.Rev. 1031; Hill, The Erie Doctrine and the Constitution, 1958, 53 Nw.U.L.Rev. 427, 541; Comment, the Constitutional Power of Congress to Control Procedure in the Federal Courts, 1961, 56 Nw.U.L.Rev. 560.

2. Erie R. Co. v. Tompkins, 1938, 58 S.Ct. 817, 822, 304 U.S. 64, 77–78, 82 L.Ed. 1188.

perplexed the commentators for many years as this statement. Justice Brandeis is noted for his insistence that the Court refrain from deciding constitutional issues if any other means of disposing of the case is available.[3] Yet in Erie he seemed to go out of his way to reach the constitutional issue, since it would have been possible—if perhaps not desirable—to resolve the case as a matter of statutory construction, on the basis of what the Court believed Professor Warren's discoveries to have "established." Justice Brandeis put the decision on constitutional grounds though Justice Reed, concurring specially, was unwilling to accept such an argument, and Justice Stone, reluctant to accept all that Brandeis said about the Constitution, three years later referred to it as "unfortunate dicta." [4]

There are other remarkable features of the constitutional discussion in Erie. Though he observed that Congress has no power to declare substantive rules of common law applicable in a state, Justice Brandeis apparently recognized that Congress had not attempted to do so for he stated expressly "we do not hold unconstitutional section 34 of the Federal Judiciary Act of 1789 or any other act of Congress." [5] Instead it was the Court's own conduct that was regarded as unconstitutional. Again the Court does not say which provision of the Constitution was violated by the doctrine of Swift v. Tyson. The courts, we are told, "have invaded rights which in our opinion are reserved by the Constitution to the several states." [6] Presumably the reference is to the Tenth Amendment, but it is unusual to have a constitutional decision that avoids making specific reference to the constitutional provision involved. No authority is cited for the constitutional arguments in the decision except earlier dissents by Justices Field and Holmes, which are themselves quite cryptic as to why Swift v. Tyson is contrary to the Constitution. Finally Justice Brandeis fails to answer the argument of Justice Reed in his concurring opinion that the Judiciary Article of the Constitution and the Necessary and Proper Clause of Article I may indeed give Congress power to enact the substantive rules that are to be applied by the courts.

For 18 years after Erie the Court refrained from referring again to the Constitution in an Erie context. This silence was perhaps most

---

3. See his famous concurring opinion in Ashwander v. Tennessee Valley Authority, 1936, 56 S.Ct. 466, 482–484, 297 U.S. 288, 346–348, 80 L.Ed. 688.

4. Mason, Harlan Fiske Stone: Pillar of the Law, 1956, pp. 476–481. The reference to "unfortunate dicta" was in a letter to Justice Roberts in 1941. Id. at 480n.

5. 58 S.Ct. at 823, 304 U.S. at 79–80.

6. 58 S.Ct. at 823, 304 U.S. at 80.

Earlier in the Erie opinion there is a casual statement that Swift had "rendered impossible equal protection of the law." 58 S.Ct. at 821, 304 U.S. at 75.

It was not until many years later, however, that it was first held that the notion of equal protection binds the federal government as well as the states. Bolling v. Sharpe, 1954, 74 S.Ct. 693, 347 U.S. 497, 98 L.Ed. 884. "Needless to say, in speaking of 'equal protection,' Justice Brandeis was not referring to the fourteenth amendment (which, then, applied only to the states) or to any other constitutional limitation." Westen, After "Life for Erie"—A Reply, 1980, 78 Mich.L.Rev. 971, 980 n. 35.

significant in the Guaranty Trust case. In that major redefinition of the Erie doctrine, Justice Frankfurter referred at three separate places to the "policy" of federal jurisdiction embodied in the Erie case.[7] It is odd that what had seemed to Justice Brandeis a constitutional imperative was reduced to a mere "policy," even if an important one, in the eyes of Justice Frankfurter and the Court for which he spoke.

The next reference to the Constitution after Erie itself was in 1956 in Bernhardt v. Polygraphic Co. of America, Inc.[8] Defendant in a diversity breach of contract action moved for a stay pending arbitration, since the contract provided that all disputes under it were to be referred to arbitration. Vermont law arguably did not consider arbitration agreements enforcible, but § 3 of the United States Arbitration Act,[9] if applicable, did. Respondent argued that § 3 of the Act was applicable. The Court, through Justice Douglas, said: "If respondent's contention is correct, a constitutional question might be presented. Erie R. Co. v. Tompkins indicated that Congress does not have the constitutional authority to make the law that is applicable to controversies in diversity of citizenship cases. * * * We therefore read § 3 narrowly to avoid that issue." [10] Justice Frankfurter, concurring, said that "in view of the ground that was taken in [the Erie case] for its decision, it would raise a serious question of constitutional law whether Congress could subject to arbitration litigation in the federal courts which is there solely because it is 'between Citizens of different States' ".[11] These vague statements that it "might" or "would raise" a constitutional issue if Congress were to set out the applicable law in diversity cases in themselves cast doubt on how firmly Erie is based on the Constitution.

The only other reference to the Constitution since Erie was in Hanna v. Plumer.[12] The Court there said that "we are reminded by the Erie opinion that neither Congress nor the federal courts can, under the guise of formulating rules of decisions for federal courts, fashion rules which are not supported by a grant of federal authority contained in Article I or some other section of the Constitution; in such areas state law must govern because there can be no other law." [13] This says rather less than it appears to, because it leaves open hard questions about the extent to which the Necessary and Proper Clause of Article I or even Article III itself do support grants

7. Guaranty Trust Co. of New York v. York, 1945, 65 S.Ct. 1464, 1466, 1470, 326 U.S. 99, 101, 109, 89 L.Ed. 2079.

8. 1956, 76 S.Ct. 273, 350 U.S. 198, 100 L.Ed. 199, noted 1957, 45 Calif.L.Rev. 87, 70 Harv.L.Rev. 137.

9. 9 U.S.C.A. § 3.

10. 76 S.Ct. at 275–276, 350 U.S. at 202. It was later held that there is no Erie problem in applying the Arbitration Act to a diversity case involving matters over which Congress plainly has power to legislate, such as interstate commerce and admiralty. Prima Paint Corp. v. Flood & Conklin Mfg. Co., 1967, 87 S.Ct. 1801, 1806–1807, 388 U.S. 395, 404–405, 18 L.Ed.2d 1270.

11. 76 S.Ct. at 279, 350 U.S. at 208.

12. 1965, 85 S.Ct. 1136, 380 U.S. 460, 14 L.Ed.2d 8.

13. 85 S.Ct. at 1144, 380 U.S. at 471–472.

of federal authority. Indeed in that same passage the Court in Hanna relied on the "necessary and proper" clause as the source of the power to make rules of procedure and also to regulate matters that are rationally capable of being classified either as substance or procedure.

The earlier commentators had a great deal to say about the constitutional discussion in Erie, most of it critical. The view that the discussion was "a bit of judicial hyperbole which, having served its purpose, should not be permitted to mislead even the most literal-minded reader," [14] had been put forward by many distinguished students of federal jurisdiction,[15] but this view was never unanimous, and as time went past the constitutional framework of the Erie decision attracted more defenders.[16]

On an issue that left the scholarly writers so divided, and about which the Supreme Court has been so cryptic, it would be foolhardy to venture a confident answer. A few observations may help focus the nature of the problem. When Justice Brandeis said that Congress has no power to declare substantive rules of common law applicable in a state, there is a sense in which he is surely right. If Congress were to pass a general statute that persons walking along longitudinal pathways are to be regarded as licensees and entitled to recover for ordinary negligence, such a statute could not be binding in state court actions because Congress has no power to enact a gen-

---

14. The phrase was Professor Brainerd Currie's but he later disowned it. Compare Currie, Change of Venue and the Conflict of Laws, 1955, 22 U.Chi.L. Rev. 405, 468–469, with Currie, Change of Venue and the Conflict of Laws: A Retraction, 1960, 27 U.Chi.L.Rev. 341, 351.

15. Ahrens, Erie v. Tompkins—The Not So Common Law, 1961, 1 Washburn L.J. 343; Broh-Kahn, Amendment by Decision—More on the Erie Case, 1941, 30 Ky.L.J. 3; Clark, State Law in the Federal Courts: The Brooding Omnipresence of Erie v. Tompkins, 1946, 55 Yale L.J. 267, 273, 278; Cowan, Constitutional Aspects of the Abolition of Federal "Common Law," 1938, 1 La.L. Rev. 161; Crosskey, Politics and the Constitution in the History of the United States, 1953, pp. 563–574, 711–937; Dodd, The Decreasing Importance of State Lines, 1941, 27 A.B.A.J. 78, 83; Herriott, Has Congress the Power to Modify the Effect of Erie Railroad Co. v. Tompkins?, 1941, 26 Marq.L.Rev. 1; Keeffe et al., Weary Erie, 1949, 34 Corn.L.Q. 494, 496–497; Keeffe, In Praise of Joseph Story, Swift v. Tyson and "The" True National Common Law, 1969, 18 Amer.U.L.Rev. 316;

Kurland, Mr. Justice Frankfurter, The Supreme Court and the Erie Doctrine in Diversity Cases, 1957, 67 Yale L.J. 187, 188–204; McCormick & Hewins, The Collapse of "General" Law in the Federal Courts, 1938, 33 Ill.L.Rev. 126, 135; cf. Comment, note 1 above.

16. Bowman, The Unconstitutionality of the Rule of Swift v. Tyson, 1938, 18 B. U.L.Rev. 659; Ely, note 1 above, at 700–706; Friendly, note 1 above, at 384–398; Hart, The Relations Between State and Federal Law, 1954, 54 Col.L. Rev. 489, 509–510; Hill, note 1 above, at 541; Leathers, Erie and Its Progeny as Choice of Law Cases, 1974, 11 Hous. L.Rev. 791, 795–796; Mishkin, The Thread, 1974, 87 Harv.L.Rev. 1682; Smith, Blue Ridge and Beyond: A Byrd's-Eye View of Federalism in Diversity Litigation, 1962, 36 Tul.L.Rev. 443, 465–470; Wechsler, Federal Jurisdiction and the Revision of the Judicial Code, 1948, 13 L. & Contemp.Probs. 216, 239 n. 121; Wechsler & Lehman, note 1 above, at 338–344, 353–356; Whicher, The Erie Doctrine and the Seventh Amendment: A Suggested Resolution of Their Conflict, 1959, 37 Texas L.Rev. 549.

eral code of tort law obligatory upon the states.[17] To say this, however, is to contribute very little to a resolution of the Erie problem, since whatever Erie involved, it surely did not involve any such statute. There are at least three possible arguments for applying "general" law in the Erie situation—none of them at all like the hypothetical statute just described—that Justice Brandeis may have had in mind. It can be argued that Article III, § 2, of the Constitution gives the federal courts judicial power in cases between citizens of different states, and that judicial power itself includes the power to determine the rules of law that are to apply. Alternatively, resort may be had to that provision of Article I, § 8, that empowers Congress to make "all laws which shall be necessary and proper" for carrying into execution any power vested by the Constitution in any department of the government of the United States. Chief Justice Marshall held long ago that this does not confine Congress to those things that are absolutely necessary, but that it permits the use of any means calculated to produce the end, and is not confined to those single means without which the end would be entirely unattainable.[18] It can be argued from this that Congress does have power to adopt rules of tort law to be followed by the federal courts in their exercise of the judicial power.[19] Or it can be argued that Congress may tell the federal courts which subjects they may decide for themselves and which must be decided according to state law.

Since Justice Brandeis denounced as unconstitutional the course of conduct of the federal courts, he is surely rejecting the first of these three arguments, and perhaps all three. There has been much learned dispute as to whether his constitutional discussion is holding or dicta, but such discussion seems to miss any mark worth shooting at. The fact is that the Court made a considered statement that it would not overrule Swift v. Tyson if only a question of statutory construction were involved, and that it was overruling that decision only because it was inconsistent with the Constitution of the United States. If the Court believes it is deliberately deciding a constitutional question, it is wise to suppose that the constitutional question has been decided, unless and until some later Court suggests a different answer.[20]

Even if Erie is to be considered, as apparently it must, as deciding that neither Congress nor the Court can create tort rules to be ap-

17. In the precise situation involved in Erie, that of a railroad involved in interstate commerce, the Commerce Clause is broad enough to authorize legislation as to the tort duties of such carriers. Cf. Friendly, The Gap in Lawmaking—Judges Who Can't and Legislators Who Won't, 1963, 63 Col.L. Rev. 787, 789.

18. McCulloch v. Maryland, 1819, 4 Wheat. 316, 4 L.Ed. 579. See Shepard v. Adams, 1898, 18 S.Ct. 214, 216, 168 U.S. 618, 625, 42 L.Ed. 602.

19. Cf. Panama R. Co. v. Johnson, 1924, 44 S.Ct. 391, 264 U.S. 375, 68 L.Ed. 748; Note, From Judicial Grant to Legislative Power: The Admiralty Clause in the Nineteenth Century, 1954, 67 Harv.L.Rev. 1214.

20. See Friendly, note 1 above, at 386 n. 15.

plied in federal court in diversity cases, the constitutional questions raised by Erie are not yet resolved. Surely "judicial power" means something and the Necessary and Proper Clause means something. Suppose that in some state accustomed to moving at a more leisurely pace than are most of its sister states, the local law were to provide that defendant have six months in which to answer the complaint, and that either party might have unlimited continuances as a matter of right. Is the federal judiciary constitutionally compelled to countenance similar delays in diversity cases in that state, or is there rather constitutional power—if not indeed a constitutional duty—for the federal system to enforce its own procedures so that justice will not be delayed to the point where it is denied? There is nothing in the Erie decision that would seem to deny such constitutional power.[21]

Thus perhaps a proper conclusion is that under the Constitution only Pennsylvania can say what tort duties are to be imposed on Pennsylvania landowners, that under the Constitution only the federal government can say how the federal courts are to administer their proceedings, and that under the Constitution it is a difficult and doubtful question whether New York or the federal government should have the right to determine how promptly a suit must be brought in federal court to vindicate a right created by the state. This is not the only conceivable conclusion. The argument that the judicial article and the Necessary and Proper Clause give the federal government power to provide for "juster justice" in federal courts is a compelling one, but the Erie decision, deliberately rested on a constitutional basis, stands in the way. The conclusion here suggested is not a tidy one, but federalism is not a tidy concept.

§ 57. The Erie Doctrine—Which State's Law? [1]

An accident occurs in Pennsylvania. Suit is brought in federal court in New York. Under the Erie doctrine, the federal court is required to apply state law, but is it to apply Pennsylvania law or New York law? To Justice Brandeis the question was simple. The federal court in New York was not "free to disregard the alleged rule of

---

21. See Wayman v. Southard, 1825, 10 Wheat. 1, 6 L.Ed. 253. In the Hanna case the Court said: "For example, a plaintiff cannot then insist on the right to file subsequent pleadings in accord with the time limits applicable in state courts, even though enforcement of the federal timetable will, if he continues to insist that he must meet only the state time limit, result in determination of the controversy against him." 85 S.Ct. at 1142, 380 U.S. at 468–469.

[§ 57]

1. 19 Wright, Miller & Cooper, Jurisdiction § 4506; Cavers, Special Memorandum on Change in Choice-of-Law Thinking and Its Bearing on the Klaxon Problem, in A.L.I., Study of the Division of Jurisdiction between State and Federal Courts, Tent.Dr.No. 1, 1963, pp. 154–214; Baxter, Choice of Law and the Federal System, 1963, 16 Stan.L.Rev. 1; Weintraub, The Erie Doctrine and State Conflict of Laws Rules, 1964, 39 Ind.L.J. 228; Randall, The Erie Doctrine and State Conflict of Laws, 1965, 17 S.C.L.Rev. 494; Horowitz, Toward a Federal Common Law of Choice of Law, 1967, 14 U.C. L.A.L.Rev. 1191.

the Pennsylvania common law." [2]   The Court never explained why Pennsylvania law, rather than New York law, was to govern.   The opinion could fairly be interpreted as meaning either that the Supreme Court had made its own decision that Pennsylvania law was properly applicable, relying on a federal choice-of-law doctrine,[3] or that it had determined sub silentio that a New York state court in similar circumstances would apply Pennsylvania law. Judge Friendly has said that "a pretty good reason for having 'skimmed over the conflicts problem as if none existed' was that none did exist; counsel were agreed that if state law controlled, Pennsylvania law would govern the rights of a Pennsylvanian injured in Pennsylvania, and no one to this day has ever suggested anything else." [4]   Perhaps so, but Professor Hill has shown that while New York would feel bound to apply Pennsylvania law, it would not necessarily feel bound to follow the decisions of the Pennsylvania courts.[5]

In a case a week later, the Court expressly left open a similar question.   In noting that general conflicts doctrine looks for interpretation of an insurance contract to the law of the place where the policy is delivered, the Court, in a case arising from federal court in Pennsylvania, said: "We do not now determine which principle must be enforced if the Pennsylvania courts follow a different conflict of laws rule." [6]

The courts of appeals, left without guidance by the Supreme Court, divided on whether they were bound by the conflicts rule in the state where the district court was sitting, or whether they were free to make their own choice of law.   The best known opinion was that of Judge Magruder of the First Circuit in Sampson v. Channell.[7] In a comprehensive discussion, he concluded that the reasoning of Justice Holmes, adopted by Justice Brandeis in the Erie case, "seems

---

2.   Erie R. Co. v. Tompkins, 1938, 58 S.Ct. 817, 819, 304 U.S. 64, 71, 82 L.Ed. 1188. There are two other references in the opinion to Pennsylvania law, and no references to New York law.

See also Mutual Benefit, Health & Acc. Assn. v. Bowman, 1938, 58 S.Ct. 1056, 304 U.S. 549, 82 L.Ed. 1521, directing application of New Mexico law in a suit in federal court in Nebraska based on a New Mexico contract.

3.   "In Erie itself, Justice Brandeis seemed to assume that a federal court should think for itself on conflicts problems."   Hart, The Relations between State and Federal Law, 1954, 54 Col.L.Rev. 489, 514 n. 84.

4.   Friendly, In Praise of Erie—And of the New Federal Common Law, 1964, 39 N.Y.U.L.Rev. 383, 401.

5.   "It is important to remember that the jurisprudence of Swift v. Tyson had its votaries in the state courts as well as in the federal courts. If the state law concededly applicable to a controversy was the 'general law,' then not only the federal courts but also some of the state courts, among them the courts of New York, took it upon themselves to discover the applicable rules independently and thereby to avoid any 'errors' which might have been committed by the courts of the state whose 'law' was deemed to govern."   Hill, The Erie Doctrine and the Constitution: II, 1958, 53 Nw.U.L.Rev. 541, 598.

6.   Ruhlin v. New York Life Ins. Co., 1938, 58 S.Ct. 860, 862 n. 2, 304 U.S. 202, 208 n. 2, 82 L.Ed. 1290.

7.   Sampson v. Channell, C.C.A.1st, 1940, 110 F.2d 754, certiorari denied 60 S.Ct. 1099, 310 U.S. 650, 84 L.Ed. 1415.

to be applicable to that portion of the Massachusetts common law relating to conflict of laws quite as much as to the common law of contracts or torts. * * * If the federal court in Massachusetts or points of conflict of laws may disregard the law of Massachusetts as formulated by the Supreme Judicial Court and take its own view as a matter of 'general law,' then the ghost of Swift v. Tyson * * * still walks abroad, somewhat shrunken in size, yet capable of much mischief." [8]

It is worth noting that Judge Magruder's conclusion on this point is not an inevitable one. It is not compelled by the Erie decision, nor by the Rules of Decision Act, nor by the Constitution. In the Erie case, as has been seen, the Court directed recourse to Pennsylvania law without any attempt to demonstrate that New York choice-of-law doctrines required such a result. The Rules of Decision Act, from 1789 to the present, has referred to "the laws of the several states * * * in cases where they apply." [9] This leaves the question open of which state's law applies in a particular case. Finally, even if the Erie decision is assumed to be constitutionally compelled,[10] the Constitution does not compel a federal court to follow state conflicts doctrines. The "full faith and credit" clause of Article IV, § 1 is an affirmative grant of power to Congress, and inferentially also to the courts, to create a uniform body of conflicts principles, binding not only on the federal courts but even on the states.[11] Either from this provision, or from the implications of the grant of "judicial power" in Article III, it is possible to find a constitutional basis for independent determination by federal courts of conflicts questions.[12]

A 1941 decision of the Court seemed to point, if without considered discussion, in this direction. The issue was whether Civil Rule 35, authorizing the court to order a physical examination of a party to a lawsuit, was invalid as violating "substantive rights." The suit was brought in federal court in Illinois. That state did not then provide for physical examinations. The accident had occurred in Indiana, which did authorize such examinations. The Court held Rule 35 valid, but in the course of the decision made the interesting observation that "if the right to be exempt from such an order is one of substantive law, the Rules of Decision Act required the District Court, though sitting in Illinois, to apply the law of Indiana, the state where

8. 110 F.2d at 761.

9. 28 U.S.C.A. § 1652.

10. See § 56 above.

11. See Baxter, note 1 above, at 22–42; Cheatham, Federal Control of Conflict of Laws, 1953, 6 Vand.L.Rev. 581; Hughes v. Fetter, 1951, 71 S.Ct. 980, 341 U.S. 609, 95 L.Ed. 1212; Sutton v. Leib, 1952, 72 S.Ct. 398, 342 U.S. 402, 96 L.Ed. 448; First Nat. Bank of Chicago v. United Air Lines, 1952, 72 S.Ct. 421, 342 U.S. 396, 96 L.Ed. 441.

See also Jackson, Full Faith and Credit— The Lawyer's Clause of the Constitution, 1945, 45 Col.L.Rev. 1; Cook, The Powers of Congress Under the Full Faith and Credit Clause, 1919, 28 Yale L.J. 421.

12. See Friendly, note 4 above, at 402; Manderino, Erie v. Tompkins: A Geography Lesson, 1967, 5 Duquesne L.Rev. 465.

the cause of action arose, and to order the examination." [13] This is interesting because it is beyond belief that an Illinois court would hold that it could order such an examination if an accident had occurred in Indiana when it was the Illinois rule that such examinations could not be compelled in suits arising out of Illinois accidents. Thus the Court seemed to be saying that if the matter were not governed by a valid federal rule, the federal court should apply the practice of the place of the wrong rather than the practice, and the conflicts doctrine, of the forum state.

Before that term was over, the Court had laid any such notions to rest, and in two cases, decided the same day, held clearly that a federal court, in a case governed by the Erie doctrine, is to apply whatever law would be applied by the courts of the state in which the district court is sitting. In Klaxon Co. v. Stentor Electric Manufacturing Co., Inc.,[14] suit had been brought in Delaware federal court, because the defendant corporation was incorporated there, on a New York contract. The Third Circuit held that a New York statute providing for interest in contract actions was to be applied. In so holding, it made no examination of Delaware law, but followed what it deemed to be the better view on such an issue. The Supreme Court reversed, in an uninformative opinion. It disposed of this difficult question in a single paragraph, in which it gave, as its sole reason for holding that Delaware's choice-of-law rules must be applied, that any other ruling would do violence to the principle of uniformity within a state upon which the Tompkins decision is based.[15]

The other case decided the same day, Griffin v. McCoach,[16] is even more extreme. An administrator sued an insurance company in the district court in Texas to collect an insurance policy on the life of his decedent. The company responded with a bill of interpleader, bringing in other claimants to the policy proceeds. The policy had been taken out in New York by members of a syndicate on the life of the insured. Three of the members of the syndicate subsequently had assigned their interest in the policy to individuals not previously interested in the transaction, and these assignees had paid their proportion of the premiums after the assignments. The lower courts, considering the contract to be a New York contract, had applied New York law and awarded the proceeds to the members of the syndicate and their assignees. The Supreme Court reversed. Texas had a unique rule that an assignee of an interest in a life insurance policy

13. Sibbach v. Wilson & Co., Inc., 1941, 61 S.Ct. 422, 425, 312 U.S. 1, 10–11, 85 L.Ed. 479. The Court repeated such a statement, 61 S.Ct. at 426 n. 13, 312 U.S. at 13 n. 13.

14. 1941, 61 S.Ct. 1020, 313 U.S. 487, 85 L.Ed. 1477.

15. On remand the Third Circuit concluded that Delaware would look to New York law on interest. Stentor Elec. Mfg. Co., Inc. v. Klaxon Co., C.C.A.3d, 1942, 125 F.2d 820, certiorari denied 62 S.Ct. 1284, 316 U.S. 865, 86 L.Ed. 1757.

16. 1941, 61 S.Ct. 1023, 313 U.S. 498, 85 L.Ed. 1481.

who has no insurable interest in the life of the insured cannot collect on the policy, and arguably this was true of the assignees in the Griffin case. The Supreme Court held that if a Texas court would apply this rule to a contract made in another state, so must a federal court in Texas. The case goes beyond Klaxon, because in Griffin the assignees were made parties to a suit in federal court in Texas only by virtue of the nationwide service authorized by the Federal Interpleader Act. They could not have been made parties to an action in a Texas state court against their will, but after the long arm of the federal court had brought them to a Texas forum, they were held bound by whatever law a Texas state court would have applied to them in the unlikely event that they had appeared in a Texas state court.[17]

The Supreme Court has made it clear that the Klaxon rule is not to yield to the more modern thinking of conflicts-of-laws scholars. The premature explosion of an artillery shell in Cambodia injured a soldier from Wisconsin and killed another from Tennessee. Suit was brought for the injury and the death against the manufacturer in federal court in Texas, where the shell was manufactured. The Fifth Circuit reasoned that under Texas conflicts rules the law of Cambodia would certainly apply to the wrongful death claim and perhaps to the personal injury claim. Cambodian law would require proof of fault by the manufacturer, while Texas, Wisconsin, and Tennessee all apply strict liability to manufacturers. The Fifth Circuit held that Cambodia had no interest in this dispute between American litigants and, on this reasoning, the court felt it could apply the strict liability rule of all of the interested jurisdictions.[18] The Supreme Court summarily reversed without hearing argument.[19] It said that Klaxon was applicable and controlling. "A federal court in a diversity case is not free to engraft onto those state rules exceptions or modifications which may commend themselves to the federal court, but which have not commended themselves to the State in which the federal court sits." [20]

The insistence on uniformity with the courts of the state where the district court is sitting would seem to introduce even a further

17. On remand it was held that the Texas rule applied and that the proceeds from those interests in the policy assigned to third parties were payable to the estate of the insured. Griffin v. McCoach, C.C.A.5th, 1941, 123 F.2d 550, certiorari denied 62 S.Ct. 1270, 316 U.S. 683, 86 L.Ed. 1755.

18. Challoner v. Day and Zimmerman, Inc., C.A.5th, 1975, 512 F.2d 77.

The Fifth Circuit had taken a similar approach in Lester v. Aetna Life Ins. Co., C.A.5th, 1970, 433 F.2d 884, certiorari denied 91 S.Ct. 1382, 402 U.S. 909, 28 L.Ed.2d 650, criticised 1971, 40 U.Cin. L.Rev. 356, where it held that a federal court in Louisiana correctly applied Louisiana law, since Louisiana was the only state interested in the contract, even though Louisiana law would have looked to the law of Wisconsin, where the contract in question was made.

19. Day and Zimmerman, Inc. v. Challoner, 1975, 96 S.Ct. 167, 423 U.S. 3, 46 L.Ed.2d 3.

20. 96 S.Ct. at 168, 423 U.S. at 4.

On remand it was held that the Supreme Court of Texas would have applied the law of Cambodia. Challoner v. Day & Zimmerman, C.A.5th, 1977, 546 F.2d 26.

refinement. In a situation such as Erie, where the accident was in Pennsylvania and suit in New York, Klaxon dictates that New York principles of choice-of-law control. If New York holds that in such a situation Pennsylvania law is to govern, it would seem that the federal court is then to apply, not Pennsylvania law as the federal court understands it, but the New York conception, if any, of what the Pennsylvania law is.[21] Indeed the Supreme Court seems to have gone this far in a case where it directed the federal court to decide the relative weights, as authoritative sources for ascertaining the law of the place of the wrong, the forum state would give to direct holdings of an intermediate court of the state of the wrong and a considered dictum of relevant scope of the supreme court of that state.[22] That this may mean that a federal court in New York "is to determine what the New York courts would think the California courts would think on an issue about which neither has thought"[23] merely highlights the unreality of the process.

The Klaxon case has been criticised on two principal grounds.[24] By demanding uniformity between the federal and state courts in a particular state, it eliminates the possibility of forum-shopping among the courts sitting in that state, but at the same time opens wide the door to forum-shopping among different states. Before Erie, the substantive law that would govern the parties could not be determined until it was seen whether suit was ultimately brought in state or federal court. After Klaxon, the substantive law that will govern the parties cannot be determined until it is seen in which state suit is brought. Second, the federal courts are likely to be disinterested in questions of conflicts of laws, and are in a uniquely favorable position to develop a rational body of doctrine for that branch of law.[25] Klaxon deprives them of this power.

21. See Johnson v. Eastern Air Lines, C.A.2d, 1949, 177 F.2d 713, 714.

22. Nolan v. Transocean Air Lines, 1961, 81 S.Ct. 555, 365 U.S. 293, 5 L.Ed.2d 571.

23. See Nolan v. Transocean Air Lines, C.A.2d, 1960, 276 F.2d 280, 281.

The state with the best developed conflicts law is New York, but even in that state in 1941 there were no local authorities either way on 20.1% of the propositions stated in the Restatement of Conflict of Laws. In Tennessee there was no local authority on 73% of those propositions. Goodrich, Mr. Tompkins Restates the Law, 1941, 27 A.B.A.J. 547, 548. Thus there will be difficulty in determining the state's conflicts doctrine generally, much less in determining its conception of the law of some particular state.

For a striking example of the difficulties the Klaxon approach causes for lower

courts, see Melville v. American Home Assur. Co., D.C.Pa.1977, 443 F.Supp. 1064, reversed C.A.3d, 1978, 584 F.2d 1306.

24. See Trautman, The Relation between American Choice of Law and Federal Common Law, 1977, 41 L. & Contemp.Prob. (No. 2) 105; Horowitz, note 1 above; Cook, The Federal Courts and the Conflict of Laws, 1942, 36 Ill.L.Rev. 493; Hart, The Relations between State and Federal Law, 1954, 54 Col.L.Rev. 489, 513–515.

25. But see Cavers, note 1 above.

Weintraub, note 1 above, accepts the Klaxon principle generally but says that there must be "separate scrutiny of various diversity jurisdiction cases to determine in which circumstances the policy against intrastate forum-shopping is overcome by countervailing considerations." Id. at 248.

Even if the Klaxon doctrine is accepted, there is ground to argue that Griffin v. McCoach goes too far, and that in those situations, so far quite limited, where Congress or the federal rules have made it possible to bring a litigant into a federal court located in a state where he could not have been sued in state court, the federal court should apply its own doctrine of conflicts and determine for itself which state's law to apply.[26]

§ 58. The Erie Doctrine—The Determination of State Law [1]

Once it is agreed that on a particular issue in a particular case the federal court is to apply state law, the problem arises of determining what the state law is that is to be applied. In Erie Justice Brandeis said that the federal court was to apply state law whether "declared by its Legislature in a statute or by its highest court." [2] The Erie doctrine has advanced—or retrogressed—far beyond this comparatively simple test.

A series of decisions in 1940 held that the federal court must follow the decision of an intermediate appellate state court in the absence of other persuasive data that the highest court of the state would decide otherwise.[3] The most notorious of the cases then decided, however, did not involve an intermediate state court at all, but rather a decision at nisi prius. The case is Fidelity Union Trust Co. v. Field.[4] Prior to 1932 New Jersey law had not permitted the so-called "Totten trust," by which a person can make a deposit in a savings bank for himself as trustee for another, and create a tentative trust, revocable at any time before death. In 1932 the New Jersey legislature passed four statutes that seemed, in clearest terms, to change the prior law and permit the Totten trust. In 1935 Miss Peck made such a deposit in trust for her friend, Miss Field. She died shortly thereafter and Miss Field sued the bank, which had denied the validity of the trust, to collect the funds. In the meantime the 1932 legis-

26. ALI Study, §§ 2361(c), 2374(c); Weintraub, note 1 above, at 253–256; Boner, Erie v. Tompkins: A Study in Judicial Precedent, 1962, 40 Texas L.Rev. 509, 522; Freund, Chief Justice Stone and the Conflict of Laws, 1946, 59 Harv.L.Rev. 1210, 1236 n. 62.

But see Currie, Change of Venue and the Conflicts of Laws: A Retraction, 1960, 27 U.Chi.L.Rev. 341.

[§ 58]

1. 19 Wright, Miller & Cooper, Jurisdiction § 4507; Thomas, The Erosion of Erie in the Federal Courts: Is State Law Losing Ground?, 1977 B.Y.U.L. Rev. 1; Gibbs, How Does the Federal Judge Determine What is the Law of the State?, 1965, 17 S.C.L.Rev. 487.

2. Erie R. Co. v. Tompkins, 1938, 58 S.Ct. 817, 822, 304 U.S. 64, 78, 82 L.Ed. 1188.

3. West v. American Tel. & Tel. Co., 1940, 61 S.Ct. 179, 311 U.S. 223, 85 L.Ed. 139; Six Companies of California v. Joint Highway Dist., 1940, 61 S.Ct. 186, 311 U.S. 180, 85 L.Ed. 114; Stoner v. New York Life Ins. Co., 1940, 61 S.Ct. 336, 311 U.S. 464, 85 L.Ed. 284.

Judge Friendly refers to these decisions as "the excesses of 311 U.S. as to the respect that federal judges must pay to decisions of lower state courts * * *." Friendly, In Praise of Erie—And of the New Federal Common Law, 1964, 39 N.Y.U.L.Rev. 383, 400.

4. 1940, 61 S.Ct. 176, 311 U.S. 169, 85 L.Ed. 109.

lation came before the Court of Chancery in 1936 in two cases involving other parties and "two vice-chancellors had more respect for the law than to believe it could be made imperfect by a mere legislature, and so they had construed the statute away by decision." [5] The New Jersey Court of Chancery was a court of original jurisdiction, though it had statewide jurisdiction and a standing on the equity side comparable to that of the intermediate appellate courts on the law side. The Third Circuit, in Miss Field's case, recognized that the case before it was indistinguishable from those decided by the two vice-chancellors, and recognized that it was obliged to apply New Jersey law, but it found the 1932 legislation clearly constitutional and unambiguous and applied the statute, awarding the funds to Miss Field, rather than following the contrary decisions of the vice-chancellors. For doing so it was reversed by the Supreme Court. The decisions of the vice-chancellors would not have been binding on the New Jersey Court of Errors and Appeals, nor on any other vice-chancellor, nor even on the vice-chancellors who had made the decisions if they could be persuaded in a later case to change their mind. Nevertheless they were binding on the federal courts. Miss Field lost the money that Miss Peck wanted to leave to her because the decisions of two inferior judges, in cases to which she was not a party and in which she was not represented by counsel, were held to have, in federal court, an effect not unlike that of res judicata. It is somewhat ironical—though it can have been of little comfort to Miss Field—that later New Jersey cases followed the decision of the Third Circuit as to the 1932 statutes, which, they noted, had been "reversed on other grounds" by the Supreme Court,[6] and that New Jersey law now is what the Third Circuit thought it was, rather than what two vice-chancellors declared it to be in 1936. It is no wonder that Judge Jerome N. Frank said that federal judges were now "to play the role of ventriloquist's dummy to the courts of some particular state," [7] nor that Judge Charles E. Clark denounced the Field case as "the most troublesome, the most unsatisfying in its consequence, of all the rules based upon the Tompkins case." [8] Perhaps the highpoint of the Field doctrine came in a case where the Sixth Circuit felt obliged to follow an unreported decision of an intermediate Ohio court in the face of an Ohio statute providing that "only such cases as are hereafter reported in accordance with the provisions of this section shall be recognized by and receive the official sanction of any court within the state." [9]

5. Clark, State Law in the Federal Courts: The Brooding Omnipresence of Erie v. Tompkins, 1946, 55 Yale L.J. 267, 292.

6. Hickey v. Kahl, 1941, 19 A.2d 33, 129 N.J.Eq. 233.

7. Richardson v. C. I. R., C.C.A.2d, 1942, 126 F.2d 562, 567.

8. Clark, note 5 above, at 290.

9. Gustin v. Sun Life Assur. Co., C.C.A. 6th, 1946, 154 F.2d 961, certiorari denied 66 S.Ct. 1374, 328 U.S. 866, 90 L.Ed. 1636.

But in Southern Ry. Co. v. Foote Mineral Co., C.A.6th, 1967, 384 F.2d 224, 228, the Sixth Circuit said it was not bound by an unpublished opinion of the Tennessee Supreme Court since under Tennessee practice unpublished opinions

The first retreat from the rigidity of the Field decision came in 1948, when it was held that an unreported decision of a South Carolina Court of Common Pleas, which would not have even precedential value in any other case in that state and which could be located only with great difficulty, was entitled to "some weight" but was "not controlling" on the federal court.[10]

Unlike the the situation under Swift v. Tyson, where the federal court was free to disregard even state decisions construing state statutes if the decision came down after a lower federal court had decided the case,[11] under the Erie rule it is never too late to change in conformity to some new pronouncement of state law, and a court of appeals must rely on the latest state decisions even though they come after the federal court decision that the appellate court is reviewing.[12] This raises the question whether a federal court can anticipate a change in state law that has not yet been authoritatively announced by the state court. Some courts thought that they had this power. They held that they could disregard a decision of the state court that the state court itself had ignored in later decisions, even though the earlier decision had never been expressly overruled,[13] or that they might follow a recent dictum discrediting outdated holdings,[14] or that if the state legislature had spoken since the state court's decision in an apparent effort to change the law as declared in that decision, the legislative enactment, rather than the decision, should take precedence.[15] On all of this there was no unanimity of view. Judge Frank, of the Second Circuit, thought that the test for the federal judge was: "What would be the decision of reasonable intelligent lawyers, sitting as judges of the highest New York court, and fully conversant with New York 'jurisprudence'?"[16] But Judge Jones,

are binding only on the parties to the particular litigation.

10. King v. Order of United Commercial Travelers of America, 1948, 68 S.Ct. 488, 333 U.S. 153, 92 L.Ed. 608.

For applications of this principle, see e.g., MGM Grand Hotel, Inc. v. Imperial Glass Co., C.A.9th, 1976, 533 F.2d 486, 489 n. 5, certiorari denied 97 S.Ct. 239, 429 U.S. 887, 50 L.Ed.2d 168; U. S. v. Wyoming Nat. Bank of Casper, C.A. 10th, 1974, 505 F.2d 1064.

11. Burgess v. Seligman, 1883, 2 S.Ct. 10, 107 U.S. 20, 27 L.Ed. 359. See § 54 above.

12. Vandenbark v. Owens-Illinois Glass Co., 1941, 61 S.Ct. 347, 311 U.S. 538, 85 L.Ed. 327; Huddleston v. Dwyer, 1944, 64 S.Ct. 1015, 322 U.S. 232, 88 L.Ed. 1246; Nolan v. Transocean Air Lines, 1961, 81 S.Ct. 555, 365 U.S. 293, 5 L.Ed.2d 571.

This principle is extended in Maryland Cas. Co. v. Hallatt, C.A.5th, 1964, 326

F.2d 275, and carried to—or perhaps beyond—its limit in Pierce v. Cook & Co., C.A.10th, 1975, 518 F.2d 720, noted 1975, 7 St. Mary's L.J. 594; 1976, 29 Rutgers L.Rev. 921, 62 Va.L.Rev. 414.

13. City of Newark v. U. S., D.C.N.J. 1957, 149 F.Supp. 917, 922, affirmed C. A.3d, 1958, 254 F.2d 93; City of Stockton v. Miles & Sons, Inc., D.C.Cal.1958, 165 F.Supp. 554, 563.

14. Mason v. American Emery Wheel Works, C.A.1st, 1957, 241 F.2d 906, 908. But cf. Nolan v. Transocean Air Lines, C.A.2d, 1961, 290 F.2d 904, certiorari denied 81 S.Ct. 555, 365 U.S. 293, 5 L.Ed.2d 571.

15. U. S. v. Covington Independent Tobacco Warehouse Co., D.C.Ky.1957, 152 F.Supp. 612, 615–616.

16. Cooper v. American Airlines, Inc., C.C.A.2d, 1945, 149 F.2d 355, 359.

for the Fifth Circuit, thought that to follow such a process "would be attempting to psychoanalyze state court judges rather than to rationalize state court decisions." [17]

It now seems clear that Judge Frank was right. The Court first hinted at the answer in Bernhardt v. Polygraphic Co. of America.[18] One of the issues there was whether a 1910 Vermont decision, holding arbitration agreements unenforcible, was binding on a federal court in 1956. The Court held that the 1910 decision was controlling, but in doing so pointed out that "there appears to be no confusion in the Vermont decisions, no developing line of authorities that casts a shadow over the established ones, no dicta, doubts or ambiguities in the opinions of Vermont judges on the question, no legislative development that promises to undermine the judicial rule." [19]

The Court was even more explicit in 1967 in Commissioner v. Estate of Bosch.[20] Although the issue there was a different one, the Court drew on what it understood to be the practice where Erie is controlling as providing a useful analogy. Speaking directly to the Erie cases, the Court said that "under some conditions, federal authority may not be bound even by an intermediate state appellate court ruling.   *   *   *   [T]he underlying substantive rule involved is based on state law and the State's highest court is the best authority on its own law. If there be no decision by that court then federal authorities must apply what they find to be the state law after giving 'proper regard' to relevant rulings of other courts of the State. In this respect, it may be said to be, in effect, sitting as a state court." [21]

Two dissenters in the Bosch case stated their understanding of "the formula now ordinarily employed to determine state law in diversity cases" to be that "absent a recent judgment of the State's highest court, state cases are only data from which the law must be derived   *   *   *   ." [22]

Thus the federal judge need no longer be a ventriloquist's dummy. Instead he is free, just as his state counterpart is, to consider all the data the highest court of the state would use in an effort to determine how the highest court of the state would decide.[23] This is as it

---

17. Polk County v. Lincoln Nat. Life Ins. Co., C.A.5th, 1959, 262 F.2d 486, 489.

18. 1956, 76 S.Ct. 273, 350 U.S. 198, 100 L.Ed. 199.

19. 76 S.Ct. at 277, 350 U.S. at 205. In an interesting concurring opinion, Justice Frankfurter argued that the 1910 Vermont decision was a product of the hostility to arbitration at that time, and that the court of appeals might reasonably "estimate" that Vermont would no longer adhere to it if the question were to be raised now when arbitration is well accepted. 76 S.Ct. at 279–281, 350 U.S. at 208–212.

20. 1967, 87 S.Ct. 1776, 387 U.S. 456, 18 L.Ed.2d 886.

21. 87 S.Ct. at 1782–1783, 387 U.S. at 465.

22. 87 S.Ct. at 1788, 387 U.S. at 477.

23. Roginsky v. Richardson-Merrell, Inc., C.A.2d, 1967, 378 F.2d 832, 851. This is the view long urged by the commentators. In addition to the articles cited note 1 above, see Hart, The Relations between State and Federal Law, 1954, 54 Col.L.Rev. 489, 510; Clark, note 5 above, at 290–295; Corbin, The Laws of the Several States, 1941, 50 Yale L.J. 762.

should be. Unless this much freedom is allowed the federal judge, the Erie doctrine would simply have substituted one kind of forum-shopping for another. The lawyer whose case was dependent on an old or shaky state court decision that might no longer be followed within the state would have a strong incentive to maneuver the case into federal court, where, on the mechanical jurisprudence that the Erie doctrine was once thought to require, the state decision could not have been impeached.

If there are no holdings from state courts, high or low, on the matter that the federal court is to decide, that court must look for other indications of the state law. Though there are various remarks from federal courts about the effect of state court dicta,[24] such remarks should not be read out of context. Much depends on the character of the dictum. Mere obiter may be entitled to little weight, while a carefully considered statement by the state court, though technically dictum, must carry great weight,[25] and may even, in the absence of any conflicting indication of the law of the state, be regarded as conclusive.[26]

The opinions of a state attorney general are not part of "the laws" of the state within the meaning of the Rules of Decision Act, though they are entitled to weight in determining the legislative intent in enacting a statute.[27] Similarly the long-continued construction of a state statute by the state agency charged with administering it may be accepted by the federal court as representing the state law, even

There is an excellent statement of the process a federal judge is not to follow in determining state law in McKenna v. Ortho Pharmaceutical Corp., C.A.3d, 1980, 622 F.2d 657, 662–663, certiorari denied 101 S.Ct. 387, 449 U.S. 976, 66 L.Ed.2d 237. Even so, there is force to the argument of the dissenting judge that the majority in that case "disregards Ohio's current (though archaic) doctrine and announces a rule of law that Ohio should adopt.": 622 F.2d at 669.

See Vargus v. Pitman Mfg. Co., C.A.3d, 1982, 675 F.2d 73, where the court refused to follow an extremely recent decision of the state supreme court that appeared to abolish the defense of assumption of risk, since only three of the seven judges of the state court joined in the opinion to that effect while a fourth judge merely concurred in the result.

24. Compare Hardy Salt Co. v. Southern Pac. Transp. Co., C.A.10th, 1974, 501 F.2d 1156, 1163, and Rocky Mountain Fire & Cas. Co. v. Dairyland Ins. Co., C.A.9th, 1971, 452 F.2d 603 (state dicta binding), with Nolan v. Transocean Airlines, C.A.2d, 1961, 290 F.2d 904, certiorari denied 82 S.Ct. 177, 368 U.S. 901, 7 L.Ed.2d 96, and Walker v. Felmont Oil Corp., C.A.6th, 1957, 240 F.2d 912 (state dicta not binding).

25. Gee v. Tenneco, Inc., C.A.9th, 1980, 615 F.2d 857, 861; Hartford Acc. & Indem. Co. v. First Nat. Bank & Trust Co. of Tulsa, C.A.10th, 1961, 287 F.2d 69, 73.

26. One commentator, however, argues that if the federal court gives weight to state dicta it has substituted "stare dictis" for "stare decisis," and that the courts doing so "have departed not only from the Erie decision, but also from the very policy that they profess to serve." Boner, Erie v. Tompkins: A Study in Judicial Precedent, II, 1962, 40 Tex.L.Rev. 619, 623. See also Harnett & Thornton, Precedent in the Erie-Tompkins Manner, 1949, 24 N.Y.U.L.Q. 770.

27. Bostick v. Smoot Sand & Gravel Corp., C.A.4th, 1958, 260 F.2d 534, 541; Lowe v. Socony Mobil Oil Co., D.C.Or. 1963, 222 F.Supp. 624, 626.

where the language of the statute, to an outsider, might appear to require a different construction.[28]

Inevitably situations will arise where there is no state law of any kind on the particular point involved. It is probably still true, as clearly held in 1943, that a federal court cannot decline jurisdiction of a case simply because it is difficult to ascertain what the state courts may thereafter determine the state law to be.[29] "In the absence of a state court ruling, our duty is tolerably clear. It is to decide, not avoid, the question." [30] In vicariously creating law for a state, the federal court may look to such sources as the Restatements of Law, treatises and law review commentary, and "the majority rule." [31] The federal court must keep in mind, however, that its function is not to choose the rule that it would adopt for itself, if free to do so, but to choose the rule that it believes the state court, from all that is known about its methods of reaching decisions, is likely in the future to adopt.[32]

As a general proposition, a federal court judge who sits in a particular state and has practiced before its courts may be better able to resolve complex questions about the law of that state than is some other federal judge who has no such personal acquaintance with the law of the state. For this reason federal appellate courts have frequently voiced reluctance to substitute their own view of the state law for that of the federal judge.[33] As a matter of judicial adminis-

28. Dickinson v. First Nat. Bank in Plant City, C.A.5th, 1968, 400 F.2d 548, 558, affirmed 1969, 90 S.Ct. 337, 396 U.S. 122, 24 L.Ed.2d 312; Rosenfield, Administrative Determinations as State Law under Erie v. Tompkins, 1949, 24 N.Y.U.L.Q.Rev. 319.

But see Mogis v. Lyman-Richey Sand & Gravel Co., C.A.8th, 1951, 189 F.2d 130, certiorari denied 72 S.Ct. 168, 342 U.S. 877, 96 L.Ed. 659, criticised 1951, 36 Minn.L.Rev. 100, where the rule stated in the text was recognized but the court in fact did not follow the administrative construction.

29. Meredith v. City of Winter Haven, 1943, 64 S.Ct. 7, 320 U.S. 228, 88 L.Ed. 9. The recent burgeoning of the abstention doctrines casts some doubt on whether the Meredith case still represents an absolute rule. See § 52 above.

30. Daily v. Parker, C.C.A.7th, 1945, 152 F.2d 174, 177. See Fitzgerald, The Celebrated Case of Daily v. Parker, 1947, 15 U.Kan.City L.Rev. 120.

31. Michelin Tires (Canada) Ltd. v. First Nat. Bank of Boston, C.A.1st, 1981, 666 F.2d 673, 682; City of Aurora v. Bechtel Corp., C.A.10th, 1979, 599 F.2d 382, 386; and cases cited 19 Wright,

Miller & Cooper, Jurisdiction § 4507 nn. 49–54.

32. Tucker v. Paxson Machine Co., C.A.8th, 1981, 645 F.2d 620, 624–625; Green v. Amerada-Hess Corp., C.A.5th, 1980, 612 F.2d 212, 214, certiorari denied 101 S.Ct. 356, 449 U.S. 952, 66 L.Ed.2d 216; Kline v. Wheels by Kinney, Inc., C.A.4th, 1972, 464 F.2d 184, 187.

Two cases illustrate this process in interesting fashion. In Yost v. Morrow, C.A.9th, 1959, 262 F.2d 826, 828 n. 3, it was assumed that the Idaho court would follow decisions of its sister state, Oregon. In Pomerantz v. Clark, D.C.Mass.1951, 101 F.Supp. 341, 346, Judge Wyzanski based his estimate of what the Massachusetts court would do on his judgment that "subtle variations and blurred lines are not characteristic of that court. Principles are announced and adhered to in broad magisterial terms. The emphasis is on precedent and adherence to the older ways, not on creating new causes of action or encouraging the use of novel judicial remedies that have sprung up in less conservative communities."

33. E.g., Bernhardt v. Polygraphic Co. of America, 1956, 76 S.Ct. 273, 277, 350

tration, this seems defensible. But there is some tendency to go beyond that, and to say that if the trial court has reached a permissible
conclusion under state law, the appellate court cannot reverse even if
it thinks the state law otherwise, thus treating the question of state
law much as if it were a question of fact.[34] It would seem that a
party is entitled to review the trial court's determination of state law
just as he is of any other legal question in the case, and that the
decision of the local trial judge cannot reasonably be regarded as conclusive.[35]

An interesting variation on the problem just discussed was before
the Second Circuit in Factors Etc., Inc. v. Pro Arts, Inc.[36] In a diversity case in federal court in New York, the issue was whether Elvis
Presley's right of publicity had survived his death. All of the Second
Circuit judges agreed that New York's conflicts rules would turn to
Tennessee law for the answer to that question. No Tennessee statute or decision gave any hint of an answer, but the Sixth Circuit, in
another case, had held on policy and practical grounds that Presley's
right had not survived. The majority in the Second Circuit held that
when the court of appeals for the circuit that includes the state has
made a prediction of state law on a question of first impression within the state, the other circuits must defer to that holding "at least in
all situations except the rare instance when it can be said with conviction that the pertinent court of appeals has disregarded clear signals
emanating from the state's highest court pointing toward a different
rule."[37] It is hard to see why the decision of one court of appeals
should have more than persuasive effect on a coordinate court on an
issue as to which neither of them can speak with authority.[38] Indeed

U.S. 198, 204, 100 L.Ed. 199; Huddleston v. Dwyer, 1944, 64 S.Ct. 1015,
1018, 322 U.S. 232, 237, 88 L.Ed. 1246;
MacGregor v. State Mut. Life Assur.
Co. of Worcester, Mass., 1942, 62 S.Ct.
607, 315 U.S. 280, 281, 86 L.Ed. 846.

34. This view is expressed in many
cases from the Sixth, Ninth, and Tenth
Circuits. See cases cited in 19 Wright,
Miller & Cooper, Jurisdiction § 4507 n.
60. But as the cases cited id. at n. 61
show, there are other decisions even
from those circuits taking the view
here urged.

35. Luke v. American Family Mut. Ins.
Co., C.A.8th, 1973, 476 F.2d 1015,
1019–1020, certiorari denied 94 S.Ct.
158, 414 U.S. 856, 38 L.Ed.2d 105;
Freeman v. Continental Gin Co., C.A.
5th, 1967, 381 F.2d 459, 466.

" * * * [T]he very essence of the Erie
doctrine is that a federal judge can
find, if not make, the law almost as
well as a state judge. Certainly, if the
law is not a brooding omnipresence in
the sky over the United States, neither

is it a brooding omnipresence in the
sky of Vermont, or New York or California. The bases of state law are assumed to be communicable by lawyers
to judges, federal judges no less than
state judges." Kurland, Mr. Justice
Frankfurter, The Supreme Court and
the Erie Doctrine in Diversity Cases,
1957, 67 Yale L.J. 187, 215–218.

36. C.A.2d, 1981, 652 F.2d 278, certiorari denied 1982, 102 S.Ct. 1973, ___ U.S.
___, 72 L.Ed.2d 442, noted 1981 B.Y.
U.L.Rev. 974; 1982, 67 Cornell L.Rev.
415, 1982 Duke L.J.704, 10 Hofstra
L.Rev. 927, 15 John Marshall L.Rev.
499, 27 Vill.L.Rev. 393.

37. 652 F.2d at 283.

38. Indeed only three months after the
Second Circuit's decision, a Tennessee
court decided the issue, holding that
the Sixth and Second Circuits were
wrong and that the right did survive.
Commerce Union Bank v. Coors, Tenn.
Ch.Ct.1981, 7 Media L.Rep. 2204. The
federal district court then stayed entry
of judgment so that plaintiffs might

it is even arguable that the proper question is one not addressed either in the majority opinion or the vigorous dissent in Factors Etc.: what weight would New York's highest court have given to the Sixth Circuit's construction of Tennessee common law?

§ 59. The Erie Doctrine—Issues on Which State Law Is Controlling [1]

A central and recurring question in the application of the Erie doctrine has been how to distinguish between those issues on which state law is controlling and those on which a federal court is not bound by state law. The Supreme Court has given different answers to this question at different times over the years. Although in 1965 it gave what seemed to be a durable and reasonably clear answer, both the lower courts and the commentators have found that the answer is not as simple as the 1965 decision seemed to make it.

In the Erie case Justice Brandeis asserted that Congress is powerless to declare "substantive rules of common law applicable in a state." [2] Justice Reed, in his concurring opinion, completed the dichotomy by observing that "no one doubts federal power over procedure." [3] For seven years it was supposed that Erie drew a line between "substance" and "procedure," with the first governed by state law in diversity cases while the second was subject to a federal rule. [4] Commentators were critical of such a distinction, but it gave no undue difficulty in the early years of the Erie era, when the most notable Supreme Court decisions were those holding that the federal court must apply state rules as to burden of proof. [5] To this day the terms "substance" and "procedure" are widely used, not only by lawyers but also by courts. As has already been seen in section 55, the Erie doctrine has been substantially redefined by the Supreme Court,

petition the Second Circuit to recall its mandate and rehear the case in the light of the intervening Tennessee decision. Factors Etc., Inc. v. Pro Arts, Inc., D.C.N.Y.1982, 541 F.Supp. 231.

[§ 59]

1. 19 Wright, Miller & Cooper, Jurisdiction §§ 4508–4513. In addition to the commentaries cited § 55 n. 1 above, see Leathers, Erie and Its Progeny As Choice of Law Cases, 1974, 11 Hous.L.Rev. 791; Knowlton, The Impact of Erie upon the Federal Rules, 1965, 17 S.C.L.Rev. 480; McCoid, Hanna v. Plumer, The Erie Doctrine Changes Shape, 1965, 51 Va.L.Rev. 884; Note, The Law Applied in Diversity Cases: The Rules of Decision Act and the Erie Doctrine, 1976, 85 Yale L.J. 678.

2. Erie R. Co. v. Tompkins, 1938, 58 S.Ct. 817, 822, 304 U.S. 64, 78, 82 L.Ed. 1188.

3. 58 S.Ct. at 828, 304 U.S. at 92.

4. This line seemed to be accepted by the Supreme Court in Sibbach v. Wilson, 1941, 61 S.Ct. 422, 425, 312 U.S. 1, 10–11, 85 L.Ed. 479. See the discussion of Sibbach in Ely, The Irrepressible Myth of Erie, 1974, 87 Harv.L.Rev. 693, 733–737.

5. Cities Serv. Oil Co. v. Dunlap, 1939, 60 S.Ct. 201, 308 U.S. 208, 84 L.Ed. 196; Palmer v. Hoffman, 1943, 63 S.Ct. 477, 318 U.S. 109, 87 L.Ed. 645.

For scholarly criticism of the line, see Cook, Logical and Legal Bases of the Conflict of Laws, 1942, pp. 163–165; Tunks, Categorization and Federalism: "Substance" and "Procedure" After Erie Railroad v. Tompkins, 1939, 34 Ill. L.Rev. 271.

and it is now clear that no simple dichotomy between substance and procedure will determine the issues on which state law is to control. The trouble with such a dichotomy, as Justice Frankfurter pointed out in the Guaranty Trust case, is that " 'substance' and 'procedure' are the same keywords to very different problems. Neither 'substance' nor 'procedure' represents the same invariants. Each implies different variables depending upon the particular problem for which it is used." [6] A particular issue may be classified as substantive or procedural in determining whether it is within the scope of a court's rulemaking power, or in resolving questions of conflict of laws, or in determining whether to apply state law or federal law. These are three very different kinds of problems. Factors that are of decisive importance in making the classification for one purpose may be irrelevant for another. To use the same name for all three purposes is an invitation to a barren and misleading conceptualism by which a decision holding that a particular issue is substantive for one of these purposes would be thought controlling authority when classification for a different purpose is involved. [7]

In the Guaranty Trust case itself the issue was whether a state statute of limitations was controlling on the equity side of federal court. Much of the opinion was devoted to refuting "talk in the cases that federal equity is a separate legal system." One week after Erie it had been held that the Erie principle applied to proceedings in equity, [8] even though the Rules of Decision Act then was limited to "trials at common law." [9] This portion of the Guaranty opinion is not as clear as might be desired. In particular, there is language in the opinion that seems to suggest that the doctrine of "equitable remedial rights" persists, and that a federal court sitting in equity is free to grant or withhold remedies without regard to what a state court would do in a similar case. [10] Probably this is true where an Act of Congress has taken away jurisdiction to grant an injunction in partic-

---

6. Guaranty Trust Co. of New York v. York, 1945, 65 S.Ct. 1464, 1469, 326 U.S. 99, 108, 89 L.Ed. 2079.

"The line between 'substance' and 'procedure' shifts as the legal context changes." Hanna v. Plumer, 1965, 85 S.Ct. 1136, 1144, 380 U.S. 460, 471, 14 L.Ed.2d 8.

7. Jarvis v. Johnson, C.A.3d, 1982, 668 F.2d 740, 747. The holding here was that although Pa.R.C.P. 238, requiring prejudgment interest in certain cases, had been upheld by the Pennsylvania Supreme Court as a valid exercise of its power to make rules of "procedure," Rule 238 nevertheless must be applied by a federal court in a diversity case.

8. Ruhlin v. New York Life Ins. Co., 1938, 58 S.Ct. 860, 304 U.S. 202, 82 L.Ed. 1290. This had been the rule

even under Swift v. Tyson—see Mason v. U. S., 1923, 43 S.Ct. 200, 260 U.S. 545, 67 L.Ed. 396—except insofar as state law sought to define "equitable remedial rights." See § 54 above.

9. In the 1948 revision of the Judicial Code the Rules of Decision Act was altered, and now speaks of "civil actions." 28 U.S.C.A. § 1652.

10. "State law cannot define the remedies which a federal court must give simply because a federal court in diversity jurisdiction is available as an alternative tribunal to the State's courts. Contrariwise, a federal court may afford an equitable remedy for a substantive right recognized by a State even though a State court cannot give it." 65 S.Ct. at 1468–1469, 326 U.S. at 106.

ular cases [11] or where the constitutional right to trial by jury might be abridged.[12] It seems equally true that federal courts are free to use procedural devices made available by statutes or the Federal Rules despite the absence of similar procedures in the states.[13] Beyond such situations it is difficult to believe that the federal court is free to fashion an independent law of remedies in equitable actions.[14]

The most important, and better known, aspect of the Guaranty Trust case is its holding that a state statute of limitations must be applied by a federal court in a diversity case, even though statutes of limitations may be regarded as "procedural" for some other purposes, in order to ensure that "the outcome of the litigation in the federal court should be substantially the same, so far as legal rules determine the outcome of a litigation, as it would be if tried in a State court." [15]

It has already been pointed out that to such a principle there is no apparent stopping place.[16] It is difficult to conceive of any rule of procedure that cannot have a significant effect on the outcome of a case. Yet for some years the Supreme Court seemed committed to applying this "outcome-determinative" test to its farthest reach. Three decisions handed down on the same day in 1949 showed the deference to state law that was to be required in matters that, for other purposes, are clearly procedural. One of the decisions held that a federal court, hearing a stockholder's derivative suit based on diversity, must apply a New Jersey statute making unsuccessful plaintiffs in such litigation liable for all expenses, including attorney's fees, of the defense, and requiring security for the payment of such expenses as a condition of prosecuting the action.[17]   Clearly it

---

11. As with the Norris-La Guardia Act, 29 U.S.C.A. §§ 101 et seq.

12. In Guaranty Trust the Court cites approvingly, as illustrating this point, Whitehead v. Shattuck, 1891, 11 S.Ct. 276, 138 U.S. 146, 34 L.Ed. 873.

13. E.g., class actions, Oskoian v. Canuel, C.A.1st, 1959, 269 F.2d 311; preliminary injunctions and temporary restraining orders, System Operations, Inc. v. Scientific Games Development Corp., C.A.3d, 1977, 555 F.2d 1131, 1141; declaratory judgments, Farmers Alliance Mut. Ins. Co. v. Jones, C.A. 10th, 1978, 570 F.2d 1384, certiorari denied 99 S.Ct. 97, 439 U.S. 826, 58 L.Ed. 2d 119.

14. 19 Wright, Miller & Cooper, Jurisdiction § 4513. Thus state law has been held to govern the availability of such equitable remedies as: a permanent injunction, System Operations, Inc. v. Scientific Games Development Corp., C.A.3d, 1977, 555 F.2d 1131, 1143; specific performance, Weathersby v. Gore, C.A.5th, 1977, 556 F.2d

1247, 1257–1259; rescission, Lipsky v. Commonwealth United Corp., C.A.2d, 1976, 551 F.2d 887, 894–898; and accounting, McLeod v. Stevens, C.A.4th, 1980, 617 F.2d 1038, 1041.

But see Perfect Fit Indus., Inc. v. Acme Quilting Co., Inc., C.A.2d, 1981, 646 F.2d 800, 806.

The Supreme Court treated this as still an open question in Stern v. South Chester Tube Co., 1968, 88 S.Ct. 1332, 1334, 390 U.S. 606, 609, 20 L.Ed.2d 177.

15. 65 S.Ct. at 1470, 326 U.S. at 109. See Blume & George, Limitations and the Federal Courts, 1951, 49 Mich.L. Rev. 937.

16. See § 55 nn. 20, 21 above.

17. Cohen v. Beneficial Indus. Loan Corp., 1949, 69 S.Ct. 1221, 337 U.S. 541, 93 L.Ed. 1528. See Note, Federal Rules of Civil Procedure 23(b): Its Application under Erie R. R. v. Tompkins, 1958, 26 Ford L.Rev. 694.

Justices Douglas, Frankfurter, and Rutledge dissented.

would significantly affect the outcome if the suit would be barred in state court because of the plaintiff's inability to post such security, and on this reasoning the majority held that the policy of Guaranty Trust must apply. Three dissenters, including, interestingly, the author of the Guaranty Trust opinion, took the view that the New Jersey statute neither added to nor subtracted from the cause of action, but merely prescribed the method by which the cause of action was to be enforced, and on this reasoning said state law need not be followed.

In a second case, it was held, with three justices dissenting, that a state statute barring foreign corporations that had not qualified to do business in the state from suing in the courts of the state was effective also to bar such a corporation from bringing a diversity action in the federal court sitting in that state.[18]

Finally, in the controversial case of Ragan v. Merchants Transfer & Warehouse Co.,[19] a suit had been filed within the period of a state statute of limitations, but service was not made until after the statutory period had run, and the state law made service within the statutory period an integral part of the state's statute of limitations. It was held, with only one dissent, that the action must be dismissed in federal court, despite Federal Rule 3, which provides that an action is commenced by filing a complaint with the court.

It is interesting to note that, though in each of these cases state law was held controlling, only four members of the Court were applying a principle broad enough to encompass all three cases. Five of the justices dissented in one or another of the three cases. This failure to enunciate an understandable principle made application of the teaching of these cases more difficult. Many observers believed, however, that there was no longer much, if any, room for independent federal regulation of procedure.

Prior to 1938 the pattern in federal courts had been conformity to state law on matters of procedure, under the Conformity Act,[20] but substantial uniformity among the federal courts on substantive law, under the aegis of Swift v. Tyson.[21] This arrangement was reversed in 1938. The Federal Rules of Civil Procedure, providing a uniform system of procedure for the federal courts, were adopted by the Court on December 20, 1937, and became effective September 1, 1938.[22] The Erie case, requiring conformity to state decisional law, was decided April 25, 1938.[23]

---

18. Woods v. Interstate Realty Co., 1949, 69 S.Ct. 1235, 337 U.S. 535, 93 L.Ed. 1524.

Justices Jackson, Rutledge, and Burton dissented.

The result in this case was foreshadowed by Angel v. Bullington, 1947, 67 S.Ct. 657, 330 U.S. 183, 91 L.Ed. 832. See § 46 above.

19. 1949, 69 S.Ct. 1233, 337 U.S. 530, 93 L.Ed. 1520.

Justice Rutledge dissented.

20. See § 61 below.

21. See § 54 above.

22. See § 62 below.

23. The author of the Erie opinion, Justice Brandeis, had dissented from adop-

After the three 1949 decisions, the draftsman of the rules said that "hardly a one of the heralded Federal Rules can be considered safe from attack." [24] Several distinguished commentators urged repeal of the rules in diversity cases.[25] Other writers were more sanguine, and recognized the practical necessity of arriving at a workable policy that would permit the coexistence of the Erie doctrine and the rules.[26]

For the next nine years the lower courts were left to resolve such questions with a minimum of guidance from the Supreme Court. The only decision in that period from the Court bearing on the question held that a change in forum from a court trial to arbitration might make a radical difference in ultimate result, and thus that antiquated state court decisions, holding unenforceable contract provisions for arbitration, must be applied by the federal court.[27] Then in 1958 the well-known case of Byrd v. Blue Ridge Rural Electric Cooperative, Inc.,[28] provided a formula by which the rules might indeed coexist with the Erie doctrine. "Outcome" was no longer to be the only test. Instead it was recognized that the federal judicial system is an independent system for administering justice to litigants who properly invoke its jurisdiction. Federal policies as to how the federal courts should be run—in that case the federal policy favoring jury decisions of disputed fact questions—much be balanced against the policy of providing the same outcome in federal court as in state court.

Though Byrd was a welcome retreat from the more extreme position of Guaranty Trust, and it provided a means for continuing to apply the Civil Rules in many areas, there was considerable difficulty in applying the Byrd test. Able courts—and judges within a single court—were divided in situations that were distinguishable but perhaps not really different. The interest of the federal system in having a uniform procedure in its courts was given heavy weight by the Fifth Circuit but only "slight" weight by the Seventh Circuit.[29] The presence or absence of a specific federal statute or rule was thought decisive by Judge Friendly and a majority of the Second Circuit but

tion of the Rules of Civil Procedure. Order of Dec. 20, 1937, 302 U.S. 783.

24. Clark, Book Review, 1950, 36 Corn. L.Q. 181, 183.

25. Merrigan, Erie to York to Ragan— A Triple Play on the Federal Rules, 1950, 3 Vand.L.Rev. 711; Gavit, States' Rights and Federal Procedure, 1949, 25 Ind.L.Rev. 1, 26. A later writer proposed "thorough amendment" of the rules to avoid conflicts with state law. Hill, The Erie Doctrine and the Constitution, 1958, 53 Nw.U.L.Rev. 549, 581–584.

26. Symposium, Federal Trials and the Erie Doctrine, 1956, 51 Nw.U.L.Rev. 338; Note, The Erie Case and the Federal Rules—A Prediction, 1951, 39 Geo. L.J. 600, 612.

27. Bernhardt v. Polygraphic Co. of America, 1956, 76 S.Ct. 273, 350 U.S. 198, 100 L.Ed. 199.

28. 1958, 78 S.Ct. 893, 356 U.S. 525, 2 L.Ed.2d 953.

29. Compare Monarch Ins. Co. of Ohio v. Spach, C.A.5th, 1960, 281 F.2d 401, 408, with Allstate Ins. Co. v. Charneski, C.A.7th, 1960, 286 F.2d 238, 244.

Judge Clark of that court gave it little weight as also did the Seventh Circuit.[30]

The difficulty in applying the Byrd test probably stemmed from the fact that there is no scale in which the balancing process called for by that case can take place. There is no way to say with assurance in a particular case that the federal interest asserted is more or less important than the interest in preserving uniformity of result with the state court. Even if there were such a scale, the weights to be put in it must be whatever the judges say they are. Uniformity of procedure among the federal courts is thought "important" by one court but of only "slight" weight by another. There is no objective standard by which it can be said that one of those evaluations is "wrong" and the other "right."

Perhaps because of these difficulties, the Court again turned its attention to this problem in 1965 in Hanna v. Plumer.[31] All of the fears that the Civil Rules might be limited or made ineffective by Erie were laid to rest, as the Court denounced "the incorrect assumption that the rule of Erie R. Co. v. Tompkins constitutes the appropriate test of the validity and therefore the applicability of a Federal Rule of Civil Procedure." [32] Cases that had seemed to put the rules in jeopardy were explained on the ground that "the holding of each such case was not that Erie commanded displacement of a Federal Rule by an inconsistent state rule, but rather that the scope of the Federal Rule was not as broad as the losing party urged, and therefore, there being no Federal Rule which covered the point in dispute, Erie commanded the enforcement of state law." [33]

Thus Hanna announces a bifurcated test. If one of the Civil Rules (or a statute) is valid and if, properly construed, it speaks to the question, it is controlling and no regard need be paid to contrary state provisions. " * * * [T]he court has been instructed to apply the Federal Rule, and can refuse to do so only if the Advisory Committee, this Court, and Congress erred in their prima facie judgment that the Rule in question transgressed neither the terms of the Enabling Act nor constitutional restrictions." [34]

The matter is very different if there is no rule directly in point and the court must make "the typical, relatively unguided Erie choice." [35] Such questions cannot be resolved by a talismanic analysis of whether the outcome would be affected. Instead the problem must be

30. Compare Arrowsmith v. United Press Intl., C.A.2d, 1963, 320 F.2d 219, 226, and Iovino v. Waterson, C.A.2d, 1959, 274 F.2d 41, 48, certiorari denied 80 S.Ct. 860, 362 U.S. 949, 4 L.Ed.2d 867, with Jaftex Corp. v. Randolph Mills, Inc., C.A.2d, 1960, 282 F.2d 508, 515–516, and Allstate Ins. Co. v. Charneski, C.A.7th, 1960, 286 F.2d 238, 244.

31. 1965, 85 S.Ct. 1136, 380 U.S. 460, 14 L.Ed.2d 8.

32. 85 S.Ct. at 1143, 380 U.S. at 469–470.

33. 85 S.Ct. at 1143, 380 U.S. at 470.

34. 85 S.Ct. at 1144, 380 U.S. at 471. See 19 Wright, Miller & Cooper, Jurisdiction § 4508.

35. 85 S.Ct. at 1144, 380 U.S. at 471.

viewed in the light of "the twin aims of the Erie rule; discouragement of forum-shopping and avoidance of inequitable administration of the laws." [36]

Each half of the Hanna test leaves significant questions unanswered. The first half of the test, that a valid Civil Rule is to be applied without more, frees the federal courts from Erie concerns in many cases and, in addition, provides the Civil Rules with a presumptive validity if not quite an automatic seal of approval. At the same time this portion of Hanna creates an added burden on the Court and those who advise it in the rulemaking process. In formulating a rule the rulemakers must now consider the extent to which application of a proposed rule, in cases where state law is different, is consistent with the proper ordering of the federal system.[37] As Professor Ronan E. Degnan has put it, the implication of Hanna is not that the federal rules are valid because wise men made them, but because wise men thought carefully before making them.[38]

Under this part of Hanna, a rule is to be applied only if it is valid. Hanna seems to state an easy test: anything that is arguably procedural, in that it falls "within the uncertain area between substance and procedure," [39] is a valid rule. There is reason, however, to think that this states only the constitutional limits on the power of Congress—or the Court as its rulemaking delegate—to make rules of procedure, and that the proviso in the Rules Enabling Act that rules "shall not abridge, enlarge or modify any substantive right" [40] imposes a further, more stringent limitation.[41]

36. 85 S.Ct. at 1142, 380 U.S. at 468.

37. " * * * [A] court, in measuring a Federal Rule against the standards contained in the Enabling Act and the Constitution, need not wholly blind itself to the degree to which the Rule makes the character and result of the federal litigation stray from the course it would follow in state courts * * * ." 85 S.Ct. at 1145, 380 U.S. at 473.

Wright, Procedural Reform: Its Limitations and Its Future, 1967, 1 Ga.L.Rev. 563, 571–574.

38. Quoted in Wright, note 37 above, at 574.

See also Ely, note 4 above, arguing that the Court has failed to give sufficient meaning to the second sentence of the Rules Enabling Act, 28 U.S.C.A. § 2072, providing that the rules "shall not abridge, enlarge or modify any substantive right * * * ."

39. 85 S.Ct. at 1144, 380 U.S. at 472.

40. 28 U.S.C.A. § 2072.

41. 19 Wright, Miller & Cooper, Jurisdiction § 4509; Westen & Lehman, Is

There Life for Erie after the Death of Diversity?, 1980, 78 Mich.L.Rev. 311, 360–364; Mishkin, The Thread, 1974, 87 Harv.L.Rev. 1682; Ely, note 5 above, at 718–720; McCoid, note 1 above, at 901–903.

In a thoughtful opinion it is held that for purposes of the Enabling Act, a state rule is "substantive" only if it is one "which, if all the facts were stipulated, would be meaningful in analyzing the rights and liabilities of parties to a dispute if they were to settle it on the day of filing suit, taking into account the necessity of filing suit, but without actually filing it." Boggs v. Blue Diamond Coal Co., D.C.Ky.1980, 497 F.Supp. 1105, 1120, noted 1981, 11 Mem.St.U.L.Rev. 413. On this analysis it was held that the time allowed in Rule 25(a) for substitution after death is a valid procedural rule, "because immediately prior to filing the suit the parties would not consider this rule in evaluating their rights and liabilities." 497 F.Supp. at 1121.

But see McCollum Aviation, Inc. v. CIM Associates, Inc., D.C.Fla.1977, 438

⠄⠂⠄ A testing case—and one that has given the courts much difficulty—is Rule 15(c), which provides that if the conditions stated in it are satisfied a defendant can be added to an action by amendment even if the applicable statute of limitations has run in the interim between the filing of the original complaint and the filing of the amendment. Application of Rule 15(c) will mean in some instances that the action can go forward against the new defendant even though in state court he would have a good defense of limitations. In this situation the courts have uniformly held, and properly so, that Rule 15(c) can be applied and that to do so does not violate the "substantive rights" proviso of the Enabling Act.[42]

It is the other application of Rule 15(c) that has caused more difficulty. One of the conditions of that rule is that the party to be added must have received such notice of the institution of the original action within the limitations period that he will not be prejudiced in maintaining a defense and that he must have known or had reason to know that, except for a mistake concerning the identity of the proper party, the action would have been brought against him. Some states have more liberal views on amendments to add parties and would find the statute of limitations not to be a bar even though that condition has not been met. Here the better view is that the amendment should be allowed, as permitted by state law, even though Rule 15(c) seemingly does not authorize it.[43] If a state should provide that the filing of a complaint against the wrong defendant tolls the running of the statute of limitations against the correct defendant, a federal court would apply the state's tolling provision.[44] It would honor the state's policy decision that a potential defendant's sense of repose is not so important as to prevent resolution on the merits of state

F.Supp. 245. A Florida statute providing that a corporation transaction business in the state cannot sue in Florida courts unless it has obtained authority to transact business in the state must be applied in federal court since it is highly influential in the choice of forum and has the substantive purpose of encouraging corporation qualification for the benefit of the people of the state. Thus it controls over Rule 17(b)

42. Welch v. Louisiana Power & Light Co., C.A.5th, 1972, 466 F.2d 1344; Loudenslager v. Teeple, C.A.3d, 1972, 466 F.2d 249; Swartzwelder v. Hamilton, D.C.Pa.1972, 56 F.R.D. 606; Meredith v. United Airlines, D.C.Cal.1966, 41 F.R.D. 34, 39. See also Hageman v. Signal L. P. Gas, Inc., C.A.6th, 1973, 486 F.2d 479, 483–485.

For a highly debatable application of Rule 15(c) to allow relation back to cure lack of capacity of a plaintiff when state law would not do so, see Davis v. Piper Aircraft Corp., C.A.4th,

1980, 615 F.2d 606, certiorari dismissed 101 S.Ct. 25, 448 U.S. 911, 65 L.Ed.2d 1141.

43. Marshall v. Mulrenin, C.A.1st, 1974, 508 F.2d 39, noted 1975, 9 Akron L.Rev. 199, 50 N.Y.U.L.Rev. 952; Covel v. Safetech, Inc., D.C.Mass.1981, 90 F.R.D. 427; Carmouche v. Bethlehem Steel Corp., D.C.Nev.1978, 450 F.Supp. 1361; cf. Ingram v. Kumar, C.A.2d, 1978, 585 F.2d 566, certiorari denied 99 S.Ct. 1289, 440 U.S. 940, 59 L.Ed.2d 499.

Contra: Britt v. Arvantis, C.A.3d, 1978, 590 F.2d 57; Williams v. Avis Transport of Canada, Ltd., D.C.Nev.1972, 57 F.R.D. 53.

44. Rumberg v. Weber Aircraft Corp., D.C.Cal.1976, 424 F.Supp. 294; Williams v. U. S., D.C.La.1973, 353 F.Supp. 1226; cf. Hernas v. City of Hickory Hills, D.C.Ill.1981, 507 F.Supp. 103.

causes of action simply because of an excusable mistake in the denomination of the defendant. The result should not be different because the state has chosen to cast the same policy decision in terms of relation back of amendments rather than of tolling of the statute of limitations.[45]

Even if the Civil Rule in question is clearly valid, both in terms of the Constitution and, in the circumstances of the particular case, in terms of the Enabling Act, it still must be decided whether it speaks to the precise issue before the court. A good illustration is the controversy about the continuing vitality of the Ragan case. The holding in Ragan, it will be recalled, was that the mere filing of a complaint with the court is not enough to satisfy a state statute of limitations if the state law makes service within the statutory period essential. This holding was reached despite Rule 3, which provides that an action is commenced by filing a complaint with the court.

In Hanna the Court was at pains to distinguish Ragan as a case in which "the scope of the Federal Rule was not as broad as the losing party urged."[46] Even so, some lower courts thought that Hanna had silently overruled Ragan.[47] In 1980, in Walker v. Armco Steel Corporation,[48] the Court was confronted with facts indistinguishable from those in Ragan, and it unanimously reaffirmed Ragan. Rule 3, it reasoned, does not speak to state statutes of limitations. "There is no indication that the Rule was intended to toll a state statute of limitations, much less that it purported to displace state tolling rules for purposes of state statutes of limitations. In our view, in diversity actions Rule 3 governs the date from which various timing requirements of the federal rules begin to run, but does not affect state statutes of limitations."[49] By a similar analysis Rule 23.1 (formerly Rule 23(b)) on derivative actions does not speak to whether plaintiffs can be required to give security for expenses[50] and Rule 4, though prescribing how to serve process on a foreign corporation, is silent on when a foreign corporation is amenable to suit.[51] In each of these

---

45. 19 Wright, Miller & Cooper, Jurisdiction § 4509, pp. 152–160.

46. 85 S.Ct. at 1143, 380 U.S. at 469–470.
The Court, in drawing this distinction, relied primarily on Palmer v. Hoffman, 1943, 63 S.Ct. 477, 482, 318 U.S. 109, 117, 87 L.Ed. 645, where it had held that Rule 8(c) governs the manner of pleading affirmative defenses, but that it is silent on burden of proof and that state law controls on that issue.

47. Sylvestri v. Warner & Swasey Co., C.A.2d, 1968, 398 F.2d 598; and cases cited 19 Wright, Miller & Cooper, Jurisdiction § 4510 n. 10.

48. 1980, 100 S.Ct. 1978, 446 U.S. 740, 64 L.Ed.2d 659, noted 1981, 66 Cornell L.Rev. 842, 11 Cum.L.Rev. 709, 19 Duq.L.Rev. 557; 1981, 5 U.Puget Sound L.Rev. 307. See Diffurth, Rule 3, The Enabling Act, and Statutes of Limitations, 1981 S.Ill.U.L.J. 329.

49. 100 S.Ct. at 1985, 446 U.S. at 750–751.

50. Cohen v. Beneficial Indus. Loan Corp., 1949, 69 S.Ct. 1221, 337 U.S. 541, 93 L.Ed. 1528. See § 73 below.

51. Arrowsmith v. United Press Intl., C.A.2d, 1963, 320 F.2d 219. See § 64 below.

instances the courts, finding the Civil Rule not to be in point,[52] have gone to the second half of the Hanna test and have held that state law applies.

In the absence of a valid Civil Rule addressing the point, the second half of Hanna requires courts to consider the problem in the light of "the twin aims of the Erie rule: discouragement of forum-shopping and avoidance of inequitable administration of the laws."[53] Although many courts have simply applied the Hanna formulae without further discussion, other courts have felt that these issues require some further refinement of analysis, and that it is necessary to balance the strength of the competing federal and state interests.[54] Byrd v. Blue Ridge has not been overruled, nor its interest-balancing technique repudiated, and, when faced with the typical, relatively unguided Erie choice, its approach has been found useful.[55]

---

52. See 19 Wright, Miller & Cooper, Jurisdiction § 4510.

53. 85 S.Ct. at 1144, 380 U.S. at 471.

54. 19 Wright, Miller & Cooper, Jurisdiction § 4511. See also Redish & Phillips, Erie and the Rules of Decision Act: In Search of the Appropriate Dilemma, 1977, 91 Harv.L.Rev. 356.

"[W]e must approach a problem such as is presented by the instant case by considering how the constitutional and policy concerns that motivated the Court in Erie and its progeny are implicated by the application or nonapplication of the particular state rule at issue. * * * [T]hese concerns include (1) the effect of application of the state or federal rule on the outcome of the litigation; (2) the likelihood that divergent state and federal rules will result in forum shopping; and (3) the existence of any overriding federal interest in the application of the federal rule." Jarvis v. Johnson, C.A.3d, 1982, 668 F.2d 740, 743–744.

55. The following are a few well-known cases using some form of the approach described in the text:

Szantay v. Beech Aircraft Corp., C.A.4th, 1965, 349 F.2d 60, notes 1965, 17 S.C.L. Rev. 631, 1966, 51 Cornell L.Q. 560. The court refused to apply a state's "door-closing statute" where to do so would not further any important state policy but would frustrate the federal interest in encouraging efficient joinder in multi-party actions and the interest in providing a convenient forum for plaintiff's action. Szantay has been distinguished in two later Fourth Circuit decisions: Bumgardner v. Keene Corp., C.A.4th, 1979, 593 F.2d 572; Proctor & Schwartz, Inc. v. Rollins,

C.A.4th, 1980, 634 F.2d 738. It was followed in rather exotic circumstances in Miller v. Davis, C.A.6th, 1974, 507 F.2d 308. See Leathers, Miller v. Davis: The Sixth Circuit Applies Interest Analysis to an Erie Problem, 1975, 63 Ky.L.J. 923.

Atkins v. Schmutz Mfg. Co., C.A.4th, 1970, 435 F.2d 527, certiorari denied 91 S.Ct. 1526, 402 U.S. 932, 28 L.Ed.2d 867, noted 1971, 50 Texas L.Rev. 162, 1971 Duke L.J. 785. It was held that the pendency of suit in another federal court tolled the state statute of limitations though it would not have done so in state court. See the lucid analysis of Atkins by Professor Ward in Tribute to The Honorable Clement F. Haynsworth, Jr., 1981, 665 F.2d lxxiii, lxxxviii–xc.

Goodman v. Mead Johnson & Co., C.A.3d, 1976, 534 F.2d 566, certiorari denied 97 S.Ct. 732, 429 U.S. 1038, 50 L.Ed.2d 748. A federal jury should decide when plaintiff knew or should have known that she had an actionable claim, although the state had held that application of the "discovery" exception to the statute of limitations is for the court and not the jury. Compare Justice v. Pennzoil Co., C.A.4th, 1979, 598 F.2d 1339, certiorari denied 100 S.Ct. 457, 444 U.S. 967, 62 L.Ed.2d 380, holding that state rules governed the allocation of judge and jury functions to a question of what constitutes unreasonable use of land by a mineral owner.

Hargrave v. OKI Nursery, Inc., C.A.2d, 1980, 646 F.2d 716. A defendant brought in under a state long-arm statute on a claim of fraud must defend also other claims dealing with breach of

In his concurring opinion in Hanna Justice Harlan said: "It is unquestionably true that up to now Erie and the cases following it have not succeeded in articulating a workable doctrine governing choice of law in diversity actions." [56] This is still true even after Hanna. Quite possibly this is inevitable in the nature of the Erie problem. Erie and its progeny recognize that the choice of law to be applied in the federal courts in diversity cases is an important question of federalism, and that the constitutional power of the states to regulate the relations among their people does overlap the constitutional power of the federal government to determine how its courts are to be operated.[57] Where these interests come into conflict, there can be no wholly satisfactory answer.[58] This is hardly a problem unique to questions of jurisdiction, as anyone who has read, for example, the long line of virtually irreconcilable cases on the power of the states to tax businesses engaged in interstate commerce will attest. There may be no alternative but to leave questions such as these for the ad hoc determination of judges keenly aware of their responsibilities to two sovereigns.[59]

§ 60.   The Erie Doctrine—Federal Common Law [1]

In the Erie case, Justice Brandeis wrote: "Except in matters governed by the Federal Constitution or by acts of Congress, the law to

---

contract and warranty, although in state court jurisdiction would extend to the fraud claim only.

Feinstein v. Massachusetts Gen. Hosp., C.A.1st, 1981, 643 F.2d 880. Federal plaintiff must comply with a state statutory procedure referring malpractice claims to a special tribunal before a claimant is permitted to pursue a judicial remedy. But see Hibbs v. Yashar, D.C.R.I.1981, 522 F.Supp. 247.

56. 85 S.Ct. at 1145, 380 U.S. at 474. The test Justice Harlan proposed would be to inquire "if the choice of rule would substantially effect those primary decisions respecting human conduct which our constitutional system leaves to state regulation." 85 S.Ct. at 1146, 380 U.S. at 475. With respect, that too would be a difficult and imprecise test to apply. For a view similar to that of Justice Harlan, see Note, note 1 above.

57. See § 56 above.

58. "It is, of course, neither possible nor necessary for federal courts to be totally neutral in the adjudication of state-created rights. It is not possible simply because federal courts are not protean and are unable to transform themselves into exact replicas of their state counterparts. That state and federal judicial systems are not identical will inevitably mean that the choice of forum will have some effect upon the course of litigation. Some adoption of state court procedures by federal courts sitting in diversity may be feasible, but it may also be in conflict with fundamental interests of the federal courts in the conduct of their own business and the maintenance of the integrity of their own procedures, the legitimate interests of a federal forum *qua* forum." Atkins v. Schmutz Mfg. Co., C.A.4th, 1970, 435 F.2d 527, 536, certiorari denied 91 S.Ct. 1526, 402 U.S. 932, 28 L.Ed.2d 867.

59. The view put forward in the text has been rejected as a "free-wheeling approach" that is "too ad hoc to allow the development of meaningful legal categories by which men may judge their everyday affairs * * *." Note, The Operation of Federalism in Diversity Jurisdiction: Erie's Constitutional Basis, 1965, 40 Ind.L.J. 512, 538–539.

[§ 60]

1. 19 Wright, Miller & Cooper, Jurisdiction § 4514; Redish, Federal Jurisdiction: Tensions in the Allocation of Judicial Power, 1980, c. 4; Hill, The Law-Making Power of the Federal Courts:

be applied in any case is the law of the state. * * * There is no federal general common law." [2] On that same day, in another case, Justice Brandeis, again speaking for the Court, wrote that "whether the water of an interstate stream must be apportioned between the two States is a question of 'federal common law' upon which neither the statutes nor the decisions of either State can be conclusive." [3]

It is clear, therefore, that there is a "federal common law" even if not a "federal general common law." It is not accurate to say, however, that the law of the state is to be applied in all cases except on matters governed by the Constitution or by Act of Congress. Neither the Constitution nor any statute provides the answer to controversies between states about interstate streams, or similar interstate conflicts, nor do these sources indicate where the governing law is to be found. Yet the Court, of necessity, has developed its own body of law to govern such questions, because of the obvious unsuitability of looking to the law of a particular state when two states are in dispute.[4]

It is clear that where the Constitution, or a valid Act of Congress, provides a rule of decision, it must be applied by a federal court—and by a state court—in cases where there is concurrent jurisdiction.[5] Beyond that very little is clear. Whether state law or federal law controls on matters not covered by the Constitution or an Act of Congress is a very complicated question, which yields to no simple answer in terms of the parties to the suit, the basis of jurisdiction, or

Constitutional Preemption, 1967, 67 Col.L.Rev. 1024; Friendly, In Praise of Erie—And of the New Federal Common Law, 1964, 39 N.Y.U.L.Rev. 383; Mishkin, The Variousness of "Federal Law": Competence and Discretion in the Choice of National and State Rules for Decision, 1957, 105 U.Pa.L.Rev. 797; Hart, The Relations Between State and Federal Law, 1954, 54 Col.L. Rev. 489; Note, The Federal Common Law, 1969, 82 Harv.L.Rev. 1512.

2. Erie R. Co. v. Tompkins, 1938, 58 S.Ct. 817, 822, 304 U.S. 64, 78, 82 L.Ed. 1188.

3. Hinderlider v. La Plata River & Cherry Creek Ditch Co., 1938, 58 S.Ct. 803, 811, 304 U.S. 92, 110, 82 L.Ed. 1202.

4. Kansas v. Colorado, 1902, 22 S.Ct. 552, 185 U.S. 125, 46 L.Ed. 838; Kansas v. Colorado, 1907, 27 S.Ct. 655, 206 U.S. 46, 51 L.Ed. 956; Kentucky v. Indiana, 1930, 50 S.Ct. 275, 281 U.S. 163, 74 L.Ed. 784; Connecticut v. Massachusetts, 1931, 51 S.Ct. 286, 289–290, 282 U.S. 660, 670–671, 75 L.Ed. 602; West Virginia ex rel. Dyer v. Sims, 1951, 71 S.Ct. 557, 341 U.S. 22, 95 L.Ed. 713; Texas v. New Jersey, 1965, 85 S.Ct. 626, 379 U.S. 674, 13 L.Ed.2d

596; Illinois v. City of Milwaukee, 1972, 92 S.Ct. 1385, 406 U.S. 91, 31 L.Ed.2d 712; Note, What Rule of Decision Should Control in Interstate Controversies, 1907, 21 Harv.L.Rev. 132. See § 109 below.

See, however, the suggestion of Judge Friendly that it is indeed the Constitution that requires the federal courts to fashion law when the interstate nature of a controversy makes it inappropriate that the law of either state should govern. Friendly, note 1 above, at 408 n. 119.

There is an even more surprising suggestion by Professor Westen that the Rules of Decision Act, 28 U.S.C.A. § 1652, should be read as if it said "Acts of Congress or federal common law." Westen, After "Life for Erie"— A Reply, 1980, 78 Mich.L.Rev. 971, 989. See also Westen & Lehman, Is There Life for Erie After the Death of Diversity?, 1980, 78 Mich.L.Rev. 311, 369–370. For a forceful statement of the contrary view, see Redish, Continuing the Erie Debate: A Response to Westen and Lehman, 1980, 78 Mich.L. Rev. 959, 963–964.

5. See § 45 above.

the source of the right that is to be enforced.[6] Whenever the federal court is free to decide for itself the rule to be applied, and there are many such situations, it is applying, or making, "federal common law."

In a much-admired concurring opinion in D'Oench, Duhme & Co. v. Federal Deposit Insurance Corporation,[7] Justice Jackson said: "A federal court sitting in a non-diversity case such as this does not sit as a local tribunal. In some cases it may see fit for special reasons to give the law of a particular state highly persuasive or even controlling effect, but in the last analysis its decision turns upon the law of the United States, not that of any state. Federal law is no juridical chameleon changing complexion to match that of each state wherein lawsuits happen to be commenced because of the accidents of service of process and of the application of the venue statutes. It is found in the federal Constitution, statutes, or common law. Federal common law implements the federal Constitution and statutes, and is conditioned by them. Within these limits, federal courts are free to apply the traditional common-law technique of decision and to draw upon sources of the common law in cases such as the present." In the D'Oench, Duhme case the issue was whether the accommodation maker of a note could assert a defense of no consideration in a suit by a federal agency to which the note had been assigned. The Court was unanimous in holding that he could not, apparently as a matter of independent decision of what the federal rule should be, although the other opinions are less lucid as to the source of the governing rule than is Justice Jackson's.

A somewhat similar case, and perhaps the best known case in this area, is Clearfield Trust Co. v. United States.[8] A check issued by the United States had been stolen, and cashed on the basis of a forged endorsement. The United States sued a bank that had presented the check for payment and had guaranteed prior endorsements. Under the law of Pennsylvania, where the transaction took place, the delay of the United States in notifying the bank that the endorsement was a forgery would bar recovery from the bank, but a unanimous Court held that the rights and duties of the United States on commercial paper that it issues are governed by federal rather than local law. This does not mean that in choosing the applicable federal rule the courts may not occasionally select state law.[9] But it was thought that such a course would be singularly inappropriate in the Clearfield case. "The issuance of commercial paper by the United States is on a

6. See 19 Wright, Miller & Cooper, Jurisdiction § 4514 at notes 18–20.

7. 1942, 62 S.Ct. 676, 686, 315 U.S. 447, 471–472, 86 L.Ed. 956.

8. 1943, 63 S.Ct. 573, 318 U.S. 363, 87 L.Ed. 838.

9. See Board of County Commrs. v. U. S., 1939, 60 S.Ct. 285, 288–289, 308 U.S. 343, 351–352, 84 L.Ed. 313. It was held there that state law does not control on the right to interest in an action by the United States for taxes improperly collected from an Indian, but that as a matter of choice the state rule would be absorbed and applied as the federal law.

vast scale and transactions in that paper from issuance to payment will commonly occur in several states. The application of state law, even without the conflict of laws rules of the forum, would subject the rights and duties of the United States to exceptional uncertainty. It would lead to great diversity in results by making identical transactions subject to the vagaries of the laws of the several states. The desirability of a uniform rule is plain." [10] To find such a uniform rule the Court looked to the federal law merchant, and found from this that mere delay in giving notice of a forged endorsement does not bar recovery unless there is a clear showing that the delay in giving notice caused damage to the other party. Federal courts have made similar decisions for themselves as to what the controlling rule is to be in other cases where the United States is a party and the suit involves commercial paper issued by the United States,[11] government contracts,[12] or the effect of a federal lien.[13]

A similar principle has been applied in tort cases, with federal law held to determine whether a tortfeasor who injured a soldier is liable to the United States for hospitalization of the soldier and loss of his services.[14] The Court said in that case that the Erie decision was not intended for "broadening state power over matters essentially of federal character or for determining whether issues are of that nature." [15] Federal common law also controls the validity of a defense by a federal officer sued for having committed a tort in the course of his official duties.[16]

The Court has held that "an issue concerned with a basic choice regarding the competence and function of the Judiciary and the Na-

10. 63 S.Ct. at 575, 318 U.S. at 367.

For criticism of this passage, see Friendly, note 1 above, at 410; Note, 1969, 82 Harv.L.Rev. 1512, 1526–1531.

11. National Metropolitan Bank v. U. S., 1945, 65 S.Ct. 354, 323 U.S. 454, 89 L.Ed. 383; Comment, Federal Law of Negotiable Instruments, 1961, 6 Vill.L. Rev. 388.

It has been said that the Uniform Commercial Code should generally be considered as the federal law of commerce. In re King-Porter Co., C.A.5th, 1971, 446 F.2d 722, 732; U. S. v. Wegematic Corp., C.A.2d, 1966, 360 F.2d 674, 676, noted 1966, 20 Sw.L.J. 688; In re Quantum Development Corp., D.C.V.I.1975, 397 F.Supp. 329, 336. But courts have continued to apply the particular rule of commercial paper announced in the National Metropolitan Bank case, above, although the Uniform Commercial Code, now adopted in 49 states, lays down a different rule. U. S. v. City Nat. Bank & Trust Co., C.A.8th, 1974, 491 F.2d 851, 854; U. S. v. Bank of America Nat.

Trust & Sav. Assn., C.A.9th, 1971, 438 F.2d 1213, 1214, certiorari denied 92 S.Ct. 54, 404 U.S. 864, 30 L.Ed.2d 108.

12. U. S. v. Seckinger, 1970, 90 S.Ct. 880, 397 U.S. 203, 25 L.Ed.2d 224; Wissner v. Wissner, 1950, 70 S.Ct. 398, 338 U.S. 655, 94 L.Ed. 424; U. S. v. Standard Rice Co., 1944, 65 S.Ct. 145, 147, 323 U.S. 106, 111, 89 L.Ed. 104; Pofcher, Choice of Law, State or Federal, in Government Contracts, 1951, 12 La.L.Rev. 37; Note, 1952, 27 Ind. L.J. 279.

13. U. S. v. Kimbell Foods, Inc., 1979, 99 S.Ct. 1448, 440 U.S. 715, 59 L.Ed.2d 711; U. S. v. Brosnan, 1960, 80 S.Ct. 1108, 363 U.S. 237, 4 L.Ed.2d 1192; U. S. v. Acri, 1955, 75 S.Ct. 239, 348 U.S. 211, 99 L.Ed. 264.

14. U. S. v. Standard Oil Co., 1947, 67 S.Ct. 1604, 332 U.S. 301, 91 L.Ed. 2067.

15. 67 S.Ct. at 1608, 332 U.S. at 307.

16. Howard v. Lyons, 1959, 79 S.Ct. 1331, 1333, 360 U.S. 593, 597, 3 L.Ed.2d 1454.

tional Executive in ordering our relationships with other members of the international community must be treated exclusively as an aspect of federal law." [17]   It has consistently interpreted the grant of general admiralty jurisdiction to the federal courts as a proper basis for the development of judge-made rules of maritime law.[18]   And in Illinois v. City of Milwaukee,[19] a decision that seemed to some to go very far,[20] the Court rejected its own dictum of barely a year before [21] and held that federal common law controls in an action to abate pollution of interstate or navigable waters.   The significance of that decision proved to be short-lived.   In a later phase of the same litigation the Court held that in legislation six months after the decision Congress implicitly extinguished the common law remedy there recognized.[22]

"Federal common law also may come into play when Congress has vested jurisdiction in the federal courts and empowered them to create governing rules of law." [23]   In the best-known example of this the Court read a statute that on its face only grants jurisdiction to federal courts of suits for violation of contracts between an employer and a labor union [24] as meaning that the substantive law to apply in these suits is federal law, which the courts through judicial inventiveness are to fashion from the policy of the national labor laws.[25]

17.   Banco Nacional de Cuba v. Sabbatino, 1964, 84 S.Ct. 923, 939, 376 U.S. 398, 425, 11 L.Ed.2d 804; Hill, note 1 above, at 1042–1068; Edwards, The Erie Doctrine in Foreign Affairs Cases, 1967, 42 N.Y.U.L.Rev. 42; Moore, Federalism and Foreign Relations, 1965 Duke L.J. 248.   But see Henkin, The Foreign Affairs Power of the Federal Courts: Sabbatino, 1964, 64 Col.L.Rev. 805.

18.   Edmonds v. Compagnie Generale Transatlantique, 1979, 99 S.Ct. 2753, 443 U.S. 256, 61 L.Ed.2d 521; Cooper Stevedoring Co. v. Fritz Kopke, Inc., 1974, 94 S.Ct. 2174, 417 U.S. 106, 40 L.Ed.2d 694; Fitzgerald v. United States Lines Co., 1963, 83 S.Ct. 1646, 374 U.S. 16, 10 L.Ed.2d 720; Southern Pac. Co. v. Jensen, 1917, 37 S.Ct. 524, 244 U.S. 205, 61 L.Ed. 1086.   See Redish, note 1 above, at 97–105; Robertson, Admiralty and Federalism, 1970.

19.   1972, 92 S.Ct. 1385, 406 U.S. 91, 31 L.Ed.2d 712.   See Comment, The Expansion of Federal Common Law and Federal Question Jurisdiction to Interstate Pollution, 1972, 10 Hous.L.Rev. 121; Note, Federal Common Law and Interstate Pollution, 1972, 85 Harv.L. Rev. 1439.

20.   See Currie, Federal Courts: Cases and Materials, 2d ed. 1975, p. 882: "What's left of the Erie case now?   In one respect Milwaukee goes beyond even Swift v. Tyson; for in Swift it was possible to argue that the power to create federal law was implicit in the grant of diversity jurisdiction, while in Milwaukee the District Court's jurisdiction existed only if there was federal common law."

21.   Ohio v. Wyandotte Chemicals Corp., 1971, 91 S.Ct. 1005, 1009 n. 3, 401 U.S. 493, 498 n. 3, 28 L.Ed.2d 256.

22.   City of Milwaukee v. Illinois and Michigan, 1981, 101 S.Ct. 1784, 451 U.S. 304, 68 L.Ed.2d 114.

23.   Texas Indus., Inc. v. Radcliff Materials, Inc., 1981, 101 S.Ct. 2061, 2068, 451 U.S. 630, 642, 68 L.Ed.2d 500.

24.   29 U.S.C.A. § 185(a).

25.   Textile Workers Union of America v. Lincoln Mills of Alabama, 1957, 77 S.Ct. 912, 353 U.S. 448, 1 L.Ed.2d 972. See Bickel & Wellington, Legislative Purpose and the Judicial Process: The Lincoln Mills Case, 1957, 71 Harv.L. Rev. 1.   The decision is defended in Note, 1969, 82 Harv.L.Rev. 1512, 1531–1535.

If an issue is controlled by federal common law, this is binding on both state and federal courts.[26] A case "arising under" federal common law is a federal question case, and is within the original jurisdiction of the federal courts as such.[27]

The burgeoning of a federal common law binding on federal and state courts alike occurred at the same time as the development of the Erie doctrine, and these two simultaneous developments are probably more than coincidental. Although one distinguished commentator waxed rhapsodic in his praise of the two taken together,[28] others were less enthusiastic and fears were expressed that the doctrine of federal common law meant that "further inroads may be made upon the clear provisions of the Rules of Decision Act on vague grounds of federal interest." [29] A few extreme decisions from courts of appeals gave substance to such fears. In one it was held that the federal interest in telephone companies is so strong and the legislation regulating such companies is so comprehensive that federal common law gives a remedy for tort or breach of contract against these carriers though the statutes provide no such remedy, either expressly or implicitly.[30] Another very questionable decision from a court of appeals held that the predominant interest of the federal government in regulating the nation's airways justifies application, as a matter of federal common law, of a rule that there is a right to contribution and indem-

26. Free v. Bland, 1962, 82 S.Ct. 1089, 369 U.S. 663, 8 L.Ed.2d 180; Yiatchos v. Yiatchos, 1964, 84 S.Ct. 742, 376 U.S. 306, 11 L.Ed.2d 724, noted 1965, 38 So. Cal.L.Rev. 335; Local 174, Teamsters, Chauffeurs, Warehousemen & Helpers of America v. Lucas Flour Co., 1962, 82 S.Ct. 571, 369 U.S. 95, 7 L.Ed.2d 593; Banco Nacional de Cuba v. Sabbatino, 1964, 84 S.Ct. 923, 939, 376 U.S. 398, 426, 11 L.Ed.2d 804. See Comment, The State Courts and the Federal Common Law, 1963, 27 Albany L.Rev. 73.

27. Illinois v. City of Milwaukee, 1972, 92 S.Ct. 1385, 406 U.S. 91, 31 L.Ed.2d 712. This view had been anticipated in Ivy Broadcasting Co. v. American Tel. & Tel. Co., C.A.2d, 1968, 391 F.2d 486, 492–493. See also Comment, Federal Common Law and Article III: A Jurisdictional Approach to Erie, 1964, 74 Yale L.J. 325.

28. "The complementary concepts—that federal courts must follow state decisions on matters of substantive law appropriately cognizable by the states whereas state courts must follow federal decisions on subjects within national legislative power where Congress has so directed—seems so beautifully simple, and so simply beautiful, that we must wonder why a century and a half were needed to discover them, and must wonder even more why anyone should want to shy away once the discovery was made. We may not yet have achieved the best of all possible worlds with respect to the relationship between state and federal law. But the combination of Erie with Clearfield and Lincoln Mills has brought us to a far, far better one than we have ever known before." Friendly, note 1 above, at 422.

29. Currie, Federal Jurisdiction in a Nutshell, 2d ed. 1981, p. 244. See also Comment, The Invalid Growth of the New Federal Common Law Dictates the Need for a Second Erie, 1971, 9 Hous.L.Rev. 329.

30. Ivy Broadcasting Co. v. American Tel. & Tel. Co., C.A.2d, 1968, 391 F.2d 486, noted 1968, 37 Geo.Wash.L.Rev. 425, 82 Harv.L.Rev. 479, 43 Tul.L.Rev. 168, 1969, 47 N.C.L.Rev. 447. The commentators were generally critical, and one went so far as to call the decision "a pernicious sub rosa attack on state substantive law * * *." 35 Geo.Wash.L.Rev. at 431.

nity, on a comparative negligence basis, among joint tortfeasors in aviation collision cases.[31]

The Court, however, more recently has taken a cautious course toward the recognition of federal common law. It has emphasized that federal common law is appropriate in only a "few and restricted" instances.[32] " * * * [A]bsent some congressional authorization to formulate substantive rules of decision, federal common law exists only in such narrow areas as those concerned with the rights and obligations of the United States, interstate and international disputes implicating the conflicting rights of States or our relations with foreign nations, and admiralty cases. In these instances, our federal system does not permit the controversy to be resolved under state law, either because the authority and duties of the United States as sovereign are intimately involved or because the interstate or international na-

---

31. Kohr v. Allegheny Airlines, Inc., C.A.7th, 1974, 504 F.2d 400, certiorari denied 95 S.Ct. 1980, 421 U.S. 978, 44 L.Ed.2d 470, noted 1975, 41 J.Air L. & Comm. 347, 6 Sw.U.L.Rev. 661, 28 Vand.L.Rev. 621.

Professor Currie's comment on the Kohr decision is: "Much the same could have been said, of course, as to interstate railroads in Erie itself." Currie, Federal Jurisdiction in a Nutshell, 2d ed. 1981, p. 244. See also Redish, note 1 above, at 93–94.

It seems inconceivable that Kohr can have survived Miree v. DeKalb County, 1977, 97 S.Ct. 2490, 433 U.S. 25, 53 L.Ed.2d 557. A unanimous Court there held that state law, rather than federal common law, governed whether victims of an air crash could sue as third-party beneficiaries of a contract between the county, which owned the airport where the crash occurred, and the Federal Aviation Administration. The Court found the substantial interest of the United States in regulating aircraft travel and promoting air safety insufficient to make federal common law appropriate, and said "the issue of whether to displace state law on an issue such as this is primarily a decision for Congress. Congress has chosen not to do so in this case." 97 S.Ct. at 2495, 433 U.S. at 32. Nevertheless, Kohr is cited in Northwest Airlines, Inc. v. Transport Workers Union of America, 1981, 101 S.Ct. 1571, 1580, 451 U.S. 77, 90–91, 67 L.Ed.2d 750.

32. City of Milwaukee v. Illinois and Michigan, 1981, 101 S.Ct. 1784, 1790, 451 U.S. 304, 313, 68 L.Ed.2d 114, quoting Wheeldin v. Wheeler, 1963, 83 S.Ct.

1441, 1445, 373 U.S. 647, 651, 10 L.Ed. 2d 605.

An instructive earlier case is Bank of America Nat. Trust & Sav. Assn. v. Parnell, 1956, 77 S.Ct. 119, 352 U.S. 29, 1 L.Ed.2d 93. This was a diversity action between private parties but involving United States bonds. The bank was suing Parnell to recover money he had obtained by cashing bonds that had been stolen from the bank. One issue was whether the bonds, which were not yet to mature but which had been called by the government, were "overdue." The other issue was whether Parnell had acted in good faith in redeeming the bonds, and whether he had the burden of proving good faith or the bank had the burden of proving lack of it. It was held that whether the bonds were "overdue" concerned the interpretation of the nature of the rights and obligations created by the government bonds themselves, and was controlled by federal law, but that the burden of proof of good faith represented essentially a private transaction to be dealt with by the local law of the state where the transactions took place.

See also Wallis v. Pan American Petroleum Corp., 1966, 86 S.Ct. 1301, 384 U.S. 63, 16 L.Ed.2d 369, holding that conflicting private claims to federal lands leased under the Mineral Leasing Act of 1920 were governed by state law rather than federal law. The Court could discern "no significant threat to any identifiable federal policy or interest * * *." 86 S.Ct. at 1304, 384 U.S. at 68.

ture of the controversy makes it inappropriate for state law to control." [33]

An issue that seems quite similar to that of federal common law is determining when it is appropriate to find an implied federal right of action for damages from an Act of Congress, although the Court treats these as being "two quite different theories." [34] Although the cases are not all one way, the more recent decisions have shown a reluctance to infer remedies that Congress has not given.[35]

In federal question cases, it may be that the federal statute or constitutional provision in question sets out the applicable rule. In such a case, this rule must, of course, be applied regardless of state law. Sometimes the federal statute will direct that state law be applied, as is the case with the Federal Tort Claims Act,[36] and in such a case the state rule will control regardless of the federal interest in the matter. "The variousness of federal law," to use Professor Mishkin's apt phrase,[37] is present when the federal statute is silent on a particular issue. Here the federal court must choose whether to incorporate state law to resolve that issue, or to fashion an independent federal doctrine for it. Quite commonly, for example, federal statutes will create a right of action without stating the time within which such action must be brought. The usual rule in such situations is to apply whatever statute of limitations the state has for analogous types of suits.[38] If the case were subject to the Erie doctrine, then the state limitations doctrine would have to be applied in its full force.[39] The Erie doctrine does not apply, and the federal court has much more freedom, where the state rule has merely been absorbed

33. Texas Indus., Inc. v. Radcliff Materials, Inc., 1981, 101 S.Ct. 2061, 2067, 451 U.S. 630, 641, 68 L.Ed.2d 500.

34. Northwest Airlines, Inc. v. Transport Workers Union of America, 1981, 101 S.Ct. 1571, 1578, 451 U.S. 77, 86, 67 L.Ed.2d 750. See also Texas Indus., Inc. v. Radcliff Materials, Inc., 1981, 101 S.Ct. 2061, 2066, 451 U.S. 630, 638, 68 L.Ed.2d 500; Middlesex County Sewage Auth. v. National Sea Clammers Assn., 1981, 101 S.Ct. 2615, 2627, 453 U.S. 1, 21, 69 L.Ed.2d 435.

35. See § 17 above at note 29, 30. See also 19 Wright, Miller & Cooper, Jurisdiction § 4514, pp. 238–245.

36. 28 U.S.C.A. §§ 1346(b), 2672. As the latter section shows, Congress has rejected local law, and set out a measure of damages of its own, in those two states where punitive damages are the only damages recoverable for wrongful death. Massachusetts Bonding & Ins. Co. v. U. S., 1956, 77 S.Ct. 186, 352 U.S. 128, 1 L.Ed.2d 189.

37. Mishkin, The Variousness of "Federal Law": Competence and Discretion in the Choice of National and State Rules for Decision, 1957, 105 U.Pa.L. Rev. 797.

38. Campbell v. City of Haverhill, 1895, 15 S.Ct. 217, 155 U.S. 610, 39 L.Ed. 280; Cope v. Anderson, 1947, 67 S.Ct. 1340, 331 U.S. 461, 91 L.Ed. 1602; Johnson v. Railway Exp. Agency, Inc., 1975, 95 S.Ct. 1716, 1721–1723, 421 U.S. 454, 462–466, 44 L.Ed.2d 295; Blume & George, Limitations and the Federal Courts, 1951, 49 Mich.L.Rev. 937; Note, Federal Statutes Without Limitations Provisions, 1953, 53 Col.L. Rev. 68.

The same result may be reached where the claim is one controlled by federal common law. Intl. Union, United Automobile, Aerospace & Agric. Implement Workers v. Hoosier Cardinal Corp., 1966, 86 S.Ct. 1107, 383 U.S. 696, 16 L.Ed.2d 192.

39. Guaranty Trust Co. of New York v. York, 1945, 65 S.Ct. 1464, 326 U.S. 99, 89 L.Ed. 2079.

as the relevant federal rule. This is illustrated by Holmberg v. Arm-brecht.[40] That was a suit between private parties to enforce the liability imposed upon bank stockholders by the Federal Farm Loan Act. The suit would have been barred by the statute of limitations of New York, where it was brought, but the delay in bringing the suit had been caused by fraud on the part of the defendants. The Court held that the federal equitable rule that a statute of limitations does not begin to run until the fraud has been discovered, which would be read into even an explicit federal statutory limitation, must also be read into the state limitations statute, where suit is on a federal claim.[41]

On some issues in private federal question cases, there may be compelling reasons for ignoring state law and following an independent federal rule, as where Congress has clearly indicated a substantive policy it wishes to have followed, or there are indications of a leaning toward uniformity and there is no significant state interest to be served by absorption of the state law as the rule of decision.[42] In other cases application of the state law may seem the wiser choice.[43] De Sylva v. Ballentine [44] was such a case. The issue there was whether the illegitimate son of a copyright owner is one of the "children" of the owner within the meaning of the copyright statute. The Court recognized that the meaning of the word in the statute is a federal question, but since there is no federal law of domestic rela-

---

40. 1946, 66 S.Ct. 582, 327 U.S. 392, 90 L.Ed. 743.

41. See also Bomar v. Keyes, C.C.A.2d, 1947, 162 F.2d 136, holding that regardless of state law, filing of the complaint tolls the state statute of limitations where suit is on a federal claim. The later decision by the Supreme Court, reaching a different result in a diversity action on a state-created right, Ragan v. Merchants Transfer & Warehouse Co., 1949, 69 S.Ct. 1233, 1235, 337 U.S. 530, 533, 93 L.Ed. 1520, cited and distinguished the Bomar case on the ground that it was a suit to enforce a federal claim. But in Johnson v. Railway Exp. Agency, Inc., 1975, 95 S.Ct. 1716, 421 U.S. 454, 44 L.Ed.2d 295, the timely filing of a complaint of racial discrimination with the Equal Employment Opportunity Commission was held not to toll the state statute of limitations applicable to an action under the Civil Rights Act of 1866, 42 U.S.C.A. § 1981.

42. E.g., Deitrick v. Greaney, 1940, 60 S.Ct. 480, 309 U.S. 190, 84 L.Ed. 694; Dyke v. Dyke, C.A.6th, 1955, 227 F.2d 461. See discussion of these cases by Mishkin, note 19 above, at 814–820.

See also 19 Wright, Miller & Cooper, Jurisdiction § 4514, pp. 263–274; Comment, Adopting State Law as the Fed-eral Rule of Decision: A Proposed Test, 1976, 43 U.Chi.L.Rev. 823.

43. In the following cases it is held that federal law governs an issue but that a uniform national rule is not necessary, and state law is to be looked to so long as it is not discriminatory or in conflict with federal statutes: U. S. v. Kimbell Foods, Inc., 1979, 99 S.Ct. 1448, 440 U.S. 715, 59 L.Ed.2d 711, on remand C.A.5th, 600 F.2d 478 (priority of liens under two federal loan programs); Burks v. Lasker, 1979, 99 S.Ct. 1831, 441 U.S. 471, 60 L.Ed.2d 404 (whether disinterested directors can terminate a stockholders' suit under federal statutes); Wilson v. Omaha Indian Tribe, 1979, 99 S.Ct. 2529, 442 U.S. 653, 61 L.Ed.2d 153, (effect of the change of course of a stream on Indian title to adjoining land).

See also 42 U.S.C.A. § 1988, providing that state law is to be looked to in federal civil rights actions on issues on which the federal statutes are "deficient in the provisions necessary to furnish suitable remedies," so far as state law is not inconsistent with the federal Constitution and laws. See Robertson v. Wegmann, 1978, 98 S.Ct. 1991, 436 U.S. 584, 56 L.Ed.2d 554.

44. 1956, 76 S.Ct. 974, 351 U.S. 570, 100 L.Ed. 1415.

tions, and this is primarily a matter of state concern, the Court thought it best to draw on "the ready-made body of state law" to define what Congress meant by "children." The case shows, however, the greater flexibility that a court has when state law is absorbed, as compared to the Erie-type situations where it is controlling of its own force. The Court said that a state would not be entitled to use the word "children" in a way entirely strange to its ordinary usage, and that only to the extent that there are permissible variations in the ordinary concept of "children" would the state definition be adopted. It also indicated that the federal court is free to decide for itself which state's law is applicable—as it would not be if the Erie doctrine applied [45] —although only one state was involved in the De Sylva case and there was no need to make a conflict of laws decision.

It is frequently said that the Erie doctrine applies only in cases in which jurisdiction is based on diversity of citizenship. Indeed in an action for wrongful death caused by a maritime tort committed on navigable waters, the Court curtly dismissed Erie as "irrelevant," since the district court was exercising its admiralty jurisdiction, even though it was enforcing a state-created right.[46] The Erie doctrine itself may be irrelevant, but as has just been seen, state law is frequently quite relevant though the basis of the jurisdiction is something other than diversity.[47]

At the same time Erie is not always controlling even on clearly "substantive" issues in diversity cases. There is a limited scope for "federal common law" even within the diversity jurisdiction. This is illustrated most clearly by Francis v. Southern Pacific Co.,[48] a wrongful death action for the death of a railroad employee who was riding on a free pass when he was killed. The basis of jurisdiction was diversity. The right of action was created by Utah law, and under that law a railroad is liable for ordinary negligence even to those riding on free passes. Old federal decisions, in the era of Swift v. Tyson, had reached a different result, and had said that if no fare is paid, the railroad is liable only for gross negligence. Since the earliest of those federal decisions, federal statutes had provided extensive regulation of the giving of free passes by railroads, although these statutes are silent as to the tort duties of a railroad to the recipient of such a pass. In these circumstances a majority of the Court held that federal law controlled, and that the federal law was that defined in the old cases. Although at first it appears that here the federal

---

45. See § 57 above.

46. Levinson v. Deupree, 1953, 73 S.Ct. 914, 916, 345 U.S. 648, 651, 97 L.Ed. 1319.

47. " * * * [D]espite repeated statements implying the contrary, it is the *source* of the right sued upon, and not the ground on which federal jurisdiction is founded, which determines the governing law." Maternally Yours,

Inc. v. Your Maternity Shop, Inc., C.A. 2d, 1956, 234 F.2d 538, 540 n. 1. See also Westen & Lehman, note 4 above; 19 Wright, Miller & Cooper, Jurisdiction § 4515.

48. 1948, 68 S.Ct. 611, 333 U.S. 445, 92 L.Ed. 798.

See also Banco Nacional de Cuba v. Sabbatino, 1964, 84 S.Ct. 923, 376 U.S. 398, 11 L.Ed.2d 804.

court is not acting as "another court of the state," in fact the conflict is illusory. Utah law purported to create liability for ordinary negligence but on this point the state law had been superseded by the federal common law to the contrary.

The Francis case does not stand alone in requiring application of federal law in diversity cases. Where a patent owner sues his licensee for unpaid royalties, federal rather than state law governs as to whether the licensee is estopped from raising the defenses that the patents are invalid or that the license agreement violated the federal antitrust laws.[49] Again in an extension of the doctrine that federal law is controlling in suits involving the United States on government contracts,[50] it has been held that federal common law governs in a diversity action by a subcontractor against a government prime contractor.[51] Finally where federal law creates a right of action, but does not grant jurisdiction, and suit is brought in the federal court only on the basis of diversity, the Erie doctrine does not apply and federal law controls.[52]

It may be, as Justice Brandeis said, that there is no federal *general* common law, but there remains a substantial area for the application of federal common law.

49. Sola Elec. Co. v. Jefferson Elec. Co., 1942, 63 S.Ct. 172, 317 U.S. 173, 87 L.Ed. 165; Kelly v. Kosuga, 1959, 79 S.Ct. 429, 358 U.S. 516, 3 L.Ed.2d 475.

The same result has been reached on the assignability of a patent license agreement. Unarco Indus., Inc. v. Kelley Co., C.A.7th, 1972, 465 F.2d 1303, certiorari denied 93 S.Ct. 1365, 410 U.S. 929, 35 L.Ed.2d 590.

50. See note 12 above.

51. American Pipe & Steel Corp. v. Firestone Tire & Rubber Co., C.A.9th, 1961, 292 F.2d 640, 643–644, noted 1961, 61 Col.L.Rev. 1519, 1962, 75 Harv.L.Rev. 1656; U. S. v. Taylor, C.A.5th, 1964, 333 F.2d 633, adhered to C.A.5th, 1964, 336 F.2d 149, noted 1964, 39 Tul.L.Rev. 137.

52. Huber Baking Co. v. Stroehmann Bros. Co., C.A.2d, 1958, 252 F.2d 945, certiorari denied 79 S.Ct. 50, 358 U.S. 829, 3 L.Ed.2d 69.

CHAPTER 10

PROCEDURE IN THE DISTRICT COURTS

Analysis

A. INTRODUCTION

Sec.
61. The Conformity Act and the Equity Rules.
62. The Federal Rules of Civil Procedure.
63. Rules of Procedure in Non-civil Cases.

B. PROCESS

64. Service of Summons and Complaint.
65. Service According to State Law.

C. PLEADINGS

66. Pleadings In General.
67. One Form of Action.
68. The Theory of Modern Pleading.
69. Pleading Jurisdiction.

D. JOINDER OF CLAIMS AND PARTIES

70. Parties Classified.
71. Joinder of Parties.
72. Class Actions.
73. Stockholders' Derivative Actions.
74. Interpleader.
75. Intervention.
76. Impleader.
77. Substitution of Parties.
78. Joinder of Claims.
79. Counterclaims.
80. Cross-Claims.

E. DISCOVERY

F. TRIALS

G. JUDGMENT

A. INTRODUCTION

Analysis

§ 61. The Conformity Act and the Equity Rules [1]

Although the Judiciary Act of 1789 gave the federal courts power to make necessary rules for the orderly conduct of business in those courts,[2] another statute, enacted five days later, provided that in actions at law procedure in federal court should be the same in each state "as are now used or allowed in the supreme courts of the same." [3] Conformity to state procedure in actions at law, with inde-

[§ 61]

1. 4 Wright & Miller, Civil § 1002; Clark & Moore, A New Federal Civil Procedure: I. The Background, 1935, 44 Yale L.J. 387; Lane, Twenty Years Under the Federal Equity Rules, 1933, 46 Harv.L.Rev. 638; Comment, Ineffectiveness of the Conformity Act, 1927, 36 Yale L.J. 853.

2. Act of Sept. 24, 1789, c. 20, § 17, 1 Stat. 73, 83.

3. Act of Sept. 29, 1789, c. 21, § 2, 1 Stat. 93.

pendent federal regulation of procedure in admiralty and equity proceedings, was reaffirmed in a permanent statute adopted in 1792.[4] The conformity thus called for in actions at law was a static conformity. The state practice as of September 29, 1789, was to be followed, regardless of changes that the states might thereafter have made. Further the conformity statute made no provision for states subsequently admitted to the union; in those states the federal court could follow whatever procedure it chose. The rulemaking power, though utilized in admiralty and equity, was not employed in actions at law, where the Court considered it its duty "to yield rather than encroach" upon state practice.[5]

The static conformity required by the statute was of considerable practical importance, because it made unavailable in federal court laws enacted subsequent to 1789 by the states for the relief of debtors. The matter came to a head in 1825 in the leading case of Wayman v. Southard,[6] where the Court, through Chief Justice Marshall, held that a federal court sitting in Kentucky could not apply a Kentucky statute altering the rules as to execution on a judgment in a manner favorable to debtors. The opinion in that case contained some intimation that a dynamic conformity, by which federal courts would follow the state procedure in effect as of the time they heard a case, would be an intolerable delegation of rulemaking power to the state legislatures. The holding in Wayman v. Southard was politically unpalatable, but the congressional solution to the problem posed its own difficulties. Under an 1828 statute procedure in the federal courts sitting in the original states was still to conform to the 1789 state procedure, while procedure in states subsequently admitted was to conform to the 1828 state procedure. It was provided however that all federal courts were to follow the 1828 state procedure with regard to writs of execution and other final process issued on judgments, and that the courts might, in their discretion, alter the procedure on executions to conform to any subsequent legislative changes by the state in which they were sitting.[7] This pattern continued in effect until 1872.[8]

Static conformity was unsatisfactory. During this period many states were following the lead of the New York Code of 1848 by merging law and equity and substituting a simplified form of code pleading for the common law pleading formerly required. Under the statutes then in force, these new state procedures were not available

---

4. Act of May 8, 1792, c. 36, § 2, 1 Stat. 275, 276.

5. Fullerton v. Bank of United States, 1828, 1 Pet. 604, 614, 7 L.Ed. 280.

6. 1825, 10 Wheat. 1, 6 L.Ed. 253.

7. Act of May 19, 1828, c. 68, 4 Stat. 278.

8. In 1842 a similar statute was adopted to cover states admitted between 1828 and 1842. Act of Aug. 1, 1842, c. 109, 5 Stat. 499. For states admitted after 1842, a similar result was reached by judicial construction of language in the acts admitting them to the union. U. S. v. City Council of Keokuk, 1868, 6 Wall. 514, 516–517, 18 L.Ed. 933; Smith v. Cockrill, 1868, 6 Wall. 756, 18 L.Ed. 973.

in federal actions, which were required to proceed according to the earlier, discarded procedure of a state.

The situation was changed by the famous Conformity Act of 1872.[9] Among other things, that statute repealed the unused rulemaking power of the Supreme Court in common-law actions. Its more important accomplishment was to provide that "the practice, pleadings, and forms and modes of proceeding in civil causes, other than equity and admiralty causes, in the district courts, shall conform, as near as may be, to the practice, pleadings, and forms and modes of proceeding existing at the time in like causes in the courts of record of the State within which such district courts are held * * *."

Thus a continuing or dynamic conformity was substituted for the static conformity earlier required. In theory the lawyer would now need to know but one system of procedure, since the federal courts would follow the same procedure as that currently used in the state court. The theory was largely illusory. The state practice was required to give way to any federal statute in point.[10] The state practice did not control on questions of jurisdiction or validity of service of process.[11] The state practice did not control the conduct of the federal judge in administration of the trial, which carried with it an independent federal rule on such important matters as the right of the judge to comment on the evidence,[12] the division of function between judge and jury,[13] whether instructions must be in writing,[14] and investigation of jury misconduct.[15] The state practice did not control appellate procedure.[16] Finally even where there was conformity, it was to be "as near as may be," and this was understood by the Court to make the Conformity Act "to some extent only directory and advisory" and to permit the federal judge to disregard a state practice that would, in his view, "unwisely encumber the administration of the law, or tend to defeat the ends of justice."[17] With all these exceptions to conformity, and with the judge left somewhat at large to decide when he would conform, it is hardly surprising that the result

9. Act of June 1, 1872, c. 255, 17 Stat. 197; Rev.Stat. § 914.

10. Amy v. City of Watertown, 1889, 9 S.Ct. 530, 531, 130 U.S. 301, 304, 32 L.Ed. 946; Henkel v. Chicago, St. P., M. & O. Ry., 1932, 52 S.Ct. 223, 284 U.S. 444, 76 L.Ed. 386.

11. Davenport v. City of Dodge, 1881, 105 U.S. 237, 26 L.Ed. 1018; Southern Pac. Co. v. Denton, 1892, 13 S.Ct. 44, 146 U.S. 202, 36 L.Ed. 942; Munter v. Weil Corset Co., 1922, 43 S.Ct. 347, 261 U.S. 276, 67 L.Ed. 652.

12. Nudd v. Burrows, 1875, 91 U.S. 426, 23 L.Ed. 286; Vicksburg & M. R. Co. v.

Putnam, 1886, 7 S.Ct. 1, 118 U.S. 545, 30 L.Ed. 257.

13. Herron v. Southern Pac. Co., 1931, 51 S.Ct. 383, 283 U.S. 91, 75 L.Ed. 857.

14. City of Lincoln v. Power, 1894, 14 S.Ct. 387, 151 U.S. 436, 38 L.Ed. 224.

15. McDonald v. Pless, 1915, 35 S.Ct. 783, 238 U.S. 264, 59 L.Ed. 1300.

16. St. Clair v. U. S., 1894, 14 S.Ct. 1002, 1009, 154 U.S. 134, 153, 38 L.Ed. 936.

17. Indianapolis & St. L. Ry. Co. v. Horst, 1876, 93 U.S. 291, 300–301, 23 L.Ed. 898 (per Swayne, J.).

was, in the view of a distinguished commentator, "a mixture of conflicting decisions, which have served to cloud the whole subject in hideous confusion and shifting uncertainty." [18]

The situation in equity was better than at law, though far from perfect, as indeed no system that continued the separation of law and equity could be. The Act of 1792 had provided that procedure in equity was to be "according to the principles, rules and usages which belong to courts of equity," with power in the Supreme Court to make such alterations by rule as it thought proper.[19] Rules of equity were adopted by the Supreme Court in 1822 and again in 1842. The 1842 rules continued in effect long after events had made them obsolete, so that, in the words of Judge Learned Hand, "the rules of Equity pleading fit the pleadings no better than small clothes would suit as professional costumes for the counsel." [20] The Equity Rules of 1912 were a considerable improvement,[21] and Congress helped with a 1915 statute which took a long step toward the consolidation of law and equity by permitting transfer of actions brought on the "wrong" side of the court to the "right" side, and also authorizing equitable defenses in actions at law.[22]

§ 62. The Federal Rules of Civil Procedure [1]

In the preceding section the difficulties with procedure in federal courts prior to 1938 were described. An erratic conformity to state procedure, an anachronistic survival of the separation between law and equity, and a failure to take advantage of the possibilities of judicial rulemaking were hallmarks of the system. The last of these points, that procedure is better regulated by the courts than by legislative bodies, was seen to be the key to the problem. It is doubtful whether, as some have contended, the legislature lacks constitutional

---

18. Dobie, Federal Procedure, 1928, p. 585. See also Clark & Moore, A New Federal Civil Procedure: I. The Background, 1935, 44 Yale L.J. 387, 401–411.

19. Act of May 8, 1792, c. 36, § 2, 1 Stat. 275, 276.

20. Monarch Vacuum Cleaner Co. v. Vacuum Cleaner Co., D.C.N.Y.1912, 194 F. 172, 174.

21. Talley, The New and the Old Federal Equity Rules Compared, 1913, 18 Va.L.Rev. 663.

22. Act of March 3, 1915, c. 90, 38 Stat. 956. See Liberty Oil Co. v. Condon Nat. Bank, 1922, 43 S.Ct. 118, 260 U.S. 235, 67 L.Ed. 232.

[§ 62]

1. 4 Wright & Miller, Civil §§ 1003–1008; Tolman, Historical Beginnings of Procedural Reform, 1936, 22 A.B.A.J. 783; Sunderland, The Grant of Rule-Making Power to the Supreme Court of the United States, 1934, 32 Mich.L.Rev. 1116; Holtzoff, Origin and Sources of the Federal Rules of Civil Procedure, 1955, 30 N.Y. U.L.Rev. 1057; Clark, Two Decades of the Federal Civil Rules, 1958, 58 Col.L. Rev. 435; Chandler, Some Major Advances in the Federal Judicial System, 1922–1947, 1963, 31 F.R.D. 307, 477–516; Clark, The Role of the Supreme Court in Federal Rule-Making, 1963, 46 J.Am.Jud.Soc. 250.

power to regulate procedure.[2]   It cannot be doubted that legislative regulation is less satisfactory than regulation by court-made rules.[3]

The fight for court-made rules of civil procedure for the federal courts began in 1911 when the American Bar Association, at the instigation of Thomas Shelton, adopted a resolution favoring such a system.   For almost 20 years a bill to give the Supreme Court power to make such rules was introduced in every Congress, but never was passed, despite the gallant efforts of Mr. Shelton.   In later years, in response to a suggestion by Chief Justice Taft,[4] the bill included a provision authorizing the Court to unify law and equity.   Opposition to the bill was led by Senator Walsh of Montana, and was based in large measure on the fear that grant of the rulemaking power would result in the rather simplified code practice of the western states being superseded by the involved practice that had developed in New York.[5]   In 1930 Mr. Shelton died, and the American Bar Association lost interest, even to the point of abolishing its committee that had been pressing for this reform.

Senator Walsh was to have been appointed Attorney General in 1933, which would surely have ended, for the time at least, any hope of obtaining rulemaking power for the Supreme Court.   He died, however, on the eve of his appointment, and the new Attorney General, Homer Cummings, assumed sponsorship of the bill authorizing the court to make procedural rules and to unite law and equity.   So effective was his leadership that the bill was adopted unanimously by Congress in 1934 with very little discussion.[6]

It is a long step from a grant of rulemaking power to the adoption of effective rules.   Indeed one familiar argument against rulemaking power is that it will not be exercised.   For almost a year after the Enabling Act was passed the Supreme Court took no action with regard to it.   The Department of Justice and the Conference of Senior Circuit Judges apparently contemplated that no more would be required than the drafting of uniform rules for actions at law to supplement the existing Equity Rules of 1912.

---

2.   Compare Wigmore, Legislative Rules for Judicial Procedure are Void Constitutionally, 1928, 23 Ill.L.Rev. 276, with Kaplan & Greene, The Legislature's Relation to Judicial Rule-Making: An Appraisal of Winberry v. Salisbury, 1951, 65 Harv.L.Rev. 234.

3.   4 Wright & Miller, Civil § 1001; Clark & Wright, The Judicial Council and the Rule-Making Power: A Dissent and a Protest, 1950, 1 Syracuse L.Rev. 346; Joiner & Miller, Rules of Practice and Procedure: A Study of Judicial Rule-Making, 1957, 55 Mich.L. Rev. 623; Levin & Amsterdam, Legislative Control over Judicial Rule-Making: A Problem in Constitutional Revision, 1958, 107 U.Pa.L.Rev. 1.

4.   Taft, Three Needed Steps of Progress, 1922, 8 A.B.A.J. 34, 35; Taft, Possible and Needed Reforms in the Administration of Justice in Federal Courts, 1922, 8 A.B.A.J. 601, 604, 607.

5.   Walsh, Rule-Making Power on Law Side of Federal Practice, 1927, 13 A.B. A.J. 84.   See Clark, Code Pleading, 2d ed. 1947, p. 35.

6.   Act of June 19, 1934, c. 651, 48 Stat. 1064; 4 Wright & Miller, Civil § 1003, p. 43.   The Enabling Act, as subsequently revised, is now 28 U.S.C.A. § 2072.   See Cummings, Immediate Problems of the Bar, 1934, 20 A.B.A.J. 212.

That the reform was not so limited, that law and equity were merged under a single set of simple and effective rules, was due primarily to the efforts of William D. Mitchell, a former Attorney General of the United States, and Charles E. Clark, then Dean of the Yale Law School and later Chief Judge of the Court of Appeals for the Second Circuit. In January 1935, Dean Clark, in collaboration with James Wm. Moore, published a major article summarizing the history of federal procedure and predicting that reform would be a failure unless it included a merger of law and equity.[7] Aroused by this article, General Mitchell wrote Chief Justice Hughes, on February 9, 1935, setting forth powerfully and persuasively the need for the full reform.[8] Three months later the Chief Justice, addressing the American Law Institute, made the dramatic announcement that the rules would not be limited to common-law cases, but would unify the procedure for cases in equity and actions at law "so as to secure one form of civil action and procedure for both."[9] A few weeks later the Court appointed an Advisory Committee of the most distinguished lawyers and law professors in the country to prepare and submit a draft of unified rules. General Mitchell was named by the Court as chairman, a post he filled with distinction until his death in 1955, and Dean Clark was designated as Reporter for the Committee.[10]

The Committee circulated three printed drafts for comment and criticism by the profession. The third draft, which was the Final Report of the Committee, was submitted to the Supreme Court in November 1937, and on December 20, 1937, the Court adopted the rules proposed by the Committee with some changes of its own.[11] The rules were submitted to Congress, as the Enabling Act required, and when Congress adjourned without any adverse legislation,[12] the rules became effective September 16, 1938.

Even the best system of court rules cannot remain static. Experience under the rules, and continued scholarly thinking about problems of procedure, will disclose places in which improvement is possible. Amendment will be necessary in other instances to remove unsound judicial glosses on the rules, or to codify desirable lines of

7. Clark & Moore, A New Federal Civil Procedure: I. The Background, 1935, 44 Yale L.J. 387.

8. The letter appears in full in Mitchell, The Federal Rules of Civil Procedure, in David Dudley Field Centenary Essays, 1949, pp. 73, 76–78.

9. Address of Chief Justice Hughes, 1935, 55 S.Ct. xxxv, xxxvii, 21 A.B.A.J. 340, 12 A.L.I.Proc. 54.

10. Order of June 3, 1935, 295 U.S. 774. For a full list of members of the committee, see 4 Wright & Miller, Civil § 1003, pp. 46–47.

The contributions of Dean—later Judge—Clark are described in Smith,

Judge Charles E. Clark and The Federal Rules of Civil Procedure, 1976, 85 Yale L.J. 914.

11. Order of Dec. 20, 1937, 302 U.S. 783. Justice Brandeis dissented from adoption of the rules.

12. There was opposition to the rules in the Senate, but that body took no action, since the House of Representatives favored the rules, and concurrent action of both houses would have been required to delay or defeat adoption of the rules. See Chandler, Some Major Advances in the Federal Judicial System, 1922–1947, 1963, 31 F.R.D. 307, 505–512.

decision. It is essential, therefore, that there be a continuing body charged with the responsibility of examining the rules in action, and recommending change to the Court when this seems desirable.[13] The Advisory Committee that drafted the federal rules was reconstituted in 1942 to serve this function, and did so until its discharge in 1956. Various amendments were made by the Court, on the recommendation of that Committee, but the most significant was the set of amendments adopted in 1946, effective March 19, 1948, which reflected the results of a general study of the rules in operation.

The old Advisory Committee was discharged in 1956. In 1958 Congress amended the act creating the Judicial Conference to include among the duties of that body advising the Supreme Court with regard to necessary changes in the various rules the Court has power to make or amend.[14] An elaborate structure was created to assist the Judicial Conference, and ultimately the Court, in this task. There have been, as needed, advisory committees of practitioners, judges, and scholars for civil procedure, criminal procedure, appellate procedure, admiralty, bankruptcy, and evidence. These report to a standing Committee on Rules of Practice and Procedure and it in turn reports to the Judicial Conference.[15] The Judicial Conference transmits such of the recommendations as it approves to the Supreme Court, for under this new plan, as under that in effect from 1934 to 1956, the Court retains ultimate responsibility for the adoption of amendments to the rules.

This new machinery led to significant amendments to the Civil Rules in 1961, 1963, 1966, 1970, 1980, and 1983, and to minor corrective or conforming amendments in 1971 and 1975.

The success of the Federal Rules of Civil Procedure has been quite phenomenal. They provide for the federal courts a uniform procedure in civil actions. This in itself would be a fine accomplishment, but the rules go beyond this to create a uniform procedure that is flexible, simple, clear, and efficient. It may smack of hyperbole to say, as one commentator has, that the rules are "one of the greatest contributions to the free and unhampered administration of law and justice ever struck off by any group of men since the dawn of civilized law."[16] It is nevertheless true that the chorus of approval of

---

13. Clark, "Clarifying" Amendments to the Federal Rules, 1953, 14 Ohio St.L.J. 241; Wright, Amendments to the Federal Rules: The Function of a Continuing Rules Committee, 1954, 7 Vand.L. Rev. 521; Wright, Rule 56(e): A Case Study on the Need for Amending the Federal Rules, 1956, 69 Harv.L.Rev. 839.

14. 28 U.S.C.A. § 331, as amended by Act of July 11, 1958, 72 Stat. 356. For discussion of this amendment prior to its adoption, see Symposium, 1957, 21 F.R.D. 117.

15. The work of the new committees is described by the chairman of the Judicial Conference's Standing Committee on Rules of Practice and Procedure in Maris, Federal Procedural Rule-Making: The Program of the Judicial Conference, 1961, 37 A.B.A.J. 772. Their members are listed at 4 Wright & Miller, Civil § 1007.

16. Carey, In Favor of Uniformity, 1943, 3 F.R.D. 507, 18 Temp.L.Q. 145.

the rules by judges, lawyers, and commentators had been, until very recently, unanimous, unstinted, and spontaneous.[17] In the last few years, however, there has been questioning and reexamination of the assumptions about the proper goals of procedure that are at the heart of the Civil Rules.[18] This questioning has been sparked particularly by what some think is abuse of the discovery procedures made available by the rules.[19]

The impact of the rules has not been limited to the federal courts. The excellence of the rules is such that in more than half the states the rules have been adapted for state use virtually unchanged, and there is not a jurisdiction that has not revised its procedure in some way that reflects the influence of the federal rules.[20]

The Enabling Act declares that the rules are to regulate only "practice and procedure" and are not to "abridge, enlarge or modify any substantive rights." [21] Particular rules have been attacked as affecting matters of substance, but the Supreme Court, in a notable series of decisions, has upheld all such rules challenged before it.[22]

The success of the Civil Rules caused many to think that formulation of Federal Rules of Evidence would be desirable. An Advisory Committee on Rules of Evidence was created in 1965 and followed the methods of the committee that had drafted the Civil Rules in its work. Ultimately Federal Rules of Evidence became effective July 1, 1975, but their gestation period was as troubled as it was lengthy. As is recounted in more detail in a later section,[23] a draft of Evidence Rules was promulgated by the Supreme Court in 1972, but they caused so much controversy that Congress passed a statute providing that they could not take effect until they were expressly approved by Act of Congress. Congress then made very substantial revisions in the rules as they had been promulgated by the Supreme Court before permitting them to become effective in 1975.

17. See 4 Wright & Miller, Civil § 1008, and particularly n. 40.

18. Subrin, The New Era in American Civil Procedure, 1981, 67 A.B.A.J. 1648.

19. See §§ 81, 83 below.

20. A commentator has pointed out, however, that certain provisions in the Civil Rules respond to special problems of a federal system and of courts of constitutionally-limited jurisdiction, and that those provisions ought not be blindly adopted by the states. Rowe, A Comment on the Federalism of the Federal Rules, 1979 Duke L.J. 843.

21. 28 U.S.C.A. § 2072.

22. Sibbach v. Wilson & Co., 1941, 62 S.Ct. 422, 312 U.S. 1, 85 L.Ed. 479 (Rule 35(a)); Mississippi Pub. Co. v. Murphree, 1946, 66 S.Ct. 242, 326 U.S. 438, 90 L.Ed. 185 (Rule 4(f)); Cold Metal Process Co. v. United Engineering & Foundry Co., 1956, 76 S.Ct. 904, 351 U.S. 445, 100 L.Ed. 1311 (amended Rule 54(b)); Hanna v. Plumer, 1965, 85 S.Ct. 1136, 380 U.S. 460, 14 L.Ed.2d 8 (Rule 4(d)(1)).

It has been argued, however, that the Court has been too permissive in upholding rules that do affect substantive rights, contrary to the Enabling Act. Ely, The Irrepressible Myth of Erie, 1974, 87 Harv.L.Rev. 693. Professor Ely's view is rejected, in the course of a thoughtful decision holding that Rule 25(a) is valid, in Boggs v. Blue Diamond Coal Co., D.C.Ky.1980, 497 F.Supp. 1105, 1118–1121, noted 1981, 11 Mem.St.U.L.Rev. 413.

23. See § 93 below.

The controversy over the Evidence Rules, and a similar furor over amendments to the Criminal Rules that the Supreme Court had approved in 1974,[24] has led to some reappraisal of the rulemaking process.[25] Although the critics have not been directing themselves particularly to the Civil Rules, insofar as the criticism goes to the methods that the rulemaking committees have used over the years, they may have an impact on future amendments of the Civil Rules.

Another threat to the integrity of the Civil Rules has come from the proliferation of local rules for particular districts. Although Rule 83 authorizes local rules, it had been expected that these would be few in number and confined to purely housekeeping matters. Instead the use of local rules has been extensive and they cover a great variety of important matters.[26] This in itself is a threat to uniformity of procedure throughout the country, the local rules often provide "a series of traps" [27] for lawyers from other districts, and the very casual manner in which the judges in a district decide to adopt a rule or set of rules is in striking contrast to the care with which the Civil Rules themselves are made and amended. Almost every study of experience with local rules has demonstrated how unsatisfactory it has been.[28]

The Supreme Court sought to provide a check when it ruled in 1960 that the power to make local rules is not to be used to introduce "basic procedural innovations," [29] but it seemed to retreat from this

24. See § 63 below.

25. Weinstein, Reform of Court Rule-Making Procedures, 1977 (shorter versions of this book appeared in 1977, 63 A.B.A.J. 47, and 1976, 76 Col.L.Rev. 905). See also Wright, Book Review, 1978, 9 St. Mary's L.J. 652; Clinton, Rule 9 of the Federal Habeas Corpus Rules: A Case Study on the Need for Reform of the Rules Enabling Acts, 1977, 63 Iowa L.Rev. 15; Friedenthal, The Rulemaking Power of the Supreme Court: A Contemporary Crisis, 1975, 27 Stan.L.Rev. 673; Lesnick, The Federal Rule-Making Process: Time for Re-examination, 1975, 61 A.B.A.J. 579.

An influential member of the House Judiciary Committee had also said that "few are entirely satisfied with the present process" and suggested that Congress consider whether the Rules Enabling Acts ought to be amended. Hungate, Changes in the Federal Rules of Criminal Procedure, 1975, 61 A.B.A.J. 1203, 1207.

See generally Brown, Federal Rulemaking: Problems and Possibilities, Federal Judicial Center 1981.

26. 12 Wright & Miller, Civil § 3154.

27. Woodham v. American Cystoscope Co. of Pelham, C.A.5th, 1964, 335 F.2d 551, 552.

The difficulty in finding out what local rules are in effect is illustrated by Doran v. U. S., C.A.1st, 1973, 475 F.2d 742, where the United States attorney had no knowledge of a local rule in effect for 20 years. See also U. S. v. Ferretti, C.A.3d, 1980, 635 F.2d 1089, in which the judges in the district were uncertain about the continued existence of a local rule.

28. 12 Wright & Miller, Civil § 3152; Weinstein, note 25 above, at pp. 117–137; Note, Rule 83 and the Local Federal Rules, 1967, 67 Col.L.Rev. 1251; Note, The Local Rules of Civil Procedure in the Federal District Courts—A Survey, 1966 Duke L.J. 1011.

But see Flanders, Local Rules in Federal District Courts: Usurpation, Legislation, or Information?, 1981, 14 Loy.L.A.L.Rev. 213; Flanders, In Praise of Local Rules, 1978, 62 Judicature 28.

29. Miner v. Atlass, 1960, 80 S.Ct. 1300, 1306, 363 U.S. 641, 650, 4 L.Ed.2d 1462.

when it later held that local rules reducing the size of civil juries from 12 to six did not fall afoul of that restriction.[30]   Many local rules have been held invalid for this reason, or because they are inconsistent with the Civil Rules, an Act of Congress, or the Constitution,[31] but patently there are many other invalid local rules on the books that have escaped scrutiny in a contested case.

§ 63.   Rules of Procedure in Non-Civil Cases [1]

In the title of this section, "non-civil" is used in somewhat arbitrary fashion to refer to all federal actions governed by systems of procedure other than the Federal Rules of Civil Procedure. It is beyond the scope of this book to make a detailed examination of such other systems of procedure, and the purpose of the section is simply to note their existence.

Prior to 1966 procedure in admiralty cases was different than in "civil actions."   Conformity to state procedure was never required in admiralty, where the federal courts from the first were free to apply the procedure historically associated with the courts of admiralty. Although the Supreme Court had rulemaking power in admiralty matters since 1792, the first set of admiralty rules was not promulgated until 1844.   This was superseded by the Admiralty Rules of 1920, which, as amended, remained in effect until 1966.   In that year admiralty cases were brought within Civil Rules, and treated as civil actions, with certain minor variations for admiralty and maritime claims identified as such.[2]

Procedure in bankruptcy initially was to follow the Civil Rules "as nearly as may be" except insofar as those rules were inconsistent with the Bankruptcy Act [3] or with the General Orders in Bankruptcy,

30.   Colgrove v. Battin, 1973, 93 S.Ct. 2448, 2456 n. 23, 413 U.S. 149, 163 n. 23, 37 L.Ed.2d 522.

31.   See Carter v. Clark, C.A.5th, 1980, 616 F.2d 228; Rodgers v. United States Steel Corp., C.A.3d, 1975, 508 F.2d 152, noted 1975, 88 Harv.L.Rev. 1911; U. S. v. Columbia Broadcasting System, Inc., C.A.5th, 1974, 497 F.2d 102, 103 n. 3; and cases cited 12 Wright & Miller, Civil § 3153 nn. 53–55.

[§ 63]

1.   Admiralty: 4 Wright & Miller, Civil § 1014.   Bankruptcy, 4 id. § 1016. Copyright: 4 id. § 1018.   Criminal prosecutions: 1 Wright, Criminal 2d, §§ 1–4.   Habeas corpus, 17 Wright, Miller & Cooper, Jurisdiction § 4268. Section 2255 motions, 3 Wright, Criminal 2d §§ 597–600.

2.   Civil Rule 9(h).   The variations relate to third-party practice (Rule 14(c)), deposition procedure (Rule 26(a)), jury trial (Rule 38(e)), and venue (Rule 82). There are also six "Supplemental Rules for Certain Admiralty and Maritime Claims."   See 12 Wright & Miller, Civil §§ 3201–3256.

See generally 4 Wright & Miller, Civil § 1014; Robertson, Admiralty Procedure and Jurisdiction After the 1966 Unification, 1976, 74 Mich.L.Rev. 1627; Landers, By Sleight of Rule: Admiralty Unification and Ancillary and Pendent Jurisdiction, 1972, 51 Texas L.Rev. 50; Bradley, Admiralty Aspects of the Civil Rules, 1967, 41 F.R.D. 257; Colby, Admiralty Unification, 1966, 54 Geo.L.J. 1258; Currie, Unification of the Civil and Admiralty Rules: Why and How, 1965, 17 Maine L.Rev. 1; Note, Admiralty Practice After Unification: Barnacles on the Procedural Hull, 1972, 81 Yale L.J. 1154.

3.   Title 11, U.S.C.A.

first adopted by the Supreme Court in 1898 and frequently since amended.[4] This came to an end in 1973 when a complete set of Bankruptcy Rules was adopted.[5] These conform to the Civil Rules in large measure, with the principal differences relating to service of process and setting the dispute for trial.[6]

The Civil Rules themselves provide that they do not apply to copyright proceedings "except in so far as they may be made applicable thereto by rules promulgated by the Supreme Court of the United States."[7] That Court, since 1909, has made special rules of practice for infringement actions,[8] acting under a statute that has since been repealed as covered by the general rulemaking statute. In 1939 the Court amended Rule 1 of the Copyright Rules to provide that infringement proceedings should be governed by the Civil Rules insofar as they are not inconsistent with the Copyright Rules. Thus the Court made proper the application of the Civil Rules in infringement proceedings, which many of the courts were already doing even without the change in the Copyright Rules. This arrangement has given no difficulty. The Copyright Rules prescribe certain special procedures that at most supplement, rather than contradict, the Civil Rules, and indeed there is probably no necessity for the continued existence of separate Copyright Rules.[9]

There are a number of other kinds of cases where the Civil Rules are applicable only to the extent that they do not contradict procedures required by statute or otherwise. These are listed in Civil Rule 81(a).[10]

The most interesting of the federal procedures not regulated by the Civil Rules is that for criminal actions. The federal courts never conformed to state procedure, as such, in criminal actions. From 1789 to 1946 the uncoded federal criminal procedure was the criminal procedure followed at common law, save as modified by constitutional limitations and by fragmentary statutory changes. State procedure was occasionally looked to—as it still is—where a statute so required or where it was necessary to fill the interstices of federal procedure.

Two of the men most responsible for reform of federal civil procedure are entitled to similar credit for the reform of criminal proce-

---

4. 11 U.S.C.A. following § 53.

5. These rules were promulgated under the authority granted by 28 U.S.C.A. § 2075.

6. Kennedy, The New Bankruptcy Rules, 1974, 20 Practical Law 11; Scheerer, The New Rules in Bankruptcy, 1974, 50 N.D.L.Rev. 515; Landers, The New Bankruptcy Rules: Relics of the Past as Fixtures of the Future, 1973, 57 Minn.L.Rev. 827.

7. Civil Rule 81(a)(1).

8. 17 U.S.C.A. following § 101.

9. 4 Wright & Miller, Civil § 1018; Kaplan, Continuing Work of the Civil Committee: 1966 Amendments of the Federal Rules of Civil Procedure (II), 1968, 81 Harv.L.Rev. 591, 617–620.

10. For discussion of these, see 4 Wright & Miller, Civil §§ 1013 (review of administrative proceedings), 1015 (arbitration), 1020 (forfeiture and penalty actions), 1021 (habeas corpus, quo warranto, citizenship, and naturalization), and 1028 (miscellaneous actions and proceedings).

dure. Attorney General William D. Mitchell was instrumental in the passage of 1933 legislation that gave the Supreme Court rulemaking power with respect to criminal proceedings after verdict.[11] This power was exercised by the Court in 1934. His successor as attorney general, Homer Cummings, recommended in 1938 that the Court be given similar authority to make rules in criminal cases prior to verdict. This legislation was adopted in 1940.[12] The Supreme Court determined to adopt a single set of rules that would govern proceedings both before and after verdict. The same careful methods that had proven so successful in the formulation of the Civil Rules were employed. A distinguished Advisory Committee was appointed, with Arthur T. Vanderbilt, later Chief Justice of New Jersey, as chairman, and Professor James J. Robinson, of the Indiana Law School, as Reporter.[13] The committee circulated to the profession two printed drafts of rules. Its final draft was, with some changes, approved by the Supreme Court in 1944,[14] and the Federal Rules of Criminal Procedure became effective on March 21, 1946. The great achievement of these rules was the codification and simplification of the prior practice, although important reforms were also made.

●

The Criminal Rules have worked well. They have not been adopted by the states, however, as widely as have the Civil Rules. In recent years they have been amended so frequently that even scholars in the field find it difficult to follow the constant changes or to be certain what a particular rule provided at a particular time. Amendments were made in 1966, 1968, 1971, 1972, 1974, 1975, 1976, 1977, 1979, 1980, and 1982, and still more amendments are presently in process. In addition, it has become commonplace in the last decade for Congress to postpone the effectiveness of part or all of a set of amendments to the Criminal Rules approved by the Supreme Court, so that Congress may decide for itself whether it will allow the amendments to become effective and, if so, in what form. On occasion this has led courts to act on the basis of amendments approved by the Supreme Court, not knowing that those amendments have been disapproved by Congress.[15]

11. Act of Feb. 24, 1933, c. 119, 47 Stat. 904, now codified as 18 U.S.C.A. § 3772.

12. Act of June 29, 1940, 54 Stat. 688, now codified as 18 U.S.C.A. § 3771.

13. For the other members of the committee, see 1 Wright Criminal 2d § 2 n. 2.

14. Order of December 26, 1944, 323 U.S. 821. Justices Black and Frankfurter did not join in adoption of the rules. Rules 32 to 39 regulated proceedings after verdict, and were adopted in the exercise of the Court's power

under 18 U.S.C.A. § 3772, which, unlike 18 U.S.C.A. § 3771, does not require that rules be submitted to Congress and subject to its disapproval. Thus these rules were separately adopted by the Court by Order of Feb. 8, 1946, 327 U.S. 825, to be effective on the same day as the other rules.

15. U. S. v. Gonzalez Vargas, C.A.1st, 1978, 585 F.2d 546; Government of Virgin Islands v. Bradshaw, C.A.3d, 1978, 569 F.2d 777, certiorari denied 98 S.Ct. 3070, 436 U.S. 956, 57 L.Ed.2d 1121.

Special sets of rules govern the trial of misdemeanors before United States magistrates.[16] There are also special sets of rules for collateral attacks on criminal convictions, whether by habeas corpus for a state prisoner or by a motion under 28 U.S.C.A. § 2255 by a federal prisoner.[17]

B. PROCESS

Analysis

Sec.

§ 64. Service of Summons and Complaint

Service of process in federal actions was changed drastically in 1983. In 1982 the Supreme Court had proposed amendments to Rule 4 for this purpose. Congress first postponed the effectiveness of the Court's amendments and then rewrote those amendments before adopting them by statute to be effective February 26, 1983.[1]

In some states an action is commenced by the service of process on the defendant. This "hip-pocket" method of commencing an action, as it is known, was at one time favored by a majority of the Advisory Committee, but the committee finally took a contrary view, and provided that a civil action is commenced by filing a complaint with the court.[2] This recognizes that a law suit is a matter of public record and that there is a need for certainty with regard to the time of institution of the suit and its consequent effect upon limitations and priorities.

After the action has been commenced by filing the complaint with the clerk, the rules provide that the clerk must "forthwith" issue a summons and deliver it to the plaintiff or the plaintiff's attorney, who shall be responsible for prompt service of the summons and a copy of the complaint.[3] This mandate is not always followed, and even where

---

16. These were adopted by the Supreme Court effective June 1, 1980. They replaced the Rules of Procedure for the Trial of Minor Offenses before United States Magistrates, which had been promulgated in 1971. These appear in the volume of 18 U.S.C.A. containing the complete text of the Criminal Rules following the Criminal Rules.

17. These rules became effective in 1976, and have been amended since. The Habeas Corpus Rules appear in 28 U.S.C.A. following § 2254. The Section 2255 Rules appear in 28 U.S.C.A. following § 2255.

See Clinton, Rule 9 of the Federal Habeas Corpus Rules: A Case Study

on the Need for Reform of the Rules Enabling Acts, 1977, 63 Iowa L.Rev. 15.

[§ 64]

1. See generally 4 Wright & Miller, Civil §§ 1051–1036.

The amendments were adopted by Act of January 12, 1983, Pub.L. 97–462, 96 Stat. 2527. Their text appears at 96 F.R.D. ___. The text and Committee Note to the amendments the Supreme Court had approved appears at 93 F.R.D. 255.

2. Rule 3.

3. Rule 4(a); 4 Wright & Miller, Civil §§ 1084–1086.

it is, the passage of time between the filing of the complaint and the service of process may raise some difficult questions. Of these undoubtedly the effect of the filing alone as satisfying a controlling statute of limitations is the most important.

If suit is on a right created by federal law, filing of the complaint, as called for by Rule 3, is sufficient, without more, to satisfy the statute of limitations.[4] Despite Rule 3, however, in a suit on a state-created right plaintiff must do, before the statute of limitations has run, whatever he would be required to do in a similar suit in state court. This is the holding of Ragan v. Merchants Transfer & Warehouse Co.[5] The holding there, it will be recalled, is that a federal court sitting in diversity cannot give an action longer life than it would have had in the state court, and that if state law requires something more than filing the complaint, such as service on the defendant, within the limitations period, the same formalities must be completed for the action in federal court to be timely. Although there had been some question about the continuing vitality of the Ragan case, its holding was expressly reaffirmed in 1980 in Walker v. Armco Steel Corporation.[6]

Even where the action is commenced for purposes of the statute of limitations merely by filing the complaint, whether because the suit is governed by federal law or because the relevant state law so provides, there is an implied qualification, of equitable origin,[7] that to avoid the bar of the statute of limitations there must have been a bona fide intent to prosecute the suit diligently and no unreasonable delay in the issuance or service of the summons. The decisions turn heavily on their particular facts.[8] The decisions will be less important under new Rule 4(j), adopted in 1983.[9]

Many time periods in the rules are dated from the commencement of the action. Undoubtedly this can be abused, and plaintiff can se-

---

4. U. S. v. Wahl, C.A.6th, 1978, 583 F.2d 285; Bomar v. Keyes, C.C.A.2d, 1947, 162 F.2d 136, certiorari denied 68 S.Ct. 166, 332 U.S. 825, 92 L.Ed. 400, and cases cited 4 Wright & Miller, Civil § 1056 n. 59.

5. 1949, 69 S.Ct. 1233, 337 U.S. 530, 93 L.Ed. 1520. See 4 Wright & Miller, Civil § 1057.

6. 1980, 100 S.Ct. 1978, 446 U.S. 740, 64 L.Ed.2d 659, noted 1981, 32 S.C.L.Rev. 627.

7. See Linn & Lane Timber Co. v. U. S., 1915, 35 S.Ct. 440, 236 U.S. 574, 59 L.Ed. 725.

8. See cases cited 4 Wright & Miller, Civil § 1056 nn. 62–67.

9. Rule 4(j) provides that if the summons and complaint are not served upon a defendant within 120 days after the filing of the complaint and good cause for not making service is not shown the action shall be dismissed as to that defendant without prejudice upon motion or upon the court's own initiative. The court could enlarge the 120-day period under Rule 6(b).

cure an advantage that the rules do not intend if service is delayed for whatever cause. The alternative of measuring time periods from the date of service would cause administrative difficulties, especially where there are several defendants and service is made on different days. By contrast, the date of filing the complaint with the clerk, which is the commencement of the action, is a readily discernible and easily administered point in time.[10] The courts have ample power to protect defendant in a case where plaintiff has sought to gain an advantage from the delay in making service.[11]

In the past the summons and complaint[12] had normally been served by the marshal.[13] The principal purpose of the amendments adopted in 1983 was to end this. Because of the reduction in appropriations available to the Marshal's Service, it was thought desirable to relieve the marshals of the duty of serving summonses and complaints in private civil litigation. If the amendments become effective, a marshal will not ordinarily[14] make service and service can be by any person who is not a party and is not less than 18 years old.[15]

The methods of making service on various kinds of defendants are set out in the several subdivisions of Rule 4(d). The procedures set out for service on infants and incompetent persons, and on the United States or officers or agencies thereof, and on states and subdivisions of states, are largely self-explanatory, and have given little difficulty.[16] This cannot be said of service on individuals or corporations.

10. Edwin H. Morris & Co. v. Warner Bros. Pictures, D.C.N.Y.1950, 10 F.R.D. 236, 238.

11. See, e.g., Caribbean Constr. Corp. v. Kennedy Van Saun Mfg. & Engineering Corp., D.C.N.Y.1952, 13 F.R.D. 124; 4 Wright & Miller, Civil § 1053.

12. Much less formal methods of service have always been provided for papers subsequent to the original complaint. Subpoenas may be served by any person 18 years of age or over who is not a party to the lawsuit. Rule 45(c); 9 Wright & Miller, Civil § 2461. Service of other papers may be made on the party's attorney either by delivering a copy to him or mailing a copy to his last known address. Rule 5(b); 4 Wright & Miller, Civil §§ 1145–1147.

13. There is a little-used provision allowing the court to appoint a special person to make service where substantial savings in travel fees would result. In addition, the rule had been amended in 1980 to allow service to be made by any person authorized to serve process in the courts of the state in which the federal court was held.

14. Under the amendments a marshal can still be required to make service in

cases of paupers and seamen, or on behalf of the United States or a federal officer or agency, and in cases in which the court finds the service by the marshal or a special appointee is required in order to guarantee that service is properly effectuated. Rule 4(c)(2)(B). The marshal would continue to serve forms of process that require an enforcement presence, such as temporary restraining orders, injunctions, attachments, arrests, and orders relating to judicial sales. Rule 4(c)(1).

15. Rule 4(c)(2)(A).

16. Rule 4(d)(2), (4), (5), (6), 4 Wright & Miller, Civil §§ 1099, 1106–1110.

The rules do not deal satisfactorily with service on foreign governments or agencies thereof, and judicial inventiveness had been required to fill that gap, but the matter is now covered by the provisions of the Foreign Sovereign Immunities Act of 1976. See 28 U.S. C.A. § 1608; Kane, Suing Foreign Sovereigns: A Procedural Compass, 1981, 34 Stan.L.Rev. 385.

There is a sensible and liberal provision for service on federal officers or agencies in 28 U.S.C.A. § 1391(e). 4 Wright & Miller, Civil § 1107. It does not ap-

It should be noted immediately that the procedures of subdivisions (1) and (3) of Rule 4(d) with regard to service on individuals or corporations are merely one way by which such service can be made. Rule 4(c)(2)(C)(i)—formerly Rule 4(d)(7)—provides the alternative in such cases, discussed below in section 65, of service on defendants of this character in the manner prescribed by the law of the state in which service is made. One part of the 1983 amendments, however, allows service by mailing a copy of the summons and complaint by first-class mail, postage prepaid, as an alternative to the procedures of subdivisions (1) and (3). This will undoubtedly become the normal method of serving individuals and corporations.[17]

There are three possible methods of service on an individual, in addition to the alternatives provided by Rule 4(c)(2)(C).[18] Probably the most common, and surely the most desirable, method until 1983 had been to deliver the summons and complaint to the individual personally. Where this method is followed there can be no question whether defendant had notice of the suit. Personal service may also be made by leaving copies of the summons and complaint at defendant's dwelling house or usual place of abode with some person of suitable age and discretion then residing therein. Service that meets these tests is good even though defendant never personally receives the papers.[19] Unlike some state statutes, this rule does not require an order of court or a showing of inability to find the defendant before making service in this manner. There have been elaborate attempts to define "usual place of abode," but whether defendant actually received notice is likely to have more influence on the result than any conceptual notions of whether the place where the summons and complaint were left is the "usual place of abode." [20]

A third method of service on an individual is by delivery to an agent authorized by appointment or by law to receive process. A

---

ply to a suit against a former government official, nor to an action for money damages brought against a federal official in his individual capacity. Stafford v. Briggs, 1980, 100 S.Ct. 774, 444 U.S. 527, 63 L.Ed.2d 1, noted 1980, 49 U.Cin.L.Rev. 675.

17. Proposed Rule 4(c)(2)(C)(ii). The mailing must include two copies of a notice and acknowledgement similar to Official Form 18–A and a return envelope, postage prepaid, addressed to the sender. If the acknowledgment of service is not received by the sender within 20 days after the date of mailing, service can then be made by the other methods of subdivisions (d)(1) and (d)(3) and the person served can be required to pay the costs of personal service.

18. Rule 4(d)(1); 4 Wright & Miller, Civil §§ 1094–1098.

19. Smith v. Kincaid, C.A. 6th, 1957, 249 F.2d 243; Adams v. School Bd. of Wyoming Val. West Sch. Dist., D.C.Pa. 1971, 53 F.R.D. 267.

20. Karlsson v. Rabinowitz, C.A.4th, 1963, 318 F.2d 666, 668, noted 1964, 24 Md.L.Rev. 356, 9 Utah L.Rev. 192; Williams v. Capital Transit Co., C.A.1954, 215 F.2d 487, 94 U.S.App.D.C. 221; Minnesota Mining & Mfg. Co. v. Kirkevold, D.C.Minn.1980, 87 F.R.D. 317; 4 Wright & Miller, Civil § 1096.

person who is an agent of an individual for other purposes is not necessarily authorized to receive service of process, and thus this method of service must be used with care.[21]

An individual who is personally within the state or one who is domiciled within the state although absent therefrom is subject to the jurisdiction of the state, and may be served in federal court if the procedure for service satisfies due process requirements by providing a means reasonably calculated to give him notice of the proceeding and an opportunity to be heard.[22] There are circumstances, however, where a person within the state may be immune from service there, and this is a question that the federal courts resolve for themselves and on which they are not controlled by state law. In general the federal courts recognize the principles that parties, witnesses, and attorneys coming from another state, in order to attend court under subpoena or other process, or to represent a party, in connection with one suit are immune from service of process in another and that service on a party induced to come into the jurisdiction for the purpose by the fraud or deceit of the plaintiff is invalid.[23] The immunity is granted not for the convenience of the person seeking to invoke it but for the convenience of the court. The underlying idea of immunity is to encourage voluntary appearance to secure the better administration of justice. If a defendant is willing to enter the jurisdiction and submit to it, the court will encourage him to do so by assuring him that he will not be served with process in any other suit. Thus where the subsequent suit, in which immunity is sought, is part of, or a continuation of, the suit in which the party appeared, the courts have refused to invoke the immunity.[24] The lower courts are not in agree-

21. 4 Wright & Miller, Civil §§ 1097–1098.

Hohensee v. News Syndicate, Inc., C.A. 3d 1961, 286 F.2d 527, vacated on other grounds 1962, 82 S.Ct. 1035, 369 U.S. 659, 8 L.Ed.2d 273; Nelson v. Swift, C.A.1959, 271 F.2d 504, 106 U.S.App. D.C. 238; Impoco v. Lauro, D.C.Mass. 1955, 16 F.R.D. 522.

A contractual provision designating an agent for receipt of process is valid, even if the contract does not expressly require the agent to notify the defendant when service is made. National Equipment Rental, Ltd. v. Szukhent, 1964, 84 S.Ct. 411, 375 U.S. 311, 11 L.Ed.2d 354.

22. See Milliken v. Meyer, 1940, 61 S.Ct. 339, 311 U.S. 457, 85 L.Ed. 278. This principle is recognized in Rule 4(d)(1) by the authorization for leaving the summons and complaint at the defendant's usual place of abode.

23. Lamb v. Schmitt, 1932, 52 S.Ct. 317, 285 U.S. 222, 76 L.Ed. 720; Stewart v.

Ramsay, 1916, 37 S.Ct. 44, 242 U.S. 128, 61 L.Ed. 192; Buchanan v. Wilson, C.A.6th, 1958, 254 F.2d 849; and 4 Wright & Miller, Civil §§ 1076–1081.

Immunity is unnecessary if the person could be served in his home jurisdiction under the forum's long-arm statute. 4 Wright & Miller, Civil § 1076, pp. 321–322; Note, Long Arm Statutes and the Denial of the Immunity Privilege, 1974, 9 New Eng.L.Rev. 589.

24. Page Co. v. Macdonald, 1923, 43 S.Ct. 416, 261 U.S. 446, 67 L.Ed. 737; McDonnell v. American Leduc Petroleums, Ltd., C.A.2d, 1972, 456 F.2d 1170; Moffett v. Arabian American Oil Co., D.C.N.Y.1948, 8 F.R.D. 566. It has been thought not enough, however, that there is some similarity between the two suits and that denial of immunity would be desirable as a matter of judicial administration. Matter of Equitable Plan Co., C.A.2d, 1960, 277 F.2d 319, criticised 1961, 61 Col.L.Rev. 278; Atkinson v. Jory, C.A.10th, 1961, 292

ment, and the Supreme Court has not yet spoken, on whether a person who comes into the state to answer a criminal indictment is immune from the service of civil process. It would seem that the purpose of granting immunity is not present here, where there is nothing voluntary about the person's appearance, and thus that the better view is that denying immunity under these circumstances.[25]

Service on a corporation or other association that is subject to suit under a common name is made by delivery of the summons and complaint to an officer, a managing or general agent, or to any other agent authorized by appointment or by law to receive service of process.[26] As with an individual, other methods of service are proper where authorized by the law of the state in which service is made.

If the person served is an officer, or a managing agent, or a general agent of the corporation, service on him is proper even though he is not specifically authorized by the corporation to accept service of process.[27] Whether a person is a managing or general agent within the rule depends upon the nature of his duties and authority and not upon the name of his office. There are a great many decisions as to whether particular persons were proper agents to receive service for the corporation,[28] but the underlying principle is that service must be made on a representative so integrated with the corporation sued as to make it likely that he will realize his responsibilities and know what he should do with any legal papers served on him.[29] The required agency must exist at the time service is made, and it is important that the person served on behalf of the corporation is at the time of service acting in the capacity that permits him to accept service.[30] An officer or agent may be disqualified to receive service of process on the corporation if his interests are adverse to those of the corporation.[31]

F.2d 169. But see 4 Wright & Miller, Civil § 1080.

25. Greene v. Weatherington, C.A.1962, 301 F.2d 565, 112 U.S.App.D.C. 241, noted 1962, 48 Va.L.Rev. 1163, 1963, 12 Amer.U.L.Rev. 101, 20 Wash. & Lee L.Rev. 375; Employers Mut. Liab. Ins. Co. of Wisconsin v. Hitchcock, D.C.Mo. 1958, 158 F.Supp. 783. Contra: Alla v. Kornfeld, D.C.Ill.1959, 84 F.Supp. 823. See 4 Wright & Miller, Civil § 1081.

26. Rule 4(d)(3); 4 Wright & Miller, Civil §§ 1100–1105.

27. Bergold v. Commercial Nat. Underwriters, D.C.Kan.1945, 61 F.Supp. 639; U. S. v. Central States Theatre Corp., D.C.Neb.1960, 187 F.Supp. 114.

28. See 4 Wright & Miller, Civil § 1103.

29. Goetz v. Interlake S. S. Co., D.C. N.Y.1931, 47 F.2d 753, 757. The test

has been similarly stated in more recent cases. Montclair Electronics, Inc. v. Electra/Midland Corp., D.C.N.Y. 1971, 326 F.Supp. 839, 842; Van Hoven Co. v. Stans, D.C.Minn.1970, 319 F.Supp. 180, 182.

30. Westcott-Alexander, Inc. v. Dailey, C.A.4th, 1959, 264 F.2d 853; Granite Chem. Corp. v. Northeast Coal & Dock Corp., D.C.Me.1966, 249 F.Supp. 597; Pacific Employers Ins. Co. v. The Paul David Jones, D.C.Tex.1950, 98 F.Supp. 668, affirmed C.A.5th, 195 F.2d 372; and cases cited 4 Wright & Miller Civil § 1101 nn. 55, 56.

31. Hartsock v. Commodity Credit Corp., D.C.Iowa 1950, 10 F.R.D. 181; Bishop v. Everson Mfg. Co., D.C.N.Y. 1943, 50 F.Supp. 792.

Even if service is made on an appropriate corporate agent, it is ineffective unless the corporation is subject to suit in the state where service is made. This is an issue with a long history and considerable change of view. Concepts of jurisdiction have altered through the years and the older precedents can be regarded as authoritative only to the extent that they are consistent with what one Justice has called "the enlightened rationale of our more recent cases." [32] The Court has declared unanimously that "a trend is clearly discernible toward expanding the permissible scope of state jurisdiction over foreign corporations and other nonresidents. In part this is attributable to the fundamental transformation of our national economy over the years. Today many commercial transactions touch two or more States and may involve parties separated by the full continent. With this increasing nationalization of commerce has come a great increase in the amount of business conducted by mail cross state lines. At the same time modern transportation and communication have made it much less burdensome for a party sued to defend himself in a State where he engages in economic activity." [33]

There are conceptual difficulties in deciding whether a corporation is "in" a state other than that of its incorporation so as to be subject to process. The early cases developed fictional doctrines that the corporation had given "consent" to be sued in a state other than that of its incorporation as a condition to doing business there,[34] or that simply by doing business it was "present" there and subject to the jurisdiction of the courts of that state.[35] Such metaphysical questions naturally led to confusion in the decisions. Judge Learned Hand observed that "it is quite impossible to establish any rule from the decided cases; we must step from tuft to tuft across the morass." [36]

The first, and the most important, of the "more enlightened" recent decisions on jurisdiction over foreign corporations is International Shoe Co. v. Washington,[37] in which Chief Justice Stone reviewed comprehensively the entire problem. He adopted Judge Hand's view that talk of "presence" or "consent" is a mere fiction, used to symbolize those activities of corporate agents within a state that the courts will deem sufficient to satisfy due process, and that the corporation should be subject to suit in any state where it had certain minimum

32. Burton, J., concurring in part in Polizzi v. Cowles Magazines, Inc., 1953, 73 S.Ct. 900, 905, 345 U.S. 663, 672, 97 L.Ed. 1331.

33. McGee v. International Life Ins. Co., 1957, 78 S.Ct. 199, 201, 355 U.S. 220, 222–223, 2 L.Ed.2d 223.

This development is described in 4 Wright & Miller, Civil §§ 1064–1072.

In World-Wide Volkswagen Corp. v. Woodson, 1980, 100 S.Ct. 559, 565, 444 U.S. 286, 293, 62 L.Ed.2d 490, the Court quoted this passage from McGee, and added: "The historical developments noted in McGee, of course, have only accelerated in the generation since that case was decided."

34. Lafayette Ins. Co. v. French, 1855, 18 How. 404, 15 L.Ed. 451.

35. Philadelphia & R. Co. v. McKibbin, 1916, 37 S.Ct. 280, 243 U.S. 264, 61 L.Ed. 710.

36. Hutchinson v. Chase & Gilbert, C.C.A.2d 1930, 45 F.2d 139, 142.

37. 1945, 66 S.Ct. 154, 326 U.S. 310, 90 L.Ed. 95.

contacts such that the maintenance of the suit would not offend "traditional notions of fair play and effective justice." He went on to say: "It is evident that the criteria by which we mark the boundary line between those activities which subject the corporation to suit, and those which do not, cannot be simply mechanical or quantitative. The test is not merely, as has sometimes been suggested, whether the activity, which the corporation has seen fit to procure through its agents in another state, is a little more or a little less. * * * Whether due process is satisfied must depend rather upon the quality and nature of the activity in relation to the fair and orderly administration of the laws which it was the purpose of the due process clause to insure. * * * [T]o the extent that a corporation exercises the privilege of conducting activities within a state, it enjoys the benefits and protection of the laws of that state. The exercise of that privilege may give rise to obligations; and, so far as those obligations arise out of or are connected with activities within the state, a procedure which requires the corporation to respond to a suit brought to enforce them can, in most instances, hardly be said to be undue." [38]

In the wake of International Shoe there has been a flood of decisions, including several from the Supreme Court, undertaking to say whether the contacts of a corporation with a particular state were substantial enough to make the corporation amenable to process in that state.[39] Of these the best known, and the most important, are McGee v. International Life Insurance Company,[40] Hanson v. Denckla,[41] and World-Wide Volkswagen Corporation v. Woodson.[42] The McGee case held that a Texas insurance company was subject to process in a California state court in a suit on an insurance policy on the life of a California resident, though the company never had an office or agent in California, and never solicited or did any insurance business in that state other than the policy in question. The facts that the contract was delivered in California, that the premiums were mailed from there, and that the insured resided there when he died were held to give California sufficient interest in the transaction to require the insurer to defend there. The facts of Hanson v. Denckla defy brief summarization and both the majority and dissenting opinions have a somewhat delphic quality. The case is significant as demonstrating that the McGee case did not remove all bars against service

38. 66 S.Ct. at 159–160, 326 U.S. at 319–320.

39. See 4 Wright & Miller, Civil § 1069.

40. 1957, 78 S.Ct. 199, 355 U.S. 220, 2 L.Ed.2d 223.

41. 1958, 78 S.Ct. 1228, 357 U.S. 235, 2 L.Ed.2d 1283.

42. 1980, 100 S.Ct. 559, 444 U.S. 286, 62 L.Ed.2d 490. See Louis, The Grasp of

Long Arm Jurisdiction Finally Exceeds Its Reach: A Comment on World-Wide Volkswagen Corp. v. Woodson and Rush v. Savchuk, 1980, 58 N.C.L.Rev. 407; Note, Federalism, Due Process, and Minimum Contacts, 1980, 80 Col.L. Rev. 1341.

on a foreign corporation, and that the corporation must have done some act by which it purposefully availed itself of the privilege of conducting activities within the forum state to be subject to suit there.

World-Wide Volkswagen was a suit by the owners of a car against the dealer from whom they had bought the car in New York and its wholesaler. The suit arose out of an accident in Oklahoma. The defendants were New York corporations that did no business in Oklahoma. A divided Court held that the Oklahoma courts could not exercise jurisdiction over defendants. The requirement of minimum contacts, Justice White wrote, performs "two related, but distinguishable, functions. It protects the defendant against the burdens of litigating in a distant or inconvenient forum. And it acts to ensure that the States through their courts, do not reach out beyond the limits imposed on them by their status as coequal sovereigns in a federal system." [43] The Court put great emphasis on the notion of sovereignty as a limitation on jurisdiction, and rejected the argument that jurisdiction could rest on the fact that it was foreseeable that an automobile sold in New York might travel through Oklahoma and become involved in an accident there.[44] The Court agreed that foreseeability is not wholly irrelevant, but thought that the foreseeability that is critical is not the mere likelihood that a product will find its way into the forum state, but that the defendant's conduct and connection with the forum state must be such that he should reasonably anticipate being haled into court there.[45]

The due process limitations on the amenability of a foreign corporation to suit within a state are not peculiarly, nor even particularly,

---

43. 100 S.Ct. at 564, 444 U.S. at 291–292.

In Insurance Corp. of Ireland, Ltd. v. Compagnie des Bauxites de Guinee, 1982, 102 S.Ct. 2099, 2104, ___ U.S. ___, ___, 72 L.Ed.2d 492, however, with Justice White again writing for the Court, it was said that the personal jurisdiction requirement of the Due Process Clause "recognizes and protects an individual liberty interest. It represents a restriction on judicial power not as a matter of sovereignty, but as a matter of individual liberty." This led Justice Powell, in a concurring opinion, to express concern that the Court was abandoning the rationale of World-Wide Volkswagen and of Hanson v. Denckla, and that it was abandoning "reliance on the concept of minimum contacts as a 'sovereign' limitation on the power of States" in favor of "abstract notions of fair play." 102 S.Ct. at 2110, ___ U.S. at ___.

44. 100 S.Ct. at 566–567, 444 U.S. at 295–296. For the proposition that fore-

seeability by itself is not enough, the Court cited Hanson v. Denckla, and it also read Kulko v. California Superior Court, 1978, 98 S.Ct. 1690, 436 U.S. 84, 56 L.Ed.2d 132, as supporting that result. In Kulko it had held that California could not exercise jurisdiction in a child-support action over a former husband who had remained in New York, and in World-Wide Volkswagen the Court said that it was foreseeable that the divorced wife in Kulko would move to California from New York and that the minor child would move there with her. The Court also noted in World-Wide Volkswagen that in Shaffer v. Heitner, 1977, 97 S.Ct. 2569, 433 U.S. 186, 53 L.Ed.2d 683, it had repudiated the former rule that a creditor is subject to suit quasi in rem in any state having transitory jurisdiction over his debtor.

45. 100 S.Ct. at 567, 444 U.S. at 297.

a problem for the federal courts. Thus it is not necessary, were it possible, to spell out here what those limits are now thought by the courts to be. A substantial literature is available on this subject.[46]

There is an aspect of the problem, however, that is peculiar to the federal courts. The principles discussed so far represent federal constitutional limitations. If suit in federal court is on a federally-created right, these federal general law concepts are the sole guide as to whether a foreign corporation is amenable to process.[47] The matter is not so simple, however, where the right sued on is state-created and jurisdiction rests on diversity. The landmark jurisdictional decisions of the Supreme Court show the extent to which the states may go, consistent with due process, in making foreign corporations suable in their courts, but due process does not compel the states to go this far if they do not choose to do so.[48] If a corporation cannot be sued in state court, because the state has not gone as far as the Constitution permits, is it consistent with the Erie doctrine for a federal court to entertain a diversity action against the corporation in that state? This question led to an extraordinary debate within the Second Circuit. In Jaftex Corp. v. Randolph Mills, Inc.,[49] the majority, speaking through the draftsman of the rules, Chief Judge Charles E. Clark, said that amenability to federal process in a diversity case where service is made under Rule 4(d)(3) is governed only by a federal test. Judge Henry J. Friendly disagreed, and argued that a corporation is not suable in federal court unless it could also be sued in the courts of the state. Three years later the court, this time sitting en banc, considered the issue again, in Arrowsmith v. United Press International.[50] In that case Judge Friendly spoke for the court in holding that the state test of amenability must be satisfied, while Judge Clark was alone in dissent. The commentators thought Judge Clark had the better of the argument,[51] but the courts have accepted Judge Friendly's position. Accordingly they hold that in diversity cases

---

46. The following articles, though now dated, have been helpful to the present author: Carrington & Martin, Substantive Interests and the Jurisdiction of State Courts, 1967, 66 Mich.L.Rev. 227; Foster, Judicial Economy; Fairness and Convenience of Place of Trial: Long-Arm Jurisdiction in District Courts, 1969, 47 F.R.D. 73; Hazard, A General Theory of State-Court Jurisdiction, 1965 Sup.Ct.Rev. 241; Kurland, The Supreme Court, The Due Process Clause and the In Personam Jurisdiction of State Courts from Pennoyer to Denckla: A Review, 1958, 25 U.Chi.L. Rev. 569; Reese & Galston, Doing an Act or Causing Consequences as Bases of Judicial Jurisdiction, 1959, 44 Iowa L.Rev. 249; Thode, In Personam Jurisdiction, 1964, 42 Texas L.Rev. 279.

See also Restatement Second of Judgments, 1982, §§ 4–9, and the Reporter's Notes thereto.

47. Fraley v. Chesapeake & O. Ry., C.A.3d, 1968, 397 F.2d 1; Lone Star Package Car Co. v. Baltimore & O. R.R., C.A.5th, 1954, 212 F.2d 147; and cases cited 4 Wright & Miller, Civil § 1075 n. 26. But cf. Gkiafis v. S. S. Yiosonas, C.A.4th, 1965, 342 F.2d 546, 548–549.

48. Perkins v. Benguet Consol. Mining Co., 1952, 72 S.Ct. 413, 342 U.S. 437, 96 L.Ed. 485.

49. C.A.2d, 1960, 282 F.2d 508.

50. C.A.2d, 1963, 320 F.2d 219.

51. James, Civil Procedure, 1965, § 12.12; Comment, 1964, 64 Col.L.Rev. 685; Comment, 1964, 31 U.Chi.L.Rev. 752; Note, 1964, 49 Iowa L.Rev. 1224;

state law determines whether a corporation is subject to suit in the state, and the federal decisions are important only in ascertaining whether the state law is within constitutional bounds.[52]

Although the Supreme Court has not spoken on the Jaftex-Arrowsmith problem,[53] some commentators have thought the decision in National Equipment Rental, Ltd v. Szukhent [54] indicates that the Court may accept Judge Clark's view.[55] The holding in Szukhent is that the words "agent authorized by appointment" in Rule 4(d)(1) are to be interpreted under a federal standard. But in Szukhent the Court was dealing with manner of service, rather than amenability to process, and there is force in the argument that Rule 4 speaks to the first question but not to the second.

As has been implicit in all that has been said thus far, federal process can ordinarily be served only within the territorial limits of the state in which the court is sitting.[56] This is not a necessary limitation. Congress has power to provide for the service of process anywhere within the United States [57]—or in some circumstances in foreign countries [58]—and there are not a few instances in which it has done so.[59] These are expressly recognized as exceptions to the usual limits defined in Rule 4(f). This has never been true of process in an ordinary civil action. Indeed prior to adoption of the rules process normally ran only throughout the district, and the extension of the territorial limits to the borders of the state was challenged as going beyond the rulemaking power, but this challenge was rebuffed by a unanimous Court.[60]

Though the enlargement of the territorial limits of process effected by Rule 4(f) in 1938 was a desirable change, the need was clear for further expansion of those limits. The problem was particularly pressing in great metropolitan areas that stretch across state lines.

Note, 1964, 48 Minn.L.Rev. 1131. Contra: ALI Study, pp. 133–134.

52. See the many cases cited 4 Wright & Miller, Civil § 1075 n. 50.

53. But Judge Friendly's view in Arrowsmith is fully accepted by Justice Powell in his concurring opinion in Insurance Corp. of Ireland, Ltd. v. Compagnie des Bauxites de Guinee, 1982, 102 S.Ct. 2099, 2109, ___ U.S. ___, ___, 72 L.Ed.2d 492.

54. 1964, 84 S.Ct. 411, 375 U.S. 311, 11 L.Ed.2d 354.

55. Currie, Federal Courts—Cases and Materials, 3d ed. 1982, p. 414; James, note 51 above, at p. 654, n. 9.

56. Rule 4(f); 4 Wright & Miller, Civil § 1124.

57. Mississippi Pub. Corp. v. Murphree, 1946, 66 S.Ct. 242, 245, 326 U.S. 438, 442, 90 L.Ed. 185. See also Robertson v. Railroad Labor Bd., 1925, 45 S.Ct.

621, 623, 268 U.S. 619, 622, 69 L.Ed. 1119; U. S. v. Union Pac. R. Co., 1878, 98 U.S. 569, 604, 25 L.Ed. 143; Toland v. Sprague, 1838, 12 Pet. 300, 328, 9 L.Ed. 1093; Mariash v. Morrill, C.A.2d, 1974, 496 F.2d 1138, 1142–1143.

To the same effect, see Restatement Second of Judgments, 1982, § 4(2), and comm. f; ALI Study, pp. 437–441. But see Seeburger, The Federal Long-Arm: The Uses of Diversity, or "Tain't So, McGee," 1977, 10 Ind.L.Rev. 480; Abraham, Constitutional Limitations Upon the Territorial Reach of Federal Process, 1963, 8 Vill.L.Rev. 520.

58. Rule 4(i); 4 Wright & Miller, Civil §§ 1133–1136.

59. See 4 Wright & Miller, Civil §§ 1118, 1125.

60. Mississippi Pub. Corp. v. Murphree, 1946, 66 S.Ct. 242, 326 U.S. 438, 90 L.Ed. 185.

Under the rules prior to 1963, a person who had failed to pay alimony called for by a divorce in the District of Columbia was beyond the power of the court to compel such payment so long as he remained across the Potomac River in Virginia, since an order of commitment for civil contempt could not validly be served outside the district.[61] Third-party practice was seriously limited by the inability to implead a third party who lived in a state other than that in which the original action was brought.[62] Suit was not possible in any federal court, even though venue problems were not present or were waived, if one of two "indispensable" parties defendant lived across the state line from the other.[63]

To meet these particular problems, a 1963 amendment made a modest liberalization of Rule 4(f) to meet the most pressing needs. This amendment permits service outside the state, but within 100 miles of the place where the action is commenced or is to be tried, if necessary to bring in an additional defendant to a counterclaim under Rule 13(h), or to add a third-party defendant under Rule 14, or to join an indispensable party without whose joinder the existing action must be dismissed, or to require a person to respond to an order of commitment for civil contempt.[64] Though the amended rule will take care of the problems that exist in metropolitan areas, and has the advantage of conforming to the existing limits on service of a subpoena, the ultimate solution seems likely to be that of permitting nationwide service of process in all cases, with inconvenience to parties avoided by adjustment of the venue requirements and provision for transfer to the most convenient forum.[65]

---

61. Graber v. Graber, D.C.D.C.1950, 93 F.Supp. 281.

62. See § 76 below.

63. See § 70 below. The American Law Institute proposes to grant jurisdiction to the federal courts, with nationwide service of process, in cases where necessary parties are dispersed in different jurisdictions, so that no state court could obtain jurisdiction of all the parties. ALI Study, §§ 2371–2376.

64. 4 Wright & Miller, Civil §§ 1127–1129. Although it has been held that in a diversity case in which service is made in the 100-mile "bulge," the law of the state in which the service is made determines the defendant's amenability to suit, Coleman v. American Export Isbrandtsen Lines, Inc., C.A.2d, 1968, 405 F.2d 250, the better view is that state tests are of no significance and that it is enough that the person to be served has minimum contacts with either the forum state or the "bulge" area. Sprow v. Hartford Fire Ins. Co., C.A.5th, 1979, 594 F.2d

412; Paxton v. Southern Pennsylvania Bank, D.C.Md.1982, 93 F.R.D. 503. See also 4 Wright & Miller, Civil, pp. 314–315, 534–535; Kaplan, Amendments to the Federal Rules of Civil Procedure, 1961–1963, 1964, 77 Harv.L. Rev. 601, 633. But cf. Note, The Limits of Federal Diversity Jurisdiction Under Rule 4(f) of the Federal Rules of Civil Procedure, 1980, 68 Geo.Wash.L. Rev. 269.

The "bulge" provision of Rule 4(f) allows service "in the manner stated in paragraphs (1)–(6) of subdivision (d) of this rule." Thus proposed Rule 4(d)(8), which would allow service by registered or certified mail—see note 17 above—would not be available for service in the "bulge," though it seems that this was inadvertent on the part of the rulemakers.

65. See 4 Wright & Miller, Civil § 1127; Barrett, Venue and Service of Process in the Federal Courts—Suggestions for Reform, 1954, 7 Vand.L.Rev. 608.

§ 65. Service According to State Law [1]

As was noted in section 64, the rules provide methods of service on various classes of defendants, but they also provide, in what had been Rule 4(d)(7) and in 1983 became Rule 4(c)(2)(C)(i), that service on an individual or corporation is sufficient if the summons and complaint are served in the manner prescribed, by the law of the state in which the action is pending,[2] for the service of summons or other like process upon any such defendant in an action brought in the courts of general jurisdiction of that state. In addition, Rule 4(e) provides that whenever a statute or rule of court of the state in which the district court is held allows service on a person not an inhabitant of or found within the state, service may be made under the circumstances and in the manner prescribed by the state statute or rule. Although it is possible to draw nice distinctions about the scope and interrelation of these two provisions, it seems most reasonable simply to recognize that there is considerable overlap between them and that no useful purpose would be served by trying to bifurcate them in a mechanical fashion.[3]

The alternative of service as authorized by state law has been frequently used, ordinarily in conjunction with a state long-arm statute.[4] There has been uncertainty on whether Rule 4(c) or state law controlled on who should make service when the state procedures are used.[5] This problem was cured by amendments of Rule 4(c) effective in 1983,[6] which would allow service by any person who is 18 or over and who is not a party to the lawsuit.[7]

Frequently state law conditions use of a particular means of service, as under the nonresident motorist statutes, on the action being

[§ 65]

1. Wright & Miller, Civil §§ 1112–1116, 1119–1123; Foster, Long-arm Jurisdiction in Federal Courts, 1969 Wis.L.Rev. 9; Foster, Judicial Economy; Fairness and Convenience of Place of Trial: Long-Arm Jurisdiction in District Courts, 1969, 47 F.R.D. 73.

2. Bookout v. Beck, C.A.9th, 1965, 354 F.2d 823; Wolfe v. Doucette, C.A.9th, 1965, 348 F.2d 635.

3. Whiteley v. Nelson, D.C.La.1977, 75 F.R.D. 523. See also Navarro v. Sedco, Inc., D.C.Tex.1978, 449 F.Supp. 1355, 1357 n. 1; 4 Wright & Miller, Civil § 1114.

4. 4 Wright & Miller, Civil § 1115.

5. 4 Wright & Miller, Civil § 1092. For examples of that uncertainty, see

Veeck v. Commodity Enterprises, Inc., C.A.9th, 1973, 487 F.2d 423; U. S. for Use of Tanos v. St. Paul Mercury Ins. Co., C.A.5th, 1966, 361 F.2d 838, certiorari denied 87 S.Ct. 510, 385 U.S. 971, 17 L.Ed.2d 435; Wells v. English Elec., Ltd., D.C.La.1973, 60 F.R.D. 573, 577–578.

6. See § 64 n. 1.

7. See § 64 above at notes 12–15.

The problem of service under Rules 4(d) (7) and 4(e) had already been solved by a 1980 amendment of Rule 4(c) that allows in any case service by a person authorized to serve process in state courts. The 1983 amendment deals with the subject more sweepingly, and the 1980 language is not retained.

brought in the county in which the transaction occurred. Such restrictions on venue are not binding in federal court; instead it is enough that suit is brought in the federal district that includes the county in question.[8] It may be that there are other details relating to the manner of service as prescribed by state law that cannot be literally followed in federal court. In such cases conformity as nearly as may be with the state practice should be sufficient compliance with what is now Rule 4(c)(2)(C)(i).

The state method of service is not limited to diversity cases or to cases in which state law governs amenability to process. Rule 4(c)(2)(C)(i) and the related provisions of Rule 4 allowing this alternative means of service, are available for use in any case, whatever its jurisdictional basis.[9]

The 1963 amendments of Rule 4 resolved two matters that had been unclear about using the state manner of service. It is now clear that the state method of service, authorized by Rule 4(c)(2)(C)(i) and rule 4(e), may be used as a means of making service on someone outside the state, if the state law so permits, and that Rule 4(f) does not bar this extra-territorial service.[10] One case has held that the state method of service cannot be used to make service more than 100 miles away in those situations in which Rule 4(f) directly permits service outside the state,[11] but this is unsound. Rule 4(f) allows extraterritorial service whenever this is authorized by a valid state statute. The 100-mile "bulge" provision is stated in the rule to be "in addition" to these other methods of service.

The other former problem, now resolved, had to do with state statutes authorizing so-called "quasi-in-rem" actions. These were commenced by attachment or garnishment of property within the state, with notice to the person outside the state against whom the claims were asserted. Actions commenced in this fashion could be removed to federal court if ordinary conditions for removal were satisfied,[12] but, as a result of a historical anomaly,[13] it was repeatedly held that an original action could not be commenced in federal court in this

---

8. FDIC v. Greenberg, C.A.3d, 1973, 487 F.2d 9, 12–13; and cases cited 4 Wright & Miller, Civil § 1112 nn. 92–94.

9. U. S. v. First Nat. City Bank, 1965, 85 S.Ct. 528, 379 U.S. 378, 13 L.Ed.2d 365; and cases cited 4 Wright & Miller, Civil § 1115 n. 9.

10. See 4 Wright & Miller, Civil §§ 1113–1114. This view was generally accepted even before the 1963 amendment, despite the doubt expressed in the concurring opinion in McCoy v. Siler, C.A.3d, 1953, 205 F.2d 498, 501–502, certiorari denied 74 S.Ct. 120, 346 U.S. 872, 98 L.Ed. 380.

11. American Carpet Mills, Inc. v. Bartow, Indus. Development Corp., D.C. Ga.1967, 42 F.R.D. 1.
Contra: Adams Dairy Co. v. National Dairy Products Corp., D.C.Mo.1968, 293 F.Supp. 1164.

12. Rorick v. Devon Syndicate, Ltd., 1939, 59 S.Ct. 877, 307 U.S. 299, 83 L.Ed. 1303; Clark v. Wells, 1906, 27 S.Ct. 43, 203 U.S. 164, 51 L.Ed. 138; see 28 U.S.C.A. § 1450.

13. Currie, Attachment and Garnishment in the Federal Courts, 1961, 59 Mich.L.Rev. 337; 4 Wright & Miller, Civil § 1119.

manner.[14] Rule 4(e) was amended in 1963 to permit actions to be commenced in this fashion if state law so provides.[15]

The amendment permitting "quasi-in-rem" actions has been little used,[16] and its possible utility has been further diminished by recent Supreme Court decisions holding that the mere presence of property in a state does not establish a sufficient relationship between the owner of the property and the state to support the exercise of jurisdiction over an unrelated cause of action.[17] Thus unless there are other ties sufficient to satisfy the minimum contacts standard, there cannot be a valid exercise of jurisdiction "quasi-in-rem." [18]

C. PLEADINGS

Analysis

§ 66. Pleadings in General [1]

The draftsmen of the Civil Rules proceeded on the conviction, based on experience at common law and under the codes, that pleadings are not of great importance in a lawsuit. This is evident from

14. Big Vein Coal Co. v. Read, 1913, 33 S.Ct. 694, 229 U.S. 31, 57 L.Ed. 1053; Davis v. Ensign-Bickford Co., C.C.A. 8th, 1944, 139 F.2d 624.

15. The amendment was sharply criticized by Carrington, The Modern Utility of Quasi in Rem Jurisdiction, 1962, 76 Harv.L.Rev. 303, partly because of the limited utility it would have. Doubt whether the amendment was a valid "procedural" provision was raised by Elliott & Green, Quasi in Rem Jurisdiction in Federal Courts: The Proposed Amendments to Rule 4, 1963, 48 Iowa L.Rev. 300. But cf. 4 Wright & Miller, Civil §§ 1119, 1120. Recent Supreme Court decisions imposing due process requirements on garnishment and attachment must also now be taken into account. See 4 Wright & Miller, Civil § 1074.

16. A very restrictive reading was given to the new procedure in Dunn v. Printing Corp. of America, D.C.Pa.1965, 245 F.Supp. 875, where the court applied literally a state statute that permitted attachment of property only in the county in which the court was sitting. This restrictive reading was rejected in

FDIC v. Greenberg, C.A.3d, 1973, 487 F.2d 9, and the state attachment procedure may be used in federal court though the property is in a different county of the district than that in which the federal court sits. See 4 Wright & Miller, Civil § 1121.

17. The leading case is Shaffer v. Heitner, 1977, 97 S.Ct. 2569, 433 U.S. 186, 53 L.Ed.2d 683. See also Rush v. Savchuk, 1980, 100 S.Ct. 571, 444 U.S. 320, 62 L.Ed.2d 516.

See 4 Wright & Miller, Civil § 1070. Some of the vast literature provoked by these cases is cited, id. at n. 12.9.

18. Restatement Second of Judgments, 1982, § 8.

[§ 66]

1. See 5 Wright & Miller, Civil §§ 1181–1196 (pleadings allowed; form of motions), 1261–1278 (denials and defenses), 1321–1327 (form of pleadings), 1331–1335 (signing of pleadings), 1390–1397 (waiver of defenses or objections), and 6 Wright & Miller, Civil §§ 1471–1510 (amended and supplemental pleadings).

the basic rule, discussed later,[2] on what a pleading must contain in order to state a claim that will be heard, but it is evident also from the flexible rules on the form of pleadings and the limitation on the number of pleadings.

At common law the pleadings could continue indefinitely, until they had produced a single issue of law or fact that would then be decided. The Field Code, adopted in New York in 1848 and widely imitated, limited the pleadings to three, a complaint, an answer, and a reply. In the federal system, under Rule 7(a), normally there will be only two pleadings, a complaint and an answer, though in some cases a reply is permissible.[3] The theory is that by the complaint and the answer each of the parties will have indicated the general position he is taking in the litigation, and that further pleading is not worth the trouble.

In the complaint the plaintiff is required to set forth a short and plain statement of the claim showing that he is entitled to relief, and to demand the relief to which he deems himself entitled.[4] In the answer the defendant must admit or deny each of the allegations of the complaint, or state that he is without knowledge or information sufficient to form a belief as to the truth of the allegation, which has the effect of a denial. He must also set forth anything that constitutes an avoidance or affirmative defense.[5]

A reply is allowed in only two situations. A reply must be made where the answer contains "a counterclaim denominated as such."[6] This phrase contains two elements: the answer must in fact contain a counterclaim and it must be so denominated. If the answer contains a counterclaim not so labelled, a reply is not required and is theoretically not permitted, though under Rule 8(c) the court, on terms, may treat the pleading as if it had been properly labelled and allow a reply. Similarly, if a party labels as a counterclaim what is actually a defense, a reply is again improper, though the cautious lawyer will plead the reply rather than get involved in the maze of niceties as to what is a "counterclaim" and what a "defense." Where the answer does contain a counterclaim denominated as such, the reply, which is then mandatory, is only to the counterclaim. It should not traverse allegations of the answer which are not part of the counterclaim, but

2. See § 68 below.

3. The rule also permits an answer to a cross-claim, where such a claim has been asserted by one defendant against another, see § 80 below, and a third-party complaint and a third-party answer, if a third party is impleaded, see § 76 below.

4. Rule 8(a). See § 68 below.

5. As to denials, see Rule 8(b); 5 Wright & Miller, Civil §§ 1261–1269. That rule seriously restricts use of the time-honored general denial. See Kirby v. Turner-Day & Woolworth Handle Co., D.C.Tenn.1943, 50 F.Supp. 469; Gulf Oil Corp. v. Bill's Farm Center, Inc., D.C.Mo.1970, 52 F.R.D. 114. Failure to deny an allegation in the complaint amounts to an admission of that allegation. Rule 8(d).

As to affirmative defenses, see Rule 8(c); 5 Wright & Miller, Civil §§ 1270–1278.

6. Rule 7(a).

should respond to the counterclaim in the same fashion that an answer responds to a complaint.

Rule 7(a) also allows the court to order a reply, either on its own motion or that of a party, but occasions when this power should be or has been exercised are extremely rare.[7] Where no reply is required, allegations of the answer are deemed denied or avoided, and the plaintiff can meet such allegations at the trial in any fashion that would have been open to him had a reply been proper.[8] Thus, while occasionally a reply is ordered by the court,[9] the mere fact that the answer raises affirmative defenses is not enough reason to call for a reply.

Rule 10 makes very flexible requirements for the form of pleadings. In addition to a caption,[10] the pleading must set out the averments in numbered paragraphs, each of which is limited so far as is practicable to the statement of a single set of circumstances.[11] Claims that are founded upon separate transactions or occurrences, and defenses other than denials, are to be stated in separate counts or defenses if such a separation will facilitate the clear presentation of the matters set forth.[12] Statements in one part of a pleading may be adopted by reference in other parts.[13] It is worthy of note that the requirement of numbered paragraphs limited to a single set of circumstances applies only "as far as practicable," while claims arising out of separate transactions or occurrences need be set forth in separate counts only when such a separation will facilitate the clear presentation of the matters set forth. The emphasis is on clarity and on practicality, rather than on any mechanical rule as to form. The Supreme Court has observed: "We no longer insist upon technical rules of pleading, but it will ever be difficult in a jury trial to segregate issues which counsel do not separate in their pleading, preparation or thinking."[14] Thus the rule commands only what a lawyer who has analyzed his case clearly would do in any event.

The requirement that pleadings be verified is abolished by Rule 11, except insofar as other rules or statutes call for verification. Instead every pleading must be signed by at least one attorney of rec-

7. 5 Wright & Miller, Civil § 1185.

8. Rule 8(d); Neeff v. Emery Transp. Co., C.A.2d, 1960, 284 F.2d 432; Cowling v. Deep Vein Coal Co., C.A.7th, 1950, 183 F.2d 652; First Presbyterian Church of Santa Barbara, California v. Rabbitt, C.C.A.9th, 1941, 118 F.2d 732; 5 Wright & Miller, Civil § 1186.

9. Reynolds v. Needle, C.C.A.D.C.1942, 132 F.2d 161; Beckstrom v. Coastwise Line, D.C.Alaska 1953, 13 F.R.D. 480; Columbia Pictures Corp. v. Rogers, D.C.W.Va.1949, 81 F.Supp. 580; U. S. v. Hole, D.C.Mont.1941, 38 F.Supp. 600.

10. Rule 10(a); 5 Wright & Miller, Civil § 1321.

11. Rule 10(b); 5 Wright & Miller, Civil §§ 1322–1323; Browne, Civil Rule 10(b) and the Three Basic Rules of Form Applicable to the Drafting of Documents Used in Civil Litigation, 1978, 6 Cap.U.L.Rev. 199.

12. Rule 10(b); 5 Wright & Miller, Civil §§ 1324–1325.

13. Rule 10(c); 5 Wright & Miller, Civil § 1336.

14. O'Donnell v. Elgin, J. & E. Ry. Co., 1949, 70 S.Ct. 200, 205, 338 U.S. 384, 392, 94 L.Ed. 187.

ord in his individual name, or by the party if he is not represented by counsel. The signature of the attorney constitutes a certificate by him that he has read the pleading, that to the best of his knowledge, information, and belief there is good ground to support it, and that it is not interposed for delay.[15] If the pleading is signed with an intent to defeat the purpose of Rule 11, it may be stricken, and the action will proceed as if the pleading had not been served. For a wilful violation of this rule an attorney may be subjected to appropriate disciplinary action, but fortunately there have been very few cases in which it has been necessary even to consider such a sanction.[16]

Great freedom is allowed in amending pleadings in order to assert matters that occurred before the filing of the original pleading but were overlooked by the pleader or were unknown to him at the time.[17] A party may amend his pleading once as a matter of course at any time before a responsive pleading has been served, or within 20 days after service of his pleading, if no responsive pleading is required. A motion is not a "responsive pleading," within the meaning of rule 15(a), and thus the right to amend as of course is not defeated because the other party has filed a motion attacking the pleading.[18] Indeed even where the motion is granted, as where a complaint is dismissed for failure to state a claim on which relief can be granted, the party has the right to file an amended pleading as of course, though this right must be exercised in a reasonable time, and may amend with leave of court if he has not acted promptly.[19]

The provisions of Rule 15(a) allowing amendment as of right should control over other, more guarded, provisions of the rules. Thus, while the cases are divided, the better view is that so long as amendment as of right is possible, a party may amend to add an omit-

15. 5 Wright & Miller, Civil §§ 1332–1333; Browne, Civil Rule 11: The Signature and Signature Block, 1979, 9 Cap.U.L.Rev. 291.

A 1976 statute, 28 U.S.C.A. § 1746, abolished verification and the use of affidavits generally in the federal system.

16. In re Lavine, D.C.Cal.1954, 126 F.Supp. 39, reversed C.A.9th, 217 F.2d 190 (disbarment reversed for lack of notice and hearing); American Auto Assn., Inc. v. Rothman, D.C.N.Y.1952, 104 F.Supp. 655 (opinion setting forth facts adversely to attorney ordered indexed under attorney's name); Nichols v. Alker, D.C.N.Y.1954, 126 F.Supp. 679 (pleading stricken and motion to discipline attorney referred to chief judge).

See generally Risinger, Honesty in Pleading and Its Enforcement: Some "Striking" Problems with Fed.R.Civ.P. 11, 1976, 61 Minn.L.Rev. 1. Courts have been making awards of costs or attor-

ney fees as a sanction for sham pleadings. See cases cited 5 Wright & Miller, Civil § 1334 n. 30.1.

17. Rule 15(a); 6 Wright & Miller, Civil §§ 1473–1503.

18. LaBatt v. Twomey, C.A.7th, 1975, 513 F.2d 641; Smith v. Blackledge, C.A.4th, 1971, 451 F.2d 1201; Keene Lumber Co. v. Leventhal, C.C.A.1st, 1948, 165 F.2d 815; and cases cited 6 Wright & Miller, Civil § 1483 n. 94.

19. Exxon Corp. v. Maryland Cas. Co., C.A.5th, 1979, 599 F.2d 659, 662 n. 10; Case v. State Farm Mut. Auto. Ins. Co., C.A.5th, 1961, 294 F.2d 676; and cases cited 6 Wright & Miller, Civil § 1483, pp. 413–416.

One circuit attaches great importance to a distinction between dismissal of the complaint and dismissal of the action. E.g., Firchau v. Diamond Nat. Corp., C.A.9th, 1965, 345 F.2d 269.

ted counterclaim without satisfying the test of Rule 13(f) [20] and may add or drop parties without obtaining a court order under Rule 21.[21]

After a responsive pleading has been filed, or the time for amending as of course has otherwise expired, amendment may be made only by leave of court or with the written consent of the adverse party. The rule provides, however, that "leave shall be freely given when justice so requires," and refusal to permit amendment is an abuse of discretion in the absence of some justification for the refusal.[22] Leave to amend may be accompanied with conditions that the pleader must satisfy if there is some reason that such conditions are necessary.[23] The test whether amendment is proper is functional rather than conceptual. It is entirely irrelevant that a proposed amendment changes the cause of action or the theory of the case, or that it states a claim arising out of a transaction different from that originally sued on, or that it causes a change in parties.[24] Normally leave to amend should be denied only if it would cause actual prejudice to an adverse party, but a busy court does not abuse its discretion if it protects itself from being imposed on by the presentation of theories seriatim, and may deny a belated application to amend that makes a drastic change in the case in the absence of some good reason why the amendment is offered at a late stage.[25]

Rule 15(c) provides that whenever "the claim or defense asserted in the amended pleading arose out of the conduct, transaction, or occurrence set forth or attempted to be set forth in the original pleading the amendment relates back to the date of the original pleading." This fiction of "relation back" is of great importance in avoiding the bar of the statute of limitations. Thus where plaintiff sued for wrongful death, alleging various negligent acts that would constitute a violation of the Federal Employers' Liability Act, plaintiff was per-

20. See A. J. Indus., Inc. v. United States Dist. Court, C.A.9th, 1974, 503 F.2d 384, 388; 6 Wright & Miller, Civil § 1479, pp. 402–404. Contra: Stoner v. Terranella, C.A.6th, 1967, 372 F.2d 89.

21. McLellan v. Mississippi Power & Light Co., C.A.5th, 1976, 526 F.2d 870, citing the divided cases from the district courts. See also 6 Wright & Miller, Civil § 1479, pp. 400–402.

22. Foman v. Davis, 1962, 83 S.Ct. 227, 230, 371 U.S. 178, 182, 9 L.Ed.2d 222; Hurn v. Retirement Fund Trust, C.A. 9th, 1981, 648 F.2d 1252; 6 Wright & Miller, Civil §§ 1484, 1487.

23. E.g., Phoenix Hardware Co. v. Paragon Paint & Hardware Corp., D.C.N.Y. 1940, 1 F.R.D. 116 (limiting time of service of amended pleading); Bercovici v. Chaplin, D.C.N.Y.1944, 56 F.Supp. 417 (trial without a jury); Affron Fuel Oil v. Firemen's Ins. Co., D.C.N.Y.1955, 143 F.Supp. 38 (granting jury trial on

new issues to opposing party); Shelley v. The Maccabees, D.C.N.Y.1960, 26 F.R.D. 10 (restoration of status quo); Sherrell v. Mitchell Aero, Inc., D.C. Wis.1971, 340 F.Supp. 219 (payment of costs); Prandini v. National Tea Co., D.C.Pa.1974, 62 F.R.D. 503 (waive relation back of added claim).

24. Goodman v. Mead Johnson & Co., C.A.3d, 1976, 534 F.2d 566, certiorari denied 97 S.Ct. 732, 429 U.S. 1038, 50 L.Ed.2d 748; Polin v. Dun & Bradstreet, Inc., C.A.10th, 1975, 511 F.2d 875; Sherman v. Hallbauer, C.A.5th, 1972, 455 F.2d 1236; and cases cited 6 Wright & Miller, Civil § 1474 nn. 98–10.

25. Freeman v. Continental Gin Co., C.A.5th, 1967, 381 F.2d 459, 469. See also Bradick v. Israel, C.A.2d 1967, 377 F.2d 262, certiorari denied 88 S.Ct. 101, 389 U.S. 858, 19 L.Ed.2d 124; Coral v. Gonse, C.A.4th, 1964, 330 F.2d 997.

mitted to amend, after the statute of limitations would otherwise have run, to add a claim under the Federal Boiler Inspection Act for failure to have a locomotive properly lighted. Since the amendment related to the same general conduct, transaction, and occurrence as did the original complaint, the amendment related back even though it was based on a different legal theory than was the original complaint, and rested on facts not asserted originally.[26] In a diversity action, a federal court may apply the federal rule to allow relation back and is not bound by a more restrictive state rule on the subject. The cases were once in conflict on this point, but the decision in Hanna v. Plumer [27] should have removed any doubt about this.[28] The matter is more complicated if state law would not regard the statute of limitations as a bar to an amendment even though the conditions stated for relation back in Rule 15(c) have not been satisfied. Here the better view is that the amendment should be allowed, even though Rule 15(c) seemingly does not allow it.[29]

Rule 15(d) gives the court discretionary power to permit supplementary pleadings. A supplemental pleading deals with events that have occurred since the original pleading was filed. Thus it differs from an amended pleading, which covers matters occurring before the filing of the original pleading but overlooked at that time.[30]

There was a very strange distinction, supported by some cases, by which it was held that a supplemental complaint was improper if the original complaint was insufficient, even though it has always been

26. Tiller v. Atlantic Coast Line R. Co., 1945, 65 S.Ct. 421, 323 U.S. 574, 89 L.Ed. 465. For cases on application of relation back, see 6 Wright & Miller, Civil § 1497. A discriminating opinion, rejecting mechanical tests as to relation back, and looking instead to the interests of justice, is Green v. Walsh, D.C.Wis.1957, 21 F.R.D. 15, noted 1958, 4 How.L.J. 117. See also Smyser, Rule 15(c) Relation Back of Amendments: A Workable Test, 1978, 23 S.D.L.Rev. 55.

27. 1965, 85 S.Ct. 1136, 380 U.S. 460, 14 L.Ed.2d 8. See § 59 above.

28. Ingram v. Kumar, C.A.2d, 1978, 585 F.2d 566, 570 n. 5, certiorari denied 99 S.Ct. 1289, 440 U.S. 940, 59 L.Ed.2d 499; Welch v. Louisiana Power & Light Co., C.A.5th, 1972, 466 F.2d 1344; and cases cited 6 Wright & Miller, Civil § 1503 nn. 58, 68.

See generally Haworth, Changing Defendants in Private Civil Actions Under Federal Rule 15(c)—An Ancient Problem Lingers On, 1975 Wis.L.Rev. 552; Note, Amendments That Add Plaintiffs Under Federal Rule of Civil Procedure 15(c), 1982, 50 Geo.Wash.L.Rev. 671; Note, Federal Rule of Civil Procedure

15(c); Relation Back of Amendments, 1972, 57 Minn.L.Rev. 83.

The holding in Stoner v. Terranella, C.A. 6th, 1967, 372 F.2d 89, that Rule 15(c) does not apply to an amendment to set up an omitted counterclaim, and that state law therefore controls on relation back of such a counterclaim, seems very dubious. See 6 Wright & Miller, Civil § 1496, pp. 486–489. In Butler v. Poffinberger, D.C.W.Va.1970, 49 F.R.D. 8, the court refused to follow the Stoner case.

29. Marshall v. Mulrenin, C.A.1st, 1974, 508 F.2d 39, noted 1975, 9 Akron L.Rev. 199, 50 N.Y.U.L.Rev. 952; Covel v. Safetech, Inc., D.C.Mass.1981, 90 F.R.D. 427; Carmouche v. Bethlehem Steel Corp., D.C.Nev.1978, 450 F.Supp. 1361. Contra: Britt v. Arvantis, C.A.3d, 1978, 590 F.2d 57.

See § 59 above at notes 42–45.

30. Slavenburg Corp. v. Boston Ins. Co., D.C.N.Y.1962, 30 F.R.D. 123; Berssenbrugge v. Luce Mfg. Co., D.C.Mo.1939, 30 F.Supp. 101.

On supplemental pleadings generally, see 6 Wright & Miller, Civil §§ 1504–1510.

quite clear that an amendment is proper to cure a defective complaint. On this view, if parties were before the court on a defective complaint it was held necessary to dismiss their action and make them start again, even though events occurring after commencement of the action had made clear their right to judicial relief. Such a distinction had no support in the language of Rule 15(d) and was the kind of arbitrary and mechanical procedural barrier that the rules generally do not countenance. There was case law to the contrary, holding that a supplemental complaint was to be tested on its own merits and entertained if it stated a claim on which relief could be granted even though the complaint which it purported to supplement was defective in its statement of such a claim. In 1963 Rule 15(d) was amended to codify this latter line of cases.[31]

The case law is not clearly developed on the extent to which a supplemental complaint will be held to relate back for purposes of the statute of limitations. The problem is not likely to arise often, since a supplemental complaint is limited to events that have occurred since the filing of the original complaint and usually the claim based on these recent events will not be barred by limitations. But with delays in litigation, and a short statute of limitations, such a case can arise. Where it does arise, the supplemental complaint should be treated as an amended complaint would be. If it relies on a different transaction from that originally sued on, there should be no relation back,[32] but where, as is usual, the supplemental complaint is designed to obtain relief along the same lines, pertaining to the same cause, and based on the same subject matter or claim for relief, as set out in the original complaint, it should be held to relate back, as an amended complaint would. The defendant will have had notice from the beginning that a claim was being asserted against him arising out of this subject matter, and this is usually thought enough to satisfy the statute of limitations.[33]

In addition to the pleadings, Rule 12 authorizes a variety of motions attacking pleadings. A party may move to strike any insufficient defense or any redundant, immaterial, impertinent, or scandalous matter.[34] Such motions are not favored; the motion should be denied unless the allegations attacked have no possible relation to the controversy and may prejudice the other party.[35]

---

31. Ridgeway v. International Broth. of Elec. Workers, D.C.Ill.1979, 466 F.Supp. 595; Lynam v. Livingston, D.C.Del.1966, 257 F.Supp. 520; 6 Wright & Miller, Civil § 1505.

32. Blau v. Lamb, D.C.N.Y.1961, 191 F.Supp. 906.

33. New York Central & H. R. R. Co. v. Kinney, 1922, 43 S.Ct. 122, 123, 260 U.S. 340, 346, 67 L.Ed. 294.

A supplemental complaint is treated as an amendment, and Rule 15(c) applied, in Davis v. Piper Aircraft Corp., C.A. 4th, 1980, 615 F.2d 606, 609 n. 3, certiorari dismissed 101 S.Ct. 25, 448 U.S. 911, 65 L.Ed.2d 1141. See 6 Wright & Miller, Civil § 1508.

34. 5 Wright & Miller, Civil §§ 1380–1383.

35. E.g., U. S. Dental Institute v. American Assn. of Orthodontists, D.C.Ill. 1975, 396 F.Supp. 565, 583–584; Johnson v. American Aviation Corp., D.C. N.D.1967, 64 F.R.D. 435, 440; and

Another disfavored motion is the motion for a more definite statement. By a 1948 amendment to the rules, the old bill of particulars was abolished. The motion for more definite statement, which serves much the same function, is to be granted only where a pleading to which a responsive pleading is permitted is so vague or ambiguous that the party cannot reasonably be required to frame a responsive pleading.[36] If the pleading is sufficiently definite that the opponent can reply to it, the motion for more definite statement should be denied and any particulars that the opponent needs to prepare for trial obtained by depositions, interrogatories, and similar discovery procedures.[37] The motion is never proper where no responsive pleading is permitted,[38] nor should it be used to force the plaintiff to include additional particulars that may make the complaint vulnerable to a motion to dismiss.[39]

The most familiar motion is a motion to dismiss under Rule 12(b). This rule lists seven defenses that could be set out in the answer but that may, at the option of the pleader, be made by preliminary motion.[40] By such a motion the defendant can raise the defense that the complaint fails to state a claim upon which relief can be granted, although the liberal rules as to sufficiency of a complaint make it a rare case in which a motion on this ground should properly be granted.[41] By such a motion the defendant can also challenge whether the court has jurisdiction over the subject matter, raise the failure to join an indispensable party, and assert the dilatory defenses of lack of jurisdiction over the person, improper venue, insufficiency of process, and insufficiency of service of process.

Though these motions under Rule 12(b) are much discussed, they are of limited efficacy. A sampling made in 1962 for the information of the Advisory Committee on Civil Rules suggests that such motions are made in only about 5% of all cases, and that in fewer than 2% of all cases do such motions lead to a final termination of the action.

All motions, except those made during a hearing or trial, must be made in writing, and are to state with particularity the grounds therefor, and set forth the relief or order sought.[42] In practice the

---

cases cited 5 Wright & Miller, Civil § 1380 n. 86.

36. Rule 12(e); Kirby v. Turner-Day & Woolworth Handle Co., D.C.Tenn.1943, 50 F.Supp. 469; 5 Wright & Miller, Civil §§ 1374–1379; Comment, 1963, 61 Mich.L.Rev. 1126.

37. E.g., CMAX Inc. v. Hall, C.A.9th, 1961, 290 F.2d 736; Steinberg v. Guardian Life Ins. Co. of America, D.C.Pa.1980, 486 F.Supp. 122; Choat v. Rome Indus., Inc., D.C.Ga.1979, 480 F.Supp. 387.

38. Citizens Trust Co. v. New England Dredge & Dock Co., D.C.Conn.1966, 260 F.Supp. 800.

39. E.g., Lodge 743, Intl. Assn. of Machinists, AFL–CIO v. United Aircraft Corp., D.C.Conn.1962, 30 F.R.D. 142.

40. Wright & Miller, Civil §§ 1347–1366.

41. See § 68 below. For similar reasons a motion for judgment on the pleadings, made after the close of all the pleadings, though authorized by Rule 12(c), can rarely be granted. See 5 Wright & Miller, Civil §§ 1367–1372.

42. Rule 7(b)(1); 5 Wright & Miller, Civil §§ 1191–1193.

requirement that the grounds be stated with particularity is frequent-ly ignored. Motions to dismiss for failure to state a claim on which relief can be granted rarely, if ever, set forth the detailed grounds on which the party relies, and such motions have the support of Official Form 19, which is equally unspecific, and which, by virtue of Rule 84, is expressly made sufficient. Thus there can be no doubt that such a general motion is proper, despite the language of Rule 7(b)(1).[43] Many of the district courts have met this situation by adoption of a local rule requiring the moving party to submit a brief or memoran-dum in support of his motion, at the time the motion is made.[44]

It is now quite clear that any common law rule against "speaking motions" is ended, and that the court is not confined to the pleadings and motion in ruling, but may consider evidentiary matter presented by affidavit or otherwise. It has always been the rule that such oth-er matter is proper where jurisdiction is challenged or a dilatory de-fense is being raised.[45] Amendments to the rules in 1948 provide that where a party moves to dismiss for failure to state a claim on which relief can be granted, or moves for judgment on the pleadings, and matters outside the pleadings are presented to and not excluded by the court, the motion is to be treated as if it were a motion for sum-mary judgment under Rule 56.[46] This convenient practice has been followed in innumerable cases.[47] Where it is used, the parties are able to present to the court the merits of the case, to see if there is any genuine issue which requires trial, and they are not limited to an attack on the paper allegations.

Ordinarily a motion to dismiss or a motion for judgment on the pleadings will be heard in advance of trial, although the court has discretion to order that the hearing and determination thereof be de-ferred until the trial. If the defenses listed in Rule 12(b) are included in the answer, rather than raised by motion to dismiss, they will still be heard before trial, on application of any party, unless the court chooses to defer them.[48]

The time-honored ritual of a "special appearance" has no place un-der the rules. At an earlier time an answer on the merits was thought to be a general appearance, submitting the party to the juris-

43. Sapero v. Shackelford, D.C.Va.1944, 109 F.Supp. 321; Kirby v. Penn-sylvania R. Co., D.C.Pa.1950, 92 F.Supp. 417, 423, reversed on other grounds C.A.3d, 1951, 188 F.2d 793; Territory of Alaska v. American Can Co., D.C.Alaska 1955, 21 Fed.Rules Serv. 12b.31, Case 2. But cf. Smeed v. Carpenter, C.A.9th, 1960, 274 F.2d 414.

44. See, e.g., Local Rule 13, Northern Dist. of Illinois; Mitchell v. Public Serv. Coordinated Transp., D.C.N.J. 1952, 13 F.R.D. 96.

These local rules cannot be applied as a trap for the unwary and cause a liti-gant to be deprived of a day in court. Woodham v. American Cystoscope Co., C.A.5th, 1964, 335 F.2d 551.

45. Williams v. Minnesota Mining & Mfg. Co., D.C.Cal.1953, 14 F.R.D. 1; Central Mexico Light & Power Co. v. Munch, C.C.A.2d, 1940, 116 F.2d 85.

46. As to summary judgment, see § 99 below.

47. See 5 Wright & Miller, Civil § 1366.

48. Rule 12(d); 5 Wright & Miller, Civil § 1373.

diction of the court for all purposes. The party who wished to challenge jurisdiction without so submitting was required to come in and make a special appearance. This is no longer the law. Rule 12(b) provides that no defense or objection is waived by being joined with one or more other defenses or objections in a responsive pleading or motion.[49] There is a possible qualification of this general principle. Many cases continue to apply the former practice that a defendant waives objection to venue or jurisdiction over his person by the assertion of a counterclaim,[50] though there are cases to the contrary.[51] A finding of waiver is wholly impermissible if the counterclaim is compulsory,[52] and doubt has been expressed about the soundness of finding waiver even if the counterclaim was permissive only.[53]

If a defendant chooses to assert his defenses and objections by answer, rather than raising some of them, as he may, in a Rule 12(b) motion, he waives any defenses or objections not included in the answer, with certain exceptions noted below.[54] If the defendant chooses to make a motion to dismiss under Rule 12(b), he must include all defenses and objections then available to him that Rule 12 permits to be raised by motion, and cannot make a second motion

49. Orange Theatre Corp. v. Rayherstz Amusement Corp., C.C.A.3d, 1944, 139 F.2d 871, certiorari denied 64 S.Ct. 1057, 322 U.S. 740, 88 L.Ed. 1573; Product Promotions, Inc. v. Cousteau, C.A.5th, 1974, 495 F.2d 483, 490; 5 Wright & Miller, Civil § 1344. A defense or objection overruled by the trial court may be asserted on appeal, even though the party has gone on to defend on the merits after his objection was denied. Speir v. Robert C. Herd & Co., D.C.Md.1960, 189 F.Supp. 436; Lisle Mills v. Arkay Infants Wear, D.C. N.Y.1950, 90 F.Supp. 676.

50. North Branch Products, Inc. v. Fisher, C.A.1960, 284 F.2d 611, 109 U.S. App.D.C. 182, certiorari denied 81 S.Ct. 713, 365 U.S. 827, 5 L.Ed.2d 705; Beaunit Mills, Inc. v. Industrias Reunidas F. Matarazzo, S.A., D.C.N.Y.1959, 23 F.R.D. 654; Hook & Ackerman v. Hirsh, D.C.D.C.1951, 98 F.Supp. 477; 5 Wright & Miller, Civil § 1397. This was clearly the old rule. Merchants' Heat & Light Co. v. James B. Clow & Sons, 1907, 27 S.Ct. 285, 204 U.S. 286, 51 L.Ed. 488.

51. Knapp-Monarch Co. v. Dominion Elec. Corp., C.A.7th, 1966, 365 F.2d 175; Keil Lock Co., Inc. v. Earle Hardware Mfg. Co., D.C.N.Y.1954, 16 F.R.D. 388; Sadler v. Pennsylvania Ref. Co., D.C.S.C.1940, 33 F.Supp. 414.

52. Dragor Shipping Corp. v. Union Tank Car Co., C.A.9th, 1967, 378 F.2d 241, 244; Hasse v. American Photo-

graph Corp., C.A.10th, 1962, 299 F.2d 666, 668–669; Medicenters of America, Inc. v. T & V Realty & Equip. Corp., D.C.Va.1974, 371 F.Supp. 1180; Ryan v. Glenn, D.C.Miss.1971, 336 F.Supp. 555; 5 Wright & Miller, Civil § 1397. But see North Branch Products, Inc. v. Fisher, C.A.1960, 284 F.2d 611, 615, 109 U.S.App.D.C. 182, certiorari denied 81 S.Ct. 713, 365 U.S. 827, 5 L.Ed.2d 705, noted 1961, 63 W.Va.L.Rev. 287.

53. See Neifeld v. Steinberg, C.A.3d, 1971, 438 F.2d 423, 429 n. 13, noted 1972, 32 Md.L.Rev. 156.

54. Pila v. G. R. Leasing & Rental Corp., C.A.1st, 1977, 551 F.2d 941; Taylor v. Reo Motors, Inc., C.A.10th, 1960, 275 F.2d 699; and cases cited 5 Wright & Miller, Civil § 1391 n. 30.

The answer, like any pleading, may be amended to incorporate affirmative defenses inadvertently omitted, and this may be done either by express amendment, e.g., Groninger v. Davison, C.A. 8th, 1966, 364 F.2d 638, or by amendment to conform to the evidence, e.g., Mazer v. Lipshutz, C.A.3d, 1966, 360 F.2d 275, certiorari denied 87 S.Ct. 72, 385 U.S. 833, 17 L.Ed.2d 68. However amendment to assert the objections of lack of jurisdiction over the person, improper venue, insufficiency of process, or insufficiency of service of process may only be made if Rule 15(a) allows amendment as a matter of course. Rule 12(h)(1).

raising other such defenses or objections.[55] The rule was amended in 1966 to resolve a conflict in the cases and make it clear that a defendant who makes a motion under Rule 12(b), asserting, for example, that the complaint should be dismissed for failure to state a claim on which relief can be granted, cannot thereafter raise, either by further motion or in his answer, such dilatory defenses as lack of personal jurisdiction, improper venue, or insufficiency of process or service of process.[56]

There are four exceptions to the rule that a defense or objection is waived if not made by answer or by motion, as the case may be. Lack of jurisdiction of the subject matter is never waived, and if such lack of jurisdiction appears at any time in the case, the court must dismiss the action.[57] The defense of failure to state a claim upon which relief can be granted, the defense of failure to join an indispensable party, and the objection of failure to state a legal defense to a claim, need not be asserted at the earliest opportunity. They may be made by a later pleading, if one is permitted, or by motion for judgment on the pleadings, or at the trial.[58] It is too late, however, to raise these last three defenses and objections after trial.[59]

The Erie doctrine has very little application to pleading in federal court. A complaint is sufficient if it meets the test of Rule 8(a), though it would be subject to demurrer in state court for failure to set forth the detailed facts cherished in the state system.[60] An affirmative defense listed in Rule 8(c) must be pleaded in the answer, regardless of state law, though the state law will control the burden of proof on that defense.[61] However the state law continues to con-

---

55. Rule 12(g); 5 Wright & Miller, Civil §§ 1384–1389.

56. The amendment accepts the view previously taken in Keefe v. Derounian, D.C.Ill.1946, 6 F.R.D. 11, and rejects the view taken in Phillips v. Baker, C.C.A.9th, 1941, 121 F.2d 752, certiorari denied 62 S.Ct. 301, 314 U.S. 688, 86 L.Ed. 551. See Rowley v. McMillan, C.A.4th, 1974, 502 F.2d 1326, 1332–1333; 5 Wright & Miller, Civil § 1391.

57. Rule 12(h)(3); Savarese v. Edrick Transfer & Storage, Inc., C.A.9th, 1975, 513 F.2d 140; 5 Wright & Miller, Civil § 1393.

58. Rule 12(h)(2); Wright Farms Constr., Inc. v. Kreps, D.C.Vt.1977, 444 F.Supp. 1023; Wegwart v. Eagle Movers, Inc., D.C.Wis.1977, 441 F.Supp. 872, motion denied 1979, 467 F.Supp. 573; 5 Wright & Miller, Civil § 1392.

59. Brule v. Southworth, C.A.1st, 1979, 611 F.2d 406.

60. Bank of St. Louis v. Morrissey, C.A. 8th, 1979, 597 F.2d 1131; and cases cited 5 Wright & Miller, Civil § 1204 n. 49. Contra: Adair v. Pope & Talbot, Inc., D.C.Or.1960, 190 F.Supp. 184.

61. Palmer v. Hoffman, 1943, 63 S.Ct. 477, 482, 318 U.S. 109, 117, 87 L.Ed. 645; Glass Containers Corp. v. Miller Brewing Co., C.A.5th, 1981, 643 F.2d 308; Cincinnati, N. O. & T. P. Ry. Co. v. Eller, C.A.6th, 1952, 197 F.2d 652, certiorari denied 73 S.Ct. 105, 344 U.S. 864, 97 L.Ed. 670; Sampson v. Channell, C.C.A.1st, 1940, 110 F.2d 754, 757, certiorari denied 60 S.Ct. 1099, 310 U.S. 650, 84 L.Ed. 1415; 5 Wright & Miller, Civil § 1272. Contra: Sundstrand Corp. v. Standard Kollsman Indus., Inc., C.A.7th, 1973, 488 F.2d 807, 813.

However, if Rule 8(c) is silent about a particular defense, state law, though not controlling, is frequently looked to in deciding whether it is an affirmative defense. E.g., Seal v. Industrial Elec., Inc., C.A.5th, 1966, 362 F.2d 788; 5 Wright & Miller, Civil § 1271.

trol the substantive elements of the claim, and the pleading may be required to set forth these elements,[62] though the form of stating them is governed by a federal standard.[63]

§ 67. One Form of Action [1]

Ever since the Field Code was adopted in New York in 1848, it has been recognized that the two most prominent features of that code, the abolition of the common law forms of action and the union of law and equity, are essential to any significant procedural reform.[2] Chief Justice Taft gave impetus to such a change in the federal system,[3] and when the Supreme Court determined to exercise its rulemaking power under the Enabling Act of 1934, it decided at the outset to incorporate this change in the rules it promulgated.[4] Thus Rule 2 declares: "There shall be one form of action to be known as 'civil action.' "

The creation of a single form of action for the federal courts has been uniquely successful. The courts construed the change in a sympathetic fashion, with a clear understanding of the purposes it was intended to achieve. This was in striking contrast to "the cold, not to say inhuman, treatment"[5] that judges in many states had given to the initial Field Code nearly a century before. As a result, the single form of action has worked without difficulty, and virtually without comment, in federal court. There has been an occasional nostalgic look to the past,[6] but much more common is a glad acceptance of the fact that the old distinctions are now almost without procedural significance.[7]

62. Mitchell v. White Consol., C.A.8th, 1949, 177 F.2d 500, certiorari denied 70 S.Ct. 574, 339 U.S. 913, 94 L.Ed. 1339; Whitehall Constr. Co. v. Washington Suburban Sanitary Comm., D.C.Md. 1958, 165 F.Supp. 730.

63. In the Matter of Johns Manville/Asbestosis Cases, D.C.Ill. 1981, 511 F.Supp. 1229; Korry v. International Tel. & Tel. Corp., D.C.N.Y. 1978, 444 F.Supp. 193.

[§ 67]

1. 4 Wright & Miller, Civil §§ 1041–1045.

2. See Joiner & Geddes, The Union of Law and Equity: A Prerequisite to Procedural Revision, 1957, 55 Mich.L. Rev. 1059.

"Law and equity are two things which God has joined together but New South Wales has kept asunder. In a land where natural curiosities abound, and such anachronisms as the platypus still survive, perhaps nothing is surprising; but the continued refusal of this State to adopt the judicature system is anomalous enough to excite interest." Adam, 1951, 25 Aust.L.J. 354. Though the platypus presumably still survives in New South Wales, the separation of law and equity does not. See Law Reform (Law and Equity) Act, 1972 Stat. N.S.W. 424.

3. Taft, Three Needed Steps of Progress, 1922, 8 A.B.A.J. 34, 35; Taft, Possible and Needed Reforms in Administration of Justice in Federal Courts, 1922, 8 A.B.A.J. 601, 604, 607. See also his famous opinion in Liberty Oil Co. v. Condon Nat. Bank, 1922, 43 S.Ct. 118, 260 U.S. 235, 67 L.Ed. 232.

4. See § 62 above.

5. Winslow, C. J., in McArthur v. Moffet, 1910, 128 N.W. 445, 446, 143 Wis. 564, 567.

6. See, e.g., Frank, J., in Bereslavsky v. Caffey, C.C.A.2d, 1947, 161 F.2d 499, 500, certiorari denied 68 S.Ct. 82, 332 U.S. 770, 92 L.Ed. 355.

7. See, e.g., Arnold, J., in Groome v. Steward, C.C.A.1944, 142 F.2d 756, 79 U.S.App.D.C. 50.

The forms of action are abolished. No longer is a judgment to be reversed because the pleader chose the wrong form.[8] Law and equity are merged. There is no longer, in federal practice, such a thing as a "suit in equity." [9]

Rule 2 does not affect the various remedies that have heretofore been available. Instead the merger of law and equity and the abolition of the forms of action supply one uniform procedure by which a litigant may present his claim in an orderly manner to a court empowered to give him whatever relief is appropriate and just. The substantive principles that applied previously are not changed,[10] and it remains for the court to decide, in accordance with those principles, what form of relief is proper on the particular facts proven. Because courts can now give specific relief without interference with another independent system of courts, there is a natural tendency to grant specific relief more frequently than was true in olden days. Eventually it may well be that courts will feel free to ask only "What remedy is best adapted to making the plaintiff whole?" and will ignore the historic origins of the various remedies.[11] The rules neither hasten nor retard such a development. Their function is limited to that of supplying a procedure by which a party may present his claim in an orderly manner.

Because the creation of a single form of action is a procedural reform only, the court may still find it necessary to consider the nature of the action to determine what statute of limitations is applicable, where such statutes are couched in terms of the old distinctions.[12] The right to jury trial turns—though decreasingly so in the light of recent decisions—on the historical characterization of the action.[13] But such instances in which the old distinctions continue to rule from their graves are quite rare.[14]

"Under the rules, law and equity are procedurally combined; nothing turns now upon the form of the action or the procedural devices by which the parties happen to come before the court." Ross v. Bernhard, 1970, 90 S.Ct. 733, 739, 396 U.S. 531, 540, 24 L.Ed.2d 729.

8. C & H Air Conditioning Fan Co. v. Haffner, C.A.5th, 1954, 216 F.2d 256; 4 Wright & Miller, Civil § 1042.

9. Union Mut. Life Ins. Co. v. Friedman, C.C.A.2d, 1944, 139 F.2d 542; Rodgers v. U. S., D.C.Cal.1958, 158 F.Supp. 670; U. S. v. Rosenbluth, D.C.Ohio 1952, 102 F.Supp. 996.

10. Stainback v. Mo Hock Ke Lok Po, 1949, 69 S.Ct. 606, 614 n. 26, 336 U.S. 368, 382 n. 26, 93 L.Ed. 741; Hanson v. Aetna Life & Cas. Co., C.A.5th, 1980, 625 F.2d 573; 4 Wright & Miller, Civil § 1043.

11. See Beacon Theatres, Inc. v. Westover, 1959, 79 S.Ct. 948, 955, 359 U.S. 500, 501, 3 L.Ed.2d 988; Wright, The Law of Remedies as a Social Institution, 1955, 18 U.Det.L.J. 376; Sedler, Equitable Relief, But Not Equity, 1963, 15 J.Legal Ed. 293; Frank, Bringing Equity Up to Date, 1975, 61 A.B.A.J. 91. Compare Holtzoff, Equitable and Legal Rights and Remedies Under the New Federal Procedure, 1943, 31 Calif. L.Rev. 127.

12. Williamson v. Columbia Gas & Elec. Corp., C.C.A.3d, 1940, 110 F.2d 15, certiorari denied 60 S.Ct. 1087, 310 U.S. 639, 84 L.Ed. 1407.

13. See § 92 below.

14. See 4 Wright & Miller, Civil §§ 1044, 1045.

The one civil action under the rules is used to vindicate any civil power the district court has. The demand for judgment forms no part of the claim for relief, and does not restrict the relief to be granted against those appearing and defendant: as against such parties the final judgment must grant all the relief to which a plaintiff is entitled, whether or not demanded in the pleadings.[15] Rule 8(e)(2) authorizes a party to state as many separate claims or defenses as he has, regardless of whether they are based on legal or equitable or maritime grounds,[16] and this mandate is reinforced by Rule 18(a), which permits, either as a claim or a counterclaim, as many claims, either legal or equitable or maritime, as the party may have against an opposing party.[17]

§ 68. The Theory of Modern Pleading [1]

The keystone of the system of procedure embodied in the rules is Rule 8, and specifically subsections 8(a)(2), 8(e)(1), and 8(f). These provisions state that technical forms of pleading are not required, that pleadings are to be construed liberally so as to do substantial justice, and, most important of all, they substitute the requirement of "a short and plain statement of the claim showing that the pleader is entitled to relief" for the familiar "facts constituting a cause of action" of the codes. The other procedural devices of the rules—broad joinder, discovery, free amendment, and summary judgment—rest on these provisions about pleadings.

Historically pleadings have had four functions: (1) giving notice of the nature of a claim or defense; (2) stating the facts each party believes to exist; (3) narrowing the issues; and (4) providing a means for speedy disposition of sham claims and unsubstantial defenses. The emphasis as among these four functions varied greatly with the passage of years and from jurisdiction to jurisdiction, but both at common law and under the codes, all four were expected to be performed by the pleadings. The complaint not only gave notice to the nature of the case but also was required to state the facts constituting the cause of action. Subsequent pleadings were expected to narrow the issues until the case was ready for trial. Failure to incorporate an essential allegation might lead to a speedy end of the litigation. Since the pleadings were expected to do so much, it was natural that strict rules should develop as to them, and this in turn

---

15. Rule 54(c); Zunamon v. Brown, C.A. 8th, 1969, 418 F.2d 883, 888–889; Fanchon & Marco v. Paramount Pictures, C.A.2d, 1953, 202 F.2d 731; 4 Wright & Miller, Civil §§ 1255–1257. See also § 98 below.

16. 4 Wright & Miller, Civil §§ 1282–1285.

17. De Pinto v. Provident Sec. Life Ins. Co., C.A.9th, 1963, 323 F.2d 826, certio-rari denied 84 S.Ct. 968, 376 U.S. 950, 11 L.Ed.2d 970. See also § 78 below.

[§ 68]

1. 5 Wright & Miller, Civil §§ 1202, 1215–1226; Clark, Simplified Pleading, 1942, 2 F.R.D. 456; James, The Objective and Function of the Complaint—Common Law—Codes—Federal Rules, 1961, 14 Vand.L.Rev. 899.

meant that many cases were disposed of on pleading defects without regard to the merits of the controversy.

The rules provide techniques more efficient than pleadings for performing the last three functions.[2] The facts may be determined by discovery. The issues may likewise be narrowed by discovery or at a pretrial conference, or by "partial summary judgment" under Rule 56(d). Cases where there is no real controversy may be disposed of speedily and finally, on the merits, by summary judgment. This is not to say that the pleadings will not, in some cases, still assist in performing those functions, but rather that the pleadings no longer carry exclusive responsibility for those functions. The only function left to be performed by the pleadings alone is that of notice. For these reasons, pleadings under the rule may properly be a generalized summary of the party's position, sufficient to advise the party what the incident is for which he is being sued, sufficient to show what was decided for purposes of res judicata, and sufficient to indicate whether the case should be tried to the court or to a jury. No more is demanded of pleadings than this; history shows that no more can be successfully performed by pleadings.

At common law there was a great belief in the efficacy of pleadings. The whole grand scheme was, by rigid stages of denial, avoidance, or demurrer, eventually to reach a single issue of law or fact that would dispose of the case. This system was wonderfully scientific. It was also wonderfully slow, expensive, and unworkable. The system was better calculated to vindicate scientific rules of pleading than it was to dispense justice. The great Baron Parke is said to have boasted to Sir William Erle that he had aided in building up sixteen volumes of Meeson & Welsby, reports of the Court of Exchequer, which usually went off on procedural points. "It's a lucky thing," Sir William replied, "that there was not a seventeenth volume, because if there had been, the common law itself would have disappeared altogether amidst the jeers and hisses of mankind."[3]

Under the codes the important emphasis was on developing the facts by pleadings. The pleader was asked to give the "dry, naked, actual facts,"[4] avoiding the pitfalls of stating conclusions on the one hand and pleading evidence on the other. This requirement was based on a failure to perceive that the distinction between facts and conclusions is one of degree only, not of kind.[5] But it had a further

2. Hickman v. Taylor, 1947, 67 S.Ct. 385, 388, 329 U.S. 495, 500, 91 L.Ed. 451; Conley v. Gibson, 1957, 78 S.Ct. 99, 103, 355 U.S. 41, 47–48, 2 L.Ed.2d 80.

3. Coleridge, The Law in 1847 and The Law in 1889, 1890, 57 Contemp.Rev. 797, 799.

Perhaps the most amusing piece ever to appear in the solemn pages of the Harvard Law Review is Note, Common Law Pleading, 1896, 10 Harv.L.Rev. 238, in which the editors quote and endorse the spirited defense of the old ways by Sir Montague Crackenthorpe, Q.C.

4. Pomeroy, Code Remedies, 5th ed. 1929, p. 640.

5. Cook, Statements of Fact in Pleading Under the Codes, 1921, 21 Col.L.Rev. 416; Cook, "Facts" and "Statements of Fact," 1937, 4 U.Chi.L.Rev. 233; Gavit,

weakness. The pleader who set forth too little could be attacked by demurrer. The pleader who set forth exactly the right amount in his pleading found himself committed unreservedly to a course of action and a factual statement from which he could not deviate at the trial. Many pleaders discovered that an obvious solution was to plead too much, to include every possible allegation regardless of the unlikelihood that the evidence would support it. The result of such overpleading was "frightful expense, endless delay and an enormous loss of motion." [6]

Thus the rules do not ask more of the pleadings than can reasonably be expected. The short and plain statement of the claim showing that the pleader is entitled to relief is enough to give the opposing party fair notice of the occurrences being sued on, and other devices are provided for the other functions previously entrusted to the pleadings. A series of Official Forms appended to the rules, and expressly made sufficient by virtue of Rule 84, indicate the brevity and the simplicity that Rule 8(a) contemplates. The common law emphasized scientific symmetry and issue formulation in the pleadings. The codes emphasized statement of facts. The rules emphasize fair notice and the doing of justice. "Cases are generally to be tried on the proofs rather than the pleadings." [7]

The leading case on the pleading requirements of the rules is the decision of the Supreme Court in Conley v. Gibson.[8] This was a class suit brought by certain black members of a labor union claiming that the union had breached its statutory duty to represent fairly and without hostile discrimination all of the employees in the union. The union contended, among other things, that the complaint failed adequately to set forth a claim upon which relief could be granted. A unanimous Court, speaking through Justice Black, said: "In appraising the sufficiency of the complaint we follow, of course, the accepted rule that a complaint should not be dismissed for failure to state a claim unless it appears beyond doubt that the plaintiff can prove no set of facts in support of his claim which would entitle him to relief." [9] The complaint in question alleged that petitioners were discharged wrongfully by the railroad and that the union, acting according to plan, refused to protect their jobs as it did those of white employees or to help blacks with their grievances, all because of their race. The Court asserted that if these allegations were proven they would show a manifest breach of the union's statutory duty to repre-

Legal Conclusions, 1932, 16 Minn.L. Rev. 378; Clark, Code Pleading, 2d ed. 1947, § 38.

6. Skinner, Pre-Trial and Discovery under the Alabama Rules of Civil Procedure, 1957, 9 Ala.L.Rev. 202, 204. See also James & Hazard, Civil Procedure, 2d ed. 1977, § 2.13.

7. De Loach v. Crowley's Inc., C.C.A.5th, 1942, 128 F.2d 378, 380.

8. 1957, 78 S.Ct. 99, 355 U.S. 41, 2 L.Ed. 2d 80.

9. 78 S.Ct. at 9, 35 U.S. at 45, citing, in support of "the accepted rule," such well-known cases as Leimer v. State Mut. Life Assur. Co., C.C.A.8th, 1940, 108 F.2d 302; Dioguardi v. Durning, C.C.A.2d, 1944, 139 F.2d 774, and Continental Collieries, Inc. v. Shober, C.C.A.3d, 1942, 130 F.2d 631.

sent fairly and without hostile discrimination all of the employees in the bargaining unit.

The union also contended that the complaint failed to set forth specific facts to support its general allegations of discrimination. The Court said of this contention: "The decisive answer to this is that the Federal Rules of Civil Procedure do not require a claimant to set out in detail the facts upon which he bases his claim. To the contrary, all the Rules require is 'a short and plain statement of the claim' that will give the defendant fair notice of what the plaintiff's claim is and the grounds upon which it rests. The illustrative forms appended to the Rules plainly demonstrate this. Such simplified 'notice pleading' is made possible by the liberal opportunity for discovery and the other pretrial procedures established by the Rules to disclose more precisely the basis of both claim and defense and to define more narrowly the disputed facts and issues. Following the simple guide of Rule 8(f) that 'all pleadings shall be so construed as to do substantial justice', we have no doubt that petitioner's complaint adequately set forth a claim and gave the respondents fair notice of its basis. The Federal Rules reject the approach that pleading is a game of skill in which one misstep by counsel may be decisive to the outcome and accept the principle that the purpose of pleading is to facilitate a proper decision on the merits." [10]

In line with the general philosophy of pleading that the rules embody, six specific principles are authoritatively accepted.

(1) No distinction is to be drawn between "evidence," "ultimate facts," and "conclusions." [11] The rules permit the claim to be stated in general terms, and are intended to discourage battles over mere form of statement.[12] The former distinctions, as has already been pointed out, were quite unworkable.

(2) There is no requirement of any particular "theory of the pleadings." Contrary to the rule in some code states, the complaint is not to be dismissed because the plaintiff's lawyer has misconceived the proper legal theory of the claim, if he is entitled to any relief on any theory.[13] "A simple statement in sequence of the events which have transpired, coupled with a direct claim by way of demand for judgment of what the plaintiff expects and hopes to recover, is a measure of clarity and safety; and even the demand for judgment loses its restrictive nature when the parties are at issue, for particular legal

10. 78 S.Ct. at 103, 355 U.S. at 48.

11. U. S. v. Employing Plasterers' Assn., 1954, 74 S.Ct. 452, 454, 347 U.S. 186, 188, 98 L.Ed. 618; Garcia v. Bernabe, C.A.1st, 1961, 289 F.2d 690; Oil, Chem. and Atomic Workers Intl. Union, AFL–CIO v. Delta Ref. Co., C.A.6th, 1960, 277 F.2d 694, 697; and 5 Wright & Miller, Civil § 1218.

12. Note to Rule 8(a), Advisory Committee Report of October, 1955, reprinted at 5 Wright & Miller, Civil § 1201 n. 11.

13. Bramlet v. Wilson, C.A.8th, 1974, 495 F.2d 714; Thompson v. Allstate Ins. Co., C.A.5th, 1973, 476 F.2d 746; 5 Wright & Miller, Civil § 1219.

theories of counsel yield to the court's duty to grant the relief to which the prevailing party is entitled, whether demanded or not." [14]

(3) Pleadings are to be so construed as to do substantial justice.[15] The old rule that a pleading must be construed most strongly against the pleader is no longer followed. Instead the court will not require technical exactness or make refined inferences against the pleader but will construe the pleading in his favor if justice so requires.

(4) A complaint is not subject to dismissal unless it appears to a certainty that no relief can be granted under any set of facts that can be proved in support of its allegations.[16] This rule, which has been stated literally hundreds of times, precludes final dismissal for insufficiency of the complaint except in the extraordinary case where the pleader makes allegations that show on the face of the complaint some insuperable bar to relief.[17]

(5) The pleader may allege matters alternatively or hypothetically, and except for the good faith requirements of Rule 11, the allegations may even be inconsistent.[18] The pleader cannot be required to elect among his allegations, but is entitled to have all his claims and defenses considered by the trier of facts.[19] Similarly there is no requirement of election of remedies.[20]

(6) Once the case is tried, the pleadings lose such little significance as they had before, and judgment is to be in accordance with the evidence. This is provided by Rule 15(b), which authorizes two different procedures aimed at this common objective and both usually

---

14. Gins v. Mauser Plumbing Supply Co., C.C.A.2d, 1945, 148 F.2d 974, 976.

15. Rule 8(f); Mountain Fuel Supply Co. v. Johnson, C.A.10th, 1978, 586 F.2d 1375, 1382, certiorari denied 99 S.Ct. 2182, 441 U.S. 952, 60 L.Ed.2d 1058; Powers v. Troy Mills, Inc., D.C.N.H. 1969, 303 F.Supp. 1377, 1379; 5 Wright & Miller, Civil § 1286.

16. Conley v. Gibson, 1957, 78 S.Ct. 99, 102, 355 U.S. 41, 45, 2 L.Ed.2d 80; Hospital Bldg. Co. v. Trustees of Rex Hosp., 1976, 96 S.Ct. 1848, 1853, 425 U.S. 738, 746, 48 L.Ed.2d 338; 5 Wright & Miller, Civil §§ 1215, 1216.

Professor James has pointed out that the many statements to this effect are intended to evoke a frame of mind about pleading rather than state a precise test. James, Civil Procedure, 1965, pp. 86–88. See also James & Hazard, Civil Procedure, 2d ed. 1977, § 2.11; Hoshman v. Esso Standard Oil Co., C.A.5th, 1959, 263 F.2d 499, 501, certiorari denied 80 S.Ct. 60, 361 U.S. 818, 4 L.Ed. 2d 64; 5 Wright & Miller, Civil § 1216.

17. E.g., Leggett v. Montgomery Ward & Co., C.A.10th, 1949, 178 F.2d 436; Bach v. Quigan, D.C.N.Y.1945, 5 F.R.D. 34; 5 Wright & Miller, Civil § 1226.

18. Rule 8(e)(2); 5 Wright & Miller, Civil §§ 1282–1285.

19. Berry Ref. Co. v. Salemi, C.A.7th, 1965, 353 F.2d 721; Fidelity & Deposit Co. of Maryland v. Krout, C.C.A.2d 1945, 146 F.2d 531; McAndrews v. Goody Co., D.C.Neb.1978, 460 F.Supp. 104; 5 Wright & Miller, Civil § 1283.

20. Guy James Constr. Co. v. Trinity Indus., Inc., C.A.5th, 1981, 644 F.2d 525; Gins v. Mauser Plumbing Supply Co., C.C.A.2d, 1945, 148 F.2d 974; Bauman, Multiple Liability, Multiple Remedies, and the Federal Rules of Civil Procedure, 1962, 46 Minn.L.Rev. 729.

It is most unlikely that, as held in one case, the Erie doctrine requires application of state law as to election of remedies. Berger v. State Farm Mut. Auto. Ins. Co., C.A.10th, 1961, 291 F.2d 666, criticized 1962, 15 Okla.L.Rev. 186.

referred to as "amendments to conform to the evidence." [21]   Under
this rule the pleadings shall be deemed amended to conform to the
proof on any issues that were tried by express or implied consent of
the parties, though not raised by the pleadings.   " *   *   * [A] litigant cannot, for tactical purposes, stand by silently while evidence is
being admitted and then claim later that no relief can be given because the matter was not plead." [22]   If the litigant does raise his
voice, and timely objection is made that evidence is outside the pleadings, the court may permit the pleadings to be amended and shall do
so freely when presentation of the merits of the case will be thus
served and the opposing party will not be prejudiced by the amendment.   The first of these procedures effectively abolishes the old doctrine of "variance."   The second, liberally applied as it must be,[23] en-
sures that the pleadings will not restrict proof of the actual facts of
the case.

The simplified pleading required by the rules is not infrequently
referred to as "notice pleading."   This term, which was rejected by
the rulemakers and never employed by them, is prejudicial to a proper operation of federal procedure, because it is a pure abstraction,
without content except as injected by the immediate user, and because it suggests the absence of all pleadings.[24]   The rules require
the pleader to disclose adequate information as to the basis of his
claim for relief as distinguished from a bare averment that he wants
relief and is entitled to it.   It is true that in Conley v. Gibson the
Supreme Court referred to "simplified 'notice pleading,' " [25] but in
context it is plain that the Court's statement was one of aim rather
than definition.   Only two sentences before the phrase in question
the Court had emphasized that the rules require the complaint to give
the defendant "fair notice of what the plaintiff's claim is and the
grounds upon which it rests." [26]   Thus the Court recognized that the
rule does contemplate the statement of circumstances, occurrences,
and events in support of the claim presented, even though it permits
these circumstances to be stated with great generality.[27]

21. 6   Wright   &   Miller,   Civil
§§ 1491–1495.

22. Niedland v. U. S., C.A.3d, 1964, 338
F.2d 254, 259.   See also O'Brien v.
Moriarty, C.A.1st, 1974, 489 F.2d 941;
Note, Amendment of Pleadings to Con-
form to the Evidence, 1973, 9 Wake
Forest L.Rev. 247.

But implied consent to try new issues
cannot be derived from a failure to object to evidence that is relevant to existing issues.   U. S. v. Texas, C.A.5th,
1982, 680 F.2d 356, 361.

23. See, e.g., Robbins v. Jordan,
C.A.1950, 181 F.2d 793, 86 U.S.App.
D.C. 304, where it is held that the proper remedy for surprise from a change
of theory is a continuance, and that it

is an abuse of judicial discretion to refuse to allow the amendment.   Accord:
Green v. Baltimore & O. R. Co., C.A.
6th, 1962, 299 F.2d 837.   But cf. Ther-
mo King Corp. v. White's Trucking
Serv., Inc., C.A.5th, 1961, 292 F.2d 668;
Hargrave v. Wellman, C.A.9th, 1960,
276 F.2d 948.

24. Padovani v. Bruchhausen, C.A.2d,
1961, 293 F.2d 546, 550–551;   Clark,
Two Decades of the Federal Civil
Rules, 1958, 58 Col.L.Rev. 435,
450–451.

25. 78 S.Ct. at 103, 355 U.S. at 48.

26. Ibid.

27. City of Gainesville v. Florida Power
& Light Co., D.C.Fla.1980, 488 F.Supp.

The modern philosophy of pleading has been received with general approval, and applied with success. Reviewing its operation, after 17 years' experience, the Advisory Committee on Civil Rules said: "While there has been some minority criticism, the consensus favors the rule and the reported cases indicate that it has worked satisfactorily and has advanced the administration of justice in the district courts." [28]

Minority criticism there has been,[29] though some of it may be nostalgia by those who were expert in the old ways. The principal target for the criticism has been the decision in Dioguardi v. Durning.[30] The case itself seems but a routine application of principles that are universally accepted, but it has attracted unusual attention, perhaps because of its rather colorful facts and because the opinion is by Judge Charles E. Clark, the draftsman of the federal rules.

Dioguardi was the consignee of a shipment of "tonics," which was tied up in customs for failure of the consignee to pay some charges he claimed should have been paid by the consignor. The Collector of Customs, after holding the goods for a year, sold them at auction. Dioguardi, who had but limited ability to write and speak English, scorned the help of a lawyer and brought suit against the Collector with his own "obviously home drawn" complaint. In that complaint he alleged that on the auction day defendant "sold my merchandise to another bidder with my price of $110, and not of his price of $120." He also alleged that "three weeks before the sale, two cases, of 19 bottles each case disappeared." The United States Attorney moved to dismiss the complaint on the ground that it "fails to state facts sufficient to constitute a cause of action." The trial court granted the motion with leave to amend. Plaintiff reiterated his claims, "with an obviously heightened conviction that he was being unjustly treated", in an amended complaint, but this too was dismissed, and final judgment entered for the defendant.

The Second Circuit, speaking through Judge Clark, reversed. It said that Dioguardi had "stated enough to withstand a mere formal motion, directed only to the face of the complaint, and that here is another instance of judicial haste which in the long run makes waste. * * * We think that, however inartistically they may be stated, the plaintiff has disclosed his claims that the collector has converted

1258, 1263; Meyer v. Bell & Howell Co., D.C.Mo.1978, 453 F.Supp. 801, 802, appeal dismissed C.A.8th, 584 F.2d 291; Frank v. Mracek, D.C.Ala.1973, 58 F.R.D. 365, 369.

28. Note to Rule 8(a), Advisory Committee Report of October, 1955, reprinted in 5 Wright & Miller, Civil § 1201 n. 11.

29. McCaskill, Easy Pleading, 1941, 35 Ill.L.Rev. 28; Fee, The Lost Horizon in Pleading under the Federal Rules of Civil Procedure, 1948, 48 Col.L.Rev.

491; Claim or Cause of Action, 1951, 13 F.R.D. 253; McCaskill, Modern Philosophy of Pleading: A Dialogue Outside the Shades, 1952, 38 A.B.A.J. 123; Dawson, The Place of the Pleading in a Proper Definition of the Issues in the "Big Case," 1958, 23 F.R.D. 430; Rosen v. Texas Co., D.C.N.Y.1958, 161 F.Supp. 55 (per Dimock, J.).

30. C.C.A.2d, 1944, 139 F.2d 774, see 5 Wright & Miller, Civil § 1220.

or otherwise done away with two of his cases of medicinal tonics and has sold the rest in a manner incompatible with the public auction he had announced—and indeed required   *   *   *." [31]

It is difficult to see what the Second Circuit could have done other than reverse in the Dioguardi case. Had it affirmed the judgment below, Dioguardi would have been out of court without ever having any hearing on the merits of his claims. These claims had merit if the facts were as Dioguardi believed them to be. The Collector of Customs would have been liable had he done away with part of the merchandise, or conducted the auction other than in accordance with regulations. The trial court had no means of knowing whether the facts were as Dioguardi claimed them to be or not, for the government made a purely formal motion, rather than going to the merits by a motion for summary judgment with supporting affidavits.

The critics have made much of the fact that, after the decision here noted, the case went to trial, Dioguardi failed to prove his claims, and a judgment was entered against him and affirmed by the Second Circuit.[32] The fact, however, that a litigant ultimately loses on the merits hardly shows that he should be thrown out of court without any opportunity to prove the merits of his case.

Those who criticize the result in the Dioguardi case necessarily must believe that "good pleading" is a sufficiently important goal that even possibly meritorious claims should be dismissed if they are not properly pleaded. Indeed one of the critics says virtually this much, when he attacks the federal rules, as they have been interpreted, on the ground that they lower "the standards of pleading to fit the incompetent or lazy lawyer, instead of keeping the standards where pleadings will be of some use to the courts, and making those who wish to practice in the courts meet those standards." [33] This is an arguable position, but it is contrary to the fundamental notion of all modern procedural reform, that the object of procedure should be to secure a determination on the merits rather than to penalize litigants because of procedural blunders.

Some of the critics have read the Dioguardi case as meaning that a pleader need no longer set forth facts from which it can be seen that he has a right to relief. As the Advisory Committee has correctly pointed out, Dioguardi was not based on any such holding. "The complaint in that case stated a plethora of facts and the court so construed them as to sustain the validity of the pleading." [34] The statement by the court in Dioguardi that "under the new rules of civil

---

31.   139 F.2d at 775.

32.   Dioguardi v. Durning, C.C.A.2d, 1945, 151 F.2d 501.

33.   McCaskill, The Modern Philosophy of Pleading: A Dialogue Outside the Shades, 1952, 38 A.B.A.J. 123, 125. This expression by Professor McCaskill

is strikingly reminiscent of the views of Sir Montague Crackenthorpe, Q.C., cited note 3 above.

34.   Note to Rule 8(a), Advisory Committee Report of October, 1955, reprinted 5 Wright & Miller, Civil § 1201 n. 11.

procedure, there is no pleading requirement of stating 'facts sufficient to constitute a cause of action', but only that there be 'a short and plain statement of the claim showing that the pleader is entitled to relief,' " [35] seems but an obvious truth, which many decisions have announced, pointing up the fact that a different standard now applies than did formerly, and that the language of the United States Attorney's motion in the trial court in Dioguardi was unfortunate.[36]

Even some of those who agree that Judge Clark was basically right in the Dioguardi case and his critics basically wrong have voiced the view that he was ill-advised to choose the Dioguardi case as a vehicle to set forth his pleading theories. It is hard to understand what is meant by this criticism. The Dioguardi opinion is not a treatise on pleading, nor does it purport to be. Indeed it confines itself very closely to the problem presented by the particular case and discusses pleading theory only to the extent needed to dispose of that case. It does not enter into a discussion of pleading philosophy at all comparable to that, say, of the Supreme Court in Conley v. Gibson. Perhaps Conley v. Gibson will bring to a close the unnecessary controversy that some have raised about the Dioguardi case, both because Dioguardi is cited with approval by the Supreme Court in Conley [37] and because the Court in Conley lends ringing endorsement to the principles for which the Dioguardi decision stands.

Despite the general acceptance of modern pleading, there is always a tendency to imagine that strict pleading rules will save judicial work. This has been seen in recent years with regard to antitrust litigation, stockholders' derivative actions, and similar protracted lawsuits, now popularly referred to as "the big case." These cases do impose a heavy burden on the courts, and a number of district judges have sought to discourage them at the outset by applying strict rules as to the contents of the complaint. In fact such efforts usually resulted only in waste of time and much longer pleadings, without any corresponding gain. The sad truth is that, tedious and laborious as these cases are likely to prove, there is no real substitute for trial. Recognizing this, several courts of appeals have written strong opinions pointing out that the same liberal pleading rules that apply in ordinary litigation are applicable to the "big case." [38]

35.   139 F.2d at 775.

36.   5 Wright & Miller, Civil § 1216.

37.   78 S.Ct. at 102 n. 5, 355 U.S. at 41 n. 5.

The Dioguardi case is also cited with approval in Haines v. Kerner, 1972, 92 S.Ct. 594, 596, 404 U.S. 519, 521, 30 L.Ed.2d 652. See also Estelle v. Gamble, 1976, 97 S.Ct. 285, 295, 429 U.S. 97, 113, 50 L.Ed.2d 251, (Stevens, J., dissenting).

38.   Nagler v. Admiral Corp., C.A.2d, 1957, 248 F.2d 319; New Home Appliance Center, Inc. v. Thompson, C.A. 10th, 1957, 250 F.2d 881; Austin v. House of Vision, Inc., C.A.7th, 1967, 385 F.2d 171; Control Data Corp. v. International Business Machines Corp., C.A.8th, 1970, 421 F.2d 323; Royal Farms, Inc. v. Breakstone Food Div., Nat. Dairy Products Corp., D.C.N.Y. 1967, 11 F.R.Serv.2d 44. See 5 Wright & Miller, Civil § 1221; Clark, Special

Similarly it is tempting to think that the flood of petitions and complaints filed by prisoners, most of them wholly without merit, could be quickly disposed of by strict pleading rules. The Civil Rules, after all, are based "on the working assumption that powerful extra-judicial constraints would operate to screen out most claims completely lacking factual or legal merit before the judicial process was invoked." [39] These constraints are ordinarily of no effect on those in prison.[40] Even so, the Supreme Court has insisted that pro se complaints must be tested by "less stringent standards than formal pleadings drafted by lawyers." [41] Procedures have been devised that ease the task of identifying those habeas corpus and § 2255 cases that deserve an evidentiary hearing.[42] For other cases brought by prisoners, the courts have broad discretion to dismiss suits brought in forma pauperis if "the action is frivolous or malicious," [43] and there are other promising remedies for prisoners' suits that are worth exploring.[44]

Rule 9 contains special provisions, which are largely self-explanatory, as to pleading such matters as capacity, fraud or other condition of mind, conditions precedent, official document or act, judgment, time and place, and special damage.[45] Of these provisions, the only one that has given any difficulty is Rule 9(b), which says that in all

Pleading in the "Big Case", 1957, 21 F.R.D. 45; Dawson, The Place of the Pleading in a Proper Definition of the Issues in the "Big Case," 1958, 23 F.R.D. 430; Clark, Comment on Judge Dawson's Paper, 1958, 23 F.R.D. 435; Freund, The Pleading and Pre-Trial of an Anti-Trust Claim, 1961, 46 Corn. L.Q. 555.

The problems of "the big case" may require the court to make special provisions concerning discovery and otherwise to control the case more closely than in ordinary litigation. See Manual for Complex Litigation, 5th ed. 1982, 15 Wright, Miller & Cooper, Jurisdiction §§ 3861, 3868.

39. Phillips, Foreword, 1982, 39 Wash. & Lee L.Rev. 425, 427–428.

40. Judge Phillips has accurately described the situation of prisoners, "without benefit of responsible legal counseling, largely uninhibited by concerns of expense or diversion of energies, under no general compunction of prudence or restraint, and certainly under no particular compulsion to be scrupulously fair and careful in advancing and framing legal and factual allegations against officials of the adversary state." Phillips, note 39 above, at 428.

41. Haines v. Kerner, 1972, 92 S.Ct. 594, 596, 404 U.S. 519, 520, 30 L.Ed.2d 652.

See also Boag v. MacDougall, 1982, 102 S.Ct. 700, 701, ___ U.S. ___, ___, 70 L.Ed.2d 551. See cases cited 5 Wright & Miller, Civil § 1230 n. 58. Even so, some circuits continue to require civil rights complaints to be pleaded with some factual specificity. See U. S. v. City of Philadelphia, C.A.3d, 1980, 644 F.2d 187, 204 n. 26, and cases there cited.

42. The petition or motion can be on a model form, which is readily available to prisoners. It is appended to the Habeas Corpus Rules and the Section 2255 Rules. Those sets of rules make provision for summary judgment and for "a variety of measures in an effort to avoid the need for an evidentiary hearing." Blackledge v. Allison, 1977, 97 S.Ct. 1621, 1633, 431 U.S. 63, 81, 52 L.Ed.2d 136. See 3 Wright, Federal Practice and Procedure: Criminal 2d, §§ 598, 599; 17 Wright, Miller & Cooper, Jurisdiction § 4268.

43. 28 U.S.C.A. § 1915(d). See Boag v. MacDougall, 1982, 102 S.Ct. 700, 701, n. *, ___ U.S. ___, ___ n. *, 70 L.Ed.2d 551.

44. See Phillips, note 39 above, at 429; Report of the Study Group on the Caseload of the Supreme Court, 1972, 57 F.R.D. 573, 586–588.

45. 5 Wright & Miller, Civil §§ 1291–1315.

averments of fraud or mistake, the circumstances constituting fraud or mistake shall be stated with particularity. Occasional cases have read this as if it were in a vacuum, and have given it a strict application that fails to take into account the general simplicity of pleadings contemplated by the rules.[46] Rule 9(b) must be read in the light of Rule 8(a). While fraud must be particularized, the allegations must still be as short, plain, simple, concise, and direct as is reasonable under the circumstances.[47] If the allegations of fraud are not sufficiently particularized, the remedy is not to dismiss the complaint, but to require a more definite statement or to permit defendant to ascertain the facts by discovery.[48] In these special matters, as generally, the aim of the rules to deemphasize the pleadings and to try the case on the proofs must be kept in mind.

§ 69. Pleading Jurisdiction [1]

The general requirements for pleading have been stated in the three sections preceding. In the federal system, however, there is an additional requirement not commonly found in the states. Rule 8(a) (1) requires that a pleading setting forth a claim for relief contain a short and plain statement of the grounds upon which the court's jurisdiction depends, unless the court already has jurisdiction and the claim needs no new grounds of jurisdiction to support it. The reason for the rule is clear. The federal courts are courts of limited jurisdiction.[2] There is no presumption in favor of jurisdiction, and the basis for jurisdiction must be affirmatively shown.[3] In the past, some decisions have taken a quite technical view as to the sufficiency of jurisdictional allegations. One extreme case held that an allegation that a party was "a citizen of London, England" was not a sufficient allegation that the party was an alien.[4] Since such decisions are on the books, care is indicated in jurisdictional allegations, though Rule 8(f), requiring pleadings to be construed so as to do substantial justice, applies as well to jurisdictional allegations as to other portions of the complaint.[5]

---

46. Cases holding particular allegations sufficient or insufficient are set out in 5 Wright & Miller, Civil §§ 1297–1298.

47. McGinty v. Beranger Volkswagen, Inc., C.A.1st, 1980, 633 F.2d 225, 228–229; Walling v. Beverly Enterprises, C.A.9th, 1973, 476 F.2d 393, 397; Gilbert v. Bagley, D.C.N.C.1980, 492 F.Supp. 714, 726.

48. Glus v. Brooklyn Eastern Dist. Terminal, 1959, 79 S.Ct. 760, 763, 359 U.S. 231, 235, 3 L.Ed.2d 770. See 5 Wright & Miller, Civil § 1300.

[§ 69]

1. 5 Wright & Miller, Civil §§ 1206–1214.

2. See § 7 above.

3. Hanford v. Davies, 1896, 16 S.Ct. 1051, 163 U.S. 273, 41 L.Ed. 157; Smith v. McCullough, 1926, 46 S.Ct. 338, 270 U.S. 456, 70 L.Ed. 682; Bowman v. White, C.A.4th, 1968, 388 F.2d 756; Le Mieux Bros. v. Tremont Lumber Co., C.C.A.5th, 1944, 140 F.2d 387; Carroll v. General Medical Co., D.C.Neb.1971, 53 F.R.D. 349.

4. Stuart v. City of Easton, 1895, 15 S.Ct. 268, 156 U.S. 46, 39 L.Ed. 341.

5. Neagle v. Johnson, C.A.8th, 1967, 381 F.2d 9; Bartle v. Markson, C.A.2d, 1966, 357 F.2d 517; Holy Eagle v. Towle, D.C.S.D.1963, 32 F.R.D. 591; 5 Wright & Miller, Civil § 1206.

Official Form 2, appended to the rules, gives illustrative forms for the pleading of jurisdiction. Where jurisdiction is based on diversity, the complaint should allege the citizenship of each of the parties. An allegation of residence is insufficient.[6] Nor is it enough to allege that plaintiff is a citizen of state X and that defendant is not a citizen of state X, since this leaves open the possibility that defendant may be a citizen of the United States but not of any state, or that he may have no citizenship.[7]

A corporation is not a citizen of any state, though it is treated for jurisdictional purposes as if it were.[8] Thus an allegation that a corporate party is a citizen of state X will not do.[9] Instead it must be alleged that the party is a corporation incorporated under the laws of state X and having its principal place of business in state Y. Though this is always the preferable method of allegation where there is a corporate party, it may be that plaintiff will not know the principal place of business of a corporate defendant. In this case, Official Form 2 permits the following form of allegation: "Plaintiff is a citizen of the state of Connecticut and defendant is a corporation incorporated under the laws of the state of New York having its principal place of business in a state other than the state of Connecticut." [10]

Where jurisdiction is based on the existence of a federal question, the jurisdictional allegation should state that the action arises under a particular statute or provision of the Constitution "as hereinafter more fully appears", and the body of the complaint must state facts showing that the case does in fact arise under federal law. Failure to cite the federal law involved is not fatal, if the balance of the complaint shows that a federal question is involved,[11] and correspondingly a general allegation of a federal question will not suffice if it is not

6. Robertson v. Cease, 1878, 97 U.S. 646, 648, 24 L.Ed. 1057; Southern Pac. Co. v. Denton, 1892, 13 S.Ct. 44, 146 U.S. 202, 36 L.Ed. 942; Prescription Plan Serv. Corp. v. Franco, C.A.2d, 1977, 552 F.2d 493, 498 n. 6.

This defect, however, is often disregarded if it is clear that citizenship was intended. E.g., National Farmers Union Property & Cas. Co. v. Fisher, C.A.8th, 1960, 284 F.2d 421; Holm v. Shilensky, D.C.N.Y.1967, 269 F.Supp. 359, affirmed C.A.2d, 1968, 388 F.2d 54.

7. Cameron v. Hodges, 1888, 8 S.Ct. 1154, 127 U.S. 322, 32 L.Ed. 132; Bryant v. Harrelson, D.C.Tex.1960, 187 F.Supp. 738. See § 24 above.

8. 28 U.S.C.A. § 1332(c). See § 27 above.

9. Thomas v. Board of Trustees of Ohio State Univ., 1904, 25 S.Ct. 24, 195 U.S. 207, 49 L.Ed. 160; Fifty Associates v.

Prudential Ins. Co., C.A.9th, 1970, 446 F.2d 1187. But cf. 5 Wright & Miller, Civil § 1208, p. 89.

10. McAndrews v. Goody Co., D.C.Neb. 1978, 460 F.Supp. 104; Kurtz v. Draur, D.C.Pa.1977, 434 F.Supp. 958; Gorman v. King, D.C.Wis.1970, 50 F.R.D. 195.

But an allegation that plaintiff was a citizen of South Dakota and that defendants were corporations that were incorporated and had their principal places of business in states other than South Dakota was held insufficient. McGovern v. American Airlines, Inc., C.A.5th, 1975, 511 F.2d 653.

11. Schlesinger v. Councilman, 1975, 95 S.Ct. 1300, 1306 n. 9, 420 U.S. 738, 744 n. 9, 43 L.Ed.2d 591; Blue v. Craig, C.A.4th, 1974, 505 F.2d 830, 844 n. 31; and cases cited 5 Wright & Miller, Civil § 1209 n. 13.

supported by the matters constituting the claim for relief as set forth in the complaint.[12]

With respect to jurisdictional amount, where this is required,[13] an allegation that the matter in controversy exceeds, exclusive of interest and costs, the sum of $10,000 is sufficient unless the other allegations of the complaint show that less than that amount is involved.[14]

All of these rules as to pleading jurisdiction must be read in the light of the principle that the whole record may be looked to, for the purpose of curing a defective jurisdictional allegation, and that where diversity is the basis of jurisdiction it is sufficient if the requisite citizenship is anywhere expressly averred in the record, or facts are there stated that in legal intendment constitute such allegation.[15]

Defective allegations of jurisdiction may be amended. Indeed a statute permits such amendment, on terms, in the trial or appellate court.[16] If the plaintiff, fearful that he is losing on the merits and preferring a dismissal without prejudice for want of jurisdiction, refuses to make such an amendment, the defendant may present the needed amendment to show the existence of jurisdiction.[17] The statute permitting amendment of jurisdictional allegations has been of particular importance since the adoption of the 1958 statute making diversity, with regard to a corporate party, dependent on its principal place of business as well as on the state of its incorporation. Many pleaders have failed to allege the principal place of business of a corporate party, and amendment has frequently been allowed, even on appeal, to cure such an allegation.[18] Some cases have refused to allow an amendment to show the principal place of business in a removed case after the time for removal has run,[19] but the statute per-

12. See note 2 to Official Form 2; Mantin v. Broadcast Music, Inc., C.A.9th, 1957, 244 F.2d 204; Fountain v. New Orleans Public Serv., Inc., D.C.La.1967, 265 F.Supp. 630; North Allegheny Joint Sch. System v. Secretary of Health, Educ. and Welfare, D.C.Pa. 1961, 196 F.Supp. 144.

13. See § 32 above.

14. KVOS, Inc. v. Associated Press, 1936, 57 S.Ct. 197, 299 U.S. 269, 81 L.Ed. 183; Beneficial Indus. Loan Corp. v. Kline, C.C.A.8th, 1943, 132 F.2d 520; Maryland Cas. Co. v. Baker, D.C.Ky.1961, 196 F.Supp. 234. See 5 Wright & Miller, Civil § 1213; Note, Good Faith Pleading of Jurisdictional Amount, 1963, 48 Iowa L.Rev. 426.

15. Pittsburgh, C. & St. L. R. Co. v. Ramsey, 1874, 22 Wall. 322, 326, 22 L.Ed. 823; Sun Printing & Pub. Co. v. Edwards, 1904, 24 S.Ct. 696, 194 U.S. 377, 48 L.Ed. 1027.

The complaint alone must be looked to in determining the existence of a federal question. See § 18 above.

16. 28 U.S.C.A. § 1653; Miller v. Stanmore, C.A.5th, 1981, 636 F.2d 986, 990; Miller v. Davis, C.A.6th, 1974, 507 F.2d 308; and cases cited 6 Wright & Miller, Civil § 1474 n. 89.

17. Keene Lumber Co. v. Leventhal, C.A.1st, 1948, 165 F.2d 815; Maryland Cas. Co. v. Baker, D.C.Ky.1961, 196 F.Supp. 234.

18. McCurdy v. Greyhound Corp., C.A.3d, 1965, 346 F.2d 224; Burkhardt v. Bates, C.A.8th, 1961, 296 F.2d 315; Niagara Fire Ins. Co. v. Dyess Furniture Co., C.A.5th, 1961, 292 F.2d 232; cf. Wymard v. McCloskey & Co., C.A. 3d, 1965, 342 F.2d 495, certiorari denied 86 S.Ct. 52, 382 U.S. 823, 15 L.Ed. 2d 68.

19. See Richmond, F. & P. R. Co. v. Intermodal Services, Inc., D.C.Va.1981, 508 F.Supp. 804; and cases cited 14

mitting amendment of jurisdictional allegations is broad enough to permit this, and other cases allow the amendment, even on appeal.[20]

It is never too late for a party, or the court on its own motion, to assert lack of jurisdiction over the subject matter.[21] If the defect is curable, as where diversity is destroyed by the presence of a party who is not indispensable, it is possible to cure the defect by dropping the nondiverse party. There is a variety of view, and as yet no settled answer, as to the proper procedure where the defect comes to light on appeal after judgment for the plaintiff. Some courts allow the plaintiff to drop a nondiverse defendant even at this stage.[22] The question is whether there must then be a new trial, or whether judgment can be entered against the remaining defendants on the basis of the record of the first trial. There are three possible positions, all with case support. It can be held that a new trial is always required, since the district court lacked jurisdiction to hold the former trial.[23] It can be held that the case should be remanded to the district court, with discretion in that court either to grant a new trial or to enter judgment on the former record, if it is satisfied that the remaining parties have not been prejudiced.[24] Finally it can be held that if the appellate court can see for itself that there has been no prejudice to the remaining parties, it can order judgment on the basis of the old record.[25]

If the jurisdictional allegations are challenged, they must be proved,[26] and the party invoking federal jurisdiction has the burden of proof.[27] Where there is such a challenge, the court has discretion either to decide the question itself or to submit it to a jury,[28] though

Wright, Miller & Cooper, Jurisdiction § 3733 n. 12.

20. E.g., Stanley Elec. Contractors, Inc. v. Darin & Armstrong Co., D.C.Ky. 1980, 486 F.Supp. 769; Board of Educ. of Charles County v. Travelers Indem. Co., D.C.Md.1980, 486 F.Supp. 129; and cases cited 14 Wright, Miller & Cooper, Jurisdiction § 3733 n. 13.

21. See § 7 above at notes 12 to 17.

22. E.g., Reed v. Robilio, C.A.6th, 1967, 376 F.2d 392; Anderson v. Moorer, C.A.5th, 1967, 372 F.2d 747. Contra: Universal Underwriters Ins. Co. v. Wagner, C.A.8th, 1966, 367 F.2d 866, 870, n. 5.

23. Dollar S.S. Lines v. Merz, C.C.A.9th, 1934, 68 F.2d 594; Atchison, T. & S. F. Ry. v. Francom, C.C.A.9th, 1941, 118 F.2d 712.

24. Fifty Associates v. Prudential Ins. Co., C.A.9th, 1970, 446 F.2d 1187, 1192–1193; Alderman v. Elgin, J. & E. Ry., C.C.A.7th, 1942, 125 F.2d 971; International Ladies' Garment Workers' Union v. Donnelly Garment Co., C.C.A.

8th, 1941, 121 F.2d 561 (new trial ordered); Levering & Garrigues Co. v. Morrin, C.C.A.2d, 1932, 61 F.2d 115, 121.

25. Finn v. American Fire & Cas. Co., C.A.5th, 1953, 207 F.2d 113, certiorari denied 74 S.Ct. 476, 347 U.S. 912, 98 L.Ed. 1069, noted 1954, 39 Iowa L.Rev. 681, 38 Minn.L.Rev. 406, 32 Texas L.Rev. 457, 7 Vand.L.Rev. 717, 40 Va. L.Rev. 348. Cf. Camp v. Gress, 1919, 39 S.Ct. 478, 250 U.S. 308, 63 L.Ed. 997.

26. Roberts v. Lewis, 1892, 12 S.Ct. 781, 144 U.S. 653, 36 L.Ed. 579.

27. McNutt v. General Motors Acceptance Corp., 1935, 56 S.Ct. 780, 298 U.S. 178, 80 L.Ed. 1135; Grafon Corp. v. Hausermann, C.A.7th, 1979, 602 F.2d 781; Ramsey v. Mellon Nat. Bank & Trust Co., C.A.3d, 1965, 350 F.2d 874.

28. Gilbert v. David, 1915, 35 S.Ct. 164, 235 U.S. 561, 59 L.Ed. 360; Williamson v. Tucker, C.A.5th, 1981, 645 F.2d 404, 412–415; Berardinelli v. Castle & Cooke, Inc., C.A.9th, 1978, 587 F.2d 37;

the most common practice has been for the court to determine the jurisdictional facts itself.

D. JOINDER OF CLAIMS AND PARTIES

Analysis

§ 70. Parties Classified [1]

Three different, but easily confused, concepts must be kept in mind in considering joinder of parties in federal court. Only the real party in interest can be a party. This is governed by Rule 17(a). A person must have capacity to sue or be sued. This is governed by Rule 17(b) and (c). If these tests are met, the relation of a particular person to the suit must be examined in order to determine whether his joinder ought to be compelled by Rule 19 or is permitted by Rule 20.

Rule 17(a), stating that every action shall be brought in the name of the real party in interest, follows the usual code formula. It was intended to change the common law rule, which permitted suit to be brought only in the name of the person having the legal title to the right of action, and thus precluded suit by persons who had only equitable or beneficial interests. Under the rule the "real party in interest" is the party who, by the substantive law, possesses the right sought to be enforced,[2] and not necessarily the person who will ulti-

---

Seideman v. Hamilton, C.A.3d, 1960, 275 F.2d 224, certiorari denied 80 S.Ct. 1258, 363 U.S. 820, 4 L.Ed.2d 1517.

See also Shaffer v. Coty, Inc., D.C.Cal. 1960, 183 F.Supp. 662. See Note, Trial by Jury of Preliminary Jurisdictional Facts in Federal Cases, 1963, 48 Iowa L.Rev. 471.

[§ 70]

1. 6 Wright & Miller, Civil §§ 1543–1558 (real party in interest), 1559–1569 (capacity to sue or be sued); 7 Wright & Miller, Civil §§ 1604–1608 (parties classified).

2. E.g., Lubbock Feed Lots, Inc. v. Iowa Beef Processors, Inc., C.A.5th, 1980, 630 F.2d 250, 256–258; Mason-Rust v. Laborers' Intl. Union, Local 42, C.A.8th, 1970, 435 F.2d 939, 943–944; and cases cited 6 Wright & Miller, Civil § 1543 n. 46.

The concept of real party in interest should not be confused with the concept of standing. The standing question arises in the realm of public law, when governmental action is attacked on the ground that it violates private rights or some constitutional principle. See § 13 above. " 'Real party in inter-

mately benefit from the recovery.[3] This is illustrated by the further language stating that executors, administrators, and other named representatives may sue in their own name without joining with them the party for whose benefit the action is brought. This further language is not an exception to the real party in interest provision, but was inserted as a precautionary measure in order that the "real party in interest" would not be confined to the person beneficially interested.[4] Indeed of late the existence of such a rule has come in for severe criticism. The critics argue that if the effect of the rule is merely to provide that the person who has the substantive right shall sue, the rule itself is unnecessary and the same results can be reached simply by application of the substantive law.[5] About the best that can be said for the rule is that "it conveys a certain amount of correct information about naming plaintiffs, but to the average reader innocent of history it probably suggests as much or more that is quite incorrect. It does stand as a warning, which is perhaps unnecessary, that the defendant can insist upon a plaintiff who will afford him a setup providing good res judicata protection if the struggle is carried through on the merits to the end."[6]

Since the rule does direct attention to the person with the substantive right sought to be enforced, state law must be looked to in diversity cases to see who this person is, although the federal rule then governs on the procedural question of joinder.[7] Despite the criti

est' is very different from standing." Kent v. Northern California Regional Office of American Friends Serv. Committee, C.A.9th, 1974, 497 F.2d 1325, 1329. Unfortunately, as shown by the cases cited in 13 Wright, Miller & Cooper, Jurisdiction 2d § 3531 n. 2, in recent cases confusion between standing on the one hand and real party in interest or capacity on the other has been increasing.

3. Proctor v. Gissendaner, C.A.5th, 1978, 579 F.2d 876, 880; Armour Pharmaceutical Co. v. Home Ins. Co., D.C. Ill.1973, 60 F.R.D. 592; Allen v. Baker, D.C.Miss.1968, 327 F.Supp. 706; James & Hazard, Civil Procedure, 2d ed. 1977, § 9.2; Clark & Moore, A New Federal Civil Procedure, 1935, 44 Yale L.J. 1291, 1310–1312.

4. Horwich v. Price, D.C.Mich.1960, 25 F.R.D. 500; Clark, Code Pleading, 2d ed. 1947, p. 190.

5. Kennedy, Federal Rule 17(a): Will the Real Party in Interest Please Stand?, 1967, 51 Minn.L.Rev. 675, 724; Atkinson, The Real Party in Interest Rule: A Plea for its Abolition, 1957, 32 N.Y.U.L.Rev. 926; Louisell & Hazard, Cases and Materials on Pleading and Procedure, 1962, pp. 652–653. See also

Jefferson v. Ametek, Inc., D.C.Md. 1980, 86 F.R.D. 425, 427.

6. Kaplan, Continuing Work of the Civil Committee: 1966 Amendments of the Federal Rules of Civil Procedure, 1967, 81 Harv.L.Rev. 356, 412.

This understanding that the modern function of the rule is the negative one of protecting the defendant against a subsequent action by the party actually entitled to recover and insuring that the judgment will have its proper effect as res judicata was first enunciated by Judge Hutcheson in Celanese Corp. v. John Clark Indus., Inc., C.A. 5th, 1954, 214 F.2d 551, 556, and has had wide acceptance. E.g., Prevor-Meyorsohn Caribbean, Inc. v. Puerto Rico Marine Management, Inc., C.A. 1st, 1980, 620 F.2d 1, 4; and cases cited 6 Wright & Miller, Civil § 1541 n. 9.

7. Dubuque Stone Products Co. v. Fred L. Gray Co., C.A.8th, 1966, 356 F.2d 718; McNeil Constr. Co. v. Livingston State Bank, C.A.9th, 1962, 300 F.2d 88; American Fidelity & Cas. Co. v. All American Bus Lines, C.A.10th, 1950, 179 F.2d 7; White Hall Bldg. Corp. v. Profexray Div. of Litton Indus., Inc., D.C.Pa.1974, 387 F.Supp. 1202; 6 Wright & Miller, Civil § 1544.

cisms directed at the text of the rule itself, whether a person with a particular relation to a case is "the real party in interest" has been worked out in many specific contexts,[8] and generally quite satisfactorily.

The most important application of the rule is with regard to assignment and subrogation. One of the main purposes of the provision is to allow the assignee of a chose in action to sue upon it in his own name instead of in the name of the assignor. It is now quite settled that the assignee is a real party in interest,[9] and that an assignor who has assigned his entire claim is not a real party in interest.[10] Where there has been a partial assignment, both assignor and assignee are real parties in interest; in order to avoid a split judgment, the defendant, on motion, may be able to compel both to be joined as parties plaintiff.[11]

Except as relevant state law may require a different treatment, the same results are reached in cases of subrogation as in cases of assignment. The most common situation is that of the insurer that has paid its insured and thus is subrogated to the insured's right against some third party. If the insurer has paid the entire loss, it is the real party in interest and must sue in its own name.[12] The insured, who no longer has any interest in the recovery, cannot sue.[13] If the insurer has paid only part of the loss, either the insured or the insurer may sue, but the defendant may be able to compel joinder of the other in order to avoid being subjected to a multiplicity of suits.[14]

---

8. 6 Wright & Miller, Civil §§ 1545–1553.

9. Fox-Greenwald Sheet Metal Co. v. Markowitz Bros., Inc., C.A.1971, 452 F.2d 1346, 147 U.S.App.D.C. 14; La-Tex Supply Co. v. Fruehauf Trailer Div., Fruehauf Corp., C.A.5th, 1971, 444 F.2d 1366, certiorari denied 92 S.Ct. 287, 404 U.S. 942, 30 L.Ed.2d 256; and cases cited 6 Wright & Miller, Civil § 1545 n. 73.

This result is not changed by the fact that the assignment was for collection only. Staggers v. Otto Gerdau Co., C.A.2d, 1966, 359 F.2d 292.

10. Borough of Nanty-Glo to Use of Westinghouse Credit Corp. v. Fireman's Fund Ins. Co., D.C.Pa.1966, 250 F.Supp. 329; Horwich v. Price, D.C. Mich.1960, 25 F.R.D. 500.

11. Hoeppner Constr. Co. v. U. S. for Use of Mangum, C.A.10th, 1960, 287 F.2d 108; Hurd v. Sheffield Steel Corp., C.A.8th, 1950, 181 F.2d 269; McWhirter v. Otis Elevator Co., D.C.S.C. 1941, 40 F.Supp. 11. See 6 Wright & Miller, Civil § 1545, pp. 655–656.

12. U. S. v. Aetna Cas. & Sur. Co., 1949, 70 S.Ct. 207, 215, 338 U.S. 366, 380, 94

L.Ed. 171; Hilbrands v. Far East Trading Co., C.A.9th, 1975, 509 F.2d 1321; and cases cited 6 Wright & Miller, Civil § 1546 n. 69.

13. American Fidelity & Cas. Co. v. All American Bus Lines, C.A.10th, 1950, 179 F.2d 7; McCoy v. Wean United, Inc., D.C.Tenn.1973, 67 F.R.D. 491.

14. U. S. v. Aetna Cas. & Sur. Co., 1949, 70 S.Ct. 207, 338 U.S. 366, 94 L.Ed. 171; Public Serv. Co. of Oklahoma v. Black & Veatch, C.A.10th, 1972, 467 F.2d 1143; 6 Wright & Miller, Civil § 1546, pp. 659–661; Note, 1974, 27 Okl.L.Rev. 86. The position taken in the text and in these cases is rejected, however, in Dudley v. Smith, C.A.5th, 1974, 504 F.2d 979, 983.

Joinder of the insurer will not be compelled if this would destroy diversity and the insurer will be bound by the judgment. Virginia Elec. & Power Co. v. Westinghouse Elec. Corp., C.A.4th, 1973, 485 F.2d 78, 84–85, certiorari denied 94 S.Ct. 1450, 415 U.S. 935, 39 L.Ed.2d 493.

The deference to state law precluding involuntary joinder of the insurer in Race v. Hay, D.C.Ind.1961, 28 F.R.D.

If instead of paying the loss the insurer makes a loan to the insured under an agreement whereby the loan is to be repaid only out of any recovery which may be obtained from the third person, the insured rather than the insurer is usually, but not always, considered to be the real party in interest.[15]

Though the two concepts are sometimes confused, there is a clear distinction between "real party in interest," governed by Rule 17(a), and "capacity," governed by Rule 17(b) and (c).[16] A litigant could be the real party in interest and yet lack capacity to sue, as for example a person who has become mentally incompetent. A person could have capacity to sue and yet not be the real party in interest, as for example a plaintiff who has assigned away all his interest in the claim before suit is brought. The distinction has procedural significance since the burden is on plaintiff to show that he has a substantive right to recover and thus that he is the real party in interest, while Rule 9(a) requires a specific negative averment if defendant wishes to object that plaintiff lacks capacity to sue.

The capacity of an individual, other than one acting in a representative capacity, to sue or be sued is determined according to the law of the individual's domicile.[17] The capacity of a corporation is determined by the law under which it was organized.[18] The capacity of a representative is determined by the law of the state where the district court is held.[19] This is usually the test, also, for determining the

354, seems to be unsound. See, e.g., Gas Service Co. v. Hunt, C.A.10th, 1950, 183 F.2d 417; White Hall Bldg. Corp. v. Profexray Div. of Litton Indus., Inc., D.C.Pa.1974, 387 F.Supp. 1202; Hughey v. Aetna Cas & Sur. Co., D.C.Del.1963, 32 F.R.D. 340.

15. E.g., R. J. Enstrom Corp. v. Interceptor Corp., C.A.10th, 1975, 520 F.2d 1217; Ketona Chemical Corp. v. Globe Indem. Co., C.A.5th, 1968, 404 F.2d 181; Export Leaf Tobacco Co. v. American Ins. Co., C.A.4th, 1958, 260 F.2d 839; See v. Emhart Corp., D.C.Mo. 1977, 444 F.Supp. 71; Watsontown Brick Co. v. Hercules Powder Co., D.C. Pa.1962, 201 F.Supp. 343.

Contra: Executive Jet Aviation, Inc. v. U. S., C.A.6th, 1974, 507 F.2d 508; City Stores Co. v. Lerner Shops, Inc., C.A. 1969, 410 F.2d 1010, 133 U.S.App.D.C. 311; McNeil Constr. Co. v. Livingston State Bank, C.A.9th, 1962, 300 F.2d 88; F. L. Crane Co. v. Cessna Aircraft Co., D.C.Miss.1977, 74 F.R.D. 414; Boynton, The Myth of the "Loan Receipt" Revisited Under Rule 17(a), 1966, 18 S.C.L.Rev. 624.

16. The concepts are discriminatingly distinguished, under rules based on the federal rules, in Catalfano v. Higgins, 1962, 182 A.2d 637. 4 Storey 548, vacated on other grounds, Del.1962, 188 A.2d 357, 5 Storey 470. The concepts were confused in, e.g., E. Brooke Matlack, Inc. v. Walrath, D.C.Md.1959, 24 F.R.D. 263.

See generally Kennedy, Federal Civil Rule 17(b) and (c): Qualifying to Litigate in Federal Court, 1968, 43 Notre Dame Law. 273; 6 Wright & Miller, Civil § 1542.

17. Rule 17(b); Donnelly v. Parker, C.A. 1973, 486 F.2d 402, 158 U.S.App.D.C. 335; 6 Wright & Miller, Civil § 1560.

18. Rule 17(b); 6 Wright & Miller, Civil §§ 1561–1563.

But see Woods v. Interstate Realty Co., 1949, 69 S.Ct. 1235, 337 U.S. 535, 93 L.Ed. 1524; McCollum Aviation, Inc. v. CIM Associates, Inc., D.C.Fla.1977, 438 F.Supp. 245.

19. Rule 17(b); 6 Wright & Miller, Civil § 1565.

capacity of partnerships and unincorporated associations,[20] but such an association may sue or be sued in its common name, even though it lacks capacity under state law, where the suit is to enforce a substantive right existing under the Constitution or laws of the United States.[21]

Rule 17(c) [22] provides that if an infant or incompetent person has a representative, such as a general guardian, the representative may sue or defend in behalf of his ward. If there is no such representative, suit may be brought by the next friend or a guardian ad litem. The court is authorized to appoint a guardian ad litem or otherwise take steps to protect an infant or incompetent not represented in an action.[23] There is some lack of clarity with regard to the relation between 17(b) and 17(c). One line of cases holds that the language of the first sentence of Rule 17(c), authorizing a guardian or other representative to sue on behalf of an infant or incompetent, is subject to Rule 17(b), which makes the capacity of a representative dependent on the law of the state where the district court is held.[24] Another line of cases permits appointment of a guardian ad litem even though the state law does not recognize such a representative.[25] It is possible to reconcile these two lines of authority by holding that state law controls where the ward already has a representative appointed and qualified by a state court, but that if the ward has no such representative, the federal court may appoint one for him regardless of state law.[26]

This is not the only respect in which the effect of state law on Rule 17(b) and (c) is unclear. The rule itself looks to state law, but looks variously, in Rule 17(b), to the domicile, the state in which a corporation was organized, and the forum. To what extent are the various provisions stated in the rule qualified if the law of the forum would require a contrary result than the rule provides? Here there is a conflict of view,[27] and in light of Hanna v. Plumer [28] it would

20. Rule 17(b); In re Vento Development Corp., C.A.1st, 1977, 560 F.2d 2; 6 Wright & Miller, Civil § 1564.

21. Rule 17(b)(1). This is a generalization of the doctrine first announced in United Mine Workers of America v. Coronado Coal Co., 1922, 42 S.Ct. 570, 259 U.S. 344, 66 L.Ed. 975, 27 A.L.R. 762.

22. 6 Wright & Miller, Civil §§ 1570–1572.

23. See Noe v. True, C.A.6th, 1974, 507 F.2d 9; Roberts v. Ohio Cas. Ins. Co., C.A.5th, 1958, 256 F.2d 35.

24. Brimhall v. Simmons, C.A.6th, 1964, 338 F.2d 702, noted 1965, 67 W.Va.L. Rev. 249; Vroon v. Templin, C.A.4th, 1960, 278 F.2d 345; Greenstreet v. Simmons, D.C.Ill.1972, 54 F.R.D. 554; Southern Ohio Sav. Bank & Trust Co.

v. Guaranty Trust Co. of New York, D.C.N.Y.1939, 27 F.Supp. 485.

25. Montgomery Ward & Co. v. Callahan, C.C.A.10th, 1942, 127 F.2d 32; Constantine v. Southwestern Louisiana Institute, D.C.La.1954, 120 F.Supp. 417.

26. Bengston v. Travelers Indem. Co., D.C.La.1955, 132 F.Supp. 512, affirmed C.A.5th, 1956, 231 F.2d 263. See also M. S. v. Wermers, C.A.8th, 1977, 557 F.2d 170, 174 n. 4; Donnelly v. Parker, C.A.1973, 486 F.2d 402, 406, 158 U.S. App.D.C. 335; 6 Wright & Miller, Civil § 1571.

27. Compare Urbano v. News Syndicate Co., C.A.2d, 1965, 358 F.2d 145, certiorari denied 87 S.Ct. 68, 385 U.S. 831,

28. See note 28 on page 457.

seem to turn on whether "capacity" in Rule 17(b) refers "only to the range of rules concerned with the administration of the judicial process or whether all limitations of the right to bring suit were covered." [29]

Once the requirements of Rule 17 have been complied with, and it has been decided that a particular individual or entity is a party in interest with capacity to sue or be sued, it is necessary to go one more step and decide whether the person has such a strong interest in the litigation that his joinder ought to be compelled. Compulsory joinder of parties is an exception to the usual practice that leaves a plaintiff free to decide who shall be parties to his lawsuit. Plaintiff cannot be permitted an unfettered choice in this respect, because there may be others, not named by plaintiff, so closely connected with the controversy that it would be desirable to have them as parties. "There are three classes of interests which may be served by requiring the presence of additional parties in an action: (1) the interests of the present defendant; (2) the interests of potential but absent plaintiffs and defendants; (3) the social interest in the orderly, expeditious administration of justice." [30] In some cases the connection of the absentees with the controversy will be so compelling that the three interests listed will dictate that the suit should not proceed without the absentees. In other cases the connection will be less close, and though it would be desirable to have them as parties, the action should proceed without them if it is impossible to obtain jurisdiction over them or if their joinder would destroy diversity and thus deprive the court of subject matter jurisdiction. The label "indispensable" is used if the connection is so close that the action should be dismissed unless the party is joined. The label "necessary" is used if the party is one who ought to be joined if this is possible. The label "proper" is used if the party is one who can be joined or not at plaintiff's option. That there should be such a tripartite classification of parties makes

---

17 L.Ed.2d 66, with McCollum Aviation, Inc. v. CIM Associates, Inc., D.C. Fla.1977, 438 F.Supp. 245.

See generally the article by Professor Kennedy cited note 16 above.

28. 1965, 85 S.Ct. 1136, 380 U.S. 460, 14 L.Ed.2d 8. See § 59 above.

29. R.C., 1969, 82 Harv.L.Rev. 708, 710–711. The notewriter thinks that "capacity" should be read in the narrower of these two senses, and thus that Rule 17(b) does not bar application of state "door-closing" statutes.

A similar thought about "door-closing" statutes is expressed in 6 Wright & Miller, Civil § 1569, but with the caveat the state rule may still yield to the federal if the state interest is significantly outweighed by the federal interest, as in: Szantay v. Beech Aircraft Corp., C.A.4th, 1965, 349 F.2d 60, noted 1965, 17 S.C.L.Rev. 631, 1966, 51 Corn. L.Q. 560; Tolson v. Hodge, C.A.4th, 1969, 411 F.2d 123; and Avondale Shipyards, Inc. v. Propulsion Systems, Inc., D.C.La.1971, 53 F.R.D. 341, noted 1972, 18 Wayne L.Rev. 1619.

30. Reed, Compulsory Joinder of Parties in Civil Actions, 1957, 55 Mich.L. Rev. 327, 330.

See also McCoid, A Single Package for Multiparty Disputes, 1976, 28 Stan.L. Rev. 707, arguing that broadened mandatory joinder is superior to expanded collateral estoppel and to compulsory intervention as a means of dealing with the problem of multiple disputes.

sense. Judicial attempts to define when one label or another is appropriate do not.

The leading case is Shields v. Barrow,[31] cited more than 300 times and vastly influential in the states as well as in federal courts. Barrow, a citizen of Louisiana, sold a plantation to Shields, also a citizen of Louisiana, and was given notes for the purchase price. The notes were endorsed by six persons, four from Louisiana and two from Mississippi. After about half the price had been paid, Shields defaulted. Later a compromise was worked out between Barrow on the one hand and Shields and the endorsers on the other. The plantation was returned to Barrow, who was allowed to keep the amount already paid, and the endorsers gave new notes for a fraction of the unpaid balance. Shortly thereafter Barrow became dissatisfied with the agreement and brought suit in federal court in Louisiana against the two Mississippi parties to rescind it. The Supreme Court held that the rights of the parties to the compromise agreement were "inseparable," and that the action could not proceed without joinder of all the parties to the agreement. Since the joinder of the Louisiana parties would defeat diversity, the result was to prevent suit in federal court, and it is quite possible that Barrow's attempt to rescind was defeated altogether, since it might have been difficult for any state court to obtain jurisdiction of all the parties.

Both the reasoning and the result in Shields v. Barrow have been criticized. Whether the result there was right or wrong is of little importance. The facts in Shields v. Barrow have been virtually forgotten. What has been remembered, and much quoted, is the language of the Court defining the classes of parties. "Indispensable" parties were defined as "persons who not only have an interest in the controversy, but an interest of such a nature that a final decree cannot be made without either affecting that interest, or leaving the controversy in such a condition that its final termination may be wholly inconsistent with equity and good conscience," while "necessary" parties were "persons having an interest in the controversy, and who ought to be made parties, in order that the court may act on that rule which requires it to decide on, and finally determine the entire controversy, and do complete justice, by adjusting all the rights involved in it * * * [but whose] interests are separable from those of the parties before the court, so that the court can proceed to a decree, and do complete and final justice, without affecting other persons not before the court." [32]

The sonorous generalities of Shields v. Barrow led, perhaps inevitably, to a jurisprudence of labels. Labels are not bad things in the law if they are understood for what they are, a shorthand way of expressing the result of a more complicated reasoning process. Labels become treacherous and misleading if they are applied as a sub-

31. 1854, 7 How. 130, 15 L.Ed. 158.
32. 17 How. at 139.

stitute for reasoning. It is perfectly appropriate to say: "this absentee has such a strong interest in this case that it would be unjust to let it go to decision in his absence. Therefore we will refer to him as 'indispensable.' " It is not appropriate to say, as many courts seemed to do, that "this person is 'indispensable.' Therefore we will not let the case go to decision in his absence." The latter reasoning—or nonreasoning—suggests that absent parties wear labels indicating their relation to a controversy [33] and obscures the pragmatic examination of all the circumstances that is required in the light of the very particular facts of a particular case. This jurisprudence of labels reached its high point in a decision suggesting that the category of "indispensable" parties formed such a rigid class that it had become a matter of "substantive" law and could not be altered through the process of judicial rulemaking.[34]

Rule 19, as it stood from 1938 to 1966, did little to improve this situation. "Persons having a joint interest" were required to be joined, but the action could proceed in their absence if they were "not indispensable." Thus the conceptual test of a "joint interest" was made the dividing line between permissive joinder and compulsory joinder, while once that line had been crossed, and it had been found that the party must be joined if possible, the rule offered no guidance on whether a particular party with a "joint interest" was "indispensable" or merely "necessary." In both respects the rule was unsatisfactory, not because it necessarily led to bad results but because it did not point to the factors properly relevant to decision.[35]

The "joint interest" test was not a workable division between compulsory joinder and permissive joinder. One would hardly expect that, under such a test, it would uniformly be held that joint tortfeasors were merely "proper" parties and their joinder was entirely optional,[36] or that joint obligees would be thought to be "indis-

33. See Wright, Recent Changes in the Federal Rules of Procedure, 1966, 42 F.R.D. 552, 561.

34. Provident Tradesmens Bank and Trust Co. v. Lumbermens Mut. Cas. Co., C.A.3d, 1966, 365 F.2d 802. The decision was heavily criticized. Kaplan, Continuing Work of the Civil Committee: 1966 Amendments of the Federal Rules of Civil Procedure, 1967, 81 Harv.L.Rev. 356, 371–375; Comment, The Mechanics of New Rule 19 and the Challenges to Its Validity, 1967, 12 St. Louis U.L.J. 119; Note, Rule 19 and Indispensable Parties, 1967, 65 Mich.L.Rev. 968. As will be seen, the Supreme Court reversed this decision.

35. Provident Tradesmens Bank & Trust Co. v. Patterson, 1968, 88 S.Ct.

733, 741 n. 12, 390 U.S. 102, 116 n. 12, 19 L.Ed.2d 936; Kaplan, Continuing Work of the Civil Committee: 1966 Amendments of the Federal Rules of Civil Procedure, 1967, 81 Harv.L.Rev. 356, 366–367.

36. Ward v. Deavers, C.A.1953, 203 F.2d 72, 76, 92 U.S.App.D.C. 167; Union Paving Co. v. Downer Corp., C.A.9th, 1960, 276 F.2d 468; 7 Wright & Miller, Civil § 1623.

The same result is reached under the amended rule. Stabilisierungsfonds Fur Wein v. Kaiser Stuhl Wine Distributors Pty. Ltd., C.A.1981, 647 F.2d 200, 207 U.S.App.D.C. 375; Bennie v. Pastor, C.A.10th, 1968, 393 F.2d 1; Tatham v. Hoke, D.C.N.C.1979, 469 F.Supp. 914, affirmed without opinion C.A.4th, 1980, 622 F.2d 587.

pensable" [37] while joint obligors were quite possibly only "proper" parties.[38] The ancient concept of "joint interest" simply made no sense when applied to questions such as whether a majority of a board of directors must be parties to a suit to compel declaration of a dividend,[39] or whether, in an action against a local federal officer, his superior in Washington must be joined.[40]

The rule was also no help at all in deciding whether an absentee, who ought to be joined if possible, had such a relation to the controversy that he should be regarded as "indispensable" and the action dismissed if he could not be joined. Behind the lofty language of Shields v. Barrow, and the attempts to reformulate the test there announced in terms of seeming precision,[41] what was really involved was the desire of the courts, on the one hand, to avoid a multiplicity of suits and to give parties their day in court before making decisions

37. Alden v. Central Power Elec. Co-op, Inc., D.C.N.D.1956, 137 F.Supp. 924; Fremon v. W. A. Sheaffer Pen Co., D.C.Iowa 1953, 111 F.Supp. 39, affirmed C.A.8th, 1954, 209 F.2d 627; McRanie v. Palmer, D.C.Mass.1942, 2 F.R.D. 479; McAulay v. Moody, C.C. Or.1911, 185 F. 144. But see Reed, Compulsory Joinder of Parties in Civil Actions, 1957, 55 Mich.L.Rev. 327, 367–374; James, Necessary and Indispensable Parties, 1963, 18 U.Miami L.Rev. 68, 83–85.

See note 38 below.

38. See Greenleaf v. Safeway Trails, C.C.A.2d, 1944, 140 F.2d 889, 892 (concurring opinion). That they were not "indispensable" was held in Camp v. Gress, 1919, 39 S.Ct. 478, 250 U.S. 308, 63 L.Ed. 997.

Under the 1966 amendment the result, with regard both to joint obligors and joint obligees, depends on a practical appraisal of the substantiality of the interest of the absentee and on other pragmatic factors rather than on the conceptual nature of the interest. See 7 Wright & Miller, Civil § 1613; Harrell & Sumner Contracting Co. v. Peabody Petersen Co., D.C.Fla.1976, 415 F.Supp. 573, 575, affirmed C.A.5th, 1977, 546 F.2d 1227.

39. Compare Kroese v. General Steel Castings Corp., C.A.3d, 1950, 179 F.2d 760, certiorari denied 70 S.Ct. 1026, 339 U.S. 983, 94 L.Ed. 1386, and Doherty v. Mutual Warehouse Co., C.A.5th, 1957, 245 F.2d 609, with Schuckman v. Rubenstein, C.A.6th, 1947, 164 F.2d 952. See 7 Wright & Miller, Civil § 1615, pp. 164–165.

Joinder of directors not amenable to process was held not required, under the

1966 amendment, in Levin v. Mississippi River Corp., D.C.N.Y.1968, 289 F.Supp. 353, 360–362.

40. See Williams v. Fanning, 1947, 68 S.Ct. 188, 332 U.S. 490, 92 L.Ed. 95. Whether the superior must be joined produced a multitude of irreconcilable decisions. See Byse, Proposed Reforms in Federal "Nonstatutory" Judicial Review: Sovereign Immunity, Indispensable Parties, Mandamus, 1962, 75 Harv.L.Rev. 1479, 1493–1499. A 1962 statute allowing a broad choice of venue and extra-territorial service of process has diminished the importance of the problem. 28 U.S.C.A. § 1391(e), added by Act of Oct. 5, 1962, Pub.L. 87–748. So too has the Act of Oct. 21, 1976, Pub.L. 94–574, amending 5 U.S. C.A. §§ 702, 703, providing a right of review of federal official action in suits seeking relief other than money damages, and further providing that those suits cannot be dismissed on the ground that the United States is an indispensable party and immune from suit.

To the extent that the problem is still of significance after passage of the 1962 statute, it must now be resolved by the balancing process called for by amended Rule 19. Compare, e.g., Washington v. Cameron, C.A.1969, 411 F.2d 705, 133 U.S.App.D.C. 391, with Chicago Teachers Union v. Johnson, C.A.7th, 1980, 639 F.2d 353. See generally 7 Wright & Miller, Civil § 1622.

41. See, e.g., Washington v. U. S., C.C.A.9th, 1936, 87 F.2d 421, 427–428; Montfort v. Korte, C.C.A.7th, 1939, 100 F.2d 615, 617.

that would affect their interests, and, on the other hand, the desire to make some judgment, if at all possible, rather than leaving the parties without a remedy because, if the absentees could be ordered in, a better decision might be reached.[42]

Because of the need to reconcile these conflicting interests, the courts, though they rarely articulated it, commonly strained hard to classify a missing party was not "indispensable" if the alternative was to dismiss the action and perhaps preclude the present parties from any effective relief.[43] Only an occasional statement in the cases revealed the true nature of the problem. The Supreme Court said, for example, that "there is no prescribed formula for determining in every case whether a person is an indispensable party," [44] and again that "indispensability of parties is determined on practical considerations." [45] Other courts reached sound results by anomalous reasoning, as where a party was expressly characterized as "indispensable" but the court nevertheless proceeded to judgment in his absence because justice so required.[46]

Modern scholarship exposed the inadequacies of Rule 19, and of the traditional approach to compulsory joinder of parties,[47] and the rule was extensively amended in 1966 to reflect this thinking. The amended rule was held valid, and given a discriminating and sympathetic reading, in Provident Tradesmens Bank & Trust Co. v. Patterson.[48] The amended rule, as the Supreme Court said, "was not intended as a change in principles." [49] Instead it sought to "eliminate the confusion which has long surrounded the old Rule 19 by eliminat-

---

42. Comment, The Litigant and the Absentee in Federal Multiparty Practice, 1968, 116 U.Pa.L.Rev. 531, 532.

43. An excellent example is Kroese v. General Steel Castings Corp., C.A.3d, 1950, 179 F.2d 760, certiorari denied 70 S.Ct. 1026, 339 U.S. 983, 94 L.Ed. 1386, where a holding that a majority of the directors were indispensable in an action to compel declaration of a dividend would have barred any relief in any forum. See also Standard Oil Co. of Texas v. Marshall, C.A.5th, 1959, 265 F.2d 46, 56, certiorari denied 80 S.Ct. 259, 361 U.S. 915, 4 L.Ed.2d 185; New England Mut. Life Ins. Co. v. Brandenburg, D.C.N.Y.1948, 8 F.R.D. 151.

44. Niles-Bement-Pond Co. v. Iron Moulders' Union Local No. 68, 1920, 41 S.Ct. 39, 41, 254 U.S. 77, 80, 65 L.Ed. 145.

45. Shaugnessy v. Pedreiro, 1955, 75 S.Ct. 591, 595, 349 U.S. 48, 54, 99 L.Ed. 868.

See also Roos v. Texas Co., C.C.A.2d, 1927, 23 F.2d 171, 172, certiorari denied

48 S.Ct. 434, 277 U.S. 587, 72 L.Ed. 1001.

46. Parker Rust-Proof Co. v. Western Union Tel. Co., C.C.A.2d, 1939, 105 F.2d 976, certiorari denied 60 S.Ct. 128, 308 U.S. 597, 84 L.Ed. 500; Benger Laboratories Ltd. v. R. K. Laros Co., Inc., D.C.Pa.1959, 24 F.R.D. 450.

47. Reed, Compulsory Joinder of Parties in Civil Actions, 1957, 55 Mich.L. Rev. 327, 483; Hazard, Indispensable Party: The Historical Origin of a Procedural Phantom, 1961, 61 Col.L.Rev. 1254; James, Civil Procedure, 1965, §§ 9.14–9.21. See also Developments in the Law—Multiparty Litigation in the Federal Courts, 1958, 71 Harv.L. Rev. 874, 879–889; Note, Indispensable Parties in the Federal Courts, 1952, 65 Harv.L.Rev. 1050.

48. 1968, 88 S.Ct. 733, 390 U.S. 102, 19 L.Ed.2d 936. See also the decision on remand C.A.3d, 1969, 411 F.2d 88.

49. 88 S.Ct. at 741 n. 12, 390 U.S. at 116 n. 12.

ing the categories and the ritual inherited from Shields v. Barrow," [50] and substituting instead "stated pragmatic considerations." [51]

Rule 19(a) defines the class of persons who are needed for just adjudication. A person falls into this class if in his absence complete relief cannot be accorded to the existing parties, or if he has some interest in the controversy and is so situated that disposition of the action in his absence might as a practical matter impair his ability to protect that interest, or if judgment in his absence would expose any of the existing parties to a substantial risk of double obligation by reason of his claimed interest. If an absentee meets this test, and if he is subject to process and his joinder will not destroy diversity, the court must require that he be joined. This class of persons needed for a just adjudication is roughly equivalent to those who would in the past have been classified as either "indispensable" or "necessary," but the old labels are not used, and old decisions applying the labels are not controlling. [52]

If the absentee is needed for just adjudication and is not subject to process or his joinder would destroy diversity, Rule 19(b) states the factors to be considered in deciding whether to proceed in his absence or to dismiss the action. The ultimate question is whether "equity and good conscience" permit the action to proceed, but in deciding this the court is required to weigh whether judgment in the absence of the person would prejudice him or those already parties, whether protective provisions in the decree might lessen or void this prejudice, whether a judgment rendered in the person's absence will be adequate, and whether the plaintiff will have a satisfactory remedy if the action is dismissed.

The decision by the Supreme Court in the Provident Tradesmens case not only upheld the validity of the amended rule, against a claim that it exceeded the rulemaking power by altering the "substantive" rights of "indispensable" parties, but also indicated how the new rule is to work. A collision between a truck and a borrowed car led to several deaths and serious injuries. The estate of one of the persons killed obtained a $50,000 judgment against the estate of the driver of the car, but the driver's estate was penniless and the judgment had not been paid. The owner of the car had $100,000 liability insurance. The estate of the person killed then brought an action for a declaratory judgment that the driver's use of the car had been with permission of the owner, and thus that the owner's insurance covered the $50,000 judgment. The defendants in the declaratory judgment ac-

50. Rippey v. Denver U. S. Nat. Bank, D.C.Colo.1966, 260 F.Supp. 704, 708. See also Haas v. Jefferson Nat. Bank of Miami Beach, C.A.5th, 1971, 442 F.2d 394, 396–397.

51. 88 S.Ct. at 736, 390 U.S. at 107.

See also Smith v. State Farm Fire & Cas. Co., C.A.5th, 1980, 633 F.2d 401, 405;

Lewis, Mandatory Joinder of Parties in Civil Proceedings: The Case for Analytical Pragmatism, 1974, 26 U.Fla.L. Rev. 381.

52. See generally 7 Wright & Miller, Civil § 1604.

tion were the insurance company and the estate of the driver. The owner was not a party and his presence would have defeated diversity if he had been a party. A jury found that the use of the car had been with the owner's permission and a declaratory judgment was entered that the policy coverage extended to the $50,000 judgment.

Though the issue had not been raised by the parties in the trial court or by the appellant on appeal, the court of appeals held that the owner was an "indispensable" party and that the action must be dismissed because he had not been joined.[53] The Supreme Court reversed. It had no trouble agreeing that the owner was a person needed for a just adjudication who should be "joined if feasible," since at the time the case went to trial there was at least a possibility that a judgment might impede his ability to protect his interest or lead to later relitigation by him. But from an appellate perspective, after a judgment following extensive litigation in which the owner's absence was not raised, it thought that the criteria of Rule 19(b) clearly required that the owner's absence be held not fatal to that judgment.

Although the Court indicated that the matter might have been different if the nonjoinder of the owner had been raised at the outset, it concluded that the only one of the factors mentioned in Rule 19(b) that might argue in favor of requiring dismissal at the appellate level because of the nonjoinder was the possibility of prejudice to the owner. The argument was that a judgment that the policy coverage protected the estate of the driver would deplete the policy proceeds available if, in later litigation by others killed or injured in the accident, the owner of the car should have a judgment entered against him on a theory of vicarious liability. The Court thought that "supposed threat neither large nor unavoidable." [54] The chance that the owner might be found vicariously liable was apparently slim, he would still be free to relitigate the issue whether the driver had had his permission and thus whether the insurance proceeds should not be credited against his personal liability, and in any event the judgment could be shaped to give him full protection. Thus "there was no reason then to throw away a valid judgment just because it did not theoretically settle the whole controversy." [55]

Other cases have made a similar practical analysis in allowing suit to proceed despite the absence of a party needed for a just adjudication.[56] There are, of course, cases in which a contrary result has

---

53. See note 34 above. See 7 Wright & Miller, Civil § 1609.

54. 88 S.Ct. at 740, 390 U.S. at 115.

55. 88 S.Ct. at 741, 390 U.S. at 116. On remand the judgment was shaped to protect the owner. C.A.3d, 1969, 411 F.2d 88, 98–99.

56. E.g., Pasco Intl. (London) Ltd. v. Stenograph Corp., C.A.7th, 1980, 637

F.2d 496; U. S. v. Allegheny-Ludlum Indus., Inc., C.A.5th, 1975, 517 F.2d 826; Virginia Elec. & Power Co. v. Westinghouse Elec. Corp., C.A.4th, 1973, 485 F.2d 78, certiorari denied 94 S.Ct. 1450, 415 U.S. 935, 39 L.Ed.2d 493; Bethell v. Peace, C.A.5th, 1971, 441 F.2d 495; Staten Island Rapid Transit Ry. Co. v. S. T. G. Constr. Co.,

been reached, particularly where there is a state forum in which joinder of all parties is possible,[57] but these cases too show the kind of pragmatic approach Rule 19 was intended to produce. If the action is dismissed for want of the absentee, he may then be referred to as "indispensable," but it is clear that the old label is now being used in a wholly conclusory sense.[58]

The Provident Tradesmens case also laid to rest one other matter that had been subject to dispute. It said that "in a diversity case the question of joinder is one of federal law. * * * To be sure, state-law questions may arise in determining what interest the outsider actually has, * * * but the ultimate question whether, given those state-defined interests, a federal court may proceed without the outsider is a federal matter." [59] This is in accord with the better earlier decisions, and is a sound resolution of the question. It seems not inconsistent with that rule to say that if, as a matter of substantive law, a state does not recognize that a plaintiff has a particular right of action unless he joins with him certain others, then the federal court in a diversity action is precluded from giving a plaintiff who fails to join those others an opportunity to proceed as though alone he had the substantive right.[60]

§ 71. Joinder of Parties [1]

The general principles as to compulsory joinder of parties have been sufficiently discussed in the preceding section. As there suggested, if an absent party is found to be needed for a just adjudication, the court will order his joinder if feasible. If his joinder is not feasible, there are some circumstances in which the action cannot pro-

C.A.2d, 1970, 421 F.2d 53, certiorari denied 90 S.Ct. 1871, 398 U.S. 951, 26 L.Ed.2d 291; Bennie v. Pastor, C.A.10th, 1968, 393 F.2d 1.

57. E.g., Kamhi v. Cohen, C.A.2d, 1975, 512 F.2d 1051; Glenny v. American Metal Climax, Inc., C.A.10th, 1974, 494 F.2d 651; Haas v. Jefferson Nat. Bank of Miami Beach, C.A.5th, 1971, 442 F.2d 394; Evergreen Park Nursing Home, Inc. v. American Equitable Assur. Co., C.A.7th, 1969, 417 F.2d 1113; Barnett v. Borg-Warner Acceptance Corp., D.C.Ark.1980, 488 F.Supp. 786; Reese v. Skelly Oil Co., D.C.Miss.1971, 53 F.R.D. 548.

The application of the four factors of Rule 19(b) is discussed in 7 Wright & Miller, Civil § 1608.

On the scope of appellate review of dismissals under Rule 19(b), see Walsh v. Centeio, C.A.9th, 1982, 692 F.2d 1239.

58. 88 S.Ct. at 742 n. 15, 390 U.S. at 118 n. 15.

59. 88 S.Ct. at 746 n. 22, 390 U.S. at 125 n. 22. There is a particularly careful discussion of this problem by Judge John Minor Wisdom in Kuchenig v. California Co., C.A.5th, 1965, 350 F.2d 551, certiorari denied 86 S.Ct. 561, 382 U.S. 985, 15 L.Ed.2d 473. See also Glacier General Assur. Co. v. G. Gordon Symons Co., Ltd., C.A.9th, 1980, 631 F.2d 131; 7 Wright & Miller, Civil § 1603.

60. Stevens v. Loomis, D.C.Mass.1963, 223 F.Supp. 534, 536, affirmed C.A.1st, 1964, 334 F.2d 775. But see Note, Rule 19 and Indispensable Parties, 1967, 65 Mich.L.Rev. 968, 980.

See generally Yonofsky v. Wernick, D.C. N.Y.1973, 362 F.Supp. 1005, 1021.

[§ 71]

1. 7 Wright & Miller, Civil §§ 1651–1660.

ceed in his absence, the absentee thus being regarded as "indispensable."

If the absentee needed for just adjudication is a defendant, the plaintiff may join him as he would any other defendant. If a person who is required to join as a party plaintiff refuses to do so, the situation is more difficult. In one particular circumstance, where the exclusive licensee of a patent or copyright wishes to sue for infringement but the patent or copyright owner refuses to join as a plaintiff, the licensee may name the owner as an "involuntary plaintiff." [2] Though this procedure is recognized in general terms in Rule 19(a), the courts have shown no tendency to permit broader use of the involuntary plaintiff device beyond the exclusive licensee situation in which it was developed. Thus it is held that the involuntary plaintiff procedure may be invoked only when the party sought to be joined has a duty to allow plaintiff to use his name in the action.[3] In other situations where one who should be a plaintiff refuses to join as such, the remedy, also recognized by Rule 19(a), is for plaintiff to name the person as a defendant and serve process upon him.[4] Presumably such a person will then be realigned as a plaintiff in determining whether diversity exists.[5]

The cases sometimes speak, and even act, as if the failure to join a party who may be regarded as "indispensable" is a "jurisdictional" defect.[6] This heresy has been rejected over and over again by authoritative cases.[7] The court has no jurisdiction of the absentee, and it cannot enter a judgment that will be legally binding on him, but it does have jurisdiction of the existing parties and has the power to make a judgment affecting their interests. It is for discretionary reasons, not for any want of jurisdiction, that the court may decline to proceed without the absentee.[8]

---

2. Independent Wireless Tel. Co. v. Radio Corp. of America, 1926, 46 S.Ct. 166, 269 U.S. 459, 70 L.Ed. 357; Ferrara v. Rodale Press, Inc., D.C.Pa.1972, 54 F.R.D. 3.

The requirements for joining an involuntary plaintiff were held not to have been met in Followay Productions, Inc. v. Maurer, C.A.9th, 1979, 603 F.2d 72.

3. Caprio v. Wilson, C.A.9th, 1975, 513 F.2d 837; Eikel v. States Marine Lines, Inc., C.A.5th, 1973, 473 F.2d 959.

See generally 7 Wright & Miller, Civil § 1606.

4. International Rediscount Corp. v. Hartford Acc. & Indem. Co., D.C.Del. 1977, 425 F.Supp. 669, 674; Dental Precision Shoulder v. L. D. Caulk Co., D.C. N.Y.1947, 7 F.R.D. 203; Hoffman v. Santly-Joy, Inc., D.C.N.Y.1943, 51 F.Supp. 778.

5. Eikel v. States Marine Lines, Inc., C.A.5th, 1973, 473 F.2d 959. See 7 Wright & Miller, Civil § 1605, and § 30 above.

6. See, e.g., Samuel Goldwyn, Inc. v. United Artists Corp., C.C.A.3d, 1940, 113 F.2d 703, 707; Agrashell, Inc. v. Hammons Products Co., C.A.8th, 1965, 352 F.2d 443, 447; Coughlin v. Ryder, D.C.Pa.1966, 260 F.Supp. 256, 257–258.

7. Elmendorf v. Taylor, 1825, 10 Wheat. 152, 166–168, 6 L.Ed. 289; Mallow v. Hinde, 1827, 12 Wheat. 193, 198, 6 L.Ed. 599; Provident Tradesmens Bank & Trust Co. v. Patterson, 1968, 88 S.Ct. 733, 744, 390 U.S. 102, 122, 19 L.Ed.2d 936; Dyer v. Stauffer, C.C.A. 6th, 1927, 19 F.2d 922, certiorari denied 48 S.Ct. 114, 275 U.S. 551, 72 L.Ed. 421.

8. Reed, Compulsory Joinder of Parties in Civil Actions, 1957, 55 Mich.L.Rev.

Rule 20 deals with permissive joinder of parties. If a party has some relation to the action, but it is not so close as to make him a person needed for just adjudication within Rule 19(a), he is a "proper" party, and the plaintiff has an option whether to join him if the tests of Rule 20 are met. The rule well exemplifies the modern philosophy of joinder. The provisions for joinder are very broad, but the court is then given discretion to order separate trials or to make such other orders as will prevent delay or prejudice.[9] In this way the scope of a civil action is made a question for the discretion of the judge, to be decided on practical considerations in a particular case, rather than a question governed by conceptual tests, as was true under some of the codes and at common law.

Rule 20(a) applies in similar terms to joinder of plaintiffs and joinder of defendants. It creates two tests for joinder. (1) There must be some question of law or fact common to all parties which will arise in the action. (2) There must be some right to relief asserted on behalf of each of the plaintiffs, and against each of the defendants, relating to, or arising out of, a single transaction or occurrence or series of transactions or occurrences. These tests are cumulative and both of them must be satisfied to permit joinder.[10]

It has been said that the phrase "questions of law" has reference to those arising upon the facts of the particular case, and not general principles of law.[11] The argument for such an interpretation is that otherwise a creditor, such as a bank, could bring a single action against all debtors whose obligations arose out of promissory notes, upon the theory that a common question of law was involved. This argument overlooks the fact that such joinder would not be permitted, even though it were said that a common question of law was presented, unless the notes involved a single transaction or series of transactions. Of course it will not be enough to permit joinder that there is some inconsequential or theoretical issue common to all the plaintiffs. As said by the New York Court of Appeals, construing a statute on which Rule 20 was based, "such common questions must

327, 332–334; Kaplan, Continuing Work of the Civil Committee: 1966 Amendments of the Federal Rules of Civil Procedure, 1967, 81 Harv.L.Rev. 356, 364; Lewis, Mandatory Joinder of Parties in Civil Proceedings: The Case for Analytical Pragmatism, 1974, 26 U.Fla.L.Rev. 381, 386; 7 Wright & Miller, Civil § 1611.

9. Rules 20(b), 42(b). See United Mine Workers of America v. Gibbs, 1966, 86 S.Ct. 1130, 1138, 383 U.S. 715, 724, 16 L.Ed.2d 218; 7 Wright & Miller, Civil § 1660; 9 Wright & Miller, Civil §§ 2387–2392.

10. Magnavox Co. v. APF Electronics, Inc., D.C.Ill.1980, 496 F.Supp. 29, 34; King v. Pepsi Cola Metropolitan Bottling Co., D.C.Pa.1979, 86 F.R.D. 4, 5. But see Note, Is Federal Rule 20(a) Too Restrictive?, 1965, 18 Okla.L.Rev. 195.

Note, however, that if there is a common question of law or fact, the cases may be consolidated for trial, under Rule 42(a), even though the "same transaction or occurrence" test is not met. Hanes Dye & Finishing Co. v. Caisson Corp., D.C.N.C.1970, 309 F.Supp. 237; 9 Wright & Miller, Civil § 2382.

11. Federal Housing Admr. v. Christianson, D.C.Conn.1939, 26 F.Supp. 419; Smith v. North American Rockwell Corp.—Tulsa Div., D.C.Okl.1970, 50 F.R.D. 515, 524.

be of substantial importance as compared with all of the issues, and * * * the question of the comparative weight and importance of common and separate issues involved in each cause of action is quite largely a matter of judgment." [12] In that case 193 persons who had been individually induced, by means of a fraudulent prospectus, to invest their money in a sham corporation were permitted to join in one action for fraud against the promoters. The common question of whether the prospectus was fraudulent was enough to justify joinder, even though there were separate issues as to whether each plaintiff saw the prospectus and relied on it to his detriment. By the same token permissive joinder of plaintiffs is quite common in automobile collision cases, where there is a common question of fact and law as to defendant's negligence, even though there are also separate questions as to damages and contributory negligence.[13] And in a suit against an employer for discrimination, the discriminatory character of defendant's conduct is common to all of the plaintiffs, even though particular plaintiffs may have suffered different effects from it.[14]

There is very little discussion in the cases as to what constitutes the same transaction or occurrence or series of transactions or occurrences. One court has suggested that there can be no hard and fast rule and that the approach must be generally whether there are enough factual concurrences that it would be fair to the parties to litigate the matters at one time, having in mind also the convenience of the court.[15] This seems a sensible approach, particularly in so far as it is reminiscent of the "logical relationship" test that the case law has developed as the meaning of "transaction or occurrence" in the compulsory counterclaim rule.[16] It is worth observing, however, that the convenience of the parties and the court can be fully protected, though joinder is allowed, by separate trials, pursuant to Rules 20(b)

---

12. Akely v. Kinnicutt, 1924, 144 N.E. 682, 684, 238 N.Y. 466, 473. See also Music Merchants, Inc. v. Capitol Records, Inc., D.C.N.Y.1957, 20 F.R.D. 462.

13. E.g., Franklin v. Shelton, C.A.10th, 1957, 250 F.2d 92, certiorari denied 78 S.Ct. 544, 355 U.S. 959, 2 L.Ed.2d 533; 7 Wright & Miller, Civil § 1656; James & Hazard, Civil Procedure, 2d ed. 1977, § 10.9.

14. Mosley v. General Motors Corp., C.A.8th, 1974, 497 F.2d 1330; Vulcan Soc'y of Westchester County v. Fire Dept. of City of White Plains, D.C.N.Y. 1979, 82 F.R.D. 379.

15. Eastern Fireproofing Co. v. U. S. Gypsum Co., D.C.Mass.1958, 160 F.Supp. 580, 581. See also Mosley v. General Motors Corp., C.A.8th, 1974, 497 F.2d 1330, 1333. Under a state statute similar to Rule 20(a), two rear-

end collisions five months apart were held to be a "series of occurrences." Ryan v. Mackolin, 1968, 237 N.E.2d 377, 14 Ohio St.2d 213, noted 1968, 20 Syracuse L.Rev. 67, 37 U.Cinc.L.Rev. 826, 1969, 1 U.Tol.L.Rev. 287.

The Supreme Court has held that a common practice among voter registrars to deny black persons their right to vote constituted a series of transactions and allowed joinder. U. S. v. Mississippi, 1965, 85 S.Ct. 808, 815–816, 380 U.S. 128, 142–143, 13 L.Ed.2d 717.

A more restrictive view is taken in Stanford v. Tennessee Valley Auth., D.C. Tenn.1955, 18 F.R.D. 152, Sun-X Glass Tinting of Mid-Wisconsin, Inc. v. Sun-X Intl., Inc., D.C.Wis.1964, 227 F.Supp. 365, 373–375, and in Kenvin v. Newburger, Loeb & Co., D.C.N.Y.1965, 37 F.R.D. 473.

16. See § 79 below.

and 42(b), and thus it seems practically desirable to give the broadest possible reading to the permissive language of Rule 20(a).[17]

A state court, construing a statute identical to Rule 20(a), has tried to differentiate between a "transaction" and an "occurrence." Certain property was allegedly destroyed by an explosion. Plaintiffs sought to join a claim against the persons who set off the dynamite causing the explosion with a claim against insurance companies that had issued explosion policies covering the property. There was a question of fact, admittedly common to all defendants, as to whether the damage had been done by an explosion or by some other cause. The court held nevertheless that joinder was not proper. It reasoned that the dynamiting was an "occurrence," the insurance was a "transaction," and thus that the claims did not arise from a single transaction nor from a single occurrence.[18] This is an undesirable over-refinement. The word "transaction" is normally defined in terms of "occurrences,"[19] and the history of the drafting of Rule 20(a)[20] suggests clearly that "occurrence" was added merely to guard against any over-restrictive definition of "transaction," and was not intended to add a new and independent concept. Such, it is believed, is the construction most courts have put upon the rule.[21]

A significant innovation made by Rule 20(a) is the provision allowing joinder even though liability is asserted severally or in the alternative, provided the "same transaction" and "common question" tests are met. This is a departure from the common law and older code rules, which restricted joinder to persons having a joint interest or liability. The classic case illustrating the need for joinder in the alternative is an English case decided under a rule that was the forerunner of Rule 20(a). An office supply company had contracted to sell to a particular customer time cards meeting certain specifications. It then contracted with a manufacturer to purchase such time cards from it. When the cards were shipped, the customer refused to pay for them, claiming that they failed to meet the required specifications. The supply company then sued the customer and the manufacturer, demanding the price from the customer, or, in the alternative, damages for breach of contract in not meeting the specifications from the manufacturer. The case presented one common question: "Did

17.   Wheat v. Safeway Stores, Inc., 1965, 404 P.2d 317, 321, 146 Mont. 105, 113. See also James & Hazard, Civil Procedure, 2d ed. 1977, pp. 480–481.

18.   State ex rel. Campbell v. James, Mo. 1954, 263 S.W.2d 402, 407.

19.   " 'Transaction' is a word of flexible meaning. It may comprehend a series of many occurrences * * *." Moore v. New York Cotton Exchange, 1926, 46 S.Ct. 367, 371, 270 U.S. 593, 610, 70 L.Ed. 750; Wheaton, A Study of the Statutes Which Contain the Term "Subject of the Action" and Which Relate to Joinder of Actions and Plaintiffs and to Counterclaims, 1933, 18 Corn.L.Q. 232, 242.

20.   The history is set out in Wright, Estoppel by Rule: The Compulsory Counterclaim Under Modern Pleading, 1954, 38 Minn.L.Rev. 423, 448–450.

21.   Decisions passing on the propriety of joinder in particular circumstances are collected in 7 Wright & Miller, Civil §§ 1656, 1657.

the goods furnished by the manufacturer conform to the specifications?" If they did, then the customer was obliged to pay the price. If they did not, then the manufacturer had breached his contract. No matter how many other questions might appear in the case, this common question was fundamental. Every instinct for procedural economy and simplicity suggests that this controversy be resolved in one suit, and the court properly permitted the joinder.[22] Similar joinder in the alternative is allowed under Rule 20(a).[23]

The only real difficulty in joinder of parties has come in cases involving both multiple parties and multiple claims. Here, as is discussed in section 78 below, there was, prior to a 1966 amendment, an unfortunate tendency in some cases to read Rule 20(a), on joinder of parties, as limiting Rule 18 on joinder of claims.

State restrictions on joinder do not limit the application of Rule 20(a) in federal court,[24] but the federal court may honor some strong state policy, such as that prohibiting joinder of an insurance company in a suit against its insured.[25] The rule, of course, does not alter usual requirements of federal jurisdiction, and with regard to this rule, unlike some of the special joinder devices to be considered later, the concept of "ancillary jurisdiction,"[26] has until recently not been applied.[27] Thus complete diversity is required between all the plaintiffs and all the defendants.[28] The requirements of the venue statutes, which usually speak in terms of all the parties on one side, must be met.[29] Normally the jurisdictional amount test must be satisfied with regard to each of the parties. Aggregation is permitted if there are several parties on one side with a common undivided interest,[30] but not if the demands for and against them are separate and dis-

---

22. Payne v. British Time Recorder Co., [1921] 2 K.B. 1 (C.A.).

23. E.g., Texas Employers Ins. Assn. v. Felt, C.C.A.5th, 1945, 150 F.2d 227 (three insurance companies joined as defendants where doubt as to which was liable for workmen's compensation); Amalgamated Packaging Indus., Ltd. v. National Container Corp., D.C. N.Y.1953, 14 F.R.D. 194 (alternative joinder as plaintiffs of purchaser and his subsequent vendee in breach of warranty action). See 7 Wright & Miller, Civil § 1654.

24. Siebrand v. Gossnell, C.A.9th, 1956, 234 F.2d 81; Doyle v. Stanolind Oil & Gas Co., C.C.A.5th, 1941, 123 F.2d 900; Sypherd v. Haeckl's Exp. Co., D.C.Ohio 1962, 31 F.R.D. 255; Campbell v. Pacific Fruit Exp. Co., D.C.Idaho 1957, 148 F.Supp. 209; Stanford v. Tennessee Val. Auth., D.C.Tenn.1955, 18 F.R.D. 152.

25. American Fidelity Fire Ins. Co. v. Hood, D.C.S.C.1965, 37 F.R.D. 17;

Globe Indem. Co. v. Teixeira, D.C.Hawaii 1963, 230 F.Supp. 444; Hoosier Cas. Co. of Indianapolis, Ind. v. Fox, D.C.Iowa 1952, 102 F.Supp. 214; Pennsylvania R. Co. v. Lattavo Bros., Inc., D.C.Ohio 1949, 9 F.R.D. 205. But cf. Plains Ins. Co. v. Sandoval, D.C.Colo. 1964, 35 F.R.D. 293. Joinder of the insurer will be allowed in federal court in states such as Louisiana and Wisconsin that permit such joinder. Cf. Lumbermen's Mut. Cas. Co. v. Elbert, 1954, 75 S.Ct. 151, 348 U.S. 48, 99 L.Ed. 59.

26. See § 9 above.

27. Olivieri v. Adams, D.C.Pa.1968, 280 F.Supp. 428.

28. See § 24 above at notes 33 to 36.

29. See § 42 above; 15 Wright, Miller & Cooper, Jurisdiction § 3807.

30. E.g., Troy Bank of Troy, Ind. v. G. A. Whitehead & Co., 1911, 32 S.Ct. 9, 222 U.S. 39, 56 L.Ed. 81. See § 36 above.

tinct.[31] Nor, on the orthodox view, may a party with a claim for less than the jurisdictional amount be joined with one who has a sufficient claim.[32] The one respect in which the final word has yet to be written is when, if at all, the concept of "pendent parties" can properly be used to allow joinder of one defendant in a nondiversity case against whom there is a jurisdictional basis with a second defendant for whom there is no independent basis of jurisdiction.[33]

Under Rule 21 the remedy for misjoinder or nonjoinder of parties is corrective action, rather than a punitive dismissal. If a party has been omitted who ought to be joined under Rule 19, the remedy is to join him, and dismissal is called for only if he cannot be served or his presence would destroy diversity.[34] If a party has been joined whose joinder is not proper under Rule 20, such party may be dropped by order of the court on motion of any party or on its own initiative at any stage of the action and on such terms as are just.[35] As was developed in an earlier section, this can be done even after verdict to eliminate from the case a party of nondiverse citizenship.[36]

§ 72. Class Actions [1]

"One of the most controversial recent developments in the law of federal procedure is the growth of the class action. The crucial event was the amendment in 1966 of Rule 23 of the Federal Rules of Civil Procedure." [2] The controversy has indeed been a hot one. The class action, as it was reformed in 1966, has been described as everything from "one of the most socially useful remedies in history" [3] to "legalized blackmail." [4] In less than two decades under the amended rule

31. E.g., Pinel v. Pinel, 1916, 36 S.Ct. 416, 240 U.S. 594, 60 L.Ed. 817. See § 36 above.

32. A number of courts of appeals had sensibly moved to a different rule on this point, but that movement seems to be wrong in the light of what the Supreme Court said in Zahn v. International Paper Co., 1973, 94 S.Ct. 505, 509, 414 U.S. 291, 295, 38 L.Ed.2d 511. See § 36 above.

33. The Supreme Court has taken a cautious attitude toward the notion of "pendent parties." Aldinger v. Howard, 1976, 96 S.Ct. 2413, 427 U.S. 1, 49 L.Ed.2d 276. See § 19 above.

34. 7 Wright & Miller, Civil § 1684.

35. 7 Wright & Miller, Civil § 1684.

36. Finn v. American Fire & Cas. Co., C.A.5th, 1953, 207 F.2d 113, certiorari denied 74 S.Ct. 476, 347 U.S. 912, 98 L.Ed. 1069; Dollar S. S. Lines v. Merz, C.C.A.9th, 1934, 68 F.2d 594. See § 69 above.

[§ 72]

1. 7 Wright & Miller, Civil §§ 1751–1771; 7A id., §§ 1772–1803;

American College of Trial Lawyers, Report of the Special Committee on Rule 23, 1972; Miller, Of Frankenstein Monsters and Shining Knights: Myth, Reality, and the "Class Action Problem," 1979, 92 Harv.L.Rev. 664; Dam, Class Actions: Efficiency, Compensation, Deterrence, and Conflict of Interest, 1975, 4 J.Legal Studies 47; Meyer, The Social Utility of Class Actions, 1975, 42 Brooklyn L.Rev. 189; Patrick & Cherner, Rule 23 and the Class Action For Damages: A Reply to the Report of the American College of Trial Lawyers, 1973, 28 Bus.Law. 1097; Note, Rule 23(b)(3) Class Actions: An Empirical Study, 1974, 62 Geo.L.J. 1123.

2. Dam, note 1 above, at 47.

3. Pomerantz, New Developments in Class Actions—Has Their Death Knell Been Sounded?, 1970, 25 Bus.Law. 1259.

4. Handler, The Shift from Substantive to Procedural Innovations in Antitrust Suits, 1971, 71 Col.L.Rev. 1, 9.

both the case law and the literature have become vast. Indeed it would be possible to write a book much larger than the present work on class actions alone,[5] and in this section it will be possible only to touch on the more important features.

"The class action was an invention of equity * * * mothered by the practical necessity of providing a procedural device so that mere numbers would not disable large groups of individuals, united in interest, from enforcing their equitable rights nor grant them immunity from their equitable wrongs. * * * By Rule 23 the Supreme Court has extended the use of the class action device to the entire field of federal civil litigation by making it applicable to all civil actions."[6] It provides a means by which, where a large group of persons are interested in a matter, one or more may sue or be sued as representatives of the class without needing to join every member of the class. This procedure is available in federal court, even in diversity actions in states that do not recognize the class suit, though the state law will define the substantive interest of the members of the class and the capacity to sue or be sued of the named representatives.[7]

As originally adopted in 1938, Rule 23 made a bold and well-intentioned attempt to encourage more frequent use of class actions. The rule made this procedure available in actions for legal relief as well as in those that were historically equitable, and it sought to give guidance on the kind of cases for which class treatment was appropriate. But, as was often pointed out,[8] and as will be referred to more specifically later in this section, a quarter century of experience demonstrated very serious defects in the original rule. Accordingly in 1966 the rule was extensively amended. The amended rule, like the companion amendments that year to Rules 19 and 24, sought to substitute functional tests for the conceptualisms of the old rule. In addition, it sought to provide better guidance on the measures that may be taken by the court in managing the class action. Unfortunately

5. The discussion of Rule 23 in 7 and 7A Wright & Miller, Civil, including the 1981 pocket parts, occupies 893 pages.

6. Montgomery Ward & Co. v. Langer, C.C.A.8th, 1948, 168 F.2d 182, 187.

See generally Yeazell, Group Litigation and Social Context: Toward a History of the Class Action, 1977, 77 Col.L.Rev. 866.

7. Minnesota v. U. S. Steel Corp., D.C. Minn.1968, 44 F.R.D. 559, 568; cf. Hanna v. Plumer, 1965, 85 S.Ct. 1136, 380 U.S. 460, 14 L.Ed.2d 8, discussed § 59 above. Compare Oskoian v. Canuel, C.A.1st, 1959, 269 F.2d 311, with Underwood v. Maloney, C.A.3d, 1958, 256 F.2d 334, certiorari denied 79 S.Ct. 93, 358 U.S. 864, 3 L.Ed.2d 97. The last

two cases are discussed, and distinguished in 7 Wright & Miller, Civil § 1758.

8. 7 Wright & Miller, Civil § 1752; Chafee, Some Problems of Equity, 1950, pp. 199–295; Advisory Committee Note to 1966 Amendment, 1966, 39 F.R.D. 98–99; Kalven & Rosenfield, The Contemporary Function of the Class Suit, 1941, 8 U.Chi.L.Rev. 684; Keeffe, Levy & Donovan, Lee Defeats Ben Hur, 1948, 33 Corn.L.Q. 327; Weinstein, Revision of Procedure: Some Problems in Class Actions, 1960, 9 Buffalo L.Rev. 433; Simeone, Procedure Problems of Class Suits, 1962, 60 Mich.L.Rev. 905.

the new rule, though generously described as "complicated," [9] still "tends to ask more questions than it answers." [10] The Supreme Court, in a series of decisions construing the amended rule, has answered some of the questions the rule poses but the effect of its decisions has been to limit its use. Finally, the amended rule is in jeopardy from those who embrace it too enthusiastically just as it is from those who approach it with distaste. Admonitions that "if there is to be an error made, let it be in favor and not against the maintenance of the class action" [11] conveyed a receptive spirit. But to the extent that they encouraged plaintiffs to bring, and the courts to allow, maintenance of class actions in controversies that are unmanageable by this device, they brought the rule into disrepute even for the cases to which it is well suited. Thus the same court that made the remark just quoted was to speak five years later of the need "to employ realism and good sense in denying class action status" and warned that Rule 23 "bears the seeds of its own destruction through unrealistic applications within its theoretical span." [12] It may well be that "it will take a generation or so before we can fully appreciate the scope, the virtues, and the vices of the new Rule 23." [13] Certainly the jury is not yet in.

9. Note, Revised Federal Rule 23, Class Actions: Surviving Difficulties and New Problems Require Further Amendment, 1967, 52 Minn.L.Rev. 509. The present author, less generously, has referred to the amended rule as "extremely complicated." Wright, Recent Changes in the Federal Rules of Procedure, 1966, 42 F.R.D. 552, 563.

10. Frankel, Some Preliminary Observations Concerning Civil Rule 23, 1967, 43 F.R.D. 39.

In a letter to the present author, the draftsman of the rule, Professor Benjamin Kaplan, has suggested that "a rule that came out looking smoother would simply have remitted a series of problems to the courts with fewer guides; and that the purpose of procedural rules of this order of difficulty must be precisely that of asking questions—I mean the right ones."

11. Esplin v. Hirschi, C.A.10th, 1968, 402 F.2d 94, 99; Green v. Wolf Corp., C.A.2d, 1968, 406 F.2d 291, 298, certiorari denied 89 S.Ct. 2131, 395 U.S. 977, 23 L.Ed.2d 766. See also Eisen v. Carlisle & Jacquelin, C.A.2d, 1968, 391 F.2d 555, 563.

12. Wilcox v. Commerce Bank of Kansas City, C.A.10th, 1973, 474 F.2d 336, 347.

13. Frankel, Some Preliminary Observations Concerning Civil Rule 23, 1967,

43 F.R.D. 39, 52, quoting Professor Benjamin Kaplan.

For a pessimistic view, see Friendly, Federal Jurisdiction: A General View, 1973, p. 120: "Something seems to have gone radically wrong with a well-intentioned effort." See also Dam, Class Action Notice: Who Needs It?, 1974 Sup.Ct.Rev. 97, 119: "In the light of Eisen the 1966 amendment becomes a clever bit of legal architecture that has collapsed."

For a more optimistic view, though written before the Supreme Court's decision in the Eisen case, see Miller, Problems of Giving Notice in Class Actions, 1973, 58 F.R.D. 313, 334: "With the passage of time and the accumulation of experience under the rule, which, after all, is only six years old at this point, I believe Rule 23 will prove to be a very valuable keystone in making federal procedure responsive to the exigencies of the Twentieth Century and particularly the needs of contemporary litigation." See also Hazard, The Effect of the Class Action Device Upon the Substantive Law, 1973, 58 F.R.D. 307, 308.

Professor Miller has suggested more recently that the period from 1964 to 1969 was one of overenthusiasm and euphoria about amended Rule 23, that a reaction set in and from 1969 to 1973 or 1974 antipathy to the class action

There are two general requirements for the maintenance of any class suit.[14] These are that the persons constituting the class must be so numerous that it is impracticable to bring them all before the court, and the named representatives must be such as will fairly insure the adequate representation of them all.

For the class to be large enough to permit a class suit, impossibility of joinder is not required. Extreme difficulty or impracticability of joinder is sufficient.[15] One court has referred to "the numbers game aspect of Rule 23," [16] but it is clear that no numerical test is possible. Groups of as many as 350 have been held too small for a class action,[17] while groups of 25 or more have been held sufficient.[18] The requirement of a numerous class is intended to protect members of a small class from being deprived of their rights without a day in court,[19] and in a particular case this object should be weighed in the light of the situation that exists.[20]

Adequacy of representation is essential. The representative must not hold interests that conflict with those of the class he seeks to represent.[21] The adequacy of representation should be scrutinized

was palpable, and that the pendulum swung again about 1974 beginning a phase, which may last until the end of the generation-long period Professor Kaplan envisioned, of increasing sophistication, restraint, and stabilization in class action practice. Miller, note 1 above, at 679–680.

In 1978 the Department of Justice proposed legislation that would have made drastic changes in class actions. See Miller, note 1 above, at 684–693; Wells, Reforming Federal Class Action Procedure: An Analysis of the Justice Department Proposal, 1979, 16 Harv.J. Legis. 543. That legislation now seems to be dead.

14. The requirement in Rule 23(a)(2) that there must be questions of law or fact common to the class will always be met when the further tests of Rule 23(b) are satisfied. Vernon J. Rockler & Co. v. Graphic Enterprises, Inc., D.C. Minn.1971, 52 F.R.D. 335, 340 n. 9; 7 Wright & Miller, Civil § 1763. The requirement in Rule 23(a)(3) that the claims or defenses of the representatives must be typical of those of the class may have some independent significance, e.g., Koos v. First Nat. Bank of Peoria, C.A.7th, 1974, 496 F.2d 1162, 1164, but in general seems only a further particularization of the requirement that the named representatives will adequately represent the entire class. See General Telephone Co. of the Southwest v. Falcon, 1982, 102 S.Ct. 2364, ___ U.S. ___, 72 L.Ed.2d

740; Degnan, Adequacy of Representation in Class Actions, 1972, 60 Calif.L. Rev. 705, 716.

15. Harris v. Palm Springs Alpine Estates, Inc., C.A.9th, 1964, 329 F.2d 909, 913–914; Smith v. Baltimore & O. R. Co., D.C.Md.1979, 473 F.Supp. 572, 580–581.

16. Phillips v. Sherman, D.C.N.Y.1961, 197 F.Supp. 866, 869.

17. Utah v. American Pipe & Constr. Co., D.C.Cal.1969, 49 F.R.D. 17. See also Minersville Coal Co. v. Anthracite Export Assn., D.C.Pa.1971, 55 F.R.D. 426 (330 members).

18. Philadelphia Elec. Co. v. Anaconda American Brass Co., D.C.Pa.1968, 43 F.R.D. 452, 463. For other cases ruling whether a particular class was large enough, see 7 Wright & Miller, Civil § 1762 nn. 38–65.

19. Matthies v. Seymour Mfg. Co., C.A.2d, 1959, 270 F.2d 365, 372, certiorari denied 80 S.Ct. 591, 361 U.S. 962, 4 L.Ed.2d 544, noted 1960, 69 Yale L.J. 816; Rippey v. Denver U. S. Nat. Bank, D.C.Colo.1966, 260 F.Supp. 704, 712.

20. Demarco v. Edens, C.A.2d, 1968, 390 F.2d 836, 845; Barnes v. Board of Trustees, Michigan Veterans Trust Fund, D.C.Mich.1973, 369 F.Supp. 1327, 1332–1333.

21. Albertson's, Inc. v. Amalgamated Sugar Co., C.A.10th, 1974, 503 F.2d 459; Schy v. Susquehanna Corp., C.A.

with particular care where suit is brought, as the rule has always permitted,[22] against a class of defendants. Plaintiffs must not be allowed to succumb to the temptation to name as representatives of the defendant class persons whose defense will be less than zealous.[23] It seems fairly obvious that the members of a class cannot be adequately represented if their interests are in conflict, but the application of this principle leads to considerable difficulty. In the leading case of Hansberry v. Lee,[24] involving the validity of a class action testing whether a restrictive agreement had been adopted by a group of landowners, it was held that landowners who sought to secure the benefits of the agreement could not be regarded as members of the same class as those who wished to challenge the agreement. In the course of the opinion Chief Justice Stone wrote, for the Court: "It is one thing to say that some members of a class may represent other members in a litigation where the sole and common interest of the class in the litigation, is either to assert a common right or to challenge an asserted obligation. * * * It is quite another to hold that all those who are free alternatively either to assert rights or to challenge them are of a single class, so that any group merely because it is of the class so constituted, may be deemed adequately to represent others of the class in litigating their interests in either alternative." [25]

There were excellent reasons for deciding Hansberry v. Lee as the Court did. The action that was claimed to bind all members of the class was a collusive action in which the crucial fact was established by a false stipulation.[26] The language of the Court, however, seems

---

7th, 1970, 419 F.2d 1112, certiorari denied 91 S.Ct. 51, 400 U.S. 826, 27 L.Ed. 2d 55; Degnan, note 14 above; Comment, Representation in Class Actions: Is Personal Interest Replacing Personal Stake?, 1981 Ariz.St.L.J. 1007; Comment, note 14 above; 7 Wright & Miller, Civil § 1768.

The class representative must be part of the class and possess the same interest and suffer the same injury as the class members. East Texas Motor Freight System Inc. v. Rodriguez, 1977, 97 S.Ct. 1891, 431 U.S. 395, 52 L.Ed.2d 453. However, the fact that the representative's claim becomes moot after the class has been certified but before the action terminates does not necessarily require dismissal of the action. Compare Sosna v. Iowa, 1975, 95 S.Ct. 553, 419 U.S. 393, 42 L.Ed.2d 532, and Zablocki v. Redhail, 1978, 98 S.Ct. 673, 434 U.S. 374, 54 L.Ed.2d 618, with Kremens v. Bartley, 1977, 97 S.Ct. 1709, 431 U.S. 119, 52 L.Ed.2d 184. See Kane, Standing, Mootness, and Federal Rule 23—Balancing Perspectives, 1976, 26 Buffalo L.Rev. 83.

22. 7 Wright & Miller, Civil § 1770; Note, Defendant Class Actions, 1978, 91 Harv.L.Rev. 630.

23. The danger is illustrated by a well-known state case, where the whole class was held bound by a suit against carefully picked members of the class with a very small financial interest who made only a token defense. Richardson v. Kelly, 1945, 191 S.W.2d 857, 144 Tex. 497, certiorari denied 67 S.Ct. 487, 329 U.S. 798, 91 L.Ed. 683, criticized in Notes, 1946, 55 Yale L.J. 831, 25 Texas L.Rev. 64, and by Chafee, Some Problems of Equity, 1950, pp. 239–242.

24. 1940, 61 S.Ct. 115, 311 U.S. 32, 85 L.Ed. 22.

25. 61 S.Ct. at 119, 311 U.S. at 44–45.

26. In the earlier case it had been stipulated that more than 95% of the owners had signed the restrictive agreement, as was required by its terms before it could take effect. In fact only 54% had signed. See Weinstein, Revision of Procedure: Some Problems in Class Actions, 1960, 9 Buffalo L.Rev. 433, 460; Keeffe, Levy & Donovan, Lee

unduly broad. In any conceivable case, some of the members of the class will wish to assert their rights while others will not wish to do so.[27] Thus the familiar case of the stockholders' derivative suit is almost invariably brought by minority stockholders to challenge action that a majority of the stockholders approve. Yet it is routinely regarded as an appropriate class suit.[28] Another familiar class suit is that in which one or more taxpayers of a community, suing on behalf of all, challenge the validity of a proposed public expenditure. It is difficult to believe that there has ever been such a case in which a good many of the taxpayers would not have preferred that their rights not be enforced, because of their interest in having the expenditure made. Yet no one has ever doubted the propriety of bringing such a suit as a class action.[29]

It has sometimes been said that a sufficient number of members of the class must appear as parties to insure a fair representation of the class,[30] but it has increasingly come to be recognized that the quality of the representation is more important than numbers, and that even a single representative of the class may be enough.[31]

Defeats Ben Hur, 1948, 33 Corn.L.Q. 327, 337–339.

27. A class action seeking more aggressive management of an investment fund was allowed to proceed in Dierks v. Thompson, C.A.1st, 1969, 414 F.2d 453, since the interests of the participants in the plan who preferred investments with little or no risk was adequately represented by the defendants. The amended rule is helpful on this point, by providing that a class may be divided into subclasses. Rule 23(c)(4)(B). See Carr v. Conoco Plastics, Inc., C.A. 5th, 1970, 423 F.2d 57, 58, certiorari denied 91 S.Ct. 241, 400 U.S. 951, 28 L.Ed.2d 257; 7A Wright & Miller, Civil § 1790.

28. See § 73 below. The suggestion that derivative suits are not actually class actions at all—see Note, Shareholder Derivative Suits: Are They Class Actions?, 1957, 42 Iowa L.Rev. 568—is heretical and unhistorical. See Louisell & Hazard, Cases on Pleading and Procedure, 1962, p. 721. See also Ross v. Bernhard, 1970, 90 S.Ct. 733, 739–740, 396 U.S. 531, 541, 24 L.Ed.2d 729.

29. E.g., Booth v. General Dynamics Corp., D.C.Ill.1967, 264 F.Supp. 465.

Thus it has been held that a class action could be brought although: some children might be happy with the childcare system in New York, despite its discriminatory character, Wilder v. Bernstein, D.C.N.Y.1980, 499 F.Supp. 980; many cancer patients have no interest in the use of laetrile, Rutherford v. U. S., D.C.Okl.1977, 429 F.Supp. 506; many users of the city water service might be indifferent or even opposed to the class relief sought by the named plaintiffs, Koger v. Guarino, D.C.Pa. 1976, 412 F.Supp. 1375, affirmed without opinion C.A.3d, 1977, 549 F.2d 795.

But compare Bailey v. Patterson, D.C. Miss.1962, 206 F.Supp. 67, an action to enjoin segregation on common carriers, in which the court found that the interest of the black plaintiffs was "antagonistic to and not wholly compatible with the interests of those whom they purport to represent," and held that the suit was not a proper class action. The decree thus provided that only the named plaintiffs were entitled to unsegregated transportation. This strange decision was properly reversed. Bailey v. Patterson, C.A.5th, 1963, 323 F.2d 201, certiorari denied 84 S.Ct. 666, 376 U.S. 910, 11 L.Ed.2d 609.

30. Knowles v. War Damage Corp., C.A.1948, 171 F.2d 15, 83 U.S.App.D.C. 388, certiorari denied 69 S.Ct. 604, 336 U.S. 914, 93 L.Ed. 1077; Pelelas v. Caterpillar Tractor Co., C.C.A.7th, 1940, 113 F.2d 629, certiorari denied 61 S.Ct. 138, 311 U.S. 700, 85 L.Ed. 454.

31. Hohmann v. Packard Instrument Co., C.A.7th, 1968, 399 F.2d 711; Eisen v. Carlisle & Jacquelin, C.A.2d, 1968, 391 F.2d 555, 562–563, noted 1968, 18 Amer.U.L.Rev. 225, 44 Notre Dame Law. 151, 43 Tul.L.Rev. 369, 21 Vand. L.Rev. 1124, 1969, 47 N.C.L.Rev. 393;

If the requirements of a sufficiently large class and adequate representation are met, it is still necessary to decide whether the action falls into one of the categories for which a class suit is permissible. The original rule permitted three kinds of class suits, popularly known as "true," "hybrid," and "spurious." The rule was cast in terms of jural relations, with a particular suit falling in one class or another according to the character of the right sought to be enforced for or against the class.[32] Thus a "true" class action was permitted if the right involved was "joint, or common or secondary in the sense that the owner of a primary right refuses to enforce that right and a member of the class thereby becomes entitled to enforce it." Where the right involved was "several" but the object of the action was adjudication of claims that did or might affect specific property involved in the action, the label "hybrid" was applied. Finally an action to enforce "several" rights, where there was a common question of law or fact affecting such rights and "common relief" was sought was a "spurious" class action.[33]

The "spurious" class action was a particularly puzzling creation. In any case in which such an action could have been brought under the former rule, it would have been possible to join all the parties under Rule 20(a). Thus it was said that the "spurious" action was only a permissive joinder device,[34] though if this were true it duplicated Rule 20(a).[35] It was thought not to have any binding effect on those who were not named as parties,[36] even though a non-binding class suit seems to involve a contradiction in terms. If the judgment were effective only with regard to the named parties, it was mere surplusage to say in the pleadings that others similarly situated were involved.

Under the old rule the limited effect given the judgment in the "spurious" action was in contrast to a "true" class suit, in which all the members of the class were bound, and the "hybrid" class suit,

Lerwill v. Inflight Services, Inc., D.C. Cal.1974, 379 F.Supp. 690; Green v. Cauthen, D.C.S.C.1974, 379 F.Supp. 361; 7 Wright & Miller, Civil § 1766.

32. "This tribute to the memory of Wesley Hohfeld would be more suitable in a law review article than in an enactment which is to guide the actions of practical men day in and day out." Chafee, Some Problems of Equity, 1950, p. 246.

A lonely minority view, finding meaning and value in the tripartite classification, was that of VanDercreek, The "Is" and "Ought" of Class Actions Under Federal Rule 23, 1963, 48 Iowa L.Rev. 273, 280–283.

33. The tripartite classification under the former rule is discussed in 7 Wright & Miller, Civil § 1752.

34. See cases cited 7 Wright & Miller, Civil § 1752 n. 85.

35. Union Carbide & Carbon Corp. v. Nisley, C.A.10th, 1961, 300 F.2d 561, 589, certiorari dismissed 1962, 83 S.Ct. 13, 371 U.S. 801, 9 L.Ed.2d 46.

36. All American Airways v. Elderd, C.A.2d, 1954, 209 F.2d 247, 248; and cases cited 7 Wright & Miller, Civil § 1789 n. 6. This was in accord with the view of Professor Moore, a view that was properly given great influence because of his important role in drafting original Rule 23. Moore, Federal Rules of Civil Procedure: Some Problems Raised by the Preliminary Draft, 1937, 25 Geo.L.J. 511; Moore & Cohn, Federal Class Actions, Jurisdiction and Effect of Judgment, 1938, 22 Ill.L.Rev. 555.

where the members of the class were bound only as to rights, if any, in the property involved. But this was not the only respect in which important consequences turned on the label applied to the class suit. Such matters as jurisdiction, venue, intervention, and tolling of the statute of limitations were all thought to vary depending on which kind of class suit was involved.

This was the most serious defect in the old rule, and was of much more consequence than the anomaly of a class suit that did not bind the class. If matters of importance turn on the classification given a particular suit, then it is vital that it be clearly understood which classification applies. The fact was that the task of determining which label was appropriate for a particular suit "baffled both courts and commentators." [37] The terms "joint," "common," and "several" had "little or no clear and ascertainable meaning in or out of the context of class actions," [38] and most persons who had to work with them shared the frustration of Professor Chafee who confessed that he was having as much trouble telling a "common" right from a "several" one as in deciding whether some ties were green or blue.[39] Cases challenging racial discrimination provided a particularly striking example. Some courts thought this a "true" class action, others called it "spurious," while most simply said that it was a permissible class action and avoided the unrewarding task of further identification.[40]

The principal reason for rewriting Rule 23 in 1966 was to get away from the conceptually-defined categories of the old rule. The amended rule does describe categories of cases that may be appropriate for class treatment, and procedural consequences may depend on which category is involved, but the new categories are described functionally rather than conceptually. Inevitably there is some overlap among the categories.[41] Because there are three categories in the new rule, just as there were in the old, there has been some tendency

---

37. Note, Federal Class Actions: A Suggested Revision of Rule 23, 1946, 46 Col.L.Rev. 818, 822. One well-known case was variously characterized as "a class bill," Deckert v. Independence Shares Corp., D.C.Pa.1939, 27 F.Supp. 763, 769, as "spurious," C.C.A.3d, 108 F.2d 51, 55, and as "hybrid," D.C.Pa. 1941, 39 F.Supp. 592, 595. Finally the court of appeals said "names are not important." Pennsylvania Co. for Insurances v. Deckert, C.C.A.3d, 1941, 123 F.2d 979, 983.

38. Kaplan, Continuing Work of the Civil Committee: 1966 Amendments of the Federal Rules of Civil Procedure, 1967, 81 Harv.L.Rev. 356, 380. See also the authorities cited note 8 above.

39. Chafee, Some Problems of Equity, 1950, p. 257.

40. See cases cited at 7 Wright & Miller, Civil § 1752 nn. 63–74.

41. Kaplan, note 38 above, at 390 n. 130. Problems that this overlap may cause are discussed in Note, Revised Federal Rules 23, Class Actions: Surviving Difficulties and New Problems Require Further Amendment, 1967, 52 Minn.L. Rev. 483, 515–527.

If an action qualifies both under subdivision (1) or (2) of Rule 23(b) and also under subdivision (3), it should be treated as being under (1) or (2) in order to obtain the widest binding effect by avoiding the "opt-out" provision applicable to (b)(3) class actions. Reynolds v. National Football League, C.A.8th, 1978, 584 F.2d 280, 284; Robertson v. National Basketball Assn., C.A.2d, 1977, 556 F.2d 682, 685; Bing v. Roadway Exp., Inc., C.A.5th, 1973, 485 F.2d 441, 447.

to suppose that the old names, "true," "hybrid," and "spurious," may still be used, though with their definitions in the rule altered.[42] This is not only wrong but dangerously wrong. Nothing in the amended rule corresponds to the former "spurious" class action, since it is expected that the judgment in a class action under the amended rule will bind all members of the class, except those who have been expressly excluded. Nor do any of the clauses of amended Rule 23(b) correspond with the old "true" or "hybrid" class actions. The amended rule must be approached on its own pragmatic terms, rather than with preconceptions derived from the old conceptual categories.[43]

Rule 23(b)(1) permits a class action where this is necessary to avoid possible adverse effects on the opponents of the class or on absent members of the class. The party opposing the class would be prejudiced if inconsistent results in individual adjudications establish incompatible standards of conduct to which he must adhere, as in a suit by taxpayers to invalidate municipal action or in a suit involving the rights and duties of riparian owners.[44] Individual members of the class would be prejudiced in individual actions "as a practical matter" impair their ability to protect their interests, as in a suit to compel reorganization of a fraternal association or a suit by stockholders to compel declaration of a dividend.[45]

Rule 23(b)(2) permits a class action where the party opposing the class has acted or refused to act on grounds generally applicable to the class. It is intended primarily for civil rights cases though there are other kinds of cases that fall within it.[46] It is expressly limited to cases in which "final injunctive relief or corresponding declaratory relief with respect to the class as a whole" will be appropriate, and thus deliberately excludes actions for damages,[47] in which it might otherwise be asserted that a party's denial of fault, and refusal to

42. E.g., La Mar v. H & B Novelty & Loan Co., C.A.9th, 1973, 489 F.2d 461, 467; Eisen v. Carlisle & Jacquelin, C.A. 2d, 1968, 391 F.2d 555, 565; Hartman v. Secretary of Dept. of Housing and Urban Development, D.C.Mass.1968, 294 F.Supp. 794, 796; see Frankel, Some Preliminary Observations Concerning Civil Rule 23, 1967, 43 F.R.D. 39, 43.

43. See Van Gemert v. Boeing Co., D.C. N.Y.1966, 259 F.Supp. 125, 129; Booth v. General Dynamics Corp., D.C.Ill. 1967, 264 F.Supp. 465, 470–471.

44. Rule 23(b)(1)(A). See Advisory Committee Note, 39 F.R.D. 98, 100; U. S. v. Truckee-Carson Irrigation Dist., D.C.Nev.1975, 71 F.R.D. 10; Guadamuz v. Ash, D.C.D.C.1973, 368 F.Supp. 1233; Booth v. General Dynamics Corp., D.C.Ill.1967, 264 F.Supp. 465; 7A Wright & Miller, Civil § 1773.

45. Rule 23(b)(1)(B). See, e.g., Robertson v. National Basketball Assn., C.A. 2d, 1977, 556 F.2d 682; Lynch Corp. v. MII Liquidating Co., D.C.S.D.1979, 77 F.R.D. 22; 7A Wright & Miller, Civil § 1774.

46. See 7A Wright & Miller, Civil §§ 1775, 1776.

47. Lukenas v. Bryce's Mountain Resort, Inc., C.A.4th, 1976, 538 F.2d 594, 595–596; Sarafin v. Sears, Roebuck & Co., D.C.Ill.1978, 446 F.Supp. 611, 615. But if the predominant purpose of the suit is for injunctive relief, an incidental award of damages or back pay is permissible. Pettway v. American Cast Iron Pipe Co., C.A.5th, 1974, 494 F.2d 211, 256–258. See generally 7A Wright & Miller, Civil § 1775 at notes 27 to 33.

pay claims against it, was a refusal to act on a ground generally applicable to a class.

The most complicated and controversial portion of the 1966 revision is Rule 23(b)(3). This authorizes a class action where the only justification for such a procedure is the presence of common questions of law or fact. Though this bears a superficial resemblance to the old "spurious" action, the "spurious" action was not really a class action at all while a suit under (b)(3) is a class action in all respects. The court has discretion whether to allow a (b)(3) action. Before permitting it to be maintained the court must find that the questions of law or fact common to the members of the class predominate over any questions affecting only individual members,[48] and that a class action is superior to other available methods for the fair and efficient adjudication of the controversy.[49] The rule itself lists four factors that the court is to consider, among others, in determining whether a class action is superior to other methods.[50]

As soon as practicable after the commencement of an action brought as a class action, the court must determine by order whether it will be allowed to proceed as a class action.[51] Discovery may be proper to obtain information relevant to whether the action ought to be certified as a class action,[52] but it is not proper to have a preliminary hearing on plaintiff's probability of success before making the de-

48. E.g., Cameron v. E. M. Adams & Co., C.A.9th, 1976, 547 F.2d 473; Payton v. Abbott Labs, D.C.Mass.1979, 83 F.R.D. 382; and cases cited 7A Wright & Miller, Civil § 1778 n. 21.

Individual issues were found to dominate in, e.g., LoCicero v. Day, C.A.6th, 1975, 518 F.2d 783; Borden, Inc. v. Universal Indus. Corp., D.C.Miss.1981, 88 F.R.D. 708; and cases cited 7A Wright & Miller, Civil § 1778 n. 35.

49. See 7A Wright & Miller, Civil § 1779. With the expansion of collateral estoppel and the demise of the requirement of mutuality, the possible binding effect of a test case must be considered in determining whether a class action is superior. Katz v. Carte Blanche Corp., C.A.3d, 1974, 496 F.2d 747, certiorari denied 95 S.Ct. 152, 419 U.S. 885, 42 L.Ed.2d 125, noted 1975, 88 Harv.L.Rev. 825, 21 Wayne L.Rev. 1195.

Although there is a decision to the contrary, Amalgamated Workers Union v. Hess Oil Virgin Islands Corp., C.A.3d, 1973, 478 F.2d 540, it would seem that the court should consider whether administrative remedies would be superior to a class action. Pattillo v. Schlesinger, C.A.9th, 1980, 625 F.2d 262.

50. As listed in Rule 23(b)(3), these are: "(A) the interest of members of the class in individually controlling the prosecution or defense of separate actions; (B) the extent and nature of any litigation concerning the controversy already commenced by or against members of the class; (C) the desirability or undesirability of concentrating the litigation of the claims in the particular forum; (D) the difficulties likely to be encountered in the management of a class action."

The listing of factors to be considered in Rule 23(b)(3) is not exhaustive and other factors may be considered. Wilcox v. Commerce Bank of Kansas City, C.A.10th, 1973, 474 F.2d 336. See generally 7A Wright & Miller, Civil § 1780.

51. Rule 23(c)(1); 7A Wright & Miller, Civil § 1785. The appealability of this determination is discussed in § 101 below and in 15 Wright, Miller & Cooper, Jurisdiction § 3912.

52. Oppenheimer Fund, Inc. v. Sanders, 1978, 98 S.Ct. 2380, 2389 n. 13, 437 U.S. 340, 351 n. 13, 57 L.Ed.2d 253.

termination about class action status.[53]   That determination is always subject to change at a later time.[54]

Predictions that not "very many actions" would be allowed to proceed under (b)(3) [55] have proved quite ill-founded. The great bulk of reported cases in which class actions have been allowed under the revised rule have been (b)(3) actions. This device has been especially popular in antitrust and securities fraud cases, where individual persons allegedly injured are in a poor position to seek redress, either because they do not know enough or because the cost of suit is disproportionate to each individual claim.[56]

In drafting the amended rule the Advisory Committee observed that a class action is "ordinarily not appropriate" in cases of mass tort, because of the likelihood that significant questions of damages, liability, and defenses to liability would affect the individuals in different ways.[57]   This view has generally been followed by the courts,[58] although the need for more efficient methods of disposing of large numbers of cases arising out of a single disaster or a single course of conduct has an increasingly insistent priority in improving judicial administration.[59]   The use of class actions for the protection of consumers or for environmental litigation was uncommon in the early days of the amended rule, but now occurs more often.[60]

53.   Eisen v. Carlisle & Jacquelin, 1974, 94 S.Ct. 2140, 2152, 417 U.S. 156, 177–178, 40 L.Ed.2d 732.

54.   Elster v. Alexander, C.A.5th, 1979, 608 F.2d 196, 197; Gerstle v. Continental Airlines, Inc., C.A.10th, 1972, 466 F.2d 1374; and cases cited 7A Wright & Miller, Civil § 1785 n. 81.

55.   Wright, Recent Changes in the Federal Rules of Procedure, 1966, 42 F.R.D. 552, 567.

56.   7A Wright & Miller, Civil § 1781.

57.   See Advisory Committee Note, 39 F.R.D. 98, 103. See generally 7A Wright & Miller, Civil § 1783.

58.   In re Northern District of California Dalkon Shield IUD Products Liab. Litigation, C.A.9th, 1982, 693 F.2d 847; McDonnell Douglas Corp. v. United States Dist. Court, C.A.9th, 1975, 523 F.2d 1083, certiorari denied 96 S.Ct. 1506, 425 U.S. 911, 47 L.Ed.2d 761; In re Three Mile Island Litigation, D.C. Pa.1980, 87 F.R.D. 433; Causey v. Pan American World Airways, Inc., D.C.Va. 1975, 66 F.R.D. 392; Yandle v. PPG Indus., Inc., D.C.Tex.1974, 65 F.R.D. 566. But see In re "Agent Orange" Product Liab. Litigation, D.C.N.Y.1980, 506 F.Supp. 762; Payton v. Abbott Labs, D.C.Mass.1979, 83 F.R.D. 382; Coburn

v. 4–R Corp., D.C.Ky.1977, 77 F.R.D. 43, mandamus denied C.A.6th, 1978, 588 F.2d 543; Bentkowski v. Marfuerza Compania Maritima, S. A., D.C.Pa. 1976, 70 F.R.D. 401; Hernandez v. Motor Vessel Skyward, D.C.Fla.1973, 61 F.R.D. 558, affirmed C.A.5th, 1975, 507 F.2d 1279.

59.   See the majority and dissenting opinions in In re Federal Skywalk Cases, C.A.8th, 1982, 680 F.2d 1175, certiorari denied 103 S.Ct. 342, ___ U.S. ___, ___ L.Ed.2d ___; 7A Wright & Miller, Civil § 1783; Comment, The Use of Class Actions for Mass Accident Litigation, 1977, 23 Loy.L.Rev. 383; Comment, Mass Accident Class Actions, 1972, 60 Calif.L.Rev. 1615.

60.   7A Wright & Miller, Civil § 1782; Miller, note 1 above, at 674–675; Schuck & Cohen, The Consumer Class Action: An Endangered Species, 1974, 12 San Diego L.Rev. 39; Note, The Products Liability Class Suit: Preventive Relief for the Consumer, 1975, 27 S.C.L.Rev. 229; Note, Consumer Class Actions Under Federal Rule 23, 1973, 25 S.C.L.Rev. 239; Comment, The Federal Class Action in Environmental Litigation: Problems and Possibilities, 1973, 51 N.C.L.Rev. 1385.

If the court permits a (b)(3) class action to be maintained, it must direct to the members of the class the best notice practicable under the circumstances, including individual notice to all members who can be identified through reasonable effort.[61] This notice is crucial to the whole scheme of (b)(3). Arguably notice is not constitutionally compelled as a condition to binding absentees. In the leading case of Hansberry v. Lee, the Supreme Court said that a judgment in a class action will bind absentees whenever the procedure adopted "fairly insures the protection of the absent parties who are to be bound by it," [62] and that even where the only circumstance defining the class is a common issue of fact or law, as in the (b)(3) action, the judgment might be made binding on all members of the class "provided that the procedure were so devised and applied as to insure that those present are of the same class as those absent and that the litigation is so conducted as to insure the full and fair consideration of the common issue."[63] Nevertheless it is clear that effective notice greatly strengthens the argument that the absentee is bound.[64]

In Eisen v. Carlisle & Jacquelin [65] the Supreme Court held that in a (b)(3) class action it is mandatory that individual notice must be provided to those members of the class who are identifiable through reasonable effort. Notice by publication is not permissible even where the cost of individual notice is prohibitively high.[66] Nor may the cost of notice be imposed on the defendant. Instead the plaintiff must pay for the cost of notice as a part of the ordinary burden of financing his own suit, and if he will not bear the cost of notice the action cannot proceed as a class action.[67]

---

61. Rule 23(c)(2); 7A Wright & Miller, Civil §§ 1786–1788; Dam, note 13 above; Ward & Elliott, The Contents and Mechanics of Rule 23 Notice, 1969, 10 B.C.Ind. & Com.L.Rev. 557.

The Supreme Court has severely restricted "gag orders" barring communications between parties or their counsel and actual or potential class members. Gulf Oil Co. v. Bernard, 1981, 101 S.Ct. 2193, 452 U.S. 89, 68 L.Ed.2d 693.

62. 61 S.Ct. at 118, 311 U.S. at 42. See also Sam Fox Pub. Co. v. U. S., 1961, 81 S.Ct. 1309, 1314, 366 U.S. 683, 691, 6 L.Ed.2d 604.

63. 61 S.Ct. at 119, 311 U.S. at 43.

64. See In re Four Seasons Securities Laws Litigation, C.A.10th, 1974, 502 F.2d 834, 842–843, certiorari denied 95 S.Ct. 516, 419 U.S. 1034, 42 L.Ed.2d 309, noted 1975 U.Ill.L.F. 280.

65. 1974, 94 S.Ct. 2140, 417 U.S. 156, 40 L.Ed.2d 732, noted 1974, 46 Colo.L. Rev. 243, 53 N.C.L.Rev. 409, 27 Okla.L. Rev. 70, 19 St.L.U.L.J. 100, 43 U.M. K.C.L.Rev. 226; 1975, 16 B.C.Ind. &

Comm.L.Rev. 254, 21 Loy.L.Rev. 228, 21 N.Y.L.F. 96. See Benett, Eisen v. Carlisle & Jacquelin: Supreme Court Calls for Revamping of Class Action Strategy, 1974 Wis.L.Rev. 801.

66. 94 S.Ct. at 2150–2152, 417 U.S. at 173–177.

67. 94 S.Ct. at 2152–2153, 417 U.S. at 177–179.

The Court has also held that the defendant cannot be required to bear the cost of compiling a list of members of the class, so that notice can be sent them, unless the expense is so insubstantial as not to warrant the effort required to calculate it and shift it to the plaintiff. A cost of $16,000 was held not to be insubstantial. Oppenheimer Fund, Inc. v. Sanders, 1978, 98 S.Ct. 2380, 437 U.S. 340, 57 L.Ed.2d 253, noted 1978, 78 Col.L.Rev. 1517; 1979, 12 Creighton L.Rev. 859, 1979 Duke L.J. 882, 18 Washburn L.J. 349. See Note, Allocation of Identification Costs in Class Actions, 1978, 66 Calif.L.Rev. 105.

The Court in Eisen was at pains to base its decision on the language of Rule 23(c)(2) and to point out that that subdivision applies only to (b)(3) class actions.[68] Rule 23(d)(2) permits, but does not require, notice to members of the class in class actions that proceed under sections of Rule 23 other than (b)(3)[69] and the better view is that there is no constitutional requirement of notice to members of the class in (b)(1) or (b)(2) actions.[70]

Notice is particularly critical in (b)(3) class actions, and is made mandatory by the rules, in part because the class members are only loosely associated by common questions of law or fact, rather than by any pre-existing or continuing legal relationship, and thus it is less certain that they will be fully protected by the named representatives. The other reason for making notice mandatory in these cases is because of the unusual procedural provisions that apply. The notice to the absentee in a (b)(3) action advises him of his rights in the action, that he may appear through his counsel if he wishes, that he will be excluded from the class if he so requests by a date and procedure specified in the notice, and that the judgment will include him if he has not requested exclusion.[71] It is only in actions that are brought under (b)(3) that absent members of the class have the unique privilege to "opt out."[72]

Critical to the entire operation of the revised rule is the effect of the judgment. It is clearly contemplated that every judgment in every class action will bind all of the members of the class, except for those who have asked to be excluded in a (b)(3) action.[73] The rule

68. 94 S.Ct. at 2152 n. 14, 417 U.S. at 177 n. 14.

69. 7A Wright & Miller, Civil § 1793.

70. Jones v. Diamond, C.A.5th, 1979, 594 F.2d 997, 1022; Society for Individual Rights, Inc. v. Hampton, C.A.9th, 1975, 528 F.2d 905, 906; and cases cited 7A Wright & Miller, Civil § 1786 n. 99. See also Comment, 1975, 24 Clev. St.L.Rev. 504.

The contrary view announced in Schrader v. Selective Serv. System Local Bd. No. 76, C.A.7th, 1972, 470 F.2d 73, 75, certiorari denied 93 S.Ct. 689, 409 U.S. 1085, 34 L.Ed.2d 672, was based on a dictum from the Second Circuit that since has been repudiated by its home court. Nevertheless it still has some scholarly support. Reno, Notice and Due Process in Federal Class Actions: A Requiem for Revised Rule 23?, 1975, 2 Hast.Const.L.Q. 479; Maraist & Sharp, Federal Procedure's Troubled Marriage: Due Process and the Class Action, 1970, 49 Texas L.Rev. 1. But see Miller, Problems of Giving Notice in Class Actions, 1973, 58 F.R.D. 313, 313–317.

71. 7A Wright & Miller, Civil § 1787.

72. Dosier v. Miami Val. Broadcasting Corp., C.A.9th, 1981, 656 F.2d 1295, 1299. If a class action meets the requirement of (b)(3) but also qualifies as a class action under (b)(1) or (b)(2), it is not treated as a (b)(3) action for purposes of the notice requirements and the "opt out" provision. See note 41 above.

Flexibility has been used in determining what a class member must do in order to "opt out." See In re Four Seasons Securities Laws Litigation, C.A.10th, 1974, 493 F.2d 1288, 1291, certiorari denied 95 S.Ct. 516, 419 U.S. 1034, 42 L.Ed.2d 309.

73. "The 1966 amendments were designed in part, * * * to assure that members of the class would be identified before trial on the merits and would be bound by all subsequent orders and judgments." American Pipe & Constr. Co. v. Utah, 1974, 94 S.Ct. 756, 763, 414 U.S. 538, 547, 38 L.Ed.2d 713. See 7A Wright & Miller, Civil § 1789.

does not say this. It says only that the judgment "shall include and describe those whom the court finds to be members of the class," and who have not asked to be excluded from a (b)(3) action.[74] This recognizes that a court conducting an action cannot predetermine its res judicata effect, and that this can be tested only in a subsequent action.[75] It recognizes, too, that even a party named in the judgment will not be bound if he has been denied due process of law.[76] But the rule is intended to provide due process to absentees and it plainly contemplates that they will be bound.

The absentee has an absolute right to be excluded from a (b)(3) action. If he does "opt out," and the judgment ultimately is favorable to the class, he should not be entitled to rely on it as collateral estoppel, in those jurisdictions that have departed from the requirement of mutuality for estoppel. To permit him to do this would make a mockery of the (b)(3) procedure, and would restore in a different form the "one way" intervention that the amended rule was expressly intended to preclude.[77] Notions of collateral estoppel are not so inexorable that a party who has affirmatively obtained exclusion from a judgment need be allowed later to claim the benefits of the judgment.[78]

Despite the fact that Rule 23(c)(2)(B) specifically states that the judgment in a (b)(3) action "will include all members who do not request exclusion," a few courts in actions involving extremely large classes of plaintiffs seeking a damage recovery have held that the court may require members of the class to take some affirmative action to remain in the class.[79] This is directly contrary to the language and the philosophy of the rule.[80] It is perfectly proper, however, af-

---

74. Rule 23(c)(3).

"This is a statement of how the judgment shall read, not an attempted prescription of its subsequent res judicata effect, although looking ahead with hope to that effect." Kaplan, note 38 above, at 393.

75. Gonzales v. Cassidy, C.A.5th, 1973, 474 F.2d 67, 74; Restatement Second of Judgments, 1982, § 42; Note, Binding Effect of Class Actions, 1954, 67 Harv.L.Rev. 1059, 1060. But see Note, 1965, 51 Va.L.Rev. 629, 655–660.

76. Gonzales v. Cassidy, C.A.5th, 1973, 474 F.2d 67; Note, Collateral Attack on the Binding Effect of Class Action Judgments, 1974, 87 Harv.L.Rev. 589.

77. Advisory Committee Note, 39 F.R.D. 98, 105–106. See American Pipe & Constr. Co. v. Utah, 1974, 94 S.Ct. 756, 762–764, 414 U.S. 538, 545–549, 38 L.Ed.2d 713.

78. Restatement Second of Judgments, 1982, § 42 ill. 6; Sarasota Oil Co. v. Greyhound Leasing & Financial Corp.,

C.A.10th, 1973, 483 F.2d 450. But see In re Transocean Tender Offer Securities Litigation, D.C.Ill.1977, 427 F.Supp. 1211. See generally George, Sweet Use of Adversity: Parklane Hosiery and the Collateral Class Action, 1980, 32 Stan.L.Rev. 655; Note, Offensive Assertion of Collateral Estoppel by Persons Opting Out of a Class Action, 1980, 31 Hastings L.J. 1189.

79. In re Antibiotic Antitrust Actions, D.C.N.Y.1971, 333 F.Supp. 267; Iowa v. Union Asphalt & Roadoils, Inc., D.C. Iowa 1968, 281 F.Supp. 391, 403, affirmed C.A.8th, 409 F.2d 1239; Minnesota v. United States Steel Corp., D.C. Minn.1968, 44 F.R.D. 559, 577; Philadelphia Elec. Co. v. Anaconda American Brass Co., D.C.Pa.1968, 43 F.R.D. 452, 459; Ward & Elliott, The Contents and Mechanics of Rule 23 Notice, 1969, 10 B.C.Ind. & Com.L.Rev. 557, 568.

80. Clark v. Universal Builders, Inc., C.A.7th, 1974, 501 F.2d 324, 340, certiorari denied 95 S.Ct. 657, 419 U.S. 1070,

ter defendant's liability has been established, to send a second notice to the class members requiring them to file statements of their individual claims by a stated date.[81]

It has long been the rule that in a class action only the citizenship of the named representatives is to be considered, and that it is no objection to jurisdiction that other members of the class, not named as parties, are of such citizenship as would defeat diversity.[82] This continues to be held under the amended rule. It is true that (b)(3) now permits persons to be bound by a judgment though they are linked only by common questions of law and fact. Nevertheless (b)(3), and perhaps the whole rule, would be totally unworkable in a diversity case if the citizenship of all members of the class, many of them unknown, had to be considered.[83] Similarly for purposes of venue only the residence of the named parties should be considered.[84]

Amount in controversy is a different matter.[85] The decisions in Snyder v. Harris[86] and in Zahn v. International Paper Co.[87] have, in effect, made class actions unavailable in those diversity cases in which more than $10,000 must be in controversy.[88]

The Snyder case held that traditional rules on aggregation of claims for purposes of jurisdictional amount[89] apply to class actions. Thus if a large class of plaintiffs each have small claims they cannot aggregate their claims to satisfy the amount requirement if their claims are "separate and distinct," even though the entire class is now bound by the judgment, the result cannot vary from one member

42 L.Ed.2d 666; Payton v. Abbott Labs, D.C.Mass.1979, 83 F.R.D. 382, 393; and cases cited 7A Wright & Miller, Civil § 1787 n. 65. See also Manual for Complex Litigation, 5th ed. 1982, § 1.45, pp. 49–50.

81. B & B Inv. Club v. Kleinert's Inc., D.C.Pa.1974, 62 F.R.D. 140, 149 n. 6; Forbes v. Greater Minneapolis Area Bd. of Realtors, D.C.Minn.1973, 61 F.R.D. 416; Harris v. Jones, D.C.Utah 1966, 41 F.R.D. 70.

It has also been held that a proof of claim can be required in a (b)(2) class action in which back pay is awarded as incidental to injunctive or declaratory relief. Kyriazi v. Western Elec. Co., C.A.3d, 1981, 647 F.2d 388.

82. Supreme Tribe of Ben Hur v. Cauble, 1921, 41 S.Ct. 338, 255 U.S. 356, 65 L.Ed. 673.

83. Friedman v. Meyers, C.A.2d, 1973, 482 F.2d 435; Illinois ex rel. Scott v. Hunt Intl. Resources Corp., D.C.Ill. 1979, 481 F.Supp. 71; 7 Wright & Miller, Civil § 1755.

This result seems to be assumed in Snyder v. Harris, 1969, 89 S.Ct. 1053, 1059, 394 U.S. 332, 340, 22 L.Ed.2d 319, but

the Court may not have been thinking of this problem.

84. Appleton Elec. Co. v. Advance-United Expressways, C.A.7th, 1974, 494 F.2d 126; Research Corp. v. Pfister Associated Growers, Inc., D.C.Ill.1969, 301 F.Supp. 497, appeal dismissed C.A. 7th, 1970, 425 F.2d 1059; 7 Wright & Miller, Civil § 1757.

85. See 7 Wright & Miller, Civil § 1756; 14 Wright, Miller & Cooper, Jurisdiction § 3705.

86. 1969, 89 S.Ct. 1053, 394 U.S. 332, 22 L.Ed.2d 319.

87. 1974, 94 S.Ct. 505, 414 U.S. 291, 38 L.Ed.2d 511. Zahn has produced extensive commentary, mostly critical in nature. See 7 Wright & Miller, Civil § 1756 nn. 32.4, 32.7, 32.8.

88. See § 32 above.

In fiscal 1977, the most recent year for which these figures have been given, 3,153 class actions were commenced in federal courts. Only 107 of these were based on diversity. Ann.Rep. of the Director of the Administrative Office of the U.S. Courts, 1977, p. 238.

89. See § 36 above.

of the class to another, and realistically the amount in controversy is the amount sought on behalf of the entire class. It is only if the claims can be regarded as "joint" or "common" that aggregation is permitted.[90] Zahn closed the door even farther. Although the named representatives have claims for more than $10,000, the action cannot go forward as a class action on behalf of absentees whose claims are for less than that amount. "Each plaintiff in a Rule 23(b)(3) class action must satisfy the jurisdictional amount, and any plaintiff who does not must be dismissed from the case—'one plaintiff may not ride in on another's coattails.' "[91] Perhaps the most surprising feature of Zahn is its failure even to discuss the argument of the dissent that the concept of ancillary jurisdiction could permit hearing the smaller claims as ancillary to those for more than $10,000.[92] That argument was surely rejected by Zahn, and there may well be good reasons for rejecting it, but the Court did not articulate them.

Although, in the passage just quoted, the Zahn Court spoke of (b)(3) class actions, there is nothing in its reasoning that would suggest that any other rule will govern other kinds of class actions. Even so, Snyder and Zahn should pose no problems in (b)(2) class actions, at least so long as those actions are to redress racial discrimination, since that kind of action can be brought without regard to amount in controversy.[93] In most (b)(1) actions aggregation is apparently permissible, but the (b)(1) action is not coextensive with the former "true" class action, and it cannot automatically be assumed that aggregation is always permissible. It will be necessary in those cases to determine whether the right involved is "joint" or "common" on the one hand, or "several" on the other, no matter how meaningless and arbitrary such a distinction may seem.[94]

In a (b)(3) action it appears that the right being enforced must always be labelled "several," and thus Snyder and Zahn preclude aggregation.[95] This will not affect federal question cases, in which no amount in controversy is required.

90. Gallagher v. Continental Ins. Co., C.A.10th, 1974, 502 F.2d 827; New Jersey Welfare Rights Organization v. Cahill, C.A.3d, 1973, 483 F.2d 723, 725 n. 3; Dierks v. Thompson, C.A.1st, 1969, 414 F.2d 453; Berman v. Narragansett Racing Assn., C.A.1st, 1969, 414 F.2d 311, certiorari denied 90 S.Ct. 682, 396 U.S. 1037, 24 L.Ed.2d 681; Cass Clay, Inc. v. Northwestern Pub. Serv. Co., D.C.S.D.1974, 63 F.R.D. 34. For other cases in which claims have been found "joint" or "common" and aggregation permitted, and for the more numerous cases in which the claims were thought "separate and distinct" and aggregation not allowed, see 7 Wright & Miller, Civil § 1756 n. 17.

91. 94 S.Ct. at 512, 414 U.S. at 301.

92. 94 S.Ct. at 512, 414 U.S. at 301–302 (Brennan, J., dissenting).

93. See § 32 above. Even where amount in controversy is required, it may be found that the plaintiffs in a (b)(2) action have a common, undivided interest so that aggregation will be allowed. Brandt v. Owens-Illinois, Inc., D.C.N.Y.1973, 62 F.R.D. 160. But see U. S. v. Southern Pac. Transp. Co., C.A.9th, 1976, 543 F.2d 676, 682–684.

94. Amen v. City of Dearborn, C.A.6th, 1976, 532 F.2d 554, 559.

95. Snow v. Ford Motor Co., C.A.9th, 1977, 561 F.2d 787.

There is no problem with regard to the statute of limitations under the amended rule. Since the judgment is now binding in all class actions, commencement of the action tolls the statute of limitations for all members of the class.[96] This result is reached even if the court, for reasons of judicial housekeeping, ultimately holds that it will not allow the suit to proceed as a class action, since otherwise members of the class would have to file a protective individual suit pending that determination.[97]

Because of the representative nature of a class action, the court has more control over it than over ordinary actions, and must assume "a more active role than it normally does."[98] Rule 23(d), added in 1966, spells out in some detail the flexible powers the court has over the conduct of the action.[99] The action may not be dismissed or compromised without the approval of the court, and notice of the proposed dismissal or compromise must be given to all members of the class in such manner as the court directs.[100] If the suit results in a recovery beneficial to the class, the court may award an attorneys' fee to the attorneys for the representatives out of the sum recovered,[101] though recent cases are taking a more restrictive approach to the size of the fee that can be awarded.[102]

96. Esplin v. Hirschi, C.A.10th, 1968, 402 F.2d 94, certiorari denied 89 S.Ct. 1194, 394 U.S. 928, 22 L.Ed.2d 459; Comment, 1968, 13 Vill.L.Rev. 370; 7A Wright & Miller, Civil § 1800.

97. American Pipe & Constr. Co. v. Utah, 1974, 94 S.Ct. 756, 414 U.S. 538, 38 L.Ed.2d 713; Wheeler, Predismissal Notice and Statute of Limitations in Federal Class Actions After American Pipe and Construction Co. v. Utah, 1975, 48 So.Cal.L.Rev. 771; Note, 1982, 67 Iowa L.Rev. 743; Comment, 1974, 12 San Diego L.Rev. 169.

98. Dolgow v. Anderson, D.C.N.Y.1968, 43 F.R.D. 472, 481.

99. Newberg, Orders in the Conduct of Class Actions: A Consideration of Subdivision (d), 1969, 10 B.C.Ind. & Com.L. Rev. 577; 7A Wright & Miller, Civil §§ 1791–1796.

100. Rule 23(e); 7A Wright & Miller, Civil § 1797; McGough & Lerach, Termination of Class Actions: The Judicial Role, 1972, 33 U.Pitt.L.Rev. 445. For the kinds of factors the court considers in passing on a settlement, see In re Corrugated Container Antitrust Litigation, C.A.5th, 1981, 643 F.2d 195; West Virginia v. Chas. Pfizer & Co., C.A.2d, 1971, 440 F.2d 1079, certiorari denied 92 S.Ct. 81, 404 U.S. 871, 30 L.Ed.2d 115.

If an action is brought as a class action, Rule 23(e) applies to its dismissal or compromise even though it has not yet been certified as a class action. Philadelphia Elec. Co. v. Anaconda American Brass Co., D.C.Pa.1967, 42 F.R.D. 324; and cases cited 7A Wright & Miller, Civil § 1797 n. 67.

If an action is dismissed by the court as a sanction for noncompliance with the discovery rules, and the absent members of the class are not given notice before the dismissal, the dismissal is not binding on them and they may bring a second suit. Papilsky v. Berndt, C.A.2d, 1972, 466 F.2d 251, certiorari denied 93 S.Ct. 689, 409 U.S. 1077, 34 L.Ed.2d 665. See Comment, Involuntary Dismissals of Class Actions, 1973, 40 U.Chi.L.Rev. 783.

101. Boeing Co. v. Van Gemert, 1980, 100 S.Ct. 745, 444 U.S. 472, 62 L.Ed.2d 676. See 7A Wright & Miller, Civil § 1803.

102. See 7A Wright & Miller, Civil § 1803; Miller, Attorneys' Fees in Class Actions, Federal Judicial Center 1980; Manual for Complex Litigation, 5th ed. 1982, § 1.47. Among the leading cases are Lindy Bros. Builders, Inc. v. American Radiator & Standard Sanitary Corp., C.A.3d, 1976, 540 F.2d 102, and Detroit v. Grinnell Corp., C.A.2d, 1974, 495 F.2d 448.

Until 1966 actions involving unincorporated associations were often brought under the general rule applicable to all class actions, in situations in which the association could not be treated as an entity under Rule 17(b).[103] In 1966 a new Rule 23.2 was adopted, permitting suit by or against the members of an unincorporated association as a class only if it appears that the members named as representatives will fairly and adequately protect the interests of the association and its members. Rule 23(d), listing orders the court may make in the conduct of a class action, is specifically incorporated by reference for unincorporated association actions, as is Rule 23(e), requiring approval of the court, after notice, for the dismissal or compromise of any class action. The explicit incorporation by reference of two subdivisions of Rule 23 suggests that the other parts of Rule 23, including notably the limitations in subdivisions (a) and (b) on when a class action may be maintained, do not apply to actions relating to unincorporated associations, but the committee note is wholly silent on this question.[104]

§ 73. Stockholders' Derivative Actions [1]

A derivative action "in essence is nothing more than a suit by a beneficiary of a fiduciary to enforce a right running to the fiduciary as such." [2] Easily the most common example of such an action is a suit by minority stockholders in a corporation who claim that the corporation has been wronged but that the majority will not seek redress on behalf of the corporation. Special requirements for this kind of suit appear in Rule 23.1.[3] This is not the only derivative action that is possible. Trust beneficiaries may bring claims derivatively on behalf of the trust if the trustee refuses to bring them, and the same general principles will apply as in stockholders' suits,[4] but the specific provisions of Rule 23.1 are not controlling.

---

103. See generally, 7A Wright & Miller, Civil § 1861.

104. Advisory Committee Note, 39 F.R.D. 108. Compare Management Television Systems, Inc. v. National Football League, D.C.Pa.1971, 52 F.R.D. 162, with Sembach v. McMahon College, Inc., D.C.Tex.1980, 86 F.R.D. 188.

[§ 73]

1. 7A Wright & Miller, Civil §§ 1821–1841; Kessler, Shareholder Derivative Actions: A Modest Proposal to Revise Federal Rule 23.1, 1973, 7 U.Mich.J.L.Reform 90; Dykstra, The Revival of the Derivative Suit, 1967, 116 U.Pa.L.Rev. 74; Sullivan, The Federal Courts as an Effective Forum in Shareholders' Derivative Actions, 1962, 22 La.L.Rev. 580.

2. Goldstein v. Groesbeck, C.C.A.2d, 1944, 142 F.2d 422, 425, certiorari denied 65 S.Ct. 36, 323 U.S. 737, 89 L.Ed. 590. As the cited case indicates, there may also be "double derivative" actions "in which the beneficiary is in his turn a fiduciary, and as such refuses to enforce the right which is his as beneficiary of the first fiduciary."

3. A similar rule, Rule 23.2, applies to suits by minority members of an unincorporated association. See 7A Wright & Miller, Civil § 1861.

4. Helm v. Zarecor, 1911, 32 S.Ct. 10, 12, 222 U.S. 32, 36, 56 L.Ed. 77; Reed v. Robilio, C.A.6th, 1967, 376 F.2d 392, 395–396; Hellenthal v. John Hancock Mut. Life Ins. Co., D.C.Wash.1929, 31 F.2d 997, 998.

It is possible to have a stockholders' derivative suit that is not also a class action, as where the minority stock is held by one person or a few persons,[5] but in almost all derivative actions the stockholder is suing on behalf of a large class of other minority stockholders similarly situated. Because of this, in the original rules these actions were treated in Rule 23(b), as a part of class actions generally. In the 1966 revision it was decided to deal independently with derivative actions by stockholders in a separate Rule 23.1. Thus the general class action rule, Rule 23, no longer applies to stockholders' derivative suits.[6] By the same token, suits by stockholders that are not derivative, in which they are asserting their individual claims against a corporation, such as suits to compel declaration of a dividend, or to restrain a merger, are not subject to Rule 23.1. If they are brought, as they usually will be, as class actions, they must meet the tests of Rule 23, and generally will come under Rule 23(b)(1).[7]

Rule 23.1 makes no change of substance in the previous rules applicable to stockholders' derivative suits. Indeed it was deliberately determined not to "disturb the procedural balance previously established in this kind of litigation."[8] Thus pre-1966 decisions remain completely authoritative.

In a stockholders' derivative suit the stockholder is suing to enforce a claim that belongs to the corporation. Accordingly the corporation must be joined as a party, and the relief granted is a judgment against third persons, also named as defendants, in favor of the corporation.[9]

Rule 23.1 requires the complaint in a derivative action to allege that a demand for action has been made on the directors and, if necessary, the stockholders, or that such a demand was excused. This is a requirement of long standing in federal practice,[10] and would lead to little difficulty except for the now-vexing question of the extent to which state law is to be controlling. Since the states universally require demand on the directors, that phase of the requirement has caused no controversy, but the states are divided on whether demand must be made also on the stockholders and on the circumstances that will excuse such a demand. That state law on this issue must be followed in a diversity case seems clearly required by the Erie doctrine.[11] While state law is looked to for the requirement of a demand,

5. Galdi v. Jones, C.C.A.2d, 1944, 141 F.2d 984, 992.

6. Kauffman v. Dreyfus Fund, Inc., C.A.3d, 1970, 434 F.2d 727, 734–736.

7. Advisory Committee Note, 39 F.R.D. 98, 101; King v. Kansas City Southern Indus., Inc., C.A.7th, 1975, 519 F.2d 20; Federal Sav. & Loan Ins. Corp. v. Huttner, D.C.Ill.1967, 265 F.Supp. 40.

8. Kaplan, Continuing Work of the Civil Committee: 1966 Amendments of the Federal Rules of Civil Procedure, 1967,

81 Harv.L.Rev. 356, 387 n. 118. See also Papilsky v. Berndt, C.A.2d, 1972, 466 F.2d 251, 257 n. 7, certiorari denied 93 S.Ct. 689, 409 U.S. 1077, 34 L.Ed.2d 665.

9. Ross v. Bernhard, 1970, 90 S.Ct. 733, 738, 396 U.S. 531, 538, 24 L.Ed.2d 729; 7A Wright & Miller, Civil § 1821.

10. Hawes v. City of Oakland, 1882, 104 U.S. 450, 26 L.Ed. 827.

11. Jacobs v. Adams, C.A.5th, 1979, 601 F.2d 176; Brody v. Chemical Bank,

the federal court is free to decide for itself whether the demand, or the reasons that excuse the failure to make a demand, have been pleaded with the particularity required by Rule 23.1.[12]

Rule 23.1 also requires the plaintiff to aver that he "was a shareholder or member at the time of the transaction of which he complains or that his share or membership thereafter devolved on him by operation of law." [13]   This requirement is based on "a sound and wholesome principle of equity," [14] in that it prevents a person from buying a lawsuit. It serves the further purpose in federal court of preventing collusive attempts to invoke federal jurisdiction,[15] and is related to the additional requirement of the rule that plaintiff allege that the action is not a collusive one to confer on a court of the United States jurisdiction of any action of which it would not otherwise have jurisdiction.[16]

The requirement that the plaintiff allege that he was a shareholder at the time of the transaction complained of is applicable in federal question cases,[17] except where a specific provision in a federal statute makes an exception to it.[18]   It has led to difficulty in diversity cases, since such a requirement is not yet universal in the states, and poses questions under the Erie doctrine. Some courts and commentators take the view that an allegation of this kind is unnecessary, and that plaintiff need not have been a shareholder at the time of the transac-

C.A.2d, 1973, 482 F.2d 1111, certiorari denied 94 S.Ct. 737, 414 U.S. 1104, 38 L.Ed.2d 559; Oldfield v. Alston, D.C. Ga.1978, 77 F.R.D. 735; GA Enterprises, Inc. v. Leisure Living Communities, Inc., D.C.Mass.1974, 66 F.R.D. 123, affirmed C.A.1st, 1975, 517 F.2d 24; Steinberg v. Hardy, D.C.Conn. 1950, 90 F.Supp. 167.

In Burks v. Lasker, 1979, 99 S.Ct. 1831, 441 U.S. 471, 60 L.Ed.2d 404, it is held that whether the disinterested directors of a corporation have power to terminate a derivative action based on the Investment Company Act and the Investment Advisers Act is a question of federal law, but that, as a matter of federal law, state law on the issue will be applied to the extent that it is consistent with the policies of the federal statutes in question. This holding would seem clearly to apply to the closely related question of whether a demand on the directors must be made before commencing the action.

12.   In re Kaufmann Mut. Fund Actions, C.A.1st, 1973, 479 F.2d 257, certiorari denied 94 S.Ct. 161, 414 U.S. 857, 38 L.Ed.2d 107; Steinberg v. Hardy, D.C. Conn.1950, 90 F.Supp. 167. See 7A Wright & Miller, Civil §§ 1831–1832, for decisions as to the sufficiency of

the pleading, the sufficiency of the demand, and the circumstances which excuse demand. See also Note, The Demand and Standing Requirements in Stockholder Derivative Actions, 1976, 44 U.Chi.L.Rev. 168.

13.   7A Wright & Miller, Civil § 1828; Harbrecht, The Contemporaneous Ownership Rule in Shareholders' Derivative Suits, 1978, 25 U.C.L.A.L.Rev. 1041.

14.   Home Fire Ins. Co. v. Barber, 1903, 93 N.W. 1024, 1029, 67 Neb. 644 (per Pound, C.). See also Bangor Punta Operations, Inc. v. Bangor & A. R. Co., 1974, 94 S.Ct. 2578, 417 U.S. 703, 41 L.Ed.2d 418.

15.   Hawes v. City of Oakland, 1882, 104 U.S. 450, 26 L.Ed. 827.

16.   Collusion was found in Amar v. Garnier Enterprises, Inc., D.C.Cal.1966, 41 F.R.D. 211. See 7A Wright & Miller, Civil § 1830; Rowe, A Comment on the Federalism of the Federal Rules, 1979 Duke L.J. 843.

17.   Surowitz v. Hilton Hotels Corp., 1966, 86 S.Ct. 845, 383 U.S. 363, 15 L.Ed.2d 807.

18.   E.g., 15 U.S.C.A. § 78p(b); Blau v. Oppenheim, D.C.N.Y.1966, 250 F.Supp. 881.

tion, if the law of the state in which suit is brought or the state of incorporation would permit him to sue without meeting this requirement.[19] Most courts and writers have thought, however, that the rule must be met regardless of state law.[20] Though the arguments both ways are strong, there seems especial force to the position that the Erie doctrine does not require the federal courts to entertain a suit, merely because such a suit might be brought in the state court.

There is a related question, not always clearly distinguished from that just discussed, about whether state or federal law determines if a person was a stockholder within the meaning of Rule 23.1. The older federal doctrine, and that of a majority of states, is that an equitable owner of shares at the time of the transactions complained of is entitled to maintain a derivative action, and a number of decisions continue to apply such a rule in federal court.[21] Other cases hold, however, that the equitable owner may maintain such an action in a diversity case only if the law of the state of incorporation permits it.[22] In support of the latter view, it may be argued that even if, as suggested above, Rule 23.1 may validly be applied regardless of state law to close the doors of federal court to suits by persons who became stockholders after the events complained of, the determination of who is a stockholder is not a mere procedural regulation and should be left to state law.

The corporation must be made a party in a derivative action, and is always named as a defendant, along with the third persons against whom the corporation has a claim. Since the ultimate interest of the corporation is similar to that of the stockholders bringing suit, it is frequently claimed that it should be realigned as a plaintiff, thus, in many cases, destroying diversity. It has been settled that if the cor-

19. Milvy v. Adams, D.C.N.Y.1954, 16 F.R.D. 105, remanded C.A.2d, 217 F.2d 647; Fuller v. American Machine & Foundry Co., D.C.N.Y.1951, 95 F.Supp. 764; Notes, 1952, 40 Calif.L.Rev. 433, 1949, 62 Harv.L.Rev. 1030, 1040.

20. Elkins v. Bricker, D.C.N.Y.1956, 147 F.Supp. 609; Kaufman v. Wolfson, D.C.N.Y.1955, 136 F.Supp. 939; Perrott v. United States Banking Corp., D.C.Del.1944, 53 F.Supp. 953; Developments in the Law—Multiparty Litigation in the Federal Courts, 1958, 71 Harv.L.Rev. 874, 964–966. See 7A Wright & Miller, Civil § 1829; 19 id. § 4509, pp. 160–162.

"Although most cases treat the requirement as one of procedure, this Court has never resolved the issue." Bangor Punta Operations, Inc. v. Bangor & A. R. Co., 1974, 94 S.Ct. 2578, 2582 n. 4, 417 U.S. 703, 708 n. 4, 41 L.Ed.2d 418.

21. De Haas v. Empire Petroleum Co., C.A.10th, 1970, 435 F.2d 1223; H. F. G.

Co. v. Pioneer Pub. Co., C.C.A.7th, 1947, 162 F.2d 536; Hurt v. Cotton States Fertilizer Co., C.C.A.5th, 1944, 145 F.2d 293, certiorari denied 65 S.Ct. 679, 324 U.S. 844, 89 L.Ed. 1406; Schupack v. Covelli, D.C.Pa.1980, 498 F.Supp. 704.

This seems clearly the law if the suit is based on a federal right of action. In re Pittsburgh & L. E. R. Co. Securities & Antitrust Litigation, C.A.3d, 1976, 543 F.2d 1058.

22. Drachman v. Harvey, C.A.2d, 1971, 453 F.2d 722; Gallup v. Caldwell, C.C.A.3d, 1941, 120 F.2d 90; Kreindler v. Marx, D.C.Ill.1979, 85 F.R.D. 612; Rosenfeld v. Schwitzer Corp., D.C.N.Y. 1966, 251 F.Supp. 758; Bankers Nat. Corp. v. Barr, D.C.N.Y.1945, 7 F.R.D. 305. See 7A Wright & Miller, Civil § 1826.

poration is under a control antagonistic to the plaintiffs, and made to act in a way detrimental to their rights, it should not be realigned, regardless of its ultimate interest.[23] A sharply divided Court has held that if the pleadings allege that the corporate management refuses to take action to undo a business transaction, or so solidly approves the transaction that any demand to rescind would be futile, this is sufficient to show that the corporation is properly aligned as a defendant, and the court is not to hear evidence to determine whether the corporation is actually under antagonistic control.[24]

In a derivative action, plaintiff recovers nothing and judgment runs in favor of the corporation. Therefore, for the purpose of jurisdictional amount, the test is the damage asserted to have been sustained by the defendant corporation.[25] Other stockholders may intervene regardless of the amount of their claim or their citizenship.[26]

Historically the derivative action was available only in equity, where there was no right to jury trial. But the issues a derivative action poses on behalf of the corporation against those who are alleged to have wronged it may well be legal in nature and of a sort that would be triable to a jury on demand of either party if the corporation had brought its own action. In a merged system it makes no sense to deny a jury right that would otherwise exist merely because the action is brought by virtue of a procedural device that was borrowed from the practice in equity.[27] In Ross v. Bernhard[28] the Supreme Court accepted this reasoning and held that there is a right to jury trial in a derivative action if the claim is one that would have been triable to a jury in a suit by the corporation.

A special statute provides that a derivative action by a stockholder on behalf of his corporation may be prosecuted in any district where the corporation might have sued the same defendants.[29] Though the statute seems clear enough, some courts have found surprising difficulty in construing it. The situation is this. Stockholders, citizens and residents of State X, bring a diversity action in State Y, naming as defendants the corporation on whose behalf they are suing, which is incorporated in State Y, as well as individuals claimed to have de-

---

23. Doctor v. Harrington, 1905, 25 S.Ct. 355, 196 U.S. 579, 49 L.Ed. 606; Koster v. (American) Lumbermens Mut. Cas. Co., 1947, 67 S.Ct. 828, 330 U.S. 518, 91 L.Ed. 1067.

24. Smith v. Sperling, 1957, 77 S.Ct. 1112, 354 U.S. 91, 1 L.Ed.2d 1205. See 7A Wright & Miller, Civil § 1822.

Realignment of the corporation as a plaintiff was ordered, in quite unusual circumstances, in Taylor v. Swirnow, D.C.Md.1978, 80 F.R.D. 79.

25. Koster v. (American) Lumbermens Mut. Cas. Co., 1947, 67 S.Ct. 828, 330 U.S. 518, 91 L.Ed. 1067; Bernstein v. Levenson, C.A.4th, 1971, 437 F.2d 756.

26. Weinstock v. Kallet, D.C.N.Y.1951, 11 F.R.D. 270. See § 75 below.

27. See 9 Wright & Miller, Civil § 2306.

28. 1970, 90 S.Ct. 733, 396 U.S. 531, 24 L.Ed.2d 729, noted 1970, 11 B.C.Ind. & Comm.L.Rev. 1016, 1970 Duke L.J. 1015, 65 Nw.U.L.Rev. 697, 45 Notre Dame Law. 524, 22 S.C.L.Rev. 482, 24 Sw.L.J. 860, 21 Syracuse L.Rev. 1282, 27 Wash. & Lee L.Rev. 344, 12 Wm. & Mary L.Rev.1970; 1971, 7 Tulsa L.Rev. 43. See also 7A Wright & Miller, Civil § 1837.

29. 28 U.S.C.A. § 1401.

frauded the corporation. Some of the individual defendants reside in State Y while others are from States A, B, and C. Under the general venue statute only State X or the district in which the claim arose would be proper venues, since there is no single state in which all of the defendants reside. But State X is an inconvenient venue for many purposes; it would be far better to entertain such litigation in State Y where the corporation is chartered and its records kept, yet it is possible that this will not be regarded as the district in which the claim arose. The language of the special venue statute for derivative actions would seem to permit laying venue in State Y. It is a district in which the corporation could have sued the individual defendants so far as venue is concerned, since it is the district where the corporation, the only plaintiff in such a hypothetical suit, resides. Most cases have so reasoned, and have held venue proper in State Y.[30] A few cases have rejected this reasoning. They have argued that the corporation could not have sued the individual defendants in State Y because diversity would be lacking between the corporation and the individual defendants.[31] This reasoning, as the leading case supporting it recognizes, introduces a jurisdictional element into a venue statute. Such a construction seems unnecessary, by denying venue in the most convenient district it leads to undesirable results, and it is hardly required by—indeed seems contrary to—the language of the statute.

Another special statute provides that in a derivative suit process may be served upon the corporation outside the district in which suit is brought.[32] This applies only where suit is brought in a district where the corporation might have sued the wrongdoers, under the other special statute just discussed, and does not apply where suit is brought in the district of the stockholders' residence.[33]

A derivative action cannot be maintained if it appears that the plaintiff does not fairly and adequately represent the interests of other shareholders similarly situated. The rule does not spell out the power of the court over conduct of the action, and relies instead on the inherent power of the court to determine the course of the proceedings and to require notice to other shareholders.[34] State provi-

30. Dowd v. Front Range Mines, Inc., D.C.Colo.1965, 242 F.Supp. 591, 594–596, noted 1966, 15 Cath.U.L.Rev. 264, 41 Notre Dame Law. 413; Saltzman v. Birrell, D.C.N.Y.1948, 78 F.Supp. 778; and cases cited 7A Wright & Miller, Civil § 1825 n. 88.

31. Schoen v. Mountain Producers Corp., C.A.3d, 1948, 170 F.2d 707, certiorari denied 69 S.Ct. 746, 336 U.S. 937, 93 L.Ed. 1095; Sale v. Pittsburgh Steel Co., D.C.Pa.1944, 57 F.Supp. 283.

32. 28 U.S.C.A. § 1695.

33. Koster v. (American) Lumbermens Mut. Cas. Co., 1947, 67 S.Ct. 828, 831 n.

2, 330 U.S. 518, 522 n. 2, 91 L.Ed. 1067; and cases cited 7A Wright & Miller, Civil § 1825 nn. 95, 96.

34. GA Enterprises, Inc. v. Leisure Living Communities, Inc., C.A.1st, 1975, 517 F.2d 24; Kauffman v. Dreyfus Fund, Inc., C.A.3d, 1970, 434 F.2d 727, certiorari denied 91 S.Ct. 1190, 401 U.S. 974, 28 L.Ed.2d 323; Note, Res Judicata in the Derivative Action: Adequacy of Representation and the Inadequate Plaintiff, 1973, 71 Mich.L.Rev. 1042; 7A Wright & Miller, Civil § 1833.

sions with regard to security for expenses must be followed in a diversity case.[35] Compromise or voluntary dismissal of the action must be with the approval of the court, and notice must be given of the proposed dismissal or compromise to all stockholders in such manner as the court may direct.[36] By its power to approve or disapprove any compromise of the suit, the court retains substantial control over the fee which may be paid to the attorneys for the plaintiff.[37]

§ 74. Interpleader [1]

Interpleader is a form of joinder open to one who does not know to which of several claimants he is liable, if he is liable at all. It permits him to bring the claimants into a single action, and to require them to litigate among themselves to determine which, if any, has a valid claim. Although the earliest records of a procedure similar to interpleader were at common law, it soon became an equitable rather than a legal procedure.[2] The contemporary importance of interpleader is in large measure due to the efforts of Professor Zechariah Chafee, Jr., who, in a notable group of articles,[3] paved the way for the series of reforms by which federal interpleader was modernized and made available in situations where no state court could provide an adequate remedy. There are two kinds of interpleader available in federal court. A statute, 28 U.S.C.A. § 1335, authorizes interpleader and makes very liberal provisions as to jurisdiction, venue, and service of process. Nonstatutory interpleader is available under Rule 22, but the jurisdictional and procedural requirements there are the same as in an ordinary civil action.

Before enactment of the federal interpleader statute, there was no effective procedure whereby rival claimants of diverse citizenship and

---

35. Cohen v. Beneficial Indus. Loan Corp., 1949, 69 S.Ct. 1221, 337 U.S. 541, 93 L.Ed. 1528; 7A Wright & Miller, Civil § 1835.

36. Rule 23.1: 7A Wright & Miller, Civil § 1839; Haudek, The Settlement and Dismissal of Stockholders' Actions, 1968, 22 Sw.L.J. 767.

This provision of Rule 23.1 does not apply if the derivative action is involuntarily dismissed by a court. Burks v. Lasker, 1979, 99 S.Ct. 1831, 1841 n. 16, 441 U.S. 471, 485 n. 16, 60 L.Ed.2d 404. See also Papilsky v. Berndt, C.A.2d, 1972, 466 F.2d 251, certiorari denied 93 S.Ct. 689, 409 U.S. 1077, 34 L.Ed.2d 665.

37. 7A Wright & Miller, Civil § 1841.

[§ 74]

1. 7 Wright & Miller, Civil §§ 1701–1721; Hazard & Moskovitz, An Historical and Critical Analysis of Interpleader, 1964, 52 Calif.L.Rev. 706;

Ilsen & Sardell, Interpleader in the Federal Courts, 1960, 35 St. John's L.Rev. 1; Comment, Deference to State Courts in Federal Interpleader Actions, 1980, 47 U.Chi.L.Rev. 824.

2. The earliest reported instance of relief similar to interpleader at law is in 1313, while the first reported bill of interpleader in equity is in 1484. See Rogers, Historical Origins of Interpleader, 1942, 51 Yale L.J. 924.

3. The following articles are all by Professor Chafee: Modernizing Interpleader, 1921, 30 Yale L.J. 814; Interstate Interpleader, 1924, 33 Yale L.J. 685; Interpleader in the United States Courts, 1932, 41 Yale L.J. 1134, 42 Yale L.J. 41; The Federal Interpleader Act of 1936, 1936, 45 Yale L.J. 963, 1161; Federal Interpleader Since the Act of 1936, 1940, 49 Yale L.J. 377; Broadening the Second Stage of Interpleader, 1943, 56 Harv.L.Rev. 541, 929.

residence could be sued in any district in federal court, while territorial limitation on service of process barred state courts from giving relief. This situation is cured by the statute, and the rule supplements the statute.

Rule 22 permits interpleader whenever there are multiple claimants whose claims are such that the plaintiff is or may be exposed to double or multiple liability. The statute requires that there be two or more adverse claimants who are claiming or may claim the same money or property. Under both the statute and the rule, the purpose is to protect against double vexation in respect to a single liability,[4] rather than to a double liability as such, and interpleader will be allowed even though one of the claims is not meritorious, so long as it is not so utterly baseless that the possibility of conflicting claims falls below a minimal threshold level of substantiality.[5]

Pomeroy's list of four restrictions on interpleader may well have been, as has recently been suggested, "the product of uncritical reading and uncritical thinking," [6] but it was widely accepted by the courts. The four restrictions Pomeroy described were: (1) The same thing, debt, or duty must have been claimed by both or all the parties against whom the relief was demanded. (2) All their adverse titles or claims must have been dependent on or be derived from a common source. (3) The person seeking relief—the plaintiff—must not have had or claimed any interest in the subject matter. (4) The plaintiff must have incurred no independent liability to either of the claimants.[7] This was the strict bill of interpleader. A bill in the nature of a bill of interpleader was available, where the plaintiff was not disinterested and had some special ground for equitable relief beyond the assertion of multiple claims against him.

The first of the four conditions, that the claims be identical, and the second, that they be of common origin, are abolished in express terms both by the rule and by the statute.[8] The third requirement, that the plaintiff be disinterested, is abolished in express terms by the rule and by fair implication in the statute. Thus one who is not disinterested can bring an action of interpleader, even without any special basis for equitable relief other than the danger of multiple vexation.[9] Indeed, interpleader will lie even where the claims are un-

---

4. State Farm Fire & Cas. Co. v. Tashire, 1967, 87 S.Ct. 1199, 1205, 386 U.S. 523, 534, 18 L.Ed.2d 270.

5. E.g., New York Life Ins. Co. v. Welch, C.A.1961, 297 F.2d 787, 111 U.S.App.D.C. 376; John Hancock Mut. Life Ins. Co. v. Kraft, C.A.2d, 1953, 200 F.2d 952. The rule stated in the text was recognized, but the possibility of conflicting claims found too remote to support interpleader, in Dunbar v. U. S., C.A.5th, 1974, 502 F.2d 506.

6. Hazard & Moskovitz, note 1 above, at 708.

7. 4 Pomeroy, Equity Jurisprudence, 5th ed. 1941, § 1322.

8. Standard Sur. & Cas. Co. of New York v. Baker, C.C.A.8th, 1939, 105 F.2d 578, 581.

9. Holcomb v. Aetna Life Ins. Co., C.A. 10th, 1955, 228 F.2d 75, certiorari denied 76 S.Ct. 473, 350 U.S. 986, 100 L.Ed. 853; Maryland Cas. Co. v. Glassell-Taylor & Robinson, C.C.A.5th, 1946,

liquidated tort claims, if the remedy is sought by an insurer with limited liability so that the claims are adverse.[10]

The situation is less clear as to whether the fourth condition on equitable interpleader, that the plaintiff must have incurred no independent liability to either of the claimants, survives in modern practice. The situation arises where one of the claimants asserts that the basis of his claim is such that he is entitled to recover even though the stakeholder may also be liable on some other basis to some other claimant or claimants. Prior to the Act of 1936 it was held that such an independent liability would bar interpleader.[11] The 1936 statute, now 28 U.S.C.A. § 1335, does not do away with the independent liability restriction in express terms, though it probably was the thought of Professor Chafee, who drafted it, that this restriction was merely a special application of the equitable requirement that the claims must be of common origin, which the statute does expressly end.[12] In England similar language abolishing the common origin restriction had been held to end the independent liability restriction,[13] but there have been some federal decisions holding that that restriction is still applicable.[14] In the courts that take this view the practice is for the court to try the facts as to independent liability. If no independent liability is found, interpleader is ordered; if such liability exists, the request for interpleader is denied.[15] Increasingly, however, a different view has been taken, and it has been thought that the independent liability restriction is no longer a bar to interpleader under either the statute or the rule.[16] This is as it should be. Contemporary procedure, with its flexible provisions for wide joinder of parties and claims, for separate trial of separate issues where necessary, and for shaping the judgment to the necessities of the case, is well adapted to disposing of interpleader cases where independent liability is asserted, and there is no reason today, under either the statute or the rule,

156 F.2d 519; Standard Sur. & Cas. Co. of New York v. Baker, C.C.A.8th, 1939, 105 F.2d 578; John Hancock Mut. Life Ins. Co. v. Kegan, D.C.Md.1938, 22 F.Supp. 326.

10.   State Farm Fire & Cas. Co. v. Tashire, 1967, 87 S.Ct. 1199, 386 U.S. 523, 18 L.Ed.2d 270. See 7 Wright & Miller, Civil § 1707.

11.   Dee v. Kansas City Life Ins. Co., C.C.A.7th, 1936, 86 F.2d 813.

12.   Chafee, Federal Interpleader Since the Act of 1936, 1940, 49 Yale L.J. 377, 412; Note, the Independent Liability Rule as a Bar to Interpleader in the Federal Courts, 1956, 65 Yale L.J. 714, 719.

13.   Ex parte Mersey Docks and Harbour Bd., [1899] 1 Q.B. 546.

14.   Equitable Life Ins. Co. of Iowa v. Gilman, D.C.Mo.1953, 14 F.R.D. 243; First State Bank of Chariton, Iowa v.

Citizens State Bank of Thedford, D.C. Neb.1950, 10 F.R.D. 424; Boice v. Boice, D.C.N.J.1943, 48 F.Supp. 183, affirmed C.C.A.3d, 135 F.2d 919. See also cases cited note 15 below.

15.   Poland v. Atlantis Credit Corp., D.C. N.Y.1960, 179 F.Supp. 863; American-Hawaiian S. S. Co. (Del.) v. Bowring & Co., D.C.N.Y.1957, 150 F.Supp. 449. But see Hurlbut v. Shell Oil Co., D.C. La.1955, 131 F.Supp. 466, 468.

16.   Dakota Livestock Co. v. Keim, C.A.8th, 1977, 552 F.2d 1302, 1306; Knoll v. Socony Mobil Oil Co., C.A. 10th, 1966, 369 F.2d 425, 428–429, certiorari denied 87 S.Ct. 1173, 386 U.S. 977, 18 L.Ed.2d 138; Builders & Developers Corp. v. Manassas Iron & Steel Co., D.C.Md.1962, 208 F.Supp. 485, 490; and cases cited 7 Wright & Miller, Civil § 1706 nn. 9–13.

for continuing to impose a restriction that has no claim to validity save that it is old.

It seems clear, though there is no case authority, that interpleader is available in federal court, under either the rule or the statute, even though the state in which the court is sitting preserves the old equitable restrictions on interpleader and would not allow it under similar circumstances.[17] However to determine the law to be applied in passing on the merits of the case, the federal court must look to the state law, including the conflicts rules of the state, despite the fact that the case is one where the state could not have obtained jurisdiction over all the parties, and that, therefore, no state court could have heard.[18] And since the basis of jurisdiction is diversity, whether suit is under the rule or the statute, there is some authority that state law is controlling on such matters as the award of an attorney's fee to the plaintiff, although on this point the better view is to the contrary.[19]

The principal difference between statutory interpleader and interpleader under the rule is in the matter of jurisdiction.[20] Statutory interpleader is available if the amount involved exceeds $500 and there are "two or more adverse claimants, of diverse citizenship."[21] Where each of the claimants is a citizen of a different state, and the stakeholder is disinterested, his citizenship is immaterial, since the actual controversy is between the claimants.[22] The courts have gone far beyond this, however, and have entertained statutory interpleader on the basis of what is called "minimal diversity:" so long as there are at least two opposing claimants of diverse citizenship, they have held that jurisdiction exists, even though there may be other claimants,[23] or a stakeholder who is not disinterested,[24] of the same citizen-

---

17. Wright & Miller, Civil § 1713, pp. 435–436; Developments in the Law— Multiparty Litigation in the Federal Courts, 1958, 71 Harv.L.Rev. 874, 926. See Perkins State Bank v. Connolly, C.A.5th, 1980, 632 F.2d 1306, 1310–1311.

18. Griffin v. McCoach, 1941, 61 S.Ct. 1023, 313 U.S. 498, 85 L.Ed. 1481. See § 57 above.

19. 7 Wright & Miller, Civil § 1719, pp. 490–492; Bank of China v. Wells Fargo Bank & Union Trust Co., C.A.9th, 1953, 209 F.2d 467; Lincoln Income Life Ins. Co. v. Harrison, D.C.Okl.1976, 71 F.R.D. 27; Minnesota Mut. Life Ins. Co. v. Gustafson, D.C.Ill.1976, 415 F.Supp. 615. Contra: Ohio Cas. Ins. Co. v. Berger, D.C.Ky.1970, 311 F.Supp. 840; Aetna Life Ins. Co. v. Johnson, D.C.Ill.1962, 206 F.Supp. 63.

In Perkins State Bank v. Connolly, C.A. 5th, 1980, 632 F.2d 1306, 1310–1311, it is held that state law does not control an award of an attorney's fee to a disinterested stakeholder but that it does control award of a fee to one of the claimants.

20. See 7 Wright & Miller, Civil § 1710: 14 Wright, Miller, & Cooper, Jurisdiction § 3636.

21. Statutory interpleader is not possible on the basis of a federal question if there is no diversity. Sun Shipbuilding & Dry-Dock Co. v. Industrial Union of Marine & Shipbuilding Workers of America, D.C.Pa.1951, 95 F.Supp. 50.

22. Treinies v. Sunshine Mining Co., 1939, 60 S.Ct. 44, 308 U.S. 66, 84 L.Ed. 85.

23. State Farm Fire & Cas. Co. v. Tashire, 1967, 87 S.Ct. 1199, 1203–1204, 386 U.S. 523, 530–531, 18 L.Ed.2d 270. An important earlier decision anticipating this result was Haynes v. Felder, C.A.5th, 1957, 239 F.2d 868.

24. Builders and Developers Corp. v. Manassas Iron & Steel Co., D.C.Md. 1962, 208 F.Supp. 485; Georgia Sav. Bank & Trust Co. v. Sims, D.C.Ga. 1971, 321 F.Supp. 307; Girard Trust

ship. This departure from the usual rule of complete diversity [25] is a healthy one. Whatever the merits may be in the continuing argument about the desirability of diversity jurisdiction in general,[26] the jurisdiction serves an important function, as here, in providing a federal forum for cases that would be beyond the jurisdiction of any state court. This function would be severely limited were complete diversity required, and it is good that the courts have recognized the power of Congress to provide by statute for less than complete diversity.

Unlike the statute, Rule 22 does not have, nor purport to have, any effect on jurisdictional requirements. Thus there must be either complete diversity of citizenship between the stakeholder on the one hand and all of the claimants on the other, with more than $10,000 in controversy,[27] or else there must be a federal question.[28] If, as the Supreme Court has held in a case of statutory interpleader,[29] a disinterested stakeholder is merely a nominal party whose citizenship might be disregarded in determining diversity, it might be argued that there is no diversity jurisdiction in an action under the rule where the plaintiff, a disinterested stakeholder, is a citizen of one state, and all the claimants, among whom the real controversy will lie, are citizens of another state. The courts have not reached this result, perhaps reasoning that the stakeholder is not merely a nominal party since he has a substantial interest in obtaining interpleader and thus avoiding the dangers of multiple liability.[30]

The jurisdictional amount, whether $500 for statutory interpleader or $10,000 for interpleader under the rule, is determined as in other cases.[31] The total amount to be distributed is the amount in controversy, and supports jurisdiction though individual claims may be for less than this amount.[32]

Co. v. Vance, D.C.Pa.1945, 5 F.R.D. 109; cf. U. S. v. Sentinel Fire Ins. Co., C.A.5th, 1949, 178 F.2d 217.

Contra: Boice v. Boice, C.C.A.3d, 1943, 135 F.2d 919.

25. Strawbridge v. Curtiss, 1806, 3 Cranch 267, 2 L.Ed. 435. See § 24 above.

26. See § 23 above.

27. Underwriters at Lloyd's v. Nichols, C.A.8th, 1966, 363 F.2d 357; John Hancock Mut. Life Ins. Co. v. Kraft, C.A. 2d, 1953, 200 F.2d 952; Lincoln Income Life Ins. Co. v. Harrison, D.C.Okl.1976, 71 F.R.D. 27.

28. Interpleader based on a federal question is largely a theoretical matter because of the requirement that a federal question appear in the well-pleaded complaint. St. Louis Union Trust Co. v. Stone, C.A.8th, 1978, 570 F.2d 833; Gardner v. Schaffer, C.C.A.8th,

1941, 120 F.2d 840; Cowan v. U. S., D.C.N.Y.1959, 172 F.Supp. 291.

29. Treinies v. Sunshine Mining Co., 1939, 60 S.Ct. 44, 308 U.S. 66, 84 L.Ed. 85.

30. Aetna Life & Cas. Co. v. Spain, C.A. 5th, 1977, 556 F.2d 747; Stewart Oil Co. v. Sohio Petroleum Co., C.A.7th, 1963, 315 F.2d 759, 762, certiorari denied 84 S.Ct. 71, 375 U.S. 828, 11 L.Ed. 2d 60; Developments in the Law—Multiparty Litigation in the Federal Courts, 1958, 71 Harv.L.Rev. 874, 922–923; 7 Wright & Miller, Civil § 1710, pp. 407–409.

31. See §§ 33–35 above.

32. Pan American Fire & Cas. Co. v. Revere, D.C.La.1960, 188 F.Supp. 474; Massachusetts Bonding & Ins. Co. v. City of St. Louis, D.C.Mo.1952, 109 F.Supp. 137; see United Benefit Life

For statutory interpleader, venue will lie in any district in which any claimant resides,[33] and process may be served anywhere in the United States.[34] Interpleader under the rule must be brought in the district in which the plaintiff resides, or in which the claim arose, or in which all defendants reside,[35] and as in ordinary civil actions, process must be served in accordance with Rule 4, which normally limits service to the borders of the state in which the court is sitting.[36] Since interpleader under the rule will be used only where all the claimants are citizens of the same state, these restrictions on venue and service should not ordinarily cause any problem.[37]

The present interpleader statute continues a provision, first adopted in 1926, authorizing a federal court that has taken jurisdiction of an interpleader action to enjoin other proceedings in state or federal court affecting the property, instrument, or obligation involved in the interpleader action.[38] Under the 1948 revision of the anti-injunction statute,[39] a similar injunction can now be issued in interpleader under the rule, since a preliminary injunction to stay state court action while the federal court determines the case is "necessary in aid of its jurisdiction," and a permanent injunction at the conclusion of the federal action is needed "to protect or effectuate its judgments."[40]

It is a condition to jurisdiction under the interpleader statute that the stakeholder deposit with the court the money or property demanded by the claimants, or that he give bond in sufficient amount that he will comply with the future order or judgment of the court.[41] Since it is no longer necessary that he be disinterested, he can do so without waiving his contention that he is not liable to any of the claimants, or that he is not liable for the full sum demanded and paid

Ins. Co. v. Leech, D.C.Pa.1971, 326 F.Supp. 598, 600.

33. 28 U.S.C.A. § 1397; Watson v. Manhattan & Bronx Surface Transit Operating Auth., D.C.N.J.1980, 487 F.Supp. 1273; 7 Wright & Miller, Civil § 1712.

34. 28 U.S.C.A. § 2361; 7 Wright & Miller, Civil § 1711.

35. 28 U.S.C.A. § 1391(a). See § 42 above.

There is considerable room for speculation—and no case law—on where the claim arises in an action for interpleader. See 7 Wright & Miller, Civil § 1712, pp. 425–426.

36. Metropolitan Life Ins. Co. v. Chase, C.A.3d, 1961, 294 F.2d 500. See § 64 above.

37. Pan American Fire & Cas. Co. v. Revere, D.C.La.1960, 188 F.Supp. 474.

But see Cordner v. Metropolitan Life Ins. Co., D.C.N.Y.1964, 234 F.Supp. 765, where the combined effect of the venue limitation on statutory interpleader and the service of process limitation on interpleader under Rule 22 was to prevent defendant from being able to counterclaim for interpleader.

38. 28 U.S.C.A. § 2361; 7 Wright & Miller, Civil § 1717.

39. 28 U.S.C.A. § 2283. See § 47 above.

40. U. S. v. Major Oil Corp., C.A.10th, 1978, 583 F.2d 1152, 1158; Pan American Fire & Cas. Co. v. Revere, D.C. La.1960, 188 F.Supp. 474, 483–485; Ilsen & Sardell, note 1 above, at 55–56. But see Boston Old Colony Ins. Co. v. Balbin, C.A.5th, 1979, 591 F.2d 1040, 1042 n. 5; Comment, note 1 above.

41. 28 U.S.C.A. § 1335(a)(2); Miller & Miller Auctioneers, Inc. v. G. W. Murphy Indus., Inc., C.A.10th, 1973, 472 F.2d 893. As to the amount of the deposit, see 7 Wright & Miller, Civil § 1716.

into court.[42] If he is in fact disinterested, the court can then dismiss him from the action.[43] A deposit is not required in interpleader under the rule, but general equitable powers of the court permit it to receive a deposit and to discharge the stakeholder if he is indifferent.[44]

If interpleader is sought by an insurance company against persons with unliquidated tort claims against its insured, such persons may be enjoined from claiming the proceeds of the insurance policy except in the interpleader proceeding, but they cannot be enjoined from establishing their claims against the insured in a forum of their own choosing.[45] In this way the difficulties that a race to judgment may pose for the insurer, and the resulting unfairness to some claimants, may be avoided without converting interpleader into "an all-purpose 'bill of peace' "[46] for mass torts.

Interpleader under the rule is not limited to an action by a plaintiff. Rule 22(1) makes it clear that a defendant exposed to a multiple liability may obtain interpleader by way of cross-claim or counterclaim.[47] The same result should be reached under the statute, though the statute is not explicit.[48] The interpleader must have some nexus with a party who is already in the case. Defendant will not be al-

---

42. United Benefit Life Ins. Co. v. Leech, D.C.Pa.1971, 326 F.Supp. 598; Moseley v. Sunshine Biscuits, Inc., D.C.Mo.1952, 110 F.Supp. 157; John Hancock Mut. Life Ins. Co. v. Yarrow, D.C.Pa.1951, 95 F.Supp. 185, But cf. Doering v. Buechler, C.C.A.8th, 1945, 146 F.2d 784.

43. 28 U.S.C.A. § 2361; Rosenberger v. Northwestern Mut. Life Ins. Co., D.C. Kan.1959, 176 F.Supp. 379; Savannah Bank & Trust Co. of Savannah v. Block, D.C.Ga.1959, 175 F.Supp. 798.

44. Bank of China v. Wells Fargo Bank & Union Trust Co., C.A.9th, 1953, 209 F.2d 467, 473, 48 A.L.R.2d 172; U. S. v. Henry's Bay View Inn, Inc., D.C.N.Y. 1961, 191 F.Supp. 632. Deposit in court is authorized by Rule 67. See 12 Wright & Miller, Civil § 2991.

45. State Farm Fire & Cas. Co. v. Tashire, 1967, 87 S.Ct. 1199, 386 U.S. 523, 18 L.Ed.2d 270; Allstate Ins. Co. v. McNeill, C.A.4th, 1967, 382 F.2d 84, certiorari denied 88 S.Ct. 2290, 392 U.S. 931, 20 L.Ed.2d 1390; 7 Wright & Miller, Civil § 1707.

46. State Farm Fire & Cas. Co. v. Tashire, 1967, 87 S.Ct. 1199, 1206, 386 U.S. 523, 535, 18 L.Ed.2d 270.

But see Comment, Promoting Judicial Economy Through the Extension of Interpleader to the Tortfeasor in the Mass Tort Area, 1971, 17 Wayne L.Rev. 1241.

Reasoning similar to that in Tashire was relied on to hold that interpleader was not available to a uranium dealer confronted with claims from utilities that it must deliver uranium to them at the contract price and the position of its supplier that it would not supply uranium to the dealer except at the current market price. General Atomic Co. v. Duke Power Co., C.A.10th, 1977, 553 F.2d 53. The court thought that the dealer was not a stakeholder and that the supplier and the utilities were not conflicting claimants. Although the court recognized the "serious problem" the dealer confronted, it held it could not "redesign the interpleader statute in order for it to accommodate this unusual lawsuit." 553 F.2d at 58.

47. U. S. v. Major Oil Corp., C.A.10th, 1978, 583 F.2d 1152; Powers v. Metropolitan Life Ins. Co., C.A.1971, 439 F.2d 605, 142 U.S.App.D.C. 95; and cases cited 7 Wright & Miller, Civil § 1708 n. 30.

48. Humble Oil & Ref. Co. v. Copeland, C.A.4th, 1968, 398 F.2d 364; and cases cited 7 Wright & Miller, Civil § 1708 n. 36.

lowed to counterclaim or cross-claim for interpleader when he is not seeking relief against any of the other parties to the action.[49]

Interpleader will not lie against the United States if it has not waived its sovereign immunity,[50] nor may a state be required to interplead contrary to the Eleventh Amendment.[51] The same principles apply here as in an ordinary civil action, and indeed the procedure in an interpleader action follows generally that of the ordinary action,[52] although there has been some confusion about the availability of counterclaims[53] and, in cases where a nonresident claimant has been brought in by extraterritorial service under statutory interpleader, cross-claims.[54]

The historic origin of interpleader in the courts of equity, coupled with a famous dictum from Chief Justice Taft,[55] had caused some courts to suppose that there was no right to jury trial in an interpleader action.[56] But interpleader today is simply a joinder device, not confined to equitable actions and not restricted by the conditions that limited its use in equity. It would raise doubts of constitutional dimension to say that the statute or rule, by making available a flexible and useful procedural tool, can deprive a party of a right to jury trial on a claim that heretofore would have been heard to a jury. Of course the "first stage of interpleader," the decision whether to require the claimants to interplead, is for the court alone.[57] But unless

49. Grubbs v. General Elec. Credit Corp., 1972, 92 S.Ct. 1344, 405 U.S. 699, 31 L.Ed.2d 612.

50. U. S. v. Dry Dock Sav. Institution, C.C.A.2d, 1945, 149 F.2d 917; U. S. v. Commercial Bank of North America, D.C.N.Y.1962, 31 F.R.D. 133; Cowan v. U. S., D.C.N.Y.1959, 172 F.Supp. 291; 7 Wright & Miller, Civil § 1721. See § 22 above.

51. Cory v. White, 1982, 102 S.Ct. 2325, ___ U.S. ___, 72 L.Ed.2d 694. States can be required to interplead in actions within the original jurisdiction of the Supreme Court, where the Eleventh Amendment is no bar. Texas v. New Jersey, 1965, 85 S.Ct. 626, 379 U.S. 674, 13 L.Ed.2d 596; Texas v. Florida, 1939, 59 S.Ct. 563, 306 U.S. 398, 83 L.Ed. 817.

52. 7 Wright & Miller, Civil §§ 1714, 1715.

53. In Liberty Nat. Bank & Trust Co. of Oklahoma City v. Acme Tool Div. of Ruckor Co., C.A.10th, 1976, 540 F.2d 1375, 1379–1381, the Tenth Circuit overruled earlier decisions in which it had held that a disinterested stakeholder was not an "opposing party" against whom a counterclaim would lie. The earlier decisions had been criticized in 7 Wright & Miller, Civil § 1715, pp.

448–449, and were not followed in Bell v. Nutmeg Airways Corp., D.C.Conn. 1975, 66 F.R.D 1.

54. Compare Marine Bank & Trust Co. v. Hamilton Bros., Inc., D.C.Fla.1972, 55 F.R.D. 505, with Dean Witter Reynolds, Inc. v. Fernandez, D.C.Fla.1979, 489 F.Supp. 434. See also Allstate Ins. Co. v. McNeill, C.A.4th, 1967, 382 F.2d 84, certiorari denied 88 S.Ct. 2290, 392 U.S. 931, 20 L.Ed.2d 1390. This problem is discussed in 7 Wright & Miller, Civil § 1715, pp. 449–453.

55. Liberty Oil Co. v. Condon Nat. Bank, 1922, 43 S.Ct. 118, 121, 260 U.S. 235, 244, 67 L.Ed. 232.

56. Bynum v. Prudential Life Ins. Co. of America, D.C.S.C.1947, 7 F.R.D. 585; Liberty Nat. Life Ins. Co. v. Brown, D.C.Ala.1954, 119 F.Supp. 920; Pennsylvania Fire Ins. Co. v. American Airlines, Inc., D.C.N.Y.1960, 180 F.Supp. 239; Plaza Exp. Co. v. Galloway, Mo. 1955, 280 S.W.2d 17, noted 1956, 54 Mich.L.Rev. 1171, 1956 Wash.U.L.Rev. 264.

57. Savannah Bank & Trust Co. of Savannah v. Block, D.C.Ga.1959, 175 F.Supp. 798; American-Hawaiian S. S. Co. (Del.) v. Bowring & Co., D.C.N.Y. 1957, 150 F.Supp. 449.

the issues are such that there would be no right of jury trial if they arose in an independent action,[58] issues among the claimants [59] and issues between the stakeholder and the claimants [60] are triable as of right to a jury.[61]

§ 75. Intervention[1]

Rule 24, permitting persons not named as parties to a lawsuit to intervene therein, provides a procedure by which one not made a party can protect himself from being excluded from an action that might be detrimental to him, or from an action where he might be able inexpensively to litigate his claim. Rule 24(a) describes situations in which intervention is "of right" while Rule 24(b) authorizes "permissive intervention" in the discretion of the court. The right to intervene in federal actions is governed by this rule and not by state law.[2]

Both before and after its amendment in 1966, Rule 24(a) has allowed intervention of right if a statute grants an absolute right of intervention. The most important such statute is that authorizing the United States or a state to intervene in cases in which the constitutionality of an Act of Congress or a state statute is in question.[3]

Prior to the 1966 amendment Rule 24(a) had recognized two other situations in which intervention might be had of right. One was where the representation of the applicant by existing parties was inadequate and he "is or may be bound by a judgment in the action."[4] The other was where the applicant was so situated that he would be adversely affected by a distribution or other disposition of property under the control of the court.[5]

---

58. Hyde Properties v. McCoy, C.A.6th, 1974, 507 F.2d 301; Edward B. Marks Music Corp. v. Wonnell, D.C.N.Y.1944, 4 F.R.D. 146.

59. Jefferson Standard Ins. Co. v. Craven, D.C.Pa.1973, 365 F.Supp. 861; Pan American Fire & Cas. Co. v. Revere, D.C.La.1960, 188 F.Supp. 474, 483; Savannah Bank & Trust Co. v. Block, D.C.Ga.1959, 175 F.Supp. 798, 801.

60. John Hancock Mut. Life Ins. Co. v. Yarrow, D.C.Pa.1951, 95 F.Supp. 185, 188.

61. See Ross v. Bernhard, 1970, 90 S.Ct. 733, 740 n. 15, 396 U.S. 531, 541 n. 15, 24 L.Ed.2d 729; 7 Wright & Miller, Civil § 1718.

[§ 75]

1. 7A Wright & Miller, Civil §§ 1901–1923; Shreve, Questioning Intervention of Right—Toward a New Methodology of Decisionmaking, 1980,

74 Nw.U.L.Rev. 894; Brunet, A Study in the Allocation of Scarce Judicial Resources: The Efficiency of Federal Intervention Criteria, 1978, 12 Ga.L.Rev. 701; Kennedy, Let's All Join In: Intervention under Federal Rule 24, 1969, 57 Ky.L.J. 329; Shapiro, Some Thoughts on Intervention Before Courts, Agencies, and Arbitrators, 1968, 81 Harv.L.Rev. 721; Comment, The Litigant and the Absentee in Federal Multiparty Practice, 1968, 116 U.Pa.L.Rev. 531.

2. Olden v. Hagerstown Cash Register, Inc., C.A.3d, 1980, 619 F.2d 271, 273–274; 7A Wright & Miller, Civil § 1905.

3. 28 U.S.C.A. § 2403, as amended by act of Aug. 12, 1976, Pub.L. 94–381, § 5, 90 Stat. 1119. See 7A Wright & Miller, Civil § 1906.

4. 7A Wright & Miller, Civil § 1907.

5. 7A Wright & Miller, Civil § 1907.

The courts had given a very loose reading to the requirement of property in the last of these categories.[6] Although this was a desirable result, it distorted the language of the rule. On the other hand the category dealing with one who might be bound by the judgment was read too narrowly. The Supreme Court had equated the language of the rule with res judicata, and said that it applied only if the would-be intervenor was "legally bound."[7] This created a dilemma, since intervention under that branch of the rule also required a showing of inadequacy of representation. An absent party cannot be legally bound by a judgment in an action in which he was inadequately represented.[8] Thus, no absentee could satisfy this reading of the rule, since no one could show both that he was inadequately represented and that he would be legally bound.[9]

The rule was amended in 1966 to avoid these defects in the former rule. The amendment was intended to substitute a practical rather than a conceptual emphasis in questions of intervention and to tie the intervention rule more closely to Rule 19, on compulsory joinder of parties, [10] and Rule 23, on class actions.[11] The amended rule substitutes a single category, Rule 24(a)(2), for the two categories just discussed in the old rule. It permits intervention of right "when the applicant claims an interest relating to the property or transaction which is the subject of the action and he is so situated that the disposition of the action may as a practical matter impair or impede his ability to protect that interest, unless the applicant's interest is adequately represented by existing parties."

Thus the amended rule requires the applicant to show three things: (1) that he has an interest relating to the property or transaction involved in the action; (2) that disposition of the action may impair his ability to protect his interest "as a practical matter"; and (3) that his interest is not adequately represented by the present parties.

6. E.g., Formulabs, Inc. v. Hartley Pen Co., C.A.9th, 1960, 275 F.2d 52; International Mortg. & Inv. Corp. v. Von Clemm, C.A.2d, 1962, 301 F.2d 857.

7. Sam Fox Pub. Co. v. U. S., 1961, 81 S.Ct. 1309, 1315, 366 U.S. 683, 694, 6 L.Ed.2d 604, noted 1962, 15 Vand.L. Rev. 647; Sutphen Estates, Inc. v. U. S., 1951, 72 S.Ct. 14, 16, 342 U.S. 19, 21, 96 L.Ed. 19.

8. Hansberry v. Lee, 1940, 61 S.Ct. 115, 311 U.S. 32, 85 L.Ed. 22.

9. Note, Intervention of Right in Class Actions: The Dilemma of Federal Rule of Civil Procedure 24(a)(2), 1962, 50 Calif.L.Rev. 89.

Some lower courts managed to escape the dilemma by brute force, refusing to believe that the Supreme Court could have meant the interpretation it gave to "bound." E.g., International Mortg. & Inv. Corp. v. Von Clemm, C.A.2d, 1962, 301 F.2d 857; Atlantic Refining Co. v. Standard Oil Co., C.A.1962, 304 F.2d 387, 113 U.S.App.D.C. 20.

10. See § 70 above.

11. See § 72 above. On the interrelation of Rules 19, 23, and 24, see Atlantis Development Corp. v. U. S., C.A. 5th, 1967, 379 F.2d 818, 824–825.

The amended rule has been criticized, however, as not being "totally faithful to the revision theory of new Rules 19 and 23. That theory is that the rules should express factors for decision rather than definitional categories." Kennedy, note 1 above, at 374.

There is as yet no consensus about the kind of "interest" that the would-be intervenor must have. Although the Supreme Court has added the gloss that Rule 24(a)(2) is referring to "a significantly protectable interest,"[12] this has not been a term of art in the law of intervention and provides little more guidance than does the bare term used in the rule itself. Some courts look to the pre-1966 decisions for guidance and continue to call for "a direct substantial, legally protectable interest"[13] while others have permitted intervention on the basis of interests that hardly seem to satisfy the adjectives just quoted.[14]

The second requirement, that the would-be intervenor must be so situated that the disposition of the action "may as a practical matter impair or impede" his ability to protect his interest has been sympathetically applied. It has been clear to all courts that the principal purpose of the amendment was to eliminate the old reading that a would-be intervenor must be legally bound, and that instead the court is to view the effect on his interest with a practical eye. Indeed it is significant that, as finally adopted, the amendment did not require, as an earlier draft would have, that the judgment must "substantially" impair or impede the applicant's ability to protect his interest. Thus, contrary to decisions under the pre-1966 rule, even the stare decisis effect of the judgment in the existing action may, in proper circumstances, create sufficient practical disadvantage to warrant intervention as of right.[15]

The Supreme Court has said that the third requirement, that the applicant not be adequately represented by the existing parties, "is satisfied if the applicant shows that representation of his interest

---

12. Donaldson v. U. S., 1971, 91 S.Ct. 534, 542, 400 U.S. 517, 531, 27 L.Ed.2d 580. The Court had seemed to take a very permissive view of the kind of interest that would justify intervention in Cascade Natural Gas Corp. v. El Paso Natural Gas Co., 1967, 87 S.Ct. 932, 386 U.S. 129, 17 L.Ed.2d 814. Both cases are heavily colored by their unusual facts and are less than conclusive on when intervention should be allowed in routine litigation. See 7A Wright & Miller, Civil § 1908, pp. 496–502; Shreve, note 1 above, at 923–924.

13. Hobson v. Hansen, D.C.D.C.1968, 44 F.R.D. 18, 24. See also In re Penn Central Commercial Paper Litigation, D.C.N.Y.1974, 62 F.R.D. 341, 346, affirmed C.A.2d, 1975, 515 F.2d 505; and cases cited 7A Wright & Miller, Civil § 1908 nn. 27, 43.

14. E.g., Idaho v. Freeman, C.A.9th, 1980, 625 F.2d 886; Smuck v. Hobson, C.A.1969, 408 F.2d 175, 132 U.S.App. D.C. 372; Brotherhood of Locomotive Firemen & Enginemen v. Louisville &

N. R. Co. C.A.6th, 1968, 400 F.2d 572, certiorari denied 89 S.Ct. 689, 393 U.S. 1050, 21 L.Ed.2d 692; Nuesse v. Camp, C.A.1967, 385 F.2d 694, 128 U.S.App. D.C. 172; U. S. v. Reserve Mining Co., D.C.Minn.1972, 56 F.R.D. 408; General Elec. Co. v. Bootz Mfg. Co., D.C.Ind. 1968, 289 F.Supp. 504, noted 1969, 17 Kan.L.Rev. 535. See 7A Wright & Miller, Civil § 1908, pp. 504–511.

15. Corby Recreation, Inc. v. General Elec. Co., C.A.8th, 1978, 581 F.2d 175; New York Public Interest Research Group, Inc. v. Regents of the Univ. of the State of New York, C.A.2d, 1975, 516 F.2d 350; Nuesse v. Camp, C.A.1967, 385 F.2d 694, 701–702, 128 U.S.App.D.C. 172, noted 1968, 18 Amer.U.L.Rev. 202; Atlantis Development Corp. v. U. S., C.A.5th, 1967, 379 F.2d 818, 828–829, noted, 1967 Duke L.J. 1251, 1968, 33 Mo.L.Rev. 655.

For other illustrations of the reading the courts have given to this requirement of the rule, see 7A Wright & Miller, Civil § 1908 nn. 60, 61.

'may be' inadequate; and the burden of making that showing should be treated as minimal."[16] If the absentee's interest will be affected, and he is not represented at all, or the existing parties are adverse to him, he must be allowed to intervene.[17] At the other extreme are cases in which the interest of the absentee is identical with that of one of the existing parties or there is a party charged by law with representing the interests of the absentee. In these situations representation will be presumed adequate unless special circumstances are shown.[18] The final situation is that in which the interests of the absentee and of the party thought to represent him are different, though perhaps similar. If there is a serious possibility that the applicant is not adequately represented in these situations, he should be allowed to intervene, rather than being obliged to test the validity of the judgment as applied to his interest by a later collateral attack.[19]

Permissive intervention may be allowed where a governmental officer or agency wishes to come into a case involving a statute or regulation.[20] The more common ground for permissive intervention is that the would-be intervenor's claim or defense and the existing action have a question of law or fact in common.[21] The intervenor need not have a direct personal or pecuniary interest in the subject of the litigation.[22] Indeed it would seem that he need not be a person who would have been a proper party at the beginning of the suit, since of the two tests for permissive joinder of parties, a common question of law or fact and some right to relief arising from the same transaction, only the former is stated as a limitation on intervention.[23]

16. Trbovich v. United Mine Workers of America, 1972, 92 S.Ct. 630, 636 n. 10, 404 U.S. 528, 538 n. 10, 30 L.Ed.2d 686. See Brunet, note 1 above, at 733–738.

"The number of recent cases denying intervention on the basis of adequate representation, however, suggests the requirement is still formidable." Shreve, note 1 above, at 919 n. 106.

17. Natural Resources Defense Council, Inc. v. U. S. Nuclear Regulatory Comm., C.A.10th, 1978, 578 F.2d 1341; Stallworth v. Monsanto Co., C.A.5th, 1977, 558 F.2d 257; Atlantis Development Corp. v. U. S., C.A.5th, 1967, 379 F.2d 818; and cases cited 7A Wright & Miller, Civil § 1909 nn. 76, 77.

18. McClune v. Shamah, C.A.3d, 1979, 593 F.2d 482; U. S. Postal Serv. v. Brennan, C.A.2d, 1978, 579 F.2d 188; and cases cited 7A Wright & Miller, Civil § 1909 nn. 78–95.

19. Johnson v. San Francisco Unified Sch. Dist., C.A.9th, 1974, 500 F.2d 349; Wilderness Soc'y v. Morton, C.A.1972, 463 F.2d 1261, 150 U.S.App.D.C. 170; Nuesse v. Camp, C.A.1967, 385 F.2d

694, 702–704; and cases cited 7A Wright & Miller, Civil § 1909 nn. 96–3.

20. Rule 24(b)(2); Securities and Exchange Comm. v. U. S. Realty & Improvement Co., 1940, 60 S.Ct. 1044, 310 U.S. 434, 84 L.Ed. 1293; Miami Health Studios, Inc. v. City of Miami Beach, C.A.5th, 1974, 491 F.2d 98; Nuesse v. Camp, C.A.1967, 385 F.2d 694, 704–706, 128 U.S.App.D.C. 172. But cf. Philadelphia Elec. Co. v. Westinghouse Elec. Corp., C.A.2d, 1962, 308 F.2d 856, certiorari denied 83 S.Ct. 883, 372 U.S. 936, 9 L.Ed.2d 767. See Berger, Intervention by Public Agencies in Private Litigation in the Federal Courts, 1940, 50 Yale L.J. 65; Note, 1951, 65 Harv.L. Rev. 319.

21. Rule 24(b)(2); 7A Wright & Miller, Civil § 1911.

22. Securities and Exchange Comm. v. U. S. Realty & Improvement Co., 1940, 60 S.Ct. 1044, 1055, 310 U.S. 434, 459, 84 L.Ed. 1293.

23. Usery v. Brandel, D.C.Mich.1980, 87 F.R.D. 670, 677.

Even under the pre-1966 rule, permissive intervention was often allowed where the intervenor had an economic interest in the outcome of the suit, although not a direct or a legal interest. It was on this basis that neighbors were allowed to come into an action to set aside a zoning order,[24] and that in an action in which the Brotherhood of Locomotive Engineers sought a declaratory judgment that its agreement with the railroad allowed its members to work more miles and days than they were working, the firemen's union, arguing that the more days engineers work the fewer days firemen work, was allowed to intervene.[25] Indeed, permissive intervention had even been allowed when the intervenor had little more interest than the avoiding of a precedent that might someday come back to haunt him,[26] although here the courts were more doubtful and on occasion said that the applicant could protect himself sufficiently by appearing as amicus curiae.[27] The broadened scope of intervention of right may now encompass some of these situations formerly thought appropriate for permissive intervention if the applicant's interest is not adequately represented.

All applications to intervene, whether as of right or permissively, are required to be "timely."[28] To this extent the court has discretion in all cases of intervention, because it must determine the timeliness of the application, but since in intervention of right situations the applicant may be seriously harmed if he is not permitted to intervene, courts should be especially reluctant to dismiss such applications as untimely.[29] In considering whether an application is timely, the court will look to the time element itself but will evaluate it in the light of all the circumstances of the case, and will weigh particularly whether the delay in moving for intervention has prejudiced the existing parties to the case.[30] Intervention may be disallowed where trial of the

---

24. Wolpe v. Poretsky, C.C.A.1944, 144 F.2d 505, 79 U.S.App.D.C. 141, certiorari denied 65 S.Ct. 190, 323 U.S. 777, 89 L.Ed. 621.

25. Brotherhood of Locomotive Engineers v. Chicago, M., St. P. & P. R. Co., D.C.Wis.1940, 34 F.Supp. 594. See also Ruby v. Pan American World Airways, Inc., D.C.N.Y.1966, 252 F.Supp. 393, appeal dismissed C.A.2d, 1966, 360 F.2d 691.

26. Cf. Fishgold v. Sullivan Drydock & Repair Corp., 1946, 66 S.Ct. 1105, 328 U.S. 275, 90 L.Ed. 1230.

27. Peterson v. U. S., D.C.Minn.1966, 41 F.R.D. 131; Jewell Ridge Coal Corp. v. Local No. 6167, United Mine Workers of America, D.C.Va.1943, 3 F.R.D. 251.

28. 7A Wright & Miller, Civil § 1916.

29. Alaniz v. Tillie Lewis Foods, C.A.9th, 1978, 572 F.2d 657, 659, certiorari denied 99 S.Ct. 123, 439 U.S. 838,

58 L.Ed.2d 134; and cases cited 7A Wright & Miller, Civil § 1916 n. 98. See Note, The Timeliness Threat to Intervention of Right, 1980, 89 Yale L.J. 586.

30. The factors to be considered are: the length of time the intervenor knew or reasonably should have known of his interest before he moved to intervene; prejudice to the existing parties due to failure to move promptly; the prejudice the intervenor would suffer if not allowed to intervene; and the existence of unusual circumstances mitigating either for or against intervention. Culbreath v. Dukakis, C.A.1st, 1980, 630 F.2d 15, 20; Stallworth v. Monsanto Co., C.A.5th, 1977, 558 F.2d 257, 264–266.

See cases cited 7A Wright & Miller, Civil § 1916 nn. 5–8.

case is about to begin,[31] but it may not be too late to intervene even after final judgment if it is necessary to preserve some right that cannot otherwise be protected.[32]

If the application comes under Rule 24(b) and is permissive, the court has a broader discretion with regard to it.[33] It is required by the rule to consider "whether the intervention will unduly delay or prejudice the adjudication of the rights of the original parties." [34] There is no such provision in subdivision (a). The rulemakers have made a judgment that in the situations described in subdivision (a) justice demands that the interest of the absentee should predominate over the interests of the original parties and of trial convenience. Thus in determining whether an application for intervention of right is timely, the court may consider whether delay in moving has prejudiced the existing parties, but except for that cannot consider prejudice under subdivision (a).[35] On an application for permissive intervention, however, the court is not so bound and may exercise its discretion in weighing the fact that additional parties always take additional time against the advantages of disposition of all the claims or defenses in one litigation.[36]

The cases as to jurisdiction were not easily reconciled prior to the 1966 amendment, and the courts have not fully considered what effect, if any, that amendment has on jurisdictional issues. The principle is clear enough: if the claim of the intervenor is so closely related to the main action that the claim can be regarded as ancillary, no independent grounds of jurisdiction need exist.[37] The difficulty comes in seeking to determine how close the relationship must be to

31. National Assn. for the Advancement of Colored People v. New York, 1973, 93 S.Ct. 2591, 2603, 413 U.S. 345, 366–369, 37 L.Ed.2d 648; Equal Employment Opportunity Comm. v. United Airlines, Inc., C.A.7th, 1975, 515 F.2d 946; Janousek v. Wells, C.A.8th, 1962, 303 F.2d 118.

32. United Airlines, Inc. v. McDonald, 1977, 97 S.Ct. 2464, 432 U.S. 385, 53 L.Ed.2d 423; Securities & Exchange Comm. v. U. S. Realty & Improvement Co., 1940, 60 S.Ct. 1044, 310 U.S. 434, 84 L.Ed. 1293; Fleming v. Citizens For Albemarle, Inc., C.A.4th, 1978, 577 F.2d 236, certiorari denied 99 S.Ct. 842, 439 U.S. 1071, 59 L.Ed.2d 37. A strong showing is required to intervene at this late stage. U. S. v. Blue Chip Stamp Co., D.C.Cal.1967, 272 F.Supp. 432, 435–438, affirmed 1968, 88 S.Ct. 693, 389 U.S. 580, 19 L.Ed.2d 781. See 7A Wright & Miller, Civil § 1916 nn. 9–14.

33. 7A Wright & Miller, Civil § 1913.

34. U. S. Postal Serv. v. Brennan, C.A.2d, 1978, 579 F.2d 188; Gerstle v. Continental Airlines, Inc., C.A.10th, 1972, 466 F.2d 1374; and cases cited 7A Wright & Miller, Civil § 1912 nn. 56, 57.

35. Stallworth v. Monsanto Co., C.A.5th, 1977, 558 F.2d 257, 265. See also Comment, note 1 above, at 542–543.

Professor Shreve has made an interesting argument that the distinction between intervention of right and permissive intervention should be ended and the courts given broad discretion, with only minimal appellate involvement, on all requests to intervene. Shreve, note 1 above.

36. Spangler v. Pasadena City Bd. of Educ., C.A.9th, 1977, 552 F.2d 1326, 1329; Pace v. First Nat. Bank of Osawatomie, D.C.Kan.1965, 277 F.Supp. 19, 20.

37. Phelps v. Oaks, 1886, 6 S.Ct. 714, 117 U.S. 236, 29 L.Ed. 888; Wichita R. & Light Co. v. Public Util. Comm. of Kansas, 1922, 43 S.Ct. 51, 260 U.S. 48, 67 L.Ed. 124; 7A Wright & Miller, Civil § 1917.

justify use of the concept of ancillary jurisdiction. Although there are cases to the contrary,[38] independent jurisdictional grounds ought to be required for permissive intervention under Rule 24(b).[39] Prior to the 1966 amendment, the view was increasingly accepted that no independent basis of jurisdiction was required if intervention was of right.[40] That is a desirable result to reach even with the broadened scope of Rule 24(a) under the 1966 amendment, and it is the result the courts are reaching,[41] but they have not discussed the implications of holding that an amendment to a procedural rule, broadening intervention of right, thus is given the incidental effect of broadening the jurisdiction of the federal courts.[42]

The procedure for intervention is set out in Rule 24(c).[43] The party desiring to intervene must serve a motion for leave to intervene upon all parties, stating the grounds for intervention and accompanied by a pleading setting forth the claim or defense for which intervention is sought.[44] Since the opposing parties are already subject to the jurisdiction of the court, personal service under Rule 4 is not required and the motion may be served as provided in Rule 5. The requirement of the former equity rule that intervention "shall be in subordination to and in recognition of the propriety of the main proceeding" was deliberately omitted from Rule 24 and should not be read back in by the courts.[45] The intervenor may assert a counter-

38. Northeast Clackamas County Elec. Co-op v. Continental Cas. Co., C.A.9th, 1955, 221 F.2d 329; Usery v. Brandel, D.C.Mich.1980, 87 F.R.D. 670, 678–682; TPI Corp. v. Merchandise Mart of South Carolina, D.C.S.C.1974, 61 F.R.D. 684; U. S. v. Local 638, D.C. N.Y.1972, 347 F.Supp. 164; Shipley v. Pittsburgh & L. E. R. Co., D.C.Pa.1947, 70 F.Supp. 870.

39. Moosehead Sanitary Dist. v. S. G. Phillips Corp., C.A.1st, 1979, 610 F.2d 49; Blake v. Pallan, C.A.9th, 1977, 554 F.2d 947, 955; Finance Co. of America v. Park Holding Corp., D.C.Pa.1973, 60 F.R.D. 504; and cases cited 7A Wright & Miller, Civil § 1917 n. 34. But see Harris v. Illinois-California Express, Inc., C.A.10th, 1982, 687 F.2d 1361.

40. Black v. Texas Employers Ins. Assn., C.A.10th, 1964, 326 F.2d 603; Formulabs, Inc. v. Hartley Pen Co., C.A.9th, 1963, 318 F.2d 485, certiorari denied 84 S.Ct. 352, 375 U.S. 945, 11 L.Ed.2d 275; East v. Crowdus, C.A.8th, 1962, 302 F.2d 645; Lenz v. Wagner, C.A.5th, 1957, 240 F.2d 666; Dickinson v. Burnham, C.A.2d, 1952, 197 F.2d 973, certiorari denied 73 S.Ct. 169, 344 U.S. 875, 97 L.Ed. 678.

41. Gaines v. Dixie Carriers, Inc., C.A. 5th, 1970, 434 F.2d 52; Babcock & Wilcox Co. v. Parsons Corp., C.A.8th,

1970, 430 F.2d 531; Hardy-Latham v. Wellons, C.A.4th, 1968, 415 F.2d 674; Omni Developments, Inc. v. Porter, D.C.Fla.1978, 459 F.Supp. 930.

42. Cf. Snyder v. Harris, 1969, 89 S.Ct. 1053, 394 U.S. 332, 22 L.Ed.2d 319, discussed § 72 above, in which the Court held that former distinctions about jurisdiction must continue to be applied despite the 1966 amendment of Rule 23.

See 7A Wright & Miller, Civil § 1917, pp. 597–601.

43. 7A Wright & Miller, Civil § 1914.

44. Courts should be liberal, however, in disregarding procedural errors by the would-be intervenor. Spring Constr. Co. v. Harris, C.A.4th, 1980, 614 F.2d 374; Montgomery v. Rumsfeld, C.A. 9th, 1978, 572 F.2d 250; 7A Wright & Miller, Civil § 1915, pp. 565–568. But cf. SEC v. Investors Security Leasing Corp., C.A.3d, 1979, 610 F.2d 175; Spangler v. Pasadena City Bd. of Educ., C.A.9th, 1977, 552 F.2d 1326.

45. Spangler v. U. S., C.A.9th, 1969, 415 F.2d 1242; Park & Tilford, Inc. v. Schulte, C.C.A.2d, 1947, 160 F.2d 984, 989 n. 1, certiorari denied 68 S.Ct. 64, 332 U.S. 761, 92 L.Ed. 347; Hartley Pen Co. v. Lindy Pen Co., Inc., D.C.Cal. 1954, 16 F.R.D. 141. But cf. Keystone

claim—and must do so if the compulsory counterclaim rule is applicable.[46] Where intervention is permissive, however, the court may refuse intervention if a counterclaim will delay or prejudice the existing parties.[47]

An order granting leave to intervene is not final and is not appealable as of right.[48] The situation is more complicated if intervention is denied. Here the traditional doctrine is that if the applicant has contended he may intervene as of right, denial of leave to intervene is appealable. The appellate court will consider the merits of the claim and will reverse if it determines that intervention was in fact a matter of right.[49] If, however, the appellate court concludes that there was no right to intervene, the common practice has been to dismiss the appeal for want of jurisdiction, on the ground that the order was not final.[50] The practical consequences to the appellant are the same as if the denial of intervention were affirmed on the merits, and there is now a strong trend toward considering all such orders appealable since the appellate court does in fact look into the merits of the claim.[51]

It is commonly said that a denial of permissive intervention may be reversed for abuse of discretion. This is an illusory doctrine. There seems to be only one case in which a district court has been reversed solely because of an abuse of discretion in denying permissive intervention.[52] It makes little sense to maintain a stated doctrine

Freight Lines v. Pratt Thomas Truck Line, D.C.Okl.1941, 37 F.Supp. 635; Dolcater v. Manufacturers & Traders Trust Co., D.C.N.Y.1938, 25 F.Supp. 637.

46. U. S. v. Martin, C.A.10th, 1959, 267 F.2d 764; Lenz v. Wagner, C.A.5th, 1957, 240 F.2d 666; Switzer Bros. v. Locklin, C.A.7th, 1953, 207 F.2d 483, noted 1954, 67 Harv.L.Rev. 1265; cf. Stewart-Warner Corp. v. Westinghouse Elec. Corp., C.A.2d, 1963, 325 F.2d 822, certiorari denied 84 S.Ct. 800, 376 U.S. 944, 11 L.Ed.2d 767. Contra: Kauffman v. Kebert, D.C.Pa.1954, 16 F.R.D. 225, appeal dismissed C.A.3d, 1955, 219 F.2d 113; E. G. Staude Mfg. Co. v. Berles Carton Co., Inc., D.C.N.Y.1939, 31 F.Supp. 178. See 7A Wright & Miller, Civil § 1921.

47. Northwest Airlines, Inc. v. Intl. Assn. of Machinists & Aerospace Workers, AFL-CIO, D.C.Minn.1970, 323 F.Supp. 107; Finck v. Gilman Bros. Co., D.C.Conn.1951, 11 F.R.D. 198; cf. Brown v. Lee, C.A.4th, 1964, 331 F.2d 142.

48. Shore v. Parklane Hosiery Co., C.A.2d, 1979, 606 F.2d 354; and cases

cited 7A Wright & Miller, Civil § 1923 n. 66.

49. Cascade Natural Gas Corp. v. El Paso Natural Gas Co., 1967, 87 S.Ct. 932, 386 U.S. 129, 17 L.Ed.2d 814; Brotherhood of R. Trainmen v. Baltimore & O. R. Co., 1947, 67 S.Ct. 1387, 1390, 331 U.S. 519, 524–525, 91 L.Ed. 1646.

50. Sam Fox Pub. Co. v. U. S., 1961, 81 S.Ct. 1309, 366 U.S. 683, 6 L.Ed.2d 604; Sutphen Estates v. U. S., 1951, 72 S.Ct. 14, 342 U.S. 19, 96 L.Ed. 19; Hines v. D'Artois, C.A.5th, 1976, 531 F.2d 726.

51. Blake v. Pallan, C.A.9th, 1977, 554 F.2d 947, 951 n. 5; Pennsylvania v. Rizzo, C.A.3d, 1976, 530 F.2d 501, 504, certiorari denied 96 S.Ct. 2628, 426 U.S. 921, 49 L.Ed.2d 375; Reedsburg Bank v. Apollo, C.A.7th, 1975, 508 F.2d 995, 997; Ionian Shipping Co. v. British Law Ins. Co., C.A.2d, 1970, 426 F.2d 186, 188–189. See Stallworth v. Monsanto Co., C.A.5th, 1977, 558 F.2d 257, 263 n. 7; 7A Wright & Miller, Civil § 1923.

52. Crumble v. Blumthal, C.A.7th, 1979, 549 F.2d 462.

that invites litigants to raise an issue on appeal when there is so little prospect that it will win them a reversal.[53]

§ 76. Impleader [1]

Rule 14 introduced into the federal civil practice the procedure of impleader, long familiar in England and in admiralty, by which a defendant [2] can bring in as a third-party defendant one claimed by the defendant to be liable to him for all or part of the plaintiff's claim against the defendant. This procedure is intended to avoid circuity of action and to dispose of the entire subject matter arising from one set of facts in one action, thus administering complete and evenhanded justice, expeditiously and economically.[3] The rule is not mandatory; defendant may refrain from impleader and assert his claim instead in an independent action if he prefers.[4]

Defendant may invoke this procedure by service of a summons and third-party complaint on the third party if he acts expeditiously. Otherwise he must obtain leave of court to bring in the third party. In either event the court has discretion whether to allow impleader. Where impleader is had promptly, and leave of court is not required, this discretion can be invoked by a motion of any party to strike the third-party claim, or for its severance or separate trial. Presumably a court, called upon to exercise its discretion as to impleader, must balance the desire to avoid circuity of actions and to obtain consistent results against any prejudice that the plaintiff might suffer from complication of the case.[5] There should be little occasion, however, to deny impleader. The power to order separate trial of separate issues, under Rule 42(b), is sufficient to prevent any harm from impleader.[6]

There have been cases in which impleader to assert a claim for indemnity, as against an employee of the original defendant, has been

53. 7A Wright & Miller, Civil § 1923, pp. 630–632. See Shreve, note 1 above, at 921–924.

[§ 76]

1. 6 Wright & Miller, Civil §§ 1441–1465; Brill, Federal Rule of Civil Procedure 14 and Ancillary Jurisdiction, 1980, 59 Neb.L.Rev. 631; Berch, The Erection of a Barrier Against Assertion of Ancillary Claims: An Examination of Owen Equipment and Erection Company v. Kroger, 1979 Ariz.St.L.J. 253; Garvey, The Limits of Ancillary Jurisdiction, 1979, 57 Texas L.Rev. 697; Fraser, Jurisdiction of the Federal Courts of Actions Involving Multiple Claims, 1978, 76 F.R.D. 525, 535–545; Comment, Ancillary Jurisdiction: The Kroger Approach and the Federal Rules, 1979, 28 Emory L.Rev. 463.

2. Or a plaintiff against whom a counterclaim has been asserted. Rule 14(b).

3. 6 Wright & Miller, Civil § 1442.

4. Union Paving Co. v. Thomas, D.C.Pa. 1949, 9 F.R.D. 612.

5. Somportex Ltd. v. Philadelphia Chewing Gum Corp., C.A.3d, 1971, 453 F.2d 435; American Fidelity & Cas. Co. v. Greyhound Corp., C.A.5th, 1956, 232 F.2d 89; Delco Wire & Cable Co. v. Keystone Roofing Co., D.C.Pa.1978, 80 F.R.D. 428; John Hopkins Univ. v. Hutton, D.C.Md.1966, 40 F.R.D. 338, 346–348; 6 Wright & Miller, Civil § 1443.

6. Schwab v. Erie Lackawanna R. Co., C.A.3d, 1971, 438 F.2d 62, 71–72; Caplen v. Sturge, D.C.Pa.1964, 35 F.R.D. 176. See also cases cited note 8 below.

refused.[7] If the proposed third-party defendant lacks the financial ability to indemnify the original defendant, the courts have thought that the third party would be a straw man, and that the only purpose of impleading him would be to induce the jury to proceed on the false supposition that the employee might have to pay the judgment. The feeling that using impleader for this purpose is improper is realistic and persuasive, though in most cases sufficient protection can be given by ordering a separate trial of the third-party claim.[8]

A third-party complaint may be served only against one not already a party to the action. Counterclaims and cross-claims under Rule 13 are the appropriate procedure for asserting a claim against one already a party.[9] Under the rule as it was amended in 1948, the claim must be that the third party is liable over to defendant for all or part of plaintiff's claim against defendant. Except where the original claim is maritime in nature, and the special provisions of Rule 14(c) apply, it is no longer possible, as it was theoretically prior to 1948, to implead a third party claimed to be solely liable to the plaintiff.[10] Third-party practice is typically used to assert claims for indemnity, subrogation, contribution, and for breach of warranty.[11] The third-party claim need not be based on the same theory as the main claim; one sued for negligence, for example, may implead a third party against whom he has a contractual right of indemnity.[12]

Prior to amendments of the rules in 1966, there was uncertainty about the extent to which a defendant could join other claims he might have against a third-party defendant with the claim for liability over that formed the basis of impleader, and whether he might demand damages in excess of those plaintiff was seeking from him.[13]

---

7. Goodhart v. U. S. Lines Co., D.C.N.Y. 1960, 26 F.R.D. 163; Sox v. Hertz Corp., D.C.S.C.1967, 262 F.Supp. 531.

Impleader has also been refused where the same insurance company would have to pay the judgment whether it were against the defendant employer or the third-party defendant employee. List v. Roto-Broil Corp. of America, D.C.Pa.1966, 40 F.R.D. 31; Buchholz v. Michigan Motor Freight Lines, Inc., D.C.Mich.1956, 19 F.R.D. 407.

8. Lankford v. Ryder Truck System, Inc., D.C.S.C.1967, 41 F.R.D. 430; Smith v. Moore-McCormack Lines, Inc., D.C.N.Y.1962, 31 F.R.D. 239.

9. Horton v. Continental Can Co., D.C. Neb.1956, 19 F.R.D. 429; cf. Field v. Volkswagenwerk AG, C.A.3d, 1980, 626 F.2d 293, 298 n. 9; 6 Wright & Miller, Civil § 1446, pp. 255–256.

10. McCain v. Clearview Dodge Sales, Inc., C.A.5th, 1978, 574 F.2d 848; Parr v. Great Lakes Exp. Co., C.A.7th, 1973, 484 F.2d 767.

See Comment, Impleader of Nonmaritime Claims Under Rule 14(c), 1968, 47 Texas L.Rev. 120.

11. 6 Wright & Miller, Civil § 1446 nn. 32–36; § 1448.

12. E.g., U. S. for Use of Payne v. United Pac. Ins. Co., C.A.9th, 1973, 472 F.2d 792, certiorari denied 93 S.Ct. 2273, 411 U.S. 982, 36 L.Ed.2d 958; Southern R. Co. v. Fox, C.A.5th, 1964, 339 F.2d 560; Judd v. General Motors Corp., D.C.Pa.1974, 65 F.R.D. 612.

13. Compare Noland Co. v. Graver Tank & Mfg. Co., C.A.4th, 1962, 301 F.2d 43, and Ruckman & Hansen, Inc. v. Contracting & Material Co., C.A.7th, 1964, 328 F.2d 744, with U. S. v. Scott, D.C. N.Y.1955, 18 F.R.D. 324, C. W. Humphrey Co. v. Security Aluminum Co., D.C.Mich.1962, 31 F.R.D. 41, and Gebhardt v. Edgar, D.C.Pa.1966, 251 F.Supp. 678.

Rule 18(a), as amended in 1966, now states explicitly that "a party asserting a claim to relief as * * * [a] third-party claim, may join, either as independent or as alternate claims, as many claims * * * as he has against an opposing party." Thus it is now clear that, as a matter of pleading, once a defendant has asserted a claim suitable for impleader under Rule 14(a), he may join with it all of his other claims against the third-party defendant.[14] But questions of federal jurisdiction may still limit this kind of joinder. There must be an independent basis for federal jurisdiction of the additional claims unless they arise out of the same transaction or occurrence as the original claim, and thus can be considered to be within the ancillary jurisdiction of the court.[15]

Impleader is proper only where there is a substantive right to the relief sought. In diversity actions the law of the state governs on the existence of such substantive rights, and if, for example, the state recognizes no substantive right to contribution in particular circumstances, impleader for contribution cannot be allowed in federal court.[16]

Impleader itself, however, is not governed by state law, and is available in federal court, if there is a substantive right to the relief sought, though in state court an independent action would be required to vindicate that substantive right.[17]

One of the most important features of Rule 14 is that it permits impleader of one "who is or may be liable" to the defendant. The express use of the words "may be" indicates, as has been repeatedly held, that the rule permits impleader where liability is only contin-

14. Crompton-Richmond Co., Inc., Factors v. U. S., D.C.N.Y.1967, 273 F.Supp. 219. See also 6 Wright & Miller, Civil § 1452.

15. U. S. for Use of Payne v. United Pac. Ins. Co., C.A.9th, 1973, 472 F.2d 792, certiorari denied 93 S.Ct. 2273, 411 U.S. 982, 36 L.Ed.2d 958. See also Nishimatsu Constr. Co., Ltd. v. Houston Nat. Bank, C.A.5th, 1975, 515 F.2d 1200; Schwab v. Erie Lackawanna R. Co., C.A.3d, 1971, 438 F.2d 62. There is language in the last two cases cited that it is enough that the additional claim arises out of the same transaction or occurrence as the claim for liability over. This is rejected both in the Payne case and in Note, 1971, 46 N.Y. U.L.Rev. 634 where it is argued that the additional claim must be ancillary to the original claim of the plaintiff and not to the defendant's claim of liability over.

Professor Brill has considered whether the Owen Equipment case, discussed below, casts doubt on using the ancillary jurisdiction concept for an additional claim joined with the third-party claims. His conclusion is that Owen Equipment does not automatically compel the reversal of cases in which ancillary jurisdiction has been upheld in these circumstances, but it makes the extension of those cases less likely Brill, note 1 above, at 649–659.

16. The leading cases are Brown v. Cranston, C.C.A.2d, 1942, 132 F.2d 631, certiorari denied 63 S.Ct. 1028, 319 U.S. 741, 87 L.Ed. 1698, and Goldlawr, Inc. v. Shubert, C.A.3d, 1960, 276 F.2d 614. See also Pinzer v. Wood, D.C.Tenn. 1979, 82 F.R.D. 607; and cases cited 6 Wright & Miller, Civil § 1446 nn. 37, 42.

17. D'Onofrio Constr. Co. v. Recon Co., C.A.1st, 1958, 255 F.2d 904. The D'Onofrio case is cited with approval in Hanna v. Plumer, 1965, 85 S.Ct. 1136, 1145 n. 16, 380 U.S. 460, 473 n. 16, 14 L.Ed.2d 8. See also Tormo v. Yormark, D.C.N.J.1975, 398 F.Supp. 1159, 1175 n. 20.

gent, and thus can accelerate the determination of liability.[18] The court may issue a conditional judgment, where impleader is on a contingent liability.[19] Thus if state law gives a substantive right to contribution or indemnity, this may be asserted by impleader even though the state has no procedure for determination of such liability until it has been fixed by judgment, with the form of the judgment shaped to reflect the state law.[20] A particularly important application of this principle is that when an insurance company denies liability on the policy and refuses to defend its insured, he may implead the insurer in the tort action against him and have the issue of policy coverage decided in the same case as is the issue of tort liability.[21] The usual "no action" clause of insurance policies, which bars suit against the insurer until the liability of the insured has been determined by a judgment, does not bar impleader, because Rule 14 is intended to accelerate the determination of liability.[22] Separate trial of the third-party claim may be ordered, if this is in the interest of sound judicial administration, but the courts have viewed skeptically contentions that separate trials should be ordered as a matter of course on the fear that the presence of the insurer as a party will prejudice the jury.[23]

There is some confusion whether a defendant may implead a third party liable over to him for plaintiff's claim when the plaintiff is under some disability that would bar him from suing the third party directly.[24] It has been held that defendant may implead plaintiff's employer, even though the state compensation act would bar the plaintiff from suing his employer.[25] There is some authority that the third party may be impleaded although the statute of limitations would bar a suit against him directly by plaintiff.[26] Many decisions refuse to permit impleader of plaintiff's spouse for contribution, where the plaintiff could not sue the spouse directly, though the

18. Jeub v. B/G Foods, Inc., D.C.Minn. 1942, 2 F.R.D. 238; 6 Wright & Miller, Civil § 1451. Liability is contingent where the third party will be liable to the defendant only if defendant is found liable to plaintiff.

19. Williams v. Ford Motor Credit Co., C.A.8th, 1980, 627 F.2d 158, 160; Travelers Ins. Co. v. Busy Elec. Co., C.A. 5th, 1961, 294 F.2d 139, 145.

20. Glens Falls Indem. Co. v. Atlantic Bldg. Corp., C.A.4th, 1952, 199 F.2d 60; Huggins v. Graves, D.C.Tenn.1962, 210 F.Supp. 98, 105, affirmed C.A.6th, 1964, 337 F.2d 486.

21. 6 Wright & Miller, Civil § 1449.

22. Colton v. Swain, C.A.7th, 1975, 527 F.2d 296; Jordan v. Stephens, D.C.Mo. 1945, 7 F.R.D. 140.

23. Baker v. Moors, D.C.Ky.1971, 51 F.R.D. 507, 510; Schevling v. Johnson, D.C.Conn.1953, 122 F.Supp. 87, 89–90, affirmed on the opinion below C.A.2d, 1954, 213 F.2d 959; and cases cited 6 Wright & Miller, Civil § 1449 n. 6.

24. 6 Wright & Miller, Civil § 1447.

25. Atella v. General Elec. Co., D.C.R.I. 1957, 21 F.R.D. 372; Whitmarsh v. Durastone Co., D.C.R.I.1954, 122 F.Supp. 806; Corrao v. Waterman S. S. Corp., D.C.N.Y.1948, 75 F.Supp. 482; Severn v. U. S., D.C.N.Y.1946, 69 F.Supp. 21, Contra: Cox v. E. I. Du Pont de Nemours & Co., D.C.S.C.1965, 39 F.R.D. 47.

26. Keleket X-Ray Corp. v. U. S., C.A.1960, 275 F.2d 167, 107 U.S.App. D.C. 138; Adam v. Vacquier, D.C.Pa. 1942, 48 F.Supp. 275.

cases on this point are quite divided.[27] And the United States may implead a state even though the Eleventh Amendment would bar the plaintiff from suing the state.[28]

Even though it is no longer possible, except in maritime cases falling within Rule 14(c), for defendant to implead a third party as solely liable to plaintiff, where a third party has been properly brought in, plaintiff may, if he chooses, assert directly against the third-party defendant either by amendment or by new pleading any claim he may have against the third party arising out of the transaction or occurrence that is the subject matter of the plaintiff's claim against the original defendant.[29] Even if no formal amendment is made, Rule 15(b), on amendments to conform to the evidence, is relevant, and the plaintiff will be considered to have asserted such a claim where the parties have treated themselves as adverse.[30]

The third-party defendant may always assert any defenses he has to the original defendant's claim over against him, and he may also assert any defenses that the original defendant has to plaintiff's claim. This protects the third-party defendant if the original defendant fails or neglects to assert a proper defense to the plaintiff's claim on which the third party may be liable over.[31] The third-party defendant also has the right to assert directly against the plaintiff any claim arising out of the transaction or occurrence that is the subject matter of the plaintiff's claim against the original defendant.[32]

Joinder of claims and of parties in federal court always raises two questions that seem similar but are completely independent. Is the particular joinder procedurally proper? Is it jurisdictionally proper? If Hart of Massachusetts and Wechsler of New York are injured when the car in which they are riding is hit by a car driven by Bator of Massachusetts, they could join as plaintiffs in a suit against Bator. The joinder would be procedurally proper under Rule 20.[33] It would

27. Yellow Cab Co. of D. C. v. Dreslin, C.A.1950, 181 F.2d 626, 19 A.L.R.2d 1001; Koenigs v. Travis, 1956, 75 N.W.2d 478, 246 Minn. 466; Guerriero v. U-Drive-It Co. of N. J., 1952, 92 A.2d 140, 22 N.J.Super. 588; Norfolk Southern R. Co. v. Gretakis, 1934, 174 S.E. 841, 162 Va. 597. Contra: Gray v. Hartford Acc. & Indem. Co., D.C.La. 1940, 31 F.Supp. 299; Slavics v. Wood, D.C.Pa.1964, 36 F.R.D. 47; Smith v. Southern Farm Bureau Cas. Ins. Co., 1965, 174 So.2d 122, 247 La. 695; Bedell v. Reagan, 1963, 192 A.2d 24, 159 Me. 292; Fisher v. Diehl, 1945, 40 A.2d 912, 156 Pa.Super. 476. Other cases seemingly in point are distinguishable because of different state rules as to contribution or as to inter-spousal immunity.

28. U. S. v. Illinois, C.A.7th, 1971, 454 F.2d 297, 301, certiorari denied 92 S.Ct. 1767, 406 U.S. 918, 32 L.Ed.2d 117.

29. 6 Wright & Miller, Civil § 1459.

30. Falls Indus. Inc. v. Consolidated Chem. Indus., Inc., C.A.5th, 1958, 258 F.2d 277; see Patton v. Baltimore & O. R. Co., C.A.3d, 1952, 197 F.2d 732, 743; Feldman, A Puzzle under the Federal Impleader Rule, 1959, 34 Tul.L.Rev. 77.

31. Glick v. White Motor Co., C.A.3d, 1972, 458 F.2d 1287; F & D Property Co. v. Alkire, C.A.10th, 1967, 385 F.2d 97; 6 Wright & Miller, Civil § 1457.

32. Stahl v. Ohio River Co., C.A.3d, 1970, 424 F.2d 52; Grace v. United Founders Life Ins. Co., D.C.Okl.1971, 53 F.R.D. 8; 6 Wright & Miller, Civil § 1458.

33. See § 71 above.

fail jurisdictionally, however, because of the requirement of complete diversity.[34]

This distinction between what is procedurally proper and what is jurisdictionally proper is particularly important with regard to impleader. As has just been seen, Rule 14 makes very generous provision for impleading third parties and for assertion of claims on all three sides of the resulting lawsuit. While a great deal is thus procedurally proper, the limitations on jurisdiction and venue in the federal courts would make impleader of little utility there if the courts had not given a commodious scope to the concept of ancillary jurisdiction[35] when applied to Rule 14. Indeed the Supreme Court's first full-dress examination of the ancillary jurisdiction concept came in a Rule 14 context.

The case is Owen Equipment and Erection Co. v. Kroger.[36] Kroger was electrocuted when the boom of a steel crane next to which he was walking came too close to a high-tension power line. His widow, a citizen of Iowa, sued the Omaha Public Power District (OPPD), a Nebraska corporation, claiming that it had negligently operated the power line. The utility then impleaded Owen Equipment, a Nebraska corporation that owned the crane. OPPD claimed a right of contribution against Owen Equipment for negligence. Mrs. Kroger then amended her complaint, as Rule 14 allows, to state a claim directly against Owen Equipment for negligence.

Thereafter summary judgment was granted to OPPD on Mrs. Kroger's claim against it. It did not own the power line and under the applicable Iowa law had no duty to maintain it. The case then went to trial on Mrs. Kroger's claim against the third-party defendant, Owen Erection. During the third day of trial it was disclosed that Owen Erection's principal place of business was Iowa, not Nebraska, and that Mrs. Kroger and Owen Equipment were, therefore, both citizens of Iowa. The trial court refused to dismiss the action, and the jury returned a substantial verdict for Mrs. Kroger, but the Supreme Court held that there was no jurisdiction of this claim by one citizen of Iowa against another and set the judgment aside.

In his opinion for the Court, Justice Stewart recognized that "the exercise of ancillary jurisdiction over nonfederal claims has often been upheld in situations involving impleader, cross-claims or counterclaims."[37] He thought, however, that it is one thing to extend ancillary jurisdiction to the original defendant's claim against a third party and something quite different to apply it, as was sought in the case

---

34. See § 24 above.

35. See § 9 above.

36. 1978, 98 S.Ct. 2396, 437 U.S. 365, 57 L.Ed.2d 274, noted 1978, 62 Marq.L. Rev. 89; 1979, 28 Drake L.Rev. 182, 46 Tenn.L.Rev. 865, 31 U.Fla.L.Rev. 442, 18 Washburn L.J. 357. See also the articles and Comment cited note 1 above.

37. 98 S.Ct. at 2403, 437 U.S. at 375. In footnote 18, at this point, the Court cited with apparent approval cases that had applied ancillary jurisdiction to compulsory counterclaims, impleader, cross-claims, and intervention of right.

before the Court, to the original plaintiff's claim against a third-party defendant. "First, the nonfederal claim in this case was simply not ancillary to the federal one in the same sense that, for example, the impleader by a defendant of a third-party defendant always is. A third-party complaint depends at least in part upon the resolution of the primary lawsuit. * * * Its relation to the original complaint is thus not mere factual similarity but logical dependence. * * * [Mrs. Kroger's] claim against [Owen Equipment], however, was entirely separate from her original claim against OPPD, since [Owen Equipment's] liability to her depended not at all upon whether or not OPPD was also liable. Far from being an ancillary and dependent claim, it was a new and independent one.

"Second, the nonfederal claim here was asserted by the plaintiff, who voluntarily chose to bring suit upon a state-law claim in a federal court. By contrast, ancillary jurisdiction typically involves claims by defending party haled into court against his will, or by another person whose rights might be irretrievably lost unless he could assert them in an ongoing action in a federal court. A plaintiff cannot complain if ancillary jurisdiction does not encompass all of his possible claims in a case such as this one, since it is he who has chosen the federal rather than the state forum and must thus accept its limitations."[38]

It had been well settled before Owen Equipment that there is ancillary jurisdiction over the claim by the original defendant against the third-party defendant, and that there need be nò independent jurisdictional grounds for such a claim if there was diversity between the original parties or if plaintiff's claim against the original defendant raised a federal question.[39] This is still clearly the law.[40] Such a claim, the Court said in Owen Equipment, "always is" ancillary.[41] Dismissal or settlement of the main action does not require dismissal of the third-party complaint, even though there are no independent grounds of jurisdiction for the third-party claim,[42] but if considerations of convenience will be equally well served, the court has discretion in such a situation to dismiss the third-party proceeding and leave these ancillary matters to be determined in the state courts.[43]

---

38. 98 S.Ct. at 2404, 437 U.S. at 376.

39. 6 Wright & Miller, Civil § 1444 at notes 68 to 79.

40. Field v. Volkswagenwerk AG, C.A.3d, 1980, 626 F.2d 293, 298–299; Curtis v. Radiation Dynamics, Inc., D.C.Md.1981, 515 F.Supp. 1176.

41. 98 S.Ct. at 2404, 437 U.S. at 376.

42. Nishimatsu Constr. Co., Ltd. v. Houston Nat. Bank, C.A.5th, 1975, 515 F.2d 1200, 1204 n. 2; Bowen v. Evanuk, D.C.R.I.1976, 423 F.Supp. 1341; and cases cited 6 Wright & Miller, Civil § 1444 n. 1.

43. Propps v. Weihe, Black & Jeffries, C.A.4th, 1978, 582 F.2d 1354; Duke v. RFC, C.A.4th, 1954, 209 F.2d 204, certiorari denied 74 S.Ct. 777, 347 U.S. 966, 98 L.Ed. 1108; Point of Americas Condominium Apartments, Inc.—Phase II v. General Builders Corp., D.C.Fla. 1976, 424 F.Supp. 1322; Maryland for Use and Benefit of Wood v. Robinson, D.C.Md.1947, 74 F.Supp. 279, 281–282.

See generally 6 Wright & Miller, Civil § 1444, pp. 235–237; Note, Disposition of Third Party Claims when the Primary Claim Has Been Dismissed, 1971, 23 S.C.L.Rev. 261; cf. Waste Systems,

A few cases refused to extend the ancillary concept to questions of venue, and refused to allow impleader unless venue was proper as to the third-party defendant.[44] It would be quite extraordinary to hold that the third-party claim is sufficiently ancillary to avoid the constitutional limits on jurisdiction, but that the statutory venue privilege must still be respected, and there is now much authority to the contrary.[45] If there is really a showing of great inconvenience to the third party, the court can consider this in its discretion in deciding whether to allow impleader.[46]

Before Owen Equipment was decided, the cases were divided on whether independent jurisdictional grounds were required if plaintiff exercised his right to assert a claim against the third-party defendant. In that case the Supreme Court endorsed what had been the more usual view of the lower courts and held that ancillary jurisdiction does not extend to this situation.[47] Naturally this will be followed in cases similar to Owen Equipment.[48] It is possible, however, that a different result may be reached, and that plaintiff will be allowed to assert a claim against the third-party defendant without an independent jurisdictional ground, if, unlike Mrs. Kroger, plaintiff did not voluntarily choose to bring suit in federal court. Thus if plaintiff's original claim was one within the exclusive jurisdiction of the federal court, allowing the use of ancillary jurisdiction for plaintiff's claim against the third party is the only alternative to having a wasteful second suit in state court.[49] There is also an argument, though less compelling, that the Owen Equipment rule should not be applied if plaintiff sued in state court and the suit was removed by defendant

Inc. v. Clean Land Air Water Corp., C.A.5th, 1982, 683 F.2d 927.

44. Lewis v. United Air Lines Transport Corp., D.C.Conn.1939, 29 F.Supp. 112; King v. Shepherd, D.C.Ark.1938, 26 F.Supp. 357. This view is supported by Developments in the Law—Multiparty Litigation in the Federal Courts, 1958, 71 Harv.L.Rev. 874, 912.

45. Lesnik v. Public Indus. Corp., C.C.A. 2d, 1944, 144 F.2d 968; Keiffer v. Southern Pac. Transp. Co., D.C.Tex. 1980, 486 F.Supp. 798; Tcherepnin v. Franz, D.C.Ill.1977, 439 F.Supp. 1340; Moncrief v. Pennsylvania R. Co., D.C. Pa.1947, 73 F.Supp. 815; and cases cited 6 Wright & Miller, Civil § 1445 n. 14.

46. U. S. v. Acord, C.A.10th, 1954, 209 F.2d 709, certiorari denied 74 S.Ct. 786, 347 U.S. 975, 98 L.Ed. 1115; Manley v. Standard Oil Co. of Tex., D.C.Tex. 1948, 8 F.R.D. 354. Great inconvenience must be shown. Brown v. U. S., C.A.9th, 1959, 270 F.2d 80; Globig v. Greene & Gust Co., D.C.Wis.1960, 184

F.Supp. 530; Gore v. U. S., D.C.Mass. 1959, 171 F.Supp. 136.

47. See 6 Wright & Miller, Civil § 1444, pp. 229–232.

48. West v. U. S., C.A.8th, 1979, 592 F.2d 487; Gunnell v. Amoco Oil Co., D.C.Mich.1980, 490 F.Supp. 67. But cf. Burleson v. Coastal Recreation, Inc., C.A.5th, 1978, 572 F.2d 509, and the dissent therefrom, 1979, 595 F.2d 332.

49. It was so held in Ortiz v. U. S. Government, C.A.1st, 1979, 595 F.2d 65. See Brill, note 1 above, at 673–675.
"When the grant of jurisdiction to a federal court is exclusive, for example, as in the prosecution of tort claims against the United States under 28 U.S.C. § 1346, the argument of judicial economy and convenience can be coupled with the additional argument that *only* in a federal court may all of the claims be tried together." Aldinger v. Howard, 1976, 96 S.Ct. 2413, 2422, 427 U.S. 1, 18, 49 L.Ed.2d 276.

to federal court.[50] In those situations in which plaintiff is able to assert a claim against the third party, either because there is an independent jurisdictional ground or because some exception to the Owen Equipment rule allows the use of ancillary jurisdiction, this additional claim need not meet the venue tests of an original action. When the third-party defendant is already participating in a lawsuit at a particular forum, there is no added inconvenience to him in requiring him to defend an additional claim arising from the same transaction, and venue should be held proper.[51]

Though the cases were divided, the better view had been that no independent jurisdictional ground was required if the third-party defendant exercised his right under Rule 14 to assert a claim against the plaintiff arising out of the transaction sued on by the plaintiff.[52] Although the matter is not free of doubt, this should still be the result reached after Owen Equipment.[53] Though there are no cases in point, the claim by the third party against the plaintiff should also be treated as ancillary for purposes of venue.

Although subject-matter jurisdiction, and the extent of ancillary jurisdiction, have attracted most attention under Rule 14, personal jurisdiction must also be obtained over the third-party defendant. The third-party summons and complaint ordinarily cannot be served outside the territorial limits of the state in which the main action is brought,[54] except where there is statutory authority for wider service,[55] and on occasion this has been an effective limitation on the use of Rule 14. The 1963 amendment of Rule 4(f) eased this problem somewhat by permitting service of the third-party complaint outside the state within 100 miles of the place where the action is to be tried.[56]

---

50. Ayer v. General Dynamics Corp., D.C.N.Y.1979, 82 F.R.D. 115, 122. See Brill, note 1 above, at 672 n. 224.

51. Season-All Indus., Inc. v. Merchant Shippers, D.C.Pa.1974, 385 F.Supp. 517; and cases cited 6 Wright & Miller, Civil § 1445 n. 23. Contra: Habina v. M. A. Henry Co., D.C.N.Y.1948, 8 F.R.D. 52.

52. Mayer Paving & Asphalt Co. v. General Dynamics Corp., C.A.7th, 1973, 486 F.2d 763, certiorari denied 94 S.Ct. 899, 414 U.S. 1146, 39 L.Ed.2d 102; Revere Copper & Brass Inc. v. Aetna Cas. & Sur. Co., C.A.5th, 1970, 426 F.2d 709, noted 1971, 59 Ky.L.J. 506, 49 N.C.L. Rev. 503; and cases cited 6 Wright & Miller, Civil § 1444 n. 90.

But see James King & Son, Inc. v. Indemnity Ins. Co. of North America, D.C.N.Y.1959, 178 F.Supp. 146, and

Shverha v. Maryland Cas. Co., D.C.Pa. 1953, 110 F.Supp. 173. The result in these cases is criticized in Note, 1971, 57 Va.L.Rev. 265, 275–282.

53. See Brill, note 1 above, at 661–669; Berch, note 1 above, at 260–261.

54. James Talcott, Inc. v. Allahabad Bank, Ltd., C.A.5th, 1971, 444 F.2d 451, certiorari denied 92 S.Ct. 280, 404 U.S. 940, 30 L.Ed.2d 253; and cases cited 6 Wright & Miller, Civil § 1445 nn. 9, 10.

55. Moreno v. U. S., C.C.A.1st, 1941, 120 F.2d 128; Brandt v. Olson D.C.Iowa 1959, 179 F.Supp. 363.

56. See § 64 above; Sprow v. Hartford Ins. Co., C.A.5th, 1979, 594 F.2d 412; Lee v. Ohio Cas. Ins. Co., D.C.Del. 1978, 445 F.Supp. 189.

§ 77. Substitution of Parties [1]

Rule 25 provides, in four subsections, for substitution of parties where a party has died, become incompetent, transferred his interest, or where a public officer has been suceeded by someone else. Where a change of parties is desired for some other reason, Rule 15, on amendment, Rule 21, on adding or dropping parties, and Rule 24, on intervention, must be looked to rather than Rule 25.

Rule 25, as it stood prior to 1961, was not satisfactory. The time limits it provided for substitution, enforced rigorously as they were, often proved to be traps for the unwary, and led to harsh results contrary to the beneficial purposes stated in Rule 1. The requirement of substitution of public officers was at best a time-consuming formality and at worst a cause of positive injustice. Rule 25(d), as it stood before the 1961 amendment, enjoyed what is probably the unique distinction of having been criticised editorially by a lay newspaper. Thus it is not surprising that there were persistent attempts to amend the rule. In 1961 Rule 25(d), on substitution of public officers, was amended, and in 1963 amendment was made to Rule 25(a), on substitution after death of a party. These amendments have removed most, if not all, of the earlier difficulties.

Whether an action abates on the death of a party or survives to his personal representative is not governed by the rules. State law must be looked to in a diversity action [2] and federal law and federal decisions in a federal question case.[3] Rule 25(a) provides the mechanics of substitution if the action survives, and is controlling regardless of what the state law as to such mechanics may be.[4]

The original Rule 25 provided that substitution could only be made within two years after the death of a party, and that the action must be dismissed if substitution was not so made. Such a rigid bar led to harsh results. Thus in one case the Supreme Court noted that it was

---

[§ 77]

1. 7A Wright & Miller, Civil §§ 1951–1962; Comment, Federal Civil Procedure: Substitution Under Amended Rule 25(a)(1), 1963 Duke L.J. 733.

2. E.g., McManus v. Lykes Bros. S. S. Co., D.C.La.1967, 275 F.Supp. 361; 7A Wright & Miller, Civil §§ 1952, 1954.

3. Roberson v. N. V. Stoomvaart Maatschappij, C.A.5th, 1975, 507 F.2d 994; Note, Survival of Actions Brought Under Federal Statutes, 1963, 63 Col.L. Rev. 290.

On occasion federal law adopts the law of the state on whether an action survives. E.g., Robertson v. Wegmann, 1978, 98 S.Ct. 1991, 436 U.S. 584, 56 L.Ed.2d 554, on remand C.A.5th, 545 F.2d 980.

4. Iovino v. Waterson, C.A.2d, 1959, 274 F.2d 41, certiorari denied 80 S.Ct. 860, 362 U.S. 949, 4 L.Ed.2d 867, approved 1960, 60 Col.L.Rev. 738, 73 Harv.L. Rev. 1618; Hofheimer v. McIntee, C.A.7th, 1950, 179 F.2d 789; Boggs v. Blue Diamond Coal Co., D.C.Ky.1980, 497 F.Supp. 1105, noted 1981, 11 Mem. St.U.L.Rev. 413; Millich v. Schlesinger, D.C.Ind.1957, 156 F.Supp. 658; Commercial Solvents Corp. v. Jasspon, D.C. N.Y.1950, 92 F.Supp. 20.

See, however, the more complicated analysis made in Ransom v. Brennan, C.A. 5th, 1971, 437 F.2d 513, certiorari denied 91 S.Ct. 2205, 403 U.S. 904, 29 L.Ed.2d 680, discussed in 7A Wright & Miller, Civil § 1952, pp. 644–650.

through no lack of diligence that the plaintiff, who was seeking to enforce assessments against more than 5,000 stockholders, failed to learn of the deaths of a few of these stockholders until more than two years after the event. Nevertheless his failure to move for substitution within two years of the deaths was held to bar further action against the estates of the dead stockholders.[5]

An amendment to Rule 25(a), adopted in 1963, cures such injustice. The amendment eliminates the two year time limit. A party, or the successors or representatives of the deceased party, may now move for substitution at any time, subject to two limitations. First, either a party, or the successors or representatives of a deceased party, may suggest on the record the fact of death. Where such a suggestion is made on the record, the action will be dismissed unless a motion to substitute is made within 90 days after service of the suggestion of death, or such extended time as the court may allow under Rule 6(b).[6] Second, substitution may be denied, even though the time limit has not run, if circumstances have arisen rendering it unfair to allow substitution, as where settlement and distribution of the estate of a deceased defendant is far advanced by the time the motion for substitution is made.[7] Thus it is still the safe course to move for substitution as soon as the fact of death becomes known, rather than waiting indefinitely for the suggestion of death upon the record.

The former Rule 25(d), on substitution of public officers, produced incredible results. It required substitution within six months of the time a public officer replaced another person who, as such officer, had been a party to a lawsuit.[8] Where the public officer was plaintiff, this led to much needless formality, as in the making of formal orders of substitution in thousands of pending cases whenever there was a change in the person who was charged with enforcing price controls. The consequences where the public officer was defendant were even worse. The remarkable decision of Snyder v. Buck[9] illustrates the problem. Mrs. Snyder sued Admiral Buck, then Paymaster General of the Navy, to collect an allowance she claimed was due her

5. Anderson v. Yungkau, 1947, 67 S.Ct. 428, 329 U.S. 482, 91 L.Ed. 436.

6. Compare Staggers v. Otto Gerdau Co., C.A.2d, 1966, 359 F.2d 292 (belated substitution should have been permitted), with Graham v. Pennsylvania R. Co., C.A.1964, 342 F.2d 914, 119 U.S. App.D.C. 335, certiorari denied 85 S.Ct. 1446, 381 U.S. 904, 14 L.Ed.2d 286 (not error to refuse enlargement of time). See 7A Wright & Miller, Civil § 1955.

See also Anderson v. Republic Motor Inns, Inc., C.A.3d, 1971, 444 F.2d 87, where no motion to substitute had been filed but a pretrial memorandum filed within the 90-day period that set forth the intention to substitute was held adequate to comply with Rule 25(a).

In the only reported case under the amended rule in which substitution was denied on this ground, though it was made within the time limits of the rule, the appellate court reversed. Saylor v. Bastedo, C.A.2d, 1980, 623 F.2d 230.

7. See Anderson v. Yungkau, 1947, 67 S.Ct. 428, 430–431, 329 U.S. 482, 485–486, 91 L.Ed. 436.

8. 7A Wright & Miller, Civil § 1959.

9. 1950, 71 S.Ct. 93, 340 U.S. 15, 95 L.Ed. 15.

as the widow of a member of the naval service. On January 30, 1948, the district court entered judgment in her favor for $1365. The suit, as all members of the Supreme Court explicitly recognized, was in form against Buck but in substance against the United States. Government attorneys defended the suit; government funds would have been used to satisfy the judgment. On March 18th notice of appeal was filed in the name of Rear Admiral W. A. Buck, Paymaster General of the Navy. Unfortunately Admiral Buck had retired on March 1st and had been succeeded as Paymaster General by Admiral Foster. A bare majority of the Supreme Court held that the action abated when Buck retired and no substitution was made within six months. "Petitioner loses her judgment and must start over," the Court said.[10] As a distinguished commentator put it, "the principle of justice seems to be that when one party's attorneys (or their stenographer) are at fault in failing to substitute the name of the successor officer, the court should penalize the opposing party."[11]

The lower courts were not happy with such a doctrine. One court called it "a trap for unsuspecting litigants which seems unworthy of a great government."[12] Another commented that "it all seems so foolish."[13] But in later cases the Supreme Court adhered to the doctrine, if indeed it did not expand it.[14] Finally in 1961 Rule 25(d) was amended to put substitution of public officers on a more sensible basis.

The amended rule does two things. It provides for automatic substitution of public officers, and it also permits suit by the official title of the officer rather than by name.[15] The rule should operate without difficulty where the public officer is the plaintiff, and will eliminate the needless formality of numerous orders of subtitution where a public officer, who has instituted a great many actions, dies or resigns. The matter is more complex where the officer is defending the action. Here the substitution of public officers becomes entangled with notions of sovereign immunity and with fictional devices the courts have developed to avoid those barriers to suit.

The new rule applies in any case in which "a public officer is a party to an action in his official capacity." The old law made a distinction, so confused as to be quite unworkable, between suits nominally against officers personally but in reality against the government, and suits nominally against officers in their official capacity

---

10. 71 S.Ct. at 97, 340 U.S. at 22.

11. Davis, Government Officers as Defendants: Two Troublesome Problems, 1955, 104 U.Pa.L.Rev. 69, 83.

12. Vibra Brush Corp. v. Schaffer, C.A.2d, 1958, 256 F.2d 681, 684.

13. Rossello v. Marshall, D.C.N.Y.1952, 12 F.R.D. 352, 355.

14. E.g., Blackmar v. Guerre, 1952, 72 S.Ct. 410, 342 U.S. 512, 96 L.Ed. 534;

McGrath v. National Assn. of Mfrs., 1952, 73 S.Ct. 31, 344 U.S. 804, 97 L.Ed. 627; Klaw v. Schaffer, 1958, 78 S.Ct. 1369, 357 U.S. 346, 2 L.Ed.2d 1368. The cases are described in 7A Wright & Miller, Civil § 1959 at nn. 51–55.

15. 7A Wright & Miller, Civil §§ 1960, 1961.

but in reality against the government.[16]   Rule 25(d) will be ineffective if this distinction governs its applicability; it should be read, as the Civil Rules Committee clearly intended, to apply to all suits that are against the government in reality, regardless of this old distinction.[17] Of course a public officer may commit torts, make or break contracts, or otherwise get involved in litigation that has nothing to do with his official duties, and in which any judgment must be satisfied from his personal assets.   Rule 25(d) has no application to such cases.[18]

The new rule makes substitution automatic.   Though an order of substitution can be made at any time, misnomers are to be disregarded and the litigation will be valid, unless the substantial rights of the parties are affected even though no substitution is ever made.[19] Thus such a result as in Snyder v. Buck is not possible under the amended rule.

Since substitution is now automatic, the new rule does not contain the requirement of the old rule that a showing be made of a substantial need for continuing and maintaining the action against the successor officer.   It thus purports to end a requirement that, in the case of state officers at least, may well be of constitutional origin. In Ex parte LaPrade [20] the Supreme Court said that "it is to be borne in mind that Congress had authority to direct the conduct of federal officers in proceedings brought by or against them as such and may ordain that they may sue or be sued as representatives of the United States and stand in judgment on its behalf   *   *   *   but that Congress is not so empowered as to state officers."   That case was a suit against a state attorney general to restrain enforcement of an allegedly unconstitutional statute.   Though substitution was clearly authorized by the then-applicable statute, the Court held substitution improper since the successor officer was not liable on account of anything done or threatened by his predecessor "individually."   The Court was here loyal to the fiction permitting suits against state officers despite the Eleventh Amendment, which pretends that the officer is stripped of his official character and may be proceeded against individually if he threatens to act unconstitutionally.[21]   A later case held that the successor state officer might be substituted if he adopted the attitude of his predecessor and was proceeding or threatening to proceed to enforce an unconstitutional statute.[22]

16.   Davis, Government Officers as Defendants: Two Troublesome Problems, 1955, 104 U.Pa.L.Rev. 69, 87.

17.   7A Wright & Miller, Civil § 1960 at nn. 74–80.

18.   Moran v. Commanding Gen. of the United States Army Fin. Center, C.A. 7th, 1966, 360 F.2d 920.

19.   Gonzalez Torres v. Toledo, C.A.1st, 1978, 586 F.2d 858; Lucas v. Gardner, C.A.4th, 1972, 453 F.2d 1255, 1256 n. 1; Barnett v. Rodgers, C.A.1969, 410 F.2d 995, 997 n. 2, 133 U.S.App.D.C. 296; Lankford v. Gelston, C.A.4th, 1966, 364 F.2d 197, 205 n. 9.

20.   1933, 53 S.Ct. 682, 686, 289 U.S. 444, 458, 77 L.Ed. 1311.

21.   Ex parte Young, 1908, 28 S.Ct. 441, 209 U.S. 123, 52 L.Ed. 714.   See § 48 above.

22.   Allen v. Regents of Univ. System of Georgia, 1938, 58 S.Ct. 980, 304 U.S. 439, 82 L.Ed. 1448.

Accordingly, original Rule 25(d) required a showing of substantial need for continuing the action, and made this requirement applicable to all suits against public officers, whether state or federal, though in the light of Ex parte LaPrade it could have been limited to state officers. The amended rule does not require such a showing in any case. With federal officers the situation would seem now to be the same as it was when Ex parte LaPrade was decided. The rule has as much force as an Act of Congress and authorizes automatic substitution of a successor federal officer in all cases. If the successor does in fact disavow the policy of his predecessor, he can make such a showing, and if this does make the suit moot by usual standards, it should be dismissed as such. The burden will be on the officer to show that the suit is moot.

Where the suit is against a state officer, however, the mere fact that the rule purports to authorize substitution cannot make such substitution proper, any more than did the statute in force when Ex parte LaPrade was decided. Substitution will still be within the letter of the rule, and will avoid much waste motion in the judicial process, but here the action must be dismissed as moot unless the plaintiff makes the needed showing that the officer threatens to continue the policy of his predecessor.[23]

Rule 25(d)(2) provides that when a public officer sues or is sued in his official capacity, he may be described as a party by his official title rather than by name.[24] Encouragement of this practice will minimize formal proceedings to change the name on the pleadings. Wherever automatic substitution is possible under Rule 25(d)(1) there will be no difficulty. The successor will be deemed to have been substituted and the action will continue under his official title just as it began under his predecessor's official title. But where Rule 25(d)(1) is ineffective without more to work a substitution, the action cannot be continued simply because the title of the officer, rather than his name, is contained on the pleadings. Thus it has been seen that if LaPrade succeeds Peterson as Attorney General of Arizona, the suit, for constitutional reasons, cannot be continued against LaPrade in the absence of a showing that he intends to continue Peterson's policy of enforcement of the challenged statute. The same result would have to be reached even if the litigation had originally been entitled "Atchison, T. & S. F. R. Co. v. Attorney General of Arizona," rather than naming Peterson as defendant. Indeed to caption the suit as against the Attorney General, rather than against Peterson, would expose so conspicuously the fiction on which suits against state of-

23. Spomer v. Littleton, 1974, 94 S.Ct. 685, 414 U.S. 514, 38 L.Ed.2d 694; Four Star Publications, Inc. v. Erbe, C.A.8th, 1962, 304 F.2d 872; Hirsch v. Green, D.C.Md.1974, 382 F.Supp. 187. Comment, Substitution Under Federal Rule of Civil Procedure 25(d): Mootness and Related Problems, 1975, 43 U.Chi.L.Rev. 151, takes the position that it is for the successor to show that the case is moot rather than for plaintiff to show that it is not. This seems unsound in principle and inconsistent with the cases.

24. 7A Wright & Miller, Civil § 1961.

ficers rest that it may well be doubted whether use of the title, rather than the name, is ever proper in such a suit.

§ 78. Joinder of Claims [1]

At common law the joinder of claims was limited by the system of the forms of action. With certain limited exceptions only those claims that fell under the same form might be joined. Joinder was much freer in equity, with the discretion of the court in permitting joinder limited only by a vague doctrine of avoiding "multifariousness," although there were statements from the chancellors that the claims joined should arise out of the same transaction or transactions connected with the same subject matter. Because of the separate systems of law and equity, it was not possible in either court to join a legal claim with an equitable claim. The Field Code attempted to combine the legal and equitable rules on joinder. It listed a number of classes of claims that might be joined. These permitted joinder of claims based on legal similarities, and resembled, though they did not follow, the joinder permitted at law under the forms of action. In addition a final class permitted joinder of all claims that arose out of the same transaction or transactions connected with the same subject of action, and thus incorporated what was thought to be the equitable rule. These provisions were not satisfactory. The specified classes were entirely arbitrary and little used, while the "same transaction" clause suffered from its own vice of being so vague as to defy definition.

The rules, in accord with later developments under more modern codes, proceed on an entirely different basis. All the restrictions on joinder of claims are abrogated. Rule 18 must be read, however, in connection with Rule 42(b), which permits the court to order separate trial of any claim or any issue. Thus joinder of claims is no longer a matter rigidly restricted at the pleading stage, but instead is made a matter of the court's discretion in shaping the trial.

Under Rule 18(a) it is true that "where the claims are against the same defendants, certainly there can be no misjoinder of claims in a civil action." [2] It is equally true that there can be no misjoinder of claims on behalf of the same plaintiffs. The rule permits joinder of legal claims with equitable claims, of claims resting on different legal theories, and even of inconsistent claims. [3]

Rule 18(b) expressly authorizes joinder of two claims though heretofore one of them would have been cognizable only after the other

[§ 78]

1. 6 Wright & Miller, Civil §§ 1581–1594; James & Hazard, Civil Procedure, 2d ed. 1977, §§ 10.1–10.6. Bauman, Multiple Liability, Multiple Remedies, and the Federal Rules of Civil Procedure, 1962, 46 Minn.L.Rev.

729; Note, Joinder of Actions, 1952, 40 Ky.L.Rev. 105.

2. Atlantic Lumber Corp. v. Southern Pac. Co., D.C.Or.1941, 2 F.R.D. 313–314 (per Fee, J.).

3. 6 Wright & Miller, Civil § 1582.

claim had been prosecuted to a conclusion. This is particularly intended to permit joinder of a claim for a sum of money and a claim to set aside a fraudulent conveyance of property that would be subject to the money judgment except for the conveyance.[4] On its face it would seem to permit joinder of a claim against a tortfeasor with a claim against his liability insurer but the courts generally have refused to permit such joinder under the rule.[5]

Rule 18 permits joinder. It does not compel it. Some commentators have suggested that for efficient dispatch of litigation there should be compulsory joinder of all claims one litigant has against another,[6] but the rules do not go so far.[7] However the doctrine of res judicata—or "claim preclusion," as it is now known—prevents "splitting" and requires all grounds upon which a single claim is based to be asserted and concluded in one action, on pain of being barred from separate suit.[8]

Whether joinder is permitted is governed by Rule 18 regardless of what state law may be.[9] Federal jurisdictional requirements must of course be observed in joining claims, but these will not usually be restrictive.[10] If there is diversity between the parties permitting suit on one claim, the same diversity will exist for all other claims that may be joined. In a suit between a single plaintiff and a single defendant, the claims may be aggregated in determining the amount in

4. Nowell v. Dick, C.A.5th, 1969, 413 F.2d 1204; Graff v. Nieberg, C.A.7th, 1956, 233 F.2d 860; Nelson v. Maiden, D.C.Tenn.1975, 402 F.Supp. 1307; 6 Wright & Miller, Civil §§ 1590–1593.

5. E.g., Headrick v. Smoky Mountain Stages, Inc., D.C.Tenn.1950, 11 F.R.D. 205; Pennsylvania R. Co. v. Lattavo Bros., Inc., D.C.Ohio 1949, 9 F.R.D. 205; Pitcairn v. Rumsey, D.C.Mich. 1940, 32 F.Supp. 146. Contra: U. S. v. Cisco Aircraft, Inc., D.C.Mont.1972, 54 F.R.D. 181; cf. Millers' Nat. Ins. Co., Chicago, Ill. v. Wichita Flour Mills Co., C.A.10th, 1958, 257 F.2d 93, 104. See 6 Wright & Miller, Civil § 1594.

6. Blume, Required Joinder of Claims, 1947, 45 Mich.L.Rev. 797, 812; Clark, Cases on Modern Pleading, 1952, p. 730; Schopflocher, What Is A Single Cause of Action for the Purpose of the Doctrine of Res Judicata?, 1942, 21 Ore.L.Rev. 319; Hyde, J., in Chamberlain v. Mo.-Ark. Coach Lines, Inc., 1945, 189 S.W.2d 538, 540, 354 Mo. 461, 467.

7. Fowler Mfg. Co. v. Gorlick, C.A.9th, 1969, 415 F.2d 1248, 1254 n. 4, certiorari denied 90 S.Ct. 571, 396 U.S. 1012, 24 L.Ed.2d 503; Leimer v. Woods, C.A. 8th, 1952, 196 F.2d 828. But see Shel-

ley v. The Maccabees, D.C.N.Y.1961, 191 F.Supp. 742, 745.

8. Restatement Second of Judgments, 1982, §§ 24–26. Section 24(1) defines the "claim" as including "all rights of the plaintiff to remedies against the defendant with respect to all or any part of the transaction, or series of connected transactions, out of which the action arose." Section 24(2) goes on to say that what factual groupings constitute a "transaction" or a "series" are to be "determined pragmatically, giving weight to such considerations as to whether the facts are related in time, space, origin, or motivation, whether they form a convenient trial unit, and whether their treatment as a unit conforms to the parties' expectations or business understanding or usage." See 18 Wright, Miller & Cooper, Jurisdiction §§ 4407, 4408.

9. Har-Pen Truck Lines, Inc. v. Mills, C.A.5th, 1967, 378 F.2d 705, 708–709; Huntress v. Huntress' Estate, C.A.7th, 1956, 235 F.2d 205; cf. Provident Tradesmens Bank & Trust Co. v. Patterson, 1968, 88 S.Ct. 733, 746 n. 22, 390 U.S. 102, 125 n. 22, 19 L.Ed.2d 936.

10. 6 Wright & Miller, Civil § 1588.

controversy.[11] Where the basis of jurisdiction is a federal claim, however, plaintiff may not join with it a separate and distinct nonfederal claim, unless diversity exists.[12] If, however, the two claims are closely enough related on their facts, the court has power to exercise "pendent jurisdiction" over the nonfederal claim if it chooses to do so.[13]

The only difficult problem the courts discovered was where there were both multiple claims and multiple parties. This problem was resolved by amendments of Rules 18 and 20 in 1966. The problem is clearly presented by the case of Federal Housing Administrator v. Christianson,[14] decided soon after the rules went into effect. Plaintiff held two promissory notes, each of which had been made and endorsed to it the same day. Three persons, whom it joined as defendants, were liable to plaintiff on one of the notes, while two of the same three persons were liable on the other note. The court held that there was no question of law or fact common to both notes and that the joinder was improper. Accordingly it ordered the claims severed under Rule 21. The case was probably too restrictive in its understanding of what is a common question,[15] but for present purposes the significant feature of the case was its assumption that the question of law or fact must be common to the claims joined, rather than to the parties. This was similar to the assumption of some courts and writers that multiple claims could be joined in a multiple party case only if the claims arose out of the same transaction, occurrence, or series of transactions or occurrences.

This kind of problem arose in many cases. Probably a majority of them took the same approach as in Christianson, and applied the limitations of Rule 20 to the claims sought to be joined rather than the parties. There is good reason to think that this was an incorrect construction of the former rules as they stood.[16] However that may be, it surely was an undesirable result since it put a limitation on joinder at the pleading stage and thus provided "a ready-made issue to be wrangled over upon the pleadings."[17] It makes much more sense to

11. Griffin v. Red Run Lodge, Inc., C.A. 4th, 1979, 610 F.2d 1198, 1204; Hales v. Winn-Dixie Stores, Inc., C.A.4th, 1974, 500 F.2d 836, 846; MGD Graphic System, Inc. v. A & A Bindery, Inc., D.C.Pa.1977, 76 F.R.D. 66. See § 36 above.

This result has been reached even when plaintiff holds the claims in different capacities. DeLorenzo v. Federal Deposit Ins. Corp., D.C.N.Y.1966, 259 F.Supp. 193, 197, or is the assignee of some of the claims, La-Tex Supply Co. v. Fruehauf Trailer Div., C.A.5th, 1971, 444 F.2d 1366, certiorari denied 92 S.Ct. 287, 404 U.S. 942, 30 L.Ed.2d 256.

12. Delman v. Federal Products Corp., C.A.1st, 1958, 251 F.2d 123; Eisen-

mann v. Gould-Nat. Batteries, Inc., D.C.Pa.1958, 169 F.Supp. 862; Darwin v. Jess Hickey Oil Corp., D.C.Tex.1957, 153 F.Supp. 667.

13. United Mine Workers of America v. Gibbs, 1966, 86 S.Ct. 1130, 383 U.S. 715, 16 L.Ed.2d 218. See § 19 above.

14. D.C.Conn.1939, 26 F.Supp. 419.

15. See § 71 above.

16. For complete analysis of the cases under the former rule, see Wright, Joinder of Claims and Parties under Modern Pleading Rules, 1952, 36 Minn. L.Rev. 580, 604–611.

17. Kaplan, Continuing Work of the Civil Committee: 1966 Amendments of the

allow joinder in a case like Christianson and then allow the court to decide whether to order separate trials under Rule 42(b). Indeed in Christianson itself the court, after ordering severance, held open the possibility that both claims would later be consolidated for trial.

The 1966 amendments make clear beyond any doubt that the desirable result is to be reached in situations like Christianson. Rule 20(a) was amended to speak of "these persons" and of "defendants" rather than "of them," and thus the restrictions of that rule cannot even colorably be read as applying to the claims joined rather than the parties. But it was thought that the principle went beyond the precise situation involved in Christianson, in which unrelated claims are asserted affecting fewer than all parties permissively joined under Rule 20, and that it should apply to claims against any opposing party, no matter what the basis for joining him. Accordingly Rule 18 was completely rewritten and now makes it clear that any party who has asserted a claim for relief against an opposing party or parties may join with it whatever other claims he may have, regardless of their nature, against any opposing party.[18]

§ 79. Counterclaims [1]

The provisions of Rule 13 dealing with counterclaims permit any claim that defendant has against the plaintiff to be asserted as a counterclaim, thereby avoiding multiplicity of actions. It is immaterial whether the counterclaim is legal or equitable, in contract or in tort, or even whether it has any connection with plaintiff's claim. As with the other joinder rules, the theory is to allow unlimited joinder at the pleading stage, with power in the court to order separate trial of a particular issue if this is in fact more convenient or desirable.[2] The rule does not interfere with the right of jury trial. Despite some fears expressed at the time Rule 13 was adopted, it is now settled that the pleading of a legal counterclaim, whether compulsory or permissive, in an equitable action does not waive defendant's right to jury trial on his counterclaim.[3]

Federal Rules of Civil Procedure (II), 1968, 81 Harv.L.Rev. 591, 595.

18. Id. at 595–598.

See First Nat. Bank of Cincinnati v. Pepper, C.A.2d, 1972, 454 F.2d 626, 635 (cross-claims); Schwab v. Erie Lackawanna R. Co., C.A.3d, 1971, 438 F.2d 62, 68–72 (additional claim against third-party defendant). Although the joinder of all of these claims is now proper as a pleading matter, there may be questions whether independent jurisdictional grounds are needed for the added claims. See U. S. for Use of Payne v. United Pac. Ins. Co., C.A.9th, 1973, 472 F.2d 792, certiorari denied 93 S.Ct. 2273, 411 U.S. 982, 36 L.Ed.2d 958. See also § 76 n. 15 above.

[§ 79]

1. 6 Wright & Miller, Civil §§ 1401–1430, 1434–1437; Kennedy, Counterclaims Under Federal Rule 13, 1974, 11 Hous.L.Rev. 255; Wright, Estoppel by Rule: The Compulsory Counterclaim under Modern Pleading, 1954, 38 Minn.L.Rev. 423, 39 Iowa L.Rev. 255; Green, Federal Jurisdiction over Counterclaims, 1953, 48 Nw.U.L.Rev. 271.

2. Rules 13(i), 42(b): 6 Wright & Miller, Civil § 1437.

3. Beacon Theatres, Inc. v. Westover, 1959, 79 S.Ct. 948, 359 U.S. 500, 3 L.Ed.2d 988; Beaunit Mills v. Eday Fabric Sales Corp., C.C.A.2d, 1942, 124

The rules recognize two different kinds of counterclaims. If defendant's claim falls under Rule 13(a), it is a "compulsory counterclaim" and must be asserted as such or be forever barred. Any claim defendant has against plaintiff that does not fit the definition of Rule 13(a) is a "permissive counterclaim"; Rule 13(b) permits defendant to assert such a claim as a counterclaim but does not compel him to do so.

In an action in personam [4] a claim defendant has against plaintiff is a compulsory counterclaim if it meets four conditions. It must: (1) arise "out of the transaction or occurrence that is the subject matter of the opposing party's claim;" (2) be matured and owned by the pleader at the time he serves his pleading;[5] (3) not require for its adjudication the presence of third parties of whom the court cannot acquire personal jurisdiction;[6] and (4) not have been, at the time the original action was commenced, the subject matter of another pending action.[7]

Of these tests only the first, that the claim arise out of the transaction or occurrence that is the subject of the opposing party's claim, has given difficulty. It leaves at large the critical question of what is a "transaction or occurrence." The courts quite wisely have refrained from attempting to define this phrase; such definitions are so abstract as to be of little practical value.[8] Instead they have preferred to suggest tests by which the compulsory or permissive nature of a specific counterclaim can be determined.

It has been said that the test is whether the issues of fact and law on the counterclaim are largely the same.[9] Such a test would be unworkable, since it is impossible to know what the issues will be until

---

F.2d 563; 6 Wright & Miller, Civil § 1405.

4. Under a 1963 amendment to Rule 13(a), a counterclaim is not compulsory if the plaintiff brought suit upon his claim by attachment or other process by which the court did not acquire jurisdiction to render a personal judgment on the claim.

5. Though not stated in terms, this requirement is fairly implied from Rule 13(e). Stahl v. Ohio River Co., C.A.3d, 1970, 424 F.2d 52; Bose Corp. v. Consumers Union of the U. S., Inc., D.C. Mass.1974, 384 F.Supp. 600; 6 Wright & Miller, Civil § 1411, pp. 55–57.

If the action is terminated before defendant serves a pleading, the compulsory counterclaim rule never becomes operative. Martino v. McDonald's System, Inc., C.A.7th, 1979, 598 F.2d 1079, certiorari denied 100 S.Ct. 455, 444 U.S. 966, 62 L.Ed.2d 379; Lawhorn v. Atlantic Ref. Co., C.A.5th, 1962, 299 F.2d 353.

6. Rule 13(a) says only "cannot acquire jurisdiction," but since the bringing in of additional parties to respond to a compulsory counterclaim does not destroy diversity jurisdiction, regardless of their citizenship, see note 63 below, the rule must have reference to personal jurisdiction. United Artists Corp. v. Masterpiece Productions, Inc., C.A.2d, 1955, 221 F.2d 213.

7. Southern Constr. Co. v. Pickard, 1962, 83 S.Ct. 108, 371 U.S. 57, 9 L.Ed. 2d 31; See Union Paving Co. v. Downer Corp., C.A.9th, 1960, 276 F.2d 468, 470.

8. See the definition attempted in Williams v. Robinson, D.C.D.C.1940, 1 F.R.D. 211, 213: "* * * whatever may be done by one person which affects another's rights and out of which a cause of action may arise."

9. See Nachtman v. Crucible Steel Co. of America, C.A.3d, 1948, 165 F.2d 997, 999.

after the plaintiff has replied to the counterclaim, if then. In addition, it would require discarding many authoritative decisions as wrongly decided. In the leading case of Moore v. New York Cotton Exchange,[10] the issue on plaintiff's claim was whether defendants were violating the antitrust laws by refusing to give him ticker service, while the issue on the counterclaim was whether plaintiff was purloining quotations from defendant's exchange and using them for a "bucket shop" operation. Yet the Supreme Court held the counterclaim compulsory.

Again it is said that "everyone agrees" that the "acid test" in distinguishing compulsory from permissive counterclaims is whether the counterclaim would be barred by res judicata if there were no compulsory counterclaim rule.[11] This is no test at all, for the authoritative doctrine is that, absent a compulsory counterclaim rule, a pleader is not barred from suing independently on a claim that he refrained from pleading as a counterclaim in a prior action.[12]

A third test suggested by some courts is whether substantially the same evidence will support or refute the plaintiff's claim and the counterclaim.[13] It is hard to imagine a case where such an identity exists in which the counterclaim should not be held to be compulsory; indeed the purpose of compelling counterclaims, to prevent relitigation of the same set of facts, requires that the counterclaim be held compulsory where it does turn on the same evidence as plaintiff's claim. But the converse proposition is not equally obvious. Repeatedly a counterclaim has been held compulsory where it arises from the same events as does plaintiff's claim, even though the evidence needed to prove the opposing claims may be greatly different.[14] In the very simplest situation, a suit to void an insurance policy for fraud with a counterclaim for the amount of the loss, the evidence of fraud is likely to be entirely different from the evidence as to the loss and amount; yet there can be no sound reason for permitting two suits to settle this one controversy between the parties.[15]

---

10. 1926, 46 S.Ct. 367, 270 U.S. 593, 70 L.Ed. 750.

11. Frank, J., dissenting in Libbey-Owens-Ford Glass Co. v. Sylvania Indus. Corp., C.C.A.2d, 1946, 154 F.2d 814, 817; Big Cola Corp. v. World Bottling Co., C.C.A.6th, 1943, 134 F.2d 718; American Samec Corp. v. Florian, D.C.Conn.1949, 9 F.R.D. 718, 719; Non-Ferrous Metals, Inc. v. Saramar Aluminum Co., D.C.Ohio 1960, 25 F.R.D. 102, 105; see Beach v. KDI Corp., C.A.3d, 1974, 490 F.2d 1312, 1321 n. 16.

12. Restatement Second of Judgments, 1982, § 22. A very limited exception to the rule stated in the text is set forth in subsection (2)(b) of § 22. The exception was found to be applicable in

Martino v. McDonald's System, Inc., C.A.7th, 1979, 598 F.2d 1079, certiorari denied 100 S.Ct. 455, 444 U.S. 966, 62 L.Ed.2d 379.

13. Williams v. Robinson, D.C.D.C.1940, 1 F.R.D. 211, 213; Kuster Laboratories v. Lee, D.C.Cal.1950, 10 F.R.D. 350, 351; American Samec Corp. v. Florian, D.C.Conn.1949, 9 F.R.D. 718, 719; Non-Ferrous Metals, Inc. v. Saramar Aluminum Co., D.C.Ohio 1960, 25 F.R.D. 102, 105; cf. Hoosier Cas. Co. of Indianapolis, Ind. v. Fox, D.C.Iowa 1952, 102 F.Supp. 214, 227.

14. See cases cited 6 Wright & Miller, Civil § 1410 nn. 52–56.

15. Mercury Ins. Co. v. Verea, D.C.N.Y. 1949, 12 Fed.Rules Serv. 13a.11, case 2.

Finally there is what has been correctly called "the one compelling test of compulsoriness."[16] Any claim a party has against an opposing party that is logically related to the claim the opposing party is suing on, and that is not within the exceptions listed in the rule, is a compulsory counterclaim. Under the former equity rule from which Rule 13(a) is derived, the Supreme Court had said that " 'transaction' is a word of flexible meaning. It may comprehend a series of many occurrences, depending not so much upon the immediateness of their connection as upon their logical relationship."[17] There is now an immense body of decisions accepting this test of logical relation as controlling under the present rule.[18] Most other decisions, though not stating such a test in terms, seem entirely consistent with it.[19] Indeed the very fewness of cases, and these from inferior courts, where counterclaims that meet the test of logical relation have been held not compulsory is itself instructive.[20] There is one Supreme Court dictum that is difficult to reconcile with this test,[21] but it has been sharply criticized [22] and the lower courts have refused to regard it as precedent for other that its own limited facts.[23]

16. Rosenthal v. Fowler, D.C.N.Y.1952, 12 F.R.D. 388, 391. See also Pipeliners Local Union No. 798 v. Ellerd, C.A.10th, 1974, 503 F.2d 1193, 1199, where it is called "the most controlling" test.

17. Moore v. New York Cotton Exchange, 1926, 46 S.Ct. 367, 371, 270 U.S. 593, 610, 70 L.Ed. 750.

18. Baker v. Gold Seal Liquors, Inc., 1974, 94 S.Ct. 2504, 2506 n. 1, 417 U.S. 467, 469 n. 1, 41 L.Ed.2d 243; and cases cited 6 Wright & Miller, Civil § 1410 n. 45. But see Bose Corp. v. Consumers Union of the U. S., Inc., D.C.Mass.1974, 384 F.Supp. 600, 603, where the logical relation test is criticized for its uncertainty of application and potential overbreadth.

19. See generally 6 Wright & Miller, Civil § 1410, and the cases discussed therein.

20. Such cases are Big Cola Corp. v. World Bottling Co., C.C.A.6th, 1943, 134 F.2d 718; Dundee Wine & Spirits, Ltd. v. Glenmore Distilleries Co., D.C. N.Y.1965, 238 F.Supp. 283; Kuster Laboratories v. Lee, D.C.Cal.1950, 10 F.R.D. 350; Marks v. Spitz, D.C.Mass. 1945, 4 F.R.D. 348; and cf. Williams v. Robinson, D.C.D.C.1940, 1 F.R.D. 211.

21. See Mercoid Corp. v. Mid-Continent Inv. Co., 1944, 64 S.Ct. 268, 273–274, 320 U.S. 661, 670–672, 88 L.Ed. 376, where the Supreme Court said, quite unnecessarily, that in an action for patent infringement, defendant's claim for damages for conspiracy to create a monopoly by means of the patents is not a compulsory counterclaim.

22. See Lewis Mfg. Co. v. Chisholm-Ryder Co., D.C.Pa.1979, 82 F.R.D. 745, 750; Douglas v. Wisconsin Alumni Research Foundation, D.C.Ill.1948, 81 F.Supp. 167, 170; 6 Wright & Miller, Civil § 1412, pp. 61–64.

23. U. S. v. Eastport S. S. Corp., C.A.2d, 1958, 255 F.2d 795, 805; Dolfi Music, Inc. v. Forest Inn, Inc., D.C.Wis.1973, 59 F.R.D. 5. See also Addressograph-Multigraph Corp. v. Cooper, C.C.A.2d, 1946, 156 F.2d 483, 488 (dissenting opinion).

But an attitude similar to that taken in the Mercoid case is evident in recent decisions that have held that in a suit by a borrower under the Truth in Lending Act, 15 U.S.C.A. § 1601 et seq., the lender's claim for the underlying debt is not a compulsory counterclaim. Valencia v. Anderson Bros. Ford, C.A.7th, 1980, 617 F.2d 1278, 1290–1292, reversed on other grounds 1981, 101 S.Ct. 2266, 452 U.S. 205, 68 L.Ed.2d 783; Whigham v. Beneficial Fin. Co., C.A.4th, 1979, 599 F.2d 1322. The Fifth Circuit holds the claim compulsory. Plant v. Blazer Financial Services, Inc., C.A.5th, 1979, 598 F.2d 1357, noted 1979, 10 Mem.St.L.Rev. 169.

It is entirely accepted that failure to assert a claim as a compulsory counterclaim precludes the party from later bringing an independent action on the claim, though the rules nowhere so provide, and the theoretical basis of this result is not clear. There is talk in the literature of "res judicata," of "merger," of "bar," and of "waiver,"[24] but the soundest analysis is that of a state court, interpreting rules virtually the same as the federal rules, which said that Rule 13 does not create the absolute bar of res judicata but is "a bar created by rule * * * which logically is in the nature of an estoppel arising from the culpable conduct of a litigant in failing to assert a proper counterclaim."[25] Such an analysis affords a means, if it be thought desirable, of extricating from the rigors of the compulsory rule the defendant who has never knowingly refrained from asserting his claim,[26] a situation that is particularly important where an insurance company has controlled the defense of the first action,[27] and it is a more flexible tool for handling the cases of a default judgment or a consent judgment or a dismissal after a compromise agreement.[28]

Considering the great number of jurisdictions that compel counterclaims, it is remarkable that there have been so few cases in which a party has actually been held to be barred because of his failure to plead his claim as a counterclaim in a prior action.[29] The reason is obvious: jurisdictions that make some counterclaims compulsory almost invariably provide, as in the federal rules, that any other counterclaim, not compulsory, may be pleaded. Thus the careful attorney can and will plead all his client's claims as counterclaims if there is any reason at all to think that they may be compulsory. Further, under Rule 13(f), the courts have power, which has been liberally exercised, to permit amendment to assert a compulsory counterclaim

24. See 6 Wright & Miller, Civil § 1417, nn. 33–35.

25. House v. Hanson, 1955, 72 N.W.2d 874, 877, 245 Minn. 466, 470. See also Dindo v. Whitney, C.A.1st, 1971, 451 F.2d 1, 3; Reynolds v. Hartford Acc. & Indem. Co., D.C.N.Y.1967, 278 F.Supp. 331, 332–333; Wright, Estoppel by Rule: The Compulsory Counterclaim under Modern Pleading, 1954, 38 Minn. L.Rev. 423, 428–436; Vestal, Claim Preclusion by Rule, 1968, 2 Indiana Leg.J. 25; Kennedy, note 1 above, at 260.

26. LaFollette v. Herron, D.C.Tenn. 1962, 211 F.Supp. 919.

27. Compare Reynolds v. Hartford Acc. & Indem. Co., D.C.N.Y.1967, 278 F.Supp. 331, with Kennedy v. Jones, D.C.Va.1968, 44 F.R.D. 42. See Dindo v. Whitney, C.A.1st, 1971, 451 F.2d 1.

28. Compare Benjamin v. U. S., 1965, 348 F.2d 502, 172 Ct.Cl. 118 and Doug-las v. Wisconsin Alumni Research Foundation, D.C.Ill.1948, 81 F.Supp. 167, with Schott v. Colonial Baking Co., D.C.Ark.1953, 111 F.Supp. 13, and Firemen's Ins. Co. of Newark v. L. P. Steuart & Bro., Inc., D.C.Mun.App. 1960, 158 A.2d 675.

29. The only federal cases so holding seem to be: New Britain Mach. Co. v. Yeo, C.A.6th, 1966, 358 F.2d 397; U. S. v. Eastport S. S. Corp., C.A.2d, 1958, 255 F.2d 795; Twin Disc, Inc. v. Lowell, D.C.Wis.1975, 69 F.R.D. 64; Kennedy v. Jones, D.C.Va.1968, 44 F.R.D. 52; Reconstruction Fin. Corp. v. First Nat. Bank of Cody, D.C.Wyo.1955, 17 F.R.D. 397; and Schott v. Colonial Baking Co., D.C.Ark.1953, 111 F.Supp. 13. State cases reaching this result are listed in Wright, Estoppel by Rule: The Compulsory Counterclaim under Modern Pleading, 1954, 38 Minn.L.Rev. 423, 432 n. 53.

that has been omitted.[30] In a deserving case it is even possible to reopen the judgment, under Rule 60(b), and allow pleading of the omitted compulsory counterclaim after the first action has been terminated.[31]

Several cases have held that the bar created by the compulsory counterclaim rule applies only after the first action has gone to judgment, and that the fact that a claim should have been asserted as a counterclaim in an action then pending is not ground for abatement of a second action in which it is sued on independently.[32] These decisions seem inconsistent with the purposes of Rule 13(a) since they permit duplicative litigation of the sort the rule is intended to prevent.[33]

The compulsory counterclaim rule is applicable even though state law has no such requirement.[34] A more difficult question is whether the states must refuse to hear a suit that would be barred in federal court for failure to have pleaded it as a compulsory counterclaim. It is held that a federal court may not enjoin prosecution in a state court of what should be a compulsory counterclaim in a pending federal action,[35] but this is because of the general reluctance of federal

30. E.g., Safeway Trails v. Allentown & Reading Transit Co., C.A.4th, 1950, 185 F.2d 918 (lawyer had never read federal rules); 6 Wright & Miller, Civil § 1430.

31. Williams v. Blitz, C.A.4th, 1955, 226 F.2d 463.

32. ACF Indus., Inc. v. Hecht, D.C.Kan. 1967, 284 F.Supp. 572; Local Union 499, Intl. Broth. of Elec. Workers, AFL–CIO v. Iowa Power & Light Co., D.C.Iowa 1964, 224 F.Supp. 731; Bellmore Sales Corp. v. Winfield Drug Stores, Inc., D.C.N.Y.1960, 187 F.Supp. 161. But cf. Semmes Motors, Inc. v. Ford Motor Co., C.A.2d, 1970, 429 F.2d 1197 (second action stayed).

33. See United Broadcasting Co. v. Armes, C.A.5th, 1975, 506 F.2d 766, certiorari denied 95 S.Ct. 1953, 421 U.S. 965, 44 L.Ed.2d 452, holding that a federal court may enjoin prosecution in another federal court of an action that should have been asserted as a compulsory counterclaim. See 6 Wright & Miller, Civil § 1418.

34. G & M Tire Co. v. Dunlop Tire & Rubber Corp., D.C.Miss.1964, 36 F.R.D. 440; Note, The Erie Doctrine and Federal Rule 13(a), 1962, 46 Minn. L.Rev. 913; cf. Sinkbeil v. Handler, D.C.Neb.1947, 7 F.R.D. 92; O'Donnell v. Archie's Motor Exp., D.C.Pa.1959, 176 F.Supp. 36. But cf. Intra-Mar Shipping (Cuba) S. A. v. John S. Emery & Co., D.C.N.Y.1951, 11 F.R.D. 284.

Indeed a counterclaim is compulsory under Rule 13 even though under relevant state law the party would lack capacity to bring an independent action on the claim. Tolson v. Hodge, C.A. 4th, 1969, 411 F.2d 123; Avondale Shipyards, Inc. v. Propulsion Systems, Inc., D.C.La.1971, 53 F.R.D. 341, noted 1972, 26 Sw.L.J. 437, 18 Wayne L.Rev. 1619.

35. Counter v. Bedford, D.C.Ark.1976, 420 F.Supp. 927; Nolen v. Hammet Co., D.C.S.C.1972, 56 F.R.D. 361; L. F. Dommerich & Co. v. Bress, D.C.N.J. 1968, 280 F.Supp. 590, 599; Reines Distributors, Inc. v. Admiral Corp., D.C. N.Y.1960, 182 F.Supp. 226; Fantecchi v. Gross, D.C.Pa.1957, 158 F.Supp. 684, appeal dismissed C.A.3d, 1958, 255 F.2d 299; Red Top Trucking Corp. v. Seaboard Freight Lines, D.C.N.Y.1940, 35 F.Supp. 740. See 6 Wright & Miller, Civil § 1418.

But if the federal action has gone to judgment, the federal court can enjoin a state action on what should have been a compulsory counterclaim under the exception to the Anti-Injunction Act, 28 U.S.C.A. § 2283, allowing a federal court to enjoin state proceedings where necessary to protect and effectuate its judgment. Brown v. McCormick, C.A.10th, 1979, 608 F.2d 410. See § 47 above.

courts to enjoin state actions, and does not suggest that the states are free to disregard the failure of the pleader to put forward his federal counterclaim.

There are some cases in which state courts managed to find means of allowing the second suit, without passing on the general question of whether a federal procedure rule can bar a party from bringing a suit in state court.[36] And in one case a state court held that failure to plead what would plainly have been a compulsory counterclaim in federal court did not prevent later suit on the claim in state court, but did so on the basis of a quite erroneous notion that the pleader would not have been barred from independent suit in federal court.[37]

If Rule 13(a) is a mere rule of procedure, then, on well-understood principles of conflicts of laws, it should have no extra-territorial effect.[38] But if it defines the scope of the cause of action to which res judicata will apply, or if it sets up an estoppel against the party who does not comply with it, the defendant should be barred no matter where he attempts to sue. The effect of a judgment as res judicata is "substantive" and other jurisdictions must regard it as being as broad and conclusive as it would be in the jurisdiction in which it was rendered. So too if a party so conducts himself as to erect an estoppel against prosecution of his claim, the estoppel is personal to him and may be asserted against him wherever he sues. On such reasoning a number of state courts have properly held a claim barred for failure to plead it as a counterclaim in a federal action.[39]

Any claim whatever that a party against whom a claim is made has against an opposing party may be pleaded as a permissive counterclaim, if its assertion is not compelled as a compulsory counterclaim.[40] There are a few apparent court-made exceptions. On grounds of a public policy in having such proceedings decided swiftly

36. Campbell v. Ashler, 1946, 70 N.E.2d 302, 320 Mass. 475, criticized 1948, 15 U.Chi.L.Rev. 446; Detroit, T. & I. R. Co. v. Pitzer, 1943, 61 N.E.2d 93, 42 Ohio Law Abst. 494.

37. Phoenix Ins. Co. v. Haney, 1959, 108 So.2d 227, 235 Miss. 60, certiorari denied 79 S.Ct. 1435, 360 U.S. 917, 3 L.Ed.2d 1534, criticized 1960, 73 Harv. L.Rev. 1410.

38. In Chapman v. Aetna Fin. Co., C.A.5th, 1980, 615 F.2d 361, it was held that the Georgia compulsory counterclaim rule is "essentially procedural," and that the Full Faith and Credit statute, 28 U.S.C.A. § 1738, does not require a federal court to dismiss a suit that would have been barred in state court for failure to interpose the claim as a counterclaim in an earlier state action. Nevertheless the court held that

as a matter of comity the federal court should refuse to hear a suit that both under state law and under Rule 13(a) should have been a compulsory counterclaim in an earlier suit.

39. London v. City of Philadelphia, 1963, 194 A.2d 901, 412 Pa. 496; Horne v. Woolever, 1959, 163 N.E.2d 378, 170 Ohio St. 178, certiorari denied 80 S.Ct. 861, 362 U.S. 951, 4 L.Ed.2d 868, noted 1960, 21 Ohio St.L.J. 251; Meacham v. Haley, 1954, 270 S.W.2d 503, 38 Tenn. App. 20; Conrad v. West, 1950, 219 P.2d 477, 98 Cal.App.2d 116; Jocie Motor Lines v. Johnson, 1950, 57 S.E.2d 388, 231 N.C. 367. See Vestal, Claim Preclusion by Rule, 1968, 2 Indiana Leg.J. 25; 6 Wright & Miller, Civil § 1417, pp. 101–102.

40. 6 Wright & Miller, Civil §§ 1420, 1421.

and without becoming ensnarled with counterclaims, it has been held that counterclaims are not permissible in an informer's qui tam action.[41] And there has been a variance of view as to whether a counterclaim must or may be pleaded where it is a type of claim that is usually required to be asserted in an independent action.[42] Such decisions as these add to the confusion of the lawyer in understanding an essentially simple rule. They would not be necessary if it is remembered that the counterclaim rule affects only the pleadings; whatever advantages there may be in independent actions can be retained through the power of the court to order separate trials, and, if need be, to enter a final judgment on the plaintiff's claim before proceeding to consider the counterclaim. Here, as elsewhere, it is dangerous to push to the pleading stage a question that properly has to do only with the method of trial.[43]

A similar approach would be desirable on the question, which has vexed the courts and led to a variety of conflicting decisions, of the capacity in which a party sues or is sued.[44] For example, in an action against the administrator of an estate for negligence of his deceased, may the defendant counterclaim for wrongful death of his intestate? A state court held that he cannot, reasoning that the administrator is sued in his capacity as the representative of the estate for the benefit of creditors, while he brings the wrongful death claim for the benefit of the statutory beneficiaries of such a claim.[45] All this is true, and can easily be taken care of in shaping the form of the judgment. But to reason from this to the conclusion that the administrator when sued is not the same person as the administrator when prosecuting a wrongful death claim, and to close with ringing declarations against "depriving of his cause of action a person who was never a party to litigation",[46] is, in the words of a commentator, "to pursue a legal fiction to an absurd extreme."[47] In this same situation other courts have refused to bemuse themselves with fiction, and have held the counterclaim permitted or compelled as the case might be.[48]

---

41. U. S. ex rel. Rodriquez v. Weekly Publications, D.C.N.Y.1947, 74 F.Supp. 763. The same result has been reached in an action to recover short-swing profits from corporate insiders. Epstein v. Shindler, D.C.N.Y.1960, 26 F.R.D. 176.

42. Compare Jewish Consumptives Relief Soc'y v. Rothfeld, D.C.N.Y.1949, 9 F.R.D. 64 (action to test title to office), and Paxton v. Desch Bldg. Block Co., Inc., D.C.Pa.1956, 146 F.Supp. 32 (replevin), with John R. Alley & Co. v. Federal Nat. Bank of Shawnee, Shawnee County, Okl., C.C.A.10th, 1942, 124 F.2d 995 (usury).

43. 6 Wright & Miller, Civil § 1425.

44. 6 Wright & Miller, Civil § 1404, pp. 15–19.

45. Campbell v. Ashler, 1946, 70 N.E.2d 302, 320 Mass. 475.

46. 70 N.E.2d at 305, 320 Mass. at 481.

47. 1948, 15 U.Chi.L.Rev. 446, 447.

48. Sams v. Beech Aircraft Corp., C.A.9th, 1980, 625 F.2d 273; Moore-McCormack Lines, Inc. v. McMahon, C.A. 2d, 1956, 235 F.2d 142; Newton v. Mitchell, Fla.1949, 42 So.2d 53, approved 1950, 4 Miami L.Q. 251; Morgan v. Rankin, 1938, 122 S.W.2d 555, 197 Ark. 119. See Tolson v. Hodge, C.A.4th 1969, 411 F.2d 123.

See also Scott v. U. S., 1965, 354 F.2d 292, 173 Ct.Cl. 650 (counterclaim against individual partner in suit by partnership); Matter of Penn Central Transp. Co., D.C.Pa.1976, 419 F.Supp. 1376 (similar).

There is more reason to draw a distinction when one claim runs for or against a party in a representative capacity and he is involved in the proposed counterclaim in an individual capacity. In those situations the counterclaim is not allowed.[49]

The rule allows a counterclaim only against an opposing party. Even one who is not formally a party of record has been found to be an opposing party within the rule,[50] but the courts are divided on whether a counterclaim will lie against members of a class who are not named as plaintiffs in a class action.[51] Even though a disinterested stakeholder is named as a plaintiff in an interpleader action, there is division on whether a counterclaim will lie against him.[52]

Another unsettled question is whether the filing of an action tolls the statute of limitations, so as to permit assertion of a counterclaim that would otherwise be barred. Probably this question is to be resolved by state law.[53] The usual doctrine, with respectable common law origins, is that an unrelated counterclaim is barred by the statute of limitations.[54] A counterclaim that arises out of the transaction or occurrence on which the action is founded may be asserted for purposes of recoupment to prevent or reduce a judgment for plaintiff but

49. E.g., Pioche Mines Consol., Inc. v. Fidelity-Philadelphia Trust Co., C.A. 9th, 1953, 206 F.2d 336, certiorari denied 74 S.Ct. 225, 346 U.S. 899, 98 L.Ed. 400; and cases cited 6 Wright & Miller, Civil § 1404 nn. 39–41.

Similarly in a suit against members of a school board as individuals it was held that a claim of the board itself against the plaintiff could not be asserted as a counterclaim. Dunham v. Crosby, C.A. 1st, 1970, 435 F.2d 1177. The Third Circuit has properly reversed a district that carried this to a fictional extreme, and had held that a state Attorney General, sued on the fiction that he was acting as an individual in enforcing an allegedly unconstitutional statute—see § 48 above—could not counterclaim on behalf of the state for enforcement of the law. Aldens, Inc. v. Packel, C.A.3d, 1975, 524 F.2d 38, 50–51.

Except in the case of closely held corporations, a counterclaim will not lie against a stockholder who brings a derivative action. Twardzik v. Sepauley, D.C.Pa.1968, 45 F.R.D. 529.

50. Legate v. Maloney, C.A.1st, 1965, 348 F.2d 164; Automated Datatron, Inc. v. Woodcock, D.C.D.C.1979, 84 F.R.D. 408.

51. Counterclaim allowed: National Super Spuds, Inc. v. New York Mercantile Exchange, D.C.N.Y.1977, 75 F.R.D. 40; Herrmann v. Atlantic Rich-

field Co., D.C.Pa.1976, 72 F.R.D. 182; Weit v. Continental Illinois Nat. Bank & Trust Co., D.C.Ill.1973, 60 F.R.D. 5; Partain v. First Nat. Bank of Montgomery, D.C.Ala.1973, 59 F.R.D. 56. Not allowed: AAMCO Automatic Transmissions, Inc. v. Tayloe, D.C.Pa. 1975, 67 F.R.D. 440; Donson Stores, Inc. v. American Bakeries Co., D.C. N.Y.1973, 58 F.R.D. 485, noted 1973, 87 Harv.L.Rev. 470; Cotchett v. Avis Rent A Car System, Inc., D.C.N.Y. 1972, 56 F.R.D. 549.

52. Counterclaim allowed: Bell v. Nutmeg Airways Corp., D.C.Conn.1975, 66 F.R.D. 1. See also 7 Wright & Miller, Civil § 1715, pp. 448–449. Not allowed: Erie Bank v. U. S. Dist. Court for Dist. of Colo., C.A.10th, 1966, 362 F.2d 539; First Nat. Bank in Dodge City v. Johnson County Nat. Bank & Trust Co., C.A.10th, 1964, 331 F.2d 325.

53. Bose Corp. v. Consumers Union of the U. S., Inc., D.C.Mass.1974, 384 F.Supp. 600; Azada v. Carson, D.C.Hawaii 1966, 252 F.Supp. 988; Keckley v. Payton, D.C.W.Va.1958, 157 F.Supp. 820. Contra: O'Donnell v. Archie's Motor Exp., D.C.Pa.1959, 176 F.Supp. 36.

54. U. S. v. Southern Cal. Edison Co., D.C.Cal.1964, 229 F.Supp. 268; McGovern v. Martz, D.C.D.C.1960, 182 F.Supp. 343; Clark, Code Pleading, 2d ed. 1947, p. 666.

affirmative relief will not be given on such a counterclaim.[55]   There are conflicting decisions on whether a counterclaim under the Federal Tort Claims Act may be asserted against the government after the two year statute has run; a majority of the decisions take the harsh view that the two year limitation is a condition on the remedy and do not permit such a counterclaim, even for recoupment.[56]   If the statute of limitations has not run on a counterclaim at the time suit is commenced, the counterclaim ought to be allowed for all purposes even though the statutory period expires between the filing of the claim and the assertion of the counterclaim.[57]

It is well settled that a compulsory counterclaim requires no independent jurisdictional grounds and is to be considered within the ancillary jurisdiction of the court.[58]   It has been argued that permissive counterclaims should be similarly treated,[59] but the courts have not accepted this argument.   They have required that a permissive counterclaim be supported by independent grounds of federal jurisdiction.[60]   The one limited exception to this is that no independent jurisdictional grounds are required for a permissive counterclaim if it is in the nature of a set-off and is used to reduce plaintiff's judgment rather than as a basis of affirmative relief.[61]

55.   Stone v. White, 1937, 57 S.Ct. 851, 301 U.S. 532, 81 L.Ed. 1265; Hartford v. Gibbons & Reed Co., C.A.10th, 1980, 617 F.2d 567; ALI Study, pp. 258–259.

56.   U. S. v. Wilkes-Barre Transit Corp., D.C.Pa.1956, 143 F.Supp. 413; U. S. v. Webb Trucking Co., D.C.Del.1956, 141 F.Supp. 573; U. S. v. W. H. Pollard Co., D.C.Cal.1954, 124 F.Supp. 495. Contra: U. S. v. Southern Pac. Co., D.C.Cal.1962, 210 F.Supp. 760; U. S. v. Capital Transit Co., D.C.D.C.1952, 108 F.Supp. 348.

57.   Azada v. Carson, D.C.Hawaii 1966, 252 F.Supp. 988. See Hartford v. Gibbons & Reed Co., C.A.10th, 1980, 617 F.2d 567, 570; 6 Wright & Miller, Civil § 1419, pp. 109–110.

58.   Baker v. Gold Seal Liquors, Inc., 1974, 94 S.Ct. 2504, 2506, n. 1, 417 U.S. 467, 469 n. 1, 41 L.Ed.2d 243; Moore v. New York Cotton Exchange, 1926, 46 S.Ct. 367, 270 U.S. 593, 70 L.Ed. 750; and cases cited 6 Wright & Miller, Civil § 1414 n. 55.

59.   Green, Federal Jurisdiction over Counterclaims, 1953, 48 Nw.U.L.Rev. 271, 282–285. Another commentator suggests that a permissive counterclaim need not satisfy the requirement of amount in controversy. Fraser, Ancillary Jurisdiction and the Joinder of Claims in the Federal Courts, 1963, 33 F.R.D. 27, 28–31.

In a concurring opinion in U. S. for Use & Benefit of D'Agostino Excavators, Inc. v. Heyward-Robinson Co., C.A.2d, 1970, 430 F.2d 1077, 1088, Judge Friendly said that he "would now reject the conventional learning" and would hold that a permissive counterclaim does not require independent jurisdictional grounds. It is doubtful if Judge Friendly would renew that suggestion after Owen Equipment & Erection Co. v. Kroger, 1978, 98 S.Ct. 2396, 2403, 437 U.S. 365, 374–375, 57 L.Ed.2d 274. The Court there rejected the notion that a common nucleus of operative fact is enough for the exercise of ancillary jurisdiction. A permissive counterclaim would not even have such a common nucleus.

60.   Federman v. Empire Fire & Marine Ins. Co., C.A.2d, 1979, 597 F.2d 798, 812–813; Sue & Sam Mfg. Co. v. B–L–S Constr. Co., C.A.4th, 1976, 538 F.2d 1048, 1071; and cases cited 6 Wright & Miller, Civil § 1422 n. 26.

61.   Curtis v. J. E. Caldwell & Co., D.C. Pa.1980, 86 F.R.D. 454; Binnick v. Avco Financial Services of Nebraska, Inc., D.C.Neb.1977, 435 F.Supp. 359; and cases cited 6 Wright & Miller, Civil § 1422 n. 31. See also Fraser, note 59 above, at 31–34.

Venue is no problem with regard to counterclaims. The venue statutes speak of where a suit may be "brought." The courts construe this literally, holding that the suit is already brought by the plaintiff, and that defendant may assert his counterclaims even though the venue would not be proper if they were prosecuted in an independent action.[62]

Rule 13(h) permits bringing in additional parties to respond to a counterclaim if their joinder on the claim is required by Rule 19 or permitted by Rule 20. This is a revision of the rule made in 1966 to remove an implication in the prior rule that only those who would in the past have been called "indispensable" or "necessary" parties may be brought in as additional parties to a counterclaim. Of course the rule does not alter ordinary requirements of jurisdiction or venue, but if the counterclaim is compulsory, it will be treated as within the ancillary jurisdiction of the court.[63] A contrary result is reached, and the ordinary rules of jurisdiction and venue apply, if the counterclaim is permissive only.[64] In either event, additional persons can be made parties only if the court is able to obtain personal jurisdiction over them by service of process.[65]

§ 80.　Cross-Claims [1]

A cross-claim is defined by Rule 13(g) as a "claim by one party against a co-party arising out of the transaction or occurrence that is the subject matter of the original action or of a counterclaim therein or relating to property which is the subject matter of the original action." The courts have not always distinguished clearly between a cross-claim and a counterclaim, and have used one name where the other is proper under the rules,[2] perhaps because in some states, and in the old equity practice, the term cross-complaint or cross-bill is used for what the rules regard as a counterclaim. Under Rule 13 a counterclaim is a claim against an opposing party, while a cross-claim

---

62. 6 Wright & Miller, Civil §§ 1416, 1424.

63. H. L. Peterson Co. v. Applewhite, C.A.5th, 1967, 383 F.2d 430; United Artists Corp. v. Masterpiece Productions, C.A.2d, 1955, 221 F.2d 213; Note, 1956, 56 Col.L.Rev. 130.

Professor Fraser is skeptical of this rule as applied to an additional party whose joinder is not compelled by Rule 19. Fraser, note 59 above, at 34–36.

64. Chance v. County Bd. of Sch. Trustees, C.A.7th, 1964, 332 F.2d 971; Reynolds v. Maples, C.A.5th, 1954, 214 F.2d 395.

65. Garfield Gas Gathering Co. v. Indiana-Ohio Pipe Co., D.C.Colo.1961, 29 F.R.D. 8. The 100-mile "bulge" provision of Rule 4(f) applies to service of process in this situation.

[§ 80]

1. Wright & Miller, Civil §§ 1431–1433.

2. E.g., Farr v. Detroit Trust Co., C.C.A.6th, 1941, 116 F.2d 807, 811; Keller Research Corp. v. Roquerre, D.C.Cal.1951, 99 F.Supp. 964, 965. If the parties use the wrong terminology, the court should disregard the error. Missouri-Kansas-Texas R. Co. v. Early, D.C.Okl.1977, 74 F.R.D. 60; Falciani v. Philadelphia Transp. Co., D.C.Pa.1960, 189 F.Supp. 203.

Courts have also confused a third-party claim, under Rule 14(a), with a cross-claim under Rule 13(g). E.g., Fogel v. United Gas Improvement Co., D.C.Pa. 1963, 32 F.R.D. 202. The distinction is correctly stated in Schwab v. Erie Lackawanna R. Co., C.A.3d, 1971, 438 F.2d 62, 65–67.

is against a co-party. Further there is not the same freedom in asserting cross-claims that the rules provide as to counterclaims. An unrelated claim against an opposing party may be asserted as a permissive counterclaim, but only claims related to the subject matter of the original action, or property involved therein, are appropriate as cross-claims. There is an obvious reason for this difference. When plaintiff brings suit against a defendant, there is no harm to him if defendant asserts some unrelated claim that he has against the plaintiff, but he could be prejudiced if defendants could raise in that action an unrelated claim that one defendant has against the other and in which plaintiff has no interest. Nevertheless the rule should be given a broad construction, and the test of logical relation, now authoritatively accepted as the measure of "transaction or occurrence" in Rule 13(a), should be equally applicable to that phrase where it appears in Rule 13(g).[3] As with the other joinder rules, it is more desirable to permit broad joinder at the pleading stage, and order separate trials if sound judicial administration so dictates. Even though the test for a cross-claim is similar to that for a compulsory counterclaim, it is always discretionary with a party to assert his claim as a cross-claim or to reserve it for later independent litigation.[4]

A cross-claim must state a claim for relief that the cross-claimant has against a co-party. Consider the various possibilities that may arise in a tort action against two defendants: if the parties are jointly liable, one of them may cross-claim against the other for contribution, provided that he has a substantive right to such relief under the relevant state law.[5] The rule specifically provides that a cross-claim will lie if the party against whom it is asserted "is or may be liable to the cross-claimant for all or part" of the original plaintiff's claim. The use of the words "may be" means, as with the same language in Rule 14, on impleader,[6] that the claim may be of a contingent nature with the judgment shaped accordingly.[7] If one of the parties is only secondarily liable, he may cross-claim against the primarily liable defendant for indemnity against any amount he may have to pay—the demand for indemnification is a "claim for relief."[8] But finally there is the situation, quite frequently encountered now that joinder in the alternative is permissible, where one defendant wishes to assert that he is blameless and that his co-defendant is solely liable. In this cir-

---

3. LASA Per L'Industria Del Marmo Societa Per Azioni v. Alexander, C.A.6th, 1969, 414 F.2d 143; Allstate Ins. Co. v. Daniels, D.C.Okl.1978, 87 F.R.D. 1, 4–5; and cases cited 6 Wright & Miller, Civil § 1432 nn. 16, 18.

See § 79 n. 18 above. But see Hoosier Cas. Co. of Indianapolis, Ind. v. Fox, D.C.Iowa 1952, 102 F.Supp. 214, 227.

4. Augustin v. Mughal, C.A.8th, 1975, 521 F.2d 1215.

5. Dennier v. Dodge Transfer Corp., D.C.Conn.1962, 201 F.Supp. 431; cf.

Linkenhoger v. Owens, C.A.5th, 1950, 181 F.2d 97.

6. See § 76 nn. 18–20 above.

7. Smith v. Whitmore, C.A.3d, 1959, 270 F.2d 741, 746; Providential Development Co. v. U. S. Steel Co., C.A.10th, 1956, 236 F.2d 277; Chicago, R. I. & P. R. Co. v. Chicago, B. & Q. R. Co., D.C. Ill.1972, 55 F.R.D. 209.

8. Callahan v. Cheramie Boats, Inc., D.C.La.1974, 383 F.Supp. 1217; Atlantic Aviation Corp. v. Estate of Costas, D.C.N.Y.1971, 332 F.Supp. 1002.

cumstance a cross-claim will not be permissible, since it asks for no relief from the party against whom it is asserted.[9] Facts that show that the would-be cross-claimant is blameless will be a complete defense as to him, but they raise no issue between him and the other defendant.

Although the rule does not so provide in terms, it has been held that only parties against whom a claim has been made can cross-claim against each other. Thus though two plaintiffs are co-parties, and within the literal language of the rule, one plaintiff may not assert a cross-claim against his fellow plaintiff.[10] Presumably the result would be different if there were a counterclaim against the two plaintiffs, and they then could cross-claim with regard to the subject matter of the counterclaim.

The courts have disagreed about whether in a suit by a liability insurer for a declaratory judgment of non-coverage, brought against its insured and an injured person who is suing him, the injured person may assert in that action a cross-claim against the insured for his injuries. Where the company is seeking to avoid the policy on the ground of fraud in its procurement, it is possible to argue that such a claim of fraud is not related to the injured person's claim of damages for negligence, and thus to hold that the cross-claim is not within Rule 13(g).[11] But a cross-claim to recover for damages to proper in a declaratory judgment action where there is a logical relation between the claim and the cross-claim, as where the insurer is claiming non-liability on the ground that the car in question was not under the control of its insured at the time of the accident, and the insured is raising the same defense as against the injured person.[12]

There is also a variety of views on whether cross-claims may be raised among the defendants in an action for condemnation.[13] To

9. Washington Bldg. Realty Corp. v. Peoples Drug Stores, C.C.A.1947, 161 F.2d 879, 82 U.S.App.D.C. 119.

10. Danner v. Anskis, C.A.3d, 1958, 256 F.2d 123. In 6 Wright & Miller, Civil § 1432, pp. 173–174, this case is discussed and it is suggested that the result, though the one intended by the draftsmen of the rules, is contrary to the explicit and unqualified language of Rule 13(g).

11. Allstate Ins. Co. v. Daniels, D.C.Okl. 1978, 87 F.R.D. 1; Fireman's Fund Ins. Co. v. Trobaugh, D.C.Okl.1971, 52 F.R.D. 31; American Fidelity Fire Ins. Co. v. Hood, D.C.S.C.1965, 37 F.R.D. 17; Globe Indem. Co. v. Teixeira, D.C. Hawaii 1963, 230 F.Supp. 444; Hoosier Cas. Co. of Indianapolis, Ind. v. Fox, D.C.Iowa 1952, 102 F.Supp. 214; Temperance Ins. Exchange v. Carver, 1961, 365 P.2d 824, 83 Idaho 487. Contra: Allstate Ins. Co. v. Smith, D.C.Mich.

1959, 169 F.Supp. 374, mandamus refused C.A.6th, 1959, 264 F.2d 38. See generally Note, Insurance Litigation: Counterclaims and Cross-Claims under the Federal Declaratory Judgment Act, 1967, 52 Iowa L.Rev. 671.

12. Collier v. Harvey, C.A.10th, 1949, 179 F.2d 664; cf. U. S. Fidelity & Guar. Co. v. Janich, D.C.Cal.1943, 3 F.R.D. 16; Plains Ins. Co. v. Sandoval, D.C. Colo.1964, 35 F.R.D. 293; cf. R. E. Linder Steel Erection Co., Inc. v. Alumisteel Systems, Inc., D.C.Md.1980, 88 F.R.D. 629.

13. Compare U. S. v. Merchants Matrix Cut Syndicate, Inc., C.A.7th, 1955, 219 F.2d 90, certiorari denied 75 S.Ct. 873, 349 U.S. 945, 99 L.Ed. 1271 (permitting cross-claim), with U. S. v. 76.15 Acres of Land, More or Less, D.C.Cal.1952, 103 F.Supp. 478 (refusing to permit cross-claim).

permit such procedure would be desirable, since it would avoid circuity of litigation, but it appears to be prohibited by Rule 71A(e).[14]

By definition cross-claims must be closely related to the existing action. Thus they are commonly treated as within the ancillary jurisdiction of the court. Independent jurisdictional grounds are not required and there can be no venue objection.[15] Additional persons may be brought in to defend against a cross-claim, and here too the ancillary jurisdiction concept should be applicable.[16] All of this is well enough if the cross-claimant is stating a claim derived from the plaintiff's claim against him, as for liability over. But if the cross-claimant attempts to assert an independent claim on his own behalf, or in effect joins in the plaintiff's original claim, it may be necessary to realign the cross-claimant as a party plaintiff in determining whether diversity exists,[17] at least with regard to the cross-claim.[18]

E. DISCOVERY

Analysis

§ 81. The Scope of Discovery [1]

Discovery was the Cinderella of the changes in procedure made by the Civil Rules. Now there are those who are saying that the carriage has turned into a pumpkin, and that major changes are needed if it is to be a carriage again.

14. See 6 Wright & Miller, Civil § 1432, pp. 176–177.

15. LASA Per L'Industria Del Marmo Societa Per Azioni v. Alexander, C.A. 6th, 1969, 414 F.2d 143; Scott v. Fancher, C.A.5th, 1966, 369 F.2d 842; and cases cited 6 Wright & Miller, Civil § 1433 n. 33.

16. Cf. United Artists Corp. v. Masterpiece Productions, C.A.2d, 1955, 221 F.2d 213.

17. See § 30 above.

18. Farr v. Detroit Trust Co., C.C.A.6th, 1941, 116 F.2d 807; Main v. Festa, D.C. Pa.1965, 37 F.R.D. 227. But cf. Belcher v. Grooms, C.A.5th, 1968, 406 F.2d 14. The Main case is criticized at 6 Wright & Miller, Civil § 1432, p. 174.

[§ 81]

1. 8 Wright & Miller, Civil §§ 2007–2020, 2029–2034; Connolly, Holleman & Kuhlman, Judicial Controls and the Civil Litigative Process: Discovery, Federal Judicial Center 1978; Glaser, Pretrial Discovery and the Adversary Process, 1968; Cutner, Discovery—Civil Litigation's Fading Light: A Lawyer Looks at the Federal Discovery Rules After Forty Years of Use, 1979, 52 Temp.L.Q. 933.

The broad and flexible provisions in Rules 26 to 37 for discovery were the most significant innovation in civil procedure when the rules were adopted in 1938. These rules rested on a philosophy that prior to trial every party to a civil action is entitled to the disclosure of all relevant information in the possession of any person, unless the information is privileged.[2] No longer are civil trials to be "carried on in the dark."[3] Use of the discovery rules is intended to "make a trial less a game of blind man's buff and more a fair contest with the basic issues and facts disclosed to the fullest practicable extent."[4] The "sporting theory of justice" was rejected.[5] Victory is intended to go to the party entitled to it, on all the facts, rather than to the side that best uses its wits. It was thought that surprise, dearly cherished by an earlier generation of trial lawyers, would be minimized or ended altogether.[6] The discovery rules complement the rules on pleadings. The pleadings are now not much emphasized, since the discovery rules provide better means for performing the functions formerly demanded of the pleadings.[7]

For more than three decades the discovery rules remained fundamentally unchanged. There continued to be controversy about them, and criticism from those who thought that the rules could be used to compel one lawyer to prepare the other's case or that elimination of surprise would open the door to perjury.[8] Despite these fears, the discovery rules were widely used and copied in many states, and the conclusion that "the present federal discovery rules enjoy the predominant support of the Bar"[9] seemed entirely justified.

Experience, however, did disclose details of the discovery rules that could be improved. In 1970 these rules were extensively amended. The amendments, which were based on an extensive empirical study of the operation of the discovery rules made by the Project for Effective Justice at Columbia University, rearranged the rules and made a number of substantive changes in them.[10]

2. 8 Wright & Miller, Civil § 2001.

3. Hickman v. Taylor, 1947, 67 S.Ct. 385, 388, 329 U.S. 495, 500, 91 L.Ed. 451.

4. U. S. v. Procter & Gamble Co., 1958, 78 S.Ct. 983, 987, 356 U.S. 677, 683, 2 L.Ed.2d 1077.

5. Tiedman v. American Pigment Corp., C.A.4th, 1958, 253 F.2d 803, 808.

6. Holtzoff, The Elimination of Surprise in Federal Practice, 1954, 7 Vand.L. Rev. 576; Frank, Pretrial Conferences and Discovery—Disclosure or Surprise, 1965 Ins.L.J. 661.

One study suggests that discovery does not reduce surprise and, if anything, may be associated with more surprise. Glaser, note 1 above, at pp. 105–109.

7. See § 68 above.

8. E.g., Hawkins, Discovery and Rule 34: What's So Wrong about Surprise?, 1953, 39 A.B.A.J. 1075; Knepper, Some Suggestions for Limiting Discovery, 1967, 34 Ins.Couns.J. 398; Gooch, Book Review, 1964, 42 Texas L.Rev. 764, 765.

9. Glaser, note 1 above, at p. 225. See also, e.g., Virtue, Sweet Are the Uses of Discovery: A Reply to Mr. Hawkins, 1954, 40 A.B.A.J. 303; Wright, Wegner & Richardson, The Practicing Attorney's View of the Utility of Discovery, 1952, 12 F.R.D. 97; Frost, The Ascertainment of Truth by Discovery, 1960, 28 F.R.D. 89.

10. The 1970 amendments, and the Advisory Committee Notes explaining them, are set out at 48 F.R.D. 459. The study by the Project for Effective

In the late 1970s, however, a new wave of criticism of discovery began, and this time the criticism was both more vigorous and from more influential sources. As the Supreme Court said in 1979: "There have been repeated expressions of concern about undue and uncontrolled discovery, and voices from this Court have joined the chorus."[11] For some in the profession it became an article of faith—though with little empirical proof—that discovery is being widely abused.[12] Others asserted that there is abuse of discovery, and that it is a serious thing when it occurs, but that it does not occur commonly.[13] From these conflicting viewpoints came contrasting suggestions on what, if anything, should be done. Some called for extensive changes in the rules,[14] while others argued that the rules already contain "ample powers of the district judge to prevent abuse" [15] and that strong judicial management of cases and use of the powers already there is an adequate answer to the problem.[16]

Justice is described, and its findings set out, in Glaser, note 1 above.

Those amendments are discussed in Blair, A Guide To The New Federal Discovery Practice, 1971, 21 Drake L.Rev. 58, and in Cooper, Work Product of the Rulesmakers, 1969, 53 Minn. L.Rev. 1269.

11. Herbert v. Lando, 1979, 99 S.Ct. 1635, 1649, 441 U.S. 153, 177, 60 L.Ed. 2d 115.

Bar dissatisfaction with discovery today is surveyed in Brazil, Civil Discovery: How Bad Are the Problems?, 1981, 67 A.B.A.J. 450.

See generally Segal, Survey of Literature on Discovery From 1970 to the Present: Expressed Dissatisfactions and Proposed Reforms, Federal Judicial Center 1978.

12. "Delay and excessive expense now characterize a large percentage of all civil litigation. The problems arise in significant part, as every judge and litigator knows, from abuse of the discovery procedures available under the Rules." Powell, J., joined by Stewart, J. and Rehnquist, J., dissenting from Order of April 29, 1980, Amending Civil Rules, 446 U.S. 997, 999.

See also, e.g., the two Reports of the ABA Special Committee for the Study of Discovery Abuse. October 1977 Report, reprinted 92 F.R.D. 149; November 1980 Report, reprinted 92 F.R.D. 137.

13. "The Committee believes that abuse of discovery, while very serious in certain cases, is not so general as to require such basic changes in the rules that govern discovery in all cases." Advisory Committee Note to 1980

amendment of Rule 26(f), 85 F.R.D. 521, 526.

See also, e.g., Levine, "Abuse" of Discovery: or Hard Work Makes Good Law, 1981, 67 A.B.A.J. 565; Friedenthal, A Divided Supreme Court Adopts Discovery Amendments to the Federal Rules of Civil Procedure, 1981, 69 Calif.L. Rev. 806, 813; Pollack, Discovery—Its Abuse and Correction, 1978, 80 F.R.D. 219, 222; Schroeder & Frank, The Proposed Changes in the Discovery Rules, 1978 Ariz.St.L.J. 475, 476–478, 492; Wright, New Civil Discovery Rules—A "No" Vote, Virginia Law Weekly, Oct. 13, 1978, pp. 1, 3–4.

14. See the dissent of Justice Powell and the two Reports of the ABA Special Committee, all cited note 12 above. See also Flegal & Umin, Curbing Discovery Abuse in Civil Litigation: We're Not There Yet, 1981 B.Y.U.L.Rev. 597; Umin, Discovery Reform: A New Era or Business as Usual?, 1979, 65 A.B. A.J. 1050; Smith, The Concern Over Discovery, 1979, 28 Drake L.Rev. 51; Lundquist & Schechter, The New Relevancy: An End to Trial by Ordeal, 1978, 64 A.B.A.J. 59.

15. Herbert v. Lando, 1979, 99 S.Ct. 1635, 1649, 441 U.S. 153, 177, 60 L.Ed. 2d 115.

16. Connolly, Holleman & Kuhlman, note 1 above; Brazil, note 11 above, at 456; Levine, note 13 above; Rosenberg & King, Curbing Discovery Abuse in Civil Litigation: Enough is Enough, 1981 B.Y.U.L.Rev. 579, 588–589; Sherman & Kinnard, Federal Court Discovery in the 80s—Making the Rules Work, 1981, 2 Rev. Litigation 9; Pollack, note 13 above, at 227; Cutner,

The term "discovery abuse" has been used as if it were a single concept, but it includes several different things. Thus it is useful to subdivide "abuse" into "misuse" and "overuse." What is referred to as "misuse" would include not only direct violation of the rules, as by failing to respond to a discovery request within the state time limit, but also more subtle attempts to harass or obstruct an opponent, as by giving obviously inadequate answers or by requesting information that clearly is outside the scope of discovery. By "overuse" is meant asking for more discovery than is necessary or appropriate to the particular case.[17] "Overuse," in turn, can be subdivided into problems of "depth" and of "breadth," with "depth" referring to discovery that may be relevant but is simply excessive and "breadth" referring to discovery requests that go into matters too far removed from the case.[18] Although most of the problems of abuse of discovery are discussed in a later section,[19] concerns about the breadth of discovery are related to the discussion in this section.

In 1980 some rather modest amendments to the discovery rules were adopted, over the objection of three Justices that the amendments "fall short of those needed to accomplish reforms in civil litigation that are long overdue" and that they were only "tinkering changes."[20] Those amendments made changes in Rules 33 and 34 to prevent misuse of those rules [21] and also sought to strengthen judicial control of the discovery process by authorizing a discovery conference to frame a discovery plan for a particular case.[22] Presently the Advisory Committee on Civil Rules is considering other amendments that would seek to limit discovery, on pain of sanctions against the offending party or lawyer, to matters that are "not unreasonable or unduly burdensome or expensive, given the nature and complexity of the case, the discovery already had in the case, the amount in contro-

---

note 1 above; Comment, Preventing Abuse of Discovery in Federal Courts, 1981, 30 Cath.U.L.Rev. 273.

But see Flegal & Umin, note 14 above, at 603–604; Nordenberg, The Supreme Court and Discovery Reform: The Continuing Need for an Umpire, 1980, 31 Syracuse L.Rev. 543.

17. This terminology, and the examples of its meaning, are borrowed from Lundquist & Flegal, Discovery Abuse—Some New Views About an Old Problem, 1981, 2 Rev. Litigation 1, and from Friedenthal, note 13 above, at 810–812.

18. This terminology is borrowed from Rosenberg & King, note 16 above, at 586–587. Those authors think that depth is the serious problem, while Flegal & Umin, note 14 above, at 601–603, argue that breadth is at least as serious a problem.

19. See § 83 below.

20. See the dissent, cited note 12 above, 446 U.S. at 997–998, 1000. The full text of the 1980 amendments, and of the dissent from their adoption, is reprinted also at 85 F.R.D. 521. For the history of those amendments, and of an earlier proposal by the Advisory Committee of more drastic changes, echoing those recommended in the October 1977 Report of the ABA Special Committee, cited note 12 above, see 8 Wright & Miller, Civil § 2002.

See generally Watkins, 1980 Amendments to the Federal Rules of Civil Procedure, 1980, 32 Baylor L.Rev. 533.

21. See §§ 86, 87 below.

22. Rule 26(f); 8 Wright & Miller, Civil § 2051. See Watkins, note 20 above, at 541–544; Sherman & Kinnard, note 16 above, at 38–39.

versy, and other values at stake in the litigation."[23] What will come of these proposals, and what the ultimate resolution will be of the present controversy about discovery, remains to be seen. For now it is necessary to examine the discovery rules as they stand.

The central notion of the discovery practice set out in the rules is that the right to take statements and the right to use them in court must be kept entirely distinct. By this method discovery at the pretrial stage is not fettered with the rules as to admissibility that apply at a trial, and the utmost freedom is here allowed, but restrictions are imposed on the use of the products of discovery in order to preserve traditional methods of trial.[24]

The rules provide a number of different procedures for compelling disclosure of information. These cannot be read in isolation, but are to be regarded as an integrated mechanism for narrowing the issues and ascertaining the facts.[25] To all of these devices Rule 26 is basic. It contains the central provisions as to the scope of discovery, which, with one exception,[26] are incorporated by reference in the other discovery rules.

The scope of discovery contemplated by Rule 26 is extremely broad.[27] "No longer can the time-honored cry of 'fishing expedition' serve to preclude a party from inquiring into the facts underlying his opponent's case."[28] Discovery may extend to matters relating to the claim or defense of any party,[29] unlike the former equity practice that limited discovery to matters in support of the proponent's case. It is no objection that the examining party already knows the facts as to which he seeks discovery, since one of the purposes of discovery is to

---

23. Preliminary Draft of Proposed Amendments to the Federal Rules of Civil Procedure, June 1981, reprinted 90 F.R.D. 451. The language quoted in the text is taken from a proposed new Rule 26(g), and see the related amendment proposed to Rule 26(b), 90 F.R.D. at 478–480. These proposals follow closely the recommendations in the November 1980 Report of the ABA Special Committee, cited note 12 above. For critical discussion of them see Schroeder & Frank, Discovery Reform: Long Road to Nowheresville, 1982, 66 A.B.A.J. 572; Rosenberg & King, note 16 above; Sherman & Kinard, note 16 above, at 46–56.

24. Independent Productions Corp. v. Loew's Inc., D.C.N.Y.1962, 30 F.R.D. 377, 381; Drum v. Town of Tonawanda, D.C.N.Y.1952, 13 F.R.D. 317, 319; Pike & Willis, The New Federal Deposition-Discovery Procedure, 1938, 38 Col.L.Rev. 1179, 1187.

25. Hickman v. Taylor, 1947, 67 S.Ct. 385, 391, 329 U.S. 495, 505, 91 L.Ed.

451; Clark, Special Problems in Drafting and Interpreting Procedural Codes and Rules, 1950, 3 Vand.L.Rev. 493, 502.

26. Rule 27, authorizing depositions before action is commenced or while an appeal is pending, is intended for perpetuation of testimony, rather than as a discovery device, and the scope of examination is less broad than under other discovery procedures. Ash v. Cort, C.A.3d, 1975, 512 F.2d 909, 912; In re Killian, D.C.Mass.1953, 14 F.R.D. 471; Petition of Johanson Glove Co., D.C. N.Y.1945, 7 F.R.D. 156. But see Martin v. Reynolds Metals Corp., C.A.9th, 1961, 297 F.2d 49, 55, noted 1962, 41 Texas L.Rev. 330. See 8 Wright & Miller, Civil § 2071.

27. 8 Wright & Miller, Civil § 2007.

28. Hickman v. Taylor, 1947, 67 S.Ct. 385, 392, 329 U.S. 495, 507, 91 L.Ed. 451.

29. Rule 26(b); 8 Wright & Miller, Civil § 2011.

ascertain the position of the adverse party on the controverted issues.[30]

Impeaching material has caused controversy. It should be clear that one party may obtain by discovery evidence that will impeach witnesses for the other party.[31] The controversy has been whether a party who has obtained on his own evidence that will impeach his adversary is required to disclose the existence of that evidence. Surveillance movies of an injured plaintiff that the defense has had made are the most common example. There is some support for the view that evidence of this kind is to be disclosed if the defendant intends to use it substantively but that he need not disclose it if he intends to use it only to impeach the plaintiff's testimony.[32] There are two difficulties with this. It ignores the fact that much evidence of this kind—and surveillance movies are an excellent example—has both impeaching and substantive aspects and that there is no way to prevent a jury from giving substantive effect to the evidence supposedly offered only for impeachment.[33] Further these proposals seem to assume that evidence used for impeachment is intrinsically more trustworthy than any other kind of evidence and therefore does not need the explanation or refutation that advance knowledge will permit.[34] For these reasons, it is thought that the better view is to read Rule 26 as it is written and not carve out of its broad scope any exception for impeaching material,[35] although many courts do require that the plaintiff submit to a deposition before discovery of the surveillance movies will be required.[36]

30. Weiner v. Bache Halsey Stuart, Inc., D.C.Fla.1977, 76 F.R.D. 624; Baim & Blank, Inc. v. Philco Distributors, Inc., D.C.N.Y.1957, 25 F.R.D. 86; 8 Wright & Miller, Civil § 2014.

31. E.g., Mellon v. Cooper-Jarrett, Inc., C.A.6th, 1970, 424 F.2d 499; U. S. v. International Business Machines Corp., D.C.N.Y.1974, 66 F.R.D. 215; and cases cited 8 Wright & Miller, Civil § 2015 nn. 31–38. But see Wharton v. Lybrand, Ross Bros. & Montgomery, D.C.N.Y.1966, 41 F.R.D. 177, 179.

32. Bogotay v. Montour R. Co., D.C.Pa. 1959, 177 F.Supp. 269; Leach v. Chesapeake & O. Ry. Co., D.C.Mich.1964, 35 F.R.D. 9; cf. Hikel v. Abousy, D.C.Md. 1966, 41 F.R.D. 152; Mort v. A/S D/S Svendborg, D.C.Pa.1966, 41 F.R.D. 225; see Zimmerman v. Superior Court, 1965, 402 P.2d 212, 217, 98 Ariz. 85; Frank, Pretrial Conferences and Discovery—Disclosure or Surprise?, 1965 Ins.L.J. 661, 664–667; Comment, 1966, 7 Ariz.L.Rev. 283.

33. Zimmerman v. Superior Court, 1965, 402 P.2d 212, 98 Ariz. 85; Cooper, note 10 above, at 1317.

34. Boldt v. Sanders, 1961, 111 N.W.2d 225, 227–228, 261 Minn. 160; Cooper, note 10 above, at 1314–1315.

35. In addition to the cases cited note 36 below, see Boldt v. Sanders, 1961, 111 N.W.2d 225, 261 Minn. 160, noted 1962, 47 Minn.L.Rev. 289; Suezaki v. Superior Court, 1962, 373 P.2d 432, 23 Cal. Rptr. 368, 58 Cal.2d 166; Zimmerman v. Superior Court, 1965, 402 P.2d 212, 98 Ariz. 85, noted 1966, 51 Iowa L.Rev. 765; Cooper, note 10 above, at 1310–1318; Gourley, Effective Pretrial Must Be the Beginning of Trial, 1960, 28 F.R.D. 165, 169; Chandler, Discovery and Pre-Trial Procedure in Federal Courts, 1959, 12 Okla.L.Rev. 321, 324.

The issue is fully discussed in 8 Wright & Miller, Civil § 2015.

36. Martin v. Long Island R. Co., D.C. N.Y.1974, 63 F.R.D. 53; Blyther v. Northern Lines, Inc., D.C.Pa.1973, 61 F.R.D. 610; Snead v. American Export-Isbrandtsen Lines, Inc., D.C.Pa.1973, 59 F.R.D. 148, noted 1973, 18 How.L.J. 228; Smith v. Central Linen Serv. Co., D.C.Md.1966, 39 F.R.D. 15; McCoy v. General Motors Corp., D.C.Pa.1963, 33

Rule 26(b) specifically allows discovery of the identity and location of persons having knowledge of discoverable matter. The traditional principle prior to the rules was that a party could not be required to disclose the names of his witnesses, in order that there should be no opportunity to tamper with them. The rules rest on the different premise that persons having knowledge of the relevant facts are not necessarily the witnesses of any particular party. Thus it is routinely held that a party may be required to disclose the names of occurrence witnesses of whom he has knowledge.[37] A party cannot refuse, on the ground of attorney-client privilege, to divulge the names of witnesses his attorney has located.[38] To hold otherwise would defeat the purposes of the discovery rules.

A distinction must be drawn between witnesses to the occurrences in question, and witnesses who will be called for trial by the adverse party. The names of occurrence witnesses may always be obtained by discovery. It is usually held that a party is not entitled to find out, by discovery, which witnesses his opponent intends to call at the trial,[39] although the court may require disclosure of this information at a pre-trial conference.[40]

Under Rule 26(b) discovery is also proper as to the existence and location of books, documents, and other tangible things.[41] If the object itself is properly the subject of discovery, the party, having ascertained its location, may endeavor to require production under Rule 34, but he is entitled to learn of the existence and location of tangible things even though the thing itself is one that he cannot compel to be produced.[42]

The extent to which the reports and opinions of experts are subject to discovery has undergone considerable change. The early cases, though divided, ordinarily refused to allow discovery, and in 1946 the Advisory Committee proposed an amendment, which the Su-

---

F.R.D. 354; Parla v. Matson Navigation Co., D.C.N.Y.1961, 28 F.R.D. 348.

37. Bell v. Swift & Co., C.A.5th, 1950, 283 F.2d 407; Hikel v. Abousy, D.C. Md.1966, 41 F.R.D. 152; 8 Wright & Miller, Civil § 2013.

38. Duffy v. Dier, C.A.8th, 1972, 465 F.2d 416; Harrison v. Prather, C.A.5th, 1968, 404 F.2d 267; Edgar v. Finley, C.A.8th, 1963, 312 F.2d 533; and cases cited 8 Wright & Miller, Civil § 2013 n. 16. Contra: Walczak v. Detroit-Pittsburgh Motor Freight, Inc., D.C.Ind. 1956, 140 F.Supp. 10, criticized 1957, 45 Geo.L.J. 701.

39. Brennan v. Engineered Products, Inc., C.A.8th, 1974, 506 F.2d 299; Wirtz v. Continental Fin. & Loan Co. of West End, C.A.5th, 1964, 326 F.2d 561; and cases cited 8 Wright & Miller, Civil § 2013 nn. 18, 19. But see U.S. EEOC

v. Metropolitan Museum of Art, D.C. N.Y.1978, 80 F.R.D. 317.

Rule 26(b)(4)(A) makes an exception to this rule for expert witnesses who will be called at trial. See 8 Wright & Miller, Civil § 2030.

40. Wirtz v. Hooper-Holmes Bureau, Inc., C.A.5th, 1964, 327 F.2d 939; Globe Cereal Mills v. Scrivener, C.A. 10th, 1956, 240 F.2d 330; Lloyd v. Cessna Aircraft Co., D.C.Tenn.1976, 434 F.Supp. 4.

41. 8 Wright & Miller, Civil § 2012.

42. Cox v. E. I. DuPont de Nemours & Co., D.C.S.C.1965, 38 F.R.D. 396; Pressley v. Boehlke, D.C.N.C.1963, 33 F.R.D. 316; Harvey v. Eimco Corp., D.C.Pa.1961, 28 F.R.D. 380; Margeson v. Boston & M. R. R., D.C.Mass.1954, 16 F.R.D. 200.

preme Court did not adopt, that would have created an absolute immunity from discovery for the conclusions of an expert. In later years the decisions, though still divided, were much more liberal in allowing discovery.[43] The problem is now addressed in Rule 26(b)(4), as amended in 1970, which is a rather conservative codification of the later cases.[44] The new rule speaks only to facts known and opinions held by experts that were "acquired or developed in anticipation of litigation or for trial." It distinguishes sharply between those experts the opposing party expects to call as witnesses at the trial and those he does not expect to call. A party may learn by interrogatories the names of the experts his opponent expects to call, the subject matter on which the expert is expected to testify, and the substance of the facts and opinions to which the expert will testify. In addition, he is entitled to a summary of the grounds for each opinion.[45] It is further provided that the court on motion may order further discovery by other means. Presumably this will ordinarily be by taking the deposition of the expert.[46] If the court orders further discovery of this kind, it may restrict the scope of the examination if it deems this appropriate. Thus it could restrict the deposition to the opinions that the expert is expected to give on direct examination at trial, and in this way prevent the discovering party from using the deposition to establish his own affirmative case,[47] but the court is not required to do so. If further discovery beyond the interrogatories is ordered the court is authorized to make appropriate provision about paying for the expert's time and, if it chooses, may require the discovering party to reimburse his opponent for a portion of the fee the opponent has paid to the expert.[48]

---

43. 8 Wright & Miller, Civil § 2029. The later cases were heavily influenced by the arguments made in Friedenthal, Discovery and Use of an Adverse Party's Expert Information, 1962, 14 Stan. L.Rev. 455.

44. See Comment, Ambiguities After the 1970 Amendments to the Federal Rules of Civil Procedure Relating to Discovery of Experts and Attorney's Work Product, 1971, 17 Wayne L.Rev. 1145.

45. Rule 26(b)(4)(A)(i). See In re Folding Carton Antitrust Litigation, D.C.Ill. 1979, 83 F.R.D. 256; Bailey v. Meister Brau, Inc., D.C.Ill.1972, 57 F.R.D. 11; 8 Wright & Miller, Civil § 2030.

46. Rule 26(b)(4)(A)(ii). Courts vary widely in how they have applied this portion of the rule. 8 Wright & Miller, Civil § 2031; Connors, A New Look at an Old Concern—Protecting Expert Information from Discovery Under the Federal Rules, 1980, 18 Duq.L.Rev.

271; Graham, Discovery of Experts Under Rule 26(b)(4) of the Federal Rules of Civil Procedure: Part One, An Analytical Study, 1976 U.Ill.L.F. 895; Comment, Discovery of Expert Information Under the Federal Rules, 1976, 10 U.Rich.L.Rev. 706. In addition, there is evidence that full discovery, rather than the two-step procedure of the rule, is what normally happens in practice with regard to experts. See Graham, Discovery of Experts Under Rule 26(b)(4) of the Federal Rules of Civil Procedure: Part Two, An Empirical Study and a Proposal, 1977 U.Ill. L.F. 169.

47. See Bailey v. Meister Brau, Inc., D.C.Ill.1972, 57 F.R.D. 11, 14; Connors, note 46 above, at 277–280.

48. Rule 26(b)(4)(C); Keith v. Van Dorn Plastic Machinery Co., D.C.Pa.1980, 86 F.R.D. 458; Worley v. Massey-Ferguson, Inc., D.C.Miss.1978, 79 F.R.D. 534; 8 Wright & Miller, Civil § 2034.

Expert witnesses who are not expected to testify are treated very differently. With the exception of an examining physician,[49] facts or opinions may be obtained from an expert who has been retained or specially employed by another party in anticipation of litigation or preparation for trial, but who is not expected to be called at the trial, only "upon a showing of exceptional circumstances under which it is impracticable for the party seeking discovery to obtain facts or opinions on the same subject by other means."[50] Most cases have refused to find the exceptional circumstances that will justify this discovery.[51] If a party merely seeks to obtain the names of experts retained by his opponent who will not be called at trial, and does not seek to obtain discovery from those experts, the better view is that the requirement of exceptional circumstances does not apply and the discovery should be allowed,[52] but there is significant authority to the contrary.[53] In the rare cases in which discovery is ordered with regard to a non-testifying expert, the court is normally required to make the party obtaining discovery reimburse the party who retained the expert for a portion of his fee.[54]

Rule 26(b)(4) makes no provision whatever for discovery with regard to an expert who was informally consulted in preparation for trial but who was never retained or specially employed. Therefore neither the names of these persons nor their information are subject to discovery.[55] On the other hand the rule does not limit discovery from an expert whose information was not acquired in preparation for trial but because he was an actor or viewer with respect to the transactions that are the basis of the lawsuit. The deposition of this kind of expert may be taken merely by notice, in the same fashion as with any other fact witness.[56]

---

49. Rule 35(b). See § 88 below.

50. Rule 26(b)(4)(B); 8 Wright & Miller, Civil § 2032.

51. Galella v. Onassis, C.A.2d, 1973, 487 F.2d 986; Arco Pipeline Co. v. S/S Trade Star, D.C.Pa.1978, 81 F.R.D. 416; and cases cited 8 Wright & Miller, Civil § 2302 n. 86. But see Roesberg v. Johns-Manville Corp., D.C.Pa.1980, 85 F.R.D. 292; Pearl Brewing Co. v. Jos. Schlitz Brewing Co., D.C.Tex.1976, 415 F.Supp. 1122.

52. Roesberg v. Johns-Manville Corp., D.C.Pa.1980, 85 F.R.D. 292, 303; In re Folding Carton Antitrust Litigation, D.C.Ill.1979, 83 F.R.D. 256, 258; Arco Pipeline Co. v. S/S Trade Star, D.C.Pa. 1978, 81 F.R.D. 416, 417; Weiner v. Bache Halsey Stuart, Inc., D.C.Fla. 1977, 76 F.R.D. 624, 628; Baki v. B. F. Diamond Constr. Co., D.C.Md.1976, 71 F.R.D. 179, 182; Sea Colony, Inc. v. Continental Ins. Co., D.C.Del.1974, 63 F.R.D. 113, 114; Comment, Discovery of the Nonwitness Expert Under Fed-eral Rule of Civil Procedure 26(b)(4)(B), 1982, 67 Iowa L.Rev. 349, 360–372.

53. Ager v. Jane C. Stormont Hosp. & Training Sch. for Nurses, C.A.10th, 1980, 622 F.2d 496, 502–504; Perry v. W. S. Darley & Co., D.C.Wis.1971, 54 F.R.D. 278, 280; Graham, note 46 above, at 201.

54. Rule 26(b)(4)(C); 8 Wright & Miller, Civil § 2034.

55. Ager v. Jane C. Stormont Hosp. & Training Sch. for Nurses, C.A.10th, 1980, 622 F.2d 496, 501; 8 Wright & Miller, Civil § 2033. It is often difficult to decide whether an expert was "informally consulted" or was "retained or specially employed." See Comment, Note 52 above, at 355–360.

56. Keith v. Van Dorn Plastic Machinery Co., D.C.Pa.1980, 86 F.R.D. 458; Virginia Elec. & Power Co. v. Sun Shipbuilding & Dry Dock Co., D.C.Va.1975, 68 F.R.D. 397, 406–410; Rodrigues v.

The scope of discovery is governed entirely by the federal rules. State law on scope of discovery is of no force in federal court.[57]

The rules recognize only three limitations on the broad scope of discovery thus far indicated. The matter sought to be discovered must be relevant to the subject matter of the action, it must not be privileged, and it must not be the "work product" of an attorney.

The boundaries defining information that is relevant to the subject matter involved in the action are necessarily vague and it is practically impossible to state a general rule by which they can be drawn. Though some early decisions purported to require relevancy to "the issues" in the case, this is unduly restrictive, and it is clear that all that is required is relevancy to the "subject matter." Discovery cannot be limited to evidence that would be relevant at the trial. The concept at the discovery stage is much broader, as was made specific by a 1946 amendment to Rule 26(b), stating that it is not ground of objection that the testimony will be inadmissible at the trial if the testimony sought appears reasonably calculated to lead to the discovery of admissible evidence.[58] Certainly the requirement of relevancy should be construed liberally and with common sense, rather than in terms of narrow legalisms. Indeed in its most recent statement about this the Supreme Court said that the relevancy requirement "has been construed broadly to encompass any matter that bears on, or that reasonably could lead to other matter that could bear on, any issue that is or may be in the case."[59] The ABA Special Committee for the Study of Discovery Abuse thinks that this broad definition of relevancy is a major source of discovery abuse. At one time the committee proposed that Rule 26(b) be amended to limit discovery to matters "relevant to the issues raised by the claim or defense of any party."[60] More recently it has proposed to eliminate the words "the subject matter involved in the pending action," so that the rule would then require relevance to the claims or defenses of any party.[61]

Hrinda, D.C.Pa.1972, 56 F.R.D. 11; 8 Wright & Miller, Civil § 2033.

57. Dixon v. 80 Pine St. Corp., C.A.2d, 1975, 516 F.2d 1278; Hosie v. Chicago & N.W. Ry. Co., C.A.7th, 1960, 282 F.2d 639, certiorari denied 81 S.Ct. 695, 365 U.S. 814, 5 L.Ed.2d 693; 8 Wright & Miller, Civil § 2005.

State law will be applicable, by virtue of Evidence Rule 501, in determining what information is privileged on those matters as to which state law supplies the substantive rule of decision. State law is also available as an alternative to the federal rules for discovery in aid of execution after judgment. See Civil Rule 69.

58. 8 Wright & Miller, Civil §§ 2008, 2009.

59. Oppenheimer Fund, Inc. v. Sanders, 1978, 98 S.Ct. 2380, 2389, 437 U.S. 340, 351, 57 L.Ed.2d 253. Justice Powell went on to write: "Consistently with the notice-pleading system established by the Rules, discovery is not limited to issues raised by the pleadings, for discovery itself is designed to help define and clarify the issues. * * * Nor is discovery limited to the merits of a case, for a variety of fact-oriented issues may arise during litigation that are not related to the merits."

60. October 1977 Report, reprinted 92 F.R.D. 149, 157. Compare with this what the Supreme Court said in the Oppenheimer case, quoted note 59 above.

61. November 1980 Report, reprinted 92 F.R.D. 137, 140.

These proposals have not attracted a significant following. The general view is that depth, rather than breadth, of discovery is more likely to be a problem,[62] and that if protection is needed against unduly broad discovery, it can better be provided by the discretionary powers of the court to issue protective orders rather than by a constricting concept of relevance.

A principal battleground on relevance had been whether the extent of defendant's liability insurance, if any, is subject to discovery. Though much was written on the question, the federal courts were hopelessly divided, as were also the state courts and the commentators.[63] Rule 26(b)(2), adopted in 1970, resolved this long controversy by making the existence and contents of a liability insurance agreement subject to discovery. A rule one way or the other on this point was badly needed. It was wasteful to have this simple issue litigated repeatedly before many different district judges. The decision to adopt a rule permitting discovery was based on the view that knowledge of insurance limits will lead to more realistic negotiation and thus to more settlements.[64]

A second limitation on discovery is that it may extend only to matters "not privileged." Matter is privileged from discovery if it would be privileged at trial under the applicable rules of evidence.[65] On issues on which the court must look to the state law for the substantive rule of decision, it must apply also the state law of privilege.[66] If the arguably privileged communication was made, or the deposition is to be taken, in a state other than that in which the action is pending, it would seem that the federal court must apply whichever state's rule of privilege would be applied by the courts of the state in which the district court is held.[67] Thus if, for example, in a diversity action pending in Pennsylvania there is a claim that a communication made in Ohio was privileged, the federal court must look to see whether the Pennsylvania state courts would apply their own rules of privilege to

62. See note 18 above.

63. Compare, e.g., Hughes v. Groves, D.C.Mo.1969, 47 F.R.D. 52, and Jenkins, Discovery of Automobile Insurance Limits: Quillets of the Law, 1965, 14 Kan.L.Rev. 59, with Beal v. Zambelli Fireworks Mfg. Co., D.C.Pa. 1969, 46 F.R.D. 449, and Frank, Discovery and Insurance Coverage, 1959 Ins. L.J. 281. The authorities are fully set out at 8 Wright & Miller, Civil § 2010.

64. See Clauss v. Danker, D.C.N.Y. 1967, 264 F.Supp. 246; Cook v. Welty, D.C.D.C.1966, 253 F.Supp. 875; Glaser, Pretrial Discovery and the Adversary System, 1969, pp. 127–128.

The validity of the rule allowing discovery of the existence of insurance was upheld in Helms v. Richmond-Peters-

burg Turnpike Auth., D.C.Va.1971, 52 F.R.D. 530.

65. Evidence Rule 1101(c); U. S. v. Reynolds, 1953, 73 S.Ct. 528, 531, 345 U.S. 1, 6, 97 L.Ed. 727.

66. Evidence Rule 501. See § 93 below.

67. The Third Edition of this book took the view that the privilege rule should be that of the state whose substantive law is to govern. Wright, Federal Courts, 3d ed. 1976, p. 404. On further reflection the author has become convinced that the view now stated in the text is the proper view. See Wellborn, The Federal Rules of Evidence and the Application of State Law in Federal Courts, 1977, 55 Texas L.Rev. 371, 448; 23 Wright & Graham, Evidence § 5435.

such a communication or would apply the Ohio notions of privilege.[68] On issues governed by federal law, the federal court applies the principles of the common law, as they have been modified in the light of reason and experience, in deciding questions of privilege.[69]

Finally there is a court-made qualified immunity from discovery of matter gathered by a lawyer in anticipation of litigation or preparation for trial, known as the lawyer's "work product." In practice this is the most difficult and controversial of all the limits on discovery, and it is discussed in the following section.

Most of the law on discovery comes from the district courts, because there is little opportunity to obtain appellate review of discovery rulings. Such rulings are not final orders and are not appealable as such.[70] They can be reviewed on appeal from a final judgment, but by then the matter will probably be moot and in any event the broad discretion the discovery rules vest in the trial courts will bar reversal save under very unusual circumstances.[71] Occasionally there will be review from a sanction imposed under Rule 37,[72] and in a few instances an interlocutory appeal has been allowed under 28 U.S.C.A. § 1292(b),[73] although normally a question about discovery

68. Samuelson v. Susen, C.A.3d, 1978, 576 F.2d 546. See also Miller v. Transamerican Press, Inc., C.A.5th, 1980, 621 F.2d 721, certiorari denied 101 S.Ct. 1759, 450 U.S. 1041, 68 L.Ed.2d 238.

69. Evidence Rule 501. See § 93 below; 8 Wright & Miller, Civil §§ 2016–2020.

The United States is subject to the discovery rules, but it has a number of privileges available to it that are not enjoyed by private litigants. Id. at § 2019. One point now settled in the cases is that income tax returns are not privileged, and their disclosure can be required in a civil case. Id. at § 2019, pp. 162–164.

The application of the privilege against self-incrimination to discovery in a civil case is not yet satisfactorily resolved in the case law. Id. at § 2018. However, there is a dictum in Baxter v. Palmigiano, 1976, 96 S.Ct. 1551, 1558, 425 U.S. 308, 318, 47 L.Ed.2d 810, that "the Fifth Amendment does not forbid adverse inferences against parties to civil actions when they refuse to testify in response to probative evidence offered against them * * *." See the explanation of that dictum in Lefkowitz v. Cunningham, 1977, 97 S.Ct. 2132, 2137 n. 5, 431 U.S. 801, 808 n. 5, 53 L.Ed.2d 1.

70. The fullest statement of the reason for the rule is in American Exp. Ware-

housing, Ltd. v. Transamerica Ins. Co., C.A.2d, 1967, 380 F.2d 277, 280. See also Browning Debenture Holders' Committee v. DASA Corp., C.A.2d, 1975, 524 F.2d 811, 817; and cases cited 8 Wright & Miller, Civil § 2006 n. 65, and 15 Wright, Miller & Cooper, Jurisdiction § 3914 n. 84.

There are a few unusual situations in which the order is final and appealable. E.g., Republic Gear Co. v. Borg-Warner Corp., C.A.2d, 1967, 381 F.2d 551; U. S. v. McWhirter, C.A.5th, 1967, 376 F.2d 102; Martin v. Reynolds Metals Corp., C.A.9th, 1960, 297 F.2d 49.

71. See, e.g., Voegeli v. Lewis, C.A.8th, 1977, 568 F.2d 89, 96, stating the rule as set out in the text, but finding that reversal was required on the particular facts before it. See 8 Wright & Miller, Civil § 2006 nn. 86–89.

72. Hickman v. Taylor, 1947, 67 S.Ct. 385, 329 U.S. 495, 91 L.Ed. 451; Cooke v. New Mexico Junior College Bd., C.A. 10th, 1978, 579 F.2d 568; David v. Hooker, Ltd., C.A.9th, 1977, 560 F.2d 412. But cf. Cromaglass Corp. v. Ferm, C.A.3d, 1974, 500 F.2d 601.

73. E.g., Duplan Corp. v. Moulinage et Retorderie de Chavanoz, C.A.4th, 1973, 487 F.2d 480; Baker v. F and F Inv., C.A.2d, 1972, 470 F.2d 778, certiorari denied 93 S.Ct. 2147, 411 U.S. 966, 36 L.Ed.2d 686; and cases cited 8 Wright & Miller, Civil § 2006 n. 72.

would not satisfy the rigid criteria of that statute.[74] In the states the writs of mandamus and prohibition are often used for this purpose and the federal courts have sometimes allowed them to be used to review a discovery order,[75] although this continues to be the exception rather than the rule.[76]

§ 82. The Rule of Hickman v. Taylor [1]

The best-known, and most important, decision on discovery in federal court is that of the Supreme Court in Hickman v. Taylor.[2] The tug "John M. Taylor" sank on February 7, 1943, while helping to tow a car float across the Delaware River at Philadelphia. Five of the nine crewmen, including Norman Hickman, drowned. Three days later the owners of the tug retained a lawyer to defend them in whatever litigation might arise. On March 4th a public hearing was held before the United States Steamboat Inspectors, at which the four survivors testified. This testimony was recorded and made available to all interested parties. Shortly thereafter the lawyer interviewed the survivors privately, and obtained statements from them about the sinking, which they signed on March 29th. He also interviewed other persons believed to have some information relating to the accident and in some cases he made memoranda of what they told him. Seven months after the sinking Hickman's administrator brought suit under the Jones Act against the tugowners and the owner of the car float.

One year after this lawsuit was commenced plaintiff served 39 interrogatories upon the tugowners. All of these were answered except one, interrogatory 38, which read: "State whether any statements of the members of the crews of the Tugs 'J. M. Taylor' and 'Philadelphia' or of any other vessel were taken in connection with the towing of the car float and the sinking of the Tug 'John M. Taylor.' Attach hereto exact copies of all such statements if in writing,

---

74. Xerox Corp. v. SCM Corp., C.A.2d, 1976, 534 F.2d 1031; U. S. v. Woodbury, C.A.9th, 1959, 263 F.2d 784. See also 16 Wright, Miller & Cooper, Jurisdiction § 3931.

75. Schlagenhauf v. Holder, 1964, 85 S.Ct. 234, 379 U.S. 104, 13 L.Ed.2d 152; Colonial Times, Inc. v. Gasch, C.A. 1975, 509 F.2d 517, 166 U.S.App.D.C. 184; Heathman v. U. S. Dist. Court for Central Dist. of California, C.A.9th, 1974, 503 F.2d 1032; and cases cited 8 Wright & Miller, Civil § 2006 n. 80. See also 16 Wright, Miller & Cooper, Jurisdiction §§ 3934, 3935.

76. Kerr v. U. S. Dist. Court of Northern Dist. of California, 1976, 96 S.Ct. 2119, 426 U.S. 394, 48 L.Ed.2d 725. National Right to Work Legal Defense v. Richey, C.A.1975, 510 F.2d 1239, 167 U.S.App.D.C. 18, certiorari denied 95

S.Ct. 2631, 422 U.S. 1008, 45 L.Ed.2d 671; American Exp. Warehousing, Ltd. v. Transamerica Ins. Co., C.A.2d, 1967, 380 F.2d 277; and cases cited 8 Wright & Miller, Civil § 2006 n. 75.

[§ 82]

1. 8 Wright & Miller, Civil §§ 2021–2028. The literature is large but the definitive treatment is Cooper, Work Product of the Rulesmakers, 1969, 53 Minn.L.Rev. 1269. See also Comment, Ambiguities After the 1970 Amendments to the Federal Rules of Civil Procedure Relating to Discovery of Experts and Attorney's Work-Product, 1971, 17 Wayne L.Rev. 1145.

2. 1947, 67 S.Ct. 385, 329 U.S. 495, 91 L.Ed. 451. See Freedman, Discovery as an Instrument of Justice, 1948, 22 Temp.L.Q. 174.

and if oral, set forth in detail the exact provisions of any such oral statements or reports." The defendants also refused to answer certain supplemental interrogatories that called for copies of any other oral or written statements defendants had obtained as to the accident.

The five judges of the district court, sitting en banc, overruled defendants' objection to interrogatory 38 and the supplemental interrogatories, and ordered them answered.[3] The court held that statements of a third party obtained by an attorney are not within the attorney-client privilege, and that discovery of non-privileged material would be granted when asked unless under the circumstances of a particular case the court was satisfied that the administration of justice would be in some way impeded. It did agree that the lawyer's memoranda of oral statements made to him could be submitted to the court, and so much of these memoranda as contained his mental impressions, opinions, legal theories, or other collateral matter would be deleted.

The tugowners and the lawyer refused to produce these statements, and the court ordered them imprisoned for contempt of court. Their appeal from the contempt conviction was twice heard by the Court of Appeals for the Third Circuit, sitting en banc. It unanimously held that the order of production was improper and that the contempt conviction should be reversed.[4] It created a broadened attorney-client privilege, applicable in discovery proceedings, and held that the "work product of the lawyer," the results of his use of his tongue, his pen, and his head, for his client, fell within this broadened privilege.

The Supreme Court unanimously affirmed the holding of the court of appeals that the discovery ordered, and the resulting contempt conviction, were improper, but it did so on a rather different analysis from that employed by either of the lower courts. In a sweeping opinion by Justice Murphy, the Court illuminated many of the dark and controversial areas of the discovery rules.

In a much-quoted passage, the Court called for a broad and liberal treatment of the discovery rules.[5] And it agreed with the plaintiff that the materials sought were not protected by the attorney-client privilege,[6] apparently considering, as it later explicitly held,[7] that "privilege" in the discovery rules is to be given the same meaning as

---

3. Hickman v. Taylor, D.C.Pa.1945, 4 F.R.D. 479.

4. Hickman v. Taylor, C.C.A.3d, 1945, 153 F.2d 212.

It has been commonly supposed that the order was for criminal contempt and appealable on that ground. See § 101 below. But see Southern Ry. Co. v. Lanham, C.A.5th, 1969, 408 F.2d 348, 350 n. 2 (Brown, J., dissenting).

5. 67 S.Ct. at 392, 329 U.S. at 507. See also Herbert v. Lando, 1979, 99 S.Ct. 1635, 1649, 441 U.S. 153, 177, 60 L.Ed. 2d 115.

6. 67 S.Ct. at 392, 329 U.S. at 508.

7. U. S. v. Reynolds, 1953, 73 S.Ct. 528, 531, 345 U.S. 1, 6, 97 L.Ed. 727.

it has generally in the law of evidence. Even though the material sought was not privileged, the Court held that discovery was not proper. "Here is simply an attempt, without purported necessity or justification, to secure written statements, private memoranda and personal recollections prepared or formed by an adverse party's counsel in the course of his legal duties. As such, it falls outside the arena of discovery and contravenes the public policy underlying the orderly prosecution and defense of legal claims. Not even the most liberal of discovery theories can justify unwarranted inquiries into the files and the mental impressions of an attorney."[8]

This did not mean, the Court said, that all written materials obtained or prepared by a lawyer with an eye to litigation are necessarily free from discovery in all cases. "Where relevant and non-privileged facts remain hidden in an attorney's file and where production of those facts is essential to the preparation of one's case, discovery may properly be had. Such written statements and documents might, under certain circumstances, be admissible in evidence or give clues as to the existence or location of relevant facts. Or they might be useful for purposes of impeachment or corroboration. And production might be justified where the witnesses are no longer available or can be reached only with difficulty."[9] The burden, though, was on the party seeking discovery of the lawyer's "work product" to establish adequate reasons to justify such production.

A different rule was said to apply to the oral statements made by witnesses to the lawyer. To require him to state what he remembers or what he saw fit to write down as to the remarks of a witness would carry additional dangers not involved when the lawyer is merely asked to turn over a statement that the witness has signed. Thus as to such oral statements, the Court said, "we do not believe that any showing of necessity can be made under the circumstances of this case so as to justify production."[10]

Finally on the facts before it the Court noted that searching interrogatories had been directed to defendants and that full and honest answers to such broad inquiries would necessarily have included all pertinent information gleaned by the lawyer through his interviews with the witnesses. Thus plaintiff already had the facts that he needed, and his stated reason for seeking production of the statements, that he wanted them to help prepare himself to examine witnesses and to make sure that he had overlooked nothing, was an insufficient showing of necessity and justification for the discovery sought.[11]

Hickman v. Taylor adopted a middle position between that of the district court, which would have made the work product of lawyers normally subject to discovery, and that of the court of appeals, which,

---

8. 67 S.Ct. at 393, 329 U.S. at 510.

9. 67 S.Ct. at 394, 329 U.S. at 511.

10. 67 S.Ct. at 394, 329 U.S. at 512–513.

11. 67 S.Ct. at 395, 329 U.S. at 513.

by calling such material privileged, would have barred all discovery no matter how pressing the need. The Supreme Court gave the lawyer's work product a qualified immunity from discovery. Such material was discoverable only on a substantial showing of "necessity or justification."[12] The Court also made a distinction, presaged both by the decision of the district court and by an amendment to Rule 30(b) proposed by the Advisory Committee in 1946 but never adopted, by which so much of the work product as may reflect the mental impressions or opinions of the lawyer was for practical purposes, absolutely immune from discovery.

An absolute rule, either permitting or barring all discovery, would be simple to administer. A qualified rule, which requires a balancing of competing interests in each case, necessarily is not. Thus there was much litigation and many reported decisions subsequent to Hickman v. Taylor in which courts sought to apply that qualified rule.

It is probably no exaggeration to say, as one court did, that Hickman v. Taylor had opened "a veritable Pandora's Box."[13] Many states, otherwise adopting the federal discovery rules, had undertaken to solve the problems raised by the decision in a detailed rule,[14] but for more than 20 years the matter was left in the federal system to adjudication on a case-by-case basis. It was not until 1970 that a new Rule 26(b)(3) was adopted in the federal system to cover this problem. That rule accepts the notion of a qualified immunity for work product, as the Hickman case had announced, but it speaks to details on which Hickman was silent and has resolved questions on which the lower courts were in disagreement.

Thus Hickman's holding that the work product of a lawyer has a qualified immunity from discovery can be applied only when it is known what constitutes a lawyer's work product. Prior to the 1970 amendment there were repeated questions about who is a "lawyer" for purposes of the work product immunity, and about what classes of materials obtained by such persons are entitled to this qualified immunity.[15]

One question of much practical importance is whether the work product immunity extends only to statements and other material obtained by trial counsel, or whether it gives a qualified protection also to statements obtained by claim agents or investigators, which may ultimately be used by counsel. In the Hickman case the Court was concerned only with statements obtained by the defendants' lawyer. Thus the holding of Hickman necessarily went only that far. The Third Circuit, however, in the important Alltmont case, said that "its

---

12. 67 S.Ct. at 393, 329 U.S. at 510.

13. Viront v. Wheeling & L. E. Ry. Co., D.C.Ohio 1950, 10 F.R.D. 45, 47.

"No subject had been more disputed or had received more conflicting judicial interpretation than the discovery of lawyers' work product * * *." Glaser, Pretrial Discovery and the Adversary System, 1968, p. 128.

14. The state provisions are cited in 8 Wright & Miller, Civil § 2022 n. 98.

15. 8 Wright & Miller, Civil § 2024.

rationale has a much broader sweep and applies to all statements of prospective witnesses which a party has obtained for his trial counsel's use."[16] There is obvious force to the arguments made in Alltmont, but arguments could be made for an opposite result and the lower court decisions were quite divided.[17] Rule 26(b)(3) resolves this conflict in the direction taken by Alltmont. It defines work product as "documents and tangible things * * * prepared in anticipation of litigation or for trial by or for another party or by or for that other party's representative (including his attorney, consultant, surety, indemnitor, insurer, or agent) * * *."[18] Thus it is now clear that the immunity, when it is otherwise applicable, does not turn on whether an attorney obtained a document but extends to material obtained by anyone representing a party,[19] including the party's insurer.[20]

The one area to which the work product immunity had always clearly applied was to material obtained by a lawyer. Even here it was thought that there was a qualified immunity only if the material was the result of a basic professional relationship between the lawyer who obtained the material and the party, or that it required the training, skill, and knowledge of a lawyer, or the essential integrity implicit in the lawyer-client relationship.[21] These limitations are ended under Rule 26(b)(3) since it reaches any representative of the party.

Rule 26(b)(3) codifies the prior decisions in providing that no matter who has obtained the material, the immunity attaches only if the material was "prepared in anticipation of litigation or for trial." Some of the prior cases had attached significance to whether a document was obtained before or after litigation was commenced, but this cannot be sound. Prudent parties anticipate litigation and begin preparation prior to the formal commencement of an action. Thus the test should be whether, in light of the nature of the document and the factual situation in the particular case, the document can fairly be said to have been prepared or obtained because of the prospect of

---

16. Alltmont v. U. S., C.C.A.3d, 1949, 177 F.2d 971, 976, certiorari denied 70 S.Ct. 999, 339 U.S. 967, 94 L.Ed. 1375.

17. See cases cited 8 Wright & Miller, Civil § 2024 nn. 37, 38.

18. "The sole issue in Hickman related to materials prepared by an attorney, and courts thereafter disagreed over whether the doctrine applied as well to materials prepared on his behalf. * * * Necessarily, it must. This view is reflected in the Federal Rules of Civil Procedure, see Rule 26(b)(3) * * *." U. S. v. Nobles, 1975, 95 S.Ct. 2160, 2170 n. 13, 422 U.S. 225, 239 n. 13, 45 L.Ed.2d 141, on remand C.A.9th, 522 F.2d 1274. See also Cooper, note 1 above, at 1327.

19. Almaguer v. Chicago, R. I. & P. R. Co, D.C.Neb.1972, 55 F.R.D. 147; Bunting v. Gainsville Machine Co., D.C. Del.1971, 53 F.R.D. 594; U. S. v. Maryland Shipbuilding & Drydock Co., D.C. Md.1970, 51 F.R.D. 159; Dingler v. Halcyon Lijn N. V., D.C.Pa.1970, 50 F.R.D. 211.

20. Bredice v. Doctors Hosp. Inc., D.C. D.C.1970, 50 F.R.D. 249, adhered to D.C.D.C.1970, 51 F.R.D. 187, affirmed C.A.1973, 479 F.2d 920, 156 U.S.App. D.C. 199; cf. Bunting v. Gainsville Machine Co., D.C.Del.1971, 53 F.R.D. 594.

21. U. S. v. Anderson, D.C.Colo.1963, 34 F.R.D. 518, 521; Bifferato v. States Marine Corp. of Delaware, D.C.N.Y. 1951, 11 F.R.D. 44, 46.

litigation.[22] But the converse of this is that even though litigation is already in prospect, there is no work product immunity for documents prepared in the regular course of business rather than for purposes of the litigation.[23] Although the earlier decisions are not wholly consistent, and to the extent that the amended rule seems to speak to the question it gives unsatisfactory answers,[24] it ought to be held, as the Fourth Circuit has in an important decision,[25] that material prepared in anticipation of one lawsuit enjoys the qualified immunity even in another unrelated lawsuit.

Even if the work product doctrine applies, it protects only documents and tangible things. It does not protect facts learned from the documents or things. There is no shield against discovery, by interrogatories or by deposition, of the facts that the opponent has acquired, or the persons from whom he obtained the facts, or the existence or nonexistence of documents, even though the documents themselves have a qualified immunity from discovery.[26]

Even if, on the tests just described, a document or other tangible thing is found to be a part of the work product, this does not mean that it is not subject to discovery. Rule 26(b)(3), like the Hickman decision, creates only a qualified immunity and allows discovery of work product material if "the party seeking discovery has substantial need of the materials in the preparation of his case and * * * he is unable without undue hardship to obtain the substantial equivalent of the materials by other means."

Undoubtedly the single most important factor in determining whether to allow discovery of work product information is whether the information in question is otherwise available to the party seeking discovery. This factor is deftly captured in the formula of Rule 26(b)(3). On this principle discovery of the statements of witnesses is

---

22. In re Grand Jury Proceedings, C.A.3d, 1979, 604 F.2d 798, 803; Indian Law Resource Center v. Department of Interior, D.C.D.C.1979, 477 F.Supp. 144, 148; and cases cited 8 Wright & Miller, Civil § 2024 n. 24.

See Comment, Access to Work Product of Disqualified Counsel, 1979, 46 U.Chi.L.Rev. 443; Note, The Availability of the Work Product of a Disqualified Attorney: What Standard?, 1979, 127 U.Pa.L.Rev. 1607.

A remote possibility of litigation is not enough. Garfinkle v. Arcata Nat. Corp., D.C.N.Y.1974, 64 F.R.D. 688.

23. U. S. v. Brown, C.A.7th, 1973, 478 F.2d 1038; Westhemeco Ltd. v. New Hampshire Ins. Co., D.C.N.Y.1979, 82 F.R.D. 702; and cases cited 8 Wright & Miller, Civil § 2024 n. 25.

24. See 8 Wright & Miller, Civil § 2024, pp. 200–202.

25. Duplan Corp. v. Moulinage et Retorderie de Chavanoz, C.A.4th, 1973, 487 F.2d 480, noted 1974, 27 Vand.L. Rev. 826.

See also Duplan Corp. v. Moulinage et Retorderie de Chavanoz, C.A.4th, 1974, 509 F.2d 730, certiorari denied 95 S.Ct. 1438, 420 U.S. 997, 43 L.Ed.2d 680; Hercules Inc. v. Exxon Corp., D.C.Del. 1977, 434 F.Supp. 136, 153; Note, Discovery of an Attorney's Work Product in Subsequent Litigation, 1974 Duke L.J. 799.

26. Hickman v. Taylor, 1947, 67 S.Ct. 385, 390, 329 U.S. 495, 504, 91 L.Ed. 451; In re Murphy, C.A.8th, 1977, 560 F.2d 326, 336 n. 20; Ford v. Phillips Electronics Instruments Co., D.C.Pa. 1979, 82 F.R.D. 359; 8 Wright & Miller, Civil § 2023, pp. 194–196.

usually denied if it is possible for the party to interview the witnesses himself or to take their depositions.[27] The fact that this will cause added expense for the party seeking discovery is not usually, in itself, enough to constitute necessity or justification for discovery.[28] The corollary is that if the witness is no longer available, so that the moving party cannot obtain his version of the facts, production of his statements will be required.[29]

The fact that the witness is available does not bar a finding that discovery should be had. As one important decision put it, "the real question is whether the movant can obtain the *facts* without production of the documents containing the original statements. Therefore, the likelihood that the movant, even though he presently can obtain statements from the witnesses by deposition, will not obtain the substantial equivalent of the prior statements he seeks to obtain through production should also be considered."[30] This view is accepted in Rule 26(b)(3).

The party cannot obtain the substantial equivalent of a prior statement of a witness, and discovery must be allowed, if by the time the party interviews him or takes his deposition his memory is faulty and he no longer recalls details of the event.[31] Indeed, though there are cases to the contrary,[32] there is now substantial authority for the proposition that statements taken from witnesses close to the time of the occurrence are unique, in that they provide an immediate impression of the facts. On this view, mere lapse of time is in itself enough to justify discovery.[33] On the face of it, the Hickman case itself might seem to the contrary, since the statements sought unsuccessfully in that case were contemporaneous statements. But Hickman may be distinguishable on this point, since in Hickman plaintiff did have access to the testimony of the survivors before an investigating board, and this testimony was even closer to the date of the accident sued for than were the statements obtained by defendants' lawyer. Thus in Hickman both parties did have access to a more or less con-

27. Miles v. Bell Helicopter Co., D.C.Ga. 1974, 385 F.Supp. 1029, 1032; U. S. v. Real Estate Bd. of Metropolitan St. Louis, D.C.Mo.1973, 59 F.R.D. 637; Arney v. Geo. A. Hormel & Co., D.C. Minn.1971, 53 F.R.D. 179; and cases cited 8 Wright & Miller, Civil § 2025 n. 72.

28. See 8 Wright & Miller, Civil § 2025 nn. 73, 74.

29. In re Grand Jury Investigation, C.A.3d, 1979, 599 F.2d 1224, 1231–1232; Rackers v. Siegfried, D.C.Mo.1971, 54 F.R.D. 24; and cases cited 8 Wright & Miller, Civil § 2025 nn. 75–78.

30. Southern Ry. Co. v. Lanham, C.A.5th, 1968, 403 F.2d 119, 127.

31. McDougall v. Dunn, C.A.4th, 1972, 468 F.2d 468, 474; Xerox Corp. v. International Business Machines Corp., D.C.N.Y.1977, 79 F.R.D. 7; and cases cited 8 Wright & Miller, Civil § 2025 n. 82.

32. First Wisconsin Mortg. Trust v. First Wisconsin Corp., D.C.Wis.1980, 86 F.R.D. 160, 166–167; and cases cited 8 Wright & Miller, Civil § 2025 n. 84.

33. McDougall v. Dunn, C.A.4th, 1972, 468 F.2d 468, 474; Southern R. Co. v. Lanham, C.A.5th, 1968, 403 F.2d 119, 127–131; Teribery v. Norfolk & W. Ry. Co., D.C.Pa.1975, 68 F.R.D. 46; Advisory Committee Note, 48 F.R.D. 485, 501; and cases cited 8 Wright & Miller, Civil § 2025, n. 83.

temporaneous record of events.[34] The notion that the statement taken nearest to the event will most accurately reflect the perception the witness had of the event is amply supported by psychological studies,[35] as well as by common sense. This fact lends strong support to the argument that lapse of time in itself creates necessity or justification for the production of statements taken near the time of the event.

It is not enough to obtain discovery of work product material that the party cannot get the information he is seeking by other means. He must also satisfy the court that he has "substantial need of the materials in the preparation of his case."[36] A mere surmise that the material sought may be useful is not a sufficient showing.[37]

If information that otherwise is subject to discovery may be obtained in no other way, it may be had from the opposing party's attorney.[38] In ordering discovery, however, Rule 26(b)(3) codifies the teaching of the cases when it says that the court "shall protect against disclosure of the mental impressions, conclusions, opinion, or legal theories of an attorney or other representative of a party concerning the litigation."[39] This protection is absolute and "no showing of relevance, substantial need or undue hardship should justify compelled disclosure of an attorney's mental impressions, conclusions, opinions or legal theories."[40]

---

34. See Guilford Nat. Bank of Greensboro v. Southern Ry. Co., C.A.4th, 1962, 297 F.2d 921, 926.

35. Gray et al., Psychology in Use, 2d ed. 1951, p. 242; Dallenbach, The Relation of Memory Error to Time Interval, 1913, 20 Psych.Rev. 323; Hutchins & Schlesinger, Some Observations on the Law of Evidence—Memory, 1928, 41 Harv.L.Rev. 860, 864–867; Gardner, The Perception and Memory of Witnesses, 1933, 18 Cornell L.Q. 391, 393–394. See Southern Ry. Co. v. Lanham, C.A.5th, 1968, 403 F.2d 119, 128 n. 7.

This point is subject to the qualification, however, stated by Judge Rubin in Hamilton v. Canal Barge Co., Inc., D.C. La.1974, 395 F.Supp. 975, 977–978, that only statements taken almost immediately after an event have this unique value.

36. Compare Augenti v. Cappellini, D.C. Pa.1979, 84 F.R.D. 73, and Wheeling-Pittsburgh Steel Corp., v. Underwriters Laboratories, Inc., D.C.Ill.1978, 81 F.R.D. 8, with Breedlove v. Beech Aircraft Corp., D.C.Miss.1972, 57 F.R.D. 202, and Hodgson v. General Motors Acceptance Corp., D.C.Fla.1972, 54 F.R.D. 445. See 8 Wright & Miller, Civil § 2025 nn. 88–93.

37. Stephens Produce Co. v. NLRB, C.A.8th, 1975, 515 F.2d 1373, 1377; Hauger v. Chicago, R. I. & P. R. Co., C.A.7th, 1954, 216 F.2d 501, 508; U. S. v. Chatham City Corp., D.C.Ga.1976, 72 F.R.D. 640, 643.

38. Xerox Corp. v. International Business Machines Corp., D.C.N.Y.1974, 64 F.R.D. 367; In re Penn Central Commercial Paper Litigation, D.C.N.Y. 1973, 61 F.R.D. 453; and cases cited 8 Wright & Miller, Civil § 2026 nn. 95, 96.

39. Hickman v. Taylor, 1947, 67 S.Ct. 385, 394–395, 329 U.S. 495, 512–513, 91 L.Ed. 451; 8 Wright & Miller, Civil § 2026.

40. Duplan Corp. v. Moulinage et Retorderie de Chavanoz, C.A.4th, 1974, 509 F.2d 730, 734, certiorari denied 95 S.Ct. 1438, 420 U.S. 997, 43 L.Ed.2d 680. See also Upjohn Co. v. U. S., 1981, 101 S.Ct. 677, 686–689, 449 U.S. 383, 397–402, 66 L.Ed.2d 584; Comment, The Potential for Discovery of Opinion Work Product under Rule 26(b)(3), 1978, 64 Iowa L.Rev. 103; Note, Protection of Opinion Work Product under the Federal Rules of Civil Procedure, 1978, 64 Va.L.Rev. 333.

Although there was considerable confusion on the matter, prior to 1970 the courts had come increasingly to the view that a statement given by a party himself to his opponent stood in a different category from other work product material and that the party should be allowed to obtain a copy of his own statement without making any special showing.[41] The statement of a party differs significantly from the statement of an ordinary witness. The statement of the witness is hearsay, normally usable at the trial, if at all, only for purposes of impeachment. The statement of the party, on the other hand, may be introduced as substantive evidence by his opponent as an admission. Decisions that had refused to require production of a party's statement had failed to give full effect to the important principle, stated by Justice Jackson in his concurring opinion in the Hickman case, that "it seems clear and long has been recognized that discovery should provide a party access to anything that is evidence in his case."[42]

The 1970 amendments wrote the better view on this question into the rules. Under the second paragraph of Rule 26(b)(3) a party may obtain as a matter of right a statement concerning the action or its subject matter that he has previously made.[43]

The new rule, however, goes even farther. In addition to allowing a party access to a copy of his own statement it also creates a procedure by which any person who has given a statement concerning the action or its subject matter may request a copy from the person to whom it was given and may obtain a court order compelling delivery of the copy if the request is refused.[44] The compelling arguments for requiring discovery of a party's statement are applicable only in part to a statement of a person not a party. The strongest argument for this new procedure is one simply of fairness, that it is unfair to take a statement from a person without providing him with a copy of it. It must be emphasized that this provision creates a right only in the person who gave the statement and does not allow a party to the lawsuit to obtain, as of right, the statement of some other person. It well may be, however, that this portion of Rule 26(b)(3) is a step in the direction of ultimately making all statements of witnesses freely discoverable.[45] If the rulemakers should ever go all the way in that direction, it would greatly reduce the controversy about the work product doctrine and the bulk of the litigation it has caused.

The Supreme Court has recently said that "the concerns reflected in the work-product doctrine do not disappear once trial has begun.

---

41. 8 Wright & Miller, Civil § 2027.

42. 67 S.Ct. at 396, 329 U.S. at 515.

43. Dingler v. Halcyon Lijn N. V., D.C. Pa.1970, 50 F.R.D. 211.

44. 8 Wright & Miller, Civil § 2028. This portion of the new rule has not been mentioned in any reported case and it is impossible to tell to what extent it is being used in practice.

45. See Miller v. Harpster, Alaska, 1964, 392 P.2d 21; Monier v. Chamberlain, 1966, 221 N.E.2d 410, 35 Ill.2d 351; Cooper, note 1 above, at 1318–1328.

Disclosure of an attorney's efforts at trial, as surely as disclosure during pretrial discovery, could disrupt the orderly development and presentation of his case."[46] The Court found it unnecessary in that case to delineate the scope of the doctrine at trial, but the very suggestion that the doctrine applies at trial was surprising to two concurring Justices who had shared the common understanding that the Hickman rule is solely a limitation on pretrial discovery.[47]

§ 83. Preventing Abuse of Discovery [1]

Liberal discovery procedures are an important advance in the litigation process but it cannot be thought that they are an unmixed blessing. Any device, however salutary, can be abused and there are undoubtedly instances in which a party will seek to use discovery in a way that will oppress his opponent,[2] although studies have shown that these instances are relatively uncommon.[3]

The rules provide remedies against abuse of discovery. Rule 26(c) authorizes the court to make orders for the protection of parties and persons from whom discovery is being sought. The Supreme Court has said that this provides "ample powers of the district judge to prevent abuse" and that "[w]ith this authority at hand, judges should not hesitate to exercise appropriate control over the discovery process."[4]

---

46. U. S. v. Nobles, 1975, 95 S.Ct. 2160, 2170, 422 U.S. 225, 239, 45 L.Ed.2d 141. The holding of the case is that the work product doctrine applies in criminal litigation as well as civil.

47. 95 S.Ct. at 2172–2176, 422 U.S. at 242–254 (White, J., joined by Rehnquist, J., concurring).

[§ 83]

1. 8 Wright & Miller, Civil §§ 2035–2044; Levine, "Abuse" of Discovery: or Hard Work Makes Good Law, 1981, 67 A.B.A.J. 565; Pollack, Discovery—Its Abuse and Correction, 1979, 80 F.R.D. 219; Comment, Preventing Abuse of Discovery in Federal Courts, 1981, 30 Cath.U.L.Rev. 273.

2. In a 1975 securities case, the Supreme Court said: "The potential for possible abuse of the liberal discovery provisions of the federal rules may likewise exist in this type of case to a greater extent than they do in other litigation. The prospect of extensive deposition of the defendant's officers and associates and the concomitant opportunity for extensive discovery of business documents, is a common occurrence in this and similar types of litigation. To the extent that this process eventually produces relevant evidence which is useful in determining the merits of the claims asserted by the parties, it bears the imprimatur of the Federal Rules of Civil Procedure and of the many cases liberally interpreting them. But to the extent that it permits a plaintiff with a largely groundless claim to simply take up the time of a number of other people, with the right to do so representing an *in terrorem* increment of the settlement value rather than a reasonably founded hope that the process will reveal relevant evidence, it is a social cost rather than a benefit." Blue Chip Stamps v. Manor Drug Stores, 1975, 95 S.Ct. 1917, 1928, 421 U.S. 723, 741, 44 L.Ed. 2d 539.

3. Connolly, Holleman & Kuhlman, Judicial Controls and the Civil Litigative Process: Discovery, Federal Judicial Center 1978, p. 35; Glaser, Pretrial Discovery and the Adversary System, 1968, pp. 117–123, 129–134; Schroeder & Frank, The Proposed Changes in the Discovery Rules, 1978 Ariz.St.L.J. 475, 476–478, 492.

4. Herbert v. Lando, 1979, 99 S.Ct. 1635, 1649, 441 U.S. 153, 177, 60 L.Ed. 2d 115.

Prior to the 1970 amendments what is now Rule 26(c) was Rule 30(b), and purported to apply only to oral deposi-

A motion for a protective order may be made by any party to the case or by the person from whom discovery is sought.[5] Ordinarily the motion must be addressed to the court in which the action is pending, though Rule 26(c) also allows application to the court in the district where a deposition is to be taken on matters relating to that deposition.[6] The motion should be timely, a limitation that is interpreted with reference to the circumstances of the particular case and the discovery sought.[7] The moving party must show good cause for a protective order, which puts the burden on him to show some adequate reason for the order.[8]

Rule 26(c) provides that the court may make any order that justice requires to protect from annoyance, embarrassment, oppression, or undue burden or expense. It then specifies eight particular types of protective orders that a court may make. The court may order that the discovery not be had, although in view of the freedom of discovery that the rules provide, motions for such relief are usually denied.[9] Witnesses cannot ordinarily escape examination by claiming that they have no knowledge of any relevant facts, since the party seeking to take the deposition is entitled to test their lack of knowledge.[10]

The court may order that discovery be had only on specified terms and conditions, and may designate the time or place for discovery.[11] As a normal rule plaintiff will be required to submit to a deposition in

---

tions, though it was incorporated by reference in some other discovery rules and had been read by the courts into the others.

5. Caisson Corp. v. County West Bldg. Corp., D.C.Pa.1974, 62 F.R.D. 331; Norris Mfg. Co. v. R. E. Darling Co., D.C.Md.1961, 29 F.R.D. 1; Central Hide & Rendering Co. v. B–M–K Corp., D.C.Del.1956, 19 F.R.D. 296. Other parties have no standing to claim protection of a purely personal nature for a witness or party who makes no such claim for himself. Commercial Laundry v. Linen Supply Assn. of Greater N. Y., D.C.N.Y.1950, 90 F.Supp. 470.

6. The courts prefer to have the court in which the action is pending pass on these matters. Socialist Workers Party v. Attorney Gen. of U. S., D.C.Md. 1977, 73 F.R.D. 699; E. I. du Pont de Nemours & Co. v. Deering Milliken Research Corp., D.C.Del.1976, 72 F.R.D. 440.

7. Until 1970 the rule required that the motion be "seasonably" made. The present form of the rule does not include that requirement but the courts consider to look to the timeliness of the

motion. See cases cited 8 Wright & Miller, Civil § 2035 nn. 12–17.

8. In re Halkin, C.A.1979, 598 F.2d 176, 183, 194 U.S.App.D.C. 257; Blankenship v. Hearst Corp., C.A.9th, 1975, 519 F.2d 418. See Comment, note 1 above, at 285–297, for discussion of how courts decide whether this burden has been carried.

9. Salter v. Upjohn Co., C.A.5th, 1979, 593 F.2d 649, 651; Apco Oil Corp. v. Certified Transp., Inc., D.C.Mo.1969, 46 F.R.D. 428, 431; 8 Wright & Miller, Civil § 2037.

10. Amherst Leasing Corp. v. Emhart Corp., D.C.Conn.1974, 65 F.R.D. 121; Less v. Taber Instrument Corp., D.C. N.Y.1971, 53 F.R.D. 645; and cases cited 8 Wright & Miller, Civil § 2037 n. 52.

A different result is often reached if the proposed deponent is a busy government official. Shirley v. Chestnut, C.A.10th, 1979, 603 F.2d 805; Kyle Engineering Co. v. Kleppe, C.A.9th, 1979, 600 F.2d 226; and cases cited 8 Wright & Miller, Civil § 2037 n. 53.

11. Rule 26(c)(2); 8 Wright & Miller, Civil §§ 2038, 2111, 2112.

the district in which he has brought suit.[12] Since he has selected the forum, he will not be heard to complain about having to appear there for a deposition. But this is at best a general rule, and is not adhered to if the plaintiff can show good cause for not being required to come to the district where the action is pending. Thus a protective order will be granted if the plaintiff is physically and financially unable to come to the forum,[13] or if to do so would cause unusual and serious hardship to the plaintiff.[14] The general principle that the plaintiff must come to the forum he has chosen loses force if he had no choice of forum to begin with.[15] Commonly if a sufficient showing is made that examination at the designated place will cause undue hardship, the court makes an order in the alternative, providing that the examination be held at some other place or that the party seeking the examination pay travel expenses for the deponent to the place he has chosen or that the deposition be taken on written questions rather than orally, thus leaving the choice of method to the party who wishes the examination.[16]

The court has power, however, in any case to order that discovery be had only by a method of discovery other than that selected by the party seeking discovery. In the past this has most often involved a motion asking that a deposition be taken only on written questions rather than by oral examination. Usually the court will not interfere with the choice made by the party seeking discovery,[17] but if the examination will be brief or simple, or there are other reasons why written questions will suffice in the particular case, the court will order that the deposition be taken in that fashion.[18]

The court may order that certain matters not be inquired into, or that the scope of the discovery be limited to certain matters. Ever since the days of the former equity bill of discovery there has been applied to discovery "the principle of judicial parsimony," by which, where one issue may be determinative of a case, the court has discre-

---

12. Collins v. Wayland, C.C.A.9th, 1944, 139 F.2d 677, certiorari denied 64 S.Ct. 1151, 322 U.S. 744, 88 L.Ed. 1576; Hunter v. Riverside Community Memorial Hosp., D.C.Wis.1972, 58 F.R.D. 218; and cases cited 8 Wright & Miller, Civil § 2112 n. 85.

13. Sullivan v. Southern Pac. Co., D.C. N.Y.1947, 7 F.R.D. 206; cf. Rifkin v. United States Lines Co., D.C.N.Y.1959, 177 F.Supp. 875. The showing of inability was held insufficient in Dalmady v. Price Waterhouse & Co., D.C.Puerto Rico 1973, 62 F.R.D. 157.

14. Hyam v. American Export Lines, C.A.2d 1954, 213 F.2d 221; Powell v. International Foodservice System, Inc., D.C.Puerto Rico 1971, 52 F.R.D. 205; and cases cited 8 Wright & Miller, Civil § 2112 n. 87.

15. Ellis Air Lines v. Bellanca Aircraft Corp., D.C.Del.1955, 17 F.R.D. 395; Endte v. Hermes Export Corp., D.C. N.Y.1957, 20 F.R.D. 162; cf. O'Hara v. United States Lines Co., D.C.N.Y.1958, 164 F.Supp. 549.

16. E.g., Boone v. Wynne, D.C.D.C. 1947, 7 F.R.D. 22; 8 Wright & Miller, Civil § 2112, pp. 411–417.

17. E.g., National Life Ins. Co. v. Hartford Acc. & Indem. Co., C.A.3d, 1980, 615 F.2d 595, 599–600.

18. Rule 26(c)(3); Colonial Capital Co. v. General Motors Corp., D.C.Conn.1961, 29 F.R.D. 514; Moore v. George A. Hormel & Co., D.C.N.Y.1942, 2 F.R.D. 340; 8 Wright & Miller, Civil § 2039.

tion to stay discovery on other issues until the critical issue has been decided.[19] An obvious application of this principle—salutary if applied sparingly and with real discretion rather than as an absolute rule—is that courts may stay discovery on the merits of an action until challenges to jurisdiction have been resolved.[20] Similarly where an issue is to be tried separately the court may limit discovery to that issue.[21] But in many instances such a limitation could lead to wasted effort, by requiring two depositions from the same witness, and the court is well justified in refusing such a limitation.[22] The scope of depositions in a federal civil action may also be limited in cases where it is contended that the depositions are intended for discovery in another case, such as a closely related criminal action [23] or an action in state court.[24] Again if the information sought is relevant to the pending action and the transactions involved are so interrelated that a limitation of examination to specific matters would frustrate the inquiry, limitation should be denied.[25]

The court may order that discovery be conducted with no one present except persons designated by the court.[26] Under the pre-1970 rule the court lacked power to order the exclusion of a party or an officer of a corporate party, but this language was not carried into the 1970 amendment and courts now hold that they can exclude a party.[27] A related provision permits an order that after being sealed,

19. Sinclair Ref. Co. v. Jenkins Petroleum Process Co., 1933, 53 S.Ct. 736, 289 U.S. 689, 77 L.Ed. 1449.

20. Investment Properties Intl., Ltd. v. IOS, Ltd., C.A.2d, 1972, 459 F.2d 705; McDonnell Douglas Corp. v. Polin, C.A. 3d, 1970, 429 F.2d 30; and cases cited 8 Wright & Miller, Civil § 2040 n. 86.

21. Brennan v. Local Union No. 639, C.A.1974, 494 F.2d 1092, 161 U.S.App. D.C. 173; Joseph v. Donover Co., C.A. 9th, 1959, 261 F.2d 812; Defensive Instruments, Inc. v. RCA Corp., D.C.Pa. 1974, 385 F.Supp. 1053; and cases cited 8 Wright & Miller, Civil § 2040 nn. 87, 88.

22. Vollert v. Summa Corp., D.C.Hawaii 1975, 389 F.Supp. 1348; Technitrol Inc. v. Digital Equipment Corp., D.C.Ill. 1973, 62 F.R.D. 91; and cases cited 8 Wright & Miller, Civil § 2040 n. 90.

23. Campbell v. Eastland, C.A.5th, 1962, 307 F.2d 478, certiorari denied 83 S.Ct. 502, 371 U.S. 955, 9 L.Ed.2d 502; Dienstag v. Bronsen, D.C.N.Y.1970, 49 F.R.D. 327; Hiss v. Chambers, D.C.Md. 1948, 8 F.R.D. 480; cf. McSurely v. McClellan, C.A.1970, 426 F.2d 664, 138 U.S.App.D.C. 187. See Note, 1968, 66 Mich.L.Rev. 738.

24. Sperry Rand Corp. v. Rothlein, C.A.2d, 1961, 288 F.2d 245, noted 1962,

110 U.Pa.L.Rev. 751; In re Coronet Metal Products Corp., D.C.N.Y.1948, 81 F.Supp. 500. See also 8 Wright & Miller, Civil § 2040, pp. 291–295.

25. E.g., Waldbaum v. Worldvision Enterprises, Inc., D.C.N.Y.1976, 84 F.R.D. 95; Johnson Foils, Inc. v. Huyuck Corp., D.C.N.Y.1973, 61 F.R.D. 405; and cases cited 8 Wright & Miller, Civil § 2040 nn. 95, 96. See Comment, Federal Discovery in Concurrent Criminal and Civil Proceedings, 1978, 52 Tul.L. Rev. 769.

26. Rule 26(c)(5); 8 Wright & Miller, Civil § 2041.

Neither the public nor representatives of the press have a right to be present at the taking of a deposition. Times Newspapers Ltd. (of Great Britain) v. McDonnell Douglas Corp., D.C.Cal. 1974, 387 F.Supp. 189. But there must be compelling reasons for denying access to the public. American Tel. & Tel. Co. v. Grady, C.A.7th, 1979, 594 F.2d 594, certiorari denied 99 S.Ct. 213, 439 U.S. 875, 58 L.Ed.2d 190.

27. Galella v. Onassis, C.A.2d, 1973, 487 F.2d 986; Beacon v. R. M. Jones Apartment Rentals, D.C.Ohio 1978, 79 F.R.D. 141. Compare Evidence Rule 615, which precludes barring a party or

as required by Rule 30(f), the deposition shall be opened only by order of court.[28] In the absence of such a protective order the deposition is a public document and is freely open to inspection after it is filed by the clerk.[29]

The court may order that a trade secret or other confidential research, development, or commercial information not be disclosed or be disclosed only in a designated way.[30] There is no true privilege for trade secrets [31] and disclosure will be ordered if the issues cannot be fairly adjudicated without such information,[32] but the court must exercise its discretion to avoid unnecessary disclosure of the information, and it may make conditions about the disclosure in order to protect the party compelled to disclose.[33]

The court may order that the parties simultaneously file specified documents or information enclosed in sealed envelopes to be opened as directed by the court.[34]

The provisions for confidentiality in Rule 26(c) may have to be reevaluated if, as has recently been suggested, an order limiting access to and use of material obtained by discovery is a form of prior restraint that must be justified by First Amendment standards.[35] There is already substantial literature appraising the implications of this suggestion.[36]

the officer of a corporate party from being present at the trial.

28. Martindell v. International Tel. & Tel. Corp., C.A.2d, 1979, 594 F.2d 291; OKC v. Williams, D.C.Tex.1978, 461 F.Supp. 540. Such an order was refused in Teplitzky v. Boston Ins. Co., D.C.Pa.1971, 52 F.R.D. 160.

29. See Burnham Chem. Co. v. Borax Consol., Ltd., D.C.Cal.1947, 7 F.R.D. 341; 8 Wright & Miller, Civil § 2042.

Rules 5(d) and 30(f)(1) were amended in 1980 to allow the court, on motion of a party or on its own initiative, to provide that discovery materials not be filed. See 4 Wright & Miller, Civil § 1152.

30. Rule 26(c)(7); 8 Wright & Miller, Civil § 2043.

31. Federal Open Market Committee v. Merrill, 1979, 99 S.Ct. 2800, 2813, 443 U.S. 340, 362, 61 L.Ed.2d 587.

32. Carter Products, Inc. v. Eversharp, Inc., C.A.7th, 1966, 360 F.2d 868; Covey Oil Co. v. Continental Oil Co., C.A. 10th, 1965, 340 F.2d 993, certiorari denied 85 S.Ct. 1110, 380 U.S. 964, 14 L.Ed.2d 155; Olympic Ref. Co. v. Carter, C.A.9th, 1964, 332 F.2d 260, certiorari denied 85 S.Ct. 186, 379 U.S. 900, 13 L.Ed.2d 175; and cases cited 8 Wright & Miller, Civil § 2043 n. 24.

33. A. H. Robins Co. v. Fadley, C.A.5th, 1962, 299 F.2d 557; Chemical & Indus. Corp. v. Druffel, C.A.6th, 1962, 301 F.2d 126; Downs v. U. S., D.C.Tenn. 1974, 382 F.Supp. 713; Nader v. Butz, D.C.D.C.1974, 372 F.Supp. 175; and cases cited 8 Wright & Miller, Civil § 2043 nn. 29–32.

34. Rule 26(c)(8); 8 Wright & Miller, Civil § 2044.

35. In re Halkin, C.A.1979, 598 F.2d 176, 194 U.S.App.D.C. 257, noted 1979, 48 U.Cin.L.Rev. 900, 92 Harv.L.Rev. 1550, 52 Temp.L.Q. 1197, 21 Wm. & Mary L.Rev. 331; 1980, 48 Geo.Wash. L.Rev. 486, 55 Notre Dame Law. 424. See also In re San Juan Star Co., C.A. 1st, 1981, 662 F.2d 108.

But see International Products Corp. v. Koons, C.A.2d, 1963, 325 F.2d 403, 407: "we entertain no doubt as to the constitutionality of a rule allowing a federal court to forbid the publication, in advance of trial, of information obtained by one party from another by use of the court's processes."

36. Dore, Confidentiality Orders—The Proper Role of the Courts in Providing Confidential Treatment for Information Disclosed Through the Pre-Trial Discovery Process, 1978, 14 New England L.Rev. 1; Note, Nonparty Access to Discovery Materials in the Federal

The eight specific types of orders listed in Rule 26(c) are merely illustrative of the general power of the court to make any order justice requires to protect from annoyance, embarrassment, oppression, or undue burden or expense.[37] This emphasizes the complete control that the court has over the discovery process. It is impossible to set out in a rule all the circumstances that may require limitations on discovery or the kinds of limitations that may be needed. The rules, instead, permit the broadest scope of discovery and leave it to the enlightened discretion of the district court to decide what restrictions may be necessary in a particular case. The harassment or oppression should be unreasonable to justify restriction on discovery,[38] but even very slight inconvenience may be unreasonable if there is no showing of need for the discovery sought.[39]

A provision appearing for the first time in 1970 in Rule 26(c) authorizes the court, in denying a motion for a protective order, to go a step further and issue an affirmative order compelling the discovery objected to. This will bring into play the sanctions of Rule 37 if the party against whom discovery is sought continues to refuse to provide it.[40] In addition the court has discretion under proposed Rules 26(c) and 37(a)(4) to require the losing party on the motion to pay expenses incurred in relation to the motion.

In 1981 the Advisory Committee on Civil Rules circulated a proposal to give the court still further power to prevent abuse of discovery. As part of an attack on the problem of overuse of discovery in terms of depth,[41] this would provide that the court, on its own initiative or pursuant to a motion, could limit discovery when it is unreasonably cumulative, when the information could be obtained more economically elsewhere, when there has been abundant opportunity for the discovery, and when the discovery is unduly burdensome or expensive, taking into account such factors as the needs of the case, the amount in controversy, limitations on the parties' resources, and the importance of the issue.[42] Although the draft of the proposed amendment

Courts, 1981, 94 Harv.L.Rev. 1085; Note, Rule 26(c) Protective Orders and the First Amendment, 1980, 80 Col.L. Rev. 1465; Comment, Protective Orders Prohibiting Dissemination of Discovery Information: The First Amendment and Good Cause, 1980 Duke L.J. 766.

37. Herbert v. Lando, 1979, 99 S.Ct. 1635, 1649, 441 U.S. 153, 177, 60 L.Ed. 2d 115.

38. U. S. v. International Business Machines Corp., D.C.N.Y.1979, 83 F.R.D. 92; Alliance to End Repression v. Rochford, D.C.Ill.1977, 75 F.R.D. 441; and cases cited 8 Wright & Miller, Civil § 2036 n. 34.

39. United Air Lines, Inc. v. U. S., D.C. Del.1960, 26 F.R.D. 213.

40. See § 90 below.

41. See § 81 above at notes 11 to 23.

42. Preliminary Draft of Proposed Amendments to the Federal Rules of Civil Procedure, June 1981, 90 F.R.D. 451, 478–480. The provision described in the text would be an amendment of Rule 26(b). A companion proposed amendment would add a Rule 26(g) authorizing sanctions against an attorney or party who requests discovery going beyond the limits set out in the proposed subdivision (b), or on an attorney who makes a discovery request, response, or objection for an improper purpose. Two knowledgeable commentators are enthusiastic about the proposal for (b) but very critical of the proposed new (g). Schroeder & Frank,

puts this in terms of a limit on the scope of discovery, an order of this kind would be similar in purpose and operation to the protective orders with which the courts have long been familiar.[43]

§ 84.   Oral Depositions [1]

The most important of the discovery devices is the oral deposition. It is used far more often than any other device, despite the fact that it is the most expensive, because lawyers can accomplish more purposes by oral depositions than by the other devices.[2] It is the only significant discovery device that may be directed against any person, and is not confined to parties to the action.   It is the only discovery device that permits examination and cross-examination of a live witness by counsel, where there is no opportunity to reflect and carefully shape the information given.   Thus, despite its expense, it is the most valuable device if the deponent has important information.

When the rules were originally adopted, the basic rule governing oral depositions was Rule 26.   As a part of the rearrangement of the discovery rules in 1970, Rule 26 was made a general rule on the scope of discovery and the provisions for depositions were transferred, with very little change in substance, so that Rule 30 now contains the provisions dealing with the procedure for taking an oral deposition while Rule 32 has the provisions on use of a deposition.

An oral deposition may be taken in any civil action, and any person, whether or not a party to the suit, may be required to give such a deposition.   Indeed a party may even take his own deposition.[3] When an oral deposition is sought, the party wishing to take such a deposition must give reasonable notice in writing to every other party to the action, stating the time and place where the deposition is to be taken and the name and address of the deponent.[4] If the deposition is to be of a party, this notice is sufficient to compel his attendance.[5] A subpoena must be served on a person not a party whose deposition is to be taken.[6]

Discovery Reform: Long Road to Nowheresville, 1982, 68 A.B.A.J. 572, 573.

43. A suggested modification of the proposal would tie it directly to the protective order provision.   See Rosenberg & King, Curbing Discovery Abuse in Civil Litigation: Enough is Enough, 1981 B.Y.U.L.Rev. 579, 594.

[§ 84]

1. 8   Wright   &   Miller,   Civil §§ 2101–2120, 2141–2157.

2. Glaser, Pretrial Discovery and the Adversary System, 1968, pp. 52–54, 63–67.

3. Richmond v. Brooks, C.A.2d, 1955, 227 F.2d 490; Van Sciver v. Rothen-

sies, C.C.A.3d, 1941, 122 F.2d 697; 8 Wright & Miller, Civil § 2102 n. 16.

4. Rule 30(b)(1); 8 Wright & Miller, Civil § 2106.

5. E.g., Chages v. U. S., C.A.5th, 1966, 369 F.2d 643; 8 Wright & Miller, Civil § 2107.

6. El Salto, S. A. v. PSG Co., C.A.9th, 1971, 444 F.2d 477, certiorari denied 92 S.Ct. 273, 404 U.S. 940, 30 L.Ed.2d 253; Cleveland v. Palmby, D.C.Okl.1977, 75 F.R.D. 654.   On issuing a subpoena to a witness for the taking of his deposition, see Rule 45(d)(1); 9 Wright & Miller, Civil § 2458.

Obviously it is not literally possible to take the deposition of a corporation; instead, where a corporation is involved, the information sought must be obtained from natural persons who can speak for the corporation. It is equally obvious that, since the deposition of any person can be taken, any person connected with the corporation or acquainted with the facts may be examined. A problem that has arisen frequently in the cases is the extent to which the corporation is responsible for producing such persons to have their deposition taken, and whether what they say may be used against the corporation.[7]

These questions are not specifically answered in the rules but the courts have worked out satisfactory answers from other rules. An action may be dismissed, or a default judgment entered, if a party or an officer, director, or managing agent of a party wilfully fails to appear for the taking of his deposition after being served with proper notice.[8] Thus the corporation is responsible for producing its officers, directors, and managing agents if notice is given, a subpoena for their appearance is unnecessary, and sanctions may be imposed against the corporation if one of these persons fails to appear. Another provision allows introduction into evidence by an adverse party of the deposition of any one who at the time of taking the deposition was an officer, director, or managing agent of a corporation, partnership, or association.[9] Thus the depositions of persons who fit these categories may be used against the corporate party. It is in this sense, in respect of the responsibility to produce the deponent and of the usability of the deposition, that it is said that the deposition of the corporation is "taken through" the particular individual.

The meaning of the terms "officer" and "director" has caused no difficulty, but "managing agent" has required definition. Though the question of whether a particular person is a "managing agent" is to be answered pragmatically on an ad hoc basis,[10] the courts look to see if the individual involved is invested by the corporation with general powers to exercise his discretion and judgment in dealing with corporate matters,[11] whether he can be depended upon to carry out his employer's direction to give testimony at the demand of a party engaged in litigation with the employer,[12] and whether he can be expected to identify himself with the interests of the corporation rather than with those of the other parties.[13] The determination will be made by the trial court, when the deposition is sought to be introduced or sanctions are asked because the person failed to appear for

7. Note, Discovery Against Corporations Under the Federal Rules, 1962, 47 Iowa L.Rev. 1006.

8. Rule 37(d). This differs from the former rule only by including "director."

9. Rule 32(a)(2).

10. Petition of Manor Inv. Co., D.C.N.Y. 1967, 43 F.R.D. 299; U. S. v. The Dorothy McAllister, D.C.N.Y.1959, 24 F.R.D. 316.

11. Kolb v. A. H. Bull S.S. Co., D.C.N.Y. 1962, 31 F.R.D. 252; Krauss v. Erie R. Co., D.C.N.Y.1954, 16 F.R.D. 126.

12. Bernstein v. N. V. Nederlandsche-Amerikaansche Stoomvaart-Maatschappij, D.C.N.Y.1953, 15 F.R.D. 37.

13. Independent Productions Corp. v. Loew's, Inc., D.C.N.Y.1959, 24 F.R.D. 19; Rubin v. General Tire & Rubber Co., D.C.N.Y.1955, 18 F.R.D. 51.

the taking of his deposition,[14] on the basis of these three tests.[15] Normally the corporation is accountable for a person only if he was an officer, director, or managing agent at the time the deposition was taken. This is to protect the party from the admissions of disgruntled former officers or agents,[16] and is applied in the light of its purpose where the person retains such a connection with the corporation as to be loyal to it.[17]

There is frequent difficulty in designating in the notice the name of the deponent where the party is a corporation, and the opposing party does not know which corporate officer or agent has the needed information. Most cases had refused to permit a notice that called on the corporation to produce such of its officers and managing agents as have knowledge of the facts.[18] Here it would seem that the corporate party is much better able to make this determination than is its opponent, and that the requirement that the party seeking the deposition make a specific designation is a technical and unnecessary stumbling block, serving only to delay and make more expensive the discovery to which he is entitled.

Rule 30(b)(6), added in 1970 and amended in 1971, provides a procedure to meet this problem. A party seeking the deposition of a corporation or other organization may still name a particular deponent and proceed as before, but the new rule makes an alternative available. The party seeking discovery may simply name the corporation, or other organization, as the deponent and designate with reasonable particularity the matters on which examination is requested.[19] It is then the duty of the corporation to name one or more persons who consent to testify on its behalf and these persons must testify about matters known or reasonably available to the corporation. This new procedure applies to corporations and other organizations whether or not they are a party to the suit, but if the organization is not a party mere notice is not enough and it must be served with a subpoena.[20]

14. Hughes Bros., Inc v. Callanan Road Improvement Co., D.C.N.Y.1967, 41 F.R.D. 450; Curry v. States Marine Corp. of Del., D.C.N.Y.1954, 16 F.R.D. 376.

15. Terry v. Modern Woodmen of America, D.C.Mo.1972, 57 F.R.D. 141; Newark Ins. Co. v. Sartain, D.C.Cal. 1957, 20 F.R.D. 583, 586; 8 Wright & Miller, Civil § 2103, pp. 376–379.

16. Curry v. States Marine Corp. of Delaware, D.C.N.Y.1954, 16 F.R.D. 376; Independent Productions Corp. v. Loew's, Inc., D.C.N.Y.1959, 24 F.R.D. 19; Sykes Intl., Ltd. v. Pilch's Poultry Breeding Farms, Inc., D.C.Conn.1972, 55 F.R.D. 138; see Cameo-Parkway Records, Inc. v. Premier Albums, Inc., D.C.N.Y.1967, 43 F.R.D. 400, 401.

17. Independent Productions Corp. v. Loew's, Inc., D.C.N.Y.1962, 30 F.R.D. 377; Fay v. U. S., D.C.N.Y.1958, 22 F.R.D. 28. Compare Proseus v. Anchor Line, Ltd., D.C.N.Y.1960, 26 F.R.D. 165, with U. S. v. The Dorothy McAllister, D.C.N.Y.1959, 24 F.R.D. 316.

18. E.g., Budget Dress Corp. v. Joint Bd. of Dress and Waistmakers' Union of Greater New York, D.C.N.Y.1959, 24 F.R.D. 506; U. S. v. Gahagan Dredging Corp., D.C.N.Y.1959, 24 F.R.D. 328; 8 Wright & Miller, Civil § 2110.

19. Scovill Mfg. Co. v. Sunbeam Corp., D.C.Del.1973, 61 F.R.D. 598.

20. Cates v. LTV Aerospace Corp., C.A.5th, 1973, 480 F.2d 620. The sub-

Rule 30(a) provides that leave of court must ordinarily be obtained if a deposition is to be taken by plaintiff within 30 days after the service of the summons and complaint upon any defendant. The purpose of the leave requirement is to protect a defendant who has not yet retained counsel. This is reflected by another provision, new in 1970, dispensing with the requirement of leave after the defendant has served a notice of taking deposition or has otherwise sought discovery.[21] Finally there is another new provision, responsive to the needs of the admiralty bar but applicable in all cases, permitting a deposition to be taken without leave at the outset of the action if plaintiff's attorney certifies that the deponent is about to go away and will be unavailable for examination after the expiration of the 30-day period. If a deposition is taken without leave under this last provision, it cannot be used against a party who subsequently shows that he was unable through the exercise of diligence to obtain counsel to represent him at the taking of the deposition.[22]

As originally adopted, the rules were silent about the order in which depositions were to be taken or other discovery was to be held. There developed, however, very substantial case authority for the proposition that, as a general rule, the party who first made service of a notice of taking depositions was entitled to priority.[23] The rule of priority led to a race of diligence in serving notice, though how frequently such a race occurred is a matter of dispute.[24] If it ever occurs, it is an abuse of the discovery rules.[25] The courts have always had ample power in this regard—though they often seemed reluctant to use it—and Rule 26(d), adopted in 1970, codifies that power and allows both sides to proceed with discovery unless the court has otherwise ordered.

Under the new rule, as formerly, the courts may give priority as the circumstances of a particular case require.[26] They may stay the

poena to a non-party organization must advise the organization of its duty to designate someone to testify for it. See 8 Wright & Miller, Civil § 2103, pp. 371–373.

21. Rule 30(a)(1); 8 Wright & Miller, Civil § 2104.

22. Rule 30(b)(2).

23. 8 Wright & Miller, Civil § 2045; Younger, Priority of Pretrial Examinations in the Federal Courts—A Comment, 1959, 34 N.Y.U.L.Rev. 1271.

24. E.g., Stover v. Universal Moulded Products Corp., D.C.Pa.1950, 11 F.R.D. 90; Sanib Corp. v. United Fruit Co., D.C.N.Y.1955, 19 F.R.D. 9.

The extent of this problem is minimized in Glaser, Pretrial Discovery and the Adversary System, 1969, pp. 212–219.

25. Note, Discovery: Boon or Burden?, 1952, 36 Minn.L.Rev. 364, 376; Com-

ment, Tactical Use and Abuse of Depositions, 1949, 59 Yale L.J. 117, 134–136; Caldwell-Clements, Inc. v. McGraw Hill Pub. Co., D.C.N.Y.1951, 11 F.R.D. 156, 157–158; International Commodities Corp. v. International Ore & Fertilizer Corp., D.C.N.Y.1961, 30 F.R.D. 58, 63.

26. E.g., Boxer v. Smith, Kline and French Laboratories, D.C.N.Y.1967, 43 F.R.D. 25; Kaeppler v. Jas. H. Matthews & Co., D.C.Pa.1961, 200 F.Supp. 229; Deep South Oil Co. of Texas v. Metropolitan Life Ins. Co., D.C.N.Y. 1958, 21 F.R.D. 340; Morrison Export Co. v. Goldstone, D.C.N.Y.1952, 12 F.R.D. 258.

The lower court was criticized, however, in George C. Frey Ready-Mixed Concrete, Inc. v. Pine Hill Concrete Mix Corp., C.A.2d, 1977, 554 F.2d 551, for giving priority to defendant rather

beginning of one examination until after the completion of another.[27] They may provide that each party examine the other for alternating periods of equal duration.[28]   In the absence of a court order the parties will be free to proceed when and how they choose.

A deposition may be taken before any person authorized to administer oaths who has no disqualifying interest in the case.[29]   Normally a court reporter will be selected by the party giving notice of the deposition, and he will administer the oath to the deponent as well as record the testimony. However Rule 30(b)(4), added in 1970, permits the court on motion to order that the testimony be recorded by other than stenographic means, as by videotape or a tape recorder. An important decision of the District of Columbia Circuit held that experimentation with this new procedure should be encouraged rather than blocked and that the discretion of the trial court in passing on a motion to record the testimony by nonstenographic means is limited to those actions needed to ensure accuracy and trustworthiness.[30]

At the taking of a deposition, the witness will be examined and cross-examined by counsel for the parties in the same fashion as at a trial, with one important exception. If there is objection to a question, the reporter will simply note the objection in the transcript and the witness will answer the question despite the objection.[31]   The court can consider the objection if the deposition is offered at the trial, and at that time will refuse to allow reading of the answer to any question which was properly objectionable. If the witness refuses to answer a question put at a deposition, the examination may be adjourned, or completed on other matters, and application then made to the court to compel an answer. This is undesirable, since it delays the deposition and brings the court into a process that is intended to

than allowing both parties to proceed simultaneously.

27. Kahn v. Eaststates Gas Producing Co., D.C.Ohio 1973, 59 F.R.D. 132. A stay was refused in Black v. Sheraton Corp. of America, D.C.D.C.1974, 371 F.Supp. 97.

28. Planning and Investing Co., S. A. v. Hemlock, D.C.N.Y.1970, 50 F.R.D. 48; Caldwell-Clements, Inc. v. McGraw-Hill Pub. Co., D.C.N.Y.1951, 11 F.R.D. 156.

29. Rule 28; 8 Wright & Miller, Civil §§ 2081–2084. See, also the provision as to stipulations in Rule 29, 8 Wright & Miller, Civil §§ 2091–2094.

30. Colonial Times, Inc. v. Gasch, C.A. 1975, 509 F.2d 517, 166 U.S.App.D.C. 184, noted 1975, 26 S.C.L.Rev. 753. See also Champagne v. Hygrade Food Products, Inc., D.C.Wash.1978, 79 F.R.D. 671.

But see United Auto., Aerospace & Agr. Implement Workers of America v. Na-

tional Caucus of Labor Committees, C.A.2d, 1975, 525 F.2d 323; Barham v. IDM Corp., D.C.Ohio 1978, 78 F.R.D. 340.

These conflicting views were noted, but no choice among them expressed, in In re Sessions, C.A.5th, 1982, 672 F.2d 564.

See generally 8 Wright & Miller, Civil § 2115; Graham, Nonstenographic Recording of Depositions: The Empty Promise of Federal Rule 30(b)(4), 1977, 72 Nw.U.L.Rev. 566; Note, Videotape Depositions: An Analysis of Use in Civil Cases, 1978, 9 Cum.L.Rev. 195.

In another triumph of modern technology, Rule 30(b)(7) was amended in 1980 to allow the taking of testimony at a deposition by telephone, if the court so orders or on stipulation by the parties.

31. Rule 30(c); 8 Wright & Miller, Civil § 2113.

work largely without judicial supervision. For this reason, it is provided that expenses and attorneys' fees may be assessed if the refusal to answer was unjustified, or if there was no substantial justification for the motion to compel an answer.[32]

Most errors and irregularities in the taking of a deposition are waived unless prompt objection is made.[33] This gives the erring party an opportunity to correct the mistake, and prevents waste of time and money by a subsequent claim to suppress a deposition because of some technical error long before. But objections to competency, relevancy, or materiality that could not have been corrected if made at the time need not be made, and are not waived.[34] They may be made for the first time at the trial.[35]

The provision for protective orders gives the parties and witnesses protection before a deposition begins.[36] Continued protection during the course of the examination is provided by Rule 30(d). Thus at any time during the taking of the deposition, on motion of the deponent or of any party,[37] and upon a showing that the examination is being conducted in bad faith or in such manner as unreasonably to annoy, embarrass, or oppress the deponent or party, the court may order the termination of the examination, or may limit the scope and manner of the taking of the deposition.[38] The order may be made either by the court in which the action is pending or by the court for the district where the deposition is being taken.[39] On such a motion the only question is whether the examination is being conducted properly, and the fact that counsel did not wish further cross-examination of the deponent is not a ground for termination of the examination.[40] Grounds for terminating or limiting an examination include insistent questioning on privileged matters,[41] or that the examination has gone too far afield,[42] or that unwarranted attempts are being made to pry into a party's preparation for trial.[43] The physical condition of the

---

32. Rule 37(a)(4); 8 Wright & Miller, Civil § 2288.

33. Rule 32(d); 8 Wright & Miller, Civil §§ 2153–2157.

34. Rule 32(d)(3)(A); Glenwillow Landfill, Inc. v. City of Akron, D.C.Ohio 1979, 485 F.Supp. 671, 674; 8 Wright & Miller, Civil § 2156.

35. Rule 32(b).

36. See § 83 above.

37. De Wagenknecht v. Stinnes, C.A.1957, 243 F.2d 413, 100 U.S.App. D.C. 156, certiorari denied 78 S.Ct. 44, 355 U.S. 830, 2 L.Ed.2d 43.

38. 8 Wright & Miller, Civil § 2116.

39. Shawmut, Inc. v. American Viscose Corp., D.C.N.Y.1951, 11 F.R.D. 562.

40. Broadbent v. Moore-McCormack Lines, Inc., D.C.Pa.1946, 5 F.R.D. 220.

Motions to terminate depositions were also denied in In re Master Key Litigation, C.A.9th, 1974, 507 F.2d 292, and in Paiewonsky v. Paiewonsky, D.C.V.I. 1970, 50 F.R.D. 379.

41. Vulcan Detinning Co. v. Continental Can Co., D.C.N.Y.1951, 12 F.R.D. 74; Lever Bros. Co. v. Proctor & Gamble Mfg. Co., D.C.Md.1941, 38 F.Supp. 680; Lewis v. United Air Lines Transport Co., D.C.Pa.1940, 32 F.Supp. 21.

42. Pittsburgh Plate Glass Co. v. Allied Chem. Workers of America, Local Union No. 1, D.C.Ohio 1951, 11 F.R.D. 518; Macrina v. Smith, D.C.Pa.1955, 18 F.R.D. 254.

43. Schweinert v. Insurance Co. of North America, D.C.N.Y.1940, 1 F.R.D. 247.

witness and the adequacy of the examination which has already taken place are other factors that may be considered.[44]

A deposition must be transcribed, submitted to the witness for examination and signature by him, certified by the officer before whom the deposition was taken, and, unless otherwise ordered by the court, filed with the court.[45]

The provisions governing the use of a deposition at a trial or hearing are in Rule 32(a). Even if the requirements of that rule are met the deposition can be used only to the extent that the matters contained in it are admissible under the rules of evidence "applied as though the witness were then present and testifying." The quoted language did not appear in the pre-1970 rule. It recognizes that the rule for use of depositions is itself an exception to the hearsay rule. Thus a deposition that satisfies Rule 32(a) is not objectionable on the ground that it is hearsay. Instead it is tested as if the witness were giving his answers orally. An answer that itself contains hearsay would be subject to that rule of evidence, but the fact that the witness himself was not testifying in court would not permit a hearsay objection.[46]

Rule 32(a)(1) permits use of any deposition by any party to contradict or impeach the testimony of deponent as a witness.[47] As amended in 1980 it also allows use of the deposition for any other purpose permitted by the Federal Rules of Evidence.[48]

Under Rule 32(a)(2) the deposition of a party, the officer, director, or managing agent of a party, or of a person designated by an organization to testify on its behalf, may be used by an adverse party for any purpose.[49]

---

44. De Wagenknecht v. Stinnes, C.A.1957, 243 F.2d 413, 100 U.S.App. D.C. 156, certiorari denied 78 S.Ct. 44, 355 U.S. 830, 2 L.Ed.2d 43.

45. Rule 30(c), (e), (f); 8 Wright & Miller, Civil §§ 2117–2119. See Bernstein v. Brenner, D.C.D.C.1970, 51 F.R.D. 9.

The witness may change his answers when the transcript is presented to him for signing but his original answers must remain part of the record. Rogers v. Roth, C.A.10th, 1973, 477 F.2d 1154.

Rules 5(d) and 30(f)(1) were amended in 1980 to give the court power to order that a deposition need not be filed. However the tempestuous history of this amendment strongly suggests that this is a power to be exercised only in a particular case when strong public or private interests compel waiving the filing requirement. See 4 Wright & Miller, Civil § 1152.

46. 8 Wright & Miller, Civil § 2143. See also Evidence Rules 802 and 804(b) (1).

47. Merchants Motor Freight v. Downing, C.A.8th, 1955, 227 F.2d 247; Lewis v. United Air Lines Transport Corp., D.C.Conn.1939, 27 F.Supp. 946; 8 Wright & Miller, Civil § 2144.

48. Evidence Rule 801(d)(1)(A) excludes a deposition of a witness who testifies at the trial from the definition of hearsay, and thus the contradictory statements in the deposition may be given substantive effect. In addition, Evidence Rule 801(d)(2) makes the statement of an agent or servant admissible against the principal under the circumstances stated in that rule.

49. Coughlin v. Capitol Cement Co., C.A.5th, 1978, 571 F.2d 290, 308; Fey v. Walston & Co., Inc., C.A.7th, 1974, 493 F.2d 1036; 8 Wright & Miller, Civil § 2145. Under Evidence Rule 801(d)(2) this use of a deposition is defined as not being hearsay.

Rule 32(a)(3) authorizes use of the deposition of any witness, whether a party or not, by any party for any purpose if one of five conditions is met.[50] Such use is permitted if the witness is dead, or if he is more than 100 miles from the place of trial and his absence was not procured by the party offering the deposition, or if the witness is unable to attend or testify because of age, sickness, infirmity or imprisonment, or if the party offering the deposition has been unable to procure the attendance of the witness by subpoena. The fifth of the conditions permitted by this rule is that a deposition may be used if, upon application and notice, the court finds that such exceptional circumstances exist as to make it desirable, in the interest of justice and with due regard to the importance of presenting the testimony of witnesses orally in open court, to admit the deposition. This provision has been regarded as an attempt at liberalization of the hearsay rule [51] but it has hardly ever been used.[52] Rule 32(a)(3)(B), 32(a)(3), allowing a party who is more than 100 miles from the place of trial to introduce his own deposition,[53] is also a liberalization of traditional notions of the hearsay rule.

Rule 32(a) has always purported to state the circumstances in which a deposition taken in one action can be used in another action. In fact, the rule was quite misleading and the courts allowed depositions to be used in these circumstances more broadly than the rule seemed to indicate. Since 1975 this matter has been covered also by Evidence Rule 804(b)(1), which allowed depositions taken in other actions to be used more often than Civil Rule 32(a) had seemed to permit, though arguably less often than what the courts had been allowing in practice. Rule 32(a) was amended in 1980 to make it as broad as the Evidence Rule.[54]

If one party offers in evidence part of a deposition, an adverse party may require him to introduce any other part of it that ought in fairness to be considered with the part introduced, and any party may introduce any other parts.[55] This guards against giving a distorted picture of the deponent's testimony by introducing only a part of it.

---

50. 8 Wright & Miller, Civil § 2146.

51. Weinstein, Probative Force of Hearsay, 1961, 46 Iowa L.Rev. 331, 340.

52. Huff v. Marine Tank Testing Corp., C.A.4th, 1980, 631 F.2d 1140; Lebeck v. William A. Jarvis, Inc., D.C.Pa.1956, 145 F.Supp. 706, 724–725; Hart v. Friedman, D.C.Pa.1961, 29 F.R.D. 2. Hostility of a witness was held insufficient for application of this provision. Klepal v. Pennsylvania R. Co., C.A.2d, 1956, 229 F.2d 610.

53. E.g., Stewart v. Meyers, C.A.7th, 1965, 353 F.2d 691; Richmond v. Brooks, C.A.2d, 1955, 227 F.2d 490; Houser v. Snap-On Tools Corp., D.C. Md.1962, 202 F.Supp. 181. But cf. Vevelstad v. Flynn, C.A.9th, 1956, 230 F.2d 695, certiorari denied 77 S.Ct. 40, 352 U.S. 827, 1 L.Ed.2d 49. See Note, Offering Plaintiff's Deposition in Evidence, 1956, 69 Harv.L.Rev. 1503; 8 Wright & Miller, Civil § 2147.

54. See 8 Wright & Miller, Civil § 2150.

55. Rule 32(a)(4); Ikerd v. Lapworth, C.A.7th, 1970, 435 F.2d 197; Mangual v. Prudential Lines, Inc., D.C.Pa.1971, 53 F.R.D. 301; 8 Wright & Miller, Civil § 2148.

The otherwise similar provision of Evidence Rule 106 says "which ought in fairness to be considered contemporaneously with it." The word "contemporaneously" does not appear in Civil Rule 32(a)(4).

Until 1975 Rule 32(c) provided that a party did not make a person his own witness for any purpose by taking his deposition.[56] This was repealed in 1975, on the ground that it was no longer needed in the light of the adoption of the Evidence Rules that year. This over-looked the fact that the Evidence Rules were substantially changed in Congress, and, as finally adopted, continued to recognize state rules of incompetency such as Dead Man's Acts in many cases.[57] Thus to the extent that Rule 32(c) had been significant with regard to incompetency, it should not have been repealed. The saving grace with regard to the mistaken repeal of Rule 32(c) is that it shed almost no light on questions of waiver of incompetency, and, in particular, it was not settled whether the estate of a deceased party waived the protection of a Dead Man's Act by taking a deposition of the survivor. A powerful argument can be made in favor of waiver in this situation,[58] but the fact is that the rules are silent on the question and incompetency, when it exists at all under Rule 601, exists only because of a state rule of incompetency. Since the initial protection comes solely from state law, the conditions on which it is waived must also depend on state law.[59]

§ 85. Depositions on Written Questions [1]

Rule 31 specifies the procedure to be followed in taking depositions by written questions. This is an alternative to the taking of depositions by oral examination provided by Rule 30. The advantage of a deposition on written questions is that counsel for the parties need not go to some distant place to be present at the taking of the deposition. Instead they serve on each other questions and cross questions—and even redirect and recross questions—that they wish to have put to the deponent.[2] These are then sent to the officer who is to take the deposition. He puts the questions to the witness, records the answers, and transcribes and files the deposition as with an oral deposition.[3] The officer is merely to record what the witness says in response to the various questions propounded to him. Comments by the officer as to the demeanor of the witness or as to remarks he made before the questions were put are improper and will be stricken.[4]

---

56. 8 Wright & Miller, Civil § 2152; Keeton, Proprietorship over Deponents, 1955, 68 Harv.L.Rev. 600.

57. Evidence Rule 601. See § 93 below.

58. Degnan, The Evidence Law of Discovery: Exclusion of Evidence Because of Fear of Perjury, 1965, 43 Texas L.Rev. 435.

59. Prior to the repeal of Rule 32(c) and the adoption of the Evidence Rules, the cases were divided on this point. See cases cited 8 Wright & Miller, Civil § 2152 nn. 11, 14.

[§ 85]

1. 8 Wright & Miller, Civil §§ 2131–2133; Schmertz, Written Depositions under Federal and State Rules as Cost-Effective Discovery at Home and Abroad, 1970, 16 Vill.L.Rev. 7.

2. Rule 31(a); 8 Wright & Miller, Civil § 2132.

3. Rule 31(b); 8 Wright & Miller, Civil § 2133.

4. Gill v. Stolow, D.C.N.Y.1954, 16 F.R.D. 9.

Though Rule 31 appears to offer a saving in expense where the deposition is to be taken at some faroff place,[5] its advantages are largely illusory. The procedure is more cumbersome than an oral examination, and is less suitable for a complicated inquiry, or for a searching interrogation of a hostile or reluctant witness. Thus Justice Whittaker, while still a district judge, commented: "From my long experience at the Bar, I can readily agree that the device of taking a deposition upon written interrogatories under Rule 31, except for the proof of formal matters, is a tool of discovery very inferior to oral examination."[6]

The court may make protective orders where a deposition is to be taken on written questions, and in particular may order that the deposition not be taken except upon oral examination.[7] It also may authorize oral cross-examination though the deposition is otherwise to be taken on written questions.[8] Usually such authorization is denied and the party is required to attempt first to conduct his examination by cross-questions, with leave to apply for oral examination if it appears that further cross-examination is necessary.[9]

As originally adopted the procedure provided by Rule 31 was known as a "deposition upon written interrogatories." This was an invitation to confusion with Rule 33, providing for the use of interrogatories to parties. These are quite different devices, with different purposes and different procedures and they are applicable to different persons.[10] Rule 31, as it was amended in 1970, changed the name of the device to "deposition upon written questions" and thus avoided this confusion.

§ 86. Interrogatories to Parties [1]

Rule 33 provides a procedure by which a party may require another party to give written answers under oath to written questions relevant to the subject matter of the action. Where the person who has the information sought is a party, whether to use interrogatories or to take the party's deposition is a choice dependent on practical considerations.[2]

---

5. See J. C. Nichols Co. v. Mid-States Freight Lines, D.C.Mo.1949, 9 F.R.D. 553, 554.

6. Perry v. Edwards, D.C.Mo.1954, 16 F.R.D. 131, 133.

7. Rule 26(c)(3); Smith v. Morrison-Knudsen Co., Inc., D.C.N.Y.1958, 22 F.R.D. 108; Lago Oil & Transport Co., Ltd. v. U. S., D.C.N.Y.1951, 97 F.Supp. 438. But cf. J. C. Nichols Co. v. Mid-States Freight Lines, D.C.Mo.1949, 9 F.R.D. 553; Kiachif v. Philco Intl. Corp., D.C.N.Y.1950, 10 F.R.D. 277; 8 Wright & Miller, Civil § 2039.

8. Winograd Bros., Inc. v. Chase Bank, D.C.N.Y.1939, 31 F.Supp. 91.

9. Wheeler v. West India S.S. Co., D.C. N.Y.1951, 11 F.R.D. 396; U. S. v. National City Bank of New York, D.C. N.Y.1940, 1 F.R.D. 367.

10. Smith v. Morrison-Knudsen Co., D.C.N.Y.1958, 22 F.R.D. 108. See § 86 below.

[§ 86]

1. 8 Wright & Miller, Civil §§ 2161–2182; Haydock & Herr, Interrogatories: Questions and Answers, 1981, 1 Rev.Litigation 263.

2. 8 Wright & Miller, Civil § 2163; Haydock & Herr, note 1 above, at 264–265.

Inevitably much of the efficacy that attaches to oral examination on deposition is lost when Rule 33 interrogatories are used. At the very outset, the interrogated party is fully apprised of all the questions that will be addressed to him. He is accorded time to ponder and reflect on his answers and to formulate them in writing with exactness and caution. He may take the advice of counsel and secure the assistance of other persons in framing his replies, benefits that he does not enjoy at a rapid oral examination. Moreover, the examining party is handicapped by the fact that he is required to formulate all of his questions in advance of receiving answers to any of them. Attempts at evasion, which might be met by a persistent oral examination, cannot be easily dealt with. The flexibility and the potency of oral depositions is in large part lacking in written interrogatories to an adverse party.

Nevertheless, Rule 33 interrogatories fulfill important functions. They are much less expensive than a deposition, either orally or on written questions, where the answers must be stenographically recorded and transcribed. They are useful in narrowing the issues as to items that though formally denied in the pleadings are not seriously disputed. Resort may successfully be had to Rule 33 for the purpose of obtaining details as to matters concerning which the allegations of the pleadings are general in character. Interrogatories constitute a simple mode of obtaining names and addresses of persons having knowledge of pertinent facts, and information as to the existence of documentary evidence. After Rule 33 has been used to obtain such information, the depositions of the witnesses may be taken, or production of documents may be required under Rule 34. An attempt may even be made to secure damaging admissions by taking the depositions of a party whose answers to interrogatories are disingenuous. His replies to interrogatories may be used for purposes of impeachment if the oral examination leads to contradiction.

Despite these advantages, "interrogatories are the most unpopular device because they can embody either the best or worst qualities of discovery: some pursue information too skillfully, others too crudely." [3] Disputes over interrogatories frequently must be resolved by the court and this has been burdensome and irritating to the judges. The amendments to Rule 33 adopted in 1970 were intended to remedy some of the defects in the prior rule and to reduce the

---

3. Glaser, Pretrial Discovery and the Adversary System, 1968, p. 149. The reasons for this are spelled out, id. at pp. 149–153. See also Flegal & Umin, Curbing Discovery Abuses in Civil Litigation: We're Not There Yet, 1981 B.Y.U.L.Rev. 597, 604–606; Schroeder & Frank, The Proposed Changes in the Discovery Rules, 1978 Ariz.St.L.J. 475, 478.

But compare Haydock & Herr, note 1 above, at 307: "We do know that rule 33 provides an efficient, effective, and economical discovery tool. Implementations of this system requires attorneys to submit only those interrogatories necessary to obtain essential information and to respond in good faith to properly submitted interrogatories."

number of cases involving interrogatories that the courts must pass upon.

The scope of examination under Rule 33 is the same as that for the other discovery devices, as defined in Rule 26 and already discussed.[4] The only problems as to scope that are peculiar to Rule 33 are whether interrogatories may be used to ascertain opinions, contentions, and conclusions of the adverse party, and whether he may be required to answer interrogatories where he lacks personal knowledge of the matter or is required to do research to prepare his answers.

Prior to the 1970 amendments of Rule 33, the decisions on the propriety of interrogatories inquiring about opinions, contentions, and conclusions had been extremely numerous and quite inconsistent.[5] The better view, however, was that "the line between fact and conclusion is frequently an uncertain and illogical one," [6] and that an interrogatory was proper, regardless of its label, if it would serve any substantial purpose, either in leading to evidence or in clarifying the issues in the case.[7]

This better view was written into Rule 33(b) in the 1970 amendments. It now provides that an otherwise proper interrogatory "is not necessarily objectionable merely because an answer to the interrogatory involves an opinion or contention that relates to fact or the application of law to fact * * *." The word "merely" is significant and should not be overlooked. The interrogatory may still be objectionable because in the circumstances of the particular case an answer to the interrogatory will not serve any useful purpose.[8] But there is no longer any automatic rule that an interrogatory must be disallowed merely because it calls for an opinion or a contention.

The rule is limited to opinions and contentions that relate to "fact or the application of law to fact." It does not authorize interrogatories calling for legal conclusions as such.[9] But many legal conclusions do require the application of law to fact and are the proper subject of interrogatories under the amended rule.[10]

---

4. See § 81 above.

5. 8 Wright & Miller, Civil § 2167.

6. B. & S. Drilling Co. v. Halliburton Oil Well Cementing Co., D.C.Tex.1959, 24 F.R.D. 1, 7.

7. Hartsfield v. Gulf Oil Corp., D.C.Pa. 1962, 29 F.R.D. 163, 165; and cases cited 8 Wright & Miller, Civil § 2167 n. 21.

8. Scovill Mfg. Co. v. Sunbeam Corp., D.C.Del.1973, 357 F.Supp. 943; Comment, Civil Procedure—Opinion Interrogatories After the 1970 Amendment to Federal Rule 33(b), 1975, 53 N.C.L. Rev. 695, 705.

9. Advisory Committee Note, 48 F.R.D. 487, 524; O'Brien v. International Broth. of Elec. Workers, D.C.Ga.1977, 443 F.Supp. 1182; Union Carbide Corp. v. Travelers Indem. Co., D.C.Pa.1973, 61 F.R.D. 411; Sargent-Welch Scientific Co. v. Ventron Corp., D.C.Ill.1973, 59 F.R.D. 500.

10. Union Carbide Corp. v. Travelers Indem. Co., D.C.Pa.1973, 61 F.R.D. 411; Sargent-Welch Scientific Co. v. Ventron Corp., D.C.Ill.1973, 59 F.R.D. 500; Ballard v. Allegheny Airlines, Inc., D.C.Pa.1972, 54 F.R.D. 67; Joseph v. Norman's Health Club, Inc., D.C.Mo.

The more liberal cases permitting interrogatories as to the contentions of the opponent are not always an unmixed blessing. To the extent that they put an end to attempted distinctions between facts and conclusions, they are desirable. But an argument has been made by a distinguished critic that the cases allowing interrogatories as to contentions have revived, under a different name, the unlamented bill of particulars, which was abolished in 1948.[11] The generalized pleading permitted by the rules has significance beyond the pleading rules themselves. It represents a broad determination that it is not desirable or feasible to tie a party down at an early stage to a particular theory as to the case, and that judgment must be allowed to go according to the facts as they develop at the trial, not limited by the belief of the party before the trial as to what the facts may be.

Amended Rule 33(b) seeks to meet this objection by providing that the court may order than an interrogatory calling for an opinion or contention need not be answered until after designated discovery has been completed, or at a pre-trial conference, or at some other later time. Thus if a malpractice plaintiff is sent an interrogatory asking him to specify the respects in which he claims defendant was negligent, and he does not know as yet because he was under anesthesia at the time, he should not be required to answer the interrogatory until he has ample opportunity through discovery of his own to see if he can prove specific acts of negligence.[12] The power to defer answers is useful, since it enables the court to protect a party from being tied down before he has had an opportunity fully to explore the case,[13] but it is a power that should not be exercised automatically but only in appropriate cases.[14]

As a general rule a party in answering interrogatories must furnish information that is in his possession and can be given without undue labor and expense.[15] He cannot generally be forced to prepare his opponent's case.[16] Consequently interrogatories that require a party to make investigations, research, or compilation of data are in many circumstances improper.[17] Even if the records containing the desired information are in the possession of the interrogated party,

---

1971, 336 F.Supp. 307. See Haydock & Herr, note 1 above, at 283–286.

11. James, The Revival of Bills of Particulars under the Federal Rules, 1958, 71 Harv.L.Rev. 1473.

12. A rather different result was reached on these facts under the former rule in Bynum v. U. S., D.C.La. 1964, 36 F.R.D. 14.

13. Dow Corning Corp. v. Surgitek, Inc., D.C.Wis.1973, 61 F.R.D. 578; Diamond Crystal Salt Co. v. Package Masters, Inc., D.C.Del.1970, 319 F.Supp. 911. See James & Hazard, Civil Procedure, 2d ed. 1977, § 6.12.

14. Diversified Products Corp. v. Sports Center Co., D.C.Md.1967, 42 F.R.D. 3, 5.

15. Flour Mills of America, Inc. v. Pace, D.C.Okl.1977, 75 F.R.D. 676; Cinema Amusements v. Loew's Inc., D.C.Del. 1947, 7 F.R.D. 318.

16. Olmert v. Nelson, D.C.D.C.1973, 60 F.R.D. 369; La Chemise Lacoste v. Alligator Co., Inc., D.C.Del.1973, 60 F.R.D. 164; Kainz v. Anheuser-Busch, Inc., D.C.Ill.1954, 15 F.R.D. 242.

17. E.g., Deering Milliken Research Corp. v. Tex-Elastic Corp., D.C.S.C. 1970, 320 F.Supp. 806; and cases cited 8 Wright & Miller, Civil § 2174 n. 91.

his adversary cannot use interrogatories to evade the burden of compiling data at his own expense if the records are available for his inspection under Rule 34 or with the consent of the interrogated party.[18] Rule 33(c) now gives the party on whom an interrogatory is served the option to make available his records from which an answer can be found [19] in any case in which the burden of finding the answer is substantially the same for the party serving the interrogatory as for the party served.[20] Rule 33(c) was amended in 1980 to provide that a party exercising this option must specify the records from which the answer can be found in sufficient detail to permit the interrogating party to locate and to identify them as readily as can the party served.[21]

The objection that preparing an answer would require research by the interrogated party is not enough to bar interrogatories in every case. In order to justify sustaining an objection to such an interrogatory—except where the option provided by Rule 33(c) has been availed of—it must be shown that the research is unduly burdensome and oppressive.[22] The party seeking to avoid answering the interrogatories carries the burden of showing that the information sought is not readily available to him,[23] and where there is conflict the court will make its own determination as to the cost and inconvenience of answering the interrogatories, rather than relying on bare assertions as to this by the party.[24]

Some cases say that a party who has no personal knowledge of an incident may not be required to search out information and answer interrogatories on the basis of such hearsay,[25] but such statements are too broad. A party is charged with knowledge of what his agents know, or what is in records available to him, or even, for purposes of Rule 33, what others have told him on which he intends to rely in his suit.[26] Nor can he refuse to answer interrogatories on the ground

18. See cases cited 8 Wright & Miller, Civil § 2174 nn. 94, 95.

19. 8 Wright & Miller, Civil § 2178. See Harlem River Consumers Co-op., Inc. v. Associated Grocers of Harlem, Inc., D.C.N.Y.1974, 64 F.R.D. 459; Concept Indus. Inc. v. Carpet Factory, Inc., D.C.Wis.1973, 59 F.R.D. 546; Ballard v. Allegheny Airlines, Inc., D.C. Pa.1972, 54 F.R.D. 67.

20. Daiflon, Inc. v. Allied Chem. Corp., C.A.10th, 1976, 534 F.2d 221, certiorari denied 97 S.Ct. 239, 429 U.S. 886, 50 L.Ed.2d 168; Mid-America Facilities, Inc. v. Argonaut Ins. Co., D.C.Wis. 1978, 78 F.R.D. 497.

21. This does not mean that exact documents must be identified. See Sherman & Kinnard, Federal Court Discovery in the 80s—Making the Rules Work, 1981, 2 Rev.Litigation 9, 14–21.

22. Roesberg v. Johns-Manville Corp., D.C.Pa.1980, 85 F.R.D. 292; Rogers v. Tri-State Materials Corp., D.C.W.Va. 1970, 51 F.R.D. 234; and cases cited 8 Wright & Miller, Civil § 2174 nn. 97, 98.

23. Sherman Park Community Assn. v. Wauwatosa Realty Co., D.C.Wis.1980, 486 F.Supp. 838; Martin v. Easton Pub. Co., D.C.Pa.1980, 85 F.R.D. 312.

24. Tivoli Realty v. Paramount Pictures, D.C.Del.1950, 10 F.R.D. 201; State ex rel. Gamble Constr. Co. v. Carroll, Mo. 1966, 408 S.W.2d 34.

25. E.g., Robinson v. Tracy, D.C.Mo. 1954, 16 F.R.D. 113; Bullard v. Universal Millwork Corp., D.C.N.Y.1960, 25 F.R.D. 342.

26. Miller v. Doctor's General Hosp., D.C.Okl.1977, 76 F.R.D. 136; Stonybrook Tenants Assn., Inc. v. Al-

that the information sought is solely within the knowledge of his attorney.[27]

It is clear, from Rule 26(b), that interrogatories may properly be used to ascertain the existence and location of documents or tangible things.[28] In the past it was not clear whether such interrogatories might require that copies of documents be attached to the answers, or whether a subsequent Rule 34 motion was required for production. A 1949 decision said, correctly at the time, that there was "irreconcilable conflict" among the decisions on this point.[29] The conflict has vanished in the more recent decisions, which are in agreement that copies of documents may not be obtained by interrogatories.[30]

Amendments to Rule 33 were made in 1948 to resolve two questions on which the decisions had been conflicting. Some courts had set an arbitrary limit on the number of interrogatories a party might submit. The amendment provided that "the number of interrogatories or of sets of interrogatories to be served is not limited except as justice requires to protect the party from annoyance, expense, embarrassment, or oppression." [31] Another amendment made at the same time provided that interrogatories may be served after a deposition has been taken, and a deposition may be sought after interrogatories have been answered, subject to the power of the court to make a protective order if justice so requires.[32] Thus under the amended rules the two procedures were clearly regarded as complementary. A party could use both depositions and interrogatories, either consecutively or simultaneously, so long as the other party could not show some hardship or injustice from use of the two procedures. These 1948 amendments were dropped from Rule 33 when it was further amended in 1970, on the ground that they were now covered by general provisions, applicable to all discovery devices. Rule 26(a) says that in the absence of a protective order "the frequency of use of these methods is not limited," and Rule 26(d) permits methods of discovery to be used in any sequence.[33]

pert, D.C.Conn.1961, 29 F.R.D. 165; and cases cited 8 Wright & Miller, Civil § 2177 n. 22.

27. Hickman v. Taylor, 1947, 67 S.Ct. 385, 390, 329 U.S. 495, 504, 91 L.Ed. 451; General Dynamics Corp. v. Selb Mfg. Co., C.A.8th, 1973, 481 F.2d 1204, certiorari denied 94 S.Ct. 926, 414 U.S. 1162, 39 L.Ed.2d 116; Shapiro, Some Problems of Discovery in an Adversary System, 1979, 63 Minn.L.Rev. 1055, 1071–1072.

28. U. S. v. Becton-Dickinson & Co., D.C.N.J.1962, 30 F.R.D. 132; Chatman v. American Export Lines, D.C.N.Y. 1956, 20 F.R.D. 176; Gaynor v. Atlantic Greyhound Corp., D.C.Pa.1948, 8 F.R.D. 302.

29. Alfred Pearson & Co. v. Hayes, D.C. N.Y.1949, 9 F.R.D. 210.

30. Alltmont v. U. S., C.A.3d, 1949, 177 F.2d 971, certiorari denied 70 S.Ct. 999, 339 U.S. 967, 94 L.Ed. 1375; Miller v. Doctor's Hosp., D.C.Okl.1977, 76 F.R.D. 136; and cases cited 8 Wright & Miller, Civil § 2166 n. 82.

31. 8 Wright & Miller, Civil § 2168, pp. 519–521.

32. E.g., Rogers v. Tri-State Materials Corp., D.C.W.Va.1970, 51 F.R.D. 234, 241. See 8 Wright & Miller, Civil § 2169.

33. Advisory Committee Note, 48 F.R.D. 487, 524. See Hine v. Superior Court, 1972, 504 P.2d 509, 18 Ariz.App. 568.

Until 1970 Rule 33 provided that interrogatories could be served only on an "adverse party." Presumably this requirement of adversity was intended to compensate for the absence from Rule 33 of any provision for notice or opportunity for cross-examination.[34] This limitation to "adverse" parties was an undesirable one. It was difficult to apply,[35] and in many circumstances barred use of the least expensive and most convenient means of discovery. The decision in the 1970 amendments to drop the word "adverse" and thus to allow a party to serve interrogatories on any other party was a sound one.[36] Under the rule as it had been in the past, answers to interrogatories had always been admissible at trial when offered by the interrogating party, as an admission of a party opponent.[37] Now that it is possible to have interrogatories answered by someone who is not a party opponent it will be necessary to see if the answers fall into some other exception to the hearsay rule, since Rule 33(b) states that answers are admissible "to the extent permitted by the rules of evidence."

Amendments in 1970 to Rule 33(a) made small but significant changes in the procedure for use of interrogatories. Leave of court is unnecessary and the amended rule allows interrogatories to be served with the complaint. The party interrogated ordinarily has 30

Despite this, many districts have adopted local rules limiting the number of interrogatories that may be served without leave of court. Haydock & Herr, note 1 above, at 269–271. In 1978 the Advisory Committee on Civil Rules circulated a proposed amendment that would have authorized districts to adopt local rules of this kind, but in 1979 it withdrew that proposal, explaining that it had attracted virtually no support. See 85 F.R.D. 521, 543–544; 8 Wright & Miller, Civil § 2169. Nevertheless, such local rules have become even more numerous and there is continued pressure to adopt a numerical limitation on the national basis. Some commentators who had opposed numerical limits in 1978 have now changed their mind. Compare Schroeder & Frank, note 3 above, at 486–487, with Schroeder & Frank, Discovery Reform: Long Road to Nowheresville, 1982, 68 A.B. A.J. 572, 574. For a contrary view, see Sherman & Kinnard, note 21 above, at 31–38.

34. In re City of Coral Gables, D.C.Fla. 1941, 1 F.R.D. 600; Cooke v. Kilgore Mfg. Co., D.C.Ohio 1954, 15 F.R.D. 465.

35. See Powell v. Willow Grove Amusement Park, D.C.Pa.1968, 45 F.R.D. 274; Carey v. Schuldt, D.C.La.1967, 42 F.R.D. 390; 8 Wright & Miller, Civil § 2171.

36. Carey v. Schuldt, D.C.La.1967, 42 F.R.D. 390, 396; Note, 1968, 68 Col.L. Rev. 271, 286–287.

There has been some disagreement on whether members of a class who are not named as parties can be required to respond to discovery under Rules 33 and 34. A consensus seems now to have developed that if discovery from absent members of the class is permissible at all, it should be sharply limited and allowed only on a strong showing of justification. Dellums v. Powell, C.A.1977, 566 F.2d 167, 187, 184 U.S. App.D.C. 275, certiorari denied 1978, 98 S.Ct. 3146, 438 U.S. 916, 57 L.Ed.2d 1161, rehearing denied 1979, 99 S.Ct. 234, 439 U.S. 886, 58 L.Ed.2d 201; Clark v. Universal Builders, Inc., C.A. 7th, 1974, 501 F.2d 324, 340, certiorari denied 95 S.Ct. 657, 419 U.S. 1070, 42 L.Ed.2d 666, on remand D.C.Ill.1978, 409 F.Supp. 1274; Note, Obtaining Discovery from Absent Class Members in Federal Rule of Civil Procedure 23(b) (3) Class Actions, 1981, 30 Drake L.Rev. 347.

37. 8 Wright & Miller, Civil § 2180.

It is held in Treharne v. Callahan, C.A.3d, 1970, 426 F.2d 58, that there are circumstances in which a party may introduce his own answers to interrogatories submitted to him by his opponent.

days in which to serve his answers and his objections, if any.[38] Objections to interrogatories are waived if they are not timely [39] or if the party has voluntarily answered the interrogatory.[40] If a party fails to answer, or objects to an interrogatory, the burden is now put on the party serving the interrogatory to make a motion under Rule 37(a) to compel an answer, and the expense sanction of that rule is applicable.

Interrogatories must be answered separately and fully under oath and signed by the person making the answers.[41] If a party fails entirely to serve answers or objections he is subject to the sanctions provided by Rule 37(d).[42] The rules had made no explicit provision for a remedy against incomplete, evasive, or false answers, but the courts uniformly and properly held that a motion would lie to compel further answers in such a case.[43] This is now dealt with explicitly in Rules 33(a) and 37(a)(3), as amended in 1970, which allow a motion under Rule 37(a) in these circumstances.

Although answers to interrogatories may limit the issues and define the contentions of the parties, the party should not be held irrevocably to them. The court has discretion to limit the proof in the light of the answers to the interrogatories,[44] but this is a discretion that should be exercised with attention to the fact that the great goal of the rules is that judgment be given on the facts as they actually exist. A party may be embarrassed by his answer to a pretrial interrogatory in which he took a position different from that he asserts at the trial, and it is right that he should have to explain his change of position, but his answer to the interrogatory should not be a conclusive bar to asserting a different view at the trial.[45]

---

38. This is a longer period than the unrealistic times formerly set for objections and for answers. See Glaser, Pretrial Discovery and the Adversary System, 1968, pp. 222–224.

Under no circumstances is a defendant to be required to answer or object less than 45 days after service of the summons and complaint upon him.

39. Antico v. Honda of Camden, D.C.Pa. 1979, 85 F.R.D. 34; and cases cited 8 Wright & Miller, Civil § 2173 n. 68. But cf. Shenker v. Sportelli, D.C.Pa. 1979, 83 F.R.D. 365.

40. Meese v. Eaton Mfg. Co., D.C.Ohio 1964, 35 F.R.D. 162; Cardox Corp. v. Olin Mathieson Chem. Corp., D.C.Ill. 1958, 23 F.R.D. 27, approved 1959, 6 Utah L.Rev. 429.

41. McDougall v. Dunn, C.A.4th, 1972, 468 F.2d 468; 8 Wright & Miller, Civil §§ 2172, 2177.

42. See § 90 below. 8 Wright & Miller, Civil § 2291.

43. E.g., Robinson v. Jordan, D.C.Mass. 1961, 27 F.R.D. 493; Brown v. United States Lines Co., D.C.N.Y.1953, 15 F.R.D. 127; Kraft v. Washington & Jefferson College, D.C.Pa.1951, 11 F.R.D. 503; 8 Wright & Miller, Civil §§ 2177, 2285.

44. Maryland to Use of Summerlin v. Kemp, D.C.Md.1961, 194 F.Supp. 838; Zielinski v. Philadelphia Piers, Inc., D.C.Pa.1956, 139 F.Supp. 408; Newsum v. Pennsylvania R. Co., D.C.N.Y. 1951, 97 F.Supp. 500.

45. Victory Carriers, Inc. v. Stockton Stevedoring Co., C.A.9th, 1968, 388 F.2d 955, 959; Ray v. J. C. Penney Co., C.A.10th, 1959, 274 F.2d 519, 521; Mangual v. Prudential Lines, Inc., D.C. Pa.1971, 53 F.R.D. 301; Pressley v. Boehlke, D.C.N.C.1963, 33 F.R.D. 316, 317; 8 Wright & Miller, Civil § 2181.

Not infrequently it will happen that an answer to an interrogatory, though full and truthful to the best of the party's knowledge at the time it is made, will become incomplete or misleading in the light of later information he finds. Is he under any duty to amend his answer and advise the party who submitted the interrogatory of his new information? This question had caused the courts difficulty.[46] For a party to sit idly by, knowing that a previous answer he has given to an interrogatory is not truthful in the light of his present information, seems inconsistent with the purpose of the rules to avoid surprise and with the standards expected of a learned and honorable profession.[47] At the same time it must be recognized that in a large and busy law practice the lawyer may honestly not realize that information he has just acquired is inconsistent with an answer he has given months or years before to an interrogatory.

A compromise was struck in 1970 in Rule 26(e), which applies to all discovery devices but is most important with regard to interrogatories.[48] It provides that a party is under a duty to supplement an earlier response in only two situations. He is under such a duty with regard to any question in which he was asked to give the name and address of persons having knowledge of discoverable matters or the name and the subject matter of an expert he expects to call at trial. This is thought justified because of the obvious importance of the information and because it is information that comes routinely to the attention of the lawyer in charge of the case. Second, he is under a duty to amend a prior response if either he obtains information from which he knows that the response was incorrect when made or he knows that a response correct when made is no longer true and the circumstances are such that a failure to amend the response would amount to a knowing concealment.[49]

If a party fails to give his opponent added information when he is under a duty to do so the court may refuse to allow an unnamed witness to testify, or may grant a continuance or a new trial, or otherwise follow whatever course seems just.[50]

46. 8 Wright & Miller, Civil § 2048.

47. Comment, The "Continuing" Nature of Discovery Techniques, 1957, 42 Iowa L.Rev. 579.

Texas & P. Ry. v. Buckles, C.A.5th, 1956, 232 F.2d 257, 260, certiorari denied 76 S.Ct. 1052, 351 U.S. 984, 100 L.Ed. 1498; Abbatemarco v. Colton, 1954, 106 A.2d 12, 31 N.J.Super. 181; D'Agostino v. Schaffer, 1957, 133 A.2d 45, 45 N.J.Super. 395.

48. See Rogers v. Tri-State Materials Corp., D.C.W.Va.1970, 51 F.R.D. 234, 244–245; 8 Wright & Miller, Civil §§ 2049, 2050.

49. See Havenfield Corp. v. H & R Block, Inc., C.A.8th, 1975, 509 F.2d 1263, certiorari denied 95 S.Ct. 2395, 421 U.S. 999, 44 L.Ed.2d 665.

50. Voegeli v. Lewis, C.A.8th, 1977, 568 F.2d 89 (new trial); Holiday Inns, Inc. v. Robertshaw Controls Co., C.A.7th, 1977, 560 F.2d 856 (testimony excluded); Frankel v. Stake, D.C.Pa.1963, 33 F.R.D. 1 (statement suppressed); Wembley, Inc. v. Diplomat Tie Co., D.C.Md.1963, 216 F.Supp. 565, 573–574 (continuance). See 8 Wright & Miller, Civil § 2050.

§ 87. Production of Documents [1]

Rule 34 authorizes the broadest sweep of access, inspection, examination, copying, and photographing of documents or objects in the possession or control of another party.[2] The scope of discovery under this rule is the same as that under the discovery rules generally.[3] The rule includes production of documents and things so that the other party may inspect them,[4] allowing a party to make drawings or photographs of the objects in question,[5] and entry upon premises for inspection of objects.[6] As amended in 1970, the rule even makes provision for production or inspection of computerized information.[7]

Rule 34 runs only against a party to a pending action,[8] though production and inspection can be had against a person not a party in many instances by a subpoena duces tecum for the taking of his deposition,[9] and Rule 34(c) makes it clear that the rule does not have a preemptive effect and does not bar an independent action in the nature of a bill of discovery against a person not a party.[10]

A party can be required to produce only such documents or things as "are in his possession, custody, or control." [11] The basic test of

[§ 87]

1. 8 Wright & Miller, Civil §§ 2201–2218.

2. Morales v. Turman, D.C.Tex.1972, 59 F.R.D. 157.

3. See § 81 above. For application of the principles there developed to Rule 34, see 8 Wright & Miller, Civil § 2206.

4. Even the taking of urine specimens from cattle and doing post-mortems on dead cattle had been said to be within the concept of "inspection." Martin v. Reynolds Metals Corp., C.A.9th, 1961, 297 F.2d 49, noted 1962, 41 Texas L.Rev. 330. This result was made explicit by the inclusion in amended Rule 34(a) of the words "test, or sample." See Sladen v. Girltown, Inc., C.A.7th, 1970, 425 F.2d 24; Sperberg v. Firestone Tire & Rubber Co., D.C.Ohio 1973, 61 F.R.D. 80.

5. Diapulse Corp. of America v. Curtis Pub. Co., C.A.2d, 1967, 374 F.2d 442; Rosenthal v. Compagnie-Generale Transatlantique, D.C.N.Y.1953, 14 F.R.D. 336; Prosperity Co. v. St. Joe Machines, D.C.Mich.1942, 2 F.R.D. 299.

6. A sufficient showing for entry on land was held not to have been made in Belcher v. Bassett Furniture Indus., Inc., C.A.4th, 1978, 588 F.2d 904. Inspection was allowed in Morales v. Turman, D.C.Tex.1972, 59 F.R.D. 157. See generally Hughes & Anderson, Discovery: A Competition Between the Right of Privacy and the Right to Know, 1971, 23 U.Fla.L.Rev. 289.

7. National Union Elec. Corp. v. Matushita Elec. Indus. Co., Ltd., D.C. Pa.1980, 494 F.Supp. 1257; Pearl Brewing Co. v. Jos. Schlitz Brewing Co., D.C.Tex.1976, 415 F.Supp. 1122; Adams v. Dan River Mills, Inc., D.C. Va.1972, 54 F.R.D. 220; Sherman & Kinnard, The Development, Discovery, and Use of Computer Support Systems in Achieving Efficiency in Litigation, 1979, 73 Col.L.Rev. 267; 8 Wright & Miller, Civil § 2218.

8. Hickman v. Taylor, 1947, 67 S.Ct. 385, 390, 329 U.S. 495, 504, 91 L.Ed. 451; In re Franklin Nat. Bank Securities Litigation, C.A.2d, 1978, 574 F.2d 662; 8 Wright & Miller, Civil § 2208.

For possible application of Rule 34 to unnamed members of a class, see § 86 n. 36 above.

A person who expects to be a party to an action may proceed under Rule 27 and obtain any relief that would be proper in a pending action under Rule 34. Martin v. Reynolds Metals Corp., C.A. 9th, 1961, 297 F.2d 49, noted 1962, 41 Texas L.Rev. 330.

9. See Rules 30(f)(1) and 45(d)(1); 8 Wright & Miller, Civil § 2108.

10. See 8 Wright & Miller, Civil § 2209; Note, Rule 34(c) and Discovery of Non-party Land, 1975, 85 Yale L.J. 112.

11. 8 Wright & Miller, Civil § 2210.

the rule is "control." [12] Frequently inspection will be ordered where the party against whom the order runs has the legal right to obtain the document, even though in fact he has no copy,[13] and regardless of whether the document is beyond the jurisdiction of the court.[14] Thus a party cannot escape discovery by turning the document over to his attorney or his insurer.[15] Where the party has no legal right to the thing in question, he has been held not required to produce,[16] even though the thing was in his possession.[17] However the Supreme Court has held that a foreign corporation is in "control" of certain records, and thus may be ordered to produce them, even though penal laws of the country where it is located limit its ability to satisfy the production order.[18] The effect of those laws is considered in determining what sanction to impose for noncompliance with the order, rather than regarded as a reason for refusing to order production.[19]

As originally adopted in 1938 Rule 34 required a court order on a showing of "good cause." Rule 34(b), as it was amended in 1970, changed this and provided a mechanism that is intended ordinarily to operate extra-judicially. This simply recognizes what was in fact happening under the former rule. In practice lawyers rarely went to court to invoke Rule 34 and proceeded instead by informal agreement. Thus the amended rule permits the party seeking inspection to proceed by a simple request, describing what it is he wishes to see and specifying a reasonable time, place, and manner for this to be accomplished.[20] The party on whom the request is served must re-

12. Bifferato v. States Marine Corp. of Delaware, D.C.N.Y.1951, 11 F.R.D. 44, 46; Note, Meaning of "Control" in F.R. C.P. 34, 1958, 107 U.Pa.L.Rev. 103.

13. E.g., In re Folding Carton Antitrust Litigation, D.C.Ill.1977, 76 F.R.D. 420 (corporate documents in hands of former employees); Herbst v. Able, D.C. N.Y.1972, 63 F.R.D. 135 (SEC testimony); Schwartz v. Travelers Ins. Co., D.C.N.Y.1954, 17 F.R.D. 330 (hospital records); Reeves v. Pennsylvania R. Co., D.C.Del.1948, 80 F.Supp. 107 (income tax returns).

14. First City Nat. Bank of New York v. IRS, C.A.2d, 1959, 271 F.2d 616, certiorari denied 80 S.Ct. 402, 361 U.S. 948, 4 L.Ed.2d 381, rehearing denied 1960, 80 S.Ct. 609, 362 U.S. 906, 4 L.Ed.2d 557.

15. Bingle v. Liggett Drug Co., D.C. Mass.1951, 11 F.R.D. 593; Simper v. Trimble, D.C.Mo.1949, 9 F.R.D. 598; Kane v. News Syndicate Co., D.C.N.Y. 1941, 1 F.R.D. 738; State Farm Ins. Co. v. Roberts, 1965, 398 P.2d 671, 97 Ariz. 169; cf. Wilson v. David, D.C. Mich.1957, 21 F.R.D. 217.

16. Fisher v. U. S. Fidelity & Guar. Co., C.A.7th, 1957, 246 F.2d 344; Reeves v.

Pennsylvania R. Co., D.C.Del.1948, 80 F.Supp. 107.

17. U. S. v. Kyle, D.C.N.Y.1957, 21 F.R.D. 163; In re Harris, D.C.N.Y. 1939, 27 F.Supp. 480.

18. Societe Internationale Pour Participations Industrielles et Commerciales, S. A. v. Brownell, 1958, 78 S.Ct. 1087, 357 U.S. 197, 2 L.Ed.2d 1255, noted 1958, 107 U.Pa.L.Rev. 103.

19. In re Westinghouse Elec. Corp. Uranium Contracts Litigation, C.A.10th, 1977, 563 F.2d 992, noted 1978 Utah L.Rev. 361; SEC v. Banca Della Svizzera Italiana, D.C.N.Y.1981, 92 F.R.D. 111; In re Uranium Antitrust Litigation, D.C.Ill.1979, 480 F.Supp. 1138; Restatement of the Foreign Relations Law of the United States Revised, Tent.Dr. No. 3, 1982, § 420; Lowenfeld, Bank Secrecy and Insider Trading: The Banca Della Svizzera Italiana Case, 1982, 15 Rev.Sec.Reg. 942.

20. 8 Wright & Miller, Civil § 2212. See proposed Official Form 24 for the form of such a request.

spond, ordinarily within 30 days, either saying that inspection will be permitted or stating reasons for objections to the request. If objection is made, the party seeking discovery may move under Rule 37(a) to compel the inspection sought.

In a request for inspection under amended Rule 34, just as in a motion under the prior rule, the party seeking discovery must designate the things he wishes to inspect. There has been considerable discussion as to how specifically these must be designated.[21] The discussion has centered on two familiar cases that seem to reflect varying views on this point. In one case Judge Woolsey said that a "designation in a motion under Rule 34 must be sufficiently precise in respect to each document or item of evidence sought to enable the defendant to go to his files and, without difficulty, to pick the document or other item requested out and turn to the plaintiff saying 'Here it is.' "[22] In a later case Judge Rifkind held that it is sufficient to demand all the documents under defendant's control pertaining to a particular subject matter.[23]

It is not unnatural, in the light of these differing constructions of the rule, that commentators and courts should speak of the cases as if they represent a narrow view and a broad view as to the specificity of designation.[24] Yet it is not clear that the decisions cannot be reconciled. As many cases have said, and probably all courts would agree, the things to be produced for inspection must be described with reasonable particularity.[25] Particularity of designation, however, like so many other matters in life and law, is a matter of degree, dependent upon a pragmatic consideration of the circumstances in each case. Necessarily the test must be a relative one, turning on the amount of knowledge that a party has as to the documents he requests.[26] In some cases he has such exact and definite knowledge that he can designate, identify, and enumerate with precision the documents to be produced, in which event he should do so. This is the ideal designation, but the ideal is not always attainable, and the rule does not require the impossible. The goal is that the description be sufficient to apprise a man of ordinary intelligence what documents are required, and that the court be able to ascertain whether the re-

21. 8 Wright & Miller, Civil § 2211; Roman, Designation of Documents under Rule 34, 1958, 25 Ins.Couns.J. 313; Newport, "Designation" as used in Rule 34 of the Federal Rules of Civil Procedure on Discovery and Production of Documents, 1950, 35 Iowa L.Rev. 422.

22. U. S. v. American Optical Co., D.C. N.Y.1942, 2 F.R.D. 534, 536.

23. U. S. v. U. S. Alkali Export Assn., Inc., D.C.N.Y.1946, 7 F.R.D. 256.

24. See U. S. v. National Steel Corp., D.C.Tex.1960, 26 F.R.D. 607, 611.

25. Roebling v. Anderson, 1958, 257 F.2d 615, 620, 103 U.S.App.D.C. 237; U. S. v. Certain Parcels of Land, etc., D.C.Cal.1953, 15 F.R.D. 224, 228; Hefter v. National Airlines, D.C.N.Y. 1952, 14 F.R.D. 78, 79; Olson Transp. Co. v. Socony-Vacuum Oil Co., D.C. Wis.1944, 7 F.R.D. 134, 136.

26. Tiedman v. American Pigment Corp., C.A.4th, 1958, 253 F.2d 803, 809; Roebling v. Anderson, C.A.1958, 257 F.2d 615, 621, 103 U.S.App.D.C. 237; Mitsui & Co. (U.S.A.) Inc. v. Puerto Rico Water Resources Auth., D.C.Puerto Rico 1978, 79 F.R.D. 72.

quest has been complied with.[27] This notion is well captured in amended Rule 34(b); it provides that the request may describe either individual items or categories and that it must "describe each item and category with reasonable particularity."

Easily the most difficult and controversial requirement of Rule 34 as originally adopted was the showing of "good cause." It was clear, as the Supreme Court said, that the requirement was "not a mere formality" but rather "a plainly expressed limitation on the use of that Rule." [28] The requirement was certainly plainly expressed but its meaning was far from plain and its application was uncertain.[29]

Probably the principal accomplishment of amended Rule 34 was that it eliminated the requirement of good cause. This was possible because an empirical study showed that the "good cause" requirement in fact had little effect on the use of inspections.[30] The cases in which its meaning had been litigated dealt almost exclusively with trial preparation materials, in which the work product concept was close to the surface even if technically the documents did not come within the concept. Inspection of documents and things not obtained in anticipation of litigation or preparation for trial was routinely granted. The 1970 amendments brought the rules into conformance with actual practice. Rule 26(b)(3) gives substantial protection to trial preparation materials [31] while amended Rule 34 allows inspection without any showing of good cause, of other documents and things that are relevant to the subject matter of the action and not privileged.[32]

A minor amendment to Rule 34 was made in 1980. It provides that a party who produces documents for inspection shall produce them as they are kept in the usual course of business or shall organize and label them to correspond with the categories in the request.[33] Although the amendment is ambiguous on this point, it should not be read as giving the party from whom the discovery is sought an absolute option to produce records as kept in the usual course of business. He should be required to produce them in a form that will make reasonable use of them possible.[34]

27. Scuderi v. Boston Ins. Co., D.C.Del. 1964, 34 F.R.D. 463, 466; U. S. v. National Steel Corp., D.C.Tex.1960, 26 F.R.D. 607, 610; Dean v. Superior Court, 1958, 324 P.2d 764, 84 Ariz. 104.

28. Schlagenhauf v. Holder, 1964, 85 S.Ct. 234, 242, 379 U.S. 104, 118, 13 L.Ed.2d 152.

29. See 8 Wright & Miller, Civil § 2205, discussing the varying views of good cause taken in the pre-1970 cases and the elimination of that requirement by the amendments in that year.

30. Glaser, Pretrial Discovery and the Adversary System, 1968, p. 221.

31. See § 82 above.

32. Galambus v. Consolidated Freightways Corp., D.C.Ind.1974, 64 F.R.D. 468, 474; Mallinckrodt Chem. Works v. Goldman, Sachs & Co., D.C.N.Y.1973, 58 F.R.D. 348, 354; Herbst v. Able, D.C.N.Y.1972, 63 F.R.D. 135.

33. "It is apparently not rare for parties deliberately to mix crucial documents with others in the hope of obscuring significance." Advisory Committee Note, 85 F.R.D. 521, 532.

34. Sherman & Kinnard, Federal Court Discovery in the 80s—Making the Rules Work, 1981, 1 Rev.Litigation 9, 21–25; Watkins, 1980 Amendments to

§ 88. Physical Examination [1]

Under Rule 35, whenever the physical or mental condition of a party is in controversy, the court in which the action is pending may require him to submit to an examination by a physician. Prior to the adoption of the rules a federal court could not order such an examination unless express authority therefor was granted by the laws of the state in which the court sat.[2] The leading Supreme Court decision so holding posed the issue squarely. To the majority the issue was one of sanctity of the person, which it thought as much invaded by a compulsory stripping, and exposure, as by a blow,[3] while the dissenters considered "truth and justice * * * more sacred than any personal consideration." [4] Most of the states believed that the invasion of the person involved in a physical examination was outweighed by the need for such examinations in the interest of truth and justice.[5] Relying on this experience, Rule 35 was adopted, providing for such examinations in federal court. The Supreme Court, by a five-to-four vote, held the rule valid and applicable regardless of the law of the state in which the district court was sitting,[6] and in the more recent case of Schlagenhauf v. Holder,[7] though the Court was divided on other issues, there was no dissent from the proposition that "Rule 35, as applied to either plaintiffs or defendants to an action, is free of constitutional difficulty and is within the scope of the Enabling Act." [8]

The rule purports to apply to "any action in which the mental or physical condition of a party is in controversy." [9] An early case refused to allow an examination in a libel case, where defendant was claiming he had spoken truthfully in attributing various physical and mental conditions to the plaintiff.[10] The court thought that the rule looked only to personal injury litigation where the condition was in issue "immediately and directly" rather than "incidentally and collat-

the Federal Rules of Civil Procedure, 1980, 32 Baylor L.Rev. 533, 550.

[§ 88]

1. 8 Wright & Miller, Civil §§ 2231–2239; Barnet, Compulsory Medical Examinations Under the Federal Rules, 1955, 41 Va.L.Rev. 1059; Draper, Medical Examinations of Adversary Parties, 1953, 25 Rocky Mtn.L. Rev. 163; King, A Study of Rule 35 of the Federal Rules of Civil Procedure, 1959, 11 S.C.L.Rev. 183; Note, Court-Ordered Mental and Physical Examinations: A Survey of Federal Rule 35 and Illinois Rule 215, 1980, 11 Loy.U.L.J. 725.

2. Union Pac. R. Co. v. Botsford, 1891, 11 S.Ct. 1000, 141 U.S. 250, 35 L.Ed. 734; Camden & Suburban R. Co. v. Stetson, 1900, 20 S.Ct. 617, 77 U.S. 172, 44 L.Ed. 721.

3. Union Pac. R. Co. v. Botsford, 1891, 11 S.Ct. 1000, 1001, 141 U.S. 250, 251–252, 35 L.Ed. 734.

4. 11 S.Ct. at 1004, 141 U.S. at 259.

5. The almost universal acceptance of physical examinations in the states is discussed in 8 Wright & Miller, Civil § 2231, pp. 665–666.

6. Sibbach v. Wilson & Co., Inc., 1941, 61 S.Ct. 422, 312 U.S. 1, 85 L.Ed. 479.

7. 1964, 85 S.Ct. 234, 379 U.S. 104, 13 L.Ed.2d 152, noted 1965, 14 Cath.U.L. Rev. 278, 65 Col.L.Rev. 715, 69 Dick.L. Rev. 326, 3 Hous.L.Rev. 133, 51 Iowa L.Rev. 242, 16 Syracuse L.Rev. 668, 32 Tenn.L.Rev. 317.

8. 85 S.Ct. at 240, 379 U.S. at 114.

9. 8 Wright & Miller, Civil § 2232.

10. Wadlow v. Humberd, D.C.Mo.1939, 27 F.Supp. 210.

erally." Fortunately such a restrictive construction did not long prevail. The rule was soon held to permit blood tests in a paternity action,[11] and since then it has not been doubted that the rule means what it says in referring to "any action."

The rule authorizes examination only of a "party." In the Schlagenhauf case the Supreme Court said that this means what it says; it authorizes examination either of a plaintiff or a defendant and there is no requirement that the examination be sought by a party who is opposed to the party to be examined.[12] The Court found it unnecessary to determine "to what extent, if any, the term 'party' includes one who is a 'real party in interest' although not a named party to the action." [13] As amended in 1970, Rule 37(a) allows examination of "a person in the custody or under the legal control of a party," [14] but it now seems clear that examination of strangers to an action is not authorized, no matter how useful the examination might be in deciding a case.[15]

An order under Rule 35 may be made only on motion and a showing of good cause. In practice, the showing is very perfunctory, in personal injury cases at least, and in almost all cases the examination is arranged by stipulation of the attorneys.[16] The Supreme Court said in Schlagenhauf that the requirements that the condition be "in controversy" and that "good cause" for the examination be shown are satisfied from the pleadings alone if a plaintiff claims mental or physical injury or a defendant asserts his mental or physical condition as a defense to a claim.[17] But if a party does not put his own condition in issue, and the issue is raised by some other party who seeks an examination, a more discriminating decision is required. In this instance neither conclusory allegations of the pleadings nor mere relevance to the case are enough. Instead there must be "an affirmative showing by the movant that each condition as to which the exam-

---

11. Beach v. Beach, C.A.1940, 114 F.2d 479, 72 App.D.C. 318. This result was codified in a 1970 amendment of Rule 37(a). The rule does not apply if no action is pending. Tarlton v. U. S., C.A. 5th, 1970, 430 F.2d 1351.

12. 85 S.Ct. at 239–242, 379 U.S. at 112–116.

13. 88 S.Ct. at 241 n. 12, 379 U.S. at 115 n. 12. As an example of the situation it had in mind, the Court cited Beach v. Beach, C.A.1940, 114 F.2d 479, 72 U.S. App.D.C. 318, in which a blood test was ordered on an infant who would benefit from her mother's separate maintenance action.

14. Beckwith v. Beckwith, D.C.App. 1976, 355 A.2d 537, appeal after remand 1978, 379 A.2d 955, certiorari de-

nied 98 S.Ct. 2239, 436 U.S. 907, 56 L.Ed.2d 405 (child in custody of defendant in a divorce action).

15. Scharf v. U. S. Attorney Gen., C.A.9th, 1979, 597 F.2d 1240 (parents of person claiming citizenship); Schuppin v. Unification Church, D.C.Vt.1977, 435 F.Supp. 603 (adult child of party), affirmed C.A.2d, 573 F.2d 1295; Kropp v. General Dynamics Corp., D.C.Mich. 1962, 202 F.Supp. 207 (employee). See 8 Wright & Miller, Civil § 2233.

16. Liechty v. Terrill Trucking Co., D.C. Tenn.1971, 53 F.R.D. 590; Glaser, Pretrial Discovery and the Adversary System, 1968, pp. 54–55. See generally 8 Wright & Miller, Civil § 2234.

17. 85 S.Ct. at 243, 379 U.S. at 119.

ination is sought is really and genuinely in controversy and that good cause exists for ordering each particular examination." [18]

Examination by more than one doctor is permissible,[19] and more than one examination may be ordered, though the court will require a stronger showing of necessity before ordering repeated examinations.[20] Usually the court will name a doctor suggested by the moving party to make the examination.[21] The court has the power to make the ultimate decision, however,[22] and will consider any serious objection that the person to be examined may have to the doctor suggested by the moving party.[23]

In determining what kinds of examination to permit, the court must balance the desire to insure the safety and freedom from pain of the party to be examined against the need for the facts in the interest of truth and justice. The showing of the medical acceptance and safety of the particular procedure is important. Where an adequate foundation is laid as to the need for the procedure and its safety, even novel and painful procedures may be ordered.[24] It is commonly provided that the examined party may have his own physician present during the examination if he wishes to do so.[25] In some states the person may also have his attorney present, but this is hardly necessary under ordinary circumstances, and a more sensible rule is that the attorney cannot be present as a matter of right, but only with permission of the court granted for good reason.[26]

18. 88 S.Ct. at 242–243, 379 U.S. at 118. See Stuart v. Burford, D.C.Okl.1967, 42 F.R.D. 591. Plaintiff's physical and mental condition were held not in controversy in Winters v. Travia, C.A.2d, 1974, 495 F.2d 839. A sufficient showing for a mental examination of defendant was not made in Marroni v. Matey, D.C.Pa.1979, 82 F.R.D. 371.

It is held in Bodnar v. Bodnar, C.A.5th, 1971, 441 F.2d 1103, that a court has power to order mental examination of a plaintiff to determine if plaintiff is mentally competent to understand the nature and effect of the litigation.

19. Little v. Howey, D.C.Mo.1963, 32 F.R.D. 322, 323; Marshall v. Peters, D.C.Ohio 1962, 31 F.R.D. 238, 239; cf. Stuart v. Burford, D.C.Okl.1967, 42 F.R.D. 591, 593.

20. Ishler v. Cook, C.A.7th, 1962, 299 F.2d 507; Benning v. Phelps, C.A.2d, 1957, 249 F.2d 47; Vopelak v. Williams, D.C.Ohio 1967, 42 F.R.D. 387; cf. Rutherford v. Alben, D.C.W.Va.1940, 1 F.R.D. 277.

21. Postell v. Amana Refrigeration, Inc., D.C.Ga.1980, 87 F.R.D. 706; Gale v. National Transp. Co., D.C.N.Y.1946, 7 F.R.D. 237.

22. Liechty v. Terrill Trucking Co., D.C. Tenn.1971, 53 F.R.D. 590; Leach v. Greif Bros. Cooperage Corp., D.C.Miss. 1942, 2 F.R.D. 444. Contra: Wasmund v. Nunamaker, 1967, 151 N.W.2d 577, 277 Minn. 52.

23. Stuart v. Burford, D.C.Okl.1967, 42 F.R.D. 591; Gitto v. Societá Anonima Di Navigazione, Genova, D.C.N.Y.1939, 27 F.Supp. 785.

24. E.g., Klein v. Yellow Cab Co., D.C. Ohio 1949, 7 F.R.D. 169 (cystoscopy and phylegrams); 8 Wright & Miller, Civil § 2235.

25. Dziwanoski v. Ocean Carriers Corp., D.C.Md.1960, 26 F.R.D. 595; Klein v. Yellow Cab Co., D.C.Ohio, 1944, 7 F.R.D. 169; see Warrick v. Brode, D.C. Del.1969, 46 F.R.D. 427, 428. But see Sanden v. Mayo Clinic, C.A.8th, 1974, 495 F.2d 221; Swift v. Swift, D.C.N.Y. 1974, 64 F.R.D. 440.

26. Brandenberg v. El Al Israel Airlines, D.C.N.Y.1978, 79 F.R.D. 543; Warrick v. Brode, D.C.Del.1969, 46 F.R.D. 427; Dziwanoski v. Ocean Carriers Corp., D.C.Md.1960, 26 F.R.D. 595; 8 Wright & Miller, Civil § 2236.

Under Rule 35(b)(1) the party examined has an absolute right to receive from the party who caused the examination to be made a copy of the report of the findings of the examining physician. Not infrequently a party submits to an examination voluntarily, prior to retaining counsel, and does not stipulate that he is to receive a copy of the report. Rule 35(b)(3), added in 1970, codifies a result the courts had already reached and provides that the same right to receive, on a request, a copy of the report of the findings exists in this situation as exists when the examination is pursuant to a court order.[27]

Rule 35(b)(2) provides that by requesting and obtaining a report of the examination made pursuant to Rule 35, the party examined waives any privilege he may have in that action regarding the testimony of every other person who has examined or may thereafter examine him with regard to the same mental or physical condition. He must turn over to his adversary his own medical reports.[28] Literally the rule applies only if the person examined has requested a copy of the report,[29] but if the physician-patient privilege is not applicable, the examined person's reports may be subject to discovery under Rule 34 or otherwise,[30] and the deposition of the doctor can be taken if the requirements of Rule 26(b)(4) are satisfied.[31]

If a party fails to comply with a court order requiring him to submit to a physical examination, all of the sanctions of Rule 37(b)(2) are available,[32] with the important exception that the party may not be imprisoned for contempt.[33]

There has been much interest in the last few years in proposals to provide for impartial medical examinations in appropriate cases,[34] and

27. 8 Wright & Miller, Civil § 2237, pp. 690–691.

Even if the examining physician has not made a written report, the court can require the party who moved for the examination to obtain a report to give to the party examined. Salvatore v. American Cyanamid Co., D.C.R.I.1982, 94 F.R.D. 156.

28. Weir v. Simmons, D.C.Neb.1964, 233 F.Supp. 657; Lindsay v. Prince, D.C. Ohio, 1948, 8 F.R.D. 233; 8 Wright & Miller, Civil § 2237, pp. 687–688.

29. Sher v. De Haven, C.A.1952, 199 F.2d 777, 91 U.S.App.D.C. 257, certiorari denied 73 S.Ct. 797, 345 U.S. 936, 97 L.Ed. 1363; Galloway v. National Dairy Products Corp., D.C.Pa.1959, 24 F.R.D. 362; Shepherd v. Castle, D.C. Mo.1957, 20 F.R.D. 184; cf. Benning v. Phelps, C.A.2d, 1957, 249 F.2d 47.

30. Rule 35(b)(3), added in 1970; Buffington v. Wood, C.A.3d, 1965, 351 F.2d 292; Leszynski v. Russ, D.C.Md.1961, 29 F.R.D. 10; see Cox v. Fennelly, D.C. N.Y.1966, 40 F.R.D. 1, 2.

It is held in Hardy v. Riser, D.C.Miss. 1970, 309 F.Supp. 1234, that testimony of a physician who has examined a party under Rule 35 is admissible even though the state would recognize a physician-patient privilege and there has been no waiver of the privilege.

31. See the discussion of Rule 26(b)(4) in § 81 above. See generally Comment, Discovery and the Doctor: Expansion of Rule 35(b), 1973, 34 Mont.L.Rev. 257.

32. See § 90 below.

33. See Rule 37(b)(2)(D), (E). See also Sibbach v. Wilson & Co., Inc., 1941, 61 S.Ct. 422, 312 U.S. 1, 85 L.Ed. 479; 8 Wright & Miller, Civil § 2238.

34. 8 Wright & Miller, Civil § 2239; Comment, The Doctor in Court: Impartial Medical Testimony, 1967, 40 So.Cal. L.Rev. 728; Symposium on the Impartial Medical Expert, 1961, 34 Temp.L.Q. 357; Comment, Impartial Medical Testimony Plans, 1961, 55 Nw.U.L.Rev. 700; Comment, Impartial Medical Testimony—A New Horizon, 1959, 32

some federal courts had followed the lead of certain state courts in providing by local rule for such examinations. Such rules appear to codify the common law power of the judge to call his own witnesses where this is necessary.[35] Although there has been controversy about the idea of impartial medical examinations,[36] the issue is now resolved by Evidence Rule 706, effective in 1975. It authorizes court appointment of expert witnesses on any subject, not merely for medical matters, and makes provision for the compensation of experts so appointed. The court is given discretion to authorize disclosure to the jury of the fact that the court appointed the expert witness.[37]

§ 89. Requests for Admissions [1]

Rule 36(a) provides that a party to an action may serve upon any other party a written request for the admission by the latter of the genuineness of any relevant documents described in the request or of the truth of any matter set forth in the request that is within the general scope of discovery defined in Rule 26(b).[2] The party on whom such a request is served may file written objections to the request, if he thinks it improper under the rule, or he may file an answer denying specifically the matters of which an admission is requested or setting forth in detail the reasons why he cannot truthfully admit or deny those matters.[3] If he fails to respond to the request, the matters set out in the request are deemed admitted,[4] though the court has discretion to avoid the admission if there is an untimely answer.[5] If the party fails to admit the matters set out in the request, and the party requesting the admission later proves the truth of the matter, the court, on application, will order the party failing to admit to pay the reasonable expenses incurred in proving the matter, including reasonable attorney's fees, unless the court has previously sustained an objection to the request, or the court finds that the admission was not of substantial importance, or the party failing to admit had reasonable ground to believe that he might prevail on

Temp.L.Q. 193; Peck, Impartial Medical Testimony: A Way to Better and Quicker Justice, 1958, 22 F.R.D. 21; Association of the Bar of the City of New York, Impartial Medical Testimony, 1956.

35. Scott v. Spanjer Bros., Inc., C.A.2d 1962, 298 F.2d 928; McCormick, Evidence, Cleary et al. ed. 1972, § 17.

36. See Levy, The Impartial Medical Expert System: The Plaintiff's Point of View, 1961, 34 Temp.L.Q. 416.

37. Evidence Rule 706(c).

[§ 89]

1. 8 Wright & Miller, Civil §§ 2251–2265.

2. On the general scope of discovery, see § 81 above.

3. 8 Wright & Miller, Civil §§ 2260–2262.

4. Luick v. Graybar Elec. Co., Inc., C.A. 8th, 1973, 473 F.2d 1360; and cases cited 8 Wright & Miller, Civil § 2259, pp. 724–726.

5. U. S. v. Lake Killarney Apartments, Inc., C.A.5th, 1971, 443 F.2d 1170; Hadra v. Herman Blum Consulting Engineers, D.C.Tex.1977, 74 F.R.D. 113; and cases cited 8 Wright & Miller, Civil § 2257 nn. 71–75.

The standard for withdrawal of an admission is higher after trial. Brook Village North Associates v. General Elec. Co., C.A.1st, 1982, 686 F.2d 66.

the matter, or there was some other good reason for the failure to admit.[6]

An admission is for the purpose of Rule 36 only and cannot be used against the party in any other proceeding.[7] It is a binding admission in that proceeding, however, except insofar as the court permits the admission to be amended or withdrawn.[8]

Strictly speaking Rule 36 is not a discovery procedure at all, since it presupposes that the party proceeding under it knows the facts or has the document and merely wishes his opponent to concede their genuineness.[9] Thus the purpose of this rule is to expedite the trial and to relieve the parties of the cost of proving facts that will not be disputed at the trial and the truth of which can be ascertained by reasonable inquiry.[10]

As originally adopted Rule 36 spoke of admissions as to "relevant" documents and "relevant" matters of fact. It was generally agreed that this was to be given the same broad meaning as in the other discovery rules, and that relevancy to the subject matter of the action, rather than admissibility in evidence, was the test.[11] There was some authority taking a different view, and suggesting that admissibility was the key,[12] but this was doubtful at the time and such a construction cannot survive the amendments of Rule 36 adopted in 1970 in which the word "relevant" was deleted and requests allowed of any matters within the scope of proposed Rule 26(b), the general rule on scope of discovery.

Some cases had refused to recognize the privilege against self-incrimination because of the provision of Rule 36(b) that an answer to a

6. Rule 37(c); 8 Wright & Miller, Civil § 2290. Sanctions have not often been imposed in the past. Glaser, Pretrial Discovery and the Adversary System, 1968, pp. 211–212. Payment of costs was ordered in Bradshaw v. Thompson, C.A.6th, 1972, 454 F.2d 75, certiorari denied 93 S.Ct. 130, 409 U.S. 878, 34 L.Ed.2d 131.

7. Rule 36(b).

8. The language to this effect in amended Rule 36(b) codified what the courts were already holding. See McSparran v. Hanigan, D.C.Pa.1963, 225 F.Supp. 628, affirmed, C.A.3d, 1965, 356 F.2d 983; 8 Wright & Miller, Civil § 2264, pp. 741–746; Finman, The Request for Admissions in Federal Civil Procedure, 1962, 71 Yale L.J. 371, 418–426.

9. McHugh v. Reserve Min. Co., D.C. Ohio, 1961, 27 F.R.D. 505; Driver v. Gindy Mfg. Corp., D.C.Pa.1959, 24 F.R.D. 473; Knowlton v. Atchison, T.

& S. F. Ry. Co., D.C.Mo.1951, 11 F.R.D. 62.

10. Champlin v. Oklahoma Furniture Mfg. Co., C.A.10th, 1963, 324 F.2d 74; Syracuse Broadcasting Corp. v. Newhouse, C.A.2d, 1959, 271 F.2d 910; Burns v. Phillips, D.C.Ga.1970, 50 F.R.D. 187. See Shapiro, Some Problems of Discovery in an Adversary System, 1979, 63 Minn.L.Rev. 1055, 1079.

11. Goldman v. Mooney, D.C.Pa.1959, 24 F.R.D. 279; Knowlton v. Atchison, T. & S. F. Ry. Co., D.C.Mo.1951, 11 F.R.D. 62; Finman, note 8 above, at 386–394; Developments in the Law— Discovery, 1961, 74 Harv.L.Rev. 940, 969.

12. U. S. v. Watchmakers of Switzerland Information Center, Inc., D.C. N.Y.1960, 25 F.R.D. 203; Johnstone v. Cronlund, D.C.Pa.1960, 25 F.R.D. 42; Waider v. Chicago, R. I. & P. R. Co., D.C.Iowa, 1950, 10 F.R.D. 376.

request for admission may not be used in any other proceeding.[13] This seems to overlook the possibility that the answer, though not usable in itself, may be a link in an incriminating chain. Thus the better, and now accepted, view is that a party in answering a request for admissions is entitled to the same constitutional protection as if he were called as a witness.[14]

As amended in 1970, Rule 36(a) speaks directly to several points on which there were differences of view under the original rule. Thus it allows a request to go to any matters "that relate to statements or opinions of fact or of the application of law to fact." This recognizes that the test should be whether a response will assist in narrowing the proof, rather than a nice exercise in probing the shadowy borderline of what is a "fact." [15] Though the earlier cases were surely not all one way, and many decisions held objectionable requests calling for admissions as to opinions or conclusions of law, admissions as to factual conclusions had frequently been required, as were requests calling for the admission of facts that would support legal conclusions.[16] Under the amended rule, it is still not proper to request an admission of a pure matter of law,[17] but admissions can be requested on matters of factual opinions and the application of law to fact.[18]

Again amended Rule 36(a) provides that a request is not objectionable solely on the ground that the party on whom it is served thinks that it presents a genuine issue for trial. If this is the situation he is to deny the matter or set forth reasons why he cannot admit or deny it. This accords with the view of some of the earlier cases[19] and the commentators[20] that Rule 36 is not confined to securing admissions as to peripheral facts and may properly be addressed to matters that are crucial to the outcome of the case or are "controversial" or "dis-

---

13. Woods v. Robb, C.A.5th, 1948, 171 F.2d 539; U. S. v. LaFontaine, D.C.R.I. 1952, 12 F.R.D. 518; U. S. v. Lewis, D.C.N.J.1950, 10 F.R.D. 56.

14. Gordon v. FDIC, C.A.1970, 427 F.2d 578, 581, 138 U.S.App.D.C. 308; Le Blanc v. Spector, D.C.Conn.1974, 378 F.Supp. 310; FDIC v. Logsdon, D.C. Ky.1955, 18 F.R.D. 57; U. S. v. Fishman, D.C.N.Y.1953, 15 F.R.D. 151; In re Stein, D.C.Ill.1942, 43 F.Supp. 845; see Village of Brookfield v. Pentis, C.C.A.7th, 1939, 101 F.2d 516, 522; Finman, note 8 above, at 383–386; Note, The Constitutional Limits of Discovery, 1960, 35 Ind.L.J. 337, 346.

15. Photon, Inc. v. Harris Intertype, Inc., D.C.Mass.1961, 28 F.R.D. 327, 328; Finman, note 8 above, at 409–418.

16. 8 Wright & Miller, Civil § 2255.

17. Williams v. Krieger, D.C.N.Y.1973, 61 F.R.D. 142.

18. Lumpkin v. Meskill, D.C.Conn.1974, 64 F.R.D. 673. See the earlier cases cited 8 Wright & Miller, Civil § 2255 n. 47.

19. U. S. ex rel. Seals v. Wiman, C.A.5th, 1962, 304 F.2d 53, 61–64; Ranger Ins. Co. v. Culberson, D.C.Ga. 1969, 49 F.R.D. 181, 182–183; Tillman v. Fickencher, D.C.Pa.1960, 27 F.R.D. 512, 513; and cases cited 8 Wright & Miller, Civil § 2256 n. 56.

Under the amended rule an admission may be requested on "ultimate facts." City of Rome v. U. S., D.C.D.C.1978, 450 F.Supp. 378, 383, affirmed 1980, 100 S.Ct. 1548, 446 U.S. 156, 64 L.Ed. 2d 119, rehearing denied 100 S.Ct. 3003, 447 U.S. 916, 64 L.Ed.2d 865.

20. Finman, note 1 above, at 394–402; Comment, The Dilemma of Rule 36, 1961, 56 Nw.U.L.Rev. 679, 684–685.

puted." There were cases to the contrary under the original rule,[21] but these seemed too confining since it cannot be told when a request is served, whether a particular fact is actually disputed, and a party should not be able to avoid an answer, simply because a matter is disputable, if he has no intention of disputing it.

Finally, amended Rule 36(a) states that a party may not give lack of information or knowledge as a reason for failure to admit or deny unless he has made reasonable inquiry and the information known or readily obtainable by him is insufficient for him to admit or deny.[22] Some cases had imposed no duty on a party in this circumstance, but the better view had been that a good faith effort to ascertain the truth of the matter was required of a litigant when the sources of corroboration were readily at hand.[23]

Requests under Rule 36 should be simple and direct, so that the answering party in a few words can admit, deny, or explain why he can do neither.[24] Similarly answers should fairly meet the substance of the requested admission,[25] and an evasive denial or an insufficient statement of reasons why the party cannot either admit or deny will have the effect of an admission.[26] An alternative remedy is for the court, on motion of the party making the request, to order further answers if the original answers are inadequate. This is now expressly authorized by amended Rule 36(a). It provides that if, on motion, the court finds that an answer does not comply with the requirements of the rule it may order either that the matter is admitted or that an amended answer be served.[27]

§ 90. Sanctions for Failure to Make Discovery [1]

Rule 37 deals with the consequences of failure to make discovery. It refers back to all the rules relating to depositions and discovery.

21. Pickens v. Equitable Life Assur. Socy., C.A.5th, 1969, 413 F.2d 1390, 1393–1394; Syracuse Broadcasting Corp. v. Newhouse, C.A.2d, 1959, 271 F.2d 910, 917; and cases cited 8 Wright & Miller, Civil § 2256 n. 55.

22. Lumpkin v. Meskill, D.C.Conn.1974, 64 F.R.D. 673; Alexander v. Rizzo, D.C.Pa.1971, 52 F.R.D. 235.
It has been persuasively argued, however, that regardless of what a party believes or should believe, he is not required to make an admission if there is reasonable ground for concluding, on the basis of all the admissible evidence known to him, that the proponent who is seeking the admission may not prevail at trial. Shapiro, note 10 above, at 1078–1092.

23. See cases cited 8 Wright & Miller, Civil § 2261 nn. 26, 27.

24. Havenfield Corp. v. H & R Block, Inc., D.C.Mo.1975, 67 F.R.D. 93; and cases cited 8 Wright & Miller, Civil § 2258 n. 85.

25. U. S. v. American Tel. & Tel. Co., D.C.D.C.1979, 83 F.R.D. 323, 333; 8 Wright & Miller, Civil § 2260.

26. U. S. ex rel. Seals v. Wiman, C.A.5th, 1962, 304 F.2d 53, 64; Southern Ry. Co. v. Crosby, C.A.4th, 1953, 201 F.2d 878, 880. But see Finman, note 8 above, at 404–409.

27. Havenfield Corp. v. H & R Block, Inc., D.C.Mo.1975, 67 F.R.D. 93; Alexander v. Rizzo, D.C.Pa.1971, 52 F.R.D. 235. See 8 Wright & Miller, Civil § 2263.

[§ 90]

1. 8 Wright & Miller, Civil §§ 2281–2293; Rodes, Ripple & Mooney, Sanctions Imposable for Violations of the

The general scheme of the rule is that sanctions can be imposed only for failure to comply with an order of the court. Thus where the discovery procedure itself requires a court order, as under Rule 35, or permits a court order, as when there has been a discovery conference under Rule 26(f) or a protective order has been denied under Rule 26(c), failure to obey the order can be punished immediately by any of the sanctions listed in Rule 37(b)(2). Where the discovery procedure is one set in motion by the parties themselves without court order, the party seeking discovery must first obtain an order under Rule 37(a) requiring the recalcitrant party or witness to make the discovery sought; it is only violation of this order that is punishable under Rule 37(b).[2] There are three exceptions to this general scheme: Rule 37(d) permits an immediate sanction against parties, and those who speak for corporate or other organization parties, for a willful failure to appear for a deposition or to answer interrogatories or to respond to a request for inspection under Rule 34; Rule 37(c) authorizes imposition of expenses for an unjustified refusal to admit under Rule 36; and Rule 37(g) authorizes imposition of expenses for failure to participate in good faith in the framing of a discovery plan when required to do so under Rule 26(f)(5).

Without adequate sanctions, the procedure for discovery would be ineffectual. Under Rule 37 a party who seeks to evade or thwart a full and candid discovery incurs the risk of serious consequences that may include imprisonment for contempt of court,[3] the entry of an order that designated facts be taken to be established,[4] the entry of an order refusing the disobedient party the right to support or oppose designated claims or defenses,[5] striking out pleadings or parts of

---

Federal Rules of Civil Procedure, Federal Judicial Center 1981; Renfrew, Discovery Sanctions: A Judicial Perspective, 1981, 1 Rev.Litigation 71; Werner, Survey of Discovery Sanctions, 1979 Ariz.St.L.J. 229; Epstein et al., An Up-Date on Rule 37 Sanctions, 1979, 84 F.R.D. 145; Comment, Preventing Abuse of Discovery in Federal Courts, 1981, 30 Cath.U.L.Rev. 273, 298–305.

2. Schleper v. Ford Motor Co., C.A.8th, 1978, 585 F.2d 1367, 1371; SEC v. Research Automation Corp., C.A.2d, 1975, 521 F.2d 585, 588–589; Cates v. LTV Aerospace Corp., C.A.5th, 1973, 480 F.2d 620, 624. Contra: Airtex Corp. v. Shelley Radiant Ceiling Co., C.A.7th, 1976, 536 F.2d 145, 155.

3. Rules 37(b)(1), 37(b)(2)(D); Hodgson v. Mahoney, C.A.1st, 1972, 460 F.2d 326, certiorari denied 93 S.Ct. 519, 409 U.S. 1039, 34 L.Ed.2d 488; and cases cited 8 Wright & Miller, Civil § 2289 n. 71.

Contempt requires a court order and is not available as a sanction under Rule 37(d). Schleper v. Ford Motor Co., C.A.8th, 1978, 585 F.2d 1367, 1371 n. 3. The elaborate argument to the contrary in the dissent in that case founders not only on the absence of a court order but also on the fact that Rule 37(d) incorporates by reference the sanctions available under paragraphs (A), (B), and (C) of Rule 37(b)(2) and does not incorporate paragraph (D), which provides for contempt.

4. Rule 37(b)(2)(A); Insurance Corp. of Ireland, Ltd. v. Compagnie des Bauxites de Guinee, 1982, 102 S.Ct. 2099, ___ U.S. ___, 72 L.Ed.2d 492; and cases cited 8 Wright & Miller, Civil § 2289 n. 63, § 2291 n. 31.

5. Rule 37(b)(2)(B); U. S. v. Sumitomo Marine & Fire Ins. Co., Ltd., C.A.9th, 1980, 617 F.2d 1365; and cases cited 8 Wright & Miller, Civil § 2289 nn. 64, 65, § 2291 nn. 32, 33. This sanction was applied on unusually colorful facts

pleadings,[6] rendering judgment by default,[7] dismissal of claims or defenses,[8] or assessment of costs and attorneys' fees.[9]

The rule is flexible. Under Rule 37(b) the court makes such orders "as are just." The addition of this language in amended Rule 37(d) only codifies a result that the courts had already reached and that the Constitution would in any event require.[10] Amended Rule 37(d) eliminated the former stated requirement [11] that a failure be willful. Even a negligent failure may be ground for imposition of sanctions though the willfulness of the failure is a role in the choice of sanctions. This is in accord with the construction that the Supreme Court had previously given Rule 37(b). It held that a mere failure, whether or not willful, was a "refusal," in the language of the rule as it then stood, but that if the failure to comply is because of inability to do so, rather than because of willfulness, bad faith, or any fault of the party, the action should not be dismissed and less drastic sanctions provided by the rule should be invoked.[12]

Typically the courts have given the delinquent party another opportunity to comply with the rules and the orders of the court.[13] This

in Rubenstein v. Kleven, D.C.Mass. 1957, 150 F.Supp. 47.

6. Rule 37(b)(2)(C); General Dynamics Corp. v. Selb Mfg. Co., C.A.8th, 1973, 481 F.2d 1204, certiorari denied 94 S.Ct. 926, 414 U.S. 1162, 39 L.Ed.2d 116; and cases cited 8 Wright & Miller, Civil § 2289 n. 66, § 2291 n. 34.

7. Rule 37(b)(2)(C); Haskins v. Lister, C.A.8th, 1980, 626 F.2d 42; Anderson v. Air West, Inc., C.A.9th, 1976, 542 F.2d 1090; and cases cited 8 Wright & Miller, Civil § 2289 n. 70, § 2291 n. 37.

8. Rule 37(b)(2)(C); National Hockey League v. Metropolitan Hockey Club, Inc., 1976, 96 S.Ct. 2778, 427 U.S. 639, 49 L.Ed.2d 747; Atlantic Cape Fisheries v. Hartford Fire Ins. Co., C.A.1st, 1975, 509 F.2d 577; and cases cited 8 Wright & Miller, Civil § 2289 nn. 68, 69, § 2291 n. 36.

9. Rule 37(a)(4). See also Rules 37(b), (c), and (d); David v. Hooker, Ltd., C.A. 9th, 1977, 560 F.2d 412; Powerlock Systems, Inc. v. Duo-Lok, Inc., D.C. Wis.1972, 56 F.R.D. 50; and cases cited 8 Wright & Miller, Civil § 2289 n. 62, § 2291 n. 38. See also id. at § 2288.

10. The requirement that any sanction must be just "represents the general due process restrictions on the court's discretion." Insurance Corp. of Ireland, Ltd. v. Compagnie des Bauxites de Guinee, 1982, 102 S.Ct. 2099, 2107, ___ U.S. ___, ___, 72 L.Ed.2d 492.

11. E.g., Patterson v. C. I. T. Corp., C.A.10th, 1965, 352 F.2d 333, 336; U.

S. v. 3963 Bottles, C.A.7th, 1959, 265 F.2d 332, 337, certiorari denied 79 S.Ct. 1448, 360 U.S. 931, 3 L.Ed.2d 1544. But cf. Milewski v. Schneider Transp. Co., C.A.6th, 1956, 238 F.2d 397.

12. Societe Internationale Pour Participations Industrielles et Commerciales, S. A. v. Brownell, 1958, 78 S.Ct. 1087, 357 U.S. 197, 2 L.Ed.2d 1255, noted 1958, 46 Calif.L.Rev. 836, 107 U.Pa.L. Rev. 103; 1959 Duke L.J. 278. This is reaffirmed in National Hockey League v. Metropolitan Hockey Club, Inc., 1976, 96 S.Ct. 2778, 2779, 427 U.S. 639, 640, 49 L.Ed.2d 747, rehearing denied 97 S.Ct. 197, 429 U.S. 874, 50 L.Ed.2d 158.

Simple negligence does not warrant dismissal. Marshall v. Segona, C.A.5th, 1980, 621 F.2d 763. Gross professional negligence may. Cine Forty-Second St. Theatre Corp. v. Allied Artists Picture Corp., C.A.2d, 1979, 602 F.2d 1062. See Note, Defining a Feasible Culpability Threshold for the Imposition of Severe Discovery Sanctions, 1980, 65 Minn.L.Rev. 137.

13. E.g., Bates v. Firestone Tire & Rubber Co., D.C.S.C.1979, 83 F.R.D. 535; Culp v. Devlin, D.C.Pa.1978, 78 F.R.D. 136; and cases cited 8 Wright & Miller, Civil § 2284 nn. 72, 73.

"The typical pattern of sanctioning that emerges from the reported cases is one in which the delay, obfuscation, contumacy, and lame excuses on the part of litigants and their attorneys are toler-

may be less common as a result of the Supreme Court's decision in 1976 in National Hockey League v. Metropolitan Hockey Club, Inc.[14] The important holding of the case is that in reviewing sanctions appellate courts are not to ask whether the sanction is one that they as an original matter would have imposed but only whether the district court abused its discretion in imposing the sanction.[15] But in an important dictum the Court spoke to the purposes of sanctions, saying that "the most severe in the spectrum of sanctions provided by statute or rule must be available to the district court in appropriate cases, not merely to penalize those whose conduct may be deemed to warrant such a sanction, but to deter those who might be tempted to such conduct in the absence of such a deterrent. If the decision of the Court of Appeals remained undisturbed in this case, it might well be that *these* respondents would faithfully comply with all future discovery orders entered by the District Court in this case. But other parties to other lawsuits would feel freer than we think Rule 37 contemplates they should feel to flout other discovery orders of other district courts."[16] There is evidence, though not yet conclusive, that the emphasis in National Hockey on the deterrent effect of sanctions on other litigants has caused courts to impose sanctions more readily, and to impose more severe sanctions than in the past.[17] There is also evidence, however, that some courts of appeals have not fully heeded the holding of National Hockey and continue to exercise considerable freedom in setting aside or altering sanctions imposed by the district courts.[18]

In applying the sanctions permitted by Rule 37, it must be remembered that there are constitutional limitations upon the power of courts, even in aid of their own valid processes, to dismiss an action without affording a party the opportunity for a hearing on the merits of his cause.[19] In the early case of Hovey v. Elliott[20] it was

---

ated without any measured remedial action until the court is provoked beyond endurance. At that point the court punishes one side or the other with a swift and final termination of the lawsuit by dismissal or default. This 'all or nothing' approach to sanctions results in considerable laxity in the day-to-day application of the rules. Attorneys are well aware that sanctions will be imposed only in the most flagrant situations." Rodes, Ripple & Mooney, note 1 above, at 85.

14. 1976, 96 S.Ct. 2778, 427 U.S. 639, 49 L.Ed.2d 747.

15. 96 S.Ct. at 2780, 427 U.S. at 642. See also Insurance Corp. of Ireland, Ltd. v. Compagnie des Bauxites de Guinee, 1982, 102 S.Ct. 2099, 2107, ___ U.S. ___, ___, 72 L.Ed.2d 492.

16. 96 S.Ct. at 2781, 427 U.S. at 643.

17. Werner, note 1 above, at 316. See Rodes, Ripple & Mooney, note 1 above, at 31.

See also Cine Forty-Second St. Theatre Corp. v. Allied Artists Pictures Corp., C.A.2d, 1979, 602 F.2d 1062, 1066, noted 1980, 53 Temp.L.Q. 140; G-K Properties v. Redevelopment Agency of City of San Jose, C.A.9th, 1978, 577 F.2d 645, 647; and cases cited 8 Wright & Miller, Civil § 2284 n. 67.4; Note, The Emerging Deterrence Orientation in the Imposition of Discovery Sanctions, 1978, 91 Harv.L.Rev. 1033.

18. See Epstein et al., note 1 above, at 169–170.

19. 8 Wright & Miller, Civil § 2283; Rodes, Ripple & Mooney, note 1 above, at 80–84; Note, cited note 17 above, at 1041–1043, 1052–1055; Note, Sanctions for Enforcement of Discovery—Consti-

20. See note 20 on page 599.

held that due process had been denied a defendant where, because of his refusal to obey a court order pertinent to the suit, his answer was stricken and a decree pro confesso entered against him. This holding was substantially modified 12 years later in Hammond Packing Co. v. Arkansas.[21] There it was held not to be a denial of due process to strike defendant's answer, and render a default judgment against him, where he refused to produce documents in accordance with a pretrial order. In Hammond the Court explained the Hovey case on the basis that there defendant had been denied his right to defend "as a mere punishment," while in Hammond, it reasoned, the state was merely relying on a reasonable presumption that defendant's failure to produce the documents was an admission that there was no merit to his defense. The modern Court reads the two cases as showing that it would at least raise "substantial constitutional questions" were a pleading to be stricken for noncompliance with a discovery order where the party had made a good faith effort to comply.[22] Thus an adequate excuse for noncompliance, barring dismissal, was found where, under foreign law, controlling on the party in the case before the Court, it would be committing a crime if it made the disclosure sought. More recently the Court has said that due process is violated only if the behavior of the defendant will not support the Hammond presumption, and that a proper application of Rule 37(b)(2) will, as a matter of law, support such a presumption.[23] Even so it emphasized that the Hammond rule requires; that "the sanction must be specifically related to the particular 'claim,' which was at issue in the order to provide discovery." [24] Although Rule 37 sweeps broadly, some courts had looked to other sources, such as Rule 41, or local rules, or inherent power, to justify imposition of sanctions for failure to disclose. Usually this resort to other authority is unnecessary, and in 1958 the Court held that Rule 37 is the exclusive authority for sanctions for the discovery procedures.[25] There are other rules with their own provisions for sanctions [26] and there are some violations of the discovery rules that are not within the compass of Rule 37. For these latter matters courts continue to exercise inherent power.[27]

tutionality of Rule 37, 1962, 37 Wash. L.Rev. 175; Note, The Constitutional Limits of Discovery, 1960, 35 Ind.L.J. 337, 348–350.

20. 1897, 17 S.Ct. 841, 167 U.S. 409, 42 L.Ed. 215.

21. 1909, 29 S.Ct. 370, 212 U.S. 322, 53 L.Ed. 530.

22. Societe Internationale Pour Participations Industrielles et Commerciales, S. A. v. Brownell, 1958, 78 S.Ct. 1087, 1095, 357 U.S. 197, 210, 2 L.Ed.2d 1255.

23. Insurance Corp. of Ireland, Ltd. v. Compagnie des Bauxites de Guinee, 1982, 102 S.Ct. 2099, 2106, ___ U.S. ___, ___, 72 L.Ed.2d 492.

24. 102 S.Ct. at 2107, ___ U.S. at ___.

25. Societe Internationale Pour Participations Industrielles et Commerciales, S. A. v. Brownell, 1958, 78 S.Ct. 1087, 1093, 357 U.S. 197, 207, 2 L.Ed.2d 1255.

26. Rule 30(g); 8 Wright & Miller, Civil § 2120. Rule 45(f); 9 Wright & Miller, Civil § 2462.

See also the proposed amendments, circulated in 1981, to Rules 7(b), 11, 16(f), and 26(g). 90 F.R.D. 451, 458–480.

27. Courts have considered that they have inherent power to devise a sanction against a party who has ignored the duty under Rule 26(e) to supplement answers. See 8 Wright & Miller, Civil § 2050.

When the discovery rules were amended in 1970, it was thought that one reason courts at that time were reluctant to impose sanctions was that the sanctions then described in the rule were so drastic. Amended Rule 37 sought to alter this by making more generally available the sanction of requiring a party or his attorney to pay to his opponent the reasonable expenses incurred by the failure to make discovery.[28] This broadened a provision long in the rules with regard to an unjustified refusal to answer questions at a deposition or an unjustified attempt to obtain an order to compel answers to questions. The amended rule made this generally available for many discovery devices and shifted the emphasis by saying that the court "shall" order payment of expenses unless it finds that the failure to make discovery or the attempt to secure an order compelling discovery was substantially justified or that other circumstances make an award of expenses unjust. Although an award of expenses has been made in many cases,[29] there are those who think that the award of expenses should be made almost automatic.[30]

A motion for imposition of sanctions should not provide an occasion to test the propriety of the discovery sought. Amended Rule 37(d) is explicit that sanctions under that subsection cannot be avoided on the ground that the discovery sought was objectionable unless the party failing to act had applied for a protective order as provided by Rule 26(c). This had already been the usual view of the courts prior to the amendment.[31] This result seems implicit also in Rule 37(b), since the sanctions there provided for come into play only when a party has failed to comply with a court order to allow discovery. Any question of the propriety of the discovery will have been re-

See also U. S. v. American Tel. & Tel. Co., D.C.D.C.1980, 86 F.R.D. 603, 656; U. S. v. Moss-American, Inc., D.C.Wis. 1978, 78 F.R.D. 214.

In narrowly defined circumstances federal courts have inherent power to assess attorney's fees against counsel. Roadway Exp., Inc. v. Piper, 1980, 100 S.Ct. 2455, 2463–2464, 447 U.S. 752, 764–767, 65 L.Ed.2d 488.

28. Rules 37(a)(4), 37(b), 37(d). A very similar expense sanction was made available by Rule 37(g), added in 1980, for failure to participate in good faith in the framing of a discovery plan when required by Rule 26(f)(5). See Watkins, 1980 Amendments to the Federal Rules of Civil Procedure, 1980, 32 Baylor L.Rev. 533, 550–552.

29. E.g., Weigel v. Shapiro, C.A.7th, 1979, 608 F.2d 268; EEOC v. Carter Carburetor, Div. of ACF Indus., Inc., D.C.Mo.1977, 76 F.R.D. 143, mandamus issued C.A.8th, 577 F.2d 43, certio-

rari denied 99 S.Ct. 865, 439 U.S. 1081, 59 L.Ed.2d 52; and cases cited 8 Wright & Miller, Civil § 2288 n. 40.

There have also been a few cases in which the courts have exercised their power to make an award personally against the delinquent attorney. U. S. v. Sumitomo Marine & Fire Ins. Co., Ltd., C.A.9th, 1980, 617 F.2d 1365; Ogletree v. Keebler Co., D.C.Ga.1978, 78 F.R.D. 661; and cases cited 8 Wright & Miller, Civil § 2288 n. 43. See Comment, Sanctions Imposed by Courts on Attorneys Who Abuse the Judicial Process, 1977, 44 U.Chi.L.Rev. 619.

30. Schroeder & Frank, Discovery Reform: Long Road to Nowheresville, 1982, 68 A.B.A.J. 572, 574.

31. Collins v. Wayland, C.C.A.9th, 1944, 139 F.2d 677, certiorari denied 64 S.Ct. 1151, 322 U.S. 744, 88 L.Ed. 1576; and cases cited 8 Wright & Miller, Civil § 2291 nn. 22, 23.

solved when the court entered its order.[32]   Though it is less clear, this would seem the proper result also under amended Rule 37(c), dealing with requests for admissions.   Since Rule 36 was amended in 1970 to provide a mechanism for judicial determination of the sufficiency of answers or objections to requests, a party should be required to use that procedure rather than contending after trial that his objection was a good one.[33]

F. TRIALS

Analysis

Sec.
91. Pretrial Conference.
92. The Right to Jury Trial.
93. Evidence.
94. Submission to the Jury.
95. Attacks on a Verdict.
96. Trial to the Court.
97. Control by the Judge.

§ 91. Pretrial Conference [1]

Rule 16, authorizing the pretrial conference, has been easily the most popular of the rules.   Similar provisions have been adopted in almost all of the states.   Rule 16 provides a means by which the court and counsel confer about a case in advance, and endeavor to eliminate unnecessary issues, analyze and settle the pleadings by amendments if desirable or necessary, eliminate matters of proof by admissions or stipulations, limit the number of expert witnesses, ascertain whether issues in jury cases may be referred to a master for findings, and discuss other matters that may expedite the disposition of the action.[2]

The pretrial conference is an important adjunct of the other procedural devices provided by the rules.   The simplified pleading permitted by Rule 8 is possible because the issues can be defined at the pretrial conference.   The unlimited joinder of claims and parties that other rules allow is made workable by the availability of a pretrial

---

32. Interstate Cigar Co. v. Consolidated Cigar Co., C.A.2d, 1963, 317 F.2d 744, 746; Kozlowski v. Sears, Roebuck & Co., D.C.Mass.1976, 71 F.R.D. 594, 597, motion denied 73 F.R.D. 73. Independent Productions Corp. v. Loew's, Inc., D.C.N.Y.1962, 30 F.R.D. 377, 380. But see Roberson v. Christoferson, D.C. N.D.1975, 65 F.R.D. 615, 620.

33. See 8 Wright & Miller, Civil § 2290, p. 804.

[§ 91]

1. 6   Wright   &   Miller,   Civil §§ 1521–1530; Rosenberg, The Pretrial Conference and Effective Justice, 1964; Pollack, Pretrial Procedures More Effectively Handled, 1974, 65 F.R.D. 475; Walker & Thibaut, An Experimental Examination of Pretrial Conference Techniques, 1971, 55 Minn.L.Rev. 1113; Note, Pretrial Conference: A Critical Examination of Local Rules Adopted in Federal District Courts, 1978, 64 Va.L. Rev. 467.

2.   6 Wright & Miller, Civil § 1522.

conference at which the court can decide on the form and order of the trial.

Though the pretrial conference has been promoted on the ground that it will improve the quality of the trial, the main reason for its wide popularity has been a belief that it will help reduce court congestion by increasing the number of cases that are settled and by shortening the trial in those cases that are tried. In an eloquent tribute to the device of the pretrial conference, the Second Circuit, speaking through Judge Clark, said that it leads to "better justice more shortly and efficiently obtained." [3] This would be marvelous if true—but there is convincing evidence suggesting that it is not wholly true. An exhaustive empirical study by Professor Maurice Rosenberg shows that pretrial does indeed improve the quality of those cases that are tried, but that to require a pretrial conference in every case leads to a net loss in judicial time because there is no saving in the trial time demands a case makes to compensate for the time required to conduct conferences.[4] Thus pretrial should be justified on the ground that it leads to better justice rather than because justice will be more shortly and efficiently obtained.

Rule 16 does not make a pretrial compulsory in every case in federal court.[5] In some districts only selected cases are pretried, generally on the application of counsel, though many districts do provide by local rule for pretrial as a matter of routine in every case. It is left to the court to determine at what time to have the pretrial conference. The most usual practice is to hold it shortly before trial, when both parties will be fully informed as to the case and will have made full use of discovery techniques. In a complicated case, however, it may be desirable to have the conference, or the first conference, at an early day, so that discovery and other pretrial proceedings may be shaped under the guidance of the court. There is no limit on the number of conferences that may be ordered in a particular case. In one "big" case, the court noted that it had held 23 pretrial conferences.[6]

The pretrial conference should be attended by at least one attorney on each side who will participate in the trial.[7] While it is not compulsory upon the court to call a pretrial conference, it is compulsory upon counsel to attend when the court does call one. A divided Supreme Court has held that where the excuse of counsel for failure to attend a pretrial conference was inadequate, and the history of the litigation suggested that plaintiff had been deliberately proceeding in

3. Padovani v. Bruchhausen, C.A.2d, 1961, 293 F.2d 546, 550.

4. Rosenberg, note 1 above, at 28–29.

5. McCargo v. Hedrick, C.A.4th, 1976, 545 F.2d 393.

6. See Life Music Inc. v. Broadcast Music Inc., D.C.N.Y.1962, 31 F.R.D. 3, 4.

See also Manual for Complex Litigation, 5th ed. 1982, § 0.40.

7. Burton v. Weyerhaeuser Timber Co., D.C.Or.1941, 1 F.R.D. 571; Stanley v. City of Hartford, 1954, 103 A.2d 147, 140 Conn. 643; James & Hazard, Civil Procedure, 2d ed. 1977, p. 216.

a dilatory fashion, the court has inherent power to dismiss because of the failure to attend.[8]

At the pretrial conference counsel must make full and fair disclosure of their views as to what the real issues of the trial will be.[9] They may be required at that time to disclose the names of the witnesses they plan to call at the trial.[10] In many districts, local rules require parties to exchange pretrial memoranda prior to the conference, which commonly are expected to contain a very detailed statement of the case from each party's point of view.[11] The courts have put teeth into such local rules by holding the parties quite closely to what they have set forth in such a memorandum.[12] But these rules must be administered with considerable circumspection. "Not without careful planning were the federal rules designed to eliminate the evils of special pleading, and they should not be brought back under the guise of pre-trial." [13]

How pretrial is carried on varies from court to court, indeed from judge to judge. Some are extremely formal, with elaborate hearings in open court attended by litigants and counsel resulting in a memorial order wrapping up the whole proceeding. Some are carried on in chambers, with no record kept save the final pretrial order, which may be simple or may be complex, while others are in chambers with a court reporter present. There is also much difference of view on whether the judge should take part directly in seeking to achieve a settlement of the case at the pretrial conference.[14] The whole process, however carried on, is aimed at trying to reduce the forthcom-

---

8. Link v. Wabash R. Co., 1962, 82 S.Ct. 1386, 370 U.S. 626, 8 L.Ed.2d 734.

See also Beshear v. Weinzapfel, C.A.7th, 1973, 474 F.2d 127; Hyler v. Reynolds Metal Co., C.A.5th, 1970, 434 F.2d 1064, certiorari denied 91 S.Ct. 2219, 403 U.S. 912, 29 L.Ed.2d 689.

See Vestal, The Pretrial Conference and the Recalcitrant Attorney: A Study in Judicial Power, 1963, 48 Iowa L.Rev. 761; Note, Federal Pre-Trial Practice: A Study of Modification and Sanctions, 1963, 51 Geo.L.J. 309; Note, Power of Federal Courts to Discipline Attorneys for Delay in Pre-Trial Procedure, 1963, 38 Notre Dame Law. 158; Note, 1969, 47 Texas L.Rev. 1198.

9. Payne v. S. S. Nabob, C.A.3d, 1962, 302 F.2d 803; Marble v. Batten & Co., D.C.D.C.1964, 36 F.R.D. 693.

10. Morgan v. Commercial Union Assur. Companies, C.A.5th, 1979, 606 F.2d 554; Wirtz v. Hooper-Holmes Bureau, Inc., C.A.5th, 1964, 327 F.2d 939; Globe Cereal Mills v. Scrivener, C.A.10th, 1956, 240 F.2d 330; and cases cited 6 Wright & Miller, Civil § 1525 n. 82.

11. 6 Wright & Miller, Civil § 1524, pp. 581–582.

12. E.g., Payne v. S. S. Nabob, C.A.3d, 1962, 302 F.2d 803, noted 1962, 36 Temp.L.Q. 101; Johnson v. Geffen, C.A.1960, 294 F.2d 197, 111 U.S.App. D.C. 1; Frankel v. Todd, D.C.Pa.1966, 260 F.Supp. 772.

13. Padovani v. Bruchhausen, C.A.2d, 1961, 293 F.2d 546, 549. See also McCargo v. Hedrick, C.A.4th, 1976, 545 F.2d 393, 401–402; James & Hazard, note 7 above, at 216–217; Clark, To an Understanding Use of Pre-Trial, 1961, 29 F.R.D. 454.

14. Brennan, Introduction to the Problem of the Protracted Case, 1958, 23 F.R.D. 276, 278–279; Clark, Objectives of Pre-Trial Procedure, 1956, 17 Ohio St.L.J. 163, 167. The view that the court should take an active role in settlement negotiations is stated by Judge J. Skelly Wright in The Pre-Trial, Conference, 1960, 28 F.R.D. 141, 145–147.

ing trial to its simplest terms consistent with the full preservation of the basic positions and rights of the litigants.[15]

Stipulations and statements of counsel at a pretrial conference are binding on the parties,[16] but if the court should relieve the party of the statement, as Rule 16 permits, the statement is out of the case and is neither binding nor admissible as evidence of the facts stated.[17]

The pretrial conference and the motion for summary judgment complement one another, and each serves its own special purpose.[18] It has been said: "A pre-trial conference is more than a mere conference at which the court seeks to eliminate groundless allegations or denials and the court has the power to compel the parties to agree to all facts concerning which there can be no real issue."[19] It has also been held, in an extreme case, that the court could itself define what the issues were between the parties where the parties, despite extensive effort, had never been able to agree on the issues.[20] In considering such cases, however, the purpose of the rule must be kept in mind. The draftsman of the federal rules, speaking for the Second Circuit, has said: "That rule calls for a *conference* of counsel with the court to *prepare* for, not to avert, trial, leading to an order which shall recite the 'agreements made by the parties as to any of the matters considered.' It is subordinate and conciliatory, rather than compulsive, in character. Nothing in the rule affords basis for clubbing the parties into admissions they do not willingly make; but it is the way of advancing the trial ultimately to be had by setting forth the points on which the parties are agreed after a conference directed by a trained judge."[21]

After the pretrial conference, the court makes an order reciting the action taken at the conference. This order, unless modified, controls the subsequent course of the case.[22] The order may be modified

---

15. Laird v. Air Carrier Engine Serv., Inc., C.A.5th, 1959, 263 F.2d 948, 954.

16. Air-Exec, Inc. v. Two Jacks, Inc., C.A.10th, 1978, 584 F.2d 942; Funding Systems Leasing Corp. v. Pugh, C.A. 5th, 1976, 530 F.2d 91; and cases cited 6 Wright & Miller, Civil § 1527 nn. 24–26.

17. Laird v. Air Carrier Engine Serv., Inc., C.A.5th, 1959, 253 F.2d 948; see Smith Contracting Corp. v. Trojan Constr. Co., C.A.10th, 1951, 192 F.2d 234, 236.

18. Wirtz v. Young Elec. Sign Co., C.A. 10th, 1963, 315 F.2d 326; Irving Trust Co. v. U. S., C.A.2d, 1955, 221 F.2d 303, certiorari denied 76 S.Ct. 59, 350 U.S. 828, 100 L.Ed. 740; 6 Wright & Miller, Civil § 1529, pp. 621–624.

19. Holcomb v. Aetna Life Ins. Co., C.A. 10th, 1958, 255 F.2d 577, 580, certiorari

denied 79 S.Ct. 118, 358 U.S. 879, 3 L.Ed.2d 110.

20. Life Music Inc. v. Edelstein, C.A.2d, 1962, 309 F.2d 242, noted 1962, 72 Yale L.J. 383.

21. Padovani v. Bruchhausen, C.A.2d, 1961, 293 F.2d 546, 548, noted 1961, 60 Mich.L.Rev. 223, 1962, 110 U.Pa.L.Rev. 446, 35 Temp.L.Q. 342.

See also Identiseal Corp. of Wisconsin v. Positive Identification Systems, Inc., C.A.7th, 1977, 560 F.2d 298, 302; McCargo v. Hedrick, C.A.4th, 1976, 545 F.2d 393, 401–402.

The court cannot require a party to agree to a stipulation of facts. J. F. Edwards Constr. Co. v. Anderson Safeway Guard Rail Corp., C.A.7th, 1976, 542 F.2d 1318.

22. Hodgson v. Humphries, C.A.10th, 1972, 454 F.2d 1279; Federal Deposit

by the court to prevent manifest injustice,[23] and it will be deemed modified to conform to evidence admitted without objection.[24] It is discretionary with the court whether to permit modification of the order. Since the pretrial conference is held shortly before trial and at a time when each side should usually know what it intends to prove, the court may, if it thinks it best, refuse to permit modification.[25] But as with all rules problems, the dominant purpose of the courts must be to do justice rather than to vindicate procedural rules, and an unswerving insistence upon every provision of a pretrial order may, under certain circumstances, cause injustice.[26]

In 1981 the Advisory Committee on Civil Rules circulated for consideration by the profession a proposed revision of Rule 16 that would greatly expand the rule and also change its thrust. The proposed amendment would alter the thrust of the rule to encourage pretrial management and scheduling through a series of pretrial conferences. The proposed rule would also authorize sanctions against an attorney who is substantially unprepared to participate in a conference or fails to participate in good faith.[27]

§ 92. The Right to Jury Trial [1]

The Seventh Amendment to the Constitution provides: "In suits at common law, where the value in controversy shall exceed twenty

Ins. Corp. v. Glickman, C.A.9th, 1971, 450 F.2d 416; and cases cited 6 Wright & Miller, Civil § 1527 nn. 36–42.

23.   Stahlin v. Hilton Hotels Corp., C.A. 7th, 1973, 484 F.2d 580; Jeffries v. U. S., C.A.9th, 1973, 477 F.2d 52; Clark v. Pennsylvania R. Co., C.A.2d, 1964, 328 F.2d 591, 593–595, certiorari denied 84 S.Ct. 1943, 377 U.S. 1006, 12 L.Ed.2d 1054; 6 Wright & Miller, Civil § 1527, pp. 608–613.

In an extreme case it is an abuse of discretion not to relieve a party from pretrial stipulations. U. S. v. Texas, C.A. 5th, 1982, 680 F.2d 356, 370.

24.   Perfection-Cobey Co., Div. of Harsco Corp. v. City Tank Corp., C.A.4th, 1979, 597 F.2d 419; Wallin v. Fuller, C.A.5th, 1973, 476 F.2d 1204; and cases cited 6 Wright & Miller, Civil § 1257 nn. 54–57.

25.   Payne v. S. S. Nabob, C.A.3d, 1962, 302 F.2d 803, noted 1962, 36 Temp.L.Q. 101; Hoeppner Constr. Co. v. U. S. for Use of Mangum, C.A.10th, 1960, 287 F.2d 108; Note, Variance from the Pre-Trial Order, 1951, 60 Yale L.J. 175.

26.   Scott v. Spanjer Bros., Inc., C.A.2d, 1962, 298 F.2d 928, 931.

27.   Preliminary Draft of Proposed Amendments to the Federal Rules of Civil Procedure, June 1981, 90 F.R.D. 451, 466–478. See Sherman & Kinnard, Federal Court Discovery in the 80s—Making the Rules Work, 1981, 1 Rev.Litigation 9, 42–46. The proposal is sharply criticized in Schroeder & Frank, Discovery Reform: Long Road to Nowheresville, 1982, 68 A.B.A.J. 572.

[§ 92]

1.   9 Wright & Miller, Civil §§ 2301–2307; James, Right to a Jury Trial in Civil Actions, 1963, 72 Yale L.J. 655; Rothstein, Beacon Theatres and the Constitutional Right to Jury Trial, 1965, 51 A.B.A.J. 1145; McCoid, Procedural Reform and the Right to Jury Trial: A Study of Beacon Theatres, Inc. v. Westover, 1967, 116 U.Pa.L. Rev. 1; Wolfram, The Constitutional History of the Seventh Amendment, 1973, 57 Minn.L.Rev. 639; Redish, Seventh Amendment Right to Jury Trial: A Study in the Irrationality of Rational Decision Making, 1975, 70 Nw.U.L. Rev. 486; Rendleman, Chapters of the Civil Jury, 1977, 65 Ky.L.J. 769; Comment, From Beacon Theatres to Dairy Queen to Ross: The Seventh Amendment, The Federal Rules, and a Receding Law-Equity Dichotomy, 1971, 48

dollars, the right of trial by jury shall be preserved, and no fact tried by a jury shall be otherwise re-examined in any Court of the United States, than according to the rules of the common law." Rule 38(a) states that the right of trial by jury as declared by the Seventh Amendment, or as given by a federal statute, "shall be preserved to the parties inviolate."

The right of trial by jury is of ancient origin.[2] To Blackstone it was "the glory of the English law" and "the most transcendent privilege which any subject can enjoy."[3] In Justice Story's view "the Constitution would have been justly obnoxious to the most conclusive objection if it had not recognized and confirmed it in the most solemn terms"[4] The Supreme Court itself has voiced similar eulogies to the jury.[5]

Today these views are not universally accepted. Assertions are made that trial by jury is "expensive and dilatory—perhaps anachronistic."[6] In federal courts, at least, the Seventh Amendment writes into the basic charter the belief that trial by jury is the normal and preferable mode of disposing of issues of fact in civil cases involving legal relief as well as in criminal cases. Despite the critics, there is still a general professional view that maintenance of the jury as a factfinding body is of such importance and occupies so firm a place in our history and jurisprudence that any seeming curtailment of the right to jury trial should be scrutinized with the utmost care.[7] The Supreme Court has been zealous to safeguard, perhaps even to enlarge, the function of the jury.

Though there had been some divergence of opinion on this point,[8] it is now wholly clear that the right of jury trial in federal court is governed entirely by federal law, and that state law may be disregarded. Three different situations may exist. State law may deny a jury trial in a case where the Seventh Amendment requires a jury

J.Urban Law 459. There is a large literature on this subject, but, with the exception of the authorities just cited, and of those cited note 45 below, it antedates recent Supreme Court decisions that have made all that was written before obsolete and probably misleading.

2. Henderson, The Background of the Seventh Amendment, 1966, 80 Harv.L. Rev. 289.

3. 3 Bl.Comm.*379.

4. 2 Story, Commentaries on the Constitution, 1833, § 1779.

5. E.g., Sioux City & P. Ry. Co. v. Stout, 1874, 17 Wall. 657, 664, 21 L.Ed.2d 745.

6. James, Trial by Jury and the New Federal Rules of Procedure, 1936, 45 Yale L.J. 1022, 1026. See also, e.g.,

Frank, Courts on Trial, 1949; Devitt, Should Jury Trial Be Required in Civil Cases? A Challenge to the Seventh Amendment, 1982, 47 J.Air L. & Comm. 495; Redish, note 1 above, at 502–508; Shapiro & Coquillette, The Fetish of Jury Trial in Civil Cases: A Comment on Rachal v. Hill, 1971, 85 Harv.L.Rev. 442; Peck, Do Juries Delay Justice?, 1956, 18 F.R.D. 455.

7. Dimick v. Schiedt, 1934, 55 S.Ct. 296, 300, 293 U.S. 474, 485, 79 L.Ed. 603.

See Kalven, The Dignity of the Civil Jury, 1964, 50 Va.L.Rev. 1055; Summers, Some Merits of Civil Jury Trials, 1964, 39 Tul.L.Rev. 3; DeParcq, Thoughts on the Civil Jury, 1965, 3 Tulsa L.J. 1.

8. See authorities cited 9 Wright & Miller, Civil § 2303 nn. 64–66.

trial. In this situation the federal court must allow a jury trial.[9] The language of the Rules of Decision Act [10] cannot prevail over the clear command of the Seventh Amendment. Even if Justice Brandeis's controversial view that the Erie holding was constitutionally required be accepted,[11] it cannot alter the result in this situation, for Congress not only has explicit constitutional authority to provide a jury trial in common law cases but indeed is prohibited from denying such a trial.

The second situation is that in which the state law denies jury trial but federal courts customarily permit such trial though not required to do so by the Seventh Amendment. The Court decided Byrd v. Blue Ridge Rural Electric Cooperative [12] as if it were such a case, expressly refusing to determine whether the right of jury trial there involved was constitutionally protected,[13] and held that, at least where the state rule is not bound up with rights and obligations, the federal policy favoring jury decisions of disputed fact questions should prevail over the contrary state rule.

Finally there is the situation in which state law would provide trial by jury as to an issue that, in the federal system, would normally be decided by the judge. This was essentially the situation involved in Herron v. Southern Pacific Co.,[14] where a unanimous Court held that a federal court might direct a verdict on the ground of contributory negligence despite a state constitutional provision that that defense "shall, in all cases whatsoever, be a question of fact and shall, at all times, be left to the jury." There was room to doubt whether the Herron rule had survived the subsequent announcement of the Erie doctrine, but the holding and language of Herron were heavily relied on in the post-Erie decision of Byrd v. Blue Ridge, and it now seems established that in this third situation trial should be to the judge in a federal court regardless of the contrary state rule.

The same result should be reached, and state law disregarded, in determining the sufficiency of the evidence to go to the jury. The state may have a more liberal standard than the federal courts in permitting an issue to go to the jury. It may be that a certain issue in state practice is always for the jury, as with the Arizona constitutional provision involved in the Herron case, or the state rule may be, as in Alabama, that a scintilla of evidence is enough to create a jury issue. The Herron case would seem to have settled that the state rule is not controlling in such circumstances. Conversely the state may demand a higher quantum of proof than would the federal court,

9. Simler v. Conner, 1963, 83 S.Ct. 609, 610–611, 372 U.S. 221, 222, 9 L.Ed.2d 691; Parsons v. Bedford, Breedlove & Robeson, 1830, 3 Pet. 433, 7 L.Ed. 732; U. S. v. Williams, C.A.5th, 1971, 441 F.2d 637, 643–644; Green, Protection of Jury Trial in Diversity Cases against State Invasions, 1957, 35 Texas L.Rev. 768.

10. 28 U.S.C.A. § 1652.

11. See § 56 above.

12. 1958, 78 S.Ct. 893, 356 U.S. 525, 2 L.Ed.2d 953. See § 55 above.

13. 78 S.Ct. at 901 n. 10, 356 U.S. at 537 n. 10.

14. 1931, 51 S.Ct. 383, 283 U.S. 91, 75 L.Ed. 857.

and may authorize a directed verdict where a federal court would normally submit the matter to a jury. The Seventh Amendment itself would seem to bar resort to state law here, since to follow the state rule would deprive the party of the verdict of a jury under circumstances where, at common law, he would have been entitled to go to the jury.

Doubt was cast upon this analysis by the decision of the Supreme Court in Stoner v. New York Life Ins. Co.[15] A federal trial judge, sitting without a jury, held that a person was totally disabled within the meaning of an insurance policy. The circuit court of appeals reversed, finding that the evidence established that the person was not totally disabled. In two actions still pending, the state intermediate appellate court had held, with regard to the same evidence and the same parties, that there was sufficient evidence to create a jury issue as to total disability. In this situation the Supreme Court held that the Erie doctrine required the federal courts to accept the state holdings that the evidence would support a finding of total disability.

In Byrd v. Blue Ridge, in 1958, the Supreme Court referred to its decision in Stoner as having "held that the federal court should follow the state rule defining the evidence sufficient to raise a jury question whether the state-created right was established."[16] Some courts of appeals had read Stoner in this same way, though a majority were to the contrary and applied the federal standard of sufficiency of the evidence.[17] It is hard to believe that Stoner held what the Court later said it held. The Stoner decision may be regarded as merely a peculiar application of the doctrine of "law of the case."[18] Or it may be thought that the state court decisions defined what constituted total disability under the law of that state, and that the circuit court of appeals had erred in applying a different definition.[19] The one thing that Stoner did not hold is that state law controls as to when a verdict may be directed. In Stoner itself trial was to the court and no jury problem arose. Neither the circuit court, the Supreme Court, nor the parties in their briefs in Stoner ever mentioned the Herron case or the Seventh Amendment.

The Court, which thought the question settled in 1958, spoke more fully to the point in 1959, and in rather a different tone. Without even referring to Stoner, the Court called the issue here discussed as to the effect of state law in defining the sufficiency of the evidence an "important question" that should be left for decision to a case in which it was properly briefed and argued.[20] Thus the question is now

15. 1940, 61 S.Ct. 336, 311 U.S. 464, 85 L.Ed. 284.

16. 78 S.Ct. at 902 n. 15, 356 U.S. at 540 n. 15.

17. See cases cited 9 Wright & Miller, Civil § 2525 n. 69.

18. See Note, 1953, 66 Harv.L.Rev. 1516, 1524.

19. See Notes, 1956, 51 Nw.U.L.Rev. 338, 348–350, 1953, 66 Harv.L.Rev. 1516, 1524–1525.

20. Dick v. New York Life Ins. Co., 1959, 79 S.Ct. 921, 926, 359 U.S. 437, 444–445, 3 L.Ed.2d 935. The Court also left the question open in Mercer v.

explicitly an open one in the federal system, but, for reasons already indicated, it would be very surprising if state law were held controlling on this point.[21]

The Seventh Amendment creates a historical test for trial by jury. The practice of the common law in 1791, when the amendment was adopted, is made the standard, although this practice must be read in the light of the decisions between 1791 and 1938, when law and equity were merged. This historical test does not exhaust the situations in which trial by jury can be had. Congress has given a right to jury trial in certain matters not within the Seventh Amendment, and it seems quite settled that there is no constitutional right to a nonjury trial in a case outside the Seventh Amendment.[22]

Because the test under the Seventh Amendment is historical, it will not always be easy to apply. Courts have complained of being held in "historical bondage," [23] and have apologized for an analysis that "may seem to reek unduly of the study." [24] But the number of cases in which existence of a jury right will be difficult to determine is very small. In many cases jury trial will not be demanded. Where it is demanded, in most instances it will be obvious that there is or is not a right to trial by jury. Thus the vast and controversial literature that has developed as to the scope of the jury right is, fortunately, not in proportion to the practical importance of the problem in the actual working of the courts.

Theriot, 1964, 84 S.Ct. 1157, 377 U.S. 152, 12 L.Ed.2d 206.

21.   9 Wright & Miller, Civil § 2525; 19 Wright, Miller & Cooper, Jurisdiction § 4511, pp. 177–178; cf. Cooper, Directions for Directed Verdicts: A Compass for Federal Courts, 1971, 55 Minn. L.Rev. 903, 972–989. Contra: Moore, A Century Old Problem: Federal or State Law as Determinative of a Directed Verdict in a Federal Court, 1970, 4 U.Rich.L.Rev. 282; Comment, Arizona Constitutional Law Derailed in Federal Diversity Court: A Reevaluation of Herron v. Southern Pacific Co., 1974, 16 Ariz.L.Rev. 208.

Although the lower courts are not yet in agreement on the point, there are especially forceful statements of the arguments for a federal test by Chief Judge Haynsworth in Wratchford v. S. J. Groves & Sons Co., C.A.4th, 1969, 405 F.2d 1061, 1064–1066, and by Chief Judge Tuttle in Planters Mfg. Co. v. Protection Mut. Ins. Co., C.A.5th, 1967, 380 F.2d 869, 870–871, certiorari denied 88 S.Ct. 293, 389 U.S. 930, 19 L.Ed.2d 282.

See also Donovan v. Penn Shipping Co., Inc., 1977, 97 S.Ct. 835, 837, 429 U.S.

648, 649, 51 L.Ed.2d 112: "The proper role of the trial and appellate courts in the federal system in reviewing the size of jury verdicts is * * * a matter of federal law."

The Sixth Circuit, which had long held that state law controls, has indicated a disposition to reexamine the question. Gold v. National Sav. Bank, C.A.6th, 1981, 641 F.2d 430, 434 n. 3. The Seventh Circuit, therefore, may be the last to adhere to a general rule that state law controls. Lykos v. American Home Ins. Co., C.A.7th, 1979, 609 F.2d 314, 315, certiorari denied 100 S.Ct. 1030, 444 U.S. 1079, 62 L.Ed.2d 762.

22.   Beacon Theatres, Inc. v. Westover, 1958, 79 S.Ct. 948, 359 U.S. 500, 3 L.Ed.2d 988; Note, The Right to a Non-jury Trial, 1961, 74 Harv.L.Rev. 1176.

23.   Gefen v. U. S., C.A.5th, 1968, 400 F.2d 476, 479, certiorari denied 89 S.Ct. 990, 393 U.S. 1119, 22 L.Ed.2d 123.

24.   Damsky v. Zavatt, C.A.2d, 1961, 289 F.2d 46, 48. A dissenter would have added "if not of the museum." Id. at 59.

In general there is no right to a trial by jury of claims that historically were "equitable," such as actions for injunction, specific performance, and the like.[25] There is a right to trial by jury in actions that historically would have been considered "legal," of which actions for money damages for tort or breach of contract are the most familiar examples.[26] If new causes of action are created unknown at common law, the courts must look to the nearest historical analogy to decide whether there is a right to a jury.[27]

The discussion thus far has assumed, as has been common in the literature, that the test of jury trial is entirely historical, and that the task of the court is to determine whether the claim is, or may be considered analogous to, a claim that would have been triable to a jury prior to the merger of law and equity and the adoption of the rules. The Supreme Court has cast doubt on this assumption. In Beacon Theatres, Inc. v. Westover,[28] the Court said: "Since in the federal courts equity has always acted only when legal remedies were inadequate, the expansion of adequate legal remedies provided by the Declaratory Judgment Act and the Federal Rules necessarily affects the

---

25. 9 Wright & Miller, Civil §§ 2302, 2308, 2309.

26. 9 Wright & Miller, Civil §§ 2302, 2316.

27. E.g., right to jury: Lorillard v. Pons, 1978, 98 S.Ct. 866, 434 U.S. 575, 55 L.Ed.2d 40, noted 1978, 62 Harv.L. Rev. 270 (suit for lost wages under the Age Discrimination in Employment Act); Pernell v. Southall Realty, 1974, 94 S.Ct. 1723, 416 U.S. 363, 40 L.Ed.2d 198 (summary action for repossession of real property); Curtis v. Loether, 1974, 94 S.Ct. 1005, 415 U.S. 189, 39 L.Ed.2d 260 (action for damages and injunctive relief for violation of fair housing provisions of the Civil Rights Act of 1968); Fleitmann v. Welsbach Street Lighting Co., 1916, 36 S.Ct. 233, 240 U.S. 27, 60 L.Ed. 505 (private antitrust actions).

No right to jury: Lehman v. Nakshian, 1981, 101 S.Ct. 2698, 2702 n. 9, 453 U.S. 156, 162 n. 9, 69 L.Ed.2d 548 (suit against the United States); Katchen v. Landy, 1966, 86 S.Ct. 467, 382 U.S. 323, 15 L.Ed.2d 391 (summary action in bankruptcy court); Luria v. U. S., 1913, 34 S.Ct. 10, 15, 231 U.S. 9, 27–28, 58 L.Ed. 101 (statutory action to cancel naturalization).

The Seventh Amendment does not prevent Congress from creating new statutory public rights and allowing an administrative agency to enforce them by civil penalties without jury trial. Atlas Roofing Co. v. Occupational Safety and Health Review Commn., 1977, 97 S.Ct. 1261, 430 U.S. 442, 51 L.Ed.2d 464; NLRB v. Jones & Laughlin Co., 1937, 57 S.Ct. 615, 629, 301 U.S. 1, 48, 81 L.Ed. 893. See Kirst, Administrative Penalties and the Civil Jury: The Supreme Court's Assault on the Seventh Amendment, 1978, 126 U.Pa.L.Rev. 1281.

The lower courts have held that a suit against a foreign sovereign pursuant to the Foreign Sovereign Immunities Act is not a suit at common law and that the statute barring jury trial in such actions, 28 U.S.C.A. § 1330(a), is valid. E.g., Rex v. Cia. Pervana De Vapores, S. A., C.A.3d, 1981, 660 F.2d 61; Williams v. Shipping Corp. of India, C.A.4th, 1981, 653 F.2d 875; Note, Jurisdiction and Jury Trials in Actions Against Foreign Government Owned Corporations, 1981, 38 Wash. & Lee L.Rev. 1211.

28. 1959, 79 S.Ct. 948, 956, 359 U.S. 500, 509–510, 3 L.Ed.2d 988. Professor James finds the Beacon Theatres case "cloudy and ambiguous and susceptible of an interpretation which would go far to abolish the historical test altogether and extend jury trial over most of the former domain of equity." James, note 1 above, at 687. Professors Rothstein and McCoid, in the articles cited note 1 above, find these fears unjustified and take a favorable view of Beacon Theatres.

scope of equity. Thus, the justification for equity's deciding legal issues once it obtains jurisdiction, and refusing to dismiss a case, merely because subsequently a legal remedy becomes available, must be re-evaluated in the light of the liberal joinder provisions of the Federal Rules which allow legal and equitable causes to be brought and resolved in one civil action. Similarly the need for, and therefore, the availability of such equitable remedies as Bills of Peace, Quia Timet and Injunction must be reconsidered in view of the existence of the Declaratory Judgment Act as well as the liberal joinder provision of the Rules. This is not only in accord with the spirit of the Rules and the Act but is required by the provision in the Rules that '(t)he right to trial by jury as declared by the Seventh Amendment to the Constitution or as given by a statute of the United States shall be preserved * * * inviolate.' "

The historical test, to the extent it is still applicable, works without undue difficulty where the case presents but a single claim for relief. The jurisdictional line that divided Westminster Hall was drawn largely, if not exclusively, in terms of the remedy sought. If but a single claim is presented and a single remedy demanded, the action can rationally be classified as one that historically would have been either legal or equitable. Modern procedure, however, not only permits but encourages more complicated actions that had no precise analogue in the ancient practice, and it is these that pose the most complex problems as to a jury right.

One kind of case is that in which the parties, by joinder of claims and counterclaims, are asserting several claims for relief, or are demanding several remedies arising out of a single claim for relief. If the claims, or the remedies, are either all legal or all equitable, the matter is no more difficult than in a simple suit. If the matters raised are entirely independent, again there is no difficulty. There is no waiver of jury trial by joining "legal" and "equitable" claims and counterclaims in one action.[29] Those claims historically legal will be tried to a jury; those claims historically equitable will be tried to the court. Frequently, however, the matters will not be independent; there will be, instead, one or more issues common to both the legal and equitable claims and determinative of each. In this instance the order of trial becomes important, for the determination of the first factfinder, whether court or jury, will be binding on the other. The clear holding of Beacon Theatres is that, in all conceivable situations of this sort, the legal claim should be tried first, in order to avoid depriving the party of a determination by a jury on the common issue.[30]

29. Kennedy v. Lakso Co., Inc., C.A.3d, 1969, 414 F.2d 1249; Thermo-Stitch, Inc. v. Chemi-Cord Processing Corp., C.A.5th, 1961, 294 F.2d 486; Ring v. Spina, C.C.A.2d, 1948, 166 F.2d 546, certiorari denied 69 S.Ct. 30, 335 U.S. 813, 93 L.Ed. 368; 9 Wright & Miller, Civil § 2305.

30. 9 Wright & Miller, Civil § 2338.

Another difficult situation is where a party has a single claim for relief, but demands various remedies, some available at law and some available only in equity. Thus a party may ask damages for past harm and an injunction against continuing the wrongful conduct in the future, or he may pray alternatively for specific performance of a contract or for damages for its breach. In some of these situations there is historical precedent by which equity took the whole case and awarded damages in addition to or in lieu of the equitable relief demanded.[31] Such precedent is fairly limited, and in any event it is not clear that this practice, which was justified historically only to avoid multiplicity of litigation, should be continued in a system where such multiplicity can be avoided without depriving the parties of a jury.

This problem had perplexed the courts and bemused the commentators. They suggested variously that the whole case should be labelled as "basically legal" or "basically equitable," or that the court should be guided by plaintiff's preferred remedy, or that history should be resorted to for a determination as to which party could have controlled whether the case would have gone to a jury in the old practice, or that a certain issue should be identified as "basic" and the right to a jury trial made to turn on its characteristics.[32]

All such tests must fail. They attempt to use a historical test, of one form or another, to classify a hybrid form of lawsuit that could never have existed in the ancient days. If the problem cannot be solved by history, resort must be had to policy, and the relevant policy, expressed in the Seventh Amendment, is favorable to jury trial. This was clearly indicated by the Supreme Court in Dairy Queen, Inc. v. Wood,[33] in which it carried further the doctrines first suggested in Beacon Theatres. The theory of the complaint in Dairy Queen was not clear. Defendant had been licensed by contract to use plaintiffs' trademark, and continued to do so after plaintiffs, claiming material breach of the contract, told it to desist. The complaint could be read as one for breach of contract, or for infringement of trademark, or both, but in any event plaintiffs wished to enjoin defendant from doing business using plaintiffs' mark, and they sought a money judgment, styled a demand for an "accounting," for sums due them in the past. The district court regarded the claim for a money judgment as "incidental" to the injunctive relief sought, and struck defendant's demand for jury trial. The Supreme Court held that the court of appeals erred in refusing to grant a writ of mandamus to require jury trial.

31. E.g., Denton v. Stewart, Ch.1786, 1 Cox Ch. 258, 29 Eng.Rep. 1156; Gulbenkian v. Gulbenkian, C.C.A.2d, 1945, 147 F.2d 173; Levin, Equitable Clean-Up and the Jury: A Suggested Orientation, 1951, 100 U.Pa.L.Rev. 320.

32. E.g., Fraser v. Geist, D.C.Pa.1940, 1 F.R.D. 267; Innersprings, Inc. v. Joseph Aronauer, Inc., D.C.N.Y.1961, 27 F.R.D. 32; and articles cited 9 Wright & Miller, Civil § 2302 n. 35.

33. 1962, 82 S.Ct. 894, 369 U.S. 469, 8 L.Ed.2d 44.

The Court first laid to rest the erroneous notion that if a "basic" equitable issue can be discovered, there is no right to jury trial on other legal issues. "Our previous decisions," it said, "make it plain that no such rule may be applied in the federal courts." [34] In particular it read Beacon Theatres as requiring that any legal issue for which a trial by jury is timely and properly demanded be submitted to a jury, and said: "That holding, of course, applies whether the trial judge chooses to characterize the legal issues presented as 'incidental' to equitable issues or not." [35]

Thus if the claim for a money judgment was triable to a jury, it must still be so tried although it was asserted in a suit where the basic relief sought was equitable. The Court then had to consider whether there was a right to jury trial on the money claim. It held that whether the claim be construed as one for debt allegedly due on a contract, or for damages based on a charge of trademark infringement, it was a legal claim, triable to a jury. The fact that the complaint styled the claim as one for an accounting was held not controlling, for "the constitutional right to trial by jury cannot be made to depend upon the choice of words used in the pleadings." [36] Citing Beacon Theatres, the Court restated the rule that equitable relief is available only where the remedy at law is inadequate, and it repeated the accepted proposition that the legal remedy is inadequate, and an equitable accounting available, only where the accounts are of such a complicated nature that a court of equity alone is able satisfactorily to unravel them.[37] The Court noted the procedure under Rule 53(b) by which a master can be appointed to assist the jury in those exceptional cases that are too complicated for the jury,[38] and said that in view of this the burden of showing that the legal remedy is inadequate and that an equitable accounting is required "is considerably increased and it will indeed be a rare case in which it can be met." [39] The case before it was not such a rare case, and defendant was entitled to a trial by jury on the issues involved in the claim for a money judgment. Since those issues were common to the plaintiffs' claim for equitable relief, the Beacon Theatres rule was held to require that the legal claims be determined prior to any final court determination of the equitable claims.

34. 82 S.Ct. at 896, 369 U.S. at 470.

35. 82 S.Ct. at 897, 369 U.S. at 473.
See also Nunez v. Superior Oil Co., C.A. 5th, 1978, 572 F.2d 1119; National Life Ins. Co. v. Silverman, C.A.1971, 454 F.2d 899, 147 U.S.App.D.C. 56; Simmons v. Avisco, Local 713, Textile Workers Union of America, C.A.4th, 1965, 350 F.2d 1012. But cf. Crane Co. v. American Standard Inc., C.A.2d, 1973, 490 F.2d 332.

36. 82 S.Ct. at 900, 369 U.S. at 477–478.
See 9 Wright & Miller, Civil § 2304.

37. See Kirby v. Lake Shore & M. S. R. Co., 1887, 7 S.Ct. 430, 432, 120 U.S. 130, 134, 30 L.Ed. 569.

38. See § 97 below.

39. 82 S.Ct. at 900, 369 U.S. at 478.
See also Bradshaw v. Thompson, C.A.6th, 1972, 454 F.2d 75, certiorari denied 93 S.Ct. 130, 409 U.S. 878, 34 L.Ed.2d 131; and cases cited 9 Wright & Miller, Civil § 2310 n. 76.

Still another variant of the problem arises when a party is seeking relief that would by itself be legal in nature but he invokes a procedural device, such as interpleader, a class suit, or a derivative action, that historically had been available only in equity. This came to the Court in 1970 in Ross v. Bernhard.[40] The holding there is that in a stockholders' derivative action, a type of action that historically could only have been brought in equity, there is now a right to jury trial on those issues as to which the corporation, if it had been suing in its own right, would have been entitled to a jury. This seems a necessary result from the doctrines announced in Beacon Theatres and Dairy Queen, and it is the result that should be reached in all situations in which a party is seeking relief that would by itself pose legal issues but is doing so by a procedural device historically available only in equity.[41] Indeed the Court itself seemed to indicate this when it said in the Ross opinion that "nothing turns now upon * * * the procedural devices by which the parties happen to come before the court."[42]

The Court did make one surprising statement in Ross. In a footnote, in which it cited no authority for this proposition, it said: "As our cases indicate, the 'legal' nature of an issue is determined by considering, first, the pre-merger custom with reference to such questions; second, the remedy sought; and third, the practical abilities and limitations of juries."[43] The third of the factors mentioned in that footnote was surprising since it seems to invite a balancing approach to the right to jury trial, while the accepted learning has been that that balance was already struck by the Seventh Amendment. But "the footnote is so cursory, conclusory and devoid of cited authority or reasoned analysis that it is difficult to believe it could have been intended to reject such established historical practice or Supreme Court precedent."[44]

For the most part the lower courts have ignored the Ross footnote, or cited it as a makeweight reference to support results that would have been reached had the footnote never been written. But it has helped to fire one very lively controversy that is still not resolved. As part of the general questioning of the utility of the civil jury, there has been a narrower argument that juries should not be used in the complex cases of great duration that are a part of contemporary

40. 1970, 90 S.Ct. 733, 396 U.S. 531, 24 L.Ed.2d 729. See Note, Ross v. Bernhard: The Uncertain Future of the Seventh Amendment, 1971, 81 Yale L.J. 112.

41. 9 Wright & Miller, Civil § 2307.

See 7 Wright & Miller, Civil § 1718 (interpleader); 7A id. §§ 1801 (class actions), 1837 (derivative suits), 1910 (intervention).

This principle was recognized in Hyde Properties v. McCoy, C.A.6th, 1974,

507 F.2d 301, but it was held that there was no right to a jury when the underlying issue in an interpleader action was equitable in nature.

42. 90 S.Ct. at 739, 396 U.S. at 540.

43. 90 S.Ct. at 738 n. 10, 396 U.S. at 538 n. 10.

44. Redish, note 1 above, at 526. See also Wolfram, note 1 above, at 644–645; Note, 1971, 81 Yale L.J. 112, 126–130.

litigation. Much has been written on every side of this argument.[45] The case for a "complexity exception" to the Seventh Amendment has proceeded on three fronts. First, it has been sought to justify such an exception on historical grounds. Scholars have searched the pre-1791 English precedents and some of them believe that they have found there evidence that cases otherwise legal were given to the chancellor for trial if the issues were too complex for a jury. Other scholars disagree. Second, there is an argument from the Ross footnote. It is claimed that regardless of what may have been the historical practice, "the practical abilities and limitations of juries" dictate that trial be to the court in complex patent or antitrust cases and other litigation of this scope. Finally, it is claimed that a party is denied due process of law if its rights are decided by a jury unable to understand the case and decide it rationally, and that the Due Process Clause of the Fifth Amendment overrides the Seventh Amendment when the two are in conflict.

The Ninth Circuit has rejected all of these arguments and held that there is no complexity exception.[46] The Third Circuit rejected the historical argument and the argument from the Ross footnote, but accepted, in guarded form, a complexity exception based on the due process argument.[47] Finally, the Fifth Circuit has expressed no opinion on whether there can be a complexity exception, but has held that if such an exception exists, it cannot reach a case where the trial court finds only that "it would be most difficult, if not impossible, for

45. Lempert, Civil Juries and Complex Cases: Let's Not Rush to Judgment, 1981, 80 Mich.L.Rev. 68; Loo, A Rationale for an Exception to the Seventh Amendment Right to a Jury Trial, 1981, 30 Cleve.St.L.Rev. 647; Jorde, The Seventh Amendment Right to Jury Trial of Antitrust Issues, 1981, 69 Calif.L.Rev. 1; Devlin, Jury Trial of Complex Cases: English Practice at the Time of the Seventh Amendment, 1980, 80 Col.L.Rev. 43; Arnold, A Historical Inquiry into the Right to Trial by Jury in Complex Civil Litigation, 1980, 128 U.Pa.L.Rev. 829; Campbell, Complex Cases and Jury Trials: A Reply to Professor Arnold, 1980, 128 U.Pa.L.Rev. 965; Arnold, A Modest Replication to a Lengthy Discourse, 1980, 128 U.Pa.L. Rev. 986; Lynch, The Case for Striking Jury Demands in Complex Antitrust Litigation, 1980, 1 Rev.Litigation 3; Blecher & Daniels, In Defense of Juries in Complex Antitrust Litigation, 1980, 1 Rev.Litigation 47; Note, Unfit for Jury Determination: Complex Civil Litigation and the Seventh Amendment Right of Trial by Jury, 1979, 20 B.C.L. Rev. 511; Note, Preserving the Right to Jury Trial in Complex Civil Cases, 1979, 32 Stan.L.Rev. 99; Comment,

The Right to An Incompetent Jury: Protracted Commercial Litigation and the Seventh Amendment, 1978, 10 Conn.L.Rev. 775; Note, The Right to Trial by Jury in Complex Litigation, 1978, 20 Wm. & Mary L.Rev. 329.

46. In re U. S. Financial Securities Litigation, C.A.9th, 1979, 609 F.2d 411, certiorari denied 100 S.Ct. 1866, 446 U.S. 929, 64 L.Ed.2d 281. Judge Kilkenny dissented, but without indicating which of the arguments for an exception persuaded him. 609 F.2d at 432.

47. "The complexity of a suit must be so great that it renders the suit beyond the ability of a jury to decide by rational means with a reasonable understanding of the evidence and applicable legal rules." In re Japanese Electronic Products Antitrust Litigation, C.A.3d, 1980, 631 F.2d 1069, 1088, noted 1980, 35 U.Miami L.Rev. 164; 1981, 42 U.Pitts.L.Rev. 693. Judge Gibbons dissented, arguing that "there is no case in which properly separated claims for relief cognizable at common law would be so complex that trial by jury would amount to a violation of due process." 631 F.2d at 1093.

a jury to reach a rational decision."[48]   It is obvious that this is an issue that the Supreme Court will have to resolve, but it may be wise for the Court to refrain from doing so until there has been more discussion of the issue in the lower courts.

In Fitzgerald v. United States Lines Co.[49] a suit was brought seeking money damages under the Jones Act and also for maintenance and cure. The Jones Act remedy is "legal" and there is a right of trial by jury. The remedy of maintenance and cure is of admiralty origin, and by itself would not be tried to a jury.[50]   In practice, however, injured seamen routinely join both claims, as well as an admiralty claim for unseaworthiness. The Supreme Court held that when the claims arise from a single set of facts, practical convenience requires that they be submitted to a single trier of fact, and since a jury must hear the Jones Act claim, the other claims must therefore also be submitted to the jury. In the opinion the Court made the suggestive statement that: "Only one trier of fact should be used for the trial of what is essentially one lawsuit to settle one claim split conceptually into separate parts because of historical developments."[51]   This would suggest that where legal and equitable claims arise from a single set of facts, it may be held not only that the legal claim must be tried first, as previously required by Beacon Theatres, but also that the whole case must be submitted to the jury. However the Fitzgerald case has had no generative force outside the maritime area and it is doubtful that the Court meant to go beyond the particular issue the case presented.

There can be no right to trial by jury if there are no issues of fact to be tried.[52] This principle was controlling in Parklane Hosiery Co. v. Shore.[53] A class action for damages was brought against Parklane and some of its officers and directors for issuing false proxy statements. The Securities and Exchange Commission brought a separate action against the same defendants for a declaratory judgment, and it was successful. Plaintiffs in the class action then claimed Parklane was precluded from relitigating in their action the issues that had

48. Cotten v. Witco Chem. Corp., C.A.5th, 1981, 651 F.2d 274, 276. Judge Tate, concurring, thought that the result should have been based on a square holding that the constitutional right of jury trial cannot be abrogated on the grounds of complexity of inconvenience. 651 F.2d at 277.

49. 1963, 83 S.Ct. 1646, 374 U.S. 16, 10 L.Ed.2d 720.

50. The strange distinctions governing right to a jury in actions arising from a maritime transaction were preserved when admiralty and civil procedure were merged. See Rules 9(h), 38(e); 9 Wright & Miller, Civil § 2315. The American Law Institute proposes a simpler and more rational standard to govern the right to jury. See ALI Study, § 1319 and Commentary thereto.

51. 83 S.Ct. at 1650, 374 U.S. at 21.

52. Ex parte Peterson, 1920, 40 S.Ct. 543, 547, 253 U.S. 300, 310, 64 L.Ed. 919.

53. 1979, 99 S.Ct. 645, 439 U.S. 322, 58 L.Ed.2d 552, noted 1979, 48 U.Cin.L. Rev. 611, 64 Cornell L.Rev. 1002, 10 Cum.L.Rev. 619, 57 Denver L.J. 115, 9 Stetson L.Rev. 182, 52 Temp.L.Q. 1221, 14 Tulsa L.J. 744; 1980, 29 Cath.U.L. Rev. 509, 10 Seton Hall L.Rev. 681.

been determined adversely to it in the SEC action. The Supreme Court agreed, rejecting Parklane's argument that to do so deprived it of its right to trial by jury on these issues. At common law a litigant was not entitled to have a jury determine issues that had previously been adjudicated by a chancellor in equity, and it is immaterial that the scope of collateral estoppel, or issue preclusion as it is now called,[54] has recently been greatly broadened. In 1791 a litigant could not have been precluded unless the parties were the same in both actions. Today's notions of issue preclusion allow preclusion against Parklane, since it was a party to both suits, even though it is the stockholders, who were not parties to the SEC suit, who are now claiming the benefit of preclusion. "[M]any procedural devices developed since 1791 that have diminished the civil jury's historic domain have been found not to be inconsistent with the Seventh Amendment," [55] and the broadened concept of issue preclusion is merely one of these.

The provision for a jury trial preserved by Rule 38 is not self-executing. A party desiring trial by jury must serve a timely written demand therefor not later than ten days after the service of the last pleading directed to the issue he wishes tried to a jury.[56] Once such a demand has been made, other parties may rely on it, and it cannot be withdrawn without the consent of all parties.[57] Failure to make a timely demand for jury trial waives the right to this form of trial,[58] though the court has discretion, on motion,[59] to order jury trial despite the waiver.[60] A considerable number of decisions take a very strict view, and refuse to relieve a party from his waiver of jury trial unless there are special circumstances excusing the failure to make a timely demand. Thus one court boasts that "it has been the unbending practice of this Court for many years not to order a jury trial once it has been waived." [61] Such decisions put the emphasis in the wrong place. Technical insistence upon imposing a penalty for inadvertence by denying a jury trial is not in the spirit of the rules. If the issue is one that normally should be tried by a jury, the court should grant relief from waiver in the absence of compelling reasons to the contrary.[62]

54. See § 100A below.

55. 99 S.Ct. at 654, 439 U.S. at 336.

56. Rule 38(b), (c); 9 Wright & Miller, Civil §§ 2318–2320.

57. Calnetics Corp. v. Volkswagen of America, Inc., C.A.9th, 1976, 532 F.2d 674, certiorari denied 97 S.Ct. 355, 429 U.S. 940, 50 L.Ed.2d 309; and cases cited 9 Wright & Miller, Civil § 2318 n. 8.

58. Rule 38(d); 9 Wright & Miller, Civil § 2321.

59. Mesa Petroleum Co. v. Coniglio, C.A.5th, 1980, 629 F.2d 1022; and cases cited 9 Wright & Miller, Civil § 2334 nn. 27, 28.

60. 9 Wright & Miller, Civil § 2334.

61. Ligouri v. New York, N. H. & H. R. Co., D.C.Conn.1961, 26 F.R.D. 565, 568, criticized 1962, 47 Iowa L.Rev. 759; and cases cited 9 Wright & Miller, Civil § 2334 nn. 33–37.

62. Cox v. C. H. Masland & Sons, Inc., C.A.5th, 1979, 607 F.2d 138, 143–144; AMF Tuboscope, Inc. v. Cunningham, C.A.10th, 1965, 352 F.2d 150, 155; Rodriguez v. Schweiger, D.C.Ill.1982, 534 F.Supp. 229; In re N–500L Cases, D.C. Puerto Rico 1981, 517 F.Supp. 821; Pawlak v. Metropolitan Life Ins. Co., D.C.Mass.1980, 87 F.R.D. 717; and

In the absence of a demand for jury trial, or if there has been a demand but the case is not one triable to a jury as of right, the case will be tried to the court.[63] The court may, if it wishes, submit an issue to an advisory jury on its own initiative, but the verdict of such a jury is advisory only, and the ultimate responsibility for finding the facts remains with the court.[64] In an action not triable to a jury as of right, the court may, with the consent of both parties, order a trial with a jury whose verdict has the same effect as if trial by jury had been a matter of right.[65]

§ 93. Evidence [1]

The Federal Rules of Evidence became effective on July 1, 1975.[2] They have such a wide impact that it is not possible to discuss them comprehensively in the present work. Instead resort must be had to the standard textbooks on evidence [3] and to the writing that has been produced and will be produced in direct response to the Evidence Rules.[4] No more can be attempted here than to describe the background of the new rules and to suggest one or two problems raised by the new rules that have general implications on the law applied in the federal courts.

Prior to 1975, Criminal Rule 26 had provided for uniform rules of evidence in federal criminal cases. The admissibility of evidence and

cases cited 9 Wright & Miller, Civil § 2334 nn. 32, 38–40.

The narrower view, that something more than mere inadvertence is required, was announced in Noonan v. Cunard S. S. Co., C.A.2d, 1967, 375 F.2d 69, noted 1967, 36 U.Cin.L.Rev. 714, and is supported, in varying degrees, in: Rhodes v. Amarillo Hosp. Dist., C.A.5th, 1981, 654 F.2d 1148, 1154; Aetna Cas. & Sur. Co. v. Jeppesen & Co., C.A.9th, 1981, 642 F.2d 339, 341; and Littlefield v. Fort Dodge Messenger, C.A.8th, 1980, 614 F.2d 581, 585, certiorari denied 100 S.Ct. 1342, 445 U.S. 945, 63 L.Ed.2d 779.

63. See § 96 below.

64. Rule 39(c); Hyde Properties v. McCoy, C.A.6th, 1974, 507 F.2d 301; Hurwitz v. Hurwitz, C.A.1943, 136 F.2d 796, 78 U.S.App.D.C. 66; (American) Lumbermen's Mut. Cas. Co. v. Timms & Howard, Inc., C.C.A.2d, 1939, 108 F.2d 497; 9 Wright & Miller, Civil § 2335.

65. Rule 39(c); Security Mut. Cas. Co. v. Affiliated FM Ins. Co., C.A.8th, 1972, 471 F.2d 238; Stockton v. Altman, C.A.5th, 1970, 432 F.2d 946, certiorari denied 91 S.Ct. 1232, 401 U.S. 994, 28 L.Ed.2d 532; 9 Wright & Miller, Civil § 2333.

[§ 93]

1. See volumes 21 et seq., Wright & Graham, Evidence.

2. The text of the rules as finally adopted appears at 65 F.R.D. 131, but there have been four amendments since that time.

At particularly helpful publication is Federal Rules of Evidence Annotated, 1975, a compilation by the Federal Judicial Center. This presents in connection with each rule the original Advisory Committee Note and the legislative history of the rule, including material from committee reports and floor debate dealing with the rule. It makes it easy to see what changes, if any, Congress made in a rule as it had been proposed by the Supreme Court, and why those changes were made.

3. E.g., McCormick, Evidence, Cleary et al. ed. 1972.

4. E.g., Wright & Graham, Evidence; Weinstein, Evidence: United States Rules, 1975; Symposium, The Federal Rules of Evidence, 1975, 36 La.L.Rev. 59; Comment, A Practitioner's Guide to the Federal Rules of Evidence, 1975, 10 U.Rich.L.Rev. 169.

the competency and privileges of witnesses were governed, in the absence of a federal statute providing otherwise, "by the principles of the common law as they may be interpreted by the courts of the United States in the light of reason and experience." [5] There is empirical evidence that the courts were faithful to this principle and made almost no use of state rules of evidence in criminal cases.[6]

The situation in civil cases was very different prior to 1975. Although the Civil Rules made some provisions on evidentiary matters—and some of these, including Rule 43(e) on evidence on motions,[7] Rule 44 on proof of official records,[8] and Rule 44.1 on determination of foreign law,[9] have survived the adoption of the Evidence Rules—the basic provision was former Rule 43(a). It created a three-pronged test, allowing the admission of evidence if it fell into any one of the three categories described in the rule:

(1) Evidence was admissible if statutes of the United States so provided. There were not many such statutes.[10]

(2) Evidence was admissible "under the rules of evidence heretofore applied in the courts of the United States on the hearing of suits in equity." Read literally, this was of limited usefulness, because there were very few decisions on the admissibility of evidence under the old equity procedure.[11] However the courts showed considerable inventiveness, holding that the federal judge could put himself in the shoes of a chancellor prior to 1938 and search the sources for guidance that a chancellor of that day would have used.[12] Another formulation was that a rule could be deduced from general principles and related federal decisions, although there was no stated equity precedent available.[13]

---

5. 2 Wright, Criminal 2d § 402.

6. Sherman, Appendix, 1969, 69 Col.L. Rev. 377.

7. 9 Wright & Miller, Civil § 2416.

8. 9 Wright & Miller, Civil §§ 2431–2437.

9. 9 Wright & Miller, Civil §§ 2241–2247; Sass, Foreign Law in Federal Courts, 1981, 1 Amer.J.Comp. L. 97; Baade, Proving Foreign and International Law in Domestic Tribunals, 1978, 18 Va.J.Intl.L. 619; Miller, Federal Rule 44.1 and the "Fact" Approach to Determining Foreign Law: Death Knell for a Die-Hard Doctrine, 1967, 65 Mich.L.Rev. 613; Comment, Determination of Foreign Law Under Rule 44.1, 1975, 10 Texas Intl.L.J. 67.

10. The most important was the business records act, 28 U.S.C.A. § 1732, now superseded by Evidence Rule 803(6).

11. Callahan & Ferguson, Evidence and the New Federal Rules of Civil Procedure: I, 1936, 45 Yale L.J. 622, 625.

12. Monarch Ins. Co. of Ohio v. Spach, C.A.5th, 1960, 281 F.2d 401, 411; Hope v. Hearst Consol. Publications, Inc., C.A.2d, 1961, 294 F.2d 681, 684, certiorari denied 82 S.Ct. 399, 368 U.S. 956, 7 L.Ed.2d 388, noted 1962, 15 Vand.L. Rev. 1330; New York Life Ins. Co. v. Harrington, C.A.9th, 1962, 299 F.2d 803, 808; Comment, 1962, 62 Col.L. Rev. 1049; Note, 1962, 48 Va.L.Rev. 939.

A particularly interesting illustration of this process is United Services Auto. Assn. v. Wharton, D.C.N.C.1965, 237 F.Supp. 255.

13. Butler v. Southern Pac. Co., C.A.5th, 1970, 431 F.2d 77; Treharne v. Callahan, C.A.3d, 1970, 426 F.2d 58; 9 Wright & Miller, Civil § 2403.

(3) Evidence was admissible "under the rules of evidence applied in the courts of general jurisdiction of the state in which the United States court is held."

Thus unless evidence fell under one of the first two branches of Rule 43(a)—or could be brought by an inventive view of what the federal equity rule had been into the second of those branches—admissibility was dependent on the rules of evidence of the state in which the federal court was sitting. The courts disagreed on whether they could admit evidence if it would not come in under any of the three prongs of Rule 43(a),[14] but that disagreement is a matter of ancient history in the light of the adoption of the Evidence rules. There were also problems of the application of the Erie doctrine in a diversity case if evidence would be excluded in a state court but could be admitted under the first or second branches of Rule 43(a).[15] This problem, too, takes on such a different form with the adoption of the Evidence rules that it would be unprofitable to examine the former views about it.

Rule 43(a) was a stop-gap.[16] It was intended to provide a liberal and flexible rule for the admissibility of evidence, pending the adoption of a detailed set of evidence rules for the federal courts. There was dispute about how successful it was as a stop-gap.[17] Although the desirability of a uniform set of federal evidence rules, to be applied in all cases, civil or criminal, continued to be recognized,[18] and distinguished authorities concluded that the task was a feasible one,[19] it was not until 1965 that Chief Justice Warren appointed an advisory committee to formulate these rules. Preliminary drafts were circulated by the committee in 1969 [20] and 1971,[21] and in 1972 the Supreme Court reported to Congress a set of Federal Rules of Evidence, to take effect in 1973.[22] These provoked considerable controversy, with disagreement about the power of the Supreme Court to adopt rules of evidence, about the utility of uniform federal rules of evidence, and about the desirability of particular provisions in the rules as approved by the Supreme Court, with particular emphasis on the proposed

14. Compare, e.g., Wright v. Wilson, C.C.A.3d, 1946, 154 F.2d 616, 619, certiorari denied 67 S.Ct. 50, 329 U.S. 743, 91 L.Ed. 640, with Dallas County v. Commercial Union Assur. Co., Ltd., C.A.5th, 1961, 286 F.2d 388. See 9 Wright & Miller, Civil § 2404.

15. 9 Wright & Miller, Civil § 2405.

16. Clark, Foreword to Symposium on the Uniform Rules of Evidence, 1956, 10 Rutgers L.Rev. 479, 482.

17. 9 Wright & Miller, Civil § 2401.

18. Estes, The Need for Uniform Rules of Evidence in the Federal Courts, 1960, 24 F.R.D. 331; Joiner, Uniform Rules of Evidence for the Federal Courts, 1957, 20 F.R.D. 429.

19. Rules of Evidence: A Preliminary Report on the Advisability and Feasibility of Developing Uniform Rules of Evidence for the United States District Courts, 1962, 30 F.R.D. 73; Degnan, The Law of Federal Evidence Reform, 1962, 76 Harv.L.Rev. 275; Degnan, The Feasibility of Rules of Evidence in Federal Courts, 1960, 24 F.R.D. 341; Ladd, Uniform Evidence Rules in the Federal Courts, 1963, 49 Va.L.Rev. 692. Morgan, Rules of Evidence—Substantive or Procedural, 1957, 10 Vand.L.Rev. 467.

20. 46 F.R.D. 161.

21. 51 F.R.D. 315.

22. 56 F.R.D. 183.

rules of privilege.[23] Prior to the date on which the rules were to have taken effect, Congress adopted a statute providing that the rules should have no effect except as they might be expressly approved by Act of Congress.[24] The proposed rules were carefully studied in both Houses, and many significant changes were made in the draft the Supreme Court had approved before Congress adopted the Federal Rules of Evidence by statute, effective July 1, 1975.[25]

The aspect of the Evidence Rules, as at last adopted, that is within the scope of the present work is their impact on state law, particularly in diversity cases and in other cases in which state law provides the substantive rule of decision. Since the rules were finally adopted by Act of Congress rather than by the Supreme Court, any question whether rules of evidence were within the scope of the Enabling Act was mooted.[26] In Hanna v. Plumer,[27] the Court said: "Erie and its offspring cast no doubt on the long-recognized power of Congress to prescribe housekeeping rules for federal courts even though some of those rules will inevitably differ from comparable state rules."[28] Thus it would seem that the Evidence Rules are to be applied without regard to the Erie doctrine, although the Court in Hanna did add the caution that in determining the validity of a particular rule, a court "need not wholly blind itself to the degree to which the Rule makes the character and result of the federal litigation stray from the course it would follow in state courts * * * ."[29]

At the same time, the implication of Hanna is not that the federal rules are valid because wise men made them, but because wise men thought carefully before making them.[30] A major reason for the critical reaction in Congress to the draft prepared by the advisory committee and approved by the Court was a feeling that insufficient thought had been given to the presuppositions of federalism, and to the value of deference to state policies, in the formulation of that draft.

As Judge Weinstein and Professor Degnan had most fully developed,[31] evidence rules are of three kinds. Most rules are of a house-

---

23. E.g., Moore & Bendix, Congress, Evidence and Rulemaking, 1974, 84 Yale L.J. 9; Weinberg, Choice of Law and the Proposed Federal Rules of Evidence: New Perspectives, 1974, 122 U.Pa.L.Rev. 594; Note, Separation of Powers and the Federal Rules of Evidence, 1975, 26 Hast.L.J. 1059; Comment, Rules of Evidence and the Federal Practice: Limits on the Supreme Court's Rulemaking Power, 1974 Ariz. St.L.J. 77.

24. Act of March 30, 1973, Pub.L. 93–12, 87 Stat. 9.

25. Act of Jan. 2, 1975, Pub.L. 93–595, 88 Stat. 1926.

26. 19 Wright, Miller & Cooper, Jurisdiction § 4512. These questions were probably insubstantial in any event. See note 19 above. Some of the authorities cited note 23 above took a different view.

27. 1965, 85 S.Ct. 1136, 380 U.S. 460, 14 L.Ed.2d 8. See § 59 above.

28. 85 S.Ct. at 1145, 380 U.S. at 473.

29. Id.

30. The phrase was suggested to the author by Professor Ronan E. Degnan.

31. Weinstein, The Uniformity-Conformity Dilemma Facing Draftsmen of Federal Rules of Evidence, 1969, 69 Col.L. Rev. 353; Degnan, The Law of Federal

keeping nature and are merely intended to make efficient use of the court's time and to assist in reaching the truth by preventing the jury from being confused or mislead. These matters should be settled by the federal courts for themselves. They commonly had been in diversity cases [32] and there was no reason to defer to state practices in formulating rules of this kind for the future.

Next there are rules that in form only regulate evidence but in fact are closely associated with substantive rights. The most obvious of these are rules dealing with burden of proof and presumptions respecting facts that are elements of a claim or defense. The federal courts had always applied state rules on these matters in diversity cases in the past,[33] and the rules wisely will continue to do so.[34] Here, however, there are grey areas. Is a dead man's statute, for example, intended to provide substantive protection for estates or to guard against misleading the jury by untruthful testimony of an interested party that cannot be rebutted? The cases had held that a state statute of this kind must be followed; [35] it would not have been followed under the rules as proposed by the Court but Congress restored the former understanding on this point.[36] Other situations are even more murky. A state rule prohibiting opinion evidence on whether a defamatory article was understood to refer to a particular person appears to be a routine rule of evidence but it may reflect a state policy to discourage this kind of disfavored action.[37]

Evidence Reform, 1962, 76 Harv.L.Rev. 275.

This subject is brilliantly explored in a later article, Wellborn, The Federal Rules of Evidence and the Application of State Law in the Federal Courts, 1977, 55 Texas L.Rev. 371.

32. E.g., Haddigan v. Harkins, C.A.3d, 1971, 441 F.2d 844, 851–852 (admissibility of expert testimony); U. S. v. 60.14 Acres of Land, C.A.3d, 1966, 362 F.2d 660 (competency of expert witness); Croom v. Fiedler, C.A.6th, 1965, 341 F.2d 909 (hearsay); Hambrice v. F. W. Woolworth Co., C.A.5th, 1961, 290 F.2d 557 (relevancy); United Services Auto. Assn. v. Wharton, D.C.N.C.1965, 237 F.Supp. 255 (hearsay); Een v. Consolidated Freightways, D.C.N.D.1954, 120 F.Supp. 289, affirmed C.A.8th, 1955, 220 F.2d 82. See generally 9 Wright & Miller, Civil § 2405.

33. Cities Serv. Oil Corp. v. Dunlap, 1939, 60 S.Ct. 201, 308 U.S. 208, 84 L.Ed. 196 (burden of proof); Dick v. New York Life Ins. Co., 1959, 79 S.Ct. 921, 359 U.S. 437, 3 L.Ed.2d 935 (presumptions).

The misnamed "parol evidence rule" is not a rule of evidence at all, and state doctrine must be followed. Freeman v. Continental Gin Co., C.A.5th, 1967, 381 F.2d 459. This continues to be true under the Evidence Rules. E.g., Southern Stone Co., Inc. v. Singer, C.A.5th, 1982, 665 F.2d 698; Betz Labs, Inc. v. Hines, C.A.3d, 1981, 647 F.2d 402.

34. Evidence Rule 302.

35. First Nat. Bank & Trust Co. v. McKeel, C.A.10th, 1967, 387 F.2d 741; Wright v. Wilson, C.C.A.3d, 1946, 154 F.2d 616, certiorari denied 67 S.Ct. 50, 329 U.S. 743, 91 L.Ed. 640.

36. Evidence Rule 601 makes state law govern questions of the competency of a witness in civil actions with respect to which state law supplies the substantive rule of decision.

37. Both Weinstein, note 31 above, at 367–368, and Degnan, note 31 above, at 294, raise questions on this ground about Hope v. Hearst Consol. Publications, Inc., C.A.2d, 1961, 294 F.2d 681, certiorari denied 82 S.Ct. 399, 368 U.S. 956, 7 L.Ed.2d 388, in which this kind of evidence was held admissible though the state would have excluded it.

This grey area is illustrated by Conway v. Chemical Leaman Tank Lines, Inc.,[38] one of the first decisions of significance to apply the Evidence rules. That was a Texas wrongful death case, brought in federal court on the basis of diversity. A Texas statute provides that in a wrongful death action evidence of the remarriage of the surviving spouse is admissible, but the Texas courts continue to hold that the fact of the remarriage may not be considered in mitigation of damages.

The Fifth Circuit held that the evidence of the plaintiff's remarriage was admissible in Conway, not because of the Texas statute but because of the Evidence Rules. Rules 401 and 402 on relevancy, it said, were specifically intended to provide that background evidence is admissible.[39] But the court, with obvious regret, held that since under Erie state law governs the measures of damages, including admissibility and jury consideration of particular issues, the jury must be instructed that it could not consider plaintiff's remarriage for the purpose of mitigating damages.

This clearly seemed to mean that evidence of remarriage would be admissible in a wrongful death case, not only in Texas, which has so provided by statute, but in each of the states of the Fifth Circuit, even though other states have no such statute. The rule that the spouse's remarriage is not to be considered in mitigation of damages is plainly a rule of substantive law that must be honored in a diversity case. Yet if a state considers this policy so important that it enforces it by not allowing the evidence for any purpose, and thus avoids the considerable risk that a jury would disregard a limiting instruction, the federal diversity court, by virtue of the Evidence Rules, would give the policy less protection than the state thinks it merits. To achieve this under the guise of a housekeeping rule on relevancy would be a severe blow to the values of federalism.

Fortunately the panel of the Fifth Circuit that had decided Conway wrote again on the case on an application for rehearing. There the court held that the evidence of remarriage is admissible because the Texas statute was more than a rule of evidence; it was a part of the state law of wrongful death, which federal courts must follow under Erie.[40] Evidence Rule 402 was not mentioned. This strongly

38. C.A.5th, 1976, 525 F.2d 927, on rehearing C.A.5th, 1976, 540 F.2d 837, noted 1977, 55 Texas L.Rev. 557. See 22 Wright & Graham, Evidence § 5201, pp. 235–237; Wellborn, note 31 above, at 376–384, 415–417.

39. "Although the Rules do not deal specifically with proof of a surviving spouse's remarriage, their treatment of comparable issues suggests that the evidence is admissible for background and perhaps various other limited purposes. See Fed.R.Evid. 407 (admissibility of subsequent remedial measures); Fed.R.Evid. 411 (admissibility of liability insurance coverage)." 525 F.2d at 930.

40. "These determinations, though in a sense matters of evidence-law, are embedded in Texas substantive law and policy, and we adopt them as part of the Texas wrongful death act for application in federal trials of actions brought thereunder." 540 F.2d at 839.

suggests that a federal court should exclude the evidence in a state that would do so,[41] and this appears to be the desirable result.[42]

Finally there are state rules of evidence that are deliberately adopted to effectuate some extrinsic policy of the state. The problem is seen most clearly where the state has adopted an evidentiary privilege for confidential communications that was unknown at common law, or it has given an established privilege greater scope than it traditionally has had.

Prior to 1975 there was considerable confusion on the applicability of state privileges in federal actions, with both the decisions and the commentators divided.[43] Though there were many variations and inconsistencies, in general the courts applied state privileges in diversity cases [44] but did not do so in actions in which the United States was seeking to enforce federal law.[45] In private federal question cases the situation was quite unclear.[46]

As a matter of policy it seems appropriate that the states should not be permitted to say when the federal courts must refrain from hearing useful testimony in a matter involving federal law. A different result seems most tenable in diversity litigation. Privileges for confidential communications are created because the state thinks a particular relationship—attorney-client, husband-wife, journalist-source—is sufficiently important that it should be fostered by preserving confidentiality in the relationship even at the cost of losing evidence that would help to determine the truth in later litigation.[47] Thus privilege differs from most rules of evidence, which are intended to facilitate getting at the truth of a matter, not deliberately block it. The state's effort to encourage these relationships will be hampered if the secrets of the marriage bed or the attorney's office can

41. In Estate of Spinosa, C.A.1st, 1980, 621 F.2d 1154, the district court was affirmed in excluding evidence of remarriage of the spouse in a diversity wrongful death case. The appellate court looked only to the fact that it believed this evidence would be excluded in state court. It made no reference to the Evidence Rules.

42. Wellborn, note 31 above, at 416–417; Case note, 1977, 55 Texas L.Rev. 557, 566–567.

A failure to consider state policies that may be substantive in nature may have occurred in Cann v. Ford Motor Co., C.A.2d, 1981, 658 F.2d 54. The court there construed Evidence Rule 407 as excluding evidence of post-accident design cases in a strict liability action, and on that construction held the evidence properly excluded in a New York diversity case. The New York Court of Appeals had held very recently that such evidence is admissible. The Sec-

ond Circuit's only reference to the state decision was a citation to the dissent.

43. 9 Wright & Miller, Civil § 2408.

44. See Lukee Enterprises, Inc. v. New York Life Ins. Co., D.C.N.M.1971, 52 F.R.D. 21; and cases cited 9 Wright & Miller, Civil § 2408 nn. 2–5.

45. See U. S. v. Kansas City Lutheran Home & Hosp. Assn., D.C.Mo.1969, 297 F.Supp. 239; and cases cited 9 Wright & Miller, Civil § 2408 n. 94.

There was some reason for believing that more deference was paid to state privileges in the courtroom than in the reported decisions. See Weinstein, note 31 above, at 372 n. 82.

46. The fullest examination of the problem was in Garner v. Wolfinbarger, C.A.5th, 1970, 430 F.2d 1093, 1098–1100.

47. 8 Wigmore, Evidence (McNaughton rev. 1961), § 2285.

be kept secret in state court but disclosed where, because of the accident of diversity, suit is brought in federal court. Since the litigation is on a state-created right, there is no federal interest that justifies such an interference with the state's decision that the relation is more important than the litigation.

The Advisory Committee on Rules of Evidence reached a contrary conclusion. In its proposed rules it defined those privileges it thought should be recognized and expressly refused to honor broader state privileges.[48] The wisdom of making such a serious intrusion on state policies was highly doubtful,[49] and this treatment of privilege was a major factor in the controversy that developed about the proposed rules as they were approved by the Supreme Court.

As finally adopted by Congress, the detailed set of rules of privilege that had been proposed for the Evidence Rules was scrapped, and the subject is covered by Rule 501, which provides: "Except as otherwise required by the Constitution of the United States or provided by Act of Congress or in rules prescribed by the Supreme Court pursuant to statutory authority, the privilege of a witness, person, government, State, or political subdivision thereof shall be governed by the principles of the common law as they may be interpreted by the courts of the United States in the light of reason and experience. However, in civil actions and proceedings, with respect to an element of a claim or defense as to which State law supplies the rule of decision, the privilege of a witness, person, government, State, or political subdivision thereof shall be determined in accordance with State law." [50]

Evidence Rule 501, as rewritten by Congress, adopts what had been the common understanding prior to enactment of the rules. On matters governed by federal substantive law—and this will generally be true in criminal cases, civil actions brought by the United States, and private federal question cases—federal courts are to apply and develop a federal common law of privilege.[51] In determining what this is to be, the federal courts may consider state privilege law [52] but

---

48. Proposed Evidence Rule 501. The Committee Note defending this course is set out at 51 F.R.D. 356–360. For a full examination of this history, see 23 Wright & Graham, Evidence § 5421.

49. See the articles by Judge Weinstein and Professor Degnan cited note 31 above. See also Wright, Procedural Reform: Its Limitations and Its Future, 1967, 1 Ga.L.Rev. 563, 571–574; Note, The Constitutionality of Federal Abrogation of State Created Rules of Privilege in Diversity Cases: Proposed Federal Rule of Evidence 501, 1973, 34 Ohio St.L.J. 400.

50. The rule as finally adopted is analyzed in 23 Wright & Graham, Evi-

dence §§ 5421–5438. See also Kaminsky, State Evidentiary Privileges in Federal Civil Litigation, 1975, 43 Ford. L.Rev. 923, 949–962.

51. U. S. v. Gillock, 1980, 100 S.Ct. 1185, 445 U.S. 360, 63 L.Ed.2d 454; Trammel v. U. S., 1980, 100 S.Ct. 906, 445 U.S. 40, 63 L.Ed.2d 186; 23 Wright & Graham, Evidence § 5425.

52. E.g., Socialist Workers Party v. Grubusic, C.A.7th, 1980, 619 F.2d 641, 643; Riley v. City of Chester, C.A.3d, 1979, 612 F.2d 708, 715; U. S. v. H. E. Crain, C.A.9th, 1979, 589 F.2d 996, 999.

are not bound by it,[53] and may look also for guidance to the rules of privilege that were proposed by the Advisory Committee on Rules of Evidence but not adopted.[54]

With regard to elements of a claim or defense as to which state law supplies the rule of decision, the state law of privilege must be applied.[55] To the extent that federal law provides the rule of decision in federal question cases and state law provides the rule of decision in diversity cases, Evidence Rule 501 will work without difficulty. But though the pattern just described is usually true, it is not always true. At times state law is looked to in federal question cases and at times federal law is controlling on some issues in diversity cases.[56] Thus the application of Rule 501 depends on the rule of decision that applies to a particular issue in a particular case and cannot be mechanically resolved by looking to the basis for jurisdiction of the case.[57]

In federal question cases in which a federal court adopts or incorporates state law to fill interstices in federal statutory phrases, federal privilege law will be applied. In these cases in which a federal court chooses to absorb state law, it is applying the state law as a matter of federal common law. Thus the rule of decision is not state law, even though the rule may be derived from state decisions.[58]

There are instances in which federal statutes or common law provide the rule of decision in diversity cases.[59] In those instances the federal common law of privilege will be applied.

Finally, there are federal question cases in which the court also may hear a related state law claim as pendent to the federal claim.[60] In these instances the federal law of privilege would apply on the federal claim and the state law of privilege on the state claim.[61] Oft-

53. U. S. v. Gillock, 1980, 100 S.Ct. 1185, 1191, 445 U.S. 360, 368, 63 L.Ed.2d 454; Memorial Hosp. for McHenry County v. Shadur, C.A.7th, 1981, 664 F.2d 1058.

54. U. S. v. Meagher, C.A.5th, 1976, 531 F.2d 752, 753; U. S. v. Allery, C.A.8th, 1975, 526 F.2d 1362, 1365–1367. See 23 Wright & Graham, Evidence § 5422, pp. 691–693.

55. 23 Wright & Graham, Evidence §§ 5432–5434.

56. See § 60 above at notes 46 to 52.

57. The version of Rule 501 approved in the Senate would have made privilege turn on the jurisdictional basis of the suit. It was wisely rejected by the conference committee in favor of the House version, which appears in the rule as finally adopted. See Federal Judicial Center, Federal Rules of Evidence Annotated, 1975, pp. 45–46.

58. E.g., De Sylva v. Ballentine, 1956, 76 S.Ct. 974, 351 U.S. 570, 100 L.Ed.

1415; Holmberg v. Armbrecht, 1946, 66 S.Ct. 582, 327 U.S. 392, 90 L.Ed. 743; D'Oench, Duhme & Co. v. Federal Deposit Ins. Corp., 1942, 62 S.Ct. 676, 686, 315 U.S. 447, 471–472, 86 L.Ed. 956 (Jackson, J., concurring).

59. E.g., Francis v. Southern Pac. Co., 1948, 68 S.Ct. 611, 333 U.S. 445, 92 L.Ed. 798; Sola Elec. Co. v. Jefferson Elec. Co., 1942, 63 S.Ct. 172, 317 U.S. 173, 87 L.Ed. 165; Huber Baking Co. v. Stroehmann Bros. Co., C.A.2d, 1958, 252 F.2d 945, certiorari denied 79 S.Ct. 50, 358 U.S. 829, 3 L.Ed.2d 69.

60. See § 19 above.

61. 2 Louisell & Mueller, Federal Evidence, 1978, pp. 503–504; see Scott v. McDonald, D.C.Ga.1976, 70 F.R.D. 568, 571. But cf. 23 Wright & Graham, Evidence § 5434, where it is recognized that Professor Graham and the present author differ on this issue.

en the federal and state rules of privilege will be the same, and no problem will be created. If the privilege rules differ, it would be anomalous if evidence were held admissible on one claim and privileged on the related claim. But the possibility of jury confusion is a recognized reason for refusing to exercise jurisdiction over a pendent state claim,[62] and this is the course the court should follow when contradictory rules of privilege will apply to the two claims.

Rule 501 has raised another interesting problem, one that was never considered by the Advisory Committee or by Congress. If state law is to furnish the rule of privilege under the proviso to the rule, to which state's law is the federal court to look if it is sitting in one state but the arguably privileged communication was made in some other state? Although there are several answers to this question for which reasonable arguments can be made,[63] the wisest course seems to be to hold that the general principle of the Klaxon case[64] applies, and that the federal court is to do whatever the courts of the state in which it is sitting would do under that state's notions of conflict of laws.[65]

§ 94. Submission to the Jury[1]

The Seventh Amendment preserves the essential elements of trial by jury, rather than particular details.[2] Among the essential elements that are preserved is the requirement that the jury must be an impartial cross-section of the community, without systematic and in-

In Wm. T. Thompson Co. v. General Nutrition Corp., C.A.3d, 1982, 671 F.2d 100, 104, the court held that "when there are federal law claims in a case also presenting state law claims, the federal rule favoring admissibility, rather than any state law privilege, is the controlling rule. * * * [O]ur holding is consistent with the legislative history of Rule 501 and the decisions of a number of trial courts." In support of its reference to legislative history, the court quoted the Senate Report, apparently overlooking that the Conference Committee deliberately rejected the Senate version of Rule 501, which would have made the question of privilege turn on the jurisdictional basis of the action rather than which body of law furnishes the rule of decision. See note 57 above.

62. United Mine Workers v. Gibbs, 1966, 86 S.Ct. 1130, 1139, 383 U.S. 715, 727, 16 L.Ed.2d 218.

63. See 23 Wright & Graham, Evidence § 5435.

64. Klaxon v. Stentor Elec. Mfg. Co., 1941, 61 S.Ct. 1020, 313 U.S. 487, 85 L.Ed. 1477. See § 57 above.

65. Miller v. Transamerican Press, Inc., C.A.5th, 1980, 621 F.2d 721, certiorari denied 101 S.Ct. 1759, 450 U.S. 1041, 68 L.Ed.2d 238; Samuelson v. Susen, C.A. 3d, 1978, 576 F.2d 546; and cases cited 23 Wright & Graham, Evidence § 5435 n. 24.

In the Third Edition of the present work, the author took the view that the law of privilege of the state whose substantive law is being applied should be the applicable law. Wright, Federal Courts, 3d ed. 1976, p. 462. This would have the advantage that in a single sentence of the rule in which "State law" is used twice, it would not mean two different things. Further reflection persuaded him, however, that the more complicated Klaxon approach is the proper one.

[§ 94]

1. 9 Wright & Miller, Civil §§ 2481–2485, 2491–2492, 2501–2513, 2521–2536, 2551–2558.

2. Parklane Hosiery Co., Inc. v. Shore, 1979, 99 S.Ct. 645, 654, 439 U.S. 322, 336–337, 58 L.Ed.2d 552.

tentional exclusion of any economic, social, religious, racial, political, or geographical group.[3] Although it had long been supposed that another of these essential elements of trial by jury was, except as waived by the parties, a unanimous verdict of 12 jurors, the Supreme Court has upheld local rules providing for civil juries of fewer than 12,[4] and whether a unanimous verdict is constitutionally required is now a matter of doubt.[5]

The case need not be submitted to the jury at all. The court has the power to direct a verdict [6] if the evidence is such that reasonable men could not differ as to the result. A verdict may be directed for the plaintiff, though this is much less common than a directed verdict for the defendant.[7] A 1963 amendment to the rules put an end to the embarrassing practice by which the jurors were required to sign a directed verdict, though it was in no sense their own free act.[8] Now it is clear that the order of the court granting the motion is effective without any assent of the jury. In most circumstances the court wisely will reserve decision on the motion for directed verdict, submit the case to the jury, and then pass on the legal sufficiency of the evidence on a motion for judgment notwithstanding verdict. This course avoids the need for a second trial if an appellate court should

3. Thiel v. Southern Pac. Co., 1946, 66 S.Ct. 984, 328 U.S. 217, 90 L.Ed. 1181; Ballard v. U. S., 1946, 67 S.Ct. 261, 329 U.S. 187, 91 L.Ed. 181. This is implemented by the careful procedures required by the Jury Selection and Service Act of 1968, 28 U.S.C.A. §§ 1861–1874. See 2 Wright, Criminal 2d § 375.

4. Colgrove v. Battin, 1973, 93 S.Ct. 2448, 413 U.S. 149, 37 L.Ed.2d 522, noted 1974, 28 Ark.L.Rev. 270, 23 DePaul L.Rev. 753, 43 Tul.L.Rev. 439. See Bieser & Varrin, Six-member Juries in the Federal Courts, 1975, 58 Judicature 425; Zeisel & Diamond, "Convincing Empirical Evidence" on the Six-Member Jury, 1974, 41 U.Chi.L.Rev. 281; Fisher, The Seventh Amendment and the Common Law: No Magic in Numbers, 1973, 56 F.R.D. 507; 9 Wright & Miller, Civil § 2491.

5. The Seventh Amendment was held to require a unanimous verdict in American Pub. Co. v. Fisher, 1897, 17 S.Ct. 618, 619, 166 U.S. 464, 468, 41 L.Ed. 1079. More recently the Court has held that the Fourteenth Amendment does not require a unanimous verdict in a state criminal case, Apodaca v. Oregon, 1972, 92 S.Ct. 1628, 406 U.S. 404, 32 L.Ed.2d 184, but that the Sixth Amendment requires a unanimous verdict in a federal prosecution. 92 S.Ct. at 1635, 406 U.S. at 366 (Powell, J.,

concurring). There are no recent opinions on the requirement of unanimity in civil cases, but if the issue should arise, it seems very likely that the Court would hold that unanimity is not required.

6. Galloway v. U. S., 1943, 63 S.Ct. 1077, 319 U.S. 372, 87 L.Ed. 1458; Blume, Origin and Development of the Directed Verdict, 1950, 48 Mich.L.Rev. 555; Chadbourn, Trial by Jury under the Seventh Amendment, 1943, 92 U.Pa.L.Rev. 92; McBaine, Trial Practice, Directed Verdicts, Federal Rule, 1943, 31 Calif.L.Rev. 454.

On the problems of a directed verdict generally, see the very helpful article, Cooper, Directions for Directed Verdicts: A Compass for Federal Courts, 1971, 55 Minn.L.Rev. 903.

7. Delaware, L. & W. R. Co. v. Converse, 1890, 11 S.Ct. 569, 139 U.S. 469, 35 L.Ed. 213; Chesapeake & O. R. Co. v. Martin, 1931, 51 S.Ct. 453, 283 U.S. 209, 75 L.Ed. 983; Service Auto Supply Co. of Puerto Rico v. Harte & Co., Inc., C.A.1st, 1976, 533 F.2d 23; Comment, Directing the Verdict in Favor of the Party with the Burden of Proof, 1972, 50 N.C.L.Rev. 843; 9 Wright & Miller, Civil § 2535.

8. Rule 50(a); 9 Wright & Miller, Civil § 2533, p. 583.

hold, contrary to the view of the trial court, that the evidence was sufficient to raise a jury issue.[9] The standard of sufficiency of the evidence is the same whether on a motion for directed verdict or a motion for judgment notwithstanding the verdict, and is discussed in the following section.

In the manner and method of instructing the jury, federal courts follow their own rules, regardless of state practice and legislation. Substantially the federal courts follow the common law practice inherited from the English courts, where it still prevails. The judge instructs the jury orally at the conclusion of the trial after the summing up arguments of counsel to the jury. Where a state-created right is to be enforced, of course the state law must be looked to for the substance of the instructions, but the form of instructions and the method of objecting to them are procedural questions as to which the federal court is not bound by state concepts.[10] Thus the federal judge retains the common law power to comment on the evidence, which is no longer available in many of the states.[11] He is not limited to summarizing the applicable rules of law, but may also summarize, discuss, and comment on the facts and the evidence, provided he indicates to the jury that they are not bound by his discussion of the evidence. The power to comment on the evidence has its own inherent limitations. The judge's discretion is not unbridled but is a judicial discretion to be exercised in conformity with the standards governing the judicial office. In commenting upon the testimony the judge may not assume the role of a witness. He may analyze and dissect the evidence, but may not destroy it or add to it.[12] He should not hesitate to clear away false issues and lead the jury to a proper understanding of the facts. His comments, however, should be fair and not arguments for either party. He should not assume the role of counsel or say anything that might prejudice either party.[13]

In another respect the federal practice on instructions differs from that common in the states. Rule 51 precludes a claim of error for giving an improper instruction, or failure to give a proper one,

9. Mattivi v. South African Marine Corp., "Huguenot", C.A.2d, 1980, 618 F.2d 163, 166 n. 2; Tackett v. Kidder, C.A.8th, 1980, 616 F.2d 1050, 1052–1053; and cases cited 9 Wright & Miller, Civil § 2533 n. 98.

10. Nudd v. Burrows, 1875, 91 U.S. 426, 23 L.Ed. 286; Barrett v. Virginian R. Co., 1919, 39 S.Ct. 540, 250 U.S. 473, 63 L.Ed. 1092; Barger v. Charles Machine Works, Inc., C.A.8th, 1981, 658 F.2d 582, 586; Batesole v. Stratford, C.A.6th, 1974, 505 F.2d 804, 807; 9 Wright & Miller, Civil § 2555, pp. 651–652.

11. Vicksburg & M. Ry. v. Putnam, 1886, 7 S.Ct. 1, 2, 118 U.S. 545, 553, 30 L.Ed. 257; Capital Traction Co. v. Hof, 1899, 19 S.Ct. 580, 174 U.S. 1, 43 L.Ed. 873; Evans v. Wright, C.A.4th, 1974, 505 F.2d 287; County of Todd, Minnesota v. Loegering, C.A.8th, 1961, 297 F.2d 470, 480–481; Chesnut, Instructions to the Jury, 1943, 3 F.R.D. 113, 117.

12. Quercia v. U. S., 1933, 53 S.Ct. 698, 289 U.S. 466, 77 L.Ed. 1321; McCullough v. Beech Aircraft Corp., C.A.5th, 1979, 587 F.2d 754.

13. Callen v. Pennsylvania R. Co., 1947, 68 S.Ct. 296, 332 U.S. 625, 92 L.Ed. 242; 9 Wright & Miller, Civil § 2557.

unless an objection has been taken, stating distinctly the grounds of the objection, before the jury retires.[14] Thus the judge is made aware of the supposed defect in the instructions while he still has an opportunity to correct it. This avoids the necessity of a retrial where by design or through oversight a party has remained silent despite error in the instructions.[15] There is a good deal of dicta from appellate courts that they have power to consider "plain error" in the instructions, even though the instructions were not objected to.[16] In recent years there has been an increased number of cases in which such power has been exercised, and a reversal ordered.[17] To allow reversal for plain error in the instructions is not only inconsistent with what Rule 51 says,[18] but burdens the appellate courts with having to review afterthought claims of error, which counsel parade forward under the banner of plain error. If there is to be an exception of this kind, it should be confined to the exceptional case where the error has seriously affected the fairness, integrity, or public reputation of judicial proceedings.[19]

In most federal cases, the traditional general verdict is used, by which the jury merely finds for one or the other of the parties. Two other procedures are made available by the rules. Under Rule 49(b) the court may, in its discretion, submit along with the general verdict one or more issues of fact upon which the verdict necessarily depends. This course requires the jury to give close attention to the

---

14. 9 Wright & Miller, Civil §§ 2553, 2554.

Even though it is reversible error in Colorado state courts not to instruct that plaintiff can recover nothing under the comparative negligence statute if he is found to be more than 50% negligent, it is not error to omit this instruction in federal court if plaintiff fails to object. Platis v. Stockwell, C.A.7th, 1980, 630 F.2d 1202.

15. Atlantic Coast Line R. Co. v. Bennett, C.A.4th, 1958, 251 F.2d 934; Paschal, A Plea for a Return to Rule 51 of the Federal Rules of Civil Procedure in North Carolina, 1957, 36 N.C.L.Rev. 1.

16. E.g., Shearson Hayden Stone, Inc. v. Leach, C.A.7th, 1978, 583 F.2d 367, 370; Batesole v. Stratford, C.A.6th, 1974, 505 F.2d 804, 808; and cases cited 9 Wright & Miller, Civil § 2558 n. 40.

17. Rodrigue v. Dixilyn Corp., C.A.5th, 1980, 620 F.2d 537, certiorari denied 1981, 101 S.Ct. 923, 449 U.S. 1113, 66 L.Ed.2d 842; MacEdward v. Northern Elec. Co., Ltd., C.A.2d, 1979, 595 F.2d 105; Pritchard v. Liggett & Myers Tobacco Co., C.A.3d, 1965, 350 F.2d 479,

certiorari denied 1966, 86 S.Ct. 549, 382 U.S. 987, 15 L.Ed.2d 475, amended C.A. 3d, 1966, 370 F.2d 95, certiorari denied 1967, 87 S.Ct. 1350, 386 U.S. 1009, 18 L.Ed.2d 436; and cases cited 9 Wright & Miller, Civil § 2558 n. 41.

18. Compare the third sentence of Civil Rule 51 with Criminal Rule 52(b), which specifically permits a consideration of "plain errors."

19. Liner v. J. B. Talley and Co., Inc., C.A.5th, 1980, 618 F.2d 327, 329, rehearing denied 623 F.2d 711; Cohen v. Franchard Corp., C.A.2d, 1973, 478 F.2d 115, 125, certiorari denied 94 S.Ct. 161, 414 U.S. 857, 38 L.Ed.2d 106; Sowizral v. Hughes, C.A.3d, 1964, 333 F.2d 829, 837; Figge Auto Co. v. Taylor, C.A.8th, 1964, 325 F.2d 899, 907; Troupe v. Chicago, Duluth & Georgia Bay Transit Co., C.A.2d, 1956, 234 F.2d 253, 260. See U. S. v. Atkinson, 1936, 56 S.Ct. 391, 392, 297 U.S. 157, 160, 80 L.Ed. 555.

Nor can a party claim that an instruction was plain error if the party invited the error by requesting that instruction. Herman v. Hess Oil Virgin Islands Corp., C.A.3d, 1975, 524 F.2d 767, 771.

more important issues and their answers serve to check the propriety of the general verdict.[20]

A more drastic, and controversial, procedure is made available by Rule 49(a). When this is used, the jury returns no general verdict at all but makes special written findings on each issue of fact. Special verdicts were known at common law, but rarely used, because of a rigid rule that the findings of the jury had to cover every material issue, at pain of judgment against the party carrying the burden of proof.[21] Rule 49(a), building on experience in North Carolina, Wisconsin, and Texas, avoids this particular pitfall by providing that a party waives his right to jury trial of any omitted issue unless he demands its submission before the jury retires. The judge may make a finding on such an omitted issue, or if he does not do so he will be deemed to have made a finding in accord with the judgment he orders entered.[22]

The use of special verdicts is intended to emphasize the facts, prevent the jury from acting on bias, and make the law more scientific.[23] Little is gained, however, by making the law more scientific if, in the process, it becomes harder to achieve substantial justice. Some of the most famous students of the judicial process have argued that one of the purposes of the jury system is to permit the jury to temper strict rules of law by the demands and necessities of substantial justice, thereby adding a much needed element of flexibility.[24] Those who share this conception of the role of the jury rightly fear that it will be limited or defeated by the special verdict practice, and thus oppose widespread use of special verdicts.

---

20. Guinn, The Jury System and Special Verdicts, 1970, 2 St. Mary's L.J. 175; Note, The Case for Interrogatories Accompanying a General Verdict, 1964, 52 Ky.L.J. 852; 9 Wright & Miller, Civil §§ 2511–2513.

The Fifth Circuit, however, believes that use of Rule 49(b) is "fraught with many pitfalls." Weymouth v. Colorado Interstate Gas Co., C.A.5th, 1966, 367 F.2d 84, 93 n. 1.

21. Graham v. Bayne, 1855, 18 How. 60, 15 L.Ed. 265; Stinson, Special Verdicts and Interrogatories, 1942, 7 Mo.L.Rev. 105, 142.

There is an excellent discussion of the background and application of the rule in Comment, Special Verdicts: Rule 49 of the Federal Rules of Civil Procedure, 1965, 74 Yale L.J. 483.

22. Hyde v. Land-of-Sky Regional Council, C.A.4th, 1978, 572 F.2d 988; John R. Lewis Inc. v. Newman, C.A.5th,

1971, 446 F.2d 800; 9 Wright & Miller, Civil § 2507.

23. Driver, The Special Verdict—Theory and Practice, 1951, 26 Wash.L.Rev. 21; Driver, A Consideration of the More Extended Use of the Special Verdict, 1950, 25 Wash.L.Rev. 43; Rossman, The Judge-Jury Relationship, 1943, 3 F.R.D. 98; Lipscomb, Special Verdicts Under The Federal Rules, 1940, 25 Wash.U.L.Q. 185. See 9 Wright & Miller, Civil § 2503.

24. Wigmore, A Program For the Trial of a Jury Trial, 1929, 12 J.Am.Jud.Soc. 166, 170; Pound, Law in Books and Law in Action, 1910, 44 Am.L.Rev. 12, 18–19; Wyzanski, A Trial Judge's Freedom and Responsibility, 1952, 65 Harv.L.Rev. 1281, 1286; Traynor, Fact Skepticism and the Judicial Process, 1958, 106 U.Pa.L.Rev. 635, 640; Holmes, Collected Legal Papers, 1920, pp. 237–238. See also Comment, 1965, 74 Yale L.J. 483, 495–497.

The use of special verdicts is always in the discretion of the trial judge.[25] The use he makes of this procedure is likely to depend on his view of its utility, and his conception of the role of the jury. At one extreme, the late Judge Jerome N. Frank, a brilliant and outspoken critic of the jury system, hailed the special verdict as "usually preferable to the opaque general verdict," and urged that the use of Rule 49 be made compulsory in all civil cases.[26] At the other extreme, those who look on the jury as a means by which the law is made to speak the voice of the man in the street urge that the special verdict should be used rarely.[27] Indeed Justices Hugo L. Black and William O. Douglas call Rule 49 "but another means utilized by courts to weaken the constitutional power of juries" and argue for its repeal.[28]

Many experienced judges take a middle position, holding that special verdicts may often be useful but pointing out that in some areas they cause more difficulties than they solve. Thus Judge Learned Hand, in a concurring opinion in the case in which Judge Frank called for compulsory use of Rule 49, was willing to say only that "it would be desirable to take special verdicts more often." [29] Judge Gunnar H. Nordbye, who had written sympathetically on Rule 49, agreed that "in may cases, it seems that little is to be gained from the use of the special verdict procedure," and pointed to the ordinary personal injury suit as a type of case in which special verdicts are not helpful.[30] Judge Charles E. Clark similarly observed that "this often-desirable practice should be resorted to with discrimination and foresight; it should never be used for mere cross-examination of the jury to create error for the record. Its purpose and best achievement is to enable errors already potential because of confusions of fact or law 'to be localized so that the sound portions of the verdict may be saved.' * * * It is hence best available, when, as the judge can foresee, the issues can be thus clearly and simply differentiated, to save an appeal on at least that portion which cannot be questioned; it is of

25. Bartak v. Bell-Galyardt & Wells, Inc., C.A.8th, 1980, 629 F.2d 523, 531; 9 Wright & Miller, Civil § 2505. But see Comment, note 22 above, at 508, 517–522, which is critical of the broad discretion given the trial courts.

26. Skidmore v. Baltimore & O. R. Co., C.A.2d, 1948, 167 F.2d 54, 67, certiorari denied 69 S.Ct. 34, 335 U.S. 816, 93 L.Ed. 371.

Chief Judge John R. Brown, though recognizing that there are pitfalls in Rule 49(a), has enthusiastically praised the rule and called for its more frequent use. Brown, Federal Special Verdicts: The Doubt Eliminator, 1967, 44 F.R.D. 245. See also Guidry v. Kem Mfg. Co., C.A.5th, 1979, 598 F.2d 402, 405–407, rehearing denied 604 F.2d 320, certiorari denied 1980, 100 S.Ct. 1318, 445

U.S. 929, 63 L.Ed.2d 763 (per Alvin B. Rubin, J.).

27. Thayer, A Preliminary Treatise on Evidence at the Common Law, 1898, p. 218; James, Sufficiency of the Evidence and Jury-Control Devices Available Before Verdict, 1961, 47 Va.L.Rev. 218, 246–248.

28. 1963, 83 S.Ct. 43, 45, 31 F.R.D. 617, 619 (dissenting from adoption of the 1963 amendments to the Civil Rules).

29. Skidmore v. Baltimore & O. R. Co., C.A.2d, 1948, 167 F.2d 54, 70, certiorari denied 69 S.Ct. 34, 335 U.S. 816, 93 L.Ed. 371.

30. Nordbye, Comments on Selected Provisions of the New Minnesota Rules, 1952, 36 Minn.L.Rev. 672, 683.

more doubtful value in a relatively simple factual situation   *   *   * where the details asked for may not be the whole story." [31]

§ 95.   Attacks on a Verdict [1]

The party dissatisfied with a jury verdict, as the losing party usually is, may attack it in either of two ways. He may assert that the proceeding was in some fashion so tainted with error that he should be given a new trial, or he may assert that his opponent's evidence failed to create an issue on which reasonable men could differ, and that as a matter of law the dissatisfied party should be awarded judgment notwithstanding the verdict. Though these two motions are very different in what they seek, and in the standard to be applied in passing on them, the losing party may, and usually does, move in the alternative for both kinds of relief.

Rule 59 does not list the grounds for which a new trial may be granted, but says only that this action may be taken for any of the reasons for which new trials have heretofore been granted in actions at law in federal courts. The usual grounds for a new trial are that the verdict is against the weight of the evidence, that the damages are excessive, or that, for other reasons, the trial was not fair, and the motion may also raise questions of law arising out of substantial errors in the admission or rejection of evidence or the giving or refusal of instructions.[2] As to most of these grounds there is little controversy, save for a quite surprising suggestion in one case that where the judge believes he has erred on a controlling question of law, he should nevertheless deny the motion for a new trial and leave the error to the appellate court to cure.[3]

The power to order a new trial because the judge deems the verdict to be against the weight of the evidence—or the very similar power to order a new trial because the damages are excessive—is more controversial. The power is supported by clear precedent at common law and has long been regarded as an integral part of trial by jury. In a famous passage, Justice Gray long ago said: " 'Trial by

---

31.   Morris v. Pennsylvania R. Co., C.A.2d, 1951, 187 F.2d 837, 841. See also Wright, The Use of Special Verdicts in Federal Court, 1965, 38 F.R.D. 199. The same philosophic difference that causes varying views on how frequently special verdicts should be used leads to differing opinions on whether the court should advise the jury of the legal effect of its answers. See Comment, Informing the Jury of the Legal Effect of Special Verdict Answers in Comparative Negligence Actions, 1981 Duke L.J. 824; Note, Informing the Jury of the Effect of Its Answers to Special Verdict Questions—The Minnesota Experience, 1974, 58 Minn.L.Rev. 903; 9 Wright & Miller, Civil § 2509.

[§ 95]

1.   9   Wright   &   Miller,   Civil §§ 2521–2532,   2537–2540;   11   id., §§ 2801–2821; James & Hazard, Civil Procedure, 2d ed. 1977, §§ 7.16–7.22; Cooper, Directions for Directed Verdicts: A Compass for Federal Courts, 1971, 55 Minn.L.Rev. 903.

2.   Montgomery Ward & Co. v. Duncan, 1940, 61 S.Ct. 189, 194, 311 U.S. 243, 251, 85 L.Ed. 147; 11 Wright & Miller, Civil §§ 2805–2810.

3.   Steele v. Wiedemann Machine Co., C.A.3d, 1960, 280 F.2d 380, discussed 11 Wright & Miller, Civil § 2803, pp. 33–35.

jury,' in the primary and usual sense of the term at the common law and in the American constitutions * * * is a trial by a jury of twelve men in the presence and under the superintendence of a judge empowered to instruct them on law and to advise them on the facts, and (except on acquittal of a criminal charge) to set aside their verdict if, in his opinion, it is against the law or the evidence." [4] It has long been understood that if the trial judge is not satisfied with the verdict of a jury, he has the right—and indeed the duty—to set the verdict aside and order a new trial.[5]

Despite the historical background, there is still some feeling that when the trial court grants a new trial because of dissatisfaction with the verdict it has, to an extent, substituted its judgment of the facts and the credibility of the witnesses for that of the jury, and that "such an action effects a denigration of the jury system and to the extent that new trials are granted the judge takes over, if he does not usurp, the prime function of the jury as the trier of the facts."[6] This uneasiness about such grants of a new trial is reflected in the varying views as to the standard a trial court should apply in passing on a motion seeking such relief. At one extreme is a decision saying that a new trial should not ordinarily be granted on the ground that the verdict was against the weight of the evidence if the evidence was conflicting and the jury might have found for either party.[7] If this is right, a new trial can never be granted on this ground, since unless the jury could reasonably have found for either party, the court should enter judgment as a matter of law. At the other extreme are cases that seem to give the trial court virtually unlimited discretion in granting or denying a new trial.[8] In the middle is a large group of cases that use varying adjectives, but agree in general that the trial court should not interfere with the verdict unless it is quite clear that the jury has reached a seriously erroneous result, and that it should

4. Capital Traction Co. v. Hof, 1899, 19 S.Ct. 580, 585, 174 U.S. 1, 13–14, 43 L.Ed. 873.

5. A leading case is Aetna Cas. & Sur. Co. v. Yeatts, C.C.A.4th, 1943, 122 F.2d 350, 352–354. See also Tidewater Oil Co. v. Waller, C.A.10th, 1962, 302 F.2d 638, 643; Riddell, New Trial at the Common Law, 1916, 26 Yale L.J. 49.

If the judge considers a verdict excessive he need not grant a new trial but may deny it on condition that plaintiff consent to a remittitur of the excess. Dimick v. Schiedt, 1935, 55 S.Ct. 296, 293 U.S. 474, 79 L.Ed. 603; 11 Wright & Miller, Civil § 2815. However the Dimick case held that the Seventh Amendment prohibits a conditional additur if the judge thinks the verdict inadequate. 11 Wright & Miller, Civil § 2816. Contra: McCoy v. Wean United, Inc., D.C.Tenn.1975, 67 F.R.D. 495.

The Supreme Court has resolved a conflict in the circuits by holding that a plaintiff who has consented to a remittitur under protest cannot obtain appellate review of the remittitur order. Donovan v. Penn Shipping Co., Inc., 1977, 97 S.Ct. 835, 429 U.S. 648, 51 L.Ed.2d 112. See generally Comment, Remittitur Practice in the Federal Courts, 1976, 76 Col.L.Rev. 299.

6. Lind v. Schenley Indus. Inc., C.A.3d, 1960, 278 F.2d 79, 90, certiorari denied 81 S.Ct. 58, 364 U.S. 835, 5 L.Ed.2d 60, criticized 1961 Duke L.J. 308.

7. Snyder v. Macaluso, D.C.Pa.1962, 204 F.Supp. 370, 373.

8. Murphy v. U. S. District Court, C.C.A.9th, 1944, 145 F.2d 1018, 1020; Grayson v. Deal, D.C.Ala.1949, 85 F.Supp. 431.

not set the verdict aside merely because the court, as finder of fact, would have come to a different conclusion.[9] It may be doubted whether there is any verbal formula that will be of much use to trial courts in passing on motions of this type. Necessarily all such formulations are couched in broad and general terms that furnish no unerring litmus for a particular case. On the one hand, the trial judge does not sit to approve miscarriages of justice. On the other hand, a decent respect for the collective wisdom of the jury, and for the function entrusted to it in our system, certainly suggests that in most cases the judge should accept the findings of the jury, regardless of his own doubts in the matter. Probably all that the judge can do is to balance these conflicting principles in the light of the facts of the particular case. If, having given full respect to the jury's findings, the judge on the entire evidence is left with the definite and firm conviction that a mistake has been committed, it is to be expected that he will grant a new trial.[10]

In theory the trial court could continue to set aside verdicts for the same party until the case finally went to a jury that agreed with the judge. This is almost entirely theoretical. When two juries have reached substantially the same result, the possibility of a miscarriage of justice is very slight, and thus "courts rarely grant a new trial after two verdicts upon the facts in favor of the same party." [11]

A motion for a new trial, stating grounds therefore, must be made within 10 days after the entry of judgment.[12] Though the tendency has been to apply this strictly, and to hold that neither waiver nor estoppel nor acquiescence by the opposing party can permit the court to act on an untimely motion,[13] a doctrine has developed allowing relief where a party has been misled by action of the court purporting to enlarge the time, even though the court lacks power to make such an order.[14] It is held also that the court cannot grant new trial on its

9. E.g., Conway v. Chemical Leaman Tank Lines, Inc., C.A.5th, 1980, 610 F.2d 360, 362–363; Firemen's Fund Ins. Co. v. Aalco Wrecking Co., Inc., C.A.8th, 1972, 466 F.2d 179, 187, certiorari denied 93 S.Ct. 1371, 410 U.S. 930, 35 L.Ed.2d 592; Werthan Bag Corp. v. Agnew, C.A.6th, 1953, 202 F.2d 119, 122; 11 Wright & Miller, Civil § 2806.

10. Kerry Coal Co. v. United Mine Workers of America, D.C.Pa.1980, 488 F.Supp. 1080, 1095, affirmed C.A.3d, 1981, 637 F.2d 957; Anglo-American General Agents v. Jackson Nat. Life Ins. Co., D.C.Cal.1979, 83 F.R.D. 41, 43; Klein v. Auto Owners Ins. Co., D.C.Minn.1965, 39 F.R.D. 24, 26.

11. Louisville & N. R. Co. v. Woodson, 1890, 10 S.Ct. 628, 631, 134 U.S. 614, 623, 33 L.Ed. 1032. The authorities in point are marshaled in Frank v. Atlantic Greyhound Corp., D.C.D.C.1959, 177 F.Supp. 922, affirmed C.A.1960, 280 F.2d 628, 108 U.S.App.D.C. 80.

12. Rules 59(b), (d); 11 Wright & Miller, Civil §§ 2812, 2813.

It is the time of service of the motion, not the time of filing, that is critical. Allen v. Ault, C.A.5th, 1977, 564 F.2d 1198.

13. Leishman v. Associated Wholesale Elec. Co., 1943, 63 S.Ct. 543, 317 U.S. 612, 87 L.Ed. 714; Hulson v. Atchison, T. & S. F. Ry. Co., C.A.7th, 1961, 289 F.2d 726, certiorari denied 82 S.Ct. 61, 368 U.S. 835, 7 L.Ed.2d 36; Nugent v. Yellow Cab Co., C.A.7th, 1961, 295 F.2d 794, certiorari denied 82 S.Ct. 844, 369 U.S. 828, 7 L.Ed.2d 793.

14. Thompson v. Immigration and Naturalization Service, 1964, 84 S.Ct. 397, 375 U.S. 384, 11 L.Ed.2d 404; Wolfsohn v. Hankin, 1964, 84 S.Ct. 699, 376

own initiative more than 10 days after judgment,[15] and, until 1966, it was the law that even if there was a timely motion the court could not grant the new trial on a ground not stated in the motion.[16] These restrictions caused the new trial rule to be buried under confusing technicalities. It is right that there should be only a brief period in which to attack a verdict. The difficulty came from confusion as to the specificity with which grounds for a new trial had to be stated. Where counsel has made a good faith attempt to state the grounds on which he is seeking a new trial, and has put the grounds as specifically as his trial notes or his memory of the supposed errors permits, there is no reason for the court to view the motion with the hostile eye of a Baron Parke in deciding what it is the moving party sought to allege. The motion should be given a broad construction, and reasonable specification of grounds held sufficient.[17] The problem is greatly eased by a 1966 amendment to Rule 59(d) providing that if there is a timely motion, the court may grant a new trial on a ground not stated in the motion.[18]

The law as to the reviewability of orders granting or denying a new trial is in a state of flux. Normally an order granting a new trial is not appealable,[19] except where the trial court has lacked power to grant the new trial.[20] The order is reviewable, however, and on

U.S. 203, 11 L.Ed.2d 636; Fairway Center Corp. v. U. I. P. Corp., C.A.8th, 1974, 491 F.2d 1092; Eady v. Foerder, C.A.7th, 1967, 381 F.2d 980.

15. Peterman v. Chicago, R. I. & P. R. Co., C.A.8th, 1974, 493 F.2d 88, certiorari denied 94 S.Ct. 3072, 417 U.S. 947, 41 L.Ed.2d 667; Tsai v. Rosenthal, C.A. 8th, 1961, 297 F.2d 614; Hunter v. Thomas, C.A.10th, 1949, 173 F.2d 810, noted 1949, 47 Mich.L.Rev. 1018; and cases cited note 16 below.

16. Russell v. Monongahela R. Co., C.A.2d, 1958, 262 F.2d 349; Freid v. McGrath, C.A.1942, 133 F.2d 350, 76 U.S.App.D.C. 388; Kanatser v. Chrysler Corp., C.A.10th, 1952, 199 F.2d 610, certiorari denied 73 S.Ct. 388, 344 U.S. 921, 97 L.Ed. 710; Marshall's U. S. Auto Supply, Inc. v. Cashman, C.C.A.10th, 1940, 111 F.2d 140, certiorari denied 61 S.Ct. 26, 311 U.S. 667, 85 L.Ed. 428; cf. Jackson v. Wilson Trucking Corp., C.A.1957, 243 F.2d 212, 100 U.S.App.D.C. 106, criticized 1957, 33 Notre Dame L.Rev. 126, 1958, 71 Harv. L.Rev. 552.

17. Tsai v. Rosenthal, C.A.8th, 1961, 297 F.2d 614, 619; General Motors Corp. v. Perry, C.A.7th, 1962, 303 F.2d 544.

18. Since the court can now grant a new trial on a ground not stated in the motion, it is difficult to understand recent

cases that have said that a new trial motion cannot be amended more than 10 days after judgment. Arkwright Mut. Ins. Co. v. Philadelphia Elec. Co., C.A.3d, 1970, 427 F.2d 1273, 1275; Conrad v. Graf Bros., Inc., C.A.1st, 1969, 412 F.2d 135, 137, certiorari denied 90 S.Ct. 215, 396 U.S. 902, 24 L.Ed.2d 178. "[I]t would be a strange rule which deprived a judge of power to do what was asked when made by the person most concerned, and yet allowed him to act without petition." U. S. v. Smith, 1947, 67 S.Ct. 1330, 1333, 331 U.S. 469, 474–475, 91 L.Ed. 1610.

19. Allied Chem. Corp. v. Daiflon, Inc., 1980, 101 S.Ct. 188, 190, 449 U.S. 33, 34, 66 L.Ed.2d 193. This case holds also that such an order will rarely, if ever, justify issuance of mandamus.

20. Phillips v. Negley, 1886, 6 S.Ct. 901, 117 U.S. 665, 29 L.Ed. 1013; Stradley v. Cortez, C.A.3d, 1975, 518 F.2d 488; Demeretz v. Daniels Motor Freight, Inc., C.A.3d, 1962, 307 F.2d 469; Jackson v. Wilson Trucking Corp., C.A. 1957, 243 F.2d 212, 100 U.S.App.D.C. 106; cf. U. S. v. Mayer, 1914, 35 S.Ct. 16, 235 U.S. 55, 59 L.Ed. 129; Kanatser v. Chrysler Corp., C.A.10th, 1952, 199 F.2d 610, certiorari denied 73 S.Ct. 388, 344 U.S. 921, 97 L.Ed. 710.

appeal from the final judgment following the second trial, the appellant may claim error in the grant of the new trial and seek reinstatement of the verdict at the first trial.[21] An order denying a new trial is technically not appealable. Appeal must be taken from the final judgment and on that appeal the erroneous denial of the new trial, if reviewable at all, may be considered.[22] However if the party mistakenly purports to appeal from denial of the new trial, the appeal will be considered as if from the final judgment.[23]

Where the grant or denial of a new trial is claimed as error in an appeal from an appealable judgment, it is reviewable, and the order below can be reversed, if the trial court has made an error of law. There is vast disagreement, however, as to whether the appellate court can review the trial court's exercise of discretion with regard to such factual issues as whether the verdict is excessive or against the weight of the evidence.[24]

As recently as 1945 the Third Circuit said: "The members of the Court think the verdict is too high. But they also feel very clear there is nothing the Court can do about it." [25] This was the accepted view, supported by famous opinions of Justices Holmes and Brandeis,[26] which have never been overruled. Yet by 1962, when the Eighth Circuit, which had been the last to cling to the accepted view, succumbed,[27] every one of the eleven courts of appeals had either held or said that it had power to do something about excessive verdicts.[28] Such power has been claimed far more often than it has been exercised, and the Supreme Court has made it clear that it is a power to be exercised, if at all, only in the most extreme case.[29]

Both on the issue of the size of the verdict and on the related issue whether the verdict is against the weight of the evidence a distinction should be recognized between an order denying a new trial and one granting a new trial. If a new trial is denied, the trial judge

21. Conway v. Chemical Leaman Tank Lines, Inc., C.A.5th, 1980, 610 F.2d 360; and cases cited 11 Wright & Miller, Civil § 2818 nn. 41, 42. For the interesting sequel to the Conway case, see C.A.5th, 1981, 644 F.2d 1059.

22. Mattox v. U. S., 1892, 13 S.Ct. 50, 146 U.S. 140, 36 L.Ed. 917; Montgomery Ward & Co. v. Duncan, 1940, 61 S.Ct. 189, 311 U.S. 243, 85 L.Ed. 147.

23. Foman v. Davis, 1962, 83 S.Ct. 227, 371 U.S. 178, 9 L.Ed.2d 222; Hennessy v. Schmidt, C.A.7th, 1978, 583 F.2d 302; and cases cited 11 Wright & Miller, Civil § 2818 n. 46.

24. Compare Note, Appealability of Rulings on Motion for New Trial in the Federal Courts, 1950, 98 U.Pa.L.Rev. 575, with Wright, The Doubtful Omniscience of Appellate Courts, 1957, 41

Minn.L.Rev. 751. See 11 Wright & Miller, Civil §§ 2819, 2820.

25. Scott v. Baltimore & O. R. Co., C.C.A.3d, 1945, 151 F.2d 61, 64.

26. Southern Ry. Carolina Div. v. Bennett, 1914, 34 S.Ct. 566, 233 U.S. 80, 58 L.Ed. 860; Fairmount Glass Works v. Cub Fork Coal Co., 1933, 53 S.Ct. 252, 287 U.S. 474, 77 L.Ed. 439.

27. Bankers Life & Cas. Co. v. Kirtley, C.A.8th, 1962, 307 F.2d 418. See Solomon Dehydrating Co. v. Guyton, C.A. 8th, 1961, 294 F.2d 439, 446–448.

28. See cases cited 11 Wright & Miller, Civil § 2820 n. 84.

29. Grunenthal v. Long Island R. Co., 1968, 89 S.Ct. 331, 393 U.S. 156, 21 L.Ed.2d 309; Neese v. Southern Ry. Co., 1955, 76 S.Ct. 131, 350 U.S. 77, 100 L.Ed. 60.

has accepted the verdict of the jury and there are the most compelling reasons for an appellate court not to interfere. But if a new trial is granted, the verdict of the jury has gone for naught and the appellate court can interfere more freely to resolve the difference between the judge and the jury.[30]

There is a developing body of dicta claiming a power to set aside the determination of the trial judge that a verdict is not against the weight of the evidence, and at least two cases in which an appellate court has actually reversed on this ground.[31] Again this is in the face of a long line of authority from the Supreme Court and elsewhere that the action of the trial judge on a motion for a new trial on the ground that the verdict was against the weight of the evidence "would not be subject to review." [32] The recent claims that there can be such review are probably also in the face of the Seventh Amendment, which prohibits re-examination of any "fact tried by jury * * * than according to the rules of the common law."

Various attempts have been made to reconcile appellate review of the weight of the evidence with the Seventh Amendment.[33] The most popular argument rests on the practice, at common law, by which the trial was conducted by a single judge at nisi prius, while motions for a new trial were heard by the court sitting en banc at Westminster. It is argued that this review by the court en banc, though it was not appellate review, is more like present American appellate practice than it is like our motion for a new trial, addressed to the single judge who presided at the trial.[34] The argument oversimplifies the historical data. An exhaustive examination of the early English cases has led one writer to conclude that there is not a single reported case where an English court at common law ever granted a new trial, as being against the weight of the evidence, unless the judge or judges who sat with the jury stated in open court, or certified, that

---

30. Conway v. Chemical Leaman Tank Lines Co., C.A.5th, 1980, 610 F.2d 360, 363; Borras v. Sea-Land Serv., Inc., C.A.1st, 1978, 586 F.2d 881, 887; Taylor v. Washington Terminal Co., C.A. 1969, 409 F.2d 145, 133 U.S.App.D.C. 110, certiorari denied 90 S.Ct. 93, 396 U.S. 835, 24 L.Ed.2d 85, on remand D.D.C.1970, 308 F.Supp. 1152. See Lind v. Schenley Indus., Inc., C.A.3d, 1960, 278 F.2d 79, 90, certiorari denied 81 S.Ct. 58, 364 U.S. 835, 5 L.Ed.2d 60; Note, Appellate Review in the Federal Courts of Orders Granting New Trial, 1961, 13 Stan.L.Rev. 383.

31. U. S. v. Simmons, C.A.5th, 1965, 346 F.2d 213; Georgia-Pacific Corp. v. U. S., C.A.5th, 1959, 264 F.2d 161.

The dicta asserting a power to reverse but not exercising it are collected in 11 Wright & Miller, Civil § 2819 n. 59.

32. U. S. v. Socony-Vacuum Oil Co., 1940, 60 S.Ct. 811, 856, 310 U.S. 150, 248, 84 L.Ed. 1129; U. S. v. Laub, 1838, 12 Pet. 1, 4, 9 L.Ed. 977; Southern Pac. Co. v. Guthrie, C.A.9th, 1951, 186 F.2d 926, 932–933; Portman v. American Home Products Corp., C.A.2d, 1953, 201 F.2d 847, 848; Snead v. New York Central R. Co., C.A.4th, 1954, 216 F.2d 169, 172.

33. 11 Wright & Miller, Civil § 2819, pp. 123–125.

34. Blume, Review of Facts in Jury Cases—The Seventh Amendment, 1936, 20 J.Am.Jud.Soc. 130, 131; Notes, 1951, 30 Tex.L.Rev. 242, 1950, 98 U.Pa.L.Rev. 575, 579; Corcoran v. City of Chicago, 1940, 27 N.E.2d 451, 373 Ill. 567; see Dagnello v. Long Island R. Co., C.A.2d, 1961, 289 F.2d 797, 802–805.

the verdict was against the evidence and that he was dissatisfied with the verdict.[35] Assuming the accuracy of the historical conclusion, the common law system was one in which the verdict could be set aside only if the judge who had presided at the trial and heard the witnesses deemed the verdict to be unjustified, and even then, only if he could persuade his brethren at Westminster to this view. Thus we have already liberalized the granting of new trials beyond that known at common law, since under the present American system, the trial judge can set aside the verdict on this ground without getting the approval of any other judge. To allow appellate review of his refusal to do so would mean that the verdict could be set aside solely by judges who were not present at the trial even though the trial judge, by denying the motion for a new trial, has found that the verdict is not contrary to the clear weight of the evidence. This would be a complete reversal of the common law practice, and does not seem consistent with the Seventh Amendment.

Though the power to order a new trial is based on a long historical foundation, the power to order judgment notwithstanding the verdict is not. In the much-criticized case of Slocum v. New York Life Insurance Co.,[36] the Supreme Court in 1913 held that entry of a judgment contrary to the verdict was a violation of the Seventh Amendment. That rule was qualified in 1935 in Baltimore & Carolina Line v. Redman.[37] In the Redman case the district court had expressly reserved its decision on motions for directed verdicts and had submitted the case to the jury subject to its opinion on the questions reserved, without objection by either party. The Supreme Court held that this practice was recognized at common law and that on appeal from a judgment entered on the verdict the circuit court of appeals might reverse the judgment and direct the entry of a judgment notwithstanding the verdict. This case was distinguished from the Slocum case on the ground that in Slocum the submission to the jury had been absolute and not subject to the court's reservation of decision of the question of law raised by the motion for directed verdict. Rule 50(b) has substituted a fiction for the reservation that was held to distinguish Slocum from Redman. Under that rule whenever a motion for a directed verdict made at the close of all the evidence is denied or for any reason is not granted, the court is deemed to have submitted the action to the jury subject to a later determination of the legal questions raised by the motion, and the court can subsequently order judgment notwithstanding the verdict, or can order judgment if the jury fails to agree.[38] The motion for a directed verdict is an absolute prerequisite to a subsequent grant of judgment n.o.v. If no motion for a directed verdict was made, neither the trial

35. Weisbrod, Limitations on Trial by Jury in Illinois, 1940, 19 Chi.-Kent L.Rev. 91, 92.

36. 1913, 33 S.Ct. 523, 228 U.S. 364, 57 L.Ed. 879.

37. 1935, 55 S.Ct. 890, 295 U.S. 654, 79 L.Ed. 1636.

38. 9 Wright & Miller, Civil § 2522.

nor the appellate court can order judgment n.o.v.[39] It is not necessary that the trial court expressly reserve decision on the motion for a directed verdict. It can do so if it wishes, but the fiction that it has reserved decision is held sufficient to permit the post-verdict motion even though the motion for a directed verdict was expressly denied.[40] A motion must be made after verdict, however, for judgment n.o.v. Even where the trial court had expressly reserved decision on the motion for a directed verdict, it was held that the appellate court was powerless to order judgment n.o.v. where the moving party had failed to make a specific motion for such judgment after the verdict.[41] Where proper motions have been made, the court is not required to order judgment n.o.v., even though the case is appropriate for such an order, but has discretion to order a new trial instead if it believes that this, rather than a final termination of the case, would better serve the ends of justice.[42]

The motion for judgment n.o.v., like the motion for directed verdict, raises only the legal question whether there was enough evidence to make an issue for the jury. It differs from the motion for a new trial, where the court has a discretion to set aside a verdict and grant a new trial even if the verdict is supported by substantial evidence. The motion for judgment n.o.v., on the other hand, must be denied if there is any substantial evidence supporting the verdict. The credibility of witnesses and weight of the evidence, proper considerations on a motion for a new trial, are not the concern of the court on a motion for a directed verdict or for judgment n.o.v. The evidence must be viewed in the light most favorable to the party against whom the motion is made, he must be given the benefit of all legitimate inferences that may be drawn in his favor from that evidence, and the motion must be denied if, so viewed, reasonable men might differ as to the conclusions of fact to be drawn.

The rules set out in the foregoing paragraph have been stated and restated, in many forms, by the courts.[43] Though the matter is not yet definitely settled, the better view is that they represent a federal

---

39. E.g., Martinez Moll v. Levitt & Sons of Puerto Rico, Inc., C.A.1st, 1978, 583 F.2d 565; Rawls v. Daughters of Charity of St. Vincent De Paul, Inc., C.A. 5th, 1974, 491 F.2d 141, certiorari denied 95 S.Ct. 513, 419 U.S. 1032, 42 L.Ed.2d 307; and cases cited 9 Wright & Miller, Civil § 2537 nn. 31–33.

40. E.g., Lowden v. Denton, C.C.A.8th, 1940, certiorari denied 60 S.Ct. 1100, 310 U.S. 652, 84 L.Ed. 1417.

41. Johnson v. New York, N. H. & H. R. Co., 1952, 73 S.Ct. 125, 344 U.S. 48, 97 L.Ed. 77. Accord: Cone v. West Virginia Pulp & Paper Co., 1947, 67 S.Ct. 752, 330 U.S. 212, 91 L.Ed. 849; Globe Liquor Co. v. San Roman, 1948, 68 S.Ct. 246, 332 U.S. 571, 92 L.Ed. 177.

42. Cone v. West Virginia Pulp & Paper Co., 1947, 67 S.Ct. 752, 755, 330 U.S. 212, 215, 91 L.Ed. 849; cf. Iacurci v. Lummus Co., 1967, 87 S.Ct. 1423, 387 U.S. 86, 18 L.Ed.2d 581. See 9 Wright & Miller, Civil § 2539.

43. 9 Wright & Miller, Civil § 2524.
As good a statement of the test as any is in Simblest v. Maynard, C.A.2d, 1970, 427 F.2d 1, 4: "Simply stated, it is whether the evidence is such that, without weighing the credibility of the witnesses or otherwise considering the weight of the evidence, there can be but one conclusion as to the verdict that reasonable men could have reached."

test of sufficiency of evidence that must be followed even if state law sets up some other standard.[44] No one disagrees with the rules but only as to their application in a particular case. There are three questions about the rules, however, that are not yet resolved.

It is said that a party is entitled to the benefit of all "legitimate" inferences that may be drawn in his favor from the evidence, and that even if the facts are undisputed, the case must go to the jury if conflicting inferences may legitimately be drawn from the facts. Unfortunately there is no sure test to distinguish between the legitimate inference, to which the party opposing the motion is entitled, and the unreasonable inference, to which he is not. Courts endeavor to state a test for distinguishing the two in terms of probability. They say that the inference is legitimate only where the evidence offered makes the existence of the fact to be inferred more probable than the nonexistence of the fact, and they warn that any lesser test would permit the jury to rest its verdict on speculation and conjecture.[45] Any attempt to suggest mathematical precision in the weighing of probabilities is spurious; rarely does the court have any way of knowing what the mathematical probabilities are.[46] And it may be that the purported test overstates the quantum of proof required, as one court has suggested.[47] The Supreme Court itself has said that "whenever facts are in dispute or the evidence is such that fair-minded men may draw different inferences, a measure of speculation and conjecture is required on the part of those whose duty it is to settle the dispute by choosing what seems to them to be the most reasonable inference." [48]

In determining whether there is a submissible issue, it is not settled whether the court is to look only to the evidence favorable to the party against whom the motion is made, or whether it is to consider all the evidence. A party may have produced weak evidence that, in itself, would be sufficient for a finding in his favor, but that is overwhelmed by his opponent's evidence to the contrary. The earlier cases reflect a practice of examining all the evidence in order to affirm direction of a verdict or grant of judgment n.o.v. in these circumstances,[49] and this practice has scholarly support.[50] The Supreme

44. See § 92 above at notes 15–21.

45. Haldeman v. Bell Tel. Co. of Pennsylvania, C.A.3d, 1967, 387 F.2d 557; Sherman v. Lawless, C.A.8th, 1962, 298 F.2d 899; Commercial Standard Ins. Co. v. Feaster, C.A.10th, 1958, 259 F.2d 210; Ford Motor Co. v. McDavid, C.A. 4th, 1958, 259 F.2d 261, certiorari denied 79 S.Ct. 234, 358 U.S. 908, 3 L.Ed. 2d 229; and cases cited 9 Wright & Miller, Civil § 2528 n. 19.

46. James, Sufficiency of the Evidence and Jury-Control Devices Available Before Verdict, 1961, 47 Va.L.Rev. 218, 221–222.

47. Gutierrez v. Public Serv. Interstate Transp. Co., C.A.2d, 1948, 168 F.2d 678, 680.

48. Lavender v. Kurn, 1946, 66 S.Ct. 740, 744, 327 U.S. 645, 653, 90 L.Ed. 916. See also Cooper, note 1 above, at 955–958; 9 Wright & Miller, Civil § 2528, pp. 565–569.

49. Pennsylvania R. Co. v. Chamberlain, 1933, 53 S.Ct. 391, 288 U.S. 333, 77 L.Ed. 819; Southern Ry. Co. v. Walters, 1931, 52 S.Ct. 58, 284 U.S. 190, 76 L.Ed. 239.

50. Blume, Origin and Development of the Directed Verdict, 1950, 48 Mich.L.

Court has apparently adopted a different rule, though without expressly rejecting the older cases. Thus in one case it noted that there was evidence from which a jury could have reached a contrary conclusion, but said: "There was evidence from which a jury could reach the conclusion that petitioner was totally and permanently disabled. That was enough." [51] In a later case the Court said: "it is the established rule that in passing upon whether there is sufficient evidence to submit an issue to the jury we need look only to the evidence and reasonable inferences which tend to support the case of a litigant against whom a peremptory instruction has been given." [52] Despite these decisions from the Supreme Court, many lower courts continue to follow the older practice.[53]

The correct rule seems to be that the court may consider all of the evidence favorable to the position of the party opposing the motion as well as any unfavorable evidence that the jury is required to believe. Thus it may take into account evidence supporting the moving party that is uncontradicted and unimpeached, at least to the extent that this evidence comes from disinterested witnesses.[54]

Finally, consideration must be given to the well-known, and highly controversial, series of decisions in which the Supreme Court has reversed judgments of lower courts that have taken cases away from the jury in actions arising under the Federal Employers' Liability Act and the Jones Act. Although these decisions do not clearly articulate the test of sufficiency of the evidence which the Court is applying, it appears that the Court is holding that so long as there is evidence from which an inference might rationally be drawn, whether as to how the accident happened or whether defendant's conduct was negligent, it is for the jury to accept or reject that inference, even though the inference may be quite an improbable one and some other inference highly probable.[55] It is of much practical importance to know

Rev. 555, 576–581; Comment, 1949, 47 Mich.L.Rev. 974. But see Comment, 1964, 42 Texas L.Rev. 1053, 1060–1061.

51. Berry v. U. S., 1941, 61 S.Ct. 637, 640, 312 U.S. 450, 456, 85 L.Ed. 945.

52. Wilkerson v. McCarthy, 1949, 69 S.Ct. 413, 415, 336 U.S. 53, 57, 93 L.Ed. 497.

53. Oldenburg v. Clark, C.A.10th, 1974, 489 F.2d 839, 841; Boeing Co. v. Shipman, C.A.5th, 1969, 411 F.2d 365, 375 n. 16; Stief v. J. A. Sexauer Mfg. Co., C.A.2d, 1967, 380 F.2d 453, 455, certiorari denied 88 S.Ct. 220, 389 U.S. 897, 19 L.Ed.2d 216; Smith v. U. S., C.A.9th, 1964, 337 F.2d 237, 238; Dehydrating Process Co. v. A. O. Smith Corp., C.A.1st, 1961, 292 F.2d 653, 656 n. 6, certiorari denied 82 S.Ct. 368, 368 U.S. 931, 7 L.Ed.2d 194; Hanson v. Ford Motor Co., C.A.8th, 1960, 278

F.2d 586, 590; and cases cited 9 Wright & Miller, Civil § 2529 n. 49.

Contra: Simpson v. Skelly Oil Co., C.A. 8th, 1967, 371 F.2d 563, 567; Lohr v. Tittle, C.A.10th, 1960, 275 F.2d 662, 664 n. 1; Weir v. Chicago Plastering Institute, C.A.7th, 1959, 272 F.2d 883, 885; and cases cited 9 Wright & Miller, Civil § 2529 n. 48.

54. Simblest v. Maynard, C.A.2d, 1970, 427 F.2d 1, 5; Negron v. Ward, D.C. N.Y.1978, 458 F.Supp. 748, 756; Cooper, note 1 above, at 948–953; 9 Wright & Miller, Civil § 2529.

55. E.g., Lavender v. Kurn, 66 S.Ct. 740, 743–744, 327 U.S. 645, 652–653, 90 L.Ed. 916; Tennant v. Peoria & P. U. Ry. Co., 1944, 64 S.Ct. 409, 412, 321 U.S. 29, 35, 88 L.Ed. 520; Rogers v. Missouri Pac. R. Co., 1957, 77 S.Ct. 443, 448, 352 U.S. 500, 506, 1 L.Ed.2d

whether these decisions are confined to the particular statutory actions in which they have been handed down, or whether they represent a construction of the Seventh Amendment that is controlling in all jury cases in federal courts. Arguments can be made that these decisions are to be confined to FELA and Jones Act litigation, and many lower courts and commentators have so understood them.[56] The most powerful argument to the contrary is that the opinions announcing the rule as to sufficiency of the evidence in these cases refer to "the jury's historic function"[57] and to the Seventh Amendment,[58] and the Supreme Court itself has cited these cases as representing the "federal test of sufficiency of the evidence to support a jury verdict where federal jurisdiction is rested on diversity of citizenship."[59] For these reasons other courts and commentators have held the test laid down in the FELA cases applicable in all cases.[60]

Rule 50(b) permits a party to move in the alternative for judgment n.o.v. or for a new trial. In such a case if the trial court grants the motion for judgment n.o.v. but fails to rule upon the alternative motion for a new trial, and the appellate court finds that the entry of judgment n.o.v. was erroneous, it is necessary to remand the case to the trial court for a decision on the motion for a new trial. In Mont-

493. See 9 Wright & Miller, Civil § 2526.

For a suggestion that the Court is taking a more conservative approach today in FELA cases, see Note, Federal Employers' Liability Act: Apostasy of Sufficiency of Evidence Policy, 1971, 42 Miss.L.J. 418.

56. E.g., Missouri-K.-T. Ry. v. Hearson, C.A.10th, 1970, 422 F.2d 1037, 1040; Boeing Co. v. Shipman, C.A.5th, 1969, 411 F.2d 365, 370–373; Dehydrating Process Co. v. A. O. Smith Corp., C.A. 1st, 1961, 292 F.2d 653, 656 n. 6, certiorari denied 82 S.Ct. 368, 368 U.S. 931, 7 L.Ed.2d 194; Zegan v. Central R. Co. of N. J., C.A.3d, 1959, 266 F.2d 101, 104; Gibson v. Elgin, J. & E. R. Co., C.A.7th, 1957, 246 F.2d 834, 840, certiorari denied 78 S.Ct. 270, 355 U.S. 897, 2 L.Ed.2d 193; Cahill v. New York, N. H. & H. R. Co., C.A.2d, 1955, 224 F.2d 637, 640 (Frank, J., dissenting); Cooper, note 1 above, at 924–927; Note, 58 Col.L.Rev. 517, 523 n. 47.

57. Lavender v. Kurn, 1947, 66 S.Ct. 740, 744, 327 U.S. 645, 652, 90 L.Ed. 916. See also Davis v. Virginian R. Co., 1960, 80 S.Ct. 387, 389, 361 U.S. 354, 356–357, 4 L.Ed.2d 366.

58. Atlantic and Gulf Stevedores, Inc. v. Ellerman Lines, Ltd., 1962, 82 S.Ct. 780, 784, 369 U.S. 355, 360, 7 L.Ed.2d

798; Harris v. Pennsylvania R. Co., 1959, 80 S.Ct. 22, 24, 361 U.S. 15, 17, 4 L.Ed.2d 1 (Douglas, J., concurring). See also Rogers v. Missouri Pac. R. Co., 1957, 77 S.Ct. 443, 449–450 n. 18, 352 U.S. 500, 508 n. 18, 1 L.Ed.2d 493.

59. Dick v. New York Life Ins. Co., 1959, 79 S.Ct. 921, 926 n. 8, 359 U.S. 437, 445 n. 8, 3 L.Ed.2d 935; Continental Ore Co. v. Union Carbide & Carbon Corp., 1962, 82 S.Ct. 1404, 1409 n. 6, 370 U.S. 690, 696 n. 6, 8 L.Ed.2d 777.

60. Wratchford v. S. J. Groves & Sons Co., C.A.4th, 1969, 405 F.2d 1061, 1066 n. 14; Lones v. Detroit, Toledo & Ironton R. Co., C.A.6th, 1968, 398 F.2d 914, 919; see Bruce Lincoln-Mercury, Inc. v. Universal C. I. T. Credit Corp., C.A. 3d, 1963, 325 F.2d 2, 22; Anglen v. Braniff Airways, C.A.8th, 1956, 237 F.2d 736, 740; Radio v. Chernack, D.C. R.I.1963, 217 F.Supp. 33, 35.

See also Green, Jury Trial and Mr. Justice Black, 1956, 65 Yale L.J. 482, 490 n. 17; Green, Protection of Jury Trial in Diversity Cases Against State Invasions, 1957, 35 Tex.L.Rev. 768; DeParcq, The Supreme Court and the Federal Employers' Liability Act, 1958–1959 Term, 44 Minn.L.Rev. 707, 716–717; Comment, 1964, 42 Texas L.Rev. 1053, 1064–1071.

gomery Ward & Co. v. Duncan [61] the Supreme Court pointed out this difficulty and held that in such a case the trial court should rule upon both motions, making its grant or denial of a new trial conditional upon reversal of its decision on the motion for judgment n.o.v. Though this practice is desirable in avoiding an unnecessary remand, it is extremely unrealistic in asking the trial judge to make a conditional ruling on the assumption that, for reasons which he cannot know, his ruling on the motion for judgment is held to be erroneous.[62] Further, with all the possibilities present when the court may either grant or deny either or both branches of the alternative motion, the practice is necessarily very complicated, and has often been misunderstood by courts and counsel.[63] In 1963 subdivisions (c) and (d) were added by amendment to Rule 50, spelling out the procedure to be followed for conditional rulings on the alternative motion. The amendment may lessen the confusion in applying this procedure, but it cannot lessen the unreality of it. And Supreme Court decisions construing the 1963 additions [64] have received sharp criticism from the commentators, who assert that they have created new uncertainty about the procedure and that they have lessened the protection formerly provided for the party in whose favor the verdict had run.[65]

§ 96. Trial to the Court [1]

Fewer than 10% of the civil actions commenced in federal court are actually disposed of by trial. Of those that do go to trial, the majority are tried to a judge, rather than to a jury,[2] either because no right of jury trial exists or because the parties have waived such right. Though trial to the court is statistically the more significant method of disposing of cases, it raises many fewer procedural problems than does trial to a jury.

Consider, for example, the question of evidence. The rules of evidence are, in large part, the product of the jury system. They apply,

61. 1940, 61 S.Ct. 189, 195, 311 U.S. 243, 253, 85 L.Ed. 147.

62. See Momand v. Universal Film Exchange, Inc., D.C.Mass.1947, 72 F.Supp. 469, 483.

63. See 9 Wright & Miller, Civil §§ 2539, 2540.

64. Neely v. Martin K. Eby Constr. Co., 1967, 87 S.Ct. 1072, 386 U.S. 317, 18 L.Ed.2d 75; Iacurci v. Lummus Co., 1967, 87 S.Ct. 1423, 387 U.S. 86, 18 L.Ed.2d 581.

65. Note, Post-Verdict Motions Under Rule 50: Protecting the Verdict Winners, 1968, 53 Minn.L.Rev. 358; Note, Disposition of Cases by the Court of Appeals after Granting Judgment Notwithstanding the Verdict, 1968, 47 N.C.L.Rev. 162.

These decisions are defended in Louis, Post-Verdict Rulings on the Sufficiency of the Evidence: Neely v. Martin K. Eby Construction Co. Revisited, 1975 Wis.L.Rev. 503.

[§ 96]

1. 9 Wright & Miller, Civil §§ 2371, 2412, 2571–2591.

2. In the fiscal year 1981, of 172,942 civil actions terminated in district courts, only 11,416 were disposed of by trial. Of these, 6,714, or 59%, were tried to a judge, while 4,702 were tried to a jury. Ann.Rep. of the Director of the Administrative Office of the U. S. Courts, 1981, p. 381.

nevertheless, in nonjury actions as well.[3] Rules of privilege, which represent an extrinsic policy determination that protection of a confidential relation is more important than obtaining all relevant evidence in the particular case, are applied in nonjury cases with as much vigor as in jury cases. The importance of such other rules as the hearsay rule, the misnamed "best evidence" rule, and the rule against opinions, is minimized in nonjury cases, though the rules remain applicable. The erroneous admission of evidence will not often be the basis of reversal, since the appellate courts indulge the gracious presumption that the trial judge relied only on the evidence that was properly admitted in making his findings.[4] Thus in a nonjury case the court should be slow to keep out evidence challenged under one of the exclusionary rules. The attitude now governing has been strongly stated by the Eighth Circuit: "In the trial of a nonjury case, it is virtually impossible for a trial court to commit reversible error by receiving incompetent evidence, whether objected to or not. * * * On the other hand, a trial judge, who, in the trial of a nonjury case, attempts to make strict rulings on the admissibility of evidence, can easily get his decision reversed by excluding evidence which is objected to but which, on review, the appellate court believes should have been admitted." [5]

In a nonjury case a motion for dismissal for insufficiency of the evidence, under Rule 41(b), takes the place of the motion for a directed verdict in a jury case.[6] There is little point in such a motion at the close of all the evidence, since at that stage the judge will determine the facts in any event, and the significance of the motion is that it may be made at the close of the plaintiff's case. In a jury case, when a motion for a directed verdict is made, the judge is required to consider the evidence in the light most favorable to the party against whom the motion is directed, in order to prevent any infringement on the function of the jury.[7] No such limitation applies in a nonjury case. In 1948, resolving a conflict that had developed in the cases, Rule 41(b) was amended to provide that on a motion to dismiss at the close of plaintiff's evidence in a nonjury case, the court may weigh the evidence, and may give judgment against plaintiff or may decline to render any judgment until the close of all the evidence.[8] This provision has come in for severe attack from a noted scholar, who con-

3. On evidence in federal court, see § 93 above.

4. See New York Life Ins. Co. v. Harrington, C.A.9th, 1962, 299 F.2d 803, 806; and cases cited 9 Wright & Miller, Civil § 2412 n. 89. See also Davis, Hearsay in Nonjury Cases, 1970, 83 Harv.L.Rev. 1362.

5. Builders Steel Co. v. C. I. R., C.A.8th, 1950, 179 F.2d 377, 379. See also SEC v. Glass Marine Indus. Inc., D.C.Del. 1961, 194 F.Supp. 879, 884; cf. Samuel H. Moss, Inc. v. FTC, C.C.A.2d, 1945,

148 F.2d 378, 380. See generally Davis, An Approach to Rules of Evidence for Nonjury Cases, 1964, 50 A.B.A.J. 723. A contrary view is stated in Note, Improper Evidence in Nonjury Trials: Basis for Reversal, 1965, 79 Harv.L.Rev. 407.

6. 9 Wright & Miller, Civil § 2371.

7. See § 95 above.

8. Weissinger v. U. S., C.A.5th, 1970, 423 F.2d 795; and cases cited 9 Wright & Miller, Civil § 2371 nn. 55–60.

tends that it is artificial to speak of weighing the evidence when nothing has been heard from the other side against which plaintiff's evidence can be weighed, and argues that where plaintiff has made out a prima facie case, the court should hear all the evidence from both parties, and thus have the whole controversy before it, prior to determining which side should win.[9]

When the judge decides the case, either on a motion for dismissal or at the close of all the evidence, he must make findings of fact and state separately his conclusions of law, though these may be contained in an opinion if one is written.[10] Such findings are intended to aid the appellate court by affording it a clear understanding of the basis of the trial court's decision, and to make definite what was decided for purposes of res judicata and estoppel. Finally, the requirement of findings should evoke care on the part of the trial judge in ascertaining the facts.[11] Some judges prepare their own findings, while others ask winning counsel to submit proposed findings for the court to adopt.[12] Though it is settled that findings do not carry less weight on appeal because they were prepared in the first instance by counsel rather than the court,[13] findings that represent the independent study of the district judge are more helpful to the appellate court.[14]

A motion to amend the findings is authorized by Rule 52(b) and may be joined with a motion for a new trial. Though this bears a surface similarity to the motion for new trial in a jury case, in practice it is not much used and has a different function. Such a motion is not required as a prerequisite to appeal.[15] In a jury case, a new trial will be before a different, and, it is hoped, more favorable, jury, while in the nonjury case the motion to amend or for a new trial goes to the same judge who has already decided the case. Thus the primary purpose of Rule 52(b) is to enable the appellate court to obtain a

9. Steffen, The Prima Facie Case in Non-Jury Trials, 1959, 27 U.Chi.L.Rev. 94. This view was accepted in substance, in application of a similar state rule in Rogge v. Weaver, Alaska 1962, 368 P.2d 810, 813. But see Mackey-Woodard, Inc. v. Citizens State Bank, 1966, 419 P.2d 847, 860, 197 Kan. 536.

10. Rule 52(a); 9 Wright & Miller, Civil §§ 2571–2582.

11. Lemelson v. Kellogg Co., C.A.2d, 1971, 440 F.2d 986, 988; Featherstone v. Barash, C.A.10th, 1965, 345 F.2d 246, 249; Nordbye, Improvements in Statement of Findings of Fact and Conclusions of Law, 1940, 1 F.R.D. 25.

12. 9 Wright & Miller, Civil § 2578.

13. U. S. v. Crescent Amusement Co., 1944, 65 S.Ct. 254, 260, 323 U.S. 173, 184–185, 89 L.Ed. 160; Schwerman Trucking Co. v. Gartland S. S. Co., C.A.

7th, 1974, 496 F.2d 466. But see Roberts v. Ross, C.A.3d, 1965, 344 F.2d 747, 752, noted 1966, 51 Corn.L.Q. 567.

14. U. S. v. El Paso Natural Gas Co., 1964, 84 S.Ct. 1044, 1047, 376 U.S. 651, 656–657, 12 L.Ed.2d 12; Kelson v. U. S., C.A.10th, 1974, 503 F.2d 1291, 1294–1295; Roberts v. Ross, C.A.3d, 1965, 344 F.2d 747, 752, noted 1966, 51 Corn.L.Q. 567; Lorenz v. General Steel Products Co., C.A.5th, 1964, 337 F.2d 726, 727 n. 3; U. S. v. Forness, C.C.A. 2d, 1942, 125 F.2d 928, 942, certiorari denied 62 S.Ct. 1293, 316 U.S. 694, 86 L.Ed. 1764; and cases cited 9 Wright & Miller, Civil § 2577 nn. 18–20.

15. E.g., Twentieth Century Fox Film Corp. v. Goldwyn, C.A.9th, 1964, 328 F.2d 190, certiorari denied 85 S.Ct. 143, 379 U.S. 880, 13 L.Ed.2d 87; 9 Wright & Miller, Civil § 2582.

correct understanding of the factual issues determined by the trial court.[16]

Probably no provision of the federal rules has been quoted and cited more often than the famous sentence in Rule 52(a) that says: "Findings of fact shall not be set aside unless clearly erroneous, and due regard shall be given to the opportunity of the trial court to judge of the credibility of the witnesses." This provision represents a statement of what was considered to be the federal equity practice in the years just prior to merger of law and equity. Before adoption of the rules, in a legal action in which jury trial was waived, the findings of fact of the court were not reviewable,[17] just as the fact determination of a jury could not be reviewed. Equity practice had departed from the broad de novo review of ancient chancery, and the rule had developed that the findings of the trial court had great weight with the appellate court, though they were not conclusive.[18] It was thought desirable to have a single standard of review apply to all nonjury cases, whether historically legal or equitable, and the broader equity review was adopted.[19] Thus findings of fact by the trial court are not conclusive on appeal, but there is a heavy burden on the party who seeks to overturn them.[20] In the colorful phrase of one court, the findings "come here well armed with the buckler and shield" of Rule 52(a).[21] The rule is usually cited to justify refusal to interfere with the fact findings made in the trial court. It is settled that a finding is clearly erroneous, within the meaning of Rule 52(a), when "although there is evidence to support it, the reviewing court on the entire is left with the definite and firm conviction that a mistake has been committed." [22]

On one question of construction of Rule 52(a), the authorities are indescribably confused. Even within a single circuit, decisions vacillate inexplicably from one position to another. This question is whether the deference that must normally be paid to the findings by the trial court applies where the finding rests on an inference drawn from documentary evidence or undisputed facts.[23]

Where the trial judge has seen and heard the witnesses, he has the benefit, which the appellate court does not, of being able to observe their demeanor, and the rule recognizes this by adding to the "clearly erroneous" test the statement "and due regard shall be giv-

16. Heikkila v. Barber, D.C.Cal.1958, 164 F.Supp. 587; Nordbye, Comments on Selected Provisions of the New Minnesota Rules, 1952, 36 Minn.L.Rev. 672, 690.

17. Dooley v. Pease, 1900, 21 S.Ct. 329, 331, 180 U.S. 126, 131, 45 L.Ed. 457.

18. U. S. v. United States Gypsum Co., 1948, 68 S.Ct. 525, 542, 333 U.S. 364, 395, 92 L.Ed. 746.

19. 9 Wright & Miller, Civil § 2571.

20. 9 Wright & Miller, Civil § 2585.

21. Horton v. U. S. Steel Corp., C.A.5th, 1961, 286 F.2d 710, 713.

22. U. S. v. United States Gypsum Co., 1948, 68 S.Ct. 525, 542, 333 U.S. 364, 395, 92 L.Ed. 746, rehearing denied 68 S.Ct. 788, 333 U.S. 869, 92 L.Ed. 1147. See also Inwood Laboratories, Inc. v. Ives Laboratories, Inc., 1982, 102 S.Ct. 2182, 2189, ___ U.S. ___, ___, 72 L.Ed. 2d 606.

23. 9 Wright & Miller, Civil § 2587.

en to the opportunity of the trial court to judge of the credibility of the witnesses." Some courts have reasoned from this that where the trial court did not see the witnesses the appellate court can more readily hold the trial court's finding to be clearly erroneous.[24] Other decisions have gone on to reason from this gloss, rather than from the rule itself, and to say that the appellate court is not bound at all, and that review is de novo with no presumption in favor of the trial court's findings, where the evidence below was not oral.[25] This process was carried to its ultimate in an opinion by the late Judge Jerome N. Frank in which he set out a number of narrowly-defined classes, turning on the kind of case and the proportion of testimony that was oral, and asserted that the freedom of review is dependent upon the class in which a particular case falls.[26]

Though the cases pointing to broader review where the finding is not based on conflicting oral testimony have been widely followed, there are at least as many cases, often coming from the same courts, that apply a contrary rule. The most fully considered such decision is from the Ninth Circuit, which, in a forthright and scholarly opinion, holds that both history and the explicit language of Rule 52(a) show that the "clearly erroneous" test is applicable even though the trial judge has not had the opportunity to judge the credibility of the witnesses.[27] Despite the confusion in the case law, it seems clear that this is the correct construction of the rule. No matter what the nature of the evidence or the basis of the finding, an appellate court may set it aside only where it is convinced that the finding is clearly erroneous, and it must be especially reluctant so to regard the finding below where it rested, in part, on the opportunity of the trial judge to observe the demeanor of the witnesses. Such a construction is required by the language of the rule itself, by the Committee Notes to the rule,[28] and by the clear and consistent rulings to this effect of the

24. Toms v. Country Quality Meats, Inc., C.A.5th, 1980, 610 F.2d 313, 315 n. 5; Emmco Ins. Co. v. Wallenius Caribbean Line, S.A., C.A.5th, 1974, 492 F.2d 508, 512; Best Medium Pub. Co. v. National Insider, Inc., C.A.7th, 1967, 385 F.2d 384, 386, certiorari denied 88 S.Ct. 1052, 390 U.S. 955, 19 L.Ed.2d 1150; Caradelis v. Refineria Panama, S.A., C.A.5th, 1967, 384 F.2d 589, 593–594; Hicks v. U. S., C.A.4th, 1966, 368 F.2d 626, 630–631.

25. E.g., Swanson v. Baker Indus., Inc., C.A.8th, 1980, 615 F.2d 479, 483; U. S. ex rel. Lasky v. LaVallee, C.A.2d, 1973, 472 F.2d 960, 963; Stokes v. U. S., C.C.A.2d, 1944, 144 F.2d 82, 85; and cases cited 9 Wright & Miller, Civil § 2587 n. 30.

26. Orvis v. Higgins, C.A.2d 1950, 180 F.2d 537, 539–540, certiorari denied 71

S.Ct. 37, 340 U.S. 810, 95 L.Ed. 595, criticized 1950, 2 Stan.L.Rev. 784.

27. Lundgren v. Freeman, C.A.9th, 1962, 307 F.2d 104, 113–115, noted 1963, 41 Texas L.Rev. 935. Another comprehensive and thoughtful discussion of the question, reaching the same result, is in Alaska Foods, Inc. v. American Mfrs. Mut. Ins. Co., Alaska 1971, 482 P.2d 842, 843–848. See also New York v. Nuclear Regulatory Comm., C.A.2d, 1977, 550 F.2d 745, 51 n. 6; and the many cases cited 9 Wright & Miller, Civil § 2587 n. 33; Note, Rule 52(a): Appellate Review of Findings of Fact Based on Documentary or Undisputed Evidence, 1963, 41 Texas L.Rev. 935.

28. The Committee Note to the original rule, reprinted 12 Wright & Miller, Civil pp. 490–491, said that the "clearly er-

Supreme Court.[29] It is required even more clearly by the essential
nature of trial courts as distinguished from appellate courts. Even in
instances where an appellate court is in as good a position to decide
as the trial court, it should not disregard the trial court's finding, for
to do so impairs confidence in the trial courts and multiplies appeals
with attendant expense and delay.[30] The matter was clearly stated
by Judge John B. Sanborn for the Eighth Circuit: "The entire responsibility for deciding doubtful fact questions in a nonjury case should
be, and we think it is, that of the district court. The existence of any
doubt as to whether the trial court or this Court is the ultimate trier
of fact issues in nonjury cases is, we think, detrimental to the orderly
administration of justice, impairs the confidence of litigants and the
public in the decisions of the district courts, and multiplies the number of appeals in such cases." [31]

It is well understood that the "clearly erroneous" rule applies on
issues of fact, but not on questions of law,[32] and there is much authority that it does not apply to rulings on mixed questions of law
and fact.[33] Such expressions may be misleading. If an error of law
has impaired the judgment of the trial judge on such a mixed question, then his finding should be set aside,[34] but this should not be true
where his finding involves the application of a correct principle of law
to the facts.[35] Thus the Supreme Court has held that the "clearly
erroneous" test applies to a finding of negligence,[36] and to the deter-

roneous" test applied "whether the
finding is of a fact concerning which
there was conflict of testimony, or of a
fact deduced or inferred from uncontradicted testimony." See also the
1955 note to Rule 52(a), id. at pp.
609–611.

29. U. S. v. United States Gypsum Co.,
1948, 68 S.Ct. 525, 541, 333 U.S. 364,
394, 92 L.Ed. 746; Graver Tank & Mfg.
Co. v. Linde Air Products Co., 1950, 70
S.Ct. 854, 857, 339 U.S. 605, 609–610,
94 L.Ed. 1097; C. I. R. v. Duberstein,
1960, 80 S.Ct. 1190, 1200, 363 U.S. 278,
291, 4 L.Ed.2d 1218; U. S. v. Singer
Mfg. Co., 1963, 83 S.Ct. 1773, 1784 n. 9,
374 U.S. 174, 194 n. 9, 10 L.Ed.2d 823.

30. Lundgren v. Freeman, C.A.9th,
1962, 307 F.2d 104, 114; Alaska Foods,
Inc. v. American Mfrs. Mut. Ins. Co.,
Alaska 1971, 482 P.2d 842, 847; Navajo
Freight Lines, Inc. v. Liberty Mut. Ins.
Co., 1970, 471 P.2d 309, 312, 12 Ariz.
App. 424; Wright, The Doubtful Om-
niscience of Appellate Courts, 1957, 41
Minn.L.Rev. 751, 764–771, 778–782.
But see Godbold, Fact Finding by Ap-
pellate Courts—An Available and Ap-
propriate Power, 1982, 12 Cum.L.Rev.
365; Carrington, The Power of District
Judges and the Responsibility of

Courts of Appeals, 1969, 3 Ga.L.Rev.
507.

31. Pendergrass v. New York Life Ins.
Co., C.A.8th, 1950, 181 F.2d 136, 138.

32. 9 Wright & Miller, Civil § 2588.

33. See Pullman-Standard v. Swint,
1982, 102 S.Ct. 1781, 1790 n. 19, ___
U.S. ___, ___ n. 19, 72 L.Ed.2d 66; and
cases cited 9 Wright & Miller, Civil
§ 2589 nn. 55–61.

34. U. S. v. Singer Mfg. Co., 1963, 83
S.Ct. 1773, 1784 n. 9, 374 U.S. 174, 194
n. 9, 10 L.Ed.2d 823; and cases cited 9
Wright & Miller, Civil § 2585 n. 7.

35. A contrary view is taken in Karavos
Compania Naviera S. A. v. Atlantica
Export Corp., C.A.2d, 1978, 588 F.2d 1,
7–9, and in Weiner, The Civil Nonjury
Trial and the Law-Fact Distinction,
1967, 55 Calif.L.Rev. 1020.

36. McAllister v. U. S., 1954, 75 S.Ct. 6,
348 U.S. 19, 99 L.Ed. 20.

The Second Circuit persists in a contrary
view, Mamiye Bros. v. Barber S. S.
Lines, Inc., C.A.2d, 1966, 360 F.2d 774,
776–778, certiorari denied 87 S.Ct. 80,
385 U.S. 835, 17 L.Ed.2d 70, though it
seems to be softening its position.
E.g., In re Seaboard Shipping Corp.,
C.A.2d, 1971, 449 F.2d 132, 136, certio-

mination of whether a payment to a taxpayer was a "gift." [37] Lower courts have held Rule 52(a) applicable on many questions that surely have elements of law involved in them.[38] In view of this array of precedent any attempt to make nice distinctions between fact and law, so as to broaden the scope of review of determinations that can better be made by the trial court, seems doomed to fail. The "clearly erroneous" test should apply whenever the finding is based on the "fact-finding tribunal's experience with the mainsprings of human conduct." [39]

Occasionally it is said that a finding based on substantial evidence cannot be held clearly erroneous,[40] or that the appellee must be given the benefit of all favorable inferences that may reasonably be drawn from the evidence.[41] Such statements go too far, and equate the review of findings in a nonjury case with the test that applies in jury cases.[42] In a nonjury case the appellate court can reject inferences it deems clearly erroneous and can reverse a finding, though supported by substantial evidence, if the court is convinced on the whole record that the finding does not reflect the truth and right of the case.[43] This issue was resolved when the rule was adopted and the broader equity review accepted in preference to the narrower scope of review applicable to findings of fact in actions at law.[44]

Some commentators believed that they detected a recent tendency among the courts of appeals to depart from Rule 52(a) and to review fact determinations by the trial judge more broadly than that rule had intended.[45] If there was such a tendency, two Supreme Court decisions in 1982 should have put an end to it. In one, the Court held

rari denied 92 S.Ct. 2038, 406 U.S. 949, 32 L.Ed.2d 337. Decisions in the Third and Fourth Circuits go both ways. The other circuits accept the view that findings of negligence cannot be disturbed unless clearly erroneous. See 9 Wright & Miller, Civil § 2590.

37. C. I. R. v. Duberstein, 1960, 80 S.Ct. 1190, 363 U.S. 278, 4 L.Ed.2d 1218, criticized as typical of "excessive deference to triers of fact." Griswold, Of Time and Attitudes—Professor Hart and Judge Arnold, 1960, 74 Harv.L. Rev. 81, 86–91. The decision is criticized also in Carrington, note 30 above, at 521–523.

38. See generally 9 Wright & Miller, Civil § 2589. On the review of findings in patent cases, see id. at § 2591.

39. C. I. R. v. Duberstein, 1960, 80 S.Ct. 1190, 1198, 363 U.S. 278, 289, 4 L.Ed.2d 1218.

40. E.g., Jackson v. Hartford Acc. & Indem Co., C.A.8th, 1970, 422 F.2d 1272, 1275, certiorari denied 91 S.Ct. 86, 400 U.S. 855, 27 L.Ed.2d 92; and cases cited 9 Wright & Miller, Civil § 2585 n. 9.

41. E.g., Aunt Mid, Inc. v. Fjell-Oranje Lines, C.A.7th, 1972, 458 F.2d 712, 718–719, certiorari denied 93 S.Ct. 130, 409 U.S. 877, 34 L.Ed.2d 131; and cases cited 9 Wright & Miller, Civil § 2585 n. 95.

42. It is expressly stated in Minnesota Amusement Co. v. Larkin, C.A.8th, 1962, 299 F.2d 142, 146, and Kaiser Motors Corp. v. Savage, C.A.8th, 1956, 229 F.2d 525, 526, that the scope of review of fact findings is the same as of jury verdicts.

43. See Jackson v. Hartford Acc. & Indem. Co., C.A.8th, 1970, 422 F.2d 1272, 1275–1278 (concurring opinion); 9 Wright & Miller, Civil § 2585 n. 10.

44. 9 Wright & Miller, Civil § 2585, pp. 730–731.

45. Nangle, The Ever Widening Scope of Fact Review in Federal Appellate Courts—Is the "Clearly Erroneous Rule" Being Avoided?, 1981, 59 Wash. U.L.Q. 409; Note, Federal Rule of Civil Procedure 52(a) and the Scope of Appellate Fact Review: Has Application of the Clearly Erroneous Rules Been

that a finding that the differential impact of a seniority system did not reflect an intent to discriminate on account of race "is a pure question of fact, subject to Rule 52's clearly erroneous standard. It is not a question of law and not a mixed question of law and fact." [46] The Court emphatically rejected the notion that there can be broader review of "ultimate" facts than of "subsidiary" facts.[47]

In the other case the court of appeals had not held the findings of the district court to be clearly erroneous but even so it had set them aside. The court of appeals thought that the trial court had failed to give sufficient weight to certain evidence. This, the Supreme Court said, was error. "Determining the weight and credibility of the evidence is the special province of the trier of fact." [48] The court of appeals had further held that the evidence was "clearly sufficient" to establish a violation of the statute, and the Supreme Court said that this was also improper. "An appellate court cannot substitute its interpretation of the evidence for that of the trial court simply because the reviewing court 'might give the facts another construction, resolve the ambiguities differently, and find a more sinister cast to actions which the District Court apparently deemed innocent.' " [49]

§ 97. Control by the Judge [1]

A federal judge is a very puissant figure. "In a trial by jury in a federal court, the judge is not a mere moderator, but is the governor of the trial for the purpose of assuring its proper conduct and of determining questions of law." [2] He retains the powers that judges had at common law, including notably the power to comment on the evidence,[3] though one of the results of Jacksonian democracy was to deny such powers to judges in most states. He is appointed for life, and need not justify his record to the electorate at regular intervals.

Clearly Erroneous?, 1977, 52 St. John's L.Rev. 68.

But see Godbold, Fact Finding by Appellate Courts—An Available and Appropriate Power, 1982, 12 Cum.L.Rev. 365.

46. Pullman-Standard v. Swint, 1982, 102 S.Ct. 1781, 1789, ___ U.S. ___, ___, 72 L.Ed.2d 66.

See also Rogers v. Lodge, 1982, 102 S.Ct. 3272, ___ U.S. ___, ___ L.Ed.2d ___, holding that Rule 52(a) applied to a district court's finding that the at-large system for electing a county board was being maintained for discriminatory purposes.

47. "It does not divide facts into categories; in particular, it does not divide findings of fact into those that deal with 'ultimate' and those that deal with 'subsidiary' facts." 102 S.Ct. at 1789, ___ U.S. at ___.

48. Inwood Laboratories v. Ives Laboratories, 1982, 102 S.Ct. 2182, 2189, ___ U.S. ___, ___, 72 L.Ed.2d 606.

49. 102 S.Ct. at 2190, ___ U.S. at ___. The internal quotation is from U. S. v. Real Estate Boards, 1950, 70 S.Ct. 711, 717, 339 U.S. 485, 495, 94 L.Ed. 1007.

[§ 97]

1. 9 Wright & Miller, Civil §§ 2361–2376 (dismissal of actions), 2381–2392 (consolidation or separate trials), 2601–2615 (reference to master).

2. Herron v. Southern Pac. Co., 1931, 51 S.Ct. 383, 384, 283 U.S. 91, 95, 75 L.Ed. 857.

The Fourth Circuit has restated this somewhat less elegantly in saying that "a United States district judge is not a bump on a log. Nor is he a referee at a prize fight." Evans v. Wright, C.A. 5th, 1974, 505 F.2d 287, 289.

3. See § 94 above.

In many respects he is given power unknown at common law, because one of the principal ideas embodied in the rules is that it is wise to leave many details of procedure to the informed discretion of the judge, acting in the circumstances of the particular case, rather than regulating such details by rigid provisions.

Joinder of claims and parties is a good example of this thesis. At common law and under the codes joinder was measured by conceptual tests and was narrowly confined. Under the rules joinder is virtually unlimited. But Rule 42(b) then gives the judge power to order a separate trial of any claim or issue, as he thinks necessary to further convenience, to avoid prejudice, and to promote expedition and economy.[4] The judge, acting with an eye to all the circumstances of the particular case, has been able to regulate the joint or separate trial of issues far better than was done under the former systems.

There is still some question whether issues can be ordered tried before different juries. There is no doubt that the court can order separate trials of issues, with the same jury sitting in each trial,[5] and it seems to be accepted that the better and preferred practice is to use the same jury for all issues, even though it may hear the issues at different times.[6] The issue can thus be narrowed to whether the preferred procedure is constitutionally required. It has been held, on sound ground, that the Seventh Amendment is not violated by the separate submission of the issues to a single jury.[7] Is there a violation of the constitutional provision if issues are separately submitted to separate juries? The answer rather clearly must be in the negative. Where a single jury has passed on all issues, but error has tainted its verdict on one of the issues, it is quite settled that there may be a new trial before a second jury limited to that single issue, provided that the error requiring a new trial has not affected the determination of any other issue.[8] In this instance the result is that different juries ultimately resolve the issues. An argument that two

4. 9 Wright & Miller, Civil §§ 2388–2389; Schwartz, Severance— A Means of Minimizing the Role of Burden and Expense in Determining the Outcome of Litigation, 1967, 20 Vand.L.Rev. 1197; Note, Liberal Joinder of Issues and the Sequence of Trial, 1958, 34 Ind.L.J. 97; Note, Separate Trial of a Claim or Issue in Modern Pleading: Rule 42(b) of the Federal Rules of Civil Procedure, 1955, 39 Minn.L.Rev. 743.

5. Moss v. Associated Transport, Inc., C.A.6th, 1965, 344 F.2d 23; Shoreham Village Inc. v. Bush Constr. Co., D.C. Pa.1960, 185 F.Supp. 534.

6. Martin v. Bell Helicopter Co., D.C. Colo.1980, 85 F.R.D. 654, 659; O'Donnell v. Watson Bros. Transp. Co., D.C.Ill.1960, 183 F.Supp. 577, 580.

7. Hosie v. Chicago & N. W. R. Co., C.A.7th, 1960, 282 F.2d 639, 642–643, certiorari denied 81 S.Ct. 695, 365 U.S. 814, 5 L.Ed.2d 693, noted 1961, 74 Harv.L.Rev. 781, 1961 U.Ill.L.Forum 194.

8. Gasoline Products Co., Inc. v. Champlin Refining Co., 1931, 51 S.Ct. 513, 283 U.S. 494, 75 L.Ed. 1188; Woods Exploration & Producing Co., Inc. v. Aluminum Co. of America, C.A. 5th, 1975, 509 F.2d 784; Pritchard v. Liggett & Myers Tobacco Co., C.A.3d, 1966, 370 F.2d 95, certiorari denied 87 S.Ct. 1350, 386 U.S. 1009, 18 L.Ed.2d 436. See 11 Wright & Miller, Civil § 2814.

juries may be used if one jury has first passed on all the issues—though its verdict as to one of them has gone out of the case—but that two juries may not be used in the first instance, seems untenable.[9] The great guaranty of the Seventh Amendment will hardly support such a gossamer distinction.

There is a limitation that must not be overlooked. In the case stating that a partial new trial may under some circumstances be used, the Supreme Court held that this practice cannot be resorted to unless it clearly appears that the issue to be retried is so distinct and separable from the others that a trial of it alone may be had without injustice.[10] Similarly separate trial of a particular issue cannot be ordered in the first instance where the issue is so interwoven with the other issues that it cannot be submitted to the jury independently of the others without confusion and uncertainty that would amount to a denial of a fair trial.[11] But this problem goes beyond the question of whether two juries are to be used. In the circumstances described, separate trial, even to the same jury, would be erroneous. Applying these principles to a matter that is of much current interest, separate trial of the issues of damages and of liability in a personal injury case, even to separate juries, is not improper where the two issues are distinct and separate. Whether such separate trials should be ordered as a routine matter is a different, and highly controversial, question.[12] When it is seen that defendants win 42% of the cases tried routinely, but that they win 79% of the cases in which the liability issue is submitted alone, there is reason to believe that this procedural reform, though it does alleviate court congestion, has made a drastic change in the nature of jury trial itself.[13]

9. Arthur Young & Co. v. U. S. District Court, C.A.9th, 1977, 549 F.2d 686, certiorari denied 98 S.Ct. 109, 434 U.S. 829, 54 L.Ed.2d 88; Martin v. Bell Helicopter Co., D.C.Colo.1980, 85 F.R.D. 654; In re Gap Store Securities Litigation, D.C.Cal.1978, 79 F.R.D. 283, 305 n. 22; In re Folding Carton Antitrust Litigation, D.C.Ill.1977, 75 F.R.D. 727, 736 n. 10.

10. Gasoline Products Co., Inc. v. Champlin Ref. Co., 1931, 51 S.Ct. 513, 515, 283 U.S. 494, 500, 75 L.Ed. 1188. See 11 Wright & Miller, Civil § 2814.

11. Franchi Constr. Co. v. Combined Ins. Co. of America, C.A.1st, 1978, 580 F.2d 1, 7–8; United Air Lines, Inc. v. Wiener, C.A.9th, 1961, 286 F.2d 302, certiorari denied 81 S.Ct. 1352, 366 U.S. 924, 6 L.Ed.2d 384; McClain v. Socony-Vacuum Oil Co., D.C.Mo.1950, 10 F.R.D. 261; U. S. ex rel. Rodriguez v. Weekly Publications, Inc., D.C.N.Y. 1949, 9 F.R.D. 179.

12. The following commentators are critical of such practice: Weinstein, Routine Bifurcation of Jury Negligence Trial: An Example of the Questionable Use of Rule Making, 1961, 14 Vand.L.Rev. 831; Comment, 1961, 46 Iowa L.Rev. 815; Notes, 1961, 36 Notre Dame Law. 388, 1955, 39 Minn.L. Rev. 743, 760–761. But see: Miner, A New Approach to Court Congestion, 1959, 45 A.B.A.J. 1265; Zeisel & Callahan, Split Trials and Time Saving: A Statistical Analysis, 1963, 76 Harv.L. Rev. 1606; Notes 1964, 26 U.Pitt.L. Rev. 99; 1962, 48 Va.L.Rev. 99, 46 Minn.L.Rev. 1059.

See generally 9 Wright & Miller, Civil § 2390.

13. Rosenberg, Court Congestion: Status, Causes, and Proposed Remedies, in The Courts, The Public, and The Law Explosion, 1965, pp. 29, 45; Wright, Procedural Reform: Its Limitations and Its Future, 1967, 1 Ga.L. Rev. 563, 569–570.

Just as the judge may order separate trials of the issues in a single case under Rule 42(b), he is empowered by Rule 42(a) to order joint trial of two separate actions, and may even order such actions consolidated.[14] Here again he has a broad discretion, and efficient judicial administration is the principal goal, but in one respect his discretion to order joint trial or consolidation is limited. He may do this only if the actions involve a common question of law or fact.[15] Thus the power of the judge to order consolidation is narrower than the power of the parties to join claims against each other, since there the claims may be entirely unrelated, but it is broader than the power to join parties to an action, where both a common question of law or fact and some claim arising out of the same transaction or occurrence must be present.[16]

The judge also has considerable power over the taking of a voluntary dismissal, or nonsuit, by the plaintiff. The right to take a nonsuit was far-reaching at common law. It is limited by Rule 41(a) to the period before defendant has answered or moved for summary judgment, although a few cases suggest that if the parties have joined issue on the merits of the controversy, regardless of the formal status of the pleadings, plaintiff's right to dismiss is ended.[17] After the period for dismissal as of right has expired, plaintiff, except on stipulation with the other parties, can dismiss without prejudice only with the consent of the court and upon such terms and conditions as are just. The discretion of the court does not go merely to the terms and conditions, but extends to whether to permit a nonsuit at all.[18] Dismissal will normally be allowed unless the defendant will

---

14. 9 Wright & Miller, Civil §§ 2382–2386; Comment, Consolidation in Mass Tort Litigation, 1963, 30 U.Chi. L.Rev. 373; Note, Federal District Court Consolidation Orders and the Final Judgment Rules, 1962, 38 Ind.L.J. 86.

15. St. Paul Fire & Marine Ins. Co. v. King, D.C.Okl.1968, 45 F.R.D. 519; Holiday Inns of America, Inc. v. Lussi, D.C.N.Y.1967, 42 F.R.D. 27; Oliver v. Humble Oil & Ref. Co., D.C.La.1963, 225 F.Supp. 536.

16. See Stanford v. Tennessee Val. Auth., D.C.Tenn.1955, 18 F.R.D. 152, ordering consolidation on the basis of a common question though the court had found misjoinder of parties since independent transactions were involved.

17. Harvey Aluminum, Inc. v. American Cyanamid Co., C.A.2d, 1953, 203 F.2d 105, certiorari denied 73 S.Ct. 949, 345 U.S. 964, 97 L.Ed. 1383; Tele-Views News Co. v. S. R. B. TV Pub. Co., D.C. Pa.1961, 28 F.R.D. 303; Robertson v. Limestone Mfg. Co., D.C.S.C.1957, 20 F.R.D. 365. See Note, Absolute Dismissal under Federal Rule 41(a): The Disappearing Right of Voluntary Nonsuit, 1954, 63 Yale L.J. 738; Note, Right of a Plaintiff to Take a Voluntary Nonsuit or to Dismiss His Action Without Prejudice, 1951, 37 Va.L.Rev. 969.

Most cases have refused to write a judge-made exception into the rule and have held that until an answer or motion for summary judgment has been filed plaintiff has an absolute right to dismiss. See cases cited 9 Wright & Miller, Civil § 2363 n. 38. Indeed the Second Circuit itself has noted that Harvey Aluminum "has not been well received" and has refused to extend it beyond its own extreme facts. Thorp v. Scarne, C.A.2d, 1979, 599 F.2d 1169, 1174–1176.

18. E.g., Grivas v. Parmalee Transp. Co., C.A.7th, 1953, 207 F.2d 334, 336–337, overruling an earlier decision of the same court to the contrary.

The court cannot prevent plaintiff from dismissing with prejudice if dismissal will dispose of all aspects of the action.

suffer some plain legal prejudice other than the mere prospect of a second lawsuit.[19] It is no bar to dismissal that plaintiff may obtain some tactical advantage thereby,[20] but he will not be permitted to dismiss where this is unjust, as where the evidence has been concluded and the judge has indicated he is about to rule for the defendant.[21] It has been held that voluntary dismissal under Rule 41 applies only to dismissal of an entire controversy, and that Rules 15(a) or 21 must be used for dismissal of particular parties or fewer than all of the claims.[22] The same considerations apply, however, no matter which of these rules is invoked,[23] and more recent cases have not applied this limitation on Rule 41.[24]

The judge also has the power to dismiss the case involuntarily for want of prosecution by the plaintiff, or for failure of the plaintiff to comply with the rules or any order of court.[25] Such a dismissal is normally with prejudice. This is a drastic sanction, and though the courts have the power and must have the power if they are to discharge their responsibility to prevent undue delay in litigation, it is a power that should be exercised only in extreme situations.[26] Thus in one case dismissal with prejudice was held to be an abuse of discretion where plaintiff had delayed for more than two years in making service on a defendant who was at all times amenable to service, the court saying that "the doom entered below seems altogether too final

Compare Smoot v. Fox, C.A.6th, 1964, 340 F.2d 301, with Hudson Engineering Co. v. Bingham Pump Co., D.C. N.Y.1969, 298 F.Supp. 387.

19. Ex parte Skinner & Eddy Corp., 1924, 44 S.Ct. 446, 265 U.S. 86, 68 L.Ed. 912; Cone v. West Virginia Pulp & Paper Co., 1947, 67 S.Ct. 752, 755, 330 U.S. 212, 217, 91 L.Ed. 849; Note, Voluntary Dismissal by Order of Court—Federal Rules of Civil Procedure Rule 41(a)(2) and Judicial Discretion, 1972, 48 Notre Dame Law. 446; 9 Wright & Miller, Civil § 2364.

20. E.g., Hoffmann v. Alside, Inc., C.A. 8th, 1979, 596 F.2d 822; and cases cited 9 Wright & Miller, Civil § 2364 nn. 70–76. But cf. Noonan v. Cunard S. S. Co., C.A.2d, 1967, 375 F.2d 69, noted 1967, 36 U.Cinc.L.Rev. 714.

21. Piedmont Interstate Fair Assn. v. Bean, C.A.4th, 1954, 209 F.2d 942; International Shoe Co. v. Cool, C.C.A.8th, 1946, 154 F.2d 778.

22. Harvey Aluminum, Inc. v. American Cyanamid Co., C.A.2d, 1953, 203 F.2d 105, certiorari denied 73 S.Ct. 949, 345 U.S. 964, 97 L.Ed. 1383; Kerr v. Compagnie De Ultramar, C.A.2d, 1958, 250

F.2d 860; Robertson v. Limestone Mfg. Co., D.C.S.C.1957, 20 F.R.D. 365. Contra: Young v. Wilky Carrier Corp., C.C.A.3d, 1945, certiorari denied 66 S.Ct. 470, 326 U.S. 786, 90 L.Ed. 477.

23. Johnston v. Cartwright, C.A.8th, 1966, 355 F.2d 32, 39; Altman v. Liberty Equities Corp., D.C.N.Y.1972, 54 F.R.D. 620; Note, 1961 Wis.L.Rev. 160.

24. Plains Growers, Inc. v. Ickes-Braun Glasshouses, Inc., C.A.5th, 1973, 474 F.2d 250; and cases cited 9 Wright & Miller, Civil § 2362 n. 10.

25. Rule 41(b); 9 Wright & Miller, Civil §§ 2369–2373.

26. Moore v. St. Louis Music Supply Co., Inc., C.A.8th, 1976, 539 F.2d 1191; Syracuse Broadcasting Corp. v. Newhouse, C.A.2d, 1959, 271 F.2d 910; and cases cited 9 Wright & Miller, Civil § 2369 nn. 67–75. See also Comment, The Demise (Hopefully) of an Abuse: The Sanction of Dismissal, 1971, 7 Calif.West.L.Rev. 438. But cf. Link v. Wabash R. Co., 1962, 82 S.Ct. 1386, 370 U.S. 626, 8 L.Ed.2d 734, noted 1963, 65 W.Va.L.Rev. 187, 72 Yale L.J. 819; Frank, Book Review, 1963, 76 Harv.L. Rev. 1704, 1707–1708.

and definitive" and that plaintiff should not "face a permanent bar for a delay which in our congested trial courts is hardly unusual." [27]

Where the judge requires help in a case, he may refer it to a master, under Rule 53, but this is a power to be exercised only in rare cases.[28] The procedural advantage from a reference must be weighed against the fact that it deprives litigants of their traditional right to have their case passed upon, in the first instance, by a court or jury. And even the supposed procedural advantage must be considered in the light of the "unbelievably long" delay and the increased expense to which the litigants will be subjected by a reference.[29] In a jury case Rule 53 purports to make it sufficient for reference that the issues are complicated, since the report of the master is merely evidence, which the jury is free to disregard, and there is no danger that the master will displace the court in making the decision. Reference is as expensive and as time-consuming in a jury case as in any other, it is always disfavored for that reason, and the Supreme Court has indicated that it represents an inroad on trial by jury that should be made, if at all, only when unusual circumstances exist.[30]

In a nonjury case the findings of the master must be accepted by the court unless they are clearly erroneous, and thus there is added reason to refuse reference in such a case. Accordingly the rule has always required an "exceptional condition" to justify reference in a nonjury case. In La Buy v. Howes Leather Co.[31] the Court held that neither calendar congestion, nor complexity of the issues, nor the great length of time trial would take were exceptional conditions justifying reference. With a few minor exceptions, it is hard to conceive of any reference of a nonjury case that will meet the rigid standard of the La Buy decision.[32]

Recently a new use has developed for masters that is quite different from what was contemplated when Rule 53 was written. New kinds of complex litigation that are now coming to the courts have

27. Lyford v. Carter, C.A.2d, 1960, 274 F.2d 815, 816.

28. 9 Wright & Miller, Civil §§ 2601–2615.

29. Adventures in Good Eating v. Best Places to Eat, C.C.A.7th, 1942, 131 F.2d 809, 815; Vanderbilt, Cases and Materials on Modern Procedure and Judicial Administration, 1952, pp. 1240–1241; Kaufman, Masters in the Federal Courts: Rule 53, 1958, 58 Col. L.Rev. 452; 9 Wright & Miller, Civil § 2603.

30. Dairy Queen, Inc. v. Wood, 1962, 82 S.Ct. 894, 900, 369 U.S. 469, 478, 8 L.Ed.2d 44.

31. 1957, 77 S.Ct. 309, 352 U.S. 249, 1 L.Ed.2d 290.

32. See Kaufman, Masters in the Federal Courts: Rule 53, 1958, 58 Col.L.Rev. 452, 459. For cases in which a reference has been found proper, see 9 Wright & Miller, Civil § 2605 n. 56.

The Supreme Court has held that reference of all Social Security benefit cases to United States magistrates for preparation of a recommended decision is permissible. It was at pains to distinguish the La Buy case and to say that "the important premises from which the La Buy decision proceeded are not threatened here." Mathews v. Weber, 1976, 96 S.Ct. 549, 556, 423 U.S. 261, 275, 46 L.Ed.2d 483.

emphasized the need for aggressive management of the case on behalf of the court at the pretrial stages. In some cases of this kind, the use of a master to supervise discovery or otherwise act as a class manager has been found helpful.[33]

Because the federal judge is given such extensive power over litigation before him, it is especially important that he not only be but seem impartial. To be sure that this is the case, there are statutory provisions requiring the judge to disqualify himself if a timely and sufficient affidavit has been filed that he has a personal bias or prejudice against a party or in favor of an adverse party.[34] Another statute, which was completely rewritten in 1974, requires a judge to disqualify himself in any proceeding in which his impartiality might reasonably be questioned, or if he is related to the case in any of a number of ways specified in the statute.[35]

G. JUDGMENT

Analysis

§ 98. Judgments in General [1]

A judgment, as defined by Rule 54(a), "includes a decree and any order from which an appeal lies." It is the final decisive act of a court defining the rights of the parties. The rule contemplates "a simple form of judgment * * * eschewing the lengthy recitals familiar in state practice," [2] and Official Forms 31 and 32 illustrate the simplicity that is permissible.

Where judgment is by default, the relief given cannot be different from or in excess of that demanded in the complaint. This is the traditional view, based on the fundamental unfairness of giving

---

33. See In re "Agent Orange" Product Liab. Litigation, D.C.N.Y.1982, 94 F.R.D. 173; Brazil, Special Masters in the Pretrial Development of Big Cases: Potential and Problems, 1982 A.B.A. Res.J. 287; Hazard & Rice, Judicial Management of the Pretrial Process in Massive Litigation: Special Masters as Case Managers, 1982 A.B.A.Res.J. 375.

34. 28 U.S.C.A. § 144; 13 Wright, Miller & Cooper, Jurisdiction § 3551.

35. 28 U.S.C.A. § 455; 13 Wright, Miller & Cooper, Jurisdiction §§ 3541–3544, 3546–3550, 3552–3553.

Another statute, 28 U.S.C.A. § 47, prohibits a judge from sitting on an appeal from the decision of a case or issue tried by him. See Swann v. Charlotte-Mecklenburg Bd. of Educ., C.A.4th, 1970, 431 F.2d 135 (memorandum of Craven, J.); 13 Wright, Miller & Cooper, Jurisdiction § 3545.

[§ 98]

1. 10 Wright, Miller & Kane, Civil 2d §§ 2651–2664, 2681–2702; 11 Wright & Miller, Civil §§ 2781–2787, 2851–2873.

2. U. S. v. Wissahickon Tool Works, C.A.2d, 1952, 200 F.2d 936, 938. See 10 Wright, Miller & Kane, Civil 2d § 2652.

greater or different relief in a judgment from that of which the defendant was given notice by the complaint, in cases where he does not appear and defend against the action.[3] A different principle is stated, however, in Rule 54(c), for non-default cases. Here the judgment is not limited in kind or amount by the demand for relief, but may include whatever relief the successful party is entitled to, regardless of the demand. This is in accord with the general theory of Rule 15(b), that in a contested case the judgment is to be based on what has been proved rather than what has been pleaded. It is a necessary rule in a merged system of law and equity; indeed the difficulties some states have had in implementing such a merger stems from a failure to grasp and to apply this principle.[4] Any rule other than that stated in the second sentence of Rule 54(c) would mean preservation of the distinctions between law and equity and of the various forms of action that these rules are intended to abolish.

Thus the rule provides that the demand for judgment loses much of its restrictive force if the case is at issue.[5] Particular legal theories of counsel then are subordinated to the court's right and duty to grant the relief to which the prevailing party is entitled whether demanded or not.[6] The party may be awarded damages in excess of those he demanded in his pleading,[7] or may be awarded a different kind of relief than he requested.[8] This does not mean that the court will force relief on the parties against their wishes where there is nothing in the case to indicate a need therefor,[9] nor will it give the successful party relief, though he may be entitled to it, where the

---

3. Thomson v. Wooster, 1885, 5 S.Ct. 788, 114 U.S. 104, 29 L.Ed. 105; Fong v. U.S., C.A.9th, 1962, 300 F.2d 400, 412–413, certiorari denied 82 S.Ct. 1584, 370 U.S. 938, 8 L.Ed.2d 807; National Discount Corp. v. O'Mell, C.A. 6th, 1952, 194 F.2d 452, 455–456. See 10 Wright, Miller & Kane, Civil 2d § 2663.

4. Note, Law and Equity in New York— Still Unmerged, 1946, 55 Yale L.J. 826; Clark & Wright, The Judicial Council and the Rule-Making Power: A Dissent and a Protest, 1950, 1 Syracuse L.Rev. 346, 353–357. See Rosden v. Leuthold, C.A.1960, 274 F.2d 747, 750, 107 U.S.App.D.C. 89; Fitzharris v. Phillips, 1958, 333 P.2d 721, 723, 74 Nev. 371.

5. Bowles v. J. J. Schmitt & Co., C.A.2d, 1948, 170 F.2d 617.

6. Massachusetts Bonding & Ins. Co. v. State of New York, C.A.2d, 1958, 259 F.2d 33; Hamill v. Maryland Cas. Co., C.A.10th, 1954, 209 F.2d 338; and cases cited 10 Wright, Miller & Kane, Civil 2d § 2664 n. 2. But see In re Lin-

da Coal & Supply Co., C.A.3d, 1958, 255 F.2d 653, 656–657.

7. E.g., Steinmetz v. Bradbury Co., Inc., C.A.8th, 1980, 618 F.2d 21; Bail v. Cunningham Bros., Inc., C.A.7th, 1971, 452 F.2d 182; Riggs, Ferris & Geer v. Lillibridge, C.A.2d, 1963, 316 F.2d 60; and cases cited 10 Wright, Miller & Kane, Civil 2d § 2664 nn. 10–13. Though the rule is thoroughly settled, its desirability is questioned in Frank, Book Review, 1963, 76 Harv.L.Rev. 1704, 1707.

8. E.g., Fitzgerald v. Sirloin Stockade, Inc., C.A.10th, 1980, 624 F.2d 945 (reinstatement ordered though only monetary relief sought); Blazer v. Black, C.A. 10th, 1952, 196 F.2d 139 (constructive trust where damages asked); Garland v. Garland, C.C.A.10th, 1948, 165 F.2d 131 (specific performance where rescission demanded); Truth Seeker Co. v. Durning, C.C.A.2d, 1945, 147 F.2d 54 (damages where injunction demanded).

9. Mercury Oil Ref. Co. v. Oil Workers Intl. Union, C.I.O., C.A.10th, 1951, 187 F.2d 980.

propriety of such relief was not litigated and his opponent had no opportunity to assert defenses to such relief.[10]

The federal statute makes mandatory the allowance of interest, at a rate tied to the yield on Treasury bills, from the date of entry of the judgment, and the judgment must make provision for such interest regardless of whether it was demanded in the complaint.[11] Whether the judgment is to include interest from the time of the wrong to the entry of judgment is a question of the measure of damages, to be resolved by state law or by any applicable federal statute or in the discretion of the court, as the case may be.[12]

Rule 54(d) provides that, except as against the United States or when a statute or the rules are otherwise controlling, costs shall be allowed as of course to the prevailing party unless the court otherwise directs. The court retains a considerable discretion on whether costs should be allowed,[13] and on review of taxation of the costs by the clerk, may pass on whether particular items are properly included as costs, and the amounts to be allowed for them. The Supreme Court has said that the courts should exercise their discretion sparingly in taxing as costs expenses not specifically allowed by statute.[14]

Many important matters, including notably the time in which to appeal or to make post-trial motions, turn on the date of entry of the judgment. This had been a source of considerable confusion.[15] Rule 58 was amended in 1963 to remove that confusion. The amended rule recognizes two classes of cases. Where there is a general verdict of a jury, or where the court has decided that a party shall recover only money or costs or that all relief shall be denied, the clerk, unless oth-

---

10. Armstrong Cork Co. v. Lyons, C.A.8th, 1966, 366 F.2d 206; Brotherhood of Locomotive Firemen and Enginemen v. Butte, A. & P. Ry. Co., C.A. 9th, 1961, 286 F.2d 706, certiorari denied 81 S.Ct. 1650, 366 U.S. 929, 6 L.Ed.2d 388; Rosenfeld v. Lion Mfg. Corp., C.A.7th, 1958, 253 F.2d 90.

11. 28 U.S.C.A. § 1961(a), as amended by Act of April 2, 1982, Pub.L. 97–164, § 301, 96 Stat. 55.

12. Lytle v. Freedom Intl. Carrier, S.A., C.A.6th, 1975, 519 F.2d 129; Phillips Petroleum Co. v. Adams, C.A.5th, 1975, 513 F.2d 355; and cases cited 10 Wright, Miller & Kane, Civil 2d § 2664 nn. 54–57.

13. Fishgold v. Sullivan Drydock & Repair Corp., 1946, 66 S.Ct. 1105, 1110, 328 U.S. 275, 283–284, 90 L.Ed. 1230; 10 Wright, Miller & Kane, Civil 2d § 2668.

Costs and attorneys' fees can be taxed against the United States as provided by 28 U.S.C.A. § 2412. See 10 Wright, Miller & Kane, Civil 2d § 2672.

Rule 68 allows a defending party to cut off the further running of costs against him if he makes an offer of judgment and the judgment ultimately obtained by his opponent is not more favorable than the offer. The rule does not come into play if the judgment is for the defending party rather than for his opponent but in an amount less than the offer. Delta Air Lines, Inc. v. August, 1981, 101 S.Ct. 1146, 450 U.S. 346, 67 L.Ed.2d 287, noted 1981, 9 Fla.St.U.L.Rev. 671, 51 Miss. L.J. 599; 1982, 47 J.Air L. & Comm. 625.

14. Farmer v. Arabian American Oil Co., 1964, 85 S.Ct. 411, 416, 379 U.S. 227, 235, 13 L.Ed.2d 248. The relevant statute is 28 U.S.C.A. § 1920. See generally 10 Wright, Miller & Kane, Civil 2d §§ 2675–2678.

15. E. g., U. S. v. F. & M. Schaefer Brewing Co., 1958, 78 S.Ct. 674, 356 U.S. 227, 2 L.Ed.2d 721; Jung v. K. & D. Mining Co., 1958, 78 S.Ct. 764, 356 U.S. 335, 2 L.Ed.2d 806; 11 Wright & Miller, Civil §§ 2781, 2782.

erwise ordered by the court, will forthwith prepare, sign, and enter the judgment without awaiting any direction by the court. On the other hand, where the court orders some other relief, or there is a special verdict or a general verdict accompanied by answers to interrogatories, the court must promptly approve the form of the judgment, and the clerk will then enter it. The amended rule states specifically that the judgment is to be set forth on a separate document,[16] and declares that entry of judgment is not to be delayed for the taxing of costs and that "attorneys shall not submit forms of judgment except upon direction of the court, and these directions shall not be given as a matter of course."

The amended rule has much to commend it, and has operated without difficulty in practice. The requirement of a separate document gives a readily determinable date as to when judgment was entered, while the requirements that the clerk act "forthwith," where the power is his, and that the court act "promptly," where it must approve the form of judgment, indicate that the process is not to be a dilatory one. Finally the provision that attorneys are not to submit forms of judgment bars a practice, formerly followed by custom in some districts and required by local rules in others, that had served only to delay the end of litigation.[17]

Under the 1963 amendment, as before, a judgment is not effective until it has been noted on the docket.[18] Ample power is given the trial court and the appellate court to stay the effectiveness of the judgment after that date on proper conditions.[19] When the court has made a final decision with regard to fewer than all of the parties or the claims in a case that involves multiple parties or claims, it may order judgment as to the part that it has decided, without awaiting decision of the remainder of the case, but must make an express determination that there is no just reason for delay and an express direction for the entry of judgment.[20]

If a party against whom a claim has been asserted fails to plead or otherwise defend as provided in the rules, the clerk, on a showing of this fact, will enter his default.[21] Thereafter a default judgment may be entered. In some situations the clerk may enter the default judgment, as where the claim is for a sum certain or a sum that can

---

16. An appellate court cannot disregard a failure to set forth the judgment on a separate document. The 1963 amendment requiring the judgment to be on a separate document is "a 'mechanical change' that must be mechanically applied * * *." U. S. v. Indrelunas, 1973, 93 S.Ct. 1562, 1565, 411 U.S. 216, 222, 36 L.Ed.2d 202.

17. Roberts v. Ross, C.A.3d, 1965, 344 F.2d 747, 753; Matteson v. U. S., C.A.2d, 1956, 240 F.2d 517, 518–519. See 11 Wright & Miller, Civil § 2786.

18. Brown v. U. S., C.A.8th, 1955, 225 F.2d 861; McAlister v. C. J. Dick Towing Co., C.A.3d, 1949, 175 F.2d 652. See Rule 79(a); 12 Wright & Miller, Civil §§ 3102, 3103.

19. Rule 62; 11 Wright & Miller, Civil §§ 2901–2909.

20. Rule 54(b); 10 Wright, Miller & Kane, Civil 2d §§ 2653–2661. See § 101 below.

21. Rule 55(a); Fisher v. Taylor, D.C. Tenn.1941, 1 F.R.D. 448; 10 Wright, Miller & Kane, Civil 2d § 2682.

be made certain by computation,[22] but in most cases application for judgment to be entered on the default must be to the court, and proof will be required as to the damages sought or other relief to be given.[23] The rules provide for setting aside a default, or a judgment entered thereon, in the discretion of the court.[24] In exercising this discretion the court will be guided by the fact that default judgments are not favored in the law.[25] Courts exist to do justice, and are properly reluctant to lend their processes to the enforcement of an unjust judgment. At the same time, the rules that require responsive pleadings within a limited time serve important social goals, and a party should not be permitted to flout them with impunity. In balancing these policies, the court will not reopen a default judgment merely because the party in default requests it, but should require the party to show both that there was good reason for the default and that he has a meritorious defense to the action.[26]

Any judgment, whether by default or after trial, may be altered or amended by the court on motion made and served within 10 days after entry of the judgment.[27] Thereafter the judgment may be attacked, other than by appeal, only as provided in Rule 60. That rule allows clerical mistakes arising from oversight or omission to be corrected at any time, either on motion or at the court's initiative.[28] The rule is more restrictive as to other grounds for relief from a judgment. Where relief is sought because of mistake, inadvertence, surprise, or excusable neglect, or because of newly-discovered evidence that could not have been discovered in time to be brought forward on motion for a new trial, or because of fraud or other misconduct of the adverse party, the motion must be made within a reasonable time,

22. Rule 55(b)(1); Thorpe v. Thorpe, C.A.1966, 364 F.2d 692, 124 U.S.App. D.C. 299; 10 Wright, Miller & Kane, Civil 2d § 2683.

It has been held that the clerk cannot enter a judgment by confession and that court approval is required where defendant confesses judgment rather than defaulting. Virgin Islands Nat. Bank v. Tropical Ventures, Inc., D.C. V.I.1973, 358 F.Supp. 1203.

23. Rule 55(b)(2); 10 Wright, Miller & Kane, Civil 2d §§ 2684–2688.

24. Rules 55(c), 60(b); American & Foreign Ins. Assn. v. Commercial Ins. Co., C.A.1st, 1978, 575 F.2d 980, 982 n. 3; 10 Wright, Miller & Kane, Civil 2d § 2693.

25. Schwab v. Bullock's Inc., C.A.9th, 1974, 508 F.2d 353, 355; and cases cited 10 Wright, Miller & Kane, Civil 2d § 2693 nn. 18, 20.

26. McGrady v. D'Andrea Elec., Inc., C.A.5th, 1970, 434 F.2d 1000, 1001; Gomes v. Williams, C.A.10th, 1970, 420

F.2d 1364, 1366; Consolidated Masonry & Fireproofing Inc. v. Wagman Constr. Corp., C.A.4th, 1967, 383 F.2d 249; Zaro v. Strauss, C.C.A.5th, 1948, 167 F.2d 218.

27. Rule 59(e); Boaz v. Mutual Life Ins. Co. of New York, C.C.A.8th, 1944, 146 F.2d 321; Scola v. Boat Frances, R., Inc., C.A.1st, 1980, 618 F.2d 147; 11 Wright & Miller, Civil § 2817.

A post-judgment request for an attorney's fee under 42 U.S.C.A. § 1988 is not a motion to alter or amend a judgment and need not be made within the time limit of Rule 59(e). White v. New Hampshire Dept. of Employment Sec., 1982, 102 S.Ct. 1162, ___ U.S. ___, 71 L.Ed.2d 325.

28. Rule 60(a); Fluoro Elec. Corp. v. Branford Associates, C.A.2d, 1973, 489 F.2d 320; Jackson v. Jackson, C.A. 1960, 276 F.2d 501, 107 U.S.App.D.C. 255; 11 Wright & Miller, Civil §§ 2854–2856.

and in any event not more than one year after the judgment.[29] This time limit does not apply if it is claimed that the judgment is void, or that it is no longer equitable, or if the claim is based on "any other reason justifying relief from the operation of the judgment."[30] It is now settled that the language just quoted and the other reasons stated in Rule 60(b) are mutually exclusive, and that that language cannot without more be used as an escape from the time limits that usually apply to such a motion.[31] At the same time the concepts involved are sufficiently flexible that a court that finds the equities so compelling that it wishes to reopen the judgment will have little difficulty in discerning that the moving party has presented "something more" than the grounds stated in the first three clauses of Rule 60(b), and that he thus has brought himself within the broad reach of Rule 60(b) (6).[32]

The court has considerable discretion in motions for relief from judgments, and the teaching of experience is that the courts will not permit technicalities to prevent them from remedying injustice. Laudable as this goal is, the rule requires the courts to balance it against the desire to achieve finality in litigation.[33] The cases show that the courts have exercised their discretion under the rule with a scrupulous regard for the aims of finality.[34] They have required that the motion be made within a "reasonable time," even though the stated time limit has not expired.[35] They have prevented the needless protraction of litigation by requiring the moving party to show a good claim or defense.[36] They have been astute to consider the hardship that a reopening of the judgment might cause to other persons.[37]

29. Rule 60(b); 11 Wright & Miller, Civil §§ 2858–2861, 2866. See Morgan, Delayed Attacks on Final Judgments, 1980, 33 Okla.L.Rev. 45; Note, Attacking Fraudulently Obtained Judgments in the Federal Courts, 1963, 48 Iowa L.Rev. 398; Comment, Federal Rule 60(b): Finality of Civil Judgments v. Self-Correction by District Court of Judicial Error of Law, 1967, 43 Notre Dame Law. 98; Comment, Rule 60(b): Survey and Proposal for General Reform, 1972, 60 Calif.L.Rev. 531.

30. Rule 60(b); 11 Wright & Miller, Civil §§ 2862–2864, 2866.

31. Klapprott v. U. S., 1948, 69 S.Ct. 384, 335 U.S. 601, 93 L.Ed. 266; Ackermann v. U. S., 1950, 71 S.Ct. 209, 340 U.S. 193, 95 L.Ed. 207; Goland v. C.I.A., C.A.1978, 607 F.2d 339, 372–373, 197 U.S.App.D.C. 25, certiorari denied 1980, 100 S.Ct. 1312, 445 U.S. 927, 63 L.Ed.2d 759; and cases cited 11 Wright & Miller, Civil § 2864 n. 39.

32. Compare the two opinions in U. S. v. Karahalias, C.A.2d, 1953, 205 F.2d 331.

See also 11 Wright & Miller, Civil § 2864, pp. 218–223. But cf. Kane, Relief from Federal Judgments: A Morass Unrelieved by a Rule, 1978, 30 Hastings L.J. 41.

33. In re Casco Chem. Co., C.A.5th, 1964, 335 F.2d 645, 651; 11 Wright & Miller, Civil § 2857.

34. See Kane, note 32 above, at 67.

Indeed it has been argued that the courts have been too strict. Wham, Federal District Court Rule 60(b): A Humane Rule Gone Wrong, 1963, 49 A.B.A.J. 566.

35. Security Mut. Cas. Co. v. Century Cas. Co., C.A.10th, 1980, 621 F.2d 1062; Schildhaus v. Moe, C.A.2d, 1964, 335 F.2d 529; Goldfine v. U. S., C.A.1st, 1964, 326 F.2d 456; Rhodes v. Houston, D.C.Neb.1966, 258 F.Supp. 546; and cases cited 11 Wright & Miller, Civil § 2866 nn. 70, 72.

36, 37. See notes 36–37 on page 663.

A district court cannot grant relief from a judgment while a case is pending on appeal.　There are some older holdings that where grounds for relief appear while the appeal is pending, the party should present them to the appellate court, which may then remand the case for consideration of the motion for relief from the judgment.[38]　Recent cases have suggested a different, and preferable procedure, by which the application is made to the district court.　If it indicates that it would grant the motion, the appellate court will then remand for that purpose.[39]

After the appellate court has decided a case, a lower court has no power to deviate from the decision of the appellate court so far as it goes.[40]　This does not bar the district court, however, from entertaining a Rule 60(b) motion.　Although a number of lower courts had said that leave from the appellate court was required before a Rule 60(b) motion could be considered to set aside a judgment that had been affirmed by the appellate court, the Supreme Court has widely ruled to the contrary, saying that a requirement of appellate leave "adds to the delay and expense of litigation and also burdens the increasingly scarce time of the federal appellate courts."[41]

§ 99.　Summary Judgment [1]

Rule 56 permits any party to a civil action to move for a summary judgment upon a claim, counterclaim, or cross-claim as to which there is no genuine issue of material fact and upon which the moving party

36.　Universal Film Exchanges, Inc. v. Lust, C.A.4th, 1973, 479 F.2d 573; Madsen v. Bumb, C.A.9th, 1969, 419 F.2d 4; and cases cited 11 Wright & Miller, Civil § 2857 n. 85.

37.　Menashe v. Sutton, D.C.N.Y.1950, 90 F.Supp. 531; McCawley v. Fleischmann Transp. Co., D.C.N.Y.1950, 10 F. R.D. 624; Albion-Idaho Land Co. v. Adams, D.C.Idaho, 1945, 58 F.Supp. 579.

38.　Baruch v. Beech Aircraft Corp., C.A.10th, 1949, 172 F.2d 445; Zig Zag Spring Co. v. Comfort Spring Corp., C.A.3d, 1953, 200 F.2d 901; Schempp v. Sch. Dist. of Abington Twp., Pennsylvania, D.C.Pa.1959, 184 F.Supp. 381, remand ordered 1960, 81 S.Ct. 268, 364 U.S. 298, 5 L.Ed. 89.

39.　Smith v. Pollin, C.A.1952, 194 F.2d 349, 90 U.S.App.D.C. 178; Ferrell v. Trailmobile, Inc., C.A.5th, 1955, 223 F.2d 697; Binks Mfg. Co. v. Ransburg Electro-Coating Corp., C.A.7th, 1960, 281 F.2d 252; Greear v. Greear, C.A.9th, 1961, 288 F.2d 466; Ryan v. United States Lines Co., C.A.2d, 1962, 303 F.2d 430; Aune v. Reynders, C.A. 10th, 1965, 344 F.2d 835; Iannarelli v. Morton, C.A.3d, 1972, 463 F.2d 179;

Puerto Rico v. SS Zoe Colocotroni, C.A. 1st, 1979, 601 F.2d 39; Note, Disposition of Federal Rule 60(b) Motions During Appeal, 1956, 65 Yale L.J. 708; 11 Wright & Miller, Civil § 2873, pp. 265–266.

40.　Briggs v. Pennsylvania R. Co., 1948, 68 S.Ct. 1039, 334 U.S. 304, 92 L.Ed. 1403; U. S. v. Cato Bros. Inc., C.A.4th, 1959, 273 F.2d 153, certiorari denied 80 S.Ct. 753, 362 U.S. 927, 4 L.Ed.2d 746.

41.　Standard Oil Co. of California v. U. S., 1976, 97 S.Ct. 31, 32, 429 U.S. 17, 19, 50 L.Ed.2d 21.

[§ 99]

1.　10 and 10A Wright, Miller & Kane, Civil 2d §§ 2711–2742; Asbill & Snell, Summary Judgment under the Federal Rules—When an Issue of Fact is Presented, 1953, 51 Mich.L.Rev. 1143; Bauman, A Rationale of Summary Judgment, 1958, 33 Ind.L.J. 467; Clark, The Summary Judgment, 1952, 36 Minn.L.Rev. 567; Guiher, Summary Judgments—Tactical Problem of the Trial Lawyer, 1962, 48 Va.L.Rev. 1263; Lemley, Summary Judgment Proce-

is entitled to prevail as a matter of law. The motion may be made as to all or a part of a claim of defense. It may be made on the pleadings or the record or it may be supported by affidavits. The motion strikes at the heart of the claim. In effect it argues that as a matter of law upon admitted or established facts the moving party is entitled to prevail.

The motion lies whenever there is no genuine issue as to any material fact. It follows that a formal denial in an answer should not necessarily defeat such a motion as otherwise the rule could be rendered nugatory at will. To take a simple example, in an action on a promissory note, the defendant in his answer denies the making of the note. Plaintiff moves for summary judgment, accompanying his motion with an affidavit of a person who swears that he saw the defendant sign the note. If the defendant does not file an opposing affidavit, raising a genuine issue as to this fact, summary judgment should be rendered for plaintiff. On the other hand, if the defendant files an affidavit to the effect that his purported signature is a forgery, or that it was affixed by a person who was not authorized to do so, a genuine issue as to a material fact is created, and the case must go to trial.[2]

Summary judgment procedure "is not a catch-penny contrivance to take unwary litigants into its toils and deprive them of a trial, it is a liberal measure, liberally designed for arriving at the truth. Its purpose is not to cut litigants off from their right of trial by jury if they really have evidence which they will offer on a trial, it is to carefully test this out, in advance of trial by inquiring and determining whether such evidence exists."[3] On a motion for summary judgment the court cannot try issues of fact. It can only determine whether there are issues to be tried. So conceived, it is a salutary and efficient instrumentality for expedition of the business of the courts.[4] Rule 56 builds on a procedure that had been used in England for more than 50 years, and adopted in a number of states.[5] It goes beyond earlier procedures of this sort in that it is available to both

dure under Rule 56 of the Federal Rules of Civil Procedure—Its Use and Abuse, 1957, 11 Ark.L.Rev. 138; Louis, Federal Summary Judgment Doctrine: A Critical Analysis, 1974, 83 Yale L.J. 745; McDonald, The Effective Use of Summary Judgment, 1961, 15 Sw.L.J. 365; Pyle, Appraisal of Summary Judgment Practice under Rule 56, 1960, 31 Miss.L.J. 1960.

2. See Fugate v. Mayor & City Council of Town of Buffalo, Wyo.1959, 348 P.2d 76, 81; Epps v. Remmel, 1963, 373 S.W.2d 141, 237 Ark. 391; New Hampshire York Co. v. Titus Constr. Co., 1966, 219 A.2d 708, 710, 107 N.H. 223.

3. Whitaker v. Coleman, C.C.A.5th, 1940, 115 F.2d 305, 307 (per Hutcheson, J.).

4. Freeman v. Continental Gin Co., C.A. 5th, 1967, 381 F.2d 459, 469; Minnesota Mining & Mfg. Co. v. U. S. Rubber Co., C.A.4th, 1960, 279 F.2d 409, 415.

5. Clark & Samenow, The Summary Judgment, 1929, 38 Yale L.J. 423; Bauman, Evolution of the Summary Judgment Procedure, 1956, 31 Ind.L.J. 329; see Weather-Rite Sportswear Co. v. U. S., Customs Ct.1969, 298 F.Supp. 508, 510–516.

plaintiffs and defendants in all forms and kinds of civil actions to which the Civil Rules apply.[6]

Though the procedure is freely available in all types of litigation, it is obvious that some kinds of cases lend themselves more readily to summary adjudication than do others. It is as much for functional reasons as for historical that statistics show motions for summary judgment granted more frequently in actions on notes, and for debts than in other kinds of cases.[7] Thus summary judgment will not usually be as feasible in negligence cases, where the standard of the reasonable man must be applied to conflicting testimony, as it is in other kinds of litigation, but there have been unusual cases in which grant of summary judgment, either for defendant or for plaintiff, has been held proper in a negligence case.[8] It is probably true, as five members of the Supreme Court said over a strong dissent, that summary judgment "should be used sparingly in complex antitrust litigation where motive and intent play leading roles, the proof is largely in the hands of the alleged conspirators, and hostile witnesses thicken the plot."[9] Yet there are decisions, including some from the Supreme Court, in which summary judgment has been granted in cases of this type.[10] Probably it usually is not feasible to resolve on motion for summary judgment cases involving state of mind,[11] or in which the

6. Engl v. Aetna Life Ins. Co., C.C.A.2d, 1943, 139 F.2d 469.

7. Note, Use of Summary Judgment by Type of Case, 1952, 36 Minn.L.Rev. 515.

8. Flying Diamond Corp. v. Pennaluna & Co., Inc., C.A.9th, 1978, 586 F.2d 707; Crum v. Continental Oil Co., C.A. 5th, 1973, 471 F.2d 784; Littleton v. Mardigan, C.A.7th, 1972, 458 F.2d 251; Bland v. Norfolk & S. R. Co., C.A.4th, 1969, 406 F.2d 863; Marsden v. Patane, C.A.5th, 1967, 380 F.2d 489; Berry v. Atlantic Coast Line R. Co., C.A.4th, 1960, 273 F.2d 572, certiorari denied 80 S.Ct. 1060, 362 U.S. 976, 4 L.Ed.2d 1011; American Airlines, Inc. v. Ulen, C.A.1949, 186 F.2d 529, 87 U.S.App. D.C. 307.

See 10A Wright, Miller & Kane, Civil 2d § 2729; Forkosch, Summary Judgment in Automobile Negligence Cases: A Procedural Analysis and Suggestions, 1968, 53 Corn.L.Q. 814.

9. Poller v. Columbia Broadcasting System, Inc., 1962, 82 S.Ct. 486, 491, 368 U.S. 464, 473, 7 L.Ed.2d 458. The view of the dissenters on this point is stated 82 S.Ct. at 493, 368 U.S. at 478. See also Fortner Enterprises, Inc. v. United States Steel Co., 1969, 89 S.Ct. 1252, 1257, 394 U.S. 495, 500, 22 L.Ed.2d 495.

In a later case the Court said: "Summary judgments have a place in the anti-

trust field, as elsewhere, though as we warned in Poller v. Columbia Broadcasting System, * * * they are not appropriate 'where motive and intent play leading roles.' Some of the law in this area is so well developed that where, as here, the gist of the case turns on documentary evidence, the rule at times can be divined without a trial." White Motor Co. v. U. S., 1963, 83 S.Ct. 696, 700, 372 U.S. 253, 259, 9 L.Ed.2d 738.

10. E.g., First Nat. Bank of Arizona v. Cities Serv. Co., 1968, 88 S.Ct. 1575, 391 U.S. 253, 20 L.Ed.2d 569; Morton Salt Co. v. G. S. Suppiger Co., 1942, 62 S.Ct. 402, 314 U.S. 488, 315 U.S. 788, 86 L.Ed. 363; Joe Regueira, Inc. v. American Distilling Co., Inc., C.A.5th, 1981, 642 F.2d 826; and cases cited 10A Wright, Miller & Kane, Civil 2d § 2732.1.

11. See Alabama Great Southern R. Co. v. Louisville & N. R. Co., C.A.5th, 1955, 224 F.2d 1, 5; Hart v. Johnston, C.A.6th, 1968, 389 F.2d 239; Croley v. Matson Navigation Co., C.A.5th, 1970, 434 F.2d 73, 77, adhered to C.A.5th, 1971, 439 F.2d 788. But cf. Orvis v. Brickman, C.A.1952, 196 F.2d 762, 90 U.S.App.D.C. 266; Washington Post Co. v. Keogh, C.A.1966, 365 F.2d 965, 967–968, 125 U.S.App.D.C. 32, certiorari denied 87 S.Ct. 708, 385 U.S. 1011, 17

facts are peculiarly within the knowledge of the moving party, [12] but it would be wrong to generalize from this and say that summary judgment never can be granted in such cases.[13] The rule permits summary judgment in any case, and the inquiry must be whether such a judgment is appropriate in the particular case, a question that cannot be resolved by some broad judicial gloss on the rule.

The rule requires that the moving party show that he "is entitled to judgment as a matter of law." One court made the mistake of reasoning from this that summary judgment is never proper in an equitable action, where judgment is in the discretion of the court rather than a matter of right.[14] This is an obvious misconstruction of the rule, contrary to a multitude of cases in which summary judgment for specific performance or injunction has been granted without comment, [15] and it has been expressly repudiated several times by other courts.[16]

It is frequently said that summary judgment should not be granted if there is the "slightest doubt" as to the facts.[17] Such statements are a rather misleading gloss on a rule that speaks in terms of "genuine issue as to any material fact," and would, if taken literally, mean that there could hardly ever be a summary judgment, for at least a slight doubt can be developed as to practically all things human.[18] A better formulation would be that the party opposing the motion is to

L.Ed.2d 548; Treutler v. Meredith Corp., C.A.8th, 1972, 455 F.2d 255, 257.

12. See Subin v. Goldsmith, C.A.2d, 1955, 224 F.2d 753; Alvado v. General Motors Corp., C.A.2d, 1956, 229 F.2d 408; Cochran v. U. S., D.C.Conn.1954, 123 F.Supp. 362, noted 1956, 41 Iowa L.Rev. 452. But cf. Dyer v. MacDougall, C.A.2d, 1952, 201 F.2d 265; Radio City Music Hall Corp. v. U. S., C.C.A. 2d, 1943, 135 F.2d 715.

13. See 10A Wright, Miller & Kane, Civil 2d § 2730.

14. Seaboard Sur. Co. v. Racine Screw Co., C.A.7th, 1953, 203 F.2d 532.

15. E.g., U. S. v. W. T. Grant Co., 1953, 73 S.Ct. 894, 345 U.S. 629, 97 L.Ed. 1303; 10A Wright, Miller & Kane, Civil 2d § 2731.

16. Booth v. Barber Transp. Co., C.A.8th, 1958, 256 F.2d 927, 931; Holmes v. Government of the Virgin Islands, D.C.V.I.1974, 370 F.Supp. 715, 718; Moore v. Texas Reserve Life Ins. Co., D.C.Tex.1962, 214 F.Supp. 925, 928, affirmed C.A.5th, 1963, 314 F.2d 948; Thickman v. Schunk, Wyo.1964, 391 P.2d 939, 944; Elias v. Manis, Tex. Civ.App.1956, 292 S.W.2d 836, 838, error refused.

17. E.g., Doehler Metal Furniture Co. v. U. S., C.C.A.2d, 1945, 149 F.2d 130,

135; Armco Steel Corp. v. Realty Inv. Co., C.A.8th, 1960, 273 F.2d 483, 484; Morrissey v. Procter & Gamble Co., C.A.1st, 1967, 379 F.2d 675, 677; Dolgow v. Anderson, C.A.2d, 1970, 438 F.2d 825, 830, affirmed C.A.3d, 464 F.2d 437; Tomalewski v. State Farm Life Ins. Co., C.A.3d, 1974, 494 F.2d 882, 884; Clark v. West Chemical Products, Inc., C.A.5th, 1977, 557 F.2d 1155, 1157.

18. See DeLuca v. Atlantic Ref. Co., C.A.2d, 1949, 176 F.2d 421, 423, certiorari denied 70 S.Ct. 423, 338 U.S. 943, 94 L.Ed. 581; Carlander v. Dubuque Fire & Marine Ins. Co., D.C.Ark.1949, 87 F.Supp. 65, 69; Clark, Special Problems in Drafting and Interpreting Procedural Code and Rules, 1950, 3 Vand.L.Rev. 493, 504.

"Since courts are composed of mere mortals they can decide matters only on the basis of probability, never on certainty. The 'slightest doubt' test, if it is taken seriously, means that summary judgment is almost never to be used—a pity in this critical time of overstrained legal resources." Chubbs v. City of New York, D.C.N.Y.1971, 324 F.Supp. 1183, 1189.

See also Frank, American Law: The Case for Radical Reform, 1969, pp. 146–152.

be given the benefit of all reasonable doubts in determining whether a genuine issue exists.[19]   Again it is sometimes said, rather opprobriously, that Rule 56 does not permit "trial by affidavits."[20]   The correct principle, which the epithet tends to conceal, is that affidavits may be used on a motion for summary judgment, but that the court may not resolve disputed fact issues by reference to the affidavits.[21]

Allegations in the pleadings do not create an issue as against a motion for summary judgment supported by affidvits. The very object of the summary judgment procedure, as then-Judge Cardozo said long ago, is "to separate what is formal or pretended in denial or averment from what is genuine and substantial, so that only the latter may subject a suitor to the burden of a trial."[22] Indeed there would be no point to Rule 56 if it did not permit a party to pierce the allegations of fact in his opponent's pleadings, for it would then merely duplicate the old common-law demurrer. Though this principle was accepted in every other circuit,[23] the Third Circuit held resolutely to the rule that pleading allegations did create an issue barring summary judgment,[24] and it was necessary to amend Rule 56(e), in 1963, to state explicitly that when the moving party has supported his motion with proper affidavits or other materials, his opponent, to defeat summary judgment, must set forth by affidavits or otherwise specific facts showing that there is a genuine issue for trial.[25]

The obligation created by amended Rule 56(e) exists only if the papers submitted by the moving party show initially the absence of a

---

19. E.g., U. S. v. Farmers Mut. Ins. Assn. of Kiron, Iowa, C.A.8th, 1961, 288 F.2d 560, 562; Chesapeake & O. Ry. Co. v. International Harvester Co., C.A.7th, 1959, 272 F.2d 139, 142; Heyward v. Public Housing Adm'n, C.A. 5th, 1956, 238 F.2d 689, 696; Begnaud v. White, C.A.6th, 1958, 170 F.2d 323, 327; Mickle v. Lipstock, D.C.S.C.1965, 39 F.R.D. 58, 61.

"Appellate courts should not look the other way to ignore the existence of the genuine issues of material facts, but neither should they strain to find the existence of such genuine issues where none exist." Mintz v. Mathers Fund, Inc., C.A.7th, 1972, 463 F.2d 495, 498.

20. Poller v. Columbia Broadcasting System, Inc., 1962, 82 S.Ct. 486, 491, 368 U.S. 464, 473, 7 L.Ed.2d 458; Redman v. Warrener, C.A.1st, 1975, 516 F.2d 766, 768; Colby v. Klune, C.A.2d, 1949, 178 F.2d 872, 873; Turner v. McWhirter Material Handling Co., D.C.Ga.1964, 35 F.R.D. 560, 563.

21. E.g., U. S. ex rel. Jones v. Rundle, C.A.3d, 1971, 453 F.2d 147, 150; F. A.

R. Liquidating Corp. v. Brownell, C.A. 3d, 1954, 209 F.2d 375; Lane Bryant, Inc. v. Maternity Lane, Ltd. of California, C.A.9th, 1949, 173 F.2d 559.

22. Richard v. Credit Suisse, 1926, 152 N.E. 110, 111, 242 N.Y. 346, 350.

23. See cases cited 10 Wright, Miller & Kane, Civil 2d § 2711 n. 19.

24. Frederick Hart & Co. v. Recordgraph Corp., C.C.A.3d, 1948, 169 F.2d 580; Reynolds Metals Co. v. Metals Disintegrating Co., C.A.3d, 1949, 176 F.2d 90; Bragen v. Hudson County News Co., C.A.3d, 1960, 278 F.2d 615.

25. First Nat. Bank of Arizona v. Cities Serv. Co., 1968, 88 S.Ct. 1575, 1592–1593, 391 U.S. 253, 289, 20 L.Ed. 2d 569; Dressler v. MV Sandpiper, C.A.2d, 1964, 331 F.2d 130, 131–135; Robin Constr. Co. v. U. S., C.A.3d, 1965, 345 F.2d 610, 614–615; Wright, Rule 56(e): A Case Study on the Need for Amending the Federal Rules, 1956, 69 Harv.L.Rev. 839; Note, Summary Judgment Under Federal Rule of Civil Procedure 56—A Need for a Clarifying Amendment, 1963, 48 Iowa L.Rev. 453.

genuine issue concerning any material fact.[26] It is only after this initial showing has been made by the movant that the party opposing the motion has a duty to respond. A continuance can be ordered to permit the opposing party to obtain additional facts, or he can defeat the motion by demonstrating that evidence exists that he would have at the trial but cannot, for some good reason, produce on the motion.[27] Despite all that may be shown, the court always has the power to deny summary judgment if, in its sound judgment, it believes for any reason that the fair and just course is to proceed to trial rather than to resolve the case on a motion.[28]

Finally, it is always true that, whether or not the non-moving party has submitted affidavits or similar material, the burden is on the moving party to establish that there is no genuine issue as to any material fact and that he is entitled to judgment as a matter of law.[29] The moving party is not entitled to the benefit of favorable inferences to be drawn from his moving papers.[30] Instead the matters presented in connection with the motion must be construed most favorably to the party opposing the motion.[31] That it may be surmised that the non-moving party is unlikely to prevail at the trial is not sufficient to authorize summary judgment against him.[32]

Much of the confusion in the case law as to the showing required to defeat a motion for summary judgment stems from the differing views various judges have as to the utility and application of this procedural device. These differences are most dramatically illustrated

26. Adickes v. S. H. Kress & Co., 1970, 90 S.Ct. 1598, 398 U.S. 144, 26 L.Ed.2d 142. See the discussion of this case in 10A Wright, Miller & Kane, Civil 2d § 2739, and the cases there cited.

As is true on all motions for summary judgment, affidavits, both in support of and in opposition to the motions may be considered only if they are made on personal knowledge, set forth facts that would be admissible in evidence, and show affirmation that the affiant is competent to testify to the matters stated in the affidavits. Rule 56(e); Automatic Radio Mfg. Co.v. Hazeltine Research, 1950, 70 S.Ct. 894, 339 U.S. 827, 94 L.Ed. 1312; Pension Benefit Guar. Corp. v. Heppenstall Co., C.A.3d, 1980, 633 F.2d 293; Dyer v. MacDougall, C.A.2d, 1952, 201 F.2d 265; 10A Wright, Miller & Kane, Civil 2d § 2738.

27. Rule 56(f); Taylor v. Rederi A/S Volo, C.A.3d, 1967, 374 F.2d 545; Slagle v. U. S., C.A.5th, 1956, 228 F.2d 673; Moore v. Kibbee, D.C.N.Y.1974, 385 F.Supp. 765; 10A Wright, Miller & Kane, Civil 2d §§ 2740, 2741.

28. Kennedy v. Silas Mason Co., 1948, 68 S.Ct. 1031, 334 U.S. 249, 92 L.Ed. 1347; McLain v. Meier, C.A.8th, 1979,

612 F.2d 349, 356; 10A Wright, Miller & Kane, Civil 2d § 2728.

29. Adickes v. S. H. Kress & Co., 1970, 90 S.Ct. 1598, 1608, 398 U.S. 144, 157, 26 L.Ed.2d 142; Mack v. Cape Elizabeth Sch. Bd., C.A.1st, 1977, 553 F.2d 720; and cases cited 10A Wright, Miller & Kane, Civil 2d § 2727 n. 1.

Louis, note 1 above, would impose a lesser burden on a motion for summary judgment by a party who would not have the burden of proof at a trial. This proposal is quite contrary to the settled rule in the cases.

30. Cochran v. U. S., D.C.Conn.1954, 123 F.Supp. 362, noted 1956, 41 Iowa L.Rev. 452.

31. E.g., U. S. v. Diebold, Inc., 1962, 82 S.Ct. 993, 369 U.S. 654, 8 L.Ed.2d 176; Cole v. Cole, C.A.4th, 1980, 633 F.2d 1083, 1090; and cases cited 10A Wright, Miller & Kane, Civil 2d § 2727 n. 5.

32. E.g., Hayden v. First Nat. Bank of Mt. Pleasant, C.A.5th, 1979, 595 F.2d 994, 997; Jobson v. Henne, C.A.2d, 1966, 355 F.2d 129, 133; Harl v. Acacia Mut. Life Ins. Co., C.A.1963, 317 F.2d 577, 115 U.S.App.D.C. 166.

by divergent opinions from the Court of Appeals for the Second Circuit, with Judge Charles E. Clark, the principal draftsman of the federal rules, the spokesman for those sympathetic to Rule 56, and Judge Jerome N. Frank representing the point of view of the rule's critics.[33] The conflict appeared most sharply in the well-known case of Arnstein v. Porter,[34] a copyright infringement action termed by a historian of the art "one of the most absurd plagiarism suits on record."[35] There was an issue whether defendant could have had access in order to copy plaintiff's composition. Each party took the deposition of the other. The defendant categorically denied access or copying and the plaintiff admitted that he had no evidence to support his contention on this point. The court, speaking through Judge Frank, characterized much of plaintiff's testimony as "fantastic,"[36] but held nevertheless that the grant of summary judgment for defendant was error, since defendant's credibility was a question of fact and plaintiff might be able to discredit defendant's denial by cross-examination before a jury. In a vigorous dissent Judge Clark spoke of "the anti-intellectual and book-burning nature" of the majority opinion, which, in his view, amounted to a "novel method of amending" Rule 56. He said: "Of course it is error to deny trial when there is a genuine dispute of facts; but it is just as much error—perhaps more in cases of hardship, or where impetus is given to strike suits—to deny or postpone judgment where the ultimate legal result is clearly indicated."[37]

The Arnstein decision is difficult to reconcile with earlier decisions from the Second Circuit, in which, however, Judge Frank either dissented or did not participate.[38] It is even more difficult to reconcile it with the later case of Dyer v. MacDougall,[39] a slander action in which defendant presented affidavits from the persons to whom the slanders were supposedly uttered, denying that the slanderous remarks were made. Judge Frank concurred in affirmance of the grant of summary judgment on this showing. Nevertheless subsequent cases from the Second Circuit seem to echo Judge Frank's views on summary judgment.[40]

On a motion for summary judgment, it may appear that there is some genuine issue as to a material fact, which requires denial of the motion, but that there is no substantial controversy as to a number of

---

33. See 10A Wright, Miller & Kane, Civil 2d § 2727.

34. C.C.A.2d, 1946, 154 F.2d 464, noted 1946, 55 Yale L.J. 810.

35. Spaeth, A History of Popular Music, 1948, p. 553.

36. 154 F.2d at 469.

37. 154 F.2d at 478, 479, 480.

38. E.g., Engl v. Aetna Life Ins. Co., C.C.A.2d, 1943, 139 F.2d 469; Madeirense Do Brasil S/A v. Stulman-

Emrick Lumber Co., C.C.A.2d, 1945, 147 F.2d 399, certiorari denied 65 S.Ct. 1201, 325 U.S. 861, 89 L.Ed. 1982. See Melville, Summary Judgment and Discovery: The Amended Rules Will Add to Their Usefulness, 1948, 34 A.B.A.J. 187.

39. C.A.2d, 1952, 201 F.2d 265.

40. E.g., Dolgow v. Anderson, C.A.2d, 1970, 438 F.2d 825; Louis, note 1 above, at 760–762.

other material facts. In that situation the court may make an entry specifying the facts that appear without substantial controversy, and these facts will be deemed established on the trial of the action.[41] Such an order is frequently referred to as a "partial summary judgment." This phrase is misleading, since a "judgment" is, by definition, appealable,[42] while the order here contemplated is not appealable unless it makes final disposition as to some claim or party and is certified as final by the court under Rule 54(b).[43]

§ 100. Declaratory Judgment [1]

In an earlier section, it was seen that for some years the Supreme Court had raised serious doubts about whether an action for a declaratory judgment was a "case or controversy" within the jurisdiction of the federal courts.[2] The Court changed its view in 1933, and this was followed immediately in 1934 by the adoption of the Federal Declaratory Judgment Act, now 28 U.S.C.A. §§ 2201, 2202. Rule 57 implements the provisions of that Act and specifies that the procedure in an action for a declaratory jdugment is to be in accord with the rules. The validity of the Act was settled quite early.[3]

Actions for declaratory judgments represent a comparatively recent development in American jurisprudence. Much of the credit for this development is due to Professors Edwin Borchard, of Yale, and Edson Sunderland, of Michigan, who crusaded for more than 30 years for a uniform state and federal declaratory relief procedure,[4] a goal that has now been substantially achieved. The traditional and conventional concept of the judicial process had been that the courts may act only in case a litigant is entitled to a coercive remedy, such as a

---

41. Rule 56(d); National Life Ins. Co. v. Silverman, C.A.1971, 454 F.2d 899, 147 U.S.App.D.C. 56; Parmelee v. Chicago Eye Shield Co., C.C.A.8th, 1946, 157 F.2d 582; Brager & Co. v. Leumi Securities Corp., D.C.N.Y.1979, 84 F.R.D. 220; Hedrick v. S. Bonaccurso & Sons, Inc., D.C.Pa.1978, 466 F.Supp. 1025; 10A Wright, Miller & Kane, Civil 2d § 2737.

42. Rule 54(a). See § 98 above.

43. Liberty Mut. Ins. Co. v. Wetzel, 1976, 96 S.Ct. 1202, 424 U.S. 737, 47 L.Ed.2d 435; Reliance Ins. Co. v. Luke, C.A.5th, 1979, 608 F.2d 1020; Clark v. Kraftco Corp., C.A.2d, 1971, 447 F.2d 933; and cases cited 10 Wright, Miller & Kane, Civil 2d § 2715 nn. 14–23.

Under appropriate circumstances the order might be certified under Rule 54(b). Norris Mfg. Co. v. R. E. Darling Co., C.A.4th, 1963, 315 F.2d 633.

[§ 100]

1. 10A Wright, Miller & Kane, Civil 2d §§ 2751–2771; Borchard, Declaratory Judgments, 2d ed. 1941; Zamir, The Declaratory Judgment Revisited, 1977, 30 Current Legal Problems 43.

2. See § 12 above, discussing the cases of Liberty Warehouse Co. v. Grannis, 1927, 47 S.Ct. 282, 273 U.S. 70, 71 L.Ed. 541, and Willing v. Chicago Auditorium Assn., 1928, 48 S.Ct. 507, 277 U.S. 274, 72 L.Ed. 880, raising such doubts, and Nashville, C. & St. L. Ry. Co. v. Wallace, 1933, 53 S.Ct. 345, 288 U.S. 249, 77 L.Ed. 730, which resolved them.

3. Aetna Life Ins. Co. v. Haworth, 1937, 57 S.Ct. 461, 300 U.S. 227, 81 L.Ed. 617.

4. Clark, Code Pleading, 2d ed. 1947, § 53, p. 333. See Sunderland, A Modern Evolution in Remedial Rights, 1917, 16 Mich.L.Rev. 69; Borchard, The Declaratory Judgment—A Needed Procedural Reform, 1918, 28 Yale L.J. 1, 105.

judgment for damages or an injunction. Until a controversy had matured to a point at which such relief was appropriate and the person entitled thereto sought to invoke it, the courts were powerless to act. At times, however, there may be an actual dispute as to the rights and obligations of the parties, and yet the controversy may not have ripened to a point at which an affirmative remedy is needed. Or this stage may have been reached, but the party entitled to seek the remedy may fail to take the necessary steps. For example, the maker of a promissory note may have stated to the payee that the instrument would not be honored at maturity, because, perhaps, his signature is claimed to have been forged or procured by fraud or affixed without his authority. The payee had to wait until payment was due before appealing to the courts. It might well have been important for him to ascertain in advance whether the note was a binding obligation and whether he might rely on it and list it among his assets. Nevertheless, he could receive no judicial relief until the instrument became due and was dishonored. Or it might have been necessary for a person to determine whether he was bound by some contractual provision that he deemed void. In that event, if he desired to contest the matter, he had to assume the risk and to hazard the consequences of committing a breach and then await a suit.[5] Or the owner of a patent might assert that a manufacturer was infringing his monopoly, while the latter contended that his product was not an infringement or that the patent was invalid. The manufacturer was helpless, however, to secure an adjudication of the issue, but had to pursue his course of action and await suit for infringement, unless he preferred to yield and discontinue his activity.

In all of these situations the declaratory judgment procedure provides a useful solution. It creates a means by which rights and obligations may be adjudicated in cases involving an actual controversy that has not reached the stage at which either party may seek a coercive remedy, or in which the party entitled to such a remedy fails to sue for it.

The critical question in each case is whether the facts averred under the existing circumstances present a real controversy between parties having adverse legal interests of such immediacy and reality as to warrant a declaratory judgment.[6] The Act, as required by the Constitution, is limited to cases that present an "actual" controversy.[7]

5. This is strikingly illustrated by Willing v. Chicago Auditorium Assn., 1928, 48 S.Ct. 507, 277 U.S. 274, 72 L.Ed. 880, in which the lessee under a long-term lease was not able to get any judicial declaration as to whether he would forfeit the lease if he tore down an unprofitable auditorium and built an office building. Compare the use of a declaratory judgment in such a situation in the cases cited note 11 below.

6. Lake Carriers Assn. v. MacMullan, 1972, 92 S.Ct. 1749, 406 U.S. 498, 32 L.Ed.2d 257; Golden v. Zwickler, 1969, 89 S.Ct. 956, 394 U.S. 103, 22 L.Ed.2d 113; Altvater v. Freeman, 1943, 63 S.Ct. 1115, 319 U.S. 359, 87 L.Ed. 1450; Maryland Cas. Co. v. Pacific Coal & Oil Co., 1941, 61 S.Ct. 510, 312 U.S. 270, 85 L.Ed. 826.

7. Aetna Life Ins. Co. v. Haworth, 1937, 57 S.Ct. 461, 300 U.S. 227, 81 L.Ed.

Necessarily the difference between an abstract question and an actual controversy is one of degree, and where there is a substantial dispute touching some real and proximate interest of the party, the fact that he has taken action in order to provoke a test case does not make the case inappropriate for a declaratory judgment.[8]

It has been suggested by distinguished scholars that there may be a difference between suit for a declaration about the legal consequences of past conduct and a suit in which a declaration is sought about the legal consequences of future conduct. The latter situation, it is said, is "doubly contingent,"[9] since the future conduct may not take place and if it does the other party may not challenge it. Of course a court should not "express legal opinions on academic theoreticals which might never come to pass."[10] But the number of contingencies that can be found in a particular situation seems largely a verbal matter, and the practical likelihood that the contingencies will occur and that the controversy is a real one should be decisive in determining whether an actual controversy exists. The courts have ordinarily not used the language of single or double contingency and they have issued declaratory judgments about the legal consequences of future conduct.[11]

Declaratory judgments are probably sought most often in insurance and patent litigation, but they are available and are used in all types of civil litigation[12] with two exceptions. Controversies over federal taxes are expressly excluded from the Declaratory Judgment Act,[13] while the Tax Injunction Act,[14] though in terms only prohibiting federal courts from enjoining the collection of state taxes if a plain,

617; Eccles v. People's Bank of Lakewood Village, 1948, 68 S.Ct. 641, 333 U.S. 426, 92 L.Ed. 784; Golden v. Zwickler, 1969, 89 S.Ct. 956, 394 U.S. 103, 22 L.Ed.2d 113; 10A Wright, Miller & Kane, Civil 2d § 2757.

8. Evers v. Dwyer, 1958, 79 S.Ct. 178, 358 U.S. 202, 3 L.Ed.2d 222, noted 1959, 30 Miss.L.J. 329. See also International Longshoremen's Assn. v. Seatrain Lines, Inc., C.A.2d, 1964, 326 F.2d 916, 918–919.

9. Hart & Wechsler, The Federal Courts and the Federal System, Bator, Mishkin, Shapiro & Wechsler ed. 1973, p. 132.

10. American Fidelity & Cas. Co. v. Pennsylvania Threshermen & Farmers Mut. Cas. Ins. Co., C.A.5th, 1960, 280 F.2d 453, 461. See also Hendrix v. Poonai, C.A.11th, 1981, 662 F.2d 719, 722.

11. E.g., Steffel v. Thompson, 1974, 94 S.Ct. 1209, 415 U.S. 452, 39 L.Ed.2d 505, conformed to C.A.5th, 494 F.2d 691; Super Products Corp. v. D P Way Corp., C.A.7th, 1976, 546 F.2d 748;

Technical Tape Corp. v. Minnesota Mining & Mfg. Co., C.A.2d, 1952, 200 F.2d 876.

Courts have refused to entertain the case if the future events are not sufficiently real or immediate. E.g., International Harvester Co. v. Deere & Co., C.A.7th, 1980, 623 F.2d 1207, 1215–1217; Wembley, Inc. v. Superba Cravats, Inc., C.A.2d, 1963, 315 F.2d 87; Enka B. V. of Arnhem, Holland v. E. I. duPont de Nemours & Co., D.C.Del.1981, 519 F.Supp. 356.

The "doubly contingent" language is used in McCahill v. Borough of Fox Chapel, C.A.3d, 1971, 438 F.2d 213, 218.

12. 10A Wright, Miller & Kane, Civil 2d §§ 2760–2765.

13. See Bob Jones Univ. v. Simon, 1974, 94 S.Ct. 2038, 2045 n. 7, 416 U.S. 725, 732 n. 7, 40 L.Ed.2d 496; and cases cited 10A Wright, Miller & Kane, Civil 2d § 2762 nn. 3, 4.

14. 28 U.S.C.A. § 1341. See § 51 above.

speedy, and efficient remedy is available in the courts of the state, has recently been read as also barring declaratory judgments about state taxes if an injunction would be barred.[15]

It is always discretionary with the court whether to entertain an action for a declaratory judgment.[16] It may refuse to give such relief where the judgment sought would not settle the controversy between the parties,[17] or would cause inconvenience to some of them,[18] or where the declaratory judgment action is being used for "procedural fencing."[19] At the same time, as Rule 57 specifically provides, the existence of another adequate remedy,[20] or even the pendency of another suit in state or federal court,[21] does not bar an otherwise appropriate action for a declaratory judgment. The determinative factor is whether the declaratory action will probably result in a just and more expeditious and economical determination of the entire controversy.[22]

15. California v. Grace Brethren Church, 1982, 102 S.Ct. 2498, ___ U.S. ___, 73 L.Ed.2d 93.

16. Brillhart v. Excess Ins. Co. of America, 1942, 62 S.Ct. 1173, 1175, 316 U.S. 491, 494, 86 L.Ed. 1620; Public Affairs Associates, Inc. v. Rickover, 1962, 82 S.Ct. 580, 582, 369 U.S. 111, 112, 7 L.Ed.2d 604; Borchard, Discretion to Refuse Jurisdiction of Actions for Declaratory Judgments, 1942, 26 Minn.L.Rev. 677; 10A Wright, Miller & Kane, Civil 2d § 2759.

"In the exercise of their sound discretion to entertain declaratory actions the district courts may not decline on the basis of whim or personal disinclination; but they may take into consideration the speculativeness of the situation before them and the adequacy of the record for the determination they are called upon to make, as well as other factors, such as whether there is a pending procedure in state court in which the matters in controversy between the parties may be fully litigated." Hollis v. Itawamba County Loans, C.A.5th, 1981, 657 F.2d 746, 750.

17. Aetna Cas. & Sur. Co. v. Quarles, C.C.A.4th, 1937, 92 F.2d 321; Williams v. Ball, C.A.2d, 1961, 294 F.2d 94, certiorari denied 82 S.Ct. 598, 368 U.S. 990, 7 L.Ed.2d 526.

18. Kozol v. Lumbermens Mut. Cas. Co., D.C.Mass.1962, 201 F.Supp. 718; Ohio Cas. Ins. Co. v. Richards, D.C.Or.1939, 27 F.Supp. 18; Lumbermens Mut. Cas. Co. of Illinois (American) v. Cieri, D.C. Pa.1938, 23 F.Supp. 435.

19. Hanes Corp. v. Millard, C.A.1976, 531 F.2d 585, 593 n. 5, 174 U.S.App. D.C. 253; Shell Oil Co. v. Frusetta,

C.A.9th, 1961, 290 F.2d 689, 692; Franklin Life Ins. Co. v. Johnson, C.C.A.10th, 1946, 157 F.2d 653, 656.

It has been held that a prospective negligence action defendant should not be able to obtain a declaratory judgment of nonliability since this would force the injured party to litigate his claim at a time and place of the alleged tortfeasor's choosing. Cunningham Bros., Inc. v. Bail, C.A.7th, 1969, 407 F.2d 1165; UNC Resources, Inc. v. Benally, D.C.Ariz.1981, 518 F.Supp. 1046, 1049; Frito-Lay, Inc. v. Dent, D.C.Miss.1974, 373 F.Supp. 771. But an interesting state court case shows that there are circumstances in which a declaratory judgment may be useful in negligence litigation. Ditzler v. Spee, 1970, 180 N.W.2d 178, 288 Minn. 314. See 10A Wright, Miller & Kane, Civil 2d § 2765, pp. 729–731.

20. E.g., Scott-Burr. Stores Corp. v. Wilcox, C.A.5th, 1952, 194 F.2d 989; Mutual Life Ins. Co. of New York v. Krejci, C.C.A.7th, 1942, 123 F.2d 594; U. S. Fidelity & Guar. Co. v. Koch, C.C.A.3d, 1939, 102 F.2d 288; New York Life Ins. Co. v. Roe, C.C.A.8th, 1939, 102 F.2d 28.

21. E.g., Provident Tradesmens Bank & Trust Co. v. Patterson, 1968, 88 S.Ct. 733, 746–747, 390 U.S. 102, 125–128, 19 L.Ed.2d 936; Peabody Coal Co. v. Erwin, C.A.6th, 1971, 453 F.2d 398; Western Cas. & Sur. Co. v. Teel, C.A.10th, 1968, 391 F.2d 764; Tyrill v. Alcoa S. S. Co., D.C.N.Y.1958, 172 F.Supp. 363, affirmed C.A.2d, 1959, 266 F.2d 27.

22. Maryland Cas. Co. v. Boyle Constr. Co., C.C.A.4th, 1941, 123 F.2d 558, 565. See also Guardian Life Ins. Co. of America v. Kortz, C.C.A.10th, 1945,

The Supreme Court has frequently, although not invariably, indicated a very marked reluctance to have important issues of public law resolved by declaratory judgments.[23] It has said that declaratory judgment procedure should not be used to preempt and prejudge issues that are committed for initial decision to an administrative body or special tribunal,[24] and warned against grant of a declaratory judgment involving an important question of public law on the basis of a sparse and inadequate record.[25] The Court has said also that questions of the scope and constitutionality of legislation must not be decided "in advance of its immediate adverse effect in the context of a concrete case."[26]

Despite these repeated cautions, it is clear that declaratory judgments play an important part in litigation of constitutional issues and other issues of public law. The Supreme Court has held that declaratory relief was appropriate in a case raising a constitutional issue of the utmost importance and sensitivity [27] and it has expressed a willingness to have declaratory actions used to challenge the constitutionality of state laws if no state proceeding is pending.[28]

The Declaratory Judgment Act is not a grant of jurisdiction to the federal courts. It merely makes available an additional remedy in

151 F.2d 582, 586; Smith v. Vowell, D.C.Tex.1974, 379 F.Supp. 139, 162, affirmed without opinion C.A.5th, 504 F.2d 759; Western v. McGehee, D.C. Md.1962, 202 F.Supp. 287, 294; 10A Wright, Miller & Kane, Civil 2d § 2758.

The factors to be considered are enlighteningly discussed in National Union Fire Ins. Co. v. Lippert Bros., Inc., D.C.Neb.1964, 233 F.Supp. 650. See also Puerto Rico Intl. Airlines, Inc. v. Silva Recio, C.A.1st, 1975, 520 F.2d 1342.

For recent illustrations of situations in which it was concluded that the court properly exercised its discretion in deferring to another action, see Fay v. Fitzgerald, C.A.2d, 1973, 478 F.2d 181, and PPG Indus., Inc. v. Continental Oil Co., C.A.5th, 1973, 478 F.2d 674, noted 1973, 51 Texas L.Rev. 1252.

23. E.g., United Public Workers v. Mitchell, 1946, 67 S.Ct. 556, 330 U.S. 75, 91 L.Ed. 754; Eccles v. Peoples Bank of Lakewood Village, 1948, 68 S.Ct. 641, 333 U.S. 426, 92 L.Ed. 784; Golden v. Zwickler, 1969, 89 S.Ct. 956, 394 U.S. 103, 22 L.Ed.2d 113; 10A Wright, Miller & Kane, Civil 2d § 2763.

24. Public Serv. Comm. of Utah v. Wycoff Co., 1952, 73 S.Ct. 236, 344 U.S. 237, 97 L.Ed. 291, noted 1953, 3 Utah L.Rev. 388; cf. A. L. Mechling

Barge Lines, Inc. v. U. S., 1961, 82 S.Ct. 337, 368 U.S. 324, 7 L.Ed.2d 317. Compare Toilet Goods Assn. v. Gardner, 1967, 87 S.Ct. 1520, 387 U.S. 158, 18 L.Ed.2d 697, with Abbott Laboratories v. Gardner, 1967, 87 S.Ct. 1507, 387 U.S. 136, 18 L.Ed.2d 681.

25. A. L. Mechling Barge Lines, Inc. v. U. S., 1962, 82 S.Ct. 337, 368 U.S. 324, 7 L.Ed.2d 317; Public Affairs Associates, Inc. v. Rickover, 1962, 82 S.Ct. 580, 369 U.S. 111, 7 L.Ed.2d 604; Askew v. Hargrave, 1971, 91 S.Ct. 856, 401 U.S. 476, 28 L.Ed.2d 196.

26. International Longshoremen's and Warehousemen's Union v. Boyd, 1954, 74 S.Ct. 447, 448, 347 U.S. 222, 224, 98 L.Ed. 650.

See also Zemel v. Rusk, 1965, 85 S.Ct. 1271, 381 U.S. 1, 14 L.Ed.2d 179; McCahill v. Borough of Fox Chapel, C.A. 3d, 1971, 438 F.2d 213; Dickson, Declaratory Remedies and Constitutional Change, 1971, 24 Vand.L.Rev. 257.

27. Powell v. McCormack, 1969, 89 S.Ct. 1944, 395 U.S. 486, 23 L.Ed.2d 491.

28. Steffel v. Thompson, 1974, 94 S.Ct. 1209, 415 U.S. 452, 39 L.Ed.2d 505. See § 52A above and Note, Federal Declaratory Relief and the Non-pending State Criminal Suit, 1974, 34 Md.L.Rev. 87.

cases of which they have jurisdiction by virtue of diversity and the requisite amount in controversy, or because of a federal question.[29] Similarly the procedure in a declaratory judgment action is the same as that in any other action. Only two difficult procedural questions have arisen. These concern the effect of a declaratory action on the burden of proof and on the right to jury trial.

The answer to the question about jury trial is now clear. Although it is sometimes said that an action for a declaratory judgment is "equitable in nature,"[30] other cases have spoken of an action for a declaratory judgment as "essentially legal."[31] The truth is that "a declaratory judgment action is a statutory creation, and by its nature is neither fish nor fowl, neither legal nor equitable."[32] The new remedy may be sought both in cases that historically would have been legal and those that historically would have been equitable. Of course the availability of this new procedure cannot be used to erode a constitutional right to a jury that would have existed if there were no such procedure.[33] The solution the courts have worked out is to look to the kind of action in which the issue involved would have been decided if there were no declaratory judgment procedure.[34] Thus in one typical case an insurance company sought a declaratory judgment that an accident in which its insured was involved was not within the coverage of the policy. There were three ways in which this issue of coverage could have been litigated were there no declaratory judgment procedure. The insured could have paid a judgment against him and sued the insurer for the amount due him by way of indemnity. This would be a simple action for the recovery of money only, which at common law would have been tried in debt or assumpsit and which thus would be triable to a jury today. If the insured failed to pay the judgment, the injured person, under the relevant state statutes, could have brought an independent action against the insurer for the amount of the judgment, which would be triable to a jury, or at his option he could have garnished the insurer, and the garnishment proceeding would be tried, in the state in question, with-

29. 10A Wright, Miller & Kane, Civil 2d §§ 2766, 2767. The jurisdictional questions are particularly complex in a federal question case. See § 18 above.

30. Abbott Laboratories v. Gardner, 1967, 87 S.Ct. 1507, 1519, 387 U.S. 136, 155, 18 L.Ed.2d 681.

31. Simler v. Conner, 1963, 83 S.Ct. 609, 611, 372 U.S. 221, 223, 9 L.Ed.2d 691.

32. American Safety Equipment Corp. v. J. P. Maguire & Co., C.A.2d, 1968, 391 F.2d 821, 824. In this case the right of interlocutory appeal depended on whether the action was regarded as legal or equitable. See also Wallace v. Norman Indus. Inc., C.A.5th, 1972, 467 F.2d 824.

33. Simler v. Conner, 1963, 83 S.Ct. 609, 611, 372 U.S. 221, 223, 9 L.Ed.2d 691; Beacon Theatres v. Westover, 1959, 79 S.Ct. 948, 359 U.S. 500, 3 L.Ed.2d 988; Fraser, Jury Trials in Declaratory Judgment Actions, 1967, 52 Iowa L.Rev. 609; Comment, The Right to Trial by Jury in Declaratory Judgment Actions, 1971, 3 Conn.L.Rev. 564; 9 Wright & Miller, Civil § 2313.

34. Pacific Indem. Co. v. McDonald, C.C.A.9th, 1939, 107 F.2d 446, 448, 131 A.L.R. 208; (American) Lumbermens Mut. Cas. Co. of Illinois v. Timms & Howard, Inc., C.C.A.2d, 1939, 108 F.2d 497; James v. Pennsylvania General Ins. Co., C.A.1965, 349 F.2d 228, 121 U.S.App.D.C. 251.

out a jury. Since the issues of coverage would, then, usually be tried to a jury, and would only be tried without a jury if the injured person so elected by using garnishment rather than bringing an independent action, the court held that in the declaratory judgment action it was error to deny trial by jury over a demand for jury trial by the injured person.[35]

The question of burden of proof is not yet settled. It arises when, as in the example just described, the parties are reversed by virtue of the declaratory judgment action. If there were no declaratory judgment procedure, the issue of policy coverage would come up when the injured person or the insured sued the insurer, and in such a suit that person, as plaintiff, would have the burden of proof on this issue. There is strong support for the view that he still has the burden of proof even though the insurer has instituted the action.[36] Though this is consistent with the result as to jury trial just described, the case law is in much confusion,[37] and there is a good deal to be said for the view that the party who brings a law suit—in the example given, the insurer—should carry the burden.[38] Even if the view first described should prevail, it is substantially qualified in practice by a well-developed line of authority that holds that if the plaintiff in the declaratory judgment action voluntarily goes forward and attempts to prove its case, it will be held to have assumed the risk of nonpersuasion.[39]

There is not much law on whether the availability of a declaratory judgment in a diversity case should depend on state law, probably because virtually all states have statutes similar to the federal act. If a state simply does not provide for declaratory judgments, it would seem that a federal court is nevertheless free to grant such relief, which may be regarded as "procedural" and is expressly authorized by Act of Congress.[40] It has been held, however, that where a state, though permitting declaratory judgments generally, refuses to permit them in one particular situation in order to further a unique state policy, the state rule must be followed and similar declaratory judg-

35. Johnson v. Fidelity & Cas. Co. of New York, C.A.8th, 1956, 238 F.2d 322.

36. Fireman's Fund Ins. Co. v. Videfreeze Corp., C.A.3d, 1976, 540 F.2d 1171, certiorari denied 97 S.Ct. 767, 429 U.S. 1053, 50 L.Ed.2d 770; Preferred Acc. Ins. Co. of New York v. Grasso, C.A.2d, 1951, 186 F.2d 987; Travelers Ins. Co. v. Greenough, 1937, 190 A. 129, 88 N.H. 391; Borchard, note 1 above, at pp. 404–409; cf. Royal Indem. Co. v. Wingate, D.C.Md.1973, 353 F.Supp. 1002, affirmed without opinion C.A.4th, 1973, 487 F.2d 1398.

37. See the cases cited 10A Wright, Miller & Kane, Civil 2d § 2770.

38. See Developments in the Law—Declaratory Judgments, 1949, 62 Harv.L. Rev. 787, 836–838.

39. Liberty Mut. Ins. Co. v. Sweeney, C.A.3d, 1954, 216 F.2d 209, 210; Pacific Portland Cement Co. v. Food Machinery & Chem. Corp., C.A.9th, 1949, 178 F.2d 541, 547; Bauer v. Clark, C.C.A. 7th, 1949, 161 F.2d 397, 401; Hartford Acc. & Indem. Co. v. Lougee, 1938, 196 A. 267, 89 N.H. 222.

40. See M. Swift & Sons, Inc. v. Lemon, D.C.N.Y.1959, 24 F.R.D. 43, 45. There is also a dictum to this effect in Skelly Oil Co. v. Phillips Petroleum Co., 1950, 70 S.Ct. 876, 880, 339 U.S. 667, 674, 94 L.Ed. 1194.

ments refused in federal courts in that state in diversity actions.[41] That decision was questionable when it was handed down, and its authority has been eroded by the later decision in Hanna v. Plumer.[42] The fact that the right of action is state-created, and that the state would not allow a declaratory judgment suit under the circumstances, may, however, be an appropriate factor for the court to consider in exercising its discretion whether to hear the declaratory action.

A judgment in a declaratory judgment action is conclusive in a subsequent action between the parties as to the matters declared and, in accordance with the usual rules of issue preclusion, as to any issues actually litigated and determined.[43] Further necessary or proper relief based on a declaratory judgment may be granted, after reasonable notice and hearing, against any adverse party whose rights have been determined by the judgment.[44] Although the Supreme Court has voiced some uncertainty about the res judicata effect to be given to a federal declaratory judgment by a state court,[45] the Court's concern apparently is limited to the special situation in which a federal declaration that a state statute is unconstitutional may interfere with state law enforcement.[46]

41. Allstate Ins. Co. v. Charneski, C.A. 7th, 1960, 286 F.2d 238. See § 59 above. For varying views of this decision, compare Comment, The Constitutional Power of Congress to Control Procedure in the Federal Courts, 1961, 56 Nw.U.L.Rev. 560, with Smith, Blue Ridge and Beyond: A Byrd's Eye View of Federalism in Diversity Litigation, 1962, 36 Tul.L.Rev. 443.

42. 1965, 85 S.Ct. 1136, 380 U.S. 460, 14 L.Ed.2d 8. See § 55 above.

Post-Hanna cases have held that federal law determines whether a federal court can give a declaratory judgment. Farmers Alliance Mut. Ins. Co. v. Jones, C.A.10th, 1978, 570 F.2d 1384, certiorari denied 99 S.Ct. 97, 439 U.S. 826, 58 L.Ed.2d 119; Beacon Constr. Co. v. Matco Elec. Co., Inc., C.A.2d, 1975, 521 F.2d 392, 397–399; American Motorists Ins. Co. v. Mack, D.C.Pa. 1965, 248 F.Supp. 1016.

43. Restatement Second of Judgments, 1982, § 33; 18 Wright, Miller & Cooper, Jurisdiction, § 4446; Note, The Res Judicata Effect of Declaratory Relief

in the Federal Courts, 1973, 45 S.Cal.L. Rev. 803.

44. 28 U.S.C.A. § 2202; Powell v. McCormack, 1969, 89 S.Ct. 1944, 1952, 395 U.S. 486, 499, 23 L.Ed.2d 491; 10A Wright, Miller & Kane, Civil 2d § 2771.

45. Steffel v. Thompson, 1974, 94 S.Ct. 1209, 1221, 415 U.S. 452, 470–471, 39 L.Ed.2d 505. See also id., 94 S.Ct. at 1224–1225, 415 U.S. at 477 (White, J., concurring); 94 S.Ct. at 1227 n. 3, 415 U.S. at 482 n. 3 (Rehnquist, J., concurring).

See also U. S. ex rel. Lawrence v. Woods, C.A.7th, 1970, 432 F.2d 1072, certiorari denied 91 S.Ct. 1658, 402 U.S. 983, 29 L.Ed.2d 148; Comment, The Binding Effect of Federal Declaratory Judgments on State Courts, 1973, 51 Texas L.Rev. 743.

46. Shapiro, State Courts and Federal Declaratory Judgments, 1979, 74 Nw. U.L.Rev. 759; Restatement Second of Judgments, Reporter's Note to § 33 comm. b.

§ 100A. Effect of a Prior Judgment [1]

"The defense of res judicata is universally respected, but actually not very well liked." [2] So wrote one of America's greatest proceduralists, Judge Charles E. Clark, in a 1945 dissent. Compare with that a 1981 decision in which a court of appeals had held that "simple justice" dictated that it should not hold a party barred by res judicata. Justice Rehnquist answered for the Supreme Court that "we do not see the grave injustice which would be done by the application of accepted principles of res judicata. 'Simple justice' is achieved when a complex body of law developed over a period of years is evenhandedly applied. The doctrine of res judicata serves vital public interests beyond any individual judge's ad hoc determination of the equities in a particular case." [3]

The new attitude toward res judicata, toward the various ways in which a judgment in one action will have a binding effect in another, has certainly been influenced by the flood of cases that have come into the courts. Courts today are having difficulty giving a litigant one day in court. To allow that litigant a second day is a luxury that cannot be afforded. But "it is clear that more than crowded dockets is involved." [4] Modern scholarship had looked hard at the rules of res judicata and found that they had failed to keep pace with the rules of procedure that they complement. [5]

The central proposition of res judicata remains, as it has always been, that "a party who has had a full opportunity to present a contention in court ordinarily should be denied permission to assert it on some subsequent occasion." [6] What has only recently been grasped is that the traditional rules of res judicata had developed at a time when the common law system of pleading and procedure was still in vogue. Modern procedural notions, found in the Federal Rules of Civil Procedure and in most of the states, have greatly expanded the opportunity to present all of the contentions a party has in a single action. Joinder of claims is no longer restricted by the forms of action and the separation of law and equity. Joinder of parties has been liberal-

[§ 100A]

1. 18 Wright, Miller & Cooper, Jurisdiction, c. 13; Restatement Second of Judgments, 1982; Casad, Res Judicata in a Nutshell, 1976; James & Hazard, Civil Procedure, 2d ed. 1977, c. 11.

2. Riordan v. Ferguson, C.C.A.2d, 1945, 147 F.2d 983, 988.

3. Federated Department Stores, Inc. v. Moitie, 1981, 101 S.Ct. 2424, 2429, 452 U.S. 394, 401, 69 L.Ed.2d 103, noted 1982, 59 U.Det.J.Urb.L. 440, 30 U.Kan. L.Rev. 455.

4. Blonder-Tongue Laboratories, Inc. v. University of Illinois Foundation, 1971, 91 S.Ct. 1434, 1442, 402 U.S. 313, 328, 28 L.Ed.2d 788.

"To preclude parties from contesting matters that they have had a full and fair opportunity to litigate protects their adversaries from the expense and vexation attending multiple lawsuits, conserves judicial resources, and fosters reliance on judicial action by minimizing the possibility of inconsistent decisions." Montana v. U. S., 1979, 99 S.Ct. 970, 973–974, 440 U.S. 147, 153–154, 59 L.Ed.2d 210.

5. Vestal, Res Judicata/Preclusion, 1969; Hazard, Res Nova in Res Judicata, 1971, 44 S.Cal.L.Rev. 1036; Cleary, Res Judicata Reexamined, 1948, 57 Yale L.J. 339.

6. Hazard, note 5 above, at 1043.

ized so that a lawsuit need not be merely a two-party matter but can include persons interested in a controversy from many sides. Pleadings no longer need be precise, and modern rules on amendment allow them to be changed as the case develops. The rules on discovery give a party the ability to learn fully about his case. Modern procedure has expanded the scope of the initial opportunity to litigate and this has made inevitable the narrowing of the situations in which a second opportunity to litigate need be given.[7]

This modern thinking about res judicata has not only produced new and more restrictive rules on when relitigation will be allowed, but it has also produced rules that are cast in practical and empirical terms. It is no longer necessary to resort to "the question-begging and illusorily definite conceptual categories of 'cause of action,' 'privity,' and 'on the merits.' "[8] The new approach has been enthusiastically accepted by the United States Supreme Court and by many state courts.[9] The acceptance this approach has had in the courts has made it possible to bring together the current analysis of problems of preclusion in an elegant Restatement Second of Judgments, which is likely to be immensely influential.[10]

It has been said that the changes in this area of the law "are clearly evolutionary rather than revolutionary."[11] This may be true; but only those who cannot distinguish between a monkey and a man will think that the changes are less marked for that reason.

Space limitations make it impossible to give here any kind of comprehensive overview of res judicata.[12] The present section can do no

---

7. James & Hazard, note 1 above, at 531.

The relation is neatly put in Restatement Second of Judgments, 1982, c. 1, at p. 10: "The rules of res judicata in modern procedure therefore may fairly be characterized as illiberal toward the opportunity for relitigation. Their rigor contrasts sharply with the liberality of the rules governing the original event, which is the theme of the Federal Rules of Civil Procedure and similar systems.   *   *   *

"That difference does not represent a contradiction or ambivalence in procedural policy. Rather, it reflects the relationship between rules of original procedure and rules of res judicata. Inasmuch as the former are now generally permissive, the latter are correspondingly restrictive."

8. Hazard, note 5 above, at 1043.

9. Indeed a principal impetus toward the new way of thinking was the pathbreaking opinion by Chief Justice Roger J. Traynor in Bernhard v. Bank of America Nat. Trust & Sav. Assn., 1942,

122 P.2d 892, 19 Cal.2d 807. See below at note 57.

10. There is a useful Symposium on Restatement Second, 1981, 66 Cornell L.Rev. 401. See also Casad, Two Important Books on Res Judicata, 1982, 80 Mich.L.Rev. 664.

Even before Restatement Second was finally approved, courts had often cited and followed formulations contained in Tentative Drafts of that project. The numbering of sections is not the same in the Official Draft as in the Tentative Drafts. Helpful tables in the rear of the second volume of the Official Draft make it easy to identify provisions there with their counterparts in a Tentative Draft.

11. Martin, The Restatement (Second) of Judgments: An Overview, 1981, 66 Cornell L.Rev. 404, 405.

12. Volume 18 of Wright, Miller & Cooper, Jurisdiction devotes 801 pages to current federal law on the subject without purporting to get into the rich and often divergent strands of state law.

more than to inform the reader that this is now a lively and important part of adjective law, to explain the new terminology that is now being used, and to mention a few of the special problems that come from having parallel systems of state and federal courts.

"Res judicata" has been used in this section as a general term referring to all of the ways in which one judgment will have a binding effect on another. That usage is and doubtless will continue to be common, but it lumps under a single name two very different effects of judgments. The first is the effect of foreclosing any litigation of matters that never have been litigated, because of the determination that they should have been advanced in an earlier suit. The second is the effect of foreclosing relitigation of matters that have once been litigated and decided. The first of these, preclusion of matters that were never litigated, has gone under the name, "true res judicata,"[13] or the names, "merger" and "bar."[14] The second doctrine, preclusion of matters that have once been decided, has usually been called "collateral estoppel."[15] Professor Allan Vestal has long argued for use of the names "claim preclusion" and "issue preclusion" for these two doctrines,[16] and this usage is increasingly employed by the courts as it is by Restatement Second of Judgments.[17]

The general rule of claim preclusion is that a valid and final judgment on a claim precludes a second action on that claim or any part of it.[18] The judgment must be final,[19] but an otherwise final judgment of a trial court is regarded as final even though an appeal from it is pending.[20] Cases continue to say that the judgment has a preclusive effect only if it is "on the merits,"[21] but that terminology has been avoided in Restatement Second "because of its possibly misleading connotations."[22] It is sufficient that in the first litigation there

13. E.g., White v. World Fin. of Meridian, Inc., C.A.5th, 1981, 653 F.2d 147, 150 n. 5; Ross v. International Broth. of Elec. Workers, C.A.9th, 1980, 634 F.2d 453, 457 n. 6.

14. Restatement Second of Judgments, 1982, Introductory Note before § 24; Kaspar Wire Works, Inc. v. Leco Engineering & Machine, Inc., C.A.5th, 1978, 575 F.2d 530, 535. The Kaspar case has a highly useful summary of the major variations in terminology.

15. E.g., Lawlor v. National Screen Serv. Corp., 1955, 75 S.Ct. 865, 867, 349 U.S. 322, 326, 99 L.Ed. 1122.

16. E.g., Vestal, Rationale of Preclusion, 1964, 9 St.L.U.L.J. 29.

17. 18 Wright, Miller & Cooper, Jurisdiction § 4402; Casad, note 1 above, § 1–2.

18. Restatement Second of Judgments, 1982, §§ 18, 19; 18 Wright, Miller & Cooper, Jurisdiction §§ 4406–4409.

19. Restatement Second of Judgments, 1982, § 13; 18 Wright, Miller & Cooper, Jurisdiction § 4432.

20. Restatement Second of Judgments, 1982, § 13, comm. f; 18 Wright, Miller & Cooper, Jurisdiction § 4433. Even if the first judgment is ultimately reversed, this does not automatically mean nullification of the judgment in a second action in which the first judgment was given preclusive effect. Reed v. Allen, 1932, 52 S.Ct. 532, 286 U.S. 191, 76 L.Ed. 1054; Restatement Second of Judgments, 1982, § 16.

21. E.g., Kremer v. Chemical Constr. Corp., 1982, 102 S.Ct. 1883, 1889 n. 6, ___ U.S. ___, ___ n. 6, 72 L.Ed.2d 262.

22. Restatement Second of Judgments, 1982, § 19, comm. a. See James & Hazard, note 1 above, § 11.15.

was an opportunity to get to the merits. Those situations in which plaintiff was unable to get to the merits in the first action because of some procedural barrier are now identified and made exceptions to the general rule of claim preclusion.[23]

Claim preclusion applies "not only as to every matter which was offered and received to sustain or defeat the claim or demand, but as to any other admissible matter which might have been offered for that purpose."[24] Indeed the principal distinction between claim preclusion and issue preclusion is, as noted earlier, that the former forecloses litigation of matters that never have been litigated. This makes it important to know the dimensions of the "claim" that is foreclosed by bringing the first action, but unfortunately no precise definition is possible. Restatement Second has taken a pragmatic approach that looks to the transaction from which the action arose. The claim extinguished "includes all rights of the plaintiff to remedies against the defendant with respect to all or any part of the transaction, or series of connected transactions, out of which the action arose," and what constitutes a "transaction" or a "series" is "to be determined pragmatically, giving weight to such considerations as whether the facts are related in time, space, origin, or motivation, whether they form a convenient trial unit, and whether their treatment as a unit conforms to the parties' expectations or business understanding or usage."[25] That formulation defines a process rather than an absolute concept. The test thus stated is fully consistent with the clear rules that control the vast run of ordinary litigation and suggests the approach that should be taken in unusual litigation.[26] It applies to extinguish a claim by the plaintiff against the defendant even though the plaintiff is prepared in the second action to present evidence or grounds or theories of the case not presented in the first action, or to seek remedies or forms of relief not demanded in the first action.[27] For many common kinds of cases the rules on what is or is not a single claim are already well worked out in the decisions.[28] For those situations where this is not true, the test is imprecise, but no more so than the test for determining which counterclaims are compulsory.[29] Here, as with the compulsory counter-

---

23. Restatement Second of Judgments, 1982, § 20, listing such situations as where the first judgment was for lack of jurisdiction, improper venue, non-joinder or misjoinder of parties, prematurity, failure to satisfy a precondition to suit, or dismissal without prejudice. See 18 Wright, Miller & Cooper, Jurisdiction §§ 4435–4447.

24. Cromwell v. County of Sac, 1877, 94 U.S. 351, 352, 24 L.Ed. 195.

25. Restatement Second of Judgments, 1982 § 24.

26. 18 Wright, Miller & Cooper, Jurisdiction § 4407.

27. Restatement Second of Judgments, 1982, § 25. See. e.g., Constantini v. Trans World Airlines, C.A.9th, 1982, 681 F.2d 1199; Comment, The Res Judicata Implications of Pendent Jurisdiction, 1981, 66 Cornell L.Rev. 608.

28. 18 Wright, Miller & Cooper, Jurisdiction §§ 4408–4411; Casad, note 1 above, §§ 3–9 to 3–25; James & Hazard, note 1 above, §§ 11.9–11.12. The illustrations to §§ 24 and 25 of Restatement Second also show many of the areas for which there are clear rules.

29. See § 59 above.

claim rule, the safe course is to bring forward in the first action any-thing that might later be thought to have arisen out of the same transaction.   There are also a number of exceptions to the general rule of claim preclusion, such as consent or acquiescence by the de-fendant to the bringing of two actions, limitations on the first pro-ceeding that made it impossible to sue on the entire claim, and con-flict with other public policies.[30]

The general rule of issue preclusion is that if an issue of fact or law was actually litigated and determined by a valid and final judg-ment, the determination is conclusive in a subsequent action between the parties, whether on the same or a different claim.[31] The determi-nation must have been essential to the first judgment, however, and if the court has determined two issues, either of which standing inde-pendently would be sufficient to support the result, it cannot be said that either determination was essential to the judgment and thus it will not be conclusive with respect to either issue.[32] The requirement that there have been a final judgment in the first action is applied less rigidly to issue preclusion than to claim preclusion. For pur-poses of issue preclusion, a final judgment includes any prior adjudi-cation of an issue in another action that is "determined to be suffi-ciently firm to be accorded conclusive effect."[33]

Suppose, by way of example, that Paul sues Davis, claiming that a widget manufactured by Davis infringes a patent held by Paul. The court finds that Paul's patent is valid and that it is being infringed, and gives judgment for Paul. Subsequently Davis retools his plant and begins manufacture and sale of "New! Improved! Widget II." Paul thinks that this is as much an infringement of his patent as was the original device and brings a second suit. Claim preclusion does not apply, since Widget II did not exist at the time of the first ac-tion.[34] Davis is fully free to litigate in the second suit whether Wid-

30. Restatement Second of Judgments, 1982, § 26; 18 Wright, Miller & Coop-er, Jurisdiction §§ 4412, 4413, 4415; Casad, note 1 above, §§ 3–19 to 3–24.

31. Restatement Second of Judgments, 1982, § 27; 18 Wright, Miller & Coop-er, Jurisdiction §§ 4416–4419.

An often-difficult question in issue pre-clusion, the existence of which can only be noted here, is defining the dimen-sions of the issue that is precluded. There need not be total identity be-tween the particular matter presented in the second action and that presented in the first. Restatement Second of Judgments, 1982, § 27 comm. c; 18 Wright, Miller & Cooper, Jurisdiction § 4417. Thus, if A claims that B was negligent in driving at an excessive rate of speed, and that issue is deter-mined in B's favor, in a subsequent suit by B against A, A is precluded

from defending on the ground of con-tributory negligence, even though he now wishes to claim negligence in re-spects other than excessive speed. Re-statement Second of Judgments, 1982, § 27, ill. 4.

32. Restatement Second of Judgments, 1982, § 27 comm. h, i, j. The result is different, however, and both of the al-ternative determinations are conclu-sive, if an appellate court upholds both of those determinations. Id., § 27 comm. o. See 18 Wright, Miller & Cooper, Jurisdiction § 4421.

33. Restatement Second of Judgments, 1982, § 13; 18 Wright, Miller & Coop-er, Jurisdiction § 4434.

34. Cf. illustrations 7 and 8 to Restate-ment Second of Judgments, 1982, § 24. If Davis had been manufacturing both devices at the time of the original suit,

get II infringes the patent. That issue has never been litigated, and there is no issue preclusion with regard to it. As between Paul and Davis, however, it has been determined that Paul's patent is valid. That issue was actually litigated and determined in the first suit, and that determination was essential to the judgment. Therefore Davis cannot again contest the validity of the patent.

The situation would be quite different if judgment had gone for Davis in the first suit, with the court finding that Paul's patent was invalid, but also that it was not infringed. If Paul then brings a second action concerning Widget II, no issue is precluded. There has never been a determination whether Widget II infringes, and although it was determined in the first action that Paul's patent was not valid, that was only an alternative determination by a court of first instance. Since the judgment for Davis could have rested solely on the finding that his device did not infringe the patent, the further holding that the patent was invalid was not essential to the judgment and has no preclusive effect.[35]

Neither claim preclusion nor issue preclusion can apply unless the party against whom preclusion is asserted had a "full and fair opportunity" to litigate the claim or issue in the first action.[36] This is recognized in the exceptions to the rule of claim preclusion.[37] There are also exceptions to the rule of issue preclusion, and these are somewhat more flexible than are the exceptions to claim preclusion, although it is not often that they need to be applied. There is no issue preclusion if appellate review could not have been obtained of the judgment in the first action,[38] or the issue is one of law and there has been a change in the legal context or the claims are substantially unrelated,[39] or because a new determination of the issue is warranted by differences in the quality or extensiveness of the procedure followed in the two courts[40] or there is a significant difference in the burden

---

Paul might have been required by the rules of claim preclusion to assert that each was infringing. See 18 Wright, Miller & Cooper, Jurisdiction § 4409.

35. Restatement Second of Judgments, 1982, § 27 ill. 14. But if the first judgment had been appealed, and the appellate court upheld both determinations by the trial court, the determination of invalidity of the patent would be preclusive in the second suit. See note 32 above.

Although the position taken in the text is supported by Restatement Second, the federal cases on the point are in disarray. See 18 Wright, Miller & Cooper, Jurisdiction, § 4421, pp. 203–209.

36. Kremer v. Chemical Constr. Corp., 1982, 102 S.Ct. 1883, 1897 n. 22, ___ U.S. ___, ___ n. 7, 72 L.Ed.2d 262 (claim preclusion); Allen v. McCurry,

1980, 101 S.Ct. 411, 415, 449 U.S. 90, 95, 66 L.Ed.2d 308 (issue preclusion).

37. See note 30 above.

38. Restatement Second of Judgments, 1982, § 28(1). But see the surprising decision to the contrary in Chemetron Corp. v. Business Funds, Inc., C.A.5th, 1982, 682 F.2d 1149, 1187–1192, and the dissent therefrom at 1200–1203.

39. Restatement Second of Judgments, 1982, § 28(2); 18 Wright, Miller & Cooper, Jurisdiction § 4425.

This exception is recognized, but found inapplicable, in Montana v. U. S., 1979, 99 S.Ct. 970, 978, 440 U.S. 147, 162–163, 59 L.Ed.2d 210.

40. Restatement Second of Judgments, 1982, § 28(3); 18 Wright, Miller & Cooper, Jurisdiction § 4423.

of persuasion on the issue in the two actions.[41] Finally, in exceptional cases a new determination may be needed because of considerations of the public interest or of fairness to persons who were not parties to the first action, or because it was not sufficiently foreseeable at the time of the initial action that the issue would arise in the context of a subsequent action.[42]

Once the basic rules are mastered, it remains necessary to identify the persons affected by preclusion. This question arises in determining both who is bound by a judgment and who may take advantage of it. Analysis begins with the proposition that parties are bound and that ordinarily nonparties are not bound.[43] Even actual parties may escape preclusion, however, if they appear in a different capacity in the second action than in the first.[44] Parties who were on the same side in the first litigation ordinarily are not bound if they are adversaries in the second suit, but issue preclusion will apply if the issue was actually litigated between them in the first suit.[45]

There are many situations in which a nonparty will be bound. Traditionally it was said that a judgment bound the parties and persons in "privity" with them. Current decisions look directly to the reasons for holding a nonparty bound by a judgment. The most obvious justification for preclusion of a nonparty is that the person was a nonparty in name only, and participated so actively in the first litigation that he assumed a de facto role as an actual party.[46] A more attenuated justification is found in the slowly emerging possibility

---

"Redetermination of issues is warranted if there is reason to doubt the quality, extensiveness, or fairness of procedures followed in prior litigation." Montana v. U. S., 1979, 99 S.Ct. 970, 979 n. 11, 440 U.S. 147, 164 n. 11, 59 L.Ed.2d 210.

That the second action will be tried to a jury and the first action was tried to the court is not sufficient to bring this exception into play. Parklane Hosiery Co., Inc. v. Shore, 1979, 99 S.Ct. 645, 652 n. 19, 439 U.S. 322, 332 n. 19, 58 L.Ed.2d 552.

41. Restatement Second of Judgments, 1982, § 28(4); 18 Wright, Miller & Cooper, Jurisdiction § 4422.

Thus an acquittal in a criminal case does not have a preclusive effect against the government in a civil forfeiture proceeding, where the government must prove its case only by a preponderance of the evidence. One Lot Emerald Cut Stones and One Ring v. U. S., 1972, 93 S.Ct. 489, 492, 409 U.S. 232, 234–235, 34 L.Ed.2d 438.

42. Restatement Second of Judgments, 1982, § 28(5); 18 Wright, Miller & Cooper, Jurisdiction §§ 4424, 4426;

James & Hazard, note 1 above, § 11.30.

43. Restatement Second of Judgments, 1982, § 34; 18 Wright, Miller & Cooper, Jurisdiction § 4449.

44. Restatement Second of Judgments, 1982, § 36; 18 Wright, Miller & Cooper, Jurisdiction § 4454.

45. Restatement Second of Judgments, 1982, § 38; 18 Wright, Miller & Cooper, Jurisdiction § 4450.

46. Restatement Second of Judgments, 1982, § 39; 18 Wright, Miller & Cooper, Jurisdiction § 4451.

The United States directed a federal contractor to bring suit challenging a state tax. The United States paid the attorney fees and costs and directed the course of the litigation. After the highest state court upheld the tax, and the contractor, at the instance of the United States, dropped an appeal to the Supreme Court, the United States was bound by the judgment and issue preclusion prevented it from again challenging the tax. Montana v. U. S., 1979, 99 S.Ct. 970, 440 U.S. 147, 59 L.Ed.2d 210.

that nonparties may at times be precluded because they had some duty either to become a party or to give notice that they intended to pursue separate litigation.[47] A second major concept is found in a variety of rules that extend preclusion to persons who somehow were represented in the first litigation. Thus, trust beneficiaries are bound by the judgment in a suit by the trustee, and absent members of a class are bound by the judgment in a class action.[48] Finally, there is a third set of rules defining when preclusion results because of some substantive legal relationship between the person who was a party to the suit and the person who was not. Persons holding successive interests in the same property or claim can often preclude each other, while persons holding concurrent interests in the same property ordinarily do not. These rules apply in a variety of commercial and property law contexts, and arise as much from the needs of the substantive branches of law involved as they do from the values of preclusion by judgment.[49]

These various kinds of rules on when nonparties are bound are, for the most part, quite well settled. It is highly likely that courts and lawyers will continue to use the term "privity" when speaking of them. There is no reason why they should not do so, just as the terms "substance" and "procedure" are still used in an Erie context [50] and the label "indispensable" is still used in connection with compulsory joinder of parties.[51] The old names are harmless so long as they are recognized for what they are, a convenient means of expressing conclusions that are supported by independent analysis. So it is with "privity."

There has not been much major change in the rules on who is bound by a judgment. There has been a great deal of change in the rules on when a nonparty can take advantage of a judgment. At one time the Supreme Court could accurately describe the usual rule when it said: "It is a principal of general elementary law that the estoppel of a judgment must be mutual."[52] This meant that if the circumstances were such that a nonparty was not bound by a previous judgment, he could not assert it as preclusive against one who was bound by it. Although Jeremy Bentham long ago had made the scathing comment that the rule of mutuality was "a maxim which one would suppose to have found its way from the gaming-table to the

47. Restatement Second of Judgments, 1982, § 62; James & Hazard, note 1 above, § 11.31. A guarded view is taken of this development in 18 Wright, Miller & Cooper, Jurisdiction §§ 4452–4453.

48. Restatement Second of Judgments, 1982, §§ 41–42; 18 Wright, Miller & Cooper, Jurisdiction §§ 4454–4458.

49. Restatement Second of Judgments, 1982, §§ 43–61; 18 Wright, Miller & Cooper, Jurisdiction §§ 4459–4462.

50. See § 59 above.

51. See § 70 above.

52. Bigelow v. Old Dominion Copper Mining & Smelting Co., 1912, 32 S.Ct. 641, 642, 225 U.S. 111, 127, 56 L.Ed. 1009.

bench,"[53] and though no satisfactory rationalization was ever offered for the rule, it was widely followed for many years.[54]

Thus, suppose that in Paul's suit against Davis for patent infringement, described earlier in this section, judgment goes for Davis solely on the ground that Paul's patent is invalid. That determination will have preclusive effect in any future suit between Paul and Davis involving that same patent. But what if Paul brings suit for infringement of that same patent against another widget manufacturer, Triplett? If Paul's suit against Davis had resulted in a finding of validity, that could not be preclusive against Triplett.[55] The rule of mutuality meant that since Triplett could not be bound by an adverse determination in the first action, he could not take advantage of a favorable determination there.[56] This permitted the unattractive result that the patent might be found valid and enforceable against Triplett though invalid and unenforceable against Davis. It also meant that Paul, who had had a full and fair opportunity to litigate the issue in his suit against Davis, was now given a second opportunity to litigate the same issue all over again.

It is rare that a major change in established legal doctrine can be identified with a single decision and judge, but there is no doubt that Chief Justice Traynor's decision in Bernhard v. Bank of America [57] was the turning point that brought about the demise of mutuality.

---

53. 3 Bentham, Rationale of Judicial Evidence, 1827, p. 579, reprinted in 7 Bowring, Works of Jeremy Bentham 1843, p. 171.

See also the witty, but also penetrating, opinion by the then-Master of the Rolls, Lord Denning, in McIlkenny v. Chief Constable, [1980] 1 Q.B. 283, 317–318 (C.A.): "Today we go into a room described as estoppel per rem judicatam: in which there is an alcove which has sometimes passed unnoticed. It is called issue estoppel. In this room there are several chairs to sit on. One is called the doctrine of privity. The other is the doctrine of mutuality. The two look all right but they are both a bit rickety. * * *

"Now although those two chairs look all right to start with, you will soon find that they are quite unsafe. Jeremy Bentham as long ago as 1827 told people not to rely on them. * * *

"Our friends in the United States have been just as scathing as Jeremy Bentham. They have rejected the doctrine of mutuality altogether: and they have limited the doctrine of privity."

Lord Denning's result was affirmed, but on grounds of abuse of process rather than issue estoppel, in Hunter v. Chief

Constable of the West Midlands Police, [1981] 3 W.L.R. (H.L.).

54. 18 Wright, Miller & Cooper, Jurisdiction § 4463. See 18 id. § 4464, pp. 581–585, for citations to the literature on the subject and for consideration of the arguments for and against mutuality in modern litigation, when opportunities for complex litigation among multiple parties in disparate forums are commonly available.

Rules about mutuality were a favorite with 19th Century legal thinkers. The announcement by one commentator that there is a requirement of mutuality for specific performance of a contract led to what has been described as "one of the most hilarious misadventures in legal history." Wright, Cases on Remedies, 1955, p. 234.

55. "Due process prohibits estopping them despite one or more existing adjudications of the identical issue which stand squarely against their position." Blonder-Tongue Laboratories, Inc. v. University of Illinois Foundation, 1971, 91 S.Ct. 1434, 1443, 402 U.S. 313, 329, 28 L.Ed.2d 788.

56. Triplett v. Lowell, 1936, 56 S.Ct. 645, 297 U.S. 638, 80 L.Ed. 949.

57. 1942, 122 P.2d 892, 19 Cal.2d 807.

His powerful reasoning proved persuasive to other courts and, in 1971 in the Blonder-Tongue case,[58] the United States Supreme Court joined the courts that had abandoned the requirement of mutuality. The Supreme Court did so in a patent setting similar to that of the example just given, holding that the determination of invalidity in Paul's suit against Davis could be used defensively in the subsequent suit against Triplett.

The Blonder-Tongue decision could have been limited to patent cases, but there was language in the opinion that seemed to indicate that the Court was announcing a broader principle, applicable in any lawsuit. The lower courts so read Blonder-Tongue, and subsequent Supreme Court decisions have proved them right in doing so. In addition, Blonder-Tongue involved "defensive" use of issue preclusion, meaning that a plaintiff was precluded from asserting a claim that it had previously litigated and lost against another defendant. There was more hesitation about "offensive" use of issue preclusion, in which a plaintiff is seeking to preclude a defendant from relitigating the issues that the defendant had previously litigated and lost against another plaintiff. In the case of a mass disaster, for example, if one plaintiff sues the common defendant and loses, this would have no preclusive effect in a suit by another plaintiff, while if offensive use of issue preclusion is proper, a victory by any plaintiff effectively establishes defendant's liability to all the remaining plaintiffs. It has been pointed out that this means that each case is essentially a test case for the defendant, but not for the remaining plaintiffs, and leads to great disparity in litigating risks.[59]

The Supreme Court was not unaware of these concerns in 1979 in the Parklane Hosiery case.[60] Nevertheless it held that "the preferable approach for dealing with these problems in the federal courts is not to preclude the use of offensive collateral estoppel, but to grant trial courts broad discretion to determine when it should be applied."[61] This is also the approach taken in Restatement Second. It abandons mutuality across the board by stating that a party precluded from relitigating an issue with an opposing party is also precluded from doing so with another person unless the fact that he lacked full and fair opportunity to litigate the issue in the first action or other circumstances justify according him an opportunity to relitigate the

58. Blonder-Tongue Laboratories, Inc. v. University of Illinois Foundation, 1971, 91 S.Ct. 1434, 402 U.S. 313, 28 L.Ed.2d 788.

59. James & Hazard, note 1 above, § 11.24, at pp. 580–581.

60. Parklane Hosiery Co. v. Shore, 1979, 99 S.Ct. 645, 439 U.S. 322, 58 L.Ed.2d 552, noted 1979, 48 U.Cin.L.Rev. 611, 64 Cornell L.Rev. 1002, 10 Cum.L.Rev. 619, 57 Den.L.J. 115, 9 Stetson L.Rev.

182, 52 Temp.L.Q. 1221, 14 Tulsa L.J. 744; 1980, 29 Cath.U.L.Rev. 509, 10 Seton Hall L.Rev. 681. See Kempkes, Issue Preclusion: Parklane Hosiery Co. v. Shore Revisited, 1981, 31 Drake L.Rev. 111; Callen & Kadue, To Bury Mutuality Not to Praise It: An Analysis of Collateral Estoppel After Parklane Hosiery Co. v. Shore, 1980, 31 Hastings L.J. 755.

61. 99 S.Ct. at 651, 439 U.S. at 331.

issue.[62] Any of the circumstances that would justify an exception to the issue preclusion if the second suit were between the parties to the first suit [63] will also justify an exception to the nonmutual use of issue preclusion, by one who was not a party to the prior suit, but in addition there are many other factors that may tip the scales against nonmutual preclusion, and especially against offensive nonmutual preclusion, that would not apply to defeat preclusion between the original parties.[64] No clear logical ordering can be found for the various factors that Restatement Second lists or that courts have considered in particular cases, but they run from broad concerns about such general matters as choice of forum, party joinder, incentive to litigate, and foreseeability, through more pointed inquiries as to the nature of the initial forum and litigation, and into very individualized concerns with the competence of counsel, appearance of compromise, and the like.[65] The burden of avoiding preclusion is on the party who asserts lack of a full and fair opportunity to litigate in the first action.[66]

The problems discussed thus far in this section are matters that could arise within a single legal system. They take on an added dimension because of the special problems that come from having two systems of courts, state and federal. What rules of claim and issue preclusion is a federal court to apply if a state court judgment is the source of the supposed preclusion? What preclusion rules apply to a federal judgment in a second federal action? What preclusion rules apply to a federal judgment in a state court action? The recent change in thinking about preclusion generally has been paralleled by an even more recent change in thinking, both scholarly and judicial, on these questions, a change that has been heavily influenced by Professor Degnan's seminal article.[67]

Both the Constitution and a statute enacted so near in time to the Constitution that it has been described as "contemporaneous" [68] are important in approaching these questions. Article IV, § 1, of the Constitution says: "Full Faith and Credit shall be given in each State to the public Acts, Records, and judicial Proceedings of every other State. And the Congress may by general Laws prescribe the Manner in which such Acts, Records and Proceedings shall be proved, and the

---

62. Restatement Second of Judgments, 1982, § 29.

63. Restatement Second of Judgments, 1982, § 28. See text above at notes 38 to 42.

64. Restatement Second of Judgments, 1982, § 29.

65. See 18 Wright, Miller & Cooper, Jurisdiction § 4465.

Compare e.g., Carr v. District of Columbia, C.A.1980, 646 F.2d 599, 207 U.S. App.D.C. 264, in which offensive nonmutual preclusion was allowed, with

Hardy v. Johns-Manville Sales Corp., C.A.5th, 1982, 681 F.2d 334, and Rufenacht v. Iowa Beef Processors, Inc., C.A.5th, 1981, 656 F.2d 198, in which it was held that offensive preclusion would be "unfair."

66. The Blonder-Tongue case so held, 91 S.Ct. at 1443, 402 U.S. at 329.

67. Degnan, Federalized Res Judicata, 1976, 85 Yale L.J. 741.

68. McElmoyle for use of Bailey v. Cohen, 1839, 13 Pet. 312, 325, 10 L.Ed. 177.

Effect thereof." The statute, first adopted in 1790 and not significantly altered since then in the matters here relevant,[69] provides that "[t]he records and judicial proceedings of any court" of "any State, Territory, or Possession of the United States" shall have "the same full faith and credit in every court within the United States and its Territories and Possessions as they have by law or usage in the courts of such State, Territory or Possession from which they are taken."[70] It is worth noting that the Constitution speaks only of the effect "in each State" of the "Proceedings of every other State." Probably because it was not clear when the Constitution was drawn that there would be lower federal courts,[71] Article IV, § 1, says nothing about them. By 1790 Congress had created a system of lower federal courts. A lower federal court is surely a "court within the United States" that is required to give full faith and credit, but only the proceedings of courts of a state, territory, or possession are listed as those to which full faith and credit must be given. Thus the statute speaks to the effect in a federal court of a state court judgment, but it says nothing about the effect in a state court of a federal court judgment.

To the first question, what rules of claim and issue preclusion is a federal court to apply if a state court judgment is the source of the supposed preclusion, the basic answer is clear. It is to give the state court judgment the same full faith and credit as it would have in the courts of the state in which it was entered. This is the command of the 1790 statute, now 28 U.S.C.A. § 1738. The Supreme Court merely stated what had long been well settled in Allen v. McCurry [72] when it said: "though the federal courts may look to the common law or to the policies supporting res judicata and collateral estoppel in assessing the preclusive effect of decisions of other federal courts, Congress has specifically required all federal courts to give preclusive effect to state-court judgments whenever the courts of the State from which the judgments emerged would do so."[73] All that was involved in Allen was issue preclusion, and the Court was careful to limit its decision to that, but two years later, in Kremer v. Chemical Construction Corp.,[74] the Court was speaking also of claim preclusion when it said: "It has long been established that § 1738 does not allow federal courts to employ their own rules of res judicata in determining the effect of state judgments. Rather, it goes beyond the common law and commands a federal court to accept the rules chosen by the state from which the judgment is taken."[75] Neither issue nor

---

69. Act of May 26, 1790, c. XI, 1 Stat. 122. The language in the statute on how the first judgment should be proved was added in 1804.

70. 28 U.S.C.A. § 1738.

71. See § 1 above.

72. 1980, 101 S.Ct. 411, 449 U.S. 90, 66 L.Ed.2d 308.

73. 100 S.Ct. at 415, 449 U.S. at 96.

74. 1982, 102 S.Ct. 1883, ___ U.S. ___, 72 L.Ed.2d 262.

75. 102 S.Ct. at 1897, ___ U.S. at ___. See generally 18 Wright, Miller & Cooper, Jurisdiction § 4469.

claim preclusion can attach to a judgment unless there was a "full and fair opportunity" to litigate the claim or issue,[76] but in the context of a state court judgment being relied on in a federal action, this apparently means very little. State rules on what is a "full and fair opportunity," and on any of the other usual exceptions to preclusion,[77] will be applied, but beyond that, as Kremer put it, "where we are bound by the statutory directive of § 1738, state proceedings need do no more than satisfy the minimum procedural requirements of the Fourteenth Amendment's Due Process Clause in order to qualify for the full-faith-and-credit guaranteed by federal law."[78]

There is still room to argue that full faith and credit embraces the central doctrines of claim and issue preclusion but that it does not incorporate every minute detail. On this view full faith and credit would be limited to the rules that support the core values of finality, repose, and reliance, as well as some of the rules that facilitate control by the first court over its own procedure, but the statute does not demand obeisance to other aspects of preclusion doctrine that are incidental to the central role of preclusion and that may intrude on substantial interests of later courts.[79] Such arguments have been made more difficult, however, by Allen and Kremer.

It is generally assumed that the command of § 1738 "is to give to the state judgment the same effect—no more and no less—that the state courts would give it."[80] Nevertheless the central purpose of § 1738 seems to be to assure that state judgments are respected elsewhere, and it would not offend this policy to give the judgment greater effect than it would have in the rendering state.[81] A testing case of current importance is where the judgment is from a state that retains the old rule that mutuality is required for issue preclusion. The federal courts, to the extent that they are free to decide these matters independently, have abandoned that rule and now allow both offensive and defensive use of nonmutual preclusion.[82] The few cases in point are divided on whether the federal court could hold a party bound by nonmutual preclusion if he would not be bound in the state from which the judgment comes,[83] but the better view is that

76. Allen, 101 S.Ct. at 415, 449 U.S. at 95; Kremer, 102 S.Ct. at 1897 n. 22, ___ U.S. at ___ n. 22.

77. Allen, 101 S.Ct. at 415 n. 7, 449 U.S. at 95 n. 7.

78. 102 S.Ct. at 1897, ___ U.S. at ___.

79. 18 Wright, Miller & Cooper, Jurisdiction § 4467, pp. 636–648.

80. Prosise v. Haring, C.A.4th, 1981, 667 F.2d 1133, 1138 n. 4, certiorari granted 103 S.Ct. 205, ___ U.S. ___, 74 L.Ed.2d 164.

"As the judgment pleaded had no force or effect in the Tennessee state courts other than as a bar to the identical taxes litigated in the suit, the courts of

the United States can accord it no greater efficacy." Union & Planters' Bank of Memphis v. City of Memphis, 1903, 23 S.Ct. 604, 606, 189 U.S. 71, 75, 47 L.Ed. 712.

81. Currie, Res Judicata: The Neglected Defense, 1978, 45 U.Chi.L.Rev. 317, 326–327. This possibility is noted, but no position taken on it, in Restatement Second of Judgments, 1982, § 86 comm. g.

82. See above at notes 52 to 66.

83. Compare Clyde v. Hodge, C.A.3, 1969, 413 F.2d 48, 50 (denying nonmutual preclusion), with In re Transocean Tender Offer Securities Litiga-

the interest of the federal court in this situation in avoiding relitigation is not sufficient to impose preclusion at the expense of the state court's interest in limiting the effect of its own proceedings.[84]

That all states have not yet abandoned mutuality illustrates another aspect of the problem that has given the courts unnecessary difficulty. Suppose that Nebraska has abandoned mutuality but that South Carolina has not. Suppose further that a diversity action is brought in federal court in South Carolina in which one party urges that the other party is precluded by a determination adverse to him in a Nebraska state court proceeding to which the other was a party. Some courts have supposed that this is an Erie problem and that it must look to see whether a South Carolina state court would apply its own rule denying preclusion or the Nebraska rule allowing preclusion to a Nebraska judgment.[85] This approach is incorrect. Section 1738 requires both the South Carolina state courts and the federal court to give the Nebraska judgment the effect it would have in Nebraska.[86] Erie has no application, since it is rested on the Rules of Decision Act [87] and that Act does not apply when an Act of Congress otherwise requires or provides. Section 1738 is such an Act of Congress and it is its command, not that of the Rules of Decision Act, that must be honored.[88]

The American Law Institute completed action on Restatement Second of Judgments in June, 1980. It stated the general rule on the effect of a state court judgment in a subsequent action in federal court as it has been described here, but it noted that claim preclusion does not apply if the federal claim arises under a scheme of federal remedies that contemplates that the federal claim may be asserted notwithstanding the adjudication in state court, and that issue preclusion does not apply if it would be incompatible with a scheme of federal remedies that contemplates that the federal court may make an independent determination of the issue in question.[89] The Comment said: "Whether a scheme of federal remedies implies an exception to 28 U.S.C. § 1738 in any particular case is a matter of statutory interpretation. However, the intention of Congress to make such an exception should not be readily inferred."[90] Decisions in the next two

tion, D.C.Ill.1978, 455 F.Supp. 999, 1005–1006 (allowing preclusion.)

84. See 18 Wright, Miller & Cooper, Jurisdiction § 4465, pp. 616–617, and § 4467, pp. 647–648.

85. E.g., Adzigan v. Harron, D.C.Pa. 1969, 297 F.Supp. 1317, 1323; Eisel v. Columbia Packing Co., D.C.Mass. 1960, 181 F.Supp. 298, 299; and cases cited Degnan, note 67 above, at 753 n. 49.

86. E.g., Braselton v. Clearfield State Bank, C.A.10th, 1979, 606 F.2d 285, 287 n. 1; Hazen Research, Inc. v. Omega Minerals, Inc., C.A.5th, 1974, 497 F.2d 151, 153 n. 1; J. Aron & Co., Inc. v.

Service Transp. Co., D.C.Md.1981, 515 F.Supp. 428, 435–439; 18 Wright, Miller & Cooper, Jurisdiction § 4472 n. 13.

87. 28 U.S.C.A. § 1652. See § 54 above.

88. Degnan, note 67 above, at 750–755; J. Aron & Co., Inc. v. Service Transp. Co., D.C.Md.1981, 515 F.Supp. 428, 438–439.

89. Restatement Second of Judgments, 1982, § 86.

90. Restatement Second of Judgments, 1982, § 86, comm. d.

years showed that the Institute was wise to take so guarded a position on possible exceptions to the general rule.

There had been extensive arguments in the literature in the 1970s on why there should be an exception to issue preclusion or claim preclusion or both in federal civil rights actions under 42 U.S.C.A. § 1983, and some lower courts, though they were distinctly in the minority, had so held.[91] Allen v. McCurry, decided six months after the Institute acted, rejected those arguments. The Court there could find nothing in the language or the legislative history of § 1983 to "in any clear way suggest that Congress intended to repeal or restrict the traditional doctrines of preclusion."[92] A supposed analogy to habeas corpus, where usual notions of preclusion do not apply, was dismissed.[93] Finally, the argument that every person asserting a federal right is entitled to one unencumbered opportunity to litigate that right in a federal district court, regardless of the legal posture in which the federal claim arises, was found unsupported by authority, and to rest on what is "hardly a legal basis at all, * * * a general distrust of the capacity of the state courts to render correct decisions on constitutional issues."[94] The Court made it clear it did not share this distrust.

It was possible after Allen to suppose that even though § 1983 did not create an implied exception to § 1738, perhaps modern, more specific, civil rights statutes do. The provisions against employment discrimination in Title VII of the Civil Rights Act of 1964[95] were thought to be a likely candidate.[96] The Supreme Court rejected that possibility in Kremer. The Kremer Court relied on Allen for the proposition that an exception to § 1738 will not be recognized unless a later statute contains an express or implied partial repeal.[97] Title VII does not expressly repeal § 1738 and the Court could not find in Title VII or in the legislative debates giving rise to it the "clear and manifest" intention of Congress that is required before an implied repeal will be found.[98]

---

91. The literature and the cases are discussed in 18 Wright, Miller & Cooper, Jurisdiction § 4471.

92. 101 S.Ct. at 416–417, 449 U.S. at 97–98.

93. 101 S.Ct. at 417 n. 12, 449 U.S. at 98 n. 12.

The rule announced in England v. Louisiana State Bd. of Medical Examiners, 1964, 84 S.Ct. 461, 375 U.S. 411, 11 L.Ed.2d 440, that when the parties are required to go to state court for decision of an issue of state law after Pullman-type abstention has been ordered, either party may reserve the federal issue and return to federal court for its determination—see § 52 above—was

distinguished as based on the purposes of abstention and as having "no bearing in the present case." 101 S.Ct. at 418 n. 17, 449 U.S. at 101 n. 17.

94. 101 S.Ct. at 420, 449 U.S. at 105.

95. 42 U.S.C.A. § 2000e et seq.

96. See 18 Wright, Miller & Cooper, Jurisdiction § 4471, pp. 721–725. But see Jackson, Matheson & Piskorski, The Proper Role of Res Judicata and Collateral Estoppel in Title VII Suits, 1981, 79 Mich.L.Rev. 1485.

97. 102 S.Ct. at 1890, ___ U.S. at ___.

98. 102 S.Ct. at 1890–1896, ___ U.S. at ___.

There is one area of uncertainty still remaining after Allen and Kremer. This is whether a state court defendant will be precluded from bringing a federal civil rights action based on constitutional arguments that he could have used as a defense, but did not, in state court. The notion that there may be a third kind of preclusion, defendant preclusion, that bars later litigation of matters that could have been used as a defense but in fact were not litigated is still in embryonic form.[99] If there is not to be preclusion here, however, special care must be taken to avoid later federal actions that will jeopardize the stability of the state judgment in any significant way.[100] The case law is still in a very unsatisfactory condition on the related question of whether anything is "actually litigated," so that issue preclusion will follow, by plea of guilty.[101]

Another issue that was considered by the American Law Institute when it took its guarded position in 1980 on possible exceptions to the usual rules of preclusion was whether an exception is justified because the federal courts have exclusive jurisdiction of the proceeding in which it is argued that a state court judgment has some preclusive effect. As recently as 1978 three members of the Supreme Court had joined in a dissent in which Justice Brennan, though calling it "an unresolved and difficult issue," had said: "For myself, I confess to serious doubt that it is ever appropriate to accord res judicata effect to a state-court determination of a claim over which the federal courts have exclusive jurisdiction; for surely state-court determinations should not disable federal courts from ruling de novo on purely legal questions surrounding such federal claims."[102] Such case law as there is on the point is divided and inconclusive.[103] After Kremer, however, it would seem that there is at least a framework for analy-

99. 18 Wright, Miller & Cooper, Jurisdiction § 4414. See, e.g., Southern Jam, Inc. v. Robinson, C.A.5th, 1982, 675 F.2d 94.

100. Wright, Miller & Cooper, Jurisdiction § 4471, pp. 716–717.

101. 18 Wright, Miller & Cooper, Jurisdiction § 4474, pp. 759–761; Restatement Second of Judgments, 1982, § 85 comm. b; Prosise v. Haring, C.A.4th, 1981, 667 F.2d 1133, certiorari granted 103 S.Ct. 205, ___ U.S. ___, 74 L.Ed.2d 164. Compare Vestal, The Restatement (Second) of Judgments: A Modest Dissent, 1981, 66 Cornell L.Rev. 464, 478–483, with Hazard, Revisiting the Second Restatement of Judgments: Issue Preclusion and Related Problems, 1981, 66 Cornell L.Rev. 564, 576–584.

102. Will v. Calvert Fire Ins. Co., 1978, 98 S.Ct. 2552, 2563–2564, 437 U.S. 655, 675–676, 57 L.Ed.2d 504. Justices Marshall and Powell joined in the dissent. Chief Justice Burger joined the

dissent generally, but wrote separately to note that he thought it unnecessary to determine how preclusion applies in cases of exclusive jurisdiction.

103. Compare, e.g., SEC v. United Financial Group, Inc., C.A.9th, 1978, 576 F.2d 217, 220–221 (preclusion applies), with RX Data Corp. v. Department of Social Services, C.A.2d, 1982, 684 F.2d 192, and United States Fidelity & Guar. Co. v. Hendry Corp., C.A.5th, 1968, 391 F.2d 13, 18, certiorari denied 89 S.Ct. 446, 393 U.S. 978, 21 L.Ed.2d 439 (preclusion does not apply). See 18 Wright, Miller & Cooper, Jurisdiction § 4470; Comment, Exclusive Federal Court Jurisdiction and State Judgment Finality—The Dilemma Facing the Federal Courts, 1980, 10 Seton Hall L.Rev. 848; Note, The Collateral Estoppel Effects of Prior State Court Findings in Cases Within Exclusive Federal Jurisdiction, 1978, 91 Harv.L. Rev. 1281.

sis. The issue will be whether for a particular grant of exclusive jurisdiction there is "clear and manifest" evidence of an intention on the part of Congress to make an implied partial repeal of § 1738. Each area of law in which federal jurisdiction is exclusive will present its own unique problems; there can be no general rule that the usual rules do or do not apply to cases of which the federal courts have exclusive jurisdiction.[104] Given the rigorous showing that Kremer requires to establish an implied partial repeal of § 1738, the situations in which there is an exception to the usual rules are likely to be few, if any.[105]

The second of the special problems of preclusion that arise from having two systems of courts was what preclusion rules apply to a federal judgment in a second federal action. The third asked what rules apply to a federal judgment in a state court action. They may usefully be considered together, since it turns out that there is a single answer to both questions, although the means of reaching that answer differ. Restatement Second of Judgments declares the answer as a matter of black-letter law: "Federal law determines the effects under the rules of res judicata of a judgment of a federal court."[106]

If the judgment was in federal court, and the second action is also in federal court, full faith and credit does not apply but res judicata does.[107] It has been less clear what gives a federal judgment preclusive effect if the second action is in state court. The suggestion that state courts should be free to disregard the judgments of federal courts is so unthinkable that the rule rejecting any such suggestion has been stated in an unbroken line of cases that do not offer any clear judicial thought or explanation. Many of the cases talk as if § 1738 requires state courts to honor federal judgments, but as was noted at the outset of this discussion, the face of the statute itself makes this conclusion preposterous. Perhaps what these cases are saying is that this is something that Congress would have intended when it enacted § 1738 if only it had thought about it.[108]

There is a better explanation for why state courts are bound. Article III limits the federal judicial power to cases and controversies. To decide a case or controversy implies some binding effect. Proceedings that do not have at least the potential effect of precluding later relitigation of the same claims and issues would constitute something other than the exercise of the judicial power. Once it is accepted that Article III and its implementing legislation have created courts with the power to issue judgments that will have preclusive

---

104. 18 Wright, Miller & Cooper, Jurisdiction § 4470, pp. 689–693.

105. See Currie, note 81 above, at 347–348.

106. Restatement Second of Judgments, 1982, § 87.

107. Baldwin v. Iowa State Traveling Men's Assn., 1931, 51 S.Ct. 517, 283 U.S. 522, 524, 75 L.Ed. 1244. See 18 Wright, Miller & Cooper, Jurisdiction § 4466.

108. See 18 Wright, Miller & Cooper, Jurisdiction § 4468, pp. 648–654.

effects in other litigation, the Supremacy Clause of Article VI mandates that those preclusive effects are binding on state courts.[109]

The conclusion that both federal and state courts are obliged to honor the preclusive effects of federal court judgments does not automatically identify the body of rules that measure those effects. The early cases often said that a federal court judgment had the same effect as would judgments of the state in which the federal court was sitting in a like case and under similar circumstances.[110] These cases were decided at a time when the Conformity Act required federal courts to conform to state procedure.[111] Language from those older cases has been repeated by modern courts without taking into account the facts that the Conformity Act has long since been repealed and federal courts are now governed by their own independent system of procedure. Thus the scope of the preclusive effect to be given to a judgment today should be recognized as a question of federal law, on which the federal courts are free to adopt their own doctrines.[112]

This is now well recognized if the federal judgment has decided some question of federal law.[113] There are still many cases that say that when the federal court is exercising its diversity jurisdiction, the law of the state where it sits determines the preclusive effect of its judgment.[114] This is wrong on two counts. If there is to be a distinction of this kind, it should have nothing to do with the jurisdictional basis of the suit, but with whether the particular issue is one on which state law or federal law provides the rule for decision.[115] Those decisions are more fundamentally wrong because there ought not be such a distinction. As Judge Medina wrote in a well-known decision: "One of the strongest policies a court can have is that of determining the scope of its own judgments. * * * It would be destructive of the basic principles of the Federal Rules of Civil Procedure to say that the effect of a judgment of a federal court was governed by the law of the state where the court sits simply because the source of federal jurisdiction is diversity. * * * [W]e think it would be strange doctrine to allow a state to nullify the judgments of federal courts constitutionally established and given power also to enforce state created rights. The Erie doctrine * * * is not applica-

109. Degnan, note 67 above, at 742–749, 768–769; 18 Wright, Miller & Cooper, Jurisdiction § 4468, pp. 649–650.

110. Dupasseur v. Rochereau, 1874, 21 Wall. 130, 135, 22 L.Ed.2d 588; and cases cited 18 Wright, Miller & Cooper, Jurisdiction § 4468 n. 24.

111. See § 61 above.

112. Degnan, note 67 above, at 760–773.

113. Blonder-Tongue Laboratories, Inc. v. University of Illinois Foundation, 1971, 91 S.Ct. 1434, 1440 n. 12, 402 U.S. 313, 324 n. 12, 28 L.Ed.2d 788; and

cases cited 18 Wright, Miller & Cooper, Jurisdiction § 4466 nn. 8, 9.

114. Schneider v. Lockheed Aircraft Corp., C.A.1981, 658 F.2d 835, 851 n. 17, ___ U.S.App.D.C. ___; Provident Tradesmens Bank & Trust Co. v. Lumbermens Mut. Cas. Co., C.A.3d, 1969, 411 F.2d 88; and cases cited 18 Wright, Miller & Cooper, Jurisdiction § 4472 n. 27.

115. 18 Wright, Miller & Cooper, Jurisdiction § 4466, pp. 623–624.

ble here   *   *   * ." [116]   Many cases have now taken the view that state law cannot control the preclusive effects of a federal court judgment, regardless of the nature of the case the federal court was deciding.[117]

To say this is not to suggest that federal courts are to ignore important state interests or that the preclusive effect of federal judgments is monolithic. It has become very common in other areas to hold that a particular subject matter is governed by federal law, but that a uniform national rule is not necessary and state law is to be looked to so long as it is not discriminatory or in conflict with federal statutes.[118] Some aspects of preclusion reflect primarily procedural policies and go to the essence of the judicial function. These aspects of preclusion should be governed by a single uniform federal rule. Other aspects of preclusion reflect policies that seem more distinctively substantive. It was pointed out earlier that many of the rules on when nonparties are bound turn on substantive legal relationships stemming from property law and commercial law.[119] If state law governs the substantive relationship, then it would be appropriate to adopt the law of the state as the federal rule for determining the effect of the judgment on others. This is the position taken in Restatement Second of Judgments.[120] The implications of this will have to be worked out as the courts become more familiar with the notion that federal law governs the effect of federal judgments.

116. Kern v. Hettinger, C.A.2d, 1962, 303 F.2d 333, 340. See also Aerojet-General Corp. v. Askew, C.A.5th, 1975, 511 F.2d 710, 717, certiorari denied 96 S.Ct. 210, 423 U.S. 908, 46 L.Ed.2d 137.

117. See cases cited 18 Wright, Miller & Cooper, Jurisdiction § 4472 nn. 32, 36, 42.

118. See § 60 above.

119. See above at note 49.

120. Restatement Second of Judgments, 1982, § 87, comm. b. See also 18 Wright, Miller & Cooper, Jurisdiction § 4472, pp. 733–741.

CHAPTER 11

THE APPELLATE JURISDICTION OF THE COURTS OF APPEALS

Analysis

Sec.
101. Review of Final Decisions.
102. Review of Interlocutory Orders.
103. Review of Administrative Determinations.
104. Appellate Procedure.

§ 101. Review of Final Decisions[1]

The historic policy of the federal courts has been that appeal will lie only from a final decision.[2] This policy was first declared in the Judiciary Act of 1789, and is carried forward today in the provision of the Judicial Code giving the courts of appeals "jurisdiction of appeals from all final decisions of the district courts * * *."[3] Though there are varying judgments about the wisdom of this policy,[4] in general it has seemed to be sound. Interlocutory appeals add to the delay of litigation. This delay can be justified only if it is outweighed by the advantage of settling prior to final decision an important issue

[§ 101]

1. 15 Wright, Miller & Cooper, Jurisdiction §§ 3905–3917; Redish, The Pragmatic Approach to Appealability in the Federal Courts, 1975, 75 Col.L.Rev. 89; Note, Toward a More Rational Final Judgment Rule: A Proposal to Amend 28 U.S.C. § 1292, 1979, 67 Geo.L.J. 1025.

2. Cobbledick v. U. S., 1940, 60 S.Ct. 540, 541, 309 U.S. 323, 324, 84 L.Ed. 783; Andrews v. U. S., 1963, 83 S.Ct. 1236, 1240, 373 U.S. 334, 340, 10 L.Ed. 2d 383. See 15 Wright, Miller & Cooper, Jurisdiction § 3906.

3. 28 U.S.C.A. § 1291.

But if a direct appeal will lie to the Supreme Court—see § 105 below—the courts of appeals lack jurisdiction to hear an appeal. Donovan v. Richland County Assn. for Retarded Citizens, 1982, 102 S.Ct. 713, ___ U.S. ___, 70 L.Ed.2d 570.

Section 1291 is not limited to civil actions and includes appeals by defendants from final decisions in criminal cases. See 15 Wright, Miller & Cooper, Jurisdiction § 3918. The government may also appeal to the courts of appeals in criminal cases. It may appeal from interlocutory orders suppressing or excluding evidence, and also from any order dismissing an indictment or information "as to any one or more counts, except that no appeal shall lie where the double jeopardy clause of the United States Constitution prohibits further prosecution." 18 U.S.C.A. § 3731. See 15 Wright, Miller & Cooper, Jurisdiction § 3919.

4. See 15 Wright, Miller & Cooper, Jurisdiction § 3907; Redish, note 1 above; Crick, The Final Judgment as a Basis for Appeal, 1932, 41 Yale L.J. 539.

In Firestone Tire & Rubber Co. v. Risjord, 1981, 101 S.Ct. 669, 673, 449 U.S. 368, 374, 66 L.Ed.2d 571, the Court said that the finality requirement preserves the independence and the special role of the district judge, avoids the potential harassment and cost of a succession of separate appeals, and "serves the important purpose of promoting efficient judicial administration." See also the thoughtful opinion by Judge Adams in Bachowsky v. Usery, C.A.3d, 1976, 545 F.2d 363.

in the case. In most cases such advantage is not present; the interlocutory issue that seems crucial at the time may fade into insignificance as the case progresses, and in any event the district courts are right in their resolution of most such issues.

Nevertheless, it is not feasible to bar all appeals save from final decisions. In some cases important rights of a party will be irremediably destroyed if he is unable to secure prompt review, and in others an issue is so readily separable from the balance of the case that there is no advantage in postponing review of that issue, and thus holding in abeyance the trial court's resolution of it, until the remainder of the case has been decided. For these reasons there are certain statutory provisions, discussed in the next section, permitting review of interlocutory orders, and there are a variety of court-made rules by which particular orders are treated as "final" and appealable as such.

Indeed even if it were to be agreed that only "final" orders might be reviewed, there would be no sure test as to what is meant by "final." We are told that "a 'final decision' generally is one which ends the litigation on the merits and leaves nothing for the court to do but execute the judgment."[5] It is hardly clear from such a definition that an order in a condemnation case decreeing title in the United States but leaving open the question of compensation is not "final" and not appealable,[6] while an order in an antitrust case finding a violation of the statutes and ordering divestiture, though leaving open the question as to how such divestiture would be accomplished, is "final" and thus appealable.[7] It is not surprising that the Court should have said long ago that the cases on finality "are not altogether harmonious",[8] nor that more than eighty years later it should have said: "No verbal formula yet devised can explain prior finality decisions with unerring accuracy or provide an utterly reliable guide for the future."[9] The source of the difficulty is that the Court, torn between the usual wisdom of the final judgment rule and its inappropriateness in certain unusual situations, has followed "a pragmatic approach to the question of finality."[10] In general this has worked out well in practice, whatever theoretical problems it may raise, though it is hard not to

5. Catlin v. U. S., 1945, 65 S.Ct. 631, 633, 324 U.S. 229, 233, 89 L.Ed. 911. This formulation has been much quoted. E.g., Coopers & Lybrand v. Livesay, 1978, 98 S.Ct. 2454, 2457, 437 U.S. 463, 467, 57 L.Ed.2d 351.

6. Catlin v. U. S., 1945, 65 S.Ct. 631, 324 U.S. 229, 89 L.Ed. 911; cf. The Palmyra, 1825, 10 Wheat. 502, 6 L.Ed. 375; Taylor v. Board of Educ. of City Sch. Dist. of City of New Rochelle, C.A.2d, 1961, 288 F.2d 600.

7. Brown Shoe Co. v. U. S., 1962, 82 S.Ct. 1502, 370 U.S. 294, 8 L.Ed.2d 510, noted 1962, 42 B.U.L.Rev. 559.

8. McGourkey v. Toledo & O. Central R. Co., 1892, 13 S.Ct. 170, 172, 146 U.S. 536, 545, 36 L.Ed. 1079.

9. Eisen v. Carlisle & Jacquelin, 1974, 94 S.Ct. 2140, 2149, 417 U.S. 156, 170, 40 L.Ed.2d 732. See also Dickinson v. Petroleum Conversion Corp., 1950, 70 S.Ct. 322, 338 U.S. 507, 508, 94 L.Ed. 299.

10. Brown Shoe Co. v. U. S., 1962, 82 S.Ct. 1502, 1513, 370 U.S. 294, 306, 8 L.Ed.2d 510. See Freeman v. Califano, C.A.5th, 1978, 574 F.2d 264, 266–267; Redish, note 1 above.

feel sympathy for the litigant who appeals from what is styled "Final Decree," only to learn that a decree a year earlier, on its face only a partial disposition of the case, was final as to that particular litigant, and thus his later appeal was untimely.[11] The saving grace of the imprecise rule of finality is that in almost all situations it is entirely clear, either from the nature of the order or from a crystallized body of decisions, that a particular order is or is not final.[12] No one would doubt that a judgment awarding money damages to plaintiff on the only claim involved in the case is a final judgment. No one would doubt that an order denying a motion to dismiss under Rule 12(b)(6) is interlocutory and not final.[13] The case in which there is real doubt about the finality of an order is extremely rare, although recent cases broadening the concept of finality have created new uncertainties.

Rule 54(b) contributes clarity in one recurring situation that, absent the rule, would be either confusing, or unworkable, or both. Before the adoption of the federal rules, a judgment was thought appealable only if it made final disposition with regard to all the parties and all the claims involved in the suit.[14] The rules have liberalized joinder of claims and of parties, and there now are cases in which it is desirable to put into effect, or to permit appeal from, an order that disposes of some of the claims or parties, without waiting for decision of the remainder of the case. If this is to be done, it must be clear when the decision is final as to the partial disposition, in order that an unwary litigant will not let the time for appeal go by without action. This is accomplished by Rule 54(b), though it has taken two amendments of the rule to perfect it. Under the rule as it now stands, when more than one claim for relief is presented in an action, or when multiple parties are involved, the court may direct the entry of judgment as to one or more but fewer than all of the claims or parties only upon (1) an express determination that there is no just reason for delay, and (2) an express direction for the entry of judgment. A partial disposition of the case is not final in the absence of such a determination and direction by the court.[15]

The rule lends a welcome certainty to the appellate procedure. In cases within the scope of the rule, a litigant need not appeal an interlocutory order not certified as required by Rule 54(b) to guard against the possibility that it may be held to have been a final deci-

---

11. Dickinson v. Petroleum Conversion Corp., 1950, 70 S.Ct. 322, 338 U.S. 507, 94 L.Ed. 299. Later amendments to Rule 54(b) will prevent recurrence of this particular problem, but others like it will surely arise. E.g., Howze v. Arrow Transp. Co., C.A.5th, 1960, 280 F.2d 403, certiorari denied 81 S.Ct. 285, 364 U.S. 920, 5 L.Ed.2d 260, criticized 1961, 35 Tul.L.Rev. 444.

12. See Note, Appealability in the Federal Courts, 1961, 75 Harv.L.Rev. 351, 354.

13. Save the Bay, Inc. v. U. S. Army, C.A.5th, 1981, 639 F.2d 1100, 1103; see Catlin v. U. S., 1945, 65 S.Ct. 631, 635, 324 U.S. 229, 236, 89 L.Ed. 911.

14. Collins v. Miller, 1920, 40 S.Ct. 347, 252 U.S. 364, 64 L.Ed. 616.

15. 10 Wright, Miller & Kane, Civil 2d § 2654.

sion. When the court does make the requisite certificate, the litigant is put on notice that it is time to take his appeal.

A Rule 54(b) certificate is not conclusive on the finality of the order below. If an order is in fact interlocutory, and does not actually make a final disposition of some of the claims or as to some of the parties, appeal from it will be dismissed even though the trial court has certified the order as final.[16] Further, the certificate of the trial judge does not conclude the appellate court on whether there were actually multiple claims presented, and thus on whether Rule 54(b) has any application. If the complaint presents only variants of a single claim, appeal cannot be taken from an order dealing with some of these variants, even though the order has been duly certified.[17] The determination of whether there are multiple claims rests on whether the underlying factual bases for recovery state a number of different claims, not mutually exclusive, that could have been separately enforced.[18]

The appellate court is not limited to determining whether the order actually falls within Rule 54(b). It may also consider whether the trial court abused its discretion in finding that there was no just reason for delay. On this point, however, the discretionary judgment of the trial court must be given substantial deference and the reviewing court may disturb the trial court's assessment of the equities only if it can say that the judge's conclusion was clearly unreasonable.[19]

If a case falls within Rule 54(b), an appeal must be dismissed if the trial court has not made the requisite certificate.[20] If the case is not within Rule 54(b), as where the court has ordered entry of judgment as to all the claims and parties involved in the action, or there

16. E.g., Cinerama, Inc. v. Sweet Music, S.A., C.A.2d, 1973, 482 F.2d 66, affirmed 1974, 493 F.2d 1397; Haverhill Gazette Co. v. Union Leader Corp., C.A.1st, 1964, 333 F.2d 798, certiorari denied 85 S.Ct. 329, 379 U.S. 931, 13 L.Ed.2d 343; 10 Wright, Miller & Kane, Civil 2d § 2655.

17. Liberty Mut. Ins. Co. v. Wetzel, 1976, 96 S.Ct. 1202, 424 U.S. 737, 47 L.Ed.2d 435.

18. Local P–171, Amalgamated Meat Cutters & Butcher Workmen of N. America v. Thompson Farms Co., C.A. 7th, 1981, 642 F.2d 1065, 1070; Rieser v. Baltimore & O. R. Co., C.A.2d, 1955, 224 F.2d 198, 199, affirmed 228 F.2d 563, certiorari denied 1956, 76 S.Ct. 651, 350 U.S. 1006, 100 L.Ed. 868; Note, Federal Rule 54(b): The Multiple Claims Requirement, 1957, 43 Va.L. Rev. 229; 10 Wright, Miller & Kane, Civil 2d § 2657.

19. Curtiss-Wright Corp. v. General Elec. Co., 1980, 100 S.Ct. 1460, 446 U.S. 1, 64 L.Ed.2d 1. In that case the Court rejected, as neither workable nor entirely reliable as a benchmark for appellate review, expressions that had appeared in some lower court decisions that Rule 54(b) is to be reserved for "the infrequent harsh case." 100 S.Ct. at 1466, 446 U.S. at 9. See 10 Wright, Miller & Kane, Civil 2d § 2659.

20. E.g., U. S. v. Taylor, C.A.5th, 1980, 632 F.2d 530; In the Matter of Licek Potato Chip Co., C.A.7th, 1979, 599 F.2d 181; 10 Wright, Miller & Kane, Civil 2d § 2660. But cf. Riggle v. California, C.A.9th, 1978, 577 F.2d 579, 581 n. A; Browning Debenture Holders' Committee v. DASA Corp., C.A.2d 1975, 524 F.2d 811, 814 n. 4.

has been judgment as to the only claim in a case not involving multiple parties, the judgment is appealable without such a certificate.[21]

For many years there was controversy as to the validity of Rule 54(b). No one doubted the validity of the "negative aspect" of the rule, by which the refusal to certify barred appeal from orders which would have been appealable before the adoption of the rule. The controversy centered about the other aspect of the rule, by which the court, through issuance of its certificate, made its order final and appealable though that order might not have been regarded as a final decision before the rules.[22] It was thought by some that this was an impermissible extension by rule of the jurisdiction of the appellate courts. This argument was rejected by the Supreme Court, which held that the rule scrupulously recognizes the statutory requirement of a "final decision" as a basic requirement for an appeal, and merely provides a practical means of permitting an appeal to be taken from one or more final decisions on individual claims without waiting for final decisions to be rendered on all the claims in the case.[23] Thus the validity of the rule is now clearly settled.

The Supreme Court has long recognized, though it defined only in 1949, a small class of orders, now referred to as "collateral orders," which are offshoots from the principal litigation in which they are issued, and which are immediately appealable, as "final decisions," without regard to the posture of the principal litigation. The leading case is Cohen v. Beneficial Industrial Loan Corporation.[24] That case was a stockholders' suit in which the defendant corporation, pursuant to New Jersey law, moved to require plaintiff to post security for defendant's costs, including attorney's fees, and appealed from denial of the motion. The Supreme Court held unanimously that the order denying the motion was appealable, saying that it fell within "that small class which finally determine claims of right separable from, and collateral to, rights asserted in the action, too important to be denied review and too independent of the cause itself to require that appellate consideration be deferred until the whole case is adjudicated. * * * We hold this order appealable because it is a final disposition of a claimed right which is not an ingredient of the cause of

---

21. Shafer v. Children's Hosp. Soc'y of Los Angeles, C.A.1959, 265 F.2d 107, 105 U.S.App.D.C. 123; General Time Corp. v. Padua Alarm Systems, C.A.2d, 1952, 199 F.2d 351, certiorari denied 73 S.Ct. 728, 345 U.S. 917, 97 L.Ed. 1351.

22. Compare the several opinions in Pabellon v. Grace Line, C.A.2d 1951, 191 F.2d 169, certiorari denied 72 S.Ct. 201, 342 U.S. 893, 96 L.Ed. 669, and Bendix Aviation Corp. v. Glass, C.A.3d, 1952, 195 F.2d 267.

23. ·Sears, Roebuck & Co. v. Mackey, 1956, 76 S.Ct. 895, 899–901, 351 U.S.

427, 435–438, 100 L.Ed. 1297, noted 1956, 44 Calif.L.Rev. 952, 42 Va.L.Rev. 982; 10 Wright, Miller & Kane, Civil 2d § 2653.

24. 1949, 69 S.Ct. 1221, 337 U.S. 541, 93 L.Ed. 1528. See 15 Wright, Miller & Cooper, Jurisdiction § 3911.

If the "collateral orders" doctrine is applicable, the better view is that a certificate under Rule 54(b) is not required. See Swanson v. American Consumer Indust., Inc., C.A.7th, 1975, 517 F.2d 555; 10 Wright, Miller & Kane, Civil 2d § 2658.

action and does not require consideration with it."[25] The Court emphasized also that the new doctrine does not permit appeal of orders that are "tentative, informal or incomplete,"[26] and that it was applicable only if the issue raised by appeal "presents a serious and unsettled question."[27]

Since the Cohen case the Supreme Court has held that the "collateral order" doctrine makes an order vacating an attachment in admiralty appealable, although suggesting that appeal would not have been available if the order had sustained the attachment.[28] It also held that denial of a petition to proceed in forma pauperis was appealable as a "collateral order,"[29] as was an order challenging the amount of bail [30] and an order imposing on the defendants 90% of the costs of notifying members of a class.[31]

The Court reviewed the "collateral order" doctrine again in 1978 in Coopers & Lybrand v. Livesay.[32] The holding there was that a determination that an action may not go forward as a class action is not appealable as a matter of right, either under the "collateral order" doctrine or any other. "To come within the 'small class' of decisions excepted from the final-judgment rule by Cohen, the order must conclusively determine the disputed question, resolve an important issue completely separate from the merits of the action, and be effectively unreviewable on appeal from a final judgment."[33] An order decertifying a previously certified class action met none of those requirements. It is inherently nonfinal and subject to revision before final judgment, it is inherently enmeshed in the facts of the individual case, and it is subject to effective review after final judgment either at the behest of the named plaintiff or of intervening class members.

---

25. 69 S.Ct. at 1225–1226, 337 U.S. at 546–547.

26. 69 S.Ct. at 1225, 337 U.S. at 546.

27. 69 S.Ct. at 1226, 337 U.S. at 547.

28. Swift & Co. Packers v. Compania Colombiana Del Caribe, 1950, 70 S.Ct. 861, 339 U.S. 684, 94 L.Ed. 1206.

Subsequent lower courts cases on orders relating to attachment, or similar forms of security, are in some disarray. Appeal has sometimes been allowed from orders granting security or refusing to quash it, while there have been occasions in which an order refusing security has been held unappealable. See cases cited at 15 Wright, Miller & Cooper, Jurisdiction § 3911 nn. 61–67.

29. Roberts v. U. S. Dist. Court, 1950, 70 S.Ct. 954, 339 U.S. 844, 94 L.Ed. 1326.

Although the Roberts case can be read narrowly, some lower courts have understood it to mean that all orders denying leave to proceed in forma pauperis are immediately appealable. See Flowers v. Turbine Support Div., C.A.5th, 1975, 507 F.2d 1242; 15 Wright, Miller & Cooper, Jurisdiction § 3911 at nn. 14–16.

30. Stack v. Boyle, 1951, 72 S.Ct. 1, 342 U.S. 1, 96 L.Ed. 3. Bail orders are now ordinarily reviewed pursuant to 18 U.S. C.A. § 3147(b).

31. Eisen v. Carlisle & Jacquelin, 1974, 94 S.Ct. 2140, 2148–2150, 417 U.S. 156, 169–172, 40 L.Ed.2d 732.

32. 1978, 98 S.Ct. 2454, 437 U.S. 463, 57 L.Ed.2d 351.

33. 98 S.Ct. at 2458, 437 U.S. at 468.

The general requirements for a "collateral order" appeal have been neatly summarized as "separability, finality, urgency, and importance." U. S. v. Alcon Labs., C.A.1st, 1981, 636 F.2d 876, 884, certiorari denied 101 S.Ct. 3005, 451 U.S. 1017, 69 L.Ed.2d 388.

The Coopers & Lybrand formulation was repeated by the Court three years later, in the course of holding that an order refusing to disqualify opposing counsel in a civil case, is not appealable.[34] The Court thought that the order before it met the first part of the test, since it conclusively determined the question, and it assumed that this is an important issue separate from the merits, but it held that the order failed the third part of the Coopers & Lybrand test, since the order was one that could be effectively reviewed after a final judgment.

There had been a tendency to expand the "collateral order" doctrine, but more recently the courts have been emphasizing the need to use the doctrine sparingly, lest an expanded "collateral order" doctrine swallow the basic finality requirement and the courts become swamped with appeals.[35] The most recent Supreme Court decisions reinforce this more recent approach.

Another, though related, court-made exception to the usual requirement of finality, although not stated as such, is that a judgment directing immediate delivery of physical property is appealable, if necessary in order to avoid irreparable injury, even though the court has also ordered an accounting that has not yet taken place.[36] Civil contempt orders against a person not a party to the case are considered final and appealable, since that person could not appeal a final judgment in the case.[37] Criminal contempt orders also are regarded

---

34. Firestone Tire & Rubber Co. v. Risjord, 1981, 101 S.Ct. 669, 674, 449 U.S. 368, 375, 66 L.Ed.2d 571.

The Court left open whether appeal would lie if a trial court granted a disqualification order, or if it denied a disqualification order in a criminal case. 101 S.Ct. at 672 n. 8, 449 U.S. at 372 n. 8. Several courts have subsequently held that grant of disqualification in a civil case is appealable. In re Coordinated Pretrial Proceedings in Petroleum Products Antitrust Litigation, C.A. 9th, 1981, 658 F.2d 1355; Glueck v. Jonathan Logan, Inc., C.A.2d, 1981, 653 F.2d 746; Duncan v. Merrill Lynch, Pierce, Fenner & Smith, Inc., C.A.5th, 1981, 646 F.2d 1020. But grant of a motion to disqualify defense counsel in a criminal case was held not appealable in U. S. v. Greger, C.A.9th, 1981, 657 F.2d 1109.

35. E.g., Minnesota v. Picklands Mather & Co., C.A.8th, 1980, 636 F.2d 251, 254–255; Ruiz v. Estelle, C.A.5th, 1980, 609 F.2d 118, 119; Cullen v. New York State Civil Serv. Comm., C.A.2d, 1977, 566 F.2d 846, 848; Rodgers v. United States Steel Corp., C.A.3d, 1976, 541 F.2d 365, 369; Weit v. Continental Illi-

nois Nat. Bank & Trust Co., C.A.7th, 1976, 535 F.2d 1010, 1014; Blackie v. Barrack, C.A.9th, 1975, 524 F.2d 891, 897, certiorari denied 97 S.Ct. 57, 429 U.S. 816, 50 L.Ed.2d 75; U. S. v. Lansdown, C.A.4th, 1972, 460 F.2d 164, 170. See 15 Wright, Miller & Cooper, Jurisdiction § 3911.

36. Forgay v. Conrad, 1848, 6 How. 201, 12 L.Ed. 404; Radio Station WOW v. Johnson, 1945, 65 S.Ct. 1475, 1478–1480, 326 U.S. 120, 124–127; 89 L.Ed. 2092; Pioche Mines Consol. v. Fidelity-Philadelphia Trust Co., C.A.9th, 1951, 191 F.2d 399; Kasishke v. Baker, C.C.A.10th, 1944, 144 F.2d 384; 15 Wright, Miller & Cooper, Jurisdiction § 3910.

37. Lamb v. Cramer, 1932, 52 S.Ct. 315, 285 U.S. 217, 76 L.Ed. 715; Fenton v. Walling, C.C.A.9th, 1944, 139 F.2d 608, certiorari denied 64 S.Ct. 938, 321 U.S. 798, 88 L.Ed. 1086.

The rule is otherwise if a party is found in civil contempt. McCrone v. U. S., 1939, 59 S.Ct. 685, 307 U.S. 61, 83 L.Ed. 1108. For criticism of this view, see 15 Wright, Miller & Cooper, Jurisdiction § 3917.

as severable from the main action and appealable before final judgment in that action.[38]

Decisions granting or denying class action status have caused pressure for immediate review that had led some courts to accept a "death knell" doctrine as a new expansion of the requirement of finality. In an important early case the Second Circuit held that appeal would lie from an order denying class action status in a case in which the individual plaintiff's claim was only for $70 and if the action were not permitted to proceed on a class basis it would surely not proceed at all. "Where the effect of a district court's order, if not reviewed, is the death knell of the action, review should be allowed."[39] This doctrine had been accepted in some circuits though rejected in others. A few cases had even reasoned by analogy to the "death knell" doctrine to hold that an order granting class action status was appealable, even though such an order surely does not bring an action to an end.[40]

It was pointed out earlier that in the Coopers & Lybrand case the Court held that refusal to allow a suit to be maintained as a class action could not be appealed as a "collateral order." In that same case the Court sounded the death knell for the "death knell" doctrine. "A threshold inquiry of this kind," it said, "may, it is true, identify some orders that would truly end the litigation prior to final judgment; allowing an immediate appeal from those orders may enhance the quality of justice afforded a few litigants. But this incremental benefit is outweighed by the impact of such an individualized jurisdictional inquiry on the judicial system's overall capacity to administer justice."[41] It held, therefore, that the fact that an interlocutory order may induce a party to abandon his claim before final judgment is not a sufficient reason for considering it a "final decision" within the meaning of the statute.[42] If there is to be immediate review of a class certification ruling, it must be by allowance of an interlocutory appeal under 28 U.S.C.A. § 1292(b).[43] It is true that this requires a

---

38. Bray v. U. S., 1975, 96 S.Ct. 307, 423 U.S. 73, 46 L.Ed.2d 215; Bessette v. W. B. Conkey Co., 1904, 24 S.Ct. 665, 194 U.S. 324, 48 L.Ed. 997.

On the distinction between civil contempt and criminal contempt, see 3 Wright Criminal 2d § 704.

39. Eisen v. Carlisle v. Jacquelin, C.A.2d, 1966, 370 F.2d 119, 120–121, certiorari denied 87 S.Ct. 1487, 386 U.S. 1035, 18 L.Ed.2d 598.

40. 15 Wright, Miller & Cooper, Jurisdiction § 3912.

41. 98 S.Ct. at 2460, 437 U.S. at 473.

42. 98 S.Ct. at 2462, 437 U.S. at 477.

On the same day as the Coopers & Lybrand decision, the Court also held that denial of class action status cannot be appealed under 28 U.S.C.A. § 1292(a)(1) on the theory that the refusal to allow class status restricted the permanent injunctive relief that might ultimately be awarded. Gardner v. Westinghouse Broadcasting Co., 1978, 98 S.Ct. 2451, 437 U.S. 478, 57 L.Ed.2d 364.

43. See § 102 below.

"* * * [O]ur ruling in Livesay was not intended to preclude motions under 28 U.S.C. § 1292(b) seeking discretionary interlocutory appeal for review of the certification ruling. * * * In some cases such an appeal would promise substantial savings of time and resources or for other reasons should be viewed hospitably." Deposit

certificate from the trial judge but few district judges are likely to be so eager to suffer the burdens of class action litigation that they will deny certification of orders that offer a genuine basis for a plausible appeal.[44]

Generalizing from the various situations in which the courts have treated as "final" an order that is not a complete disposition of a case, the Fifth Circuit once said that "an order, otherwise nonappealable, determining substantial rights of the parties which will be irreparably lost if review is delayed until final judgment may be appealed immediately under section 1291."[45] Though the Supreme Court has never said as much in terms, its decisions do point in such a direction. In recent years the Court has relaxed considerably the requirement of finality. Although the most striking of these decisions have come in considering what is a "final judgment" for purposes of review in the Supreme Court of a state court decision,[46] the Court apparently considers that a "final judgment" is the same thing in all contexts and treats precedents under the various statutes that use those words as interchangeable.[47]

The sharpest departure from traditional notions of finality for review by a court of appeals of a district court decision came in Gillespie v. United States Steel Corp.[48] In a Jones Act case the district court struck portions of the complaint adding claims under state law and also struck all references in the complaint to recovery for the benefit of relatives of the decedent other than his mother. The court refused to certify its order for interlocutory appeal under 28 U.S.C.A. § 1292(b). Plaintiff took an appeal despite this and the court of appeals decided the appeal on its merits. It found that it had jurisdiction to decide the case on the intriguing theory that the plaintiff had

Guar. Nat. Bank v. Roper, 1980, 100 S.Ct. 1166, 1173 n. 8, 445 U.S. 326, 336 n. 8, 63 L.Ed.2d 427.

44. Hackett v. General Host Corp., C.A.3d, 1972, 455 F.2d 618, 624, certiorari denied 92 S.Ct. 2460, 407 U.S. 925, 32 L.Ed.2d 812.

45. U. S. v. Wood, C.A.5th, 1961, 295 F.2d 772, 778, certiorari denied 82 S.Ct. 933, 369 U.S. 850, 8 L.Ed.2d 9, noted 1962, 62 Col.L.Rev. 901, 48 Va.L.Rev. 390, 1963, 76 Harv.L.Rev. 638.

46. See § 107 below.

47. Thus, at one key point in Brown Shoe Co. v. U. S., 1962, 82 S.Ct. 1502, 1515, 370 U.S. 294, 309, 8 L.Ed.2d 510, on direct appeal from a district court to the Supreme Court, the Court, in determining what was a "final judgment" within the meaning of the Expediting Act, 15 U.S.C.A. § 29, cited three cases. Two of the cases were concerned with whether there was a "final judgment" of a district court within 28

U.S.C.A. § 1291 permitting appeal to a court of appeals, while the third involved the meaning of "final judgment" in 28 U.S.C.A. § 1257, providing for review of state court decisions in the Supreme Court. And in determining whether a state court decision is final for purposes of review the Court commonly cites decisions on finality for review of district court decisions by a court of appeals. E.g., Local No. 438 Constr. & Gen. Laborers' Union, AFL–CIO v. Curry, 1963, 83 S.Ct. 531, 536, 371 U.S. 542, 549, 9 L.Ed.2d 514; Cox Broadcasting Corp. v. Cohn, 1975, 95 S.Ct. 1029, 1037 n. 7, 420 U.S. 469, 478 n. 7, 43 L.Ed.2d 328; National Socialist Party of America v. Village of Skokie, 1977, 97 S.Ct. 2205, 2206, 432 U.S. 43, 44, 53 L.Ed.2d 96.

48. 1964, 85 S.Ct. 308, 379 U.S. 148, 13 L.Ed.2d 199, noted 1966, 51 Cornell L.Q. 369.

sought such a decision, by taking the appeal, and defendant was not harmed by it, since the appellate court agreed with the defendant on the merits.[49] The Supreme Court also reached the merits, though on a different theory than that of the court of appeals. It thought that the appeal raised questions fundamental to the further conduct of the case, that it would save time and money to have them settled, and that "the Court of Appeals properly implemented the same policy Congress sought to promote in § 1292(b) by treating this obviously marginal case as final and appealable under 28 U.S.C.A. § 1291."[50]

Even a commentator who favors a pragmatic approach to appealability has said that the Gillespie opinion "is astounding for its clouded reasoning and enigmatic conclusions. It is unfortunate that a decision which may represent a truly significant adjustment of the entire philosophy of appealability is so devoid of any persuasive analysis."[51] The explanation offered by the Court in Gillespie for holding the order appealable suggests at least two positive and two negative justifications for finding that a fundamental change had been wrought in all prior approaches to finality. The positive justifications lie in the apparent invitation to weigh the benefits and costs of immediate appeal on an individualized basis, and the statement that appeal should be available from orders fundamental to the further conduct of the case. The negative justifications were in the assertion of a fictitious severability analogy, and in the incredible suggestion that the purposes of § 1292(b) were fulfilled by simply ignoring the deliberate statutory choice to require a certificate from the district court.

There are lower court cases that have seized on each of these four justifications of the Gillespie opinion as a basis for permitting review.[52] Nevertheless, for the most part Gillespie has either been ignored by the courts of appeals or invoked to justify appeals that could have been explained on more traditional notions of finality.[53] Indeed in Coopers & Lybrand the Court itself said: "If Gillespie were

---

49. Gillespie v. United States Steel Corp., C.A.7th, 1963, 321 F.2d 518, 520–522.

50. 85 S.Ct. at 312, 379 U.S. at 154.

51. Redish, note 1 above, at 118.

52. Balancing approach: Mahaley v. Cuyahoga Metropolitan Housing Auth., C.A.6th, 1974, 500 F.2d 1087, 1090 n. 3, certiorari denied 95 S.Ct. 781, 419 U.S. 1108, 42 L.Ed.2d 805; Fox v. City of West Palm Beach, C.A.5th, 1967, 383 F.2d 189. Fundamental to further conduct: Thoms v. Heffernan, C.A.2d, 1973, 473 F.2d 478, 481–482, vacated on other grounds 1974, 94 S.Ct. 3199, 418 U.S. 908, 41 L.Ed.2d 1154. Severability: Wescott v. Impresas Armadoras, S. A. Panama, C.A.9th, 1977, 564 F.2d 875, 879–881; Jetco Electronic Indus., Inc. v. Gardiner, C.A.5th, 1973, 473

F.2d 1228, 1231. Policies of § 1292(b): Nelson v. Heyne, C.A.7th, 1974, 491 F.2d 352, 354 n. 2, certiorari denied 94 S.Ct. 3183, 417 U.S. 976, 41 L.Ed.2d 1146.

Another possible explanation of Gillespie is that the Court was attempting to formulate a rule that would allow disposition on the merits of appeals that had been mistakenly taken from nonfinal decisions. Compare Clark v. Kraftco Corp., C.A.2d, 1971, 447 F.2d 933, 935–936, with Robert M. v. Benton, C.A.8th, 1980, 622 F.2d 370, 372 n. 2, and U. S. v. Estate of Pearce, C.A.3d, 1974, 498 F.2d 847, 850.

53. 15 Wright, Miller & Cooper, Jurisdiction § 3913; Redish, note 1 above, at 120–124.

extended beyond the unique facts of that case, § 1291 would be stripped of all significance."[54]

Justice Harlan was a consistent, and usually a lonely, dissenter from the line of cases expanding the notion of finality. There is surely force in his remark in one of his dissents that these decisions throw "the law of finality into a state of great uncertainty and will, I am afraid, tend to increase further efforts at piecemeal review."[55]

§ 102. Review of Interlocutory Orders[1]

There are four situations, by now well-established, in which the courts of appeals have statutory jurisdiction to review interlocutory orders of the district court. They may review:

1. Interlocutory orders granting, continuing, modifying, refusing, or dissolving injunctions, or refusing to dissolve or modify injunctions, except where a direct review may be had in the Supreme Court.[2]

2. Interlocutory orders appointing receivers, or refusing orders to wind up receiverships or to take steps to accomplish purposes such as directing sales or other disposals of property.[3]

3. Interlocutory decrees determining the rights and liabilities of the parties to admiralty cases in which appeals from final decrees are allowed.[4]

4. Judgments in civil actions for patent infringement that are final except for accounting.[5]

Until recently the courts of appeals also could review either interlocutory or final judgments, orders, or decrees in bankruptcy, but the 1978 Bankruptcy Act has provided a new, and virtually incomprehensible, scheme for appellate review of bankruptcy matters.[6]

---

54. 98 S.Ct. at 2462 n. 30, 437 U.S. at 477 n. 30.

Nevertheless in American Export Lines, Inc. v. Alvez, 1980, 100 S.Ct. 1673, 446 U.S. 274, 64 L.Ed.2d 284, the Court relied on Gillespie to establish finality for review of a state court in circumstances that stretch the finality doctrine to or beyond the limit. See 16 Wright, Miller & Cooper, Jurisdiction § 4010.

55. Mercantile Nat. Bank at Dallas v. Langdeau, 1963, 83 S.Ct. 520, 531, 371 U.S. 555, 575, 9 L.Ed.2d 523.

[§ 102]

1. 16 Wright, Miller & Cooper, Jurisdiction §§ 3920–3936.

2. 28 U.S.C.A. § 1292(a)(1). See 16 Wright, Miller & Cooper, Jurisdiction §§ 3921–3924. With regard to the exception, see § 105 below.

3. 28 U.S.C.A. § 1292(a)(2). See 16 Wright, Miller & Cooper, Jurisdiction § 3925.

4. 28 U.S.C.A. § 1292(a)(3); Rule 9(h). See Slatton v. Martin K. Eby Constr. Co., C.A.8th, 1974, 491 F.2d 707; 16 Wright, Miller & Cooper, Jurisdiction § 3927.

5. 28 U.S.C.A. § 1292(a)(4). Under this provision, unlike the provision in § 1292(a)(1) for preliminary injunctions, appeal will lie only if the judgment below is final except for the accounting. American Cyanamid Co. v. Lincoln Laboratories Inc., C.A.7th, 1968, 403 F.2d 486. See 16 Wright, Miller & Cooper, Jurisdiction § 3928.

6. 28 U.S.C.A. § 1293. See 16 Wright, Miller & Cooper, Jurisdiction § 3926; Levin, Bankruptcy Appeals, 1980, 58 N.C.L.Rev. 967.

These exceptions from the usual requirement of finality, the Court has said, "seem plainly to spring from a developing need to permit litigants to effectually challenge interlocutory orders of serious, perhaps irreparable consequence. When the pressure rises to a point that influences Congress, legislative remedies are enacted."[7] Of these traditional grounds for interlocutory appeals, that involving injunctions is of the most general interest and has caused the most difficulty.

Ordinarily the scope of appellate review under 28 U.S.C.A. § 1292(a)(1) of an order granting or refusing an injunction is confined to the issues necessary to determine the propriety of the interlocutory order itself. Nevertheless, review quite properly extends to all matters inextricably bound up with the remedial decision and the court, if it sees fit, may consider and decide the merits of the case and may order dismissal of the action.[8] It is settled, too, that orders granting or denying a preliminary injunction are appealable,[9] while similar orders involving a temporary restraining order are not.[10] In applying this distinction the label put on the order by the trial court is not decisive.[11] Instead the courts look to such factors as the duration of the order, whether it was issued after notice and hearing, and the type of showing made in obtaining the order.[12] Application of these tests is not easy to fathom. In one case an order labelled "temporary restraining order" was issued after a hearing at which both parties were represented, on a showing similar to what would have been

---

7. Baltimore Contractors v. Bodinger, 1955, 75 S.Ct. 249, 252, 348 U.S. 176, 181, 99 L.Ed. 233.

A modern example of Congressional response to pressures of this kind was the 1968 amendment of 18 U.S.C.A. § 3731 allowing the United States to appeal from an order suppressing or excluding evidence or requiring the return of seized property in a criminal proceeding. See 3 Wright, Criminal 2d § 678.

8. Smith v. Vulcan Iron Works, 1897, 17 S.Ct. 407, 165 U.S. 518, 41 L.Ed. 810; Myers v. Bethlehem Shipbuilding Corp., 1938, 58 S.Ct. 459, 303 U.S. 41, 82 L.Ed. 638; Aerojet-General Corp. v. American Arbitration Assn., C.A.9th, 1973, 478 F.2d 248, 252–253; 16 Wright, Miller & Cooper, Jurisdiction § 3921.

Jurisdiction of the interlocutory appeal is in large measure jurisdiction to deal with all aspects of the case that have been sufficiently illuminated to enable decision by the court of appeals without further trial court development. Energy Action Educational Foundation v. Andrus, C.A.1980, 654 F.2d 735, 745 n. 54, 210 U.S.App.D.C. 20.

For cases in which the appellate court follows the more usual practice of limiting itself to review of the order concerning the injunction, see 11 Wright & Miller, Civil § 2962 n. 28.

9. Deckert v. Independence Shares Corp., 1941, 61 S.Ct. 229, 311 U.S. 282, 85 L.Ed. 189.

10. Drudge v. McKernon, C.A.4th, 1973, 482 F.2d 1375; Connell v. Dulien Steel Products, Inc., C.A.5th, 1957, 240 F.2d 414, certiorari denied 78 S.Ct. 1008, 356 U.S. 968, 2 L.Ed.2d 1074; Schainman v. Brainard, C.C.A.9th, 1925; 8 F.2d 11; and cases cited 16 Wright, Miller & Cooper, Jurisdiction § 3922 n. 10.

11. Sampson v. Murray, 1974, 94 S.Ct. 937, 951, 415 U.S. 61, 86–87, 39 L.Ed.2d 166; Western Union Tel. Co. v. U. S. & Mexican Trust Co., C.C.A.8th, 1915, 221 F. 545, 553.

12. Sampson v. Murray, 1974, 94 S.Ct. 937, 951, 415 U.S. 61, 86–87, 39 L.Ed.2d 166; Melanson v. John J. Duane Co., Inc., C.A.1st, 1979, 605 F.2d 31, 33; Dilworth v. Riner, C.A.5th, 1965, 343 F.2d 226, 229; Austin v. Altman, C.A.2d, 1964, 332 F.2d 273, 275; Grant v. U. S., C.A.2d, 1960, 282 F.2d 165, 167.

made to obtain a preliminary injunction, and was to last for 28 days. But the appellate court held that since it "barely extended" beyond the 20 day limit for temporary restraining orders [13] it was not a preliminary injunction and was not appealable.[14]

The cases seem to be edging slowly toward a principle that rulings with respect to temporary restraining orders are appealable on a sufficiently strong showing of potentially irreparable injury.[15] It has been held also that the trial court may not avoid review of its determination that a preliminary injunction should not issue merely by refusing to make a formal ruling on the motion for such an injunction. Its refusal to act will be held equivalent to denial of the preliminary injunction, and appealable as such.[16]

An order need not refuse an injunction in terms in order to be immediately appealable under § 1292(a)(1). But if the order has the practical effect of refusing an injunction, it is only appealable if the order has serious, perhaps irreparable, consequences that can be effectually challenged only by immediate appeal. On this analysis appeal was allowed from a refusal to approve a consent decree that would have barred racial discrimination in hiring,[17] but appeal was not allowed from denial of a plaintiff's motion for summary judgment in a case seeking permanent injunctive relief [18] nor was it allowed from denial of class certification in a similar case.[19]

In Enelow v. New York Life Insurance Co.,[20] decided before law and equity were merged by adoption of the federal rules, and, more surprisingly, in Ettelson v. Metropolitan Life Insurance Co.,[21] decided after adoption of the rules, the Supreme Court held that if an action is brought that is triable to a jury, and defendant asserts a defense or

13.   Rule 65(b); 11 Wright & Miller, Civil § 2953.

14.   Connell v. Dulien Steel Products, Inc., C.A.5th, 1957, 240 F.2d 414, noted 1958, 71 Harv.L.Rev. 550. Cf. Pennsylvania Motor Truck Assn. v. Port of Philadelphia Marine Terminal Assn., C.A.3d, 1960, 276 F.2d 931.

15.   In some instances the order is considered a final decision and appealable under 28 U.S.C.A. § 1291. See § 101 n. 50 above. Other cases consider that the effect of the ruling on the temporary restraining order is sufficiently grave to make it, in effect, the grant or denial of a preliminary injunction and thus appealable under 28 U.S.C.A. § 1292(a)(2). E.g., Environmental Defense Fund v. Andrus, C.A.9th, 1980, 625 F.2d 861; Levesque v. Maine, C.A.1st, 1978, 587 F.2d 78. See 16 Wright, Miller & Cooper, Jurisdiction § 3922 at nn. 24–28.

16.   U. S. v. Lynd, C.A.5th, 1962, 301 F.2d 818, certiorari denied 83 S.Ct. 187,

371 U.S. 893, 9 L.Ed.2d 125; McCoy v. Louisiana State Bd. of Educ., C.A.5th, 1964, 332 F.2d 915; cf. Empire Nat. Bank of Clarksburg v. Penfield Coal & Coke Co., C.A.3d, 1966, 354 F.2d 873.

17.   Carson v. American Brands, Inc., 1981, 101 S.Ct. 993, 450 U.S. 79, 67 L.Ed.2d 59. See 16 Wright, Miller & Cooper, Jurisdiction § 3924.

18.   "Orders that in no way touch on the merits of the claim but only relate to pretrial procedures are not in our view 'interlocutory' within the meaning of § 1292(a)(1)." Switzerland Cheese Assn., Inc. v. E. Horne's Market, Inc., 1966, 87 S.Ct. 193, 195, 385 U.S. 23, 25, 17 L.Ed.2d 23.

19.   Gardner v. Westinghouse Broadcasting Co., 1978, 98 S.Ct. 2451, 437 U.S. 478, 57 L.Ed.2d 364.

20.   1935, 55 S.Ct. 310, 293 U.S. 379, 79 L.Ed. 440.

21.   1942, 63 S.Ct. 163, 317 U.S. 188, 87 L.Ed. 176.

a counterclaim not triable to a jury, the decision of the trial court to try the nonjury issues before the jury issues is appealable. The theory was that such an order had the effect of an injunction staying prosecution of the legal action, a theory that bore little resemblance to reality in 1935 and none in 1942, when the merger of law and equity had been completed. A converse situation arose a few years later in City of Morgantown v. Royal Insurance Co.[22] There it was the plaintiff who sued for reformation of an insurance policy, a claim not triable to a jury, and the defendant who counterclaimed to recover on the policy, a claim on which there is a right of jury trial. The court struck defendant's demand for a jury and ordered trial to the court. This order was held not to be appealable. The Court refused to accept analogies to pre-merger practice, and said that this was not an injunction, but simply a judge making a ruling as to the manner in which he would try one issue in a civil action pending before himself. The dissenters complained that the decision was a silent overruling of Enelow and Ettelson. Indeed the theory of the Court seemed to have this effect, and the commentators were hopeful that this was the result. Unfortunately the Enelow and Ettelson decisions were resuscitated in Baltimore Contractors, Inc. v. Bodinger.[23] The result there is surely sound. It was held that the refusal, in a nonjury case, to order a stay for arbitration "was simply a ruling in the only suit pending, actual or fictional. It was a mere order and not an injunction as that word is understood through the Enelow and the Ettelson cases as a stay through equitable principles of a common-law action."[24] In its reasoning, however, the Court accepted a distinction that had been offered by one concurring justice in the City of Morgantown case, by which a stay of the jury issues is appealable where the "law" action is brought first but not where the original action is "equitable" and the "legal" claim comes in as a counterclaim. The Court recognized the "incongruity" of such a distinction, and said that it "has elements of fiction" and "springs from the persistence of outmoded procedural differentiations,"[25] but felt that any change must come from Congress.

If Congress were aware of the travail this obsolete and fictional distinction is causing the courts of appeals, relief would surely be forthcoming. Indeed it is not too much to hope that the Supreme Court itself may reconsider its decision to preserve the distinction pending action by Congress. A rule that causes confusion at best and injustice at worst can hardly be justified. It has been correctly pointed out that "the decisions of the lower federal courts, sometimes within the same circuit, are not easily reconcilable."[26] Courts are

---

22. 1949, 69 S.Ct. 1067, 337 U.S. 254, 93 L.Ed. 1347.

23. 1955, 75 S.Ct. 249, 348 U.S. 176, 99 L.Ed. 233, noted 1955, 43 Geo.L.J. 498, 23 Geo.Wash.L.Rev. 780.

24. 75 S.Ct. at 254, 348 U.S. at 184.

25. Ibid.

26. Standard Chlorine of Delaware, Inc. v. Leonard, C.A.2d, 1967, 384 F.2d 304, 307–308.

forced to results that they themselves recognize as "anomalous."[27] Under some circumstances the Baltimore Contractors rule "tolerates opposite results depending upon the pure fortuity of the outcome of the race to the courthouse."[28]

There has been general acceptance of the formulation of the rule developed by the Fifth Circuit: "An order staying or refusing to stay proceedings in the District Court is appealable under § 1292(a)(1) only if (A) the action in which the order was made is an action which, before the fusion of law and equity, was by its nature an action at law; *and* (B) the stay was sought to permit the prior determination of some *equitable* defense or counterclaim."[29] That rule itself is extremely difficult to apply. When, as is true in most cases, the complaint seeks both legal and equitable relief, it presents "an essentially insolvable problem."[30]

In addition to the four situations in which the statute has for years permitted interlocutory review, the potential availability of such review by means of the so-called "extraordinary writs" of mandamus and prohibition has been an additional avenue of escape from the final judgment rule. Traditionally the use of these writs in the federal courts has been sharply limited.[31] In one case the Court said: "We are unwilling to utilize them as substitutes for appeals. As extraordinary remedies, they are reserved for really extraordinary

---

27. Mansbach v. Prescott, Ball & Turben, C.A.6th, 1979, 598 F.2d 1017, 1022; Wallace v. Norman Indus., Inc., C.A.5th, 1972, 467 F.2d 824, 827; Penoro v. Rederi A/B Disa, C.A.2d, 1967, 376 F.2d 125, 129, certiorari denied 88 S.Ct. 78, 389 U.S. 852, 19 L.Ed.2d 122; Travel Consultants, Inc. v. Travel Management Corp., C.A.1966, 367 F.2d 334, 338, 125 U.S.App.D.C. 108, certiorari denied 87 S.Ct. 861, 386 U.S. 912, 17 L.Ed.2d 785.

28. Chapman v. International Ladies' Garment Workers' Union, C.A.4th, 1968, 401 F.2d 626, 628, commenting on the situation presented in A. & E. Plastik Pak Co., Inc. v. Monsanto Co., C.A. 9th, 1968, 396 F.2d 710.

29. Jackson Brewing Co. v. Clarke, C.A.5th, 1962, 303 F.2d 844, 845, certiorari denied 83 S.Ct. 190, 371 U.S. 891, 9 L.Ed.2d 124 (emphasis in original). See generally Note, Appealability of Stay Orders in the Federal Courts, 1963, 47 Minn.L.Rev. 1099; 16 Wright, Miller & Cooper, Jurisdiction § 3923.

It has been held that the Baltimore Contractors rule does not apply at all, and there is no appeal, if the action stayed is an admiralty proceeding. Penoro v. Rederi A/B Disa, C.A.2d, 1967, 376 F.2d 125, certiorari denied 88 S.Ct. 78, 389 U.S. 852, 19 L.Ed.2d 676.

30. Schine v. Schine, C.A.2d, 1966, 367 F.2d 685, 688 (Friendly, J., concurring). See also Mellon Bank, N. A. v. Pritchard-Keang Nam Corp., C.A.8th, 1981, 651 F.2d 1244; Danford v. Schwabacher, C.A.9th, 1973, 488 F.2d 454, 457; Thompson v. House of Nine, Inc., C.A. 5th, 1973, 482 F.2d 888, 890; Chapman v. International Ladies' Garment Workers' Union, C.A.4th, 1968, 401 F.2d 626, 628–629, noted 1969, B.U.L.Rev. 355; Alexander v. Pacific Maritime Assn., C.A.9th, 1964, 332 F.2d 266, certiorari denied 85 S.Ct. 150, 379 U.S. 882, 13 L.Ed.2d 88.

The same thing is true in actions for a declaratory judgment, where the courts are "in the unenviable position not only of solving modern procedural problems by the application of labels which have no currency, but also of considering the nature of law suits which were never brought." Diematic Mfg. Corp. v. Packaging Indus., Inc., C.A.2d, 1975, 516 F.2d 975, 978, certiorari denied 96 S.Ct. 217, 423 U.S. 913, 46 L.Ed.2d 141.

31. 16 Wright, Miller & Cooper, Jurisdiction §§ 3932, 3933.

cases."[32] Though their use was said to be in the sound discretion of the courts of appeals, the Supreme Court would not hesitate to reverse, without reference to any discretion below, if it considered that a writ had been used as a substitute for appeal.[33] The usual federal doctrine was summarized as follows by the Supreme Court in 1956: "Such writs may go only in aid of appellate jurisdiction. 28 U.S.C.A. § 1651. The power to issue them is discretionary and it is sparingly exercised. * * * This is not a case where a court has exceeded or refused to exercise its jurisdiction, see Roche v. Evaporated Milk Ass'n, 319 U.S. 21, 26, 63 S.Ct. 938, 941, 87 L.Ed. 1185, nor one where appellate review will be defeated if a writ does not issue, cf. Maryland v. Soper, 270 U.S. 9, 29–30, 46 S.Ct. 185, 189, 70 L.Ed. 449. Here the most that could be claimed is that the district courts have erred in ruling on matters within their jurisdiction. The extraordinary writs do not reach to such cases; they may not be used to thwart the congressional policy against piecemeal appeals."[34]

A bare majority of the Supreme Court found these principles inapplicable, however, in a 1957 case, and held that a writ of mandamus was properly issued by a court of appeals to overrule the determination of a district judge that "exceptional conditions" existed, within the meaning of Rule 53(b), justifying appointment of a master.[35] Though the Court cautioned that by its holding it did not intend "to authorize the indiscriminate use of prerogative writs as a means of reviewing interlocutory orders,"[36] its conclusion that "supervisory control of the District Courts by the Courts of Appeals is necessary to proper judicial administration in the federal system"[37] certainly appeared to make the writs more freely available.[38]

Mandamus is now routinely used to require jury trial where it has been improperly denied.[39] The writ has been held appropriate also where there was a substantial allegation of usurpation of power by the trial court and the issue was one of first impression requiring application of one of the Civil Rules in a new context.[40] It has been

32. Ex parte Fahey, 1947, 67 S.Ct. 1558, 1559, 332 U.S. 258, 260, 91 L.Ed. 2041.

33. Roche v. Evaporated Milk Assn., 1943, 63 S.Ct. 938, 319 U.S. 21, 87 L.Ed. 1185.

34. Parr v. U. S., 1956, 76 S.Ct. 912, 917, 351 U.S. 513, 520, 100 L.Ed. 1377.

35. La Buy v. Howes Leather Co., 1957, 77 S.Ct. 309, 352 U.S. 249, 1 L.Ed.2d 290. See the critical discussion of this case in Wright, The Doubtful Omniscience of Appellate Courts, 1957, 41 Minn.L.Rev. 751, 771–778. A favorable view is taken in Carrington, The Power of District Judges and the Responsibility of Courts of Appeals, 1969, 3 Ga.L.Rev. 507, 508–517.

36. 77 S.Ct. at 314, 352 U.S. at 255.

37. 77 S.Ct. at 315, 352 U.S. at 259–260. See 16 Wright, Miller & Cooper, Jurisdiction § 3934; Note, Supervisory and Advisory Mandamus Under the All Writs Act, 1973, 86 Harv.L.Rev. 595.

38. See 16 Wright, Miller & Cooper, Jurisdiction § 3935.

39. Beacon Theatres, Inc. v. Westover, 1959, 79 S.Ct. 948, 957, 359 U.S. 500, 511, 3 L.Ed.2d 988; Dairy Queen, Inc. v. Wood, 1962, 82 S.Ct. 894, 901, 369 U.S. 469, 480, 8 L.Ed.2d 44.

40. Schlagenhauf v. Holder, 1964, 85 S.Ct. 234, 238–239, 379 U.S. 104, 109–112, 13 L.Ed.2d 152.

See also Colonial Times, Inc. v. Gasch, C.A.1975, 509 F.2d 517, 166 U.S.App. D.C. 184.

held appropriate also where a district court remanded a case removed from state court on improper grounds.[41]   On the other hand, the Court has held that mandamus will not issue to test a pretrial discovery order in a criminal case.[42]   Although there is much emphasis in the opinion on the "extraordinary" nature of the writ and the reluctance with which it should be used, the particular case was heavily influenced by the fact that it was a criminal case and that normally the government has no right to appeal in a criminal matter.[43]   However later cases have relied on that decision in a civil context,[44] and most recently, in the course of holding that the grant of a new trial by the district court will rarely, if ever, justify the issuance of a writ of mandamus, the Court said that "[o]nly exceptional circumstances, amounting to a judicial usurpation of power, will justify the invocation of this extraordinary remedy."[45]   Thus the Court seems to have retreated considerably from the expanded use of mandamus that it had seemed to sanction in 1957.

The entire pattern of interlocutory review in federal civil cases was drastically altered by the Interlocutory Appeals Act of 1958, which grants discretion to the courts of appeals to review any interlocutory order whatever in a civil case if the trial judge, in making the order, has stated in writing that the order involves a controlling question of law as to which there is substantial ground for difference of opinion and that an immediate appeal from the order may materially advance the ultimate termination of the litigation.[46]   This statute, 28 U.S.C.A. § 1292(b), was recommended by the Judicial Conference of the United States as a compromise between those who opposed any broadening of interlocutory review and those who favored giving the appellate courts discretion to entertain any interlocutory appeal they wished regardless of certification by the trial judge.[47]

The 1958 statute is an addition to prior methods of securing interlocutory review; it does not replace them.   Thus orders of the four types already described, which were appealable by statute prior to 1958, are still appealable without the certificate required by

41. Thermtron   Products,   Inc.   v. Hermansdorfer, 1976, 96 S.Ct. 584, 423 U.S. 336, 46 L.Ed.2d 542.

42. Will v. U. S., 1967, 88 S.Ct. 269, 389 U.S. 90, 19 L.Ed.2d 305.

43. 88 S.Ct. at 274–275, 389 U.S. at 96–98.   But see 16 Wright, Miller & Cooper, Jurisdiction § 3936.

44. Kerr v. U. S. Dist. Court, 1976, 96 S.Ct. 2119, 426 U.S. 394, 48 L.Ed.2d 725; Will v. Calvert Fire Ins. Co., 1978, 98 S.Ct. 2552, 437 U.S. 655, 57 L.Ed.2d 504 (plurality opinion), on remand C.A. 7th, 586 F.2d 12.

45. Allied Chem. Corp. v. Daiflon, Inc., 1980, 101 S.Ct. 188, 190, 449 U.S. 33, 35, 66 L.Ed.2d 193.

46. 16 Wright, Miller & Cooper, Jurisdiction §§ 3929–3931; Bourdeaux, Federal Interlocutory Appeals Act—A Five Year View, 1963, 35 Miss.L.J. 55; Note, Interlocutory Appeals in the Federal   Courts   under   28   U.S.C.A. § 1292(b), 1975, 88 Harv.L.Rev. 607.

Section 1292(b) has no application in a criminal case.   General Motors Corp. v. U. S., C.A.6th, 1978, 584 F.2d 1366, certiorari denied 99 S.Ct. 1277, 440 U.S. 934, 59 L.Ed.2d 492, criticized Note, 1979, 92 Harv.L.Rev. 931, 939–942.

47. See Gottesman v. General Motors Corp., C.A.2d, 1959, 268 F.2d 194, 196.

§ 1292(b). Matters previously appealable as "final decisions," such as "collateral orders," judgments in multiple claims cases certified as final under Rule 54(b), and the like,[48] are still appealable as final decisions under § 1292 and do not require a § 1292(b) certificate. Although it is preferable to use Rule 54(b) rather than § 1292(b) in those cases within the rule, an order that disposes of fewer than all of the parties or claims is interlocutory in the absence of a Rule 54(b) certificate. Thus it is within the terms of the statute, and the appellate court can take the case if a § 1292(b) certificate is made.[49] The statute should reduce the number of cases in which the extraordinary writs are used, since a condition for issuance of those writs has been the absence of any other adequate remedy,[50] but the writs remain available in the extraordinary cases where the trial judge has refused to give a § 1292(b) certificate and the case is of that rare sort that is properly reviewable by mandamus or prohibition.[51]

For the statute to apply there must be a "controlling question of law." Many cases have held a § 1292(b) appeal not proper on matters that lie within the discretion of the district court.[52] Ordinarily a district court should refuse to certify such matters, not only because of the low probability of reversal, but also because the recognition of discretion results from a studied determination that appellate courts should not generally interfere. But the key consideration is not whether the order involves the exercise of discretion, but whether it truly implicates the policies underlying § 1292(b).[53]

There must also be "substantial ground for difference of opinion" about the controlling question of law. One court held that this precluded it from certifying a question governed by clear precedent in its own circuit, though five other circuits were to the contrary.[54] Final-

48. See § 101 above.

49. DeMelo v. Woolsey Marine Indus., Inc., C.A.5th, 1982, 677 F.2d 1030; Local P-171, Amalgamated Meatcutters and Butcher Workmen of North America v. Thompson Farms Co., C.A. 7th, 1981, 642 F.2d 1065, 1069 n. 4; Sass v. District of Columbia, C.A.1963, 316 F.2d 366, 114 U.S.App.D.C. 365; 16 Wright, Miller & Cooper, Jurisdiction § 3929.

50. In re Centrotextil, C.A.8th, 1980, 620 F.2d 690; Mohasco Indus., Inc. v. Lydick, C.A.9th, 1972, 459 F.2d 959; Ex parte Watkins, C.A.5th, 1958, 260 F.2d 548; and cases cited 16 Wright, Miller & Cooper, Jurisdiction § 3929 n. 54.

51. Japan Line Ltd. v. Sabre Shipping Corp., C.A.2d, 1969, 407 F.2d 173, certiorari denied 89 S.Ct. 1774, 395 U.S. 922, 23 L.Ed.2d 239; Holub Indus., Inc. v. Wyche, C.A.4th, 1961, 290 F.2d 852; In re Watkins, C.A.5th, 1959, 271 F.2d 771, 76 A.L.R.2d 1113. But see Roach

v. Churchman, C.A.8th, 1972, 457 F.2d 1101, 1105.

52. E.g., Phelps v. Burnham, C.A.2d, 1964, 327 F.2d 812 (setting amount of security for costs); City of Burbank v. General Elec. Co., C.A.9th, 1964, 329 F.2d 825 (refusal to strike portion of a pleading); Standard v. Stoll Packing Corp., C.A.3d, 1964, 315 F.2d 626 (refusal to change venue); Rippey v. Denver U. S. Nat. Bank, D.C.Colo.1966, 260 F.Supp. 704 (determination parties not "indispensable"); Seven-Up Co. v. O-So Grape Co., D.C.Ill.1959, 179 F.Supp. 167 (separate trial of a particular issue).

53. Katz v. Carte Blanche Corp., C.A.3d, 1974, 496 F.2d 747, 756, certiorari denied 95 S.Ct. 152, 419 U.S. 885, 42 L.Ed.2d 125; and cases cited 16 Wright, Miller & Cooper, Jurisdiction § 3930 nn. 18–20.

54. Berger v. U. S., D.C.N.Y.1959, 170 F.Supp. 795, noted 1960, 108 U.Pa.L.

ly, it must be thought that immediate appeal "may materially advance the ultimate termination of the litigation." On this theory interlocutory appeal has been held inappropriate from orders involving sufficiency of the pleadings, since if the pleading were held insufficient it could be amended.[55] Also appeal has not been allowed where the case must go to trial in any event against other parties regardless of the correctness of the challenged ruling.[56] Generalizing from this statutory language, and from the legislative history of the statute, there is a good deal of authority for the proposition that § 1292(b) should not be used in "run-of-the-mill" cases and is intended for "exceptional cases" where appeal may avoid "protracted and expensive litigation."[57] The Fifth Circuit, however, has expressly disapproved statements from other courts calling for a strict construction of § 1292(b), or suggesting that it should be restricted to exceptional cases,[58] though in recent cases it has taken a narrower view of when the statute is properly used.[59]

If the appellate court agrees to hear a case that the district court has certified under § 1292(b), the appellate court is not limited to the question or questions the district court has certified. All questions material to the order below are properly before the court.[60]

Though a great deal has been written about § 1292(b), numerically the statute has not been of great importance. In the fiscal year 1981 26,362 appeals were taken to the eleven courts of appeals.[61] By contrast trial court certificates under § 1292(b) are made in only

Rev. 601. But cf. Corabi v. Auto Racing, Inc., C.A.3d, 1959, 264 F.2d 784 (appeal allowed where other circuits held a view contrary to that of court allowing appeal on controlling question of law).

55. City of Burbank v. General Elec. Co., C.A.9th, 1964, 329 F.2d 825; Gottesman v. General Motors Corp., C.A. 2d, 1959, 268 F.2d 194, noted 1959, 45 Va.L.Rev. 1236, 48 Geo.L.J. 594. Contra: Jewel Tea Co., Inc. v. Local Unions, etc., C.A.7th, 1960, 274 F.2d 217.

56. Bowling Machines, Inc. v. First Nat. Bank of Boston, C.A.1st, 1960, 283 F.2d 39; Speir v. Robert C. Herd & Co., D.C.Md.1960, 189 F.Supp. 436. Contra: Schnell v. Peter Eckrich & Sons, Inc., C.A.7th, 1960, 279 F.2d 594.

57. Lear Siegler, Inc. v. Adkins, C.A.9th, 1964, 330 F.2d 595, 598. See also Paschall v. Kansas City Star Co., C.A.8th, 1979, 605 F.2d 403, 406; Cardwell v. Chesapeake & O. R. Co., C.A.6th, 1974, 504 F.2d 444, 446–447; Fisons Ltd. v. U. S., C.A.7th, 1972, 458 F.2d 1241, 1248, certiorari denied 92 S.Ct. 1312, 405 U.S. 1041, 31 L.Ed.2d 581; In re Heddendorf, C.A.1st, 1959,

263 F.2d 887, 888; Milbert v. Bison Laboratories, Inc., C.A.3d, 1958, 260 F.2d 431, 433.

But see Note, Interlocutory Appeals in the Federal Courts under 28 U.S.C.A. § 1292(b), 1975, 88 Harv.L.Rev. 607; 16 Wright, Miller & Cooper, Jurisdiction § 3929.

58. Hadjipateras v. Pacifica, S.A., C.A. 5th, 1961, 290 F.2d 697, 702–703.

59. Alabama Labor Council v. Alabama, C.A.5th, 1972, 453 F.2d 922, 924; Garner v. Wolfinbarger, C.A.5th, 1970, 433 F.2d 117. In the Garner case even the dissenting judge expressed "concern that we have been too lax in allowing § 1292(b) appeals." 433 F.2d at 123.

60. Nuclear Engineers Co. v. Scott, C.A. 7th, 1981, 660 F.2d 241, 245–246; Murphy v. Heppenstall Co., C.A.3d, 1980, 635 F.2d 233, 235 n. 1; Note, note 57 above, at 628–629; 16 Wright, Miller & Cooper, Jurisdiction § 3929 at nn. 31–36.

61. Ann.Rep. of the Director of the Administrative Office of the U. S. Courts, 1981, p. 346.

about 100 cases a year and the courts of appeals allow interlocutory appeal in about half of those 100 cases.[62]

§ 103. Review of Administrative Determinations[1]

Two principal statutory patterns for judicial review of orders of federal administrative agencies have been commonly employed in the past, in addition to the "nonstatutory" review available by suit in the district court against the officer or agency involved.[2] The first pattern, originally adopted for the Interstate Commerce Commission in the Hepburn Act of 1906[3] and reenacted as the Urgent Deficiencies Act of 1913,[4] permitted suit to enjoin a commission order before a three-judge district court, with such suit given precedence over all other cases, and appeal as of right to the Supreme Court. The other pattern is that of the Federal Trade Commission Act of 1914.[5] It gave exclusive jurisdiction to affirm, enforce, modify, or set aside orders of that commission to the then-circuit courts of appeals, with discretionary review in the Supreme Court by certiorari.

In subsequent years each pattern of review was chosen by Congress for particular agencies. Review of some or all orders of the Federal Communications Commission, the Maritime Commission, the Packers and Stockyards Administration, and the Perishable Agricultural Commodities Administration was by a three-judge district court, under the procedure of the Urgent Deficiencies Act. Review by a court of appeals, under the pattern of the Federal Trade Commission Act, was written into most other regulatory statutes. Often it was difficult to fathom why Congress chose one form of review rather than another. Thus in the Packers and Stockyards Act of 1921 it was provided that orders of the Secretary of Agriculture under the "Packers" part of the act were to be reviewed in the court of appeals, while those under the "Stockyards" part of the act were to be reviewed by a three-judge district court.[6]

There were substantial reasons for preferring review by a court of appeals to review by a three-judge district court. It was always difficult to bring together two district judges and a judge of the court of appeals to make up a statutory three-judge district court,[7] while the court of appeals was readily available for review. In addition,

---

62. Note, note 46 above, at 607 n. 5.

[§ 103]

1. 16 Wright, Miller & Cooper, Jurisdiction §§ 3940–3944; 3 Davis, Administrative Law Treatise, 1958 and 1970 Supp., § 23.03; Currie & Goodman, Judicial Review of Federal Administrative Action: Quest for the Optimum Forum, 1975, 75 Col.L.Rev. 1.

2. The scope of "nonstatutory" review was greatly broadened when 5 U.S. C.A. §§ 702, 703, were amended in

1976. See 14 Wright, Miller & Cooper, Jurisdiction § 3655.

3. Act of June 29, 1906, c. 3591, § 5, 34 Stat. 584, 590.

4. Act of Oct. 22, 1913, c. 32, 38 Stat. 219; 28 U.S.C.A. §§ 1336, 2321–2325.

5. Act of Sept. 26, 1914, c. 311, § 5, 38 Stat. 717, 720; 15 U.S.C.A. § 45.

6. Act of Aug. 15, 1921, c. 64, §§ 204, 316, 42 Stat. 159, 162, 168.

7. See § 50 above.

the direct appeal to the Supreme Court from three-judge courts forced that Court to review many cases where the questions involved were of only minor importance, but where lengthy records and extreme technicalities added heavily to the burden of the Court. Accordingly in 1950 Congress, recognizing that review by a court of appeals "is the more modern method and is generally considered to be the best method for the review of orders of administrative agencies,"[8] adopted that means of review for all agencies except the Interstate Commerce Commission.[9] Review is obtained under the 1950 statute by filing a petition for review with the court of appeals for the circuit where the party or parties seeking review reside or have their principal office, or with the Court of Appeals for the District of Columbia.[10] Review will ordinarily be on the record made at the hearing before the administrative agency,[11] with the findings of fact by the agency accepted if they are supported by substantial evidence in the light of the whole record.[12]

It was wholly anomalous that Interstate Commerce Commission orders were not made reviewable in the courts of appeals when this was accomplished for other agencies in the 1950 legislation.[13] Fortunately this reform was finally accomplished in 1975.[14] Actions to enforce an ICC order or to enjoin or suspend an order of the ICC for the payment of money or the collection of fines, penalties, or forfeitures are heard by a single judge in the district court.[15] All other review of ICC orders is now in the courts of appeals to be handled in the same fashion as review of other agencies.[16]

8. H.Rep. No. 2122, 81st Cong., 2d Sess. 1950; 1950 U.S.Code Cong.Serv., pp. 4303, 4306. See also D. L. Piazza Co. v. West Coast Line, Inc., C.A.2d, 1954, 210 F.2d 947, 949.

9. Act of Dec. 29, 1950, c. 1189, 64 Stat. 1129; 28 U.S.C.A. §§ 2341–2352. The act is not all-inclusive. Other statutes providing for review by a court of appeals remain, and are not superseded by the 1950 statute. For such other statutes, see 16 Wright, Miller & Cooper, Jurisdiction § 3941.

10. 28 U.S.C.A. §§ 2342, 2343. There is a provision for transfer if petitions for review of the same order are filed in several courts of appeals. 28 U.S.C.A. § 2112(a). See 16 Wright, Miller & Cooper, Jurisdiction § 3944; Comment, A Proposal to End the Race to the Court House in Appeals from Federal Administrative Orders, 1968, 68 Col.L. Rev. 166.

11. 28 U.S.C.A. § 2347. See also Appellate Rules 15–20.

12. 5 U.S.C.A. § 706(2)(E); Universal Camera Corp. v. N. L. R. B., 1951, 71 S.Ct. 456, 340 U.S. 474, 95 L.Ed. 456; 4 Davis, Administrative Law Treatise, 1958 and 1970 Supp., cc. 29, 30.

13. Report of the Study Group on the Caseload of the Supreme Court, 1972, 57 F.R.D. 573, 597. The Supreme Court had said that the statutes on review of ICC orders were "an historical patchwork * * * surely ripe for congressional consideration * * *." Interstate Commerce Comm. v. Atlantic Coast Line R. Co., 1966, 86 S.Ct. 1000, 1007 n. 4, 383 U.S. 576, 586 n. 4, 16 L.Ed.2d 109.

14. Act of Jan. 2, 1975, Pub.L. 93–584, 88 Stat. 1917; Boskey & Gressman, Recent Reforms in the Federal Judicial Structure—Three-Judge District Courts and Appellate Review, 1975, 67 F.R.D. 135, 154–156.

15. 28 U.S.C.A. § 1336(a).

16. 28 U.S.C.A. §§ 2321–2323, 2342(5).

§ 104. Appellate Procedure [1]

One of the most striking achievements in the federal rules from the first has been the simplified procedures they introduced for taking appeals. These matters were dealt with until 1968 by Civil Rules 73 to 76 and Criminal Rules 37 to 39. In that year the Federal Rules of Appellate Procedure were adopted, applicable to all cases, and the former civil and criminal provisions were repealed. The Appellate Rules incorporate in general the portions of the Civil Rules and Criminal Rules that they replaced but they also make uniform provision for a number of other matters of appellate practice that prior to 1968 were dealt with in varying ways by the rules of the eleven courts of appeals, though the uniformity that was hoped for has been greatly compromised by the proliferation of local rules for particular circuits.

Under the rules the timely filing of a simple notice of appeal is the only step required to take an appeal. Such former devices as writs of errors, bills of exceptions, summons and severance, petitions for allowance of appeal, citations, assignments of errors, and similar vestiges of procedural antiquity have been "consigned, without mourners, to the legal limbo."[2]

It is true that an appellant who has filed a notice of appeal cannot then sit back and do nothing until his case is called for argument. He must file a cost bond (in a civil case),[3] file the record on appeal,[4] docket the appeal,[5] and file his brief and appendix,[6] but none of these steps is jurisdictional.[7] The appeal may be dismissed for failure to take these further steps at the proper time, but the matter is within the discretion of the court of appeals. It need not dismiss the appeal and ordinarily will not do so in the absence of prejudice to the appellee.[8]

The only exceptions to this general pattern are interlocutory appeals under 28 U.S.C.A. § 1292(b) and certain bankruptcy appeals. In these instances the party seeking to appeal must petition the appellate court and his petition must be allowed before the appeal may proceed further.[9]

[§ 104]

1. 16 Wright, Miller & Cooper, Jurisdiction §§ 3945–3994. The principal author of this portion of volume 16 was Professor Eugene Gressman of the University of North Carolina Law School. See also Ward, The Federal Rules of Appellate Procedure, 1968, 28 Fed.B.J. 100.

2. Cf. Wiener, The Supreme Court's New Rules, 1954, 68 Harv.L.Rev. 20, 59.

3. Appellate Rule 7.

4. Appellate Rules 10, 11, 12(b).

5. Appellate Rule 12(a).

6. Appellate Rules 28, 30–32.

7. Appellate Rule 3(a).

8. Compare Savard v. Marine Contracting, Inc., C.A.2d, 1972, 471 F.2d 536, 543, certiorari denied 93 S.Ct. 2778, 412 U.S. 943, 37 L.Ed.2d 404, and Mikkelson v. Young Men's Christian Assn. of Chicago, C.A.7th, 1963, 317 F.2d 78, with PAAC v. Rizzo, C.A.3d, 1974, 502 F.2d 306, 309 n. 3, certiorari denied 95 S.Ct. 780, 419 U.S. 1108, 42 L.Ed.2d 804, and Johnson v. Danielson, C.A.9th, 1961, 295 F.2d 12.

9. 28 U.S.C.A. § 1292(b). The procedure for petitioning is set out in Appellate Rules 5 and 6.

The notice of appeal, as described in Appellate Rule 3(c), is an extremely simple document.[10] Some notice of appeal, regarded as sufficient by the appellate court, must be filed, for the notice of appeal is the one jurisdictional prerequisite to an appeal.[11] The courts are very liberal, however, in entertaining an appeal even where the notice fails to comply with the rule. The notice should not be used as a technical trap for the unwary draftsman, and a defective notice of appeal should not warrant dismissal for want of jurisdiction if the intention to appeal from a specific judgment may be reasonably inferred from the text of the notice and the defect has not materially misled the appellee.[12] This has been fully understood by the courts. As noted by the Ninth Circuit, "there is a considerable body of authority indicating that in determining whether an attempted appeal has been accomplished, most informally drawn papers and improperly labeled documents have been held sufficient to accomplish the apparent objective of taking an appeal. * * * The rationale of the cases relating to informal or irregular appeals is that notwithstanding the papers filed were inaptly worded, or labeled, or even failed to use the word "appeal, or were filed in the wrong court, yet they sufficed to show the party intended to appeal."[13] The Supreme Court has endorsed this liberality in passing on the sufficiency of a notice of appeal.[14]

In civil cases the notice of appeal must be filed within 30 days after entry of judgment except where the United States is a party to the suit, in which case 60 days is allowed.[15] In a criminal case the notice must be filed within ten days.[16] Prior to 1966 the time could be extended for 30 days in a civil case only because the party, through excusable neglect, had failed to learn of the entry of the judgment.[17] In criminal cases there could be no extension for any reason.[18] These provisions were changed in 1966 and in both civil and

The rule on bankruptcy appeals is obsolete since the drastic changes made by the 1978 Bankruptcy Act. See § 102 n. 6.

10. See Official Form 1 of the Appellate Rules.

11. U. S. v. Robinson, 1960, 80 S.Ct. 282, 285, 361 U.S. 220, 224, 4 L.Ed.2d 259; Federal Deposit Ins. Corp. v. Congregation Poiley Tzedeck, C.C.A.2d, 1946, 159 F.2d 163, 166.

12. Williams v. General Motors Corp., C.A.5th, 1981, 656 F.2d 120, 125–126; Vargas v. McNamara, C.A.1st, 1979, 608 F.2d 15, 21; Scherer v. Kelley, C.A.7th, 1978, 584 F.2d 170, 174–175, certiorari denied 99 S.Ct. 1511, 440 U.S. 964, 59 L.Ed.2d 778; Donovan v. Esso Shipping Co., C.A.3d, 1958, 259 F.2d 65, 68, certiorari denied 79 S.Ct. 583, 359 U.S. 907, 3 L.Ed.2d 572; Crump v. Hill, C.C.A.5th, 1939, 104 F.2d 36, 38.

13. Yanow v. Weyerhaeuser S. S. Co., C.A.9th, 1959, 274 F.2d 274, 282–283, certiorari denied 80 S.Ct. 671, 362 U.S. 919, 4 L.Ed.2d 739.

14. Foman v. Davis, 1962, 83 S.Ct. 227, 371 U.S. 178, 9 L.Ed.2d 222. See also Sanabria v. U. S., 1978, 98 S.Ct. 2170, 2180 n. 21, 437 U.S. 54, 67 n. 21, 57 L.Ed.2d 43. But see Griggs v. Provident Consumer Discount Co., 1982, 103 S.Ct. 400, ___ U.S. ___, ___ L.Ed.2d ___.

15. Appellate Rule 4(a)(1).

16. Appellate Rule 4(b).

17. E.g., Watson v. Providence Washington Ins. Co., C.A.4th, 1953, 201 F.2d 736.

18. Berman v. U. S., 1964, 84 S.Ct. 1895, 378 U.S. 530, 12 L.Ed.2d 1012; U. S. v. Robinson, 1960, 80 S.Ct. 282, 361 U.S. 220, 4 L.Ed.2d 259.

criminal cases the time for noticing the appeal may now be extended an additional 30 days for "excusable neglect" of any kind.[19] If the trial court finds excusable neglect, and grants an extension, the appellate court should not second-guess this determination and thus defeat the appeal, though some courts have done do.[20] On the other hand, some courts have given a surprisingly permissive reading to the provision. This has come in cases in which the appellant never seeks an extension from the trial court but simply files his notice of appeal during the period to which the time could have been extended. Several courts in these circumstances have remanded the case, long after the time for extension has run, so that the trial court may determine whether there was excusable neglect and if so grant a nunc pro tunc extension.[21]

It is important to observe that it is the "filing" of the notice within the designated time that is required. Service on the opposing party will not do.[22] Neither will deposit in the mail if the notice is not actually received in the clerk's office within the designated time,[23] though an exception has been made in extreme cases.[24] If the clerk actually receives the notice, however, he cannot refuse to file it on the ground that his fee has not been paid.[25]

Certain post-trial motions suspend the finality of the judgment and the time for giving notice of appeal runs from the decision of the motions. In criminal cases a motion for a new trial, under Criminal Rule 33, or a motion for arrest of judgment, under Rule 34, has this effect,[26] though curiously a motion for judgment of acquittal under Rule 29(c) does not.[27] In civil cases the time is extended by: a motion

19. As further amended in 1979, the rule now allows extension of time in a civil case for either excusable neglect or good cause. Appellate Rule 4(a)(5). Only excusable neglect will suffice in a criminal case. Appellate Rule 4(b). See 16 Wright, Miller & Cooper, Jurisdiction § 3950.

20. Pellegrino v. Marathon Bank, C.A.5th, 1981, 640 F.2d 696; Fase v. Seafarers Welfare & Pension Plan, C.A.2d, 1978, 574 F.2d 72; and cases cited 16 Wright, Miller & Cooper, Jurisdiction § 3950 n. 15.

21. U. S. v. McKnight, C.A.3d, 1979, 593 F.2d 230; U. S. v. Umfress, C.A.5th, 1977, 562 F.2d 359; Stirling v. Chem. Bank, C.A.2d, 1975, 511 F.2d 1030; Reed v. Michigan, C.A.6th, 1968, 398 F.2d 800; Evans v. Jones, C.A.4th, 1966, 366 F.2d 772.

22. Federal Deposit Ins. Corp. v. Congregation Poiley Tzedeck, C.C.A.2d, 1946, 159 F.2d 163.

23. Allen v. Schnuckle, C.A.9th, 1958, 253 F.2d 195; Kahler-Ellis Co. v. Ohio

Turnpike Comm., C.A.6th, 1955, 225 F.2d 922; Lejeune v. Midwestern Ins. Co. of Oklahoma City, Okla., C.A.5th, 1952, 197 F.2d 149.

24. Fallen v. U. S., 1964, 84 S.Ct. 1689, 378 U.S. 139, 12 L.Ed.2d 760; Da'Ville v. Wise, C.A.5th, 1973, 470 F.2d 1364, certiorari denied 94 S.Ct. 40, 414 U.S. 818, 38 L.Ed.2d 50, and 94 S.Ct. 170, 414 U.S. 818, 38 L.Ed.2d 50; Hegler v. Board of Educ. of Bearden Sch. Dist., C.A.8th, 1971, 447 F.2d 1078.

25. Parissi v. Telechron, Inc., 1955, 75 S.Ct. 577, 349 U.S. 46, 99 L.Ed. 867. But see Stirling v. Chem. Bank, C.A.2d, 1975, 511 F.2d 1030.

See also Aldabe v. Aldabe, C.A.9th, 1980, 616 F.2d 1089, holding the appeal timely where the notice was received by the clerk on the last day even though it was not "filed" for another two weeks.

26. Appellate Rule 4(b).

27. 2 Wright, Criminal 2d § 465.

for judgment notwithstanding the verdict, under Civil Rule 50(b); a motion to amend the findings, under Rule 52(b); a motion for a new trial, under Rule 59; a motion to alter or amend the judgment, under Rule 59(e).[28] A motion for relief from the judgment or order under Rule 60(b) does not affect the finality of the judgment and thus does not affect the time to appeal.[29] A post-trial motion must itself be timely if it is to extend the time for appeal.[30]

An appellee may defend a judgment on any ground consistent with the record, even if rejected in the lower court.[31] But he cannot attack the decree with a view either to enlarging his own rights thereunder or to lessening the rights of his adversary unless he files a cross appeal, whether what he seeks is to correct an error or to supplement the decree with respect to a matter not dealt with below.[32] Until 1966 the appellee was given no additional time in which to file notice of his cross-appeal and might be trapped if he did not learn of his opponent's appeal until the time for appeal has elapsed. The rule now provides that if one party files a timely notice of appeal, any other party may file a notice of appeal within 14 days of the filing of the first notice or within the time in which he might otherwise have given notice of appeal, whichever period last expires.[33]

Ordinarily the appellant cannot seek reversal upon a ground not raised in the trial court, but this is only a rule of practice and may be relaxed if the public interest so requires.[34]

Appellate Rules 10 and 11 prescribe how the record on appeal is to be prepared and transmitted to the appellate court. The record on appeal is defined as being "the original papers and exhibits filed in the district court, the transcript of proceedings, if any, and a certified copy of the docket entries prepared by the clerk."[35] When the Civil

---

28. Appellate Rule 4(a)(4).

29. Textile Banking Co., Inc. v. Rentschler, C.A.7th, 1981, 657 F.2d 844, 848–850; Hardy v. St. Paul Fire & Marine Ins. Co., C.A.5th, 1979, 599 F.2d 628, 629; 11 Wright & Miller, Civil § 2871 n. 90.

30. Hulson v. Atchison, T. & S. F. Ry. Co., C.A.7th, 1961, 289 F.2d 726, certiorari denied 82 S.Ct. 61, 368 U.S. 835, 7 L.Ed.2d 36; John E. Smith's Sons Co. v. Lattimer Foundry & Machine Co., C.A.3d, 1956, 239 F.2d 815; Albers v. Gant, C.A.5th, 1970, 435 F.2d 146.

31. Colautti v. Franklin, 1979, 99 S.Ct. 675, 686 n. 16, 439 U.S. 379, 397 n. 16, 58 L.Ed.2d 596; Massachusetts Mut. Life Ins. Co. v. Ludwig, 1976, 96 S.Ct. 2158, 426 U.S. 479, 48 L.Ed.2d 784; Kennecott Copper Corp. v. Curtiss-Wright Corp., C.A.2d, 1978, 584 F.2d 1195, 1206; In re Henderson, C.A.5th, 1978, 577 F.2d 997.

32. Morley Constr. Co. v. Maryland Cas. Co., 1937, 57 S.Ct. 325, 327–328, 300 U.S. 185, 191–192, 81 L.Ed. 593; Alexander v. Cosden Pipe Line Co., 1934, 54 S.Ct. 292, 293–294, 290 U.S. 484, 487–488, 78 L.Ed. 452; Third Nat. Bank of Nashville v. U. S., C.A.6th, 1972, 454 F.2d 689; Stern, When to Cross-Appeal or Cross-Petition—Certainty or Confusion?, 1974, 87 Harv.L. Rev. 763.

33. Appellate Rule 4(a)(3). The rule reaches "any other party" and is not limited to a cross-appeal. Kurdziel v. Pittsburgh Tube Co., C.A.6th, 1969, 416 F.2d 882.

34. Wratchford v. S. J. Groves & Sons Co., C.A.4th, 1969, 405 F.2d 1061; Green v. Brown, C.A.2d, 1968, 398 F.2d 1006; New York, N. H. & H. R. Co. v. Reconstruction Fin. Corp., C.A.2d, 1950, 180 F.2d 241, 244.

35. Appellate Rule 10(a).

Rules were originally adopted a certified copy of the record on file in the district court was made and sent to the appellate court. This was a wasteful burden and expense.[36] In 1948 the Civil Rules were amended to permit a court of appeals, if it wished, to provide by rule that the original district court record could be used as the record on appeal and by 1962 every circuit had exercised this sensible option.

In addition to the record, of which only a single copy is required, some provision must be made for putting into the hands of each of the judges who will hear the appeal those portions of the record that are of particular significance. This document, known as the appendix, "is exactly what its name implies: an addendum to the briefs for the convenience of the judges."[37] What is to go into it and how it is to be prepared is of great significance because it forms a large part of the cost of appellate review. Rule 32(a) makes an important contribution by permitting briefs and appendices to be produced "by standard typographic printing or by any duplicating or copying process which produces a clear black image on white paper." Thus modern copying methods may be used and the parties are no longer confined to printing or offset duplicating.[38]

The question of the contents and preparation of the appendix was more controversial than any other question in the preparation of the Appellate Rules and at one point three different drafts were distributed for consideration by the profession.[39] The rule finally adopted contemplates that there will be filed with the appellant's brief a single appendix, prepared by the appellant, and containing all the portions of the record to which either the appellant or the appellee wishes "to direct the particular attention of the court."[40] The rule makes it very clear that the parties and the court may rely on portions of the record that are not included in the appendix[41] and it cautions that "in designating parts of the record for inclusion in the appendix, the parties shall have regard for the fact that the entire record is always available to the court for reference and examination and shall not engage in unnecessary designation."[42]

---

36. See Dean, Proposed Rule for Hearing of Appeals on Original Papers, 1948, 8 F.R.D. 143, 148.

37. Ward, note 1 above, at 108.

38. "In 1964 the cost of a single page of the brief or of the reproduction of the record by standard letterpress printing was approaching $4.00 per page; the cost of a page by offset duplicating, the only other method generally permitted by the circuits, was approximately $2.80 per page." Ward, note 1 above, at 108. See also Wilcox, Karlen & Roemer, Justice Lost—By What Appellate Papers Cost, 1958, 33 N.Y.U.L. Rev. 934.

39. Drafts of Proposed Rule 30, Uniform Rules of Federal Appellate Procedure, December 1966, 41 F.R.D. 311.

40. Appellate Rule 30. See Alger v. Hayes, C.A.8th, 1972, 452 F.2d 841; Slade, The Appendix to the Briefs: Rule 30 of the Federal Rules of Appellate Procedure, 1968, 28 Fed.B.J. 116.

41. Appellate Rule 30(a).

42. Appellate Rule 30(b).

Rule 11(c), 1st Cir. Rules, provides: "Notwithstanding the provisions of FRAP Rule 30 the court may decline to refer to portions of the record omitted from the Appendix, except by inadvertence, unless leave be granted prior to argument." The rule seems plainly in-

Rule 30(c) also provides that in some circumstances the appendix may be deferred until after the briefs have been prepared and filed 21 days after the brief of the appellee. The thought is that if the appendix is not prepared until after the briefs are completed the parties will be able to see precisely what the issues are, and what parts of the record need to be reproduced, and that this will encourage smaller appendices. In large cases the deferred appendix will be advantageous though the procedure for preparing it and referring to the appendix in the briefs is quite complicated. The rule was amended in 1970 to provide that the deferred appendix may be used only if the court has provided by rule for classes of cases or by order in the specific case.

Finally Rule 30(f) somewhat grudgingly provides that a court of appeals may dispense with the requirement of an appendix altogether and permit appeals to be heard on copies of the relevant parts of the original record. It has been estimated that such a procedure, taking advantage of inexpensive modern copying machines, can cut the cost of reproduction by two-thirds and also eliminate most of the lawyer time otherwise required for preparation of the record.[43] This has been standard procedure in the Ninth Circuit since 1962 [44] and a number of other circuits now permit use of the original record and two copies of it in many kinds of cases.

As other circuits obtain experience with the Ninth Circuit practice in limited classes of cases, they are likely to become aware of its usefulness and to make it applicable in all cases. Just as in 14 years every circuit exercised the option given it and elected to adopt the original papers as the record on appeal, so too the option provided in Rule 30(f) is likely in a short time to have been exercised universally. Although a distinguished authority has said flatly of the Ninth Circuit practice that "it is not workable as a practical matter,"[45] the Advisory Committee Note to Rule 30(f) states that "the judges of the Court of Appeals for the Ninth Circuit have expressed complete satisfaction with the practice there in use and have suggested that attention be called to the advantages which it offers in terms of reducing cost."[46]

The major change in appellate procedure in the last 15 years has been with regard to oral argument and publication of opinions. In the face of overwhelming caseloads, most courts of appeals have felt the need to institute screening procedures to decide which cases merit oral argument and how much time should be allowed for it. In addition, many cases are now disposed of by summary orders.[47] Even

valid as inconsistent with Appellate Rule 30(b).

43. Joiner, Lawyer Attitudes Toward Law and Procedural Reform, 1966, 50 Judicature 23, 25.

44. Rule 4(b), 9th Cir. Rules.

45. Prettyman, The New Federal Rules of Appellate Procedure, 1968, 28 Fed. B.J. 97, 99.

46. 1967, 43 F.R.D. 61, 150.

47. Appellate Rule 34(a); Commission on Revision of the Federal Court Appellate System, Structure and Internal

when an opinion is written, it is frequently designated as not for publication and frequently is regarded as without precedential effect.[48] If these drastic reforms had not been instituted, the federal courts of appeals would have collapsed under the pressure of docket congestion. Even so, there is concern for the implications these new devices may have for the quality of justice administered by the appellate courts.[49]

Procedures: Recommendations for Change, 1975, 67 F.R.D. 195, 247–260; Wasby, Oral Argument in the Ninth Circuit: The View from Bench and Bar, 1981, 11 Golden Gate L.Rev. 21; Haworth, Screening and Summary Procedures in the United States Courts of Appeals, 1973 Wash.U.L.Q. 257.

48. Reynolds & Richman, An Evaluation of Limited Publication in the United States Courts of Appeals, 1981, 48 U.Chi.L.Rev. 573; Reynolds & Richman, The Non-Precedential Precedent—Limited Publication and No-Citation Rules in the United States Courts of Appeals, 1978, 78 Col.L.Rev. 1167; Newbern & Wilson, Rule 21: Unprecedent and the Disappearing Court, 1978, 32 Ark.L.Rev. 37; Stern, The Enigma of Unpublished Opinions, 1978, 64 A.B.A.J. 1191; Walther, The Noncitation Rule and the Concept of Stare Decisis, 1978, 61 Marq.L.Rev.

581; Gardner, Ninth Circuit's Unpublished Opinions: Denial of Equal Justice, 1975, 61 A.B.A.J. 1224; Note, Unreported Decisions in the United States Courts of Appeals, 1977, 63 Cornell L.Rev. 128.

49. Compare Carrington, Ceremony and Realism: Demise of Appellate Procedure, 1980, 66 A.B.A.J. 860, with Godbold, Improvements in Appellate Procedure: Better Use of Available Facilities, 1980, 66 A.B.A.J. 863.

The extent to which screening procedures and dispositions without published opinions are being used in each circuit is examined by the Senate Judiciary Committee in S.Rep. No. 94–404, 1975, and concern expressed that "our concept of due process imposes limits on the nature and on the extent of permissible short-cuts in the appellate process * * *." Id. at 25.

CHAPTER 12

THE APPELLATE JURISDICTION OF THE SUPREME COURT

Analysis

§ 105. Review of Decisions of the District Courts [1]

A principal purpose of the Evarts Act of 1891, which created the circuit court of appeals, of the Judicial Code of 1911, which abolished the old circuit courts, and of the Judges' Bill of 1925, limiting appeals to the Supreme Court and substituting the discretionary writ of certiorari,[2] was to lessen the burden on the Supreme Court and to put control of its docket in its hands by substituting an intermediate appellate court to which most appeals would go and that would, in most cases, speak the final word.

That goal is highly desirable, yet on various occasions in the first part of this century the view became accepted that there were particular classes of cases of great public moment that required prompt review as a matter of right in the highest court of the land. Responding to these pressures, Congress made provision in four classes of cases for direct review by appeal from a district court to the Supreme Court.

Experience has demonstrated the unwisdom of these provisions. The Supreme Court is forced to decide these cases without the guidance of a decision from a court of appeals. These cases take up a disproportionate amount of the limited time the Court has for oral argument.[3] That burden would be even greater if the Court did not dispose of many of them by summary orders, without full briefs or oral argument, but summary disposition increases the risk that the Court may act erroneously. Many of these cases come to the Court on an inadequate record. Uncertainty about when direct appeal will

[§ 105]

1. 17 Wright, Miller & Cooper, Jurisdiction §§ 4039–4040; Stern & Gressman, Supreme Court Practice, 5th ed. 1978, §§ 2.9–2.17.

2. See § 1 above.

3. In an average term, 22% of the cases argued orally in the Supreme Court were direct appeals from three-judge courts though these cases made up only 2.7% of the Court's docket. Report of the Study Group on the Caseload of the Supreme Court, 1972, 57 F.R.D. 573, 598. The virtual elimination of three-judge courts in 1976—see § 50 above—has remedied this unhappy situation.

lie and what the scope of review is has added wasteful complications to the process.

For all of these reasons direct appeal from district courts has been a failure. Where prompt decision by the Supreme Court is truly important, it is possible for the Supreme Court to bypass the courts of appeals by granting certiorari before judgment in those courts.[4] Even this is not always necessary, because a prompt determination can be had even though there is review in a court of appeals prior to Supreme Court review.[5] These arguments against direct review have come to be accepted,[6] and in the last six years there has been great progress toward eliminating direct appeal.

The earliest of the direct appeal statutes was the Expediting Act of 1903,[7] which was intended originally to provide expeditious determination of actions brought by the United States under the antitrust laws and the Interstate Commerce Act, but was extended also to cover actions under the common carriers sections of the Communications Act.[8] The Expediting Act had two features. In any case falling within the act the Attorney General could certify that the case was of general public importance. Upon such certification, the case had to be heard at the earliest practicable date by a three-judge district court. The other feature of the Expediting Act was that in actions it covered an appeal from the final judgment of the district court would lie only to the Supreme Court. It must be noticed that these features were independent. Certification by the Attorney General, which required a three-judge court, was not much used in recent years. Direct appeal ran from the final judgment, however, even though the case was not so certified, and accordingly was heard by a single judge.

The intricacies of the Expediting Act—and they were many—need not be explored because it is now a matter of past history. Responding to criticisms from the Court itself that direct review had proven "unsatisfactory" in Expediting Act cases,[9] Congress responded in

4. 28 U.S.C.A. § 1254(1).

The disadvantages is not having an opinion from the court of appeals are described in the separate opinion of Justices Burton and Frankfurter in Youngstown Sheet & Tube Co. v. Sawyer, 1952, 72 S.Ct. 775, 343 U.S. 937, 96 L.Ed. 1344.

5. See § 106 n. 13 below.

6. Report of the Study Group on the Caseload of the Supreme Court, 1972, 57 F.R.D. 573, 596–602; Buskey & Gressman, Recent Reforms in the Federal Judicial Structure—Three-Judge Courts and Appellate Review, 1975, 67 F.R.D. 135, 143–147.

7. Act of Feb. 11, 1903, c. 544, 32 Stat. 823.

8. Prior to their amendment or repeal by the Antitrust Procedures and Penalties Act of 1974, Pub.L. 93–528, 88 Stat. 1706, the relevant statutes were: 15 U.S.C.A. §§ 28, 29; 49 U.S.C.A. §§ 44, 45; 47 U.S.C.A. § 401(d).

9. U. S. v. Singer Mfg. Co., 1963, 83 S.Ct. 1773, 1774 n. 1, 374 U.S. 174, 175 n. 1, 10 L.Ed.2d 823. Most commentators agreed. ALI Study, p. 324; Gesell, A Much Needed Reform—Repeal the Expediting Act for Anti-trust Cases, 1961 N.Y.S.B.A. Antitrust Law Symposium 98; Comments, 1968, 81 Harv.L.Rev. 1558; 1965, 63 Mich.L. Rev. 1240; 1964, 13 DePaul L.Rev. 261; 1964, 39 N.Y.U.L.Rev. 319.

For a contrary view, see Kirkpatrick, Antitrust to the Supreme Court: The Ex-

1974 by substantially abolishing the Act.[10]   The rarely-used right of
the Attorney General to require a three-judge court was ended and
so, for the most part, was direct appeal to the Supreme Court.[11]   The
only direct appeal that remains is in civil actions brought by the United States seeking equitable relief for violation of the antitrust laws
or to enforce certain provisions of the Interstate Commerce Act.[12]   In
these cases both appeals from final judgments and interlocutory appeals go to the courts of appeals, with one exception.   An appeal
from a final judgment may still go directly to the Supreme Court if,
on application of any party, the district judge makes an order "stating that immediate consideration of the appeal by the Supreme Court
is of general public importance in the administration of justice."
Even when such an order is made, the Supreme Court is given discretion either to hear the appeal or to deny the direct appeal and remand
the case to the court of appeals.[13]

The second class of direct appeals from district courts was under
the Criminal Appeals Act of 1907, as amended over the years.[14]   The
Supreme Court had held in 1892 that the act creating the circuit
courts of appeals, passed the preceding year, had left the United
States without any right of review in criminal cases, even where the
defendant had not been put in jeopardy.[15]   For years successive attor-
neys-general asked that this omission be rectified, but their appeals
were unheeded.   The impetus that led to adoption of the Act of 1907
came from the action of a single district judge who directed a verdict
for the individual defendants in an antitrust case of importance to the
Roosevelt administration.[16]   President Theodore Roosevelt accordingly pressed successfully for passage of a law giving the government
the right of appeal, and providing that such appeal would be to the
Supreme Court.   It is somewhat ironic that the Act of 1907 would not
have provided relief in the case that led to the legislation, since in
that case defendants had been put in jeopardy.   As the Act was successively amended, it defined some kinds of appeals that could be tak-
en to the Supreme Court and others that went to the courts of ap-

pediting Act, 1969, 37 Geo.Wash.L.Rev.
746; Celler, Case in Support of Application of the Expediting Act to Antitrust Suits, 1964, 14 DePaul L.Rev. 29;
Solomon, Repeal of the Expediting
Act—A Negative View, 1961, N.Y.
S.B.A. Antitrust Law Symposium 94.

10. Antitrust Procedures and Penalties
Act of 1974, Pub.L. 93–528, 88 Stat.
1706.

11. See Boskey & Gressman, note 6
above.

12. 15 U.S.C.A. § 29, 49 U.S.C.A. § 45.

13. Boskey & Gressman, note 6 above,
at 148–154.

An eminent authority has ventured the
prophecy that "it seems highly unlike-

ly" that there will be many such antitrust cases in which both the district
judge and the Supreme Court will find
that there should be immediate review
by the Supreme Court.   Boskey,
West's Federal Forms, 1976 Supp.,
§ 121 at p. 39.   That prophecy is repeated in Boskey, West's Federal
Forms, 3d ed. 1982, p. 230.   There has
been no such case as of the present
writing.

14. Act of March 2, 1907, c. 2564, 34
Stat. 1246; 18 U.S.C.A. § 3731.

15. U. S. v. Sanges, 1892, 12 S.Ct. 609,
144 U.S. 310, 36 L.Ed. 445.

16. U. S. v. Armour & Co., D.C.Ill.1906,
142 F. 808.

peals, with provision for transfer if, as not infrequently happened, the government appealed to the wrong court.

In 1928 Professors Frankfurter and Landis wrote: "The reasons which impelled the enactment of the Act of 1907 remain. They will continue to be controlling. Congress is not apt to give the power of invalidating its legislation wholly to the inferior federal courts without an appeal as of right to the Supreme Court, and Congress is still less likely to do this with regard to criminal legislation. The criminal law is increasingly resorted to, for the 'achievement of some social betterment rather than the punishment of the crimes as in cases of mala in se.' The defeat of these purposes is not likely to be entrusted to any tribunal other than the Supreme Court." [17] This view was not accepted by more recent commentators, who thought it undesirable to burden the Supreme Court with an obligatory appeal in these cases, many of them of little consequence save to the parties.[18] The narrow scope of review made such appeals quite artificial,[19] and the circumstances in which the statute allowed appeal were defined in archaic terms that made the right of appeal quite uncertain.[20] In 1970 the Supreme Court called the Criminal Appeals Act "a failure," [21] and Congress responded in less than a year with drastic revision. The language of the former statute was much simplified, the right of appeal by the government was extended to all cases in which the Constitution permits appeal, and all appeals now go to the courts of appeals rather than to the Supreme Court.[22]

A third class of cases in which there is direct review is from an order granting or denying, after notice and hearing, an interlocutory or permanent injunction in any civil action, suit or proceeding required by any Act of Congress to be heard and determined by a district court of three judges.[23] There had been such a three-judge court, with direct appeal to the Supreme Court, since 1903 in certain cases under the Expediting Act, since 1906 in cases to enjoin orders

17. Frankfurter & Landis, The Business of the Supreme Court, 1928, p. 120. Justice Frankfurter took the same view as had Professor Frankfurter. In a letter to the present author on June 17, 1959, he said: "I have of course not been unmindful that some of the cases which automatically come here under the Criminal Appeals Act of 1907 don't belong here, but that reflection has always been checked by the considerations that led to direct review of the invalidation or misconstruction of an important criminal statute."

18. Kurland, The Mersky Case and the Criminal Appeals Act: A Suggestion for Amendment of the Statute, 1961, 28 U.Chi.L.Rev. 419; Friedenthal, Government Appeals in Federal Criminal Cases, 1959, 12 Stan.L.Rev. 71.

19. See U. S. v. Borden Co., 1939, 60 S.Ct. 182, 186, 308 U.S. 188, 193, 84 L.Ed. 181. See also U. S. v. Cores, 1958, 78 S.Ct. 875, 356 U.S. 405, 2 L.Ed.2d 873; U. S. v. Harriss, 1954, 74 S.Ct. 808, 347 U.S. 612, 98 L.Ed. 989.

20. E.g., U. S. v. Sisson, 1970, 90 S.Ct. 2117, 399 U.S. 267, 26 L.Ed.2d 608; U. S. v. Mersky, 1960, 80 S.Ct. 459, 361 U.S. 431, 4 L.Ed.2d 423.

21. U. S. v. Sisson, 1970, 90 S.Ct. 2117, 2139, 399 U.S. 267, 307, 26 L.Ed.2d 608.

22. 18 U.S.C.A. § 3731, as amended by Act of Jan. 2, 1971, Pub.L. 91–644, Title III, § 14(a), 84 Stat. 1890. See 15 Wright, Miller & Cooper, Jurisdiction § 3919.

23. 28 U.S.C.A. § 1253; 17 Wright, Miller & Cooper, Jurisdiction § 4040.

of the Interstate Commerce Commission, since 1910 in cases seeking to restrain enforcement of a state statute or administrative order, and since 1937 in cases seeking to restrain enforcement of a federal statute. The circumstances in which a three-judge court was required and the bewildering rules on when the orders of such a court were appealable directly to the Supreme Court and when they had to go to a court of appeals have been considered in an earlier section.[24] As indicated there, Congress responded in 1974 and 1976 to the widespread dissatisfaction with three-judge courts by ending them for Expediting Act and ICC cases and by virtually eliminating them for constitutional cases.

The final class of cases in which direct appeal to the Supreme Court is permitted was enacted as part of the Judiciary Act of 1937. It permits appeal to the Supreme Court from an interlocutory or final judgment of any court of the United States holding an Act of Congress unconstitutional in any civil action, suit, or proceeding to which the United States or any of its agencies, or any officer or employee thereof, as such officer or employee, is a party.[25] Unlike the provision for review of three-judge courts, there is no requirement here of an injunction to restrain enforcement of the act in question. Instead it is enough that an Act of Congress has been held unconstitutional, even as a matter of defense in a proceeding to enforce the act.[26] Direct review is available even though the act is held unconstitutional only as applied to a particular person, with its constitutionality in general not questioned.[27] The statute applies only if the act is held unconstitutional. If the district court decides in favor of the act, review must be in the court of appeals as in any other case. Nor can there be direct review if the lower court has construed a statute narrowly to avoid a possible constitutional question.[28] When direct appeal lies under this statute, it brings the whole case before the Supreme Court, and permits the Court to pass on all the questions in the case.[29]

Direct appeal is not provided, though an Act of Congress is held unconstitutional, in purely private litigation. The United States, or an agency, officer, or employee thereof, must be a party to the suit.

24. See § 50 above.

25. Act of Aug. 24, 1937, c. 754, §§ 2, 5, 50 Stat. 752, 753, as amended; 28 U.S. C.A. § 1252.

Appeal lies under § 1252 even if the district court lacked jurisdiction. McLucas v. DeChamplain, 1975, 95 S.Ct. 1365, 421 U.S. 21, 43 L.Ed.2d 699; Weinberger v. Salfi, 1975, 95 S.Ct. 2457, 2466 n. 8, 422 U.S. 749, 763 n. 8, 45 L.Ed.2d 522.

The statute is permissive. The government is not required to appeal from an interlocutory order. U. S. v. Clark, 1980, 100 S.Ct. 895, 445 U.S. 23, 63 L.Ed.2d 171.

26. Fleming v. Rhodes, 1947, 67 S.Ct. 1140, 331 U.S. 100, 91 L.Ed. 1368, noted 1947, 47 Col.L.Rev. 1231.

27. U. S. v. Darusmont, 1981, 101 S.Ct. 549, 449 U.S. 292, 66 L.Ed.2d 549.

28. U. S. v. Christian Echoes Nat. Ministry, Inc., 1972, 92 S.Ct. 663, 404 U.S. 561, 30 L.Ed.2d 716.

29. McLucas v. DeChamplain, 1975, 95 S.Ct. 1365, 421 U.S. 21, 43 L.Ed.2d 699; U. S. v. Raines, 1960, 80 S.Ct. 519, 362 U.S. 17, 4 L.Ed.2d 524.

However this must be read in the light of another provision of the Judicial Code [30] that requires certification to the Attorney General when a constitutional question is raised in a case to which the United States is not a party, and permits intervention by the United States in such a case as a matter of right. If the United States chooses to intervene in such circumstances, and the Act of Congress is held unconstitutional, the direct appeal provision becomes applicable, even though the United States was not a party originally.[31] Usually it will be the United States that will take the appeal, but a federal officer may also appeal under these circumstances.[32]

This statute has not yet been repealed, but it should be. After 1937 there had been very few instances in which district courts had held Acts of Congress unconstitutional, and thus the appeal statute had been little used. In the last few years, however, appeals from district court decisions under this statute have been coming to the Court with some frequency.[33] Regardless of that, the statute ought to be repealed on the general principle that appeal by right is an anachronism and that the Supreme Court should have control over its own docket.[34]

If a final decision of a district court is one where a direct review may be had in the Supreme Court, under what survives of the statutes just described, the appeal can go only to the Supreme Court. The court of appeals lacks jurisdiction of such a case.[35]

It is conceivable—though it apparently has happened only once—that in a case where direct appeal to the Supreme Court is provided, that Court will be unable to muster six qualified judges to constitute a quorum. Though appeal is not constitutionally required, there is a strong tradition that a party should be able to obtain appellate review in at least one court. Accordingly in 1944 a statute was passed to meet this situation when the Supreme Court could not muster a quorum to hear an appeal under the Expediting Act in an important antitrust case.[36] In the 1948 revision of the Judicial Code this special statute was made applicable to all cases where there is direct appeal from a district court to the Supreme Court and a quorum is lacking.[37]

30. 28 U.S.C.A. § 2403.

31. International Ladies' Garment Workers' Union v. Donnelly Garment Co., 1938, 58 S.Ct. 875, 304 U.S. 243, 82 L.Ed. 1316.

32. Reid v. Covert, 1956, 76 S.Ct. 880, 351 U.S. 487, 100 L.Ed. 1352, on rehearing, 1957, 77 S.Ct. 1222, 354 U.S. 1, 1 L.Ed.2d 1148.

33. See 17 Wright, Miller & Cooper, Jurisdiction § 4039 n. 15.

34. See Gressman, Requiem for the Supreme Court's Obligatory Jurisdiction, 1979, 65 A.B.A.J. 1325; Report of the Study Group on the Caseload of the Supreme Court, 1972, 57 F.R.D. 573, 601–602.

35. 28 U.S.C.A. § 1291; Donovan v. Richland County Assn. for Retarded Citizens, 1982, 102 S.Ct. 713, ___ U.S. ___, 70 L.Ed.2d 570.

36. Act of June 9, 1944, c. 239, 58 Stat. 272; U. S. v. Aluminum Co. of America, 1944, 64 S.Ct. 1281, 322 U.S. 716, 88 L.Ed. 1557. A later phase of the same proceeding is reported in U. S. v. United States Dist. Court, 1948, 68 S.Ct. 1035, 334 U.S. 258, 92 L.Ed. 1351.

37. 28 U.S.C.A. § 2109.

It provides that in such cases the case may be remitted to the court of appeals for the circuit in which the case arose, to be considered either by the three senior judges of that court of appeals or by the court en banc. The decision of the court of appeals in such a case is final and conclusive.

§ 106. Review of Decisions of the Courts of Appeals [1]

The usual method for review in the Supreme Court of decisions of the courts of appeals is by the statutory writ of certiorari. The statute authorizing such review is sweeping. The Court, in its discretion, may issue the writ "upon the petition of any party to any civil or criminal case, before or after rendition of judgment or decree." [2] Review of decisions of state courts necessarily is more limited [3] for in most such cases there is no basis for federal jurisdiction. Cases in the courts of appeals, on the other hand, must involve at least a claim of federal jurisdiction to have reached those courts and thus are within the constitutional limits of the appellate jurisdiction of the Supreme Court. Thus, as the Court said of an earlier form of the present statute for review by certiorari to the courts of appeals, "the generality of this provision was not a mere matter of accident. It expressed the thought of Congress distinctly and clearly, and was intended to vest in this court a comprehensive and unlimited power." [4]

The Court may issue a writ of certiorari to a court of appeals regardless of the subject matter of the case, the citizenship of the parties, or the amount in controversy. [5] It may issue such a writ although the decision of the court of appeals is not a final judgment. The lack of finality may be a factor that will induce the Court to deny certiorari. It has said that it should not review interlocutory orders of the courts of appeals "unless it is necessary to prevent extraordinary inconvenience and embarrassment to the conduct of the cause." [6] But in the very case in which it said this it did in fact review the order below, though it was not final, and this power to review interlocutory orders of the courts of appeals has been exercised in many cases. [7] A party is not required to petition for certiorari to

[§ 106]

1. 17 Wright, Miller & Cooper, Jurisdiction §§ 4035–4038; Stern & Gressman, Supreme Court Practice, 5th ed. 1978, §§ 2.1–2.8.

2. 28 U.S.C.A. § 1254(1).

3. See § 107 below.

4. Forsyth v. City of Hammond, 1897, 17 S.Ct. 665, 668, 166 U.S. 506, 513, 41 L.Ed. 1095.

5. Whitney v. Dick, 1906, 26 S.Ct. 584, 202 U.S. 132, 50 L.Ed. 963.

6. American Constr. Co. v. Jacksonville, T. & K. W. R. Co., 1893, 13 S.Ct. 758, 763, 148 U.S. 372, 384, 37 L.Ed. 486.

See also Brotherhood of Locomotive Firemen and Enginemen v. Bangor & Aroostook R. Co., 1967, 88 S.Ct. 437, 438, 389 U.S. 327, 328, 19 L.Ed.2d 560, in which the Court, in denying certiorari, said that the fact that the court of appeals had remanded the case for further proceedings made the case "not yet ripe for review by this Court."

7. 17 Wright, Miller & Cooper, Jurisdiction § 4036, pp. 21–25. For an elaborate justification of the power of the Court to do so, see Forsyth v. Hammond, 1897, 17 S.Ct. 665, 166 U.S. 506, 41 L.Ed. 1095.

review an interlocutory order, and the fact that he did not petition, or that his petition was denied, does not bar the Court from granting certiorari after final judgment in the case and then considering the supposedly erroneous interlocutory order.[8]

The Court has power under the statute to grant certiorari before judgment in the court of appeals, so long as the case has been docketed in a court of appeals,[9] but "this is a power not ordinarily to be exercised." [10] The Court has granted such writs where the case involved an important constitutional question, or some other matter of great national significance, on which a speedy decision from the Supreme Court was important.[11] Even in these situations, there have been protests from justices who felt that a considered opinion from the court of appeals would be of sufficient assistance to the Court to justify such delay as it would cause.[12] In other instances, it has been demonstrated that it need not delay a case unduly to await decision in the court of appeals before granting certiorari.[13] The power to grant certiorari before judgment is also used to bring up a case that involves an issue also presented by a case then pending before the Court.[14] There is some question, never yet resolved, whether the Court has power to grant certiorari before judgment below where the court of appeals is reviewing an administrative order. The argument is that, unless there has been some order by a court that the Supreme

8. E.g., Washington v. Washington State Commercial Passenger Fishing Vessel Assn., 1979, 99 S.Ct. 3055, 3067 n. 19, 443 U.S. 658, 672 n. 19, 61 L.Ed. 2d 823; Hughes Tool Co. v. Trans World Airlines, Inc., 1973, 93 S.Ct. 647, 650 n. 1, 409 U.S. 363, 365 n. 1, 34 L.Ed.2d 577; City of Indianapolis v. Chase Nat. Bank, 1941, 62 S.Ct. 15, 314 U.S. 63, 86 L.Ed. 47; Toledo Scale Co. v. Computing Scale Co., 1923, 43 S.Ct. 458, 261 U.S. 399, 67 L.Ed. 719; Hamilton-Brown Shoe Co. v. Wolf Brothers & Co., 1916, 36 S.Ct. 269, 240 U.S. 251, 50 L.Ed. 629; Panama R. Co. v. Napier Shipping Co., 1897, 17 S.Ct. 572, 574, 166 U.S. 280, 284, 41 L.Ed. 1004.

9. Gay v. Ruff, 1934, 54 S.Ct. 608, 292 U.S. 25, 78 L.Ed. 1099.

10. The Three Friends, 1897, 17 S.Ct. 495, 497, 166 U.S. 1, 49, 41 L.Ed. 897.

11. E.g., Dames & Moore v. Regan, 1981, 101 S.Ct. 2972, 453 U.S. 654, 69 L.Ed.2d 918; U. S. v. Nixon, 1974, 94 S.Ct. 3090, 418 U.S. 683, 41 L.Ed.2d 1039; Wilson v. Girard, 1957, 77 S.Ct. 1409, 354 U.S. 524, 1 L.Ed.2d 1544; Youngstown Sheet & Tube Co. v. Sawyer, 1952, 72 S.Ct. 863, 865, 343 U.S. 579, 584, 96 L.Ed. 1153; U. S. v. United Mine Workers, 1947, 67 S.Ct. 677, 684, 330 U.S. 258, 269, 91 L.Ed. 884; Ex parte Quirin, 1942, 63 S.Ct. 1, 6–7, 317

U.S. 1, 19–20, 87 L.Ed. 3; Carter v. Carter Coal Co., 1936, 56 S.Ct. 855, 298 U.S. 238, 80 L.Ed. 1160.

12. Youngstown Sheet & Tube Co. v. Sawyer, 1952, 72 S.Ct. 775, 343 U.S. 937, 96 L.Ed. 1344 (separate opinion of Justices Burton and Frankfurter).

13. In an important case involving a nationwide steel strike, the judgment of the district court was entered October 21st. The appeal was argued before the Third Circuit on October 22nd and decided by that court on October 27th. The case was argued before the Supreme Court on November 3d and decided November 7th. United Steelworkers of America v. U. S., 1959, 80 S.Ct. 1, 361 U.S. 39, 4 L.Ed.2d 12. See also Aaron v. Cooper, 1958, 78 S.Ct. 1189, 357 U.S. 566, 2 L.Ed.2d 1544.

A less happy example of judicial speed, at least according to the dissenters, is New York Times Co. v. U. S., 1971, 91 S.Ct. 2140, 403 U.S. 713, 29 L.Ed.2d 822.

14. E.g., Taylor v. McElroy, 1959, 79 S.Ct. 1428, 1429, 360 U.S. 709, 710, 3 L.Ed.2d 1528; Brown v. Board of Educ., 1952, 73 S.Ct. 1, 2, 344 U.S. 1, 3, 97 L.Ed. 3; cf. Turner v. City of Memphis, 1962, 82 S.Ct. 805, 807, 369 U.S. 350, 353–354, 7 L.Ed.2d 762.

Court can affirm, reverse, or modify,[15] review of the administrative decision in the first instance by the Supreme Court would be an unconstitutional exercise of original jurisdiction.[16]

The Court may grant certiorari on petition of "any party." In some cases where certiorari has been granted prior to judgment in the court of appeals it has been the United States, which was successful in the district court, that has sought speedy review by petitioning for certiorari.[17] There seems to be no case in which the Court has granted certiorari at the instance of a party who has been successful in the court of appeals.[18]

There are a few instances in which review of decisions of a court of appeals is by appeal rather than by certiorari. This is true where the court has held an Act of Congress unconstitutional in a case to which the United States is a party, since the statute authorizing appeal to the Supreme Court in such cases applies to decisions in any court of the United States.[19] There is specific provision for appeal to the Supreme Court when a court of appeals has held a state statute to be repugnant to the Constitution, laws, or treaties of the United States. Taking of such an appeal precludes review by writ of certiorari, and the review on appeal is restricted to the federal questions presented.[20] For purposes of this provision, as is true also of the statute dealing with review of state court decisions,[21] a "state statute" includes a municipal ordinance,[22] the order of a state administrative agency if it is legislative in nature,[23] and any other enactment to which the state gives the force of law.

The statute says, as has been noted, that an appeal under it precludes the appellant from seeking review of the same decision by certiorari. However, the Court sensibly held that this applies only where appeal in fact lies, and that where an appeal was erroneously

---

15. There was such an order in Ickes v. Associated Indus., 1943, 64 S.Ct. 74, 320 U.S. 707, 88 L.Ed. 414.

16. Cf. U. S. v. Rice, 1946, 66 S.Ct. 835, 837, 327 U.S. 742, 747, 90 L.Ed. 982.

This question was presented, but not decided, in Chandler v. Judicial Council of the Tenth Circuit, 1970, 90 S.Ct. 1648, 398 U.S. 74, 26 L.Ed.2d 100.

17. U. S. v. Nixon, 1974, 94 S.Ct. 3090, 418 U.S. 683, 41 L.Ed.2d 1039; Youngstown Sheet & Tube Co. v. Sawyer, 1952, 72 S.Ct. 863, 343 U.S. 579, 96 L.Ed. 1153; U. S. v. United Mine Workers, 1947, 67 S.Ct. 677, 330 U.S. 258, 91 L.Ed. 884; U. S. v. Bankers' Trust Co., 1935, 55 S.Ct. 407, 410, 294 U.S. 240, 294, 79 L.Ed. 885.

18. Cf. Public Serv. Comm. of Missouri v. Brashear Freight Lines, Inc., 1939,

59 S.Ct. 480, 482, 306 U.S. 204, 206, 83 L.Ed. 806.

19. 28 U.S.C.A. § 1252, discussed § 105 above. See Parker v. Levy, 1974, 94 S.Ct. 2547, 417 U.S. 733, 41 L.Ed.2d 439.

20. 28 U.S.C.A. § 1254(2). The limitation on the scope of review and the preclusion of review by certiorari seem illadvised. See 17 Wright, Miller & Cooper, Jurisdiction § 4037, pp. 40–45.

21. See § 107 below.

22. City of New Orleans v. Dukes, 1976, 96 S.Ct. 2513, 2516, 427 U.S. 297, 301, 49 L.Ed.2d 511.

23. Cf. Lake Erie & W. R. Co. v. State Public Utilities Comm., 1919, 39 S.Ct. 345, 346, 249 U.S. 422, 424, 63 L.Ed. 684.

taken, certiorari could be granted on a timely petition.[24] More recently Congress has provided that if an appeal is improvidently taken in a case where the proper method of review is by certiorari, the appeal papers shall be acted upon as a petition for a writ of certiorari.[25]

The Supreme Court has twice held that an appeal under this provision may only be taken from a final judgment.[26] Many recent cases have expressly suggested the need to reconsider the question, but have avoided reconsideration either by finding a final judgment or by dismissing the appeal and granting certiorari.[27] If the Court should ever have to resolve the matter, arguments can be made both ways on whether finality should be a requirement.[28]

It is not clear whether the provision that review by appeal shall be restricted to the federal questions involved permits review of all federal questions in the case, or only those concerned with the invalidity of the statute in question.[29] In any event it clearly precludes review on that appeal of state law questions that may be in the case.[30] For this reason counsel may be well advised to petition for certiorari, even where an appeal could be taken, and to assign as one of the reasons why certiorari should be granted that they were forced to forego their privilege of appeal in order to bring all the questions before the Court.[31]

A third method of taking cases from a court of appeals to the Supreme Court is by certificate. The court of appeals may certify at any time any question of law in any civil or criminal case as to which instructions are desired.[32] The power is that of the court of appeals, and it has been said to be improper for the parties to move for certification.[33] Certification is limited to questions of law, and the ques-

24. Bradford Elec. Light Co. v. Clapper, 1931, 52 S.Ct. 118, 284 U.S. 221, 76 L.Ed 254.

25. 28 U.S.C.A. § 2103, as amended Act of Sept. 19, 1962, Pub.L. 87–669, § 1, 76 Stat. 556. E.g., City of El Paso v. Simmons, 1965, 85 S.Ct. 577, 580–581, 379 U.S. 497, 501–503, 13 L.Ed.2d 446.

26. Slaker v. O'Connor, 1929, 49 S.Ct. 158, 278 U.S. 188, 73 L.Ed. 258; South Carolina Elec. & Gas Co. v. Flemming, 1956, 76 S.Ct. 692, 351 U.S. 901, 100 L.Ed. 1439.

27. City of Chicago v. Atchison, T. & S. F. Ry., 1958, 78 S.Ct. 1063, 357 U.S. 77, 2 L.Ed.2d 1174; City of El Paso v. Simmons, 1965, 85 S.Ct. 577, 580, 379 U.S. 497, 502, 13 L.Ed.2d 446; Doran v. Salem Inn, Inc., 1975, 95 S.Ct. 2561, 2565–2566, 422 U.S. 922, 927, 45 L.Ed. 2d 562; City of New Orleans v. Dukes, 1976, 96 S.Ct. 2513, 2516, 427 U.S. 297, 301–302, 49 L.Ed.2d 511.

28. See 17 Wright, Miller & Cooper, Jurisdiction § 4037, pp. 36–39, concluding

that if the question should be forced to decision, it might be better to retain the finality requirement.

29. Such scant evidence as exists suggests that the Court is willing to review any federal question presented by the case. 17 Wright, Miller & Cooper, Jurisdiction § 4037, pp. 40–41.

30. City of Mesquite v. Aladdin's Castle, Inc., 1982, 102 S.Ct. 1070, ___ U.S. ___, 71 L.Ed.2d 152.

31. This was done in Williams v. Mayor and City of Baltimore, 1933, 53 S.Ct. 431, 289 U.S. 36, 77 L.Ed. 1015, and in Village of Schaumburg v. Citizens for a Better Environment, 1980, 100 S.Ct. 826, 444 U.S. 620, 63 L.Ed.2d 73.

32. 28 U.S.C.A. § 1254(3).

33. Louisville, N. A. & C. Ry. Co. v. Pope, C.C.A.7th, 1896, 74 F. 1; Cella v. Brown, C.C.A.8th, 1906, 144 F. 742; Rutherford v. American Medical Assn., C.A.7th, 1967, 379 F.2d 641.

tions must be distinct and definite.[34] The Court will dismiss a certificate in which the questions are so broad that in effect they bring up the whole case,[35] although when a case has been certified the Court may itself require that the entire record be sent up for decision of the entire matter in controversy.[36] The statute purports to make it obligatory for the Supreme Court to consider questions certified to it, but there are so many grounds on which the Court may find the certificate improper that its jurisdiction over certificates is in fact discretionary.[37]

Certification has a long history in federal practice. The old circuit courts could certify a case when the two judges before whom it was heard were divided in opinion, and frequently the judges would disagree deliberately in order to bring a question to the Supreme Court. This practice is no longer considered proper. The courts of appeals recognize that certificates should be granted only when they are in fact in doubt on a question.[38] In recent years the practice has become even more restrictive. For many years the Second Circuit has refused to certify questions except in cases where the point was involved in another appeal, already pending in the Supreme Court.[39] The Supreme Court seems to have endorsed this policy, saying that it is "the task of a Court of Appeals to decide all properly presented cases coming before it, except in the rare instances, as for example the pendency of another case before this Court raising the same issue, when certification may be advisable in the proper administration and expedition of judicial business." [40]

Although writers have detected value in the certification process, and urged its more frequent use,[41] there are two very strong arguments against certification. Certificates bring to the Court abstract questions of law, divorced from a complete factual setting in which they may be more carefully explored. Further, it should not be for the courts of appeals to decide what matters are of enough importance to require decision by the Supreme Court. The control of that

34. U. S. v. Mayer, 1914, 35 S.Ct. 16, 235 U.S. 55, 59 L.Ed. 129; Warner v. City of New Orleans, 1897, 17 S.Ct. 892, 167 U.S. 467, 42 L.Ed. 239; U. S. v. Union Pac. Ry. Co., 1897, 18 S.Ct. 167, 168 U.S. 505, 42 L.Ed. 559.

35. News Syndicate Co. v. New York Cent. R. Co., 1927, 48 S.Ct. 39, 275 U.S. 179, 72 L.Ed. 225; Chicago B. & Q. Ry. Co. v. Williams, 1907, 27 S.Ct. 559, 205 U.S. 444, 51 L.Ed. 875.

36. 28 U.S.C.A. § 1254(3); Loewe v. Lawlor, 1908, 28 S.Ct. 301, 208 U.S. 274, 52 L.Ed. 488.

37. E.g., National Labor Relations Bd. v. White Swan Co., 1941, 61 S.Ct. 751, 313 U.S. 23, 85 L.Ed. 1165; Busby v. Electric Utilities Employees Union, 1944, 65 S.Ct. 142, 323 U.S. 72, 89 L.Ed. 78. See also Rule 25.2, 1980 Sup.Ct.Rules.

38. Glynn v. Krippner, C.C.A.8th, 1932, 60 F.2d 406; Williams v. Order of Commercial Travelers of America, C.C.A. 6th, 1930, 41 F.2d 745, certiorari denied 51 S.Ct. 80, 282 U.S. 876, 75 L.Ed. 774.

39. Taylor v. Atlantic Maritime Co., C.A.2d 1950, 181 F.2d 84, 85.

40. Bernard, Certified Questions in the Supreme Court: In Defense of an Option, 1978, 83 Dick.L.Rev. 31; Moore & Vestal, Present and Potential Role of Certification in Federal Appellate Procedure, 1949, 35 Va.L.Rev. 1; Comment, 1958, 43 Iowa L.Rev. 432.

41. Wisniewski v. U. S., 1957, 77 S.Ct. 633, 634, 353 U.S. 901, 902, 1 L.Ed.2d 658, noted 1958, 43 Iowa L.Rev. 432.

Court's docket should rest exclusively in its own hands.[42] The power of the Court to grant certiorari before judgment in the court of appeals permits of expedition where this is required. For these reasons, the power to certify cases to the Supreme Court seems an anachronism that the courts of appeals should not use, and that Congress should repeal.[43]

§ 107. Review of State Court Decisions [1]

The Constitution does not, in terms, authorize the Supreme Court to review decisions of state courts. It does, however, extend the judicial power of the United States to defined classes of cases, some of which are as likely to arise in the courts of a state as in a federal court, and it gives to the Supreme Court appellate jurisdiction over all such cases, other than those within the original jurisdiction of the Court, with such exceptions and under such regulations as the Congress shall make.[2] It is unusual for the court of one sovereign to have appellate jurisdiction over the courts of other sovereigns, but federalism itself is—or was when the Constitution was adopted—an unusual system, and the Supremacy Clause is a sufficient basis on which to rest the appellate jurisdiction over state court decisions. Thus the First Congress, in the famous section 25 of the Judiciary Act of 1789, authorized such review.[3] That it did so can hardly have been surprising at the time. At the Constitutional Convention, in the ratifying debates, and again in the debates over the Judiciary Act in the First Congress, the issue was not whether the Supreme Court

---

42. See Taylor v. Atlantic Maritime Co., C.A.2d 1950, 181 F.2d 84, 85.

43. See 17 Wright, Miller & Cooper, Jurisdiction § 4038.

The only three instances in modern times in which the Supreme Court has accepted a certificate are highly exceptional cases that prove the rule. In U. S. v. Barnett, C.A.5th, 1963, 316 F.2d 236, the Fifth Circuit was sitting as a court of original jurisdiction, rather than as an appellate court, the members of that court were equally divided in opinion, and the question was one that had to be resolved before the proceedings could continue. The question was answered in U. S. v. Barnett, 1964, 84 S.Ct. 984, 376 U.S. 681, 12 L.Ed.2d 23.

In Moody v. Albemarle Paper Co., 1974, 94 S.Ct. 2513, 417 U.S. 622, 41 L.Ed.2d 358, the certified question was whether 28 U.S.C.A. § 46(c) permits a senior circuit judge who has participated in the decision of a panel to vote on whether the case should be heard by the court en banc. Whether a rehearing was granted or denied turned on whether

votes of senior judges are to be counted and here, as in Barnett, the question was one that had to be resolved before the proceedings could continue.

In Iran National Airlines Corp. v. Marschalk Co., Inc., 1981, 101 S.Ct. 3154, 453 U.S. 919, 69 L.Ed.2d 1002, the questions decided on certificate involved issues that had been decided the same day on a petition for certiorari before judgment in the court of appeals in another case. Even so three justices dissented, urging that the certificate should have been dismissed.

[§ 107]

1. 16 Wright, Miller & Cooper, Jurisdiction §§ 4006–4033; Stern & Gressman, Supreme Court Practice, 5th ed. 1978, c. 3.

2. See Berger, Congress v. Supreme Court, 1969, pp. 225–296; Merry, Scope of the Supreme Court's Appellate Jurisdiction: Historical Basis, 1962, 47 Minn.L.Rev. 53.

3. Act of Sept. 24, 1789, § 25, 1 Stat. 73, 85.

should be allowed to review state court decisions, but whether there need be any inferior federal courts. Those who were opposed to a strong federal government saw no need for such courts, and argued that the judicial power of the United States could be exercised sufficiently by the Supreme Court, which would review decisions of the state courts raising questions within the federal judicial competence.[4] In the earliest years of our history this jurisdiction of the Supreme Court was accepted without question.[5] Controversy first arose when the Virginia court refused to obey a mandate of the Supreme Court on the ground that the Supreme Court had no jurisdiction over it. Justice Story's opinion in 1816 in Martin v. Hunter's Lessee,[6] if no longer satisfactory in all its reasoning, was a full and forceful defense of the jurisdiction. It was not the final answer. Criticism of this appellate jurisdiction continued over the years [7]—indeed even today it is not entirely stilled—and famous opinions by Chief Justices Marshall and Taney [8] were required to restate the principles of Martin v. Hunter's Lessee.

From 1789 to 1914 the jurisdiction over state courts was limited to cases in which the state court had held some federal act invalid, or had upheld the validity of a state act against a claim based on the federal Constitution or laws. The Supreme Court could not review a state court decision that upheld the federal claim and found a state act invalid. Indeed this was true even after an 1867 statute had in important ways extended the jurisdiction.[9] The reason for such a distinction was clear enough. When the state court had yielded to the authority of the federal government, and had held its own statute invalid, appeal to the Supreme Court was thought unnecessary to protect the federal government in the exercise of its rightful powers.[10] Review was not broadened in this respect until 1914, when the Supreme Court was for the first time permitted to hear cases in which the state court has sustained the federal claim.[11] The impetus for the 1914 statute was an unpopular New York decision a few years before holding a state workmen's compensation statute invalid as violating

4. See § 1 above.

5. Between 1790 and 1815, 17 cases from state courts had been before the Supreme Court. Frank, Historical Bases of the Federal Judicial System, 1948, 13 L. & Contemp.Prob. 3, 16.

6. 1816, 1 Wheat. 304, 4 L.Ed. 97. See 2 Crosskey, Politics and the Constitution in the History of the United States, 1953, 785–817.

7. See Warren, Legislative and Judicial Attacks on the Supreme Court of the United States—a History of the Twenty-Fifth Section of the Judiciary Act 1913, 47 Am.L.Rev. 1, 161.

8. Cohens v. Virginia, 1821, 6 Wheat. 264, 5 L.Ed. 257; Ableman v. Booth,

1859, 21 How. 506, 16 L.Ed. 169. The Ableman case, written on the eve of the Civil War and involving the constitutionality of the Fugitive Slave Act, is particularly dramatic. For a full account, see Swisher, History of the Supreme Court of the United States: The Taney Period, 1836–1864, 1974, pp. 653–675.

9. Act of Feb. 5, 1867, § 2, 14 Stat. 385, 386.

10. Commonwealth Bank of Kentucky v. Griffith, 1840, 14 Pet. 56, 58, 10 L.Ed. 352.

11. Act of Dec. 23, 1914, c. 2, 38 Stat. 790.

both the state and federal constitutions.[12] Rather ironically, the 1914 amendment would have furnished no relief in the case that led to its enactment, since, on principles developed later in this section, the decision that it violated the New York constitution would have precluded review of the determination that it also violated the United States Constitution.[13]

The 1914 amendment, with only a little further refinement,[14] defined the scope of Supreme Court review of state court decisions that still exists today. Under the present statute review is possible of the final judgment of the highest court of a state in which a decision could be had in any case where the validity of a treaty or statute of the United States is drawn in question or where the validity of a state statute is drawn in question on the ground of its being repugnant to the Constitution, treaties, or laws of the United States, or where any title, right, privilege, or immunity is specially set up or claimed under the Constitution, treaties, or statutes of, or commission held or authority exercised under, the United States.[15] The jurisdiction does not depend on the amount in controversy [16] or the citizenship of the parties.[17] It rests entirely on the existence of what is always referred to as a "federal question" in the case. The distinction that persisted from 1789 to 1914 between cases where the state court had rejected the federal claim and cases in which it had honored it still remains, as will be seen, in distinguishing those cases where an appeal may be taken from those that are reviewable only on petition for certiorari.

The state court decision to be reviewable must be that of the highest court of the state in which a decision could be had. This by no means restricts review to decisions of the highest state court. Even a trial court decision is reviewable in the United States Supreme Court if there is no higher state court to which the party can resort. In a well-known case certiorari was granted to review a decision of the Police Court of Louisville, Kentucky, where the fines imposed were so small that no review was available in any Kentucky court.[18] If discretionary review is available in some higher state court, such review must be sought, no matter how unlikely it may seem that it

12. Ives v. South Buffalo Ry., 1911, 94 N.E. 431, 201 N.Y. 271.

13. This is not unusual with jurisdictional reforms. Thus the Criminal Appeals Act of 1907 would not—and could not—have permitted appeal from the directed verdict in the antitrust case that led to its enactment. See § 105 above.

14. Act of Feb. 13, 1925, c. 229, § 1, 43 Stat. 937.

15. 28 U.S.C.A. § 1257(3).

16. Buel v. Van Ness, 1823, 8 Wheat. 312, 5 L.Ed. 624.

17. French v. Hopkins, 1888, 8 S.Ct. 589, 124 U.S. 524, 31 L.Ed. 536.

18. Thompson v. City of Louisville, 1960, 80 S.Ct. 624, 362 U.S. 199, 4 L.Ed.2d 654. In Cohens v. Virginia, 1821, 6 Wheat. 264, 5 L.Ed. 257, the judgment reviewed was that of the Quarterly Session Court for the Borough of Norfolk, Virginia. Decision of a magistrate was reviewed in Stanford v. Texas, 1965, 85 S.Ct. 506, 379 U.S. 476, 13 L.Ed.2d 431. In Brown v. Texas, 1979, 99 S.Ct. 2637, 443 U.S. 47, 61 L.Ed.2d 357, the judgment was from the El Paso County Court.

will be granted.[19] The attempt to secure further review will extend the time in which to resort to the Supreme Court, but if discretionary further review is refused, the judgment is that of the court below that rendered it, and it is this that must be taken to the Supreme Court.[20] However if the higher state court takes action that amounts to an affirmance of what has been done below, it is the judgment of the higher court that must be taken to the Supreme Court.[21]

Review can only be had of "final judgments or decrees." Obviously there can be no final judgment unless there has been a judgment. Here however the Court has been liberal, and has even been willing to regard a letter from the clerk of the state court to the appellant, refusing to docket his appeal, as being a judgment of the state court.[22] In some states the highest court sits in divisions. If, after decision by a division, the party may obtain review by the whole court as a matter of right, the decision of the division is not a final judgment of the court and is not reviewable.[23] But if reconsideration by the whole court is discretionary, the decision of the division will be regarded as a final judgment, and reviewable, even though the party did not seek reconsideration by the whole court.[24] On the same principle, a party need not petition for rehearing by a court in order to have a final judgment of that court,[25] though if he does so unsuccessfully the pendency of his petition extends the time in which to seek review in the Supreme Court of the original decision.[26]

The limitation of review to "final" judgments is consistent with the general aversion of the federal courts to piecemeal review.[27] Thus the same principles that determine what is a final judgment of a district court, reviewable in a court of appeals [28] or, in some in-

19. Costarelli v. Massachusetts, 1975, 95 S.Ct. 1534, 421 U.S. 193, 44 L.Ed.2d 76; Banks v. California, 1969, 89 S.Ct. 1901, 395 U.S. 708, 23 L.Ed.2d 653; Gotthilf v. Sills, 1963, 84 S.Ct. 187, 375 U.S. 79, 11 L.Ed.2d 159; Stratton v. Stratton, 1915, 36 S.Ct. 26, 239 U.S. 55, 60 L.Ed. 142.

20. Michigan-Wisconsin Pipe Line Co. v. Calvert, 1954, 74 S.Ct. 396, 347 U.S. 157, 98 L.Ed. 583; Minneapolis, St. P. & S. S. M. Ry. Co. v. Rock, 1929, 49 S.Ct. 363, 279 U.S. 410, 73 L.Ed. 766; Virginian Ry. Co. v. Mullens, 1926, 46 S.Ct. 526, 271 U.S. 220, 70 L.Ed. 915.

21. Tumey v. Ohio, 1926, 47 S.Ct. 437, 273 U.S. 510, 71 L.Ed. 749.

22. Burns v. Ohio, 1959, 79 S.Ct. 1164, 360 U.S. 252, 3 L.Ed.2d 1209. Orders characterized as "informal" were held reviewable in Smith v. Hooey, 1969, 89 S.Ct. 575, 576, 393 U.S. 374, 375, 21 L.Ed.2d 607, and in In re Summers, 1945, 65 S.Ct. 1307, 1309, 325 U.S. 561, 564, 89 L.Ed. 1795.

23. Gorman v. Washington Univ., 1942, 62 S.Ct. 962, 316 U.S. 98, 86 L.Ed. 1300.

24. Local 174, Teamsters, Chauffeurs, Warehousemen and Helpers of America v. Lucas Flour Co., 1962, 82 S.Ct. 571, 369 U.S. 95, 7 L.Ed.2d 593.

25. Southern Ry. Co. v. Clift, 1922, 43 S.Ct. 126, 260 U.S. 316, 67 L.Ed. 283; cf. Market St. Ry. Co. v. Railroad Comm. of California, 1945, 65 S.Ct. 770, 324 U.S. 548, 89 L.Ed. 1171.

26. Chicago G. W. R. Co. v. Basham, 1919, 39 S.Ct. 213, 249 U.S. 164, 63 L.Ed. 534.

But a motion to clarify the mandate by certifying that a federal question was decided does not extend the time. Department of Banking, State of Nebraska v. Pink, 1942, 63 S.Ct. 233, 317 U.S. 264, 87 L.Ed. 254.

27. See Crick, The Final Judgment as a Basis for Appeal, 1932, 41 Yale L.J. 539.

28. See § 101 above.

stances, directly in the Supreme Court, are generally applied in determining what is a final judgment of a state court.[29] Indeed quite commonly the precedents are cited interchangeably.[30]

It might be supposed that the requirement of finality would be given stricter application in reviewing state court decisions, since they involve potential conflict between the courts of two different governments and thus, as the Court has several times said, the requirement "is not one of those technicalities to be easily scorned. It is an important factor in the smooth working of our federal system."[31] There is no evidence, however, of any significant difference of this sort.

The Court decides for itself whether the decision of the state court is a final judgment. State law and state practice are of importance in determining what has been done and what may still be done within the state judicial system, but the Court will then make its own determination of whether under such circumstances the judgment has that finality requisite for Supreme Court review.[32] Although the early practice was contrary, and did not permit the Court even to consider the opinion of the state court in determining whether the state decision was final,[33] it is now quite settled that the Court may look not only to the opinion but also to any other relevant matter, in or out of the record, in determining finality.[34] The test, as in other instances where finality must be determined, is increasingly a pragmatic one. A judgment is final for purposes of review if it leaves only ministerial acts, such as entry of judgment accordingly in the lower court, to be done.[35] The traditional rule has been that a judgment is not final for

---

29. See generally 16 Wright, Miller & Cooper, Jurisdiction §§ 4008–4010; Note, The Finality Rule for Supreme Court Review of State Court Orders, 1978, 91 Harv.L.Rev. 1004.

30. See § 101 n. 47 above.

31. Radio Station WOW v. Johnson, 1945, 65 S.Ct. 1475, 1478, 326 U.S. 120, 124, 89 L.Ed. 2092; Montgomery Bldg. & Constr. Trades Council v. Ledbetter Erection Co., Inc., 1952, 73 S.Ct. 196, 197, 344 U.S. 178, 180, 97 L.Ed. 204. See also Cox Broadcasting Corp. v. Cohn, 1975, 95 S.Ct. 1029, 1050–1951, 420 U.S. 469, 502, 503, 43 L.Ed.2d 328 (Rehnquist, J., dissenting).

But see Dyk, Supreme Court Review of Interlocutory State-Court Decisions: "The Twilight Zone of Finality," 1967, 19 Stan.L.Rev. 907, 939–946, arguing that the Court should have discretion to review interlocutory state judgments.

32. Department of Banking, State of Nebraska v. Pink, 1942, 63 S.Ct. 233, 317 U.S. 264, 87 L.Ed. 254; Cole v. Violette, 1943, 63 S.Ct. 1204, 319 U.S. 581,

87 L.Ed. 1599; Richfield Oil Corp. v. State Bd. of Equalization, 1946, 67 S.Ct. 156, 329 U.S. 69, 91 L.Ed. 80.

33. E.g., Haseltine v. Central Nat. Bank, 1901, 22 S.Ct. 49, 183 U.S. 130, 46 L.Ed. 117. This rule was abandoned in Clark v. Williard, 1934, 54 S.Ct. 615, 292 U.S. 112, 78 L.Ed. 1160.

34. Gospel Army v. City of Los Angeles, 1947, 67 S.Ct. 1428, 1430, 331 U.S. 543, 547, 91 L.Ed. 1662; Local No. 438 Constr. & General Laborers' Union, AFL–CIO v. Curry, 1963, 83 S.Ct. 531, 537, 371 U.S. 542, 551, 9 L.Ed.2d 514.

35. Board of Commrs. of Tippecanoe County v. Lucas, 1876, 93 U.S. 108, 23 L.Ed. 822; Department of Banking, State of Nebraska v. Pink, 1942, 63 S.Ct. 233, 317 U.S. 264, 87 L.Ed. 254; Cole v. Violette, 1943, 63 S.Ct. 1204, 319 U.S. 581, 87 L.Ed. 1599.

A judgment that terminates original proceedings in a state appellate court, in which the only issue decided concerns the jurisdiction of a lower state court, is final even if further proceedings are to be had in the lower court. Fisher v.

purposes of review, though it settles the important issue in the case, if it leaves open something not merely ministerial that might itself raise a federal question.[36]

In recent years the Court has departed strikingly from this traditional view. As it said in Cox Broadcasting Corp. v. Cohn,[37] "as the cases have unfolded, the Court has recurringly encountered situations in which the highest court of a State has finally determined the federal issue present in a particular case, but in which there are further proceedings in the lower state courts to come. There are now at least four categories of such cases in which the Court has treated the decision on the federal issue as a final judgment for the purposes of 28 U.S.C. § 1257 and has taken jurisdiction without awaiting the completion of the additional proceedings anticipated in the lower state courts."

The first of these categories, as defined by the Court in Cox, includes those cases in which there are further proceedings yet to occur in the state courts but for one reason or another the federal issue is conclusive or the outcome of further proceedings preordained.[38] The second category is the cases in which the federal issue, finally decided by the highest court in the state, will survive and require decision regardless of the outcome of future state proceedings.[39] The third category is those situations in which the federal claim has been finally decided, with further proceedings on the merits in the state courts

District Court of Sixteenth Judicial Dist., 1976, 96 S.Ct. 943, 424 U.S. 382, 47 L.Ed.2d 106. See 16 Wright, Miller & Cooper, Jurisdiction § 4009, pp. 578–581.

36. Republic Natural Gas Co. v. Oklahoma, 1948, 68 S.Ct. 972, 334 U.S. 62, 92 L.Ed. 1212; Washington ex rel. Grays Harbor Logging Co. v. Coats-Fordney Logging Co., 1917, 37 S.Ct. 295, 243 U.S. 251, 61 L.Ed. 702; Houston v. Moore, 1818, 3 Wheat. 433, 4 L.Ed. 428.

For recent applications of this rule, see, e.g., O'Dell v. Espinoza, 1982, 102 S.Ct. 1865, ___ U.S. ___, 72 L.Ed.2d 237; San Diego Gas & Elec. Co. v. City of San Diego, 1981, 101 S.Ct. 1287, 450 U.S. 621, 67 L.Ed.2d 551.

37. 1975, 95 S.Ct. 1029, 1037, 420 U.S. 469, 502–503, 43 L.Ed.2d 328, noted 1975 Ariz.St.L.J. 627.

38. 95 S.Ct. at 1038, 420 U.S. at 479. As examples the Court cited Organization for a Better Austin v. Keefe, 1971, 91 S.Ct. 1575, 1577 n. 1, 402 U.S. 415, 418 n. 1, 29 L.Ed.2d 1; Mills v. Alabama, 1966, 86 S.Ct. 1434, 384 U.S. 214, 16 L.Ed.2d 484; Local No. 438 v. Curry, 1963, 83 S.Ct. 531, 536–537, 371 U.S. 542, 550–551, 9 L.Ed.2d 514; Pope v. Atlantic C. L. R. Co., 1953, 73 S.Ct.

749, 750, 345 U.S. 379, 382, 97 L.Ed. 1094; Richfield Oil Corp. v. State Bd. of Equalization, 1946, 67 S.Ct. 156, 158–159, 329 U.S. 69, 73–74, 91 L.Ed. 80.

See also City of Philadelphia v. New Jersey, 1978, 98 S.Ct. 2531, 2533 n. 3, 437 U.S. 617, 620 n. 3, 57 L.Ed.2d 475.

But in Minnick v. California Dept. of Corrections, 1981, 101 S.Ct. 2211, 452 U.S. 105, 68 L.Ed.2d 706, the state judgment was held not final despite the argument of plaintiffs that all of the evidence they could produce was already in the record and the outcome of any further proceedings was preordained.

39. 95 S.Ct. at 1038–1039, 420 U.S. at 480–481. As examples the Court cited Brady v. Maryland, 1963, 83 S.Ct. 1194, 1195 n. 1, 373 U.S. 83, 85 n. 1, 10 L.Ed. 2d 215; Radio Station WOW, Inc. v. Johnson, 1945, 65 S.Ct. 1475, 1479–1480, 326 U.S. 120, 126–127, 89 L.Ed. 2092; Carondelet Canal & Navigation Co. v. Louisiana, 1914, 34 S.Ct. 627, 233 U.S. 362, 58 L.Ed. 1001; Forgay v. Conrad, 1848, 6 How. 201, 47 U.S. 201, 12 L.Ed. 404.

See also New York v. Cathedral Academy, 1977, 98 S.Ct. 340, 343 n. 4, 434 U.S. 125, 128 n. 4, 54 L.Ed.2d 346.

to come, but in which later review of the federal issue cannot be had, whatever the ultimate outcome of the case.[40]

The fourth of the Cox categories was described by the Court as "those situations where the federal issue has been finally decided in the state courts with further proceedings pending in which the party seeking review here might prevail on the merits on nonfederal grounds, thus rendering unnecessary review of the federal issue by this Court, and where reversal of the state court on the federal issue would be preclusive of any further litigation on the relevant cause of action rather than merely controlling the nature and character of, or determining the admissibility of evidence in, the state proceedings still to come. In these circumstances, if a refusal immediately to review the state court decision might seriously erode federal policy, the Court has entertained and decided the federal issue, which itself has been finally determined by the state courts for purposes of the state litigation." [41]

The Cox case itself was held reviewable as falling in the fourth category. The state court had rejected a federal constitutional challenge to a state law authorizing damage suits against the press for publishing the names of rape victims. The state court had sent the case back for trial. The defendants might win at trial on nonfederal grounds, but if the statute was unconstitutional there should be no trial at all. Even if defendants won at trial, this would leave on the books the unreviewed decision of the highest state court rejecting the constitutional challenge. Delaying final decision of the constitutional

---

40. 95 S.Ct. at 1039–1040, 420 U.S. at 481–482. As examples the Court cited North Dakota State Bd. of Pharmacy v. Snyder's Drug Stores, Inc., 1973, 94 S.Ct. 407, 414 U.S. 156, 38 L.Ed.2d 379; California v. Stewart, 1966, 86 S.Ct. 1602, 1640 n. 71, 384 U.S. 436, 498 n. 71, 16 L.Ed.2d 694 (decided sub nom. Miranda v. Arizona).

41. 95 S.Ct. at 1041, 420 U.S. at 482–483. As examples the Court cited Miami Herald Pub. Co. v. Tornillo, 1974, 94 S.Ct. 2831, 2834 n. 6, 418 U.S. 241, 247 n. 6, 41 L.Ed.2d 730; Hudson Distributors v. Eli Lilly, 1964, 84 S.Ct. 1273, 1276 n. 4, 377 U.S. 386, 389 n. 4, 12 L.Ed.2d 394; Local No. 438 v. Curry, 1963, 83 S.Ct. 531, 536, 371 U.S. 542, 550, 9 L.Ed.2d 514; Mercantile Nat. Bank v. Langdeau, 1963, 83 S.Ct. 520, 522, 371 U.S. 555, 558, 9 L.Ed.2d 523.

See also Shaffer v. Heitner, 1977, 97 S.Ct. 2569, 2575 n. 12, 433 U.S. 186, 195 n. 12, 53 L.Ed.2d 683.

But in Flynt v. Ohio, 1981, 101 S.Ct. 1958, 451 U.S. 619, 68 L.Ed.2d 489, a bare majority of the Court to review, as not final, a judgment of the highest state court that reversed dismissal of a criminal complaint on the ground of selective and discriminatory prosecution. Even a claim of selective prosecution that drew from First Amendment rights did not present the kind of "identifiable federal statutory or constitutional rights which would * * * [be] undermined by the continuation of the litigation in the state courts" that would justify a finding of finality. 101 S.Ct. at 1960, 451 U.S. at 621.

In two other recent cases the Court has found a state judgment sufficiently final for review though the judgment was hardly final in any traditional sense and does not seem to fit into any of the four Cox categories. See National Socialist Party of America v. Village of Skokie, 1977, 97 S.Ct. 2205, 432 U.S. 43, 53 L.Ed.2d 96, and American Export Lines, Inc. v. Alvez, 1980, 100 S.Ct. 1673, 446 U.S. 274, 64 L.Ed.2d 284, discussed in 16 Wright, Miller & Cooper, Jurisdiction § 4010.

claim until after trial would leave unanswered an important question about freedom of the press, while if the Supreme Court took the case and sustained the constitutional claim—as it in fact did—the litigation would be at an end.

There is one unusual procedure required by the final judgment rule in combination with the rule that only the decision of the highest state court in which review can be had is reviewable. Suppose, for example, that a defendant demurs to a complaint, arguing that some provision of federal law makes the claim improper. The trial court sustains the demurrer, but the state appellate court reverses, rejecting the federal claim and remanding the case for trial. This is not a final judgment—unless the circumstances of the particular case bring it within one of the four categories defined in Cox—since it leaves something more than merely ministerial to be done. After trial judgment is entered for plaintiff. This is not immediately reviewable by the Supreme Court since it is not the judgment of the highest state court in which decision can be had. It may be that defendant can claim no error except the earlier overruling of his demurrer. He is required, however, to appeal to the state appellate court, even though that court will refuse to consider his only claimed error on the ground that its earlier decision of the federal question is now law of the case. Only after the judgment has been affirmed on this useless appeal is review in the Supreme Court possible.[42] However on review of this second judgment of the state appellate court the Supreme Court will consider the federal question raised and decided on the first appeal, even though the state court has refused to consider it on the second appeal, or appellant has not raised it on the second appeal.[43]

Under the statute there must be a federal question in order to invoke the jurisdiction of the Supreme Court. Whether there is such a question in the case is a matter that the Supreme Court must decide for itself.[44] The mere presence of a federal question will not permit review, however, unless that federal question is "substantial." [45] Even though a question as to federal law has been raised, if it appears that the question is wholly formal, or is so absolutely devoid of merit as to be frivolous, or has been explicitly foreclosed by a decision or decisions of the Supreme Court so as to leave no room for real

42. Great Western Tel. Co. v. Burnham, 1896, 16 S.Ct. 850, 162 U.S. 339, 40 L.Ed. 991.

43. Hathorn v. Lovorn, 1982, 102 S.Ct. 2421, 2426, ___ U.S. ___, ___, 72 L.Ed. 2d 824; Reece v. Georgia, 1955, 76 S.Ct. 167, 169, 350 U.S. 85, 87, 100 L.Ed. 77; Urie v. Thompson, 1949, 69 S.Ct. 1018, 1025–1026, 337 U.S. 163, 171–173, 93 L.Ed. 1282.

44. Angel v. Bullington, 1947, 67 S.Ct. 657, 330 U.S. 183, 91 L.Ed. 832.

45. 16 Wright, Miller & Cooper, Jurisdiction § 4014; Ulman & Spears, "Dismissed for Want of a Substantial Federal Question", 1940, 20 B.U.L.Rev. 501; Note, The Supreme Court Dismissal of State Court Appeals for Want of Substantial Federal Question, 1982, 15 Creighton L.Rev. 749.

controversy, the Court will not hear the case.[46]   At an earlier time
when all cases were argued, this was of no real significance, since it
did not make any difference whether the Court, after argument, affirmed the decision of the state court or whether it dismissed the appeal for want of a substantial federal question.   Since 1928, however,
both on certiorari and appeal, it has been necessary to file a printed
statement in advance of argument showing the basis for jurisdiction,
and if, on the basis of this statement, the Court finds the federal
question insubstantial, it will dismiss the appeal, or deny certiorari,
without hearing oral argument.[47]

The substantial federal question must have been raised in a proper and timely manner in the state courts.   "No particular form of
words or phrases is essential, but only that the claim of invalidity and
the ground therefor be brought to the attention of the state court
with fair precision and in due time.   And if the record as a whole
shows either expressly or by clear intendment that this was done, the
claim is to be regarded as having been adequately presented." [48]

The timeliness with which the federal question is raised in the
state court is critical.   This is largely a matter for the state to regulate by its own procedural rules.   Failure to raise the question at the
stage of the proceedings required by state law will preclude review,[49]

46.   Equitable Life Assur. Soc'y v.
Brown, 1902, 23 S.Ct. 123, 187 U.S.
308, 47 L.Ed. 190; Zucht v. King, 1922,
43 S.Ct. 24, 260 U.S. 174, 67 L.Ed. 194.

47.   See § 108 below.

48.   New York ex rel. Bryant v. Zimmerman, 1928, 49 S.Ct. 61, 63, 278 U.S. 63,
67, 73 L.Ed. 184; Street v. New York,
1969, 89 S.Ct. 1354, 1360–1362, 394
U.S. 576, 581–585, 22 L.Ed.2d 572;
PruneYard Shopping Center v. Robins,
1980, 100 S.Ct. 2035, 2043 n. 9, 447 U.S.
74, 85 n. 9, 64 L.Ed.2d 741.

The Court held that it lacked jurisdiction
to review a state judgment when the
petitioner had used the phrase "full
faith and credit" several times in the
proceedings below, but had never cited
the federal Constitution or any of the
cases relying on it.   Webb v. Webb,
1981, 101 S.Ct. 1889, 451 U.S. 493, 68
L.Ed.2d 392.

Ordinarily the Court will not consider
questions that were not raised at all in
the state court.   Tacon v. Arizona,
1973, 93 S.Ct. 998, 410 U.S. 351, 35
L.Ed.2d 346.   But the Court has
claimed a power to consider plain error
though not raised below.   Wood v.
Georgia, 1981, 101 S.Ct. 1097, 1100 n.
5, 450 U.S. 261, 265 n. 5, 67 L.Ed.2d
220; Stern & Gressman, note 1 above,
at p. 460.

49.   Edelman v. California, 1953, 73 S.Ct.
293, 344 U.S. 357, 97 L.Ed. 387; Bar-
bour v. Georgia, 1919, 39 S.Ct. 316, 249
U.S. 454, 63 L.Ed. 704; Mutual Life
Ins. Co. v. McGrew, 1903, 23 S.Ct. 375,
188 U.S. 291, 47 L.Ed. 480.

Whether the federal question has been
sufficiently and timely raised in the
state court is itself a federal question
that the Supreme Court can decide for
itself.   Street v. New York, 1969, 89
S.Ct. 1354, 1361, 394 U.S. 576, 583, 22
L.Ed.2d 572;   Douglas v. Alabama,
1965, 85 S.Ct. 1074, 1078–1079, 380
U.S. 415, 420–423, 13 L.Ed.2d 934;
Wright v. Georgia, 1963, 83 S.Ct. 1240,
1243–1245, 373 U.S. 284, 289–291, 10
L.Ed.2d 349; Carter v. Texas, 1900, 20
S.Ct. 687, 689, 177 U.S. 442, 447, 44
L.Ed. 839.   See, e.g., Chambers v. Mississippi, 1973, 93 S.Ct. 1038, 1043 n. 3,
410 U.S. 284, 290 n. 3, 35 L.Ed.2d 297,
holding that the federal question was
timely raised on a motion for a new trial since the challenge—that the cumulative effect of several rulings on evidence denied fundamental fairness in
the trial—was not one that was available until the evidence had been concluded.

See 16 Wright, Miller & Cooper, Jurisdiction § 4022.

unless the state rule is regarded as an attempt to evade decision of the federal question or permits no fair opportunity to assert the question.[50] The course of safety is to raise the federal question at every step in the proceedings in the state courts.[51] Even if the question has been properly raised in the trial court, the party may be held to have waived it by failing to preserve it on appeal [52] or by appealing to the wrong court.[53] It is too late to raise a federal question by petition for rehearing to the state appellate court,[54] except where the decision of that court has unexpectedly given rise to a federal question that the party seeking review has had no previous opportunity to assert and could not fairly have anticipated.[55]

To all of these rules as to when and how the federal question must be presented in the state court, there is a salutary and sensible exception. If the highest court of the state in which decision could be had actually decides the federal question, it is reviewable in the Supreme Court regardless of when it was first presented. "There can be no question as to the proper presentation of a federal claim when the highest state court passes on it." [56]

The most important, and most difficult, limitation on Supreme Court review of state court decisions has been well stated by Justice Jackson: "This Court from the time of its foundation has adhered to the principle that it will not review judgments of state courts that rest on adequate and independent state grounds. * * *   The

---

50. National Mut. Bldg. & Loan Assn. v. Brahan, 1904, 24 S.Ct. 532, 193 U.S. 635, 48 L.Ed. 823; Reece v. Georgia, 1955, 76 S.Ct. 167, 350 U.S. 85, 100 L.Ed. 77. But cf. Michel v. Louisiana, 1955, 76 S.Ct. 158, 350 U.S. 91, 100 L.Ed. 83.

51. See Wiener, Wanna Make a Federal Case Out of It?, 1962, 48 A.B.A.J. 59.

52. Beck v. Washington, 1962, 82 S.Ct. 955, 960–962, 369 U.S. 541, 549–553, 8 L.Ed.2d 98.

53. Parker v. Illinois, 1948, 68 S.Ct. 708, 333 U.S. 571, 92 L.Ed. 886; Central Union Tel. Co. v. City of Edwardsville, 1925, 46 S.Ct. 90, 269 U.S. 190, 70 L.Ed. 229.

54. Herndon v. Georgia, 1935, 55 S.Ct. 794, 295 U.S. 441, 79 L.Ed. 1530; Bilby v. Stewart, 1918, 38 S.Ct. 264, 246 U.S. 255, 62 L.Ed. 701; Forbes v. Virginia State Council, 1910, 30 S.Ct. 295, 216 U.S. 396, 54 L.Ed. 534.

55. Missouri ex rel. Missouri Ins. Co. v. Gehner, 1930, 50 S.Ct. 326, 281 U.S. 313, 74 L.Ed. 870; Brinkerhoff-Faris Trust & Sav. Co. v. Hill, 1930, 50 S.Ct. 451, 281 U.S. 673, 74 L.Ed. 1107; cf. Saunders v. Shaw, 1917, 37 S.Ct. 638, 244 U.S. 317, 61 L.Ed. 1163.

56. Raley v. Ohio, 1959, 79 S.Ct. 1257, 1265, 360 U.S. 423, 436, 3 L.Ed.2d 1344. See also Orr v. Orr, 1979, 99 S.Ct. 1102, 1109, 440 U.S. 268, 274–275, 59 L.Ed.2d 306, noted 1980, 23 Howard L.J. 559, 41 Ohio St.L.J. 1061, 54 Tul.L. Rev. 500; Cox Broadcasting Corp. v. Cohn, 1975, 95 S.Ct. 1029, 1036–1037, 420 U.S. 469, 502–503, 43 L.Ed.2d 328. Boykin v. Alabama, 1969, 89 S.Ct. 1709, 1711, 395 U.S. 238, 241–242, 23 L.Ed.2d 274. Manhattan Life Ins. Co. of New York v. Cohen, 1914, 34 S.Ct. 874, 877, 234 U.S. 123, 134, 58 L.Ed. 1245; Grannis v. Ordean, 1914, 34 S.Ct. 779, 234 U.S. 385, 58 L.Ed. 1363; San Jose Land & Water Co. v. San Jose Ranch Co., 1903, 23 S.Ct. 487, 189 U.S. 177, 47 L.Ed. 765.

It has also been held that the Court need not consider whether the federal question was properly raised in the state courts if the state, as a party to the case, states in the Supreme Court that it is prepared to meet the federal question on its merits. Gomez v. Perez, 1973, 93 S.Ct. 872, 874 n. 2, 409 U.S. 535, 537 n. 2, 35 L.Ed.2d 56.

reason is so obvious that it has rarely been thought to warrant statement. It is found in the partitioning of power between the state and federal judicial systems and in the limitations of our own jurisdiction. Our only power over state judgments is to correct them to the extent that they incorrectly adjudge federal rights. And our power is to correct wrong judgments, not to revise opinions. We are not permitted to render an advisory opinion, and if the same judgment would be rendered by the state court after we corrected its views of federal laws, our review could amount to nothing more than an advisory opinion." [57]

In the early years such a limitation was imposed on the Court by the proviso to section 25 of the Judiciary Act of 1789, which said: "But no other error shall be assigned or regarded as a ground of reversal in any such case as aforesaid, than such as appears on the face of the record, and immediately respects the before mentioned questions of validity or construction of the said constitution, treaties, statutes, commissions, or authorities in dispute." This proviso was eliminated when that section of the statute was amended in 1867.[58] It seems entirely plausible that Congress intended by eliminating the proviso to open the whole case for review by the Supreme Court, if there is a federal question in the case sufficient to take the case to the Supreme Court. Such a broad review may well be constitutional. When cases are brought in a district court because they arise under the Constitution, laws, or treaties of the United States, the district court, and the Supreme Court in reviewing the judgment, decides all the issues in the case, and is not limited to the federal question that provides the basis for jurisdiction.[59] In normal understanding the amendment of a statute to remove a limitation on it suggests that such limitation is no longer to apply. Such a course seems wholly consistent with the temper of the times, and with the other purposes of the 1867 act. The Supreme Court, however, took a different view. In the landmark case of Murdock v. Memphis [60] the Court held that no such drastic change in its jurisdiction had been accomplished by the 1867 revision. This case, and others that have built on it,[61] lay down two fundamental propositions. The Court will not review a case, even though it contains a federal question, if there is an adequate state ground that supports the decision of the state court.

57. Herb v. Pitcairn, 1945, 65 S.Ct. 459, 463, 324 U.S. 117, 125–126, 89 L.Ed. 789.

See 16 Wright, Miller & Cooper, Jurisdiction §§ 4019–4032.

58. Act of Feb. 5, 1867, § 2, 14 Stat. 385, 386.

59. Osborn v. Bank of United States, 1824, 9 Wheat. 738, 823, 6 L.Ed. 204; Siler v. Louisville & N. R. Co., 1909, 29 S.Ct. 451, 213 U.S. 175, 53 L.Ed. 753. See § 19 above.

60. 1875, 20 Wall. 590, 22 L.Ed. 429. See 16 Wright, Miller & Cooper, Jurisdiction § 4020, pp. 662–665.

61. Eustis v. Bolles, 1893, 14 S.Ct. 131, 150 U.S. 361, 37 L.Ed. 1111; Berea College v. Kentucky, 1908, 29 S.Ct. 33, 211 U.S. 45, 53 L.Ed. 81; Enterprise Irrigation Dist. v. Farmers' Mut. Canal Co., 1917, 37 S.Ct. 618, 243 U.S. 157, 61 L.Ed. 644; Fox Film Corp. v. Muller, 1935, 56 S.Ct. 183, 296 U.S. 207, 80 L.Ed. 158.

Further, the Court will accept as binding upon it the state court's decision of questions of state law.

There has been an elaborate argument made that the framers of the Constitution intended that the Supreme Court would speak authoritatively on questions of state law as well as on questions of federal law.[62] The historical evidence for this proposition is unconvincing, and the uniform practice of the Court has been to the contrary. It has considered that the state courts speak with final authority on questions of state law.[63] The exceptions to this principle are very few. Decisions of the state court as to state law are only persuasive, rather than controlling, where state law is incorporated by reference in a federal statute,[64] or where protection of a federal constitutional right would be thwarted if the state had the last word on state questions, as in determining whether there is a "contract" within the meaning of the clause of the Constitution prohibiting impairment of the obligation of contracts,[65] or where the state court interpretation of state law appears to be an "obvious subterfuge to evade consideration of a federal issue." [66]

The other aspect of the rule of Murdock v. Memphis is that the Supreme Court cannot review a state decision at all if that decision rests on an adequate state ground. Thus there can be no review if the state court has decided the case exclusively on some ground of state law, and has never reached a federal question present in the case.[67] Nor can there be review where the state court has decided both the state and federal questions, if its decision of the federal question was unnecessary in the light of its disposition of the state question.[68] But if the state court has decided the case entirely on the federal question presented, the Supreme Court can review, even

62. 2 Crosskey, Politics and the Constitution in the History of the United States, 1953, cc. 23–26.

63. E.g., Mullaney v. Wilbur, 1975, 95 S.Ct. 1881, 1885–1886, 421 U.S. 684, 689, 44 L.Ed.2d 508; Scripto, Inc. v. Carson, 1960, 80 S.Ct. 619, 362 U.S. 207, 4 L.Ed.2d 660; Sutter Butte Canal Co. v. R. Comm. of California, 1929, 49 S.Ct. 325, 279 U.S. 125, 73 L.Ed. 637; American Ry. Exp. Co. v. Kentucky, 1927, 47 S.Ct. 353, 273 U.S. 269, 71 L.Ed. 639; Murdock v. Memphis, 1875, 20 Wall. 590, 22 L.Ed. 429; cf. Caldarola v. Eckert, 1947, 67 S.Ct. 1569, 332 U.S. 155, 91 L.Ed. 1968. See 16 Wright, Miller & Cooper, Jurisdiction § 4021, pp. 687–692.

64. Reconstruction Fin. Corp. v. Beaver County, 1946, 66 S.Ct. 992, 328 U.S. 204, 90 L.Ed. 1172.

65. Indiana ex rel. Anderson v. Brand, 1938, 58 S.Ct. 443, 303 U.S. 95, 82 L.Ed. 685.

66. Radio Station WOW, Inc. v. Johnson, 1945, 65 S.Ct. 1475, 1480, 326 U.S. 120, 129, 89 L.Ed. 2092; Ward v. Board of County Commrs. of Love County, 1920, 40 S.Ct. 419, 253 U.S. 17, 64 L.Ed. 751; Terre Haute & I. R. Co. v. Indiana ex rel. Ketcham, 1904, 24 S.Ct. 767, 194 U.S. 579, 48 L.Ed. 1124.

This was held not to be the situation when the pronouncement of state law by the state court, even if novel, would not frustrate consideration of the federal issue. Mullaney v. Wilbur, 1975, 95 S.Ct. 1881, 1886 n. 11, 421 U.S. 684, 691 n. 11, 44 L.Ed.2d 508.

67. McCoy v. Shaw, 1928, 48 S.Ct. 519, 277 U.S. 302, 72 L.Ed. 891; Johnson v. New Jersey, 1966, 86 S.Ct. 1772, 1782, 384 U.S. 719, 735, 16 L.Ed.2d 882.

68. Fox Film Corp. v. Muller, 1935, 56 S.Ct. 183, 296 U.S. 207, 80 L.Ed. 158; Jankovich v. Indiana Toll Road Comm., 1965, 85 S.Ct. 493, 379 U.S. 487, 13 L.Ed.2d 439. But see Sandalow, Hen-

though there was a state question in the case that could have been the basis for decision.[69]   In such a case, if the state court's resolution of the federal question is erroneous, the Supreme Court will remand the case to the state court, which can then pass on the state question.[70]   And it is held, though on shaky theoretical ground, that where a state statute incorporates federal law by reference, the Supreme Court may review a state court decision as to that statute, pass on the federal question that is incorporated by reference, and remand for the state court to reconsider its interpretation of the statute in the light of the Supreme Court's interpretation of the underlying federal law.[71]

In order to bar Supreme Court review, the state ground must be "adequate." [72]   If there is no fair and substantial support in the facts for the state court's ruling on the state ground, the Supreme Court can disregard it.[73]   A new state rule cannot be invented for the occa-

ry v. Mississippi and the Adequate State Ground: Proposals for a Revised Doctrine, 1965 Sup.Ct.Rev. 187, 201–203.

69. United Air Lines, Inc. v. Mahin, 1973, 93 S.Ct. 1186, 410 U.S. 623, 35 L.Ed.2d 545; Beecher v. Alabama, 1967, 88 S.Ct. 189, 190 n. 3, 389 U.S. 35, 37 n. 3, 19 L.Ed.2d 35; International Steel & Iron Co. v. National Sur. Co., 1936, 56 S.Ct. 619, 297 U.S. 657, 89 L.Ed. 961; Red Cross Line v. Atlantic Fruit Co., 1924, 44 S.Ct. 274, 275–276, 264 U.S. 109, 120, 68 L.Ed. 582.

70. Orr v. Orr, 1979, 99 S.Ct. 1102, 1109–1110, 1114, 440 U.S. 268, 275–277, 283–284, 59 L.Ed.2d 306, noted 1980, 23 Howard L.J. 559, 41 Ohio St.L.J. 1061, 54 Tul.L.Rev. 500; Indiana ex rel. Anderson v. Brand, 1938, 58 S.Ct. 443, 303 U.S. 95, 82 L.Ed. 685. See Evans v. Newton, 1966, 86 S.Ct. 486, 490, 382 U.S. 296, 303, 15 L.Ed.2d 373 (White, J., concurring).   For the later history of that case, see Evans v. Abney, 1970, 90 S.Ct. 628, 396 U.S. 435, 24 L.Ed.2d 634.

Cf. Stanton v. Stanton, 1975, 95 S.Ct. 1373, 421 U.S. 7, 43 L.Ed.2d 688; United Air Lines, Inc. v. Mahin, 1973, 93 S.Ct. 1186, 1192, 410 U.S. 623, 632, 35 L.Ed.2d 545.

71. Standard Oil Co. of California v. Johnson, 1942, 62 S.Ct. 1168, 316 U.S. 481, 86 L.Ed. 1611; cf. St. Martin Evangelical Lutheran Church v. South Dakota, 1981, 101 S.Ct. 2142, 2147 n. 9, 451 U.S. 772, 780, 68 L.Ed.2d 612; State Tax Comm. v. Van Cott, 1939, 59 S.Ct. 605, 306 U.S. 511, 83 L.Ed. 950,

criticized 1939, 39 Col.L.Rev. 1043. See 16 Wright, Miller & Cooper, Jurisdiction § 4031; Greene, Hybrid State Law in the Federal Courts, 1970, 83 Harv.L.Rev. 289; Note, Supreme Court Review of State Interpretations of Federal Law Incorporated by Reference, 1953, 66 Harv.L.Rev. 1498.

72. 16 Wright, Miller & Cooper, Jurisdiction §§ 4025–4028; Bice, Anderson and the Adequate State Ground, 1972, 45 S.Cal.L.Rev. 750; Hill, The Inadequate State Ground, 1965, 65 Col.L. Rev. 943; Sandalow, Henry v. Mississippi and the Adequate State Ground: Proposals for a Revised Doctrine, 1965 Sup.Ct.Rev. 187; Note, State Constitutional Guarantees as Adequate State Ground: Supreme Court Review and Problems of Federalism, 1976, 13 Am. Crim.L.Rev. 737; Note, A Clarification of the Adequate State Ground Doctrine, 1971 Wash.U.L.Q. 485. Comment, Supreme Court Treatment of State Procedural Grounds Relied on in State Courts to Preclude Decision of Federal Questions, 1961, 61 Col.L.Rev. 255; Note, The Untenable Nonfederal Ground in the Supreme Court, 1961, 74 Harv.L.Rev. 1376.

73. Ward v. Board of County Commrs. of Love County, 1920, 40 S.Ct. 419, 253 U.S. 17, 64 L.Ed. 751; Ancient Egyptian Arabic Order of Nobles of the Mystic Shrine v. Michaux, 1929, 49 S.Ct. 485, 279 U.S. 737, 73 L.Ed. 931; Creswill v. Grand Lodge, Knights of Pythias of Georgia, 1912, 32 S.Ct. 822, 225 U.S. 246, 56 L.Ed. 1074.

sion in order to defeat the federal claim.[74] It has been said that if the state court's refusal to consider the merits of a case is based on a rule "more properly deemed discretionary than jurisdictional" this does not bar review in the Supreme Court.[75] Even a state procedural rule of general applicability may be thought not an adequate state ground if it is so strict that it interferes unduly with the presentation of federal questions.[76] In the familiar words of Justice Holmes, "whatever springes the State may set for those who are endeavoring to assert rights that the State confers, the assertion of Federal rights, when plainly and reasonably made, is not to be defeated under the name of local practice." [77]

Review will not be defeated by a state court decision that a case that otherwise would turn on a federal question is moot or that the party lacked standing to raise the federal claim.[78] The Court considers that these are not state grounds at all but rather questions of federal law on which only it can pronounce final judgment.

74. NAACP v. Alabama ex rel. Flowers, 1964, 84 S.Ct. 1302, 1306–1311, 377 U.S. 288, 293–302, 12 L.Ed.2d 325; NAACP v. Alabama ex rel. Patterson, 1958, 78 S.Ct. 1163, 357 U.S. 449, 2 L.Ed.2d 1488; Staub v. City of Baxley, 1958, 78 S.Ct. 277, 355 U.S. 313, 2 L.Ed.2d 302; see Parrot v. City of Tallahassee, 1965, 85 S.Ct. 1322, 381 U.S. 129, 14 L.Ed.2d 263. See generally 16 Wright, Miller & Cooper, Jurisdiction § 4027.

75. Sullivan v. Little Hunting Park, Inc., 1969, 90 S.Ct. 400, 396 U.S. 229, 24 L.Ed.2d 386. This doctrine had been suggested in Justice Black's dissent in Henry v. Mississippi, 1965, 85 S.Ct. 564, 571–573, 379 U.S. 443, 455–457, 13 L.Ed.2d 408. In the Sullivan case three members of the Court agreed that there was no adequate state ground but relied on a ground very different from that announced by the majority.

It is argued that this possible implication in the Sullivan opinion is unwarranted. 16 Wright, Miller & Cooper, Jurisdiction § 4026, pp. 733–736.

In Hathorn v. Lovorn, 1982, 102 S.Ct. 2421, ___ U.S. ___, 72 L.Ed.2d 824, the state court arguably had refused to decide a federal question because it found it untimely when it was first raised in a petition for rehearing. The Supreme Court held that even if this was the explanation for the state court's action, it was not a bar to review. The Court found that the state court does not consistently preclude

consideration of issues raised for the first time on rehearing, and said: "State courts may not avoid deciding federal issues by invoking procedural rules that they do not apply evenhandedly to all similar claims." 102 S.Ct. at 2426, ___ U.S. at ___. For analysis of this confusing decision, which could mean a great deal but is better read as meaning very little, see 16 Wright, Miller & Cooper, Jurisdiction § 4028.

76. Brown v. Western Ry. of Alabama, 1949, 70 S.Ct. 105, 338 U.S. 294, 94 L.Ed. 100, noted 1949, 35 Va.L.Rev. 1098, 1950, 50 Col.L.Rev. 385, 21 Tenn. L.Rev. 324, 28 Tex.L.Rev. 972; Douglas v. Alabama, 1965, 85 S.Ct. 1074, 1078–1079, 380 U.S. 415, 420–423, 13 L.Ed.2d 934. See Comment, Procedural Protection for Federal Rights in State Courts, 1961, 30 U.Cin.L.Rev. 184; 16 Wright, Miller & Cooper, Jurisdiction § 4023, pp. 708–713, § 4027, pp. 740–742.

Professor Hill, in the article cited note 72 above, at 971–977, argues that neither the Brown case, nor any other, supports the proposition stated in the text.

77. Davis v. Wechsler, 1923, 44 S.Ct. 13, 14, 263 U.S. 22, 24, 68 L.Ed. 143.

78. Liner v. Jafco, Inc., 1964, 84 S.Ct. 391, 375 U.S. 301, 11 L.Ed.2d 347; Cramp v. Board of Public Instruction, 1961, 82 S.Ct. 275, 368 U.S. 278, 7 L.Ed.2d 285; Allied Stores of Ohio, Inc. v. Bowers, 1959, 79 S.Ct. 437, 358 U.S. 522, 3 L.Ed.2d 480.

The question of the adequate state ground was much confused by the decision in Henry v. Mississippi.[79] Although the majority in that case spoke of applying "settled principles," [80] three of the dissenters thought that the decision "portends a severe dilution, if not complete abolition, of the concept of 'adequacy' as pertaining to state procedural grounds," [81] while a commentator suggests that "the implication that a change in doctrine is under consideration is manifest, yet the holding is sufficiently narrow that retreat is not foreclosed." [82]

It is difficult to determine what was held in Henry, much less what effect, if any, it has on previous notions of the adequate state ground. Henry's conviction was affirmed by the Mississippi Supreme Court, despite the admission of evidence that arguably had been illegally obtained, on the ground that his counsel had failed to object to the evidence when it was introduced, as normally required by state procedure.

The Court first recognized the adequate state ground rule but drew a distinction between state substantive grounds and state procedural grounds, and declared it to be settled that "a litigant's procedural defaults in state proceedings do not prevent vindication of his federal rights unless the State's insistence on compliance with its procedural rule serves a legitimate state interest." [83] This indicates that the Court could review the case if it found that the state rule served no legitimate state interest. The Court immediately agreed that the state requirement of a contemporaneous objection clearly serves a legitimate state interest, but it pointed out other ways in which Henry's counsel had made his position known at a time when corrective action was possible. In those circumstances, the Court said, the delay in making the objection could not have frustrated the state's interest in avoiding delay and waste of time. Thus to enforce the contemporaneous objection rule would be to force resort to an arid ritual rather than to serve a substantial state interest.[84]

At this point it sounded as if the Court was prepared to declare the state ground inadequate and consider the merits, but it then expressly stated that it was not holding that the state ground was inadequate nor was it looking into the merits.[85] It saw some reason to think that counsel might have withheld objection to the evidence in

79. 1965, 85 S.Ct. 564, 379 U.S. 443, 13 L.Ed.2d 408. The case is extensively considered in the articles by Hill and Sandalow, note 72 above. See also 16 Wright, Miller & Cooper, Jurisdiction § 4020, pp. 671–675.

80. 85 S.Ct. at 568, 379 U.S. at 449.

81. 85 S.Ct. at 572, 379 U.S. at 457.

82. Sandalow, note 72 above, at 197.

83. 85 S.Ct. at 567, 379 U.S. at 447. One commentator thinks this proposition "amply supported by previous case law," Sandalow, note 72 above, at

229, while another can find "no suggestion" of it in the earlier cases, Hill, note 72 above, at 988. The distinction between substantive and procedural grounds is said to be insignificant in Wechsler, The Appellate Jurisdiction of the Supreme Court: Reflections on the Law and the Logistics of Direct Review, 1977, 34 Wash. & Lee L.Rev. 1043, 1054.

84. 85 S.Ct. at 568, 379 U.S. at 448–449.

85. 85 S.Ct. at 568, 379 U.S. at 449.

question as a matter of strategy. If he had deliberately bypassed the opportunity to make timely objection, Henry would be deemed to have forfeited his state court remedies.[86] The case was, accordingly, remanded to the state court to determine whether there had been such a waiver.

If there had been a waiver, that would bar Henry from a decision on the merits of his federal claim either in state or federal court. But if the state court found no waiver, it was still free to insist on its procedural requirements and could, if it wished, again affirm the conviction. In that case, however, Henry "could have a federal court apply settled principles to test the effectiveness of the procedural default to foreclose consideration of his constitutional claim." [87] Whether the federal court referred to was the Supreme Court, on direct review, or a district court, on habeas corpus, was not made clear.

Subsequent developments in the Henry case shed no additional light. In the course of three more years of litigation, the state court found that there had been a deliberate waiver by Henry and his counsel, and it again affirmed his conviction.[88] The Supreme Court denied certiorari "without prejudice to the bringing of a proceeding for relief in federal habeas corpus." [89] The case clearly must be studied in any consideration of the doctrine of the adequate state ground but the few obscure cases in which it has since been invoked go in opposite directions [90] and suggest that Henry was not a significant break with the past but only an unusual case heavily influenced by its facts.[91]

86. 85 S.Ct. at 568–569, 379 U.S. at 450–452.

87. 85 S.Ct. at 570, 379 U.S. at 452.

88. Henry v. State, Miss.1967, 198 So.2d 213; id., 202 So.2d 40.

89. Henry v. Mississippi, 1968, 88 S.Ct. 2276, 392 U.S. 931, 20 L.Ed.2d 1389.

A federal court subsequently held that there had been no waiver and that Henry was entitled to relief on habeas corpus. Henry v. Williams, D.C.Miss. 1969, 299 F.Supp. 36.

90. See Camp v. Arkansas, 1971, 92 S.Ct. 307, 404 U.S. 69, 30 L.Ed.2d 223, in which the Supreme Court reversed because of remarks by the prosecutor in his summation, though no objection had been made in the trial court. The state court refused to consider the point because of the lack of objection but the Supreme Court cited Henry for the proposition that "petitioner's alleged procedural default does not bar consideration of his constitutional claim in the circumstances of this case."

Compare Monger v. Florida, 1972, 92 S.Ct. 1163, 405 U.S. 958, 31 L.Ed.2d 236, where the state court's dismissal of an appeal because notice of appeal had been given after the oral entry of judgment but before the written order was expressly held to be an adequate state ground, over the dissent of three justices who relied on Henry.

Henry was cited, in circumstances that did nothing to clarify its meaning, in Chambers v. Mississippi, 1973, 93 S.Ct. 1038, 1043 n. 3, 410 U.S. 284, 290–291 n. 3, 35 L.Ed.2d 297.

These seem to be the only cases in which the Court has discussed Henry with regard to its power to review state law decisions.

Professor Hill has observed that "Henry has never been overruled, but seems relatively moribund." Hill, The Forfeiture of Constitutional Rights in Criminal Cases, 1978, 78 Col.L.Rev. 1050, 1052.

91. "* * * [E]ven though not mentioned by the Court, is it really immaterial that the petitioner was not merely a man charged with disturbing the peace, but Aaron Henry, a Negro resident of Clarksdale, Mississippi, and president of both the Coahoma County Branch of the National Association for

It is often difficult to determine whether there is an adequate state ground that bars Supreme Court review because of failure of the state decision to indicate with sufficient clarity whether that court was relying on a federal ground or a state ground. This can occur either where the state court has not written an opinion or where its opinion is ambiguous. It is not surprising that there should be such ambiguous state decisions. The state courts have power to pass on both state and federal questions, and there is no need for them to draw a sharp distinction between the two. The matter is, of course, very different when review is sought in the Supreme Court.[92] One remedy in such a situation is for counsel to seek clarification from the state court, either by amendment of its judgment [93] or by a certificate from the court, or the presiding judge.[94] If the state court does give such clarification, and it appears from it that decision rested on the federal ground, review can then be had.

Where there is no such clarification from the state court, four techniques are available to the Supreme Court: (1) since the burden is on the party invoking the jurisdiction of the Supreme Court to establish that that Court has jurisdiction, it may dismiss if its jurisdiction is ambiguous;[95] (2) it may vacate the judgment below and remand so that the state court will have an opportunity to clarify what it has ruled;[96] (3) it may continue the case to give the parties an opportunity to apply to the court below for clarification;[97] or (4) if it considers

---

the Advancement of Colored People and of its State Conference of Branches? It is, moreover, immaterial that the prosecution was commenced in 1962 in Mississippi and not at another time and in another place?" Sandalow, note 72 above, at 190.

92. See 16 Wright, Miller & Cooper, Jurisdiction § 4032; Note, Supreme Court Treatment of State Court Cases Exhibiting Ambiguous Grounds of Decision, 1962, 62 Col.L.Rev. 822.

93. E.g., Kedroff v. St. Nicholas Cathedral of Russian Orthodox Church in North America, 1952, 73 S.Ct. 143, 145, 344 U.S. 94, 97, 97 L.Ed. 120.

94. E.g., Allenberg Cotton Co., Inc. v. Pittman, 1974, 95 S.Ct. 260, 262 n. 2, 419 U.S. 20, 23 n. 2, 42 L.Ed.2d 195. Indiana ex rel. Anderson v. Brand, 1938, 58 S.Ct. 443, 445, 303 U.S. 95, 99, 82 L.Ed. 685; cf. Marvin v. Trout, 1905, 26 S.Ct. 31, 199 U.S. 212, 50 L.Ed. 157; Wolfson & Kurland, Certificates by State Courts of the Existence of a Federal Question, 1949, 63 Harv.L. Rev. 111. A letter from the clerk of the court is insufficient for this purpose. Dixon v. Duffy, 1952, 73 S.Ct. 193, 194, 344 U.S. 143, 145, 97 L.Ed. 153.

95. E.g., Johnson v. Risk, 1890, 11 S.Ct. 111, 137 U.S. 300, 34 L.Ed. 683; Lynch v. New York ex rel. Pierson, 1934, 55 S.Ct. 16, 293 U.S. 52, 79 L.Ed. 191; Stembridge v. Georgia, 1952, 72 S.Ct. 834, 343 U.S. 541, 96 L.Ed. 1130; Durley v. Mayo, 1956, 76 S.Ct. 806, 351 U.S. 277, 100 L.Ed. 1178; Black v. Cutter Laboratories, 1956, 76 S.Ct. 824, 351 U.S. 292, 100 L.Ed. 1188; Fuller v. Oregon, 1974, 94 S.Ct. 2116, 2123 n. 11, 417 U.S. 40, 50 n. 11, 40 L.Ed.2d 642; cf. Jankovich v. Indiana Toll Road Comm., 1965, 85 S.Ct. 493, 379 U.S. 487, 13 L.Ed.2d 439.

96. The practice originated in Minnesota v. National Tea Co., 1940, 60 S.Ct. 676, 309 U.S. 551, 84 L.Ed. 920. The many cases in which it has since been followed are collected in 16 Wright, Miller & Cooper, Jurisdiction § 4032 n. 28.

97. E.g., Herb v. Pitcairn, 1945, 65 S.Ct. 459, 324 U.S. 117, 89 L.Ed. 789, noted 1946, 94 U.Pa.L.Rev. 251; Loftus v. Illinois, 1948, 68 S.Ct. 1212, 334 U.S. 804, 92 L.Ed. 1737; Lynumn v. Illinois, 1961, 82 S.Ct. 190, 368 U.S. 908, 7 L.Ed.2d 128.

that any state ground that might be advanced for the decision is insubstantial, or that the federal question seems necessarily to have been decided, it may take jurisdiction and decide the federal question.[98] Although there has been no coherent pattern in the Court's choice of one device rather than another,[99] the second course seems to be the one followed most often in recent cases.

The statute for review of state court decisions in the Supreme Court permits review by certiorari in any case within its terms, but allows review by appeal if the state court has held a statute or treaty of the United States invalid[100] or if the state court has held valid a statute of the state against a claim that it is repugnant to the Constitution, treaties or laws of the United States.[101] In order to be entitled to appeal under these provisions it is not necessary that the statute be challenged in its entirety. It is enough that there is a claim that the statute is invalid as applied to a particular situation.[102] This somewhat doubtful rule gives rise to extremely subtle distinctions. Thus appeal does not lie, and review is only on certiorari, if the claim is that there is an erroneous exercise of authority under a valid statute,[103] or that a statute is being applied in a constitutionally discriminatory fashion.[104] Fortunately these distinctions are not of very great practical importance. Though the chance of obtaining review is better on appeal than on certiorari, and counsel would prefer appeal for that reason, both modes of review are now essentially discretionary.[105] In addition, since 1925 there has been a statutory provision that if appeal has been improvidently taken in a case in which the proper mode of review is by certiorari, the papers on which the appeal was taken shall be considered as if they were a petition for certiorari.[106] Thus it is not uncommon for the Court to dismiss the appeal but grant certiorari.[107]

98. E.g., Neilson v. Lagow, 1851, 12 How. 98, 110, 13 L.Ed. 909; Williams v. Kaiser, 1945, 65 S.Ct. 363, 323 U.S. 471, 89 L.Ed. 398; Konigsberg v. State Bar of California, 1957, 77 S.Ct. 722, 723–726, 353 U.S. 252, 254–258, 1 L.Ed. 2d 810; Oregon v. Hass, 1975, 95 S.Ct. 1215, 420 U.S. 714, 43 L.Ed.2d 570; Zacchini v. Scripps-Howard Broadcasting Co., 1977, 97 S.Ct. 2849, 433 U.S. 562, 53 L.Ed.2d 965, on remand 1978, 376 N.E.2d 582, 54 Ohio St.2d 286; Oregon v. Kennedy, 1982, 102 S.Ct. 2083, ___ U.S. ___, 72 L.Ed.2d 416.

99. Note, note 92 above, at 847–850.

100. 28 U.S.C.A. § 1257(1).

101. 28 U.S.C.A. § 1257(2).

102. Dahnke-Walker Milling Co. v. Bondurant, 1921, 42 S.Ct. 106, 257 U.S. 282, 66 L.Ed. 239. See also Japan Line, Ltd. v. County of Los Angeles, 1979, 99 S.Ct. 1813, 441 U.S. 434, 60 L.Ed.2d 336; 16 Wright, Miller & Cooper, Jurisdiction § 4012, pp. 613–615.

103. Philadelphia & R. Coal & Iron Co. v. Gilbert, 1917, 38 S.Ct. 58, 245 U.S. 162, 62 L.Ed. 221; Ireland v. Woods, 1918, 38 S.Ct. 319, 246 U.S. 323, 62 L.Ed. 745; Hanson v. Denckla, 1958, 78 S.Ct. 1228, 1234, 357 U.S. 235, 244, 2 L.Ed.2d 1283.

104. Zucht v. King, 1922, 43 S.Ct. 24, 260 U.S. 174, 67 L.Ed. 194; Charleston Federal Sav. & Loan Assn. v. Alderson, 1945, 65 S.Ct. 624, 324 U.S. 182, 89 L.Ed. 857.

105. See § 108 below.

106. 28 U.S.C.A. § 2103.

107. E.g., Richmond Newspapers, Inc. v. Virginia, 1980, 100 S.Ct. 2814, 2820 n. 4, 448 U.S. 555, 562 n. 4, 65 L.Ed.2d 973; Palmore v. U. S., 1973, 93 S.Ct. 1670, 411 U.S. 389, 36 L.Ed.2d 342; Garrity v. New Jersey, 1967, 87 S.Ct.

For purposes of appeal, the term "statute" refers to every enactment, legislative in character, to which the state gives the force of law.[108] These range from the state constitution, on the one hand,[109] to a municipal ordinance, on the other,[110] and include such things as an order by the regents of the state university,[111] a traffic regulation promulgated by the city police commissioner,[112] and a court order establishing an integrated bar.[113]

§ 108. Procedures in the Supreme Court [1]

To bring a case to the Supreme Court it is necessary to make timely application. In civil cases, whether from state or federal courts, the application must be made within 90 days of the entry of the judgment sought to be reviewed, with some lesser periods for direct appeals from district courts.[2] Sixty days is normally the time allowed in criminal cases, but 90 days is permitted if the case is coming from a state court by appeal rather than by certiorari.[3] An extension of time for petitioning for certiorari can be obtained, for good cause, from a justice of the Supreme Court, but no extension is permissible if review is by appeal.[4]

616, 618, 385 U.S. 493, 496, 17 L.Ed.2d 562; Slagle v. Ohio, 1961, 81 S.Ct. 1076, 1079, 366 U.S. 259, 264, 6 L.Ed.2d 277.

108. Williams v. Bruffy, 1877, 96 U.S. 176, 182–183, 24 L.Ed. 716.

Although 28 U.S.C.A. § 1257 provides that "highest court of a State" includes the District of Columbia Court of Appeals, it has been held that a statute adopted by Congress but applicable in the District of Columbia only is neither "a statute of any state" within the meaning of § 1257(2), Palmore v. U. S., 1973, 93 S.Ct. 1670, 411 U.S. 389, 36 L.Ed.2d 342, nor a "statute of the United States" within the meaning of § 1257(2), Key v. Doyle, 1977, 98 S.Ct. 280, 434 U.S. 59, 54 L.Ed.2d 238, rehearing denied 98 S.Ct. 753, 434 U.S. 1025, 54 L.Ed.2d 773. Thus decision of the District of Columbia Court of Appeals can be reviewed only by certiorari. See 16 Wright, Miller & Cooper, Jurisdiction § 4013.

109. E.g., Railway Exp. Agency v. Virginia, 1931, 51 S.Ct. 201, 282 U.S. 440, 75 L.Ed. 450.

110. E.g., Erznoznik v. City of Jacksonville, 1975, 95 S.Ct. 2268, 422 U.S. 205, 45 L.Ed.2d 125.

111. Hamilton v. Regents of the Univ. of California, 1934, 55 S.Ct. 197, 293 U.S. 245, 79 L.Ed. 343.

112. Railway Exp. Agency v. New York, 1949, 69 S.Ct. 463, 336 U.S. 106, 93 L.Ed. 533.

113. Lathrop v. Donohue, 1961, 81 S.Ct. 1826, 1828–1829, 367 U.S. 820, 824–827, 6 L.Ed.2d 1191.

[§ 108]

1. 16 Wright, Miller & Cooper, Jurisdiction §§ 4003–4005; Stern & Gressman, Supreme Court Practice, 5th ed. 1978, cc. 4–7; Boskey & Gressman, The Supreme Court's New Rules for the Eighties, 1980, 85 F.R.D. 487.

2. 90 days: 28 U.S.C.A. § 2101(c); Rules 11.2, 20.2, 1980 Sup.Ct.Rules.

60 days: direct appeal of a final judgment of a district court in a civil case, 28 U.S.C.A. § 2101(b); Rule 11.2, 1980 Sup.Ct.Rules.

30 days: direct appeal from federal decision holding Act of Congress unconstitutional, 28 U.S.C.A. § 2101(a); direct appeal of an interlocutory order of a district court in a civil case, 28 U.S. C.A. § 2101(b). See Rule 11.2, 1980 Sup.Ct.Rules.

3. The court has power to prescribe the time by rule for federal cases, 18 U.S. C.A. § 3772, and for state cases, 28 U.S.C.A. § 2101(d). It has prescribed 60 days, Rule 20.1, 1980 Sup.Ct.Rules, except for appeals from state courts, Rule 11.1, 1980 Sup.Ct.Rules.

4. 28 U.S.C.A. § 2101(c); Rule 20.1, 1980 Sup.Ct.Rules.

The time limits for seeking Supreme Court review have commonly been thought to be jurisdictional [5] though it has been argued persuasively that review should not be barred if the delay was wholly caused by circumstances entirely beyond the applicant's control.[6] The Court has also held that it has discretion to entertain an untimely petition for certiorari to a court of appeals in a criminal case,[7] on the theory that this time limit is imposed solely by a rule of the Court and not by statute. A similar argument can be made with regard to an application for review of a state court judgment in a criminal case.[8]

Questions of procedure in the Supreme Court, other than in part the time in which to apply for review, are governed by the 1980 Supreme Court Rules.[9] If the party is petitioning for certiorari, he must file with the Supreme Court a petition for certiorari, accompanied by a docket fee and the entry of appearance of counsel, within the time permitted.[10] If the mode of review is appeal, the party must file within the required time a notice of appeal with the clerk of the lower court. Thereafter he has either 60 or 90 days in which to docket the case with the Supreme Court by filing there a document known as a jurisdictional statement accompanied by the docket fee and appearance, as in certiorari cases.[11] The Court may dismiss an appeal if it is not docketed within the time allowed by the rules,[12] but it is not required to do so and may overlook the defect if it chooses.[13]

Perhaps the most widely held misconception of the work of the Supreme Court is the notion that appeal is a matter of right, while

---

5. E.g., Gibson Distributing Co. v. Downtown Development Assn., 1978, 99 S.Ct. 606, 439 U.S. 1000, 58 L.Ed.2d 674; FTC v. Minneapolis-Honeywell Regulator Co., 1952, 73 S.Ct. 245, 344 U.S. 206, 97 L.Ed. 245; Parker v. Illinois, 1948, 68 S.Ct. 708, 333 U.S. 571, 92 L.Ed. 886; Toledo Scale Co. v. Computing Scale Co., 1923, 43 S.Ct. 458, 261 U.S. 399, 67 L.Ed. 719.

6. Teague v. Regional Commr. of Customs, 1969, 89 S.Ct. 1457, 1460–1463, 394 U.S. 977, 981, 984, 22 L.Ed.2d 756 (dissenting opinion).

7. Sanabria v. U. S., 1978, 98 S.Ct. 2170, 2177 n. 12, 437 U.S. 54, 62 n. 12, 57 L.Ed.2d 43; Schacht v. U. S., 1970, 90 S.Ct. 1555, 1559–1560, 398 U.S. 58, 63–65, 26 L.Ed.2d 44.

8. See 28 U.S.C.A. § 2101(d); Stone v. Powell, 1976, 96 S.Ct. 3037, 3070, 428 U.S. 465, 482, 49 L.Ed.2d 1067, on remand C.A.9th, 539 F.2d 693, rehearing denied 97 S.Ct. 197, 429 U.S. 874, 50 L.Ed.2d 158 (Brennan, J., dissenting); Stern & Gressman, note 1 above, at pp. 389–395.

9. See Boskey & Gressman, note 1 above.

The text of the 1980 Rules appears at 85 F.R.D. 435, but note that Rule 28.1 was amended later in 1980. See Boskey & Gressman, The Supreme Court's 1980 Rules—The First Addendum, 1980, 87 F.R.D. 513.

10. Rule 19.3, 1980 Sup.Ct.Rules. The procedure for seeking a stay of the decision below pending review in the Supreme Court is set out in Rule 44, 1980 Sup.Ct.Rules.

11. Rule 12, 1980 Sup.Ct.Rules.

12. U. S. v. Cotton, 1970, 90 S.Ct. 816, 397 U.S. 45, 25 L.Ed.2d 43; Stein v. Luken, 1970, 90 S.Ct. 756, 396 U.S. 555, 24 L.Ed.2d 747.

13. Johnson v. Florida, 1968, 88 S.Ct. 1713, 1714 n. *, 391 U.S. 596, 598 n. *, 20 L.Ed.2d 838.

See also Communist Party of Indiana v. Whitcomb, 1974, 94 S.Ct. 656, 660 n. 4, 414 U.S. 441, 446 n. 4, 38 L.Ed.2d 635, rehearing denied 94 S.Ct. 1476, 415 U.S. 952, 39 L.Ed.2d 568; Stern & Gressman, note 1 above, at pp. 512–513.

certiorari is in the discretion of the Court. This is literally true—but seriously misleading. There is no doubt about the discretionary nature of certiorari. Rule 17.1 of the 1980 Rules states clearly that "a review on writ of certiorari is not a matter of right, but of judicial discretion, and will be granted only when there are special and important reasons therefor." The rule then lists six factors that, among others, indicate the kind of reasons that may induce the Court to grant certiorari.[14]

When certiorari is granted, it almost always means either that the petitioner will get the relief he seeks, or that he will at least be heard by the Supreme Court in support of such relief. It does not mean that he will always be heard. Despite trenchant criticism,[15] the Court in a number of cases summarily reverses the decision below on the basis of the petition for certiorari and brief in opposition thereto, without hearing oral argument.[16] Though occasionally the Court will grant certiorari and affirm summarily,[17] this is less common.

Even of those cases that come to the Court by appeal, oral argument is heard in only a small fraction.[18] The other cases brought to

---

14. 16 Wright, Miller & Cooper, Jurisdiction § 4004.

Unfortunately there are no current statistics that distinguish between cases coming on certiorari and by appeal. The last available figures show that in the decade from 1958 to 1968, certiorari was granted in 13.4% of the cases by petitions paying docket fees and 4.5% of those by indigent petitioners. The percentage of certiorari petitions that are granted has steadily declined. In the 1971 Term the Court granted 8.9% of the paid petitions and 3.3% of those from indigents. Report of the Study Group on the Caseload of the Supreme Court, 1972, 57 F.R.D. 573, 615.

In the 1980 Term the Court granted review in 10.6% of the paid cases and 1.4% of the indigent cases, but this includes both certiorari and appeal. The Supreme Court—1980 Term, 1981, 95 Harv.L.Rev. 17, 342.

15. See Brown, Process of Law, 1958, 72 Harv.L.Rev. 77; Note, Supreme Court Per Curiam Practice: A Critique, 1956, 69 Harv.L.Rev. 707; The Supreme Court, 1960 Term, 1961, 75 Harv.L.Rev. 40, 92–99.

The practice has frequently been criticized from within the Court. See, e.g., the dissent of Justice Blackmun, in which Justices Brennan and Marshall joined, in U. S. v. Hollywood Motor Car Co., Inc., 1982, 102 S.Ct. 3081, 3086, ___ U.S. ___, ___, 73 L.Ed.2d 754: "The Court, it seems to me, has shown a dis-

turbing tendency of late to dispose of difficult cases by summary per curiam reversals. I must assume that this tendency is prompted, at least in part, by the growing pressures of the Court's calendar and an ill-conceived conviction that we must stay ahead of the increasing workload whatever the costs may be. I regret this pattern, for I think it demeans the Court and its work and surely tends to lessen the quality of its legal product."

But see Wright, Miller & Cooper, Jurisdiction § 4004, pp. 525–526.

16. E.g., U. S. v. Hollywood Motor Car Co., Inc., 1982, 102 S.Ct. 3081, ___ U.S. ___, 73 L.Ed.2d 754; Stone v. Graham, 1980, 101 S.Ct. 192, 449 U.S. 39, 66 L.Ed.2d 199; Idaho Dept. of Employment v. Smith, 1977, 98 S.Ct. 327, 434 U.S. 100, 54 L.Ed.2d 324; Day and Zimmerman, Inc. v. Challoner, 1975, 96 S.Ct. 167, 423 U.S. 3, 46 L.Ed.2d 3.

17. E.g., Kaufer v. U. S., 1969, 89 S.Ct. 1223, 394 U.S. 458, 22 L.Ed.2d 414; Taglianetti v. U. S., 1969, 89 S.Ct. 1099, 394 U.S. 316, 22 L.Ed.2d 302; Fuller v. Alaska, 1968, 89 S.Ct. 61, 393 U.S. 80, 21 L.Ed.2d 212.

18. In the 1971 Term the figure was 18%. Report of the Study Group on the Caseload of the Supreme Court 1972, 57 F.R.D. 573, 622. This figure seems to have been fairly steady for at least the next five years. See Stern & Gressman, note 1 above, at p. 318.

the Court by appeal are disposed of summarily. Some appeals will not be heard because of procedural defects in taking the appeal, or because the case is not one in which appeal will lie, but in most cases the Court summarily affirms, or dismisses the appeal for want of a substantial federal question. Thus while such dispositions represent decisions on the merits, they are of scant comfort to the appellant who has obtained no relief.

Six justices constitute a quorum of the Court.[19] The decision to grant or deny certiorari, or to hear or make summary disposition of an appeal, is made by the whole Court. The Court does not function by committees, or by dividing applications for review among the justices. Each justice studies the application individually and casts his vote at conference on whether to hear the case.[20] Under the well-settled "rule of four", certiorari is granted whenever four justices vote for a grant, and the Court will then hear the case even though five justices consider the case not worthy of the attention of the Supreme Court.[21] A similar practice applies on appeals. The case will be heard, rather than summarily disposed of, if four justices so vote.[22] Plainly it is important that the petition for certiorari, or the jurisdictional statement, be carefully drafted in order to attract the interest of at least four members of the Court.[23]

Denial of certiorari, as has frequently been explained, imports nothing as to the merits of the case. All it means is that, for whatever reason, there were not four members of the Court who wished to hear the case.[24] Summary disposition of an appeal, however, either

19. 28 U.S.C.A. § 1. Disposition of a case in which a quorum of qualified justices cannot be mustered is governed by 28 U.S.C.A. § 2109. Ordinarily in this situation the judgment below is affirmed with the same effect as an affirmance by an equally divided court. Sloan v. Nixon, 1974, 95 S.Ct. 218, 419 U.S. 958, 42 L.Ed.2d 174. If the case has come to the Court on direct appeal from a district court, the case may be remitted to the court of appeals for the circuit including the district in which the case arose. See § 105 above at notes 36–37.

20. See Furness, Withy & Co. v. Yang-Tsze Ins. Assn., 1917, 37 S.Ct. 141, 142, 242 U.S. 430, 434, 61 L.Ed. 409; Brennan, State Court Decisions and the Supreme Court, 1960, 21 Pa.B.A.Q. 393, 400–406; Stern & Gressman, note 1 above, §§ 5.1, 5.2.

21. Rogers v. Missouri Pac. R. Co., 1957, 77 S.Ct. 443, 352 U.S. 500, 1 L.Ed.2d 493. See Leiman, The Rule of Four, 1957, 57 Col.L.Rev. 975; Note, 1957, 105 U.Pa.L.Rev. 1084. There have been cases that the Court has re-

fused to hear over three dissents though only seven justices participated. See 16 Wright, Miller & Cooper, Jurisdiction § 4004, pp. 512–516.

22. Ohio ex rel. Eaton v. Price, 1959, 79 S.Ct. 978, 360 U.S. 246, 3 L.Ed.2d 1200 (opinion of Brennan, J.).

23. Despite its title, even experienced practitioners will benefit from the excellent article, Prettyman, Petitioning the United States Supreme Court—A Primer for Hopeful Neophytes, 1965, 51 Va.L.Rev. 582. See also the equally helpful article, Prettyman, Opposing Certiorari in the United State Supreme Court, 1975, 61 Va.L.Rev. 197.

24. Hughes Tool Co. v. Trans World Airlines, 1973, 93 S.Ct. 647, 650 n. 1, 409 U.S. 363, 365 n. 1, 34 L.Ed.2d 577; Brown v. Allen, 1953, 73 S.Ct. 397, 437–441, 344 U.S. 443, 489–497, 97 L.Ed. 469; Maryland v. Baltimore Radio Show, 1950, 70 S.Ct. 252, 338 U.S. 912, 94 L.Ed. 562 (opinion of Frankfurter, J.); Linzer, The Meaning of Certiorari Denials, 1979, 79 Col.L.Rev. 1227.

by affirmance or by dismissal for want of a substantial federal question, is a disposition on the merits.[25]   An affirmance by an equally divided Court leaves the judgment below in effect but it is not of any precedential value.[26]

In cases coming from state courts, whether by appeal or by certiorari, review in the Supreme Court is limited, as has been seen, to the properly presented federal questions.[27]   This is true also of appeals to the Supreme Court from a court of appeals.[28]   On direct appeals from district courts, and on certiorari from a court of appeals, no such limitations apply.   The writ brings the whole case before the Supreme Court [29] and it may consider all issues in the case that have been properly raised below.[30]   However, though the Court has on occasion departed from the rule,[31] on certiorari, whether to a federal or state

---

25. As such it is binding on lower courts, Hicks v. Miranda, 1975, 95 S.Ct. 2281, 2289, 422 U.S. 332, 344–345, 45 L.Ed.2d 223, although for the Supreme Court itself "summary actions do not have the same authority" as decisions rendered after plenary consideration. Metromedia, Inc. v. City of San Diego, 1981, 101 S.Ct. 2882, 2888, 453 U.S. 490, 500, 69 L.Ed.2d 800.   See Note, The Precedential Effect of Summary Affirmances and Dismissals for Want of a Substantial Federal Question, 1978, 64 Va.L.Rev. 117; Note, The Precedential Weight of a Dismissal by the Supreme Court for Want of a Substantial Federal Question: Some Implications of Hicks v. Miranda, 1976, 76 Col.L.Rev. 508.   The practical difficulties for the lower courts in giving binding effect to summary dispositions are apparent from Mandel v. Bradley, 1977, 97 S.Ct. 2238, 432 U.S. 173, 53 L.Ed.2d 199, on remand D.C.Md. 1978, 449 F.Supp. 983.

26. Neil v. Biggers, 1972, 93 S.Ct. 375, 378–379, 409 U.S. 188, 190–192, 34 L.Ed.2d 401.   Thus it is not an actual adjudication that would bar habeas corpus under 28 U.S.C.A. § 2244(c). Habeas corpus is barred on issues on which the Supreme Court has dismissed an appeal for want of a substantial federal question but not on issues on which certiorari has been denied.   Howell v. Jones, C.A.5th, 1975, 516 F.2d 53.

If the Court is able to reach a decision, but no majority can agree on the reason, it is difficult for lower courts to know how to regard the decision as precedent.   See Note, The Precedential Value of Supreme Court Plurality Decisions, 1980, 80 Col.L.Rev. 756.

27. See § 107 above.

If the Court notes probable jurisdiction without making any restriction in a case coming by appeal from a state court, this is understood as a grant of certiorari on any non-appealable federal questions that are properly presented in the case.   Gomez v. Perez, 1973, 93 S.Ct. 872, 874 n. 2, 409 U.S. 535, 537 n. 2, 35 L.Ed.2d 56.

28. 28 U.S.C.A. § 1254(2).   See § 106 above.

29. Lutcher & Moore Lumber Co. v. Knight, 1910, 30 S.Ct. 505, 217 U.S. 257, 54 L.Ed. 757.

30. FTC v. Travelers Health Assn., 1960, 80 S.Ct. 717, 362 U.S. 293, 4 L.Ed.2d 724; Marconi Wireless Tel. Co. of America v. Simon, 1918, 38 S.Ct. 275, 277, 246 U.S. 46, 57, 62 L.Ed. 568.

Writ dismissed where question was not raised in state court.   Cardinale v. Louisiana, 1969, 89 S.Ct. 1162, 394 U.S. 437, 22 L.Ed.2d 398.

31. E.g., Vachon v. New Hampshire, 1974, 94 S.Ct. 664, 414 U.S. 478, 38 L.Ed.2d 666; Blonder-Tongue Laboratories, Inc. v. University of Illinois Foundation, 1971, 91 S.Ct. 1434, 1438 n. 6, 402 U.S. 313, 320 n. 6, 28 L.Ed.2d 788; Terminiello v. City of Chicago, 1949, 69 S.Ct. 894, 337 U.S. 1, 93 L.Ed. 1131, noted 1950, 59 Yale L.J. 971. The Court has more freedom in going beyond the questions presented in the writ where review is of a federal court decision.   See Piper Aircraft Co. v. Reyno, 1981, 102 S.Ct. 252, 261 n. 12, __ U.S. __, __ n. 12, 70 L.Ed.2d 419; McGoldrick v. Compagnie Generale Transatlantique, 1940, 60 S.Ct. 670, 672–673, 309 U.S. 430, 434, 84 L.Ed. 849.   A famous example is Erie R. Co. v. Tompkins, 1938, 58 S.Ct. 817, 304

court, the Court will normally consider only those issues presented in the petition [32] and it may limit review still further by granting certiorari only as to some of the questions set out in the petition.[33]

The Supreme Court does not ordinarily sit to decide questions of fact. If the facts have been found by a jury, the Court is precluded from reexamination of them by the Seventh Amendment.[34] Even where there is no such constitutional bar, the Court usually should not decide fact questions for its special competence is in questions of law. Accordingly the Court follows rules of self-limitation with regard to questions of fact. In civil cases coming from a court of appeals, the so-called "two court rule" applies, and the Court will not review findings of fact concurred in by two courts below in the absence of a very obvious and exceptional showing of error.[35] On review of decisions of state courts, the stated rule is that "all those matters which are usually termed issues of fact are for conclusive determination by the State courts and are not open for reconsideration by this Court. Observance of this restriction in our review of State courts calls for the utmost scruple."[36] Perhaps this is so, but only by an ingenious redefinition of what constitutes a question of fact.[37] Only a year before the statement just quoted a unanimous Court had said: "The duty of this Court to make its own independent

U.S. 64, 82 L.Ed. 1188, 114 A.L.R. 1487. See § 55 n. 4 above.

32. Rule 21.1(a), 1980 Sup.Ct.Rules; General Talking Pictures Corp. v. Western Elec. Co., 1938, 58 S.Ct. 849, 304 U.S. 175, 82 L.Ed. 1273; Irvine v. California, 1954, 74 S.Ct. 381, 347 U.S. 128, 129–130, 98 L.Ed. 561.

The rules on when the winning party below must cross-petition or cross-appeal are the same as apply to appeals to the courts of appeals. See § 104 above at notes 31–32.

33. E.g., Dennis v. U. S., 1951, 71 S.Ct. 857, 871, 341 U.S. 494, 516, 95 L.Ed. 1137; Beck v. Washington, 1962, 82 S.Ct. 955, 962, 369 U.S. 541, 554, 8 L.Ed.2d 98. See Bice, The Limited Grant of Certiorari and the Justification of Judicial Review, 1975 Wis.L. Rev. 343; 16 Wright, Miller & Cooper, Jurisdiction § 4004, pp. 516–518.

34. Chicago, B. & Q. R. Co. v. Chicago, 1897, 17 S.Ct. 581, 166 U.S. 226, 41 L.Ed. 979. But it is not barred from determining whether there were sufficient facts to require submission to the jury. The Supreme Court's willingness to accept cases of this sort, particularly arising under the Federal Employers' Liability Act and the Jones Act, was the subject of debate within and without the Court. See e.g., Wilkerson v. McCarthy, 1949, 69 S.Ct. 413, 336 U.S.

53, 93 L.Ed. 497; Note, Supreme Court Certiorari Policy in Cases Arising Under the FELA, 1956, 69 Harv.L.Rev. 1441. Compare Hart, The Time Chart of the Justices, 1959, 73 Harv.L.Rev. 84, with Arnold, Professor Hart's Theology, 1960, 73 Harv.L.Rev. 1298.

35. Graver Tank & Mfg. Co. v. Linde Air Products Co., 1949, 69 S.Ct. 535, 538, 336 U.S. 271, 275, 93 L.Ed. 672; Pick Mfg. Co. v. General Motors Corp., 1936, 57 S.Ct. 1, 299 U.S. 3, 81 L.Ed. 4. But cf. Baumgartner v. U. S., 1944, 64 S.Ct. 1240, 322 U.S. 665, 88 L.Ed. 1525.

The Court has indicated that the "two court" rule does not apply in habeas corpus cases where the dispute between the parties is not so much over the elemental facts as over the constitutional significance to be attached to them. Neil v. Biggers, 1972, 93 S.Ct. 375, 379 n. 3, 409 U.S. 188, 193 n. 3, 34 L.Ed.2d 401.

36. Watts v. Indiana, 1949, 69 S.Ct. 1347, 1348, 338 U.S. 49, 50, 93 L.Ed. 1801; Wolfe v. North Carolina, 1960, 80 S.Ct. 1482, 1492, 364 U.S. 177, 196, 4 L.Ed.2d 1650.

37. Such a redefinition is attempted in Comment, Supreme Court Review of State Findings of Fact in Fourteenth Amendment Cases, 1962, 14 Stan.L. Rev. 328.

examination of the record when federal constitutional deprivations are alleged is clear, resting, as it does, on our solemn responsibility for maintaining the Constitution inviolate."[38] In making such an independent examination the Court recognizes that it is reviewing the facts. It has said that "this Court will review the finding of facts by a State court where a Federal right has been denied as the result of a finding shown by the record to be without evidence to support it; or where a conclusion of law as to a Federal right and a finding of fact are so intermingled as to make it necessary, in order to pass upon the Federal question, to analyze the facts."[39] Since cases do not come to the Supreme Court from the state courts unless they involve some claim of a federal right, the exceptions seem quite broad enough to swallow up the announced rule against review of state court fact determinations.

When the Supreme Court has disposed of a case coming to it from a federal court, it ordinarily reverses with directions to enter a particular judgment or to follow a particular course of action. Occasionally a lower federal court may prove recalcitrant, but the Court can issue a writ of mandamus to compel the action that it has previously held proper.[40] It is more likely to be a state court that refuses to comply with the Supreme Court's judgment.[41] The problem of evasion of Supreme Court mandates by state courts is as old as Martin v. Hunter's Lessee [42] and as current as NAACP v. Alabama.[43] In cases

---

38. Napue v. Illinois, 1959, 79 S.Ct. 1173, 1178, 360 U.S. 264, 271, 3 L.Ed.2d 1217.

39. Fiske v. Kansas, 1927, 47 S.Ct. 655, 656, 274 U.S. 380, 385–386, 71 L.Ed. 1108. See also Norris v. Alabama, 1935, 55 S.Ct. 579, 580, 294 U.S. 587, 590, 79 L.Ed. 1074; Niemotko v. Maryland, 1951, 71 S.Ct. 325, 327, 340 U.S. 268, 271, 95 L.Ed. 267; Kern-Limerick, Inc. v. Scurlock, 1954, 74 S.Ct. 403, 410, 347 U.S. 110, 121, 98 L.Ed. 546; Vachon v. New Hampshire, 1974, 94 S.Ct. 664, 414 U.S. 478, 38 L.Ed.2d 666.

See 16 Wright, Miller & Cooper, Jurisdiction § 4033.

In Giles v. Maryland, 1967, 87 S.Ct. 793, 797, 386 U.S. 66, 74, 17 L.Ed.2d 737 (opinion of Brennan, J.), remand was ordered on the basis of facts not part of the record that first were disclosed in the Supreme Court.

40. U. S. v. Haley, 1962, 83 S.Ct. 11, 371 U.S. 18, 9 L.Ed.2d 1. As is customary in such matters, the Court followed the nicety of holding that the party was entitled to mandamus but not actually issuing a formal writ on the assumption that the district court would now do what the Court thought should be done.

41. Beatty, State Court Evasion of United States Supreme Court Mandates during the Last Decade of the Warren Court, 1972, 6 Valp.L.Rev. 260; Schneider, State Court Evasion of United States Supreme Court Mandates: A Reconsideration of the Evidence, 1973, 7 Valp.L.Rev. 191; Note, Remand to State Courts and its Effect on the Dual-Sovereign System, 1962, 50 Geo.L.J. 819; Note, Evasion of Supreme Court Mandates in Cases Remanded to State Courts Since 1941, 1954, 67 Harv.L. Rev. 1251; Note, State Court Evasion of United States Supreme Court Mandates, 1947, 56 Yale L.J. 574.

42. 1816, 1 Wheat. 304, 4 L.Ed. 97.

43. 1959, 79 S.Ct. 1001, 360 U.S. 240, 3 L.Ed.2d 1205. For a later stage in the same proceeding, in which federal habeas corpus was used to force compliance with the 1958 and 1959 mandates, see NAACP v. Gallion, 1961, 82 S.Ct. 4, 368 U.S. 16, 7 L.Ed.2d 85. Even this was not the end. The Supreme Court was compelled to act again, in NAACP v. Alabama ex rel. Flowers, 1964, 84 S.Ct. 1302, 377 U.S. 288, 12 L.Ed.2d 325, before the state court finally complied. 1964, 167 So.2d 171, 277 Ala. 89.

coming from state courts the Supreme Court normally does not issue a mandate calling for specific action, but remands for proceedings not inconsistent with its opinion. The state court is deliberately left free to pass on any state questions that may still be open in the case.[44] A litigant, however, may disagree as to whether the subsequent disposition of the case by the state court is in fact consistent with the Supreme Court's opinion. In such a case the Supreme Court can review, by appeal or by certiorari as is appropriate, the second judgment of the state court and reverse again. This was the course followed in both Martin v. Hunter's Lessee and NAACP v. Alabama.[45] If the state court should still refuse to conform, the Court has statutory power to direct the entry of such appropriate judgment decree, or order, or require such further proceedings to be had as may be just under the circumstances.[46] It may send its mandate directly to the state trial court,[47] or issue its own execution.[48] It would even seem that the judges of the state court might be punished for contempt for refusal to obey a lawful order of the Supreme Court,[49] but fortunately no case has arisen that has required such drastic action.[50]

The Supreme Court, like all other courts established by Congress, is authorized to issue "all writs necessary or appropriate in aid of their respective jurisdictions and agreeable to the usages and principles of law."[51] The Court cannot be given original jurisdiction to issue such writs except in cases within its original jurisdiction as defined in the Constitution.[52] But where a case is within the appellate jurisdiction of the Supreme Court, it may issue the common law writs of mandamus, prohibition, and certiorari in aid of the appellate jurisdiction that might otherwise be defeated by the unauthorized action of the court below.[53] The question is not one of power to issue the writ but of discretion as to when it should issue,[54] and the considera-

44. E.g., Stanton v. Stanton, 1975, 95 S.Ct. 1373, 1379, 421 U.S. 7, 17, 43 L.Ed.2d 688.

45. This course is not available where the state court has simply failed to enter a final judgment in response to the Supreme Court's mandate. Lavender v. Kurn, 1946, 67 S.Ct. 111, 329 U.S. 762, 91 L.Ed. 656. In the same case leave to file a petition for a writ of mandamus was denied. Lavender v. Clark, 1946, 67 S.Ct. 108, 329 U.S. 674, 91 L.Ed. 596.

46. 28 U.S.C.A. § 2106; e.g., Poindexter v. Greenhow, 1885, 5 S.Ct. 903, 114 U.S. 270, 29 L.Ed. 185. See NAACP v. Alabama ex rel. Flowers, 1964, 84 S.Ct. 1302, 1315, 377 U.S. 288, 310, 12 L.Ed. 2d 325.

47. E.g., Williams v. Bruffy, 1880, 102 U.S. 248, 26 L.Ed. 135.

48. E.g., Tyler v. Magwire, 1873, 17 Wall. 253, 21 L.Ed. 576.

49. 18 U.S.C.A. § 401(3).

50. Cf. U. S. v. Shipp, 1909, 29 S.Ct. 637, 214 U.S. 386, 53 L.Ed. 1041; id., 1909, 30 S.Ct. 397, 215 U.S. 580, 54 L.Ed. 337 (sheriff imprisoned for contempt for complicity in lynching of a prisoner after Supreme Court had granted a stay of execution).

51. 28 U.S.C.A. § 1651(a). See 16 Wright, Miller & Cooper, Jurisdiction § 4005.

52. Marbury v. Madison, 1803, 1 Cranch 137, 2 L.Ed. 60.

53. McClellan v. Carland, 1910, 30 S.Ct. 501, 503, 217 U.S. 268, 280, 54 L.Ed. 782.

54. Ex parte Republic of Peru, 1943, 63 S.Ct. 793, 318 U.S. 578, 87 L.Ed. 1014; Ex parte Fahey, 1947, 67 S.Ct. 1558, 332 U.S. 258, 91 L.Ed. 2041; Wolfson, Extraordinary Writs in the Supreme

tions that govern the exercise of this discretion are similar to those that control when a court of appeals is asked to issue an extraordinary writ to a district court.[55]

It was long unclear whether the Court may issue these writs to a state court, but recent cases seem to settle that controversy by holding that the writ can issue, at least where the case has actually been within the jurisdiction of the Supreme Court.[56] There is no doubt that, to protect its appellate jurisdiction, the Supreme Court can issue a writ, even before a case has come to it, to a court of appeals, or to a district court in a case that is reviewable directly in the Supreme Court,[57] although there may be sharp differences of view as to the propriety of exercise of this power in a particular case.[58] Further it is agreed that in a case that a court of appeals has refused to review, and that has therefore never been "in" the court of appeals so as to permit the Supreme Court to grant a statutory writ of certiorari, the Court may issue a common-law writ of certiorari on which it can review the action of the court of appeals in refusing to allow appeal, and can even determine the merits of the case.[59] Finally, the Court has held that it has power to issue one of the extraordinary writs to a district court, in a case where appeal would be to the court of appeals, and that while ordinarily application for such a writ should be made first to the court of appeals, it can be made directly to the Supreme Court in a case of public importance and exceptional character.[60]

The Supreme Court, or any justice thereof, also has power to issue a writ of habeas corpus.[61] The statute, however, authorizes the application to be transferred to the district court having jurisdiction to en-

Court Since Ex parte Peru, 1951, 51 Col.L.Rev. 997.

See Chandler v. Judicial Council of the Tenth Circuit, 1970, 90 S.Ct. 1648, 1654–1656, 398 U.S. 74, 86–89, 26 L.Ed. 2d 100.

55. See § 102 above.

56. Deen v. Hickman, 1958, 79 S.Ct. 1, 358 U.S. 57, 3 L.Ed.2d 28; Bucolo v. Adkins, 1976, 96 S.Ct. 1086, 424 U.S. 641, 47 L.Ed.2d 301.

57. Ex parte Northern Pac. Ry., 1929, 50 S.Ct. 70, 280 U.S. 142, 74 L.Ed. 233; United States Alkali Export Assn. v. U. S., 1945, 65 S.Ct. 1120, 325 U.S. 196, 89 L.Ed. 1554.

58. E.g., De Beers Consol. Mines v. U. S., 1945, 65 S.Ct. 1130, 325 U.S. 212, 89 L.Ed. 1566.

59. House v. Mayo, 1945, 65 S.Ct. 517, 324 U.S. 42, 89 L.Ed. 739; In re 620 Church Street Bldg. Corp., 1936, 57 S.Ct. 88, 299 U.S. 24, 81 L.Ed. 16.

There is lively controversy within the Court, however, on whether the com-

mon-law writ of certiorari remains available in a case in which a habeas corpus petitioner has been denied a certificate of probable cause, so that the case was never "in" the court of appeals and could not be reviewed by the statutory writ of certiorari. Compare the concurring and dissenting opinions in Davis v. Jacobs, 1981, 102 S.Ct. 417, 454 U.S. 911, 70 L.Ed.2d 226. See 17 Wright, Miller & Cooper, Jurisdiction § 4036 n. 13.

60. Ex parte Republic of Peru, 1943, 63 S.Ct. 793, 318 U.S. 578, 87 L.Ed. 1014. See Wolfson, note 54 above.

61. 28 U.S.C.A. § 2241. See Oaks, The "Original" Writ of Habeas Corpus in the Supreme Court, 1962 Sup.Ct.Rev. 153. See also Locks v. Commanding General, Sixth Army, 1968, 89 S.Ct. 31, 21 L.Ed.2d 78 (opinion of Circuit Justice Douglas), raising question about the power of an individual justice to issue the writ.

tertain it, and the practice of the Court is not to exercise its power to grant habeas corpus, save in exceptional circumstances,[62] where an adequate remedy may be had in a lower federal court or if there are state remedies that have not been exhausted.[63]

An important, but little-noticed, part of practice in the Supreme Court involves applications to an individual justice for a stay or for other forms of interim action. An individual justice has no power to dispose of cases on the merits,[64] but may make a variety of interim orders, sometimes of literally life-and-death significance.[65]

62. Ex parte Hudgings, 1919, 39 S.Ct. 337, 249 U.S. 378, 63 L.Ed. 656; cf. Hirota v. MacArthur, 1948, 69 S.Ct. 157, 335 U.S. 876, 93 L.Ed. 418.

63. Ex parte Abernathy, 1943, 64 S.Ct. 13, 320 U.S. 219, 88 L.Ed. 3. See Rule 27.3, 1980 Sup.Ct.Rules.

64. Locks v. Commanding General, Sixth Army, 1968, 89 S.Ct. 31, 32, 21 L.Ed.2d 78 (opinion of Circuit Justice Douglas).

65. Stern & Gressman, note 1 above, c. 17; Note, The Powers of the Supreme Court Justice Acting in an Individual Capacity, 1964, 112 U.Pa.L.Rev. 981; Boner, Index to Chambers Opinions of Supreme Court Justices, 1972, 65 L.Lib.J. 213; 16 Wright, Miller & Cooper, Jurisdiction § 4005 n. 55.

CHAPTER 13

THE ORIGINAL JURISDICTION OF
THE SUPREME COURT

Analysis

§ 109.   Cases in Which a State Is a Party [1]

Article III, § 2 of the Constitution defines the judicial power of the United States. It then provides: "In all Cases Affecting Ambassadors, other public Ministers and Consuls, and those in which a State shall be Party, the supreme court shall have original Jurisdiction." It has always been understood that this provision is self-executing, and that it is itself a grant of jurisdiction to the Supreme Court [2] that Congress can neither restrict nor enlarge.[3] In fact ever since 1789 statutes have purported to describe the original jurisdiction of the Supreme Court. The present statute [4] does not list all the cases to which the constitutional grant of jurisdiction extends, but in the unlikely event that a case were to be brought that is within the constitu-

---

[§ 109]

1.   17 Wright, Miller & Cooper, Jurisdiction §§ 4042–4049, 4051–4054; Wagner, Original Jurisdiction of National Supreme Courts, 1959, 33 St. John's L.Rev. 217; Barnes, Suits Between States in the Supreme Court, 1954, 7 Vand.L.Rev. 494; Wagner, The Original and Exclusive Jurisdiction of the United States Supreme Court, 1952, 2 St. Louis U.L.J. 111; Note, Exclusive Original Jurisdiction of the United States Supreme Court: Does It Still Exist?, 1982 B.Y.U.L.Rev. 727; Note, The Original Jurisdiction of the United States Supreme Court, 1959, 11 Stan.L. Rev. 665.

Cases within the original jurisdiction are not a statistically significant part of the work of the Court. In the ten years from 1960–1969 the Court disposed of 33 cases on its original docket, and this included disbarments. Ann. Rep. of the Director of the Administrative Office of the U. S. Courts, 1970, p. 204. After that year the Administrative Office discontinued publishing statistics on the work of the Supreme Court, but in the 1980 Term the Court

disposed of seven cases brought within its original jurisdiction, only one with full opinion. The Supreme Court, 1980 Term, 1981, 89 Harv.L.Rev. 17, 342–343.

2.   Chisholm v. Georgia, 1793, 2 Dall. 419, 1 L.Ed. 440; Florida v. Georgia, 1854, 17 How. 478, 492, 15 L.Ed. 181; Kentucky v. Dennison, 1860, 24 How. 66, 16 L.Ed. 717.

3.   Marbury v. Madison, 1803, 1 Cranch 137, 2 L.Ed. 60; Wisconsin v. Pelican Ins. Co., 1888, 8 S.Ct. 1370, 1379, 127 U.S. 265, 300, 32 L.Ed. 239; California v. Southern Pac. R. Co., 1895, 15 S.Ct. 591, 604, 157 U.S. 229, 261, 39 L.Ed. 683.

In California v. Arizona, 1979, 99 S.Ct. 919, 924, 440 U.S. 59, 66, 59 L.Ed.2d 144, the Court thought it "extremely doubtful" that Congress could limit original jurisdiction by waiving the sovereign's immunity to suit but limiting suit against it to district courts. It was able to avoid the question by finding that the statute was not intended to exclude Supreme Court jurisdiction.

4.   28 U.S.C.A. § 1251.

tional grant but not within the statute [5] it seems clear that the Court would have jurisdiction of the case.

Chief Justice Marshall thought that the jurisdiction of the Supreme Court was exclusive in cases within its original jurisdiction.[6] The statutes, from 1789 to the present, have proceeded on a different theory, and have distinguished between situations in which the Supreme Court is given exclusive jurisdiction and those in which its jurisdiction is concurrent with the lower federal courts. The validity of such a division is now settled.[7]

The provision for original jurisdiction does not extend the judicial power of the United States as defined in the preceding language of Article III, § 2. Instead the latter language merely distributes the judicial power as previously defined.[8] Thus the original jurisdiction of the Supreme Court does not reach to all cases to which a state is party, but only to cases within the judicial power to which a state is party. A suit by the United States against a state is within the judicial power, since it is a "Controversy to which the United States shall be a party," and it is within the original jurisdiction, since it is one "in which a state shall be Party." On this analysis it was held that such a suit can be brought in the Supreme Court.[9] A suit by a state against one of its own citizens is not ordinarily within the judicial power at all, and thus cannot be brought in the Supreme Court even though the state is a party.[10] It would seem that a suit by a state against one of its citizens that arises under the Constitution, laws, or treaties of the United States would be within the judicial power, and that the presence of the state as a party would permit invoking the original jurisdiction. The Supreme Court held to the contrary, however, without reasoned discussion and on the basis of earlier cases in which it did not appear that a federal question was present.[11]

Since the case must be within the judicial power of the United States, the usual tests of case or controversy, standing, political questions, and the like,[12] are applicable.[13] The Court has also held that its

5. As for example, a suit by a foreign government against a state to which the state has consented.

6. Marbury v. Madison, 1803, 1 Cranch 137, 174, 2 L.Ed. 60.

7. Bors v. Preston, 1884, 4 S.Ct. 407, 111 U.S. 252, 28 L.Ed. 419; Ames v. Kansas ex rel. Johnston, 1884, 4 S.Ct. 437, 111 U.S. 449, 28 L.Ed. 482; Plaquemines Tropical Fruit Co. v. Henderson, 1898, 18 S.Ct. 685, 170 U.S. 511, 42 L.Ed. 1126.

8. Pennsylvania v. Quicksilver Mining Co., 1870, 10 Wall. 553, 19 L.Ed. 998; Duhne v. New Jersey, 1920, 40 S.Ct. 154, 251 U.S. 311, 64 L.Ed. 280.

9. U. S. v. Texas, 1892, 12 S.Ct. 488, 143 U.S. 621, 36 L.Ed. 285. See 17 Wright, Miller & Cooper, Jurisdiction § 4048.

10. California v. Southern Pac. R. Co., 1895, 15 S.Ct. 591, 157 U.S. 229, 39 L.Ed. 683; Minnesota v. Northern Securities Co., 1902, 22 S.Ct. 308, 184 U.S. 199, 46 L.Ed. 499.

11. Texas v. ICC, 1922, 42 S.Ct. 261, 258 U.S. 158, 66 L.Ed. 531.

12. See §§ 12–15 above.

13. E.g., Mississippi v. Johnson, 1867, 71 U.S. 475, 4 Wall. 475, 18 L.Ed. 437; Georgia v. Stanton, 1868, 6 Wall. 50, 18 L.Ed. 721; Massachusetts v. Mellon, 1923, 43 S.Ct. 597, 262 U.S. 447, 67 L.Ed. 1078. See 17 Wright, Miller & Cooper, Jurisdiction § 4051.

original jurisdiction is limited to civil cases.[14]   It will not hear a case by which a state seeks to enforce a judgment for a penalty, even though the case is not criminal in the usual sense.[15]

Under the statute suits by one state against another are within the original and exlusive jurisdiction of the Supreme Court.[16]   Such suits are the most numerous class of suits heard by the Court in its original jurisdiction.[17]   The need for the Supreme Court as a tribunal for such suits is apparent.   The states of the union are not at liberty to wage war against each other.   Controversies between them, which when they were independent would have been resolved by diplomatic negotiation or by force, are now peacefully settled by a neutral court. No consent of the state is required.   It is deemed to have consented by accepting the Constitution, which grants jurisdiction of "Controversies between two or more States."[18]   This jurisdiction has been especially useful in resolving disputes as to boundaries [19] or water rights,[20] but it has been used also to enforce a financial obligation of one state to another,[21] or to provide a forum where two or more states are claiming a right to tax or escheat a fund that is insufficient to satisfy all the claims against it.[22]

The Supreme Court has original but not exclusive jurisdiction of actions by the United States against a state.[23]   Again consent of the

---

14. See Chisholm v. Georgia, 1793, 2 Dall. 419, 431–432, 1 L.Ed. 440; Cohens v. Virginia, 1821, 6 Wheat. 264, 399, 5 L.Ed. 257.

15. Wisconsin v. Pelican Ins. Co., 1888, 8 S.Ct. 1370, 127 U.S. 265, 32 L.Ed. 239.   But a suit on a judgment for taxes is not considered penal.   Milwaukee County v. M. E. White Co., 1935, 56 S.Ct. 229, 296 U.S. 268, 80 L.Ed. 220.

16. 28 U.S.C.A. § 1251(a)(1).   A political subdivision of a state is not the state for purposes of this statute.   Illinois v. City of Milwaukee, 1972, 92 S.Ct. 1385, 406 U.S. 91, 31 L.Ed.2d 712.

17. For a complete list of all such cases as of that time in which the Supreme Court had written an opinion, see Note, 1959, 11 Stan.L.Rev. 665, 708–718.

18. See New Jersey v. New York, 1831, 5 Pet. 284, 291, 8 L.Ed. 127.

19. E.g., Rhode Island v. Massachusetts, 1838, 12 Pet. 657, 9 L.Ed. 1233; Nebraska v. Iowa, 1972, 92 S.Ct. 1379, 406 U.S. 117, 31 L.Ed.2d 733; Ohio v. Kentucky, 1980, 100 S.Ct. 588, 444 U.S. 335, 62 L.Ed.2d 530, rehearing denied 100 S.Ct. 1307, 445 U.S. 939, 63 L.Ed. 2d 756.

20. E.g., Kansas v. Colorado, 1902, 22 S.Ct. 552, 185 U.S. 125, 46 L.Ed. 838; id., 1907, 27 S.Ct. 655, 206 U.S. 46, 51

L.Ed. 956; Idaho ex rel. Evans v. Oregon and Washington, 1980, 100 S.Ct. 616, 444 U.S. 380, 62 L.Ed.2d 564.

21. E.g., South Dakota v. North Carolina, 1904, 24 S.Ct. 269, 192 U.S. 286, 48 L.Ed. 448; Virginia v. West Virginia, 1907, 27 S.Ct. 732, 206 U.S. 290, 51 L.Ed. 1068.

22. Right to tax: Texas v. Florida, 1939, 59 S.Ct. 563, 306 U.S. 398, 83 L.Ed. 817; California v. Texas, 1982, 102 S.Ct. 2335, ___ U.S. ___, 72 L.Ed.2d 755.   But cf. Massachusetts v. Missouri, 1939, 60 S.Ct. 39, 308 U.S. 1, 84 L.Ed. 3.

Escheat: Texas v. New Jersey, 1965, 85 S.Ct. 626, 379 U.S. 674, 13 L.Ed.2d 596; see Western Union Tel. Co. v. Pennsylvania, 1961, 82 S.Ct. 199, 202–204, 368 U.S. 71, 77–80, 7 L.Ed.2d 139.

23. 28 U.S.C.A. § 1251(b)(2).   It is held that the jurisdiction can validly be conferred on a district court in Case v. Bowles, 1946, 66 S.Ct. 438, 441, 327 U.S. 92, 97, 90 L.Ed. 552.   In a suit by the United States against a state, citizens of the state may be joined as defendants.   U. S. v. West Virginia, 1935, 55 S.Ct. 789, 295 U.S. 463, 79 L.Ed. 1546; U. S. v. Wyoming, 1947, 67 S.Ct. 1319, 331 U.S. 440, 91 L.Ed. 1590.

state is not required.[24]   Here it is not so easy to find consent in the state's acceptance of the Constitution, since the literal words of the Constitution might seem to preclude such jurisdiction,[25] but the alternative is the unthinkable one that controversies between the United States and a state would have to be resolved by force. This is an argument, however, that has been allowed to run only one way. Suit by a state against the United States is not permitted,[26] except in those instances where the United States has consented to be sued.[27]

The Constitution purports to grant jurisdiction of controversies between a state and a foreign country. Such a suit could not be brought against the foreign country without its consent, which surely would not be given. It would seem however, that the foreign government could bring suit in the Supreme Court against a state, on the same principle that permits a state to be made a defendant where a sister state or the United States is plaintiff. This was the prediction of a distinguished authority, at a time when the question was unresolved.[28] The Court later held, however, that such a suit cannot be brought against a state where it has not consented to be sued.[29] Presumably such a suit could be brought where the state consented— indeed unless this is permissible, the constitutional grant of jurisdiction over such cases is meaningless—but the present statute makes no mention of such a suit.[30]

In a very early case it was held that the Supreme Court had original jurisdiction of a suit against a state by a citizen of another state.[31] The Eleventh Amendment was immediately adopted to bar such a result.[32] As the Amendment has been construed, it prohibits suit against a state by a citizen of another state, a citizen of the state

24. U. S. v. Texas, 1892, 12 S.Ct. 488, 143 U.S. 621, 36 L.Ed. 285; U. S. v. Louisiana, 1950, 70 S.Ct. 914, 915, 339 U.S. 699, 701–702, 94 L.Ed. 1216.

Nor is consent required if the suit is brought in a district court. U. S. v. Illinois, C.A.7th, 1971, 454 F.2d 297, certiorari denied 92 S.Ct. 1767, 406 U.S. 918, 32 L.Ed.2d 117; U. S. v. California, C.A.9th, 1964, 328 F.2d 729, certiorari denied 85 S.Ct. 34, 379 U.S. 817, 13 L.Ed.2d 29; Williams v. U. S., D.C.N.Y. 1967, 42 F.R.D. 609.

25. See Frankfurter, J., dissenting in Ex parte Republic of Peru, 1943, 63 S.Ct. 793, 804, 318 U.S. 578, 598, 87 L.Ed. 1014.

26. Oregon v. Hitchcock, 1906, 26 S.Ct. 568, 202 U.S. 60, 50 L.Ed. 935; Kansas v. U. S., 1907, 27 S.Ct. 388, 204 U.S. 331, 51 L.Ed. 510; Hawaii v. Gordon, 1963, 83 S.Ct. 1052, 373 U.S. 57, 10 L.Ed.2d 191.

27. Minnesota v. Hitchcock, 1902, 22 S.Ct. 650, 185 U.S. 373, 46 L.Ed. 954. See also Utah v. U. S., 1969, 89 S.Ct. 761, 394 U.S. 89, 22 L.Ed.2d 99; California v. Arizona, 99 S.Ct. 919, 440 U.S. 59, 59 L.Ed.2d 144.

28. Dobie, Federal Procedure, 1928, pp. 526–528.

29. Principality of Monaco v. Mississippi, 1934, 54 S.Ct. 745, 292 U.S. 313, 78 L.Ed. 1282. See Lenoir, Suit by a Foreign State Against the Union: Monaco v. Mississippi, 1934, 7 Miss.L.J. 134.

30. See 28 U.S.C.A. § 1251.

31. Chisholm v. Georgia, 1793, 2 Dall. 419, 1 L.Ed. 440.

32. Mathis, The Eleventh Amendment: Adoption and Interpretation, 1968, 2 Ga.L.Rev. 207; 13 Wright, Miller & Cooper, Jurisdiction § 3524; Jacobs, The Eleventh Amendment and Sovereign Immunity, 1972.

itself, or an alien,[33] except where the state has consented to suit.[34] It is a different matter where the state is plaintiff. The Supreme Court has original but not exclusive jurisdiction of all actions by a state against the citizens of another state or against aliens.[35] There is no jurisdiction if a citizen of another state is joined as defendant with a citizen of the plaintiff state, [36] presumably because the case is no longer "between a State and Citizens of another State" as the Constitution requires. As has already been pointed out, it is held, with doubtful logic and no discussion, that the same result applies where the case arises under the federal law and there is thus another basis of jurisdiction.[37] Since the jurisdiction of the Supreme Court is not exclusive if a state is suing a citizen of another state, the action can be brought in a district court, rather than the Supreme Court, if there is a statutory basis for jurisdiction in the district court.[38] This may induce the Supreme Court to refuse to permit filing of an original action, leaving the state to its remedy in the district court or in a state court, but there is no fixed rule on this point and the Court has entertained original actions in cases that could have been brought in a district court.[39]

In Ohio v. Wyandotte Chemicals Corp.,[40] the Supreme Court held that it had jurisdiction of a suit by a state against citizens of other states and another country for abatement of a nuisance allegedly caused by dumping mercury into streams that ultimately run into Lake Erie. In the exercise of its discretion, however, it refused to entertain the case, holding that the complex scientific issues presented by the case were inappropriate for the Supreme Court to consider

33. Ex parte Ayers, 1887, 8 S.Ct. 164, 123 U.S. 443, 31 L.Ed. 216; Hans v. Louisiana, 1890, 10 S.Ct. 504, 134 U.S. 1, 33 L.Ed. 842; Ex parte New York, 1921, 41 S.Ct. 588, 256 U.S. 490, 65 L.Ed. 1057; Employees of Dept. of Public Health & Welfare v. Department of Public Health & Welfare, 1973, 93 S.Ct. 1614, 411 U.S. 279, 36 L.Ed.2d 251.

34. See § 46 n. 6 above.

35. 28 U.S.C.A. § 1251(b)(3).

36. California v. Southern Pac. Co., 1895, 15 S.Ct. 591, 157 U.S. 229, 39 L.Ed. 683.

37. Texas v. ICC, 1922, 42 S.Ct. 261, 258 U.S. 158, 66 L.Ed. 531. Dean Dobie, who had apparently not noticed this case, thought that a different result would be reached in this situation. Dobie, Federal Procedure, 1928, p. 531.

38. 28 U.S.C.A. § 1251(b)(3) is not itself a grant of jurisdiction. Ohio v. Wyandotte Chemicals Corp., 1971, 91 S.Ct. 1005, 1009 n. 3, 401 U.S. 493, 498 n. 3, 28 L.Ed.2d 256. A state is not a citizen of a state within the grant of diversity

jurisdiction. Ibid. Suits to abate pollution of interstate waters had been held to be governed by federal common law and thus to come within federal question jurisdiction. Illinois v. City of Milwaukee, 1972, 92 S.Ct. 1385, 406 U.S. 91, 31 L.Ed.2d 712. It has been held, however, that an Act of Congress passed shortly after the decision just cited has preempted federal common law for this kind of case. City of Milwaukee v. Illinois and Michigan, 1981, 101 S.Ct. 1784, 451 U.S. 304, 68 L.Ed. 2d 114.

39. Georgia v. Pennsylvania R. Co., 1945, 65 S.Ct. 716, 324 U.S. 439, 89 L.Ed. 1051.

40. 1971, 91 S.Ct. 1005, 401 U.S. 493, 28 L.Ed.2d 256. See Woods & Reed, The Supreme Court and Interstate Environmental Quality; Some Notes on the Wyandotte Case, 1970, 12 Ariz.L.Rev. 691; Ficken, Wyandotte and Its Progeny, The Quest for Environmental Protection Through the Original Jurisdiction of the Supreme Court, 1974, 78 Dick.L.Rev. 429.

as an original matter. It said: "we may decline to entertain a complaint brought by a State against the citizens of another State or country only where we can say with assurance that (1) declination of jurisdiction would not disserve any of the principal policies underlying the Article III jurisdictional grant and (2) the reasons of practical wisdom that persuade us that this Court is an inappropriate forum are consistent with the proposition that our discretion is legitimated by its use to keep this aspect of the Court's functions attuned to its other responsibilities."[41] Since that decision the Court has exercised its discretion to deny leave to file not only in other actions brought by states against citizens of other states,[42] but also in actions between the United States and two states [43] and between two states.[44]

A state cannot sue unless it is the real party in interest. In one leading case New Hampshire attempted to avoid the limitations of the Eleventh Amendment by providing by statute that it would bring suit in its name for the benefit of its citizens who held bonds of another state. This was not permitted.[45] Nor can a state invoke the original jurisdiction to prosecute claims on behalf of particular citizens of the state even where the debtor is a citizen of another state and the Eleventh Amendment is no bar.[46] But where a state has been given bonds of another state absolutely, and is suing for its own benefit rather than as an assignee for collection, suit in the original jurisdiction will lie.[47] Similarly a state can sue to protect its own property interests.[48]

41. 91 S.Ct. at 1010, 401 U.S. at 499. See 17 Wright, Miller & Cooper, Jurisdiction § 4053.

42. Illinois v. City of Milwaukee, 1972, 92 S.Ct. 1385, 406 U.S. 91, 31 L.Ed.2d 712; Washington v. General Motors Corp., 1972, 92 S.Ct. 1396, 406 U.S. 109, 31 L.Ed.2d 727.

43. U. S. v. Nevada and California, 1973, 93 S.Ct. 2763, 412 U.S. 534, 37 L.Ed.2d 132; cf. California v. Nevada, 1980, 100 S.Ct. 2064, 447 U.S. 125, 65 L.Ed.2d 1.

44. Arizona v. New Mexico, 1976, 96 S.Ct. 1845, 425 U.S. 794, 48 L.Ed.2d 376; California v. West Virginia, 1981, 102 S.Ct. 561, 454 U.S. 1027, 70 L.Ed. 2d 470. Dissenting from denial of leave to file, Justice Stevens said that in Ohio v. Wyandotte Chemicals the Court had explained why it will decline to exercise its nonexclusive jurisdiction over cases in which only one of the parties is a state, but "that explanation is inapplicable to cases in which our jurisdiction is exclusive." 102 S.Ct. at 562, 454 U.S. at 1028.

The Court went to great lengths in Maryland v. Louisiana, 1981, 101 S.Ct. 2114,

451 U.S. 725, 68 L.Ed.2d 576, to explain why exercise of its exclusive original jurisdiction was "appropriate" in that case but was inappropriate in Arizona v. New Mexico, cited above.

See the Brigham Young Note, cited note 1 above.

45. New Hampshire v. Louisiana, 1883, 2 S.Ct. 176, 108 U.S. 76, 27 L.Ed. 656; cf. North Dakota v. Minnesota, 44 S.Ct. 138, 139, 263 U.S. 365, 374–376, 68 L.Ed. 342. See also Pennsylvania v. New Jersey, 1976, 96 S.Ct. 2333, 426 U.S. 660, 49 L.Ed.2d 124.

46. Oklahoma ex rel. Johnson v. Cook, 1938, 58 S.Ct. 954, 304 U.S. 387, 82 L.Ed. 1416, noted 1938, 25 Va.L.Rev. 236; cf. Oklahoma v. Atchison, T. & S. F. R. Co., 1911, 31 S.Ct. 434, 220 U.S. 277, 55 L.Ed. 465.

47. South Dakota v. North Carolina, 1904, 24 S.Ct. 269, 192 U.S. 286, 48 L.Ed. 448.

48. Pennsylvania v. Wheeling & B. Bridge Co., 1852, 13 How. 518, 559, 14 L.Ed. 249.

Under some circumstances a state has been permitted to sue as parens patriae to restrain conduct injurious to the health or welfare of the state's population as a whole.[49] Thus suit by Missouri to restrain Illinois from discharging the sewage of Chicago through a canal running into the Mississippi river was held to lie in the original jurisdiction.[50] Georgia was permitted to enjoin a private corporation in Tennessee from emitting noxious gases which drifted into Georgia.[51] Pennsylvania was allowed to sue West Virginia to enjoin it from distributing natural gas produced in that state in such a fashion as to diminish the supply available for Pennsylvania consumers.[52] In the most far-reaching case of this type, Georgia v. Pennsylvania R. Co.,[53] the state was permitted to file an action under the antitrust laws against 20 railroad companies that were alleged to have conspired to set rates that gave northern shippers an advantage over those in Georgia, and thus retarded the economic growth of that state.

There had been thought to be one clear limitation on the parens patriae doctrine. Although a state may in some circumstances be permitted to sue in this capacity to protect its citizens against harm threatened by another state or by private persons, it cannot represent them in this way in a challenge of federal action. The citizens of a state are also citizens of the United States, and it is the United States to which they must look as parens patriae where federal law is involved. This was the holding of the well-known case of Massachusetts v. Mellon,[54] in which the state was held not able to sue on behalf of its citizens to restrain the Secretary of the Treasury from carrying out an allegedly unconstitutional Act of Congress.

---

49. 17 Wright, Miller & Cooper, Jurisdiction § 4047; Note, note 1 above, at 671–678.

50. Missouri v. Illinois, 1901, 21 S.Ct. 331, 344, 180 U.S. 208, 241, 45 L.Ed. 497.

51. Georgia v. Tennessee Copper Co., 1907, 27 S.Ct. 618, 619, 206 U.S. 230, 237, 51 L.Ed. 1038.

52. Pennsylvania v. West Virginia, 1923, 43 S.Ct. 658, 663, 262 U.S. 553, 592, 67 L.Ed. 1117, 32 A.L.R. 300.

Pennsylvania v. West Virginia was relied upon to establish standing in Maryland v. Louisiana, 1981, 101 S.Ct. 2114, 451 U.S. 725, 68 L.Ed.2d 576. There eight states were allowed to sue to enjoin a tax imposed by Louisiana on natural gas. The incidence of the tax fell not on a small group of citizens but on a great many citizens, and there was no clear alternative remedy.

53. 1945, 65 S.Ct. 716, 722–723, 324 U.S. 439, 450–452, 89 L.Ed. 1051, noted

1945, 58 Harv.L.Rev. 741, 93 U.Pa.L. Rev. 442, 1946, 31 Iowa L.Rev. 283. The Court distinguished, with questionable success, Oklahoma v. Atchison, T. & S. F. R. Co., 1911, 31 S.Ct. 434, 220 U.S. 277, 55 L.Ed. 465, which had held that a state could not sue in the Supreme Court to enjoin carriers from charging unreasonable rates for transportation.

In Hawaii v. Standard Oil Co. of California, 1972, 92 S.Ct. 885, 405 U.S. 251, 31 L.Ed.2d 184, it was held that a claim by a state in a district court as parens patriae is not for an injury to its "business or property" as is required for a treble damage action under § 4 of the Clayton Act, 15 U.S.C.A. § 15. That result has since been changed by statute.

54. 1923, 43 S.Ct. 597, 262 U.S. 447, 67 L.Ed. 1078.

Doubt is cast on this proposition by the more recent case of South Carolina v. Katzenbach.[55] There a state was seeking to restrain the Attorney General from enforcing portions of the Voting Rights Act of 1965. The Court held that the state lacked standing to challenge the statute under the Due Process Clause of the Fifth Amendment or the Bill of Attainder Clause of Article I, citing Massachusetts v. Mellon.[56] But the Court did consider and reject the state's claim that the statute violated the Fifteenth Amendment. It said: "Original jurisdiction is founded on the presence of a controversy between a State and a citizen of another State under Art. III, § 2, of the Constitution."[57] For this proposition it cited Georgia v. Pennsylvania R. Co. That there was jurisdiction is hardly doubtful, but the Court's failure to explain why the state has standing to raise the Fifteenth Amendment objection but not the others is mystifying.[58]

Where a state is suing in a representative capacity on behalf of its citizens, individual citizens within the state will not be permitted to intervene and advance a position contrary to that of the state, unless they can show some compelling interest in their own right apart from the interest that they have in common with all citizens.[59]

Actions within the original jurisdiction are almost always equitable in nature. A statute purports to give a right to trial by jury in original actions in the Supreme Court against citizens of the United States,[60] but no such jury trial has been had since the 18th century.[61] The Supreme Court has held that the Seventh Amendment and the statute, if they extend to original jurisdiction cases at all, are applicable only to actions at law.[62] Normally cases within the original jurisdiction that cannot be resolved as a matter of law are referred to a master.[63] Pleadings and motions in original actions are governed by the Federal Rules of Civil Procedure, and those rules are "a guide"

55. 1966, 86 S.Ct. 803, 383 U.S. 301, 15 L.Ed.2d 769.

56. 86 S.Ct. at 816, 383 U.S. at 323–324.

57. 86 S.Ct. at 807, 383 U.S. at 307.

58. See Bickel, The Voting Rights Cases, 1966 Sup.Ct.Rev. 79, 80–93.

The Court decided, without discussing jurisdiction or standing, a challenge by a state to a federal statute concerning voting in Oregon v. Mitchell, 1970, 91 S.Ct. 260, 400 U.S. 112, 27 L.Ed.2d 272. It said only: "No question has been raised concerning the standing of the parties or the jurisdiction of this Court." 91 S.Ct. at 261 n. 1, 400 U.S. at 117 n. 1. See also 91 S.Ct. at 279 n. 1, 400 U.S. 152 n. 1 (opinion of Harlan, J.).

59. Kentucky v. Indiana, 1930, 50 S.Ct. 275, 281 U.S. 163, 74 L.Ed. 784; New Jersey v. New York, 1953, 73 S.Ct. 689, 345 U.S. 369, 97 L.Ed. 1081.

Cases in which individuals have been allowed to intervene are cited in 17 Wright, Miller & Cooper, Jurisdiction § 4054 n. 16.

60. 28 U.S.C.A. § 1872. See 17 Wright, Miller & Cooper, Jurisdiction § 4054, pp. 197–198.

61. There was a jury trial in Georgia v. Brailsford, 1794, 3 Dall. 1, 1 L.Ed. 483, and in two other unreported cases in 1795 and 1797. Carson, The Supreme Court of the United States: Its History, 1891, p. 169 n. 1.

62. U. S. v. Louisiana, 1950, 70 S.Ct. 914, 917, 339 U.S. 699, 706, 94 L.Ed. 1216.

63. In Maryland v. Louisiana, 1981, 101 S.Ct. 2114, 2122, 451 U.S. 725, 734, 68 L.Ed.2d 576, the Court noted that "as is usual, we appointed a Special Master to facilitate handling of the suit."

on other procedural questions that may arise,[64] but the procedure remains not very well defined.[65] Commonly such cases are protracted and expensive, but it is likely that the importance, and the technical nature, of the issues that typically arise in original cases to which a state is a party are such that no system of procedure could prevent such delay and expense.

In deciding suits between states—and apparently in all other cases to which a state is a party, though the matter is not clearly settled—the Court applies "federal common law."[66] The source of such law, and its precise content, have never been clearly specified. Sitting, as it were, as an international, as well as a domestic tribunal, the Court draws on federal law, state law, and international law, as the exigencies of the particular case may demand.[67] While the municipal law relating to like questions between individuals is taken into account, it is not deemed to have controlling effect.[68] In such cases, as in cases involving the validity or construction of interstate compacts, the Court is free to decide questions of local law for itself if need be.[69]

It is not clear how a judgment against a state would be enforced if a state were to prove recalcitrant. In the lengthy litigation between Virginia and West Virginia over some 12 million dollars owed by the latter to the former, the Court at one point wrote a strong opinion saying that the judgment was enforceable but not deciding precisely how it might be enforced.[70] It did not have to solve that question

---

64. Rule 9.2, 1980 Sup.Ct.Rules. The Civil Rules are a guide only "where their application is appropriate." See Utah v. U. S., 1969, 89 S.Ct. 761, 765, 394 U.S. 89, 95, 22 L.Ed.2d 99. See also Ohio v. Kentucky, 1973, 93 S.Ct. 1178, 1180, 410 U.S. 641, 644, 35 L.Ed. 2d 560.

65. 17 Wright, Miller & Cooper, Jurisdiction § 4054; Stern & Gressman, Supreme Court Practice, 5th ed. 1978, §§ 10.8–10.14; Note, note 1 above, at 685–690.

66. Hinderlider v. La Plata River & Cherry Creek Ditch Co., 1938, 58 S.Ct. 803, 811, 304 U.S. 92, 110, 82 L.Ed. 1202, rehearing denied, 59 S.Ct. 55, 305 U.S. 668, 83 L.Ed. 433. See 17 Wright, Miller & Cooper, Jurisdiction § 4052; Stanford Note, note 1 above, at 680–685.

67. Kansas v. Colorado, 1902, 22 S.Ct. 552, 560, 185 U.S. 125, 146, 46 L.Ed. 838; id., 1907, 27 S.Ct. 655, 206 U.S. 46, 51 L.Ed. 956. See Note, What Rule of Decision Should Control in Interstate Controversies, 1907, 21 Harv.L.Rev. 132.

68. Connecticut v. Massachusetts, 1931, 51 S.Ct. 286, 289, 282 U.S. 660, 670, 75 L.Ed. 602.

69. Kentucky v. Indiana, 1930, 50 S.Ct. 275, 281 U.S. 163, 74 L.Ed. 784; Petty v. Tennessee-Missouri Bridge Comm., 1959, 79 S.Ct. 785, 359 U.S. 275, 3 L.Ed.2d 804; Nebraska v. Iowa, 1972, 92 S.Ct. 1379, 1380 n. 1, 406 U.S. 117, 118 n. 1, 31 L.Ed.2d 733; Vermont v. New York, 1974, 94 S.Ct. 2248, 2252, 417 U.S. 270, 277, 41 L.Ed.2d 61. See Zimmerman & Wendell, The Interstate Compact and Dyer v. Sims, 1951, 51 Col.L.Rev. 931. But see Engdahl, Construction of Interstate Compacts: A Questionable Federal Question, 1965, 51 Va.L.Rev. 987.

70. Virginia v. West Virginia, 1918, 38 S.Ct. 400, 246 U.S. 565, 59 L.Ed. 1272. See Coleman, The State as Defendant under the Federal Constitution: the Virginia-West Virginia Debt Controversy, 1917, 31 Harv.L.Rev. 210; Powell, Coercing a State to Pay a Judgment: Virginia v. West Virginia, 1918, 17 Mich.L.Rev. 1; Fischer, Enforcement of a Money Judgment against a State, 1927, 12 St. Louis L.Rev. 57; Stanford Note, note 1 above, at 690–694.

because West Virginia ultimately paid the judgment.[71]   In another case that was before the Court a number of times, Wyoming sought to have Colorado held in contempt for violation of an earlier decree, but the Court found room for misunderstanding in the earlier decree and clarified Colorado's duties, rather than punishing the state.[72]   Patience by the Court, and the moral suasion of its decree, are likely to be more satisfactory in resolving these delicate interstate controversies than is a more coercive attitude.

§ 110.   Cases Affecting Ambassadors, Other Public Ministers, and Consuls [1]

In addition to cases in which a state is a party, the Constitution provides for original jurisdiction in the Supreme Court "in all Cases affecting Ambassadors, other public Ministers and Consuls."   From the time of the First Judiciary Act on, a distinction was drawn by statute.   The Supreme Court was given original and exclusive jurisdiction of proceedings against ambassadors and other public ministers or their domestics, or domestic servants, and original but not exclusive jurisdiction of suits brought by ambassadors or other public ministers, or in which a consul or a vice consul was a party.[2]   This ancient distinction was abandoned in 1978.   The statute was amended in that year so that there is no longer exclusive original jurisdiction of suits against ambassadors.   Instead the Supreme Court now has original but not exclusive jurisdiction of all actions or proceedings to which ambassadors, other public ministers, consuls, or vice consuls of foreign states are parties.[3]   Another statute gives the district courts jurisdiction, exclusive of the courts of the states, of all civil actions against consuls or vice consuls of foreign states or members of a mission or members of their families.[4]

It is reassuring to know that the Supreme Court is no longer required to hear all actions against ambassadors, but Congress hardly

---

In South Dakota v. North Carolina, 1904, 24 S.Ct. 269, 277, 192 U.S. 286, 321–322, 48 L.Ed. 448, the bonds of the defendant state on which suit was brought were secured by certain railroad stock.   The Court ordered the Supreme Court marshal to hold a public sale of the state's interest in the stock if the state failed to pay the judgment.

71.   W.Va.Acts, 1919 Ext.Sess., c. 10, p. 19.

72.   Wyoming v. Colorado, 1940, 60 S.Ct. 765, 769, 309 U.S. 572, 582, 84 L.Ed. 954.

[§ 110]

1.   17 Wright, Miller & Cooper, Jurisdiction § 4050; Note, The Original Jurisdiction of the United States Supreme Court, 1959, 11 Stan.L.Rev. 665, 667–668.

2.   Act of Sept. 24, 1789, c. 20, § 13, 1 Stat. 73, 80–81.

3.   28 U.S.C.A. § 1251(b)(1).

4.   28 U.S.C.A. § 1351.   See also 28 U.S. C.A. § 1364 (one of three separate statutes all numbered § 1364) giving the district courts original and exclusive jurisdiction of direct actions against insurers of members of diplomatic missions and their families.

Under an earlier version of what is now 28 U.S.C.A. § 1351, it was held that a suit against a consul for divorce cannot be brought in district court, and must be brought in state court.   Ohio ex rel. Popovici v. Agler, 1930, 50 S.Ct. 154, 280 U.S. 379, 74 L.Ed. 489.   See § 25 above.

needed to bother changing the law. The grant of original jurisdiction in suits affecting ambassadors, ministers, and consuls has almost never been used. Only three cases have come to the Supreme Court in which it was sought to invoke that jurisdiction. In one early case it was held that suit would not lie against a consul where the claim was against his government rather than against the consul individually.[5] In another case the Court held, as the statute now provides, that the original jurisdiction extends only to diplomatic and consular representatives accredited to the United States by foreign powers, and not to those who represent the United States in other countries.[6] Finally there is one case in which, without discussing any jurisdictional question, the Court heard an action in debt against a vice-consul and gave judgment for plaintiff.[7] The diplomatic immunity that attaches to ambassadors and other public ministers,[8] though not to consuls, probably explains why there has been so little use of this head of original jurisdiction. There have been a few cases in which the grant of original jurisdiction has been construed because of unsuccessful attempts of parties to claim that the case was one "affecting" a diplomat, though he was not a party, and thus not properly brought in the lower court.[9]

5. Jones v. Le Tombe, 1798, 3 Dall. 384, 1 L.Ed. 647.

6. Ex parte Gruber, 1925, 46 S.Ct. 112, 269 U.S. 302, 70 L.Ed. 280.

7. Casey v. Galli, 1877, 94 U.S. 673, 24 L.Ed. 168.

8. 22 U.S.C.A. § 252. See Bergman v. De Sieyes, C.C.A.2d 1948, 170 F.2d 360;

Pooley v. Luco, D.C.Cal.1896, 76 Fed. 146; Gittings v. Crawford, C.C.D.Md. 1838, 10 Fed.Cas. 447, No. 5,465.

9. U. S. v. Ortega, 1826, 11 Wheat. 467, 6 L.Ed. 521; Ex parte Hitz, 1884, 4 S.Ct. 698, 111 U.S. 766, 28 L.Ed. 592; In re Baiz, 1890, 10 S.Ct. 854, 135 U.S. 403, 34 L.Ed. 222.

TABLE OF CASES

References are to Pages

TABLE OF CASES

N

TABLE OF STATUTES AND COURT RULES

References are to Pages

---

840 TABLE OF STATUTES

POPULAR NAME ACTS

Administration Procedure Act

Sec.	Wright Fed.Courts Page
10	117

Arbitration Act

Sec.	Wright Fed.Courts Page
3	361

Bankruptcy Act

Sec.	Wright Fed.Courts Page
25a	177

Civil Rights Act of 1866

Sec.	Wright Fed.Courts Page
2	121

Judiciary Act

Sec.	Wright Fed.Courts Page
11	165
25	5
	736
34	347
	360

Regional Rail Reorganization Act

Sec.	Wright Fed.Courts Page
209	18

Rules of Decision Act

Sec.	Wright Fed.Courts Page
34	5

Taft-Hartley Act

Sec.	Wright Fed.Courts Page
301	110

DISTRICT OF COLUMBIA CODE ENCYCLOPEDIA

D.C.C.E. Sec.	Wright Fed.Courts Page
31–101(a)	48

SUPREME COURT OF THE UNITED STATES

R.R. Rule	Wright Fed.Courts Page
9.2	772
11.2	754
12A	755
17.1	756
19.3	755
20.1	754
20.2	754
21.1(a)	759
25.2	735
27.3	763

FEDERAL RULES OF CIVIL PROCEDURE

F.R.C.P. Rule	Wright Fed.Courts Page
1	518
2	436
	437
3	380
	385
	411
	412
4	385
	411
	421
	424
	498
	507
4(a)	297
	412
4(c)	423
4(c)(2)(A)	413
4(c)(2)(B)	413
4(c)(2)(C)(i)	423
	424
4(c)(2)(C)(ii)	414
4(d)	413
4(d)(1)	358
	406
	414
	415
	421
4(d)(1)–4(d)(6)	422
4(d)(2)	413
4(d)(3)	414

*

INDEX

References are to Pages.

INDEX

†